1. Features to make reading more interesting

FEATURE	DESCRIPTION		PAGE REF
Opening vignettes	Each chapter begins with a short article on some m keting research practice or an example illustrating chapter content such as the survey that changed su vey sampling for all time!	re ho	
Current insights from industry professionals	"War stories" and recommendations from seasoned practitioners of marketing research	Ill ap	
Global applications	Examples of global marketing research in action	F re	
Ethical applications	Situations that show how ethical marketing researchers behave	R	
Practical applications	"Nuts and bolts" examples of how marketing research is performed		

2. Features to help you study for exams

FEATURE	DESCRIPTION	
Chapter objectives	Bulleted items listing the major topics and issues addressed in the chapter	
Marginal notes	One-sentence summaries of key concepts	
Chapter summaries	Summaries of the key points in the chapter	
Key terms	Important terms defined within the chapter and listed at the end of the chapter.	
Review questions	Assessment questions to challenge your understanding of the theories and topics covered within the chapter	
Companion website	The student resources on this website include chapter out lines, case study hints, online tests, and PowerPoint slides	...on ...m/

3. Elements that help you apply the knowledge you've gain...

FEATURE	DESCRIPTION		PAGE REF
End-of-chapter cases	Case studies that ask you to apply the material you've learned in the chapter	Helps you learn how to use the material that some-times must be customized for a particular marketing research case	p.400
Synthesize your learning	Exercises that ask you to apply and integrate material from across three to four chapters	• Overcomes the "silo effect" of studying chapters in isolation • Enhances learning by showing you how topics and concepts are related across chapters	p. 396-397
Integrated case	A case study running throughout the book which you study through end-of-chapter exercises	• Simulates a real-world marketing research project running across all of the steps in the marketing research process • Shows you the execution of an entire marketing research project	p. 112
Integration of SPSS 17.0 Student Version	The most widely adopted statistical analysis program in the world, with annotated screenshots and output, plus step-by-step "how to do it" instructions	Teaches you the statistical analysis program that is the standard of the marketing research industry.	p. 451-452
Online SPSS datasets	SPSS data sets for four different cases in the textbook, including the integrated case	• Offers easy access to SPSS datasets that you can use without worrying about setting up or cleaning up • Provides good models for SPSS datasets	www.pearson highered.com/ burns
Qualtrics	Qualtrics survey software is the most robust survey tool available	You'll gain experience in creating and launching an online questionnaire using software that you will use throughout your career	p. 325-328
SPSS student assistant	Stand-alone modules with animation and annotated screen shots to show you how to use many SPSS features	Handy reference for many SPSS functions and fea-tures, including statistical analyses	p. 269

Marketing Research

Sixth Edition

Alvin C. Burns
Louisiana State University

Ronald F. Bush
University of West Florida

Prentice Hall

Boston Columbus Indianapolis New York San Francisco Upper Saddle River
Amsterdam Cape Town Dubai London Madrid Milan Munich Paris Montreal Toronto
Delhi Mexico City Sao Paulo Sydney Hong Kong Seoul Singapore Taipei Tokyo

Library of Congress Cataloging-in-Publication Data

Burns, Alvin C.

   Marketing research / Alvin C. Burns, Ronald F. Bush. — 6th ed.
      p. cm.
   Includes bibliographical references.
   ISBN-13: 978-0-13-602704-1
   ISBN-10: 0-13-602704-0
   1. Marketing research.   2. SPSS for Windows.   I. Bush, Ronald F.   II. Title.
   HF5415.2.B779 2009
   658.8'3—dc22

                                 2009015613

Editorial Director: Sally Yagan
Editor in Chief: Eric Svendsen
Acquisitions Editor: James Heine
Editorial Project Manager: Ashley Santora
Editorial Assistant: Karin Williams
Director of Marketing: Patrice Lumumba Jones
Marketing Manager: Anne Falhgren
Senior Managing Editor: Judy Leale
Project Manager: Becca Richter
Senior Operations Supervisor: Arnold Vila
Operations Specialist: Ilene Kahn
Senior Art Director: Janet Slowik
Interior and Cover Designer: Wanda Espana
Cover Photos: Palto/Shutterstock; Geopaul/iStockphoto
Manager, Visual Research: Beth Brenzel
Photo Researcher: Heather Donofrio
Manager, Rights and Permissions:
Zina Arabia

Image Permission Coordinator: Debbie Hewitson
Manager, Cover Visual Research
& Permissions:
Karen Sanatar
Media Project Manager, Editorial:
Denise Vaughn
Media Project Manager, Production:
Lisa Rinaldi
Full-Service Project Management and
Composition: GGS Higher Education
Resources, a Division of PreMedia
Global, Inc.
Printer/Binder: Courier/Kendallville
Cover Printer:Lehigh-Phoenix
Color/Hagerstown
Text Font: 10/12 Times

Credits and acknowledgments borrowed from other sources and reproduced, with permission, in this textbook appear on appropriate page within text (or on page 655).

Microsoft® and Windows® are registered trademarks of the Microsoft Corporation in the U.S.A. and other countries. Screen shots and icons reprinted with permission from the Microsoft Corporation. This book is not sponsored or endorsed by or affiliated with the Microsoft Corporation.

Many of the designations by manufacturers and seller to distinguish their products are claimed as trademarks. Where those designations appear in this book, and the publisher was aware of a trademark claim, the designations have been printed in initial caps or all caps.

Prentice Hall
is an imprint of

www.pearsonhighered.com

10 9 8 7 6 5 4 3 2
ISBN 10:   0-13-602704-0
ISBN 13: 978-0-13- 602704-1

Only we know how much our wives, Jeanne and Libbo, have sacrificed during the times we have been devoted to this book. We are fortunate in that, for both of us, our wives are our best friends and smiling supporters.

Al Burns,
Louisiana State University

Ron Bush,
University of West Florida

Brief Contents

Contents

Chapter 13   Determining the Size of a Sample   372

Chapter 14   Dealing with Field Work and Data Quality Issues   400

Preface to the Sixth Edition

What's New in the Sixth Edition?
Integrated Case

Our new case, *Advanced Automobile Concepts (AAC)*, focuses on a new manager who must determine the type of automobiles that the auto market will demand in the future. By using this case you will learn how to examine attitudes and opinons (for example, attitudes about global warming and future fuel prices) that are important in consumer choice, how to determine the most preferred models, and how to identify market segment differences between the different models. You are shown how SPSS tools can aid in analyzing case data to make important decisions. We have included at least one integrated case in every chapter.

Fresh Cases Contributed by Marketing Research Professors

We found several professors who had excellent case ideas they were willing to contribute to the Sixth Edition. The following are all new:

Case 4.1 The Civic Agency Initiatives Project

This case was contributed by Pushkala Raman, Ph.D., of Texas Woman's University.

Case 7.1 Entertainment Research

This case was contributed by Anthony Patino, Ph.D., Assistant Professor of Marketing; Velitchka D. Kaltcheva,Ph.D., Assistant Professor of Marketing; and Annie H. Liu, Ph.D., Associate Professor of Marketing, all of Loyola Marymount University.

Case 8.1 The College Experience

This case was provided by Professor Daniel Purdy, Ph.D., Assistant Director of the MBA Program and Professor Wendy Wilhelm, Ph.D., Professor of Marketing, both of Western Washington University.

Case 8.2 Integrated Case: Advanced Automobile Concepts

This case was provided by Professor Philip Trocchia, Ph.D., Associate Professor of Marketing, University of South Florida, St. Petersburg, Florida.

Case 11.2 The SteakStop Restaurant: What is Wrong with These Questions?

This case was contributed by Tulay Girard, Ph.D., Assistant Professor of Marketing, Pennsylvania State University–Altoona.

Case 12.2 How to Become Involved in Politics Using a Sampling Design

This case was provided by Robert W. Armstrong, Ph.D., Professor of Marketing, University of North Alabama.

Case 15.1 SafeScope Case Study: Market Research to Validate a New Business

This case was contributed by U. N. Umesh, Ph.D., Professor of Marketing and Entrepreneurship, Washington State University, Vancouver, and Ash Gupte, Partner, Key West Technologies, LLC.

Chapter 16 Synthesize Your Learning: Blood Bank of Delmarva and Optimal Strategix, LLC

This case was provided by Anu Sivaraman, Ph.D., Assistant Professor of Marketing, Alfred Lerner College of Business & Economics, University of Delaware, and R. Sukumar, President and CEO, Optimal Strategix Group, Inc., Newtown, PA.

Chapter 4 Rewritten to Reflect Today's Practice

We started over from square one when we wrote Chapter 4, "Defining the Problem and Determining Research Objectives." We have taken a complex topic and sequenced the issues in logical succession. We do not pretend that what we've developed is simple, but we do add some order to the process.

New Section in Chapter 11 on Specific Use of Qualtrics Online Surveying Software

For those of you who wish to use this software, you will find easy-to-follow instructions in our chapter on questionnaire design, Chapter 11. Following our explanation of keystrokes for SPSS, we provide annotated screen captures for using Qualtrics.

Integration of SPSS 17.0

You are holding the first textbook to fully integrate SPSS. We started this integration in 1995, and we enhance the integration of SPSS by offering you step-by-step screen captures that help you learn the keystrokes in SPSS. This allows you to spend more time teaching what the analysis technique is, when to use it, and how to interpret it. Illustrated keystrokes for the latest edition of SPSS are presented in this text with clear, easy-to-follow instructions.

NEW! Current Insights from Industry Professionals

Being involved as researchers for many years ourselves and as authors of a marketing research textbook, we have developed many relationships with those who practice in the industry every day. Our friends provide us with insights that only those working daily in the industry can have, and we pass those along to you in every chapter. You will find many of these insights in the opening chapter vignettes and Marketing Research Insight boxes throughout the book. For example, we bring you insights from the CEO of Maritz Research, Herb Sorensen of TNS-Sorensen, executives from IPSOS, and many other leading companies. We also sought out several marketing researchers who recently graduated from college to give you their perspectives on the industry.

New! Expanded Insights on Marketing Research as a Career

At the end of Chapter 3 we offer an appendix on marketing research as a career. We cover the usual topics here—job outlook, salaries, and job requirements. However, we decided to personalize the Sixth Edition by asking people in the industry to give you their opinions about a career in marketing research. What are people hiring in the industry looking for? Also, we include some extensive coverage of people who have recently entered the industry. These boxes are included in the body of the chapter as well as in the appendix.

In addition, some of you may be thinking about a master's degree. We offer a listing of master's degree programs in marketing research with links to sites enabling you to find out more about these programs. In this edition we worked closely with Dr. Madhav Segal, Director of Southern Illinois University Edwardsville's MMR program. This is one of the leading MMR programs in the country, and the material we assembled can help you assess the benefits of a specialized degree program in marketing research.

NEW! Synthesize Your Learning

We added this feature to help you synthesize the knowledge you have gained across several chapters. The exercises require you to go back to previous chapters and integrate material into answers for the exercise. The following "Synthesize Your Learning" exercises are included in the Sixth Edition:

The First Interview: Synthesize Your Learning, page 71

AAC: Synthesize Your Learning, page 198

Starting a Business: Synthesize Your Learning, page 232
Moe's Tortilla Wraps: Synthesize Your Learning, page 328
Niagara Falls Tourism Association: Synthesize Your Learning, page 394
Blood Bank of Delmarva and Optimal Strategix, LLC: Synthesize Your Learning, page 491
Alpha Airlines: Synthesize Your Learning, page 600

NEW! Guidelines on Reporting Statistical Analyses to Clients

We have noticed that after teaching our students to properly conduct a statistical analysis using SPSS, they have trouble when it comes to writing down what they have done. We decided to add an element in our Sixth Edition that would address this problem. In our data analysis chapters we include information on how to write up the findings for the client. We offer easy-to-follow guidelines and examples. This should make you better research report writers.

NEW! The iReportWriting Assistant

When our students write up reports for their marketing research projects, we find ourselves answering the same kinds of questions over and over. "How do you properly reference a journal article?" "What about referencing an online source of information?" "What do you have to reference and what do you not have to reference?" "When I write the introduction to the research report, what are some of the topics I need to cover and how do I word them?" So, we asked a business communications expert, Dr. Heather Donofrio, to develop an online resource that would help you answer these questions. With the new *iReportWriting Assistant*, available online at the website www.pearsonhighered.com/burns, you can now go online for assistance:

- What to do prior to writing?
- Templates to help get started writing
- Help with grammar
- Help with citations
- Example reports

You are either given information on these topics or linked to sites that specialize in a particular issue relevant to report writing.

NEW! New Global Applications

We have many new examples that illustrate the global dimensions of marketing research.

NEW! New Ethical Applications

We have new examples of the ethical issues facing both marketing research suppliers and buyers. We make every effort to ensure that your students are sensitized to the ethical issues they are likely to confront in their careers.

To the Student

WHAT IS THIS COURSE ABOUT? This course is about gathering information in order to make better decisions. You've learned in your fundamentals of marketing course that managers must make decisions. Sometimes these decisions are routine and can be made easily. Other decisions require a different approach. Sometimes managers are faced with a decision that (a) is important, (b) has severe negative consequences if made incorrectly, and (c) requires the decision maker to gather additional information. When any one of these conditions occurs, managers often turn to marketing research. In this course you will learn about the basic process marketing researchers use to provide managers with the information they need to make better decisions.

WHY IS THIS COURSE IMPORTANT FOR YOUR MAJOR? If you are a marketing major, you should definitely understand the role marketing research plays in the marketing process. You've learned that marketing strategy essentially involves selection of a target market and development of a marketing "mix" tailored to meet the needs of that target market. Think about the decisions that marketing managers must make in order to plan, implement, and control a marketing strategy. First, what is the market? How can the market be segmented? Which segments' needs are currently being met by competitors? Which segments' needs are not being met? Would it be profitable to serve any of those segments? These are just a few of the decisions marketers must make, and we haven't even started talking about the decisions necessary to develop the right "mix" to serve the segment we select as our target market. Decisions, decisions, decisions! Understanding the process of gathering information to help make these decisions through marketing research will be important to you in your business career. In fact, many non-marketing majors take this course. All majors in business benefit from it as well as such closely related majors as advertising and public relations.

TIME-TESTED APPROACH. We mentioned the basics of marketing strategy earlier, and we used that same concept in developing this book. After conducting and teaching marketing research at the university level for many years, we realized there was a market segment whose needs were not being met by competitive textbooks. Our target market is "undergraduate students who are taking their first course in marketing research."

THE MARKET REACTION TO THIS BOOK HAS CONFIRMED OUR APPROACH. Many students around the world have learned the basics of marketing research using this book. The book is published in English, Dutch, and Chinese and has special editions in Canada and the Philippines. We have been advised by our publisher that we have had the top-selling book in marketing research for over a decade. We hope you find our book as interesting and informative as the many thousands of students who have preceded you in learning about marketing research. But, you will have to do your part in this course in order to learn as much as you can.

WHAT'S EXPECTED OF YOU. For the vast majority of you, this will be your one chance at acquiring knowledge about the basic function and process of marketing research. Take advantage of this opportunity! You will be better prepared to learn this material if you've had the prerequisite courses we recommend. Your instructor will make the final decision about what your prerequisites are for the course. Still, we recommend that you have already studied fundamentals of marketing and elementary statistics. Why? If you haven't had the fundamentals of a marketing course, you will probably have experienced some problems already in interpreting what we've been saying about marketing strategy and the "mix." Marketing research is part of marketing, so it will help if you understand marketing first. Also, we know that many students do not recall all they learned in elementary statistics. However, having had the course, you will be surprised at what concepts come back to you as you begin to learn the basics of data analysis in this book. Just being familiar with concepts like the "area under the normal distribution" and "z scores" will help you pick up the concepts we present.

Finally, in terms of what's expected of you . . . go to class. Someone once said that "80% of being successful is just showing up." There is a lot of truth in this remark. Do not miss class. Get there early so you can hear important announcements and listen to what is being discussed. Get involved and enjoy learning about marketing research.

HOW SHOULD YOU STUDY THIS BOOK? By now you know the "secrets" of learning. Listen carefully to what your professor has to say. Read your assignments. To this we add another suggestion that seems to work: Get interested in the subject matter. You will find that being interested is a very effective catalyst in helping you learn. How do you do it? We recommend that you look through the chapter you have been assigned. Pay attention to the headings and subheadings. Ask yourself: "Do I already know what the authors mean by this?" Probably not. Ask: "What could this topic be about and how will I be able to use this in the future?" Now, you should have some interest in what you are about to read. Try it!

TIPS FOR SUCCESS! We would love for you to take advantage of our numerous years of teaching to help you become a better student. Want to know what we see in "better" students? Always attend class. Sit near the front. Pay close attention. Ask questions if you don't understand something (do not be embarrassed to ask!). Print PowerPoint slides in Handout form before class and take notes. Find someone else with whom to study. Make up test questions and ask the study mate to do the same. Take each other's test and compare your answers. Read the book as we have suggested above. Do these things and you will see your grade point average go up.

How to Get the Most Out of This Textbook

Here are our recommendations on how to read a chapter in this textbook to maximize your memory and your understanding of the concepts and material.

- **Read the Learning Objectives.** They list the major topics in the chapter.
- **Figure out where we are.** Use the "Where we are" element to locate the step in the marketing research process that the chapter pertains to. It will help you to comprehend how this chapter topic fits with other chapter topics you have learned.
- **Read the opening vignette.** It illustrates how the topic in the chapter is actually used in marketing research.
- **Read the chapter content.** It contains all the specifics on the chapter's topics.
- **Do the Active Learning exercises.** They require you to apply some material in the chapter that you will subsequently retain in memory.
- **Read the Marketing Research Insights.** These are practical examples, global cases, or ethical issues associated with selected topics in the chapter. They will expand your knowledge of these topics.
- **Study the figures and tables.** These are visual aids and/or an organized presentation of crucial material in the chapter that will help you to remember or understand the material.
- **Write up your solution to Synthesize Your Learning!** This exercise requires that you integrate material from the present chapter and from one or two prior chapters into an organized solution to a marketing research problem.
- **Read the chapter summary.** It will remind you of the key points in the chapter.
- **Review the key terms.** You should be able to recount the definitions of these important items.
- **Answer the review questions.** Answering these questions will assist you in memorizing important aspects of the chapter.
- **Answer the applications questions.** Preparing answers to these questions will help you to understand and apply important aspects of the chapter.
- **Answer questions for the end-of-chapter cases.** The cases are situations where you need to apply important concepts from the chapter to come up with solutions. Deciding what concepts are relevant and molding them to the case situation enhances your understanding of these concepts.

Helpful Hints on How to Utilize This Text in Exam Preparation

- When assigned by your instructor, read each chapter using our "How to Get the Most Out of This Textbook" recommendations.
- 5–7 days before the exam, for each chapter . . .
  - Review the marginal notes
  - Review the key terms
  - Reread the chapter summaries
  - Review the Active Learning exercises that you performed
  - Review your answers to the review and application questions
  - Review your "Synthesize Your Learning" answers
  - Review end-of-case solutions you wrote
  - Take note of those chapters or chapter topics where you do not feel adequately prepared for the exam at this time
- 3–5 days before the exam, for all chapters . . .
  - Reread the chapter or chapter section
  - Review areas you highlighted when you read the chapter (or you may have made notes on the highlights)
  - Use the Companion Website to review chapter outlines and key terms
  - Review all PowerPoint slides
  - Test your knowledge with the online tests
  - Take note of those chapters or chapter topics where you do not feel adequately prepared for the exam at this time
- 2–3 days before the exam, for each chapter or chapter topic where you feel you need additional preparation . . .
  - Reread the chapter or topic in the chapter
  - Review the specific areas you identified where you are weak (key terms, review questions, etc.)
- 1 day before the exam, for each chapter . . .
  - Review the marginal notes
  - Review the key terms
  - Reread the chapter summaries
  - Review all PowerPoint slides
  - For any topic where you feel weak, reread the topic coverage in the chapter
- On the day of the exam, relax and feel confident that you are prepared to perform well on it.

Tools That Come with This Book to Help You

INTEGRATION OF SPSS 17.0.   In this course you will learn the latest edition of the most widely used statistical analysis software used by marketing research firms, SPSS 17.0. SPSS allows you to analyze data sets using a variety of data analysis techniques. Our basic approach is to teach you when to use the technique, how to run it in SPSS, how to interpret your SPSS output, and how to write the results in your report. We use annotated screen captures taken from SPSS to help you easily learn the keystrokes necessary to become proficient. We also have an online tutorial, *SPSS Student Assistant*, which is shown under items you can access through your Companion Website to this book at www.pearsonhighered.com/burns.

GLOBAL AND ETHICAL APPLICATIONS.   In the book you will read about global and ethical applications in marketing research. Why? First, all of business has been affected by globalization. This is certainly true for marketing research, as you will learn in this book. Second, we are often reminded how ethics should play a role in bettering the world. Unfortunately, we usually read what goes wrong when ethics are forgotten. Executives at WorldCom, HealthSouth, Enron, Arthur Andersen, and many of the financial institutions such as AIG and Lehman Brothers have set a poor example of ethical behavior. We cannot teach you right from wrong, but we can make you sensitive to ethical issues as either a buyer or supplier of marketing research.

MARKETING RESEARCH INSIGHTS.   In every chapter we offer you several special features we call Marketing Research Insights, which illustrate how marketing research professionals apply the material we are addressing at that point in the text.

OPENING CHAPTER VIGNETTES.   We have opening chapter vignettes, where we show you what marketing research professionals have to say about what you are about to read. Take advantage of these vignettes because, in almost all cases, they were written specifically for this Sixth Edition. The subject matter of the vignette is directly related to the subject matter in the chapter and will give you a better understanding of the material.

ACTIVE LEARNING.   In every chapter we will alert you to an Active Learning exercise. These are intended to make you an active learner. For example, it's one thing to read about the Nielsen TV Index and quite another to go to its website and see which TV shows were the most watched shows of the week. Through these exercises we try to raise your interest because we know that learning is highly associated with interest.

AN INTEGRATED CASE AND END-OF-CHAPTER CASES.   We created one case that runs throughout this book. *Advanced Automobile Concepts* (AAC) is written for today's world. An automobile manufacturer needs information to help the company make decisions about the auto models that will be demanded by future car buyers. An installment of the case appears at the end of each chapter. Your instructor will tell you whether or not you will be using the case. Also, many end-of-chapter cases are included in the book. Each of these was especially written for this text so that you may learn how to apply concepts presented in the chapter in a case setting.

THE COMPANION WEBSITE.   By going to www.pearsonhighered.com/burns you will have several resources available to you.

- **Study quizzes** are available for each chapter. Want a tip? Read the chapter first, then take the quiz. Use the quiz as feedback to tell you how well you've learned the chapter material.
- **PowerPoint presentations** for each chapter. Whether or not your instructor uses these PowerPoint slides, you would benefit by studying them, as they will help you learn the material in this book.
- **Case Study hints** for each chapter. If your instructor assigns you any of the cases at the end of the chapters, you can get some useful ideas by reading these hints.
- **SPSS Student Assistant.** We developed this tutorial to teach you step-by-step how to learn SPSS.
- **Dataset downloads.** Once you learn SPSS, you may be assigned to use it on data provided for the cases in this book. You can access these datasets on the Companion Website and download them to your computer. Datasets available are:
  - *Advanced Automobile Concepts* (AAConcepts.sav)—integrated case dataset used in Chapters 15–20
  - *Blood Bank of Delmarva and Optimal Strategix, LLC* (BBDDonor.sav)—synthesized learning case used in Chapter 16
  - *Hobbit's Choice* (Hobbit.sav)—end-of-chapter case used in Chapters 15–19
  - *Friendly Market* (Friendly.sav)—the end-of-chapter case in Chapter 18
- *IReportWriter Assistant.* We developed an online resource for you to use when you have to write a marketing research report. The iReportWriter Assistant offers the following:
  - What to do prior to writing?
  - Templates to help you get started writing
  - Help with grammar

- Help with citations
- Example reports
- ■ **Online data analysis modules.** We provide you with the basic tools of data analysis in the book. However, from time to time your instructor may want you to gain some familiarity with some other tools. We have provided some additional data analysis techniques online. These tools are in two categories: nonparametric tests and multivariate techniques. Your instructor will tell you if you need any of these.
  - When to Use Nonparametric Tests
  - Nonparametric: Chi-square Goodness-of-Fit Test
  - Nonparametric: Mann-Whitney *U* Test
  - Nonparametric: Wilcoxon Test
  - Nonparametric: Kruskal Wallis *H* Test
  - When to Use Multivariate Techniques
  - Factor Analysis
  - Cluster Analysis
  - Conjoint Analysis

STUDY GUIDE AND TECHNOLOGY MANUAL. This supplement enables you to study more effectively. It also gives detailed instructions for running the various data analysis procedures using SPSS.

COURSESMART ETEXTBOOKS. CourseSmart eTextbooks Online cost less than the suggested list price of the print text. Simply select your eText by title or author and purchase immediate access to the content for the duration of the course using any major credit card. With a CourseSmart eText, you can search for specific keywords or page numbers, make notes online, print out reading assignments that incorporate lecture notes, and bookmark important passages for later review. For more information or to purchase a CouseSmart eTextbook, visit www.coursesmart.com.

Acknowledgments

Few people realize just how many people are involved in writing and producing a book. We are fortunate to have so many friends and colleagues who support us with each edition of *Marketing Research*. First, we want to thank the professional staff at Pearson/Prentice Hall. This was our first edition with our new editorial director, Mrs. Sally Yagan, and our new editor, James Heine. We thank them both for their philosophy concerning book revisions, which we share, as well as their encouragement. Mrs. Ashley Santora is Product Development Manager and has worked closely with us on this edition. She has done a superb job of managing the myriad of details necessary to produce a new edition. Thank you, Ashley, for your professional management style and pleasant demeanor. Ms. Becca Richter is Project Manager, Production. A big "300 dpi thank you" to Becca for handling all those details necessary to get us through the production process. Thank you as well to Heidi Allgair at GGS; Anne Fahlgren, Senior Marketing Manager; Karin Williams, Editorial Assistant; and Judy Leale, Senior Managing Editor. We also appreciate the professional support and positive attitude of Pearson's marketing representatives. We think Pearson Education has the most professional representatives in the industry.

We are thankful for our colleagues at our universities. They support our efforts with constructive criticism. We thank our deans, Dean Eli Jones of LSU and Dean Ed Ranelli of UWF, for providing us with an environment conducive to pursuing knowledge in our discipline. Shari Johnson is the business reference librarian at the University of West Florida. Ms. Johnson updated secondary information sources for Chapter 6 and helps us keep up with the many changes going on with secondary data providers. Thanks also go to Rafael Lisboa for his research assistance on a variety of topics.

There are always a few people who make special contributions to a book writing project. Working with outside organizations, setting up schedules, discussing contributions of other individuals, and acquiring permissions to reprint information are but a few of the unseen tasks. We have been fortunate to have someone who not only is very knowledgeable about research and has taught the course but who has excellent time management skills. Dr. Heather H. Donofrio serves as the authors' "managing editor." As always, Dr. Donofrio did an outstanding job. We offer special thanks to Mrs. Ashley Roberts. Ashley has worked with us on a previous edition and was involved with many of the details involved in writing the Sixth Edition.

We could not write a book about the marketing research industry without a great deal of input from those who practice marketing research daily. We are fortunate to have developed many friendships and relationships in the industry. We call on these people, ranging from CEO's to highly specialized technicians, to provide our readers with current practice in the industry. Often these individuals share their knowledge of new techniques they are developing as well as evaluations of their use based upon experiences with clients. Often, we ask them to read our manuscripts and give us their reactions. Time and again, our friends spend hours reading our manuscript and penning new information based on their special insights. Many of the contributions made to the Sixth Edition came from:

Anne Donohoe, *Arbitron, KCSA Strategic Communications*; Ted Donnelly, *Baltimore Research;* Ron Tatham, *Burke, Inc.*; Patrick Glaser, *CMOR;* Jerry W. Thomas, *Decision Analyst*; Cristi Allen, *Decision Analyst*; Brent Roderick, *ESRI;* Molly Turner-Lammers, *Fieldwork, Inc.*; Jon Last, *Golf Digest*; Keith Price, *Greenfield-Ciao Surveys*; Janice Caston, *Greenfield-Ciao Surveys*; Shelley Hughes, *IRI*; Jennifer Dale, *InsideHeads*; Jack Honomichl, *Inside Research*; Laurence N. Gold, *Inside Research*; Jenny R. Donohue, *InsightExpress*; Richard Homans, *Ipsos Forward Research*; Paul Abbate, *Ipsos Public Affairs*; Alison Babcock, *Ipsos Public Affairs*; Kathryn Blackburn, *Irwin Research*; Erica Demme, *Knowledge Networks*; Velitchka D. Kaltcheva, *Loyola Marymount University*; Annie H. Liu, *Loyola Marymount University*; Anthony Patino, *Loyola Marymount University*; Michael Brereton, *Maritz Research*; Tom Evans, *Maritz Research*; Jennifer Cattel, *Marketing Research Association*; Lawrence J. Brownell, *Marketing Research Association*; Jeff Minier, *Merial Limited*; Doss Struss, *Momentum Market Intelligence*; Colleen Moore Mezler, *Moore Research Services*; Holly Ford, *MRSI*; Nick Thomas, *MrWeb Ltd.*; Fred Miller, *Murray State University*; Marilyn Raymond, *New Product Works*; Penny Wamback, *New Product Works*; Stephen F. Moore, *Nielsen Claritas*; Tulay Girard, *Pennsylvania State University- Altoona*; Hal Meier, *TAi* Companies; Holly M. O'Neill, *Talking Business*; Farnaz Badie, *The Thought Bubble*; Jennifer Frighetto, *The Nielsen Company*; Alana Johnson, *The Nielsen Company*; Sandra Parrelli, *The Nielsen Company*; Matt Senger, *The Nielsen Company*; Tina Taylor, *ProQuest*; Steve Richardson, *QRCA;* Scott M. Smith, *Qualtrics Survey Software*; Ryan Smith, *Qualtrics Survey Software*; James Quirk, *Quirk's Marketing Research Review*; William D. Neal, *SDR Consulting*; Bill MacElroy, *Socratic Technologies*; Madhav N. Segal, *Southern Illinois University Edwardsville*; Jim Follet, *Survey Sampling International*; Diane Urso, *Survey Sampling International*; Pushkala Raman, *Texas Woman's University*; Herb Sorensen, *TNS-Sorensen*; U.S. Census Bureau; Clifford D. Scott, *University of Arkansas, Ft. Smith*; Philip Trocchia, *University of South Florida*; Harriette Bettis-Outland, *University of West Florida*; Daniel Purdy, *Western Washington University*; and Wendy Wilhelm, *Western Washington University.*

We wish to thank the many individuals who served as reviewers for this book. Reviewers for the Sixth Edition were:

Joel Saegert, The University of Texas at San Antonio

Nancy Bush, Wingate University

Tung-Zong Chang, Metropolitan State College

Kathryn Cort, North Carolina A & T State University

Joshua Fogel, Brooklyn College

Yancy Edwards, University of South Florida

Stanley Garfunkel, Queensborough Community College

Ronald Goldsmith, FSU

Perry Haan, Tiffin University

Stacey Hills, Utah State University

Karl Kampschroeder, St. Mary's University

Thomas O'Connor, University of New Orleans

Jean Powers, Ivy Tech Community College

Scott Swain, Boston University

Bernard Weidenaar, Dordt College

Carrie White, West Liberty State College

Beverly Wright, East Carolina University

Eric Yorkston, Neeley School of Business, TCU

We also thank those who reviewed the first five editions, as many of their suggestions and insights have been incorporated from these earlier editions:

Manoj Agarwal, Binghamton University

Linda Anglin, Mankato State University

Silva Balasubramanian, Southern Illinois University

Ron Beall, San Francisco State University

Jacqueline J. Brown, University of Nevada, Las Vegas

Joseph D. Brown, Ball State University

E. Wayne Chandler, Eastern Illinois University

Thomas Cossee, University of Richmond

B. Andrew Cudmore, Florida Institute of Technology

Eric Freeman, Concordia University

Anthony R. Fruzzetti, Johnson & Wales University

Corbett Gaulden Jr., University of Texas of the Permian Basin

Ashok Gupta, Ohio University

Douglas Hausknecht, The University of Akron

M. Huneke, University of Iowa

Ben Judd, University of New Haven

James Leigh, Texas A&M University

Aron, Levin, Northern Kentucky University

Bryan Lilly, University of Wisconsin

Joann Lindrud, Mankato State University

Subhash Lonial, University of Louisville

Gary McCain, Boise State University

Sumaria Mohan-Neill, Roosevelt University

V. Padmanabhan, Stanford University

Diane Parente, State University of New York, Fredonia

James A. Roberts, Baylor University

Angelina M. Russell, West Virginia University of Technology

Don Sciglimpaglia, San Diego State University

Srivatsa Seshadri, University of Nebraska at Kearney

Terri Shaffer, Southeastern Louisiana University

Birud Sindhav, University of Nebraska at Omaha

Bruce L. Stern, Portland State University

John H. Summey, Southern Illinois University

Nicolaos E. Synodinos, University of Hawaii

Peter K. Tat, The University of Memphis

Dr. William Thomas, University of South Carolina

Paul Thornton, Wesley College

Jeff W. Totten, Southeastern Louisiana State University

Dr. R. Keith Tudor, Kennesaw State University

Steve Vitucci, University of Central Texas

Heiko de B. Wijnholds, Virginia Commonwealth University

Bonghee Yoo, Hofstra University

Charles J. Yoos II, Fort Lewis College

Xin Zhao, University of Utah

About the Authors

Alvin C. Burns is the Ourso Distinguished Chair of Marketing and Chairperson of Marketing in the E. J. Ourso College of Business Administration at Louisiana State University. He received his doctorate in marketing from Indiana University and an MBA from the University of Tennessee. Professor Burns has taught undergraduate and masters-level courses as well as doctoral seminars in marketing research for over 35 years. During this time, he has supervised a great many marketing research projects conducted for business-to-consumer, business-to-business, and not-for-profit organizations. His articles have appeared in the *Journal of Marketing Research*, *Journal of Business Research*, *Journal of Advertising Research*, and others. He is a Fellow in the Association for Business Simulation and Experiential Learning. He resides in Baton Rouge, Louisiana, with his wife, Jeanne.

Ronald F. Bush is Distinguished University Professor of Marketing at the University of West Florida. He received his B.S. and M.A. from the University of Alabama and his Ph.D. from Arizona State University. With over 35 years of experience in marketing research, Professor Bush has worked on research projects with firms ranging from small businesses to the world's largest multinationals. He has served as an expert witness in trials involving research methods, often testifying on the appropriateness of research reports. His research has been published in leading journals, including the *Journal of Marketing, Journal of Marketing Research, Journal of Advertising Research, Journal of Retailing,* and *Journal of Business,* among others. In 1993 he was named a Fellow by the Society for Marketing Advances. He and his wife, Libbo, live on the Gulf of Mexico, where they can often be found playing "throw the stick" with their Scottish Terrier, Maggie.

Introduction to Marketing Research

Learning Objectives

- To know the relationship of marketing research to marketing, the marketing concept and marketing strategy

- To know how to define marketing research

- To understand the purpose and uses of marketing research

- To know how to classify different types of marketing research studies

- To describe a marketing information system (MIS) and understand why marketing research occupies a place in an MIS

A Welcome to Marketing Research from the President of the Marketing Research Association

Jon Last is Vice President, Marketing, Research & Brand Development, Golf Digest Publications and President, Marketing Research Association

In this book you will learn about the role marketing research plays in providing timely and objective information that drives decision making in both the public and private sector. Throughout my career, I've been both an end user of marketing research conducted for others, and have built my own research company to assist clients in the golf, sports and leisure industries in measuring brand equity, assessing the effectiveness of marketing communications, testing concepts, evaluating the best way to price and package products and services, segmenting a market and better understanding the steps that consumers take in making purchase decisions. You will also learn about the marketing research process that Al Burns and Ron Bush conceptualize in an 11-step approach. By using this approach, you will have a basic understanding of what it takes to conduct a marketing research project.

The marketing research profession is a growing and vital industry, becoming even more important as we move through an age replete with an abundance of information and one where the opinions and behaviors of customers play an increasingly important role in determining marketplace success. The industry is supported by a number of outstanding professional associations, including the Marketing Research

Ask most marketing researchers about how they entered the profession, and many will say that it found them, as much as they pursued it. In my case, I entered the profession as a marketing generalist who became enamored with how marketing research could help any organization get to the heart of the needs, expectations or assessments of one's target market. Further, I was drawn to the way in which marketing research is at the epicenter of putting an emphasis on constituent attitudes and behaviors on key strategic business decisions.

Association (MRA), CASRO (Council of American Survey Research Organizations), CMOR (Council for Marketing & Opinion Research), IMRO (Interactive Marketing Research Organization), QRCA (Qualitative Research Consultants Association), and the American Marketing Association. The Marketing Research Association is dedicated to advancing the practical application, use, and understanding of the opinion and marketing research profession. It promotes excellence by providing members with a variety of opportunities for advancing and expanding their marketing research and related business skills. The association also acts as an advocate with appropriate governmental entities, other associations, and the public to protect the interests of the marketing research profession.

This book is a perfect launching pad for you to learn more about the importance of marketing research and to gain a baseline understanding of the complex but critical steps necessary to conduct it properly, so as to facilitate effective business decision making. We hope some of you will become so fascinated with the process and its applications that you will also choose to devote your career to this rewarding and enriching profession. You will be able to read more about careers in the industry at the end of Chapter 3.

Enjoy!

elcome to our new, Sixth Edition of Marketing Research! *As you will learn by reading this text, we strive to include the ideas and practices of those who practice daily in the marketing research industry. Mr. Jon Last, whose introduction you just read, has been one of our partners for several editions. Throughout this book you will be reading about current practices in the industry from other persons like Mr. Last. In addition to being very active in marketing research in the golf industry, Mr. Last is the president of the Marketing Research Association (MRA), which you will learn about in this book. The MRA is the host of PRC (Professional Researcher Certification) as well as other associations that serve the industry.*

When you finish this book, you will have a basic understanding of marketing research, the role it plays in facilitating decision making, and a good understanding of how to conduct marketing research. You will start by learning the relationship of marketing research to marketing and why marketing research is necessary for the practice of marketing, especially for managers who have adopted the philosophy known as the marketing concept. You should learn a definition of marketing research, and we introduce you to the official definition of the American Marketing Association as well as our shorter definition. We also want you to know the purpose and uses of marketing research and the types of marketing research studies being conducted in the industry all over the globe. In this chapter, you will learn the role marketing research plays in the total marketing information systems (MIS) and how to distinguish marketing research from the other MIS components. Finally, we will introduce you to some key issues in the industry. Together, these concepts will help lay a foundation for understanding marketing research.

By knowing how marketing research is related to marketing and the marketing concept, definitions of marketing research, its uses, types of studies, and how marketing research is part of a marketing information system, you will have a good foundation for understanding marketing research.

THE RELATIONSHIP OF MARKETING RESEARCH TO MARKETING

We need to understand the relationship of marketing research to marketing. Marketing research is part of marketing, and you cannot fully appreciate marketing research and the role it plays in the marketing process unless you know how it fits into the marketing process. Though this should be a review for you, we should ask, What is **marketing**? Perhaps the shortest definition of marketing is "meeting needs profitably."[1] When Toyota designed the Prius, it met a growing need among those seeking a more fuel-efficient auto-mobile as the price of oil zoomed higher and higher. With over half the market share among hybrid cars, there is little doubt that the Prius is a profitable model for Toyota. The American Marketing Association offers us another definition:

> The American Marketing Association has defined marketing as an organizational function and a set of processes for creating, communicating and delivering value to customers and for managing customer relationships in ways that benefit the organization and its stakeholders.[2]

The way we view marketing is shifting away from thinking that we create a physical product and then optimize profits by making efficient promotion, distribution, and pricing decisions. For many years marketing focused on providing the customer with value through a physical product that emerged at the end of the distribution channel. Current thinking, proposed primarily by Vargo and Lusch (2004),[3] calls for a framework that goes beyond a "manufacturing-tangible product" view of marketing; that is, Toyoto creates value by building cars. Rather, Vargo and Lusch argue that we should adopt a service-centered view of marketing that (a) identifies core comepetencies—the fundamental knowledge and skills that may represent a potential competitive advantage; (b) identifies potential customers that can benefit from these core competencies; (c) cultivates relation-ships with these customers that allow customers to help in creating values which meet their specific needs; and (d) gauges feedback from the market, learns from the feedback, and improves the values offered to the public. One implication of this new framework is that firms must be *more* than customer oriented (making and selling what firms think cus-tomers want and need). Rather, firms must *collaborate with* and *learn from* customers, adapting to their changing needs. A second implication is that products are not viewed as separate from services. Isn't Toyota really marketing a service, a service that happens to include a by-product called a car?[4] This new framework is referred to as the "Service-Dominant Logic for Marketing."

Our point here is not to provide a discourse on how marketing thought is evolving. After all, for the present, we are trying to understand the relationship of marketing research to marketing. That relationship may best be explained by understanding that in order to practice marketing, marketing decision makers need information in order to make better decisions. And, in our opinion, current definitions and frameworks of marketing mean that information is *more* important, not less important, in today's world. For example, the "Service-Dominant Logic for Marketing" implies that decision makers need information to know what their real core competencies are; how to create meaningful relationships with customers; how to create, communicate, and deliver value to customers; how to gather feedback to gauge customer acceptance; and how to determine the appropriate responses to the feedback. Keeping these information needs in mind, think about the information needed by these succesful firms: Apple, whose iPods, iTunes, and iPhone*s* have experi-enced great success in the market; General Mill's organic food line Small Planet Foods; CBS's venerable yet still highly watched TV show *60 Minutes*; or not-for-profits such as The Red Cross, which earns donations and support by creating value in the sense that it provides donors with "peace of mind for helping others." In order to make the decisions necessary for the success of these organizations, decision makers needed information. As you will learn, marketing research provides information to decision makers.

The phrase "hearing the voice of the consumer" has been popularized to mean that companies have the information they need to effectively satisfy wants and needs in the marketplace. While we just cited some successful firms, we recognize that not all firms "hear the voice of the consumer." They do not conceive of products or services that meet the needs and wants of the market. They do not provide value, and their sales come from short-term exchanges, not enduring customer relationships. These companies produce the wrong products or services. They have the wrong price, poor advertising, or poor distribution. Then they become part of the many firms that experience product failure. GM's first electric vehicle, the *EV1,* was a failure. McDonald's veggie burger, the *MacLean* was taken off the market. GfK Strategic Innovation's NewProductWorks®, tracks and studies innovation over time in order to help clients glean ideas for successful new innovations. For example, a firm introduced scrambled eggs, frozen and in a push-up tube. The eggs came with cheese, bacon or sausage and the idea was to quickly heat it up and take it with you for a convenient, eat-on-the-go breakfast. You could have eggs and bacon while driving to work! While this sounded great in the board room, *IncrEdibles* were taken off the market as buyers found the eggs often ended up in their laps as they tried to push up another bite! There was inadequate information on how real consumers would use the product. Out! International, Inc. came up with what sounded like a cute name for a new bug spray: "Hey! There's a Monster in My Room!" What information did the company fail to pick up on? The name alone scared kids when Mommy told them there was "A monster in the room!" The product failed. Our Marketing Research Insight 1.1, illustrates some other examples of product failure supplied to us from the marketing researchers at NewProductWorks®.

Of course, it is easy to play "Monday morning quarterback," and keep in mind that all these companies have many successful products to their credit. Peter Drucker wrote that successful companies are those that know and understand the customer so well that the product conceived, priced, promoted, and distributed by the company is ready to be bought as soon as it is available.[5] Drucker's statement is, as usual, right on target, but how can a marketer know and understand how to deliver value to the customer so well? The answer, as you can now easily see by our examples, is by having information about consumers. So to practice marketing correctly, managers must have information—this is the purpose of marketing research and why we say that marketing research is a part of marketing. It provides the necessary information to enable managers to market ideas, goods, and services *properly*. But how do you market ideas, goods, and services *properly*? You have probably already learned in your studies that you must begin by having the right philosophy, followed by proper marketing strategy. We call that philosophy the "marketing concept."

> Marketing research is a part of marketing; it provides the necessary information to enable managers to market ideas, goods, and services *properly*.

The Importance of Philosophies and the Philosophy We Call "The Marketing Concept"

> Philosophies are more important to you than you may think; your philosophies dictate how you behave every day.

A philosophy may be thought of as a system of values, or principles, by which you live. Your values, or principles, are important because they dictate what you do each day. This is why philosophies are so important; your philosophy affects your day-to-day decisions. For example, you likely have a philosophy similar to this: "I believe that higher education is important because it will provide the knowledge and understanding I will need in the world to enable me to enjoy the standard of living I desire." Assuming this does reflect your philosophy regarding higher education, consider what you do every day. You go to class, listen to your professors, take notes, read this book. If you did not share the philosophy we just described, you would likely be doing something entirely different. Well, the same is true for business managers. A manager's philosophy will affect how he or she will make day-to-day decisions in the business. There are many different philosophies that managers may use to guide them in their decision making. "We are in the locomotive business; we make and run trains." Or "To be successful we must set high sales quotas and sell, sell, sell!"[6] The managers who guided their companies by these philosophies guided those companies right out of business. A much better philosophy is called the "marketing

MARKETING RESEARCH INSIGHT   *Practical Application*

1.1 Could Better Information Help to Avoid These Failures?

Ice Breakers Pacs went into distribution in November, 2007. Pacs were small dissolvable pouches with a powdered flavored sweetener inside offered in Orange and Cool Mint flavors. By January 2008, The Hershey Company stopped the production in response to criticism that the mints looked too much like the tiny heat-sealed bags used to sell powdered illegal street drugs (cocaine). Hershey stated the mints were not intended to resemble anything. CEO David West disclosed the decision to stop production. "We are sensitive to these viewpoints and thus have made the decision that we will no longer manufacture Ice Breaker Pacs." While a break-through, innovative way to deliver a mint form, the consumer behaviors towards safety (for self, community, world) made this unacceptable to the marketplace. Would better information as to the market's reaction to the packaging been helpful?

Ice Breakers Pacs

and began to market a coffee product called Mazagran. It was a lightly carbonated iced coffee beverage. Customers were willing to try it once, based on the Starbucks name alone, but the drink didn't encourage repeat sales. One question is whether it was the carbonation or the coffee that put consumers off. Since premium coffee sales have boomed and carbonated beverages are still a mainstay in the U.S. marketplace and, Coke saw that, in Japan, the combination of coffee and carbonation was popular. But, it was not a taste U.S. consumers were ready to accept. Another cause for failure may be some confusion as to when and how this type of blended beverage could meet the needs currently being provided by coffee and soda separately. Maybe consumers love their coffee and they love their colas; but they don't want a combination. Would better information, prior to launch of Blak, have been helpful?

Coca-Cola spent an estimated $30 to $50 million to promote C2, a cola-flavored beverage introduced first in Japan, then later in the United States in June 2004, in response to the low-carbohydrate diet trend. This was Coca-Cola's biggest product launch since Diet Coke in 1982.

Coca-Cola Blak

Introduced in April 2006, Blak entered the U.S. marketplace as a carbonated fusion beverage—a taste blend of Classic Coke and coffee "essence." Coke spent two years developing Blak in hopes of making inroads into consumers' growing taste for coffee and a booming premium beverage market, targeting over-30, savvy, sophisticate-achiever consumers. Weak product performance in the United States resulted in its being discontinued 17 months after launch. Coke would have benefited by taking a look at more information on product history in this category. *Blak* was not the first of its kind; similar blends were released in the past and have failed as well. Why? In 1994, Pepsi began to test market a soda called Pepsi_Kona. It tasted more like coffee than soda. In 1995, Starbucks partnered with Pepsi

Wolfgang Puck Self-Heating Latte

Despite this support, C2 (as well as its competitor Pepsi Edge) failed to meet sales expectations and was pushed out a year later. This is due, mostly, to the decline of the low-carb fad, and, partly, to the success of Coca-Cola Zero, a zero-calorie version launched within the same timeframe. Zero calorie beverages had already been established, and with the advancement in the taste of sweeteners, the combined effect made reduced-carb beverages obsolete.

Sources reported the Wolfgang Puck self-heating coffee containers technology took 10 years and $24 million to develop. The self-heating can technology is by *OnTech* and is based on a two-part container. The outer chamber holds the beverage and the inner chamber holds the Calcium Oxide and a water puck, which when its seal is broken mixes with the calcium oxide and creates a heating effect. Launched in Spring, 2005, the product was quickly picked up for distribution by Kroger, Albertsons, and Sam's Club. Less than a year later, Puck's namesake company demanded brand-licensee BrandSource Inc. pull the products from stores nationwide after complaints due to faulty technology, ranging from the product's failure to reach an appropriately hot temperature to it actually overheating, spurting product from the can and/or leaking out of the can. While self-heating and self-chilling technology could help meet the needs of many on-the-go consumers, any future use of an improvement in the technology will have to face an even higher hurdle of regaining the consumers trust.

Coca-Cola C2

Visit NewProductWorks® at www.newproductworks.com/.

Source: NewProductWorks®, the innovation resource center of GfK Strategic Innovation (formerly Arbor Strategy Group).

concept." A prominent marketing professor, Philip Kotler, has defined the marketing concept as follows:

> *The marketing concept is often referred to as "being market driven," or "having a customer orientation."*

The **marketing concept** is a business philosophy that holds that the key to achieving organizational goals consists of the company being more effective than competitors in creating, delivering, and communicating customer value to its chosen target markets.[7]

> *It has long been recognized that the philosophy known as the marketing concept is the "right philosophy." Organizations are more likely to achieve their goals if they satisfy consumers' wants and needs.*

For many years, business leaders have recognized that this is the "right philosophy." And although the marketing concept is often used interchangeably with other terms, such as *customer-oriented* or *market-driven*, the key point is that this philosophy puts the consumer first! Some scholars have added the concept of *holistic marketing*, which includes four components: relationship marketing, integrated marketing, internal marketing, and social responsibility marketing.[8] Time has proven that a philosophy focusing on the consumer is superior to one in which company management focuses on production, the product itself, or high-pressure selling. If you satisfy consumers, they will seek to do business with your company.

What does all this mean? It means that having the "right philosophy" is an important first step in being successful. But just appreciating the importance of satisfying consumer wants and needs is not enough. Firms must put together the "right strategy."

The "Right Marketing Strategy"

The term *strategy* was borrowed from military jargon and means developing plans of attack that would minimize the enemy's ability to respond. So, by strategy, we mean a plan, and one that should anticipate competitors' reactions. Firms may also have strategies in many areas other than marketing. Financial strategy, production strategy, technology strategy, for example, may be key components of a firm's overall strategy. Here, however, we focus on marketing strategy. How do we define marketing strategy?

A **marketing strategy** consists of selecting a segment of the market as the company's target market and designing the proper "mix" of product/service, price, promotion, and distribution system to meet the wants and needs of the consumers within the target market.

A marketing strategy consists of selecting a segment of the market as the company's target market and designing the proper "mix" of product/service, price, promotion, and distribution system to meet the wants and needs of the consumers within the target market.

Note that this definition of strategy assumes that we have *already* adopted the marketing concept. A manager who does not embrace the marketing concept, for example, would not be concerned whether the plan addressed any particular market segment and certainly would not be concerned with consumers' wants and needs. So, to continue, we are thinking like *enlightened* managers; we have adopted the marketing concept. Now, as we shall see, because we have adopted the marketing concept, we cannot come up with just any strategy. We have to develop the "right" strategy—the strategy that allows our firm to truly meet the wants and needs of the consumers within the market segment we have chosen. Think of the many questions we now must answer: What is the market, and how do we segment it? What are the wants and needs of each segment, and what is the size of each segment? Who are our competitors, and how are they already meeting the wants and needs of consumers? Which segment(s) should we target? Which model of a proposed product will best suit the target market? What is the best price? Which promotional method will be the most efficient? How should we distribute the product/service?

All these questions must be answered in order to develop the "right" strategy. In order to make the right decisions, managers must have objective, accurate, and timely *information*.

Today, it is more important to understand that today's strategy may not work tomorrow. We are seeing unprecedented change. Just think about issues facing firms today as they struggle to anticipate future consumer needs. How will global warming affect today's products? What new fuels will replace fossil fuels and what new products and services will the new energy environment bring about? How will governments deal with growing health care crises? What differences will we see in financial institutions' products as a result of the 2008 financial crisis? What new strategies will be needed in tomorrow's world? As environments change, business decisions must be revised again and again to produce the right strategy for the new environment. The bottom line of this entire discussion: To make the right decisions, managers continuously need information. As we shall learn next, marketing research supplies much of this information.

DEFINING MARKETING RESEARCH

Now that we have established that managers need information in order to carry out the marketing process, we need to define marketing research.

Marketing research is the process of designing, gathering, analyzing, and reporting information that may be used to solve a specific marketing problem.

Marketing research is the process of designing, gathering, analyzing, and reporting information that may be used to solve a specific marketing problem.

This definition tells us that marketing research is a process that reports information that can be used to solve a marketing problem, such as determining price, how to advertise, and so on. The focus then is on a process that results in information that will be used to make decisions. (We introduce you to this 11-step process in Chapter 2.) Notice also that our definition refers to information that may be used to solve a *specific* marketing problem. We are going to explain the importance of this later in this chapter. Ours is not the only definition of marketing research. The American Marketing Association (AMA) formed a committee several years ago to establish a definition. The AMA definition is

Marketing research is the function that links the consumer, customer, and public to the marketer through information—information used to identify and define marketing opportunities and problems; generate, refine, and evaluate marketing actions; monitor marketing performance; and improve the understanding of marketing as a process.[9]

Each of these definitions is correct. Our definition is shorter and illustrates the process of marketing research. The AMA's definition is longer because it elaborates on the function (we call it the *purpose*) as well as the *uses* of marketing research. Note that market research, a part of marketing research, refers to applying marketing research to a specific market area. One definition of **market research** is: "The systematic gathering, recording, and analyzing of data with respect to a particular market, where *market* refers to a specific customer group in a specific geographic area."[10] In the next two sections, we will talk more about the purpose and uses of marketing research.

WHAT IS THE PURPOSE OF MARKETING RESEARCH?

The purpose of marketing research is to link the consumer to the marketer by providing information that can be used in making marketing decisions.

As you now know, the purpose of marketing research has to do with providing information to make decisions. That is essentially correct, but the AMA definition includes a reference to the consumer, and so we state the formal purpose as: The **purpose of marketing research** is to link the consumer to the marketer by providing information that can be used in making marketing decisions. Some believe that the link between the consumer and marketing research is more important today than ever. Competition for the consumer has become fierce as globalization has taken hold. Consumers expect greater value in the marketplace. It is more important today than ever to learn insights from the customer in order to keep them loyal.[11] Our Active Learning exercise illustrates some marketing research reports that aid decision makers in the golf industry. Go ahead—take this opportunity to "see" some marketing research reports.

 Golf Anyone?

Media, whether electronic or print, often conduct marketing research in order to better understand their viewers, listeners, or readers. The very successful golf magazines, *Golf Digest, Golf World,* and *Golf Digest Index* make use of a vast amount of research. So much

By permission, Golf Digest Publications

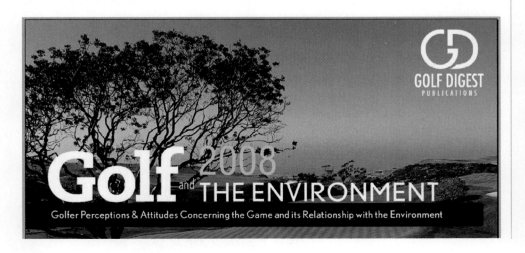

WHAT IS THE PURPOSE OF MARKETING RESEARCH?

so, in fact, that the company has its own internal marketing research entity called Golf Digest Publications Research Resource Center. In operation for over 16 years, the Golf Digest Publications Research Resource Center has evolved into the only leading full-service golf marketing research department of its kind. Clients may be golf equipment manufacturers, other media, lodging and travel firms that cater to golfers, and so on. All these clients need more and better information about golf, the industry, and the golfers themselves.

What kinds of information would such a company provide? To get an idea and to better help you understand the role that marketing research plays, go to the website at www .researchresourcecenter.com and go to DOWNLOADS. Here you can read some of the reports written by this research firm. Take a look at the contents of some of the reports. Can you think of the kinds of decisions that may be facilitated by having access to this information?

The AMA definition expands on our definition by telling us that the information provided by marketing research for decision making should represent the consumer. In fact, by mentioning the consumer, this implies that marketing research is consistent with the marketing concept because it "links the consumer . . . to the marketer." The AMA definition is normative. That is, it tells us how marketing research should be used to ensure the firm is consumer-oriented. We certainly agree with this, but what should be done is not always followed. Clancy and Krieg, in their book *Counterintuitive Marketing: Achieve Great Results Using Uncommon Sense*, argue that many failures can be attributed to managers just making "intuitive" decisions.[12] These well-known authors implore managers to use research in order to make better decisions and make a good argument for studying marketing research. The AMA definition makes the point that marketing research links the firm to the consumer; we want to point out that marketing research information is also routinely collected on entities other than the consumer: members of distribution channels, employees, and all the environments, including competitors.[13] Of course, one could argue that the point of all this research is to do a better job of satisfying consumers.

Sometimes marketing research studies lead to the wrong decisions. We should point out here that just because a manager uses marketing research does not mean that the decisions based on the research are infallible. In fact, marketing research studies are not always accurate. There are plenty of examples in which research said a product would fail, yet when the product made it to market in spite of the prognosis, it turned out to be a resounding success.

Marketing research does not produce infallible results.

Stella Artois beer appealed primarily to people in urban areas. The company's ad agency developed an ad showing a peasant selling flowers in a rural setting. The ad was 60 seconds long, and marketing research results showed it to be a failure, citing below-average brand awareness and the fact that the ad positioned the beer away from the group to which it primarily appealed. Management at Stella Artois, however, believed that the ad was good and the marketing research was flawed. The ad was so successful it is credited with helping to turn the company's product from a niche beer to one of the top-selling grocery-store beer brands in the United Kingdom.[14]

One of the classic examples of a success that marketing research predicted would be a failure is Jerry Seinfeld's popular TV program *Seinfeld*. The marketing research that was conducted on the pilot for the Jerry Seinfeld TV show stated the show was so bad that executives gave up on the idea. It was 6 months before another manager questioned the accuracy of the research and resurrected the show, which became one of the most successful shows in television history.[15] Likewise, marketing research studies also predicted that hair styling mousse and answering machines would fail if brought to market.[16]

There are also plenty of failures in cases where marketing research predicted success. Most of these failures are removed from the shelves with as little fanfare as possible. When Duncan Hines introduced its line of soft cookies, marketing research studies showed that

80% of customers who tried Soft Batch® cookies stated they would buy them in the future. They didn't.[17] An ad prepared for Sainsbury's, the U.K. grocery chain, tested favorably in marketing research testing. However, the company received negative reactions from customers and staff alike when the ad ran. Sainsbury switched ad agencies.[18]

Many start-up retailers go out of business because of "flawed" research. GrandKids, a toy store targeting grandparents, failed. The owner relied on marketing research on local school data and statistics from a company soliciting advertising. Had she conducted better research, such as examining the most recent census data, she would have discovered that there were only 3,219 families in the whole town and those 50 and over made up only 31% of town residents. There simply were not enough grandparents to support her store.[19]

Another classic example of a failure when research predicted success was Beecham's cold-water-wash product Delicare. The new product failed even though marketing research predicted it would unseat the category leader, Woolite. This failure attracted a great deal of publicity because Beecham sued the research company that predicted success.[20]

These examples illustrate that marketing research is not infallible, but that does not mean marketing research is not useful. Remember, most marketing research studies are trying to understand and predict consumer behavior, and that is a difficult task. The fact that the marketing research industry has been around for many years and is growing means that it has passed the toughest of all tests to prove its worth—the test of the marketplace. If the industry did not provide value, it would cease to exist. And for each of the examples just cited, there are tens of thousands of success stories supporting the value of marketing research.

> Though marketing research takes on the difficult task of trying to predict consumer behavior—a daunting task indeed—it has passed the test of the marketplace and is viewed as valuable by many.

WHAT ARE THE USES OF MARKETING RESEARCH?

Identify Market Opportunities and Problems

> One use of marketing research is to identify opportunities and problems in the marketplace.

Now that you understand the purpose of marketing research, let's take a closer look at the *uses* of marketing research. In our short definition we simply refer to the use of marketing research to provide information to solve a specific marketing problem; the AMA definition spells out what some of these problems may be.

For example, the *identification of market opportunities and problems* is certainly a use of marketing research. Today many managers are asking "What opportunities are in the market?" When everyone saw the music industry facing a terrible decline due to pirating of songs on the Internet, Apple saw an opportunity for iTunes. iTunes has been an overwhelming success. NewProductWorks® has a proprietary approach to identifying viable opportunities. Importantly, NewProductWorks'® approach moves beyond today's market to help firms "See the Future" through this process. Likewise, a use of marketing research is to identify problems. We will learn more about this in Chapter 4.

> You can visit NewProductWorks®, the innovation resource center of GfK Strategic Innovation (formerly Arbor Strategy Group), at www.newproductworks .com.

OPPORTUNITY IDENTIFICATION. NewProductWorks® helps clients identify strategic opportunities using the following process:

New Opportunity Identification:

- Synthesis of Internal Client Research and Product Category Knowledge—Comprehensive Situation Analysis
- Qualitative Mining of Consumer Insights—how consumers see the market and how they "experience" products
- Future Innovations Analysis—what will consumers want in the future?
- Assessment of Emerging & Future Technologies
- Opportunity Definition—where is the future white space?

Once NewProductWorks® identifies opportunities and assesses them, they move to the ideation and concept development phase, resulting in innovation that is positioned against the highest potential opportunities.

Generate, Refine, and Evaluate Potential Marketing Actions

Marketing research can also be used to generate, refine, and evaluate a potential marketing action. When the marketing "action" was evaluating proposed ads, Wrangler conducted research to determine which of several magazine ads was best.

Marketing research may be used to generate, refine, and evaluate a potential marketing action.

When the marketing "action" was designing a better product, Kimberly-Clark researchers found that the most important criterion for feminine napkins is comfort. The company designed a new product based on this information.[21] Of course, firms are constantly trying to refine their marketing mix variables. As we've stated earlier, decision makers cannot become complacent about an existing strategy. The environment is constantly changing. A car manufacturer promoting large-sized vehicles will find it needs to adjust its actions as consumers shift toward vehicles that are more fuel efficient.

Monitor Marketing Performance

Many research dollars are spent by firms to just "see where we are." They not only want to know how they are doing but they also want information about their competitors. So, marketing research may be used to monitor marketing performance. After companies have implemented their marketing strategies, they want to monitor the effectiveness of their ads, salesforce, in-store promotions, dealer effectiveness, and competitors. Of course, companies also wish to monitor their sales and market shares. This is often done through what is called "tracking research." Tracking research is used to find out how well products of companies such as Hershey, Campbell's Soup, Kellogg, and Heinz are performing in the supermarkets. These "consumer packaged goods" firms want to monitor the sales of their brands and sales of their competitor's brands as well. Research firms such as The Nielsen Company and IRI are two of several companies measuring the performance of products in supermarkets and other retail outlets. They monitor how many units of these products are being sold, through which chains, at what retail price, and so on. You will learn more about tracking studies in Chapter 7.

Marketing research is used to "see where we and our competitors are."

Improve Marketing as a Process

The AMA definition says that a use of marketing research is to improve marketing as a process. To improve our understanding of the marketing process means that some marketing research is conducted to expand our basic knowledge of marketing. Typical of such research, which is often published in journals like the *Journal of Marketing Research* or *Marketing Research,* would be attempts to define and classify marketing phenomena and to develop theories that describe, explain, and predict marketing phenomena. Much of this research is conducted by marketing professors at colleges and universities and by other organizations, such as the *Marketing Science Institute*, and could be described as the only part of marketing research that is basic research. **Basic research** is conducted to expand our knowledge rather than to solve a specific problem. Research conducted to solve specific problems is called **applied research**, and this represents the vast majority of marketing research studies. We will revisit the idea that marketing research solves specific problems a little later in this chapter.

Studies that are designed to improve our basic understanding of marketing as opposed to solving a particular problem facing a business represent a very small part of all marketing research studies, but they are still an important form of marketing research

CLASSIFYING MARKETING RESEARCH STUDIES

Now you are making progress in learning about marketing research. Let us now examine a way of classifying the different types of marketing research studies being conducted in the industry. In Table 1.1, we organize the major types of studies under the usage categories in the AMA definition. Within each of these four categories we provide example studies.

TABLE 1.1   A Classification of Marketing Research Studies

A. Identifying Market Opportunities and Problems

As the title implies, the goal of these studies is to find opportunities or to identify problems with an existing strategy. Examples of such studies include the following:

Market-demand determination

Market-segments identification

Marketing audits SWOT analysis

Product/service-use studies

Environmental analysis studies

Competitive analysis

B. Generating, Refining, and Evaluating Potential Marketing Actions

Marketing research studies may be used to generate, refine, and then evaluate potential marketing actions. Marketing actions could be as broad as a proposed marketing strategy or as narrow as a tactic (a specific action taken to carry out a strategy). Typically, these studies deal with one or more of the marketing-mix variables (product, price, distribution, and promotion). Examples include the following:

Proposed marketing-mix evaluation testing

Concept tests of proposed new products or services

New-product prototype testing

Reformulating existing product testing

Pricing tests

Advertising pretesting

In-store promotion effectiveness studies

Distribution effectiveness studies

C. Monitoring Marketing Performance

These studies are control studies. They allow a firm that already has a marketing mix in place to evaluate how well that mix is performing. Examples include the following:

Image analysis

Tracking studies

Customer-satisfaction studies

Employee-satisfaction studies

Distributor-satisfaction studies

Website evaluations

D. Improving Marketing as a Process[a]

A small portion of marketing research is conducted to expand our knowledge of marketing as a process rather than to solve a specific problem facing a company. With the knowledge generated from these studies, managers may be in a much better position to solve a specific problem within their firms. This type of research is often conducted by institutes, such as the Marketing Science Institute, or universities. Examples include the following:

How can we better understand the "new media": blogs, social networking, mobile phones, etc.?

In the age of the "new media," what is the role of the "old media": radio, TV, print?

How can companies use consumers to help them create innovative new products and services?

What are new ways to study consumer behavior, for example, through the use of virtual/simulated shopping or ethnographic studies?

How can marketers better assess investments in marketing? How can they measure the impact of marketing strategies and tactics on ROI?

How do movie reviews, posted on the Internet, affect moviegoers?

[a]These study topics were taken from the Marketing Science Institute's research priorities list and former award-winning research papers. See www.msi.org for additional studies designed to improve marketing as a process.

THE MARKETING INFORMATION SYSTEM (MIS)

In order to stay abreast of competitive markets, firms must attempt to have the right information at the right time in the right format in the hands of those who must make decisions. We have learned that this is not an easy task. In fact, one author suggests that more than 25% of critical data within *Fortune* 1000 companies is inaccurate or incomplete.[22] To manage information properly, companies develop information systems. So far, we have presented marketing research as if it were the only source of information. This is not the case, as you will understand by reading this section on marketing information systems.

Marketing decision makers have a number of sources of information available to them. We can understand these different information sources by examining the components of the **marketing information system (MIS)**. An MIS is a structure consisting of people, equipment, and procedures to gather, sort, analyze, evaluate, and distribute needed, timely, and accurate information to marketing decision makers.[23] The role of the MIS is to determine decision makers' information needs, acquire the needed information, and distribute that information to the decision makers in a form and at a time when they can use it for decision making. However, this sounds very much like marketing research—providing information to aid in decision making. We can understand the distinction by understanding the components of a MIS.

Components of an MIS

As noted previously, the MIS is designed to assess managers' information needs, to gather this information, and to distribute the information to the marketing managers who need to make decisions. Information is gathered and analyzed by the four subsystems of the MIS: internal reports, marketing intelligence, marketing decision support, and marketing research. We discuss each of these subsystems next.

INTERNAL REPORTS SYSTEM. The **internal reports system** gathers information generated by internal reports, which include orders, billing, receivables, inventory levels, stockouts, and so on. In many cases, the internal reports system is called the "accounting information system." Although this system produces financial statements (balance sheets and income statements, etc.), it generally contains insufficient detail for many marketing decisions. But the internal reports system also provides a great deal of information on both revenues and costs that can be invaluable in making decisions. It also collects other information, such as inventory records, sales calls records, and orders. A good internal reports system can tell a manager a great deal about what has happened within the firm in the past. When information is needed from sources *outside* the firm, other MIS components must be called on.

MARKETING INTELLIGENCE SYSTEM. A second component of a MIS is the **marketing intelligence system**, defined as a set of procedures and sources used by managers to obtain everyday information about pertinent developments in the environment. Such systems include both informal and formal information-gathering procedures. Informal information-gathering procedures involve activities such as scanning newspapers, magazines, and trade publications. Formal information-gathering activities may be conducted by staff members who are assigned the specific task of looking for anything that seems pertinent to the company or industry. They then edit and disseminate this information to the appropriate staff or departments. Formerly known as "clipping bureaus" (because they clipped relevant newspaper articles for clients), several online information service companies, such as Lexis-Nexis, provide marketing intelligence. To use the Lexis-Nexis service, a firm would enter key terms into search forms provided online. Information containing the search terms appears on the subscriber's computer screen as often as several times a day. By clicking on an article title, subscribers can view a full-text version of the article. In this way, marketing intelligence goes on continuously and searches a broad range of information sources in order to bring pertinent information to decision makers.

 ### Create Your Own Intelligence System

As we just noted, firms have subscribed to information services such as Lexis-Nexis for many years in order to have access to possibly important information generated outside the firm. You can do the same thing through Google, which offers a service called "Google Alert" at no charge. If you go to Googlealerts.com, you will see that Google Alerts promotes itself as helping users locate sales leads, monitor competitors, or monitor what is being said about the company . . . to safeguard its reputation. You can sign up for a free trial. If you have a term paper to write or you want to get the latest news on a particular subject, daily e-mails will be delivered containing information based on the keywords you selected for your search. You can also see what professional accounts cost. Thanks to the information age, Google Alert represents an efficient way for even small firms to maintain their own intelligence system.

MARKETING DECISION SUPPORT SYSTEM (DSS). The third component of a MIS is the decision support system. A **marketing decision support system (DSS)** is defined as collected data that may be accessed and analyzed using tools and techniques that assist managers in decision making. The large amount of information companies collect is stored in huge databases that, when accessed with decision-making tools and techniques (for example, break-even analysis, regression models, and linear programming), allow companies to ask "what-if" questions. Answers to these questions are then immediately available for decision making.

> A DSS is collected data that may be accessed and analyzed using tools and techniques that assist managers in decision making.

MARKETING RESEARCH SYSTEM. Marketing research, which we have already discussed and defined, is the fourth component of a MIS. Now that you understand the three other components of a MIS, we are ready to discuss the question we raised at the beginning of this section: If marketing research and a MIS both are designed to provide information for decision makers, how do they differ? In answering this question, we will see how marketing research differs from the other three MIS components.

> We have already defined marketing research, but now we should ask, If marketing research and an MIS both are designed to provide information for decision makers, how do they differ?

First, the **marketing research system** gathers information not gathered by the other MIS component subsystems. Marketing research studies are conducted for a *specific* situation facing the company. It is unlikely that other components of a MIS have generated the particular information needed for the specific situation.

For example, GM is working on changes in the appearance of their new electric car, the Volt. From the several design options available, will GM be able to get information from their internal reports system that will indicate what today's new-car consumer will most prefer? No. Can GM get useful information from its intelligence system? No. Can the company get information from its DSS? You could argue that GM's DSS has stored past design preference data and that this information may be helpful. Yet, when you consider the change in the car-buying public due to a renewed enthusiasm for fuel efficiency, should GM rely on old design preferences data? GM will have to use marketing research to help it design the Volt for today's consumer. When *People* magazine wants to know which of three cover stories it should use for this week's publication, can its managers obtain that information from internal reports? No. From the intelligence system or the DSS? No.

This, then, is how marketing research plays a unique role in the total information system of the firm. By providing information on a specific problem at hand, marketing research is unique among other components of the MIS. This is why persons in the industry sometimes refer to marketing research studies as "ad hoc studies." *Ad hoc* is Latin meaning "with respect to a specific purpose." (Recall that earlier in the chapter when we defined marketing research, we told you we would revisit the word *specific*. Now you see why we used that word in our definition.)

There is another notable characteristic of marketing research that differentiates it from the other MIS components, although this difference isn't the reason marketing research belongs in the MIS. Marketing research projects, unlike the other components, are not continuous—they have a beginning and an end. This is why marketing research studies are sometimes referred to as "projects." The other components are available for use on an ongoing basis. However, marketing research projects are launched only when there is a justifiable need for information that is not available from internal reports, intelligence, or the DSS.

> By providing information on a specific problem at hand, marketing research is unique among other components of the MIS.

> Because marketing research studies are not continuous; they are often referred to as "projects."

BECOMING FAMILIAR WITH THIS BOOK

Before moving on, let's take a moment to help you better understand where you are headed. Chapter 1 was written to introduce you to marketing research. At this point, you understand how marketing research is a part of the marketing process and the role marketing research plays in providing managers with information to help them make more informed decisions. You also understand the unique role marketing research plays in a firm's marketing information system, MIS. You are ready to continue learning about marketing research. In the next chapter, we will introduce you to the 11-step marketing research process from which you will gain a better understanding of the process. You will see how marketing research begins and where it ends. The remainder of this book will give you an in-depth analysis of each of the 11 steps. But before we take you through the steps, we pause in Chapter 3 to give you a look at the industry of marketing research. You will learn about the industry structure (the types and sizes of firms) and the major issues facing the industry, including the ethical challenges. You will also learn much more about the Marketing Research Association's certification program, the PRC.

Summary

Marketing research is part of marketing. So, to understand marketing research, we must understand the role it plays in marketing. The American Marketing Association (AMA) defines marketing as an organizational function and a set of processes for creating, communicating, and delivering value to customers and for managing customer relationships in ways that benefit the organization and its stakeholders. Among the new frameworks for understanding marketing is the "service-dominant logic for marketing." But regardless of the framework used to understand marketing, marketers must "hear the voice of the consumer" to determine how to create, communicate, and deliver value that will result in long-lasting relationships with customers. Some firms "hear" the voice and have success; others do not and experience product and service failures. There are many examples of product

failure, including the Irridium telephone, Coca-Cola's Blak, and McDonald's MacLean burger. In all these cases, managers would have been better off with better information.

Our philosophies guide our day-to-day decisions. Marketers should follow the philosophy known as the marketing concept—also known as being "customer-oriented" or "market-driven." The marketing concept is a philosophy that states the key to business success lies in being more effective than competitors in creating, delivering, and communicating customer value to chosen target markets. Companies whose philosophy focuses on products and selling efforts do not tend to stay around long. If a firm's management follows the marketing concept, it develops the "right" strategies, or plans, to provide consumers with value. The significance of all this is that in order to practice marketing as we have described it, managers need information in order to determine wants and needs and to design marketing strategies that will satisfy customers in selected target markets. Furthermore, environmental changes mean that marketers must constantly collect information to monitor customers, markets, and competition.

One definition of marketing research is that it is the process of designing, gathering, analyzing, and reporting information that may be used to solve a specific problem. The AMA defines marketing research as the function that links the consumer, customer, and public to the marketer through information—information used to identify and define marketing opportunities and problems; generate, refine, and evaluate marketing actions; monitor marketing performance; and improve the understanding of marketing as a process. *Market* research is different from *marketing* research. Market research is a subset of marketing research and refers to applying marketing research to a specific geographical area, or market.

To link the consumer to the marketer by providing information that can be used in making marketing decisions is the purpose of marketing research. Not all firms use marketing research, and sometimes marketing research leads to the wrong decisions. The producers of the very successful TV program *Seinfeld* were advised by marketing researchers not to air the show. But, marketing research has been around for many years and is growing—it has passed the "test of the marketplace."

The uses of marketing research are to (1) identify and define marketing opportunities and problems; (2) generate, refine, and evaluate marketing actions; (3) monitor marketing performance; and (4) improve our understanding of marketing. Most marketing research is considered to be applied research, in that it is conducted to solve specific problems. A limited number of marketing research studies are considered basic research, in that they are conducted to expand the limits of our knowledge. The four broad types of marketing research studies are (a) identifying market opportunities and problems (e.g., market demand determination studies); (b) generating, refining, and evaluating potential marketing actions (e.g., advertising pretesting); (c) monitoring marketing performance (e.g., tracking studies); and (d) improving marketing as a process (e.g., studies conducted by marketing professors that lead to better understanding marketing phenomena in general as opposed to a particular problem facing a company).

If marketing research provides information with which to make marketing decisions, why should we also have a marketing information system (MIS)? Actually, marketing research is one of the four subsystems making up a MIS. Other subsystems include internal reports, marketing intelligence, and decision support systems. Marketing research gathers information not available through the other subsystems and provides information for the specific problem at hand. Marketing research is conducted on a project basis having a beginning and an end, whereas the other MIS components operate continuously, 24/7.

Key Terms

Marketing 5
Marketing concept 8
Marketing strategy 9
Marketing research 9
Market research 10

Purpose of marketing research 10
Basic research 13
Applied research 13
Marketing information system 15
Internal reports system 15

Marketing intelligence system 15
Marketing decision support system (DSS) 16
Marketing research system 16

Review Questions/Applications

1. What are some examples of professional organizations in the marketing research field?
2. What is marketing? Explain the role of marketing research in the process of marketing management.
3. Give some examples of products that have failed.
4. Why are philosophies important to decision makers? What is the marketing concept?
5. What is strategy, and why is marketing research important to planners of strategy?
6. Define marketing research. Define market research.

7. What is the purpose of marketing research?
8. Name the uses of marketing research.
9. Which use of marketing research is considered basic research?
10. Give two examples of the types of studies in each of the four classes of marketing research studies provided in this chapter.
11. Distinguish among MIS (marketing information system), marketing research, and DSS (decision support system).
12. Explain why the phrase "specific problem" is important to the definition of marketing research and how this phrase relates to justifying the existence of marketing research in the MIS.
13. Go to your library, either in person or online, and look through several business periodicals such as *Advertising Age, Business Week, Fortune,* and *Forbes.* Find three examples of companies using marketing research.
14. Select a company in a field in which you have a career interest and look up information on this firm in your library or on the Internet. After gaining some knowledge of this company and its products and services, customers, and competitors, list five different types of decisions that you believe this company's management may have made within the past two years. For each decision, list the information the company's executives would have needed in order to make these decisions.
15. Think of the following situations. What component of the marketing information system would a manager use to find the necessary information?
    a. A manager of an electric utilities firm hears a friend at lunch talk about a new breakthrough in solar panel technology she read about in a science publication.
    b. A manager wants to know how many units of three different products the company sold during each month for the past three years.
    c. A manager wants to estimate the contribution to company return on investment earned by ten different products in the company product line.
    d. A manager is considering producing a totally new type of health food. But he would like to know if consumers are likely to purchase the new food, at which meal they would most likely eat the food, and how they would prefer the food to be packaged.
16. Assume you are the manager of a successful marketing research company located in Southern California. Discuss different types of research studies you could conduct for your clients.

CASE 1.1

MARKETING RESEARCH AND THE MOVIE INDUSTRY: STARLIGHT FILMS

There are many factors that go into making a great movie. Good scripts, directors, producers, actors, and all the support staff are fundamental to making a good movie. But for many years movies have been improved by using marketing research to gather consumer reactions. Two of the earliest users of marketing research, though primitive, were Carl Laemmie and Adolph Zukor. In the early 1900s small, neighborhood theaters, called Nickelodeons, showed films of the day; admission was a nickel. Laemmie observed audience and sales data for Hale's Tours in Chicago. He made notes on what types of people saw the films and determined the most popular hours of the day. Zukor, a Nickelodeon operator in New York, watched audience faces to see their reactions to different parts of the films and claimed he learned "feel" reactions of laughter, pleasure, and boredom. Both Laemmie and Zukor must have learned something. They created the two companies Universal and Zukor Paramount—both large motion picture giants even today.

Over the years marketing research has increasingly played a role in the making of movies. When marketing research, conducted by the Gallup organization, predicted a huge market success for the movie *Gone With the Wind*, MGM decided to price the movie between $.75 and $2.20 when the average movie ticket of the day was about $.25! This resulted in huge profits, as the Gallup predictions turned out to be correct. Marketing research has continued to be used to determine if scripts are profitable, to rate the market attractiveness of the actors and actresses, to profile the movie-going market segments, to determine the effectiveness of the advertising for the movies, and to determine which type of movie ending the audience most prefers.[24]

Daniel Lee Yarbrough is a director and producer with Starlight Films in San Francisco. As part of his normal duties as a director and producer, Daniel constantly seeks scripts that he can turn into successful movies. The movie business is strongly driven by profits. Although a few films are made for their artistic value alone, the cost of movie making is so huge today that few firms can afford to make movies that do not earn a respectable ROI for their investors. Yarbrough knows he must make "good" decisions, those that will result in a film that will attract sufficient audience numbers to earn a good return.

Yarbrough has recently received a manuscript by a successful author, Warren St. John. St. John wrote the highly successful book *Rammer Jammer Yellow Hammer* (a book about football fans following their team in RVs). Recently, St. John turned out another manuscript about a boy's soccer team that gained Yarbrough's interest. As he reads through the manuscript, Yarbrough begins thinking about decisions he will need to make if he wants to turn the manuscript into a movie.

How much should he offer St. John for the manuscript rights? Yarbrough knows the manuscript is very good and he assumes other film companies are going to make offers. While he has paid for manuscripts in the past, it has been about three years since he was actively involved in bidding for an author's script. Though the amount paid the author will be a small part of the total cost of the movie, it could still be a significant amount of money.

Casting decisions must be made early because they could greatly influence costs. Who should play the lead roles? Supporting roles? As always, there is a plentiful stock of talented, yet unknown, actors available. On the other hand, there are "hot" actors who are very popular and draw audiences just due to name recognition.

Yarbrough's filmmaking experience allows him to adequately predict many of his costs. He knows, for example, what it takes to film on location versus in a studio. He also knows the costs of equipment and costs of various personnel, such as cameramen, grips, and copyeditors. However, of all the issues facing Daniel Yarbrough, the most important one will be how many people will buy a ticket to see this movie? Emmy's are great, but to make the needed ROI, Yarbrough knows he needs people to go to movie theaters to see his movies. Of course, although this number can be estimated, no one can assure the director of the exact number. But he can get some good estimates on whether samples of an audience like the script.

1. Do you think Daniel Yarbrough needs to conduct some research? Why, or why not?
2. Just based on the case material alone, list decisions that Yarbrough needs to make.
3. For each decision you list in question 2, provide a description of the information you think Yarbrough needs in order to make the decision.

CASE 1.2 **Your Integrated Case**

ADVANCED AUTOMOBILE CONCEPTS

Nick Thomas is a CEO of Advanced Automobile Concepts (AAC), a new division of a large automobile manufacturer, ZEN Motors. ZEN is a multinational manufacturer headquartered in the United States and has multiple divisions representing several auto and truck brands. ZEN's divisions have been slowly losing market share to other competitors. AAC was created to revive the aging ZEN automobile brands by either reengineering existing models or developing totally new models that are more in tune with today's changing automobile market.

Nick is very familiar with the automobile industry; his entire adult life has been spent in the automobile business. He follows trade publications carefully and believes ZEN's most significant losses are due to the growing popularity of several foreign brands, particularly brands from Japan and Korea. As CEO of ACC, Nick has been given the authority to do what he believes is needed to revive the company's brands and help return ZEN to prominence in automobile manufacturing. Nick has retrieved company sales data for all ZEN models for the last decade from ZEN's Internal Reports System, part of ZEN's MIS. He has accessed the Intelligence System to obtain trade industry articles written about the market, including evaluations of many of the top competitors' models.

He notices that several highly evaluated models are small and fuel efficient. He also has recognized that foreign competition has severely eroded the market share of ZEN's only large, luxury car brand. ZEN's brand has been around for many years and just can't seem to compete with the newer luxury car models on the market. but ZEN has been reluctant to move into the very small and highly fuel-efficient market for a couple of reasons. First, historically, ZEN has earned higher profits on larger vehicles. Every ZEN division has a large and extra-large SUV model. Historically, these SUV models, ZEN's large trucks, and its larger, family cars have been very profitable. Secondly, as sales have eroded in recent years, ZEN has been reluctant to invest the funds needed to develop designs radically different from those models that have been its "bread and butter" for decades. However, in recent months, ZEN's sales have plummeted as fuel prices have soared. ZEN management realizes it must innovate and that is why it created the AAC division.

Nick Thomas realizes that he must come up with some innovations in automobile design and engineering, but he is not certain in which direction he should guide his division. He realizes that, for now, oil prices are high and understands the increases in sales of fuel-efficient gasoline, diesel and electric hybrids. However, Nick has seen these environmental changes come and go. He tells some of his younger VPs, "I've seen these fuel crises come and go. When the crises are over, the car-buying public wants big vehicles and we have earned our standing in the industry by giving the market what they wanted." Nick wonders to himself if this oil crisis is here to stay. He has also been concerned about the prospects of real global warming. He's read the reports on climate change and is confused. He doesn't know whether to believe Al Gore or Rush Limbaugh. Nick also isn't certain about the future of alternative fuels. Will the U.S. government really encourage reducing the country's dependence on foreign energy? He vividly recalls this being an issue in the 1970s and President Carter calling for a switch to alternative fuels. He also knows that the country didn't follow through on this at the time. Nick wonders if today's promises by politicians of reducing dependence on foreign energy will be forgotten just as it was in the past. Nick is not sure what will happen, but he knows that continued high prices for fuel and increasing evidence of global warming will affect consumer behavior with regard to automobiles.

1. Should Nick Thomas use marketing research?
2. What components of ZEN's MIS will Nick Thomas need?

Explaining the Marketing Research Process

Learning Objectives

- To gain insights into marketing research by learning the steps in the marketing research process
- To understand the caveats associated with "a process"
- To know when marketing research may be needed and when it may not be needed
- To know which step is the most important in the marketing research process
- To have a framework for understanding the topics to be covered in the rest of this book

Where We Are

1 Establish the need for marketing research
2 Define the problem
3 Establish research objectives
4 Determine research design
5 Identify information types and sources
6 Determine methods of accessing data
7 Design data-collection forms
8 Determine the sample plan and size
9 Collect data
10 Analyze data, and
11 Prepare and present the final research report.

Marketing Research Practitioners View Marketing Research as a Process

Colleen Moore-Mezler, PRC and President, Moore Research Services, Inc.

I n this chapter you will learn how to look at the marketing research process in the form of a series of steps. Marketing research is fascinating and complex. Here at Moore Research, we deal with different types of problems, varying client industries, changes in our clients' markets as their customers and competition adjust to seemingly constant environmental changes. To help us deal with this complexity, researchers have a stabilizing framework upon which we rely to help us sort out each client situation. We do not all share the same framework, but many of us agree that there is great value in viewing marketing research as a series of steps making up the process. Some of us define the steps differently and some use fewer or more steps, but there is value in having this framework to help us conceptualize a path to obtaining the right information to solve a client's problem. For example, from having knowledge of this framework, I know that we will have to spend several hours visiting with a client to ensure that we properly define the client's problem and the research objectives for the project. If we know that the project entails collecting primary data, we know the general steps we will need to follow and this knowledge gives us a basis for planning the project. Without that general framework, coping with each client's situation would be much more difficult. In this chapter, Burns and Bush will present you with an 11-step process to help you develop a framework that will allow you to better understand marketing research. When you finish this chapter, you will have a better understanding of marketing research. In addition, the 11 steps you will learn here will serve you well as a framework for the entire book.

—*Colleen Moore-Mezler, PRC and President Moore Research Services, Inc.*

Visit Moore Research at http://moore-research.com/

Colleen Moore-Mezler's comments illustrate the importance of knowing the steps necessary to carry out a marketing research project. Just by having this "framework" of the process, Ms. Moore-Mezler is aided in her research planning by knowing the steps she will need to use in the proposed research project for her clients. Knowledge of these steps serves as a "road map" for planning, and marketing researchers are familiar with them. In this chapter, we will introduce you to these important steps, and they will serve as a framework for the rest of this book.

THE MARKETING RESEARCH PROCESS

The Process: 11 Steps

Chapter 1 taught you what marketing research is and the role it plays in aiding managers in making marketing decisions. You are now ready to learn the steps in the marketing research process. There is value in characterizing research projects in terms of successive steps. First, the steps give researchers and nonresearchers an overview of the entire process. Second, they provide a procedure, in the sense that a researcher, by referring to the steps, knows what tasks to consider and in what order. By introducing you to these steps, we are also giving you a preview of what is in store for you as you read this book. We identify the **11 steps in the marketing research process** in Figure 2.1.[1] The steps are (1) establish the need for marketing research, (2) define the problem, (3) establish research objectives, (4) determine research design, (5) identify information types and sources,

FIGURE 2.1

11 Steps in the Marketing Reearch Process

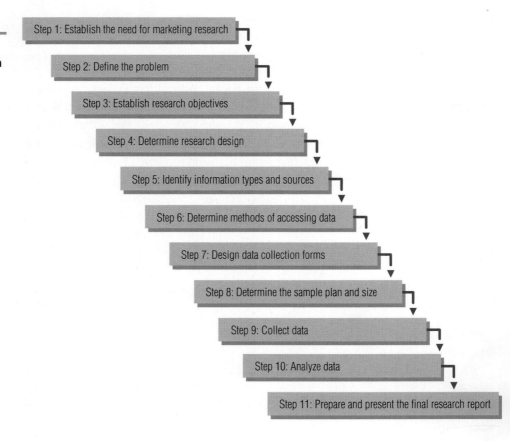

Step 1: Establish the need for marketing research

Step 2: Define the problem

Step 3: Establish research objectives

Step 4: Determine research design

Step 5: Identify information types and sources

Step 6: Determine methods of accessing data

Step 7: Design data collection forms

Step 8: Determine the sample plan and size

Step 9: Collect data

Step 10: Analyze data

Step 11: Prepare and present the final research report

(6) determine methods of accessing data, (7) design data-collection forms, (8) determine the sample plan and size, (9) collect data, (10) analyze data, and (11) prepare and present the final research report. We will discuss each of these steps in the following paragraphs, but first, you need to understand some cautions associated with using a step-by-step approach to understanding the process of marketing research.

Step-by-Step Process: Some Words of Caution

WHY 11 STEPS? You should know that not everyone presents the research process in the same way we have presented it here. First, although we conceptualize the research process in 11 steps, others may describe it in fewer steps or more steps. There is nothing sacred about 11 steps. We could, for example, present research in three steps: defining the problem, collecting and analyzing data, and presenting the results. We think this oversimplifies the process. Or, we could present you with 20-plus steps. In our opinion, this would provide more detail than is needed. We think that 11 steps are explicit enough without being overly detailed.

NOT ALL STUDIES USE ALL 11 STEPS. A second caution is that not every study requires all 11 steps. Sometimes, for example, just a review of secondary research may allow the researcher to achieve the research objectives. Our 11 steps assume that the research process examines secondary data and continues on to collect primary data.

STEPS ARE NOT ALWAYS FOLLOWED IN ORDER. Finally, our third caution is that most research projects do not follow an orderly, step-by-step process. In fact, while it is hard to understand at this point, the steps are interrelated. Sometimes, after beginning to gather data, the researcher may determine that the research objectives should be changed. Researchers do not move, robotlike, from one step to the next. Rather, as they move through the process, they make decisions as to how to proceed in the future, which may involve going back and revisiting a previous step.

Introducing "Where We Are"

You have already learned that knowing the steps in the process provides you with a framework to better understand marketing research. Colleen Moore-Mezler stated that her knowledge of these steps helps marketing researchers at Moore Research deal with the complex issues that arise. As you go through this course and this textbook, you will encounter many of those same issues. To provide you with an aid for dealing with the rest of the course material, we introduce, starting with Chapter 4, a new section at the beginning of every chapter, called "Where We Are." This feature lists the 11 marketing research steps and highlights the step presented in the chapter you are reading. So as you immerse yourself in the necessary details of marketing research, "Where We Are" will be there to show you where the material you are reading fits into the overall framework. Now, let's take a look at our first step!

At the beginning of every chapter, starting with Chapter 4, "Where We Are" will list the 11 steps and highlight the step presented in the chapter you are reading.

Step 1: Establish the Need for Marketing Research

The need for marketing research arises when managers must make decisions but have inadequate information. Fortunately, because research takes time and costs money, not all decisions will require marketing research. If they did, managers would be mired down in research instead of making timely decisions. Managers must weigh the value that may possibly be derived from conducting research and having the information at hand against the cost of obtaining that information.

Company Policy Regarding the Use of Marketing Research

Company policy toward marketing research and the role management wishes marketing research to play in the organization affects whether and how much research is conducted. For example, some managers simply do not believe in investing time and money in research and have a no-research policy. In these firms, top management believes managers are "paid to make decisions." As we already learned in Chapter 1, however, many product failures could have been avoided had the managers in charge been armed with better information. Even the best decision makers cannot make good decisions without good information. To rely solely on intuition in today's complex and rapidly changing marketplace is risky business.

Other firms use marketing research but make choices as to how much and how often marketing research will use it. For example, some firms have a policy of conducting different types of studies on a continuous basis at specified intervals. Policy may dictate, for example, that brand awareness studies of the company's brands be conducted each year. Other types of periodic studies may include customer-satisfaction studies and tracking studies of the company's brands and competitors' brands. The advantage of conducting these types of studies periodically is that they give management a method of monitoring company performance so problems can be spotted early. Management may also decide to use certain types of studies whenever a particular situation occurs. For example, when new products or services are being considered, a concept test may be conducted very early on in the company's new-product development process. Consumer use tests—conducted to observe how consumers are actually using a product—may be required once a new product concept makes it through prototype development.

Other firms may elect to conduct marketing research on an "as-needed" basis. Here, although marketing research is regarded as a useful tool, expenditures are made only when management feels the situation requires additional information. Remember, as we discussed in Chapter 1, an MIS can supply much information to management, and sometimes this information is sufficient for managers to make decisions. Coca-Cola®, for example, has information in its DSS that allows the company to predict changes in sales of soft drinks if ingredients such as carbonation or sweeteners are increased or decreased by some percentage. (The following section has more on this topic.)

Company policy regarding marketing research may also show a preference for a *type* of research. Some managers use focus groups extensively; others only rely on quantitative studies based upon large samples. Many packaged goods firms (primarily those products you see in supermarkets) make heavy use of tracking studies. They rely on data from these studies to estimate market share and as feedback on how well their strategies and tactics are working.

William D. Neal, of SDR Consulting, has suggested two broad uses of marketing research. One type of research is conducted to gather information about markets. This information is used primarily at the marketing department level to plan and assess marketing strategy. Tracking studies conducted by large firms, for example, supply this type of information. They routinely collect huge amounts of data showing sales per sku (stock keeping unit) in grocery stores, c-stores (convenience), and drug stores. Neal referred to this type of research as market research that reflected marketplace activity. Neal points out, however, that marketing research is needed at a higher level in the firm to aid top management in strategic planning. This type of research should gather information that would help managers determine the company mission, objectives and goals, growth strategy, and the business portfolio plan by providing analysis that is more focused on strategic issues: market segmentation, strategic positioning, new-product development, market forecasting, and brand value analysis.[2] Company policy toward research will determine which type (or whether both types) of research is used.

Even firms that have a proactive policy regarding marketing research sometimes determine that marketing research is not appropriate. The following section describes circumstances for which research is not needed.

When Is Marketing Research Not Needed?

THE INFORMATION IS ALREADY AVAILABLE. Many of the decisions managers make are routine and they have the experience to make the decision without any additional information. When decisions do require additional information, the manager may make use of other components of the MIS. Can the required information be obtained from the internal reports system? From the marketing intelligence system? From the decision support system? All of these systems represent ongoing sources of information, and marketing managers can access them quickly and inexpensively (low variable cost). We earlier referred to Coca-Cola's extensive database in its DSS. Any large soft-drink firm will have the data about sales levels of its different soft drinks, which will indicate what sales will be for a new soft drink with, say, 50% more caffeine than a current drink. When information is *not* available, a company should consider conducting marketing research. Marketing Research Insight 2.1 gives some examples of firms that already have the information they need to make decisions.

THE TIMING IS WRONG TO CONDUCT MARKETING RESEARCH. Often, when managers decide they need marketing research, time is critical and thus often plays a role in making the decision to use marketing research. Even though online research has sped up the process considerably, there may be simply not enough time to do it. As an example, let's just assume there are several new automobile entries in the small hybrid market. If one firm has runaway sales and has the only vehicle with a small, efficient, diesel auxiliary engine, other firms should consider moving immediately toward introducing a hybrid with a similar diesel engine. Sometimes the market is so strong, you don't need marketing research to clearly see the direction the market is headed. When Toyota introduced the Prius, it quickly became the most popular model, attracting half the market share for hybrids. Note that this doesn't happen too often: Different market segments have different wants and needs, creating subtleties in the market.

Time may also be a factor for products that are nearing the end of their life cycle. When products have been around for many years and are reaching the decline stage of their life cycle, it may be too late for research to produce valuable results.

Knowledge of the steps involved in the marketing research process serves a researcher in helping to determine how long a research project will take. As we've just mentioned, time is often critical. In the decision whether or not to conduct marketing research, a researcher's knowledge of how long it will take to perform the necessary steps should be factored in.

FUNDS ARE NOT AVAILABLE FOR MARKETING RESEARCH. The end of 2008 ushered in a new era of frugality. In many cases, firms are cutting marketing research expenditures. Small firms or firms that are having cash flow problems may not conduct marketing research simply because they cannot afford it. If conducted properly, research can be expensive: A study gathering primary data for a representative sample can cost hundreds of thousands of dollars. Also, the total cost of research is often not fully appreciated. Conducting the research is only part of the cost; for it to be useful, firms must also consider what the cost may be to *implement* the research recommendations. The owner of a pizza restaurant, for example, saved money for a research project but was then unable to fund

Company policy will dictate the use of marketing research in a firm. Some firms do not use marketing research. Others use marketing research only on an "as-needed" basis. Firms can also conduct marketing research studies at regular intervals and for certain activities, such as new-product development, assessing advertising effectiveness, or managing dealer relationships.

If the market reacts very strongly to a competitor's offering, there simply isn't time to conduct a marketing research project.

Small firms or firms having cash flow problems may not conduct marketing research simply because they cannot afford it.

MARKETING RESEARCH INSIGHT   Practical Application

2.1 Do Not Conduct Research If The Information Is Already Available

Marketing researchers John Goodman and David Beinhacker point out that many times companies execute surveys and collect data when they already have the information and that clients can save money by not doing research to measure variables that are known to be stable and when performance is high.[3] Goodman and Beinhacker also state that firms should not conduct marketing research when internal metrics are already available.

In one financial services firm, management had commissioned research to measure customer satisfaction and quality. Over a period of time, the company had developed and was administering 80 different surveys covering all of the possible customer transactions in the firm. However, upon examination, data showed that in about 30 of the 80 transactions customer expectations were being met from 98 to 99.5% of the time. Should the company be using marketing research to measure transactions in which it is consistently near-perfect? Goodman and Beinhacker concluded that relying on a traditional complaint system would be a wiser method to monitor these transactions.

Goodman and Beinhacker also tell the story of a major home repair services company that was spending large amounts on surveying customers to determine whether the repairman showed up on time. However, the company's call center already had data that tracked how many times customers were calling to complain about repairmen who were either late or didn't show up at all. For a high-involvement event like having someone in one's home, the authors reported that 90% of consumers will call when the repairman is late. So, they ask, why conduct marketing research to collect data when you already have the information needed to make the decision? In another example, a bank was surveying

Departments within a company often act as "silos," not sharing information with other departments.

customers about their satisfaction with the readiness of ATMs, since all ATMs must have some "down time" for maintenance, repair, and daily reloading of cash. But the bank already had internal metrics showing how often the ATMs were down, with data accurate to four decimal places.

Goodman and Beinhacker recommend if eight of ten transactions are being executed with little or no error, research should not be conducted on all ten transaction types. The focus should be on those that are done poorly. For example, Neiman Marcus Direct has a good reputation for handling telephone customer service. However, management identified two types of transactions that caused problems. Therefore, surveys of customers focus on these two transactions, enabling Neiman to continuously monitor and improve these trouble spots. Firms should also make certain they don't already have the data before they undertake to collect more of the same. The researchers, Goodman and Beinhacker, point out that they find many departments operate in silos; other departments in the same company already have internal metrics that will provide the information needed to make an informed decision.

any of the recommendations (should he offer drive-through and delivery service?). In this case, the research money was wasted.

COSTS OUTWEIGH THE VALUE OF MARKETING RESEARCH. Managers should always consider the cost of research and the value they expect to receive from conducting it. Although costs can be readily estimated, it is much more difficult to estimate the value that research is likely to add. As an example, consider a decision as to how best to package a new brand of toothpaste. Research on the packaging required to send a few sample boxes to a new-products trade show would certainly not be warranted; the packaging needs only to ensure safe transit. If the packaging fails, little is lost and recovery is simple. However, what about the packaging of the toothpaste itself? The toothpaste must sit on a shelf among many other brands, many of which have packaging that is easily recognized by brand-loyal customers. Chances are, a consumer quickly scanning the toothpaste section will see a favorite brand and make the purchase without even becoming aware of the new brand. If research can identify a package design that will draw greater attention and promote awareness of the brand on the shelf, sales will go up. This gives the research value. How much value? Managers must try to estimate what the impact will be on sales if 2 out of 10 shoppers are aware of the brand instead of 1 out of 20. Although placing a dollar figure on value is difficult, value *can* be estimated and a more informed decision be made justifying or not justifying marketing research. Some managers fail to compare research cost with its value, which is a mistake.[4]

When Will Research Be More Likely to Have Greater Value?   Some guidelines for answering this question are: Will the research help clarify problems or opportunities? Will research identify changes that are occurring in the marketplace among consumers and/or competitors? Will research clearly identify the best alternative to pursue among a set of proposed alternatives? Will the research help your brand establish a competitive advantage?[5] Once a decision is made that research is needed, managers (and researchers) must properly define the problem and the research objectives.

Step 2: Define the Problem

After a decision is reached to conduct marketing research, the second step is to define the problem. This is the most important step, because if the problem is incorrectly defined, all else is wasted effort. For this reason, clients and researchers must give high importance to properly defining the problem.

   To better understand the problem, consider the following questions: "Which of three proposed TV advertising commercials will generate the highest level of sales of our line of cookies?" "Which media, or combination of media, should we use to promote our line of cookies?" "What message should we use in our promotions to gain sales for our line of cookies?" "What should be our overall marketing strategy for our line of cookies?" "Should we be in the cookie business?" As you can see, problems may vary considerably from being specific and narrowly focused (e.g., Which of three TV ads should we use?) to being very general and not narrowly focused (e.g., Should we even be in the cookie business?).

Marketing research that can help a product get attention on supermarket shelves has value.

Defining the problem, though important, is often difficult. (We cover this step in detail in Chapter 4, which describes an overall process to follow.) Problems stem from two primary sources: gaps between what is *supposed* to happen and what *did* happen, and gaps between what *did* happen and what *could* have happened. When we have a gap between what is supposed to happen and what did happen, we normally refer to this as "failure to meet our objective." If our quarterly sales quota is 250 cars sold and we've sold only 98, we have a problem stemming from "failure to meet our objective." This is how we normally think of "problems." However, consider our second gap; a gap between what did happen and what could have happened. Imagine a recent scientific breakthrough that allows the manufacture of a hydrogen fuel cell that is small, extremely safe, and relatively inexpensive. Now we have a problem of a different sort. Should we try to take advantage of this new opportunity? What *could* our sales be if we did? We normally refer to this type of gap as an opportunity. What is important, in either case, is to realize we have a problem and will likely need information to help us make the right decisions to solve those problems.

A technician tinkers with a cutaway of a BMW hydrogen automobile engine. Will a new type of hydrogen engine be the "opportunity" for tomorrow's automobiles?

Problems stem from "failure to meet objectives" and "failure to take advantage of opportunities."

Step 3: Establish Research Objectives

Research objectives, although related to and determined by the problem definition, are set so that when achieved, they provide the information necessary to solve the problem. Let's consider the following example. Independent insurance agents typically belong to a state association called something like "Independent Insurance Agents of Iowa." The association is responsible for educational programs, lobbying state insurance boards, and technical advice. If the association were concerned with responding to the needs of its members, it would be reasonable for problems to be defined by these questions: (1) "Are the association's services valued by the members," and (2) "Which services should be changed?"

A good way of setting research objectives is to ask, "What information is needed in order to solve the problems?" Because the association's services are in place, the research objectives would translate as follows:

Determine the average importance level of each service.

Determine the average level of satisfaction for each service.

You should notice that these research objectives are different from the defined problems. Yet, the information gathered as a result of carrying out these research objectives solves the problems. Research objectives state what the researchers must do in order to provide the information necessary to solve the problem. By collecting the information requested by the first two research objectives, the association is in a position to rank its services based on how important they are to members, and it can identify which highly important services have low satisfaction levels and need revision. Alternatively, the association can identify services that should not be revised, that is, those receiving high satisfaction and regarded as highly important services.

Research objectives spell out exactly what information is to be collected, in what format, by what method, and from whom. Research objectives tell the researchers exactly what they must do.

Research objectives must be very detailed and specific. They spell out exactly what information should be collected, in what format, by what method, and from whom. Again, research objectives tell the researchers exactly what they must do. We will discuss research objectives in Chapter 4.

Step 4: Determine Research Design

Almost every research project is different, but they have enough similarities to enable us to categorize them by the methods and procedures used to collect and analyze data. The three categories, referred to as research designs, are (1) exploratory research, (2) descriptive research, and (3) causal research.

Exploratory research is the collection of information in an unstructured and informal manner. It is often used when little is known about a problem. Analyzing secondary data in a library or over the Internet is one of the most common ways of conducting exploratory research. An executive reading about demographic trends forecast for the next five years in *American Demographics* is conducting exploratory research, as is a manager observing the lines of customers awaiting service at a bank.

In marketing research, there are two categories: quantitative and qualitative. Quantitative research is characterized by data sets containing precise measurements of variables thought to be important to the study at hand. Analysis is often reported in terms of tests of statistical significance. Quantitative research is, as the name implies, driven by numbers. On the other hand, qualitative research is not characterized by numerical analysis, but is often used to explore; to learn more about the problem at hand. When you don't know enough about the problem to know what variables to measure, you shouldn't be using quantitative research. Qualitative research, then, is closely related to exploratory research. Exploratory research uses focus groups; one-on-one, in-depth, personal interviews; projective techniques; and other methods. We will learn more about these methods in Chapter 8, "Observation, Focus Groups, and Other Qualitative Methods."

Descriptive research designs incorporate a set of methods and procedures that describe marketing variables. Descriptive studies investigate these variables by answering who, what, where, when, and how questions. (They do not, however, answer why questions. This is done by causal research designs.) These types of research studies may describe such things as consumers' attitudes, intentions, and behaviors or the number of competitors and their strategies. Although most descriptive studies are done through surveys in which respondents are asked questions, sometimes descriptive studies are observational. They observe and record consumers' behavior in such a way as to answer the problem. When Bissell Inc. conducted marketing research on the Steam Gun, an elongated cleaning device that used steam to remove stubborn dirt, the company gave the product to families and then observed them using the product in their homes. In addition to learning that the name needed to be changed, the company learned several other important lessons that led to the successful marketing of the Steam N Clean.[6]

The final research design, **causal research**, isolates causes and effects. It answers the question of why? We call causal research designs **experiments**. Some researchers conducted an experiment on the effects of Yellow Pages ads that allowed them to conclude color is better than black and white and photos are better than line art at causing more favorable customer attitudes and perceptions of quality and credibility. The experiments also showed that these relationships varied across product categories.[7] This is powerful information to companies that spend huge sums of money on Yellow Pages ads each year. We discuss causal designs in Chapter 5.

Step 5: Identify Information Types and Sources

In order for research to provide information that helps solve problems, researchers must identify the type and sources of information they will use in Step 5. There are two types of information: **primary information** (information collected specifically for the problem at hand) and **secondary information** (information already collected). Secondary information should always be sought first since it is much cheaper and faster to collect than primary information. A company franchising car washes, for example, may use secondary data to make decisions about where to locate new car washes based on the number of vehicles per square mile and the number of existing car washes in different market areas. This is information that has been collected and is available in published sources, sometimes for a small fee. Sometimes research companies collect information and make it available to all

In marketing research, there are two categories: quantitative and qualitative.

Qualitative research is closely related to exploratory research. Exploratory research uses focus groups; one-on-one, in-depth, personal interviews; projective techniques; and other methods.

Descriptive research studies describe marketing variables such as consumers' attitudes, intentions, and behaviors or the number of competitors and their strategies.

Unlike exploratory and descriptive designs, causal research designs allow us to isolate causes and effects. Causal studies are called experiments.

Primary information is collected specifically for the problem at hand. Secondary information has already been collected by others but may be used for the problem at hand.

those wishing to pay a subscription to get the information—referred to as syndicated data. Nielsen Media Research's TV Ratings reports the numbers of persons who watch different TV programs. We discuss both types of secondary information in Chapters 6 and 7.

Sometimes, however, secondary data are inadequate. What if our car-wash franchiser wanted to know how car owners in Austin, Texas, would respond to a one-price ticket good for as many car washes as needed in a year? This information is not available. What if a particular college wanted to know what its own students felt about a proposed program? Primary data must be collected specifically for these problems. Beginning with Chapter 8, the rest of this book teaches you how to gather, analyze, and report primary data.

 ### Access Secondary Data at the Bureau of the Census

There is an amazing amount of secondary data available to you online. And much of it is free. You can access secondary data at one of the most respected sources, the U.S. Government Bureau of the Census at www.census.gov. There you will find information about the 2010 U.S. Census, FedStats, the Economic Census of Business, trade data, and more. Go to the site and check out some of the sources of information, such as some of the reports on E-Stats, which provides data related to electronic commerce. Much of the data may be downloaded as either PDF or Excel files.

WELCOME TO *E-STATS* - THE U.S. CENSUS BUREAU'S INTERNET SITE DEVOTED EXCLUSIVELY TO "MEASURING THE ELECTRONIC ECONOMY." THIS SITE FEATURES RECENT AND UPCOMING RELEASES, INFORMATION ON METHODOLOGY, AND BACKGROUND PAPERS.

Step 6: Determine Methods of Accessing Data

Accessing data may be accomplished through a variety of methods, which have been greatly improved over the past few years. Not only has the quantity of information available increased but, perhaps more significantly, the Internet has vastly improved our ability to easily and quickly retrieve information from online services and from websites of organizations providing information. Search engines like Google make online searching very effective and efficient. Still, much valuable information is available at your local library—not all information is electronic—books are still a good resource. You will learn more about secondary information sources used by marketing researchers in Chapter 6.

Although secondary data is relatively easy to access, accessing primary data is much more difficult. When the researcher must communicate with respondents, there are three main choices: (1) Have a person ask questions (i.e., conduct a personal interview using "paper and pencil" or a telephone survey); (2) use a computer-assisted method (i.e., computer-assisted telephone interview [CATI] or online survey delivered to an e-mail address); (3) allow respondents to answer questions themselves without computer assistance (i.e., mail survey); or make use of more than one method (hybrid). Within these

The most popular form of accessing data is through the Web. Furthermore, it seems as though more researchers believe their use of the Web to collect data will be increasing more than any other data collection method in the immediate future.

broad choices, there are several methods of accessing data; each of these, along with their pros and cons, are discussed in Chapter 9.

In the *2007 Confirmit Annual Market Research Survey*, a study of 233 marketing researchers in 233 firms located in 27 different countries, Wilson and Macer measured the use of different methods for collecting data by looking at the percentage of total quantitative research revenues generated by each mode. As shown in Figure 2.2, the most popular method is Web-based data collection. The study also presented data that suggest the use of Web, or online. surveys will grow the most in the immediate future. Computer-assisted telephone interviewing (CATI) was used extensively, as are paper (and pencil) surveys. In Asia-Pacific countries, paper (and pencil) was used more often because this area includes remote regions where technology is lacking. Computer-assisted personal interviewing (CAPI), using laptops or tablet PCs, generated 7.0% of total revenues; it is used less in North America than in other regions of the world. Finally, hybrid, or mixed-mode, data collection represented just less than 6% of revenues. These mixed-mode studies are mostly made up of a combination of Web (online) and CATI (telephone) data collection.[8] Figure 2.2 shows the quantitative research volume by mode of accessing data.

What if your research objective requires you to observe a consumer rather than communicate with the consumer? Then you would be using "observation" to access your data. We discuss this in Chapter 8.

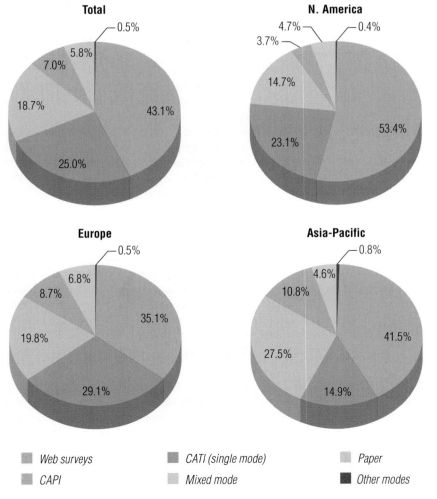

FIGURE 2.2

Source: Tim Macer and Sheila Wilson (2008, February), "Are Research Software Sales Due for an Increase?" *Quirk's Marketing Research Review,* p. 60. By permission.

qualtrics.com

Qualtrics is an example of state-of-the-art online surveying software. Visit Qualtrics at www.qualtrics.com.

The design of the data-collection form that is used to request and record information gathered in marketing research projects is critical to the success of the project.

The sample plan refers to the process used to select units from the population to be included in the sample.

The sample plan is extremely important, for it is the sample plan that determines how representative the sample is of the population.

Sample size, as the name implies, refers to determining how *many* elements of the population should be included in the sample.

The size of the sample determines the accuracy of the sample results.

Step 7: Design Data-Collection Forms

The design of the data-collection form that is used to request and record information gathered in marketing research projects is critical to the success of the project. Even when the problem has been correctly defined and the most appropriate research design planned, asking the wrong questions, or asking the right questions in the wrong order, will destroy the usefulness of the research effort.

Whether the research design requires that respondents be asked questions or that their behavior be observed, standardized forms, called questionnaires, record the information. A questionnaire's apparent simplicity (writing a list of questions) is very deceptive. Care must be taken to design a questionnaire in such a way that it will elicit objective information from the respondents. This means avoiding both ambiguous and leading questions. Additional considerations must be given to observation studies. In recent years, researchers have had access to software programs, such as *Qualtrics®*, to assist in creating surveys. Some of the newer programs allow users to post the surveys on the Web, and data are automatically downloaded into a statistical package, such as SPSS, when respondents complete answers to the questions. You will learn about preparing an objective questionnaire in Chapter 11.

Step 8: Determine Sample Plan and Size

Normally, marketing research studies are undertaken to learn about a population by taking a sample—a subset—of that population. Heinz uses a sample of homemakers to learn about the cooking preferences of all homemakers. Yanmar Diesels studies a sample of diesel mechanics in order to learn their preferences about engine design for purposes of repair and maintenance. A population consists of the entire group about which the researcher wishes to make inferences based on information provided by the sample data. A population could be "all department stores within the Portland, Oregon, metropolitan statistical area," or it could be "college students enrolled at the University of Delaware during the Spring, 2010 term." Populations should be defined by the research objectives.

The **sample plan** refers to the process used to select units or elements from the population to be included in the sample. For example, a sample plan, would specify how a researcher would draw elements from a population to be included in the study's sample. As you will learn in this book, there are different sample plans, and each has advantages and disadvantages. The sample plan is extremely important, for it determines how representative the sample is of the population. You will learn how to select a sample plan appropriate to the research objectives in Chapter 12.

Sample size, as the name implies, refers to determining how *many* units or elements of the population should be included in the sample. As a rule, the larger the sample the better, but you can have a sample that is too large, which wastes research dollars. The size of the sample determines the accuracy of the sample results. In Chapter 13 you will learn how to calculate a sample size that is just large enough to give you accurate results. There are research firms, such as Survey Sampling International and STS Samples, that help researchers with their sample plans and sample size problems. Marketing Research Insight 2.1 describes some of the services, offered globally, of Survey Sampling International.

Step 9: Collect Data

Data collection is very important because, regardless of the data analysis methods used, data analysis cannot "fix" bad data.[9] Data are usually gathered by trained interviewers who are employed by field-data-collection companies to collect primary data. Many possible errors, called **nonsampling errors** because they are attributable to factors other than sampling errors, may occur during data collection. Such errors include selecting the wrong sample elements to interview, selecting subjects who refuse to participate or are simply not at home when the

MARKETING RESEARCH INSIGHT   Global Application

2.2 Survey Sampling International Solves Sampling Problems for Marketing Researchers

Survey Sampling International is the premier global provider of sampling solutions for survey research. SSI offers access to more than 6 million consumer and business-to-business research respondents in 54 countries via the Internet, telephone, and mobile phone. Additional client services include custom profiling, survey programming and hosting, data processing, sampling consulting, and survey optimization.

SSI serves more than 1,800 clients, including nearly three-quarters of the top researchers worldwide. Founded in 1977, SSI has an international staff of more than 400 people representing 50 countries and 36 languages. The company is based in Shelton, Connecticut with additional offices in

London, Paris, Rotterdam, Stockholm, Frankfurt, Madrid, Beijing, Mumbai, Seoul, Shanghai, Sydney, Tokyo, Toronto, and La Quinta, California. Additional SSI representatives are in Guangzhou and Kuala Lumpur. For more information, visit www.surveysampling.com.

By permission.

interviewer calls, interviewing subjects who intentionally give out the wrong information, or hiring interviewers who cheat and fill out fictitious survey questionnaires. Even interviewers who honestly complete their interviews may make inadvertent nonsampling errors by copying down the wrong information on the survey form. Needless to say, good marketing researchers must be aware of the errors that may occur during data collection and should implement industry-accepted controls to reduce these errors. For example, by implementing a control called "validation," researchers may minimize the likelihood of a nonsampling error caused by a field worker cheating and making up data as reportedly coming from a respondent. Validation means that 10% (industry standard) of all respondents in a marketing research study are randomly selected, recontacted, and asked if they indeed took part in a research study. Unlike sampling error, the amount of nonsampling error that may exist in a study cannot be measured. Therefore, it is important to know the possible causes of nonsampling error so that appropriate steps, such as validation, can be taken to limit its occurrence. You will learn the causes of nonsampling errors and how to reduce those errors in Chapter 14.

Step 10: Analyze Data

Once data are collected, data analysis is used to give the raw data meaning. **Data analysis** involves entering data into computer files, inspecting the data for errors, and running tabulations and various statistical tests. The first step in data analysis is **data cleaning**, which is the process by which the raw data are checked to verify that they have been correctly input from the data-collection form to the computer software program. Typically, data analysis is conducted with the assistance of a computerized data analysis program such as SPSS. You will learn how to conduct basic descriptive data analysis in Chapter 15, how to make statistical inferences from your data in Chapter 16, how to determine if there are significant differences in Chapter 17, how to determine if there are significant associations in Chapter 18, and how to make predictions in Chapter 19. You will learn all of these types of data analysis using the SPSS software that comes with this book.

Nonsampling errors may include selecting the wrong sample elements to interview, selecting subjects who refuse to participate or are simply not at home when the interviewer calls, interviewing subjects who intentionally give out the wrong information, or hiring interviewers who cheat and fill out fictitious survey questionnaires.

You cannot measure the amount of nonsampling error. Therefore, it is important to know the possible causes of nonsampling error so that appropriate steps can be taken to limit its occurrence.

Data analysis involves entering data into computer files, inspecting the data for errors, and running tabulations and various statistical tests.

SPSS, Statistical Package for the Social Sciences, is the data analysis program most widely used by marketing researchers all over the world. You will learn how to conduct data analysis using SPSS in this book. By permission.

The final research report is very important because it is the report, or its presentation, that properly communicates the study results to the client.

Step 11: Prepare and Present the Final Research Report

The last step in the marketing research process is to prepare and present the final research report—one of the most important phases of marketing research. Its importance cannot be overstated because it is the report, or its presentation, that properly communicates the study results to the client. Sometimes researchers not only turn in a written research report to their client but also make an oral presentation of the research methods used to conduct the study as well as the research findings. In Chapter 20, we show you how to write a marketing research report, and we provide you with suggestions on how to give an oral presentation.

SOME FINAL COMMENTS ON THE MARKETING RESEARCH PROCESS

We do not mean to imply that all marketing research projects are as straightforward as we suggest with our 11 steps. And, even though many marketing research projects *are* as straightforward as we have shown here, the point we want to make is that there is great diversity among them. A research project designed to produce a new name for a new type of razor blade is very different from a research project designed to forecast sales in units for a brand-new product. Given this great diversity, your knowledge of these 11 steps in the research process will provide you with a good framework for understanding marketing research.

In Chapter 3, we continue our introduction to marketing research. You will learn about the industry itself as well as the ethical issues facing it.

Summary

There is great variability in marketing research projects. Some studies are limited to a review of secondary data; others require complex designs involving large-scale collection of primary data. But even with this diversity, projects have enough commonalities among them to enable us to characterize them in terms of "steps of the research process." There is value in characterizing research projects in terms of successive steps. First, the steps give researchers and nonresearchers an overview of the entire research process. Second, they provide a procedure, in the sense that a researcher, by referring to the steps, knows what tasks to consider and in what order. The steps are (1) establish the need for marketing research, (2) define the problem, (3) establish research objectives, (4) determine research design, (5) identify information types and sources, (6) determine methods of accessing data, (7) design data collection forms, (8) determine sample plan and size, (9) collect data, (10) analyze data, and (11) prepare and present the final research report.

There are definite advantages to presenting the marketing research process in a step-by-step fashion, but there are also caveats. First, there is nothing magic about our "11 steps." We could use fewer steps and make them more general, or we could have many more steps by increasing their specificity. Second, not all studies follow all 11 steps. Many problems may not require, for example, the collection of primary data, data analysis, and so on. Our 11 steps assume that the research process examines secondary data and continues on to collect primary data. Our third caveat is that the steps are seldom followed in the same order. Rather, the steps are more interactive. That is, after collecting some data, the researcher may decide that the problem needs to be redefined, and the process may start over.

The first step is determining the need for marketing research. Can the needed information be obtained from the internal reports system? From the marketing intelligence system? From the decision support system? All of these systems are ongoing sources of information. If these do not supply the information, marketing research may be needed. Sometimes the need to respond quickly to competition means there isn't time to conduct marketing research. And, although placing a dollar figure on value is difficult, the value of marketing research *can* be estimated and therefore a more informed decision may be made as to the justification for marketing research.

Defining the problem is the most important step, because if the problem is incorrectly defined, all else is wasted effort. Problems stem from two primary sources: gaps between what is *supposed* to happen and what *did* happen (failure to meet an objective) and gaps between what *did* happen and what *could* have happened (failure to take advantage of an opportunity). Research objectives, when achieved, provide the information necessary to solve the problem. Research objectives state what the researchers must do in order to carry out the research.

The three types of research design categories are (1) exploratory research, (2) descriptive research, and (3) causal research. Exploratory research is defined as collecting information in an unstructured and informal manner. It is often used when little is known about the problem. Descriptive research designs use a set of methods and procedures that describe marketing variables. Descriptive studies portray these variables by answering who, what, where, when, and how questions. They do not, however, answer why? Causal research allows us to isolate causes and effects. Causal designs answer the question of why? We call causal research designs "experiments."

There are two types of information: primary information (information collected specifically for the problem at hand) and secondary information (information already collected). The researcher has four main choices for accessing data from respondents: (1) a person asks the questions, (2) a computer assists in asking the questions, (3) respondents answer on their own, and (4) a fourth option—a hybrid, or mix, of the first three modes. If your research objective does not require you to communicate with the consumer, you may want to collect data by observing consumers. Care must be taken to ask the questions that will generate the information needed to solve the research objectives and to ask them clearly and without bias.

Normally, marketing research studies are undertaken to learn about a population by taking a sample—a subset—of that population. The sample plan refers to the process used to select units or elements from the population to be included in the sample. The sample plan determines how representative the sample is of the population. Sample size, as the name implies, refers to determining how many units or elements of the population should be included in the sample. As a rule, the larger the sample, the better, but a sample can be too large, which wastes research dollars. It is important that researchers know the sources of nonsampling errors and how to implement controls to minimize these errors.

Data analysis involves entering data into computer files, inspecting the data for errors, and running tabulations and various statistical tests. Data cleaning is the process by which the raw data are checked to verify that they have been correctly input from the data-collection form into the computer software program.

The last step in the marketing research process is to prepare and present the final research report—one of the most important phases of marketing research. Its importance cannot be overstated because it is the report, or its presentation, that properly communicates the study results to the client. In most cases, marketing research firms prepare a written research report and also make an oral presentation to the client and staff.

Key Terms

11 Steps in the marketing research process 24
Exploratory research 31
Descriptive research 31
Causal research 31

Experiments 31
Primary information 31
Secondary information 31
Sample plan 34
Sample size 34

Nonsampling errors 34
Data analysis 35
Data cleaning 35

Review Questions/Applications

1. What are the steps in the marketing research process?
2. Use an example to illustrate that the steps in the marketing research process are not always taken in sequence.
3. Explain why firms may not have a need for marketing research.
4. Why is defining the problem the most important step in the marketing research process?
5. Explain why research objectives differ from the definition of the problem.
6. What are the three types of research that constitute research design?
7. Which part of the research process ensures that the sample is representative?
8. Which part of the research process ensures the accuracy of the results?

9. Do a search for marketing research firms on the Internet. Look through their Web pages. Can you identify examples of what they are presenting that relate to steps in the research process?

10. Look for examples of firms conducting a marketing research study in your library's online databases or on the Internet. Many examples are reported in periodicals such as *Advertising Age, Marketing News, Business Week*, and *Forbes*. Typically, these articles will describe a few details of the research project itself. Identify as many as possible of the steps in the marketing research process that are referred to in the articles you find.

11. Observe any business in your community. Examine what it does, what products or service it provides, its prices, its promotion, or any other aspect of its business. Try to determine whether or not you, if you managed the business, would have conducted research to determine the firm's products and their design, features, prices, promotion, and so on. If you decide that you would not have conducted marketing research in a given area, explain why.

CASE 2.1

IS THERE A HYBRID AUTOMOBILE IN YOUR FUTURE?[10]

A few short years ago, hybrids were considered a fad. Few were being sold and most consumers looked upon them as a strange experimental car. Then the issue of global warming became prominent and the oil price spike of 2008 occurred. Consumers began to realize that global warming may be a real threat to Earth and certainly regarded fuel prices as a threat to their pocketbooks. Hybrids became more than a fanciful fad; they were heavily sought after. Demand for the Toyota Prius grew so dramatic during the summer of 2008 that retailers routinely charged a premium above the sticker price. Consumers willingly paid the premium. Hybrids soon had their own blogs and websites. One such website is www.hybridcars.com.

Hybridcars.com reported that it has been studying the demographics of hybrid buyers for years. It reported that J.D. Power found that hybrid owners have higher incomes than the average car buyer—an average of $100,000 annually while "other" car buyers' average income was $85,000. Another study in 2007 by Topline Strategy Group reported that Prius owners averaged incomes higher than $100,000. In the same year, a Scarborough Research Report of approximately 1,000 hybrid owners of all types showed that 42% had incomes greater than $100,000. J. D. Power and the Scarborough studies also show that hybrid buyers are older than typical car buyers. The average car buyer is 40 and the average hybrid buyer is 50.

Inside a Toyota Prius®

Research studies also show that hybrids are more popular in some states than others. California strongly outpaces all other states in terms of hybrid sales. The University of Michigan's Transportation Research Institute reports that the average education levels of hybrid buyers are the highest of any other category of vehicle owners. The same institute also reports that hybrid buyers have different attitudes and lifestyles than other car buyers. In general, they expect fuel prices to continue to increase; they are twice as likely to go skiing, hiking or practice yoga than non-hybrid buyers; they consume more organic food, yogurt, and decaffeinated coffee than the general population; they are more "tech-savvy"; and politically, 14% call themselves Republican, 38% are Democrats, and 34% percent are Independents.

Finally, these studies tend to reveal that hybrid owners are very satisfied with their hybrid car purchases. Nearly 100% of hybrid owners describe their satisfaction with their vehicle as either "very happy" or "somewhat happy."

1. Think about what you have learned in this chapter regarding the steps in the marketing research process and of the several studies about hybrids described in the case, identify what you would imagine the marketing manager's problem was that made these studies necessary. (Think of how the information described above may be used by manufacturers of hybrid automobiles.)
2. In terms of research design, how would you categorize the studies summarized in the case?
3. In terms of the sample plan used in these studies, how would you describe the sample selected for these studies?
4. Given the findings reported in the case, describe what you think were some of the basic data analysis goals of the researchers involved in the studies.

CASE 2.2   **Your Integrated Case**

ADVANCED AUTOMOBILE CONCEPTS

In Chapter 1, Case 1.2, we introduced you to Nick Thomas, who is a CEO of Advanced Automobile Concepts (AAC), a new division of the large automobile manufacturer ZEN Motors. Let's review some of the information you were given in Case 1.2.

AAC was created to revive the aging ZEN automobile brands by either reengineering existing models or developing totally new models that are more in tune with today's changing automobile market. Also recall from Case 1.2 that Nick follows trade publications carefully and believes ZEN's most significant losses are due to the growing popularity of several foreign brands, particularly brands from Japan and Korea. Nick has retrieved company sales data for all ZEN models for the last decade from ZEN's Internal Reports System. He has accessed the Intelligence System in ZEN's MIS to obtain trade industry articles written about the market, including evaluations of many of the top competitors' models. He noticed that several highly evaluated models are small and fuel efficient. ZEN has been reluctant to move into the very small and highly fuel-efficient market for a couple of reasons. First, historically, ZEN has earned higher profits on larger vehicles. Second, as sales have eroded in recent years, ZEN has been reluctant to invest the funds needed to develop designs radically different from those models that have been their "bread and butter" cars for decades.

Now ZEN must do something and this is why they have created Nick's position. Nick believes he must come up with new models that will appeal to the market, but he is concerned that the recent interest in small, fuel-efficient cars will go away, as it has done in the past, when oil prices drop. He also wonders if consumers' interest in global warming is real enough that it will affect what they purchase.

1. Review the steps in the marketing research process. How would you classify the two sources of information Nick Thomas has consulted—trade publications and information from ZEN's Internal Reports System?
2. Assume Nick Thomas decides that he must gather primary information to describe the strength of consumers' attitudes toward future oil price levels and global warming. Looking back at the 11-step process in this chapter, suggest what Nick may want to do in terms of the following:
   a. Which type of research design should Nick use?
   b. How would you describe the type of information Nick must gather?
   c. What are some of the specific questions that Nick must ask of respondents?
   d. In terms of a sample plan, who should Nick sample?

Describing Characteristics of the Marketing Research Industry

Learning Objectives

- To learn about the history and characteristics of the marketing research industry, including the professional organizations in the industry

- To learn what are the leading marketing research firms and their place in the industry structure

- To know how to classify marketing research firms

- To be aware of the challenges facing the industry and suggestions that have been made for improving the industry, including the Professional Researcher Certification (PRC)

- To understand how a researcher's philosophy might dictate behavior in ethically sensitive situations

- To learn the ethical codes and standards developed by professional associations serving the marketing research industry

- To learn about the important ethical issues facing the marketing research industry today

- To learn about careers in the marketing research industry

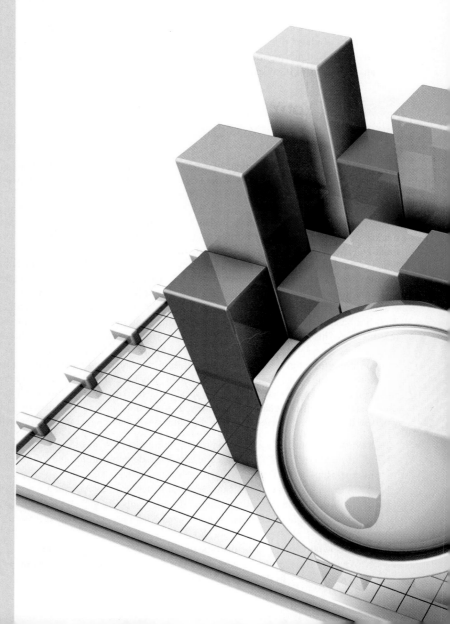

Industry Initiatives Led by the Marketing Research Association

Lawrence J. Brownell,
CEO, Marketing Research
Association.

In this chapter you are going to learn about the marketing research industry and about several associations that serve the profession. The Marketing Research Association creates and facilitates education and networking for the profession in order to create a well-informed and functional marketplace. To this end, it sponsors forums for clients and research company CEOs to advance their education and issues.

In 2005, the MRA became the certifying body in the United States for individuals involved in research. Responding to a need, MRA will also shortly become a corporate accreditation body. Providing assurances of individual and company competencies is critical to the advancement of the profession. The existing pressures in various nations could limit the use and future of research. The MRA through its initiatives and its advancement of technology as a solution agent seeks to secure good, knowledge-based decision making.

Clients and research providers have quickly adopted the Professional Researcher Certification (PRC), established in 2005. In the first three years after its inception, over 1,000 individuals qualified for the PRC. Aimed at evaluating the competencies of individuals in different areas and levels of the profession, the program vets applicants based on experience, education, and ethics. Certificates are valid for two years, and individuals must be revetted upon renewal.

In July of 2008, the MRA released PRC 2.0. In the two years since its inception, this program had expanded to include over 80 different types of

Marketing Research Association

Visit the MRA *website* at www.mra-net.org

certificate, but the PRC board agreed to pare the system down to primary categories, resulting in just 18 different certificate types at two skill levels. The revised system now includes secondary research, which is becoming a larger portion of professional activity. As a ongoing evaluative system, PRC is under constant scrutiny to ensure that certificate holders truly represent excellence in the profession.

—Larry Brownell, CEO
Marketing Research Association

E*very industry has one or more affiliated professional organization. When it intro-duced the PRC in 2005, the Marketing Research Association assumed a major lead-ership role in the marketing research industry. As CEO of the MRA Larry Brownell just stated in the opening vignette, the certification program is growing and undergoing changes to make it a living, viable program. As the number of PRCs increases every year and the program stimulates greater participation in continuing education, it will ensure industry standards remain strong.*

But there are other facets of the industry you should know about, which is the purpose of this chapter. We begin by giving a brief historical perspective on marketing research. Next, we consider the structure of the industry, examining the types of firms in the industry and firm size. We introduce you to The Honomichl Global Top 25, the top 25 marketing research firms in the world in terms of revenue. We also discuss The Honomichl Top 50, the top 50 market-ing research firms in the United States in terms of revenue earned here. We next look at some characteristics facing the industry and evaluations of the industry. How has the research industry performed, and what suggestions have been made to improve the industry? We also provide you with some detailed information on the Marketing Research Association's certifi-cation program. Finally, we examine the ethical issues facing the industry.

When you finish this chapter, you will have finished our introduction to marketing research. Some of you may have become interested in marketing research as a career. If you want to know more about a career in the industry, including seeking a master's degree in mar-keting research, we encourage you to read the Appendix on careers at the end of this chapter.

THE MARKETING RESEARCH INDUSTRY

Evolution of the Industry

It was not until the 1930s that marketing research efforts became widespread.

When the Industrial Revolution led to manufacturers producing goods for distant markets, the need for marketing research grew.

By the 1960s, marketing research had not only gained acceptance in the organization but also was recognized as being key to understanding distant and fast-changing markets and necessary for survival.

In the 1950's there was no "sense of industry."

Each year, Jack Honomichl publishes The Honomichl Global Top 25, a report on the top 25 marketing/ advertising/public opinion research services firms ranked in terms of worldwide revenues.

THE EARLY DAYS. Robert Bartels, a marketing historian, wrote that the earliest questionnaire surveys were done as early as 1824 and that in 1879 N. W. Ayers and Company conducted a study of grain production by states for a client. However, Bartels believes the first continuous and organized research was done in 1911 by **Charles Coolidge Parlin**, a schoolmaster from a small city in Wisconsin. Parlin was hired by the Curtis Publishing Company to gather information about customers and markets to help Curtis sell advertising space. Parlin was successful, and the information he gathered led to increased advertising in Curtis's *Saturday Evening Post* magazine.[1] Parlin is recognized today as the "Father of Marketing Research," and the AMA gives an award each year at the annual marketing research conference in his name.

GROWTH OF THE NEED. There are a few reported instances of the use of marketing research in the early days of the history of the United States, but it was not until the 1930s that marketing research efforts became widespread. Prior to the Industrial Revolution businesses were located close to consumers. In an economy based on artisans and craftsmen involved in barter exchange with their customers, there was not much need to "study" consumers because business owners saw their customers daily. They knew their needs and wants and their likes and dislikes. However, when the Industrial Revolution led to manufacturers producing goods for distant markets, the need for marketing research grew. Manufacturers in Boston needed to know more about the consumers, and their needs, in "faraway" places like Denver and Atlanta. In 1922, A. C. Nielsen started his research firm, and in the 1930s, colleges began to teach courses in marketing research. During the 1940s, Alfred Politz introduced statistical theory for sampling in marketing research.[2] Also during the 1940s, Robert Merton introduced focus groups, which today represent a large part of what is known as "qualitative marketing research." Computers revolutionized the industry in the 1950s.[3] By the 1960s, marketing research had not only gained acceptance in the organization but also was recognized as a key to understanding distant and fast-changing markets and necessary for survival.

A MATURING INDUSTRY. According to Jack Honomichl,[4] president of The Marketing Aid Center and publisher of *Inside Research*, the industry in the 1950s was largely composed of small, privately owned firms that didn't report their revenues.[5] There was "no sense of industry." However, according to Mr. Honomichl, the industry evolved and by the 1990s many of the smaller firms had consolidated. This trend continued into the 2000s, and today the industry structure is quite different. The industry has some "behemoths" that operate around the globe with revenues in excess of a billion dollars. Many of these firms are publicly listed or operate as subsidiaries of publicly listed parent companies and so their revenues are in the public domain, along with statements of profitability and executive remuneration. Mr. Honomichl prepares annual reports of the industry's revenues, which are described in the following section. These reports, which track industry structure and revenues, the growth of the professional organizations serving the industry, the globalization of the industry, and the introduction of certification in the industry through the PRC, are all earmarks of a maturing industry.

Tracking Revenues in the Marketing Research Industry Today

WORLD REVENUES. Each year, Jack Honomichl publishes **The Honomichl Global Top 25**, a report on the top 25 marketing/advertising/public opinion research services firms ranked in terms of worldwide revenues. The marketing research industry accounts for approximately $25.3 billion spent annually to better understand customers, markets, and competitors. In 2007, the world's top 25 marketing/advertising/public opinion firms accounted for $17.5 billion of total worldwide revenues—about 69%. The revenue growth among the top 25 firms from 2006 to 2007 was 7.7%. The industry, primarily through acquisition, continues to concentrate. In 2007, 14 firms among the top 25 acquired 55 other firms. Table 3.1 is a list of the top 25 global research organizations compiled by Jack Honomichl and reported as The Honomichl Global Top 25 annually in *Marketing News*.[6]

As we noted earlier, marketing research firms operate across the entire globe, and the top 25 firms are located all over the world, including France, Germany, Brazil, the Netherlands, the United Kingdom, Japan, and the United States. Reflecting the true global nature of marketing research, 57% of the total revenues generated by the top 25 firms in 2007 came from operations/subsidiaries outside the home country. As you can see by examining Table 3.1, the largest and one of the dominant research firm in the world is The Nielsen Company, headquartered in New York. The table also indicates that only two firms, Westat, Inc., a privately held firm, and Dentsu Research Inc., do not earn revenues outside of their headquarters country.

Jack Honomichl is president of Marketing Aid Center and founder of *Inside Research*, a trade publication serving the industry. Mr. Honomichl, a recognized authority on the marketing research industry, was inducted into the Market Research Council's Hall of Fame at the Yale Club in New York in 2002. Other members of the Hall of Fame include such notables as Arthur C. Nielsen, Sr., George Gallup, Sr., David Ogilvy, Marion Harper, Daniel Yankelovich, Daniel Starch, Ernest Dicter, Alfred Politz, and Elmo Roper.

"The Honomichl Top 50"

REVENUES OF U.S. FIRMS. Honomichl also publishes the **Honomichl Top 50** each year, which is reported in *Marketing News*.[7] This report ranks the top 50 U.S.-based firms in terms of their revenues from U.S. operations only. In 2007, Honomichl reported that the top 50 earned total revenues in the United States of $7.8 billion. Many member firms of The Council of American Survey Research Organizations (CASRO) are not large enough to make the top 50. When these 150 CASRO firms are added into the total, the revenue of the 200 U.S.-based research firms for 2007 rises to $8.6 billion, representing an increase of 6% over 2006. As Honomichl points out, these revenues do not reflect total U.S. research services, because the large sums the federal government pays to firms are not included on the list. Also, the revenues of some nonprofit research organizations affiliated with universities are not reflected, nor is the value of research companies conduct in-house.

Honomichl recognized the "sluggish economy" when he wrote the 2007 Honomichl Top 50 report (see Table 3.2). However, he had no way of anticipating the significant

The Honomichl Top 50 report is a ranking of the top 50 U.S.-based firms in terms of the revenues from U.S. operations only. In 2007, Honomichl reported that the top 50 earned total revenues in the United States of $7.8 billion.

TABLE 3.1 The Honomichl Global Top 25

The Honomichl Global Top 25 is a list of the top 25 marketing/advertising/public opinion research services firms based upon ranking worldwide revenues. By permission.

Top 25 Global Market Research Firms

Rank 2007	Rank 2006	Organization	Headquarters	Parent Country	Web Site	Number of Countries with Subsidiaries/ Branch Offices[1]	Research-Only Full-time Employees[2]	Global Research Revenue[3] (US $, in millions)	Percent Change from 2006[4]	Revenue from Outside Parent Country (US $, in millions)	Percent Revenue from Outside Home Country
1	1	The Nielsen Co.	New York	USA	nielsen.com	108	33,171	$4,220.0	12.7%	$2,047.0	48.5%
2	2	IMS Health Inc.	Norwalk, Conn.	USA	imshealth.com	76	7,950	2,192.6	6.0	1,391.6	63.5
3	3	Taylor Nelson Sofres plc	London	UK	tnsglobal.com	80	15,267	2,137.2	5.4	1,754.6	82.1
4	5	GfK AG	Nuremberg	Germany	gfk.com	63	9,070	1,593.2	5.8	1,195.3	75.0
5	4	The Kantar Group*	London & Fairfield, Conn.	UK	kantargroup.com	61	7,100	1,551.4	2.7	1,024.6	66.0
6	6	Ipsos Group SA	Paris	France	ipsos.com	56	8,088	1,270.3	9.1	1,125.5	88.6
7	7	Synovate	London	UK	synovate.com	57	5,801	867.0	7.8	813.3	93.8
8	8	IRI	Chicago	USA	infores.com	8	3,655	702.0	5.6	261.0	37.2
9	9	Westat Inc.	Rockville, Md.	USA	westat.com	1	1,906	467.8	10.4	—	—
10	10	Arbitron Inc.	New York	USA	arbitron.com	2	1,130	352.1	6.9	13.6	3.9
11	11	INTAGE Inc.**	Tokyo	Japan	intage.co.jp	2	1,666	281.1	7.5	2.5	0.9
12	12	J.D. Power and Associates*	Westlake Village, Calif.	USA	jdpa.com	8	875	260.5	12.0	76.0	29.2
13	13	Harris Interactive Inc.	Rochester, N.Y.	USA	harrisinteractive.com	7	1,336	226.8	-1.7	66.0	29.1
14	14	Maritz Research	Fenton. Mo.	USA	maritzresearch.com	4	806	223.3	3.0	35.9	16.1
15	15	The NPD Group Inc.	Port Washington, N.Y.	USA	npd.com	13	1,120	211.1	11.7	50.7	24.0
16	17	Opinion Research/ Guideline Group	Omaha, Neb.	USA	infousa.com	7	1,235	202.2	7.5	87.1	43.1
17	16	Video Research Ltd.**	Tokyo	Japan	videor.co.jp	3	386	169.6	-1.1	0.2	0.1
18	18	IBOPE Group	Sao Paulo	Brazil	ibope.com.br	16	1,743	116.5	0.4	25.0	21.5
19	19	Lieberman Research Worldwide	Los Angeles	USA	irwonline.com	4	324	87.5	11.7	16.4	18.7
20	21	comScore Inc.	Reston, Va.	USA	comscore.com	5	452	87.2	31.5	10.1	11.6
21	—	Cello Research & Consulting	London	UK	cellogroup.co.uk	2	400	79.9	11.0	38.8	48.6
22	—	Market Strategies Intl.	Livonia, Mich.	USA	marketstrategies.com	2	311	61.8	10.8	6.0	9.7
23	—	BVA Group	Paris	France	bva.fr	4	620	55.6	-0.3	2.7	4.9
24	—	OTX	Los Angeles	USA	otxresearch.com	2	191	54.5	35.6	3.7	6.8
25	22	Dentsu Research Inc.	Tokyo	Japan	dentsuresearch.co.jp	1	116	54.2	-10.4	—	—
		Total					104,719	$17,525.4	7.7%	$10,047.6	57.3%

*Estimated by Top 25 For fiscal year ending March 2008.[1] Includes countries that have subsidiaries with an equity interest or branch offices, or both.[2] Includes some nonresearch employees.[3] Total revenue that includes nonresearch activities for some companies are significantly higher. This information is given in the individual company profiles.[4] Rate of growth from year to year has been adjusted so as not to include revenue gains or losses from acquisitions or divestitures. See company profiles for explanation. Rate of growth is based on home country currency and includes currency exchange effects.

TABLE 3.2   The Honomichl Top 50

The Honomichl Top 50 is a list of the top 50 U.S.-based marketing/advertising/public opinion research services firms, ranked according to revenues earned in the United States. By permission.

Top 50 U.S. Market Research Firms

U.S. Rank 2007	2006	Organization	Headquarters	Web Site	U.S. Research Revenue[1] ($ in millions)				Percent Non-U.S. Revenue	U.S. Full-time Employees
1	1	The Nielsen Co.	New York	nielsen.com	$2,173.0	7.9%	$4,220.0	$2,047.0	48.5%	9,715
2	2	IMS Health Inc.	Norwalk, Conn.	imshealth.com	801.0	8.6	2,192.6	1,391.6	63.5	2,034
3	3	Kantar Group*	Fairfield, Conn.	kantargroup.com	526.8	3.5	1,551.4	1,024.6	66.0	2,600
4	5	Westat Inc.	Rockville, Md.	westat.com	467.8	10.4	467.8	—	—	1,935
5	4	IRI	Chicago	infores.com	441.0	2.1	702.0	261.0	37.2	1,464
6	6	TNS U.S.	New York	tnsglobal.com	379.8	2.8	2,137.2	1,757.4	82.2	2,000
7	7	Arbitron Inc.	New York	arbitron.com	338.5	6.0	352.1	13.6	3.9	1,092
8	8	GFK AG USA	Nuremberg, Germany	gfk.com	319.7	1.3	1,603.0	1,283.3	80.1	1,039
9	9	Ipsos	New York	ipsos-na.com	281.2	3.5	1,270.3	989.1	77.9	800
10	10	Synovate	London	synovate.com	250.4	6.9	867.0	616.6	71.1	832
11	11	Maritz Research	Fenton, Mo.	maritzresearch.com	187.4	5.2	223.3	35.9	16.1	632
12	13	J.D. Power and Associates*	Westlake Village, Calif.	jdpower.com	184.5	8.2	260.5	76.0	29.2	620
13	12	Harris Interactive Inc.	Rochester, N.Y.	harrisinteractive.com	161.0	-3.6	227.0	66.0	29.1	879
14	14	The NPD Group Inc.	Port Washington, N.Y.	npd.com	160.4	10.1	211.1	50.7	24.0	860
15	—	Opinion Research/Guideline Group	Omaha, Neb.	infousa.com	124.7	4.5	206.7	82.0	39.7	546
	15	*Opinion Research Corp*	*Princeton, N.J.*	*opinionresearch.com*	*97.5*	*0.7*	*179.5*	*82.0*	*45.7*	*458*
	38	*Guideline Inc.*	*New York*	*guideline.com*	*26.8*	*21.3*	*26.8*	*—*	*—*	*73*
16	18	comScore Inc.	Reston, Va.	comscore.com	77.0	26.0	87.2	10.2	11.7	370
17	20	Market Strategies Inc.	Livonia, Mich	marketstrategies.com	75.7	6.3	80.4	4.7	5.8	309
	20	*Market Strategies Inc.*	*Livonia, Mich*	*marketstrategies.com*	*53.4*	*11.0*	*58.1*	*4.7*	*8.1*	*234*
	37	*Flake-Wilkerson Market Insights*	*Little Rock, Ark.*	*fw-mi.com*	*22.3*	*-3.5*	*22.3*	*—*	*—*	*75*
18	17	Lieberman Research Worldwide	Los Angeles	lrwonline.com	71.0	12.5	87.4	16.4	18.8	208
19	—	Abt Associates Inc.	Cambridge, Mass.	abtassociates.com	55.1	-16.8	55.1	—	—	279
	19	*Abt Associates Inc.*	*Cambridge, Mass.*	*abtassociates.com*	*33.0*	*-27.5*	*33.0*	*—*	*—*	*150*
	41	*Abt SRBI Inc.*	*New York*	*srbi.com*	*22.1*	*6.8*	*22.1*	*—*	*—*	*129*
20	23	OTX	Los Angeles	otxresearch.com	50.8	32.6	54.5	3.7	6.8	184
21	21	Burke Inc.	Cincinnati	burke.com	47.0	8.0	53.1	6.1	11.5	217
22	22	MVL Group Inc.	Jupiter, Fla.	mvlgroup.com	42.3	-1.6	42.3	—	—	193
23	26	Knowledge Networks Inc.	Menlo Park, Calif.	knowledgenetworks.com	37.3	5.7	37.3	—	—	180
23	25	National Research Corp.	Lincoln, Neb.	nationalresearch.com	37.3	1.9	41.3	4.0	9.7	181
25	24	Directions Research Inc.	Cincinnati	directionsresearch.com	37.2	1.4	37.2	—	—	120
26	40	Phoenix Marketing International	Rhinebeck, N.Y.	phoenixmi.com	33.5	26.5	34.9	1.4	4.0	137
27	34	Lieberman Research Group	Great Neck, N.Y.	liebermanresearch.com	30.1	28.1	30.1	—	—	76
28	27	ICR/Int'l Communications Research	Media, Pa.	icrsurvey.com	28.8	-6.5	29.7	0.9	3.0	195

(continued)

TABLE 3.2 The Honomichl Top 50 (Continued)

The Honomichl Top 50 is a list of the top 50 U.S.-based marketing/advertising/public opinion research services firms, ranked according to revenues earned in the United States. By permission.

Top 50 U.S. Market Research Firms

U.S. Rank 2007	2006	Organization	Headquarters	Web Site	U.S. Research Revenue[1] ($ in millions)				Percent Non-U.S. Revenue	U.S. Full-time Employees
29	28	Morpace Inc.	Farmington Hills, Mich.	morpace.com	28.7	-4.7	33.2	4.5	13.6	150
30	33	MarketCast	Los Angeles	marketcastonline.com	25.1	2.0	25.1	—	—	36
31	36	Data Development Worldwide	New York	datadw.com	25.0	6.8	25.3	0.3	1.2	80
32	39	C&R Research Services Inc.	Chicago	crresearch.com	23.6	9.8	23.6	—	—	121
33	32	Informa Research Services Inc.	Calabasas, Calif.	informars.com	23.5	-6.7	23.5	—	—	189
34	31	National Analysts Worldwide	Philadelphia	nationalanalysts.com	23.3	-12.1	23.3	—	—	73
35	44	Service Management Group	Kansas City, Mo.	servicemanagement.com	22.4	22.4	23.0	0.6	2.6	134
36	34	Market Probe Inc.	Milwaukee	marketprobe.com	21.7	-3.6	41.4	19.7	47.6	115
37	—	Hitwise	New York	hitwise.com	21.6	50.0	49.9	28.3	56.7	75
38	42	Walker Information	Indianapolis	walkerinfo.com	21.2	10.4	25.5	4.3	16.9	180
39	43	KS&R Inc.	Syracuse, N.Y.	ksrinc.com	17.1	-9.5	21.0	3.9	18.6	198
40	47	Bellomy Research Inc.	Winston-Salem, N.C.	bellomyresearch.com	16.7	14.4	16.7	—	—	95
41	46	MarketVision Research Inc.	Cincinnati	marketvisionresearch.com	16.4	10.1	16.4	—	—	80
42	28	Public Opinion Strategies	Alexandria, Va.	pos.org	15.5	-48.5	15.5	—	—	33
43	—	Compete Inc.	Boston	compete.com	14.9	53.6	14.9	—	—	100
44	45	Savitz Research Companies	Dallas	savitzresearch.com	14.8	-2.6	14.8	—	—	50
45	48	RDA Group Inc.	Bloomfield Hills, Mich.	rdagroup.com	13.7	-5.5	16.8	3.1	18.5	97
46	—	Gongos Research Inc.	Auburn Hills, Mich.	gongos.com	13.3	24.3	13.3	—	—	63
47	—	Q Research Solutions Inc.	Old Bridge, N.J.	whoisq.com	13.0	8.3	13.2	0.2	1.5	77
48	49	Marketing Analysts Inc.	Charleston, S.C.	marketinganalysts.com	12.8	-3.0	13.6	0.8	5.9	39
49	50	RTi Market Research & Brand Strategy	Stamford, Conn.	rtiresearch.com	12.2	-3.9	12.2	—	—	43
50	—	The Link Group	Atlanta	the-link-group.com	11.9	5.3	13.3	1.4	10.5	39
				Total	$7,828.7	6.0%	$17,638.0	$9,809.3	55.6%	32,883
				All other (150 CASRO companies not included in the Top 50)[3]	$774.3	6.2%	$870.1	$95.8	11.0%	3,370
				Total (200 companies)	$8,603.0	6.0%	$18,508.1	$9,905.1	53.5%	36,253

[1]Estimated by Top 50.[1]U.S. and worldwide revenue may include nonresearch activities for some companies that are significantly higher. See individual company profiles for details. [2]Rate of growth from year to year has been adjusted so as not to include revenue gains or losses from acquisitions or divestitures. See company profiles for explanation. [3]Total revenue of 150 survey research companies that provide financial information on a confidential basis to the Council of American Survey Research Organizations (CASRO).

worldwide economic distress experienced in the latter part of 2008. As we go to press in early 2009, we can assume that the Honomichl reports for 2008 will reflect the growing dismal economic times. Marketing research, like most industries, will have difficulty achieving revenue growth over the previous year.

The Honomichl Top 50 firms, although based in the United States. are also highly involved in international research. While these 50 firms earned $7.8 billion in U.S.-based revenues, they earned another $9.8 billion from revenues outside the U.S. In other words, the Honomichl Top 50 U.S.-based firms earned about 55% of their total revenues from foreign operations. As you have already learned, the marketing research industry operates globally.[8]

> The Honomichl Top 50 U.S.-based firms earned about 55% of their total revenues from foreign operations; the marketing research industry operates globally.

STRONGER COMPETITION THROUGH STRATEGIC ALLIANCES. As we have noted, there have been many mergers and acquisitions in the marketing research industry. Many of these resulted in the formation of strategic alliances. **Strategic alliances** allow firms with strong expertise in one area to form partnerships with firms offering expertise in other areas. For example, a firm strong in client consultation may form an alliance with a firm specializing in data collection and with another firm specializing in data analysis. These alliances, which create higher levels of competition in the industry, are formed through acquisition, merger, or contractual agreements. For example, in 2007 Nielsen created a new division, Nielsen Mobile, by acquiring Telephia, a firm that specialized in obtaining syndicated data on consumer research for the telecom and mobile media markets.[9] IRI, long known for providing syndicated retail tracking data, has formed partnerships with IBM to deliver on-demand market intelligence; with IMS Health, Inc. to provide analytics for the Rx, OTC, and CPG markets; and with TiVo, Inc. to help advertisers better understand the impact of the DVR on consumer viewing patterns and sales of advertised brands.[10]

> Strategic alliances allow firms with strong expertise in one area to form partnerships with firms offering expertise in other areas.

> IRI has formed a strategic alliance with TiVo.

 Learn More About the Firms in the Marketing Research Industry

Not only do the two Honomichl reports, the Global Top 25 and the Top 50, give us revenues and rankings, they also provide detailed information about the firms themselves. For a good review of what is going on in each one of these firms, including any strategic alliances, partnerships, mergers, and so on, go to the American Marketing Association website at: www .marketingpower.com. At the top of the web page, choose "Resource Library." At the left margin, click on "AMA Publications" and then select "Marketing News." On the right side you should see both Honomichl reports listed. These will be pdf files that you can navigate to learn more about the research companies. If you cannot find the reports using these keystrokes, try typing in "Honomichl" in the search box at the AMA website.

Classifying Firms in the Marketing Research Industry

The marketing research industry refers to providers of marketing research information as **research suppliers**. They can be classified in several ways. We use a classification developed by Naresh Malhotra,[11] slightly modified for our purposes here. This classification system, shown in Figure 3.1, classifies suppliers as either internal or external.

> We can classify all research suppliers as either internal or external suppliers.

Internal Suppliers

An **internal supplier** is an entity within the firm that supplies marketing research. It has been estimated that firms spend roughly 1% of sales on marketing research, whether it is supplied internally or externally.[12] Most large firms, such as Kraft Foods, IBM, Kodak, General Mills, and Ford, have their own research departments. We asked Jeff Minier, director of market research and business intelligence at Merial Limited, to share his thoughts about his academic training and his responsibilities with Merial Limited in Marketing Research Insight 3.1.

> An internal supplier is an entity within the firm that supplies marketing research.

FIGURE 3.1   A Classification of Marketing Research Suppliers

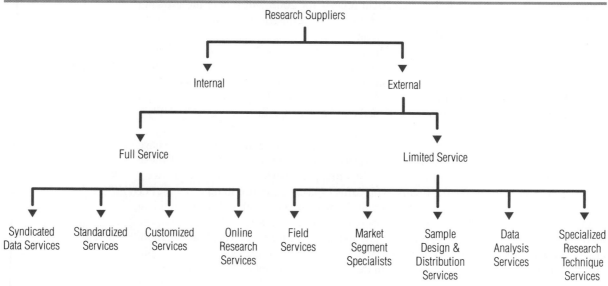

HOW DO INTERNAL SUPPLIERS ORGANIZE THE RESEARCH FUNCTION?   Internal suppliers of marketing research can elect to use several organizing methods to provide the research function. They may (1) have their own formal departments, (2) have no formal department but make at least a single individual or a committee responsible for marketing research, or (3) assign no one responsibility for conducting marketing research.

Organizing the Formal Department of Internal Suppliers.   Most large organizations have the resources to staff their own formal marketing research departments. Firms with higher sales volumes (over $500 million) tend to have their own formal marketing research departments, and many large advertising agencies have their own formal research departments.[13] Companies with their own research department must justify the large fixed costs of supporting the personnel and facilities. The advantage is that the staff is fully cognizant of the firm's operations and the changes in the industry, which may give them better insights into identifying opportunities and problems suitable for marketing research action.

Marketing research departments are usually organized according to one or a combination of the following functions: area of application, marketing function, or the research process. By "area of application," we mean these companies organize the research function around the areas to which the research is being applied. For example, some firms serve both ultimate consumers and industrial consumers. Therefore, the marketing research department may be organized into two divisions: consumer and industrial. Other areas of application may be brands or lines of products or services. Second, marketing research may be organized around functional areas (the 4 Ps), such as product research, ad research, pricing research, channel of distribution research, and so on. Finally, the research function may be organized around steps in the research process, such as data analysis or data collection.

Organizing When There Is No Formal Department.   If internal supplier firms elect not to have a formal marketing research department, there are many other organizational possibilities. When there is no formal department, responsibility for research may be assigned to such existing organizational units as departments or divisions. A problem with this method is that research activities are not coordinated; a division conducts its own research and other units of the firm may be unaware of useful information. One way to remedy this is to organize by having a committee or an individual assigned to oversee

Internal suppliers may (1) have their own formal departments, (2) have no formal department but make at least a single individual or a committee responsible for marketing research, or (3) assign no one responsibility for conducting marketing research.

Marketing research departments are usually organized according to one or a combination of the following functions: area of application, marketing function, or the research process.

When there is no formal department, responsibility for research may be assigned to such existing organizational units as departments or divisions.

MARKETING RESEARCH INSIGHT   Practical Application

3.1 Meet Jeff Minier, Director of Market Research and Business Intelligence, Merial Limited

When I entered graduate school at Southern Illinois University Edwardsville in the mid 1990s, I was very certain that I wanted to get an MBA with an emphasis in marketing. Like most students entering graduate school, I had no idea that I could get a specialized degree in Marketing Research—I had never heard about a degree like this. After starting MBA classes, it didn't take long to learn about the MMR program and figure out that it was the right path for me. In this sense, the MMR program found *me*. My undergraduate degree was a B.A. in Speech Communications from the University of Georgia, so I felt that the specificity offered by a Master's degree in Marketing Research would give me a very concrete set of skills that would prepare me to be competitive in the workforce. I also felt that it would lead me to a career that would have interesting challenges, position me at the heart of business decision-making, and be financially rewarding.

I was right about all three of these areas. Today I work as the Director of Market Research and Business Intelligence for Merial Limited's Global Strategic Marketing Team. Merial is a world-leading, innovation-driven animal health company (a joint venture between Merck & Co and sanofi-aventis) which provides a comprehensive range of products to enhance the health, well-being and performance of animals. The company operates in more than 150 countries, has more than 5,000 employees, and had 2008 sales exceeding $2.5 billion. Our largest and most well-known brands include FRONTLINE and HEARTGARD, which are used on dogs and cats to treat/prevent fleas and ticks and to control heartworm. Merial is one of the world's leaders in animal vaccine markets, and we manufacture and supply many other pharmaceutical products to ruminant, swine and avian markets.

In my role at Merial, I manage a small group of people to support the information needs of the Global Strategic Marketing team, where I oversee all market research projects in order to understand the needs of our clients: veterinarians, dog, cat and horse owners, and beef, dairy, swine and avian producers. I am also responsible for analyzing other types of market information which helps Merial executives make better decisions. Our team consists of ten brand directors who are each responsible for a specific animal species, health category, or product. They manage global marketing elements of existing brands, and provide leadership on new products and in-line extensions that are either in research or development.

Consequently, I am involved in a wide variety of qualitative and quantitative market research projects throughout the world. My role is to understand the problems, translate problems into research terms, and then to execute appropriate studies to deliver on the objectives. Obviously, I can't do it on my own. I solicit and hire many of the world's top market research companies to conduct these studies on our behalf, and I work closely with them to design and execute the most appropriate and cost-effective studies for our needs. These studies often span multiple countries, and I maintain relationships with a variety of vendors throughout the world who can bring local expertise to a project. I often have from 5 to 15 studies in progress. I might be leading a new-product concept test with horse owners in the U.S., or working on a segmentation study with veterinarians in France (trying to understand how prescribing behaviors are evolving in various segments over time), or I might be conducting a pricing study with dog owners in Australia. The variety of projects is endless.

SIUE's Master of Market Research Program did a great job in preparing me for this role. The curriculum not only exposed me to analytical tools and data collection methodologies but also prepared me to approach problem solving in a logical and productive manner. It gave me basic skills, experience and confidence to tackle any marketing research problem thrown my way. SIUE's MMR program provided a blend of academic theory and real-world experience, gained through real projects with local businesses. The best thing for me about the MMR program was its internship program. When I graduated, I had a solid degree to lean on and real experience working for a great market research firm (I served a fantastic internship at Maritz Market Research in St. Louis, MO, one of the top U.S. research firms). As a result, I had my first job offer before I even graduated. Today, I am working in an exciting position with a great career that always stays challenging. In appreciation for the positive impact the MMR program made on my career and on my life, I have maintained a close relationship with it, and currently serve as a member of its Advisory Board. My hope is that all students who have an interest in marketing, but aren't quite sure what the opportunities are in the field, would look into SIUE's MMR program (or one of the nation's other MMR programs), as a career in marketing research might be a perfect fit for them.

Jeff Minier

It is rare to find no one responsible for marketing research in large organizations; small business owners who see their customers daily conduct their own "informal" research constantly.

marketing research to ensure that all units of the firm have input into and benefit from any research activity undertaken. In some cases, committees or individuals assigned to marketing research may actually conduct some limited research, but typically their primary role is that of helping other managers recognize the need for research and coordinating the purchase of research from external research suppliers. Obviously, the advantage here is limiting fixed costs incurred by maintaining the full-time staff required for an ongoing department. In some organizations, no one may be assigned to marketing research. This is rare in large companies, but it is not at all unusual in smaller firms. In very small firms, the owner/manager plays many roles, ranging from strategic planner to salesperson to security staff. He or she must also be responsible for marketing research, making certain to have the right information before making decisions.

External Suppliers

External suppliers are outside firms hired to fulfill a firm's marketing research needs.

Go to www.greenbook .org and click on the picture of the *Greenbook*. Exploring this website will give you a better understanding of how to classify external supplier firms. Also visit the different "directory" listings at www.quirks .com.

External suppliers are outside firms hired to fulfill a firm's marketing research needs. Both large and small firms, for-profit and not-for-profit, and government and educational institutions purchase research information from external suppliers, which are listed in directories. For example, go to www.greenbook.org and click on the picture of the *Greenbook*. Exploring this website will give you a better understanding of how to classify external supplier firms by area of specialization. Also visit the different "directory" listings at www.quirks.com.

HOW DO EXTERNAL SUPPLIERS ORGANIZE? Like internal supplier firms, external supplier firms organize themselves in different ways: by function (data analysis, data collection, etc.), by type of research application (customer satisfaction, advertising effectiveness, new-product development, etc.), by geography (domestic vs. international), by type of customer (health care, government, telecommunications, etc.), or by some combination of these. Research companies also change their organizational structure to accommodate changes in the environment. For example, as online research grew in the past several years, Burke, Inc. added a division to Burke Marketing Research called Burke Interactive. Finally, many companies use multiple bases for organizing. ORC International has sectors that include business-to-business, consumer, and financial services as well as IT applications and data collection.[14]

External suppliers can be classified as either full-service or limited-service supplier firms.

CLASSIFYING EXTERNAL SUPPLIER FIRMS. As you may recall from Figure 3.1, we can classify all external supplier firms into two categories: full-service or limited-service firms. In the following paragraphs, we will define these two types of firms and give you some examples of each.

Full-service supplier firms have the ability to conduct the entire marketing research project for the buyer firms. Full-service firms can be further broken down into syndicated data services, standardized services, customized services, and online research services firms.

Full-Service Supplier Firms. **Full-service supplier firms** have the ability to conduct the entire marketing research project for the buyer firms. Full-service firms will often define the problem, specify the research design, collect and analyze the data, and prepare the final written report. Typically, these are larger firms that have the expertise as well as the necessary facilities to conduct research studies in their entirety. The Nielsen Company, for example, offers services in more than 100 countries and has more than 42,000 employees.[15] The company is a global information and media company with leading positions in marketing information, media information, business publications, trade shows, and the newspaper sector. IMS Health Inc. has approximately 8,000 full-time employees worldwide and provides services in more than 100 countries. The company offers market intelligence products and services, portfolio optimization capabilities, launch and brand management services, and managed care and consumer health offerings.[16] The Kantar Group (TKG) operates around the world and has several research businesses, including Millward Brown Group, Research International, The Ziment Group, Added Value, Kantar Media Research, Lightspeed Research, and Mattson Jack Group.[17] These divisions, among others, give TKG the ability to conduct many different forms of research. Most of the research firms found in the Honomichl Global Top 25 and Honomichl Top 50 would qualify as full-service firms.

Syndicated Data Service Firms.   **Syndicated data service firms** collect information that is made available to multiple subscribers. They supply information, or data, in standardized form (information may not be tailored to meet the needs of any one company) to a large number of companies, known as a syndicate. Therefore, these companies offer syndicated data to all subscribing members of the syndicate. IRI, formerly Information Resources, Inc., and ACNielsen, part of The Nielsen Company, are two large syndicated data services firms. We will discuss syndicated data service firms in greater detail in Chapter 7.

Standardized Service Firms.   **Standardized service firms** provide syndicated marketing research services, as opposed to syndicated data, to clients. Each client gets different data, but the *process* used to collect the data is standardized so that it may be offered to many clients at a cost less than that of a custom-designed project. Standardized service firms have the advantage of being experts in the services they offer. A firm is better off taking advantage of this expertise rather than creating its own service in-house and starting from scratch. TNS U.S., a unit of Taylor Nelson Sofres PLC, London, offers a service, TES, which focuses on information about movie theater operations.[18] Synovate's ProductQuest service assists in developing new products and improving existing products.[19] Several companies offer test marketing services. Parties involved in litigation, for example, sometimes use "mock juries" to listen to different attorney presentations. This allows the litigant's attorneys to present testimony in a way that will have greatest impact on jurors. Several marketing research firms, such as Baltimore Research, offer a "Mock Trials" service to prospective clients. Baltimore Research has a proven process for conducting this service.

Customized Service Firms.   **Customized service firms** offer a variety of research services that are tailored to meet the client's specific needs. Each client's problem is treated as a unique research project. These firms spend considerable time with a client firm to determine the problem and then design a research project to address the particular client's specific problem. For example, SDR Consulting, Inc. provides custom research to its clients. As shown by SDR's "Marketing Planning Model," the company can provide such services as market assessment, marketing-mix strategy development, implementation, and performance metrics as well as several other analytical services. (See page 52.)

Online Research Services Firms.   **Online research services firms** specialize in providing services online. First, let's clear up some terms that are used loosely when dealing with "online" research. We define **online research** as the use of computer networks, including the Internet, to assist in any phase of the marketing research process, including definition of the problem, research design, data gathering, analysis, and report distribution. Second, to distinguish between online research and **Web-based research**, we mean by the latter research that is conducted *on* Web applications. This type of research, sometimes confused with online research, may use traditional methods as well as online research methods.

Some Web-based applications would include research on the popularity of the Web pages themselves, such as "site hit counts," effectiveness studies of pop-up ads on websites, or research measuring consumers' reactions to various components of websites. Finally, online survey research, which has experienced rapid growth in the past several

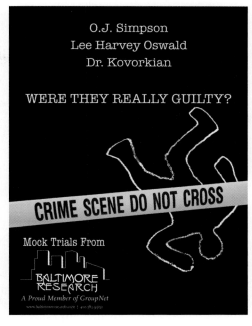

Among other services, Baltimore Research offers clients involved in litigation "Mock Trials." By permission.

Standardized service firms provide syndicated *services* as opposed to syndicated data. Each client gets different data, but the *process* used to collect the data is standardized so that it may be offered to many clients at a cost less than that of a custom-designed project.

Customized service firms offer a variety of research services that are tailored to meet the client's specific needs.

Customized service firms spend considerable time with a client firm to determine the problem and then design a research project to address the particular client's specific problem.

Marketing Planning Model

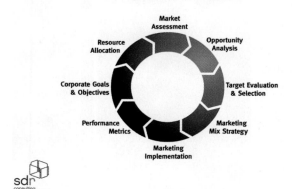

SDR Consulting, Inc. can provide services customized to fit clients' needs. Visit SDR Consulting, Inc. at http://www.sdrnet.com/. By permission.

years, is often confused with online research. Many people erroneously think online survey research is the same as online research. **Online survey research** refers to the collection of data using computer networks.

Virtually all research firms today use online research in the sense that they make use of online technology in at least one or more phases of the research process. These firms would be better categorized as one of the other types of firms shown in Figure 3.1. However, many firms *specialize* in online services. Their "reason for being" is based on the provision of services online. Affinova, for example, exists because it has proprietary software that allows consumers to design online preferred product attributes into new products. InsightExpress® was formed by NFO, Inc. in 1999 to allow clients to easily develop questionnaires and quickly conduct surveys online. The firm has grown rapidly and now offers many innovative services online. Knowledge Networks® came into being because its founders wanted to provide clients with access to probability samples online. Active Group was formed to conduct focus groups online. Greenfield Online® provides online access to panel members for marketing research firms. It specializes in maintaining an up-to-date large panel of persons who are willing to serve as study participants. Greenfield Online's service is explained in Marketing Research Insight 3.2.

Certainly, there are overlapping categories in Figure 3.1. We do not claim that the categories are mutually exclusive. In fact, we could argue that some of these, because they specialize in one step of the research process, could be placed in one of the limited-service supplier categories that follow.

LIMITED-SERVICE SUPPLIER FIRMS. **Limited-service supplier firms** specialize in one or, at most, a few marketing research activities. Firms can specialize in types of marketing research techniques, such as eye-testing and mystery shopping; or specific market segments, such as senior citizens; or certain sports segments, such as golf or tennis. The limited-service suppliers can be further classified on the basis of their specialization. These include field services, market segments, sample design and distribution, data analysis, and specialized research techniques. Many of these limited-service firms specialize in some form of online research.

Field service firms specialize in collecting data. They typically operate in a particular territory, conducting telephone surveys, focus group interviews, mall intercept surveys, or door-to-door surveys. Because it is expensive and difficult to maintain interviewers all over the country, firms will use field service firms in order to quickly and efficiently gather data. Even within firms that specialize in field services there is specialization. Some firms, for example, conduct only in-depth personal interviews; others conduct only mall-intercept surveys. Some firms, such as Mktg. Incorporated, conduct telephone surveys using CATI systems and are known as **phone banks** because they specialize in telephone surveying and have large numbers of telephone interviewers working in central locations. Irwin, located in Jacksonville, Florida, specializes in collecting data; it recruits participants for focus groups, collects data door-to-door and at in-store locations, and uses a number of other data-gathering techniques to suit the needs of clients.

Irwin is an example of a field services firm.

MARKETING RESEARCH INSIGHT   Practical Application

3.2 Greenfield Online and Ciao Surveys Would be Classified as an Online Research Services Firm

stay ahead™

Keith Price is executive vice president, Global Survey Solutions. Visit the company at: http://www.greenfield-ciaosurveys.com. By permission.

Greenfield Online-Ciao Surveys is a widely known and respected firm that would be classified in our classification system not only as an online research services firm but also as a firm that serves its customers—other marketing research firms—by providing them access to panels of respondents for online survey research.

At Greenfield Online we serve the needs of the market research industry by focusing on providing companies with access to consumer opinions globally. We engage consumers in the survey process to help companies better understand their customer in order to formulate effective product marketing strategies. Through our Greenfield Online and Ciao Surveys websites, Real-Time Sampling, just-in-time sampling methodology, and affiliate networks, we collect, organize and sell consumer opinions in the form of survey responses to marketing research companies and companies worldwide. Proprietary, innovative technology enables us to collect these opinions quickly and accurately, and to organize them into actionable form. For more information, visit www.greenfield-ciaosurveys.com.

Other limited-service firms, called **market segment specialists**, specialize in collecting data on special market segments, such as African Americans, Hispanics, children, seniors, gays, industrial customers, or on a specific geographic area within the United States or internationally. Strategy Research Corporation specializes in Latin American markets. JRH Marketing Services, Inc. specializes in marketing to ethnic markets, especially to black markets. Other firms specialize in children, mature citizens, pet owners, airlines, beverages, celebrities, college students, religious groups, and many other market segments. C&R Research has a division, called Latino Eyes, that specializes in U.S. Hispanic and Latin American markets. It has another division, called KidzEyes, specializing in kids, tweens, and teens, and another, called Sage Advice, that specializes in the 50-years-and-over market.[20] By specializing, these limited-service suppliers capitalize on their in-depth knowledge of the client's target market.

Survey Sampling Inc. and Scientific Telephone Samples (STS) are examples of limited-service firms that specialize in **sample design and distribution**. It is not uncommon, for example, for a company with an internal marketing research department to buy its sample from a firm specializing in sampling and then to send the samples and a survey questionnaire to a phone bank for completion of the survey. This way, a firm may quickly and efficiently conduct telephone surveys using a probability sample plan in markets all over the country. Survey Sampling, Inc. provides Internet samples, business-to-business samples, global samples, and samples of persons with characteristics that are hard to find (low-incidence samples).

Some limited-service marketing research firms offer **data analysis services**. Their contribution to the research process is to provide the technical assistance necessary to analyze and interpret data using the more sophisticated data analysis techniques, such as conjoint analysis. SDR Consulting, SPSS MR, and Applied Decision Analysis LLC are examples of such firms.

Specialized research technique firms provide a service to their clients by expertly administering a special technique. Examples of such firms include The PreTesting Company, which specializes in eye movement research. Eye movements are used to determine the effectiveness of ads, direct-mail pieces, and other forms of visual promotion. EyeTracking, Inc. specializes in measuring consumer attention, engagement, and affective response to new package designs and other visuals such as promotional materials. Other firms specialize in mystery shopping, taste tests, fragrance tests, creation of brand names, generating new ideas for products and services, and so on.

Survey Sampling, Inc. (SSI) is one of the oldest and best-known firms specializing in providing samples to marketing research firms. SSI is also an example of a company that uses online research. Users can design their sample plan online (see SSI SNAP) and receive their samples online. Go to www.surveysampling .com. By permission.

We know what the world is thinking.

When marketing researchers have to get it right, in more than 70 countries, they rely on SSI sampling. Knowing how to select, find, and engage research respondents has been in our DNA for 31 years. This dedication to respondent experience has earned the trust of millions worldwide across our proprietary, affiliate, and partner communities. So people are more open. Their opinions mean more. And your research is more reliable. More than 1,800 clients appreciate that.

T: +1.203.567.7200
info@surveysampling.com
surveysampling.com

Beijing • Frankfurt • La Quinta, CA • London • Madrid • Mumbai • Paris • Rotterdam • Seoul • Shanghai • Shelton, CT • Stockholm • Sydney • Tokyo • Toronto

We should not leave this section without saying that our categorization of research suppliers does not fit every situation. Many full-service firms fit neatly into more than one of our categories. TNS, for example, is a large, full-service firm. It also offers very specialized data analysis services. Also, there are other entities supplying research information that do not fit neatly into one of our categories. For example, universities and institutes supply research information. Universities sponsor a great deal of research that could be classified as marketing research.

CHALLENGES FACING THE MARKETING RESEARCH INDUSTRY

Now that you've learned some of the basics about the industry and know some of the companies themselves, we pause here to address some issues challenging the industry. Over the years, the marketing research industry has been the subject of constructive criticism and mixed reviews.[21] Earlier reviews indicated that although the marketing research industry was doing a reasonably good job, there was room for improvement.[22] More recent reviews, however, are not as complimentary.[23] The following section discusses some of the issues facing the industry, criticisms of the industry, and suggestions for remedies.

Issues with the Economy

If you were to ask a sample of marketing researchers today what their biggest concern is, it would no doubt be "the future economy." Late 2008 witnessed startling problems arising in the world economy. Forecasts are that the downturn will last several years. This will likely result in change in the marketing research industry. More than ever, marketing research firms will have to demonstrate the value that is added by their services. Research firms that can innovate and produce services that can help companies better deal with their own uncertainties and firms that can be flexible in reducing costs during hard times will survive. We will also likely see more consolidation in the industry as firms having strong expertise in one or more areas but unable to weather economic downturns will be acquired by other firms. Strategic alliances will likely grow during the next few years.

A struggling world economy will require marketing research firms to demonstrate the value that is added by their services in the years ahead.

The following quote illustrates how marketing research may be of value during economic downturns:

> When the economy weakens our first instinct is to cut back on expenditures. Few would argue with this instinct but it raises the obvious question: "Where and how much do we cut?" Managers may cut advertising at a time when advertising expenditures may be more effective than ever because competitors have cut back on advertising. Managers may cut funding for a new product roll out at a time when competitors have stopped new product introductions.
>
> When our competitors cut their marketing research and measurement expenditures, the strategic value of our marketing research information increases. With the right information, managers can make informed decisions about where and how much to cut and, in so doing, they may gain competitive advantage. At a time when budgets are expected to go farther than ever, research can actually provide the foundation for a smarter and more efficient marketing program.[24]

More than ever marketing research firms will have to demonstrate the value that is added by their services in a down economy. Research firms that can innovate and produce services that can help companies better deal with their own uncertainties and firms that can be flexible in reducing costs during hard times will survive.

The Lifeblood of the Industry—Consumer Cooperation

In addition to a struggling economy, marketing research costs have been climbing—it takes more resources than ever before to obtain samples of respondents. Response rates to requests for cooperation in research (mainly surveys) have been steadily declining for

Response rates to requests for cooperation in research (mainly surveys) have been steadily declining for several years.

several years. Because it often seeks information from consumers, marketing research is "invasive." Marketing researchers have struggled with growing consumer resentment of invasions of privacy. Weary of telemarketer and other direct marketer abuse, potential respondents have grown resentful of any attempt to gather information from them. In the *2007 Confirmit* industry survey of firms in several countries around the world, Wilson and Macer reported that the number-one "challenge" facing the marketing research industry was "falling response rates."[25] As telephone surveys response rates sank to new lows of about 7%, marketing researchers switched to online surveys. Soon after, online response rates plummeted as well. Business-to-business research has also experienced a similar decline in response rates.[26] Desperately needing respondents, research firms invested heavily in creating panels of consumers who agree to serve as research respondents.[27]

> *A worldwide industry survey reported that the number-one "challenge" facing the marketing research industry was "falling response rates."*

The long battle between marketing researchers and telemarketers has made gaining respondent cooperation more difficult. Consumer rights groups grew so powerful that the government, acting through the Federal Trade Commission (FTC), introduced a national "Do Not Call" registry in the summer of 2003 to curb telemarketer calls to anyone requesting that the calls be stopped (www.donotcall.gov). The registry has been effective, and CMOR reported that by 2008 about 145 million numbers were on the list, including both residential landlines and cell phones. Canada is implementing a DNC registry as well.[28]

> *The Do Not Call registry has been effective in the United States and is being implemented in Canada. Fortunately, the marketing research industry does not come under the ban placed on telemarketers in the Do Not Call regulations.*

Fortunately, the marketing research industry does not come under the ban placed on telemarketers in the Do Not Call regulations. However, the industry is very concerned about this trend. The Council of American Survey Research Organizations (CASRO), reporting research showing that 97% of consumers felt that telemarketers should be excluded through Do Not Call legislation, also found, alarmingly, that 64% of consumers felt the legislation should also apply to marketing researchers.[29] As an example of increasingly restrictive legislation, the FCC passed a new ruling in mid-2008 that forbids companies, including research firms, from using an automatic telephone dialing system to call a cell phone without prior consent.[30] Marketing researchers have also been paying attention to anti-spam legislation and encourage the reduction of spam. The "Can Spam" Act became effective on January 1, 2004, but it has done little to reduce spam. Increases in spam make respondents even more wary of loss of privacy, and this adversely affects legitimate requests for research information. Consumers have responded by refusing to participate in research studies.

> *Marketing researchers have also been paying attention to anti-spam legislation and encourage the reduction of spam. However, the "Can Spam" Act has done little to reduce spam.*

> *The industry must devote considerable time and effort to maintaining trusted relationships with consumer respondents, who are the "lifeblood" of the marketing research industry.*

The industry must devote considerable time and effort to maintaining trusted relationships with consumer respondents, who are the "lifeblood" of the marketing research industry. To stop growing consumer resentment, marketing research firms must treat respondents ethically.

Marketing Research No Longer Represents the "Voice of the Consumer"

Professor Emeritus Don E. Schultz of Northwestern University has claimed that marketing has lost its prominence among top management and partially blames marketing research for the decline. Why? Schultz believes that supply-chain management, by stressing economies of scale and excellence in logistics, with the assumption that lower prices will attract consumers, means that marketing's former role of representing the consumer has been lost. Marketing is now viewed as being an after-the-fact function that moves the goods, using promotional tools, at the end of the supply chain. Consumers are unimportant in the process. The assumption is that if we get the product to them at a low price, they will acquire it. Consequently, knowledge of consumers is less important. Schultz believes this is short-sighted and that marketing research must regain its role of providing top management with the "voice of the consumer."[31]

> *One critic believes marketing research must once again represent the "voice of the consumer" to top management.*

Marketing Research Is Parochial

Several critics of marketing research believe it is too parochial, that it is isolated and has a narrow focus.

Mahajan and Wind[32] and Shultz complain that managers misapply research by not having research professionals involved in high-level, strategic decision making. Marketing research professionals are left to report to lower levels in the firm and are not part of the strategic planning process. Their role is limited to routine reports and assessing promotion methods *after* the strategic decisions have been made. This occurs even when marketing research is outsourced to external suppliers. Too many executives view marketing research as a commodity to be outsourced to "research brokers," who are hired to conduct a component of the research process when they should be involved in the entire process.

Marketing research must be less parochial and must address the major strategic decisions of the firm. Mahajan and Wind suggest that marketing researchers should stop using marketing research only for testing solutions, such as testing a specific product or service. Instead, researchers should diagnose the market. For instance, consider that customers did not "ask" for a Sony Walkman or a minivan. Marketing researchers would not have known about these products by asking customers what they wanted, for without ever having seen the products, customers would have been unlikely to articulate the product characteristics. But had marketing researchers focused on diagnosing the market in terms of unserved and unarticulated needs, these products may have been discovered. The Walkman was successful because it met an unserved need for portable entertainment. The extreme popularity of Apple's iPod is a more recent example, which again, could be viewed as an extension of the market's demand for portability.

Marketing research can improve by properly diagnosing the market first, then testing alternative solutions to meet the needs discovered. Baker and Mouncey, like Mahajan and Wind, also suggest that marketing researchers should provide insight into the market and redirect their key focus to understanding the customer-brand relationship.[33]

Schultz would agree with Mahajan and Wind that marketing research has become too comfortable with providing standard reports using simple measures. Honomichl has also levied this same criticism.[34] This information, although useful, does not allow marketing research to contribute to the important central issues of determining overall strategy.

Marketing Research Operates in a "Silo"

This criticism is closely related, but different, to marketing research being too parochial. As we just learned, being too parochial means marketing research has not been addressing issues at the strategic planning level; it has been relegated to tactical issues within marketing. However, Schultz and Mahajan and Wind also believe that marketing research doesn't communicate with other entities within the firm. Shultz states that because firms are organized in a functional structure—departments of finance, operations, marketing, and so on—marketing (and marketing research) is viewed as just another function. The problem is that each function has its own knowledge and skills and operates in a "silo," with little interaction across functions. Each function reports to top management. By being just another of several functions reporting to top management, marketing has become less important as has its components, including marketing research. Consequently, marketing research has importance only within marketing. Marketers and marketing researchers have contributed to the demise of their own importance in the organization because, in recent years, they have come to view themselves not as managers, but as staff members who supply management with information. Marketing research could add value to other departments as well, but it must break down the "silos."

Several critics of marketing research believe it is too parochial, that it is isolated and has a narrow focus. Too often, marketing research professionals are left to report to lower levels of the firm and are not part of the strategic planning process.

Marketing researchers can add greater value if, instead of providing tactical reports, they provide information useful for determining and guiding the overall strategy of the firm.

Critics of marketing research believe that researchers do not adequately communicate with other entities within the firm.

Mahajan and Wind[35] feel that it is marketing researchers who have created the silos, thus separating themselves from other information. For example, by separating research into qualitative and quantitative research, researchers tend to use one or the other when, in fact, more insights may be gained by integrating the two approaches. Other silos are created when decision support systems are not linked with marketing research. Firms should integrate experiments they conduct instead of conducting one-shot projects that investigate a single issue. Mahajan and Wind also suggest greater integration of marketing research with existing databases and other information sources, such as customer complaints, other studies of product/service quality, and external databases. In other words, marketing researchers would improve their results by taking a closer look at all existing information instead of embarking on isolated research projects to solve a problem.

Marketing Research Is Too Tool-Oriented

Marketing researchers have been criticized for developing tools with which, instead of trying to diagnose the market and come up with creative solutions, they screen through issues until they find one to which they can apply one of their tools.

Critics of marketing research claim that marketing researchers develop tools with which, instead of trying to diagnose the market and come up with creative solutions, they screen through issues until they find one to which they can apply one of their tools. The problem with this is that the "cart is leading the horse." Just because the tool fits the issue doesn't mean that the chosen issue is the one that deserves attention. Schultz[36] stated that by focusing on their tools, external suppliers of marketing research have furthered this perception. Unfortunately, the research problem too often is defined in terms of being compatible with one of the existing tools ("can use conjoint analysis to solve this problem"), and researchers too readily apply a tool instead of focusing on the more complex strategic issues facing the firm. The end result is that marketing researchers have become used to supplying "ingredients" instead of being involved in making strategic decisions. Schultz believes that marketing research today provides few real insights about customers. The overused set of tools, often selected to be implemented by the lowest bidder, provides more sophisticated analysis on irrelevant data but does not help the firm hear the "voice of the consumer."[37]

Marketing Researchers Should Speed Up Marketing Research by Using Information Technology

Online research has grown significantly because it can speed up the research process.

With globalization and the outsourcing of functions to "low bidders" throughout the world, there has never been a more important time for marketing research to show value. One way to increase value is to provide the same information but at lower costs and faster. Years ago, Roger D. Blackwell, a long-time marketing consultant, stated that the marketing research cycle must be stepped up because of fierce competition.[38] Blackwell was correct and his statement is even more applicable in today's business environment. It has long been recognized that there is a trade-off between quickly producing marketing research information and doing research in a thorough manner. Marketing researchers want time to conduct projects properly. However, Mahajan and Wind point out that researchers must remember that time is money. Real dollar losses result from introducing products and services to the marketplace too late. So much so, in fact, that many companies cut many corners in the research they conduct or do not do any marketing research at all. This, labeled "death-wish" marketing, often leads, of course, to disaster.[39] The suggested remedy is for marketing researchers to make use of information technology (IT) for speed and economical efficiency, which is exactly why online research has become such a significant part of the research industry.[40] Decision Analysts, Inc. allows companies to test product concepts quickly using online respondents. Using their online technology, InsightExpress® conducts very rapid concept tests for new product and service ideas. We have already mentioned Affinova, an online research company that allows potential consumers to be involved in designing new products online in a fraction of the time it would take using standard methods. Harris Interactive, Knowledge Networks, Greenfield Online, and many others facilitate online surveys. All of these firms use IT to speed up and reduce the cost of research.

Other Criticisms of Marketing Research

Several critiques of the research industry have been issued over the years, some by knowledgeable persons and others as a result of asking buyers of marketing research studies whether the research performed by industry suppliers is worthwhile. Criticism has focused on the following areas of concern: There is a lack of creativity, the industry is too survey-oriented, the industry does not understand the real problems that need to be studied, market researchers show a lack of concern for respondents, the industry has a cavalier attitude regarding nonresponse error, the price of the research is high relative to its value, and academic marketing research should be more closely related to actual marketing management decisions.[41] Critical reviews are good for the industry. John Stuart Mill once said that "custom is the enemy of progress."[42] One entire issue of *Marketing Research*, edited by Chuck Chakrapani, was devoted to a number of articles questioning customary practices in the field.[43] The debate these articles stirred up is good for the industry. In sum, these evaluations concluded that the industry has performed well, but there is room for improvement. We discuss some of the suggestions for improvement in the following sections.

Certification and Education: Means to Improve the Industry

We must point out that although the preceding discussion focused on criticism of the industry and we fully agree with Mill that criticism is good, the marketing research industry has much to be proud of. It has performed well by the toughest of all standards, the test of the marketplace. As we noted earlier in this chapter, annual revenues in the research industry now total over $25 billion, and these revenues, with few exceptions, have increased over the years. Obviously, clients see value in the marketing research being generated. However, the industry is not complacent. Many suggest that the problems are created by a very small minority of firms, most of which are simply not qualified to deliver quality marketing research services.

A study of buyers' and suppliers' perceptions of the research industry by Dawson, Bush, and Stern found the lack of uniform quality in the industry to be a key issue—there are good suppliers and there are poor suppliers.[44] Two methods by which the industry is seeking self-improvement are certification and education.

CERTIFICATION. **Certification** indicates the achievement of some minimal standard of performance. Critics have argued for many years that marketing research attracts practitioners who are not fully qualified to provide adequate service to client firms due in large part to the fact that there have been no formal requirements in terms of education, degrees, certificates, licenses, or tests of any kind to open a marketing research business. Certainly, the staffs of a majority of research firms are thoroughly trained in research methods and have given years of excellent performance. However, many industry observers state it is those few firms with unqualified personnel and management that tarnish the industry's image. Some believe many of the problems are caused by individuals in public relations, consulting, or advertising firms who conduct marketing research without the proper training and background.

Other professions, such as accounting, real estate, and financial analysis, have learned that certification programs can raise the overall level of competence within an industry.[45] Years ago, Alvin Achenbaum[46] as well as Patrick Murphy and Gene Laczniak[47] proposed that the marketing research profession certify marketing researchers as certified public researchers (CPRs), analogous to CPAs or CFAs. Those opposed to the idea pointed out that it would be difficult, if not impossible, to agree on certification standards, particularly

Other criticisms of the industry focus on not being creative, focusing too much on survey research, not knowing the real problem of the client, not caring about respondents, not addressing the problem of nonresponse error and price being high relative to the value of the research provided.

Critical reviews have stirred debate in the marketing research industry.

Many of the problems in the research industry are created by a very small minority of firms, most of which are simply not qualified to deliver quality marketing research services.

Certification indicates the achievement of some minimal standard of performance.

MARKETING RESEARCH INSIGHT   Practical Insights

3.3 Professional Researcher Certification

On February 28, 2005, the Marketing Research Association (MRA) announced its first edition of the certification program, the Professional Researcher Certification (PRC). The new version of the certification, PRC 2.0, began on July 1, 2008. The paragraphs below contain the essentials of the program.[48]

Certification Overview

Who Designed the Certification Program?
The MRA assumed the leadership role in developing the certification program, however, to ensure widespread industry input and participation, the Certification Board included both MRA and non-MRA members. Members included representatives from the MRII, the IMRO Division of MRA, the CMOR, and the AMA. The certification board represented all segments of the marketing research industry from data collectors to end users.

What Is the Certification Designed to Do?
The certification program is designed to accomplish the following three objectives:

- reflect all segments of the marketing research profession
- be recognized by industry-related associations and experts
- meet all requirements of the NOCA (National Organization for Competency Assurance) and the IACET (CEU [continuing education unit] authorization entity)

Who Benefits from Certification?
The PRC certification program is beneficial for both the individual and the industry. For the individual, it is a means of differentiating oneself from others. A "badge" of competence gives assurance to others that the certified individual meets some minimal level of knowledge and experience. The certification program benefits the industry in that it aids in the development of a pool of well-trained, competent marketing researchers, thereby improving standards in the industry. The program also gives a face to the industry for the outside world.

Certification Recognizes the Diversity with the Industry

In order to address the diversity of the work collectively known as "survey and opinion research," job descriptions throughout the industry were analyzed and sorted into categories on the basis of levels of responsibility, levels of specialized knowledge, and levels of required knowledge. The three major segments are: Data Collection, End Users/Clients, Research Companies and Related Services. Within each segment there are two levels of certification—Expert and Practitioner—based on depth and breadth of knowledge and work experience required for the position.

Criteria for Levels of Certification

The criteria for each level of certification are the following.

Expert
Candidates are expected to have a thorough and detailed knowledge of topics classified at this level and of the corresponding positions, which may include Chief Executive Officer, Chief Operations Officer, Owner, Executive Vice-President, Senior Vice-President, Vice-President, Senior Director, and the like. Applicants must have no record of ethics complaints during the previous three years and must be a current member of at least one marketing research professional organization that adheres to a code of ethics or be a signator to the MRA's Code of Research Standards. Applicants must also have five or more years of experience in a senior-level or equivalent position and have attended at least one industry conference in the previous three years. Also, every two years those certified at the expert level must show proof of 14 completed contact hours of education and submit a renewal application to maintain proficiency in their certification category.

Practitioner
At the practitioner level, candidates are expected to have knowledge of topics that arise frequently in day-to-day professional practice. Job titles for these candidates may include Manager, Supervisor, Analyst, and Sales Staff. Applicants must

By permission, Marketing Research Association

have no record of ethics complaints during the previous three years, have three to five years of experience in the field, and be a member of at least one professional marketing research organization that adheres to a code of ethics or a signator to the MRA's Code of Research Standards. Also, every two years those certified at the practitioner level must show proof of 18 completed contact hours of education and submit a renewal application to maintain proficiency in their certification category.

Examination

All candidates who apply after December 31, 2008 must take an exam developed by the Certification Development Committee. A candidate who has taken courses within the preceding five years can include this information on their application. Exams are developed using resources within the profession and are based on topic areas directly related to the skills and knowledge required for a specific position. Once an application stating intent to apply for certification is submitted, the candidate is sent an exam handbook and information on how to prepare for a certification exam. Within two years of applying, candidates must earn the appropriate contact hours of education for their skill level and submit documentation to MRA headquarters. The MRA Certification Department will then review the documentation and set a time and place for the examination. The exams will test the candidate's comprehension of topics central to the candidate's daily professional practice.

Maintaining Certification

Knowledge and skills acquired through contact hours of education will be the primary method of maintaining certification. Individuals must accrue a specified number of these hours in the category in which they are certified. Contact hours can be earned by attending an approved educational program, such as MRA conferences and Webinars, industry association education events, or online courses that offer programming in management, research, or legal topics. Such education allows individuals to develop the skills to keep up with industry trends and techniques.

Certification versus Accreditation?

Certification applies to individuals; accreditation applies to an organization. The MRA has begun to accredit companies via the MRA Review Program, which currently covers online research and will be expanded to cover other forms of research.

Want to Learn More about Professional Researcher Certification?

Go to the PRC website at www.mra-net.org/prc.

---

for the creative aspect of the research process.[49] Professor Stephen W. McDaniel, a researcher with an interest in certification for marketing researchers, has outlined the following arguments in favor of a certification program:[50]

- **Higher level of professionalism.** Certification will raise the standards for the entire marketing research industry. The designation "Professional Researcher Certification" will communicate a level of professionalism that currently does not always exist among research practitioners.
- **More credibility.** The credibility of individual marketing researchers and the level of trust in research processes and findings will increase. Overall, marketing researchers will be more knowledgeable and qualified, and the number of incompetent researchers will no doubt be reduced.
- **Better image.** The marketing research industry will be viewed more positively and will be awarded more respect by consumers, the business community, and government regulators.
- **Higher ethical standards.** Not only will those going through the certification process be sensitive to the ethical issues involved in the research process but ethical standards can be more easily set and enforced. The threat of decertification will be a strong motivator of ethical behavior.
- **Better client service.** Those paying the bill for the research will be better served. Overall, research studies will more likely be better designed and implemented, with more valid and reliable results.

The **Professional Researcher Certification (PRC)** program was started after several years of planning by the Marketing Research Association. Marketing Research Insight 3.3 provides many of the details.

Southern Illinois University–Edwardsville offers a Master's degree that specializes in marketing research. See Appendix A for more information about this program and other educational opportunities in marketing research. By permission.

There are many opportunities for members of the marketing research industry to learn more about their profession through a wide variety of educational offerings.

Certification, by requiring CEUs, will likely have a positive effect on educational programs in the industry.

Any review of the industry would agree that it is responding to its many challenges.

Want to know what kinds of topics are taught at the Burke Institute? Go to www.burkeinstitute.com and click on "seminars."

EDUCATION. There are many opportunities for members of the marketing research industry to learn more about their profession. For many years, the marketing research industry has offered a wide variety of educational opportunities to its members. Certification, by requiring CEUs to maintain certification, will have a positive effect on educational programs in the industry. The AMA, among the several industry organizations offering programs, sponsors an annual Marketing Research Conference; the Advanced School of Marketing Research, which is a program conducted at Notre Dame University for the analyst, project supervisor, or manager of marketing research; and an annual conference that focuses on advanced analytical techniques. Several years ago the Marketing Research Association in coordination with the University of Georgia, started an introductory program on marketing research, which is designed to develop the research skills of those who have been transferred into marketing research or those who want to enter the profession. In addition, the Marketing Research Association (MRA), the Council for the Association of Survey Research Organizations (CASRO's CASRO University), the Qualitative Research Consultant's Associaton (QRCA), the Advertising Research Foundation (ARF), the British Market Research Association, the Australian Market & Social Research Society, the Market Research Society of New Zealand, and several other industry associations have many frequently scheduled, excellent training classes and programs to meet industry needs.

Several universities now offer master's-level training in marketing research. One well-regarded program is the Master of Marketing Research Program at Southern Illinois University–Edwardsville (see Appendix A at the end of this chapter). We asked Michael Brereton, president and CEO of Maritz research to describe for you the needs of the industry in terms of personnel and his experience with the Master of Marketing Research program at SIUE. His remarks, written expressly for this edition, are contained in Marketing Research Insight 3.4. Certain firms also provide excellent training for the industry. The Burke Institute, a division of Burke, Inc., has for many years provided training programs that are highly regarded in the industry. The institute conducts classes throughout the year on a number of topics, including online research, multivariate techniques, questionnaire design, focus group moderating, basic marketing research, and many others. Any review of the industry would show that the industry is responding to its many challenges.

ETHICS AND MARKETING RESEARCH

In our last edition of this book we said that "recent history has shown that ethical issues are rife in religion, government, politics and business." Unfortunately, this is still the case. The problems at Enron, WorldCom, and HealthSouth are now seemingly miniscule compared

MARKETING RESEARCH INSIGHT

Practical Insights

3.4 The President and CEO of Maritz Research Speaks on the Need for Professionals in the Marketing Research Industry

The commercial application of marketing research focuses on the capture and interpretation of the voice of the customer and employee. The resulting insight drives a market knowledge-driven process for superior decision making among business leaders.

This is a thought leadership intensive business process. Our industry is dependent upon a continuous flow of marketing professionals striving to bridge the divide between academic and theoretical research and their practical application to drive decision making in a business context.

We factor academic partnership, such as with the Southern Illinois University–Edwardsville Master of Marketing Research (MMR) program, as an integral part of our human resource planning. We consider the MMR program an important source in the development of our professional talent. This consideration is driven by the uniqueness of the program. Its cooperative format produces graduates able to quickly and significantly contribute to our organization's success.

We have been extremely impressed by the quality of MMR graduates. Looking back over a fifteen-year period, the program has consistently produced the caliber of individual that Maritz Research, and many of our clients' organizations,

Michael Brereton is president of Maritz Research and has general management responsibility for Maritz's global operations. Prior to joining Maritz, Michael was involved in advertising research, future product planning research, and corporate segmentation while employed at General Motors of Canada. He is currently a member of the Southern Illinois University–Edwardsville Master of Marketing Research Program Advisory Board and a Board Director for the Council Of American Survey Research Organizations (CASRO). Michael received a Bachelor of Science degree from General Motors Institute in Flint, Michigan and an MBA from Bowling Green State University in Ohio.

have placed in business leadership roles. We have been fortunate to hire more than twenty-five graduates of the MMR Program and have seen these graduates, without exception, achieve very high levels of performance and scholarship in the discipline of marketing research.

We credit the Southern Illinois University–Edwardsville Master of Marketing Research program, and similar such programs, with creating a generation of marketing research professionals and thereby substantially enhancing the field of applied research.

Michael Brereton, President and CEO Maritz Research
By permission.

to the unethical practices that went on in the financial industry during the last decade. Unfortunately, these were not isolated incidents involving business managers who took advantage of others for personal gain. As in most areas of business activity, there exist many opportunities in the marketing research industry for unethical (and ethical) behavior.[51] A study by the Ethics Resource Center of Washington, DC, states that the most common ethical problem in the workplace is "lying to employees, customers, vendors or the public" (26%), followed by "withholding needed information" from those parties (25%). Only 5% of those in the study reported having seen people giving or taking "bribes, kickbacks, or inappropriate gifts." Ninety percent of American workers "expect their organizations to do

As in most areas of business activity, there exist many opportunities for unethical (and ethical) behavior in the marketing research industry.

Unfortunately, the marketing research industry is not immune to ethical problems.

We think these ethical issues are so important that we call your attention to them throughout this book using the ethical issue icon that you see here.

Ethics may be defined as a field of inquiry into determining what behaviors are deemed appropriate.

what is right, not just what is profitable." But one in eight of those polled said they "feel pressure to compromise their organization's ethical standards." And among these respondents, nearly two-thirds said pressure "comes from top management, their supervisors and/or coworkers."[52] A study of MBA students reported in *USA Today* shows that 52% would buy stock on inside information; 26% would let a gift sway purchasing decisions; and 13% said they would pay someone off in order to close a business deal.[53] Unfortunately, the marketing research industry is not immune to ethical problems.[54] We introduce you here to the areas in which unethical behavior has occurred in the past and, we hope, give you a framework for thinking about how you will conduct yourself in the future when confronted with these situations. We think these ethical issues are so important that we call your attention to them throughout this book using the ethical issue icon that you see at the beginning of this section.

Ethics may be defined as a field of inquiry into determining what behaviors are deemed appropriate under certain circumstances as prescribed by codes of behavior that are set by society. Society determines what is ethical and what is not. In some cases, this code is formalized by our institutions. Some behavior, for example, is so wrongful that it is deemed illegal by statute.

Behavior that is illegal is unethical, by definition. However, there are many other behaviors that are considered by some to be unethical but that are not illegal. When these types of behaviors are not specifically identified by some societal institution (such as the justice system, the legislature, Congress, regulatory agencies such as the FTC, etc.), then the determination of whether the behaviors are ethical or unethical is open to debate.

Your Ethical Views Are Shaped by Your Philosophy: Deontology or Teleology

One's philosophy usually determines what is appropriate, ethical behavior.

One philosophy, deontology, focuses on the rights of the individual. If an individual's rights are violated, then the behavior is not ethical.

Teleology is a philosophy that focuses on the trade-off between individual costs and group benefits. If benefits outweigh costs, the behavior is judged to be ethical.

There are many philosophies that may be applied to explain one's determination of appropriate behavior given certain circumstances. In the following discussion we use the two philosophies of deontology and teleology to explain this behavior.[55] **Deontology** is concerned with the rights of the individual. Is the behavior fair and just for each individual? If an individual's rights are violated, then the behavior is not ethical.[56] For example, consider the marketing research firm that has been hired to study how consumers are attracted to and react to a new form of in-store display. Researchers, hidden from view, record the behavior of unsuspecting shoppers as they walk through a supermarket. A deontologist considers this form of research activity unethical because it violates the individual shopper's right to privacy. The deontologist would likely agree to the research provided the shoppers were informed beforehand that their behavior would be recorded, giving them the option to participate or not to participate.[57]

On the other hand, **teleology** analyzes a given behavior in terms of its benefits and costs to society. If there are costs to the individual but benefits for the group, then there are net gains, and the behavior is judged to be ethical.[58] In our example of the shopper being observed in the supermarket, the teleologist might conclude that although there is a violation of the privacy of the shoppers observed (the cost), there is a benefit if the company learns how to market goods more efficiently, thus reducing long-term marketing costs. Because this benefit ultimately is shared by many more individuals than those whose privacy was invaded during the original study, the teleologist would likely declare this research practice to be ethical.

Thus, whether you view a behavior as ethical or unethical depends on your philosophy. Are you a deontologist or a teleologist? It's difficult to answer that question until you are placed in an ethically sensitive situation. You will certainly come across ethically sensitive situations during your career. Will you recognize an ethically sensitive situation? How will you respond? We hope you will at least know when you are in such a situation in marketing research. The rest of this section is devoted to awakening your sensitivity.[59]

Ethical Behavior in Marketing Research Is a Worldwide Issue

As noted previously, a society may prescribe wanted and unwanted behaviors in many ways. In business, practices that are not illegal but are nevertheless thought to be wrong will be outlined by trade associations or professional organizations in a **code of ethical behavior**. This has been the case in marketing and, more specifically, in marketing research. The American Marketing Association (www.marketingpower.com), the Council

---

 MARKETING RESEARCH INSIGHT   *Ethical Application*

3.5 Baltimore Research Follows MRA's Code of Ethics

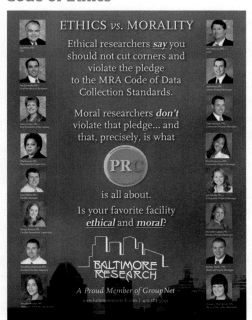

Baltimore Research is a full service marketing research firm. One of the many services we offer our clients is focus group research. There are ethical concerns with focus group facilities that "cut corners" in recruiting respondents. A given focus group will have strict specifications for the profile of qualified candidates. This can include household composition, demographics, brand and category usage, as well as a number of lifestyle and personality variables. Ideally, the focus group should be comprised of a cross section of consumers that meet the exact criteria needed by the client. For example, Frito-Lay may have a new, nutritious snack that they want to test with mothers of young children who purchase similar foods. While it takes time and effort to find the right individuals, we will only recruit the types of consumers our client expects to

have in our focus groups. Baltimore Research utilizes a number of creative methodologies to target the harder to find segments. You will read more about this concept in this book when your authors discuss "incidence rates."

Clients expect us to recruit "typical" consumers into our focus groups. There are individuals who try to get into as many focus groups as possible to make a living from participation. This presents a number of concerns to researchers. For example, they may lie in the screening process and not really be the type of consumer sought. Consequently, their experiences may not be truly relevant. For a number of other reasons, these "professional respondents" may not be representative of the average consumer. We have implemented many procedures to safeguard against professional respondents, including software to track respondent participation by a number of variables, such as frequency and research topic. At Baltimore Research, we know that our enduring profitability and existence depends on providing quality information that will help our client solve their research problems. If we give them the information that leads them to be more profitable, they will return to us when they have a future need for marketing research.

At Baltimore Research we "take the pledge" to avoid unethical shortcuts to ensure the long-term health of our industry. Many of our employees hold PRCs (Professional Researcher Certifications) from the MRA (Marketing Research Association). We are committed to continuing education for our employees and are proud custodians of the MRA's Code of Ethics.

Ted Donnelly, Ph.D., PRC, Vice President, Baltimore Research

To examine the MRA's Code of Marketing Research Standards, go to www.mra-net.org, and RESOURCES, and then CODES/FORMS and GUIDELINES.

of American Survey Research Organizations (www.casro.org), the Qualitative Research Consultants Association (www.qrca.org), the Marketing Research Association (www.mra-net.org), and the Canadian-based Professional Market Research Society (www.pmrs-aprm.com) all have codes of ethics.

The European-based ESOMAR (www.esomar.org) also has a code of ethics, referred to as "Professional Standards." ESOMAR was formed as the European Society for Opinion and Marketing Research but now refers to itself as the World Association of Opinion and Marketing Research. Most of the codes named here may be viewed online even if you are not a member of the organization.

All over the world, organizations are striving to encourage ethical behavior among practitioners of marketing research. Marketing Research Insight 3.5 illustrates how one firm follows the MRA's code of eithics.

CODES OF ETHICS.   As noted previously, The Marketing Research Association has a code of ethics. We encourage you to look over the entire code, but here are some of the issues it covers:

- prohibiting selling (sugging) or fund-raising (frugging) under the guise of conducting research
- maintaining research integrity by avoiding misrepresentation and omission of pertinent research data
- treating outside clients and suppliers fairly.

Sugging refers to "selling under the guise of a survey." Frugging refers to "fund-raising under the guise of a survey."

Sugging is illegal.

SUGGING AND FRUGGING.   Marketing researchers are prohibited from selling or fund-raising under the guise of conducting research. **Sugging** refers to "selling under the guise of a survey." Typically, sugging occurs when a "researcher" gains a respondent's cooperation to participate in a research study and then uses the opportunity to attempt to sell the respondent a good or service. Most consumers are quite willing to provide their attitudes and opinions of products and services in response to a legitimate request for this information. Suggers (and Fruggers), however, take advantage of that goodwill by deceiving unsuspecting consumers. Consumers soon learn that their cooperation in answering a few questions has led to their being subjected to a sales presentation. In sugging and frugging there is no good-faith effort to conduct a survey for the purpose of collecting and analyzing data for specific purposes. Rather, the intent of the "fake" survey is to sell or raise money. Of course, these practices have led to the decline in the pool of cooperative respondents. The Telemarketing and Consumer Fraud and Abuse Prevention Act of 1994 made sugging illegal. Under this act, telemarketers are not allowed to call someone and say they are conducting a survey and then try to sell a product or service. But even though telemarketers are not legally able to practice sugging, the act does not prohibit sugging via the mail.[60] **Frugging** is closely related to sugging; it stands for "fund-raising under the guise of a survey." Because frugging does not involve the sale of a product or service, it is not covered in the Telemarketing and Consumer Fraud and Abuse Prevention Act of 1994, but it is widely considered to be unethical. Actually, both sugging and frugging are carried out by telemarketers, who are the main offenders, or other direct marketers. But it would be rare indeed to find a researcher doing either. However, we cover this topic because both sugging and frugging are unethical treatments of potential respondents in marketing research.

Frugging is unethical.

The marketing research industry recognizes that it must attempt to influence legislation in a way that will be favorable to the industry. For example, the industry fought hard to protect consumers from sugging and frugging. Also, when Do Not Call bills were first introduced, the industry worked hard to educate lawmakers about the difference between telemarketers and researchers. Much of this work was conducted by CMOR, the Council for Marketing and Opinion Research, which was founded in 1992 by four industry associations and is now a part of the Marketing Research Association.

RESEARCH INTEGRITY. Sometimes research is not totally objective. Information may be withheld, falsified, or altered to protect vested interests. Marketing research information is often used in making significant decisions, which may have an impact on future company strategy, budgets, jobs, organization, and so forth. With so much at stake, the opportunity exists for modifying **research integrity**, defined as performing research that adheres to accepted standards. The loss of objectivity may take the form of withholding information, falsifying data, altering research results, or misinterpreting the research findings in a way that makes them more consistent with predetermined points of view. One researcher stated the consequences of maintaining integrity in these situations: "I refused to alter research results and as a result I was fired for failure to think strategically."[61]

An example illustrates that research integrity is a serious issue. Forrester Research, Inc. released a report concluding that developing and deploying Web-based portal applications is substantially less expensive using Microsoft technology than it is using a Linux/J2ee platform. When it was learned that the research was funded by Microsoft, several CEOs expressed skepticism, including one who stated, "I'm not a big fan of any of those marketing research firms. I don't believe them to be independent." Forrester CEO George Colony responded that the company was taking steps to "tighten" its internal processes and its integrity policy.[62] In another example, Hodock, when examining reasons for a product failure, addressed the issue of inflated sales forecasts that were unethically provided to upper management. Why? Because underlings knew that top management wanted a rosy picture for a new-product innovation. Hodock notes that inflating sales forecasts is an ongoing ethical issue in the business world, yet is rarely noted in college classrooms.[63]

Another example of violating the integrity of the research occurred in the automobile industry. As managers have learned that repeat sales and positive WOM (word-of-mouth) are strongly associated with customer satisfaction, they have implemented many customer satisfaction programs to track the level of customer satisfaction. These programs often offer strong incentives to dealers for "high customer satisfaction scores." However, the scores may not be an accurate reflection of true customer satisfaction. Half of the respondents to a 2007 TrueDelta Poll reported that the dealership tried to influence their survey responses by, for example, asking or begging for perfect scores, commenting the dealership would get a bonus for a perfect score, offering gifts for a perfect score, asking the customer to fill out the survey at the dealership, or even asking customers to give the blank survey to the dealership to fill out on its own.[64]

Some auto owners have reported being pressured into giving their dealer high customer-satisfaction ratings.

Either the supplier or buyer may commit a breach of research integrity. If a research supplier knows that a buyer will want marketing research services in the future, the supplier may alter a study's results or withhold information so that the study will support the buyer's wishes. Breaches of research integrity need not be isolated to those managing the research project. Interviewers have been known to make up interviews and to take shortcuts in completing surveys. In fact, there is some evidence that this is more of a problem than was once thought.[65] Maintaining research integrity is regarded as one of the most significant ethical issues in the research industry. In a study of 460 marketing researchers, Hunt, Chonko, and Wilcox found that maintenance of research integrity posed the most significant problem for one-third of those sampled.[66]

TREATING OTHERS FAIRLY. Several ethical issues in marketing research may arise from how others are treated. Suppliers, buyers, and the public may be treated unethically.

Buyers. In the Hunt, Chonko, and Wilcox study previously cited, the second most frequently stated ethical problem facing marketing researchers was fair treatment of buyer firms. Passing hidden charges to buyers, overlooking study requirements when subcontracting work out to other firms, and selling unnecessary research are examples of unfair treatment of clients. By overlooking study requirements, such as qualifying respondents on the characteristics specified or verifying that respondents were interviewed, the supplier firm may lower its cost of using the services of a subcontracting field service firm. A supplier firm may oversell research services to naive buyers by convincing them to use a more expensive research design.

> Sharing of "background knowledge" among firms raises ethical questions.

Sharing confidential and proprietary information raises ethical questions. Virtually all work conducted by marketing research firms is confidential and proprietary. Researchers build up a storehouse of this information as they conduct studies. Most ethical issues involving confidentiality revolve around how this storehouse of information, or "background knowledge," is treated. One researcher stated, "Where does 'background knowledge' stop and conflict exist [as a result of work with a previous client]?"[67] It is common practice among research firms to check their existing list of buyer-clients to ensure that there is no conflict of interest before accepting work from a new buyer.

> Marketing researchers try to avoid conflicts of interest by not working for two competitors.

Suppliers: Phony RFPs. Buyers of marketing research can also abuse suppliers. A major ethical problem arises, for example, when a firm with internal research capabilities issues a **request for proposals (RFP)** from external supplier firms but has no intention of doing the job outside. External firms spend time and money developing research designs to solve the stated problem, estimating costs of the project, and so on. Issuing a call for proposals from external firms with no intention of following through is unethical behavior.

Failure to Honor Time and Money Agreements. Often, buyer firms have obligations, such as agreeing to meetings or providing materials necessary for the research project. Buyers must fulfill these commitments in a timely fashion so supplier firms can keep to their time schedules. But buyer firms sometimes abuse their agreements to deliver personnel or other resources in the time to which they have agreed. Also, buyers sometimes do not honor commitments to pay for services. Failures to pay happen in many industries, but research suppliers do not have the ability to repossess their product, although they do, of course, have legal recourse.

> Ethical concerns arise when marketing researchers are asked to conduct research on advertising to children or on products they feel are dangerous to the public, such as certain chemicals, cigarettes, alcohol, or sugar.

The Public. Sometimes researchers are asked to do research on products thought to be dangerous to society. Ethical issues arise as researchers balance marketing requirements against social concerns, particularly in the areas of product development and advertising. For example, marketing researchers have expressed concern over conducting research on advertising to children. The objective of some advertising, for example, is increasing the total consumption of refined sugar among children via ads scheduled during Saturday-morning TV programs. Other ethical concerns involve research on products thought to be dangerous to the public, such as certain chemicals, cigarettes, alcohol, and sugar.

Some marketing research firms take a proactive approach to helping their clients implement strategies that consider ethical issues. For example, ABACO Marketing Research in Sao Paulo, Brazil, incorporates ethical considerations into its evaluations of clients' promotional materials. Their AD-VISOR® service provides ethical scores and compares them with norms, thus allowing clients to understand consumers' ethical evaluations of proposed communication messages.

RESPONDENTS. As we noted earlier in this chapter, respondents are the "lifeblood" of the marketing research industry. Respondent cooperation rates have been going down, and the industry is concerned with the ethical treatment of the existing respondent pool.[68] In 1982, some of the organizations that founded CMOR began monitoring survey response cooperation. Response rates became such a problem that CMOR created a Director of Respondent Cooperation position. (We asked him to address you for this edition; you can see what he had to say at the beginning of Chapter 14.) Marketing researchers must honor promises made to respondents that the respondent's identity will remain confidential or anonymous if they expect respondents to cooperate with requests for information in the future. Some specific respondent abuses are discussed in the following paragraphs.

Respondent cooperation rates have been going down, and the industry is concerned about the ethical treatment of the existing respondent pool.

Deception of Respondents. Historically, respondents have been deceived during the research process and this has occurred in many fields, not just marketing research.[69] Kimmel and Smith point out that **deception** may occur during subject recruitment (they are told participation will only take a "few minutes" when in fact it may take a quarter of an hour or much more; they are not told the true identity of the sponsor or of the research firm, etc.), during the research procedure itself (they are viewed without their knowledge, etc.), and during postresearch situations (there is a violation of the promise of anonymity). Also, these authors suggest that this deception has serious consequences.[70]

An example of deception in marketing research is mystery shopping. **Mystery shopping** is the practice of gathering competitive intelligence by sending people posing as customers to gather price and sales data from unsuspecting employees. Shing and Spence argue that though information collected by mystery shoppers is not confidential, it is still gathered under false pretenses.[71] Mystery shopping is widely used in industry, and many would argue that it is not unethical. Few, however, would argue that it does not involve deception. Our purpose is to make certain you know when you are dealing with an issue that is ethically sensitive. Many of the research organizations to which we have referred in this chapter have specific codes of ethics dealing with mystery shopping.

Mystery shopping is the practice of gathering competitive intelligence by sending people posing as customers to gather price and sales data from unsuspecting employees.

Many of the research organizations to which we have referred in this chapter have specific codes of ethics dealing with mystery shopping.

Confidentiality and Anonymity. One way of gaining a potential respondent's trust is by promising confidentiality or anonymity. **Confidentiality** means that the researcher knows who the respondent is but does not identify the respondent to a client by any information gathered from that respondent. So the respondent's identity is confidential information known only to the researcher. A stronger appeal may be made under conditions of **anonymity**. The respondent will be, and remain, anonymous or unknown. The researcher is interested only in gathering information from the respondent and does not know who the respondent is. Ethical issues arise when respondents are promised confidentiality and anonymity and the researcher fails to honor this promise.

Ethical issues arise when respondents are promised confidentiality and anonymity and the researcher fails to honor this promise.

Invasions of Privacy. Marketing research, by its nature, is invasive. Any information acquired from a respondent represents some degree of invasiveness. Ethical issues, some of them based in law, abound when invading others' privacy. Two areas most responsible for consumer concern are unsolicited telephone calls and spam. Marketing researchers rely heavily on telephone surveys and online survey research, and so both methods are important to the industry. As we have noted earlier in this chapter, the FTC introduced a

Marketing researchers rely heavily on telephone surveys and online survey research, and so both methods are important to the industry.

Organizations that are excluded from the "Do Not Call" legislation must understand that they cannot abuse the privilege they have gained, and marketing researchers must work especially hard to encourage consumer goodwill and to ensure that they are viewed differently from telemarketers.

The practice of sending unwanted e-mail is called *spamming.*

The practice of sending spam threatens online survey research. Potential respondents, flooded with unwanted e-mails, will come to regard all but the most personal messages as trash.

You cannot e-mail a survey to an unsuspecting person without breaking the law! Read what you must do in the codes of organizations we have introduced you to, such as the MRA, CASRO, and ESOMAR.

highly successful national "Do Not Call" registry. For now, research firms calling for consumers' opinions only have been excluded from the "Do Not Call" legislation.[72] However, organizations not covered by the "Do Not Call" legislation must understand that they cannot abuse the privilege they have gained. CMOR continues to work to keep research firms excluded and to educate research firms about their responsibilities. However, marketing researchers must work especially hard to encourage consumer goodwill and to ensure that they are viewed differently from telemarketers.

When online survey research became a possibility by accessing respondents via the Internet, some organizations viewed it as an easy, fast way to gather survey information. They were little concerned with ethical issues when obtaining e-mail lists with which to target survey recipients. They began sending out thousands of surveys to unwary persons. The practice of sending unwanted e-mail is called *spamming*. An electronic message has been defined as **spam** if (1) the recipient's personal identity and context are irrelevant because the message is equally applicable to many other potential recipients; (2) the recipient has not verifiably granted deliberate, explicit, and still revocable permission for the message to be sent; and (3) the transmission and reception of the message appear to the recipient to give a disproportionate benefit to the sender.[73] The name *spam* comes from a Monty Python skit in which a restaurant customer is deluged with many, repeated requests (sung by waiters) to order the canned luncheon meat Spam. Finally, the customer yells: "I don't want any Spam."[74] The practice of sending spam threatens online survey research. Potential respondents, flooded with unwanted e-mails, will come to regard all but the most personal messages as trash. Marketing research organizations fight to reduce spam. Although the "Can Spam Act" was passed in 2003, two years later it was estimated that 60% of all e-mail that enters in-boxes everyday is spam![75] A **"Do Not Spam" registry**, allowing citizens to register their e-mail addresses to avoid spamming, similar to the "Do Not Call" registry, has been considered by the FTC. However, in June 2004 the FTC decided not to establish such a registry, citing as the primary reason lack of an effective authentication system and the inability to enforce the registry. In fact, the FTC's report stated that there was a high likelihood such a list would be obtained by spammers and those registering would receive more spam![76] Marketing research firms have not been regarded as spam abusers and have not, thus far, been included in any anti-spam legislation. Consumer organizations, in addition to marketing research organizations, have joined the fight, such as CAUCE, Coalition Against Unsolicited Commercial Email (http://www.cauce.org/).

Since improper online surveying could be considered spam, the marketing research industry has worked hard to establish codes of ethics dealing with proper online surveying. The Interactive Marketing Research Organization (IMRO), the MRA, and CASRO have been leaders in this effort. Some of the key issues for marketing researchers to consider if they are doing online survey research are discussed in the codes of the professional associations.

Realizing that respondents are their "lifeblood," many research firms are recruiting their own panels of willing respondents, which requires a considerable investment. The value of panels, known as panel equity, may become very important in the future.

In conclusion, marketing research firms are working hard to protect the privacy of their respondents. They realize they must rely on consumer cooperation. In order to create a pool of potential cooperative respondents, marketing researchers must attempt to separate themselves from unscrupulous direct marketers. The industry has been considering developing and using an "industry identifier" such as a "Your Opinion Counts" to help consumers more easily identify legitimate marketing research firms. Although this idea has been around for several years,[77] it is being discussed again among industry leaders. As we have noted, respondent cooperation has become such a problem that research firms, realizing that respondents are their "lifeblood," have recruited their own panels of willing respondents. Recruiting and maintaining a panel requires a considerable investment. **Panel equity**, the value of readily available access to willing respondents, has become important to the operation of the industry. Marketing research firms, recognizing the value they have in panels, will make even greater efforts to ensure fair and ethical treatment of their panel respondents.

Synthesize Your Learning ─────────────────

This exercise will require you to take into consideration concepts and material from these three chapters: Chapter 1, "Introduction to Marketing Research"; Chapter 2, "The Marketing Research Process"; and Chapter 3, "The Marketing Research Industry."

The First Interview

Frank Seeger was a senior in the College of Business. His faculty advisor had told him to visit the university's Career Center to get advice during his junior year. Fortunately, he had followed that advice and knew what he needed to do in order to obtain job interviews and to prepare himself for that first interview. Since his original orientation at the Career Center, Frank had been back several times to read material in the center's library and to watch some videos of actual interviews. He had worked on his resume and had asked a couple of his professors to review it for him. He felt his resume was ready. The Career Center advisors had impressed upon Frank the need to prepare for each separate interview. "You must show the interviewers that you have a strong interest in their company by learning as much as you can about their industry and their company before you interview." The advisors had also strongly suggested that Frank develop questions, based upon the materials available to him in the Career Center, that interviewers were likely to ask.

Three weeks into his first semester as a senior, the Career Center began signing students up for interviews. Frank followed the center's website daily to keep up with the schedule and signed up for two companies that were visiting the campus in October. As a marketing major, Frank had taken a course in marketing research and was interested in the field. He was pleased to see that one of the companies visiting his campus, CMG Research, was a marketing research firm. Remembering the admonitions of the Career Center advisors, Frank started preparing himself for this important interview. He knew that what he said in the initial 30-minute interview could change his life. This gave him a few anxieties but he remembered that some anxiety was good, as it can be a strong motivator. Frank had learned the best way to deal with anxiety was to go to work immediately to reduce whatever was causing it. He went to the library and started planning for his first interview.

Frank began to contemplate the questions he would be asked. He had rehearsed answers to the introductory and background questions. He remembered one of his freshman professors saying, "Make sure you can define the course you are taking. If this is sociology, make sure you can tell me what sociology is on the first test." Frank had learned that this was good advice. In almost every course he had taken in college, one of the questions on the first test asked for a definition of the subject matter of the course. Based on this, Frank expected some of the first questions to be the following:

1. Tell me what you think marketing research is. Frank wanted to make sure he could say what marketing research was without sounding like he memorized a definition that he did not understand. He wanted to be able to converse about the meaning of the definition.

2. In this day of computer networking technology, what would you say to those who would say there is no longer a need for marketing research?

3. What do you think about the marketing research industry?

4. What about CMG Research? What do you know about us?

Frank recalled several of the professional marketing research associations named in Chapter 3 of his textbook. He remembered that several have online searchable directories, such as Quirks.com, The Greenbook, and The Bluebook. He knew he could use these directories to get more information, for example, the area of specialization of the research firm in question. He could also find out who the major competitors are for a given area of specialization.

1. Using the first three chapters of this text, outline answers to Frank's questions. For question 4, select any firm you wish from one of those listed in the Honomichl Global 25 Report.

Summary

We describe several characteristics of the marketing research industry in this chapter. We begin by introducing you to one of the industry's premier professional associations, the MRA. The chapter then gives a brief history of the evolution of the industry, beginning with studies conducted as early as the 1800s during the Industrial Revolution when the need for marketing research arose. Prior to that time, there had been little need for formal marketing research, but companies had a growing need to know more about their customers as the Industrial Revolution distanced manufacturers from consumers. This led to the growth of marketing research firms that could supply information about distant markets. Charles Coolidge Parlin, recognized as the "Father of Marketing Research," is credited with conducting the first continuous and organized research, for the Curtis Publishing Company, beginning in 1911. By the 1960s, the practice of marketing research had gained wide approval as a method for keeping abreast of fast-changing, distant markets.

The research industry today is a $25.3 billion industry, with firms operating all over the globe. The Honomichl Global Top 25 is a listing of the top 25 firms, ranked in terms of revenue generated around the world. The Honomichl Top 50 is a list of U.S.-based firms ranked by revenues generated in the United States. Strategic alliances in the industry make it very competitive.

The research industry may be broadly classified into research buyers and research suppliers. Suppliers may be internal (research is provided by an entity within the firm) or external. Internal suppliers are organized into formal departments, having a committee, an individual, or no one responsible for research. Formal departments of internal supplier firms typically organize by area of application (e.g., business-to-consumer, business-to-business, product a, product b, etc.), marketing function (product research, promotion research, etc.), or the research process (e.g., data collection, data analysis).

External supplier firms may be classified as full-service or limited-service firms. Within each type, there are several other classifications. These firms may organize by function (data analysis, data collection, etc.), by type of research application (customer satisfaction, advertising effectiveness, new-product development, etc.), by geography (domestic versus international), by type of customer (health care, government, telecommunications, etc.), or some combination of these. Full-service supplier firms have the ability to conduct the entire marketing research project for buyer firms. Limited-service supplier firms specialize in one or, at most, a few marketing research activities.

Several challenges face the marketing research industry. It must deal with what appears to be an economic downturn in the latter part of the first decade of the 2000s and with low response rates to requests for consumers to participate in research, and it must take the steps necessary to safeguard consumer cooperation, the lifeblood of the industry, and to accommodate a growing interest in consumer rights to privacy, which has resulted in "Do Not Call" and antispam legislation—for marketing research does represent an "invasion of privacy." Criticisms of marketing research are that it no longer represents the voice of the consumer, being too parochial (narrow view); that it operates in a "silo" without proper communication within the firm; that is too tool-oriented and not fast enough.

The marketing research industry launched a certification program in 2005 to ensure a minimum standard of training and experience. The Professional Researcher Certification (PRC) is coordinated by the Marketing Research Association. Professional industry organizations—CASRO, the MRA, the ARF, and the AMA—offer many varied educational programs. There are also private educational programs of excellent quality, such as the Burke Institute, and several opportunities now exist to earn a Master's degree in marketing research.

All business students should be aware of the ethical issues in marketing research. Ethics is defined as a field of inquiry into determining what behaviors are deemed appropriate under certain circumstances, as prescribed by codes of behavior set by society. How you respond to ethically sensitive situations depends on your philosophy: deontology or teleology. Several organizations in the research industry have codes of ethical behavior for both buyers and suppliers of research that prohibit such activities as sugging, which is illegal, and frugging, which is very unethical. Ethics includes research integrity and treating others (buyers, suppliers, the public, and respondents) fairly. Deception, confidentiality, and invasions of privacy, including unsolicited telephone calls and e-mail spam, are all issues concerning fairness to respondents. Several industry organizations include special standards in their codes of ethics and professional conduct for online surveys to protect the privacy of respondents.

Faced with a declining pool of willing respondents in the general public, research companies have come to rely more heavily on panels recruited specifically to respond to research requests. The value, or "panel equity," of these panels has grown, and we can expect to see even fairer treatment of panel respondents in the future.

Key Terms

Charles Coolidge Parlin 42
Honomichl Global Top 25 43
Honomichl Top 50 43
Strategic alliances 47
Research suppliers 47
Internal supplier 47
External suppliers 50
Full-service supplier firms 50
Syndicated data service firms 51
Standardized service firms 51
Customized service firms 51
Online research services firms 51
Online research 51
Web-based research 51

Online survey research 52
Limited-service supplier firms 52
Field service firms 52
Phone banks 52
Market segment specialists 53
Sample design and distribution 53
Data analysis services 54
Specialized research technique
   firms 54
Certification 59
Professional Researcher
   Certification (PRC) 61
Ethics 64
Deontology 64

Teleology 64
Code of ethical behavior 65
Sugging 66
Frugging 66
Research integrity 67
Requests for proposals (RFPs) 68
Deception 69
Mystery shopping 69
Confidentiality 69
Anonymity 69
Spam 70
"Do Not Spam" registry 70
Panel equity 70

Review Questions/Applications

1. Describe the PRC, as discussed in the opening vignette by the CEO of the Marketing Research Association.
2. Who is given credit for conducting the first continuous and organized marketing research? (He is also known as the "Father of Marketing Research.")
3. Explain why marketing research was not widespread prior to the Industrial Revolution.
4. The marketing research industry, worldwide, is about a $_____ billion industry. Marketing research in the United States is about a $_____ billion industry.
5. What is the difference between the Honomichl Global Top 25 and the Honomichl Top 50 reports?
6. What is meant by a "strategic alliance"? Give an example of one.
7. We categorized firms as internal and external suppliers of marketing research information. Explain what is meant by each category, and give an example of each type of firm.
8. Distinguish among full-service, limited-service, syndicated data services, standardized services, customized service, and online research services firms.
9. How would you categorize the following firms?
    a. A firm specializing in marketing to kids (6–12)
    b. A firm that specializes in a computerized scent generator for testing reactions to smells
    c. A firm that offers a method for conducting "mock trials"
    d. A firm that offers clients samples drawn according to the client's sample plan
    e. A firm that collects data over the Internet
10. What makes an online marketing research firm different from other marketing research firms?
11. What is the advantage of a firm having its own formal marketing research department? Explain three different ways such a department may be internally organized.
12. What are four challenges to the marketing research industry?
13. Explain how being "too tool-oriented" may hurt the marketing research industry.
14. Explain how certification and education may improve the marketing research industry.
15. What are the two levels of experience and knowledge within the PRC?
16. What are the two fundamental philosophies that can be used as a basis for making ethical decisions?
17. List where you can find some codes of ethics that are applicable to the marketing research industry.
18. Name some of the ethical issues facing the marketing research industry.
19. Explain why "sugging" and "frugging" are bad for marketing researchers.
20. Search on the websites of CASRO, the MRA, or the IMRO for their codes of ethics/professional standards. What do they have to say about doing online surveys?

21. Look up "marketing research" in your Yellow Pages directory. Given the information provided in the Yellow Pages, can you classify the research firms in your area according to the classification system of research firms we used in this chapter?

22. Comment on each practice in the following list. Is it ethical? Indicate your reasoning in each case.

    a. A research company conducts a telephone survey and gathers information that it uses later to send a salesperson to the home of potential buyers for the purpose of selling a product. It makes no attempt to sell the product over the telephone.

    b. Would your answer to part (a) change if you found out that the information gathered during the telephone survey was used in a "legitimate" marketing research report?

    c. A door-to-door salesperson finds that by telling people that he is conducting a survey they are more likely to listen to his sales pitch.

    d. Greenpeace sends out a direct-mail piece described as a survey and asks for donations as the last question.

    e. In the appendix of the final report, the researcher lists the names of all respondents who took part in the survey and places an asterisk beside the names of those who indicated a willingness to be contacted by the client's sales personnel.

    f. A list of randomly generated telephone numbers is drawn in order to conduct a telephone survey.

    g. A list of randomly generated e-mail addresses is generated using a "Spambot" (an electronic "robot" that searches the Internet looking for and retaining e-mail addresses) in order to conduct a random online research project.

    h. Students conducting a marketing research project randomly select e-mail addresses of other students from the student directory in order to conduct their term project.

CASE 3.1

ABR MARKETING RESEARCH

The authors wish to thank Dr. Harriet Bettis-Outland, Assistant Professor of Marketing, University of West Florida for revising this case.[78]

It was late Friday evening in December, and Barbara Jefferson, a senior research analyst for ABR Marketing Research, was working furiously to complete the media plan portion of the Precision Grooming Products report. PGP was considering introducing a men's hair gel, which required demographic characteristics and media habits of male hair gel users. In addition, attitudinal information about product attributes such as oiliness, stickiness, masculinity, and fragrance was needed.

The findings were to be presented Monday afternoon, and a long series of problems and delays had forced Barbara to stay late on Friday evening to complete the report. Complicating matters, Barbara felt that her boss, Michelle Barry, expected the statistical analysis to be consistent with ABR's initial recommendations to Precision. Barbara, Michelle, and David Miller, from Precision's advertising agency, were to meet Monday morning to finalize ABR's presentation to Precision.

Back in September, Barbara had recommended that 250 users of men's hair gel products be surveyed from each of 15 metropolitan areas. Phillip Parker from Precision's marketing department had argued that conclusions about local usage in each city would not be accurate unless each city's sample size was proportional to its population. In other words, sample sizes for larger cities should be larger than for smaller cities. Furthermore, Phillip feared that males in metropolitan areas differed from males in rural areas with regard to usage or other important characteristics. Barbara finally convinced Phillip that sample sizes proportional to population would mean only 25 to 50 interviews in some smaller cities, which would be too few to draw statistically valid conclusions. Furthermore, expanding the survey to include rural users would have required committing more money to the project—money Precision didn't want to spend.

In October, a Des Moines, Iowa, pretest revealed that the questionnaire's length was driving the cost per completed interview to about $18. Total expenses would be well over budget if that cost held for the 15 metro areas. If the survey costs exceeded $65,000 (counting the pilot study), then precious little money would be left for the focus groups, advertising, and packaging pretesting in ABR's contract with Precision (see Table A.1).

TABLE A.1   Proposed Budget

Phone survey (including pilot study)	$ 58,000
Focus-group study	8,000
Advertising pretesting	25,000
Package pretesting	14,000
Miscellaneous expenses	5,000
Proposed total expenses	$110,000

Since Precision was a new account with big potential, a long-term relationship with them would be valuable. (Business at ABR had been slow this past year.) Feeling "under the gun," Barbara met with Michelle and Phillip, who agreed to reduce the sample to 200 men in only 11 metropolitan areas.

In early November, a new problem arose. After surveying 8 metro areas, Barbara discovered that her assistant had accidentally deleted all questions on media habits from the questionnaire given to ABR's vendor for the phone interviews. When told of the missing-questions problem, Michelle and Phillip became visibly angry at the vendor. After much discussion, they decided there was too little time to hire a new vendor and resample the 8 areas. Therefore, they agreed to reinsert the media questions for the remaining 3 cities and just finish the survey.

Barbara's task now was to make the most of the data she had. Because responses from each of the 3 cities were reasonably similar, and each city was in a different region (East, West, and Midwest), Barbara felt confident that the 3-city data were representative. Therefore, she decided to base the media plan on the large differences between her results and the national averages for adult men—making sports magazines and newspapers the primary vehicles for Precision's advertising. (See Table A.2.)

Barbara's confidence in the media plan was bolstered by a phone conversation with David Miller. Until a short time ago, his agency had handled the advertising for Village Toiletries, so he had valuable information about this competitor's possible responses to Precision's new product. David liked Barbara's recommendations, thought Phillip would also approve, and agreed to support the media plan in Monday's meeting. Indeed, Barbara thought, David had been a big help.

TABLE A.2   Comparison of Media Habits: Three-City Sample of Male Hair Gel Users vs U.S. Adult Males

		Three-City Sample	All U.S. Men
Magazines: At least one subscription of…	News	28%	19%
	Entertainment	4%	3%
	Sports	39%	20%
	Other	9%	6%
Newspaper subscription (at least one daily)		35%	14%
Favorite radio format	Pop	41%	38%
	Country	21%	30%
	Jazz	15%	17%
	Easy listening	7%	6%
	News/talk	5%	4%
	Other	11%	5%
Hours watching television per week	Dramas	6.3	8.4
	Comedies	7.8	7.3
	News	1.1	3.9
	Other	2.3	3.9
	Total	17.5	23.5

The Precision project had put a great deal of stress on Barbara, who hated spending evenings away from her family—especially near the holidays! If the presentation went well and more business was stirred up, then Barbara suspected that she would be spending even more evenings away from her family. But if the presentation went poorly or the data-collection errors became an issue, then Precision might look elsewhere for market research, thus jeopardizing Barbara's future with ABR. Either way, she was not feeling too comfortable.

1. After you have thoroughly read the case, write down what you believe are the issues in the case.
2. For each issue you identify, indicate how important you believe the issue to be, ranging from 7 (very important) to 1 (unimportant).

CASE 3.2 Your Integrated Case

ADVANCED AUTOMOBILE CONCEPTS

In the last two chapters we introduced you to Nick Thomas, who is CEO of Advanced Automobile Concepts (AAC), a new division of a large automobile manufacturer, ZEN Motors. If you have been assigned this case, you should briefly read over the information in Cases 1.2 and 2.2. You will recall that AAC was created to revive the aging ZEN automobile brands by either reengineering existing models or developing totally new models that are more in tune with today's changing automobile market and that Nick Thomas has searched the company's MIS for information to help him make some major decisions. After reviewing these materials, Nick believes he must come up with new models that will appeal to the market, but he is concerned that the recent interest in small, fuel-efficient cars will go away as it has done in the past when oil prices drop. He also wonders if consumers' interest in global warming is real enough to affect what they purchase.

Nick knows he needs some help with additional information. ZEN Motors has its own marketing research department, and Nick is considering using professionals in that department. Also, he has made several calls and learned that CMG Research has a good reputation. However, Nick is concerned about talking with a research firm outside ZEN Motors. Having never worked with a research firm before, he is afraid of sharing information that is so vital to AAC. He is concerned that such information may be given to competitors in the industry.

1. Why should Nick Thomas use the internal supplier, his own parent company's marketing research department? Why should he not use them?
2. Nick Thomas is concerned about using an external supplier of marketing research services, CMG Research. Read the MRA's Code of Ethics and what it has to say about researchers sharing confidential information. Go to www.mra-net.org, go Resources, and then Codes, Forms and Guidelines. Then go to (Expanded) Code of Marketing Research Standards, Section A.

A Careers in Marketing Research

As you have been learning about the profession of marketing research, you may have had some thoughts about it as a career choice. There are many career opportunities in the industry, and we have prepared this appendix to give you some information about those career choices. More importantly, we give you some sources of additional information about a career in the marketing research industry. We highly recommend that you also go to the following websites:

Marketing Research Association: www.mra-net.org. Go to Education; Education; Universities offering Masters Degrees in Marketing Research.

Universities.com Distance Learning and On-Campus Colleges and Universities: www.universities.com. Search on "Marketing Research" for a list of schools offering programs in marketing research.

Visit MRWeb at
www.mrweb.com

Council of American Survey Research Organizations (CASRO) at www.casro.org. Go to "Careers in Research."

MRWeb

There are also some websites that specialize in providing career information for the marketing research industry in the U.K., the United States, Australia, and Asia. One such site we recommend you visit is: www.mrweb.com. MrWeb Ltd, an independent company established in 1998, operates the world's busiest daily news and jobs service for market research professionals, including the U.K.'s biggest marketing research recruitment medium; the world's longest-established daily marketing research news e-mail service, DRNO (Daily Research News Online) containing 4 to 8 headlines a day about the industry sent to around 5,200 subscribers; and many hundred pages of directories, links, and resources for researchers.

WHAT IS THE OUTLOOK FOR THE INDUSTRY?

Before you seek employment in any industry, you should ask about the total outlook for that industry. Buggy-whip manufacturing is not exactly a growth industry! What are the growth rates in the industry? What do the experts have to say about the future of the industry?

A good place to find this information is the *Occupational Outlook Handbook*. You can access it online at www.bls.gov/oco/home.htm. Look under the category "Professional," and then under "market and survey researchers." Or just type "marketing research" in the search box. The *Occupational Outlook Handbook* forecasts that jobs in marketing research will grow "faster than average" (20%) through 2016. Demand for qualified market research analysts should be healthy due to an increasingly competitive economy. Marketing research provides organizations valuable feedback from purchasers, allowing companies to evaluate consumer satisfaction and more effectively plan for the future. As companies seek to expand their market and consumers become better informed, the need for marketing professionals will increase.

Opportunities for market research analysts with graduate degrees should be good in a wide range of employment settings, particularly in marketing research firms, as companies find it more profitable to contract out marketing research services rather than support their own marketing department. Other organizations, including financial services organizations, health care institutions, advertising firms, manufacturing firms producing consumer goods, and insurance companies, may offer job opportunities for market research analysts.

Opportunities for survey researchers should not be as strong as for market research analysts. However, they may increase as the demand for market and opinion research increases. Employment opportunities will be especially favorable in commercial market and opinion research as an increasingly competitive economy requires businesses to more effectively and efficiently allocate advertising funds.[79]

WHAT ARE THE SALARIES?

Another question you should ask is how much the people in this profession earn. As in many professional service industries, salaries vary widely in the marketing research industry. Nevertheless, we can give you some general guidelines. The *Occupational Outlook Handbook* distinguishes between marketing research analysts and survey researchers. Its definition of survey researchers closely matches what we discuss in this chapter as field-data-collection firms (limited-service firms). The primary difference is that analysts are involved with the total research process. Median annual earnings of market research analysts in May 2006 were $58,820. The middle 50% earned between $42,190 and $84,070. The lowest 10% earned less than $32,254, and the highest 10% earned more than $112,510. Median annual earnings in the industries employing the largest numbers of market research analysts in May 2006 were as follows:

Computer systems design and related services	$76,220
Management of companies and enterprises	$62,680
Other professional, scientific, and technical services	$57,520
Management, scientific, and technical consulting services	$54,040
Insurance carriers	$53,430

Median annual earnings of survey researchers in May 2006 were $33,360. The middle 50% earned between $22,150 and $50,960. The lowest 10% earned less than $16,720, and the highest 10% earned more than $73,630. Median annual earnings of survey researchers in May 2006 were $27,440 in other professional, scientific, and technical services.[80]

Another source stated that entry-level job opportunities are dwindling in the marketing research industry because companies want people who can hit the ground running. The starting salaries for individuals with undergraduate degrees in business or statistics are around $40,000 per year. With more experience, researchers can earn six-figure salaries.[81]

WHAT KINDS OF JOBS ARE THERE?

OK, so you are still interested! What types of jobs are there in the marketing research industry? We suggest you go to the MRA website at http://www.mra-net.org and click on "Career Center," and then on "View Current Jobs in the Profession," "Career Guide Part I," and "Career Guide Part II." Once you are familiar with these guides, go to either *The Honomichl 50* table or *The Honomichl Global Top 25* table in this chapter, and then to the websites of the companies listed. Most of them will have a "Careers with Us" or similar link. Check out the types of jobs they are describing. You should, of course, go to your career center and find out what resources your college or university has to help you find the job you want.

WHAT ARE THE REQUIREMENTS?

Do you have what it takes? The traits associated with the most successful and effective marketing researchers include the following: curiosity, high intelligence, creativity, self-discipline, good interpersonal and communication skills, the ability to work under strict time constraints, and feeling comfortable working with numbers. The field is becoming gender-neutral. Information Resources, Inc. (IRI) prefers a degree in marketing or a related area. Although an undergraduate degree is required, there has been a trend in some firms toward requiring postgraduate degrees. Most universities do not offer a degree in marketing research. There are some, reported later, that are quite good. Thus, an M.B.A. with a marketing major is one of the more common combinations for people employed in marketing research. Other possibilities are degrees in quantitative methods, sociology, or economics. Undergraduate training in mathematics or the physical sciences is a very suitable (and employable) background for anyone considering a career in marketing research. Below we illustrate the background of Matt Senger. His story shows us how seemingly different fields of study and interests really can have a commonality in marketing research. Matt offers you several other insights into marketing research for those of you thinking about a career in the industry.

The Nielsen Company, BASES

EDUCATION

Bachelor of Science, Marketing '04, Illinois State University

Master of Marketing Research '06, Southern Illinois University at Edwardsville

Frank Staggers' Award Recipient for Excellence in Marketing Research

WHY IS MARKETING RESEARCH IMPORTANT TO MODERN BUSINESS? Efficiency. The commonality between marketing/business issues is that marketing resources are finite and must be used efficiently and effectively. The extent to which Marketing Research is part of the decision-making process seems to be dependent upon the level of risk a decision-maker is willing to (or has to) accept given these finite resources. It might be a simple expansion of the familiar value equation of [Benefits > Costs], whereby decision-makers seek to identify a way to [(Gain More + Lose Less) > Costs]. Expanding the definitions:

1. Lose Less—Marketing Research can help mitigate risks in marketing resource allocation.
2. Gain More—Marketing Research can help optimize strategic marketing planning.
3. Cost—The investment should deliver means to Gain More and/or Lose Less than its cost.

Matt Senger is Associate Manager, Client Consulting.

WHAT IS MY PRIMARY ROLE IN THE INDUSTRY? BASES is the new product specialist organization within Nielsen—the world's leading provider of market insights. As an Associate Manager of Client Consulting, I am in a client-facing role that helps drive our mission of helping clients grow their business through successful innovation on their brands. The mission is executed through excellent client service and a host of services which provide consumer insights spanning the new product development process—including identifying 'white space', initiative optimization and sales forecasts.

Specifically, I am part of a team dedicated to the Beverage Alcohol industry—to which BASES extended its new product expertise in 2005; however, general responsibilities are common to client/industry teams across BASES' global organization:

- Proposals—design study to meet objectives, and estimate project costs
- Analysis—develop analytical plan, and translate data into strategic recommendations
- Forecasting—construct and implement accurate forecasting plan
- Internal Communication—discuss study design and processes with internal teams
- Client Communication—consult with clients on research design and present results
- People Management—guide development of new teammates

In addition, it is important to note:

- BASES is part of an integrated Nielsen company. Nielsen's data assets are extremely valuable to our clients, but the value is further driven by sharing insights across business units. BASES, like other Nielsen companies, utilizes the competitive advantage that comes from a holistic understanding of consumer behavior in a given category/market. In addition to providing a broad toolkit, being a part of Nielsen also opens great opportunities for professional growth.
- BASES is an industry leader in terms of continuous improvement. This commitment to R&D (or, Research-on-Research) affords opportunities for exploring company- and client-level issues to remain top-of-class in terms of client consulting.

HOW DID I GET HERE? My undergraduate career was by no means a straight line to the Research industry; let's just say the "4-year plan" was not my plan. It started with the natural sciences of Chemistry and Biology—I liked the analytical nature and scientific method of exploration, but I just could not get excited about laboratories. Lucky for me, the education system needed science/math teachers, so I explored Education and Psychology—an internship teaching high school Chemistry further suggested I did not have a passion for the natural sciences, but I liked communicating complicated ideas and understanding people's motivations. Looking for a path in which communication played a central role (and not wanting to waste those years of Chemistry), I thought I could leverage my unique background to "make the big bucks" as a pharmaceutical sales rep—Marketing, here I come.

While in the business school, Marketing Strategy courses piqued my interest; but, Marketing Research hit me with an "ah ha" moment. Here it was . . . a field that connected the dots of my core values—analytical skills, the scientific method, understanding people's motivations, communicating complicated ideas and strategic business thinking. The only problem was I had no idea the Marketing Research industry existed up to this point . . .

I was interested in graduate-level study, so the decision at this point was whether to go into a general MBA program or a specialized Master of Marketing Research program. I found my passion in Marketing Research, and wanted my graduate degree to be a key differentiator in the job market—so I decided to look deeper into the specialized MMR programs. I researched the programs independently, but I did not know enough about the industry to make an educated decision on my own. So, I found contact information from as many Honomichl 50 companies as I could, and asked the leading practitioners in the US what programs they thought were best. The MMR program at SIUE consistently came up as a top recommendation.

WHAT MAKES THE MMR PROGRAM AT SIUE SPECIAL?

1. *Holistic Coverage*   The MMR program has an Advisory Board of industry-leading practitioners which helps guide the curriculum, so graduates are ready to "hit the ground running" with up-to-date knowledge of industry practices. The curriculum covers a broad spectrum of industry-specific considerations for objective-focused study design and analysis, with rigorous deep dives into high-level analytical techniques.

2. *Practical Application*   A well-established internship program provides students the opportunity to work with industry-leading partners while completing their formal education. The experience offers a street-level view of how Research fits into

the real-world—the importance of sound study design and communication, and the challenges of weaving Research into the fabric of organizational decision-making. This is a win-win for students who have the opportunity to secure an internship—real-world experience with industry-leading partners who cover the students' tuition expenses and pay a monthly stipend.

Also, throughout the MMR curriculum, students develop and execute research with real organizations—from focus groups to advertising content analyses to quantitative studies utilizing high-level statistical analyses. Most notably, the MMR program has a capstone course in which students independently engage in the research process:

- Secure a real-world client
- Identify core business issues
- Develop objective-focused proposal
- Estimate hypothetical costs
- Write and program questionnaire
- Design and obtain sample
- Blend univariate and multivariate analyses to address objectives
- Deliver formal presentation of analysis and recommendation to client

ARE YOU INTERESTED IN A MASTER'S DEGREE IN MARKETING RESEARCH?

Graduate degrees are highly recommended in the marketing research industry. If you go to the MRA website at www.mra-net.org and click on "Education," you will find "Universities Offering Masters of Market Research Programs." We have highlighted one of these, Southern Illinois University–Edwardsville, in several places in this chapter. The director of the program is Professor Madhav N. Segal, Ph.D.

Director's Welcome

Marketing research in the 21st century is a growing, challenging, and exciting field. Southern Illinois University–Edwardsville's innovative graduate program in marketing research is designed to meet business's need for skilled marketing research professionals for this new millennium. Our Master of Marketing Research (MMR) program is one of the few specialized programs in the nation that combines practical knowledge with intensive academic training resulting in excellent employment (with a near 100% placement record) and career opportunities in marketing research with leading research agencies and corporations. The program is designed to prepare students for employment as marketing research professionals for today's competitive global marketplace. The MMR program also has an active Advisory Board comprised of marketing research industry leaders from several leading research agencies and *Fortune* 500 client organizations.

Professor Madhav N. Segal, Ph.D., Director, Southern Illinois University–Edwardsville, Master of Marketing Research Program.

SIUE's MMR program is a rigorous, high-quality, and business-practice-driven program that is housed in the School of Business, which is AACSB (The Association to Advance Collegiate Schools of Business) accredited. Admission is very selective and highly competitive. The program provides an ideal blend of theoretical and analytical coursework integrated with marketing research projects and corporate-sponsored graduate internships for qualified MMR students. While providing relevant professional marketing research experience, these internships offer a monthly stipend of $1,000 along with a complete tuition waiver for the entire duration of a student's program. Several leading research agencies and corporations (e.g., Maritz Research, Forward Research Inc., Doane Marketing Research, Anheuser-Busch, Nestle Purina, Edward Jones) sponsor and support the MMR program and its related internships.

We welcome your interest in our program and look forward to your comments and questions.

Madhav Segal

Chapter 4

Defining the Problem and Determining Research Objectives

Learning Objectives

- To understand the difference between problems and research objectives

- To understand when marketing research is needed

- To understand the importance of properly defining the problem

- To learn a process that is useful in defining the problem and research objectives

- To learn the two sources of problems and how to recognize them

- To understand the role of symptoms in problem recognition

- To appreciate the role of the researcher in defining the problem

- To understand how probable causes of the symptom lead to the specification of the decision alternatives

- To appreciate how uncertainty about the consequences of decision alternatives leads to information gaps that lead to research objectives

- To appreciate the factors needed in a "good" research objective

- To know the role of the action standard and to appreciate impediments to problem definition

- To learn the components of the marketing research proposal

(continued)

Parlin Award Winner Discusses Problem Definition in Marketing Research

Ron Tatham, Ph.D., 2007 Charles C. Parlin Award Recipient, the highest honor that may be bestowed on a marketing researcher, and former president and CEO of Burke, Inc. By permission.

When I hear a manager say to a researcher, "Here is what I want to know: [fill in the blank with the manager's desired information]." To be somewhat diplomatic, I ask, "What decision are you trying to make using that information?" Most often the manager just stares at me and says, "What do you mean?" My response is along the lines of "if you aren't making a decision, you don't need the information. If you are making a decision, are you sure this is the information that will best help you make that decision?"

Choose any management request for information and the request must be predicated on a decision. The manager's job is to maintain and increase the value of his company or his brand. Every bit of knowledge acquired must be targeted at making the decisions that will lead to strengthening value. Managers cannot just "want to know something," they must want to make decisions!

Ron Tatham

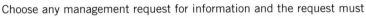

Where We Are

1 Establish the need for marketing research ◄

2 Define the problem ◄

3 Establish research objectives ◄

4 Determine research design

5 Identify information types and sources

6 Determine methods of accessing data

7 Design data-collection forms

8 Determine the sample plan and size

9 Collect data

10 Analyze data, and

11 Prepare and present the final research report.

n our opening vignette, Parlin Award winner Ron Tatham makes the point that a manager's need to make a decision should drive the need for marketing research information. In this chapter, we will discuss a process that leads to defining the problem and the research objective. In Chapter 2, we introduced you to the steps in the marketing research process. We also discussed the first step, the need for marketing research. In this chapter, we will continue looking at these steps. We will briefly revisit establishing the need for marketing research. From then on, we will assume that we need marketing research and will look at the second step in the process, which many believe is the most important of all—defining the problem. Closely associated with Step 2 is Step 3, determining research objectives, which we also cover in this chapter. We first introduce you to what we mean by "the problem" as well as by "research objectives."

Our main purpose here is to illustrate a process that explains how the researcher and manager arrive at the problem, which, as you will learn, is really a decision with alternatives. The process will also illustrate how, once decision alternatives are known, the research objectives evolve. We will also be looking at several other topics that are important, such as the role of symptoms, ITBs and RFPs, assumptions, constructs, hypotheses, and "action standards." We will also explore the role of the researcher and look at impediments to properly defining the problem. Finally, we present the elements of the research proposal.

WHAT IS "THE PROBLEM" AND THE "RESEARCH OBJECTIVE"?

The Problem

Before we go further, let's clear up what we mean by the concepts "the problem" and "research objective." First, let's understand that the context of our discussion centers around a relationship between a researcher(s) and a client, or manager. When we refer to "the problem" we are referring to the situation facing the manager or client. As we have discussed already in this book, managers must make decisions in order to manage. For our purposes here, we call **problems** situations calling for managers to make choices among alternatives. Managers make decisions because they have a problem. Sometimes these decisions are so routine and easily made on the basis of past experience that they don't really cause much of a "problem," in the sense that they are difficult and anxiety-producing. Making a decision about ordering, or not ordering, diesel fuel to run a plant's machinery is a routine, straightforward process that is normally *not* thought of as a *problem*. Nevertheless, it *is* a problem, however minor. Choices must be made and the manager must make the decision. As an example of other problems, managers must choose among alternatives to select new products, choose among advertising copy alternatives, determine the price of their products or services, select dealers, and so on. Managers face a problem when they must decide what type of business they should be in!

Notice how some of these problems can be very anxiety-producing. As we will learn in this chapter, having the right information to make the decision reduces this anxiety. We will shortly revisit problems and discuss some of their characteristics. For now, you should have a good idea as to what is meant by "the problem." Now let's take a look at that second concept in the title to this chapter, research objectives.

> Problems are situations calling for managers to make choices among alternatives.

The Research Objective

What is a research objective? Research objectives are totally dependent on the problem, but they are different in that they state what the *researcher* must do. **Research objectives** state specifically what information must be produced by the researcher so that the manager can choose the correct alternative to solve the problem. Research objectives are very specific and tell researchers exactly what information they must collect in order to solve the problem. Let's look at an example.

> Research objectives are totally dependent on the problem, but they are different in that, given the problem, research objectives state specifically what information must be produced by the researcher so that the manager can choose the correct alternative to solve the problem.

The VW *Touran* is available in Europe with a CNG engine.

Volkswagen executives recently made a decision to introduce one of their cars, the *Touran*, in Europe with a compressed natural gas (CNG) engine. CNG is cheaper than gasoline or diesel, it produces fewer greenhouse emissions, and it is safer than gasoline. Another advantage of CNG is that it is plentiful (at least in the United States) and will reduce dependence on oil from other nations. However, a drawback of CNG is that it takes up more storage space in a vehicle than the equivalent amount of gasoline or diesel. In order to keep from taking up all the trunk space to store CNG, automakers redesign vehicles to carry CNG storage tanks on the bottoms of the vehicles. This requires major retooling, so the decision to offer a CNG engine is significant. Making the decision to introduce the car in the United States will require that a U.S. factory be built and tooled to make the CNG engine and car. The *alternative* is to *not* introduce the car in the United States. VW management is faced with this decision; their problem is stated as "Will the CNG *Touran* generate enough sales in the United States to make the car profitable?"

Now, imagine you are the decision maker. What information will you need to help you make a choice between (a) introducing the *Touran* in the United States or not introducing the *Touran*? When you specify exactly what this information is, in what form, and where the information comes from, you are stating a research objective. Would you be able to make this decision if you had the following information?

Research Objective: To gather information from a sample representative of the U.S. population among those who are "very likely" to purchase an automobile within the next 6 months, which assesses preferences (measured on a 1–5 scale ranging from "very likely to buy" to "not likely at all to buy") for the model (Touran) operating on either (a) CNG, (b) gasoline, or (c) diesel at three different price levels. Such data would serve as input into a forecasting model that would forecast unit sales, by geographic regions of the country, for each combination of the model's different prices and fuel configurations.

Research objectives should be precise, detailed, clear, and operational.

Now the researcher knows what to do, and when the information is gathered, the executives at VW can make their decision. The problem has been solved. Is this research objective precise, detailed, clear, and operational? Yes, and these are the characteristics of a good research objective. In fact, the more precise and detailed the research objective, the more likely the information generated will solve the problem. We will discuss these characteristics more fully later in this chapter.

Let's look at one more example before we move on. Imagine that Joe Smith is thinking about running for Congress in his district. Joe has been a successful car dealer for many years and is well known in the area. He wants to serve his country but he doesn't want to jump into the congressional race unless there is some reasonable chance voters will perceive him as a viable candidate. He knows the incumbent will run again, and he has heard rumors that one of the lawyers in the district is likely to run. Additionally, he knows that there are several other lawyers who may throw their hats in the ring. Joe knows that people in the district don't know his platform but, aside from the incumbent, voters in the district don't know anything about the positions of the other likely candidates. But if Joe is going to run, he needs to make a decision. The alternatives are (a) run for Congress and (b) do not run for Congress. What information would Joe Smith need in order to make a good choice? After several discussions with a researcher from a marketing research firm that conducts political research, the following research objective is agreed upon:

> *Research Objective:* From a representative sample of registered voters who are "very likely" to vote in the upcoming congressional race, measure the percentage of voters who would vote for the incumbent and each of four other possible candidates, including Joe Smith, by asking, "Assuming that candidate "X" has a platform that you can accept, how likely is it that you would vote for candidate "X" on the following 1–5 scale that ranges from 'Very Likely' to 'Very Unlikely' (to vote)?" Candidates names will be randomly rotated so as to control for order bias.

From these examples, you can see more clearly what we said at the beginning of this section: Research objectives are closely related to problems. Look at the research objectives just stated. Each tells the researcher what must be done in order to help solve the client's problem. Now you should have a good idea of the difference between the problem and the research objective. Later in this chapter, we will discuss the process that should be used in order to arrive at the proper problem definition and statement of research objectives. Next, let us consider whether marketing research is even needed.

ESTABLISHING THE NEED FOR MARKETING RESEARCH

When Is Marketing Research Not Needed?

You should recall that when we presented the steps in the marketing research process in Chapter 2 we pointed out that marketing research is not needed for every decision. We also noted that this was a good thing. Otherwise, managers would constantly be involved in conducting marketing research instead of making decisions about running their companies. As a review, we said that marketing research should not be used when (a) the information is already available (remember that other components of the marketing information system provide information as well); (b) the timing is wrong, which may mean that a competitive response is needed immediately; (c) funds are not available; and (d) the costs of research are greater than the value of the information generated by the research. All of these circumstances place the manager in the situation of having to make a decision without *additional* information. Although the value of research information is hard to quantify, managers should attempt to do this before going ahead with marketing research and must determine whether or not they should make the decision without additional information. In the remainder of this chapter, we are assuming managers have decided they must seek additional information—they are going to use marketing research.

THE IMPORTANCE OF PROPERLY DEFINING THE PROBLEM

Most marketing research practitioners know the name of Lawrence D. Gibson. Not only has Mr. Gibson had a long and notable career in marketing research, he has taught many seminars to help young practitioners focus on defining the problem correctly. Mr. Gibson says:

> A problem well defined is a problem half solved says an old but still valid adage. How a problem is defined sets the direction for the entire project. A good definition is necessary if marketing research is to contribute to the solution of the problem. A bad definition dooms the entire project from the start and guarantees that subsequent marketing and marketing research efforts will prove useless. Nothing we researchers can do has so much leverage on profit as helping marketing define the right problem.[1]

It is hard to find a more impactful statement than Mr. Gibson's. Clearly, properly defining the problem is extremely important.

Other great problem solvers have recognized the importance of the need to clearly define the problem. Albert Einstein said, "(T)he formulation of a problem is often more essential that its solution. . . ."[2] John W. Tukey, the statistician, after discussing Type I and Type II errors in statistics, coined the label "Type III" for the error of solving the wrong problem![3] Tukey's Type III error illustrates why problem definition is so important. Even though you have a defined problem, there is nothing you can do in the research process to overcome the error of incorrect definition. No matter whether you use the proper sampling plan; a clear, unbiased questionnaire; achieve a very high response rate; use the proper data analysis techniques; and write a report that clearly and easily communicates to management—all is for naught. You solved the wrong problem!

Because of what we have just said, we can state that properly defining the problem is *the* most important step in the marketing research process. Note that some may state that the first step—"determining the need for marketing research" is more important, for if we need marketing research and don't use it, the consequences can be disastrous. This is true. So, we can amend our statement to say that when the decision has been made to embark on a research project, we believe defining the problem is the most important of the steps.

Let's look at a couple of examples to illustrate improper problem definition.

HOW CAN WE BEAT BURGER KING? McDonald's conducted marketing research for a new burger, the McDonald's Arch DeLuxe. The burger, targeted to adults, received a less-than-hoped-for result, even though McDonald's spent large sums of money on marketing research. What happened? The analysis points to "improper problem definition." McDonald's management was eager to match the Burger King Deluxe burger. All research was focused on measuring consumer preferences for different sizes and tastes of hamburgers. McDonald's researchers would likely have been better off not defining the problem as "How can we beat Burger King?" but, instead, focusing on adult fast-food customers' preferences and diet preferences. They may have produced a product that was better-tasting than the Burger King product, but they did not come up with a product that appealed to adults. Improperly defining the problem leads to lost time and money.[4]

HOW CAN WE WIN A TASTE TEST? Our second example is well known to researchers.[5] In the 1980s, Coke made a huge marketing mistake by introducing New Coke and taking original Coca-Cola off the market. Coke's mistake illustrates the costs and waste associated with improper problem definition.

From a market share of over 60% in the 1940s, Coke's market share declined to about 24% in the early 1980s. Coke's management focused on the rising market share of long-time rival Pepsi. Pepsi had been running a successful promotional campaign called the "Pepsi

When you define a problem incorrectly, there is nothing you can do in the research process to overcome this error.

Assuming we are going to conduct marketing research, defining the problem (and research objectives) is *the* most important step in the marketing research process.

Coke management quickly reintroduced *Classic Coke* once they learned their extensive research to introduce *New Coke* was based upon the wrong problem statement.

Challenge," in which consumers, taking part in a blind taste test, consistently chose Pepsi over Coke. Pepsi had a sweeter taste than Coke, and though Coke's original Coca-Cola still had significant market share and an established brand name, its executives defined their problem as not having a product as tasty as that of their major competitor. This led to over four years of research, during which the company developed a sweet-tasting cola. The new flavored beverage beat the competitor's cola in taste test after taste test. Thinking they had solved the "taste-test problem," Coke management dropped its old product and introduced the new, sweeter-tasting cola. To their surprise, sales plummeted and consumers, missing their old drink, protested by the thousands.

What happened? Many market experts believe Coke did not define the problem correctly. Coke defined the problem as "How can we beat the competitor in taste tests?" instead of "How can we gain market share against our competitors?" The company already had a sizable share of the market with their non-sweet-flavored traditional cola. When it stopped producing the old drink, the Coke customers could buy only the sweet-flavored beverage, which they didn't want; they had already shunned sweeter-tasting Pepsi in favor of Coke. Losing the taste tests led Coke's marketing managers to improperly define the problem; they wanted to beat their competitors. They did—but by dropping their existing product in favor of the new "better-tasting" cola, they lost their own customers. Hindsight being 20/20, they should have kept their existing Coke product and introduced a new brand to compete for the market preferring a sweeter cola. Within months, Coke management realized its mistake and reintroduced the old cola as *Coke Classic* and also kept the new, sweeter version. Management learned a hard lesson by not focusing research on the right problem and wasted much time and millions of dollars.[6]

These examples illustrate the importance of properly defining the problem. Not only does improper problem definition waste valuable resources, such as time and money, but it also eliminates the possibility of securing proper marketing research information that might set management on the right track sooner. And, as we saw in the case of Coke, improper problem definition may lose the goodwill of brand-loyal customers.

A PROCESS FOR DEFINING THE PROBLEM AND THE RESEARCH OBJECTIVES

As we mentioned at the beginning of this chapter, there is no one, universally agreed-upon process for defining the problem and research objectives. In fact, Lawrence D. Gibson, a recognized authority, wrote that "defining problems accurately is more an art than science. . . ."[7] We also told you we were going to introduce you to an approach that has been successfully used for many years by some practitioners in the marketing research industry. Figure 4.1 shows the components of this process. Remember, the process *assumes* management *is using* marketing research. We will discuss each of the components in the following paragraphs.

SOURCES OF PROBLEMS

Two Sources of Problems

FAILURE TO MEET OBJECTIVES. At the top of Figure 4.1 we see "Recognizing the Problem." Before we talk about recognizing the problem, let's look at the second topic in Figure 4.1, "Sources of Problems." Once we know what the sources of problems are, we will go back to the top of the figure and discuss how to recognize problems.

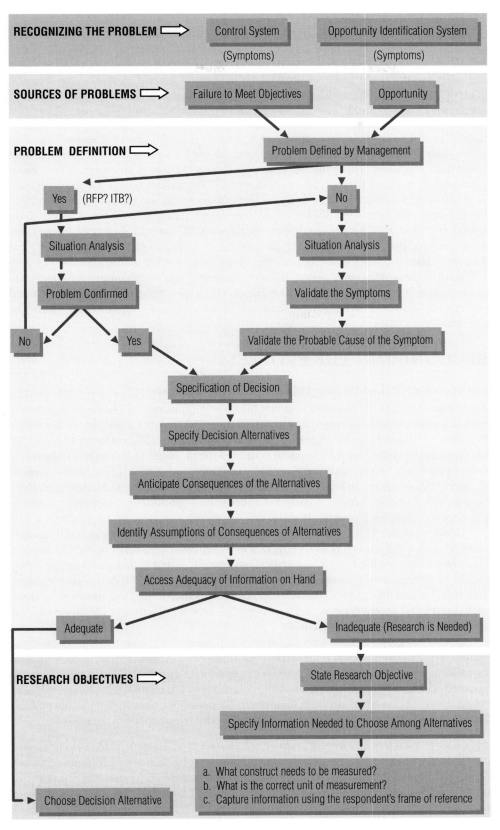

FIGURE 4.1

Defining the Problem and Determining the Research Objectives: Assuming the Use of Marketing Research

Figure 4.1 shows us there are two sources of problems: "Failure to Meet Objectives" and "Opportunity." We first recognize that we have a problem when a gap exists between what was supposed to happen and what did happen.[8] We will call this "**failure to meet an objective**." When, for example, our actual sales are below our sales objective, there is a gap between what was supposed to happen and what actually did happen. This situation is what we normally think of when we use the term *problem*. The manager must now determine what course of action to take in order to close the gap between the objective and actual performance.

OPPORTUNITY. Often the second source of a problem is not immediately recognized. This second source, called an **opportunity**, arises from the gap between what *did* happen and what *could* have happened. This situation is an opportunity because it represents a "favorable circumstance or chance for progress or advancement."[9] Put another way, an area of buyer need or potential interest in which a company can perform profitably is a marketing opportunity.[10] For example, our sales were $X but *could* have been $Y had we introduced a new, more competitive product. VW's decision to introduce a new CNG car to the U.S. market represents an opportunity. But even though there is an opportunity, managers still have a problem in that they must determine whether and how to take advantage of the opportunity.

Both of these situations, "failure to meet objectives" and "opportunity" have the same consequence for managers: They must make decisions and, hence, have what we defined earlier as a "problem." What management can do to recognize either of these sources of problems is discussed in the next section.

RECOGNIZING THE PROBLEM

Systems Needed to Recognize Sources of Problems

A CONTROL SYSTEM. It has been said that the only thing worse than having a problem is having a problem and not being aware that you have it! Now, let's go back to the top of Figure 4.1, "Recognizing the Problem." We see that there are different ways to recognize the problem depending on which source generated the problem: failure to meet objectives *or* an opportunity. We see that for "failure to meet objectives" we use a control system to recognize this problem. To help them recognize failures to meet objectives, managers must have a control system. Second, to help them recognize opportunities, managers must have a system for identifying opportunities.

Good managers will be aware of problems, or they will soon cease to hold management positions. For managers to recognize a problem when the source is "failure to meet objectives," they must be knowledgeable about objectives and actual performance. They should be setting objectives and have a control system in place to monitor performance. This is just sound management practice. To "control" is one of the basic functions of management. Unless managers have a control system, they will likely *not* identify problems arising from failure to meet objectives.

Good managers will have a control system in place that will alert them to situations in which performance is not achieving desired objectives. In fact, a good MIS will alert management to symptoms long before some stated date on which the objective is to be assessed. For example, a good sales manager will know which salespersons are "ahead," "behind," or "on schedule" to meet their quarterly sales objective *early on* in the quarter. This lead time allows them to make adjustments before failure to reach the objective.

OPPORTUNITY IDENTIFICATION SYSTEM. Look back now at Figure 4.1. How do managers recognize that they have an opportunity? Managers must be aware of opportunities; unless they have a system for monitoring opportunities—sometimes referred to as a process of **opportunity identification**—they will not likely identify these problems.[11] Kotler refers to this process as **market opportunity analysis (MOA)**.[12] We are not going to discuss MOA

Margin notes:

There are two sources of problems: "failures to meet objectives" and "opportunities."

An opportunity occurs when there is a gap between what *did* happen and what *could* have happened. This situation is an opportunity because it represents a "favorable circumstance or chance for progress or advancement."

To help them recognize failures to meet objectives, managers must have a control system. Second, to help them recognize opportunities, managers must have a system for identifying opportunities.

For managers to recognize a problem they must be knowledgeable about objectives and actual performance. They should be setting objectives and have a control system in place to monitor performance.

Managers must also be aware of opportunities; unless they have a system for monitoring opportunities—sometimes referred to as a process of opportunity identification—they will not likely identify these problems.

here, but we want to point out that if a company wishes to take advantage of opportunities it must have a system in place to help identify the opportunities when they emerge. Consider the following example. Today cell phones are common. In fact, there is growing evidence that they are on their way to replacing traditional landline phones that have been in homes since the telephone was invented. In the 1980s, when Western Electric and Bell Labs first discovered the computer switching processes that would enable the use of cell phones, a few companies applied to the FCC to obtain licenses to operate cell phone systems in the major U.S. markets. Other companies didn't learn about the potential of cell phone technology until well after the deadline passed for firms to apply to the FCC. What was the difference in these firms? Some, those that applied early (and many of whom won the license), had a system in place for early acknowledgement of technical breakthroughs. Because their system of opportunity identification worked, they were able to carry out what was necessary to enter the cell phone business. Many of their would-be competitors were "asleep" and missed a wonderful, profitable opportunity.

The Role of Symptoms in Problem Recognition

Note in Figure 4.1 that we have "symptoms" below both "Control System" and "Opportunity Identification System." What role do symptoms play in problem recognition? The classic statement "We have a problem—we are losing money" illustrates why researchers and managers, in properly defining problems, must be careful to avoid confusing symptoms with problems. The problem is not that "we are losing money." Rather, the problem may be found among all those factors that cause us to make (or lose) money; the manager, with help from the researcher, must identify all those possible causes in order to find the right problem(s). So managers must be aware that the symptoms are not the problem, but are "signals" that alert them to the fact that they have a problem.

> Symptoms are not the problem, but symptoms are those "signals" that alert us to the fact that we have a problem.

Symptoms are changes in the level of some key monitor that measures the achievement of an objective (e.g., our measure of customer satisfaction has fallen 10% in each of the past two months). In this case, the role of the symptom is to alert management to a problem; there is a gap between what should be happening and what is happening. A symptom may also be a perceived change in the behavior of some market factor that implies an emerging opportunity. A pharmaceutical company executive sees a demographic forecast that the number of teenagers will increase dramatically over the next 10 years. This may be symptomatic of an opportunity to create new drugs designed for such teen problems as acne or weight problems. One of the most successful publishing firms in college textbook history was started when Richard D. Irwin saw, while reading the *U.S. Statistical Abstract*, the rapid rise in college of business enrollments following World War II. Irwin recognized this "symptom" as an opportunity to specialize in the publication of textbooks targeted to business college students. Note that symptoms may be *negative* but still bring about opportunities. The forecast for teens is that their numbers will shrink in the next 10 years. Should the company shift R&D from developing new drugs for teens to the growing baby boomer market? Both types of symptoms should be identified by either the control system (objectives/monitoring) or by the system in place for opportunity identification. The key lesson, however, is that symptoms are not problems; their role is to serve as signals to alert managers to problems. Table 4.1 lists some examples of symptoms of the two problem sources: failures to meet objectives and opportunities.

> Symptoms are changes in the level of some key monitor that measures the achievement of an objective. A symptom may also be a perceived change in the behavior of some market factor that implies an emerging opportunity.

PROBLEM DEFINITION

Before we move on, let's state where we are and where we are headed. If we look back at the top of Figure 4.1, we can assume we can "recognize the problem" because we have a system in place to identify either of the two sources of problems: "failure to meet objectives" and/or "opportunity." Regardless of the source, when managers recognize there is a

TABLE 4.1 Problem Recognition

Sources of Problems	Example Symptoms	System Required in Order to Recognize Gap
Failure to meet objectives Gap between what is *supposed* to happen and what *did* happen	Sales calls below target number.	Control system based on setting objectives and evaluating them against actual performance.
	Sales volume below quota. Return on investment (ROI) below goal.	
Opportunities Gap between what *did* happen and what *could* happen (Should we, and how, do we take advantage of opportunities?)	Basic research opens up new technology in data transmission speed.	System for identification of opportunities
	New demographic analysis shows rapid increases in population and incomes in markets where a firm has no current distribution.	

problem, they must define it. Sometimes managers will define the problem on their own and realize they need additional information in order to make a choice among decision alternatives, thus seeking marketing research after they have defined the problem. If we look at Figure 4.1, we see this case depicted by following the "Yes" path under "Problem Defined by Management." Or, in some cases, management is aware of the symptoms and calls in the researcher to help define the problem. When we look at Figure 4.1, we see this case depicted by following the "No" path under "Problem Defined by Management."

Whether management defines the problem on its own and then calls in marketing research or management calls in marketing research to help define the problem, in *both cases* the researcher plays an important role. (Remember, we have already recognized that there are many situations in which management defines the problem and selects a decision alternative to solve it *without* marketing research. Figure 4.1 *assumes* management has decided to use marketing research.) In the next section, we will look at the role of the researcher when (a) the problem has been defined by management and (b) when it has not.

Whether management defines the problem itself or calls in marketing research to help define the problem, the marketing researcher plays an important role.

The Role of the Researcher in Problem Definition

WHEN MANAGEMENT HAS ALREADY DEFINED THE PROBLEM IN TERMS OF A DECISION TO BE MADE. Our discussion here follows the "Yes" path under "Problem Defined by Management" in Figure 4.1. In some cases, managers have defined what they think the problem is and the decision that must be made to resolve the problem. In this case, the researcher has an obligation to help managers ensure they are defining the problem correctly. This is particularly true when the researcher is called in by a manager who already has defined the problem in very specific terms. Researchers provide value at this juncture in the process by bringing in a fresh viewpoint, unhindered by the bias of recent events, trends, or influences that have informed the manager's decision-making process. The manager who thinks the problem is choosing between two proposed advertising claims has assumed that there are only two claims. Are there others that should be considered? Researchers are trained to think more broadly and should ask, "Is advertising really needed to address the problem?" The manager who has defined the problem in terms of a decision to choose a better cookie recipe may be startled to learn that total cookie sales have been falling for the past five years. Perhaps the researcher should ask the question of the manager, "Are you sure you should be in the baked

When managers have already defined the problem prior to bringing researchers in, researchers must resist the temptation to 'go along' with the first definition suggested.

cookie business?" Problem definition expert Lawrence D. Gibson wrote: "Researchers must resist the temptation to 'go along' with the first definition suggested. They should take the time to conduct their own investigation and to develop and consider alternative definitions."[13]

Look back now at Figure 4.1. When the "Yes," path is taken and management has already defined the problem for the marketing researchers to handle, researchers should conduct an additional, preliminary investigation, which may take the form of a type of exploratory research sometimes called a **situation analysis**, which is a form of exploratory research undertaken to gather background information and gather data pertinent to the problem area that may be helpful in properly defining the problem decision. (We will discuss several methods of conducting exploratory research, used in a situation analysis, when we introduce you to this type of research design in Chapter 5.) A situation analysis may reveal, for example, that the problem lies not with promotion (so we shouldn't even be discussing the two proposed advertising claims), but rather with dealer motivation. The point is that researchers have a responsibility to ensure that they are going to address the right problem, even when the problem has been previously defined by management.

At this point we need to introduce you to ITBs and RFPs, which are often used in the marketing research process. Both represent situations where the manager has predetermined the problem decision and is calling upon researchers to present a research proposal to be considered by management. (This is why we place them by the "Yes" in Figure 4.1.) We explain ITBs and RFPs in the following section.

A situation analysis is a form of exploratory research undertaken to gather background information and gather data pertinent to the problem area that may be helpful in properly defining the problem decision.

THE ROLE OF ITBS AND RFPS. **ITBs** are "invitations to bid." Alternatively, some firms use **RFPs**, which stands for "requests for proposals." Companies use these documents to alert research firms that they would like to receive bids or proposals to conduct research. In either case, the roles of the researcher and manager in the problem definition process are changed. As we have noted, when a company uses an ITB or RFP it has already defined the problem and, in some cases, the research objectives. At the very least, management has thought through many of the issues revolving around defining the problem. This means that much of the dialogue normally necessary between researchers and managers may be circumvented. For example, managers in a firm decide they need to assess customer satisfaction in a way that will allow them to prescribe remedial actions. The problem has been defined and they have specified the decision—they want to make changes to improve customer satisfaction. They submit an ITB or RFP to several research firms, who now bid on doing the necessary research. The significance of the ITB or RFP is that even when responding researchers still have an obligation to ensure that the managers have defined the decision problem correctly.

*ITBs are "invitations to bid." Alternatively, some firms use **RFPs**, which stands for "requests for proposals."*

Although each RFP and ITB is different, they all contain some common elements:

- *Introduction.* Identification of the company or organization that originates the RFP, with background information about the company.
- *Scope of proposal.* Description of the basic problem at hand.
- *Deliverables.* Specification of the tasks to be undertaken and products to be produced and delivered to the company soliciting the proposal or bid. For example, the deliverable may be "a survey of 1,000 representative recent users of the company's services, described in a report with text, tabulations, figures, and relevant statistical analyses."
- *Evaluation criteria.* The criteria or standards that will be used to judge the proposals, often set up as a point system in which the proposal is awarded a number of points for each area based on the quality of the work that is proposed.
- *Deadline.* The date by which the deliverables must be delivered.
- *Bidding specifics.* Necessary items, such as the due date for the proposal or bid, specific information required about the bidding company, proposal length and necessary elements (such as sample questions that may appear on the questionnaire), intended subcontract work, payment schedule, contact individual within the origination company, and so on.

As you may remember from our discussion of ethics in Chapter 3, ITBs and RFPs are sensitive issues in terms of appropriate ethical behavior. A firm that sends out phony ITBs (or RFPs) simply to get ideas for research is practicing highly unethical behavior.

 Want to See Some Actual RFPs and ITBs?

You can find RFPs and ITBs on the Internet, a very effective medium for broadcasting RFPs/ITBs. Supplier firms search the Web for postings of these requests and often use the Web to reply. Go to advanced search at www.google.com, "with at least one of the words," enter ITB RFP. At "with the exact phrases," enter "marketing research." You will get many hits, and that is OK. Exploring, you will find actual ITBs and RFPs. You will also find some sites designed to help you write an effective ITB or RFP.

Now let's take a look at www.marketresearchfirms.com. This takes you to a website that serves as a portal allowing buyer firms to place their RFPs on the website and research firms to review those RFPs and submit a proposal. Take a quick look at the free RFP service (top right) of the web page. Note that the form allows a buyer firm to specify the type of research firms it wishes to respond to the RFP.

If, according to the researcher, the "Problem Is Confirmed," the decision to be made is stated and we are now ready to proceed to the "Specification of the Decision," which includes stating the decision alternatives, "Specify Decision Alternatives."

Notice in Figure 4.1 that when the problem has been defined by management and after the researcher conducts a situation analysis, the researcher makes a decision as to whether or not the problem is defined correctly. If, according to the researcher, the "Problem Is Confirmed," the decision to be made is stated and we are now ready to proceed to the "Specification of the Decision," which includes stating the decision alternatives, "Specify Decision Alternatives."

However, if the researcher cannot confirm the problem as stated by management, the researcher must discuss the situation with management, providing a rationale as to why the decision specified by management is not the one that should be pursued. If management agrees, the researcher proceeds as if management did not specify the problem decision. But what if management does not agree? Certainly, the researcher should listen carefully to the arguments presented for management's position and reevaluate the decision. However, if the researcher is still convinced the problem has been defined incorrectly, this creates an ethical situation. It would certainly be easy to just conduct the research management wants to do, get paid, and move on. On the other hand, the researcher knows the client will not be satisfied with the research because it will not solve the problem. As in so many ethical dilemmas, there is a short-term reward but long-term cost. In the short run, the manager is happy and the researcher gets paid—perhaps before the manager realizes the mistake. In the long run, if researchers do not take the "high road" and do the right thing (either withdraw from the project or convince management as to the real problem), research will lose value in the eyes of management. In the long run, if research loses value, there will be no demand for marketing research!

If the researcher cannot convince the manager to abandon an ill-defined problem, the researcher is confronted with an ethical dilemma.

Whew! This is complicated! You are so right. Now you should start to appreciate why we have told you there is no one "magic" way to arrive at the problem. Yet, you know the definition of the problem and research objectives are extremely important. Let's move on! It helps to stay focused on Figure 4.1. Where are we? Look at "Problem Defined by Management" and then "No." This takes us to our following discussion.

WHEN MANAGEMENT HAS *NOT* ALREADY DEFINED THE PROBLEM IN TERMS OF A DECISION TO BE MADE. Sometimes managers call researchers when they sense that something is wrong and they need help diagnosing the situation. They may be aware of symptoms but they are not sure what the problem is and hence they are not sure what decision they should make, if any. Here, the researcher's task is more involved. Again, referring to Figure 4.1, the researcher should also undertake a situation analysis.

Conduct a Situation Analysis

We have already mentioned that researchers, even when management has previously defined the problem, should conduct a situation analysis. This is certainly important when management hasn't determined what the problem is. This step may begin with the researcher learning about the industry, the competitors, key products or services, markets, market segments, and so on. The researcher should start with the industry in order to determine if any symptoms, to be identified later, are associated with the entire industry or only with the manager's firm. The researcher should then move to the company itself: the history of the company, its performance, products/services, unique competencies, marketing plans, customers, major competitors, and so on.

The primary method of conducting a situation analysis is to review both internal and external secondary data. For internal information, as we discussed in Chapter 1, there is the internal reports system, a component of the MIS, For a full discussion of external secondary data, see Chapter 6. Other methods of conducting a situation analysis include conducting "experience surveys" (discussions with knowledgeable persons both inside and outside the firm), "case analysis" (looking at examples of former but similar situations), "pilot studies" (conducting ministudies that may reveal problem areas), and focus groups (having small groups discuss topics such as the company's product or service). We will discuss exploratory research, which would include a situation analysis, in Chapter 5.

Continuing with situation analysis, the researcher should try to find out about the manager's unique situation. Under what constraints is this manager operating? Why does this manager believe research is needed? Do other managers agree? Does this manager have a particular objective to achieve? At this stage, the researcher is gathering information and will have considerable homework to do after the first meeting with the manager. The researcher must assess what, if any, information gathered during the situation analysis conflicts with the information the manager is providing and should discuss them with the manager to resolve discrepancies.

Validate the Symptoms of the Problem

Next, the researcher should clarify or validate the symptoms. Can faith be placed in the symptoms? After all, the fact that there is a problem is based on the symptoms themselves. Are the symptoms true indicators of what they supposedly represent?

You have already learned that symptoms are important in helping to *recognize* the problem. Without symptoms, problem definition is virtually impossible. To assess the veracity of the symptoms, the researcher needs to assess the control (or opportunity identification) system in place as well as the symptoms themselves. The researcher needs to understand what the control system is or, if appropriate, whether there is a system for identifying opportunities. Companies vary greatly in terms of defining their objectives, monitoring their results, and taking corrective action. Does the company have a control system adequate to identify symptoms? Are there symptoms not identified? What are they? Are they accurate measures of performance? Are they reported in a timely fashion? Is there adequate screening of the environment to pick up on opportunities? In other words, the researcher needs to examine the process of identifying and reporting symptoms.

Second, researchers need to assess the symptoms themselves. Are these symptoms true or are they artifacts of the control (or opportunity identification) systems in place? Can the symptoms be corroborated by other factors identified in the situation analysis? Are the symptoms aberrant? Are they likely to appear again? You are no doubt beginning to realize that the researcher acts much like a detective. It is the researcher's role to explore and to question if the problem is to be defined properly. Once the symptoms have been validated, the researcher is ready to examine the causes of the symptoms.

When management has previously defined the problem, marketing researchers should conduct a situation analysis. This is certainly important when management hasn't determined what the problem is. Marketing researchers need to conduct a situation analysis to properly define the problem.

The researcher must assess what, if any, information gathered during the situation analysis conflicts with the information the manager is providing.

Next, the researcher should clarify or validate the symptoms. Can faith be placed in the symptoms?

To assess the veracity of the symptoms, the researcher needs to assess the control (or opportunity identification) system in place as well as the symptoms themselves.

Once the symptoms have been validated, the researcher is ready to examine the causes of the symptoms.

Determine the Probable Cause(s) of the Symptom

At this point, the manager and the researcher should be in agreement about which symptom or symptoms are in need of attention. Now it is time to determine what could possibly cause the symptom. To do this, we must realize that symptoms do not just pop up. There is always some **cause** or causes for the change. Profits do not go down by themselves. Sales do not drop without customers doing something differently from what they have done in the past. Satisfaction scores do not drop without some underlying cause.

First, it is important to determine *all* **possible causes**. If only a partial list of causes is compiled, it is possible that the real cause will be overlooked and the incorrect decision will be specified. To help you visualize this process, let's look at an example of an apartment complex near your university. Let's assume the management has been alerted to symptoms that show the occupancy rate declining from 100% to 80% over the last three semesters. After discussion with the researcher, all possible causes may be grouped in the following categories: (1) competitors' actions, which had drawn prospective student residents away; (2) changes in the consumers (student target population); (3) something about the apartment complex itself; and (4) general environmental factors. The researcher should discuss all these possible causes with management. There may be several possibilities within each category; for example, (1) competitors could be reducing rents or "lowering price" by providing free services such as free basic cable TV; or (2) the number of students at the university may be decreasing; or (3) the apartment building itself may not have been adequately maintained and appears to be "aging"; finally, (4) financial aid may have decreased on campus and students are less able to afford off-campus housing. The situation analysis should have identified these possible causes.

After listing all possible causes under each one of the above broad categories, the researcher and manager should narrow down the possible causes to a small set of **probable causes**, defined as the most likely factors giving rise to the symptom. In our apartment example, we can assume that the manager and researcher have eliminated many causes for the symptom. For example, there has been no change in financial aid, student enrollment is up, the apartment building's appearance is on a par, or even better, with competitive apartments, and so on. After evaluating all the other possible causes, assume the researcher and manager have reduced the probable cause down to competitors offering students free cable TV. Notice that something very important has now happened—management now has a decision to make!

Specification of the Decision

The determination that the probable cause of the symptom is "competitors offering free cable TV" creates a decision for management. From Figure 4.1, we see that we are now ready to specify the decision to be made (see "Specification of Decision"). Management must now decide what to do to win back market share. Decisions require alternatives. But what are the alternatives?

Normally, we would think this to be easy. After all, managers are decision makers, aren't they? Well, yes they are—but managers are not always clear about specifying decision alternatives. Take a look at Marketing Research Insight 4.1, which illustrates what we mean when we say that managers do not always clearly specify decision alternatives. (We also see in MRI 4.1 that managers do not always want research to help them make a decision.)

Specify Decision Alternatives That May Alleviate the Symptom

Managers have at their disposal certain resources, and these resources may provide the decision alternatives they need to address the probable cause of the symptom. Essentially, possible **decision alternatives** include any marketing action that the marketing manager thinks may resolve the problem, such as price changes, product modification or improvement, promotion of any kind, or even adjustments in channels of distribution. It is during this phase that the researcher's marketing education and knowledge fully come into play; often both the manager and the researcher brainstorm possible decision alternatives that may serve as solutions.

It is important to determine all possible causes. If only a partial list of causes is compiled, it is possible that the real cause will be overlooked and the incorrect decision will be specified.

After listing all possible causes under each of the broad categories, the researcher and manager should narrow down the possible causes to a small set of probable causes, defined as the most likely factors giving rise to the symptom.

When the "probable cause" of the symptom is identified, this triggers a decision to be made by management.

MARKETING RESEARCH INSIGHT

Practical Insights

4.1 The Decision[a]

When researchers, either internal or external, are called upon, it is because management has information needs. Managers are responsible for increasing shareholders' wealth by increasing the value of their company or brand. They cannot (should not!) request information just because they "want to know something." They should request information when they need to make decisions and need additional information in order to make a good decision. Of course, we recognize that, in some cases, managers do exactly this, and we discuss this situation below.

Not All Research Is Conducted Because Managers Want to Make a Decision

Sometimes managers want research conducted because they want to know "what is going on." This often happens when there are unplanned changes in the marketing environment—for example, gasoline prices soar, the stock market plunges, and so on—or managers may want to know the current level of customer satisfaction. In our earlier discussion of the uses of research, one use was to "monitor marketing performance." Churchill and Brown have labeled the decision driving this type of research as a "discovery-oriented decision problem," and they note that the accompanying research rarely solves a problem. Rather, the research conducted in this situation leads to insights that may help managers make better decisions.[b] But, managers do not always clearly specify decision alternatives. To illustrate this, let us look at some typical examples of decisions managers make.

Examples of Decisions

Most research is conducted because managers wish to make a decision. First, understand that *you cannot formulate the decision without specifying the alternatives* that allow the decision. If there are no alternatives, there is no decision to be made. The following examples illustrate that managers sometimes clearly specify the alternatives and sometimes do

Managers do not always clearly state decision alternatives.

not. The researcher's task is to clearly state the decision alternatives.

1. ***Example:*** *I want to choose the better of two proposed advertising claims.* Here the decision and alternatives are clear to the researcher. When the researcher specifies the research objective, the decision can still be improved on by specifying additional information, such as what makes one proposed claim "better" than another.

2. ***Example:*** *I want to choose between two formulations for my product. One formulation is more expensive but provides greater benefit to the customer. Because this is a very mature category with a very small range of prices, we believe we would have to substantially increase volume at the current price to warrant the more expensive formulation.* Here the alternatives are not provided to the researcher, but they are clear.

3. ***Example:*** *I want to choose the best way to express my product's benefit to this target market.* Here it is implicitly expressed that alternatives could exist, but they are not stated. The researcher will have more difficulty specifying the alternatives and may need to do exploratory research to determine exactly what the alternatives are.

[a] Much of this material was adapted from a conversation with Ron Tatham.
[b] Churchill, G. A., Jr. and Brown, T. J. (2004). *Basic Marketing Research.* Mason, OH: Thomson/South-Western, 62.

Once again, it is for the manager to specify *all* of the decision alternatives needed to address the probable cause of the symptom. In fact, one marketing research consultant has gone on record with this bold statement: "Unless the entire range of potential solutions is considered, chances of correctly defining the research problem are poor."[14]

Returning to our apartment complex example, assume the manager examines *all* types of television delivery systems. One alternative is to offer what the other apartments are offering: free cable TV. This is a lower-cost alternative because it does not involve offering any premium channels. The manager believes that he will at least be on a par with the competition if he elects this alternative and that he can slowly win back his market share, as all apartments are competing more or less equally. A second alternative is to try to gain a competitive advantage by offering free satellite TV with premium channels. Although this is a higher-cost option, the strategy may more than pay for itself if demand is high and the apartment complex quickly reaches full capacity.

After carefully studying the market alternatives for TV, let's assume the manager has sought out several alternatives and is considering a satellite television system such as DirecTV's Multiple Dwelling Unit Program—with its 200 channels (many of which are HD), four premium channels of HBO, Starz, Showtime, and Cinemax, plus pay-perview—as one of his likely plans of action. Now the decision alternatives become clear. If the apartment complex offers free satellite TV with premium channels, will occupancy rates go back up high enough to offset the extra cost? Or, will occupancy rates rise if the apartment complex meets competition and offers free cable TV. The unstated alternative, of course, is to do neither of these. The latter, however, is unlikely if the manager's analysis is correct. That is, he has determined that the competitors who have taken market share from him have done so because they offered free basic cable TV. However, it is possible that the alternative to offer neither free basic cable TV nor free satellite TV with premium channels could be chosen if the marketing research demonstrates that free TV service does not affect students' likelihood of selecting an apartment.

Consequences of the Alternatives

What are the most likely consequences we can anticipate with each decision alternative? If we do not know these consequences, marketing research can help us by providing information that allows us to predict the consequences.

Consequences are the results of marketing actions. What are the most likely consequences we can anticipate with each decision alternative? Note that we are *anticipating* a consequence. If we *know* the consequence, there is no need for marketing research. Assuming we don't know the consequences, then research on anticipated consequences, or most likely outcomes, of each alternative under consideration will help determine whether the alternative is correct.

Typically, the range of consequences of possible marketing decision alternatives is readily apparent. For example, if your advertising medium is changed from *People* magazine to *USA Today*, customers will either "see less," "see more," or "see the same" amount of advertising. If a nonsudsing chemical treatment is added to your swimming pool, customers will either like it "more," "less," or have "no change" in their opinions about it. If we go back to our apartment complex example, it would seem reasonable for the manager to speculate that if free satellite TV with premium channels were made available for each apartment, the consequence of this alternative would be occupancy rates that are more than enough to offset the cost of providing the service. Likewise, he is making the same assumption for free basic cable TV. But, we must ask, How certain is the manager that this will occur? Hasn't the manager made an *assumption* that providing satellite TV with premium channels will create a greater demand for the apartment complex?

Identify the Manager's Assumptions About the Consequences of the Alternatives

Decision makers make assumptions when they assign consequences to decision alternatives. Assumptions are assertions that certain conditions exist or that certain reactions will take place if the considered alternatives are implemented.

Returning to Figure 4.1, after identifying the consequences of the decision alternatives, we must address the assumptions we have made in stating these consequences. Decision makers make assumptions when they assign consequences to decision alternatives. **Assumptions** are assertions that certain conditions exist or that certain reactions will take place if the considered alternatives are implemented. For example, the manager may say, "I am positive that our lost customers will come back if we drop the price to $500," or "Our sales should go up if we gain more awareness by using advertising inserts in the Sunday paper." We will look at the certainty with which the manager makes assumptions in the following sections. However, for now, we need to make certain that we identify the assumptions being made with each decision alternative.

Assumptions deserve researcher attention because they are the glue that holds the decision process together. Given a symptom, the manager *assumes* that certain causes are at fault.

She or he further *assumes* that, by taking corrective actions (alternatives), the problem will be resolved and the symptoms will disappear. In our apartment complex example, the manager's assumption is that free satellite TV with premium channels will be a strong enough incentive to cause current students to switch apartments for the next academic year and to attract new students to select his apartments over those of competitors who only offer free basic cable TV. Another assumption is that this demand will be so much greater than the demand for apartments with free cable TV that the increase in the demand will more than offset the additional cost of providing the satellite premium channels. As we can see from Figure 4.1 our next step is to determine if we have adequate information on hand to make these assumptions. If we do not feel that information is adequate to make these assumptions, we will likely need new information. The new information will be gathered by conducting marketing research!

Even when we conduct marketing research we make assumptions. There are assumptions behind the forecasted numbers in a sales forecast. A study that segments a market will be based upon certain assumptions. Managers and researchers should be confident about those assumptions. When Campbell's Soup developed the "Souper Combo" frozen soup and a sandwich, the original sales forecast *assumed* repeat sales. Even though the marketing research department wanted more research to test if consumers would actually buy the product over and over, management made a decision based upon the assumption that sales would repeat. The assumption was wrong, and the product failed once it got to market.[15]

Assess the Adequacy of Information on Hand to Specify Research Objectives

We are almost ready to specify the research objectives. However, before we do, a key consideration is how strongly we support our own assumptions. Are we dead certain? How adequate is the information we have upon which we made the assumptions? If managers are *completely certain* that they have information adequate to support the assumptions, there is no need for research and the decision may be made. The problem may now be resolved by simply choosing the correct decision alternative (see "Choose Decision Alternative" in Figure 4.1). In this case, we don't need marketing research, do we? However, if a researcher questions a manager regarding the consequences of certain proposed alternatives, it may turn out that the manager is not really certain. It is imperative, therefore, that the manager's assumptions be analyzed for validity.

To assess validity of the manager's assumptions, the researcher assesses the existing **information state**, which is the quantity and quality of evidence a manager possesses for each assumption. During this assessment, the researcher should ask questions about the current level of information and determine the desired level of information. Conceptually, the researcher seeks to identify **information gaps**, which are discrepancies between the current level and the desired level of information at which the manager feels comfortable resolving the problem at hand. Ultimately, information gaps are the basis for establishing research objectives.

Now let's go back to the apartment complex situation and think about information gaps. Let's assume the manager felt quite confident about the accuracy of his information that free cable TV was offered by his competitors because they had advertised this new feature as well as announced this new service with signs outside their apartment complexes. Plus, we can assume that the manager was confident that students were interested in having free basic cable TV because he knew that virtually all of his tenants had basic cable TV in their apartments. However, when the researcher asked, "How do you know that students will desire the 'premium channels'," the manager stated: "Because there are great movies on these channels. My wife and I watch a movie almost every night." Now the researcher asked, "But, you don't have to study at night and you are not involved in campus activities and a fraternity or sorority, are you? How do you know that the college students will want the premium channels?" Now the manager admitted, "I really don't know. I haven't even asked any of my own tenants how many of them subscribe to premium channels." To this the researcher asked, "Would knowing that information help you make the decision? What if none of them subscribe to premium channels? Is it because they don't want premium channels or because they can't afford the premium channels?" Now the manager realized that his "certainty" had turned into high "*un*certainty." He has an information gap and he needs more information to close this gap in order to make the right decision. This situation is not unusual.

We shouldn't be too hard on our apartment manager. We often make assumptions and we are satisfied with those assumptions until we start asking ourselves hard questions. That is, we often make a lot of decisions without a perfect information state. And we have noted earlier that it is a good thing we make decisions without resorting to research, lest we all be mired down in a constant quest for additional information. But also remember what we said earlier about the cost versus value of the information. When the decision is important, it's wise to choose the right decision alternative to solve that problem. In our example, the researcher has convinced the manager that he needs more information to make sure his assumptions are correct. Exactly what information is needed in order to close the information gap? Now, we are ready to create our research objectives!

Exactly what information is needed in order to close the information gap? Now we are ready to create our research objectives!

RESEARCH OBJECTIVES

Defining Research Objectives

If the manager had the information to close the information gap we just identified, the decision alternative that will best solve the problem could be selected. Remember our discussion of research objectives back at the beginning of this chapter? Recall that we said research objectives state specifically what information must be produced by the researcher so that the manager can choose the correct decision alternative to solve the problem. It is at this point that the researcher is ready to specify the research objective. Since both the manager and the researcher agree on the type of information needed to close the information gap, they can agree on the research objective.

Sometimes hypotheses are used to guide the development of the research objective. **Hypotheses** are statements that are taken for true for the purposes of argument or investigation. In making assumptions about the consequences of decision alternatives, managers are making hypotheses. For example, a successful restaurant owner uses a hypothesis that he must use X amount of food in an entrée in order to please his customers. This restaurant owner bases his decisions on the validity of this hypothesis; he makes sure that a certain quantity of food is served on every plate regardless of the menu choice. Businesspeople make decisions every day based on statements they believe to be true. Sometimes, those decisions are very important and the person may not be confident that the hypothesis is entirely correct. This situation is very similar to our discussion of *assumptions*, isn't it? Sometimes the manager makes a specific statement (an assumption) and wants to know if there is evidence to support the statement. In these instances, we may use the term *hypothesis* to describe this "statement thought to be true for purposes of a marketing research investigation."

Hypotheses are statements that are taken for true for the purposes of argument or investigation. In making assumptions about the consequences of decision alternatives, managers are making hypotheses.

Note that not all research is conducted through hypotheses; instead a research question is often used. In this case, the question, not being a statement, is not considered a hypothesis. You will learn how to test hypotheses using the Statistical Package for Social Sciences (SPSS) later on in this book. However, for now, you should understand that when a manager makes a statement assumed to be true but is uncertain and wants the researcher to determine if there is support for the statement, we call these statements *hypotheses*. Since hypotheses are essentially statements of the decision alternative's assumed consequences, they can be very helpful in determining the research objective.

Since hypotheses are essentially statements of the decision alternative's assumed consequences, they can be very helpful in determining the research objective.

Stating the research objective is extremely important, for it defines what information will be collected from whom and in what format. The key assessment to be made of the research objective is: If this information, as stated in the research objective, is provided, can a decision alternative be selected? Before we discuss some particulars of defining research objectives, let's look back at our apartment complex example. The researcher and the manager agree that they can choose among the decision alternatives if they know whether students have a greater likelihood of signing a lease for an apartment with free satellite TV with premium channels than for an apartment with free basic cable TV. Second, they agree this information should come from a sample of students who are presently enrolled at the university, who will be returning next academic year, and who also intend to rent an off-campus apartment. An example of a research objective for our apartment complex example is:

> *Research Objective:* Conduct a survey based upon a representative sample of college students who have stated they intend to rent off-campus apartments during the next academic year to determine the likelihood (measured on a 5-point scale ranging from 1 = Very Unlikely to Rent to 5 = Very Likely to Rent) that, all factors being equal, students will rent from an apartment providing "free basic cable TV" (with channels available clearly stated) or from an apartment complex providing "free satellite TV with premium channels" (with channels available clearly stated).

Is this a good research objective? To answer this question, let's look at the following discussion of factors we should consider in defining research objectives.

FROM WHOM ARE WE GOING TO GATHER INFORMATION? Research objectives should address *who* has the information we need. Political pollsters know they must seek information from registered voters. If we are studying factors consumers use in selecting an Internet Service Provider (ISP), we should seek information from persons who have recently made this decision. We have already stated that for our apartment complex example we are seeking "students who intend to rent apartments off campus in the next academic year." Not only should the research objective specify who is to provide the information sought, it should state how these persons are to be included in the sample. Notice in our research objective above we stated that the students would be surveyed using a "representative sample." (You will learn which types of sampling plans give you a representative sample in Chapter 12.) Notice that other decisions are being made when we specify from whom we are gathering the information. We are assuming the persons specified will know the information and will provide it to us accurately. Since most students make their own decisions about where they live at college, they should know the information we need. This is not always true. A researcher who asks "anyone in the household" about details of a family's financial plans will find that usually only one person in the household is familiar enough with the plan to answer specific questions. A researcher who asks high school seniors what their preferences are for on-campus entertainment when they get to college the next year is asking the wrong people—they do not know because they haven't experienced college campus life yet. Finally, not all respondents are willing to give us the information we seek. Will a respondent be willing to give you accurate information on such sensitive topics as the number of speeding tickets they've had, the amount a family has set aside in a Roth IRA, or a host of other socially or personally sensitive topics? We must make sure we are asking for information that respondents will give us.

WHAT CONSTRUCT DO WE WISH TO MEASURE? Exactly what information do we need to choose among the decision alternatives? Recall one of the decisions to be made in Market Research Insight 4.1: "I want to choose the better of two proposed advertising claim proposals." It would be very hard to write a research objective based upon this decision statement without defining what is meant by "better." What information will tell us which claim is "better"? Is it more memorable? Is it more relevant? Is it more believable? Is the best claim the least often misinterpreted? Is it more likable? Is it the claim that is more persuasive in encouraging certain actions from the recipient? Is it the claim that is more persuasive in encouraging certain statements of intention from the recipient? Just what is "better"?[16]

We have just listed several different types of information we could collect, and each one is a separate "construct." The following constructs have been mentioned: memory, relevance, believability, understandability, likeability, and intention to purchase. A **construct** is an abstract idea inferred from specific instances that are thought to be related.[18] For example, marketers refer to the specific instances of someone buying the same brand 9 out of 10 times as a construct called *brand loyalty*. Sometimes marketing researchers call the constructs they are studying *variables*. Variables are simply constructs that can be measured, that is, quantified. They are referred to as variables because they can take on different values; that is, they can vary.[19] (Constants do not vary). A construct provides us with a mental concept that represents a real-world phenomenon. When a consumer sees an ad for a product and states, "I am going to buy that new product X," marketers would label this phenomenon as the construct called *intention to buy*. Marketers use a number of constructs to refer to phenomena that occur in the marketplace. Those just named and preference, awareness, recall, satisfaction, and so on are but a few. Table 4.2 lists constructs commonly used in marketing research.

Marketing researchers are constantly thinking of constructs as they go through the problem definition process. Once they know the construct to be measured, they can determine the proper way to go about it, which we discuss in the next section. However, before we move on, it should be noted that knowledge of constructs is also useful in developing models to explain variables involved in a phenomenon and how those variables are related. For example, a common model that marketers use to explain purchases is the "hierarchy of effects" model. This model illustrates how consumers move from (the constructs of) "awareness" to "knowledge" to "liking" to "intention" to "purchase." Since this model tells us that first "awareness" is needed to ultimately lead to "purchase," we may select "awareness" as the construct to measure in the manager's decision stated at the beginning of the previous section: "I want to choose the better of two proposed advertising claim proposals." "Better" may be defined as the advertising claim that creates the greater amount of brand "awareness." We don't wish to dwell on constructs here. What is important is that a research objective must specify which construct to measure! Managers and researchers must make this decision.

TABLE 4.2   How the "Hierarchy of Effects" Model Can Frame Research for Apartment Complex Television Decision

Hierarchy Stage	Description	Research Question
Unawareness	Not aware of your brand	What percentage of prospective student residents are unaware of satellite TV/premium channels?
Awareness	Aware of your brand	What percentage of prospective student residents are aware of satellite TV/premium channels?
Knowledge	Know something about your brand	What percentage of prospective student residents who are aware of it know that satellite TV has (1) 200 channels, (2) premium channels, and (3) pay per view?
Liking	Have a positive feeling about your brand	What percentage of prospective student residents who know something about satellite TV/premium channels feel negatively, positively, or neutral about having it in their apartment?
Intention	Intend to buy your brand next	What percentage of prospective student residents who feel positively about having satellite TV/premium channels in their apartment intend to rent an apartment with it?
Purchase*	Have purchased your brand in the past	What percentage of the market has purchased (tried) your brand in the past?
Repurchase/ Loyalty*	Purchase your brand regularly	What percentage of the market has purchased your brand more than other brands in their past five purchases?

* Not applicable to apartment complex example as satellite TV/premium channels is not currently available.

Finally, it is important to measure the *right* construct. Can you state the construct we have suggested for measurement in the research objective we stated previously for our apartment complex research project? We could call it "likelihood to rent," which is similar to "intention to rent." To illustrate why the selection of the right construct is important, let's assume we asked a sample of students to tell us what TV channels they presently "most *preferred*" to watch. Note that we would be measuring the construct "present preferences for TV channels." Can we make a decision based on this? No, we certainly can't, because students have only reported what they prefer to watch *from what is currently available* to them. Those who do not have premium TV channels, such as those being considered in our decision, will not list them, so we have no basis for making a decision as to how many students prefer them. Therefore, we can't make a decision because we measured the wrong construct. We really want to know if the presence of free satellite TV with premium channels will affect their *likelihood to rent* the apartment.

WHAT IS THE UNIT OF MEASUREMENT? Marketing researchers find constructs very helpful because, once it is determined that a specific construct is applicable to the problem, there are customary ways of *operationalizing*, or measuring, these constructs. The research objective should define how the construct being evaluated is actually measured. The definition, referred to as an **operational definition**, defines a construct, such as intention to buy or satisfaction, that describes the operations to be carried out in order for the construct to be measured empirically.[20] For example, let's take the construct "intention to buy." (This is essentially the same as our "likelihood to rent" example). This construct should represent a person's likelihood to purchase, or patronize, a particular good or service (or rent an apartment). We know that since few people know with 100% certainty that they will, or will not, purchase something, we measure this construct using a scaled response format, that is, a scale ranging from either 1 to 5, or 1 to 7, or 1 to 10. (We are not concerned about the number of scale units here; we are just illustrating that we should measure this construct using a scale of numbers, each representing a different likelihood.) This knowledge becomes very useful in properly formulating research objectives. Researchers can access sources that provide the operational definitions needed to measure many constructs.[21]

What is critical in the formulation of research objectives is that the proper unit of measurement be used for the construct. To define what is "proper," we could ask, What unit of measurement will allow the manager to choose between decision alternatives? Let's suppose that the researcher and manager have agreed to make a decision based upon a statistically significant difference between the *mean* likelihood to rent apartments with (a) cable TV versus (b) satellite TV. By measuring likelihood to rent on a 1 to 5 scale both for apartments with free cable TV and satellite TV, we can calculate the mean score for each type of TV service. We can then calculate a significant difference between the two means. This should give us the basis for choosing between the two alternatives. What if we had decided to measure "likelihood to rent" by asking students "If you had a choice between two similar apartments but one offered free satellite TV with premium channels (provide list of channels) and the other offered free basic cable TV (provide list of channels), which would you rent?" Certainly we could do this, but we now have "Yes" or "No" answers. We cannot calculate the means we said we needed in order to make our decision. Whatever the unit of measurement, the researcher and manager must agree on it *before* defining the research objectives. This will ensure that the choice among alternatives can be made after the research project.

WORD THE INFORMATION REQUESTED OF THE RESPONDENT USING THE RESPONDENT'S FRAME OF REFERENCE. Often we use jargon, which is terminology associated with a particular field. Researchers realize that when they are formulating their research objectives, the information requested of respondents must be worded using the respondent's frame of reference. A pharmaceutical manager who is about to initiate a marketing research project with physicians as respondents thinks of a particular drug in terms of dosage, form, differentiating characteristics from the nearest competitor, and so on. On the other hand, the physician, from whom they must gather information, thinks first in terms of a patient's symptoms, the disease severity, possible interaction with other drugs, willingness to comply with treatment, and so on. The pharmaceutical manager must think of the information needed in terms of the respondent-physician's frame of reference, not his own.

If we apply this concept to our apartment complex example, we could say that cable and satellite television companies often speak of "basic," "advanced basic," and "premium" channels. Consumers do not think of TV channels in these same terms. Consumers know channels by their names, such as MSNBC, CBS, Golf, or HBO. This is why it is important in our example to provide consumers with a list of the actual channels so that they can make an informed decision without having to guess as to what "premium" channels are.

Completing the Process

Turn back and look over Figure 4.1. We started out several pages back by discussing the different sources of problems ("failure to meet objectives" and "opportunity") and the systems needed to recognize those problems. We then looked at problem definition and stated that problems must be couched in terms of decisions and decisions must have alternatives. We addressed two different routes for the researcher to take in defining the decision alternatives, depending on whether or not the manager had already defined the problem. We then discussed how decision alternatives contain assumptions and that managers may be uncertain about these assumptions. Uncertainty about assumptions creates what we called information gaps, and those gaps are what research seeks to fill. The research objective specifies exactly what information the researcher must collect in order to fill the information gaps. Once this information is provided, the manager should be able to choose between the decision alternatives.

But exactly how will that decision choice be made? What must the information look like in order for a certain alternative to be selected and another not selected? This is the subject of the next section.

ACTION STANDARDS

We've seen the process of how problem definition and research objectives are developed (Figure 4.1) using our apartment complex example. However, there is another important element that we have not yet covered: action standards. An **action standard** is the predesignation in a research objective of some quantity of the attribute or characteristic being measured that must be achieved in order for a predetermined action to take place. The purpose of the action standard is to define what action will be taken given the results of the research findings.[22] In other words, by specifying the action standard, we will know, once we receive the information collected by the researcher, which decision alternative to select.

In our apartment complex case, we have determined that one research objective should be to collect information which measures *the likelihood that students will rent an apartment which offers free satellite TV service with premium channels (as well as the same for free basic cable TV)*. Recall that we stated in our research objective that we were going to measure the construct, likelihood to rent, measured on a 5-point scale ranging from 1 = Very Unlikely to Rent to 5 = Very Likely to Rent. When we get our research results, how do we know which of our three decision alternatives to select: (1) offer free satellite TV with premium channels, (2) offer free basic cable TV, or (3) do not offer either TV service? We know that we are going to get two means, one for "premium satellite" and one for "basic cable." Recall that we are asking respondents to choose an apartment, all other factors being equal, based on the provision of free "premium satellite" or "basic cable."

Let's think about the two means and create a situation where it is easy to make the decision; the "premium satellite" mean is 4.8 (high likelihood) and the "basic cable" is 1.0 (very

An action standard is the predesignation in a research objective of some quantity of the attribute or characteristic being measured that must be achieved in order for a predetermined action to take place. The purpose of the action standard is to define what action will be taken given the results of the research findings.

low likelihood) and these two means are statistically significant. Clearly, we should select the "premium satellite" decision alternative. The manager and the researcher should try to determine, prior to collecting the data, at which point they will make this decision. Let's assume they decide that if the "premium satellite" mean is above 3.5 and is statistically different from a lower mean for "basic cable," they will still go with the decision alternative of "premium satellite." In other words, they believe that with any mean of 3.5 or above and with a mean for "basic cable" significantly (statistically) lower, they believe the demand will be high enough to warrant the extra expense of providing the "premium satellite" service. A possible action standard that would warrant choosing neither would be two means that are *both below* 2. A possible action standard that would warrant installing "basic cable" would be a mean for "basic cable" that is above 3.5 and that is either not statistically different from or statistically significantly *above* the mean for "premium satellite."

Action standards require you to make important decisions before you collect your information, and they serve as clear guidelines for action once the research is over. Ron Tatham has stated,

> The action standard is an important component of the problem definition and research objective determination process because it requires the client to focus on predetermining what information he or she will need in order to take action. Using action standards helps the researcher determine the appropriate research objective because the specification of the action standards tells the researcher what information and in what format they must provide the client. Secondly, action standards allow clients to take action on research results. Without action standards, managers will often say, 'The results of the research are interesting. I learned a lot about the market but I am not sure what to do next.'[23]

Marketing Research Insight 4.2 illustrates how one well-known marketing research firm, Decision Analyst, uses action standards to help their clients test advertising.

IMPEDIMENTS TO PROBLEM DEFINITION

Now that you have an appreciation of the process that managers and researchers go through in order to properly define the problem and the research objectives, we can turn to examining why this process does not always go smoothly![24] Properly defining the problem is hampered by two factors: Managers fail to recognize the importance of communicating and interacting closely with researchers,[25] and the differences between researchers and managers may hamper communications.

Failure to Change Behavior for Problem-Definition Situations

Managers sometimes do not recognize that they need to change their normal behavior in order to properly define the problem. Managers are accustomed to dealing with outside suppliers efficiently. Suppliers are asked to present their products/services, they are evaluated against established purchasing criteria, and a decision is made. A minimum of interaction and involvement is required to make most purchasing decisions, and this is viewed as desirable; it leads to accomplishing business activities efficiently. Unfortunately, this behavior does not necessarily change when dealing with an external supplier of marketing research. Although not as probable, you could say this is true to some extent when dealing with other divisions within the same firm, as would be the case when an internal marketing research department is supplying the marketing research. Recall that we discussed marketing research acting as a "silo" in Chapter 3. Professor Sue Jones wrote:

> It is an accepted wisdom that the stage within a marketing research project of defining the problem is critical; the solution to the research design problem is derived from a full

MARKETING RESEARCH INSIGHT

Practical Insights

4.2 Decision Analyst Uses Action Standards

Decision Analyst has a database that helps it determine appropriate action standards. The following quote, supplied by Decision Analyst, explains the role action standards play when the company conducts research for their clients on the effectiveness of a given advertisement. By using an "action standard," Decision Analyst's clients know, after an advertising test, whether to run a proposed ad or kill it.

Advertising testing systems have long relied on normative data to help determine if a given advertisement is likely to be successful. "Normative data" simply means historical averages of how other advertisements in the same or similar product category have scored. If a company's new ad scores above the "norm," or average, then the advertising agency is happy and the client's marketing director is happy. However, it is Decision Analyst's position that normative data are insufficient as benchmarks. A simple average of historical test scores sets too low a standard, because the normative data includes many failed advertisements (i.e., low-scoring commercials), which pull down the historical averages. Normative data sets the bar too low.

That is why Decision Analyst focuses on "normative action standards" as the appropriate benchmarks. One might think of an "action standard" as normative data with the low-scoring advertisements removed (at a minimum). The search for a meaningful action standard is the goal of an advertising testing program. As advertisements for a brand are tested and then run or put "on air," actual sales responses are monitored to see if the ads appear to be working. Over time through trial and error, a company will begin to develop an understanding of the testing scores that correlate with positive sales response. This point at which the testing scores begin to signal an effective advertisement is where the action standard should be set. Advertisements that score near or above the action standard go forward, while ads that score below the action standard are killed.

By permission, Decision Analyst

understanding of the marketing problem. Still, it is not uncommon for initial discussions about a research project to involve relatively superficial dialog between clients and researchers; particularly if the latter are not members of the client organization.[26]

Chet Kane refers to this problem by saying that managers commission marketing research projects without being involved in them. He states that managers should be involved in designing the research and actually go out into the field and listen to some of the consumer responses first-hand. Kane says that had managers been more involved in the research, they would have known that the positive findings of research for "clear" products (clear beer, clear mouthwash, and clear cola) were based on the novelty or "fad" of the clear products. Had the managers been more involved with the research process, they would have understood this. Instead, the "clear" products were failures.[27]

Managers must understand that to find possible causes for changing symptoms or to identify and determine the likelihood of success of pursuing opportunities requires in-depth communications over an extended period of time. Often, to be effective, this process is slow and tedious. Managers often are unaware of the change required in their behavior, and this causes difficulties in identifying the real problem. Veteran researchers are well aware of this situation, and it is up to them to properly inform management of its expected role and the importance of this initial step in the research process.

Differences Between Managers and Researchers

Marketing managers and marketing researchers see the world differently because they have different jobs to perform and their backgrounds differ markedly. For example, managers possess line positions; researchers are in staff positions. Managers are responsible for generating profits; researchers are responsible for generating information. Managers are trained in general decision making, and researchers are trained in research techniques.[28] All of these differences hinder communications between two parties at a time when in-depth, continuous communications and trust are required. However, these differences have narrowed over the years. The reason is that college students today—tomorrow's managers—are in a better position to learn and have greater appreciation for the technical side of marketing research. Many of the analyses you will learn using the Statistical Package for the Social Sciences (SPSS), for example, were once available only to computer specialists who could write the code required to run these analyses on mainframe computers. You will be far better equipped to communicate with marketing researchers than your predecessors.

FORMULATE THE MARKETING RESEARCH PROPOSAL

Once a marketing researcher and client have agreed upon the problem-decision alternatives and the research objectives, the marketing researcher prepares a marketing research proposal. The purpose of the proposal is to convey to the manager, in written form, the problem and research objectives and the method that will be employed to collect and analyze the information needed to select the correct decision alternative. A **marketing research proposal** is a formal document prepared by the researcher; it serves three important functions: (1) it states the problem, (2) it specifies the research objectives, and (3) it details the research method proposed by the researcher to accomplish the research objectives. Proposals also contain (4) a timetable and (5) budget.

Problem Statement

The first step in a research proposal is to describe the problem. This section of the proposal typically identifies four factors: (1) the company, division, or principals involved; (2) the symptoms; (3) the probable causes of these symptoms; and (4) the decision alternatives. The problem statement section of the formal marketing research proposal is necessary to confirm that the researcher and the manager fully agree on these important issues.

Research Objectives

After describing the problem in the marketing research proposal, the marketing researcher must clearly spell out the specific research objectives. As we just described, the research objectives specify what information will be collected to address information gaps that must be closed in order for the manager to go about selecting the proper decision alternative to resolve the problem. The proposal provides a mechanism to ensure that the manager and researcher both agree as to exactly what information will be gathered from whom and the sample plan to be used. The research objectives should also identify the constructs to be measured and the units by which they are to be measured.

In creating research objectives, researchers must keep in mind four important qualities. Each research objective must be precise, detailed, clear, and operational. To be precise means that the terminology is understandable to the marketing manager and that it accurately captures the essence of each item to be researched. Detail is provided by elaborating, perhaps with examples, each item. The objective is clear if there is no doubt as to what will be researched and how the information will be presented to the manager. Finally, the research objective must be operational. In other words, the operational definitions of the constructs should be presented.

Detail the Proposed Research Method

Finally, the research proposal[29] will detail the proposed **research method**; that is, it will describe the sample plan, the process to be used in the development of the research instrument (questionnaire), data-collection method, safeguards to ensure against non-sampling errors, data analysis, and all other aspects of the proposed marketing research in as much detail as the researcher thinks is necessary for the manager to grasp the plan.

Timetable and Proposed Budget

The research proposal should also include a tentative timetable and specify the budget of the research undertaking. Proposals vary greatly in format and detail, but most share the basic components we have described: problem statement, research objectives, proposed research method, and the timetable and cost. We realize that you will study all of these topics in detail in chapters that follow, so we will not delve into them now.

Summary

Problems are situations calling for managers to make choices among alternatives. Research objectives state specifically what information must be produced by the researcher so that the manager can choose the correct alternative to solve the problem. Establishing the need for marketing research involves knowing when and when not to conduct marketing research. Marketing research is not needed when information to make a decision is already available, the timing is wrong, there are insufficient funds, and costs outweigh the value of doing research. Defining the problem, Step 2 in the marketing research process, though often difficult, is the most important of all the steps in the marketing research process. A bad problem definition will doom the entire project. Figure 4.1 depicts a process that may be used for defining the problem and determining the research objectives.

There are two sources of problems. One arises when there is a gap between what was *supposed* to happen and what *did* happen. This type of problem is called "failure to meet objectives." The second type of problem arises when there is a gap between what *did* happen and what *could* have happened. We refer to this type of problem as an "opportunity." Managers recognize problems either through monitoring of control systems (in the case of "failure to meet objectives") or through opportunity identification systems (in the case of opportunity). Symptoms are not problems. Rather, symptoms are changes in the level of some key monitor that measures the achievement of an objective. Symptoms alert managers to both types of problems, "failure to meet objectives" and "opportunity."

The researcher is responsible for ensuring that management has properly defined the problem even when management has already defined the problem, as in the case of ITBs or RFPs. ITBs are "invitations to bid." Alternatively, some firms use RFPs, which stands for "requests for proposals." Companies use these documents to alert research firms that they would like to receive bids or proposals to conduct research. In many cases, a situation analysis is required to help define the problem.

When defining the problem, researchers must validate the symptoms that alerted management to the problem to be certain that the symptoms are correctly reporting what they seem to report. Researchers should work with managers to determine *all possible causes* for the symptoms. Researchers should work with managers to reduce all possible causes down to probable causes. The selection of a probable cause creates the decision. The decision itself must specify alternatives that may be used to eliminate the symptom. Researchers must work with managers to clearly state the decision alternatives and to determine the consequences of each alternative. They should assess the assumptions managers have made in determining the consequences of each alternative. If the manager is completely certain about the assumptions, a decision alternative may be selected without doing any further research. However, in most cases, managers are not completely certain about their assumptions.

Lack of sufficient information creates an information gap, which is a discrepancy between the current information level and the desired information level. Information gaps are the basis for establishing research objectives. Sometimes hypotheses are stated, which helps to guide the development of the research objective. Hypotheses are statements that are taken for true for the purpose of argument or investigation. In making assumptions about the consequences of decision alternatives, managers are stating hypotheses.

Stating the research objective is extremely important, for the objective defines what information will be collected from whom and in what format. Research objectives must state what construct is to be measured and in what unit of measurement. Marketers use a number of constructs, abstract ideas inferred from specific instances that are thought to be related, to refer to phenomena that occur in the marketplace. Preference, awareness, recall, and satisfaction are but a few of these constructs. Marketing researchers find constructs very helpful because, once it is determined that a specific construct is applicable to the problem, there are customary ways of operationalizing, or measuring, it. This knowledge becomes very useful in developing the research objectives. In addition, many constructs have relationships that are explained by models, and these relationships can be useful in solving problems. Operational definitions describe the operations that must be carried out in order for a construct to measured empirically. Research objectives must define information to be requested of the respondent using the respondent's frame of reference.

Action standards refer to the predesignation of some quantity of an attribute or characteristic to be measured for a research objective that must be achieved in order for a predetermined action to take place.

Problem definition is sometimes impeded because (a) managers fail to change their normal behavior of dealing with outside suppliers in an efficient manner during problem-solving situations and (b) managers are usually generalists whereas researchers tend to be technical.

Marketing research proposals are formal documents prepared by the researcher serving the functions of stating the problem, specifying research objectives, detailing the research method, and specifying a timetable and budget.

Key Terms

Problems 84
Research objectives 84
Failure to meet objectives 90
Opportunity 90
Marketing opportunity 90
Opportunity identification 90
Market opportunity analysis 90
Symptoms 91
Situation analysis 93

ITBs 93
RFPs 93
Cause 96
Possible causes 96
Probable causes 96
Decision alternatives 96
Consequences 98
Assumptions 98
Information state 99

Information gaps 99
Hypotheses 100
Construct 102
Operational definition 103
Action standard 104
Marketing research proposal 107
Research method 108

Review Questions/Applications

1. What is meant by "the problem?"
2. What is the research objective?
3. Name the situations in which marketing research is not needed.
4. Name the situations in which marketing research is needed.
5. Explain why defining the problem is the most important step in the marketing research process.
6. Give an example of a research project that was conducted with the wrong problem definition.
7. Briefly overview the process presented in the chapter for defining the problem and the research objective.
8. What are the two sources of marketing problems?
9. Explain how managers should recognize they have a problem.
10. What is the role of symptoms in problem recognition?
11. What is the role of the researcher when management has already defined the problem?
12. What is a situation analysis and when would it likely be used when defining the problem?
13. How do ITBs and RFPs influence the problem definition process?
14. What is the role of the researcher when management has *not* already defined the problem?

15. What is meant by the researcher validating the symptoms?
16. What is the difference between (a) all possible causes and (b) probable causes?
17. Discuss why "defining the problem" is really stating the decision to be made along with the decision alternatives.
18. What are decision alternatives?
19. What is meant by "consequences" of the decision alternatives?
20. Explain how assumptions play a role in the problem definition process.
21. Using Figure 4.1, explain what happens when the information on hand is adequate.
22. Explain the information state when there are information gaps.
23. What is needed to close information gaps?
24. What is the role of a hypothesis in defining the problem?
25. What are some factors considered to be important in determining research objectives?
26. What role do constructs play in the problem definition/research objectives process?
27. What is an operational definition and where would it likely be used?
28. What is an action standard?
29. Discuss impediments to problem definition.
30. What are the components of the marketing research proposal?
31. Sony is contemplating expanding its line of 3-inch and 6-inch portable televisions. It thinks there are three situations in which this line would be purchased: (1) as a gift, (2) as a set to be used by children in their own rooms, and (3) for use at sporting events. How might the research objective be stated if Sony wished to know what consumers' preferences are with respect to these three possible uses?

32. Take the construct of channel (i.e., "brand") loyalty in the case of teenagers viewing MTV. Write at least three different definitions that indicate how a researcher might form a question in a survey to assess the degree of MTV loyalty. One example is: "Channel loyalty is determined by a stated preference to view a given channel for a certain type of entertainment."

33. You just started a new firm manufacturing and marketing MP3 players. Since your design offers more storage and several other features at two-thirds the cost of the lowest-priced competitor, your sales have been very good and it has been difficult to keep up with production. Describe the systems you need to put into place in order to detect problems your firm may have now or in the future.

34. The local Lexus dealer thinks that the four-door sedan with a list price in excess of $50,000 should appeal to Cadillac Seville owners who are thinking about buying a new automobile. He is considering a direct-mail campaign with personalized packages to be sent to owners whose Cadillac Sevilles are over two years old. Each package would contain a professional video of all the Lexus sedan's features and end with an invitation to visit the Lexus dealership. This tactic has never been tried in this market. State the marketing problem and indicate what research objectives would help the Lexus dealer understand the possible reactions of Cadillac Seville owners to this campaign.

CASE 4.1

THE CIVIC AGENCY INITIATIVES PROJECT

Alicia Kurth was frustrated. She and her fellow students—Mandi Redmon, Katie Grimes, and Betsy Ward—had spent an hour with their client, Professor Landdeck. The students had been assigned to conduct a marketing research project for Professor Landdeck, and they were still unclear about what the client needed. They had just two days to submit a research proposal and were not sure how to define their research objectives.

Dr. Landdeck was the coordinator of the Civic Agency Initiatives (CAIP) at Texas Woman's University (TWU). The focus of this three-year project was to encourage students to be civic leaders in their communities. Dr. Landdeck was pleased to have some research assistance, and when first visited by the students she told them, "Here's what I want to know. I want you to provide me with information that tells me how well I am doing as director of the TWU CAIP." She then spent most of the rest of the hour explaining how the CAIP began, how it was funded, and why she had a special interest in the program.

Pushkala Raman Assistant Professor of Marketing Texas Woman's University

One of the officers of the university first heard of the CAIP when scanning through an issue of the *Chronicle of Higher Education*, a publication that is devoted to providing news and opinions about happenings at college and universities. The officer discovered the article through one of her automatic searches on Google Alert®. She had input keywords into Google Alert to keep her informed about the higher education community; each day, the service e-mails her articles containing her keywords. When she reviewed the article about CAIP, she knew this might be a way to fulfill one of the university's mission statements regarding enriching student lives and that of the community through active civic engagement.

The four marketing research students decided they needed to have a discussion among themselves in order to get a better handle on exactly what they were supposed to write in their research proposal. Mandi stated, "We need to have some idea of what the problem is and, though we talked with Professor Landdeck for an hour, I still don't really know what the problem is." They all agreed and knew if they didn't have an understanding of the problem, they certainly couldn't write their research objectives. Katie spoke up and stated that they shouldn't tell Professor Landdeck they needed her to specify the problem so that they could write their proposal. "We need to go to the TWU online databases and search for some articles on civic engagement projects at colleges and universities." Within a couple of hours they had several recent articles that gave them a much clearer understanding of how these programs had been implemented at other colleges and universities. They emailed Dr. Landdeck and requested another appointment.

At the next meeting, the students discussed some of the civic engagement programs at other schools. Dr. Landdeck was very interested to learn that there were four main outcomes of civic engagement programs. These were:

- Volunteering
- Getting involved in community and campus government
- Caring for the environment through activities like recycling, carpooling, energy conservation
- Involvement in student organizations

Dr. Landdeck responded by stating that she wanted to accomplish all of these outcomes for students at TWU. "OK," said Betsy, "for now, let's just focus on one of them for the sake of discussion. Let's talk about involvement in student organizations." Professor Landdeck stated, "Yes. That will be one of the first things I will do." Betsy asked, "What will you do?" Professor Landdeck looked puzzled. Betsy said, "What is the decision you will need to make?" This penetrating question caused Landdeck to pause and think. "I suppose I will have to decide what methods I will use to increase involvement in student organizations." "Wait a minute!" said Alicia. "How do we know you need to increase involvement in student organizations? What if TWU is already in the 90th percentile in terms of student involvement in student organizations and is in the 10th percentile in volunteering in off-campus projects?" The students had found secondary data that showed the level of involvement at several universities in each one of the four areas. Professor Landdeck fully agreed, and the discussion centered on measuring the extent to which students are involved in each of the four areas. "My first decision should be on which of the four methods of gaining civic engagement I should concentrate my efforts."

Now the four girls' anxieties were beginning to abate. They each felt as though they were beginning to focus on the problem and that the research objectives would easily flow from the properly identified problem. As it was nearing class time, Betsy stated, "I have one last question. Let's suppose we identify that 'involvement in student organizations' at TWU is 'low.' Do you know what you will do to increase it, Professor Landdeck?" Professor Landdeck thought deeply and said, "Yes. I will ask student representatives from several organizations to make appeals in the classrooms." Quickly, the students chimed in with other alternatives: "We could have a poster campaign." "We could have a campaign targeting professors who would then encourage students to join student organizations." "We could have a contest in each college to see which student professional organizations, such as The Marketing Club, The Student Accounting Society, or the Psychology Association, could have the largest increase in student memberships." The group was still blurting out more alternative ways to increase student involvement when they realized it was time to leave for class.

As they bid farewell to Professor Landdeck and began their walk across campus, they were silent. Each was having second thoughts about the problem they defined in the meeting. Wasn't Professor Landdeck going to have to make more decisions? Which, from among all the alternatives they thought of, would be the most effective in increasing student enrollment? Their anxieties began to build once again. Mandi's parting comment was "I will be glad when this problem definition part of our project is over. This is hard!"

1. What was the source of the problem?
2. Once the students realized the client, Professor Landdeck, did not have the problem clearly formulated, what did they do? Can you identify this "step" in Figure 4.1?

3. What was the first decision identified that all agreed should be dealt with? Specify what you think the alternatives for this decision would be.

4. Assume the client's decision is stated as: "Professor Landdeck wants to improve whichever of the four methods is regarded as being 'low' at TWU." Look at Figure 4.1. Is there adequate information on hand to make this decision? What construct will need to be measured. How would you measure it, and what unit of measurement is needed?

5. As the students were about to leave from their second meeting with Professor Landdeck, they began to discuss alternative ways to increase student involvement in student organizations. Discuss the alternatives they listed in terms of the following: (a) What do we know about the client's assumptions of the consequences of these alternatives? (b) Do you think the team should try to assess the impact of different methods for increasing student involvement?

CASE 4.2 Your Integrated Case

ADVANCED AUTOMOBILE CONCEPTS

Recall that back in Case 1.2 Nick Thomas has been made CEO of Advanced Automobile Concepts (AAC), a new division of a large automobile manufacturer, ZEN Motors. ZEN is a multinational manufacturer headquartered in the United States and has multiple divisions representing several auto and truck brands. ZEN's divisions have been slowly losing market share to other competitors. AAC was created to revive the aging ZEN automobile brands by either reengineering existing models or developing totally new models that are more competitive in today's new-car market.

Nick Thomas is concerned about the strategic direction AAC should take. On the one hand, he knows the trend has been toward smaller, fuel-efficient automobiles. But he also knows that this may be a passing trend, just as it was back in the 1970s when there was a spike in fuel costs and therefore a greater demand for smaller cars and diesel engines for passenger cars. However, as soon as the OPEC countries lowered their prices, Americans for many years increasingly demanded larger cars. This eventually led to the SUV craze of the 1990s through about 2006. Now, a few years after oil prices spiked again in 2008, Nick wonders if consumers really believe oil prices will remain high. If consumers do believe this, they will probably prefer smaller, fuel-efficient vehicles. If they do not, he believes demand for smaller, fuel-efficient vehicles will be a passing fad.

A second issue that concerns Nick is the market's attitudes toward global warming. He is concerned because even though he realizes the scientific community is in reasonable agreement about global warming, there is enough controversy in the information environment to cause consumers to wonder if global warming is real. Also, Nick doesn't know how to deal with global warming in terms of the direction he should take with his automobiles. He knows consumers have several beliefs about it. Some believe global warming is a hoax. These consumers are constantly citing the record low temperatures that appear from time to time. Other consumers believe there may be global warming but it is a natural phenomenon of the Earth's temperature cycles. These consumers do not believe mankind contributes to global warming. If either of these arguments—it doesn't exist or it exists but mankind does not affect it—becomes widely accepted, then global warming will not have much effect on automobiles. On the other hand, if consumers believe their automobile exhaust affects global warming and it is a real potential threat to life on the planet Earth, there could be tremendous changes in the types of automobiles desired in the near future.

Not long after Nick was hired as CEO of AAA, he hired Marilyn Douglass. Marilyn has had many years experience working in the automotive industry and spent the last decade as director of marketing research at Nord Motors, a major competitor of ZEN. Nick wanted Marilyn on his team because he felt he needed someone to interpret consumers' future automotive needs. Nick had asked Marilyn to prepare a report summarizing what she felt were the major automobile alternatives for ZEN to consider. Marilyn's report, referred to in the company as The Douglass Report, outlined the following major alternatives.

In terms of fuels, ZEN should only consider making hybrid autos in the near future. ZEN has another division of top researchers who are investigating new fuels and engines of the future. They have spent considerable time on developing a hydrogen cell, but it will be several years before they have perfected a version that will be safe for public use. The rationale for Douglass's decision about hybrids is that some form of electric motor should be used. They are quiet, almost maintenance free, and the cost per mile is much cheaper than present internal combustion engines. But the problem with all electric vehicles is that there is a poor infrastructure to support them. For example, an all-electric car will not be useful except in very limited conditions due to restrictions on its range. For now, the range is not sufficient on the best of electric cars without widespread availability of the electrical plug-in receptacles that are needed to recharge the car. This is not something that will change overnight and even if plugs are available, they must have meters with pay receptacles allowing users to pay for the electricity consumed. This may be available in a limited way but it will be many years before such an infrastructure is available to the driving public at large.

Ms. Douglass felt that all-electric cars would find a niche in the market but that the range limitation would cap sales. She believes that several manufacturers will enter this business and will develop different vehicles for different purposes. These vehicles will differ in terms of speed, passenger space and storage payloads, range, and cost. She believes there will be many market entries, competition will be fierce, and no one will get an upper hand on the volume needed to earn respectable profits.

Douglass's report suggests that ZEN's best opportunity will reside with hybrids that use both electric power with an engine powered by gasoline, diesel, biodiesel, or even CNG. The key to the future was thought to be hybrid cars with an electric motor charged by, and alternating with, an internal combustion engine. Her preferred choice of the engine fuel for now is biodiesel, simply because diesel engines get higher mpg than gasoline and a major change in the infrastructure is not likely to be needed to make biodiesel widely available. Some form of diesel will be necessary for the trucking industry, for example, for years to come. The Douglass Report recommends that this decision be confirmed by others at ZEN.

The report stated that ZEN's competitiveness will depend on selecting the car designs (models) that meet market demand best. The underlying premise is that all vehicles will need to have high mpg ratings and that demand will differ depending on the size of the vehicles. Generally speaking, the larger the vehicle, the less the mpg, so the smallest vehicle will have "very high" mpg and the largest proposed model will have "good" mpg. Some broad choices are:

a. A very small, one-seat vehicle designed to get near maximum mpg
b. A small, two-seat vehicle designed to get high mpg
c. A larger, economy/compact-sized, four seat vehicle designed to get good mpg
d. A large, standard-size, five/six-seat vehicle with conventional trunk space designed to get reasonably good mpg

How many of these models will ZEN want to create, manufacture, and market? The Douglass Report explains that there may very well be enough demand to justify several ZEN models. It will be critical to determine which models have the greatest demand. Second, Douglass warned that just because we have an energy and environmental crisis, the car-buying public will not be satisfied with one solution. Just as is true today, there are many different market segments and each may prefer its own unique model.

Finally, The Douglass Report discusses the need to market vehicles in the future as efficiently as possible, for two reasons. First, there will be increased competition. Start-up firms will be encouraged by new government policies to produce new, energy-saving vehicles. Second, profit margins will be lower on the smaller vehicles of the future. As noted earlier, smaller cars traditionally have been priced competitively; they do not have the "higher" price points of some of the larger, luxury cars. Promotional materials will need to clearly "reach" the correct market segments without wasting dollars on market segments that are not interested in the vehicles being promoted. Media can be purchased that targets markets based upon knowledge of standard demographic data, such as gender, marital status, number of persons in household, age, level of education, job category, income, dwelling type, number of vehicles owned/leased, type of vehicle owned (economy, standard, luxury, SUV, pick-up truck, van), and so on. Also, dealer locations can be selected based upon factors such as size of the city, and so on.

Nick Thomas read The Douglass Report carefully. He felt it was a good point at which to start the decision-making process. But he needed more information.

1. How would you describe the "source" of the problem/s facing Nick Thomas?
2. Focusing on these three areas identified in The Douglass Report—(1) demand for the different basic models, (2) identification of market segment/s, and (3) marketing efficiency—describe the problems facing Nick Thomas.
3. Given the problems you have identified, describe the research objective needed to satisfy each problem.

Learning Objectives

- To understand what research design is, its significance, and types

- To learn how exploratory research design may be used and the methods to conduct exploratory research

- To know the fundamental questions addressed by descriptive research and the two major types of descriptive research

- To know the different types and uses of panels in marketing research

- To explain what is meant by causal research, experiments, and experimental design

- To know the different types of test marketing and how to select test-market cities

Where We Are

1 Establish the need for marketing research

2 Define the problem

3 Establish research objectives

4 Determine research design

5 Identify information types and sources

6 Determine methods of accessing data

7 Design data-collection forms

8 Determine the sample plan and size

9 Collect data

10 Analyze data, and

11 Prepare and present the final research report.

Research Design at Momentum Market Intelligence

Doss Struse, senior partner and CEO Momentum Market Intelligence.

Momentum Market Intelligence (MMI) is located in Portland, Oregon. The firm supplies strategic research to customers in the information technology, financial services, health care/life sciences, public utilities, and consumer packaged goods (CPG) industry sectors.[1] Doss Struse is senior partner and CEO. He has several years of high-level marketing research experience with such firms as Oscar Mayer, Carnation/Nestle, and General Mills. He also has served as an executive with ACNielsen, Research International, and Knowledge Networks. In the following paragraphs, Doss describes some different client problems and how knowledge of research design would enable

By permission, Momentum Market Intelligence.

him to make advance decisions regarding methods and procedures needed to solve the client's problem.

Research design refers to a set of advance decisions that make up the master plan specifying the methods and procedures for collecting and analyzing the information needed to solve a problem. The benefit of knowledge of research design is that, by knowing which research design is needed to solve a client's problem, a good researcher can predetermine certain procedures that will likely be needed. This not only leads to a more efficient research planning process but it enables a good researcher to advise the client early on as to the advantages and disadvantages that will be experienced with the chosen design. Let me give you some examples to illustrate my point.

Let us assume we have a client that is a consumer packaged goods manufacturer with a well-established brand name. The client has focused on manufacturing and distribution for years while the marketing program has been set on "auto pilot." All had worked fine though there was a hint of emerging problems when, in the preceding year, market share had fallen slightly. Now, let us assume our client is reviewing the current market share report and notices that over the previous 12 months their share has gradually eroded 15%. When market share falls clients are eager to learn why and to take corrective action. In these situations we know immediately the problem is that we don't know what the problem is: there are many possible causes for this slippage. In this situation we would follow a research design known as *exploratory research*, which means exactly what the name implies. We would begin to explore by examining secondary data about the industry, the market, submarkets served, and competitors. We would likely conduct some focus groups, often used in exploratory research, of both consumers and distributors. In quick order the client's problem (or problems) would begin to emerge and, once identified, we could begin solving the problem. By knowing we needed to know more about the problem itself we would know we would be using an *exploratory research* design. By knowing we needed this research design, the researcher would be in a position to select from a variety of procedures used with this design, such as secondary information search or focus groups, and make advanced decisions early in the life of the project. The client could also be apprised of the advantages and disadvantages of the procedures early on in the project.

As another example, let us assume we have a manufacturer of several baked goods products sold in grocery stores throughout the country. Marketing is divided up into five regional divisions in the U.S. The five divisions have had total autonomy over their advertising though all of them have used TV advertising almost exclusively. Each division has tried several different TV ad campaigns and some were thought to be successful and others not as successful but no one had ever formally evaluated the ad expenditures. A new Marketing VP now wants to evaluate the advertising. She's interested in knowing not only the sales of the client's products sold during the different campaigns but wants to know what happened to sales of competitors' brands. In this case, the client needs us to *describe* sales by sku (stock-keeping units) in the client's product category for each TV market and for each time period associated with each ad campaign. When we need to describe something, such as consumers' levels of satisfaction with brand X or the percentage of the target population that intends on buying a new product, we turn to *descriptive research* design. Again, by knowing we are going to be doing descriptive research, we are in a better position to determine, in advance, what methods and procedures we will be using to solve the client's problem.

To complete our discussion, let's look at one more situation. Imagine a client that is in a very competitive category with equal market share of the top three brands. Assume the client is convinced that they have changed every marketing-mix variable possible except for package design. Since the three competitive brands are typically displayed side-by-side, they want us to determine what factors of package design, i.e., size, shape, color, texture, and so on, cause an increase in awareness, preference for, and intention to buy the brand. When clients want to know if they change *x*, what happens to *y*, we know the appropriate research design is *causal research*. By knowing this we know we will be using *experimental design* research and, once again, this helps us plan many decisions in advance. You will learn more about research design by reading this chapter. After you've read the chapter, come back to this page and reread the examples I've given you. You will have a better appreciation of how important research design is to those of us in the marketing research profession.

—Doss Struse
Momentum Market Intelligence

As the examples given to us by Doss Struse illustrate, marketing research methods vary widely. One study may dictate a national telephone survey of registered voters and another requires homemakers to assemble and use a new appliance in their own kitchen. Other projects are taste tests of new, improved versions of an existing product; others are experiments of food tasting held in "kitchen-like" labs at a marketing research firm. Yet other research projects require only that we do online research of secondary data to examine existing sources of information.

How do we know which type of research project to design? Once we know the problem and we have defined our research objectives, we are in a position to determine the appropriate research design. This chapter introduces you to the three basic types of research design. You will learn about why research design is important to researchers as well as about exploratory, descriptive, and causal designs. When you complete this chapter, you should be able to determine which of the three research designs is appropriate given your research objectives.

RESEARCH DESIGN

Each type of study has certain advantages and disadvantages, and one method may be more appropriate for a given research problem than another. How do marketing researchers decide which method is the most appropriate? After thoroughly considering the problem and research objectives, researchers select a **research design**, which is a set of advance decisions that makes up the master plan specifying the methods and procedures for collecting and analyzing the needed information.

> A research design is a set of advance decisions that make up the master plan specifying the methods and procedures for collecting and analyzing the needed information.

The Significance of Research Design

Marketing researcher David Singleton of Zyman Marketing Group, Inc. believes that good research design is the first rule of good research.[2] Every research problem is unique. In fact, one could argue that given each problem's unique customer set, area of geographical application, and other situational variables, there are so few similarities among research projects that each study should be completely designed as a new and independent project. In a sense this is true; almost every research problem is unique in some way or another, and care must be taken to select the most appropriate set of approaches for the unique problem and research objectives at hand.

There are reasons to justify the significance placed on research design. First, although every problem and research objective may seem to be unique, there are usually enough similarities among problems and objectives to allow us to make some decisions in advance about the best plan to use to resolve the problem. Second, there are some basic marketing research designs that can be successfully matched to given problems and research objectives. In this way, they serve the researcher much like the blueprint serves the builder. Once the problem and the research objective are known, the researcher selects a research design. The proper research design is necessary for the researcher to achieve the research objective.

> Although every problem and research objective may seem to be unique, there are usually enough similarities among problems and objectives to allow us to make some decisions in advance about the best plan to use to resolve the problem.

> There are some basic marketing research designs that can be successfully matched to given problems and research objectives. In this way, they serve the researcher much like the blueprint serves the builder.

THREE TYPES OF RESEARCH DESIGNS

Research designs are traditionally classified into three categories: exploratory, descriptive, and causal. The choice of the most appropriate design depends largely on the objectives of the research. It has been said that research has three objectives: to gain background information and to develop hypotheses, to measure the state of a variable of interest (e.g., level of brand loyalty), or to test hypotheses that specify the relationships between two or more

The choice of the most appropriate design depends largely on the objectives of the research.

TABLE 5.1 **The Basic Research Objective and Research Design**

Research Objective	Appropriate Design
To gain background information, to define terms, to clarify problems and hypotheses, to establish research priorities	Exploratory
To describe and measure marketing phenomena	Descriptive
To determine causality, to make "if–then" statements	Causal

The choice of research design is dependent on how much we already know about the problem and research objective. The less we know, the more likely it is that we should use exploratory research.

variables (e.g., level of advertising and brand loyalty). Note also that the choice of research design is dependent on how much we already know about the problem and research objective. The less we know, the more likely it is that we should use exploratory research. Causal research, on the other hand, should be used only when we know a fair amount about the problem and are looking for causal relationships among variables associated with problem and/or research objectives. We shall see how these basic research objectives are best handled by the various research designs. Table 5.1 shows the three types of research designs and the basic research objective that would prescribe a given design.[3]

Research Design: A Caution

We pause here, before discussing the three types of research design, to warn you about thinking of research design solely in a step-by-step fashion. Some may think that it is implied in this discussion that the order in which the designs are presented—that is, exploratory, descriptive, and causal—is the order in which these designs should be carried out. This is incorrect. First, in some cases, it may be perfectly legitimate to begin with any one of the three designs and to use only that one design. Second, research is an "iterative" process—by conducting one research project, we learn that we may need additional research, and so on. This may mean that we need to use multiple research designs. We could very well find, for example, that after conducting descriptive research, we need to go back and conduct exploratory research. Third, if multiple designs are used in any particular order (if there is an order), it makes sense to first conduct exploratory research, then descriptive research, and finally causal research. The only reason for this order pattern is that each subsequent design requires greater knowledge about the problem and research objectives on the part of the researcher. Therefore, exploratory research may give one the information needed to conduct a descriptive study, which, in turn, may provide the information necessary to design a causal experiment.

All three research designs are normally used by research firms. At Ask.com, for example, researchers conduct *exploratory* research for client firms who want to know how their proposed sales strategies may work for online advertising conducted on Ask.com. Ask.com also conducts *descriptive* studies for its clients designed to describe the type of competition and characteristics of the competitors in an industry, and finally, it conducts *experiments* to determine the effects different Ask.com's marketing and advertising campaigns may have on Ask.com's brand awareness.[4]

Exploratory Research

Exploratory research is most commonly unstructured, informal research that is undertaken to gain background information about the general nature of the research problem.

Exploratory research is most commonly unstructured, informal research that is undertaken to gain background information about the general nature of the research problem. By unstructured, we mean that exploratory research does not have a predetermined set of procedures. Rather, the nature of the research changes as the researcher gains information. It is informal in that there is no formal set of objectives, sample plan, or questionnaire. Other, more formal research designs are used to test hypotheses or measure the reaction of one variable to a change in another variable. Yet, exploratory research can be accomplished by simply reading a magazine or even observing a situation. Ray Kroc, the milkshake machine salesman who created McDonald's, observed that restaurants in San Bernardino, California, run by the McDonald brothers were so busy they burned up more milkshake machines than any of his other customers. Kroc took that exploratory observation and turned it into the world-famous fast-food chain. In a more recent example, an 18-year-old college student sitting in line at McDonald's drive-through awaiting a cheeseburger saw an old dilapidated truck, loaded with junk, with a sign "Mark's Hauling." This observation set in motion Brian Scudamore's idea to launch a new type of junk service called "1-800-GOT-JUNK?" Soon he was making so much money he dropped out of college and the company was grossing revenues near $100 million.[5] A daughter talked to her dad about how messy it was to cook bacon in a microwave. They started an exploratory conversation about how to improve the process, which led to the successful creation of a microwave bacon cooking rack. Exploratory research is very flexible in that it allows the researcher to investigate any sources and to the extent necessary in order to gain a good feel for the problem at hand.

You could say that Ray Kroc's idea to start McDonald's was based on exploratory research when he began to question why the McDonald's brothers restaurants used up so many milkshake machines.

Exploratory research is usually conducted when the researcher does not know much about the problem and needs additional information or desires new or more recent information. Often, exploratory research is conducted at the outset of research projects.

Exploratory research is usually conducted when the researcher does not know much about the problem and needs additional information or desires new or more recent information.

Uses of Exploratory Research

Exploratory research is used in a number of situations: to gain background information, to define terms, to clarify problems and hypotheses, and to establish research priorities.

Exploratory research is used in a number of situations: to gain background information, to define terms, to clarify problems and hypotheses, and to establish research priorities.

GAIN BACKGROUND INFORMATION. When very little is known about the problem or when the problem has not been clearly formulated, exploratory research may be used to gain much-needed background information. It is rare even for very experienced researchers that some exploratory research is not undertaken to gain current, relevant, background information. Far too much is to be gained to ignore exploratory information.

When very little is known about the problem or when the problem has not been clearly formulated, exploratory research may be used to gain much-needed background information.

DEFINE TERMS. Exploratory research helps to define terms and concepts. By conducting exploratory research to define a question such as "What is satisfaction with service quality?" the researcher quickly learns that "satisfaction with service quality" is composed of several dimensions—tangibles, reliability, responsiveness, assurance, and empathy. Not only would exploratory research identify the dimensions of satisfaction with service quality but it could also demonstrate how these components may be measured.[6]

CLARIFY PROBLEMS AND HYPOTHESES. Exploratory research allows the researcher to define the problem more precisely and to generate hypotheses for the upcoming study. For example, exploratory research on measuring bank image reveals the issue of different groups of bank customers. Banks have three types of customers: retail customers, commercial customers, and other banks, for which services are performed for fees. This

Exploratory research helps to define terms and concepts.

Exploratory research allows the researcher to define the problem more precisely and to generate hypotheses for the upcoming study.

Exploratory research can help a firm prioritize research topics.

information is useful in clarifying the problem of the measurement of bank image because it raises the issue of for which customer group bank image should be measured.

Exploratory research can also be beneficial in the formulation of hypotheses, which are statements describing the speculated relationships among two or more variables. Formally stating hypotheses prior to conducting a research study is very important to ensure that the proper variables are measured. Once a study has been completed, it may be too late to state which hypotheses are desirable to test.

ESTABLISH RESEARCH PRIORITIES. Exploratory research can help a firm prioritize research topics. A summary account of complaint letters received by a retail store may tell management where to devote its attention. One furniture store chain owner decided to conduct research on the feasibility of carrying office furniture after some exploratory interviews with salespeople revealed that their customers often asked for directions to stores carrying office furniture.

Methods of Conducting Exploratory Research

A variety of methods are available to conduct exploratory research. These include secondary data analysis, experience surveys, case analysis, focus groups, and projective techniques.

A common method of conducting exploratory research is to examine existing information.

For some examples of secondary data often used in marketing research, see www.secondarydata.com, a website developed by Decision Analyst, Inc.

SECONDARY DATA ANALYSIS. By **secondary data analysis**, we refer to the process of searching for and interpreting existing information relevant to the research objectives. Secondary data are those that have been collected for some other purpose. Your library and the Internet are full of secondary data, which include information found in books, journals, magazines, special reports, bulletins, newsletters, and so on. An analysis of secondary data is often the "core" of exploratory research[7] because there are many benefits to examining secondary data and the costs are typically minimal. Furthermore, the costs of search time for such data are declining every day as more and more computerized databases become available. Knowledge of and ability to use these databases is already mandatory for marketing researchers. You will learn more about how to search for secondary data and also some key examples of secondary data in Chapter 6.

Exploratory research in the form of conversations with employees led a furniture store owner to add a line of office furniture.

EXPERIENCE SURVEYS. **Experience surveys** refer to gathering information from those thought to be knowledgeable on the issues relevant to the research problem. Volvo, believing that in the past autos had been designed by and for males, asked 100 women what they wanted in a car. They found some major differences between what women want and what is available, and it used this information in designing vehicles.[8] If the research problem deals with difficulties encountered when buying infant clothing, then surveys of mothers or fathers with infants may be in order. Experience surveys differ from surveys conducted as part of descriptive research in that there is usually no formal attempt to ensure that the survey results are representative of any defined group of subjects. Nevertheless, useful information can be gathered by this method of exploratory research.

> Experience surveys refer to gathering information from those thought to be knowledgeable on the issues relevant to the research problem.

CASE ANALYSIS. By **case analysis**, we mean a review of available information about a former situation(s) that has some similarities to the present research problem. Usually, many research problems have some similarities to some past situation.[9] Even when the research problem deals with a radically new product, there are often some similar past experiences that may be observed. For example, when cellular telephones were invented but not yet on the market, many companies attempted to forecast the rate of adoption by looking at adoption rates of consumer electronic products such as televisions and VCRs. A wireless communications company, 21st Century Telesis, used data from a low-power, neighborhood phone system that was very successful in Japan to help it market cellular phones to young people in Japan.[10] But researchers must be cautious in using former case examples for current problems. For example, cases dealing with technology-based products just a few years ago may be irrelevant today. The Internet and the widespread use of computers have totally changed the public's use of and attitudes toward technical products and services.

> Researchers should use former similar case situations cautiously when trying to apply them to the present research objectives.

FOCUS GROUPS. A popular method of conducting exploratory research is through **focus groups**, which are small groups of people who are brought together and guided by a moderator through an unstructured, spontaneous discussion for the purpose of gaining information relevant to the research problem.[11] Although focus groups are intended to encourage openness on the part of the participants, the moderator's task is to ensure that the discussion is "focused" on some general area of interest. For example, the Piccadilly Cafeteria chain periodically conducts focus groups all around the country. The conversation may seem "freewheeling," but the purpose of the focus group may be to learn what people think about some specific aspect of the cafeteria business, such as the perceived quality of cafeteria versus traditional restaurant food. This is a useful technique for gathering some information from a limited sample of respondents. The information can be used to generate ideas, to learn the respondents' "vocabulary" when relating to a certain type of product, or to gain some insights into basic needs and attitudes.[12]

> Focus groups are small groups of people who are brought together and guided by a moderator through an unstructured, spontaneous discussion for the purpose of gaining information relevant to the research objectives.

We will continue our discussion of focus groups in Chapter 8, but we asked a marketing researcher who specializes in focus groups, Molly Lammers of Fieldwork-Seattle, to give you some insights into the uses of focus groups here. See what Ms. Lammers has to say in Marketing Research Insight 5.1.

PROJECTIVE TECHNIQUES. Borrowed from the field of clinical psychology, **projective techniques** seek to explore hidden consumer motives for buying goods and services by asking participants to project themselves into a situation and then to respond to specific questions regarding that situation. One example of such a technique is the sentence-completion test. A respondent is given an incomplete sentence such as "John Smith would never dye his hair because. . . ." By completing the sentence, ostensibly to represent the feelings of the fictitious Mr. Smith, respondents project themselves into the situation. Another example is the "cartoon test." A respondent is given a cartoon with an empty

> Projective techniques seek to explore hidden consumer motives for buying goods and services by asking participants to project themselves into a situation and then to respond to specific questions regarding that situation.

MARKETING RESEARCH INSIGHT

Practical Application

5.1 Understanding Focus Groups

Companies and organizations constantly update, reposition, redesign or add totally new items to what they offer their constituents so that they might better serve the needs and interests of those on whom they rely. Whether they are looking for consumers to buy their products, association members to re-up for another year, stock holders to add them to their portfolios, patrons to donate, patients to bring their maladies, corporate types have long known that either you grow and flourish, or you die.

But the cost of innovation is high and the cost of errant innovation is even higher. So, today, most institutions rely on some sort of face-to-face marketing research to help them touch base with their target from time to time to make sure whatever they are working on is as compelling as they would like it to be.

Touching base, however, is easier said than done. Who, exactly, is it that you want to talk to? Where can you gain open access to such individuals? What sort of environment should you provide to make them comfortable talking about their preconceptions, desires and honest reactions to your ideas? Is

cutting-edge.

Times change. Markets evolve. Fads come and go. To keep your marketers abreast of it all, count on the state-of-the-art research capabilities of fieldwork. Our national family of focus group facilities puts the most advanced tools and techniques at your service — high-speed wireless internet, DVD recording, digital audio, usability labs, website bid requests, e-mail recruiting, video streaming/conferencing and more. All provided with fieldwork's matchless attention to detail. And did we mention catering you'll go hog-wild over?

fieldWORK

www.fieldwork.com

atlanta: 770.988.0330
boston-waltham: 781.899.3660
chicago-downtown: 312. 565.1866
chicago-north: 847.583.2911
chicago-o'hare: 773.714.8700

chicago-schaumburg: 847.413.9040
dallas: 972.866.5800
denver: 303.825.3788
east-fort lee, nj: 201.585.8200

LA-orange county: 949.252.8180
minneapolis: 952.837.8300
new york-westchester: 914.347.2145
phoenix-scottsdale: 480.443.8883

phoenix-south mountain: 602.438.2800
san francisco: 415.268.8586
seattle: 425.822.8900
seattle-downtown: 206.943.3300
multi-location projects: 1.800.TO.FIELD

it possible to have an environment with all the technology that's required today to present one's case (teleconferencing, AV-display, presentation space) that's warm enough to keep ordinary people at ease at the same time? How do you record the details of those conversations so that you can analyze what they say in pursuit of your own understanding?

Fieldwork, inc. is a company devoted to helping corporate entities of all sorts reach and relate to their constituents in a comfortable but efficient and purposeful manner. Fieldwork has three divisions. One of those divisions is comprised of a collection of focus group facilities (17) found in major metros throughout the U.S.

So what's a focus group facility and how does it work?

A focus group facility is an office comprised of interviewing suites—each of which is approximately 1,000 square feet (two large hotel rooms). Each suite has a conference room where focus groups take place and a "back room" where interested parties can observe and listen (via a piped-in sound system). Video and audio recording equipment is hard-wired into the suite so that a record of what transpires can be taken. That record goes to the client to be analyzed later. The personal identities of respondents (last names, addresses, phone numbers, etc.) are not made available unless permission has been granted ahead of time.

Finding the right people to talk to is frequently a complex task. Let me cite an example. A major restaurant chain is introducing a new line of barbequed entrees but before they go to the enormous expense of contracting with their meat vendors, printing up new menus, developing advertising and so forth, they hire a research firm to do some focus groups regarding how appealing this new line is and how well it "fits" under the current brand umbrella.

Who does the research firm want us to recruit? First of all we need people who eat out with some regularity. People who go to casual dining restaurants (the type the client has); people who aren't vegetarians. Perhaps, people who have been to one of the client's restaurants in the past six months so that they aren't totally clueless as to what the current brand umbrella really is. Furthermore, clients don't want people who are involved in any way with industries related to their own—they don't want to deal with "experts" or alert their competitors as to what they have in mind.

But there are more issues that that. They need people who are articulate in English. They need people who aren't such focus group habitués that their point of view is more like a professional respondent's than a "real" consumer's might be, But most importantly, they want people who represent a broad range of demographic, psychometric or socio-metric characteristics from that geographic area.

Keeping it all straight is the business of fieldwork. Getting the right people to show up at the right time in the right frame of mind to talk openly with strangers and doing so without violating their need for privacy is perhaps the biggest challenge a field facility has. Along the way, we have to maintain separation between client and respondent since clients frequently require that respondents be uninformed about who is sponsoring the research, not because they want to be clandestine about it, but because they don't want responses to be biased by knowing who is behind the mirror listening in.

In fact, much of what takes place in a focus group needs to be held in confidence. Every day we are dealing in intellectual property that is not only proprietary but, because these are new ideas just being considered, they are very susceptible to being picked up and perhaps utilized by competitive institutions. One of our primary tasks, then, is to have a high level of security throughout every aspect of our organization.

The recruiting process is an iterative one. The nature of the recruit may, itself, give insights and force changes into the nature of the recruiting process. We may find, for example that when we ask people in Chicago about barbequed food (where there's a strong Southern influence), they have a totally different take on what that means than do those in Seattle (where there's a strong Asian influence). Part of our job, then, is to

keep in daily contact with our clients to let them know how the recruiting process is going. It's not at all uncommon for a client to direct us to change one or more of our recruiting specifications midstream in response to what's happened so far.

After the recruiting is accomplished, we play host to various constituencies ourselves. Clients may represent a manufacturer, his ad agency and public relations associates, a design firm and a research house each represented by one or two people often flying in from several different cities. Then we have respondents who arrive hungry and need to be fed before they go in to chat for a few hours. It's a major logistic effort but, the truth is, it's our favorite part of the process—it's where we get to meet clients, hear about their efforts—it's that point in time when we get to see our hard work begin to pay off.

A focus group facility is a social place. It's full of life and full of interesting ideas floating around. Respondents may arrive with a little trepidation the first time they come to a focus group but they almost always leave with a smile and a request that they be considered in the near future for another opportunity to be a focus group participant.

Molly Turner-Lammers
Fieldwork Seattle, Inc.

balloon (used to capture statements made by cartoon characters) above a cartoon character and is asked to state what the cartoon character is saying by filling in the balloon. Marketers know that when using the cartoon test, respondents are more likely to make statements on behalf of Mr. Smith, such as "I don't care if I am dying my hair, I'm not going to look old!" Or, "I don't care if I am getting old, I'm not going to stoop to dying my hair!" More likely, if asked directly, respondents will make statements such as "some people do [dye hair] and some people don't," "I don't care what other people do." This illustrates the value of projective techniques: By talking about "others," respondents may divulge feelings about themselves that they may not divulge when questioned directly. As one marketing researcher put it: "With projective techniques, they [consumers] lay down their defenses . . . [T]he window to their psyche is opening up."[13] Projective techniques are the least used of the different types of exploratory research; nevertheless, they can play an important role given the right problem and research objective.

Our concluding word about exploratory research is that some form of it should almost always be used, at least to some extent. Why? First, exploratory research, particularly secondary data analysis, is fast. You can conduct quite a bit of exploratory research online within a matter of minutes using online databases or a search engine. Second, compared with collecting primary data, exploratory research is cheap. Finally, sometimes exploratory research either provides information to meet the research objective or assists in gathering current information necessary to construct either a descriptive or causal research design. Therefore, few researchers embark on a research project without doing some exploratory research.

> Exploratory research should almost always be used because it is fast and inexpensive, and it may help in designing the proper descriptive or causal research study.

Descriptive Research

Descriptive research is undertaken to obtain answers to questions of who, what, where, when, and how. When we wish to know *who* our customers are, *what* brands they buy and in what quantities, *where* they buy the brands, *when* they shop, and *how* they found out about our products, we turn to descriptive research. Descriptive research is also desirable when we wish to project a study's findings to a larger population. If a descriptive study's sample is representative, the findings may be used to predict some variable of interest, such as sales.

> Descriptive research is undertaken to obtain answers to questions of who, what, where, when, and how.

There are two types of descriptive studies: cross-sectional studies and longitudinal studies.

Cross-sectional studies measure units from a sample of the population at one point in time.

Because cross-sectional studies are one-time measurements, they are often described as "snapshots" of the population.

CLASSIFICATION OF DESCRIPTIVE RESEARCH STUDIES. Two basic descriptive research studies are available to the marketing researcher: cross-sectional and longitudinal. **Cross-sectional studies** measure units from a sample of the population at one point in time. A study measuring your attitude toward adding a required internship course in your degree program, for example, would be a cross-sectional study. Your attitude toward the topic is measured at one point in time. Cross-sectional studies are prevalent in marketing research, outnumbering longitudinal studies and causal studies. Because cross-sectional studies are one-time measurements, they are often described as "snapshots" of the population.

As an example of a cross-sectional study, many companies test their proposed advertising by using "storyboards." A storyboard consists of several drawings depicting the major scenes in a proposed ad as well as the proposed advertising copy. Companies can quickly and inexpensively test different ad appeals, copy, and creative elements through the use of storyboards by getting consumers' reactions to them. Consumers are shown the storyboard for a proposed ad and are then asked several questions, usually designed to measure their interest and understanding of the advertising message. Typically, a question is asked that measures the consumer's intentions to purchase the product after viewing the storyboard. Dirt Devil tested a proposed ad by using the AdInsights[SM] service offered by online research firm InsightExpress®. InsightExpress allows firms to pretest promotional messages before they spend large sums on media purchases, and promotional messages can be perfected before the messages are exposed to the competition. AdInsights may be used for all forms of promotional messages, including radio, television, and print ads. These cross-sectional studies provide client firms with useful information. In at least one situation, evaluation scores for a proposed ad were increased 219% after the ad was revised as a result of using AdInsight's cross-sectional studies. Cross-sectional studies come in many varieties, and they may be based on small or very large samples, which may or may not be representative of some larger population. When cross-sectional studies are based on fairly large sample sizes that are representative of some population, they are referred to as sample surveys.[14]

Sample surveys are cross-sectional studies whose samples are drawn in such a way as to be representative of a specific population.

Sample surveys are cross-sectional studies for which samples are drawn in such a way as to be representative of a specific population. ABC often conducts surveys on some topic of interest to report on the evening news. The surveys' samples are drawn such that ABC may report the results are representative of the population of the United States and have a "margin of error of plus or minus 3%." So sample surveys may be designed so that their results are representative and accurate, within some margin of error, of the true values in the population. (You will learn how to do this later in this book.) Sample surveys require that the samples be drawn according to a prescribed plan and a predetermined number. Later on, you will learn about these sampling plans and sample size techniques.

Longitudinal studies repeatedly measure the same sample units of a population over a period of time. Because longitudinal studies involve multiple measurements, they are often described as "movies" of the population.

Longitudinal studies repeatedly measure the same sample units of a population over a period of time. Because longitudinal studies involve multiple measurements, they are often described as "movies" of the population. Even though cross-sectional studies are far more prevalent, almost 50% of businesses use longitudinal studies in marketing research.[15] To ensure the success of the longitudinal study, researchers must have access to the same members of the sample, called a *panel*, so as to take repeated measurements. **Panels** represent sample units of the population who have agreed to answer questions at periodic intervals. Maintaining a representative panel of respondents is a major undertaking.

Panels represent sample units of the population who have agreed to answer questions at periodic intervals.

Several commercial marketing research firms develop and maintain consumer panels for use in longitudinal studies.

Several commercial marketing research firms develop and maintain consumer panels for use in longitudinal studies. Typically, these firms attempt to select a sample that is representative of some population. Firms such as Information Resources, Inc. and ACNielsen have maintained panels consisting of hundreds of thousands of households for many years. In many cases, these companies will recruit panel members so that the panel's demographic characteristics are proportionate to the demographic characteristics found in the total population according to Census Bureau statistics. Sometimes these panels will be balanced demographically not only in terms of the entire United States but also within each of various geographical regions. In this way, a client who wishes to get information from a panel of households in the Northwest can be assured that the panel is demographically matched to the total population in the states making up the northwestern region. Many companies maintain panels to target market segments, such as "dog owners," or "kids" (ages 6 to 14; see www.KidzEyes.com). Read about Knowledge Networks' panel Latino® in Marketing Research Insight 5.2. Note that panels are not limited to consumer households. Panels may consist of building contractors, supermarkets, physicians, lawyers, universities, or some other group.

Learn About Knowledge Networks' Panel

Want to learn more about panels? Go to Knowledge Networks at www.knowledgenetworks.com. Read about its panels under "Resources." Notice that Knowledge Networks first recruits panel members using probability sampling methods so as to ensure it has samples that are representative. For panel members who do not have online access, Knowledge Networks provides computer and Internet access. The ability to access probability samples (representative samples) using the speed of the Internet is a competitive advantage for Knowledge Networks.

MARKETING RESEARCH INSIGHT   Global Application

5.2 KNOWLEDGEPANEL LATINO^SM

Effective marketing and public policy making must include information from growing and distinct populations. Online survey research, as an example, must capture the Latino population, as the voices of over 45 million U.S. Latino consumers are at stake; and *Knowledge Networks (KN)* has a panel which provides clients with a full view of the Latino population. *KnowledgePanel Latino* enables clients to study attitudes and usage, opportunities for new products, reactions to changes in established brand marketing, brand landscape, and feelings about marketing and media communications. All of these must resonate with the heterogeneous Latino population, who currently represent 15% of the U.S.

KnowledgePanel Latino allows clients access to the Latino population by conducting statistically balanced online surveys of this population, covering Spanish and English speakers, as well as level of Latino identity. With *KnowledgePanel Latino*, *KN* has taken quality of representation to the next level by providing PCs and Internet service for Latinos who did not have them. By doing this, *KN* is bringing online research to a population crucial for many commercial and public policy surveys.

KN's experience shows that roughly 50% of Spanish-dominant Latinos in the U.S. do not have Internet access.

KN is known for its high quality panels and *KnowlegePanel Latino* offers several custom and syndicated options:

1. Stand-alone samples of Spanish-language and/or unassimilated households
   a. For studies representative of this portion of the Latino population reflecting Spanish-language dominance, strong Latino identity and low assimilation levels.
   b. For studies requiring large, nationally balanced Spanish-language households.
2. Inclusive studies of the U.S. Latino population.
   a. Unassimilated and/or Spanish-language households combined with existing assimilated and/or English-speaking and bilingual Latinos on *KnowledgePanel* for the most inclusive picture.
3. General population samples using *KnowledgePanel*, including unassimilated and/or Spanish-language households:
   a. For studies of the U.S. population to assure full coverage inclusive of the Latino population as part of a gen pop survey but with a readable sample.
   b. Deliver representative estimates related to Latinos and in comparison to other population segments.

By permission.

Visit Lightspeed Research at us.lightspeedpanel.com, and Greenfield Online at www.greenfield.com.

Continuous panels ask panel members the same questions on each panel measurement.

Discontinuous panels vary questions from one panel measurement to the next.

Discontinuous panels are sometimes referred to as omnibus ("including or covering many things or classes") panels.

The advantage of discontinuous (omnibus) panels are that they represent a group of persons who have made themselves available for research. The discontinuous panel provides clients with a source of information that may be quickly accessed for a wide variety of purposes.

Online research created the opportunity for several new companies to emerge that offer panels recruited to respond to online queries. Among them are C&R Research; Lightspeed Research, which offers clients panels of consumer households; and Greenfield Online, another firm that offers other marketing research firms access to its online panel of consumers.

There are two types of panels: continuous panels and discontinuous panels. **Continuous panels** ask panel members the same questions on each panel measurement. **Discontinuous panels** vary questions from one panel measurement to the next.[16] Continuous panel examples include many of the syndicated data panels that ask panel members to record their purchases using diaries or scanners. The essential point is that panel members are asked to record the *same* information (grocery store purchases) over and over. Discontinuous panels, sometimes referred to as **omnibus** ("including or covering many things or classes") **panels** may be used for a variety of purposes, and the information collected by a discontinuous panel varies from one panel measurement to the next. How longitudinal data are applied depends on the type of panel used to collect the data. Essentially, the discontinuous panel's primary usefulness is that it represents a large group—people, stores, or some other entity that is agreeable to providing marketing research information.

Discontinuous panels, like continuous panels, are also demographically matched to some larger entity, implying representativeness as well. Therefore, a marketer wanting to know how a large number of consumers, matched demographically to the total U.S. population, feels about two different product concepts may elect to use the services of an omnibus panel. The advantage of discontinuous (omnibus) panels is that they represent a group of persons who have made themselves available for research. In this way, then, discontinuous panels represent existing sources of information that may be quickly accessed for a wide variety of purposes. Marketing Research Insight 5.3 illustrates how Ipsos Public Affairs U.S. Omnibus Services can provide overnight answers to questions posed to different targets, such as teens, parents, Hispanics, U.S. online homeowners, or international markets around the world.

Ipsos' Omnibus Panel service can provide clients fast answers to their questions. By permission, Ipsos Public Affairs.

Omnibus options that fit

Need to reach targeted audiences fast? Ipsos' Omnibus team offers fast, friendly advice about the best option for getting answers to your questions from targeted respondents within your state or across North America.

For a quote or to find out more about Ipsos' Omnibus options, contact us at 1-888-289-9204 or omnibus@ipsos-na.com
www.ipsos-pa.com

Ipsos

MARKETING RESEARCH INSIGHT

Practical Application

5.3 Ipsos Public Affairs Omnibus Surveys Provide Clients Access to Discontinuous Panels

Ipsos Public Affairs U.S. Omnibus Services

Dependable, reliable, and faster than ever, Ipsos Omnibus surveys are fast turnaround research vehicles for getting the answers you need nationally, provincially, or even by market segment. Ideal for clients in the public, private and not for profit sectors, Omnibus products are reliable and accurate solutions for those who want to gauge public opinion, test advertising campaigns, set benchmarks, measure awareness and usage of brands and services, profile demographics, estimate market share, forecast trends and track reactions and opinions on specific issues.

Share the vehicle, not the results.

Think of an omnibus survey as your research car pool. You save money by sharing the vehicle (the survey) going to a common destination (the sample). The individual question results, however, are confidential and only available to you.

What Kinds of Omnibus Services are available?

Ipsos U.S. Telephone Express

Survey the U.S. marketplace quickly and cost-effectively by using Ipsos U.S. Telephone Express, a weekly poll of American opinions on social, economic and political views. This respected, timely and cost-effective survey can be used to gauge the public's response to emerging issues, identify low-incidence market segments or monitor product usage and attitudes.

Interviews for the U.S. Telephone Omnibus are conducted in Spanish as well as in English. Ipsos is the only telephone omnibus provider to complete a general population omnibus in both Spanish and English.

Ipsos U.S. Online Express

Combine the power of the web with the proven advantage of Ipsos Omnibus surveys to get the answers you need. Data is collected through random sampling of our 1,000,000+ member panel, with closed ended data returned in as little as one week. A new wave begins every business day.

Ipsos U.S. Overnight Express

Get the pulse of public opinion in just one day! The Ipsos U.S. Overnight Express Omnibus is an ideal survey instrument to gauge public opinion and reaction to issues, plan crisis communications and better understand emerging issues. Turnaround is immediate – questions confirmed by 11 a.m. (EST) on any weekday will have closed-ended data tables by 4 p.m. the next business day.

Specialty Omnibus Surveys

Ipsos US Hispanic Express Omnibus

Reach one of the fastest growing segments of the American population quickly and easily with the Ipsos U.S. Hispanic Express Omnibus. The Ipsos Hispanic Express Omnibus is the only Hispanic Omnibus that starts every week – so you don't have to wait for a new wave to start to get the answers you need.

Ipsos US Online Homeowner Express Omnibus

Every week we survey 1,000 American homeowners and find out what's on their minds. From the ABC's of their abode – the attics, basements and cupboards – to mortgages, finances, and family estate planning – the Ipsos Homeowner Online Omnibus can help you get the information you need in just five business days. A new wave begins every business day.

▶

By permission, Ipsos Public Affairs.

FIGURE 5.1

The Advantage of Longitudinal Studies vs Cross-Sectional Studies

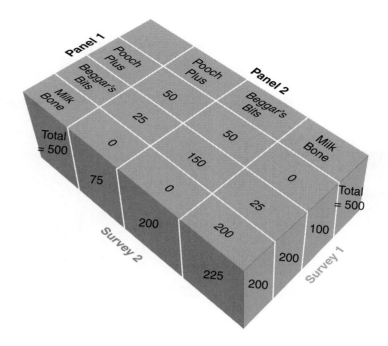

Firms are interested in using data from continuous panels because they can gain insights into changes in consumers' purchases, attitudes, and so on.

The continuous panel is used quite differently from the discontinuous panel. Usually, firms are interested in using data from continuous panels because they can gain insights into changes in consumers' purchases, attitudes, and so on. For example, data from continuous panels can show how members of the panel switched brands from one time period to the next. Studies examining how many consumers switched brands are known as **brand-switching studies**.

To illustrate the importance of using continuous panel data to gain insights into how consumers change dog treat brands, we compare longitudinal data taken from a continuous panel with data collected from two cross-sectional sample surveys. Figure 5.1 shows data collected from two separate cross-sectional studies, each having a household sample size of 500. (Cross-sectional data are referenced as "survey 1" or "survey 2.") Look at how many families used each brand in survey 1 (orange) and then see how many families used each brand in survey 2 (blue). What would we conclude about the dog-treat brands from examining these two cross-sectional studies? (1) Pooch Plus has lost market share because only 75 families indicated that they purchased Pooch Plus in the second survey as opposed to 100 Pooch Plus families in the first survey; and (2) apparently, Pooch Plus has lost out to Milk Bone dog-treat brand, which increased from 200 to 225 families. Note that Beggar's Bits remained the same. This analysis would lead most brand managers to focus on the strategies that had been used by Milk Bone (since it is "obvious" that Milk Bone took share from Pooch Plus) to increase market share for Pooch Plus.

Now, having reached a conclusion from the two cross-sectional surveys, let's look at the data, assuming we had used longitudinal research. When we examine the longitudinal data, we reach quite a different conclusion from the one we reached by looking at the two cross-sectional studies. Looking at panel 1 total (orange) and panel 2 total (blue), we see the same data that we saw in the two cross-sectional surveys.

Panel 1 totals show us that Pooch Plus had 100 families, Beggar's Bits had 200 families, and Milk Bone had 200 families. (This is exactly the same data found in our first cross-sectional survey.) Now, we later return for a second measurement of the same families in panel 2 and we find the totals are Pooch Plus, 75 families; Beggar's Bits, 200 families;

and Milk Bone, 225 families. (Again, we have the same totals as shown by survey 2 data.) But the real value of the continuous-panel longitudinal data is found in the changes that occur between panel 1 and panel 2 measurements. With longitudinal data, we can examine how each family changed from panel 1 to panel 2, and, as we shall see, the ability to measure change is very important in understanding research data. To see how the families changed, look again at panel 1 totals (orange) and then look at the data inside the figure (green) at the panel 2 results. In panel 1 (orange), we had 100 families using Pooch Plus. How did these families change by the time we asked for panel 2 information? Looking at the data on the inside of the figure (green) and reading across for Pooch Plus, we see that 50 families stayed with Pooch Plus, 50 switched to Beggar's Bits, and none of the original panel 1 Pooch Plus families switched to Milk Bone. Now look at the 200 families in panel 1 (orange) who used Beggar's Bits. In panel 2 data (green) we see that 25 of those 200 families switched to Pooch Plus, 150 stayed with Beggar's Bits, and 25 switched to Milk Bone. Finally, all of the 200 Milk Bone families in panel 1 stayed loyal to Milk Bone in panel 2.

So, what does this mean? It is clear that Pooch Plus is competing with Beggar's Bits and not with Milk Bone. Milk Bone's total shares increased but at the expense of Beggar's Bits, not Pooch Plus. The brand manager should direct attention to Beggar's Bits, not Milk Bone. This, then, is quite different from the conclusion reached by examining cross-sectional data. The key point we are making here is that because longitudinal data allow us to measure the change being made by each sample unit between time periods, we gain much richer information for analysis purposes. It is important to note, at this point, that this type of brand-switching data may be obtained only by using the continuous panel. Because different questions are asked, discontinuous panels do not allow for this type of analysis.

Another use of longitudinal data is that of market tracking. **Market tracking studies** are those that measure some variable(s) of interest, such as market share or unit sales, over time. By having representative data on brand market shares, for example, a marketing manager can "track" how the brand is doing relative to a competitor's brand performance. Every three years, the American Heart Association (AHA) conducts what it calls the "National Acute Event Tracking Study." The AHA collects data using a panel to track changes in unaided awareness of heart attack and stroke warning signs. By tracking consumers' awareness of heart attack and stroke warning signs, the AHA can determine the effectiveness of its promotional materials designed to communicate these signs to the public.[17]

> Market tracking studies are those that measure some variable(s) of interest, such as market share or unit sales, over time.

Causal Research

Causality may be thought of as understanding a phenomenon in terms of conditional statements of the form "If x, then y." These "if–then" statements become our way of manipulating variables of interest. For example, if the thermostat is lowered, then the air will get cooler. If I drive my automobile at lower speeds, then my gasoline mileage will increase. If I spend more on advertising, then sales will rise. As humans, we are constantly trying to understand the world in which we live. Likewise, marketing managers are always trying to determine what will cause a change in consumer satisfaction, a gain in market share, or an increase in sales. In one recent experiment, marketing researchers investigated how color versus noncolor and different quality levels of graphics in Yellow Page ads caused changes in consumers' attitudes toward the ad itself, the company doing the advertising, and perceptions of quality. The results showed that color and high-quality photographic materials cause more favorable attitudes. But the findings differ depending on the class of product being advertised.[18]

> Causality may be thought of as understanding a phenomenon in terms of conditional statements of the form "If x, then y." If Yellow Page ads are in color, then consumer attitudes toward the product will be more positive than if the ad is in black and white.

This illustrates how complex cause-and-effect relationships are in the real world. Consumers are bombarded on a daily and sometimes even hourly basis by a vast multitude of factors, all of which could cause them to act in one way or another. Thus, understanding

Experiments can be conducted using online research.

An experiment is defined as manipulating an independent variable to see how it affects a dependent variable, while also controlling for the effects of additional extraneous variables.

Independent variables are those that the researcher can control *and* wishes to manipulate. Independent variables could include level of advertising expenditure, type of advertising appeal, display location, method of compensating salespersons, price, and type of product.

Dependent variables are variables over which we have little or no direct control, yet we have a strong interest in manipulating them. Examples include net profits, market share, or employee or customer satisfaction.

Extraneous variables are those that may have some effect on a dependent variable but yet are not independent variables.

what causes consumers to behave as they do is extremely difficult. Nevertheless, there is a high "reward" in the marketplace for even partially understanding causal relationships. Causal relationships are determined by the use of experiments, which are special types of studies. Many companies are now taking advantage of conducting experiments online.[19]

EXPERIMENTS

An **experiment** is defined as manipulating an independent variable to see how it affects a dependent variable, while also controlling for the effects of additional extraneous variables. **Independent variables** are those that the researcher can control *and* wishes to manipulate. Some independent variables include level of advertising expenditure, type of advertising appeal (humor, prestige), display location, method of compensating salespersons, price, and type of product. **Dependent variables**, on the other hand, are variables over which we have little or no direct control, yet we have a strong interest in them. We cannot change these variables in the same way that we can change independent variables. A marketing manager, for example, can easily change the level of advertising expenditure or the location of the display of a product in a supermarket, but the manager cannot easily change sales, market share, or level of customer satisfaction. These variables are typically dependent variables. Certainly, marketers are interested in changing these variables, but because they cannot change them directly, they attempt to change them through the manipulation of independent variables. To the extent that marketers can establish causal relationships between independent and dependent variables, they enjoy some success in influencing the dependent variables.

Extraneous variables are those that may have some effect on a dependent variable but yet are not independent variables. To illustrate, let's say you and your friend wanted to know if brand of gasoline (independent variable) affected gas mileage in automobiles (dependent variable). Your "experiment" consists of filling up your two cars—one with brand A, the other with brand B. At the end of the week, you learn that brand A achieved 18.6 miles per gallon and brand B achieved 26.8 miles per gallon. Do you have a causal relationship: Brand B gets better gas mileage than brand A? Or could the difference in the dependent variable (gas mileage) be due to factors other than gasoline brand (independent variable)? Let's take a look at what these other extraneous variables may be: (1) One car is an SUV and the other is a small compact; (2) one car was driven mainly on the highway and the other was driven in the city in heavy traffic; (3) one car has never had a tune-up and the other was just tuned up. We think you get the picture.

Let's look at another example. Imagine that a supermarket chain conducts an experiment to determine the effect of type of display (independent variable) on sales of apples (dependent variable). Management records sales of the apples in its regular produce bin's position and then changes (manipulates the independent variable) the position of the apples to end-aisle displays and measures sales once again. Assume sales increased. Does this mean that if we change the display position of apples from the produce bins to end-aisle displays, sales will increase? Could there be other extraneous variables that could have affected the sales of the apples? What would happen to apple sales if the weather changed from rainy to fair? If the apple industry began running ads on TV? If the season changed from summer to fall? Yes, weather, industry advertising, and apples packed in school lunch boxes are viewed in this example as extraneous variables, having an effect on the dependent variable, yet are not themselves defined as independent variables.

As this example illustrates, it would be difficult to isolate the effects of independent variables on dependent variables without controlling for the effects of the extraneous variables. Unfortunately, it is not easy to establish causal relationships, but it can be done. In the following section we will see how different experimental designs allow us to conduct experiments.

Experimental Design

An **experimental design** is a procedure for devising an experimental setting such that a change in a dependent variable may be attributed solely to the change in an independent variable. In other words, experimental designs are procedures that allow experimenters to control for the effects on a dependent variable by an extraneous variable. In this way, the experimenter is assured that any change in the dependent variable was due only to the change in the independent variable.

An experimental design is a procedure for devising an experimental setting such that a change in a dependent variable may be attributed solely to the change in an independent variable.

Let us look at how experimental designs work. First, we list the symbols of experimental design:

O = The measurement of a dependent variable

X = The manipulation, or change, of an independent variable

R = Random assignment of subjects (consumers, stores, and so on) to experimental and control groups

E = Experimental effect, that is, the change in the dependent variable due to the independent variable

Time is assumed to be represented horizontally on a continuum.

Subscripts, such as in O_1, or O_2, refer to different measurements made of the dependent variable.

You should study the symbols of experimental design carefully. Without a good grasp of the meaning of these symbols, you will have difficulty with the following sections.

When a measurement of the dependent variable is taken prior to changing the independent variable, the measurement is sometimes called a **pretest**. When a measurement of the dependent variable is taken after changing the independent variable, the measurement is sometimes called a **posttest**.

Measurements of the dependent variable taken prior to changing the dependent variable are called *pretests* and those taken after are called *posttests*.

There are many research designs available to experimenters. In fact, entire college courses are devoted to this one topic. But our purpose here is to illustrate the logic of experimental design, and we can do this by reviewing three designs, of which only the last is a true experimental design. A **"true" experimental design** is one that truly isolates the effects of the independent variable on the dependent variable while controlling for effects of any extraneous variables. However, the first two designs we introduce you to are *not* true experimental designs. We discuss the first two designs to help you understand the real benefits of using a true experimental design. The three designs are after-only; one-group, before-after; and before-after with control group.

A "true" experimental design is one that truly isolates the effects of the independent variable on the dependent variable while controlling for effects of any extraneous variables.

AFTER-ONLY DESIGN. The **after-only design** is achieved by changing the independent variable and, after some period of time, measuring the dependent variable. It is diagrammed as follows:

$$X \quad O_1$$

where X represents the change in the independent variable (putting all of the apples in end-aisle displays) and the distance between X and O represents the passage of some time period. O_1 represents the measurement, a posttest, of the dependent variable (recording the sales of the apples). Now, what have you learned about causality? Not very much! Have sales gone up or down? We do not know because we neglected to measure sales prior to changing the display location. Regardless of what our sales are, other extraneous variables *may* have had an effect on apple sales. Managers are constantly changing things "just to see what happens" without taking the necessary precautions to properly evaluate the effects of the change. Hence, the after-only design does not really measure up to our requirement for a true experimental design.

The after-only design is achieved by changing the independent variable and, after some period of time, measuring the dependent variable. It is not a "true" experimental design.

Designs that do not properly control for the effects of extraneous variables on a dependent variable are known as **quasi-experimental designs**. Note that in the after-only design

Designs that do not properly control for the effects of extraneous variables on the dependent variable are known as quasi-experimental designs. There is no E, or "experimental effect," in quasi-experimental designs.

diagram there is no measure of E, the "experimental effect" on our dependent variable due solely to the independent variable. This is true in all quasi-experimental designs. Our next design, the one-group, before–after design, is also a quasi-experimental design, although it is an improvement over the after-only design.

ONE-GROUP, BEFORE-AFTER DESIGN. The **one-group, before-after design** is achieved by first measuring the dependent variable, then changing the independent variable, and, finally, taking a second measurement of the dependent variable. We diagram this design as follows:

$$O_1 \quad X \quad O_2$$

The obvious difference between this design and the after-only design is that we have a measurement of the dependent variable prior to and following the change in the independent variable. Also, as the name implies, we are conducting our study on only one group (a group of consumers in one store).

As an illustration of this design, let us go back to our previous example. In this design, our supermarket manager measured the dependent variable, apple sales, prior to changing the display location. Now, what do we know about causality? We know a little more than we learned from the after-only design: the change in our dependent variable from time period 1 to time period 2. We at least know if sales went up, down, or stayed the same. But what if sales did go up? Can we attribute the change in our dependent variable solely to the change in our independent variable? The answer is "no"—numerous extraneous variables, such as weather, advertising, or time of year, could have caused an increase in apple sales. With the one-group, before-after design, we still cannot accurately measure E, the "experimental effect," because this design does not control for the effects of extraneous variables on the dependent variable. Hence, the one-group, before-after design is also not a true experimental design; it is a quasi-experimental design.

Control of extraneous variables is typically achieved by the use of a second group of subjects, known as a control group. By **control group**, we mean a group whose subjects have not been exposed to the change in the independent variable. The **experimental group**, on the other hand, is the group that has been exposed to a change in the independent variable. By including these two groups in our experimental design, we can overcome many of the problems associated with the quasi-experimental designs presented thus far. We shall use the following true experimental design to illustrate the importance of the control group.

BEFORE–AFTER WITH CONTROL GROUP. The **before–after with control group** design may be achieved by randomly dividing subjects of the experiment (in this case, supermarkets) into two groups: the control group and the experimental group. A pretest measurement of the dependent variable is then made on both groups. Next, the independent variable is changed only in the experimental group. Finally, after some time period, posttest measurements are taken of the dependent variable in both groups. This design may be diagrammed as follows:

$$\text{Experimental group (R)} \quad O_1 \times O_2$$
$$\text{Control group (R)} \qquad\quad O_3 \quad O_4$$

where

$$E = (O_2 - O_1) - (O_4 - O_3).$$

In this true experimental design, there are two groups. Let's assume we have 20 supermarkets in our supermarket chain. Theoretically, if we randomly divide these stores into two groups—10 in the experimental group and 10 in the control group—then the groups should be equivalent; that is, both groups should be as similar as possible, each group having an equal number of large stores and small stores, an equal number of new stores and old stores, an equal number of stores in upper-income neighborhoods and lower-income

---

Control of extraneous variables is typically achieved by the use of a second group of subjects, known as a control group.

By control group, we mean a group whose subjects have not been exposed to the change in the independent variable.

The experimental group, on the other hand, is the group that has been exposed to a change in the independent variable.

The before-after with control group design may be achieved by randomly dividing subjects of the experiment (in this case, supermarkets) into two groups: the control group and the experimental group. It is a "true" experimental design.

Note that this design assumes that the two groups, control and experimental, are equivalent in all respects. An experimenter should take whatever steps are necessary to meet this condition of equivalency.

neighborhoods, and so on. Note that this design assumes that the two groups are equivalent in all respects. An experimenter should take whatever steps are necessary to meet this condition when using this design. There are methods for achieving equivalency other than randomization. Matching on criteria thought to be important, for example, would aid in establishing equivalent groups. When randomization or matching on relevant criteria does not achieve equivalent groups, more complex experimental designs should be used.[20]

Looking back at our design, the R indicates that we have randomly divided our supermarkets into two equal groups—one a control group, the other an experimental group. We also see that pretest measurements of our dependent variable, apple sales, were recorded at the same time for both groups of stores, as noted by O_1 and O_3. Next, we see by the X symbol that only in the experimental group of stores were the apples moved from the regular produce bins to end-aisle displays. Finally, posttest measurements of the dependent variable were taken at the same time in both groups of stores, as noted by O_2 and O_4.

Now, what information can we gather from this experiment? First, we know that $(O_2 - O_1)$ tells us how much change occurred in our dependent variable during the time of the experiment. But was this difference due solely to our independent variable, X? No, $(O_2 - O_1)$ tells us how many dollars in apple sales may be attributed to (1) the change in display location and (2) other extraneous variables, such as the weather, apple industry advertising, and so on. This does not help us very much, but what does $(O_4 - O_3)$ measure? Because it cannot account for changes in apple sales due to a change in display location (the display was not changed), then any differences in sales as measured by $(O_4 - O_3)$ must be due to the influence of other extraneous variables on apple sales. Therefore, the difference between the experimental group and the control group, $(O_2 - O_1) - (O_4 - O_3)$, results in a measure of E, the "experimental effect." We now know that if we change apple display locations, then apple sales will change by an amount equal to E. We have, through experimentation using a proper experimental design, made some progress in arriving at causality.

Now that you understand the rudiments of experimental design, you are ready to see how experiments are conducted in the marketing research industry. To illustrate a real-world marketing experiment, we asked Herb Sorensen to describe one of his experiments conducted at TNS Sorensen™. Marketing Research Insight 5.4 shows how TNS Sorensen uses the concept of control versus experimental (test) groups. Can you identify the independent and dependent variables?

As we noted earlier, there are many other experimental designs and, of course, there are almost limitless applications of experimental designs to marketing problems. An experimenter, for example, could use the before-after with control group design to measure the effects of different types of music (independent variable) on total purchases made by supermarket customers (dependent variable). Although we have demonstrated how valuable experimentation can be in providing us with knowledge, we should not accept all experiments as being valid. How we assess the validity of experiments is the subject of our next section.

How Valid Are Experiments?

How can we assess the validity of an experiment? An experiment is valid if (1) the observed change in the dependent variable is, in fact, due to the independent variable and (2) if the results of the experiment apply to the "real world" outside the experimental setting.[21] Two forms of validity are used to assess the validity of an experiment: internal and external.

Internal validity is concerned with the extent to which the change in the dependent variable was actually due to the independent variable. This is another way of asking if the proper experimental design was used and if it was implemented correctly.

To illustrate an experiment that lacks internal validity, let us return to our apple example. In the experimental design, before-after with control group, we made the point that the design assumes the experimental group and the control group are, in fact, equivalent. What would happen if the researcher did not check the equivalency of the groups? Let us suppose

---

$(O_2 - O_1)$ tells us how many dollars in apple sales may be attributed to (1) the change in display location and (2) other extraneous variables, such as the weather, apple industry advertising, and so on.

Differences in sales as measured by $(O_4 - O_3)$ are due only to the influence of extraneous variables on apple sales.

When we calculate the difference between the experimental group and the control group, $(O_2 - O_1) - (O_4 - O_3)$, the result is E, the "experimental effect." E is the amount of change we can expect in apple sales if we change apple display locations. We now have a causal understanding of the effect of changing the apple display.

An experiment is valid if (1) the observed change in the dependent variable is, in fact, due to the independent variable and (2) if the results of the experiment apply to the "real world" outside the experimental setting.

Internal validity is concerned with the extent to which the change in the dependent variable was actually due to the independent variable.

MARKETING RESEARCH INSIGHT   Practical Application

5.4 *TNS SORENSEN Uses Experiments to Increase Client's Sales in Convenience Stores*

Herb Sorensen, Ph.D.,
Global Scientific Director, TNS Retail & Shopper

A salty snack brand manufacturer thought there was a potential for increased sales in the convenience store channel. In this case, two chains of stores, widely dispersed geographically, were selected to represent the channel nationally. Obviously, there would be many variables across all the chains nationally, but understanding what drove sales in two chains could provide valuable insight for the channel. The basic experimental design here is referred to as a *controlled store test*, since two panels of matched stores were selected in each chain: Test A vs. Control A; Test B vs. Control B, where A and B are the chains.

The study began with tracking shopper behavior in stores, and interviewing them to learn more about their habits and practices in convenience stores *before* suggestions were made in terms of store design, layout and merchandising.

The PathTracker® study of where shoppers went in a few stores, how long they spent there, and what categories they visited, as well as interviews at the exits, revealed that those who buy snacks on impulse are usually coming to the store to pay for gas. The primary path in a convenience store goes from the entrance to the checkout and/or cold vault.

Review of all the data suggested that successful snack aisles will be located on the primary path to the checkout and

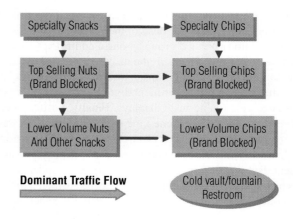

Dominant Traffic Flow

beverages and will vertically divide chips and other salty snacks (i.e., nuts). Salty Snacks will be grouped by product type and within each type items will be brand blocked.

At this point, all of the test stores had the recommended new shelf location and merchandise configuration installed, while the control stores maintained their pretest conditions. A full battery of sales data for both test and control stores, on a week-by-week basis, for the entire prior year, plus the 12 test weeks period, and 4 weeks of posttest, provides a detailed and accurate view of the impact of the changed layout and merchandising. This also allows a good understanding of other variables such as seasonality, local neighborhood, and store-specific extraneous variables that might impact the performance (causals).

The net result of this project was that sales of Chips and Nuts/Seeds increased with the new in-store execution. Other salty snacks increased only slightly. Of great interest was that although the brand manufacturer's product sales increased significantly, from the retailer's point of view, more importantly, the sales of *all* of the category brands increased.

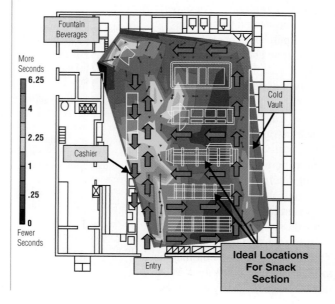

Herb is a preeminent authority on observing and measuring shopping behavior and attitudes within the four walls of the store. He has worked with *Fortune* 100 retailers and

Herb Sorensen. Ph.D.

consumer packaged goods manufacturers for more than 35 years, studying shopper behavior, motivations and perceptions at the point of purchase. Sorensen's patented shopper tracking technology PathTracker® is helping to revolutionize retail marketing strategies from a traditional "product-centric" perspective to a new "shopper-centric" focus.

Herb has conducted studies in North America, Europe, Asia, Australia, and South America. His research has been published in AMA's *Marketing Research*, *The Journal of Advertising Research*, *FMI Advantage Magazine*, *Progressive Grocer*, and *Chain Drug Review*, and he has been utilized as an expert source for

The Wall Street Journal, *Supermarket News*, and *BusinessWeek*. Additionally, he is currently a panelist of Retail Wire's "Brain Trust."

Herb was named one of the top 50 innovators of 2004 by *Fast Company Magazine* and shared the American Marketing Association's 2007 EXPLOR Award for technological applications that advance research, with Peter Fader and his group at the Wharton School of Business of the University of Pennsylvania. Herb has a Ph.D. in biochemistry.

that, by chance, the two groups of supermarkets had customers who were distinctly different with regard to a number of factors, such as age and income. The differences between the groups, then, would represent extraneous variables that had been left uncontrolled. Such an experiment would lack internal validity because it could not be said that the change in the dependent variable was due solely to the change in the independent variable. Experiments lacking internal validity have little value because they produce misleading results. Sometimes organizations will conduct studies and present them as "experiments" in order to intentionally mislead others.

> Experiments lacking internal validity have little value.

External validity refers to the extent to which the relationship observed between the independent and dependent variables during the experiment is generalizable to the real world.[22] In other words, can the results of the experiment be applied to units (consumers, stores, and so on) other than those directly involved in the experiment? Several circumstances can undermine external validity. For example, how representative is the sample of test units? Does the sample really represent the population? There are many examples of the incorrect selection of sample units for testing purposes. Executives headquartered in large cities in cold winter climates, for instance, have been known to conduct "experiments" in warmer, tropical climes during the winter. Although these experiments may be internally valid, it is doubtful that the results will be generalizable to the total population.

> If an experiment is so contrived that it produces behavior that would not likely be found in the real world, then the experiment lacks external validity.

Another threat to external validity is the artificiality of the experimental setting itself. In order to control for as many variables as possible, some experimental settings are far removed from real-world conditions.[23] If an experiment is so contrived that it produces behavior that would not likely be found in the real world, then the experiment lacks external validity.

Types of Experiments

We can classify experiments into two broad categories: laboratory and field. **Laboratory experiments** are those in which the independent variable is manipulated and measures of the dependent variable are taken in a contrived, artificial setting for the purpose of controlling the many possible extraneous variables that may affect the dependent variable.

To illustrate, let's consider a study in which subjects are invited to a theater and shown test ads, copy A or B, spliced into a TV "pilot" program. Why would a marketer want to use such an artificial setting—to control for variables that could affect the purchase of

> Laboratory experiments are those in which the independent variable is manipulated and measures of the dependent variable are taken in a contrived, artificial setting for the purpose of controlling the many possible extraneous variables that may affect the dependent variable.

Marketing researchers know how to design experiments that have both internal and external validity. Experiments enable us to know how a change in display position affects the sales of the displayed product.

Laboratory experiments are desirable when the intent of the experiment is to achieve high levels of internal validity.

products other than those in the test ads. By bringing consumers into a contrived laboratory setting, the experimenter is able to control many extraneous variables. For example, you have learned why it is important to have equivalent groups (the same kind of people watching copy A as those watching copy B commercials) in an experiment. By inviting prese-lected consumers to the TV pilot showing in a theater, the experimenter can match (on selected demographics) the consumers who view copy A with those who view copy B, thus ensuring that the two groups are equal. By having the consumers walk into an adjoining "store," the experimenter easily controls other factors, such as the time between exposure to the ad copy and shopping and the consumers' being exposed to other advertising by competitive brands. As you have already learned, any one of these factors, left uncon-trolled, could have an impact on the dependent variable. By controlling for these and other variables, the experimenter can be assured that any changes in the dependent variable were due solely to differences in the independent variable, ad copy A and B. Laboratory experi-ments, then, are desirable when the intent of the experiment is to achieve high levels of internal validity.

The advantages of laboratory experiments are that they allow for the control of extraneous variables and they may be conducted quickly and less expensively than field experiments.

There are advantages to laboratory experiments. First, as we have said, they allow the researcher to control for the effects of extraneous variables. Second, compared to field experiments, lab experiments may be conducted quickly and with less expense. Obviously, the disadvantage is the lack of a natural setting, which therefore raises concerns about the generalizability of the findings to the real world.

A disadvantage of laboratory experiments is that they are conducted in artificial settings.

For instance, blind taste tests of beer have revealed that a majority of beer drinkers favor the older beers such as Pabst, Michelob, or Coors, yet new beer brands are regularly introduced and become quite popular,[24] so the generalizability of blind taste tests is questionable.

Field experiments are those in which the independent variables are manipulated and the measurements of the dependent variable are made on test units in their natural setting.

Field experiments are those in which the independent variables are manipulated and the measurements of the dependent variable are made on test units in their natural setting. Many marketing experiments are conducted in natural settings, such as in supermarkets, malls, retail stores, and consumers' homes. Let's assume that a marketing manager con-ducts a *laboratory* experiment to test the differences between ad copy A, the company's existing ad copy, and new ad copy, copy B. The results of the laboratory experiment indi-cate that copy B is far superior to the company's present ad copy A. But before spending the money on using the new copy, the manager wants to know if ad copy B will create increased sales in the real world. She elects to actually run the new ad copy in Erie, Pennsylvania, a city noted as representative of the average characteristics of the U.S. population. By conducting this study in the field, the marketing manager will have greater confidence that the results will actually hold up in other real-world settings. Note, however, that even if an experiment is conducted in a naturalistic field setting in order to enhance external validity, it is invalid if it does not also have internal validity.

The primary advantage of the field experiment is that of conducting the study in a naturalistic setting, thus increasing the likelihood that the study's findings will also hold true in the real world. Field experiments, however, are expensive and time-consuming. Also, the experimenter must always be alert to the impact of extraneous variables, which are very difficult to control in the natural settings of field experimentation.

Erie, Pennsylvania, in the example we just cited would be called a "test market." Much of the experimentation in marketing, conducted as field experiments, is known as test marketing. For this reason, test marketing is discussed in the following section.

Even if an experiment is conducted in a naturalistic field setting in order to enhance external validity, it is invalid if it does not also have internal validity.

The primary advantage of the field experiment is that of conducting the study in a naturalistic setting, thus increasing the likelihood that the study's findings will also hold true in the real world. Field experiments, however, are expensive and time-consuming.

TEST MARKETING

Test marketing is the phrase commonly applied to an experiment, study, or test that is conducted in a field setting. Companies may use one or several geographical areas in which to conduct the test. Test markets are used (1) to test the sales potential for a new product or service and (2) to test variations in the marketing mix for a product or service.[25] Although test marketing is very expensive and time-consuming, the costs of introducing a new product on a national or regional basis routinely amount to millions of dollars. The expense of test marketing is justified if the results can improve a product's chances of success. Sometimes the test market results will be sufficient to warrant further market introductions. Sometimes the test market identifies a failure early on and allows the company to avoid huge losses. For example, the GlobalPC, a scaled-down computer targeted at novices, was tried in test markets. The parent company, MyTurn, concluded from the test market sales results that the product would not be profitable and dropped the product before the company experienced further losses.[26]

Test marketing is conducted not only to measure sales potential for a new product but also to measure consumer and dealer reactions to other marketing-mix variables. A firm may use only department stores to distribute the product in one test market and only specialty stores in another test market city to gain some information on the best way to distribute the product. Companies can also test media usage, pricing, sales promotions, and so on through test markets. Some examples of test marketing from around the world include Coke testing a new Barq's soft drink in Mississippi and Louisiana before a nationwide launch;[27] a Thailand-based furniture company conducting test marketing in India of children's furniture designed like bugs and animals;[28] Dairy Queen testing sales of irradiated ground beef patties in the United States;[29] a health care firm testing antisting jellyfish sunscreen in the United Kingdom;[30] and airlines, such as Southwest, British Midland, and Air Canada, test marketing snacks on flights around the globe.[31] Other examples of recent test marketing experiments are described in Marketing Research Insight 5.5.

Test marketing is the phrase commonly applied to an experiment, study, or test that is conducted in a field setting.

Test markets are used (1) to test the sales potential for a new product or service and (2) to test variations in the marketing mix for a product or service.

Types of Test Markets

Test markets have been classified into four types: standard, controlled, electronic, and simulated.[32] The **standard test market** is one in which the firm tests the product and/or marketing mix variables through the company's *normal* distribution channels. This type of testing takes time and exposes the new product or service to competitors, but it is a good indicator of how the product will actually perform because the testing occurs in real-world settings.

A standard test market is one in which the firm tests the product and/or marketing-mix variables through the company's normal distribution channels.

MARKETING RESEARCH INSIGHT   Practical Application

5.5 Companies Can Reduce Risks by Test Marketing First

Snoring While Driving May be Hazardous to Your Health

Specialists estimate that 20% of accidents are caused by drivers who are tired or not paying attention to the road. Moreover, statistics show that thousands of people die every year because of drivers falling asleep at the wheel. With the objective of reducing this problem, Saab is launching an in-car system called Driver Attention Warning System (DAWS) that is supposed to determine when the driver is tired or not paying enough attention to the road and to advise the driver to stop for a rest. The system consists of two cameras focused on the driver's eyes to detect when eye movements indicate drowsiness. DAWS is an innovative product in that it focuses on detecting the onset of drowsiness or inattention. Competitive products have focused on the immediate consequences of falling asleep. Saab is test marketing the system on its 9-3 Sport Wagon in Sweden; if it is successful, the idea is to introduce DAWS in other Saab models across Europe.[33]

e.l.f. Testing Online

Eyes. Lips. Face. (e.l.f.) is the brand of a company that offers good-quality, low-priced products for the eyes (shadows, liners, mascara), lips (plumpers, glosses, lipsticks), and face (powder, blusher, concealer). An urban legend had it that the company would be acquired by the retailer Nordstrom and that the new owner would sell all e.l.f. products for $1 at the website www. eyeslipsface. com. The story was not true, but the news spread quickly and resulted in an avalanche of business at the website. Now the company is using the well-known website as a test-marketing medium, trying out new products and colors before it sends products to big retail stores like Target and Kmart.[34]

Want to Stop By for Some Snacks, a Beer, and a Paternity Test?

Soreson Genomics Company has developed a do-it-yourself DNA test that allows people to discover the identity of a baby's father in a cheaper and faster way than ever before. The kit costs $29.99 and the laboratory costs are $119, representing a total cost of less than $150 instead of the $2,000 or more charged for the traditional test. The company also guarantees the results within five business days; the traditional test averages six months. The test has 99.9% certainty of establishing paternity or proving genetic links between siblings.

After a good response to the test marketing done in the Pacific coast states, Sorenson rolled out its Identigene paternity kits nationally in March 2008. Even though the test is not admissible in court (because the identity of those taking part in the at-home test cannot be verified), demand for it is high. People take the test for different reasons, but often to avoid the need to go to court. The company is promising to provide a legally sound test for about $350.[35]

McCoffee Anyone?

The number of consumers who buy a coffee drink during a quick-service food visit grew to 6.6% in 2007 from 3.5% in 2006. Looking at the fast growth of coffee consumption during snack occasions, MacDonald's has launched McCafe Specialty Coffees. The company started the launching by test marketing in six major markets, including Grand Rapids, Michigan; California's Central Coast; Kansas City, Missouri; and parts of Georgia, North Carolina, and Texas. Initial results were above expectations, but after some time had passed espresso drink sales fell off their initial pace. McDonald's is moving ahead with the new product line with the goal of adding $125.000 a year in sales per restaurant. The company plans to expand the rollout from the stores that started the test marketing to its 14,000 stores during 2009.[36]

Controlled test markets are used by outside (what we call external supplier) research firms that guarantee distribution of the product through prespecified types and numbers of distributors.

Controlled test markets are used by outside (what we call external supplier) research firms that guarantee distribution of the product through prespecified types and numbers of distributors. Companies specializing in providing this service, such as RoperASW and ACNielsen, use dollar incentives to get distributors to provide guaranteed shelf space. Controlled test markets offer an alternative to the company that wishes to gain fast access to a distribution system set up for test-market purposes. The disadvantage is that this distribution network may or may not properly represent the firm's actual distribution system. We will look at this service again in Chapter 7 on standardized services.

Electronic test markets are those in which a panel of consumers has agreed to present identification cards when buying goods and services. This type of test is conducted in only a small number of cities where local retailers have agreed to participate. The advantage of the card is that as consumers buy (or do not buy) the test product, demographic information is automatically recorded. In some cases, firms offering electronic test markets may also have the ability to link panel members to their media viewing habits as well to determine how different elements of the promotional mix affect purchases of the new product. Firms offering this service include Information Resources, Inc. and Nielsen. Obviously, electronic test marketing offers speed, greater confidentiality, and less cost than testing in standard or controlled markets. However, the test market is not the real market. Consumers in electronic test markets may be atypical just by virtue of having agreed to serve as members of the electronic panel. A user firm must evaluate this issue of representativeness, which is also raised by the fact that electronic test markets are typically situated in small cities such as Eau Claire, Wisconsin.[37]

> Electronic test markets are those in which a panel of consumers has agreed to present identification cards when buying goods and services.

Simulated test markets (STMs) use a model containing certain assumptions regarding planned marketing programs to generate likely product sales volume from a limited amount of data on consumer response to a new product Some have claimed that IBM has suffered business failures, such as the ill-fated Aptiva line of PCs, because it failed to use STM research.[38] Typical STMs have the following characteristics: (1) a sample of consumers who satisfy predetermined demographic characteristics is selected; (2) consumers are shown commercials or print ads for the test product as well as ads for competitive products; (3) consumers are given the opportunity to purchase, or not to purchase, the test product either in a real or simulated store environment; (4) consumers are recontacted after they have had an opportunity to use the product in an effort to determine likelihood of repurchase, as well as to gather other information relative to the use of the product; (5) information from this process is then fed into a computer program that calibrates assumptions about the marketing mix and other elements of the environment. The program then generates estimated sales volume, market share, and so on.[39]

STMs have many advantages. They are fast relative to standard test marketing, typically taking only 18 to 24 weeks compared to as long as 12 to 18 months for standard test marketing. STM costs are only 5 to 10% of the cost of standard test marketing, and they are confidential—competitors are less likely to know about the test. STMs can test different marketing mixes and results have shown that they can be accurate predictors of actual market response. The primary disadvantage is that they are not as accurate as full-scale test marketing; they are very dependent on the assumptions built into the models.[40]

Consumer Versus Industrial Test Markets

When we think of test marketing, we normally think of tests of consumer products. Test marketing of industrial products, however, has been growing in the business-to-business (B-to-B) market. Although the techniques used in consumer and industrial test markets differ somewhat, the results sought are the same—the timely release of profitable products.

In consumer test markets, multiple versions of a more-or-less finished product are tested by consumers. In industrial test markets, the key technology is presented to selected industrial users, who offer feedback on desired features and product performance levels. Given this information, product prototypes are then developed and placed with a select number of users. Users again provide feedback to iron out design problems. In this way, the new product is tried and tested under actual conditions before the final version is designed and produced for the total market. The negative side of this process is the time it takes to test the product from the beginning stages to the final, commercialized stages. During this period, information on the new product is leaked to competitors, and the longer the product is tested, the higher the investment costs without generating any offsetting revenues. American automakers, for example, take 48 to 60 months to design, refine, and begin production of a new car model. Japanese companies are able to do it in 30 months by using development teams made up of a combination of marketing and production people. DaimlerChrysler and 3M have experimented with this concept. In many firms, future industrial test marketing will be fully integrated with the new-product development process.[41]

"Lead Country" Test Markets

A **lead country test market** is one that seems to be good predictor of the response for an entire continent. As markets have become more global, firms are no longer interested in limiting marketing of new products and services to their domestic market.

Colgate-Palmolive used lead country test marketing when it launched its Palmolive Optims shampoo and conditioner. The company tested the product in the Philippines, Australia, Mexico, and Hong Kong. A year later, distribution was expanded to other countries in Europe, Asia, Latin America, and Africa.[42] Colgate used two countries as test markets in 1999 to test its battery-powered Actibrush for kids. These two countries brought in $10 million in sales. Colgate moved into 50 countries in 2000 and earned $115 million in sales.[43] Korea is being used as a lead country test market for digital products and services. Over the next three years in Seongnam, a middle-class Seoul suburb with a mix of high-rise apartment blocks, restaurants, and malls, municipal officials plan to transform the town of 930,000 into the world's first digital city. Multiple broadband connections will seek to do away with analog concepts—like cash and credit cards. Seongnam will start equipping citizens with digital cell phones that, in effect, pay for purchases at every store in the city. Cash-free Seongnam is one of many on-the-ground tests being launched in South Korea, a nation preoccupied with all things digital. More than half of South Korea's 15 million households have broadband service and more than 60% of Koreans carry cell phones. The country is now so wired that many companies can use entire urban populations as test markets for their latest digital products and services.[44]

Selecting Test Market Cities

There are three criteria that are useful for selecting test market cities: **representativeness**, **degree of isolation**, and **ability to control distribution and promotion**. Because one of the major reasons for conducting test marketing is to achieve external validity, the test market city should be representative of the marketing territory in which the product will ultimately be distributed. Consequently, a great deal of effort is expended to locate the "ideal" city in terms of comparability with characteristics of the total U.S. (or other country) population. The "ideal" city is, of course, the city whose demographic characteristics most closely match those of the desired total market. For instance, R. J. Reynolds chose Chattanooga, Tennessee, to test market its Eclipse "smokeless" cigarette because Chattanooga has a higher proportion of smokers than most cities and R. J. Reynolds needed to test Eclipse with smokers.[45]

When a firm test markets a product, distribution and promotion of the product are confined to a limited geographical area, such as Tulsa, Oklahoma. Advertising in the *Tulsa World* newspaper has very little "spillover" into other sizable markets. Therefore, a company, along with its dealers, competitors, and so on, is not likely to get many calls from a nearby city wanting to know why the product cannot be bought there. Distribution is restricted to the test market, Tulsa. Some markets are not so isolated. Promotions for a product test in the *Los Angeles Times* would have very large spillover in newspaper readership outside the Los Angeles geographical area. Note that this would not necessarily be a problem so long as the test is to be run in the geographical area covered by the *Los Angeles Times* and the new product is to be distributed in that area.

The ability to control distribution and promotion depends on a number of factors. Are the distributors in the city being considered available and willing to cooperate? If not, is a

A lead country test market is one that seems to be a good predictor of the response for an entire continent.

There are three criteria that are useful for selecting test market cities: representativeness, degree of isolation, and ability to control distribution and promotion.

controlled test market service company available for the city? Will the media in the city have the facilities to accommodate the test market needs? At what cost? All of these factors must be considered before selecting the test city. Fortunately, because test marketing conducted in a city brings in additional revenues, city governments as well as the media typically provide a great deal of information about their city to prospective test marketers.

A good example of the application of these three criteria is McDonald's test marketing of its all-you-can-eat breakfast bar. The test was conducted in Atlanta and Savannah, Georgia, which are representative cities in the Southeast where McDonald's has control over its outlets and where the promotional media are specific to those markets. The buffet was found to increase weekend family breakfast sales.[46]

Pros and Cons of Test Marketing

The advantages of test marketing are straightforward. Testing product acceptability and marketing-mix variables in a field setting provides the best information possible to the decision maker prior to actually going into full-scale marketing of the product, which is why Philip Kotler has referred to test markets as the "ultimate" way to test a new product.[47] Test marketing allows for the most accurate method of forecasting future sales, and it allows firms the opportunity to pretest marketing-mix variables.

Test marketing allows for the most accurate method of forecasting future sales, and it allows firms the opportunity to pretest marketing-mix variables.

There are, however, several negatives to test marketing. First, test markets do not yield infallible results. One observer noted that because they are limited geographical areas, test markets cannot really predict the diverse consumer behavior in today's global markets. This same observer questioned the short time frame in which tests are conducted. Noting that some products or services take longer to find acceptance, some products are deemed failures without adequate time to show accurate sales.[48] There have been many instances in which test market results have led to decisions that proved wrong in the marketplace. There probably have also been many "would-be successful" products withheld from the marketplace because of poor performance in test markets. Much of this problem, however, is not due to anything inherent in test marketing; rather, it is a reflection of the complexity and changeability of consumer behavior. Accurately forecasting consumer behavior is a formidable task. Another problem is that competitors intentionally try to sabotage test marketing. Often, firms will flood a test market with sales promotions if they know a competitor is test marketing a product. When PepsiCo tested Mountain Dew Sport drink in Minneapolis in 1990, Quaker Oats Company's Gatorade counterattacked with a deluge of coupons and ads. Mountain Dew Sport was yanked from the market, although Pepsi says Gatorade had nothing to do with the decision.[49] These activities make it even more difficult to forecast the normal market's response to a product.

Test markets do not yield infallible results.

Another problem with test marketing is its cost. Estimates are that the costs exceed several hundred thousand dollars even for limited testing. Test markets involving several test cities and various forms of promotion can easily reach well over six figures. Finally, test markets bring about exposure of the product to the competition. Competitors get the opportunity to examine product prototypes and to see the planned marketing strategy for the new product via the test market. If a company spends too much time testing a product, it runs the risk of allowing enough time for a competitor to bring out a similar product and to gain the advantage of being first in the market. In spite of these problems, the value of the information from test marketing makes it worthwhile.

Test marketing is expensive, exposes the new product or service to competitors, and takes time to conduct.

Test markets may create ethical problems. Companies routinely report test marketing results to the press, which allows them access to premarket publicity. But do they always report the negatives found from the test market or only the good news? Companies, eager to get good publicity, may select test market cities they think will return favorable results. Perhaps the company already has a strong brand and market power in the market. Is this method of getting publicity ethical? The *Wall Street Journal* has addressed these issues and the Advertising Research Foundation has published "Guidelines for Public Use of Market and Opinion Research" in an attempt to make reporting of test marketing more candid.[50]

Summary

Research design refers to a set of advance decisions made to develop the master plan to be used in the conduct of the research project. There are three general research designs: exploratory, descriptive, and causal. Each of these designs has its own inherent approaches. The significance of studying research design is that, by matching the research objective with the appropriate research design, a host of research decisions may be predetermined. Therefore, a research design serves as a "blueprint" for researchers.

Selecting the appropriate research design depends, to a large extent, on the research objectives and how much information is already known about the problem. If very little is known, exploratory research is appropriate. Exploratory research is unstructured, informal research that is undertaken to gain background information; it is helpful in more clearly defining the research problem. Exploratory research is used in a number of situations: to gain background information, to define terms, to clarify problems and hypotheses, and to establish research priorities. Reviewing existing literature, surveying individuals knowledgeable in the area to be investigated, relying on former similar case situations, conducting focus groups, and using projective techniques are methods of conducting exploratory research. In focus groups, a small group of persons is guided by a moderator through a spontaneous, unstructured conversation that focuses on a research problem. Exploratory research should almost always be used because it is fast, inexpensive, and sometimes resolves the research objective or is helpful in carrying out descriptive or causal research.

If concepts, terms, and so on are already known and the research objective is to describe and measure phenomena, then descriptive research is appropriate. Descriptive research measures marketing phenomena and answers the questions of who, what, where, when, and how. Descriptive studies may be conducted at one point in time (cross-sectional) or several measurements may be made on the same sample at different points in time (longitudinal). Longitudinal studies are often conducted using panels. Panels represent sample units of people who have agreed to answer questions at periodic intervals. Continuous panels are longitudinal studies in which sample units are asked the same questions repeatedly. Brand-switching tables may be prepared based on data from continuous panels. Market tracking studies may be conducted using data from continuous panels.

The second type of panel used in longitudinal research is the discontinuous panel. Discontinuous, sometimes called omnibus, panels are those in which the sample units are asked different questions. The main advantage of the discontinuous panel is that research firms have a large sample of persons who are willing to answer whatever questions they are asked. The demographics of panel members are often balanced with regard to the demographics of larger geographical areas they are to represent, such as a region or the entire United States. Marketing research firms such as IRI and ACNielsen have maintained panels for many years.

Sometimes the research objective requires the researcher to determine causal relationships between two or more variables. Causal relationships determine relationships, as in "if *x*, then *y*." Causal relationships may be discovered only through special studies called *experiments*. Experiments allow us to determine the effects of a variable, known as an independent variable, on another variable, known as a dependent variable. Experimental designs are necessary to ensure that the effect observed in the dependent variable is due, in fact, to the independent variable and not to other variables, known as extraneous variables. The validity of experiments may be assessed by internal validity and external validity.

Laboratory experiments are particularly useful for achieving internal validity, whereas field experiments are better suited for achieving external validity. Test marketing is a form of field experimentation. Test market cities are selected on the basis of their representativeness, isolation, and the degree to which market variables such as distribution and promotion may be controlled. There are various types of test markets (standard, controlled, electronic, simulated, consumer, industrial, and lead country), but, although test markets garner much useful information, they are expensive and not infallible.

Key Terms

Review Questions/Applications

1. What is the significance of knowing research design?
2. How would you match research designs with various research objectives?
3. Give some examples illustrating the uses of exploratory research.
4. What are the different methods used to conduct exploratory research?
5. Describe a focus group facility.
6. What is the rationale behind "projective" techniques?
7. What type of research design answers the questions of who, what, where, when, and how?
8. What are the differences between longitudinal studies and cross-sectional studies?
9. What is a sample survey?
10. In what situation would a continuous panel be more suitable than a discontinuous panel? In what situation would a discontinuous panel be more suitable than a continuous panel?
11. Describe an omnibus panel service.
12. Explain the key advantage of using longitudinal data for a brand-switching table.
13. Explain why studies of the "if-then" variety are considered to be causal studies.
14. What is the objective of good experimental design? Explain why certain designs are called "quasi-experimental designs."
15. Name the different types of variables involved in experimental studies and discuss each.
16. Explain why a before-after with control group experiment is a true experimental design.
17. Explain the two types of validity in experimentation and also explain why different types of experiments are better suited for addressing one type of validity versus another.
18. Distinguish among the various types of test marketing.
19. What are the pros and cons of test marketing?
20. Think of a job that you have held. List three areas in which you, or some other person in the organization, could have benefited from having information generated by research. What would be the most appropriate research design for each of the three areas of research you have listed?
21. Design an experiment. Select an independent variable and a dependent variable. What are some possible extraneous variables that may cause problems? Explain how you would control for the effects these variables may have on your dependent variable. Is your experiment a valid experiment?
22. The Maximum Company has invented an extra-strength instant coffee brand to be called "Max-Gaff" and positioned it to be stronger-tasting than any competing brands. Design a taste-test experiment that compares Max-Gaff to the two leading instant coffee brands to determine which brand consumers consider to taste the strongest. Identify and diagram your experiment. Indicate how the experiment is to be conducted and assess the internal and external validity of your experiment.
23. Coca-Cola markets PowerAde as a sports drink that competes with Gatorade. Competition for sports drinks is fierce where they are sold in the coolers of convenience stores. Coca-Cola is thinking about using a special holder that fits in a standard cooler but moves PowerAde to eye level and makes it more conspicuous than Gatorade. Design an experiment that determines whether the special

holder increases the sales of PowerAde in convenience stores. Identify and diagram your experiment. Indicate how the experiment is to be conducted and assess the internal and external validity of your experiment.

24. SplitScreen is a marketing research company that tests television advertisements. SplitScreen has an agreement with a cable television company in a medium-sized city in Iowa. The cable company can send up to four different television ads simultaneously to different households. SplitScreen also has agreements with the three largest grocery store chains, which will provide scanner data to SplitScreen. About 25% of the residents have SplitScreen scan cards that are scanned when items are bought at the grocery store and that allow SplitScreen to identify who bought which grocery products. For allowing SplitScreen access to their television hookups and their grocery purchases information, residents receive bonus points that can be used to buy products in a special points catalog. Identify and diagram the true experimental design possible using the SplitScreen system. Assess the internal and external validity of SplitScreen's system.

CASE 5.1

QUALITY RESEARCH ASSOCIATES

Sam Fulkerson of Quality Research Associates reviewed notes of meetings with his clients during the last week.

Monday/am Discussion with Janey Dean, Director of Marketing for the Hamptons Bank. Dean is interested in knowing more about a bank image study. Informed her that we had not conducted such a study but that I would meet with her in a week and discuss how to proceed. Dean wants to hire us for advice; her own staff may actually do the image study. Next meeting set for 15th at 2:30 pm.

Tuesday/pm Met with Cayleigh Rogers, Business Manager for Wesleyan College. College is considering a football team and the president wants some indication from alums if they favor it and if they would be willing to send a donation to help with start-up costs. The president of the college also wants to know if present students will support a football team. Call him back for follow up meeting.

Wednesday/am Met with Lawrence Brown of M&M Mars. Brown is brand manager for a new candy bar, and he needs advice on promotional methods in the candy bar business. Specifically, he would like to know what promotional methods have been used over the past five years by candy bar brands and how those promotions had an impact on sales. Advised Brown I would contact some other research suppliers and get back to him.

Wednesday/pm Tom Greer visited office. Tom also with M&M Mars. Company interested in going into cereal line and wants information fast on how consumers will react to candy-flavored cereal company has developed. Company's own taste tests have been favorable, but Greer wants reaction from a larger sample of consumers from around the country. Would like this information within a month. Important: Company already has the samples ready for mailing.

Thursday/am Meeting with Phyllis Detrick of McBride's Markets. McBride has a chain of 150 supermarkets in eight states. Company is spending several million dollars a year on advertising. Detrick wants to know what she can do with the advertising copy and layout of the ads that will generate the most attention. She conducted some exploratory research and found that potential consumers who were reading the paper don't recall seeing the McBride ads. Specifically, she wants to know if adding color is worth the expense. Will color ads generate greater attention? We set up joint meeting with the McBride advertising manager, who will bring in all of their newspaper ads for the past 6 months.

Thursday/pm Meeting with Carolyn Phillips, French Yarbrough, and Jeff Rogers. All three are part of a start-up company that has been working on a new toothbrush storage and sanitation device. The new product steam sanitizes the toothbrushes overnight to make them virtually germ-free. Two years ago we conducted exploratory research in the form of focus groups. We followed that up with a survey of a representative sample of households within the city. The survey showed the respondents a picture of the device and asked them if they would be willing to pay $x to buy it. Thus far, all had gone well and all studies indicated "go." Now, Phillips, Yarbrough, and Rogers think they are ready to introduce the product to the country. They have had several discussions with large retail chains. All of the chain buyers are interested, but they want more evidence that the market will accept the devices. One chain buyer said, "I want to know if people will walk in our stores and buy these off the shelf." Also, Phillips, Yarbrough, and Rogers have narrowed their national promotion campaigns down to two choices but they aren't certain which one will gain them the most customers.

Friday/am No client meetings. Work on research designs.

1. What research design do you think Sam Fulkerson should select for each of his clients?
2. For each research design you specify in Question 1, describe the reason(s) you selected it.

CASE 5.2 Your Integrated Case

ADVANCED AUTOMOBILE CONCEPTS

Nick Thomas has been considering some of the issues identified in the Douglass Report (see Case 4.2). He is considering different directions to take. First, he is a little concerned that most of the information he and AAC have based their decisions on thus far are either industry reports or opinions of persons in the company. Granted, these persons are quite knowledgeable of the automobile industry. But Thomas is concerned that he doesn't have input from some consumers. What do consumers think about global warming, future fuel costs, hybrids vs. all electric cars? He knows the media has introduced a vast amount of information on these topics to consumers, but he wonders if consumers are even aware of these issues. How important are these issues to them? What appears to be the most important . . . global warming? Fuel costs? Giving up their SUVs? He begins to realize he doesn't know very much about what consumers think about these important issues. He doesn't know how much they talk about these issues with their neighbors or even what terms they use to speak of these issues.

Second, Thomas thinks about the attitudes of consumers and car purchasing intentions. That is, will a strong belief in global warming be highly associated with buying certain types of cars? Will this vary around the country? Will these relationships exist within definable market segments?

Finally, Thomas knows that AAC can retrofit some ZEN models that will improve fuel economy without requiring drastic new technology or retooling or added costs. Nick wonders: "How much of an improvement in mpg would consumers require to buy the present ZEN models?" What percentage increase in fuel economy (mpg) in current ZEN models will be required before ZEN becomes equally preferred with some of the better-selling foreign autos?

Thomas wonders how he could find answers to these questions. He is considering talking with a marketing researcher. Imagine you are the researcher hired by Thomas to address these questions.

1. To deal with the first set of issues—determining how consumers feel about certain issues, how important these issues are to them, and what terms they use to discuss these issues—what research design would you suggest? Why?
2. Consider the second paragraph in the case. What research design would you suggest to determine all of the following: Which attitudes are strongly associated with purchase intentions of different auto models? Will these relationships vary around the country and will they exist for definable market segments? Why?
3. Nick Thomas's last question deals with determining how much of an increase in mpg will be needed for consumers to have equal preference for ZEN models as for those outselling ZEN today. What research design would you suggest and why?

Learning Objectives

- To learn how to distinguish between secondary and primary data
- To learn the uses and the classification of secondary data
- To understand both internal and external databases and their structures
- To understand the advantages and disadvantages of secondary data
- To learn how to evaluate secondary data
- To learn how to find secondary data, including strategies needed for searching online information databases
- To know the contents of some of the major sources of secondary data provided by the government and private sources

Where We Are

Marketing Researchers Use Secondary Data

Jerry W. Thomas,
President/CEO, Decision
Analyst

Here at Decision Analyst® we make certain we are fully aware of all existing information about an industry, a product category, and a company before we decide on the research objectives and methodology for a research project. Even when we are dealing with a client in an industry in which we have conducted dozens of marketing research projects, a review of current secondary data can alert us to any recent developments. Any good marketing researcher should be adept at searching for and analyzing secondary data. As you will learn in this chapter, secondary data analysis is fast and inexpensive compared to collecting primary data. Sometimes, secondary data is all we need in order to provide the

Decision Analyst, Inc.

necessary information to solve our client's problem. Also, when we need to collect primary data for our clients, we provide current, relevant secondary data to help our client better understand the implications of the primary data. We strive to add value for our clients and secondary data helps us accomplish that goal.

The Internet has been a catalyst for allowing faster searches and giving us access to more information than we thought possible just a few years ago. You have much of this information available to you through your university's databases. However, we are cautious in accepting any secondary data. Sometimes information is disseminated to serve special interests. At Decision Analyst® we use secondary data from known and trusted sources. Go to our website at www.decisionanalyst.com and click on *SecondaryData.com*. Here you will find a list of sources of secondary data. You will learn about some of these sources in this chapter, and Burns and Bush will also help you evaluate sources of secondary data.

Jerry W. Thomas

President/CEO

Decision Analyst

By permission

Marketing researcher Jerry W. Thomas's comments demonstrate the importance of secondary data and online databases to marketing researchers. As he points out, even when the project involves collecting primary data, marketing researchers also consult secondary data. He also points out how online information databases have made this task much easier for the researcher. In this chapter, you will learn how to distinguish secondary data from primary data. We will illustrate the usefulness of secondary data and discuss how it may be classified. We will introduce you to the advantages and disadvantages of secondary data. We will then introduce you to some strategies for effectively and efficiently searching for secondary data, including strategies for searching online information databases. Finally, we point out some important secondary data sources for marketing researchers.[1]

Visit Decision Analyst at www.decisionanalyst.com.

SECONDARY DATA

Primary data refers to information that is developed or gathered by the researcher specifically for the research project at hand.

Secondary data have previously been gathered by someone other than the researcher and/or for some purpose other than the research project at hand.

The evolution of the Internet has done more to bring fast and easy access of secondary data to end users than anything since Gutenberg's printing press.

Free access to secondary data via the Internet, another form of online research, will continue to grow more and more important in the marketing researcher's toolbox.

There are so many uses of secondary data that it is rare for a marketing research project to be conducted without including some of it. Some projects may be totally based on secondary data.

Visit Decision Analyst's secondary data site at www.secondarydata.com.

Primary Versus Secondary Data

As we mentioned in Chapter 2, data needed for marketing management decisions can be grouped into two types: primary and secondary. **Primary data** refers to information that is developed or gathered by the researcher specifically for the research project at hand. **Secondary data** have previously been gathered by someone other than the researcher and/or for some purpose other than the research project at hand. As commercial firms, government agencies, or community service organizations record transactions and business activities, they are creating a written record of these activities in the form of secondary data. When consumers fill out warranty cards or register their boats, automobiles, or software programs, this information is stored in the form of secondary data. It is available for someone else's secondary use.

The evolution of the Internet has done more to bring fast and easy access to secondary data to end users than anything since Gutenberg's printing press. Since the mid-1980s, virtually all documents have been electronically produced, edited, stored, and made accessible to users. For several years, firms have concentrated on bringing this information to users through specialized services, and today many of these firms offer these services via the Internet. Although some information is available only through a subscription, the Internet provides an incredible stock of free secondary data. Google®, Yahoo®, Live Search®, and ASK® account for millions of searches per day, and specialized search engines are devoted to such areas as business, real property, health, careers, news, and so on. Search engines no longer publicize how many searches are conducted daily, but Google is thought to be the largest.[2] We think secondary data access through the Internet will continue to grow and become more and more important in the marketing researcher's toolbox.

Uses of Secondary Data

There are so many uses of secondary data that it is rare for a marketing research project to be conducted without including some of it. Some projects may be totally based on secondary data. The applications of secondary data range from predicting very broad changes in a culture's "way of life" to very specific applications, such as selecting a street address location for a new car wash. As noted in our opening vignette, Decision Analyst, Inc., a marketing research firm, has a website devoted entirely to secondary data. Suggested applications include economic trends forecasting, industry information, corporate intelligence, international data, public opinion, and historical data, among others.

Marketers are very interested in having secondary demographic data to help them forecast the size of the market in a newly proposed

market territory. A researcher may use secondary data to determine the population and growth rate in almost any geographical area. Government agencies are interested in having secondary data to help them make public policy decisions. The Department of Education needs to know how many 5-year-olds will enter the public school system next year. Health-care planners need to know how many senior citizens will be eligible for Medicare during the next decade. Sometimes secondary data can be used to evaluate market performance. For example, since data on gasoline and fuel taxes collected per gallon are available in public records, petroleum marketers can easily determine the volume of fuels consumed in a county. Articles on virtually every topic are published, and this storehouse of secondary data is available to marketers who want to understand a subject more thoroughly but do not have firsthand experience.

Marketing researchers have identified certain demographic groups as market segments, in that they tend to make similar purchases, have similar attitudes, and have similar media habits.

Much secondary data are available concerning the lifestyles of demographic groups, including their purchasing habits. Marketing researchers have identified certain **demographic groups** as market segments, in that they tend to make similar purchases, have similar attitudes, and have similar media habits. The most significant of these demographic groups for decades has been the "**baby-boomer**" population, defined as those born between 1946 and 1964. As the boomers enter middle-age and senior status, marketers have turned to studying other demographic groups, such as the Gen Xers[3] and Gen Yers. Our Marketing Research Insight 6.1 illustrates how secondary data on demographic groups are important to marketers.

Much secondary data are available concerning the lifestyles of demographic groups, such as baby boomers, Gen Yers, and Gen Xers, including their purchasing habits.

MARKETING RESEARCH INSIGHT   Practical Application

6.1 If it Weren't for Demographics, Elvis Might Still Be Driving a Truck in Memphis!

Much secondary marketing research seeks demographic information. Derived from the Greek word *demos*, "demographics" refers to the study of a population. Normally included are population size, density, growth, income, ethnic background, housing, and retail sales, among other factors. Demographic analysis based on age offers many insights into the marketplace and is highly predictive. We know today how many 16-year-olds there will be in 2021! For many decades marketers followed baby boomers, persons born from 1946 to 1964 who make up a large percentage of the population, and have followed their marketplace demands through the years. In the 1950s, there was a huge demand for schools to educate boomers coming of school age. The demands for textbooks, Boy and Girl Scout uniforms, and toys experienced high growth rates. Boomers between 12 and 18 years of age wanted an alternative to their parents' preferences for Big Band and "crooner" music. Rock and roll replaced Frank Sinatra, Perry Como, and Dean Martin when the young boomers reached their teens and Elvis Presley met

Because of the youthful baby-boomer demographic, Elvis replaced Frank Sinatra on the music charts.

the demands of this new market better than anyone else. Indeed, one could argue that if it hadn't been for the young boomers demanding a change in music, Elvis would have had a normal life driving a truck in Memphis. As the boomers aged, they placed unprecedented, but predictable, demands on colleges and universities, the job market, housing, recreation, and now, retirement- and health-related goods and services.

Beyond the boomers, demographers have identified other demographic segments. Gen Y represents a group almost as large as the boomers and is expected to be as powerful a shaper of business decisions in the future. Though there is some disagreement among demographers as to the exact size, most agree that **Gen Yers** represent the 72 million Americans born between 1977 and 1994. Another group, **Gen Xers**, are the post-baby-boom generation generally represented by those born between 1965 to about 1980. The estimated spending income of the Gen Yer group is $187 billion annually. But, unlike the boomers, Gen Yers may prove to be the most unpredictable and marketing-resistant group yet faced by U.S. marketers. With many in their early 20s, a large percentage of Gen Yers are still living at home with their parents. They shun traditional media preferring video games, DVDs, and websites.

Because Gen Yers represent such a large population and still influence their younger counterparts, marketers are keenly interested in them. Honda tried to target them with its Element, which they positioned as a "dorm room on wheels." Chrysler did the same with its PT Cruiser. Gen Yers were not impressed. Both cars sold, but to a much older market. Gen Yers, however, are predictable when it comes to technology. They are heavy users of all forms of technology. Cell-phone manufacturers are watching Gen Yers closely to identify hot new trends for the rest of the market. Cell phones featuring video and speaker attachments are already available. Jupiter Research reports that 18- to 24-year-olds spend an average of 10 hours a week online, 10 hours watching TV, and 5 hours listening to the radio. They also spend considerably more online time messaging, playing games, and downloading music than their older counterparts.

Gen Yers, having been exposed to 3,000 marketing messages a day (making some 23 million in their lives thus far), are immune to traditional advertising. One advertiser said that when you do a focus group with 21-year-olds, they tell you the advertiser's strategy. In other words, they see right through the ads. Instead of viewing ads for information, as the boomers do, they view them for entertainment. Advertisers, to get their attention, must make the ads entertaining, and they feel they must use word-of-mouth and stealth marketing instead of traditional advertising media.

Gen Yers are thus viewed as being a powerful force in the market today. They not only influence their younger siblings but, surprisingly, they influence their boomer parents. For example, MTV reports that parents are watching rocker Ozzie Osbourne and his family right along with their Gen Y kids! Marketers will rely heavily on secondary data to track Gen Yers in the years ahead.[4]

Learn more about social and demographic trends by going to Social and Demographic Trends, Pew Research Center at www.pewsocialtrends.org.

CLASSIFICATION OF SECONDARY DATA

Marketing researchers should be aware of the classifications of secondary data, their advantages and disadvantages, and how to evaluate the information available.

Given that the amount of secondary information available can be overwhelming, marketing researchers must learn to handle it properly. A basic understanding of the classifications of secondary data is helpful, as well as the advantages and disadvantages of each classification and how to evaluate the information available.

Internal Secondary Data

Internal secondary data are data that have been collected within the firm. Such data include sales records, purchase requisitions, and invoices.

Secondary data may be broadly classified as either internal or external. **Internal secondary data** are data that have been collected within the firm. Such data include sales records, purchase requisitions, and invoices. Obviously, a good marketing researcher always determines what internal information is already available. You may recall from Chapter 1 that we referred to internal data analysis as being part of the internal reports system of a firm's marketing information system (MIS). Today, a major source of internal data is databases containing information on customers, sales, suppliers, and any other facet of business a firm may wish to track. Philip Kotler defines **database marketing** as ". . . the process of building, maintaining, and using customer (*internal*) databases and other (*internal*) databases (products, suppliers, resellers) for the purpose of contacting, transacting, and building relationships (italics added)".[5] The use of internal databases has continued to grow dramatically.

Internal data are part of a firm's MIS, the internal reports system, as discussed in Chapter 1.

Database marketing is defined as the process of building, maintaining, and using customer (*internal*) databases and other (*internal*) databases (products, suppliers, resellers) for the purpose of contacting, transacting, and building relationships.

Internal Databases

Before we discuss internal and external databases, we should understand that a **database** refers to a collection of data and information describing items of interest.[6] Each unit of information in a database is called a **record**. A record could represent a customer, a supplier, a competitive firm, a product, an individual inventory item, and so on. Records are composed of subcomponents of information called *fields.* As an example, a company having a database of customers would have *records* representing each customer. Typical *fields* in a customer database would include name, address, telephone number, e-mail address, products purchased, dates of purchases, locations where purchased, warranty information, and any other information the company thought was important. Although you can have a noncomputerized database, the majority of databases are computerized because they contain large amounts of information and their use is facilitated by the computer's capability to edit, sort, and analyze the mass of information.

Internal databases are databases consisting of information gathered by a company during the normal course of business transactions. Marketing managers normally develop internal databases about customers, but databases may be kept on any topic of interest, such as products, members of the salesforce, inventory, maintenance, and supplier firms. Companies gather information about customers when they inquire about a product or service, make a purchase, or have a product serviced. Think about the information you may have provided to marketing firms: your name, address, telephone number, fax number, e-mail address, credit card number, banking institution and account number, and so on. Coupled with knowledge of what products you have purchased in the past and with other information provided by government and other commercial sources, many companies know quite a bit about you. Companies use their internal databases for purposes of direct marketing and to strengthen relationships with customers, called **CRM, customer relationship management**.[7]

Internal databases can be quite large. Dealing with the vast quantities of data and managing the information in internal databases has been a problem. **Data mining** is the name for the software that is now available to help managers make sense out of seemingly senseless masses of information contained in databases.[8] However, not all databases are massive and even simple ones in small businesses can be invaluable. One study showed that almost half of retail firms have some sort of database containing information about their customers.[9]

Internal databases, built with information collected during the normal course of business, can provide invaluable insights to managers. Databases can tell managers which products are selling, report inventories, and profile customers by stock keeping unit (SKU). Coupled with geodemographic information systems (GIS), databases can provide maps of where the most profitable and least profitable customers reside by ZIP codes. We shall discuss GIS more completely in the next chapter.

What companies do with the information collected for their internal databases can present ethical problems. Should your credit card company share information on what types of goods and services you bought with anyone who wants to buy that information? Should your Internet service provider be able to store information on which Internet sites you visit? As more consumers have grown aware of these privacy issues, more companies have adopted privacy policies.[10]

A database refers to a collection of data and information describing items of interest to the database owner.

Databases are composed of records that represent a unit of information. Subcomponents of information in records are called *fields*.

Internal databases are databases consisting of information gathered by a company during the normal course of business transactions.

Companies use their internal databases for purposes of direct marketing and to strengthen relationships with customers, called CRM, customer relationship management.

Data mining is the name for the software that is now available to help managers make sense out of seemingly senseless masses of information contained in databases.

What companies do with information collected for their internal databases can present ethical problems.

 Think About this the Next Time You Order a Pizza!

Consumer activist groups are alarmed at the amount of consumer information companies have collected. The American Civil Liberties Union is one such organization that believes companies have too much access to private information. To illustrate their point, the ACLU created "Ordering a Pizza in 2010." Check it out at www.aclu.org/pizza/. What do you think? Do you have an account on Amazon.com or eBay or some other Internet retailer? Do you use that online account? Why?

MARKETING RESEARCH INSIGHT   Practical Application

6.2 A Published Source of Secondary Information: *Quirk's Marketing Research Review*

After 20 years of marketing research experience, Tom Quirk started *Quirk's Marketing Research Review* in 1986. The mission of the magazine has remained steadfast: to provide practical, valuable, and useful information to the marketing research industry. Each issue contains cases, practical examples, expert advice on research techniques, and information on the latest new-product information as well as on survey findings. Special issues address topics such as advertising research, B-to-B research, customer satisfaction, health care research, international research, Internet research and technology, among others. In addition to publishing *Quirk's Marketing*

Research Review, Quirk's also publishes nine specialty directories of research providers and a directory of all marketing research providers in the *Researcher SourceBook™*.

Tom Quirk's vision to provide information to marketing research professionals has grown to become a significant source of secondary information for researchers. Quirk's has over 16,000 subscribers in countries all over the world. You can visit Quirk's at www.quirks.com.

By permission, *Quirk's Marketing Research Review.*

External Secondary Data

PUBLISHED SOURCES. **External secondary data** are data obtained from outside the firm. There are three general sources of external data: (1) published, (2) syndicated services data, and (3) databases. **Published sources** are those prepared for public distribution and are normally found in libraries or provided by a variety of other entities, such as trade associations, professional organizations, or companies. Published sources are available in a number of formats, including print, CD-ROM, and online via the Internet. Many publications that were formerly available in print only are becoming available in electronic format, for example, magazines as e-zines and journals as e-journals. Providers of published secondary information are the government (e.g., *Census of the Population*), nonprofit organizations (e.g., chambers of commerce, colleges and universities), trade and professional associations (e.g., CASRO, AMA, IMRO, MRA), and for-profits (e.g., *Sales & Marketing Management* magazine, Prentice Hall, McGraw-Hill, and research firms). Many research firms publish secondary information in the form of books, newsletters, white papers, special reports, magazines, or journals, for example, *Quirk's Marketing Research Review*. See Marketing Research Insight 6.2.

The sheer volume of published sources makes searching this type of secondary data difficult. However, understanding the functions of the different types of publications can be of great help in successfully searching published secondary information sources. Table 6.1 depicts the different types of publications, their functions, and an example of each type.

> Published sources are those prepared for public distribution and are normally found in libraries or provided by a variety of other entities, such as trade associations, professional organizations, or companies.

How to Find Articles on Marketing Research at Quirks.com

Want to know how to search *Quirk's Marketing Research Review* to find secondary data on almost any topic in marketing research? Go to www.quirks.com and look for "Our Articles" on the menu bar. You have several search options available, including searching by topic or by industry. Quirk's allows you to search for free but if you want the most current articles, you have to subscribe to *Quirk's Marketing Research Review*.

TABLE 6.1 Understanding the Function of Different Types of Publications Can Make You a Better User of Secondary Data

Understanding the functions of the different types of publications can help you find the secondary data you need.

1. **Reference Guides**

   Function: Refer to *types* of other reference sources and recommended specific titles. Guides tell you where to look to find different types of information.
   Example: *Encyclopedia of Business Information Sources*. Detroit: Gale Group, 1970–Present.

2. **Indexes and Abstracts**

   Function: List periodical articles by subject, author, title, keyword, etc. Abstracts also provide summaries of the articles. Indexes allow you to search for periodicals by topic.
   Example: *ABI/Inform*. Ann Arbor, MI: Proquest. 1971–present.

3. **Bibliographies**

   Function: Lists various sources such as books, journals, etc. on a particular topic. Tells you what is available, in several sources, on a topic.
   Example: *Recreation and Entertainment Industries, an Information Source Book*. Jefferson, NC: Macfarland, 2000.

4. **Almanacs, Manuals, and Handbooks**

   Function: These types of sources are "deskbooks" that provide a wide variety of data in a single handy publication.
   Example: *Wall Street Journal Almanac*. New York: Ballantine Books. Annual.

5. **Dictionaries**

   Function: Define terms and are sometimes specialized by subject area.
   Example: *Concise Dictionary of Business Management*, 2nd ed. Abington, Oxon: Taylor & Francis Ltd., 2007.

6. **Encyclopedias**

   Function: Provide essays, usually in alphabetical order, by topic.
   Example: *Encyclopedia of Busine$$ and Finance*. New York: Macmillan, 2001.

7. **Directories**

   Function: List companies, people, products, organizations, etc., usually providing brief information about each entry.
   Example: *Career Guide: Dun's Employment Opportunities Directory*. Parsippany, NJ: Dun's Marketing Services. Annual.

8. **Statistical Sources**

   Function: Provide numeric data, often in tables, pie charts, and bar charts.
   Example: *Handbook of U.S. Labor Statistics*. Lanham, MD: Bernan Press. Annual.

9. **Biographical Sources**

   Function: Provide information about people. Useful for information on CEOs, etc.
   Example: *D&B Reference Book of Corporate Management*. Bethlehem, PA: Dun & Bradstreet, Annual.

10. **Legal Sources**

    Function: Provide information about legislation, regulations, and case law.
    Example: *United States Code*. Washington, DC: Government Printing Office.

Today, many libraries list their holdings of books and other publications in electronic records with fields that are searchable electronically, which allows researchers to search secondary data quickly, conveniently, inexpensively, and thoroughly. The information in most electronic libraries is available in catalogs and indexes. A **catalog** consists of a list of a library's holdings of books. (Catalogs sometimes also list the periodicals to which the library subscribes.) Therefore, catalogs are useful for finding *books* by subject, author, title, date of publication, or publisher. **Indexes** are records compiled from periodicals and contain information on the contents of periodicals recorded in fields such as author, title, keywords, date of publication, name of periodical, and so on. Sometimes an index contains the entire contents of the periodical (called *full-text* indexes). Such indexes are not normally constructed by a library. Rather, they are provided by companies that make them available to libraries or other organizations. We shall talk more about these when we discuss online information databases.

SYNDICATED SERVICES DATA. **Syndicated services data** are provided by firms that collect data in a standard format and make them available to subscribing firms. Such data are typically highly specialized and are not available in libraries for the general public. The suppliers syndicate (sell) the information to multiple subscribers, thus making the costs more reasonable for any one subscriber. Examples include Arbitron's radio listenership data, Nielsen Media Research's Television Rating Index, and IRI's InfoScan report of products sold in retail stores. In all these cases, these firms supply external secondary data to subscribing firms. We devote more attention to syndicated data services firms in Chapter 7.

EXTERNAL DATABASES. **External databases** are databases supplied by organizations outside the firm and may be used as sources of secondary data. Some of these databases are available in printed format but, in recent years, many are now available online. These **online information databases** are searchable by search engines. Some are available free of charge and are supplied as a service by a host organization. However, many online databases are compiled by commercial sources that provide subscribers password (or IP address identification) access for a fee. The number of these databases has grown dramatically since the 1980s. And although there are fewer commercial database companies since the mergers of the 1990s and early 2000s, each company is much larger, and the larger firms can offer subscribers access to billions of records of information. Often, vendors that produce the software that retrieves the information package different databases together, making it possible for a wide variety of indexes, directories, and statistical and full-text files to be searched by the same search logic. Such services, sometimes called "aggregators" or "databanks," include Factiva, Gale Group, ProQuest, First Search, LexisNexis, and Dialog, among others. Business databases comprise a significant proportion of these databanks.

ADVANTAGES OF SECONDARY DATA

Secondary Data Are Obtained Quickly

There are five main advantages of using secondary data. First, it can be obtained quickly, in contrast to collecting primary data, which may take several months from beginning to end. You can go to the Internet and quickly find a great deal of secondary data at no expense.

Secondary Data Are Inexpensive Relative to Primary Data

Second, collecting secondary data is inexpensive when compared with collecting primary data. Although there are certainly costs for collecting secondary data, they are but a fraction of the costs for collecting primary data. Primary data collection is seldom achieved without spending at least a few thousand dollars or, depending on the research objective, hundreds of thousands or even millions of dollars. Even purchasing secondary data from commercial vendors is inexpensive relative to collecting primary data.

Margin notes:

A catalog consists of a list of a library's holdings of books.

Indexes are records compiled from periodicals and contain information on the contents of periodicals recorded in fields such as author, title, keywords, date of publication, name of periodical, and so on.

Syndicated services data are provided by firms that collect data in a standard format and make them available to subscribing firms. Such data are typically highly specialized and are not available in libraries for the general public.

External databases are databases supplied by organizations outside the firm and may be used as sources of secondary data.

Online information databases are sources of secondary data searchable by search engines online. Examples include Factiva, LexisNexis, ProQuest, and Gale Group.

The five advantages of secondary data are that they can be obtained quickly and inexpensively, is usually available, enhances primary data collection, and can sometimes achieve the research objective.

Secondary Data Are Usually Available

A third advantage of secondary data is that they are usually available. No matter what the problem area may be, someone, somewhere has probably dealt with it, and some information is available that will help researchers in their task. Availability is one reason that many predict secondary data will grow in importance in marketing research applications. Not only is the amount of data growing but the ability to search billions of records to find the right data is improving with computer technology.

Secondary Data Enhance Primary Data

As our chapter-opening vignette describes, secondary data enhance existing primary data. Simply because researchers use secondary data does not mean that they will not collect primary data. In fact, in almost every case, the researcher's task of primary data collection is aided by first collecting secondary data. A secondary data search can familiarize the researcher with the industry, including its sales and profit trends, major competitors, and the significant issues facing the industry.[11] A secondary data search can identify concepts, data, and terminology that may be useful in conducting primary research. A bank's management, for example, hired a marketing research firm; together, management and the research team decided to conduct a survey measuring the bank's image among its customers. A check of the secondary information available on the measurement of bank image identified the components of bank image for the study. Also, the research team, after reviewing secondary information, determined there were three sets of bank customers: retail customers, commercial accounts, and other, correspondent banks. When the researchers mentioned this to bank management, the original objectives of the primary research were changed in order to measure the bank's image among all three customer groups.

In almost every case, the researcher's task of primary data collection is aided by first collecting secondary data.

Secondary Data May Achieve the Research Objective

Finally, not only are secondary data faster to obtain, more convenient to use, and less expensive to gather than primary research but they also may achieve the research objective! For example, if a supermarket chain marketing manager wants to allocate TV ad dollars to the 12 TV markets in which the chain owns supermarkets, a quick review of secondary data will show that data on retail food sales by TV market area are already available. Allocating the TV budget based on the percentage of food sales in a given market would be an excellent way to solve the manager's problem and satisfy the research objective.

Not only are secondary data faster to obtain, more convenient to use, and less expensive to gather than primary research, but they also may achieve the research objective! There may be no need to collect primary data.

DISADVANTAGES OF SECONDARY DATA

Although the advantages of secondary data almost always justify a search of this information, there are caveats. Five of the problems associated with secondary data include incompatible reporting units, mismatch of the units of measurement, differing definitions used to classify the data, the timeliness of the secondary data, and a lack of information needed to assess the credibility of the data reported. These problems exist because secondary data have not been collected specifically to address the problem at hand, but have been collected for some other purpose. Consequently, the researcher must determine the extent of these problems before using the secondary data, which is done by evaluating the data. We discuss the first four disadvantages in the following paragraphs. Evaluation of secondary data is discussed in the next section.

Five of the problems associated with secondary data include incompatible reporting units, mismatch of the units of measurement, differing definitions used to classify the data, the timeliness of the secondary data, and a lack of information needed to assess the credibility of the data reported.

Incompatible Reporting Units

Secondary data are provided in reporting units, such as county, city, metro area, state, region, ZIP code, or CBSA's. Core-based Statistical Areas (CBSAs) are explained in Marketing Research Insight 6.3. A researcher's use of secondary data often depends on

MARKETING RESEARCH INSIGHT   Practical Application

6.3 Geographical Reporting Units Used by the U.S. Census Bureau

What are Core-based Statistical Areas?

Core-based Statistical Areas, or CBSAs, are geographic reporting units used by the Census Bureau. CBSAs are made up of two smaller units, metropolitan and micropolitan statistical areas (SAs), which are defined in terms of whole counties or county equivalents, including the six New England states. As of June 6, 2003, there are in the United States 362 metropolitan statistical areas and 560 micropolitan statistical areas. **Metropolitan SAs** are defined by the Office of Management and Budget (OMB) as having at least one urbanized area of 50,000 or more population, plus adjacent territory that has a high degree of social and economic integration with the core as measured by commuting ties. **Micropolitan SAs** are a new set of statistical areas that have at least one urban cluster of at least 10,000 but less than 50,000 population, plus adjacent territory that has a high degree of social and economic integration with the core MSA as measured by commuting ties.

Why Do We Have Metropolitan and Micropolitan SAs?

The metropolitan area (MA) program has provided standard statistical area definitions at the metropolitan level for 50 years. In the 1940s, it became clear that the value of data produced at that level by federal government agencies would be greatly enhanced if agencies used a single set of geographic definitions for the nation's metropolitan areas. The OMB's predecessor, the Bureau of the Budget, led the effort to develop what were then called "standard metropolitan areas," also known as MSAs, in time for their use in 1950 census reports. The general concept behind an MA is that it is an area containing a large population nucleus and adjacent communities that have a high degree of integration with that nucleus. This general concept has remained essentially the same since MAs were first defined before the 1950 census. OMB establishes and maintains MAs solely for statistical purposes.[12]

Why Do MAs change?

The MA standards are reviewed and, if warranted, revised in the years preceding each decennial census. Periodic review of the MA standards is necessary to ensure their continued usefulness and relevance. The current review of the MA standards—the Metropolitan Area Standards Review Project (MASRP)—is the sixth such review; it has been especially thorough, reflecting as a first priority users' concerns with the conceptual and operational complexity of the standards that have evolved over the decades. Other key concerns behind the particularly thorough nature of MASRP's efforts have been (1) whether modifications to the standards over the years have permitted them to stay abreast of changes in population distribution and activity patterns; (2) whether advances in computer applications permit consideration of new approaches to defining areas; and (3) whether there is a practicable way to capture a more complete range of U.S. settlement and activity patterns than the current MA standards capture.

These problems exist because secondary data have not been collected specifically to address the problem at hand, but have been collected for some other purpose.

Secondary data are provided in reporting units, such as county, city, metro area, state, region, ZIP code, or CBSAs.

whether the reporting unit matches the researcher's need. For example, a researcher wishing to evaluate market areas for the purpose of considering an expansion may be pleased with data reported at the county level. A great deal of secondary data are available at the county level. But what if another marketer wishes to evaluate a 2-mile area around a street address proposed as a site location for a retail store? County data would hardly be adequate. Another marketer wishes to know the demographic makeup of each ZIP code in a major city in order to determine which ZIP codes to target for a direct-mail campaign. Again, county data would be inappropriate. Inappropriate reporting units are often a problem in using secondary data, but more and more data are available today in multiple reporting units; for example, data at the ZIP + 4 level are becoming more widely available. Also, as we will see in the next chapter, GIS offers marketers access to data in arbitrarily defined reporting units. The latter would be very useful to the marketer wishing to know the demographics within a 2-mile ring around a street address. Nevertheless, sometimes secondary data are available, but in the wrong reporting unit.

Measurement Units Do Not Match

Sometimes secondary data are reported in measurement units that do not match the measurement unit needed by the researcher. In analyzing markets, for example, marketing researchers are typically interested in income levels. Available studies of income may measure income in several ways: total income, income after taxes, household income, and per capita income. Or consider a research project that needs to categorize businesses by size in terms of square footage. Secondary data sources, however, classify businesses in terms of size according to sales volume, number of employees, profit level, and so on. Much information in the United States is recorded in American units of measurement (feet, pounds, etc.), yet most of the rest of the world uses metric units (meter, kilograms, etc.). The United States is slowly becoming metric.[13]

> Sometimes measurement units reported in secondary data sources do not match the researcher's needs. Household income may be reported when the researcher needs per capita income.

Class Definitions Are Not Usable

The class definitions of the reported data may not be usable by a researcher. Secondary data are often reported by dividing a variable among different classes and reporting the frequency of occurrence in each class. For example, suppose a source of secondary data reports the variable household income in three classes. The first class is the percentage of households having between $20,000 and $34,999, and the third class is the percentage of households having an income of $50,000 and over. For most studies, these classifications are applicable. However, imagine you are a manufacturer of high-end plumbing fixtures and you are looking to expand the number of distributorships. You have learned that your dealers are most successful in geographical areas with average household incomes above $80,000. You need another source of information since your source of secondary data only reports household incomes of $50,000 and over. What would a researcher do in this situation? Typically, if you keep looking you can find what you need, for example, other sources of secondary data with other categories.

> There is a problem when the researcher needs to know the percentage of households having income over $80,000 and the highest category in the secondary data source is $50,000 and over.

Data Are Outdated

Sometimes a marketing researcher will find information reported with the desired unit of measurement and the proper classifications; the *data*, however, *are "out-of-date."* Some secondary data are published only once. But even with secondary data published at regular intervals, the time that has passed since the last publication can be a problem when applying the data to a current problem. Ultimately, the researcher must make the decision as to whether to use the data.

EVALUATING SECONDARY DATA

We hope you have learned that not everything you read is true. In order to properly use secondary data, you must evaluate that information before you use it as a basis for making decisions. A reader must be most cautious when using an Internet source because few quality standards are applied to most Internet sites. To determine the reliability of secondary information, marketing researchers must evaluate it. This is done by answering the following five questions:

- What was the purpose of the study?
- Who collected the information?
- What information was collected?
- How was the information obtained?
- How consistent is the information with other information?[14]

A discussion of each question follows.

What Was the Purpose of the Study?

Studies are conducted for a purpose. Unfortunately, studies are sometimes conducted in order to "prove" some position or to advance the special interest of those conducting the study. Many years ago, chambers of commerce were known for publishing data that exaggerated the size and growth rates of their communities. They did this to "prove" that their communities were a good choice for new business locations. However, after a few years, they learned that few people trusted chamber data, and today chambers of commerce publish reliable and valid data. But the lesson is that you must be very careful to determine whether the entity publishing the data acted in a fair and unbiased manner.

Consider the example of disposable diapers. The disposable diaper industry was created in the 1960s. As information became available over time that it would take 50 years for the huge mountains of disposable diapers to decompose, environmental concerns became alarming. Consequently, during the late 1980s, the number of customers buying old-fashioned cloth diapers doubled. Also, more than a dozen state legislatures were considering various bans, taxes, and even warning labels on disposable diapers. Then "research studies" were produced on the environmental effects of disposable versus cloth diapers. It seemed that the "new" research proved that cloth diapers, by adding detergent by-products to the water table, were more harmful to the environment than the ever-lasting plastic disposables! Soon after several of these studies were made available to legislators, the movement against disposables was dead.

Who conducted the studies? Procter & Gamble. P&G, owning the lion's share of the market for disposable diapers, commissioned the consulting firm of Arthur D. Little, Inc. to conduct a study of disposable versus cloth diapers. The study found that disposable diapers were no more harmful to the environment than reusable cotton diapers. Another favorable study for the disposables was conducted by Franklin Associates, whose research showed disposables were not any more harmful than cloth diapers. But who sponsored this study? The American Paper Institute, an organization with major interests in disposable diapers. But wait, before you become too critical of the disposable diaper folks, let's consider some other ''scientific'' studies. In 1988, a study was published that labeled disposable diapers as "garbage" and contributing to massive buildups of waste that was all but impervious to deterioration. Who sponsored this study? The cloth diaper industry! Another study published in 1991 found cloth diapers to be environmentally superior to disposable diapers. Guess who sponsored this study?

Recently a "study" was reported in the news media citing the terrible condition of roads and bridges in the United States. Who sponsored the study? An organization representing road and bridge construction companies. It may well be that the study was objective and accurate. However, users of secondary information should be well aware of the true purpose of a study and evaluate the information accordingly. See Marketing Research Insight 6.4.

Who Collected the Information?

Research studies are often published and become a part of secondary data. However, not all research studies are conducted in a totally objective manner. You must ask who conducted the study.

Even when you are convinced that there is no bias in the purpose of the study, you should question the competence of the organization that collected the information. Why? Simply because organizations differ in terms of the resources they command and their quality control. But how do you determine the competency of the organization that collected the data? First, ask others who have more experience in a given industry. Typically, creditable organizations are well known in those industries for which they conduct studies. Second, examine the report itself. Competent firms will almost always provide carefully written and detailed explanations of the procedures and methods used in collecting the information contained in the report. Third, contact previous clients of the firm. Have they been satisfied with the quality of the work performed by the organization?

MARKETING RESEARCH INSIGHT

Ethical Issues

6.4 The Majority of Americans Want to Keep the Penny in Circulation . . . Really!

Many times, research studies report secondary data and sometimes what they report "ain't necessarily so," according to Murray, Schwartz, and Lichter's book (*It Ain't Necessarily So: How Media Make and Unmake the Scientific Picture of Reality*).[15] These authors illustrate their point by citing a study undertaken by an "activist" group called the Food Research and Action Center, whose reported aim is to highlight the problem of hunger and to increase government spending to fight hunger. Its study reported that one out of eight children had gone hungry at some point in the previous year. But the researchers did not measure "hunger" in any direct manner. Instead, they used a "proxy" measure of hunger: what people *said* about hunger. (The Census Bureau uses income as a proxy measure of hunger.) Was their measure accurate? Even if it were an accurate measure of actual hunger, the CBS Network incorrectly reported the results of the study by stating that the study found one in eight American children under the age of 12 was going hungry (tonight), which is a totally different statement from the number of children who reported being hungry in the past year.[16] For another example, some studies have reported that coffee is associated with disease, whereas others report that coffee prevents disease.[17]

Cynthia Crossen, a reporter and editor with the *Wall Street Journal*, wrote about the truthfulness of research information. She published her interesting conclusions in a book with the title *Tainted Truth: The Manipulation of Fact in America*.[18] She warned that even though Americans are fascinated by research information, we must understand that much of the "research" we use to help us buy, elect, advise, acquit, and heal has been created not to expand our knowledge, but to sell a product or advance a cause of the research sponsor. Furthermore, if the research results contradict a sponsor's agenda, they are routinely suppressed. Crossen gives some compelling evidence for her thesis, including a study that found that 62% of Americans want to keep the penny in circulation. The sponsor? The zinc industry (most pennies are made with zinc). Another study found that 70% of cellular telephone users reported that the phones made them more successful in business. The sponsor? Motorola. Even studies to test the effectiveness of new drugs are often sponsored by the pharmaceutical company selling the drug! Crossen believed that the explosion of "tainted truth" has come about because of the money involved. Money is used to "sponsor" (buy) research studies and even once independent and objective institutions such as universities have given in to the monetary pressures. Few researchers escape the pressures of gaining financial support and are influenced, whether knowingly or not, by trying to please their financial sponsors. Results can be manipulated by subtle means known to researchers.

Crossen has raised an important ethical issue for the research industry. Are research results totally independent and objective? Crossen's book is one among several that discuss research that is not objectively prepared nor presented.[19]

What Information Was Collected?

There are many studies available on topics such as economic impact, market potential, feasibility, and the like. But what exactly was measured in these studies that constitutes impact, potential, or feasibility? Many studies claim to provide information on a specific subject but, in fact, measure something quite different. Consider a study conducted by a transit authority on the number of riders on its bus line. Upon examination of the methods used in the study, the number of riders was not counted at all. Rather, the number of tokens was counted. Since a single rider may use several tokens on a single destination route requiring transfers to other buses, the study overestimated the number of "riders." Or consider a study of "advertising effectiveness." How was effectiveness measured? Was it the sales of the product the week after the ad was run? Was it the percentage of consumers who named the brand name the day after the ad was run? Is this distinction important? It may be or it may not be, depending on how the study's user intends to use the information. The important point here is that the user should discover exactly what information was collected!

It may be very important to know exactly what was measured in a report before using the results.

How Was the Information Obtained?

Evaluate the method used to collect the primary data now available to you as secondary data. You will be much better at doing this when you finish this course.

You should be aware of the methods used to obtain information reported in secondary sources. What was the sample? How large was the sample? What was the response rate? Was the information validated? As you will learn throughout this book, there are many alternative ways of collecting primary data, and each may have an impact on the information collected. Remember that even though you are evaluating secondary data, this information was gathered as primary data by some organization. Therefore, the alternative ways of gathering the data had an impact on the nature and quality of the data. It is not always easy to find out how the secondary data were gathered. However, as noted earlier, most reputable organizations that provide secondary data also provide information on their data-collection methods. If this information is not readily available and your use of the secondary data is very important to your research project, you should make the extra effort to find out how the information was obtained.

How Consistent Is the Information with Other Information?

If two or more sources of secondary data differ, you should investigate why they differ. Did they measure the same entity? Did they use different methods to collect their data?

In some cases, the same secondary data are reported by multiple, independent organizations, which provides an excellent way to evaluate secondary data sources. Ideally, if two or more independent organizations report the same data, you can have greater confidence in the validity and reliability of the data. Demographic data, for example, for metropolitan areas (MAs), counties, and most municipalities are widely available from more than one source. If you are evaluating a survey that is supposedly representative of a given geographic area, you may want to compare the characteristics of the sample of the survey with the demographic data available on the population. If you know, based on U.S. census data, that a city's population is made up of 45% males and 55% females, and a survey, which is supposed to be representative of that city, reports a sample of 46% males and 54% females, then you can be more confident about the survey data. It is indeed rare, however, for two organizations to report exactly the same results. In this case, you must look at the magnitude of the differences and determine what you should do. If all independent sources report very large differences on the same variable, then you may not have much confidence in any of the data.

You should also look carefully at what information was collected, how it was collected, and so on for each reporting source. For example, if you were to get the number of businesses in a county from Survey Sampling, Inc. and compared that number to the number of businesses reported by the governmental publication *County Business Patterns* (CBP), you would see a marked difference. Specifically, Survey Sampling's number of businesses would be much larger than the number reported by CBP. Why?[20] The answer is found by asking the questions "What information was actually collected?" and "How was this information obtained?" As it turns out, neither organization actually counts the numbers of businesses in a given area. CBP counts the number of firms submitting payroll information on their employees. Some firms may not report this information, and other small firms with "no paid employees" (whose owners are the employees) are excluded from CBP data. Therefore, the CBP surrogate indicator used to count the number of business firms is going to have a downward bias because it does not count all firms. On the other hand, Survey Sampling counts the number of business firms by adding up the number of businesses listed in the Yellow Pages. This brings up the question "What is a business firm?" One franchise organization may run the McDonald's in a city, yet the Yellow Pages lists nine locations. Is this one business or nine? Survey Sampling would list this as nine separate businesses. Therefore, Survey Sampling's estimate of the number of businesses has an upward bias. Which data source should be used? It would depend on the purpose of your study and how the information is to be used. Either source of information may be appropriate as long as you understand exactly what the information represents. The key point is that you must adequately evaluate the various data sources so that you are in a position to select the information that will give you the most valid and reliable results.

A final word about evaluating information sources is that you may be able to get some help from evaluations by others. For example, many books are the subject of published reviews. Also, many journal articles are reviewed by editorial board members to assess their quality before publication. Also, journals typically do not accept advertising and, consequently, may be more objective in accepting information for publication that may not be favorable to other interests. However, it is far more difficult to evaluate other sources of secondary data, such as magazine articles, websites, or special reports.

LOCATING SECONDARY DATA SOURCES

How does one go about the actual task of locating secondary data sources? We suggest you follow the approach outlined below.[21]

Step 1 Identify what you wish to know and what you already know about your topic. This is the most important step when searching for information. Without having a clear understanding of what you are seeking, you will undoubtedly have difficulties. Clearly define your topic: relevant facts, names of researchers or organizations associated with the topic, key papers and other publications with which you are already familiar, and any other information you may have.

Step 2 Develop a list of key terms and names. These terms and names will provide access to secondary sources. Unless you already have a very specific topic of interest, keep this initial list long and quite general. Use business dictionaries and handbooks to help develop your list. Be flexible. Every time a new source is consulted, you may have to develop a new list of terms.

In printed sources as well as databases, it is important to use correct terminology to locate the most relevant resources. In many cases, the researcher must think of related terms or synonyms for a topic. For example, one database may use the term *pharmaceutical industry*, whereas another may use the term *drug industry*. In addition, the source may require a broader term. *Pharmaceutical industry* may be listed as part of the *chemical industry*. However, a narrower term might be required. For example, if one is researching a database on the *drug industry*, it would be foolish to search on the term *drugs* because almost everything in that database would include that term. Perhaps using a specific drug may be a wiser choice.

Many databases list the terms or subject headings they assign to records of information in such sources as books or articles. These lists are called thesauri, dictionaries, or subject headings lists. In most library catalogs, the Library of Congress (LC) subject headings are used, which are standard (sometimes called *controlled*) terms for describing a particular subject. For example, the term *real property* is standard in the LC subject headings instead of the term *real estate*. Using a standard subject heading should result in a more efficient search. Marketing Research Insight 6.5 shows you how to find a standard subject heading using *ABI Inform Global*.

For searching a database, keyword searching is usually available, but using a keyword often retrieves too many false results. A keyword search means that the computer will retrieve a record that has that word anywhere in the record. For example, if someone is searching on the word *banks*, that could turn up the name of a person, a business, a type of bank, a bank of dirt (hill), or any other use of the word. Sometimes to avoid false results the searcher may simply want to search one field in the record, as described later in "Field Searching." Keywords may also be used to lead to better terms to search on. If you retrieve a long list of sources, it is wise to select an item that is relevant and examine its record to

MARKETING RESEARCH INSIGHT   Practical Application

6.5 Improve Your Searching Skills by Finding a Standard Subject Heading

Finding information on Alternative Fuel AND Automobile OR Car

How many times have you used an online information service database only to end up frustrated that you could not find what you really needed? Problems of two types occur. First, you get thousands of "hits," which requires that you read through huge amounts of information still searching for what you wanted to find in the first place. Second, you get information about articles that contain your key search terms, but the articles have nothing to do with what you really want. Sound familiar? You need to learn an important skill in searching online information databases: finding the *standard subject heading*.

Imagine that you had available several persons who were well trained in evaluating and interpreting the contents of information sources such as books, manuals, special reports, magazine articles, journal articles, and so on. Next, imagine if you told these well-trained persons to look through everything that has been published and to place all the books, articles, reports, and so on that pertained to your topic in one stack. So, you now have all the publications on your topic in one category. Now imagine that this information is all scanned into an electronic database that can be searched using any one or a combination of search strategies. Wow! Think this would improve your information search skills? The good news is that this has already been done for you. You just need to learn how to take advantage of what we shall call *standard subject headings*.

Databases have a field called the *subject* field. When a new piece of information arrives, be it a book, journal article,

or whatever, that information is evaluated to determine its subject matter. For example, let's say there is an article entitled "The Pod Squad." The title can be very misleading. In fact, if someone were doing a search about police *squads* or *iPods*, this article would appear in a results list (along with thousands of other irrelevant information sources). But why is it misleading? Because the *subject* of the article is a recent upscale restaurant design phenomenon!

Keywords are often not in the title or even the abstract of an article. If you were searching for information about restaurants, chances are you would not find the pod article using key terms in the title field of your database search engine. But because those "people who are working for you" have looked over this article and correctly placed it in the category of restaurants, we are going to find it. So, **standard subject headings** are specific words or phrases that are used to properly categorize the subject matter of records as they are entered into databases. Let's see how you would do it using ABI/INFORM Global, a popular online database owned by ProQuest.

In ABI/INFORM Global, you can use the "Basic Search" if you don't really know much about your topic. However basic searches are not very productive if you know enough about your topic to conduct a more efficient search. In fact, if you enter "automobiles" in a basic search you will get over 95,000 hits! So how do you find a "standard subject heading" in ABI/INFORM Global? First, go to "Advanced Search." Then click on the drop-down menu on the right of the first row where it presently reads "Citation and abstract." (This refers to the citation and abstract *fields* of the records in the database.) From the drop menu, select the "Subject" field. You will then see a new choice on the right—"Look up subjects." Clicking "Look up subjects" opens a dialog box that allows you to enter the words that you suspect may identify the predetermined subject category—what we call a "standard subject heading." Experiment by entering "fuel efficient autos" or "high mpg cars." You will find that these are NOT standard subject headings. You know this because when you click "Find term," your search words are not listed. But if you enter "alternative energy," you find this is a standard subject

ProQuest

| Basic | Advanced | Topics | Publications | My Research |

Databases selected: ABI/INFORM Global

Advanced Search

Tools: Search Tips   Browse Topics

Alternative energy	Subject ▼	Look up subjects
AND ▼	automobile	Citation and abstract ▼
OR ▼	car	Citation and abstract ▼

Add a row | Remove a row   **Search**   **Clear**

Database: Business - ABI/INFORM Global ▼   Select multiple databases

Date range: Last 12 months ▼

heading! Now click "Add to search" and then close the "Look up Subjects" dialog box. Notice you are now back to the advanced search screen.

If you conduct this search, you will find that you have discovered ALL records in the database that have a subject classified as "alternative fuel" even though they may not have anything to do with automobiles. To drill down and get a more focused search, let's go back to "Advanced Search" and add to "alternative energy" in the Subject field "automobile" OR "car" in the two fields each covering "Citation and Abstract." Now our search will reveal a subset of articles in the "alternative energy" subject field that have either "automobile" OR "car" either in the citation of the articles or in the

article abstracts. Finally, let's limit the search to include only articles written in the last 12 months (see "Date Range").

We are now ready to begin our search. Instead of over 95,000 hits we now have a very manageable list of 59 articles. Note the titles of some of the articles in the search; they appear to be "right on target." One is "The Car of the Perpetual Future" and another is a study of alternative fuels in vehicles. Another method of refining your search is to scroll down once you find an article that meets your search requirements and examine the Subject field from which it was drawn. You may find another standard subject heading that is even more on target than the one you've already discovered. Happy searching!

☐ 1. **Electric Car Sets Sights On Network in Australia**
   John Murphy. **Wall Street Journal (Eastern edition).** New York, N.Y.: Oct 29, 2008.
   Abstract | Full text

☐ 2. **The Election Choice: Energy**
   Joseph Rago. **Wall Street Journal (Eastern edition).** New York, N.Y.: Oct 28, 2008. p. A.17
   Abstract | Full text

☐ 3. **Thais Lead Drive to Natural-Gas Cars; Subsidies, Volatility of Oil Prices Spur Move Even as a Campaign Starts in U.S. to Get Americans to Switch**
   Patrick Barta. **Wall Street Journal (Eastern edition).** New York, N.Y.: Oct 21, 2008. p. B.1
   Abstract | Full text

☐ 4. **ALTERNATIVE BATTERIES**
   Vahan Janjigian. **Forbes.** New York: Oct 13, 2008. Vol. 182, Iss. 7; p. 134
   Abstract | Find a copy

☐ 5. **THE TOP 100**
   Richard Yerema. **Maclean's.** Toronto: Oct 13, 2008. Vol. 121, Iss. 40; p. 56 (4 pages)
   Abstract | Full text

☐ 6. **MARKET TRENDS: Fleet management**
   Nic Paton. **Employee Benefits.** London: Oct 9, 2008. p. 71
   Abstract | Full text

☐ 7. **Coping with a Persistent Oil Crisis**
   Jeffrey D Sachs. **Scientific American.** New York: Oct 2008. Vol. 299, Iss. 4; p. 38
   Abstract | Find a copy

☐ 8. **Eyes on the Road: What the U.S. Should Do To Cut Oil Consumption**
   Joseph B. White. **Wall Street Journal (Eastern edition).** New York, N.Y.: Sep 16, 2008. p. D.2
   Abstract | Full text

☐ 9. **The car of the perpetual future;**
   Anonymous. **The Economist.** London: Sep 6, 2008. Vol. 388, Iss. 8596
   Abstract | Full text

By permission, ProQuest

identify the standard subject heading assigned to that item. Submitting that subject heading should retrieve a much more relevant list of sources. (See Marketing Research Insight 6.5.)

Step 3 **Begin your search using several of the library sources, such as those listed in Table 6.2 on page 167.** If you need help in selecting the appropriate sources or databases, refer to Table 6.1 and review the functions of different types of publications.

Search Strategies Used for Searching Online Information Databases

To better understand how to search online databases, the researcher should understand how they are organized. A common vendor, also known as an aggregator or databank, may provide many databases. For example, the vendor ProQuest provides ABI/INFORM Global and the *Wall Street Journal*. An actual hierarchy exists in the organization of these databases. For example:

Top level—Databank (sometimes called "aggregator") = ProQuest

Second level—Databases = ABI/INFORM Global

Third level—Records = the units describing each item in the database

Fourth level—Fields = parts of the record, such as author, title, Standard Industrial Classification (SIC) number, and so on

Fifth level—Words or numbers = the text of the fields

Usually all databases from the same databank are searched similarly and several methods (basic, advanced, and command) of searching the databases may be available. A basic search is often sufficient when searching for books in a catalog or when searching small databases; however, it is often advisable to use the advanced mode when searching for journal articles or complex ideas so that search refinements can be used.

Most databanks use the same search features, but other databanks may use different symbols or interfaces to retrieve results. An interface is the "look and feel" of the database that actually helps the searcher know how to submit a search. Each database has a help screen, which is always useful. The following examples of search techniques are for a typical library catalog, but each databank, such as First Search, Factiva, and others, may use different searching symbols to accomplish the same results.

Boolean Logic

Boolean logic allows the establishment of relationships between words and terms in most databases. Typical words used as operators in Boolean logic are AND, OR, and NOT. The following examples illustrate:

Operator	Requirements	Examples	
AND	Both terms are retrieved	chemical AND Industry	Exxon AND financial
OR	Either term is retrieved	drug OR pharmaceutical	outlook OR forecast
NOT	Eliminates records containing the second term	Cherokee NOT jeeps	drugs NOT alcohol

Field Searching

Field searching refers to searching records in a database by one or more of its fields. Databases are collections of records, which consist of fields designated to describe certain parts of the record. Searching "by field" may make a search more efficient. For example, if a title is known, a search of the title field should find the desired record. Terms entered as "subjects" may be restricted to specific subject headings (e.g., Library of Congress subject headings in most library catalogs), depending on the database. Most databases also allow the use of keyword searching, which searches every word in a record.

Most electronic databases use the same search strategies for searching databases, but they often vary in the keystrokes designated to perform the search. For example, on the Internet, the keyword "real estate" should be submitted with quotes surrounding the phrase so that the exact sequence of words will be searched; however, to search on the same keyword phrase in some library catalogs, you would submit: "real ADJ estate." ADJ means *adjacent*.

Proximity Operators

The preceding "real estate" example demonstrates one of the proximity operators that are available to enhance keyword searching. **Proximity operators** allow the searcher to indicate how close and in which order two or more words are to be positioned within the record. Examples of proximity operators are:

Operator	Requirements	Examples
ADJ	Adjoining words in order	Electronic ADJ Commerce
NEAR	Adjoining words in any order	Bill NEAR Gates
SAME	Both terms are located in the field of the record	Microsoft SAME legal

Truncation

Another feature of database searching is **truncation**, which allows the root of the word to be submitted, retrieving all words beginning with that root. The term "forecast?" would retrieve "forecasting," "forecasts," "forecaster," and so on. The question mark is the truncation symbol in some databases; others may use an asterisk, a plus sign, a dollar sign, or other symbol. In some cases, truncation symbols may not be useful. For example, if you wanted "cat" in singular or plural, submitting "cat?" would retrieve "cat," "cats," "catch," "catastrophe," and so on. Using the search "cat OR cats" would be preferable.

Nesting

It is essential that the computer translate the search statement correctly. **Nesting** is a technique that indicates the order in which a search is to be done. For example, if you wish to search for microcomputers or personal computers in Florida, you would submit "Florida AND (microcomputer? OR personal ADJ computer?)," indicating that "Florida" should be combined with either term. The parentheses nest the two terms as one. Without the parentheses, "Florida" would be combined with "microcomputer," but every instance of the words "personal computer" would be added to the results. In search engines, there are text boxes that serve much like parentheses to aid in keeping similar terms together.

Limiting

Limiting allows for restricting searches to only those database records that meet specified criteria. For example, searches may be limited to a search of records containing a specific language, location, format, and/or date. These limitations are usually available on the database advanced search screen. When searching for current materials, the date limitation is most important in retrieving the correct results.

Step 4 **Compile the literature you have found and evaluate your findings.** Is the literature relevant to your needs? Perhaps you are overwhelmed by information. Perhaps you have found little that is relevant. Rework your list of keywords and authors. If you have had little success or your topic is highly specialized, consult specialized directories, encyclopedias, and so on, such as the ones listed in this chapter. The librarian may be able to recommend the most appropriate source for your needs.

Step 5 **If you are unhappy with what you have found or are otherwise having trouble and the reference librarian has not been able to identify sources, use an authority.** Identify some individual or organization that might know something about the topic. Publications such as *Who's Who in Finance and Industry, Consultants and Consulting Organizations Directory, Encyclopedia of Associations, Industrial Research Laboratories in the United States*, and *Research Centers Directory* may help you identify people or organizations that specialize in your topic. Do not forget university faculty, government officials, and business executives. Such individuals are often delighted to be of help.

There are several keys to a successful search. First, be well informed about the search process. Reading this chapter is a good place to start. Second, you must be devoted to the search. Do not expect information to fall into your lap; be committed to finding it. Finally, there is no substitute for a good, professional librarian. Do not be afraid to ask for advice.

Step 6 **Report results.** You may be successful in locating data, but if the information is not properly transmitted to the reader, the research is worthless. It is important to outline the paper or report, correctly compose it, and accurately reference the sources that were used. See Chapter 20 for instructions on how to properly write a research report.

KEY SOURCES OF SECONDARY DATA FOR MARKETERS

We hope you understand by now that there are thousands of sources of secondary data that may be relevant to business decisions. In Table 6.2, we list some of the major sources that are useful in marketing research. However, a few sources are so important that they deserve some extra attention. In the next few paragraphs, we give you additional information about the publications of the U.S. Census Bureau and other government publications, the North American Industrial Classification System (NAICS), which has replaced the Standard Industrial Classification (SIC) system, and an update on the "Survey of Buying Power."

The Census of the Population

The census is conducted only once every 10 years.

The U.S. decennial census, the **Census of the Population**, is considered the "granddaddy" of all market information. A new census will be taken in 2010. The census is conducted only once every 10 years and census data serve as a baseline for much marketing information that is provided in the "in-between" years. Firms providing secondary data commercially, such as ESRI, Claritas, and the "Survey of Buying Power," make adjustments each year to report current information. As we shall see in the next chapter, these commercial firms add value by providing information produced for specific uses, such as market segmentation or determining market potential. However, the Census Bureau has started an annual survey entitled The American Community Survey. You can read more about this in the next section. Besides market data, census data are used to make many governmental decisions about things such as highway construction, health care services, educational needs, and, of course, redistricting.

The Census Bureau has started an annual survey entitled The American Community Survey.

Historically, the census was composed of a short form, which every household received, and a long form, which was sent to one in six households. You can see both forms used in Census 2000 at www.census.gov/dmd/www/2000quest.html.

The taking of a census of the U.S. population began in 1790. Prior to 1940, everyone had to answer all the questions that the census used. In 1940, the long form—a form that goes out only to a sample of respondents—was introduced as a way to collect more data, more rapidly, and without increasing respondent burden. In Census 2000, the long form went to one in six housing units. As a result, much of the census data are based on statistical sampling. A great deal of effort went into promoting Census 2000 to the citizenry of the United States due to growing concerns over privacy and declining participation rates in the census since 1970.[22] You can view census data online at **www.census.gov**.

TABLE 6.2   Secondary Information Sources on Marketing

I. Reference Guides

Encyclopedia of Business Information Sources

Detroit: Gale Group, Annual. This lists marketing associations, advertising agencies, research centers, agencies, and sources relating to various business topics. It is particularly useful for identifying information about specific industries.

II. Indexes

ABI/INFORM Global

Ann Arbor, MI: ProQuest, 1971–. Available online, this database indexes and abstracts articles from major journals relating to a broad range of business topics. Electronic access to many full-text articles is also available. ABI/INFORM Global may be complemented by ABI/INFORM Archive, ABI/INFORM Dateline, and ABI/INFORM Trade & Industry and may be searched alone or in tandem with any or all of these databases at subscribing libraries.

Business File ASAP

Detroit: Gale Group, 1980–. Available online. This index covers primarily business and popular journals and includes some full-text articles.

Wilson Business Full Text

New York: H. W. Wilson, 1986. Available online. The print version is *Business Periodicals Index* (1958–). This basic index is useful for indexing the major business journals further back in time than other indexes.

III. Dictionaries and Encyclopedias

Dictionary of Marketing Terms

Hauppauge, NY: Barron's, 4th ed., 2008. Prepared by Jane Imber and Betsy Ann Toffler, this dictionary includes brief definitions of popular terms in marketing.

Encyclopedia of Consumer Brands

Detroit: St. James Press, 2005. For consumable products, personal products, and durable goods, this source provides detailed descriptions of the history and major developments of major brand names.

IV. Directories

Bradford's Directory of Marketing Research Agencies and Management Consultants in the United States and the World

Middleberg, VA: Bradford's, Biennial. Indexed by type of service, this source gives scope of activity for each agency and lists names of officers.

Broadcasting and Cable Yearbook

New Providence, NJ: R. R. Bowker, Annual. A directory of U.S. and Canadian television and radio stations, advertising agencies, and other useful information.

Directories in Print

Detroit: Gale Research, Annual. Provides detailed information on business and industrial directories, professional and scientific rosters, online directory of databases, and other lists. This source is particularly useful for identifying directories associated with specific industries or products.

Gale Directory of Publications and Broadcast Media

Detroit: Gale Research, Annual. A geographic listing of U.S. and Canadian newspapers, magazines, and trade publications, as well as broadcasting stations. Includes address, edition, frequency, circulation, and subscription and advertising rates.

V. Statistical Sources

Datapedia of the United States, 1790–2005

Lanham, MD: Bernan Press, 2001. Based on the *Historical Statistics of the United States from Colonial Times* and other statistical sources, this volume presents hundreds of tables reflecting historical and, in some cases, forecasting data on numerous demographic variables relating to the United States.

(Continued)

TABLE 6.2 *(Continued)*

Survey of Buying Power
Now available only through the website: www.surveyofbuyingpower.com/. Formerly published in print in the annual copy of *Sales & Marketing Management* magazine. Includes statistics on population, income, retail sales, effective buying income, etc., for CBSAs and media markets.

Editor and Publisher Market Guide
New York: Editor and Publisher, Annual. Provides market data for more than 1,500 U.S. and Canadian newspaper cities covering facts and figures about location, transaction, population, households, banks, autos, etc.

Market Share Reporter
Detroit: Gale Research, Annual. Provides market share data on products and service industries in the United States.

Standard Rate and Data Service
Des Plaines, IL: SRDS, Monthly. In the SRDS monthly publications (those for consumer magazine and agrimedia, newspapers, spot radio, spot television), marketing statistics are included at the beginning of each state section.

Census 2010 will be different in that only the short form will be used to collect data.

United States Census 2010

You can read about Census 2010 at www.census.gov/2010census/.

The American Community Survey provides current data about communities every year, rather than once every 10 years. Visit The American Community Survey at www.census.gov/acs/www/.

The American Community Survey will likely change the demographic landscape for marketing researchers. With reliable annual information and estimates for future years, many researchers are likely to focus on using data from this source of secondary information.

Census 2010

Census 2010 will be different in that only the short form will be used to collect data. The Census Bureau is more interested in an accurate count, which it believes is more attainable with the short form that takes only a few minutes to complete. The short form asks only for name, sex, age, date of birth, race, ethnicity, relationship, and housing tenure. Data from the long form are still needed but will be collected through the American Community Survey.

The American Community Survey

The American Community Survey provides current data about communities every year, rather than once every 10 years. It is sent to a small percentage of the population on a rotating basis throughout the decade, and no household will receive the survey more often than once every 5 years. The sample size is three million persons in the United States and Puerto Rico. The purpose of the American Community Survey is to provide more of a continuous look at U.S. demography. Instead of relying on a "snapshot" every 10 years, data from the American Community Survey will be available annually.

Data collection for The American Community Survey began in 2005 and has been building each year. Much information is available now, and in 2010 enough data will be available to provide 5-year estimates for all reporting units down to census tract and block group levels. Data will be available to report 1-year, 2-year, and 5-year estimates. The American Community Survey will likely change the demographic landscape for marketing researchers. With reliable annual information and estimates for future years, many researchers are likely to focus on using data from this source of secondary information.

Other Government Publications

The U.S. government publishes a huge volume of secondary data. Most of these publications are printed by the U.S. Government Printing Office (GPO). You can visit its website at www.gpoaccess.gov/index.html. Secondary data used by business and industry may be found at http://www.census.gov/econ/www/index.html. The **Statistical Abstract of the United States** is a convenient source of secondary statistical data, and it is now available online at www.census.gov/prod/www/statistical-abstract-us.html.

North American Industry Classification System (NAICS)

The **North American Industry Classification System (NAICS)**, pronounced "nakes," and is not actually a source in and of itself. By this, we mean that NAICS is not information per se; rather, it is a coding system that can be used to access information. All marketing research students should be familiar with it because it will be used by so many secondary data sources. NAICS is replacing the **Standard Industrial Classification (SIC)** system. (We discuss both here because data based on the SIC will be around for several years.) The SIC was created in the mid-1930s, when the government required all agencies gathering economic and industrial data to use the same system for classifying businesses. The SIC classified establishments by the type of activity in which they were engaged. Codes describing a type of business activity were used to collect, tabulate, summarize, and publish data. Each industry was assigned a code number, and all firms within that particular industry reported all activities (sales, employment, etc.) by this assigned code. The SIC divides all establishments into 11 divisions. Divisions are then subdivided into a second level of classification, "major groups." Major groups are numbered consecutively 01 through 99. Division A, for example, contains major groups 01 through 09. A major group within division A is agricultural production—crops, major group 01. Division B contains major groups 10 through 14; 10 is metal mining, 11 is coal mining, and so on. Each major group is further divided into two other categories, which provide greater specificity of classification.[23]

> NAICS is a system of coding business firms and can be used by researchers to access information stored in databases according to the NAICS codes. Visit the Census Bureau's NAICS website at www.census.gov/eos/www/naics/.

The SIC is being replaced by NAICS as a result of the North American Free Trade Agreement (NAFTA). The system will allow reports conducted by the Mexican, Canadian, and U.S. governments to share a common language for easier comparisons of international trade, industrial production, labor costs, and other statistics. NAICS will be an improvement over the SIC system and yet will allow for comparative analyses with past SIC-based data. In fact, Dun & Bradstreet is marketing software that provides a crossover from SIC codes to NAICS codes.[24] NAICS will classify businesses based on similar production processes with special attention being given to classifying emerging industries such as services and high technology, and more classifications will be assigned to certain industry groups such as eating and drinking places. Under the SIC, all restaurants—beaneries, caterers, hamburger stands, and five-star restaurants—fall under the same category: Eating and Drinking Places. NAICS will break this down into several categories, which will be more useful to researchers.[25]

> The SIC is being replaced by NAICS as a result of the North American Free Trade Agreement (NAFTA).

NAICS groups the economy into 20 broad sectors, as opposed to the 11 SIC divisions. Many of these new sectors reflect recognizable parts of the SIC, such as the Utilities and Transportation section broken out from the SIC Transportation, Communications, and Utilities division. Because the service sector of the economy has grown so much in recent years, the SIC division for Services Industries has been broken into several new sectors, including Professional, Scientific, and Technical Services; Management, Support, Waste Management, and Remediation Services; Education Services; Health and Social Assistance; Arts, Entertainment, and Recreation; and Other Services except Public Administration. Other new NAICS sectors are composed of combinations of pieces from more than one SIC division. For example, the new Information sector is made up of components from Transportation, Communications and Utilities (broadcasting and telecommunications); Manufacturing (publishing); and Services Industries (software publishing, data processing, information services, and motion pictures and sound recording).

> NAICS groups the economy into 20 broad sectors, as opposed to the 11 SIC divisions.

The NAICS uses a six-digit classification code instead of the old SIC four-digit code. The additional two digits allow for far greater specificity in identifying special types of firms. However, the six-digit code is not being used by all three NAFTA countries. The three countries agreed on a standard system using the first five digits and the sixth digit is being used by each country in a manner allowing for special user needs in each country. Note that the NAICS code does not tell you anything specific. However, knowing a NAICS number for a type of business will allow you to find all kinds of secondary information about the firms in that business.

> The NAICS uses a six-digit classification code instead of the old SIC four-digit code.
>
> Knowing a NAICS number for a type of business will allow you to find all kinds of secondary information about the firms in that business.

Survey of Buying Power

The *Survey of Buying Power* allows users to assess the marketing potential of a given geographical area using an index called the buying power index, or BPI.

For many decades the *Survey of Buying Power* was available in print format in an annual edition of *Sales & Marketing Management Magazine*. Today, the SPB is available in an online, searchable format at www.surveyofbuyingpower.com.

We noted earlier that several commercial firms provide secondary information in a format that makes the information useful for a particular application. Over the last several decades there has probably been no better example of this than the *Survey of Buying Power*, published by the Nielsen Company. As we will show you shortly, this firm combines demographic data in an index format that allows users to assess the marketing potential of a given geographical area. Prior to being purchased by The Nielsen Company, the **Survey of Buying Power** was an annual survey of demographic information published annually for many years in *Sales & Marketing Management* magazine. Today, the magazine no longer publishes the annual survey; however, the data are now available in searchable online format at www.surveyofbuyingpower.com. Access is confined to subscribers, but we encourage you to go to the site and look at the sample data. The survey contains data for the United States on population, income, and retail sales for food, eating and drinking places, appliances, and automotives. These data are provided in the following geographical reporting units: CBSA, county, metro areas, and media markets. Five-year projections are also provided. Because the data for the survey are extrapolated from census data, the data are current with each year's publication. In addition to the general data, the survey also reports the **effective buying income (EBI)** and the **buying power index (BPI)**.

EBI is defined as disposable personal income. It is equal to gross income less taxes and therefore reflects the effective amount of income available for expenditure on goods and services. This is important, because taxes differ widely depending on geographic location. BPI is an indicator of the relative market potential of a geographic area. It is based on the factors that make up a market: people, ability to buy, and willingness to buy. The BPI is an index number that represents a market's percentage of the total buying power in the United States.

HOW TO CALCULATE THE BUYING POWER INDEX (BPI). The BPI is one of the main reasons that managers and researchers find the *Survey of Buying Power* so useful. Along with all the demographic information available to marketers, the BPI uses the three factors making up a market (people, ability to buy, and willingness to buy) to calculate a quantitative index that represents the buying power of a market. We provide the formula here and illustrate how to calculate the BPI.

$$
\begin{aligned}
\text{BPI} = \ & (\text{Population of Market Area A/Total U.S. Population}) \times 2 \\
& + (\text{EBI of Market Area A/Total U.S. EBI}) \times 5 \\
& + (\text{Retail Sales of Market Area A/Total U.S. Retail Sales}) \times 3
\end{aligned}
$$

The market areas that can be selected are regions, states, counties, MSAs, cities, or DMAs (designated market areas, representing television markets). Population is the market factor *people*. EBI represents the market factor *ability to buy*. However, since *willingness to buy*, the third market factor, is a mental construct representing something consumers are going to do in the future, the *Survey of Buying Power* (SBP) uses a surrogate indicator of what consumers will buy—past retail sales, which is used because what people bought yesterday is a good indicator of what they will buy today. The foregoing formula gives you the BPI, which, as we've said, is an index number. For example, the BPI for a large market, such as Chicago or Los Angeles, may be around 3.3333. This means that 3.3333% of the nation's total buying power is within that market. Casper, Wyoming, may have a BPI around 0.026. This means that Casper has 0.026% of the nation's buying power.

A disadvantage of the BPI is that it is a general index reflecting the buying power of the total population, all income levels, and total retail sales. A manufacturer of automobiles, seeking to locate markets with the best BPI ratings for sales of upscale automobiles, may want to use different inputs to create a customized BPI. A **customized BPI** would include market factors that relate to the user's product or service. For instance, an upscale car manufacturer may select only the population "35 and older"; the income category of "$50,000 and over"; and automotive retail sales. Any one of these choices would make the customized BPI more relevant to the upscale auto market than the generalized BPI.

Over the years the *Survey of Buying Power* has been used to determine market potential, construct sales forecasts, determine promotional budgets for different geographic markets, locate distributorships, and determine sales territories with equal, or near equal, sales quotas. When it was in print format, available annually in *Sales & Marketing Management Magazine*, it was a dominant source of market demographics. The survey was dormant for three years but reappeared in 2008 in the online format.

Lifestyle Market Analyst

Another commercial source of secondary data is the **Lifestyle Market Analyst**. This printed source of information analyzes several dozen lifestyle categories, such as Avid Book Readers, Own a Cat, Take Cruise Ship Vacations, Golf, Own a Camcorder, Have Grandchildren, Shop by Catalog/Mail, Stock/Bond Investments, Improving Health, and Donate to Charitable Causes. Information is organized into sections that have different objectives. First, you can examine markets (defined as DMAs). Not only will you get some standard demographic data for the DMA but you will also be able to determine the dominant (and least dominant) lifestyles in that market. This information helps "paint a personality portrait" of a market for users who otherwise see only a sea of numbers describing markets. Another section of the book focuses on each lifestyle. There you will find the demographic profile of the participants in that lifestyle category as well as other information. For example, to understand the lifestyle of a bicycling enthusiast, you may find answers to the following questions:

- What are the demographics of bicyclists?
- In what other activities are bikers involved?
- Which markets have the heaviest concentration of bikers?
- Which magazines do bikers read?

As another example, a *Lifestyle Market Analyst* profile of boating/sailing enthusiasts reveals that they also enjoy scuba diving, snow skiing, recreation vehicles, vacation property, and fishing, but they have little interest in devotional reading or needlework. Obviously, this type of consumer is an appropriate target for outdoor equipment sales.

There are many other sources of secondary information. Visit your library to become familiar with some of these sources.

Over the years the *Survey of Buying Power* has been used to determine market potential, construct sales forecasts; determine promotional budgets for different geographic markets, locate distributorships, and determine sales territories with equal, or near equal, sales quotas.

The *Lifestyle Market Analyst* is a printed source of information that analyzes several dozen lifestyle categories, such as Avid Book Readers, Own a Cat, Take Cruise Ship Vacations, and Golf.

Ch. 6

Summary

Secondary data should be examined in virtually all marketing research projects. Data may be grouped into two categories: primary and secondary. Primary data are gathered specifically for the research project at hand. Secondary data are data that have been previously gathered for some other purpose. The access to and availability of secondary data have been greatly enhanced via the Internet. Online secondary data analysis will become a more important tool in the marketing researcher's toolbox. There are many uses of secondary data in marketing research, and sometimes secondary data are all that is needed to achieve research objectives.

Marketing researchers should be fully aware of the classifications of secondary data and their advantages and disadvantages, and researchers must know how to evaluate the information available to them. Secondary data may be internal, that is, data already gathered *within* the firm for some other purpose. Data collected and stored from sales receipts—customer names, types, quantities and prices of goods or services purchased, delivery addresses, shipping dates, salesperson making the sale, and so on—would be internal secondary data. The use of electronic databases to store internal data has become increasingly popular; these data may be used for database marketing. Companies use information recorded in internal databases for purposes of direct marketing and to strengthen relationships with customers (CRM). Data mining is the name for software now available to help managers make sense out of the seemingly senseless masses of information contained in databases. What companies do with information collected for their internal databases can present ethical problems.

External secondary data are data obtained from sources outside the firm. These data may be classified as (1) published, (2) syndicated services data, and (3) databases. The different types of published secondary data include reference guides, indexes and abstracts, bibliographies, almanacs, manuals and handbooks, and so on, and they have different functions. Understanding the different functions is useful in researching secondary data. Syndicated services data are provided by firms that collect data in a standard format and make them available to subscribing firms. Online information databases are sources of secondary data searchable by search engines. When several databases are offered under one search engine, the service is called either an aggregator or a databank.

Secondary data have the advantages of being quickly gathered, readily available, relatively inexpensive, helpful in gaining insights should primary data be needed, and sometimes all that is needed to achieve the research objective. Disadvantages are that the data are often reported in incompatible reporting units (e.g., county data are reported when ZIP code data are needed), measurement units do not match researchers' needs (e.g., household income is reported when per capita income is needed), class definitions are incompatible with the researchers' needs (e.g., income is reported in classes up to $50,000 but the researchers need to know what percentage of the population earns $80,000 or more), and the data may be out of-date. Evaluation of secondary data is important. Not all organizations are ethical in terms of reporting secondary information objectively. Users must be aware of this.

Finding secondary data involves understanding what you need to know and understanding key terms and names associated with the subject. Indexes and bibliographies may be consulted first; they list sources of secondary information by subject. Computerized data searches from databases, if available, should be conducted. Knowing how to find standard subject headings within a database is a key to successful information searching. You should understand the logic of database organization as well as be familiar with database search techniques, including Boolean logic, field searching, proximity operators, truncation, nesting, and limiting. Seek the services of a reference librarian to help you improve your searching skills.

Examples of important secondary data for business decisions are the *Census of the Population* from the U.S. Census Bureau and the *Statistical Abstract of the United States*, both of which are available online. The next census will be taken during 2010. An annual survey entitled *The American Community Survey* will provide data formerly provided from the census "long form." With reliable information provided annually along with estimates for future years, many researchers are likely to focus on using data from this source of secondary information.

NAICS is a coding system of business firms and can be used by researchers to access information stored in databases according to the NAICS codes. Because NAICS groups businesses into 20 sectors (instead of the 11 used by the SIC) and uses codes of up to six digits to classify businesses (instead of the four-digit code used by the SIC), it is much better than SIC at specifying types of industries.

A privately produced secondary data source that is useful to marketers is the *Survey of Buying Power* (SBP). The SBP is useful because it provides a quantitative index, called the buying power index (BPI), to measure the buying power of various geographical markets in the United States. The SPB is available in an online, searchable format. Another commercially available source of secondary information is the *Lifestyle Market Analyst*, a unique publication containing information on several dozen lifestyles, such as bicycling enthusiasts, dog owners, snow skiing enthusiasts, and so on. There are many other sources of secondary information. You should visit your library and become familiar with some of these sources.

Key Terms

Primary data 148	Database marketing 150	Data mining 151
Secondary data 148	Database 150	External secondary data 152
Demographic groups 149	Record 150	Published sources 152
Baby boomer 149	Fields 151	Catalog 154
Gen Yers 150	Internal databases 151	Indexes 154
Gen Xers 150	CRM, customer relationship	Syndicated services data 154
Internal secondary data 150	management 151	External databases 154

Review Questions/Applications

1. Describe how Decision Analyst® values secondary data.
2. What are secondary data, and how do they differ from primary data?
3. Describe how the Internet has affected secondary data.
4. Describe some uses of secondary data.
5. Describe what is meant by "demographic groups" and name a couple of the groups mentioned in the chapter.
6. Explain how a particular demographic group could account for the popularity of rock and roll music.
7. How would you classify secondary data?
8. What is database marketing?
9. Discuss how databases are organized.
10. What is CRM? What is data mining?
11. Explain why internal data bases could represent an ethical issue for firms.
12. What are three types of external secondary data?
13. What is the difference between a library catalog and an index?
14. What are online information databases? Name three of them.
15. Explain why it would be important to know the functions of different types of publications.
16. What are the five advantages of secondary data? Discuss the disadvantages of secondary data.
17. What is meant by geographical reporting units in the use of secondary data? What is a CBSA?
18. How would you go about evaluating secondary data? Why is evaluation important?
19. Discuss how you would go about locating secondary data in your own library.
20. What is a standard subject heading? Explain why knowing how to find a standard subject heading would help increase your information searching skills when using online information databases.

21. Explain what is meant by Boolean logic and proximity operators.
22. Why would searching by "field" help you efficiently search online information databases?
23. Name some key sources of secondary information for marketing decision makers.
24. Describe the purposes of the U.S. Census of the Population.
25. Briefly discuss what will be different about Census 2010.
26. Go to the website given in the chapter for the *Survey of Buying Power*. Describe the types of information you can retrieve from the site by examining some of the sample data.
27. Go online to your favorite search engine (e.g., Ask, Google, Yahoo, etc.) and enter "demographics." Go to some of these sites and describe the kind of information you are receiving. Why would this information be considered secondary data?
28. Access the *Statistical Abstract of the United States* online and find information relevant to any topic you are currently studying.
29. Select an industry and on the NAICS website identified in this chapter find the NAICS number that represents your industry. Discuss how you could use this number.
30. Suppose you were the marketing director for an upscale car manufacturer. Discuss what factors you would consider in building a customized BPI that could be used to evaluate markets for future dealerships.
31. Go to easidemographics.com. Explain some of the services offered and what the costs of these services are.
32. Explain how a marketer of boats could use the *Lifestyle Market Analyst*.

APPLE SUPERMARKETS, INC.

Apple Supermarkets operates 68 supermarkets in 12 states. The location philosophy has always been to cluster stores in larger cities so as to gain economies of scale through newspaper and TV advertising. All 68 stores were contained within 36 Core-based Statistical Areas. Of the total promotion budget, about 50% goes to newspapers and another 40% goes to television. The remaining 10% is normally allocated to local opportunities such as donations to sponsor a community activity such as a local Little League baseball team or a church bazaar. The newspaper budget had been allocated three months before Tony Tampary arrived, but it was time to make the allocation to the supermarket managers for the TV budget.

Tony Tampary is the new VP of Marketing for Apple Supermarkets. Historically, there had been no VP of Marketing; rather, the VP of Operations allocated funds to the local supermarket managers and let them make their own marketing decisions as to where and when to run company ads and where and when to spend money on local sponsorships of community events. Tony thought this procedure should continue; he had many other duties and didn't feel these decisions should be made centrally. He felt the managers were in the best position to know the local competition as well as the local media choices, not to mention the best community events to sponsor. However, Tony was more concerned about how the promotion budget had been allocated to the stores in the past. Essentially, the VP of Operations hadn't put a great deal of thought into this issue. Once he had received the total promotional budget figure from the CFO, he pretty much allocated the same percentage to each store that had been allocated in the past. When Tony analyzed these allocations, he realized there were some notable discrepancies. In some cases, smaller stores were receiving larger promotion budgets than much larger stores. When he asked the Operations VP how this could have happened, the reply was, "Well, I started out several years ago giving them whatever they got the previous year. But, each year I would get a call from a few managers saying they wanted more because they wanted to do some special things in the coming year. I never readjusted those budgets. Once they went up I suppose they continued getting a larger share from then on. It seemed to work OK—no one ever complained though I guess a few of the managers were pretty insistent on getting more year after year." Tony was afraid the budgets weren't allocated to the stores that had the most potential. Rather the budgets were allocated based on the "squeaky wheel gets the grease" method. The managers that learned they would get money just by asking kept asking. Other managers, not realizing this, kept operating with the funds they were allocated.

Tampary was determined to allocate the promotional budget in a way that would more likely increase the firm's ROI. He knew there wasn't much he could do about the newspaper budgets that had already been allocated, but he wanted to improve the allocation of the TV budget. He had some experience with trying to measure advertising effectiveness and knew it could be quite complex. For now, he had to make the allocation of the TV budget to the store managers and he needed to do it within the week. He really didn't have time for much research. The VP of Operations didn't have much in the way of secondary information that would be useful for marketing decisions. After work, Tony visited one of the local libraries and started looking for some useful tool that would help him make a decision. He talked with the business reference librarian. She briefed him on the contents of the census data but warned him that it was getting outdated. Tony asked her for a source of current demographic data. "I need something that is applicable to this year." She told him that for many years, the *Survey of Buying Power* had been used by local business managers and was available for a subscription at a website. The librarian showed Tony some of the information included in the *Survey of Buying Power*:

Retail Sales; reported in total and also by several categories, such as Motor Vehicle and Parts Dealers; Furniture and Home Furnishing Stores; Electronics and Appliance Stores; Food and Beverage Stores, which included Grocery Stores, Supermarkets, and Other Grocery (except Convenience Stores); Gasoline Stations; Clothing and Clothing and Accessories; and so on.

Number of business establishments
Population
Blue-collar employment
The Buying Power Index (BPI)

Effective Buying Income (EBI)
Households
Households with cars
Median age
Precent Change in Population (since the 2000 Census)
Many other items

Tampary was overwhelmed with the information but he began to focus on the geographic reporting units available to him. He noticed that data are reported by CBSA and media markets, another name for "television markets." Historically, media markets were called DMAs, or designated media markets. The concept, developed by Nielsen, categorizes geographical areas according to the market of origin of the station(s) with the largest share of viewer hours. All counties whose largest viewer share is given to stations in that same market of origin are grouped together under that particular DMA, or media market. Since broadcast signals do not conform to county boundaries, the geographical areas of media markets may cover only a portion of a given county. Essentially, then, information for a media market reports data for the geographical area covered by the broadcast signal for the market of origin TV stations.

The *Buying Power Index* (BPI) appealed to Tampary. He could take the total television budget allocated to him by the CFO and allocate it first to each of the 36 CBSAs based on each CBSA's percentage of the total BPI for all 36 CBSAs. Once he knew how much he should allocate to each CBSA, allocations to the supermarkets within the CBSA would be easy. He could base the store allocation on past sales and make adjustments if a manager planned for special promotions for the coming year. Tony would be able to gather the BPIs for each of Apple's 36 CBSAs within a few minutes.

1. Discuss the pros and cons of Tony Tampary's decision to use the BPI to allocate the TV budget to each CBSA.
2. What changes would you suggest Tony make?
3. Discuss Tony's decision to use the *Survey of Buying Power* in terms of the advantages and disadvantages of secondary data as discussed in this chapter.

CASE 6.2 Your Integrated Case

ADVANCED AUTOMOBILE CONCEPTS

Nick Thomas is very concerned. He asks himself if he is wrong about the fuel crisis this time. Is it here to stay? And is global warming as alarming as the media portrays it? As Nick considers Zen's alternatives, he realizes he needs more information than he currently has. If Zen is really going to consider more fuel-efficient cars, Nick knows he needs information on which fuel-efficient cars are selling well and which alternative fuels are the closest to being developed.

1. What types of secondary information should Nick seek?
2. Select one particular topic that you think is relevant and find in your library's databases the most appropriate "standard subject heading" for that database. List the database and the standard subject heading you found for your topic.
3. Based on your library database search, what weaknesses did you encounter in the secondary data?

Learning Objectives

- To learn how to distinguish standardized information from other types of information

- To know the differences between syndicated data and standardized services

- To understand the advantages and disadvantages of standardized information

- To see some of the various areas in which standardized information may be applied

- To understand some specific examples of standardized information sources in each of four areas of application

- To know the meaning of single-source data

The Facts about Loyalty Programs: The Maritz Poll

The Maritz poll measures consumers' attitudes and opinions.

Maritz®, one of the world leaders in research, measures public attitudes and opinions and publishes them in the Maritz Poll. Maritz studies U.S. shoppers who have made a purchase within the last 6 months in one of 11 preselected retail categories, such as apparel, home improvement, electronics, and so on. Firms in these categories, such as The Gap, Lowe's, and Best Buy, should certainly be interested in the findings and implications of this Maritz poll.

Do Members of Rewards Programs Spend More?

Maritz defined rewards programs, for the purposes of the poll, as either a store or membership program or a private or co-labeled credit card that awards customers points for purchases or other behaviors they can later redeem for various rewards, including discounts, gift certificates, merchandise, cash back, or travel. Some of the findings are: People who are members of rewards programs do spend more. Maritz notes that it may not be the rewards programs that *cause* customers to spend more. It could be that those who spend more intentionally join the rewards programs to gain the rewards. Even if rewards programs do not cause more buying, by having customers enroll in them it gives retailers a great tool because it allows them to mine the data collected from rewards programs to identify and create a dialogue with profitable customers.

Who Are the Rewards Program Members?

Maritz found that more women (62%) than men (54%) belong to rewards programs. They found that rewards program members are young. Seventy-one percent of those 25–34 belong to a program. Those who have kids are more likely to belong to a rewards program. Membership varies by region of the country, with the Northeast having the highest membership (70%) and the South having the lowest (37%).

For companies interested in keeping their most loyal customers, Maritz can help them make better decisions. Maritz has a division, Maritz Loyalty Marketing, that specializes in helping companies with these decisions.

About This Study

Maritz used a sample size of 2,178 shoppers. The study had a margin of error of ±2%. The study was published in August, 2006.

—By permission, Maritz

T*he Maritz Poll illustrates the topic of this chapter: standardized information. In this case, the Maritz Poll uses a standardized process, which ensures that consumer attitudes and opinions are properly measured and represented. Each poll addresses a different topic. The process of collecting the data remains the same, though the data generated differ with each poll. As you will learn in this chapter, this is a form of standardized information that we will call standardized services. We are going to introduce you to the different types of standardized information in this chapter: syndicated data and standardized services. We begin by defining what we mean by these types of standardized information.*

WHAT IS STANDARDIZED INFORMATION?

Standardized information is a type of secondary data in which the data collected and/or the process of collecting the data are standardized for all users. Two broad classes of standardized information are syndicated data and standardized services.

Syndicated data are data that are collected in a standard format and made available to all subscribers.

Visit the Market Evaluations, Inc. site at www.qscores.com to learn about the different Q Score studies that are available.

Standardized information is a type of secondary data in which the data collected and/or the process of collecting the data are standardized for all users. There are two broad classes of standardized information: syndicated data and standardized services. **Syndicated data** are data that are collected in a standard format and made available to all subscribers. Marketing Evaluations, Inc., for example, offers several Q Scores® services. One of its services measures the familiarity and appeal of performers in a number of categories, such as actors, actresses, authors, athletes, sportscasters, and so on. This information is used by companies to help them choose the most appropriate spokesperson for their company or help a movie producer select a performer for an upcoming movie. **Performer Q®** is the service for ratings of approximately 1,700 performers. Tom Hanks and Bill Cosby, for example, are performers who have high Q Scores. Data for all 1,700 performers studied is the same—standardized—regardless of who uses the data. Data are collected two times a year for all performers based on a sample of nearly 2,000 persons and are made available to all who subscribe, which includes advertisers, TV and movie production companies, licensing companies, talent and public relations companies, among others. Nielsen Media Research's Nielsen Television Index (NTI), another example of a syndicated data provider, supplies subscribers with data on TV viewing. The data are standardized in the sense that the same data are made available to anyone wishing to purchase it.

On the other hand, **standardized services** refers to a standardized marketing research *process* that is used to generate information for a particular user. We told you about the Maritz Poll a moment ago. The Maritz Poll uses a standardized *process* to ensure that consumer attitudes and opinions are properly measured and represented, since each poll addresses a different topic and, therefore, supplies different data, these polls are examples of a standardized service. **ESRI's Tapestry™ Segmentation** is a standardized service that uses a *process* to profile residential neighborhoods. This information is purchased by clients desiring to better understand who their customers are, where they are located, how to find them, and how to reach them. We discuss both types of information next.

Syndicated data are a form of external, secondary data supplied from a common database for a service fee to subscribers. Recall from our discussion of the types of firms in the marketing research industry in Chapter 3 that firms providing such data are called *syndicated data service firms*. These firms provide specialized, routine information needed by a given industry in the form of ready-to-use, standardized marketing data to subscribing firms. The information is typically detailed information that is not available in libraries. Firms supplying syndicated data follow standard research formats that enable them to collect the same standardized data over time. We mentioned the NTI ratings earlier. As another example, Arbitron supplies syndicated data on the number and types of listeners to the various radio stations in each radio market. This standardized information helps advertising firms reach their target markets; it also helps radio stations define audience characteristics by providing an objective, independent measure of the size and characteristics of their audiences. With syndicated data, both the process of collecting and analyzing the data and the data itself are standardized; that is, neither is varied for the client.[1] On the other hand, standardized services rarely provide clients with standardized data. Rather, it is the *process* they are marketing. The application of that standardized process will result in different data for each client. For example, a standardized service may be measurement of customer satisfaction. Instead of a user firm trying to "reinvent the wheel" by developing its own process for measuring customer satisfaction, it may elect to use a standardized service to do so. Several other marketing research services, such as test marketing, naming new brands, pricing a new product, or using mystery shoppers, are also purchased from standardized service firms.

ADVANTAGES AND DISADVANTAGES OF STANDARDIZED INFORMATION

Syndicated Data

One of the key advantages of syndicated data is shared costs. Many client firms may subscribe to the information; thus, the cost of the service is greatly reduced to any one subscriber firm. When costs are spread across several subscribers, other advantages result. Because syndicated data firms specialize in the collection of standard data and because their viability, in the long run, depends on the validity of the data, the quality of the data collected is typically very high. With several companies paying for the service, the syndicating company can as well go to great lengths to gather a great amount of data.

Another advantage of syndicated data comes from the routinized systems used to collect and process the data. This means that the data are normally disseminated very quickly to subscribers because the syndicated data firms set up standard procedures and methods for collecting the data over and over again on a periodic basis. The more current the data, the greater their usefulness.

Although there are several advantages to syndicated data, there are some disadvantages. First, buyers have little control over what information is collected. Since the research is not custom research for the buyer firm, the buyer firm must be satisfied that the information received is the information needed. Are the units of measurement

---

Margin notes:

Standardized services refers to a standardized marketing research *process* that is used to generate information for a particular user.

ESRI's Tapestry™ Segmentation is a standardized service that uses a *process* to profile residential neighborhoods. This information is purchased by clients desiring to better understand who their customers are, where they are located, how to find them, and how to reach them.

With syndicated data, the data and the process used to generate the data are standardized across all users. With standardized services, the process of collecting data is standardized across all users.

Advantages of syndicated data are shared costs, high quality of the data, and speed with which data are collected and made available for decision making.

Disadvantages of syndicated data are that there is little control over what data are collected, buyers must commit to long-term contracts, and competitors have access to the same information.

correct? Are the geographical reporting units appropriate? A second disadvantage is that buyer firms often must commit to long-term contracts when buying syndicated data. Finally, there is no strategic information advantage in purchasing syndicated data because all competitors have access to the same information. However, in many industries, firms would suffer a serious strategic disadvantage by not purchasing the information.

Standardized Services

Advantages of standardized services include using the experience of the firm offering the service, reduced cost, and increased speed of conducting the research.

The key advantage of using a standardized service is taking advantage of the experience of the research firm offering the service. Often, a buyer firm may have a research department with many experienced persons but no experience in the particular process that it needs. Imagine a firm setting out to conduct a test market for the very first time. It would take the firm several months to gain the confidence needed to conduct the test market properly. Still, lessons would be learned by trial and error. Taking advantage of others' experiences with the process is a good way to minimize potential mistakes in carrying out the research. A second advantage is the reduced cost of the research. Because the supplier firm conducts the service for many clients on a regular basis, the procedure is efficient and far less costly than if the buyer firm tried to conduct the service itself. A third advantage is speed, which is usually much faster than if the buyer firm were to conduct the service on its own. The efficiency gained by conducting a service over and over translates into reduced turnaround time from start to finish of a research project.

Disadvantages of standardized services are the inability to customize and lack of knowledge about the client's industry.

There are disadvantages to using standardized services as well. "Standardized" means "not customized." The ability to customize some projects is lacking when using a standardized service. Although some firms offer some customization, generally they cannot design a service specifically for the project at hand. Second, the company providing the standardized service may not know the idiosyncrasies of a particular industry and, therefore, the client is burdened with the responsibility of ensuring that the standardized service fits the intended situation. Client firms need to be very familiar with the service, including what data are collected on which population, how the data are collected, and how the data arc reported, before they purchase the service.

APPLICATIONS OF STANDARDIZED INFORMATION

Although many forms of standardized information may have many applications, we will illustrate four major applications in the remainder of this chapter. We will explore the use of standardized information in measuring consumer attitudes and conducting opinion polls, in defining market segments, in conducting market tracking, and in monitoring media usage and promotion effectiveness.

Measuring Consumer Attitudes and Opinion Polls

You can visit Maritz and the The Maritz Poll at www.maritz.com. Go to News & Events, Maritz Poll. Search by "topic."

Visit Yankelovich at www .Yankelovich.com. Go to Products and Services and Global MONITOR®, where you can download an in-depth description of this survey conducted in 18 different countries.

Several firms offer measurements of consumer attitudes and opinions on various issues. **The Maritz Poll** is conducted on American and European consumers on a variety of topics. Many of the past poll results are free to all those who visit the Maritz website and the results are often published in the media, including the Associated Press, *CNN Headline News*, *Business Week*, the *Financial Times*, Reuters, and *USA Today*, among many others.

The **Yankelovich Monitor**, started in 1971, measures changing social values and how these changes affect consumers. It has specialized in generational marketing and has studied mature populations, baby boomers, and Gen Xers.[2] The data are syndicated, meaning they are available to anyone who wishes to purchase, and the information can be used for a variety of marketing management decisions. Data are collected annually through 90-minute in-home interviews and a 1-hour questionnaire from 2,500 men and women aged 16 and over using a nationally representative sample.[3] A number of topics are included, such as activism, sex, nutrition, doctors, women, stress, work, television, shopping, simplification/escape, newspapers, and so on.[4] Yankelovich also measures attitudes and values of the youth, Hispanic, and African American markets.[5]

Ipsos Public Affairs® conducts 22,000 interviews in 22 countries over 22 days twice a year to produce the **Ipsos Global@dvisor®**. The purpose of the study is to allow companies to assess their risk by studying the company's proprietary audiences, who are thought to be "canaries in the global coal mine." Belgacom, the leading telecom operator in Belgium, is using Global@dvisor to help it establish benchmarks on a number of key dimensions before embarking on a repositioning of its corporate and social responsibility strategy. InBev, the global leader in beer, including brands such as Stella Artois and Anheuser-Busch, subscribes to Global@dvisor to better understand how consumers and key stakeholders view its reputation as a brand, company and industry leader. Other subscribers include Air France and Coca-Cola.[6] Read about this interesting service in Marketing Research Insight 7.1.

> Visit Ipsos Public Affairs at http://www.ipsos-pa.com/ and learn more about the Global@dvisor ® and other Ipsos Public Affairs services.

The **Harris poll** measures consumer attitudes and opinions on a wide variety of topics. Owned by Harris Interactive, the Harris poll started in 1963 and is one of the longest-running, most respected surveys of consumer opinion. Harris polls are conducted on such topics as the economy, environment, politics, world affairs, legal issues, and so on. Surveys are taken weekly and, because many of the same questions are asked over and over, the Harris poll is a good source for identifying trend lines. Since these data are standardized information, we use the Harris poll as another example of syndicated data. However, Harris Interactive will also conduct customized surveys for clients.[7]

> Companies can use Harris Interactive to receive information on consumer attitudes and opinions. Go to www.HarrisInteractive.com, "News and Events," and "The Harris Poll". Be sure to check out "Flashbacks."

The **Gallup poll** surveys public opinion, asking questions on domestic issues, private issues, and world affairs, such as "Do you consider the income tax you have to pay this year to be fair?" (Although 85% said "yes" in 1943, only 58% said "yes" in 2002.) Business executives can track attitudes toward buying private brands or attitudes toward credit by following the results from questions asked in the Gallup poll. The polls are compiled annually, and back issues are available covering each year beginning with 1935.[8] Like Harris Interactive, the Gallup Organization can conduct customized surveys for clients. However, we treat the Gallup poll here as syndicated data, since it collects attitude and opinion information and makes that information available to all who wish to purchase it. Visiting its website and viewing some poll results will give you an idea of the service provided by the Gallup Organization.

> We treat the Gallup poll here as syndicated data, since it collects attitude and opinion information and makes that information available to all who wish to purchase it. See examples of Gallup surveys at www.gallup.com.

Defining Market Segments

Defining market segments requires placing customers sharing certain attributes (age, income, stage in the family life cycle, etc.) into homogeneous groups or market segments. Marketers gather information about the market members, compiling profiles of the attributes of the consumers that make up each segment. Marketers can then decide which segments are currently being served or not served by the competition. They can also determine the size, growth trends, and profit potential of each segment. Using these data, a segment, or group of segments, can be targeted for marketing.

Several standardized information sources provide marketers with information about customers in markets. Some concentrate on members of the industrial market, and others provide information on members of the consumer market.

PROVIDING INFORMATION ON MEMBERS OF THE INDUSTRIAL MARKET. A great deal about the industrial market can be learned by using the Standard Industrial Classification (SIC) system and the North American Industry Classification System (NAICS), the government's method of classifying business firms (discussed in Chapter 6). Although it achieves the basic objectives of allowing users to identify, classify, and monitor standard

> NAICS allows marketers to define industry types more specifically than the SIC classification system does.

MARKETING RESEARCH INSIGHT   Global Application

7.1

Ipsos Public Affairs

The Ipsos Global@dvisor
Reputation Risk Identifier

22,000 interviews, in 22 countries, over 22 days, done twice a year.

We call it the Ipsos Global@dvisor *Reputation Risk Identifier.*

You'll simply call it indispensable.

You know that your reputation follows you everywhere. In today's ever increasing virtual world where your trademark is the best trustmark you have in the marketplace, you know the risk environment to your reputation is instantaneous and real.

Every time your organization finds its name in the media, in a blog or on YouTube, literally millions of people will know about it too – citizens, consumers, advocates and detractors to be sure. Add to them, your own senior management and employees, and just as easily, shareholders, investors, numerous governments and their agencies too.

So before you discover it might be too late, ask yourself this simple question: how's your reputation doing out there today?

We can help you proactively manage the risk to your organization's reputation through the Ipsos Global@dvisor *Reputation Risk Identifier* research service. Get access to this unique research service in the following countries:

US	Sweden
Canada	Netherlands
Mexico	Czech Republic
Brazil	Poland
Argentina	Turkey
UK	India
France	China
Germany	Russia
Italy	South Korea
Spain	Australia
Japan	Belgium

The Ipsos Global@dvisor *Reputation Risk Identifier* (April and October) provides in-depth feedback about the risk to your reputation and the stability of the reputational environment. We achieve this by surveying 1,000 consumer-citizen on-line respondents in each country with quotas set and balanced by gender, age, and region – standard socio-demographics – with an option for clients to add lifestyles, personal values, and other key psychographic elements to the survey instrument.

In the richly detailed, easy to grasp analysis, presentations and interactive global briefings, Ipsos' Global Public Affairs research team – with one dedicated group in each country studied – and our reputation research specialists will identify such opinion groupings and motivators as the broad elites and Global@dvisor's proprietary audience The Intelligaged, and its CSR and environmental activists, The Intelliventionists. We also show you why and how these groups are considered early portenders of risk to your reputation – proverbial canaries in the global coal mine.

The Ipsos Global@dvisor *Reputation Risk Identifier* produces a clear picture of your reputation risk environment and what it means to your reputation by analyzing public and elite opinion elements including:

- Social & Political Risk
- Country Image Barometer
- Corporate & Business Risk
- Sectoral Risk
- Brand Risk (40+ global leaders)
  - Familiarity
  - Favorability
  - Worth what paid for
  - Trust
  - Social Responsibility
  - Environmental Responsibility
  - Reputational Marketing Efficiency
- Profiles

▶

Ipsos Public Affairs

In addition to the syndicated portion of the survey, clients can add their own proprietary questions, and add countries beyond the 22 listed here. This way, the Ipsos Global@dvisor *Reputation Risk Identifier* offers clients two custom research applications that can cover research blind spots in a fast, scalable, and cost effective manner without compromising on the quality and depth of data:

- Parallel Tracking – companies, organizations, and government agencies can list their name, as well as competitor or counterpart names, to produce reputation comparisons.
- Proprietary – giving clients an opportunity to ask specific proprietary questions that further enhance the usability of the syndicated data survey sections.

For more information, please contact:

Paul Abbate
Senior Vice President
Ipsos Public Affairs
Telephone: +1.781.826.8930
Facsimile: +1.781.987.8798
Email: paul.abbate@ipsos-na.com

Ipsos Public Affairs

Ipsos is the world's third largest survey research firm with offices in 46 countries. In North America, Ipsos consists of 1,300 research professionals across 30 locations in the US and Canada, including New York City, Washington, DC, and Toronto. Ipsos Public Affairs specializes in corporate reputation, issues management, strategic communications, and sociopolitical trends, serving the needs of corporations, non-profit organizations, public relations firms, news media, and governments. Ipsos Public Affairs is well known in the US as the polling partner of The Associated Press, the world's oldest and largest news organization. In Canada, Ipsos Public Affairs is the official polling partner of CanWest News Service. Our toolbox for conducting tailor-made solutions includes rapid turnaround quantitative polling with pinpoint accuracy, qualitative focus groups, online panels, elite and stakeholder interviewing, syndicated subscriptions, and proprietary research techniques. Ipsos Public Affairs offers research programs that are creative, cost-effective, insightful, and actionable; key performance indicators developed jointly with clients; interpretive reports with clear recommendations; and workshops to facilitate action planning. To learn more, visit www.ipsos-na.com/pa/

08-01-39

statistics about certain member firms, the SIC falls short when it comes to targeting customers in a highly specific industry. NAICS partially remedies this problem by replacing the SIC's four-digit code with a six-digit code, which allows users to select more specific types of firms instead of the broad categories identifiable through SIC codes.

One standardized information service firm, Dun & Bradstreet, supplies additional information that allows subscribers to make even better use of the government's classification systems. **Dun & Bradstreet's D-U-N-S** (Data Universal Numbering System) is a 9-digit classification system that assigns an identification number to all firms. This gives D & B the ability to identify over 100 million companies around the globe. And, since Dun & Bradstreet originated as a credit reporting firm, companies willingly supplied it with detailed information about their companies and their operations. This allowed D & B to create databases containing a wide array of information on businesses for which it reported a credit rating. These databases allow D & B to offer more services, such as **Dun's Market Identifiers (DMI)**, which provides information on over 4 million firms and is updated monthly. The real benefit of DMI is its use of 8-digit codes to classify businesses. With more digits, the service can break firms down into many more categories than other classification systems. This is important if a marketer is trying to target specific business firms, however narrow their classification.

One marketing researcher, for example, worked with the manufacturing firm BasKet Kases, a manufacturer of wooden gift baskets, to secure a listing of all firms that wholesale gift baskets in order to target a marketing campaign to these wholesalers. Using the SIC Classification Manual, the researcher determined that SIC numbers with a 51 prefix were wholesalers of nondurable goods. An examinination of all 51 prefix descriptions revealed that the SIC code of 5199 represented wholesalers of "miscellaneous, nondurable goods," which included baskets. Without additional information, a list of firms with an SIC code of 5199 would have included wholesalers of all types of baskets, including wooden baskets for shipping fruit, freight, and so on. However, by using the additional codes supplied by DMI, the researcher found that the 8-digit code 51990603 represented "wholesalers of gift baskets"—exactly what the researcher was seeking. Finding the firms sharing this eight-digit code pared the list down to 83 wholesalers of gift baskets in eight states in the East Central U.S. This smaller number of market target firms made BasKet Kases' marketing job manageable.

PROVIDING INFORMATION ON MEMBERS OF THE CONSUMER MARKET. Many standardized information services are available to help marketers understand the consumer market. SRI Consulting Business Intelligence's (SRIC-BI's) **VALS**™ program segments consumers by psychographics (psychological and demographic measures).[9] The essential logic of VALS is that people express their personalities through their behaviors. Our selections of TV programs, magazines, toothpaste brand, automobile brand, stores to patronize—all are motivated by our personalities. From their answers to the "VALS Questionnaire," which measures their psychological and demographic characteristics, consumers are placed in one of eight personality segments.

The segments are Innovators, Thinkers, Believers, Achievers, Strivers, Experiencers, Makers, and Survivors. (You can read about the differences among these eight segments at http://www.sric-bi.com/VALS/. Go to "The VALS™ Types.") SRIC-BI can help a client firm determine which basic VALS segments purchase its goods or services. Knowledge of these segments helps the client firm develop a deeper understanding of its target market consumer. **GeoVALS**™ is a service that identifies at the ZIP code or census block level the major VALS segments residing in a geographical area.

When it was originally formulated in 1978, VALS stood for "values and lifestyles." However, several years later it was determined that the segmentation categories should be based on enduring personality traits rather than on values, which may change over time. The acronym, VALS, was retained, although the system is no longer based upon values and life styles. VALS is offered globally through **U.S. VALS**™, **Japan-VALS**™, and **U.K. VALS**™.

Margin notes:

The real benefit of DMI is its 8-digit codes to classify businesses. With more digits, the service can break firms down into many more categories than other classification systems.

You can visit the Dun & Bradstreet website at www.dnb.com.

VALS is a standardized service that offers a psychographic segmenting system to determine in which of eight VALS segments a consumer belongs based on psychological characteristics and demographics.

Learn more about VALS at www.sric-bi .com/VALS.

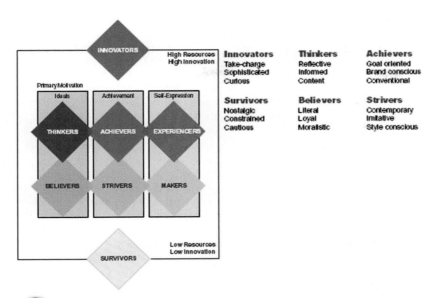

Innovators	Thinkers	Achievers	Experiencers
Take-charge	Reflective	Goal oriented	Trend setting
Sophisticated	Informed	Brand conscious	Impulsive
Curious	Content	Conventional	Variety seeking

Survivors	Believers	Strivers	Makers
Nostalgic	Literal	Contemporary	Responsible
Constrained	Loyal	Imitative	Practical
Cautious	Moralistic	Style conscious	Self-sufficient

 Active Learning

What's your VALS segment? You can determine your VALS segment by completing the VALS survey online at www.sric-bi.com/VALS/. Go to "The VALS™ Survey" and take the short survey. Based on your responses you will be assigned to your VALS segment. Then read about that segment at "The VALS™ Types."

Geodemographics is the term used to describe the classification of arbitrary, usually small, geographic areas in terms of the characteristics of their inhabitants. Aided by computer programs called **GIS** (geodemographic information systems), geodemographers can access huge databases and construct profiles of consumers residing in the geographic areas of interest to the geodemographer; that is, they are not limited to consumer information recorded by city, county, or state. Instead, geodemographers can produce information about geographic areas thought to be relevant to a given marketing application (such as a proposed site for a fast-food restaurant).

Before we give you some examples of companies that offer geodemographic services, let's take a closer look at an explanation of geodemographics and how it may be applied to marketing problems. We asked Dr. Fred L. Miller, an expert on GIS business applications and the author of *GIS Tutorial for Marketing*, to provide you an example illustrating the use of geodemographics in marketing. Dr. Miller's example, written expressly for you, appears as Marketing Research Insight 7.2.

Firms specializing in geodemographics combine census data with their own survey data or data that they gather from other sources. Nielsen Claritas (formerly Claritas Inc.) is the firm that pioneered geodemography. By accessing ZIP codes and census data regarding census tracts, census block groups, or blocks, which make up a firm's trading area(s), Nielsen Claritas can compile much information about the characteristics and lifestyles of the people within these trading areas. Or a firm may give Nielsen Claritas a descriptive profile of its target market and Nielsen Claritas can supply the firm with geographic areas that most closely match the prespecified characteristics. This service is referred to as **PRIZM** (potential ratings index for ZIP markets). The PRIZM system defines every neighborhood in the United States at the household level in terms of 66 demographically and behaviorally distinct segments. By knowing which segments make up a firm's potential customers, Nielsen Claritas can help target promotional messages to

Geodemographics is the term used to describe the classification of arbitrary, usually small, geographic areas in terms of the characteristics of their inhabitants.

Firms specializing in geodemographics combine census data with their own survey data or data that they gather from other sources. PRIZM is a standardized information service that categorizes neighborhoods at the household level into one of 66 different segments.

PRIZM defines every neighborhood in the United States based upon 66 market segments.

MARKETING RESEARCH INSIGHT   Practical Application

7.2 Understanding Customers with Geodemographic Profiling

Fred L. Miller, Ph.D., is Professor of Marketing and Telecommunications Systems Management, at Murray State University. Dr. Miller is the author of *GIS Tutorial for Marketing*.

Have you seen your home on the aerial photos in Google Earth or Virtual Earth? Printed directions from MapQuest or Google Maps? Used a GPS device for navigational purposes? Used a retailer's website to identify the closest store and find out how to get there? If so, you have some insight into the value of spatial information in personal and business decision making.

Not so long ago, geographic information system (GIS) technologies were the esoteric domain of specialists working on dedicated computers in the bowels of large organizations. Now, the consumer-oriented, Web-based experiences described above are the tip of a huge iceberg of potential GIS applications in business. A GIS is an information technology resource specifically designed to store, analyze, display, and communicate the spatial dimension of information in a wide range of disciplines. Business GIS refers to the application of these tools to business decisions.

Many business decisions are inherently spatial. Consider the following questions, each of which has a significant spatial component.

- Where do my customers live? How far are they willing to travel to my store?
- The franchise I want to buy requires 50,000 people within a five-mile radius. What sites in my home town meet this requirement?
- My manufacturing system uses JIT inventory control. Can my suppliers deliver on a timely basis? How can I

track their shipments and reroute them if necessary to maintain delivery schedules?
- My plant produces an important industrial chemical which is hazardous to humans. If we experience a leak from the plant, which areas are at risk, how many people live there, and how can we notify them?
- I am seeking a site for a new store/production site. What are the characteristics of the potential customers/employees living near that store/site?
- How large should my company's sales territories be? How can I balance sales potential and efficiency of coverage in designing them? What is the most efficient route for each sales representative's daily sales calls?

These questions form the basis for some of the most common Business GIS applications. To answer them, managers use Business GIS tools such as desktop systems, Web-based applications, or components built into enterprise information systems, including ERP, SCM, and CRM solutions. More recently, new integrated Business GIS software systems have entered the market to broaden the potential for Business GIS applications. These systems combine standard GIS software with extensive collections of geodemographic and business data, spatial analytic tools automated as software wizards, and extensive reporting capability to form powerful Business GIS solutions.

In the field of marketing research, the most beneficial application of integrated Business GIS is geodemographic customer profiling. This technique uses geographic location to infer the demographic, socioeconomic, and lifestyle characteristics of a firm's customers based on where they live. These characteristics, in turn, help marketers identify market segments and craft strategies to serve them effectively. Here's how it works.

Nature's Beauty sells herbal skin care products made from wild or organically produced plants in its suburban Minneapolis, MN retail store. The firm's loyalty club includes 400 customers who buy its products regularly. Store owner and manager, Beth Mathis, wishes to increase sales by offering club members a subscription service for the firm's new products. Each month, members would receive a moderately priced trial size of a featured product and be given the opportunity to order larger sizes as well as related products. Ms. Mathis plans to begin the new program with local media advertising to invite club members to the website dedicated to the program. In addition to current club members, she wishes to reach other prospective customers who match the club member demographic and lifestyle profile.

To assess the feasibility of this plan, Ms. Mathis wants to answer five research questions about her customers. They are:

1. What are their distinguishing characteristics, i.e., their geodemographic profile?
2. To which Tapestry™ Segmentation neighborhood segments do they belong?

3. Do they read newspapers and/or listen to radio frequently? If so, what newspaper sections and which radio formats are most popular with them?
4. How frequently do they use the Internet? Do they buy personal products online?
5. Are there concentrations of potential new customers (people with similar demographic and lifestyle characteristics) in the Minneapolis–St. Paul metropolitan area?

To answer these research questions. Ms. Mathis uses Business Analyst, an integrated Business GIS package from ESRI. She begins with an MS Excel list of club members and their purchases for the past year. Her first step is to use Business Analyst's locator tools to geocode each customer address, a process which assigns each customer record specific latitude and longitude values base on their address. These values provide the spatial reference which allows customer locations to be displayed on the map below. This enables Ms. Mathis to observe the geographic distribution of club members around her store, which is represented with a red circle. Note as well the background colors, which display values of median age at the block group level. Median age increases from light green to dark blue.

Next, Ms. Mathis uses the Spatial Overlay tool of Business Analyst to assign values for household income, median age, average household size, educational attainment, home ownership, and Tapestry™ Segmentation segment classification for each customer. In this geodemographic overlay process each customer point on the map is assigned the values for these attributes based on the census block group in which it lies. Note, these values should not be seen as precise measures for each individual, but rather as estimates based on geographic distribution. They are useful for revealing general patterns across a large number of customers, but not the precise characteristics of individual customers.

Once the Spatial Overlay operation is performed, Ms. Mathis calculates a summary table, which displays average

TABLE 7.1   Demographic Profile of Nature's Beauty Loyalty Club Members

Tapestry™ Segmentation Neighborhood Segment	Nature's Beauty Loyalty Club Members	Minneapolis/ St. Paul Metropolitan Area
Median age	31.6	35.7
Median household income	$54,762	$71,394
Average household size	1.92	2.53
%Home ownership	42%	73%
% Some college education	68%	64%

values for these measures across the customer base, and a second summary table that displays the major Tapestry™ Segmentation segments to which her customers belong. Each is useful in learning more about her customers, their media exposure, and purchasing habits.

The demographic summary Table 7.1 allows Ms. Mathis to compare her best customers with the general population of the Minneapolis–St. Paul area and to identify their distinguishing demographic characteristics. As you can see, her customers tend to be younger, with smaller family size, and lower income and home ownership levels than the area as a whole.

The Tapestry™ Segmentation summary Table 7.2 identifies the most common Tapestry™ Segmentation segments among the store's customers. As these segments include housing,

TABLE 7.2   Tapestry™ Segmentation Composition of High Purchases Segment

Tapestry™ Segmentation Neighborhood Segment	% of Nature's Beauty Loyalty Club Members	% of US Population
22: Metropolitans	26%	2.6%
27: Metro Renters	31%	2.3%
13: In Style	7%	6.1%
17: Green Acres	4%	8.7%
28: Aspiring Young Families	5%	6.1%
24: Main Street USA	2%	6.7%

[1]These figures are derived from the *2007 Community Tapestry Summary Table*, which is available as a pdf file as part of the Business Analyst Segmentation Module or from the Community Tapestry Demonstration CD. This CD is available at no charge from http://www.esri.com/data/community_data/community-tapestry/index.html

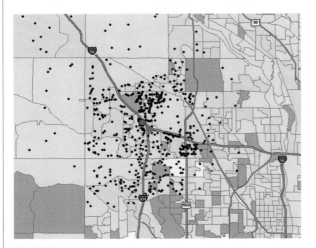

FIGURE 7.1

Nature's Beauty Loyalty Club Members

TABLE 7.3   **Tapestry™ Segmentation Composition of High Purchases Segment**

22 Metropolitans		27 Metro Renters		24 Main Street, USA	
Segment Number & Name	22 Metropolitans	**Segment Number & Name**	27 Metro Renters	**Segment Number & Name**	24 Main Street, USA
LifeMode Group	L3 Metropolis	**LifeMode Group**	L4 Solo Acts	**LifeMode Group**	L10 Traditional Living
Urbanization Group	U3 Metro Cities 1	**Urbanization Group**	U1 Principal Urban Centers 1	**Urbanization Group**	U5 Urban Outskirts 1
Household Type	Singles; Shared	**Household Type**	Singles; Shared	**Household Type**	Mixed
Median Age	37.1 Years	**Median Age**	33.6 Years	**Median Age**	36.3 Years
Income	Middle	**Income**	Middle	**Income**	Middle
Employment	Prof/Mgmt	**Employment**	Prof/Mgmt	**Employment**	Prof/Mgmt/ Skilled/Svc
Education	Some College; Bach/ Grad Degree	**Education**	Bach/Grad Degree	**Education**	Some College
Residential	Single Family; Multiunit	**Residential**	Multiunit Rental	**Residential**	Single Family; Multiunit
Race/Ethnicity	White	**Race/Ethnicity**	White; Asian	**Race/Ethnicity**	White
Preferences	Visit zoo, museum	**Preferences**	Travel by plane frequently	**Preferences**	Rent videos
	Have personal credit line		Track investments online		Own insured money mark
	Go rollerblading		Surf Internet/Shop online		Go bowling
	Listen to classical, news-talk radio		Watch Style, read fashion magazines		Watch 7th Heaven on TV
	Own/Lease station wagon		Rent car from Avis		Own/Lease compact car

spending, and lifestyle characteristics as well as demographic, they expand Ms. Mathis' understanding even further. The summary table reports the top five Tapestry™ Segmentation segments among club members, of which the top two segments account for about 57% of club members. The last segment listed, 24: Main Street USA, is a small component of the firm's customers, but is included for comparative purposes.

The value of the Tapestry™ Segmentation lifestyle segmentation system is that it reveals differences in beliefs, values, media exposure, purchasing patterns, and shopping activities that are not captured by purely demographic segmentation. In this case, the demographic profiles of the three segments, 22: Metropolitans, 27: Metro Renters, and 24: Main Street USA, are very similar. However, as you can see from the brief segment descriptions in Table 3, their purchasing patterns are quite different. By revealing these unique lifestyle characteristics, the Tapestry™ Segmentation system supports more precise targeting of marketing efforts.

The power of Tapestry™ Segmentation lifestyle segmentation is enhanced when integrated with the Market Potential

Index (MPI). MPIs are based on consumer research performed annually by MediaMark Research. They report the relative frequency with which different Tapestry™ Segmentation segments engage in specific behaviors. As Ms. Mathis is interested in newspaper readership, radio listening, and Internet shopping behaviors, these are the indexes reported in Table 7.4 on the next page. The numbers are reported as an index which reflects the behavior of that segment relative to the nation as a whole. In the "Heavy newspaper reader" row, the value of 126 for the Metropolitans segment indicates that these households are 26% more likely to be heavy newspaper readers than national households as a whole. Conversely, the value of 99 for the Main Street USA segment indicates that these households are 1% less likely than national households to do so.

Review these values relative to Ms. Mathis' research questions 3 and 4. Note as well the significant differences in media and shopping behavior between the two dominant segments in the Nature's Beauty Club and the third segment, Main Street USA. Recall that these segments have quite similar demographic profiles. Thus, for Ms. Mathis, Tapestry™

TABLE 7.4   Relevant MPI Values for Nature's Beauty Tapestry™ Segmentation Segments

Market Potential Indices: Media and Internet Buying	Tapestry™ Segmentation Segment		
	22 Metropolitans	27 Metro Renters	24 Main Street USA
Media			
Heavy newspaper reader	126	169	99
Read newspaper: business/finance section	129	105	95
Read newspaper: editorial page section	131	87	110
Read newspaper: movie listings/reviews section	120	126	114
Read newspaper: science technology section	127	121	107
Read newspaper: travel section	133	124	93
Light radio listener	88	143	87
Light-medium radio listener	112	96	98
Heavy radio listener	90	88	122
Radio format listen to: alternative	172	179	138
Radio format listen to: classical	275	197	99
Radio format listen to: news talk	209	123	111
Radio format listen to: public	240	245	69
Internet			
Use Internet more than once a day	163	220	86
Internet last 30 days: made personal purchase	154	193	91
Spent on Internet orders last 12 months: $500+	144	165	89

Source: ESRI Tapestry™ Segmentation Demonstration CD, 2005.

Segmentation lifestyle segmentation provides crucial insight into the values and behaviors of her customers that is not revealed in demographic statistics alone.

Finally, Ms. Mathis wishes to learn if there are concentrations of prospective customers in the Minneapolis–St. Paul area which match this customer profile. She uses the Customer Prospecting tool in Business Analyst to create a complex query which seeks out block groups whose characteristics fit the profile. These block groups are displayed on the map in Figure 7.2. Note that several such concentrations exist, but that they are widely distributed around the metropolitan area. This indicates that Ms. Mathis' plan to serve these potential customers through local media advertising and Web purchasing is a more cost-effective way to test this market than would be the alternative approach of opening several new stores.

To summarize, integrated Business GIS in the form of Business Analyst allowed Ms. Mathis to answer each of her research questions. To wit, her customers are younger than the metropolitan average with smaller household size and lower income and home ownership levels. Over half of them are in two Tapestry™ Segmentation segments, Metropolitans and Metro Renters. These segments are heavy newspaper readers and share interest in the movie listing, technology and travel sections. While they are moderate radio listeners, they listen to two formats, classical and public radio, frequently. They are heavy Internet users and purchasers, very willing to purchase products online. Finally, there are some concentrations of similar potential customers in several block groups distributed across the Minneapolis–St. Paul area.

On the basis of this analysis, Ms. Mathis concludes that her planned initiative is well suited to reaching and serving these customers and decides to proceed with its implementation.

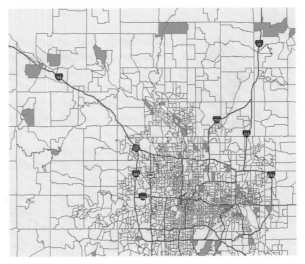

FIGURE 7.2

Block Groups Matching the Nature's Beauty Customer Profile

MARKETING RESEARCH INSIGHT   Practical Application

7.3 Nielsen Claritas Standardized Services for Market Segmentation

Since 1971, Nielsen Claritas (formerly Claritas Inc.) has been the preeminent source of accurate, up-to-date marketing information about people, households, and businesses within any geographic area in the United States. Its target marketing services are aimed at reducing the cost of customer acquisition and at growing customer value. Nielsen Claritas offers industry-leading consumer segmentation systems, consulting services, and software applications for site analysis, advertising sales, and customer targeting. Nielsen Claritas is part of the Nielsen Company, a global information and media company with leading market positions and recognized brands in marketing information (Nielsen), media information (Nielsen Media Research), business publications (*Billboard*, *The Hollywood Reporter*, *Adweek*), and trade shows. To learn more about Nielsen Claritas and Nielsen products and services visit their websites at www.claritas.com and www.nielsen.com.

With information generated through its segmentation systems and databases, Nielsen Claritas enables businesses to address key marketing issues, such as:

- Who are my best customers and prospects?
- How many are there and where do they live?
- What is the most effective way to reach them?

- Which markets, locations, or industries offer the most potential?
- How should I allocate marketing resources to maximize my return on investment?

Nielsen Claritas Products Used for Market Segmentation:

PRIZM   Defines every neighborhood in the United States at the household level in terms of 66 demographically and behaviorally distinct segments. A precision tool for lifestyle segmentation and analysis, PRIZM offers an easy way to identify, understand, and target consumers.

P$YCLE   A market segmentation system that differentiates households in terms of financial behavior. The 58-segment system predicts which households will use which types of financial/insurance products and services.

ConneXions   A classification of all U.S. households into 53 consumer segments with 10 lifestage groups to help telecommunications, Internet, cable, and satellite companies better target their rapidly expanding services.

By permission, Nielsen Claritas

consumers making up those segments. Marketing Research Insight 7.3 gives you some background information on Nielsen Claritas and describes some of its standardized services that can be used for market segmentation.

At the beginning of the chapter, we mentioned ESRI's Tapestry™ Segmentation system. ESRI® leads the global software industry in geographic information system (GIS) technology, with annual sales of more than $660 million. ESRI offers clients a market segmentation system called Tapestry Segmentation. ESRI's Tapestry Segmentation divides U.S. residential ZIP codes into 65 segments based upon selected demographic and socioeconomic characteristics. A couple of examples of the 65 segments are:[10]

Tapestry Segmentation divides U.S. residential neighborhoods into 65 distinctive segments based upon selected demographic and socioeconomic characteristics.

Top Rung   Mature, highly educated, and the wealthiest consumer market. Median age is 42.4 years; married, half households with children and half without. Only 1% of all U.S. families fall into this group. They purchase financial instruments such as stocks; they invest in home upkeep, often hiring contractors for remodeling; and own new imported luxury cars. High incidence of travel. Shop at Nordstrom's, Macy's and Eddie Bauer; purchase online and make heavy use of cell phones. Avid readers of newspapers, books and magazines. Prefer news/talk radio and watch MSNBC, The Golf Channel, CNBC, CNN, and subscribe to HBO and Showtime.

Aspiring Young Families   Young, start-up families with a mix of married couples with children or singles with children. Median age is 30.6. Ethnically diverse, most are white; 17% are black and 17% are Hispanic. About 22% have a college degree. High incidence in South and Southwest with concentrations in California, Texas and Florida. Spend baby products, children's toys and home furnishings. High use of theme parks, fish, lift weights, play basketball and visit chatrooms online. They enjoy courtroom TV shows and urban radio. Prefer family restaurants such as Tony Roma's and IHOP. Use fast foods such as Checkers and Jack-in-the-Box.

Given these descriptions, you can see how beneficial it would be to marketers to know which Tapestry Segmentation segments account for a dominant share of their target market. Knowing where these segments are located, even at the ZIP code level, knowing their demographics, knowing their media habits and purchasing preferences would give marketers keen insight into their target markets.

Visit ESRI at www.esri.com.

Conducting Market Tracking

By **tracking studies** we mean studies that monitor, or track, a variable over time. For example, companies conduct market tracking to track sales of their brands as well as sales of competitors' brands over time.[11] The "tracks" movement up and down or remaining stable serves as an important monitor of how the market is reacting to a firm's marketing mix. Many variables may be monitored in a tracking study, including market share, customer satisfaction levels, measures of promotional spending, prices, stockouts, inventory levels, and so on.

Tracking studies are those that monitor, or track, a variable such as sales or market share over time.

You may ask why a company needs to know what its own sales are. Wouldn't a company know, through sales receipts, how much it has sold of a particular product? Although a company may monitor its own sales, sales measured by a firm's own sales receipts provide an incomplete picture. By monitoring only its own sales, a firm does not know what is going on in the channel of distribution. Products are not distributed instantaneously. Rather, inventories are built up and depleted at various rates among the different distributors. Just because household sales of a product increase does not mean that a producer will experience a sales increase for that product. To really know what is happening in the industry, marketers need to monitor the movement of goods at the retail level. Recognizing this need, market tracking is conducted at both the retail-store level and at the household level. And tracking studies, as noted, also provide data on competitors' brands that otherwise would not be available to management. So, for these reasons, tracking studies are an important service provided by research firms.[12] Data are collected by scanners and by retail-store audits. We provide examples of each in the following sections.

Tracking studies can tell a firm how well its own products are selling in retail outlets around the world and also provide sales data on competitors' products.

MARKET TRACKING AT THE RETAIL LEVEL. **Nielsen Scantrack Services.**[13]   The Scantrack service is based on syndicated retail **scanning data** and is recognized as an industry standard in terms of providing tracking data gathered from stores' scanners. Each week, Nielsen collects information on millions of purchases of millions of unique items from thousands of stores—14,000+ food stores, 18,000+ drug stores, 3,000+ mass merchandisers, 2,500+ convenience stores, 450+ liquor stores, 140+ warehouse/club stores, 35+ dollar stores, plus many more collected through retailer censuses. Nielsen Scantrack Services tracks thousands of products as they move through retail stores, allowing brand managers to monitor sales and market share and to evaluate marketing strategies. Scantrack reports can be provided at many different levels of information. For example, a report may be ordered for just one category of products across the 52 U.S. markets. Or a report can be generated for one brand in a single market.

Nielsen's Scantrack services provide firms with tracking data based on scanner-collected data. Visit Nielsen at www.nielsen.com.

IRI's InfoScan Custom Store Tracking provides firms with tracking data based on scanner-collected data. Visit IRI at www.infores.com.

InfoScan Custom Store Tracking. **Information Resources, Inc. (IRI)** syndicated data service, **InfoScan Custom Store Tracking**, gathers data from scanners in supermarkets, drugstores, and mass merchandisers. InfoScan collects data weekly in over 32,000 stores and provides subscribers access to information across many InfoScan categories. Data may be analyzed across major categories as well.[14]

The primary advantage of scanning data is that the data are available very quickly to decision makers. There is a minimum delay from the time the data are collected and the time the information is available. The disadvantage is that a company may have products distributed through smaller stores that do not have scanners. This was the case a few years ago when demand for natural and organic foods began to grow. These foods were distributed through small stores, mostly independently owned and without scanners. Since this emerging market was not served by the large scanner-based services, a new firm, SPINS, emerged to track sales of natural and organic foods. Today, of course, these foods are distributed through traditional food retailers and SPINS is associated with The Neilsen Company.

Visit SPINS at www.spins.com.

In retail-store audits, auditors record merchandising information needed for tracking studies.

Retail-Store Audits. Some tracking services do not rely solely on data collected in retail stores by scanners. They use **retail-store audits** as well. In retail-store audits, auditors are sent to stores to record merchandising information needed for tracking studies. Store audits are particularly useful for smaller stores that do not have scanner equipment, such as convenience stores. Sales are estimated by calculating the following:

$$\text{Beginning Inventory} + \text{Purchases Received} - \text{Ending Inventory} = \text{Sales}$$

Auditors not only record this information for many products but also note other merchandising factors, such as the level and type of in-store promotions, newspaper advertising, out-of-stock products, and shelf facings of products. Like data collected by scanning services, data collected by audit are stored in a common database and made available to all who subscribe.

Information for tracking studies is gathered in homes using scanning devices or through the use of diaries and even home audits.

MARKET TRACKING AT THE HOUSEHOLD LEVEL. Information is gathered in homes using scanning devices, diaries, and audits. In-home scanner devices are provided to panel members who agree to scan the UPC codes on products they have purchased. Other services ask panel members to record purchases in diaries that are subsequently mailed back to the research firm. Finally, a few research firms collect data by actually sending auditors into homes to count and record information. Almost all of these methods rely on consumer household panels whose members are recruited for the purpose of recording and reporting their household purchases to one of the standardized data services firms. We shall give you some examples of each.

IRI's ScanKey Consumer Network Household Panel has members who scan products they purchase and send the data back to IRI to be used in tracking studies.

IRI ScanKey Consumer Network Household Panel. IRI (*Information Resources, Inc.*) also maintains a panel of consumer households that record purchases at outlets by scanning UPC codes on the products purchased. Using IRI's handheld ScanKey scanning wand, panel members record their purchases, and this information is transmitted via telephone link back to IRI. In the summer of 2005, IRI had 70,000 shoppers as part of its consumer panel. Like many panels, an advantage of this panel is that it provides not only information on products purchased but also purchase data that are linked to the demographics of the purchasers.[15]

Nielsen Homescan Panel. The **Homescan® Panel** recruits panel members who use handheld scanners to scan all bar-coded products purchased and brought home from all outlets, from grocery stores to wholesale clubs to convenience stores. Panel members also record the outlet at which all the merchandise was purchased and which family member made the purchase, as well as price and promotion information such as coupon usage. The

Homescan Panel consists of households that are demographically and geographically balanced and projectable to the total United States. In addition, local markets can be tracked. Nielsen's Worldwide Panel Service also provides home tracking services for 26 countries around the world.

Diary.   The use of diaries to collect data appears to be decreasing. This is likely due to falling response rates. Consumers seem to be less willing to complete diaries recording their purchases or media habits. However, some companies still offer tracking data collected in this way. Each panel member is asked to complete a **diary** containing such information as the type of product, name brand, manufacturer or producer, model number, description, purchase price, store from which the item was purchased, and information about the person making the purchase. This information can then be used to estimate important factors such as market share, brand loyalty, brand switching, and demographic profile of purchasers. The panel members are typically balanced geographically in terms of the overall United States and regions of the United States. Nielsen Media Research uses diaries to collect data on television viewing, and Arbitron, the radio ratings company, uses diaries to collect data. We will discuss both of these services in greater depth in a later section of this chapter.

Learn more about Nielsen's Homescan Panel at www.nielsen.com.

Audit.   Some companies conduct an **audit**, collecting data from households by sending auditors into homes. NPD's Complete Kitchen Audit records ingredients, kitchen utensils, and appliances in homes. The information is provided to manufacturers of kitchen products and to food producers.[16]

Some firms collect tracking data by sending auditors into panel members' homes to actually count and record data.

TURNING MARKET TRACKING INFORMATION INTO INTELLIGENCE. One of the disadvantages of today's information technology is that a user of information can easily be swamped with information, producing "information overload." You can imagine the quantity of information that could flow to a manufacturer who subscribes to tracking data. The information flows in frequently and in large quantities. Various companies have created a host of products to help decision makers use vast quantities of information to make intelligent decisions. Variously labeled "decision support systems," "data mining systems," "expert systems," and the like, these systems use analytical tools to attach meaning to data, allowing managers to make decisions in response to quickly changing market conditions. Some examples include **IRI's Builder Suite**™[17] and **Nielsen's Category Business Planner**.

Category Business Planner is a Web-based category planning tool that aids managers in making better decisions based on sales information about products in the consumer packaged goods industry. What is unique about Category Business Planner is that it allows a manufacturer to move from retailer to retailer to view how its product is performing within each retailer's proprietary view of the category containing the product. This allows a manufacturer to evaluate product performance the same way a retail customer would evaluate the manufacturer's product, allowing the manufacturer to better collaborate with retailers when developing business plans for each product category.[18]

Monitoring Media Usage and Promotion Effectiveness

Business firms typically conduct studies to measure their effectiveness, readership, listenership, and so on. This information is useful to firms contemplating advertising expenditures. To serve the need for some objective measure of promotional effectiveness, several syndicated data service companies have evolved over the years to supply such information to subscribing firms. Some of these services specialize in a particular medium; a few others conduct studies on several forms of media. A discussion of both types of these organizations follows.

TRACKING DOWNLOADED MUSIC, VIDEOS, AND RECORDED BOOKS. Nielsen's **SoundScan** tracks music and music video products downloaded online from several online music stores, such as Apple's iTunes, throughout the U.S. and Canada.[19] Likewise, Nielsen's sister company **VideoScan**, integrates point-of-sale data collected by both companies to provide information on sales of VHS and DVD videos.[20] **BookScan U.S.A.**, part of The Nielsen Company tracks the sale of over 300,000 different titles weekly. The company also has global operations as **BookScan United Kingdom, BookScan Australia,** and **BookScan New Zealand**.[21]

TELEVISION. The **Nielsen Television Index (NTI)** has been the major provider of TV ratings since 1950. Nielsen Media Research, owned by The Nielsen Company, is the provider of NTI. Television ratings data are reported by **DMAs (designated market areas)**, which were designed by The Nielsen Company to represent areas of the various geographical TV markets. There are 210 DMAs in the United States.[22]

nielsen

● ● ● ● ● ● ● ● ● ●

The Nielsen Company is a global information and media company with leading market positions in marketing and consumer information, television and other media measurement, online intelligence, mobile measurement, trade shows, and business publications (*Billboard, The Hollywood Reporter, Adweek*). The privately held company is active in more than 100 countries, with headquarters in New York, USA. For more information, visit www.nielsen.com. By permission, The Nielsen Company.

Arbitron provides syndicated data on radio station listening through representative samples of each local market it surveys. Those selected for the sample record their radio listening in diaries. Arbitron's Portable People Meter automatically records any encoded medium to which a person carrying the meter is exposed.

Few TV watchers have been unaffected by the Nielsen Television Index. Favorite shows have been canceled or, because the index showed a large audience, shows have run for many years. Obviously, firms in the TV industry are constantly trying to achieve higher viewership than their competition. High viewership allows them to charge higher prices for advertisements during the more popular programs.

In most DMAs, Nielsen Media Research uses a diary in which families record their television viewing habits. However, in 56 DMAs, television viewing is measured with the **people meter**, an electronic instrument that automatically measures when a TV set is on and who is watching which channel. Family members are asked to enter their names (by codes) into the people meter each time they watch TV. Data from the people meter are transmitted directly back to Nielsen, allowing the firm to develop estimates of the size of the audience for each program by reporting the percentage of TV households viewing a given show.[23] NTI reports a rating and a share for each program telecast. A rating is the percentage of households that have at least one set tuned to a given program for a minimum of 6 minutes for each 15 minutes the program is telecast. A share is the percentage of households with at least one set tuned to a specific program at a specific time.

The Nielsen Television Index also provides subscribers with other audience characteristic information that allows potential advertisers to select audiences that most closely match their target market's characteristics. Ratings are reported by the number of households, by whether women are employed outside the home, by age group for women (18+, 18–24, 18–34, 18–49, 25–54, 35–64, 55+), by age group for men (18+, 18–34, 18–49, 25–54, 35–65, 55+), and by age group of children (children ages 2 and older, ages 6 to 11, and teenagers).[24]

RADIO. Since 1964, radio listenership has been measured by **Arbitron Inc.** The company's national and local market samples complete diaries reporting radio listening for one week. Each local market survey is comprised of 12 weeks worth of diaries from each market. Diary keepers indicate the time of day; how long the station was tuned in; which station was on; where the listening was done (at home, in a car, at work, or other place); and the panel member's age, race/ethnicity, and gender. Although paper-and-pencil diaries are still in use, Arbitron's passive metering system, the **Portable People Meter (PPM^{SM})** system, is being used in several of the larger markets in the United States and Arbitron is aggressively moving it into additional markets.[25] The meter is the size of a mobile phone and automatically records stations listened to. (We have more to say about the PPM in the upcoming section on multimedia services.)

Data from the diaries are used to measure and report a number of variables indicative of radio listenership. Listenership is measured in 15-minute intervals and data are also reported by age and gender to aid in profiling audience characteristics. Subscribers to Arbitron Radio Market Reports can view the data electronically via software and select the output formats in which they wish to view the data. How can radio stations and businesses use this information to formulate marketing strategy? For instance, knowing where a person is listening may affect the type of message an advertiser will use. A station with a high concentration of in-car listening may appeal to car dealers, auto parts stores, transmission repair shops, and tire stores. Understanding where the listening occurs is also helpful in determining programming elements, such as traffic reports, contests, newscasts, and other information and entertainment segments. Arbitron also conducts other customized marketing research studies to suit individual clients' needs.[26]

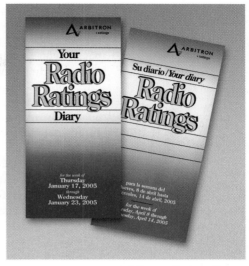

Arbitron collects radio listening data using both diaries and their Portable People Meter.
By permission.

PRINT. MRI's Starch Readership Service is known as the most widely used source for measuring the extent to which magazine ads are seen and read. Starch conducts personal interviews on a given issue of a magazine, trade publication, or newspaper. Starch readership studies are not designed to determine the number of readers who read a particular issue of a magazine. Rather, Starch determines what readers saw and read in a study issue when they first looked through it. MRI (Mediamark Research & Intelligence) Starch allows advertisers to measure impact, branding, and reader involvement. The service also allows access to several other services that provide clients with feedback about the performance of individual ads.

In addition to evaluating individual ads, Starch also analyzes the impact of many other variables on readership, such as ad size, number of pages, effect of black and white and color, special position (cover, center spread, etc.), and product category, among several others.[27] To further help marketers make decisions about what comprises a good ad, Starch also provides another syndicated data service called Adnorms. **Adnorms** provides readership scores by type of ad. Data are based upon 37,000 advertisements across 840 issues of more than 125 consumer magazines and business and

MRI's Starch Readership service provides syndicated data on magazine readership. Visit MRI Starch Readership Service at www.mediamark.com, and go to "Starch." While you are there, take a look at all the standardized services provided by MRI Starch.

The Portable People Meter is designed to be carried by panel members and records encoded signals from different media. The PPM allows Arbitron to measure media exposure to a variety of different media whether the panelist is in or out of the home.

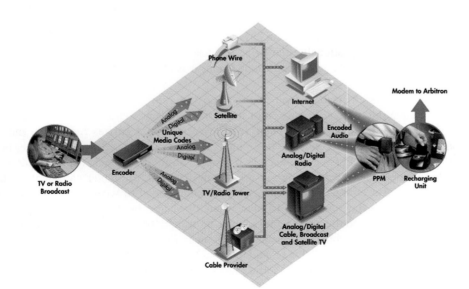

trade publications. For example, Adnorms could calculate the average readership scores for one-page, four-color computer ads appearing in *Business Week*. This allows advertisers to compare their ad scores with the norm. Adnorms lists rankings of magazines based upon engagement criteria and identifies the publications likely to generate word of mouth. In this way, subscribers can assess advertising effectiveness. Users learn the effect of ad size, color, and even copy on readership.[28] MRI Starch also does **Cover Testing, Editorial Tracking**, which identifies whether the types of editorial matter or columns read are closely aligned with a client's target market, and conducts studies of **Internet advertising**.

CONSUMER-GENERATED MEDIA. Consumer-generated media (CGM) is content created by consumers in blogs, discussion boards, forums, user groups, and other social media platforms, which post and make publicly available opinions, comments, and personal experiences on a wide range of issues, including products and brands. CGM is also referred to as *online consumer word of mouth* or *online consumer buzz*. This is a fast-growing form of media. Consumers, who value non-marketer-controlled sources of information, often seek opinion, recommendations, and product reviews from CGM. Companies desiring to keep track of the "buzz" going on in CGM about their own brands and those of their competitors may purchase a service such as BuzzMetrics from The Nielsen Company.[29] Read more about BuzzMetrics in Marketing Research Insight 7.4.

MULTIMEDIA. Some standardized information firms provide information on a number of media. **Simmons National Consumer Study** interviews about 25,000 adult consumers annually to gather information on media usage linked to product usage for over 8,000 brands. Quarterly reports reveal that media habits are related to product usage in over 450 product categories, such as apparel, automotive, computers, and travel. In addition, the company collects psychographic and demographic data. This information allows users to determine the viewing/listening media habits of users of certain product categories and brands.[30]

Earlier we discussed Arbitron in relation to radio. But Arbitron's Portable People Meter (PPM) also measures multimedia usage, including not just radio but TV, satellite radio, and the Web. The company's development of the PPM could prove to be a significant innovation in today's world, where consumers are exposed to a variety of media types in a variety of locations other than in their own living rooms. The PPM has been under development since 1992, and Arbitron has been testing the device extensively.[31] It is currently being used internationally; the BBM in Canada, for example, is using the PPM to measure French-language television. In addition, it is being used in Belgium, Norway, Singapore, and Kenya.

The PPM system is based on an encoder at a radio or television station that embeds a code into the audio portion of the signal. The encoders can also be used for audio streaming over the Web. When a survey respondent carries the meter and is exposed to a medium's broadcast, the meter captures the code identifying the exposure. Additional encoders can be used at stations with multiple feeds (digital and analog). Since the codes for the different media are different, the meter can identify the platform. In the evening, respondents, who are encouraged to wear the PPM a minimum of 8 hours a day, are asked to place their PPM in a base unit that recharges it and records the data collected so that it may be transmitted via modem to Arbitron. The PPM may allow Arbitron to measure audiences for radio, television, cable, satellite, video games, CDs, VCR tapes, and even audio on the Internet. With recent technological advances making more media alternatives available (more channels on TV,

Powerful messages are mediated through the Web in the form of blogs, recommendations on websites, viral videos, discussion forums, and so on. Companies can keep track of what is being said about them and their products by subscribing to services such as BuzzMetrics.

Simmons National Consumer Study gathers information on media usage linked to product usage. You can learn more about the services provided by Simmons by going to www.smrb.com/.

Arbitron's Portable People Meter (PPM) could prove to be a significant innovation in today's world, where consumers are exposed to a variety of media types in a variety of locations other than in their own living rooms.

MARKETING RESEARCH INSIGHT   Practical Application

7.4 What Is the *Buzz* About Your Company's Brand? Nielsen Online's BuzzMetrics® Service Can Tell You!

What is CGM? Consumer-generated media. It is the name given by Nielsen to describe the tremendous growth of online content, opinion, recommendations, word-of-mouth behavior, and buzz! CGM has been recognized as the fastest-growing media and it is unique in that consumers create it and share it among themselves. Powerful messages are mediated through the Web in the form of blogs, recommendations on websites, viral videos, discussion forums, and so on. But how can a company keep track of what is being said about them and their products? Are there negatives being disseminated? Are there

Source: www.nielsen-online.com. By permission.

advocates for the company and its products? Nielsen provides this information through the marketing research service **BuzzMetrics®**, which offers a suite of products such as BrandPulse®, Brand Association Map®, and BlogPulse®.

By using their proprietary data-mining technology, BuzzMetrics® can draw on millions of forums, discussion boards, and blogs to answer important questions for clients such as:

How do consumers feel about your brand—across a time horizon and in real time?
How many consumers are talking online, and how many other consumers are influenced by the conversation?
What specific issues are being discussed? What issues are coming around the corner?

Nielsen Online's BuzzMetrics® services can help firms identify threats as well as opportunities. For example, a Brand Association Map® can identify hostile threats associated with a client's brand or positive associations with the brand being made by third parties about whom the client has no knowledge. BlogPulse® allows client firms to track trends in the conversations occurring over millions of blogs. Through BuzzMetrics® services, client firms can keep up with what is going on in the world of CGM not only for their products/brands but those of their competitors as well.

satellite radio, wireless Internet, and so on), there is a growing demand for multimedia measurement services.[32]

SINGLE-SOURCE DATA

Single-source data are recorded continuously from a panel of respondents to measure their exposure to promotional materials (usually, TV as well as in-store promotions) and subsequent buying behavior. Armed with this information, marketers know whether consumers who saw one of their ads actually bought their product.

Several technological developments have led to the growth of single-source data, including the universal product code (UPC) and scanning equipment that electronically records and stores data gathered at the point of purchase. As we shall explain in the following paragraphs, when coupled with computer and MIS technology, powerful "single-source" databases can be built that are capable of providing a wealth of information on consumer purchases down to the UPC level.

Single-source data are data that contain information on several variables such as promotional message exposure, demographics, and buyer behavior. Single-source data can help managers determine causal relationships between types of promotions and sales. Although scanner-based databases can provide up-to-the-minute reports on the sale of virtually any consumer product by store, date, time of day, price, and so on,

Single-source data are data that contain information on several variables such as promotional message exposure, demographics, and buyer behavior. Single-source data can help managers determine causal relationships between types of promotions and sales.

Synthesize Your Learning

This exercise will require you to take into consideration concepts and material from the following chapters:

Chapter 4: Defining the Problem and Determining Research Objectives
Chapter 5: Understanding Research Design
Chapter 6: Using Secondary Data and Online Information Databases
Chapter 7: Comprehending Standardized Information Sources

J. J. Yarbrough of SBD Research had just completed the response to an RFP submitted by Advanced Automotive Concepts (AAC). AAC was interested in determining consumer response to several different vehicle designs because it was considering different types of automobiles and wanted some information on which direction consumers were likely to move. Historically, American consumers had swept up large SUVs and luxury cars from the market. AAC wanted some sense of the likelihood that consumers would actually switch demand to totally different vehicles that were almost "scooter-like" in terms of size and mpg ratings. A key issue for J. J. had been to determine how to measure consumer reaction. She had proposed measuring the construct "intention to buy" on a 7-point scale ranging from 1 "Very Unlikely to Buy" to 7 "Very Likely to Buy." J. J. worked in the automotive division of SBD research and had overseen in the past several dozen other studies measuring consumer preferences for different types of automobiles for other clients. On most of these studies she had used the same scale to measure "intention to buy."

J. J. had proposed surveying a population of potential automobile buyers to collect her "intention to buy" data. However, she had also proposed some studies that should be conducted prior to the survey that would help identify how consumers are currently thinking about autos. She wanted to do this because several environmental changes were greatly impacting the consumer's buying processes. Namely, the threat of global warming, the need to become energy independent, the escalating cost of gasoline, and the "green" movement. In years past, the percentage of consumers who had these concerns was miniscule—hence Americans' fascination with Hemis, SUVs, and Hummers. J. J. knew it would be important to get a deeper understanding of what consumers are thinking today. Most of the information about all these concerns—global warming, energy independence—J. J. had learned through the media. She knew she needed some first-hand consumer knowledge.

1. If her RFP response is accepted, how should J. J. establish an "action standard" for her 7-point scale? In other words, at what mean score should she recommend that AAC actually consider a proposed vehicle for manufacture and distribution?

2. In terms of research design, what design should J. J. use for a survey to measure "intention to buy" different models proposed by AAC? What design would be appropriate for the other studies J. J. felt were needed in order to get a current fix on what consumers' thoughts are regarding automobiles today?

3. What kind of secondary information do you think would be helpful to J. J. to better understand the current automobile customer?

4. Let's assume that J. J.'s firm, SBD Research, gets the contract from AAC and delivers a report that clearly identifies which proposed models have high "intention to buy" scores, that is, meet or exceed the action standard. Additionally, the SBD report clearly identifies the basic personality types most attracted to the different models with high "intention to buy" scores. Are there any standardized services that SBD Research should consider recommending to AAC that would help determine where these different consumer groups live and what their media preferences are?

these same powerful databases cannot tell anything about *who* bought the product. However, there are several marketing research services, such as IRI's BehaviorScan™, that can supply demographic data on purchasers.

BehaviorScan is a standardized service made up of panels of consumers in several cities around the United States who are provided with an electronic card that is scanned as they check out of participating retailers. BehaviorScan can control TV ads sent to its panel members. Knowing which ads panelists have been exposed to and also which products these same panelists have purchased gives BehaviorScan subscribers access to powerful causal data. Thus, from a single data source, a marketer may obtain information about media exposure as well as purchases. With single-source data, marketers not only have the ability to determine who is purchasing what, when, and where, but also know the media and in-store promotions to which the buyers were exposed. Therefore, from this one database (single-source) marketers should have the ability to answer cause-and-effect questions concerning how marketing mix variables actually affect sales.

Recently, we have witnessed growth in DVR services such as TiVo. **TiVo** offers compilations of reports to advertisers, including who is watching, who is interacting, and who is avoiding certain ads. Second-by-second information is also available through TiVo's Audience Research and Measurement (ARM) data. TiVo and IRI have now joined forces to produce consumer reports that compare the purchasing behavior of DVR households and non-DVR households. The IRI BehaviorScan-DVR also measures the effects of DVR's on advertising effectiveness.[33]

When the concept of single-source data was introduced several years ago, some thought it would revolutionize the marketing research industry. Others believed that it would not be so revolutionary and that there would always be a place for traditional marketing research studies. Today, single-source studies are a small part of the total, but their number is growing. ITV's tvSPAN, for example, recently expanded its single-source service from 750 households to 3,000 households.[34] As technology improves and as these systems earn the confidence of users, we are likely to see an even greater increase in single-source services.[35]

IRI's BehaviorScan is an example of a standardized service source for single-source data.

Although single-source data services have not replaced traditional marketing research studies during the past decade, their use is increasing.

Summary

Standardized information is a type of secondary data in which the data collected and/or the process of collecting the data are standardized for all users. There are two classes of standardized information. Syndicated data collected in a standard format and made available to all subscribing users. An example would be the Nielsen TV ratings. Standardized services offer a standardized marketing research process that is used to generate information for a particular user. Tapestry™ Segmentation is a system of classifying residential neighborhoods by ZIP codes into 65 different segments. That process is standardized; it is the same for all users. The information from the process is then applied to generate different data for each user. Syndicated data are the same for each user; standardized services use the same process of generating data for each user.

Syndicated data have the advantages of sharing the costs of obtaining the data among all those subscribing to the service, high data quality, and the speed with which data are collected and distributed to subscribers. Disadvantages are that buyers cannot control what data are collected, must commit to long-term contracts, and gain no strategic information advantage because the information is available to all competitors.

The advantages of standardized services are the supplier firm's expertise in the area, reduced cost, and speed with which supplier firms can perform the service. The disadvantages of standardized services are that the process cannot easily be customized, and the supplier firm may not know the idiosyncrasies of the industry in which the client firm operates.

Four major areas in which standardized information sources may be applied are measuring consumers' attitudes and opinions, defining market segments in both the industrial/business-to-business markets and the consumer market, conducting market tracking studies, and monitoring media usage and promotion effectiveness. The Harris poll is an example of a syndicated data source providing information on consumers' attitudes and opinions. Many firms offer standardized services that define consumer market segments. Examples include ESRI's Tapestry™ Segmentation, Nielsen Claritas' PRIZM, and VALS. GIS, or geodemogrphic information services, allow for the analysis of markets in arbitrarily defined units. Nielsen's Scantrack Basic Services is an example of a syndicated data source for tracking the sales of consumer product goods sold in retail stores. Other standardized services track goods by collecting data from consumer households. Arbitron radio listenership studies are an example of a syndicated data source for monitoring radio listenership.

Single-source information sources use sales data recorded by scanners that record sales at the UPC level by brand, store, date, price, and so on. Those data are then coupled with information on the buyer's demographics and media exposure. Having information on who bought what, where, and when after being exposed to promotional materials in one single database may give marketers the ability to answer important cause-and-effect questions on, for example, which marketing mix variable X caused the sale of product Y. IRI's BehaviorScan is an example of a standardized service providing single-source information. Using BehaviorScan, marketers can test the effects of different TV campaigns as well as in-store promotional materials.

Key Terms

Standardized information 178
Syndicated data 178
Performer Q® 178
Standardized services 179
ESRI's Tapestry™ Segmentation 179
The Maritz® Poll 180
Yankelovich Monitor 180
Ipsos Global@dvisor® 181
Harris poll 181
Gallup poll 181
Dun & Bradstreet's D-U-N-S 184
Dun's Market Identifiers (DMI) 184
VALS 184
GeoVALS 184
U.S. VALS 184
Japan-VALS 184
U.K. VALS 184
Geodemographics 185
GIS 185
PRIZM 185
P$YCLE 190

ConneXions 190
Top Rung 190
Aspiring Young Families 191
Tracking studies 191
Nielsen Scantrack Services 191
Scanning data 191
Information Resources, Inc. (IRI) 192
InfoScan Custom Store Tracking 192
Retail-store audits 192
ScanKey Consumer Network
  Household Panel 192
Nielsen Homescan Panel 192
Diary 193
Audit 193
IRI's Builder Suite 193
Nielsen's Category Business
  Planner 193
SoundScan 194
VideoScan 194
BookScan U.S.A. 194
BookScan United Kingdom 194

BookScan Australia 194
BooksScan New Zealand 194
Nielsen Television Index (NTI) 194
DMAs (designated market
  areas) 194
People meter 194
Arbitron, Inc. 194
Portable People Meter
  (PPM) 194
MRI's Starch Readership
  Service 195
Adnorms 195
Cover Testing 196
Editorial Tracking 196
Internet advertising 196
Simmons National Consumer
  Study 196
BuzzMetrics 197
Single-source data 197
BehaviorScan 199
TiVo 199

Review Questions/Applications

1. What is meant by "standardized information"?
2. Distinguish between syndicated data and standardized services.
3. What are the advantages and disadvantages of syndicated data?
4. What are the advantages and disadvantages of standardized services?
5. Name four broad types of applications of standardized information and give an example of each.

6. Explain how the standardized service Dun's Market Identifiers (DMI) could be helpful in a marketing research application.
7. What is geodemography, and how can it be used in marketing decisions? Give an example.
8. Explain why VALS would be considered a standardized information service.
9. What are tracking studies? Give an example of how managers would use tracking study data.

10. Describe Nielsen's Scantrack Basic Services.
11. What is a panel that gathers information from consumers by asking them to scan the UPC codes (bar codes) on goods they purchase and bring home?
12. Explain how "information overload" of tracking information can be alleviated through software also offered as standardized services.
13. Name the standardized information services designed to gather data on downloaded music, prerecorded video sales, prerecorded book sales, and natural and organic food sales.
14. What company provides syndicated data on TV ratings?
15. What is the firm that is best known for conducting studies of radio listenership? Briefly describe the service it provides.
16. What is single-source data?
17. Go to the websites of three marketing research companies. Review their list of products and services offered. Which of these are standardized services? Syndicated data? Custom research offerings?
18. Imagine you are a potential franchisee for a coffee shop franchise. Discuss how you make use of the standardized service Tapestry™ Segmentation to help you make your decision about where to locate your franchise.

19. Review the kinds of information gathered by www.gallup.com. Go to the website and look at some of the former studies. How could a marketing manager use some of this information?
20. Using a search engine like Google, Yahoo, or AskJeeves, look up "GIS." Describe some of the applications of GIS that some of the sites describe.
21. Describe how a marketing manager could make use of single-source data to make (a) pricing decisions and (b) in-store promotions decisions.
22. Contact a radio or TV station or perhaps a newspaper in your town. Ask managers how they measure listenership, viewership, or readership and for what purposes they use this information. In most cases, these firms will be happy to supply you with a standard package of materials answering these questions.
23. Given what you know about syndicated services, which firm would you call on if you had the following information needs?

   a. You want to know which types of magazine ads have the largest readership.

   b. You wish to know how attitudes have changed on several topics over the last two decades.

   c. You wish to know sales of movie DVDs.

   d. You want to know how many people listen to which radio programs in your radio market.

CASE 7.1

ENTERTAINMENT RESEARCH

Television viewing is an important pastime for many across the United States. Over 110 million households have at least one television set, and the average viewer watches over four hours of television per day. Given these facts, it is important to understand how the television industry operates. Once dominated by the three major broadcast networks, which offered a limited number of viewing options in the 1970s and 1980s, the television industry has changed today; there are significantly more broadcast and cable channels with a vast amount of programming choices to attract different audiences.

Few viewers understand the intricacies of the television landscape and the television product, also known as programs. The television landscape comprises broadcast television networks (ABC, CBS, NBC, FOX, CW), local television stations (WMAR, KABC, etc.), basic cable television networks (MTV, Lifetime, etc.), and premium cable television networks (HBO, SHOWTIME, etc.). Broadcast television networks and local television stations license and schedule television programs that target a specific audience. While the broadcast networks target individual programs for specific audiences, each cable network (all the programs on the network) is positioned to attract a specified target audience. As a result, there is a television program for anyone, whether it be *Grey's Anatomy* on ABC for females, *The Office* on NBC for young professional males, *Family Guy* on FOX for college-aged males, *The Amazing Race* on CBS for families, or *Gossip Girls* on The CW for young females. In addition, a multitude of cable stations exist for anyone's tastes, from MTV for teens and young adults to The Tennis Channel for tennis enthusiasts to TV One for black baby boomers.

Anthony Patino, Assistant Professor of Marketing, Loyola Marymount University.

Velitchka D. Kaltcheva,
Assistant Professor of
Marketing, Loyola
Marymount University.

The responsibility of a broadcast television network executive, like Les Moonves from CBS, is to schedule programs to attract an audience. Selecting and scheduling a television program can be a difficult task for these television executives. They are faced with a multitude of options, including diverse genres (situation comedies, dramas, reality programs, etc.), different actors and actresses to star in these programs, and numerous time periods to consider. The majority of the executive's time and effort is given to prime-time programming on the broadcast television networks because such programming generates the greatest share of the revenue. For instance, a 30-second spot on American Idol in the 2007–2008 prime-time season cost advertisers as much as $700,000.[1] The prime-time period, for the majority of the United States, is Monday through Saturday from 8 pm to 11 pm and Sunday from 7 pm to 11 pm.

For example, for several seasons, *The Office* has been a successful program for NBC on Thursdays at 9 pm. Consequently, to gain a greater share of the revenue, executives at NBC need to find a compatible program after *The Office* to maintain the audience levels (audience flow). When developing scheduling strategies, executives must analyze trends, the competitive environment, star power, and compatible products. The five most popular scheduling strategies are:

1. Hammocking. In hammocking, two highly rated television programs are scheduled so as to sandwich a newer, less successful television program in the hope that the same audience will view all three programs. For example, in its freshman season *Worst Week* on CBS was hammocked between *Two and a Half Men* and *CSI: Miami* on Monday nights.
2. Tent-poling. In tent-poling, a very strong program is placed in the middle of the night's prime-time schedule (i.e., 9 pm). The purpose of this is to draw the audience to the earlier program and to retain it for the later program (a spillover effect). For instance, ABC's *Grey's Anatomy* was scheduled on Thursdays at 9 pm to benefit the 8 pm program *Ugly Betty* and the 10 pm program *Life on Mars*.
3. Flow. With flow, the highly rated program is scheduled for the start of the night's prime-time schedule, usually 8 pm. Television executives believe the audience will stay throughout the evening, maintaining the audience level. Fox schedules *American Idol* at 8 pm on Tuesdays for this purpose.
4. Blocking. In blocking, programs of the same genre or theme are scheduled together to maintain a consistent theme or brand. ABC was successful with *TGIF* in the 1980s and 1990s when it scheduled family situation comedies on Fridays, and NBC was equally strong when it scheduled *Must See TV* on Thursdays. Currently, NBC has returned to its Thursday comedy roots with its 8–10 pm comedy block during the 2008–2009 prime-time schedule with *My Name is Earl*, *30 Rock*, *The Office*, and *Kath and Kim*.
5. Counter-programming. In counter-programming, television executives review the schedules of the competition and schedule a series that is of a genre different from the competition in the time period. Thus, executives are attempting to provide alternatives in the hope of attracting audiences that cannot find anything suitable to watch on the other channels. For instance, CBS schedules a reality program, *Survivor*, on Thursdays to counter comedies and dramas on the competitor networks.

Using the strategies described above, television executives study audience viewership trends. These trends are both quantitative and qualitative. Quantitatively, Nielsen releases daily television ratings[2] across households and pivotal demographics, such as adults 18–49, a valuable target for advertisers. The household ratings and demographic ratings are published on several websites, including variety.com, hollywoodreporter.com, and mediaweek.com. Qualitatively, executives screen programs, regularly conduct personal interviews with viewers, and hold focus groups to search for new ideas and to solicit feedback on their programming schedules.

Your Assignment

For this project, you have been assigned as the assistant to the executive in charge of ABC-TV's prime-time schedule. Traditionally, Thursday night is one of the most important nights for all networks because movie studios tend to spend a significant portion of their advertising budgets on upcoming motion pictures to be released the next day (Friday) and retailers want to entice weekend

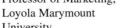

Annie H. Liu, Associate
Professor of Marketing,
Loyola Marymount
University.

[1]Advertising Age, December 17, 2007.

[2]A household television rating is the percentage of households in the United States viewing a particular program.

shoppers to their venues. Therefore, scheduling a programming lineup that appeals to a potential target audience for both weekend entertaining and weekend shopping is crucial in attracting advertisers to ensure a strong financial performance by the network.

Using data from Nielsen Entertainment available on websites (variety.com, hollywoodreporter.com, mediaweek.com) and personal interviews with relevant viewers, prepare a Thursday night prime-time schedule on ABC using each of the scheduling strategies mentioned above. All ABC programs on Thursday night have been reevaluated and can be rescheduled, except for *Grey's Anatomy*. The only television program options available to you are those currently broadcast on ABC, including the programs being reevaluated on Thursday night. (You can find all programs currently broadcast by the network on ABC.com.) You need to complete a schedule from 8 to 11 pm building on the most popular program on Thursday night, *Grey's Anatomy*. The programming time of *Grey's Anatomy* is flexible. When preparing the schedule, you need to consider popularity as measured by ratings, compatibility by genre, television program length (30 minutes or 60 minutes), as well as competitive broadcast network schedules (FOX.com, NBC.com, CBS.com, CW.com). In addition, when conducting personal interviews, it is important to select a relevant audience for the program. The following is an example of the ABC Thursday night prime-time programming schedule during the 2008–2009 season:

Time	Program
8:00 pm	*Ugly Betty (runs until 9 pm)*
8:30 pm	*Ugly Betty (runs until 9 pm)*
9:00 pm	*Grey's Anatomy (runs until 10 pm)*
9:30 pm	*Grey's Anatomy (runs until 10 pm)*
10:00 pm	*Life on Mars (runs until 11 pm)*
10:30 pm	*Life on Mars (runs until 11 pm)*

CASE 7.2

PREMIER PRODUCTS, INC.

Premier Products, Inc. (PPI) is a large, multinational firm with several product divisions, including foods, over-the-counter drugs, and household products. The firm has over 1,000 products and distributes through grocery stores, mass merchandisers, and convenience stores in the United States, Canada, and Western Europe. Products are marketed under different brand names but all are marked with the PPI family brand name. The company is headquartered in the United States and has six regional offices. There is a marketing research department with a staff of 26 people at company headquarters. The department is primarily responsible for quarterly reports and answering the information requests of divisional managers who are responsible for creating new products and ensuring profitable product performance. Each divisional manager, working with brand managers, develops his or her own marketing programs and makes all the decisions regarding product additions and deletions, pricing, distribution, and promotion of the different brands. PPI's V.P. of marketing research is Stephanie Williamson.

Dale Hair, division manager for the dairy foods line of products, met with Williamson to explain that she needed better information to help the company target customers for direct-mail campaigns consisting primarily of new-product awareness messages and cents-off coupons. Hair could describe the general demographic characteristics of her primary target market thanks to previously conducted marketing research. She needed help with this for the U.S. market.

Joy Schurr, a brand manager for a line of soups, was interested in knowing what was happening in terms of consumers' attitudes toward brand-name versus privately branded soups. PPI's brand, "Bowl-A-Soup," had been on the market for almost 35 years and was a well-established global brand. Schurr had been concerned about comments from many of the supermarket chain managers who were considering private brands. She wanted to know if consumer attitudes were shifting more in favor of private, usually less-expensive, brands versus national or global brands.

Lisa Henson, division manager, had a new product under development—a device for replacing light bulbs in ceiling fixtures that was simple to use and very effective. However, Henson was concerned that the distribution channel for this product would fall outside of PPI's present distribution network of supermarkets, mass merchandisers, and convenience stores. Although some of the company's mass-merchandiser customers would likely carry the product, she felt distribution would be too limited to ensure a profitable return. She was interested in knowing more about hardware stores as a possible distribution strategy for the new product. However, calling on hardware stores would be too expensive if PPI had only the one product to offer. Henson wanted to know if there were wholesalers of light bulbs and light-related products who called on hardware stores and other retail stores.

1. Should Stephanie Williamson assign any, or all, of these tasks to her 26-member staff?
2. Can you recommend a standardized information service that Williamson might consider for Dale Hair?
3. What would you recommend for Joy Schurr?
4. What would you recommend for Lisa Henson?

CASE 7.3 Your Integrated Case

ADVANCED AUTOMOBILE CONCEPTS

Nick Thomas of AAC was thinking ahead about the marketing of his new line of autos. He knew he couldn't rely on ZEN's existing knowledge of past consumers because his new models were going to be so different as to make any comparison erroneous. What he really needed was information on the different market segments that would be attracted to each model. Proposed models were very different, so Nick knew that he may have vastly different consumers as target markets for each model. Some models were almost "scooter-like" in nature, and others were larger models that had some similarities to some of today's foreign-car competitors, such as Toyota, Honda and Nissan.

Nick decided to contact ESRI and ask about how its standardized marketing segmentation service, Tapestry™ Segmentation, could be of help. Brent Roderick at ESRI explained the service to Nick. Brent showed Nick the following information, which depicted the general types of cars most preferred among different groupings of the 65 Tapestry segments.

Nick's interest peaked when Brent explained to him that any data collected on consumers showing their preferences or intent to buy the different proposed models could be used to determine which Tapestry™ Segments would be most associated with the target market for each vehicle model.

1. Explain how Tapestry™ Segmentation would actually work to identify the segments that would be most associated with each vehicle model.
2. Once Nick Thomas knew which Tapestry segments best described the target market for a certain vehicle, describe how this information could be used to market AAC automobiles.

Automotive Choices by Tapestry Segment

Own/Lease Luxury import with GPS

01 Top Rung
03 Conoisseurs

Own/Lease Luxury Car

15 Silver and Gold
38 Industrious Urban Fringe (SUV)
40 Military Proximity (SUV)

Own/Lease Minivan or SUV

02 Suburban Splendor
04 Boomburbs

Own/Lease Toyota

21 Urban Villages
23 Trendsetters (or Honda)
35 International Marketplace
47 Las Casas
55 College Towns

Own/Lease Station Wagon

22 Metropolitans
49 Senior Sun Seekers
58 NeWest Residents

Automotive Choices by Tapestry Segment

07 Exubanites
18 Cozy and Comfortable (minivan)

Own/Lease 3+ Vehicles

06 Sophisticated Squires

Own/Lease Imported Vehicle

10 Pleasant-Ville
44 Urban Melting Pot

Own/Lease Honda

13 In Style
16 Enterprising Professionals
39 Young and Restless
52 Inner City Tenants

Own/Lease Buick

14 Prosperous Empty Nesters
51 Metro City Edge

Own/Lease Nissan

19 Milk and Cookies
20 City Lights
59 Southwestern Families

Own/Lease Domestic Vehicle

57 Simple Living
60 City Dimensions (sedan)
62 Modest Income Homes (Dodge)
65 Social Security Set

Own/Lease All-Wheel-Drive Vehicle

37 Prairie Living

Own/Lease Ford

41 Crossroads

Own/Lease Sedan

24 Main Street USA
28 Aspiring Young Families
36 Old and Newcomers

Own Motorcycle

25 Salt of the Earth
48 Great Expectations

Own/Lease Truck

26 Midland Crowd
42 Southern Satellites

Own/Lease Pontiac

29 Rustbelt Retireees

Own/Lease Domestic Vehicle

30 Retirement Communities
32 Rustbelt Traditions
33 Midlife Junction
50 Heartland Communities
53 Home Town

Lease Vehicle

45 City Strivers

Own/Lease Compact Pickup

56 Rural Bypasses

Use Public Transportation

54 Urban Rows
61 High Rise Renters

Source: ESRI, by permission

Learning Objectives

- To understand basic differences between quantitative and qualitative research techniques

- To see how pluralistic research may be used to solve problems

- To learn the pros and cons of using observation as a means of gathering data

- To discover what focus groups are and how they are conducted and analyzed

- To become acquainted with online focus groups and their advantages

- To become familiar with other qualitative methods used by marketing researchers

Where We Are

Qualitative Research Is "Secret Sauce" in Understanding Consumer Motivation

Steve Richardson is Director of Communications, Qualitative Research Consultants Association, Qualitative Research Consultants Association is the 'Go To' Resource for Qualitative Research

When marketing a brand of personal grooming products for men on a global scale, you might also presume that American men would be leading the pack and would be first to adopt new products to improve their personal appearance. Not true. The qualitative research team working for the brand discovered that German men were engaged in some grooming activities at a much higher level than American men. Another surprise was the fact that men in the Midwestern section of the U.S. were quite open about discussing their grooming habits as opposed to men in New York City, who tended to be more uptight and reticent to discuss the topic. Thanks to qualitative research conducted in multiple international markets, the brand was able to develop a global marketing strategy that was less uniform, more segmented, and took into account regional and cultural attitudes toward male grooming.

What Is Qualitative Research?

Qualitative research is designed to reveal a target audience's range of behavior and the perceptions that drive it with reference to specific topics or issues. It uses in-depth studies of small groups of people to guide and support the construction of hypotheses. The results of qualitative research are descriptive rather than predictive. Originating in the social and behavioral sciences, today's qualitative methods in the field of marketing research include in-depth interviews with individuals, group discussions (from 2 to 10 participants is typical); diary and journal exercises; and in-context observations. Sessions may be conducted in person, by telephone, via videoconferencing and via the Internet. Here is a look at a few key qualitative research techniques.

Focus groups are a core technique in qualitative research. But thanks to frequent misuse of the term, focus groups are sometimes perceived as participants giving quantitative, rather than qualitative, responses to a project. Focus groups are popular because the vast majority are conducted with a well-defined purpose, and they elicit truthful, deep-seated emotions from participants—truths that are key to developing great brands, products, and services that resonate with consumers. You will learn all about focus groups in this chapter.

Individual depth interviews also remain popular and help guide marketers to relevant knowledge. Individual depth interviews are beneficial when respondent interaction is not needed or when it is necessary to explore each respondent's experiences and perceptions in greater depth.

Ethnography explores consumers and their natural behaviors in the context of everyday life—often in the home, but also in environments like workplaces, cars, and supermarkets. For example, rather than asking a consumer directly "What do you eat?" the researcher observes them eating and interprets those findings. Ethnography moves the research away from facilities and often elicits provocative new insights through the observation of real-life behaviors rather than planned or "socially acceptable" responses.

Online research tools like blogs, bulletin boards, and live chats are another set of tools that add dimension to observing consumer behavior. In a private blog, participants react to questions and images solely on their own or among all participants in the study. Online bulletin boards create a community experience where participants react, hear others react, and share opinions and emotions together over a course of time; the same goes for chats except they are conducted live. This can lead to rich interaction and findings that can be acted upon quickly.

Why Qualitative Research Works

Several unique aspects of qualitative research contribute to rich, insightful results:

Synergy among respondents, as they build on each other's comments and ideas.

- The dynamic nature of the interview or group discussion process, which engages respondents more actively than is possible in more structured surveys.
- The opportunity to probe ("Help me understand why you feel that way") enabling the researcher to reach beyond initial responses and rationales.
- The opportunity to observe, record, and interpret nonverbal communication (i.e., body language, voice intonation) as part of a respondent's feedback, which is valuable during interviews or discussions, and during analysis.
- The opportunity to engage respondents in "play" such as projective techniques and exercises, overcoming the self-consciousness that can inhibit spontaneous reactions and comments.

Not all qualitative techniques work for all situations. In fact, a primary role of an experienced qualitative research consultant is to help clients determine what methods work in what scenarios and how qualitative and quantitative methods can work together. When you finish this chapter, you will have a much better appreciation of the value of qualitative research.

—*Steve Richardson*
By permission, QRCA

We asked Steve Richardson of the QRCA to give you an overview of qualitative research. In his remarks, Mr. Richardson has illustrated the type of findings that you can expect from qualitative research, provided you with a brief overview of some of the qualitative research methods, and offered the rationale for why firms use qualitative research. Qualitative research methods are sometimes referred to as the "soft side" of marketing research simply because the findings are not quantitative. However, as you will learn, qualitative research is an important tool that provides clients with insights not found in quantitative research. In this chapter, you will learn how to distinguish between *qualitative and quantitative research as well as the various methods used in conducting qualitative research. You will also learn that each qualitative method has its place in the marketing research process and that each has its unique advantages and disadvantages as well. Because focus groups are a popular qualitative marketing research technique, an in-depth discussion of them is included. We begin with a discussion of quantitative, qualitative, and pluralistic research.*

QUANTITATIVE, QUALITATIVE, AND PLURALISTIC RESEARCH

Methods for collecting data during the research process can be classified into three broad categories: quantitative, qualitative, and pluralistic. The first two methods differ greatly, and it is necessary to understand their special characteristics in order to make the right selection. To start, we briefly define these two approaches, and then we describe pluralistic research.

Quantitative research, the traditional mainstay of the research industry, is sometimes referred to as "survey research." For our purposes in this chapter, **quantitative research** is defined as research involving the use of structured questions in which the response options have been predetermined and a large number of respondents are involved. When you think of quantitative research, you might envision a nationwide survey conducted by telephone interviews. That is, quantitative research often involves a sizable representative sample of the population and a formalized procedure for gathering data. The purpose of quantitative research is very specific, and it is used when the client and researcher have agreed that precise information is needed. Data format and sources are clear and well defined, and the compilation and formatting of the data gathered follows an orderly procedure that is largely numerical in nature.

Qualitative research, in contrast, involves collecting, analyzing, and interpreting data by observing what people do and say. Observations and statements are in a qualitative or nonstandardized form. Qualitative data can be quantified, but only after a translation process has taken place. For example, if you asked five people to express their opinions on a topic such as gun control or promoting alcoholic beverages to college students, you would probably get five different statements. But after studying each response, you could characterize each one as "positive," "negative," or "neutral." This translation step would not be necessary if you instructed them to choose predetermined responses such as "yes" or "no." Any study that is conducted using an observational technique or unstructured questioning can be classified as qualitative research, which is becoming increasingly popular in a number of research situations.[1]

Why would you want to use such a "soft" approach? Occasionally, marketing researchers find that a large-scale survey is inappropriate. For instance, Procter & Gamble may be interested in improving its Tide laundry detergent, so it invites a group of homemakers to sit down with some of Tide's marketing personnel and brainstorm how Tide could perform better or how its packaging could be improved or discuss other features of the detergent. Listening to the market in this way can generate excellent packaging, product design, or even product positioning ideas. As another example, if the Procter & Gamble marketing group were developing a special end-of-aisle display for Tide, they might want to test one version in an actual supermarket environment. They could place a display in a Safeway grocery store located in a San Francisco suburb and videotape shoppers as they encountered it. The marketing group would then review the videotape to see if the display generated the types of responses they hoped it would. For instance, did shoppers stop there? Did they read the copy on the display? Did they pick up the displayed product and look at it? Qualitative research techniques afford rich insight into consumer behavior.[2] Marketing Research Insight 8.1 is an example of an application of qualitative research to better understand a market segment—Latinos.

Methods of collecting data during the research process can be classified into three broad categories: quantitative, qualitative, and pluralistic.

Quantitative research is defined as research involving the use of structured questions in which the response options have been predetermined and a large number of respondents are involved.

Qualitative research involves collecting, analyzing, and interpreting data by observing what people do and say. Observations and statements are in a qualitative or nonstandardized form.

Qualitative research techniques afford rich insight into consumer behavior.

MARKETING RESEARCH INSIGHT

Global Application

8.1 You Say Hispanic, They Say Latino: Using Qualitative Research Methods to Better Understand Latino Market Segments

Many marketers refer to the "Hispanic market" unaware that this is not the term used by Latino consumers. Rather, they prefer "Latino." Another misconception is that there is a Hispanic or a Latino market. Actually, no one approach can be used to reach the Latino market because it is not a homogeneous group of people. Instead, the Latino market is a fragmented and complex tapestry of Latino backgrounds that includes more than 20 different countries of origin. According to Ricardo Lopez, president of Hispanic Research, Inc., "Latinos, like any other market segment, represent many levels of acculturation, education, income levels and ethnic influences." As an illustration of some of these differences, consider sports. Many Latinos who love baseball are primarily from the Caribbean islands of Puerto Rico, the Dominican Republic, and Cuba, as well as countries that border the Caribbean basin such as Venezuela, Colombia, Panama, and Nicaragua. But other Latinos, primarily from the rest of Latin America including Mexico, prefer soccer; baseball is not popular in those countries just as soccer is not popular in the countries that prefer baseball. Hispanic Research, Inc. used the qualitative technique of focus groups to help *Sports Illustrated* magazine understand differences among its readers for *SI Latino*, its Spanish-language magazine. In markets consisting of many Mexicans, magazine covers showing soccer did not attract much interest. As a result of the research, *SI Latino* is now printed with split covers—one to appeal to the baseball lovers and the other to appeal to the soccer fans.

Another example of using qualitative research to better understand the Latino market is provided by Rose Marie Garcia Fontana, president of Garcia Fontana Research in Half Moon Bay, California. Her company conducted 148 personal interviews with Latinos to determine perceptions, motivations, and barriers to attending, the Monterey Bay Aquarium, the company's nonprofit client. The greatest concerns of unacculturated Latinos were availability of public transportation to and from the aquarium and bilingual signage within the facility. Children

Do ALL Latino's love baseball?

were the most important motivation for going to the aquarium, and research showed that it was the father who usually made the decision, particularly in Spanish-dominant households.

Whatever the qualitative research technique researchers use, they understand that different markets require special attention. This is why the QRCA (the Qualitative Research Consultant's Association) created the Latino Special Interest Group (SIG). This group shares best practices to help researchers provide the greatest benefit to their clients. Some "best practices" already in use by SIG members include recruiting focus group members who share the same acculturation levels, being wary of using results from one Latino market in another (Miami is different from Texas which is different from California), and using an interpreter who is able to focus on picking up nuances and emotions in participants' voices.

This information was excerpted from S. Richardson (2008, June), You say Hispanic, they say Latino, *Quirk's Marketing Research Review*, 68–72. Mr. Richardson is Director of Communications for the Qualitative Research Consultant's Association (QRCA). Visit the QRCA at www.qrca.org. By permission.

In the rush toward conducting online quantitative research that produces huge amounts of data, qualitative research is sometimes overlooked.[3] However, it is our goal in this chapter to show you the value of qualitative research techniques and, as you will see very soon, to convince you that qualitative research and quantitative research should work hand in hand.

Although both qualitative and quantitative research each have their advocates, many marketing researchers have adopted a third approach, **pluralistic research**, which is defined as the combination of qualitative and quantitative research methods in order to gain the advantages of both. In pluralistic research, it is common to begin with exploratory, qualitative techniques, for example, in-depth interviews of selected dealers or a series of focus group discussions with customers in order to understand how they perceive your product and service compared with those of competitors. Even an observational study can be helpful to gaining an understanding of the problem and bringing issues to the surface. These activities often help clarify and define a problem or otherwise open researchers' eyes to factors and considerations that might have been overlooked if they had rushed into a full-scale survey. The qualitative phase serves as a foundation for the quantitative phase of the research project; it provides the researcher with firsthand knowledge. Armed with this knowledge of the problem, the researcher's design and execution of the quantitative phase are invariably superior to what they might have been without the qualitative phase. Thus, the qualitative phase serves to frame the subsequent quantitative phase. However, in some cases, qualitative methods are used *after* a quantitative study because they help the researcher understand the quantitative findings. For example, *The Arizona Republic* newspaper has used online focus groups for brainstorming, and the outcomes of these sessions are then used to devise online surveys. Through this pluralistic approach, *The Arizona Republic* has identified which topics are considered to be most important to its readers of the local news section of the paper. The information allowed the editors to make certain they covered the local news readers thought to be most important.[4]

The pluralistic approach is becoming increasingly popular, especially for emerging and complex marketing phenomena such as online shopping behavior. Marketing Research Insight 8.2 shows how a pluralistic program combined qualitative and quantitative research techniques to yield an understanding of the differences between male and female shopping behavior online and to identify gender differences in online market segments.

Observation Techniques

Qualitative techniques include **observation methods**, in which the researcher relies on observation rather than on communication in order to obtain information. Observation requires something to observe, and because our memories are faulty, researchers depend on recording devices such as videotapes, audiotapes, handwritten notes, or some other tangible record of what is observed. As we describe observation techniques, you will see that each is unique in the way it obtains data.

TYPES OF OBSERVATION. At first glance, it may seem that observation studies wouldn't require a structure. However, in order for the observations to be consistent and for comparisons or generalizations to be made without the findings being confounded by the conditions under which the observations were made, it is important to adhere to a plan. There are four general ways of organizing observation studies: (1) direct versus indirect, (2) disguised versus undisguised, (3) structured versus unstructured, and (4) human versus mechanical.

DIRECT VERSUS INDIRECT. Observing behavior as it occurs is called **direct observation**.[5] For example, if we are interested in finding out how much shoppers squeeze tomatoes to assess their freshness, we can observe people actually picking up the tomatoes. Direct observation has been used by Kellogg to understand breakfast rituals, by a Swiss chocolate maker to study the behavior of "chocoholics," and by the U.S. Post Office's advertising agency to come up with the advertising slogan "We Deliver."[6] It has also been used by General Mills to understand how children eat breakfast, leading to the launch of "Go-Gurt," a midmorning snack for schoolchildren.[7]

Pluralistic research is defined as the combination of qualitative and quantitative research methods in order to gain the advantages of both.

Often with pluralistic research, the qualitative phase serves to frame the subsequent quantitative phase.

One qualitative method is to observe others rather than communicate with them. Researchers observe behavior and record what they see.

There are four general ways of organizing observation studies: (1) direct versus indirect, (2) disguised versus undisguised, (3) structured versus unstructured, and (4) human versus mechanical. Observing behavior as it occurs is called direct observation.

MARKETING RESEARCH INSIGHT   Practical Application

8.2 Pluralistic Research Identifies Online Buyer Segments and Distinct Purchasing Behaviors

Because online purchase behavior is an emerging phenomenon, a pluralistic approach that uses both qualitative research techniques and quantitative methods is the most appropriate way to investigate it. Accordingly, market researchers combined the following research techniques in a strategy to reveal online buyer market segments.

Focus groups, which are moderated discussions conducted with groups of 8 to 12 online buyers, were used to gain a basic understanding of online buying, such as why, where, when, and how often. The focus groups uncovered basic differences between male and female online buyers.

Depth interviews, which are personal interviews lasting from 30 to 45 minutes, were then used in order to probe motivations for online purchasing, including functional as well as emotional reasons for buying online. These depth interviews also sought to tap into personal styles for online information search and processing.

An online survey was conducted via e-mail invitations to about 40,000 Internet users. The survey contained questions about demographics, lifestyle, Internet usage, preferences for Internet delivery formats, and importance of various Internet content types (such as news, entertainment, travel, family, etc.).

The online survey data were subjected to various analyses, and they resulted in the discovery of five distinct female online user segments as well as five separate male online user segments. The segments and their key differences are noted in the following table.

Online Segments and Key Differences Revealed by Pluralistic Research

Segment	Percent	Demographics	Key Online Usage	Online Favorites
Female Segments				
Social Sally	*14%*	*30–40, college educated*	*Making friends*	*Chat and personal Web space*
New Age Crusader	*21%*	*40–50, highest income level*	*Fight for causes*	*Books and government information*
Cautious Mom	*24%*	*30–45, with children*	*Nurture children*	*Cooking and medical facts*
Playful Pretender	*20%*	*Youngest, many are students*	*Role play*	*Chat and games*
Master Producer	*20%*	*Tends to be single*	*Job productivity*	*White pages and government information*
Male Segments				
Bits and Bytes	*11%*	*Young and single*	*Computers and hobbies*	*Investments, discovery, software*
Practical Pete	*21%*	*40ish, some college, above-average income*	*Personal productivity*	*Investments, company listings*
Viking Gamer	*19%*	*Young or old, least college education*	*Competing and winning*	*Games, chat, software*
Sensitive Sam	*21%*	*Highest education and income of males*	*Help family and friends*	*Investments, government information*
World Citizen	*28%*	*50 and older, most with college education*	*Connecting with world*	*Discovery, software, investments*

These are only thumbnail descriptions of these 10 different online market segments. Much more detail is provided in the original descriptions.[8] It is important to note that such complete understanding of these emerging online segments was possible only through the use of pluralistic research.

In order to observe types of hidden behavior, such as past behavior, we must rely on indirect observation. With **indirect observation**, the researcher studies the effects or results of the behavior rather than the behavior itself. Types of indirect observations include archives and physical traces.

Archives.   **Archives** are secondary sources, such as historical records, that can be applied to the present problem. These sources contain a wealth of information and should not be overlooked or underestimated. There are many types of archives. For example, records of sales calls may be inspected to determine how often salespersons make cold calls. Warehouse inventory movements can be used to study market shifts. Scanner data may afford insight into the effects of price changes, promotion campaigns, or changes in package size.

With indirect observation, the researcher studies the effects or results of the behavior rather than the behavior itself. Types of indirect observations include archives and physical traces.

Physical Traces.   **Physical traces** are tangible evidence of some event. For example, we might turn to "garbology" (observing the trash of subjects being studied) as a way of finding out how much recycling of plastic milk bottles occurs. A soft-drink company might do a litter audit in order to assess how much impact its aluminum cans have on the countryside. A fast-food company such as Wendy's might measure the amount of graffiti on buildings located adjacent to prospective sites as a means of estimating the crime potential for each site.[9]

DISGUISED VERSUS UNDISGUISED. With **disguised observation**, the subject is unaware that he or she is being observed. An example of this method might be a "mystery shopper" who is used by a retail store chain to record and report on salesclerks' assistance and courtesy. One-way mirrors and hidden cameras are a few of the other ways used to prevent subjects from becoming aware of being observed. Hiding the fact of observation is important because if subjects were aware of it, they might behave differently than they normally would, resulting in observations of atypical behavior. If you were a store clerk, how would you act if the department manager told you that he would be watching you for the next hour? You would probably be on your best behavior for the next 60 minutes. Disguised observation has proved illuminating in studies of parents and children shopping together in supermarkets.[10] Under direct questioning, parents might feel compelled to say that their children are always on their best behavior while shopping.

With disguised observation, the subject is unaware that he or she is being observed.

Sometimes it is impossible for the respondent to be unaware of the observation; this is a case of **undisguised observation**. Laboratory settings, observing a sales representative's behavior on sales calls, People Meters (Nielsen Media Research's device attached to a television set to record when and to what station a set is tuned), and Arbitron's Personal Portable Meter must all be used with the subject's knowledge. Because people might be influenced by knowing they are being observed, it is wise to always minimize the presence of the observer to the maximum extent possible.

When the respondent knows he or she is being observed, the technique is called as undisguised observation.

The use of observation raises ethical questions. Should people being observed be informed of the observation, and, if so, what changes might they make in their behavior in order to appear "normal" or conform to what they think is expected? The researcher wants to observe behavior as it actually occurs even if it is unusual or out of the ordinary. However, those being observed might feel uncomfortable about their habits or actions and try to act in more conventional ways. For instance, if a family agrees to have its television set wired so a researcher can track what programs the family watches, will the parents make sure that the children watch mainly wholesome shows, such as those on the Disney Channel? Sometimes researchers resort to deceit in order to observe people without their knowledge, but this is unethical. The ethical thing to do is to inform people ahead of time and give them an "adjustment period" or, if such a period is not feasible, to fully debrief them about the observation afterward.

The use of observation raises ethical questions. Should people being observed be informed of the observation, and, if so, what changes might they make in their behavior in order to appear "normal" or conform to what they think is expected?

STRUCTURED VERSUS UNSTRUCTURED. When using **structured observation** techniques, the researcher identifies beforehand which behaviors are to be observed and recorded. All other behaviors are "ignored." Often a checklist or a standardized observation form is used to focus the observer's attention on specific factors. Highly structured observations typically require minimum effort from the observer.

The researcher identifies beforehand which behaviors are to be observed and recorded in structured observation.

Unstructured observation places no restriction on what the observer will record. All behavior in the episode under study is monitored. The observer just watches the situation and records what seems interesting or relevant. Of course, the observer has been thoroughly

In unstructured observation, there are no predetermined restrictions on what the observer records.

briefed about the area of general concern. Unstructured observation is often used in exploratory research. For example, Black and Decker might send someone to observe carpenters working at various job sites as a means of better understanding how the tools are used and to help generate ideas on how the tools can be designed for increased safety.

HUMAN VERSUS MECHANICAL. With **human observation**, the observer is a person hired by the researcher or, perhaps, the observer is the researcher. However, it is often possible, desirable, and economical[11] to replace the human observer with some form of static observing device, as in **mechanical observation**, for accuracy, cost, or functional reasons. Auto traffic counts may be more accurate and less costly when recorded by machines that are activated by car tires rolling over them. Besides, during rush hour, a human observer could not accurately count the number of cars on most major metropolitan commuter roads. Nor would it be possible to count the number of fans entering a gate at a professional football title game, so turnstile counts are used instead. Scanning devices are used to count the number and types of products sold (see Chapter 7). Mechanical devices may also be used when it is too expensive to use human observers. For example, we mentioned earlier that the People Meter is used instead of a human observer to record families' television viewing habits for Nielsen Media Research. As these examples illustrate, mechanical observation has become a high-technology research tool through the combination of telecommunications, computer hardware, and software programs.

Appropriate Conditions for the Use of Observation

Certain conditions must be met before a researcher can successfully use observation as a marketing research tool: the event must occur during a short time interval, the observed behavior must occur in a public setting, and the possibility of faulty recall rules out collecting information by asking the person.

Short time interval means that the event must begin and end within a reasonably short time span. Examples include shopping in a supermarket, waiting in a line at a bank.

Short time interval means that the event must begin and end within a reasonably short time span. Examples include shopping in a supermarket, waiting in a line at a bank, purchasing a clothing item, or observing children as they watch a television program. Some decision-making processes can take a long time (e.g., buying a home), and it would be unrealistic in terms of the time and money required to observe the entire process. Because of this factor, observational research is usually limited to scrutinizing activities that can be completed in a relatively short time span or to observing certain phases of those activities with a long time span. *Public behavior* refers to behavior that occurs in a setting the researcher can readily observe. Actions such as cooking, playing with one's children at home, or private worshiping are not public activities and are, therefore, not suitable for observational studies such as those described here.

Public behavior refers to behavior that occurs in a setting the researcher can readily observe, such as shopping in a grocery store or shopping with children in a department store.

Observations should be used when consumers cannot recall their behaviors, such as knowing how many different web pages they accessed while shopping online. Inability to recall such behaviors is known as "faulty recall."

Faulty recall occurs when actions or activities are so repetitive or automatic that the respondent cannot recall specifics about the behavior in question. For example, people cannot recall accurately how many times they looked at their wristwatch while waiting in a long line to buy a ticket to a best-selling movie, or which FM radio station they listened to last Thursday at 2 pm. Observation is necessary under circumstances of faulty recall to fully understand the behavior at hand. Faulty recall is one of the reasons that companies have for many years experimented with mechanical devices to observe these behaviors.[12] Recall our discussion of Arbitron's new Portable People Meter in Chapter 7, another example of observing behavior under conditions of faulty recall.

Advantages of Observational Data

Observation research has the advantage of seeing what consumers actually do instead of relying on their self-report of what they think they do.

Ideally, the subjects of observational research are unaware they are being studied, so they react in a natural manner, giving the researcher insight into actual, not reported, behaviors. As previously noted, observational research methods also eliminate recall error. The subjects are not asked what they remember about a certain action; instead, they are observed while engaged in the act. In some cases, observation may be the only way to obtain accurate information. For instance, children who cannot yet verbally express their opinion of a new toy will do so by simply playing or not playing with the toy. Retail marketers commonly gather marketing intelligence about competitors and about their own employees' behaviors by hiring the services of "mystery shoppers," who pose as customers but who are actually trained observers.[13] In some situations, data can be obtained with better accuracy and less cost by using observational methods For example, observational techniques can often obtain counts of in-store traffic more accurately and less expensively than can survey techniques.

These advantages of observational research methods should not be interpreted as meaning that this technique is always in competition with other approaches. A resourceful researcher will use observation techniques to supplement and complement other methods.[14] When used in combination, each approach can serve as a check on the results obtained by other methods. Actually, anthropologists have used observation of humans in their natural context for over 100 years, and it is an accepted method of conducting marketing research.[15]

Limitations of Observational Data

The limitations of observation are those inherent in qualitative research in general. During indirect observation, typically only small numbers of subjects are studied and usually under special circumstances, so representativeness is a concern.[16] This factor, plus the subjective quality of the interpretation required to explain the observed behavior, usually forces researchers to consider their conclusions as tentative. Certainly, the greatest drawback to all observational methods is the inability to pry beneath the behavior observed and to interrogate the person as to motives, attitudes, and all of the other unseen aspects of why what was observed took place.

To recap, a limitation of observation is that motivations, attitudes, intentions, and other internal conditions cannot be observed. Only when these feelings are relatively unimportant or are readily inferred from the behavior is it appropriate to use observational research methods. For example, facial expression might be used as an indicator of a child's attitudes or preferences for various types of fruit drink flavors because children often react with conspicuous physical expressions. But adults and even children usually conceal their reasons and true reactions in public, and this fact necessitates direct questioning, because observation alone cannot give a complete picture of why and how people act the way they do.

FOCUS GROUPS

A popular method of conducting exploratory research is through **focus groups**, which are small groups of people brought together and guided by a moderator through an unstructured, spontaneous discussion for the purpose of gaining information relevant to the research problem.[17] Although focus groups are intended to encourage openness on the part of the participants, the moderator's task is to ensure the discussion is "focused" on some general area of interest. For example, the Piccadilly Cafeteria chain periodically conducts focus groups all around the country. The conversation may seem "freewheeling," but the purpose of the focus group may be to learn what people think about some specific aspect of the cafeteria business, such as the quality of cafeteria versus traditional restaurant food.

Focus groups are a useful technique for gathering some information from a limited sample of respondents. The information can be used to generate ideas, to learn the respondents' "vocabulary" in relation to a certain type of product, or to gain some insights into basic needs and attitudes.[18] Of the total amount of money spent on qualitative research 85% to 90% is spent on focus groups.[19] They have become so popular in marketing research that every large city has a number of companies that specialize in performing focus group research. You will surely encounter focus group research if you become a practicing marketing manager. "Almost nothing gets done without them,"[20] says Bill Hillsman, a successful advertising executive whose clients include the Minnesota Twins, the Dales shopping centers, and Arctic Cat snowmobiles. Focus groups are an invaluable

---

Sometimes data can be obtained at less cost and with more accuracy by using observation methods.

Even though there are several advantages to observational research, observation techniques should not be used without considering other research methods. A resourceful researcher will use observation techniques to supplement and complement other methods.

One disadvantage of observational research is that it normally observes only a few persons. Researchers must be concerned about how accurately those observed represent all consumers in the target population.

Interpretation of observed behavior is subjective.

The major disadvantage of observation research is the inability to determine consumers' motives, attitudes, and intentions.

Focus groups are small groups of people brought together and guided by a moderator through an unstructured, spontaneous discussion for the purpose of gaining information relevant to the research problem.

The focus group moderator's task is to ensure the discussion is "focused" on some general area of interest.

Information from focus groups can be used to generate ideas, to learn the respondents' "vocabulary" in relation to a certain type of product, or to gain some insights into basic needs and attitudes.

Focus groups may be either traditional or nontraditional.

Focus group facilities have a one-way mirror or cameras, which allow clients in an adjoining room to watch the focus group without influencing what the group members say and do.

It is unethical to conceal cameras or other methods of viewing or recording focus groups.

means of regaining contact with customers with whom marketers have lost touch, and they are very helpful for learning about new customer groups. You may recall reading about focus groups earlier in this book. You should go back to Chapter 5 and read what Molly Lammers of Seattle-Fieldwork has to say about the operation and use of focus groups.

How Focus Groups Work

Focus groups can be of several types. **Traditional focus groups** select about 6 to 12 persons and meet in a dedicated room, with a one-way mirror for client viewing, for about 2 hours. Recent years have seen the emergence of **nontraditional focus groups**.[21] In this format, the groups may be online and clients may observe on computer monitors from distant locations; the groups may have as many as 25 or even 50 respondents; clients may interact with participants; and sessions may last 4 or 5 hours and take part outside of traditional facilities, such as in a park. We will discuss online focus groups in more detail in the following paragraphs.

A marketing research firm offering traditional focus groups typically will have a **focus group facility**, which is a set of rooms especially designed for focus groups. The meeting is conducted in a room that seats about 10 people (optimal size is thought to be somewhere between 6 and 12 participants) and a moderator. A wall in the room has a one-way mirror, which allows clients in the adjoining room to watch the focus group without influencing what the group members say or do. Some facilities have video cameras in the focus group room, which allow clients to observe the group from another room or even a distant location. Microphones are built into the walls or ceiling or otherwise set in the center of the table, and videotape equipment often operates from an inconspicuous location.

In the past, companies tried to hide or disguise the equipment they used to record respondents' reactions in an attempt to prevent feelings of self-consciousness or awkwardness. However, such a practice is unethical, and few participants were tricked anyway. Now it is common practice to let participants know about the recording when they are recruited. If they have any objections, they can decline at that time.

Focus group participants are interviewed by **moderators**, often referred to as **Qualitative Research Consultants** (QR or QRC).[22] The training and background of the moderator or QRC is extremely important to the success of the focus group.[23] QRCs are responsible for creating an atmosphere that is conducive to openness, yet they must make certain the participants do not stray too far from the central focus of the study. A good moderator must have excellent observational, interpersonal, and communication skills to recognize and overcome threats to a productive group discussion. He or she must be prepared, experienced, and armed with a detailed list of the topics to be discussed.[24] It is also helpful if the focus group moderator can eliminate any preconceptions about the topic from his or her own mind. The best moderators are experienced, enthusiastic, prepared, involved, energetic, and open-minded.[25] An incompetent moderator can create a disaster of the focus group. Some trade secrets of successful moderators may be found in Table 8.1.

QRCs also must prepare a **focus group report** that summarizes the information provided by the focus group participants relative to the research questions. When analyzing

MRSI is a marketing research firm. Among its many services, it offers qualitative research, including focus groups. By permission.

TABLE 8.1   Focus Group Moderators' "Tricks of the Trade"

Question	Tricks of the Trade
How do you make your groups great every time?	• Be prepared. • Be energized. • Be nice but firm. • Make sure *everything* about the experience is comfortable.
How do you build rapport quickly?	• Make meaningful eye contact during each person's introduction. • Learn and remember names. • Let them create their own name cards. • Welcome folks as they come into the room, and use small talk.
How do you bring a drifting group back into focus?	• Tell them the topic is "for another group" and that they need to focus on the topic for this group. • Make a note and tell them that they will come back to this topic if there is time. • Tell them the topic is "interesting" but not the subject at hand and refer to the next question. • Suggest that they can talk about it on their own after the focus group is over.
How do you get them to talk about deeper things than top-of-the-mind answers?	• Play naïve or dumb and ask them to help you understand by explaining. • Use probes such as "Tell us more about that," or "Can you go deeper on that?" • Ask for specifics such as "Tell me about the last time that you. . . ." • Pair them up and give them 10 minutes for each pair to come up with a solution or suggestion.
What about management of the "back room" where your clients are observing?	• Orient clients with a 10-miute overview of focus groups, research objectives, and what to expect. • Check with the client(s) during breaks, written exercises, and so on to make sure things are going well. • Have an associate or colleague there to work with the client(s). • If you don't have an associate for the back room, ask the client to select one person to be the point person to communicate with you.

The above trade secrets were divulged by experienced focus group moderators at a recent panel at the annual conference of the Qualitative Research Consultants Association.[26]

the data, two important factors must be kept in mind. First, the qualitative statements of participants must be translated into categories and then the degree of consensus apparent in the focus groups must be assessed.[27] Second, the demographic and buyer behavior characteristics of focus group participants should be judged against the target market profile to assess to what degree the groups represent the target market. Information from the focus group is evaluated by an analyst who carefully observes the recorded tapes several times, transcribing any relevant statements. These statements are then subjected to closer evaluation. The evaluation is based on the analyst's knowledge of the history and statement of the problem plus his or her own interpretation of the responses. A detailed report is prepared for the client's review.

The focus group report reflects qualitative research. It lists all of the themes that have become apparent, and it notes any diversity in opinions or thoughts expressed by the participants. Numerous verbatim excerpts may be included as evidence.[28] In fact, some reports include complete transcripts of the focus group discussion. This information is then used as the basis for further research studies or even for additional focus groups, for which the client

Focus group participants are interviewed by moderators, often referred to as Qualitative Research Consultants (QR or QRC).

QRCs prepare the focus group report.

The website of the professional organization of QRCAs is www .qrca.org.

uses the first group as a learning experience, making any adjustments to the discussion topics as needed to improve the research objectives. Although focus groups alone may be used to tackle a marketing problem or question, they are also used as a starting point for quantitative research; that is, a focus group phase may be used to gain a feel for a specific survey that will ultimately generate standardized information from a representative sample.

 Qualitative Research Consultant's Association

Recall our opening vignette by Steve Richardson of QRCA. Let's learn a little about ethics in qualitative research. Go to their website at www.qrca.com. Click on "About Us" and go to "Ethics and Practices." Read the "Message from the QRCA president," "Ethics and Practices," and "Code of Member Ethics." Do you think the QRCA is interested in the ethical standards of its members? Why?

Online Focus Groups

The online focus group, a form of nontraditional focus group, is one in which the respondents and/or the clients communicate and/or observe over the Internet. Typically, online focus groups allow the participants the convenience of sitting at their own computers while the moderator operates out of an online focus group company.

The **online focus group**, a form of nontraditional focus group, is one in which the respondents and/or the clients communicate and/or observe over the Internet. Typically, online focus groups allow participants the convenience of sitting at their own computers while the moderator operates out of an online focus group company. The online focus group is "virtual" in that it communicates electronically, and there is no face-to-face contact in the traditional focus group sense. Although some experts hold that online focus groups are not equivalent to traditional focus groups, online focus groups offer many advantages and few disadvantages. The Qualitative Research Consultants Association's Online Qualitative Research Task Force published its investigations into online focus groups[29]; its major conclusions are listed in Table 8.2.

Online focus groups have the following advantages over traditional focus groups: (1) No physical setup is necessary, (2) transcripts are captured on electronic files in real time, (3) participants can be in widely separated geographic locations, (4) participants are comfortable in their home or office environments, and (5) the moderator can exchange private messages with individual participants. Innovative approaches are possible, as some researchers combine online with telephone communications for maximum effectiveness.[30] On the flip side, there are some disadvantages, such as (1) observation of participants' "body language" is not possible, (2) participants cannot physically inspect products or taste food items, and (3) participants can lose interest or become distracted.[31] Of course, as Table 8.2 indicates, both traditional and online focus groups require recruitment and compensation of participants, scheduling and notification, and a prepared and skilled moderator.

A variation of the online focus group is one conducted in a traditional setting, but with the client watching online. ActiveGroup has pioneered this research technique using streaming media and high-speed Internet connections. The focus group is conducted at a traditional focus group facility with the participants and moderator present. Several members of the client firm can observe the focus group at their own location, which saves the client firm travel expense and time. ActiveGroup provides clients with reports and a CD-ROM of the focus group. Since their introduction a few years ago, online focus groups have grown in popularity. Although they will not replace traditional focus groups, they offer a viable research method.[32]

Advantages and Disadvantages of Focus Groups

Focus groups generate fresh ideas, allow clients to observe, are applicable to a wide variety of issues, and allow researchers to obtain information from "hard-to-reach" subpopulations.

The four major advantages of focus groups are (1) they generate fresh ideas; (2) they allow clients to observe the participants; (3) they may be directed at understanding a wide variety of issues, such as reactions to a new food product, brand logo, or television ad; and (4) they allow fairly easy access to special respondent groups, such as lawyers or doctors, from whom it may be very difficult to collect a representative sample.

TABLE 8.2   Online Focus Groups FAQs[33]

Question	Answer
Can online focus groups substitute for face-to-face ones?	Yes, as long as the online environment is consistent with the study's objectives.

For what situations are online focus groups best suited?	Some are:
	  Low-incidence respondents
	  Geographically dispersed respondents
	  B-to-B professionals

What is "lost" with online focus groups?	You cannot:
	  See body language
	  Show prototypes or models of products
	  Conduct taste tests

Can I recruit online focus group participants via e-mail invitation?	Yes, if they have valid e-mail accounts that they use regularly.
What incentives should I use to recruit my focus group participants?	The going rate is about $40 in cash or the equivalent, but B-to-B participants may require twice this amount.
How many participants should I plan for in my online focus group?	A common number is 15 to 20.
How long should it last?	Up to 90 minutes is typical.
How secure is the online focus group environment?	If you use a commercial chat program, password systems can be used to maintain security.
Can my clients observe the online focus group?	Yes, there are systems in which the client(s) can observe the focus group while online at their own computers. The clients can communicate privately with the moderator online as well.
Are the moderator's skills different with an online focus group?	In addition to basic focus group moderator skills, the moderator needs to take more care in preparing the wording of the discussion topic guide to avoid misinterpretation, phrase probes to include all participants, have good typing ability, and be familiar with chat room slang.
Are participants more or less candid with online focus groups?	Participants tend to be more candid because they have anonymity. Also, they tend to compose answers to topic questions without reading others' responses, so the comments are unique to each participant.

There are three major disadvantages to focus groups. First, focus groups do not constitute representative samples and therefore, caution must be exercised in generalizing the findings. Second, it is sometimes difficult to interpret the results of focus groups; the moderator's report is based on a subjective evaluation of what was said during the session. Finally, the cost per participant is high, though the total spent on focus group research is generally a fraction of what might be spent on quantitative research.

Focus groups are not representative, and it is sometimes difficult to interpret the results of focus groups. The moderator's report is subjective, and the cost per focus group participant is high.

When to Use Focus Groups

When the research objective is to describe, rather than predict, focus groups may be an alternative to using quantitative methods. Consider the following situations: A company wants to know "how to speak" to its market; what language and terms do the customers use? What are some new ideas for an ad campaign? Will a new service it is developing have appeal to customers and how can it be improved? How can the product be packaged better?[34] In all these cases, focus groups can describe the terms customers use, their ideas for ads, why a service appeals to them, and so on. But because focus groups are based on a small number of persons who are not representative of some larger population, care must

Focus groups should be considered when the research question is one requiring something to be described.

Focus groups should not be used when the research questions requires a prediction or when a major decision, affecting the livelihood of the company, rests on the results of a focus group.

be exercised. If the research objective is to predict, focus groups should not be used. For example, if we show 12 persons in a focus group a new-product prototype and find that 6 say they are going to buy it, can we predict that 50% of the population will buy our product? Hardly. Likewise, if the results of our research are going to dictate a major, expensive decision for our company, we probably should not rely solely on focus groups. If the decision is that important, we should use research methods that are based on some large population and that have some known margin of error (quantitative research).

Some Objectives of Focus Groups

There are four main objectives of focus groups: to generate ideas; to understand consumer vocabulary; to reveal consumer needs, motives, perceptions, and attitudes about products or services; and to understand findings from quantitative studies.

Focus groups generate ideas for managers to consider.

Focus groups *generate ideas* for managers to consider. Krispy Kreme has conducted focus groups to help it design new-product choices and stores. If managers consistently hear that their customers prefer Krispy Kreme's doughnuts but go elsewhere for gourmet coffee, this gives management ideas for changing the product mix to include gourmet coffee. Mothers talking about the difficulties of strapping children into car seats give designers of these products ideas for improvements. Consumers discussing the difficulties of moving furniture gave rise to innovations in furniture designed for portability.

Focus groups may be used to understand the consumers' vocabulary, needs and motives, and attitudes.

To *understand consumer vocabulary* means to use the focus group to stay abreast of the words and phrases consumers use when describing products so as to improve communication with them about products or services. Such information may help in designing advertising copy or in preparing an instruction pamphlet, in refining the definition of a research problem, and also in structuring questions for use in later quantitative research.

To *reveal consumer needs, motives, perceptions, and attitudes* about products or services means to use the focus group to inform the marketing team about what customers really feel or think about a product or service. Or managers may need early customer reactions to changes being considered in products or services.[35] Thus focus groups are commonly used during the exploratory phase of research,[36] where it is useful in generating objectives to be addressed by subsequent research.

Focus groups may be used to better understand findings of quantitative studies.

To *understand findings from quantitative studies* means to use focus groups to better comprehend data gathered from other surveys. Sometimes a focus group can reveal why the findings came out a particular way. For example, a bank image survey showed that a particular branch consistently received lower scores on "employee friendliness." Focus group research identified the problem as being several front-line employees who were so concerned with efficiency that they appeared to be unfriendly to customers. The bank revised its training program to remedy the problem.

Warner-Lambert has successfully used focus groups to accomplish all four of the preceding objectives. Its consumer health products group, which markets over-the-counter health and beauty products as well as nonprescription drugs, makes extensive use of focus groups.[37] In fact, Warner-Lambert uses a combination of qualitative research techniques to gain background information, to reveal needs and attitudes related to health and beauty products, to interpret the results of qualitative studies, and to stimulate the brainstorming of new ideas. Focus groups have been useful to the company for understanding basic shifts in consumer lifestyles, values, and purchase patterns.

Operational Considerations

Before a focus group is conducted, certain operational questions should be addressed. It is important to decide how many people should take part, who they should be, how they will be selected and recruited, and where they should meet. We discuss general guidelines for answering these questions.

WHAT SHOULD BE THE SIZE OF A FOCUS GROUP? According to industry wisdom, the optimal size of a traditional focus group is 6 to 12 people. A small group (fewer than 6 participants) is not likely to generate the energy and group dynamics necessary for a truly beneficial focus group session. With fewer participants, it is common that 1 or 2 of the participants do most of the talking in spite of the moderator's efforts. At the same time, a small group will often produce awkward silences and force the moderator to take too active a role in the discussion just to keep it alive. Similarly, a group with over a dozen participants will ordinarily prove to be too large to be conducive to a natural discussion. As a focus group becomes larger, it tends to become fragmented. Those participating may become frustrated by the inherent digressions and side comments. Conversations may break out among 2 or 3 participants while another is talking. This situation places the moderator in the role of disciplinarian, in which he or she is constantly calling for quiet or order rather than focusing the discussion on the issues at hand.

The optimal size of a focus group is 6 to 12 people.

Unfortunately, it is often difficult to predict the exact number of people who will attend the focus group interview. Ten may agree to participate and only 4 may show up; 14 may be invited in the hope that 8 will show up, but all 14 may arrive. Of course, if this occurs, the researcher must make a judgment call as to whether or not to send some home. In the worst case, a researcher may run into a situation in which no one attends, despite promises to the contrary. There is no guaranteed method that will ensure a successful participation ratio. Incentives (which will be discussed later) are helpful but definitely not a sure way of gaining acceptance. So although 6 to 12 is the ideal focus group size, it is not uncommon to have some groups with fewer than 6 and some with more than 12.

WHO SHOULD BE IN THE FOCUS GROUP? It is generally believed that the best focus groups are ones in which the participants share homogeneous characteristics. This requirement is sometimes automatically satisfied by the researcher's need to have particular types of people in the focus group. For instance, the focus group may be comprised of executives who use satellite phones, it may involve building contractors who specialize in building residences over $500,000 in value, or it might involve a group of salespeople who are experiencing some common customer service difficulty.

Focus group members should be homogeneous.

The need for similar demographic or other relevant characteristics in the focus group members is accentuated by the fact that the focus group participants are typically strangers. In most cases, they are not friends or even casual acquaintances, and many people feel intimidated or at least hesitant to voice their opinions and suggestions to a group of strangers. But participants typically feel more comfortable once they realize they have similarities such as their age (they may all be in their early 30s), job situations (they may all be junior executives), family composition (they may all have preschool children), purchase experiences (they may all have bought a new car in the past year), or even leisure pursuits (they may all play tennis). Furthermore, by conducting a group that is as homogeneous as possible with respect to demographics and other characteristics, the researcher is assured that differences in these variables will be less likely to confuse the issue being discussed.

HOW SHOULD FOCUS GROUP PARTICIPANTS BE RECRUITED AND SELECTED? As you can guess, the selection of focus group participants is determined largely by the purpose of the group. For instance, if the purpose is to generate new ideas for improvements in digital cameras, the participants must be consumers who have used a digital camera. If the focus group is intended to elicit building contractors' reactions to a new type of central air-conditioning unit, it will be necessary to recruit building contractors. It is not unusual for companies to provide customer lists or for focus group recruiters to work from lists of potential participants. For instance, with building contractors, the list might come from the local Yellow Pages or the membership roster of a building contractor trade association. In any case, it is necessary to initially contact prospective participants by

Selection of focus group members is determined by the purpose of the group.

telephone to qualify them and then to solicit their cooperation in the focus group. Occasionally, a focus group company may recruit by requesting shoppers in a mall to participate, but this approach is rare.

As we noted earlier, "no-shows" are a problem with focus groups; researchers have at least two strategies with which to entice prospective participants. Incentives are used to encourage recruits to participate in focus groups. These range from monetary compensation for the participants' time to free products or gift certificates. Many focus group companies use callbacks during the day immediately prior to the focus group to remind prospective participants that they have agreed to take part. If one prospective participant indicates that some conflict has arisen and he or she cannot be there, it is then possible to recruit a replacement. Neither approach works perfectly, as we indicated earlier, and how many participants will show up is always a concern. Some focus group companies have a policy of overrecruiting; others have lists of people they can rely on to participate, given that they fit the qualifications.

Focus group recruiting may raise ethical issues.

The difficulties encountered by focus group companies in recruiting focus group participants have led to some unethical practices. Some people like to participate in focus groups, and a focus group company may keep them on a list of willing participants. Other participants may want to take part simply for the monetary compensation, and their names may be on the focus group company's list as well. In either case, the inclusion of people who have previously participated in numerous focus groups can lead to serious validity problems. Some researchers will explicitly forbid a focus group company to use these participants because of this concern. As a matter of policy, some focus group companies will always report the last time, if ever, that each focus group member participated in a focus group. Other companies will do so only if the client firm makes an explicit request for this information.

Focus group facilities should be comfortable, allow interaction, and not have distractions.

WHERE SHOULD A FOCUS GROUP MEET? Obviously, if a group discussion is to take place for a period of 90 minutes or more, it is important that the physical facilities be comfortable and conducive to group discussion. So focus groups ideally are conducted in large rooms set up in a format suitable to the research objective. In some cases in which it is important to have face-to-face interaction, a round-table format is ideal. Other formats are more suitable for tasting foods or beverages or for viewing video. Focus groups are held in a variety of settings. An advertising company conference room, a moderator's home, a respondent's home, the client's office, hotels, and meeting rooms at churches are all locations in which focus groups can be held. Aside from a seating arrangement in which participants can all see one another, the second critical requirement in selecting a meeting place is to find one quiet enough to permit an intelligible audiotaping of the sessions. Marketing research firms with focus group facilities like those described at the beginning of this section offer ideal settings for focus groups.

Moderators should not be hired at the last minute to run focus groups. They should thoroughly understand the research objectives.

WHEN SHOULD THE MODERATOR BECOME INVOLVED IN THE RESEARCH PROJECT? Moderators should not be viewed as robots who may be hired at the last minute to run the focus group. The group's success depends on the participants' involvement in the discussion and in their understanding of what is being asked of them. Productive involvement is largely a result of the moderator's effectiveness, which in turn is dependent on the moderator's understanding of the purpose and objectives of the interview. Unless the moderator understands what information the researcher is after and why, he or she will not be able to phrase questions effectively. It is good policy to have the moderator be part of the development of the project's goals so as to be able to guide the discussion topics. By aiding in the formation of the topics (questions), the moderator will be familiar with them and be better prepared to conduct the group.

When formulating questions, it is important that they be organized into a logical sequence and that the moderator follow this sequence to the furthest extent possible. The moderator's introductory remarks are influential; they set the tone of the entire session. All subsequent questions should be prefaced with a clear explanation of how the participants should respond, for example, how they really feel personally, not how they think they should feel. This allows the moderator to establish a rapport with participants and to lay the groundwork for the interview's structure.

REPORTING AND USE OF FOCUS GROUP RESULTS. As we noted earlier, focus groups report some of the subtle and obscure features of the relationships between consumers and products, advertising, and sales efforts. They furnish qualitative data on things such as consumer language; emotional and behavioral reactions to advertising; lifestyle; relationships; the product category and specific brand; and unconscious consumer motivations relative to product design, packaging, promotion, or any other facet of the marketing program under study. But focus group results are qualitative and not perfectly representative of the general population.

FINAL COMMENTS ON FOCUS GROUPS. The focus group approach is firmly entrenched in the world of marketing research as a mainstay technique. Focus groups are an appealing qualitative research method because their total cost is reasonable compared to that of large-scale quantitative surveys involving a thousand or more respondents, they are adaptable to managers' concerns, and they can yield immediate results. Face-to-face focus groups are becoming common worldwide, and the new capabilities of online focus groups are boosting their popularity. They are a unique research method because they permit marketing managers to see and hear the market. Managers become so engrossed in their everyday problems and crises that they find it very refreshing to see and hear their customers in the flesh. It is common for marketing managers to come away from an observation of a focus group session stimulated and energized to respond to the market's desires.

Focus group usage is growing worldwide.

OTHER QUALITATIVE RESEARCH TECHNIQUES

Although focus group interviews and many of the observation methods we have described thus far are clearly the most frequently used qualitative research techniques, they are not the only type of nonstructured research available to marketing researchers. Other popular methods include ethnographic research, depth interviews, protocol analysis, various projective techniques, and physiological measurement.

Depth Interviews

A **depth interview** is defined as a set of probing questions posed one-on-one to a subject by a trained interviewer to gain an idea of what the subject thinks about something or why the subject behaves in a certain way. The interview is conducted in the respondent's home or possibly at a central interviewing location such as a mall-intercept facility, where several respondents can be interviewed in depth in a relatively short time. The objective is to obtain unrestricted comments or opinions and to ask questions that will help the marketing researcher better understand the various dimensions of these opinions as well as the reasons for them. Of primary importance is the compilation of the data into a summary report so as to identify common themes. New concepts, designs, advertising, and promotional messages can arise from this method.[38]

A depth interview is defined as a set of probing questions posed one-on-one to a subject by a trained interviewer so as to gain an idea of what the subject thinks about something or why the subject behaves in a certain way.

There are advantages and disadvantages to in-depth interviewing. Interviewers have the ability to probe, asking many additional questions, as a result of responses, which enables the research technique to generate rich, deep, in-depth information. In-depth responses may be more revealing in some research situations than, say, responses to the predetermined, yes–no questions typical of a structured survey. If used properly, depth interviews can offer great insight into consumer behavior.[39,40] However, this advantage also leads to the major disadvantage of in-depth interviewing, which is the lack of structure in the process. Unless interviewers are well trained, the results may be too varied to give sufficient insight into the problem. Depth interviews are especially useful when the researcher wants to understand decision making on the individual level, how products are used, or the emotional and sometimes private aspects of consumers' lives.[41,42] Obviously, respondents in an in-depth interview are not influenced by others, as they would be in a focus group.

As noted, in-depth interviews should be conducted by a trained fieldworker who is equipped with a list of topics or, perhaps, open-ended questions. This is necessary because the respondent is not provided a list of set responses and then instructed to select one from the list. Rather, the respondents are encouraged to respond in their own words, and the interviewer is trained in asking probing questions: "Why is that so?" "Can you elaborate on your point?" or "Would you give me some specific reasons?" These questions are not intended to tap subconscious motivations; rather, they simply ask about conscious reasons to help the researcher form a better picture of what is going on in the respondent's head. The interviewer may record responses or may take detailed notes. Although typically depth interviews are conducted face-to-face, they can be done over the telephone when interviewees are widely dispersed.[43] Depth interviews are versatile, but they require careful planning, training, and preparation.[44]

Laddering, a technique used in in-depth interviews, attempts to discover how product attributes are associated with consumer values. Essentially, values important to consumers are first identified, such as "good health." Next, researchers determine which routes consumers take to achieve their values, such as exercise, eating certain foods, stress reduction, and so on. Finally, researchers attempt to find out which specific product attributes are viewed as a means of achieving the desired value. Through in-depth interviews researchers may learn that low-sodium foods or "white meats" are instrumental in achieving "good health."[45] The term *laddering* comes from the notion of establishing the linkages, or steps, leading from product attributes to values. We asked Professor Philip Trocchia to give you some additional insights on laddering (see Marketing Research Insight 8.3).

Protocol Analysis

Protocol analysis places people in a decision-making situation and asks them to verbalize everything they considered.

Protocol analysis involves placing people in a decision-making situation and asking them to verbalize everything they consider when making a decision. It is a special-purpose qualitative research technique that has been developed to peek into the consumer's decision-making processes. Often a recorder is used to maintain a permanent record of the person's thinking. After several people have provided protocols, the researcher reviews them and looks for commonalities, such as evaluative criteria used, number of brands considered, types and sources of information, and so forth.

Protocol studies are useful in two different purchase situations. First, they are helpful in studying purchases involving a long time frame in which several decision factors must be considered, such as when buying a house. By having people verbalize the steps they went through, a researcher can piece together the whole process. Second, when the decision process is very short, recall may be faulty and protocol analysis can be used to slow the process down. For example, most people do not give much thought to buying chewing gum, but if Dentyne wanted to find out why people buy spearmint gum, protocol analysis might provide some important insights regarding this purchasing behavior.

Projective Techniques

Projective techniques involve situations in which participants undergo (are projected into) simulated activities in the hope that they will divulge things about themselves that they might not reveal under direct questioning. Projective techniques are appropriate in situations in which the researcher is convinced that respondents will be hesitant to relate their true opinions.

Projective techniques involve situations in which participants undergo (are projected into) simulated activities in the hope that they will divulge things about themselves that they might not reveal under direct questioning. Projective techniques are appropriate in

MARKETING RESEARCH INSIGHT

Practical Application

8.3 The Laddering Interview
By *Professor Philip Trocchia*

Professor Philip Trocchia is Associate Professor of Marketing, University of South Florida, St. Petersburg. He has employed qualitative research techniques for such organizations as The Poynter Institute, Computer Renaissance, and The Honda Grand Prix of St. Petersburg. He has also written an article on the laddering technique in the Journal of Management Education.

Laddering is a type of one-on-one depth interview technique that seeks to reveal how individuals relate the features of products they purchase to their personally held beliefs. In laddering interviews, consumers are asked to describe why they purchased a particular good or service. After uncovering relevant product attributes or features influencing their purchase decisions, the interviewer probes the consumer to reveal what benefits they associate with the product feature(s) identified earlier. The interviewer then attempts to uncover why those product benefits are of importance to the consumer subject. In this portion of the interview, the consumer's personal values are revealed.

The term *laddering* refers to the series of linkages described above: relevant features of the consumer's described product purchase are related to the perceived benefits of the product. Product benefits are then linked to the individual's personal set of values. For example, suppose a consumer regularly purchases a particular cereal. The interviewer would ask her why she buys that specific cereal. She might respond that it is high in fiber, a brand attribute. The consumer would then be asked why high fiber is important, and the respondent may express health reasons as a benefit of fiber. Finally, the interviewer would ask the consumer why good health is important to her, and the respondent might indicate that she associates good health with some personal value(s), such as happiness, freedom, or pleasure. The summary ladder for this consumer would be: high fiber (attribute or feature) → good health (benefit or consequence) → freedom (value). A typical report for the series of laddering interviews would contain a summary of the common attribute-benefit-value linkages among the respondents, along with demographic characteristics of the consumers who possess common linkage patterns. This information would help marketing managers make decisions such as: ensure our cereal has high fiber; promotional messages should be developed linking freedom derived from good health derived from high-fiber diets. Demographic profiles of this target market could be used to buy media targeting this demographic group.

The summary report for the in-depth interview will look very similar to one written for a focus group study; that is, the analyst looks for common themes across several depth interview transcripts, and these are noted in the report. Verbatim responses are included in the report to support the analyst's conclusions, and any significant differences of opinion that are found in the respondents' comments are noted as well. Again, it is vital to use an analyst who is trained and experienced in interpreting the qualitative data gathered during depth interviews.

situations in which the researcher is convinced that respondents will be hesitant to relate their true opinions. Such situations may include behaviors like tipping waitresses, socially undesirable behaviors like smoking or alcohol consumption, questionable actions like littering, or even illegal practices like betting on football games. See Marketing Research Insight 8.4 for an example of the use of projective techniques with focus groups.

Five projective techniques are commonly used by marketers: the word-association test, the sentence-completion test, the picture test, the cartoon or balloon test, and role-playing activity. A discussion of each follows.

WORD-ASSOCIATION TEST. A **word-association test** involves reading words to a respondent, who then answers with the first word that comes to mind. These tests may contain over 100 words and usually combine neutral words with words being tested for ads or words involving

A word-association test involves reading words to a respondent, who then answers with the first word that comes to mind.

MARKETING RESEARCH INSIGHT　　　Practical Application

8.4 Using Projective Techniques to Discover New Insights: Turbo Charge Focus Groups with Projective & Interactive Exercises!

Focus group moderators are charged with discovering actionable insights. Marketers understand that most purchase decisions are made subconsciously and steeped with emotional imagery—both positive and negative associations. Marketers are keenly aware of the power of perception. So, how do moderators bypass the rational controls of consumers and strike up a meaningful dialogue that elicits emotions, perceptions, biases, and true buying motivations? Projective techniques and interactive exercises are the prescription here—tapping respondents' subconscious emotions and values that drive purchase behavior and shape brand relationships.

It is not enough to gather only rational thoughts in qualitative research. The challenge with pure questioning is that language is left-brain-based, the part of the brain that also processes logic, analysis, science, and math. Yet, brand relationships live in the human right brain, the part of the brain responsible for intuition, creativity, imagination, art, and music. In *How Customers Think*, author Gerald Zaltman asserts that 95% of purchase decisions are made subconsciously.

Using only structured dialogue, respondents often have difficulty expressing the sum total of their perceptions, opinions, and feelings. In a focus group that relies solely on structured dialogue, respondents can become too analytical. Therefore, moderators can use projective techniques and interactive exercises to aid respondents' verbalizing of their subconscious motivations. Interactive exercises can also uncover issues and opinions that respondents may not otherwise be able to fully verbalize, or of which they might be unaware. By increasing the variety of communication methods and modes, respondents can more easily express the whys behind their needs and feelings. As many of the techniques are tactile in nature, they promote insights from multiple senses, thus painting rich customer profiles.

According to *Qualitative Market Research* by Hy Miriampolski, projective techniques, which try to circumvent rational thinking, were adopted by the Freudians as another means of channeling into the unconscious mind. His book goes on to define projective techniques as a category of exercises that provide imagination and imagery. Other practitioners more narrowly define projectives as unstructured techniques used to project emotions onto unrelated stimuli. However, in practice, both true projective techniques and the wider class of interactive exercises bring forth deep-rooted emotions and

Holly M. O'Neill,
President

imagery associated with purchase decisions and provide marketers with exceptional, actionable insights.

Not only do projectives and interactive exercises allow marketers to uncover fresh insights, they result in a deeper level of understanding about target buyers. Further, on a tactical level, they create more engaging and productive rapport with respondents, which in turn inspires new marketing learning. By injecting creativity into the moderating process, projectives and interactive exercises keep the discussion moving and the energy level up in the room, which are also goals of the moderator. Field research has proven that when respondents are more engaged in the focus group, they are more willing and more able to open up, speak honestly, and express their inner thoughts, feelings, motivations, and biases. For the most part, respondents find these exercises to be fun, which further promotes their brains into stimulating new connections and thus providing additional learning for marketers.

Nearly all focus groups, regardless of the topic or respondent base can benefit from at least one projective or interactive exercise. Depending upon the research objectives, some focus groups can include more. Exercises can be designed for respondents to work individually, the group to work as a whole, or splitting the group into several smaller teams.

While there are literally hundreds of these types of exercises suitable for qualitative research, below you will find a few techniques that have wide applicability to different types of studies, objectives, and respondent types. Of course, each exercise should be customized, so that it is germane to the research at hand. Nonetheless, the more generic descriptions and instructions that follow are a great primer to introduce these exciting qualitative modalities.

Sort Me Up™

Sort Me Up is great for determining how target brands relate to their competition. This exercise uncovers similarities and differences across brands, product types, and product segments. It is valuable for segmentation studies, as it reveals frames of reference, thus allowing marketers to really understand what products the target brand most and least competes with. After several sorts (i.e., several focus groups), a purchase decision hierarchy emerges, which not only helps marketers understand consumer attitudes and usage patterns across different product segments but also provides an understanding of how consumers shop and consume the category under study.

To begin, the moderator places about 25 actual products on the table and asks respondents to work together as a team to sort the products into groups that make sense to them. Respondents are encouraged to create as many product groupings as they see fit. They are also instructed to give each group of items they've placed together a descriptive title. Note that for product categories where the size/shape of individual products/services is not easily brought into the focus group room (e.g., large appliances, online banking sites), Sort Me Up can be executed with cards imprinted with brand names, logos, package graphics, etc. This exercise engages respondents in a tangible way. There is visual stimulation as well as physical activity (i.e., moving the products around the table). The ensuing lively, postexercise discussion and probing provides marketers with key insights, largely unattainable through direct questioning.

Sort Me Straight™

Sort Me Straight is a variation of Sort Me Up. This variation is best implemented when the goal is to determine how the target brand and its competition perform on specific attributes. In brief, it assesses how the products under study are perceived on these specific attributes, relative to each other. It also assesses how brands perform relative to the specific attributes. Unlike Sort Me Up, this exercise is an aided technique, where consumers determine product rankings on a continuum based upon predetermined attributes. To begin, the moderator places 5–10 preselected products from the category on the table. The moderator then places pole cards on the table—opposite each other, leaving adequate room for the respondents to build the continuum. Pole cards are simply cards printed with the attributes, for example, Most Natural to Least Natural, Most Expensive to Cheapest, Masculine to Feminine, and For Guests vs. For Everyday.

Picture This, Picture That™

If a research goal is to learn about imagery and emotional associations for target brands, then Picture This, Picture That is a particularly insightful projective technique. In this exercise, pictures become metaphors for respondents to describe their perceptions. In brief, this technique allows respondents to think more broadly, frame their ideas and get over their inhibitions. The images trigger key perceptions and give consumers permission to divulge their innermost thoughts (as they project their real attitudes onto the image).

This exercise begins with about 50 preselected images that represent a wide range of emotions. It's important that the images be rich, but they can be from almost any source—magazine ads, art books, furniture catalogs, etc. It's imperative that images that are related to the topic under discussion are not included (e.g., soup for a soup study, honeymoon vacation if researching online dating). The moderator places these images on the table and asks respondents to individually select a picture that depicts how they feel about brand/category/situation. Of course, the question should be crafted to be consistent with study goals. An easy variation is to ask each respondent to select two images, for example, one that depicts the best thing and one that depicts the worst thing about brand/category/situation or one that depicts how they feel about shopping at Store A and one for Store B.

The tangible aspects of implementing this exercise, combined with the intangible aspects of the deep-seated imagery, yield insightful stories for marketers. The discussion and active probing surrounding the emotional underpinnings of these images and how they relate to the target brand reveal fresh insights, which can greatly aid the advertising team's ability to create more engaging campaigns.

Color My World™

Color My World is similar to Picture This, Picture That. Rather than utilizing rich images, this projective uses color as keys to uncovering consumer attitudes and perceptions. Here, colors become the metaphors for respondents to describe their thoughts and feelings. This quick and easy- to-implement exercise provokes storytelling and gives consumers considerable opportunity to verbalize positive and negative associations for the brand/category/situation under study.

To start, the moderator places several dozen paint chips on the table. Be sure to use a wide range of assorted colors. Again, it's imperative to exclude any category-related colors (e.g., exclude red and deep purple for a wine study). Ask respondents to choose a color that depicts how they feel when they buy or consume a brand or category, when they encounter a specific situation, etc. While this engaging exercise is suitable for most any juncture in the discussion guide, as a warm-up exercise, it has the added benefit of setting the stage for a deeper, more revealing conversation.

Dot, Dot, Dot™

This quali-quant technique helps marketers understand preferences among a set of brands, flavors, advertisements, etc. Dot, Dot, Dot yields weighted rankings, allowing marketers to iteratively narrow the range of ideas and concepts being researched. Most importantly, this exercise uncovers the functional and emotional rationale behind consumer perceptions.

This easy-to-implement technique begins with the moderator presenting respondents with a short list of choices (e.g., brands, flavors, advertisements) and 10 small, round dot stickers (think purchase tokens). Respondents are instructed to allocate the dots according to their preferences, placing as many dots as they feel appropriate (or even zero dots) on each option. Of course, they should place a greater number of dots on their preferred option(s), but how many is up to them. While the results are not statistically significant, they can be considered directional. The ensuing discussion following Dot, Dot, Dot provides fresh insights about customer preferences. When "forced" to vote their preferences, it is often easier for respondents to later divulge their needs, emotions, and biases underlying these preferences.

About Talking Business

Talking Business delivers the truth behind brands and what motivates purchase behavior—vital insights decision makers need to drive competitive marketing solutions. Offering more than focus group moderating, we specialize in innovative marketing research and strategic brand development. Our category expertise includes consumer, financial, pharmaceuticals, technology, and hospitality, with clients such as GlaxoSmithKline, Princess Cruises, and Experian. Exceeding client expectations for 12 years, Talking Business connects with target audiences to better understand brands, loud and clear. You can visit Talking Business at www.TalkingBusiness.net.

product names or services. The researcher then looks for hidden meanings or associations between responses and the words being tested on the original list to uncover people's real feelings about these products or services, brand names, or ad copy. The time taken to respond, called "response latency," and/or the respondents' physical reactions may be measured and used to make inferences. For example, if the response latency to the word *duo* is long, it may mean that people do not have an immediate association for that word.

Decision Analyst, Inc. uses word-association tests in its battery of qualitative online research services. Anywhere from 50 to 75 words are given to online respondents as stimuli. Respondents then type the first word, association, or image that comes to mind. Sample sizes are typically 100 to 200 persons, and the entire process lasts about 30 minutes. Decision Analyst states that this projective technique is very helpful in determining awareness or exploring the imagery or other associations that are linked to brands.[46]

With a sentence-completion test, respondents are given incomplete sentences and asked to complete them in their own words. The researcher then inspects these sentences to identify themes or concepts.

SENTENCE-COMPLETION TEST. With a **sentence-completion test**, respondents are given incomplete sentences and asked to complete them in their own words. The researcher then inspects these sentences to identify themes or concepts. The notion here is that respondents will reveal something about themselves in their responses. For example, suppose that Lipton Tea was interested in expanding its market to teenagers. A researcher might recruit high school students and instruct them to complete the following sentences:

Someone who drinks hot tea is _____.

Tea is good to drink when _____.

Making hot tea is _____.

My friends think tea is _____.

The researcher would attempt to identify central themes from the written responses. For instance, the theme identified from the first sentence might be "healthy," which would signify that tea is perceived as a drink for those who are health-conscious. The theme from the second sentence might be "hot," indicating that tea is perceived as a cold-weather drink, whereas the theme from the third sentence may turn out to be "messy," denoting the students' reaction to using a tea bag. Finally, the theme from the last sentence might be "okay," suggesting there are no peer pressures that would cause high school students to avoid drinking tea. Given this information, Lipton might deduce that there is opportunity to capitalize on the hot-tea market with teens. Decision Analyst, Inc. also conducts sentence-completion tests online by giving 50 to 75 respondents 50 to 60 incomplete sentences.[47]

In a picture test, participants are given a picture and are instructed to describe their reactions by writing a short story about it.

PICTURE TEST. In a **picture test**, participants are given a picture and are instructed to describe their reactions by writing a short story about it. The researcher analyzes the content of these stories to ascertain feelings, reactions, or concerns generated by the picture. Such tests are useful when testing images being considered for use in brochures, advertisements, and on product packaging. For example, a test advertisement might depict a man holding a baby, and the ad headline might say, "Ford includes driver and passenger airbags as standard equipment because you love your family." A picture test may well divulge something about the picture that is especially negative or distasteful. Perhaps unmarried male respondents cannot relate to the ad because they do not have children and have not experienced strong feelings for children. On the other hand, it may turn out that the picture has a much more neutral tone than Ford's advertising agency intended. It may be that the picture does not generate feelings of concern and safety for the family in married respondents with young children. In any case, without a picture test, it would be very difficult to determine the audience's potential reactions.

CARTOON OR BALLOON TEST. A **balloon test** is a line drawing with an empty "balloon" above the head of one of the figures. Subjects are instructed to write in the balloon what the figure is saying or thinking. The researcher then examines these responses to find out how subjects feel about the situation depicted in the cartoon. For example, shown a line drawing of a situation in which one of the characters is making the statement "Ford Explorers are on sale with a discount of $4,000 and 0% interest for 48 months," the participant is asked how the other character in the drawing would respond. Feelings and reactions of the subject are judged based on their answers.

A balloon test is a line drawing with an empty "balloon" above the head of one of the figures. Subjects are instructed to write in the balloon what the figure is saying or thinking. The researcher then examines these responses to find out how subjects feel about the situation depicted in the cartoon.

ROLE-PLAYING ACTIVITY. In a **role-playing** activity, participants are asked to pretend they are a "third person," such as a friend or neighbor, and to describe how they would act in a certain situation or react to a specific statement. By reviewing their comments, the researcher can spot latent reactions, positive or negative, conjured up by the situation. The idea is that this method will reveal some of the respondents' true feelings and beliefs because they are pretending to be another individual. For example, if Ray-Ban is thinking about introducing a new "Astronaut" sunglasses model with superior ultraviolet light filtration, space-age styling, and a price of about $200, it might use role-playing exercises to discover what consumers' initial reactions would be. Subjects could be asked to assume the role of a friend or close workmate and indicate what that person would say to a third person when learning that their friend had purchased a pair of Astronaut sunglasses. If consumers felt the Astronaut model was overpriced, this feeling would quickly surface. On the other hand, if the space-age construction and styling are consistent with these consumers' lifestyles and product desires, this fact would be divulged in the role-playing comments. A form of role playing is "walking in your customer's shoes," as illustrated by The Thought Bubble in Marketing Research Insight 8.5.

In a role-playing activity, participants are asked to pretend they are a "third person," such as a friend or neighbor, and to describe how they would act in a certain situation or react to a specific statement. By reviewing their comments, the researcher can spot latent reactions, positive or negative, conjured up by the situation.

As with depth interviews, all of these projective techniques require highly qualified professionals to interpret the results, which increases the cost per respondent compared to other survey methods. Thus, projective techniques are not used extensively in commercial marketing research, but each has its value in its special realm of application.[48]

Ethnographic Research

Ethnographic research, a technique borrowed from anthropology, is a detailed, descriptive study of a group and its behavior, characteristics, culture, and so on.[49] *Ethno* means "people" and *graphy* means "to describe."[50] Anthropologists have gained insights into human behavior by living among their subjects (called *immersion*) for prolonged periods to study their emotions, behaviors, and reactions to the demands of everyday events. Ethnography uses several different types of research, including immersion, participant observation, and informal and ongoing in-depth interviewing. Ethnographers pay close attention to words, metaphors, symbols, and stories people use to explain their lives and communicate with one another.[51] Marketers have made use of ethnographic research techniques to study consumer behavior and many believe they

Ethnographic research, a technique borrowed from anthropology, is a detailed, descriptive study of a group and its behavior, characteristics, culture, and so on.[49] *Ethno* means "people" and *graphy* means " to describe."

MARKETING RESEARCH INSIGHT

Practical Application

8.5 Walking in the Customer's Shoes Gives Insights Leading to New Ideas at The Thought Bubble

New ideas are the life blood of brands and the best ideas are those driven by consumer insights. It is the responsibility and burden of a company's marketing team to stay as close to the consumer as possible. A critical tool for getting close to the consumer is consumer research: the art of getting to know the consumer. We categorize consumer research as Quantitative or Quantitative Research. In Quantitative Research we are trying to learn answers to the *What, When,* and *Where* questions. In Qualitative Research we are attempting to answer the *Why* and *How* questions.

Farnaz Badie, Founder
and President, The
Thought Bubble

the **thought** bubble

At The Thought Bubble, a dynamic Qualitative Research consultancy, we specialize in helping marketing teams determine the best consumer-insight-driven ideas. We use client ideation sessions as well as innovative consumer interviewing techniques in order to bring out the best ideas in both clients and consumers. The Thought Bubble's typical ideation session with the client is an iterative process: it involves "walking in the consumer's shoes" as much as possible in order to define the most compelling consumer needs, wants, and insights that enable the team to ideate. Key consumers are brought in at crucial points during the ideation session in order to enhance the ideas generated. The Thought Bubble uses a number of innovative techniques in order to maximize creativity during the consumer interview sessions. The Thought Bubble team constantly challenges the status quo: from the interview room set-up to the tools used to create consumer-centric ideas. This allows us to find better ways of "peeling back the onion" to obtain more in-depth and meaningful consumer feedback.

The Thought Bubble provides fresh new ideas to clients using qualitative research.

Farnaz Badie, Founder and President
The Thought Bubble LLC
Visit The Thought Bubble at: www.thethoughtbubble.com

are doing so more frequently (see Marketing Research Insight 8.6). Unlike anthropologists, however, marketing researchers do not immerse themselves in consumers' lives for months on end. Rather, they use direct observation, interviews, and audio and video recordings of consumers conducted over time instead of at a point in time, as most other research is done. One researcher, Ann-Marie McDermott of Quaestor Research, who was working on a new chicken burger project, decided to spend time with consumers instead of using the standard research techniques. She visited their homes and watched them shop, cook, and eat.[52]

Ethnographers pay close attention to words, metaphors, symbols, and stories people use to explain their lives and communicate with one another. Marketers have increasingly used ethnographic research to study consumer behavior.

Ethnographic research is an area of ethical sensitivity. Researchers immersing themselves in others' homes, schools, and places of work and play in order to record the behaviors, comments, reactions, and emotions of persons who do not know the purposes of the research is unethical. As the technique grows more common in marketing research, researchers must become adept in the skills necessary to be "present and known" without interfering with normal behavior. Fortunately, most behaviors marketers are interested in are public behaviors—shopping and eating, for example. Such public behaviors are easily observed.

MARKETING RESEARCH INSIGHT   Practical Application

8.6 Ethnography Enjoying Resurgence as Important Qualitative Tactic

More and more companies are mandating that the marketing, research, and R&D staff get to know their consumers "up close and personal" on a regular basis. Ethnography—qualitative research that studies people in their own natural habitat—is enjoying resurgence among marketers because it provides that real-life, first-hand observation of experiences.

Ethnography differs from laboratory-based research (focus groups) because it allows the interviewer the opportunity to observe and study subjects in their own surroundings and around family and friends, if applicable. Describing how someone cleans a floor and actually watching how it is done is a completely different experience. In a Q&A format, participants may be reluctant to "spill the beans" on how much they rely on convenience food, that their kids eat sugared cereal, or that they love to eat chocolate while watching TV in the afternoon. In their homes, however, you see what is in their cupboards and refrigerator.

Some other examples of ethnographic qualitative research are:

1. Moms at home to see what they make for dinner.
2. Men at breakfast to observe what they eat and why.
3. Shopping with people at supermarkets and retail stores to observe how they shop and how they make brand decision choices.
4. "Hanging out" with teen girls as they shop and socialize in the mall.
5. Walking with seniors in their walking groups and listening to them discuss their hopes, fears, worries, health, and family/friends.
6. Watching people use a product they have been given days ago to find out how it fits into their routine (test product or a competitive product).
7. The "before and after" of someone taking a medication to observe how it makes or does not make a difference in their life.

"He told us he only ate fruit but we saw 12 packages of Twinkies in the pantry!"

Source: Qualitative Research Consultants Association
By permission: QRCA

Physiological Measurement

Physiological measurement involves monitoring a respondent's involuntary responses to marketing stimuli via the use of electrodes and other equipment. Most people who are monitored find the situation strange, and they may experience uneasiness during the monitoring. Due to this reaction and the hardware required, this measurement technique is rarely used in marketing research. However, we will briefly describe two physiological measures to round out this chapter on qualitative research: the pupilometer and the galvanometer. The **pupilometer** is a device that attaches to a person's head and determines interest and attention by measuring the amount of dilation in the pupil of the eye. It actually photographs the movement of the pupil as the subject views different pictures. The theory is that a person's pupil enlarges more when viewing an interesting image than when viewing an uninteresting one. Eye-tracking has a new application in Internet marketing. For example, AT&T has begun to use eye-tracking coupled with depth interviewing to understand how AT&T customers interact with its customer service website.[53] The **galvanometer** is a device that determines excitement levels by measuring the electrical activity in the respondent's skin. It requires electrodes or sensing pads to be taped to a

Physiological measurement involves monitoring a respondent's involuntary responses to marketing stimuli via the use of electrodes and other equipment.

The pupilometer is a device that attaches to a person's head and determines interest and attention by measuring the amount of dilation in the pupil of the eye.

The galvanometer is a device that determines excitement levels by measuring the electrical activity in the respondent's skin.

person's body in order to monitor this activity. When encountering an interesting stimulus, the electrical impulses in the body become excited.

Physiological measures are useful under special circumstances, such as testing sexually oriented stimuli, which many people are embarrassed about and so may not tell the truth, and they require special skills to be administered correctly. Their disadvantages are that the techniques are unnatural and subjects may become nervous and emit false readings and that even though the respondent reacts to the stimulus, there is no way to tell if the response is positive or negative.[54]

Other Qualitative Research Techniques

There are many qualitative research techniques other than those we have identified in this chapter.

The various techniques described thus far are in no way a complete list, for a number of other techniques are used to study human behavior. In addition, some promising analytical techniques are emerging for interpreting the marketing strategy implications of qualitative data.[55] Each new qualitative research technique requires that the researcher understand its theoretical and practical aspects in order to apply it properly, so it is often best to hire a specialist with expertise in that particular technique. Even so, companies specializing in these new techniques report that clients are cautious at first.[56] But qualitative techniques are fast and relatively inexpensive, and companies have found qualitative research to be very satisfactory when funds are low and time is short.[57] Bissell, for example, changed the name of its cleaner unit from the Steam Gun to Steam N' Clean after qualitative research found that children would want to use a Steam Gun to threaten their siblings.

 Synthesize Your Learning

This exercise will require you to take into consideration concepts and material from the following chapters:

Chapter 6:   Using Secondary Data and Online Information Databases
Chapter 7:   Comprehending Standardized Information Sources
Chapter 8:   Utilizing Exploratory and Qualitative Research Techniques

Lucy Betcher had worked as a consultant for the Small Business Administration for a number of years. Her old high school classmates and their spouses gather at least once a year to renew friendships. Judy Doyle, Mike Fuller, Adele Smith, Nancy Egolf, Joy Greer, and Jackie Reynolds had had different careers and several in the group were retiring. At their last reunion, Jackie mentioned to Lucy that she was interested in doing something else after retiring from school teaching. Adele, overhearing this conversation, said she was interested in doing something as well. Could Lucy, with all her years of helping others get started in business, help her friends?

The next morning, while sitting on Todd and Joy's comfortable balcony overlooking boats in a canal, Lucy asked the entire group, "Jackie and Adele are interested in getting into some sort of business opportunity. Do any of you have any thoughts on this?" Mike, having spent a successful career in pharmaceutical sales, said, "There are opportunities in services for senior citizens in terms of prescription drug management and administration." Mike informed them that one of the big problems for many persons living at home or even in retirement homes was making sure that their prescriptions were filled and that they took the medicines as prescribed. "It's a real problem when people get to be 85 and over. I see a growing need for a personal service that would provide this type of care."

Nancy and Judy spoke up and talked about a unique coffee shop they had patronized. The staff was very knowledgeable about different types of coffees, you could sample the different flavors, and the shop also sold different types of coffee and tea makers and books about coffee and teas. However, what they really liked was the atmosphere. Instead of having the placid and contemplative atmosphere of most coffee shops, this shop featured different exhibits every week that were actually "learning" exhibits with which you could interact and so get involved in learning something about many different topics—local history, coffee making, art, music, and readings by authors. The two classmates were fascinated with the shop and had talked to the owner about franchising the concept so they could start one in their hometowns in Pennsylvania and New York. The owner told them he had several successful franchises operating. However, their biggest problem would be locating their shops where they would attract the kind of customer who would like the shop. The owner told them he didn't know about locations outside of his own and they would need help finding the right spot.

1. Looking back at Chapter 6, what secondary data could Nancy and Judy use to identify the number of persons in different age groups in each CBSA?

2. From Chapter 7, identify a standardized services firm that would be helpful in locating a successful coffee shop locale. Assume that since the coffee shop owner has several successful franchises, he has a database of current customer information.

3. Considering either the prescription service or the coffee shop venture, what qualitative research techniques would you recommend the classmates use at this point? Why would you recommend these qualitative techniques?

Summary

This chapter described the various qualitative research techniques used by marketing researchers. Quantitative research involves predetermined structured questions with predetermined structured response options, normally with large samples. Qualitative research is much less structured than quantitative approaches. Qualitative research involves collecting, analyzing, and interpreting data by observing what people do or say. The observations and statements are in a qualitative or unstructured, nonstandardized form. The advantage of qualitative research is that it allows researchers to gather deeper, richer information from respondents. Pluralistic research involves using both qualitative and quantitative research methods.

Observation is a qualitative research technique in which researchers observe what consumers do rather than communicate with them. The four general types of observation are direct versus indirect, disguised versus undisguised, structured versus unstructured, and human versus mechanical. The circumstances most suitable to observational studies are instances of (1) short time interval, (2) public behavior, and (3) lack of recall. Ethical issues arise in observation studies when respondents are not aware they are being observed. The primary advantage of observation is that researchers record what respondents actually do instead of relying on their recall of what they think they have done. The limitations of observation studies are that they often rely on small samples, so representativeness is a concern. Another disadvantage is that subjective interpretation is required to explain the behavior observed. Researchers do not know consumers' motives, attitudes, or intentions.

Focus groups, moderated small-group discussions, are a very popular form of research. The major task of the moderator is to ensure free-wheeling and open communication that is focused on the research topic. Traditional focus groups are made up of about 6 to 12 persons who meet in a dedicated room with a one-way mirror for client viewing. In recent years, many innovations have been introduced, comprising what we call nontraditional focus groups. Online focus groups, in which clients may observe a focus group from a distant location via video streaming over the Internet, are one example of such innovations. Another form of online focus group allows the group members to participate from their homes or any remote location where they can observe and respond to others in the focus group via chat rooms. Focus groups have the following advantages: (1) they generate fresh ideas; (2) they allow clients to observe the participants; and (3) they may be directed at understanding a wide variety of issues. Disadvantages include lack of representativeness, subjective evaluation of the meaning of the discussions, and high cost per participant. Focus groups should be used when the researcher needs to describe marketing phenomena. They should not be used when the researcher needs to predict a phenomenon, such as how many persons will actually buy a new product evaluated by focus groups. Four main objectives of focus groups are to generate ideas; to understand consumer vocabulary; to reveal consumer needs, motives, perceptions, and attitudes about products or services; and to better understand findings from quantitative studies.

The chapter presented several operational issues involved in running focus groups. We noted that participants should share similar characteristics and that recruiting and selection may be problematic because of "no-shows." Focus group facilities exist in most major cities, but any large room with a central table can be used. The moderator's role is key to a successful focus group, and the moderator should be involved early on in the research project.

We wrapped up the chapter with descriptions of some of the other qualitative techniques used in marketing research. Depth interviews, for instance, have been adapted to probe consumer motivations and hidden concerns. Protocol analysis induces participants to "think aloud" so the researcher can map the decision-making process being used while a consumer goes about making a purchase decision. Projective techniques, such as word association, sentence completion, or role playing, are also useful in unearthing motivations, beliefs, and attitudes that subjects may not be able to express well verbally. Ethnographic research involves observing consumers in near-natural settings to record their behaviors, relations with others, and emotions. Finally, some physiological measurements, such as pupil movement or electrical skin activity, can be used in special circumstances to better understand consumer reactions.

Key Terms

Quantitative research 211
Qualitative research 211
Pluralistic research 212
Observation methods 213
Direct observation 213
Indirect observation 214
Archives 215
Physical traces 215
Disguised observation 215
Undisguised observation 215
Structured observation 215
Unstructured observation 215
Human observation 216
Mechanical observation 216

Focus groups 209
Traditional focus group 218
Nontraditional focus group 218
Focus group facility 218
Moderators 218
Qualitative Research
   Consultants 218
Focus group report 218
Online focus group 220
Depth interview 225
Laddering 226
Protocol analysis 226
Projective techniques 226
Word-association test 227

Sort Me Up™ 229
Sort Me Straight™ 229
Picture This, Picture That™ 229
Color My World™ 229
Dot, Dot, Dot™ 229
Sentence-completion
   test 230
Picture test 230
Balloon test 231
Role-playing 231
Ethnographic research 231
Physiological measurement 233
Pupilometer 233
Galvanometer 233

Review Questions/Applications

1. Define quantitative research. Define qualitative research. List the differences between these two research methods. What is pluralistic research?
2. What is meant by an "observation technique"? What is observed, and why is it recorded?
3. Indicate why disguised observation would be appropriate for a study on how parents discipline their children when dining out.
4. Describe a traditional focus group.
5. Describe two formats of online focus groups.
6. Describe at least three different uses of focus groups.
7. How are focus group participants recruited, and what is a common problem associated with this recruitment?
8. Should the members of a focus group be similar or dissimilar? Why?
9. Describe what a focus group company facility looks like and how a focus group would take place in one.
10. Should the client marketing manager be a focus group moderator? Why or why not?

11. Indicate how a focus group moderator should handle each of the following cases: (a) A participant is loud and dominates the conversation; (b) a participant is obviously suffering from a cold and goes into coughing fits every few minutes; (c) two participants who, it turns out, are acquaintances persist in a private conversation about their children; and (d) the only minority representative participant in the focus group looks very uncomfortable with the group and fails to make any comments.

12. What should be included in a report that summarizes the findings of a focus group?

13. Indicate the advantages and disadvantages of client interaction in the design and execution of a focus group study.

14. What is laddering? Discuss how it may be used in marketing research.

15. What is protocol analysis?

16. What is meant by the term *projective* as in *projective techniques*?

17. Describe (a) sentence completion, (b) word association, and (c) a balloon test. Create one of each test that might be used to test the reactions of mothers whose children are bed-wetters to absorbent underpants that their children would wear under their nightclothes.

18. What is ethnographic research? Discuss how a marketing researcher could get into an ethically sensitive situation using the technique.

19. What is physiological measurement? Give examples of two techniques.

20. Associated Grocery Stores (AGS) has always used paper bags for sacking groceries in its chain of retail supermarkets. Management has noticed that some competitors are offering reusable bags to their customers. AGS management isn't certain just how strongly consumers in its markets feel about recycling. Select two projective techniques and explain why you chose these techniques. Then describe in detail how your two chosen techniques would be applied to this research problem.

21. Your university is considering letting an apartment management company build an apartment complex on campus. To save money, the company proposes to include a common cooking area for every four apartments. This area would be equipped with an oven, stove-top burners, microwave oven, sink, food preparation area, garbage disposal, and individual locked mini-refrigerators for each apartment. With two students in each apartment, eight students would be using the common cooking area. You volunteer to conduct focus groups with students to determine their reactions to this concept and to brainstorm suggestions for improvements. Prepare the topics list you would use as a guide in your role as moderator.

CASE 8.1

THE COLLEGE EXPERIENCE

This case was provided by Professor Daniel Purdy, Assistant Director of the MBA Program and Professor Wendy Wilhelm, Professor of Marketing, both of Western Washington University.

Dr. Daniel Purdy, Western Washington University

The College of Business at Western University is a full-service business school at a mid-size regional university. The College of Business specializes primarily in undergraduate business education with selected graduate programs. While the college emphasizes mostly professional education, it does so within a liberal arts context. Business majors range from standards such as accounting, marketing, and finance to unique offerings such as the highly successful manufacturing and supply chain management degree.

The college is committed to a student-centered style of education, which emphasizes students not as customers per se but as equal stakeholders in the process of education. As part of its commitment to involving students as true partners, the college has recently begun the process of conducting focus groups of undergraduate and graduate students. The objective of these focus groups is to identify negative and positive attitudes about the college and develop new ideas to improve the college.

The following is an excerpt from the transcript of the first undergraduate focus group. This group was comprised of 14 students with the characteristics found in the charts on the next page.

Dr. Wendy Wilhelm, Western Washington University

Moderator: So what do you guys think are some ways that the college (not the university) can be improved?

Jeff: I really like the fact that professors are accessible, willing to help and a lot of them let us call them by their first name. Something that I think could be better is that we don't spend enough time learning how to do things but instead professors spend too much time talking about theory.

Sarah: Yea, Yea, I agree totally. It seems like most of the time we aren't learning practical skills but just talking about what we "should" do, not really learning how to do it.

Moderator: Interesting points, how would you suggest the college try to increase the amount of practical learning?

Todd: It would really be cool if we could do more real-life professional work in our classes. Things like skill-based projects that focus on doing what we would really do in our profession.

Tim: I think we should all have to do a mandatory internship as part of our major. Right now, some majors let you do it as an elective but they are really hard to find and get.

Moderator: Good ideas. Are there other things you think we could improve?

Rhonda: I agree that the professors try really hard to be open to students but the advising is really not very good. I don't know how to fix it but I know my advisor is pretty much useless.

Ariel: I know, I know. It is so frustrating sometimes. I go to my advisor and she tells me to just fill in my degree planning sheet and she'll sign it. It's like they don't even know what I should be taking or why.

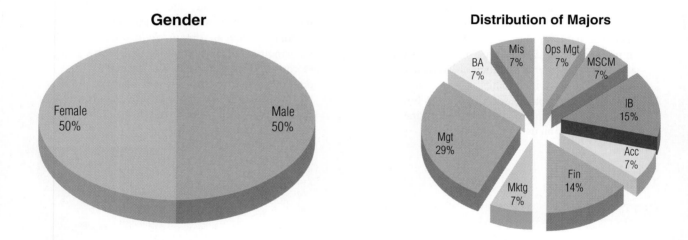

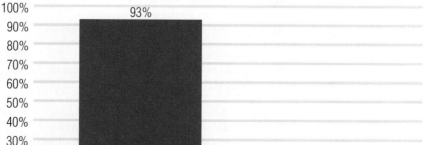

Jon: My advisor is kind of funny, he just tells me that he doesn't really know that much about classes he doesn't teach and my guess is as good as his. At least he's honest anyway.

Moderator: Ok, Ok, so the advising you are getting from the faculty leaves a little to be desired. What do you guys do to figure out how to plan your degrees if your advisors aren't helping much?

Sarah: I just ask my friends who are further along in the major than I am.

Mark: Yea, me too. In the Student Marketing Association we all give each other advice on what professors are good, what classes go good together, which have prerequisites and stuff like that. It would be cool if we could have something like that for the whole college.

Moderator: Don't you think CBE could be improved if we developed some sort of peer-advising program?

Using these excerpts as representative of the entire focus group transcript, answer the following questions.

1. Do you think focus groups were the appropriate research method in this case, given the research objectives? What other type(s) of research might provide useful data?
2. Evaluate the questions posed by the moderator in light of the research objectives/ question: (a) Are any of them leading or biasing in any way? (b) Can you think of any additional questions that could/should be included?
3. Examine the findings. How is CBE perceived? What are its apparent strengths and weaknesses?
4. Can we generalize these findings to all of the college's students? Why or why not?

CASE 8.2 **Your Integrated Case**

ADVANCED AUTOMOBILE CONCEPTS

This case was provided by Professor Philip Trocchia, Associate Professor of Marketing, University of South Florida, St. Petersburg, Florida.

Nick Thomas, CEO of Advanced Automobile Concepts has begun formulating some concepts in terms of the types of car models to pursue to bring ZEN Motors' product line back to life. He has been using a cross-functional approach to new-product development involving finance, production, R&D, marketing, and advertising in his planning. Recently, Ashley Roberts, from advertising, discussed some of the general plans for the new car models with Thomas. Nick told Ashley that he will need more marketing research information on customer preferences for different types of cars. However, he told her the broad choices will come down to different-sized vehicles with some much smaller than ZEN had ever built. One model being considered was a very small, almost scooter-like car. Other models were larger but still much smaller than ZEN's traditional line of cars in order to obtain suitable mpg ratings. Ashley knew that this meant a big change for ZEN and the way it had advertised for years. She wondered if the customers who would prefer the new, smaller models would possess different sets of salient values. Perhaps those who prefer the "scooter-like" model would value excitement and entertainment in their lives while those expressing a preference for the larger-sized, high-mpg models would place a higher priority on social recognition or harmony with the environment or some other value. If differences are found, the agency would alter the values emphasized in the ad's visuals and copy (e.g., depicting an exciting life, thrill of the drive, or sense of accomplishment, or recognition of contributing to environmental problems, etc. to suit the model of the car being promoted.

What technique identified in this chapter would help Ashley Roberts with this advertising task? Why?

Learning Objectives

- To learn the four basic alternative modes for gathering survey data

- To understand the advantages and disadvantages of each of the alternative data-collection modes

- To become knowledgeable about the details of different types of survey data-collection methods, such as personal interviews, telephone interviews, and computer-assisted interviews, including online surveys

- To comprehend the factors researchers consider when choosing a particular survey method

Where We Are

1 Establish the need for marketing research
2 Define the problem
3 Establish research objectives
4 Determine research design
5 Identify information types and sources
6 Determine methods of accessing data
7 Design data-collection forms
8 Determine the sample plan and size
9 Collect data
10 Analyze data, and
11 Prepare and present the final research report.

Situations Where Personal Interviewing Is Needed to Collect Data

Hal Meier, Owner TAi Companies.

TAi Companies specializes in collecting data. Its facilities, located in New Jersey, Tampa, and Denver, allow for focus groups and other marketing research studies. OPS, Opinion Polling Service, is a division of TAi Companies that specializes in on-site (or on-location) personal interviewing when the situation dictates using personal interviewers. We asked Hal Meier, owner, to give some examples of when it is best to personally interview consumers.

- XYZ chain restaurant regularly tests new menu items to discover if any can replace current offerings. Respondents fill out a survey form at the conclusion of their meal, so the survey is completed by real customers in the same setting in which the product is consumed commercially. Refusal rates are very low. It is impossible to duplicate this direct taste test in an artificial setting.

- XYZ bank asks their own customers why/whether they are using a new service (i.e., holiday layaway). Since the target population is their own customers, they can easily be recruited in the bank. The incidence rate is nearly 100%; almost all intercepts qualify.

- XYZ paint company distributes through a local mass merchandiser and wants to know how their paint compares with other brands, broken down by professional painters vs. home owners. By interviewing on the premises of the mass merchandiser, it is easy to identify respondents and brands they select at the paint department.

Hal Meier's basic philosophy is that, in many situations, it should be a great advantage to interview respondents in the same setting in which they will consume or purchase the product and to have them see and hold the product instead of looking at an image on a computer screen.

Visit TAi Companies at: www.taicompanies.com.

By permission, TAi Companies.

Surveys involve interviews with a large number of respondents using a predesigned questionnaire. This chapter focuses upon the data-collection methods used for surveys.

As you are learning in this course, there are many different ways of conducting marketing research studies. In previous chapters, we discussed different forms of research, such as focus groups, experiments, and surveys. There are many ways of gathering information from these various types of studies. In this chapter, our attention is on surveys. **Surveys** involve interviews with a large number of respondents using a predesigned questionnaire.[1] Communication is necessary to learn what respondents are thinking and their opinions, preferences, or intentions. Large numbers of respondents may be required in order to collect a large enough sample of important subgroups or to ensure that the study accurately represents some larger population. In this chapter, we focus on the various methods used to collect data for surveys. Often, as described in our opening vignette about the data-collection strategies used by TAi Companies, the researcher must design the data-collection method(s) around the special circumstances of the group to be surveyed in order to obtain a reasonable sample of respondents.

This chapter begins with a short discussion on why surveys are popular and advantageous. Next, it describes four basic survey modes: (1) person-administered surveys, (2) computer-assisted surveys, (3) self-administered surveys, and (4) mixed-mode, sometimes called "hybrid" surveys. We discuss the advantages and disadvantages of each of these modes and present the various alternative methods of collecting data within each of three basic data-collection modes. For example, person-administered surveys may be conducted through mall intercepts or telephone. Finally, we discuss factors a marketing researcher should consider when deciding which data-collection method to use.

ADVANTAGES OF SURVEYS

As you now know, compared to observation or other qualitative methods, survey methods allow the collection of significant amounts of data in an economical and efficient manner, and they typically involve large sample sizes. There are five advantages of using survey methods: (1) standardization, (2) ease of administration, (3) ability to tap the "unseen," (4) suitability to tabulation and statistical analysis, and (5) sensitivity to subgroup differences (see Table 9.1).

Key advantages of surveys include standardization, ease of administration, ability to tap the "unseen," suitability to tabulation and statistical analysis, and sensitivity to subgroup differences.

Surveys Provide for Standardization

Because questions are preset and organized in a particular arrangement on a questionnaire, survey methods ensure that all respondents are asked the same questions and are exposed to the same response options for each question. This uniformity is vital to the goal of high-quality information. Moreover, the researcher is assured that every respondent will be confronted with questions that address the complete range of information objectives driving the research project.

Surveys Are Easy to Administer

Sometimes surveys are conducted by an interviewer. Surveys are easily geared to such administration. On the other hand, the respondent may fill out the questionnaire unattended. In either case, the administrative aspects are much simpler than those for conducting a focus group or depth interviews. Perhaps the simplest is a survey in which a respondent answers questions online. All the researcher needs to do is design the questionnaire, publish it on the Internet, and invite prospective respondents to fill it out.

Online surveys are self-administered, the simplest form of administration for researchers.

TABLE 9.1   Five Advantages of Surveys

Advantage	Description
Provides standardization	All respondents react to questions worded identically and presented in the same order. Response options (scales) are the same, too.
Easy to administer	Interviewers read questions to respondents and record their answers quickly and easily. In many cases, the respondents read and respond to the questionnaires themselves.
Gets "beneath the surface"	Although not to the extent of depth interviews or focus groups, surveys commonly ask questions about motives, circumstances, sequences of events, or mental deliberations.
Easy to analyze	Standardization and computer processing allow for quick tallies, cross-tabulations, and other statistical analyses despite large sample sizes.
Reveals subgroup differences	Respondents can be divided into segments or subgroups (such as users versus nonusers; age groups, etc.) for comparisons in the search for meaningful differences.

Questionnaire design programs include statistical analysis packages as a natural extension of survey research.

Surveys Get "Beneath the Surface"

The four questions of what, why, how, and who reveal "unseen" data. For instance, we can ask a working parent to tell us the importance of location in the selection of a child's preschool. We can inquire how many different preschools were seriously considered, and we can easily gain an understanding of the person's financial or work circumstances with a few questions about income, occupation, and family size. Much information that marketing researchers desire is unobservable and requires direct questioning.

Surveys Are Easy To Analyze

The marketing researcher ultimately must interpret the patterns or common themes sometimes hidden in the raw data collected. Statistical analysis, both simple and complex, is the preferred means of achieving this goal and is especially suitable for large cross-sectional surveys. In contrast, determining patterns and common themes by means of qualitative methods proves much more difficult because they involve small samples, require subjective interpretation, and involve a general approach to answering questions. Questionnaire design software has made it possible to perform simple statistical analyses, such as tabulations of the answers to each question, and to create graphs to summarize these tabulations.

Surveys allow researchers to look at different types of respondents.

Surveys Reveal Subgroup Differences

Because surveys involve large numbers of respondents, it is relatively easy to "slice up" the sample into demographic groups or other subgroups and then to compare them to understand market segmentation implications. In fact, the survey sample design may be drawn up to specifically include important subgroups as a means of looking at differences among market segments.

 Experience the Advantages of Surveys

To experience the various advantages of surveys you have just read about, administer the following survey to four of your friends, two males and two females. You have the options of (1) writing or typing the questions on paper and handing them to each friend or (2) reading each question and recording the answers of each friend individually.

1. Did you watch television last night?

   _____ Yes   _____ No

2. (If yes) For about how many hours did you watch television last night?

   _____ Less than 1 _____ Between 1 and 2 _____ Between 2 and 4 _____ More than 4

3. Why do you usually watch television? (Select only one)

   _____ Entertainment (Variety, Humor, Drama, Sports, Talk)
   _____ Education (Science, News, History, Cooking)
   _____ Escape (Science Fiction, Action, Reality, Travel)

4. What is your gender?

   _____ Male _____ Female

Now that you have administered the survey, let's consider its advantages.

Standardization.

How have the response options for Questions 2 and 3 standardized the survey? In other words, what answers might have occurred if you did not give your respondents these specific response categories from which to pick?

Ease of Analysis.

What percentage of your friends who took part in the survey watched television last night? What percentage of them watched TV for 4 or more hours? How long did it take you to tabulate the answers to these questions? Also, depending on whether the respondents checked off or voiced the answers, how did this affect the task of analysis?

Ease of Administration.

How difficult was it to administer the survey? One way to answer this is to estimate how long it took you, on average, to obtain each respondent's answers.

Get Beneath the Surface.

Do your friends watch television mostly for entertainment, education, or escape? Tabulate the answers to Question 3 to find out. Notice that with a single question you have discovered the reasons (i.e., motivations) for your friends' television viewing.

Subgroup Differences.

Do the answers from the two males differ from those of the two females? Do separate percentage tabulations for each gender and compare them. In a matter of a few minutes, you can spot whether or not differences exist in the subgroups and what the differences are.

Understanding New Survey Data-Collection Methods

Surely, you have personally experienced the wave of technological advances in communications. In the case of data collection for the marketing research industry, there have been and continue to be profound changes. These are partly due to shifts in consumer preferences in communications. For example, many consumers prefer wireless telephones with caller identification and conference-calling capabilities. The changes in the industry have also come about due to technological advances that make the data-collection process faster, simpler, more secure, and even less expensive.

In Figure 9.1, we have identified the traditional or "old" methods of data collection and shown how new and better approaches have evolved. Some of the terms describing the "modern" methods in Figure 9.1 are undoubtedly unfamiliar to you. However, as you will encounter them in this chapter, learn their definitions, and come to appreciate why these methods are currently much preferred in the marketing research industry.

FOUR ALTERNATIVE MODES OF DATA COLLECTION

At the outset, we must alert you to the fact that the data-collection step in the marketing research process is undergoing great changes, for two reasons. First, in recent decades, the willingness of the general public to take part in surveys has dramatically declined; and second, significant advances in computer and telecommunications technology have opened up new, efficient ways for marketing researchers to collect data.

With respect to declining survey response rates, Roger Tourangeau[2] has identified the major reasons for this trend in a recent article. The factors underlying the growing unwillingness of the U.S. public to take part in surveys are the increasing use of "gatekeepers,"

SPSS Student Assistant:
About your SPSS Student
Assistant
Quick Tour I
Quick Tour II

FIGURE 9.1

**Impact of
Technology on
Data-Collection
Methods**

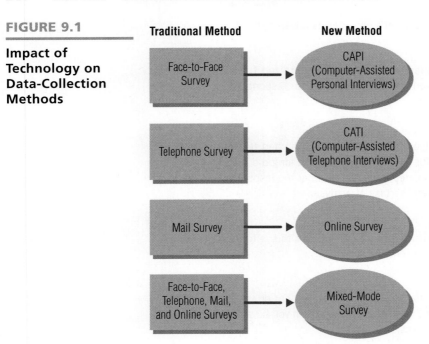

Traditional Method	New Method
Face-to-Face Survey	CAPI (Computer-Assisted Personal Interviews)
Telephone Survey	CATI (Computer-Assisted Telephone Interviews)
Mail Survey	Online Survey
Face-to-Face, Telephone, Mail, and Online Surveys	Mixed-Mode Survey

such as answering machines, caller ID, and call blocking (e.g., it is estimated that 11 million Americans use mobile phones exclusively and 64 million households are on the Federal "do-not-call list[3]); reduced amounts of free time; a decline in the public's engagement with important issues; the rising numbers of foreign-born Americans who are not fluent in English; and the growth in the elderly population, who have comprehension and expression difficulties. Americans also have a growing desire for privacy. Indeed, declining rates of cooperation have been experienced worldwide, not just in the United States. These rising nonresponse rates have caused marketing researchers to rethink the use of "traditional" data-collection methods.

Thus, although technology has opened the doors to new methods, it has not solved the nonresponse problem. In view of the rising costs of data collection (energy, personnel, and support functions) and, as just noted, consumers' adoption of new communication systems,[4] marketing research companies have sought out many types of cost-saving alternatives for data collection to remain competitive and, in some cases, to remain in business. Consumers have integrated personal, laptop, and handheld computers into their lives, and many have adopted wireless communication systems. To stay relevant, marketing research companies have necessarily had to adapt to these new communication systems.

The rapid adoption of sophisticated personal communication systems by consumers underlies the troublesome data-collection dilemma faced by marketing researchers all over the globe. As we have mentioned, response rates, meaning the percentage of individuals asked to take part in a survey who actually do so, are low and declining yearly.[5] At the same time, response rates are being "squeezed" by the increasing percentage of noncontacts, meaning the percentage of those individuals researchers attempt to contact who cannot be reached. The problem is especially significant for telephone interviewing, because land-line telephone users have effectively blocked marketing researchers with caller ID, answering devices, and the like.

We have identified four major modes of collecting survey information from respondents: (1) personal interview, either face-to-face or voice-to-voice, with no or minimal computer assistance; (2) computer-facilitated interview, in a face-to-face, voice-to-voice,

The four basic survey modes are (1) person-administered surveys, (2) computer-assisted surveys, (3) self-administered surveys, and (4) mixed-mode or "hybrid."

or self-administered survey; (3) self-administered interview, in which respondents fill out the questionnaire themselves without computer assistance; and (4) mixed-mode interview, that is some combination of two or more of the first three modes. Each data-collection mode has advantages and disadvantages, which we will describe in general before discussing the various types of surveys within each category.

Person-Administered Surveys (with No or Minimal Computer Assistance)

A **person-administered survey** is one in which an interviewer reads questions to the respondent, either face-to-face or over the telephone, and records the answers. This was the primary mode of survey administration for many years. However, as costs have increased and as computer technology has advanced, its popularity has fallen off. Nevertheless, person-administered surveys are still used, and we describe their advantages and disadvantages next.

> A person-administered survey is one in which an interviewer reads questions to the respondent, either face-to-face or over the telephone, and records the answers.

ADVANTAGES OF PERSON-ADMINISTERED SURVEYS. Person-administered surveys have four unique advantages: They offer feedback, rapport, quality control, and adaptability.[6] They also have higher response rates than telephone or mail surveys, they permit a variety of techniques (such as card sorting) that are cumbersome with other data-collection methods, and they overcome illiteracy or poor reading ability.[7]

1. Feedback. Interviewers must often respond to direct questions from respondents during an interview. Sometimes respondents do not understand the instructions, or they may not hear the question clearly, or they might become distracted during the interview. A human interviewer may be allowed to adjust the questions according to verbal or nonverbal cues. When a respondent begins to fidget or look bored, the interviewer can say, "I have only a few more questions." Or if a respondent makes a comment, the interviewer may jot it down as a side note to the researcher.

2. Rapport. Some people distrust surveys in general, or they may have some suspicions about the survey at hand. The presence of another human being can help develop some rapport with the respondent early on in the questioning, which can facilitate the process. A person can create trust and understanding that impersonal forms of data collection cannot.

> Personal interviewers can build rapport with respondents who are initially distrustful or suspicious.

3. Quality Control. An interviewer sometimes must select certain types of respondents based on gender, age, or some other distinguishing characteristic. Personal interviewers can ensure that respondents are selected correctly. Also, using a personal interviewer ensures that every question will be asked of the respondent. And some researchers feel that respondents are more likely to be truthful when they respond face-to-face.

4. Adaptability. Personal interviewers can adapt to respondent differences. It is not unusual, for instance, to find an elderly person or a very young person who initially must be helped step-by-step through the process in order to understand how to respond to questions. Interviewers are trained to ensure that they do not alter the meaning of a question by interpreting the question to a respondent. In fact, interviewers should follow precise rules on how to adapt to different situations presented by respondents.

> Personal interviewers can adapt to differences in respondents, but they must be careful not to alter the meaning of a question.

DISADVANTAGES OF PERSON-ADMINISTERED SURVEYS. The drawbacks to using human interviewers are human error, slowness, cost, and interview evaluation.

1. Humans Make Errors. Human interviewers may ask questions out of sequence, or they may change the wording of a question, which may change the meaning of the question altogether. Humans can make mistakes recording the information provided by the

> The disadvantages of person-administered surveys are: human error, slow data collection, high cost, and "interview evaluation" apprehension among respondents.

Without a personal interviewer, a respondent may fail to understand survey questions.

respondent. When they become fatigued or bored from repetition, human interviewers may make any number of errors. And, although not an "error," in the sense we are discussing, there is another drawback to using personal interviewers—cheating. Marketing Research Insight 9.1 acquaints you with this unfortunate reality associated with the use of human interviewers.

2. Slow Speed.   Collecting data using human interviewers is slower than other modes due to necessary sequential nature of the process. Although pictures, videos, and

---

MARKETING RESEARCH INSIGHT   Ethical Application

9.1 Interviewer Cheating

A concern with using the method of personal interviewing, especially in telephone interviewing where controls are sometimes difficult to put in place, is interviewer cheating. Although most telephone interviewers are honest, only minimal control and supervision can be used with this method. Consequently, there are temptations for cheating, such as turning in bogus completed questionnaires or conducting interviews with respondents who do not qualify for the survey at hand. When telephone interviewing is used, checks, which may include the following, should be more extensive[8]:

1. Have an independent party call back a sample of each interviewer's respondents to verify that they took part in the survey.

2. Have interviewers submit copies of their telephone logs to validate that the work was performed on the dates and in the time periods required.

3. If long-distance calls were made, have interviewers submit copies of their telephone bill with long-distance charges itemized to check that the calls were made properly.

4. If there is a concern about a particular interviewer's diligence, request that the interviewer be taken off the project.

A researcher should always check the accuracy and validity of interviews, regardless of the data-collection method, but because interview cheating is a well-known problem with telephone interviews, the researcher who uses this method and fails to build checks and verification procedures into the survey is not measuring up to the ethical standards of the marketing research industry.

graphics can be handled by personal interviewers, they cannot accommodate them as quickly as, say, computers can. Often, personal interviewers simply record respondents' answers using pencil and paper, which necessitates a separate data-input step to build a computer data file. For this reason, increasing numbers of data-collection companies have shifted to using laptop computers, which can immediately add the responses to a data file.

3. High Cost.   Naturally, using a face-to-face interviewer is more expensive than, say, mailing a questionnaire to respondents. Typically, personal interviewers are highly trained and skilled, which explains the expense factor. A telephone personal interviewer is less expensive but still more costly than mail or online surveys.

4. Fear of Interview Evaluation.   Another disadvantage of person-administered surveys is that the presence of another person may create apprehension,[9] called *interview evaluation*, in certain respondents. **Interview evaluation** may occur when some respondents become apprehensive that they are not answering "correctly" when responding to a personal interviewer. Even when the interviewer is a perfect stranger, some people become anxious about the possible reaction of the interviewer to their answers or how the interviewer evaluates them. Some respondents, for example, try to please the interviewer by saying what they think the interviewer wants to hear. The evaluation reaction may arise especially when the questions deal with personal topics, such as personal hygiene, political opinions, financial matters, and even age. The presence of a human interviewer may cause these respondents to answer differently than they would in an impersonal data-collection mode.

Interview evaluation occurs when the interviewer's presence creates anxieties in respondents, which may cause them to alter their normal responses.

Computer-Administered Surveys

Computer technology contributes attractive, efficient, and flexible options to survey modes, and new developments are occurring almost every day. While once person-administered surveys were the mainstay of the industry, in developed countries computer-administered survey methods have become dominant. A telephone interviewer may, for instance, read questions and record answers on a computer screen, or a questionnaire may be posted on the Internet. Basically, a **computer-administered survey** is one in which computer technology plays a central role in the interview work. Either the computer conducts the interview or the respondent interacts directly with it In the case of Internet-based questionnaires, the computer acts as the medium through which potential respondents are approached, and it is the means by which respondents submit the completed questionnaire. As with person-administered surveys, computer-administered surveys have their advantages and disadvantages.

A computer-administered survey is one in which computer technology plays a central role in the interview work.

ADVANTAGES OF COMPUTER-ADMINISTERED SURVEYS.   There are variations in computer-administered surveys. At one extreme, the respondent answers the questions on a PC, often online, and the questions are tailored to the responses to previous questions, so there are no human interviewers. At the other extreme, a telephone or personal interviewer is prompted by a computer program as to what questions to ask and in what sequence. Regardless of the amount of computer involvement, at least five advantages of computer-administered surveys are evident: speed; error-free interviews; use of pictures, videos, and graphics; real-time capture of data; and reduction of anxieties from "interview evaluation."

1. Speed.   Perhaps the greatest single advantage of computer-assisted data collection is its ability to gather survey data very quickly. The computer-administered approach is much faster than the human interview approach. A computer does not become fatigued or bored, and it can handle hundreds of respondents simultaneously. The speed factor translates into cost savings—some claim that Internet surveys cost about one-half what mail or phone surveys do.[10]

Computer-administered surveys are fast, error-free, capable of using pictures or graphics, able to capture data in real time, and less threatening to some respondents.

2. Error-free Interviews.   Properly programmed, the computer-administered approach guarantees zero interviewer errors, such as inadvertently skipping questions, asking inappropriate questions based on previous responses, misunderstanding how to pose questions, recording the wrong answer, and so forth. Moreover, a computer neither cheats nor misrepresents responses, which can happen when human interviewers are dishonest.

3. Use of Pictures, Videos, and Graphics.   Computer graphics can be integrated into questions as they are viewed on a computer screen. Rather than an interviewer pulling out a picture of a new type of window air conditioner, for instance, computer graphics can show it from various perspectives. High-quality streaming video may be programmed so the respondent can see the product in use or in a wide range of visual displays.

The real-time capture of data by computer-administered surveys is an important advantage of this data-collection mode.

4. Real-Time Capture of Data.   With online surveys, respondents interact with the computer and the information is directly entered into a computer's data storage system to be accessed for tabulation or other analyses at any time. Once the interviews are finished, final tabulations can be completed in a matter of minutes. Computer-assisted telephone interviews can store responses immediately; in other cases, the responses are periodically downloaded to a data file.

5. Reduction of "Interview Evaluation."   The respondents' worry that they won't give the "right" or "desirable" answers tends to diminish when they interact with an impersonal computer. In such cases, some researchers believe that respondents will provide more truthful answers on potentially sensitive topics.

Finally, an emerging advantage of online surveys is that those coupled to opt-in or "permission marketing" are receiving high response rates. That is, surveys sent to a panel or database of a firm's customers who have agreed to respond to a research firm's or the company's survey requests are more cooperative, are more actively involved in the survey, and do not require response inducements such as prenotifications and personalization.[11]

The disadvantages to computer-assisted data collection are of the technical skills required and the high set-up costs.

DISADVANTAGES OF COMPUTER-ADMINISTERED SURVEYS.   The primary disadvantages of computer-assisted surveys are that they require some level of technical skill and their set-up costs may be significant.

1. Technical Skills May Be Required.   Although the simplest computer-assisted methods available to marketing researchers require minimal technical skills and can be mastered by students in an hour or less, more sophisticated methods require considerable skill to ensure that the systems are operational and free of errors.

2. Set-up Costs Can Be High.   Computer technology can increase productivity, but getting some of these systems in place and operational can be costly. The most sophisticated computer-administered surveys require programming and debugging. One software evaluator estimated that a two-day setup time by an experienced programmer was fairly efficient.[12] Depending on what type of computer-administered survey is being considered, the costs, including the time factor, can render this type of delivery system less attractive relative to other data-collection options. On the other hand, there are a number of moderate- to low-cost options, such as Web-based questionnaires with user-friendly interfaces. It is these that are fueling the rush toward more and more online research around the world. A researcher can realize considerable cost savings without much effort by using a Web-based questionnaire that respondents fill out simply by going online and accessing the appropriate website.

Some types of computer-administered surveys incur relatively high set-up costs, but others are reasonably priced and easy to use.

Self-Administered Surveys (Without Computer Assistance)

A **self-administered survey** is one in which respondents complete the survey on their own. It differs from other survey modes in that there is no agent—human or computer—administering the interview.[13] So, we are referring here to the prototypical "pencil-and-paper" survey where the respondent reads the questions and responds directly on the questionnaire. Normally, respondents proceed at their own pace and often select the place and time to complete the survey. They also may decide when the questionnaire will be returned. In other words, responding to the questions is entirely under the control of the respondent. As with other survey modes, those that are self-administered have their advantages and disadvantages.

ADVANTAGES OF SELF-ADMINISTERED SURVEYS. Self-administered surveys have three important advantages: reduced cost, respondent control, and no interviewer-evaluation apprehension.

1. Reduced Cost. By eliminating the need for an interviewer or an interviewing device such as a computer program, there can be significant savings in cost.

2. Respondent Control. Respondents can control the pace at which they respond so they do not feel rushed. Ideally, a respondent should be relaxed while responding, and a self-administered survey may create this relaxed state.

3. No Interview-Evaluation Apprehension. As we noted earlier, some respondents feel apprehensive when answering questions, or the topic may be sensitive, such as gambling,[14] smoking, or dental work. The self-administered approach takes the administrator, whether human or computer, out of the picture, and respondents may feel more at ease. Self-administered questionnaires have been found to elicit more insightful information than face-to-face interviews.[15]

DISADVANTAGES OF SELF-ADMINISTERED SURVEYS. The disadvantages of self-administered surveys are respondent control, lack of monitoring, and high questionnaire requirements.

1. Respondent Control. As you can see, self-administration places control of the survey in the hands of the prospective respondent. As a result, this type of survey is subject to the possibilities that respondents will not complete the survey, will answer questions erroneously, will not respond in a timely manner, or will refuse to return the survey at all.

2. Lack of Monitoring. With self-administered surveys there is no opportunity for the researcher to monitor or interact with the respondent during the course of the interview. A monitor can offer explanations and encourage the respondent to continue. But with a self-administered survey, respondents who do not understand the meaning of a word or who are confused about how to answer a question may answer improperly or become frustrated and refuse to answer it.

3. High Questionnaire Requirements. Due to the absence of the interviewer or an internal computer check system, the burden of respondent understanding falls on the questionnaire itself. Not only must it have perfectly clear instructions, examples, and reminders throughout, the questionnaire must also entice respondents to participate and encourage them to continue answering until all questions are complete. Questionnaire design is important regardless of the data-collection mode. However, with self-administered surveys, the researcher must make sure that the questionnaire is thorough and accurate before data collection begins. You will learn more about designing questionnaires in Chapter 11.

Mixed-Mode Surveys

Mixed-mode surveys, sometimes referred to as "hybrid" surveys, use multiple data-collection modes. Mixed-mode surveys have become increasingly popular in recent years, partly due to the increasing use of online research. As more and more respondents have

---

A self-administered survey is one in which respondents complete the survey on their own; there is no agent—human or computer—administering the interview.

Self-administered surveys have three important advantages: reduced cost, respondent control, and no interviewer-evaluation apprehension.

The disadvantages of self-administered surveys are respondent control, lack of monitoring, and high questionnaire requirements.

If respondents misunderstand or do not follow directions, they may become frustrated and quit.

With self-administered surveys, the questionnaire must be especially thorough and accurate in order to minimize respondent errors.

Mixed-mode surveys, sometimes referred to as "hybrid" surveys, use multiple data-collection modes.

access to the Internet, researchers often combine online surveys, a form of computer-assisted surveying, with some other method, such as telephone surveys, a form of person-administered surveying. Another reason for the popularity of mixed-mode surveys is that marketing researchers have realized respondents should be treated like customers.[16] Basically, this realization translates into matching data-collection mode to respondent preferences insofar as possible to foster respondent goodwill[17] and maximize the quality of data collected.[18]

With a mixed-mode approach, a researcher may use two or more survey data-collection modes to access a representative sample[19] or use modes in tandem, for example, use the Internet to solicit respondents who will agree to a face-to-face interview.[20]

ADVANTAGE OF MIXED-MODE SURVEYS

The advantage of mixed-mode surveys is that researchers are able to use the advantages of each of the various modes to achieve their data-collection goals.

1. Multiple "Pluses" to Achieve Data-Collection Goal. The main benefit of mixed-mode surveys is that researchers are able to use the advantages of each of the various modes to achieve their data-collection goals. For example, one quarterly survey administered to a panel of households involves a randomly selected sample of about 800 households. Since 50% of these households have Internet service, they may be surveyed each quarter via an online survey. Administrators may access all of these panel households with the touch of a computer key, which gives them the advantages associated with online surveys. Also, as respondents open their e-mailed questionnaires and answer, their responses are automatically downloaded to a statistical package for analysis. Of course, in order to achieve a representative sample, households without Internet service must be included. These households typically have telephones. So these panel members are contacted each quarter via telephone surveys. With this mixed-mode approach, the panel administrators can take advantage of the speed and low cost of online surveying and can also reach the total household population using telephone surveys.[21]

DISADVANTAGES OF MIXED-MODE SURVEYS.

There are two primary disadvantages of using mixed-mode, or "hybrid," data collection.

A disadvantage of the mixed-mode survey is that the researcher must assess the effects the mode may have on response data.

1. The Survey Mode May Affect Response. One of the reasons that researchers in the past were reluctant to use mixed modes for gathering data was concern that the mode used might affect responses given by consumers. Would consumers responding to an in-home interview with a personal interviewer answer differently from a consumer responding to an impersonal, online survey? Some research has shown this to be so in comparisons of online surveys to telephone surveys.[22] Studies have assessed differences between data-collection methods in mixed-mode applications as well.[23] But the results of studies addressing the question of survey mode effects on respondents are not entirely consistent, so our warning to researchers is that they must assess the differences in the data collected to determine if the data-collection mode is the cause.

Multimode data collection adds to the complexities of data collection, for example, requiring different instructions and integration of data from different sources.

2. Additional Complexity. Multimode data collection adds to the complexities of data collection.[24] For example, the wording of the instructions for a multimode online and telephone survey must be different in order to accommodate those reading instructions they themselves are to follow (online respondents) versus those who are having instructions read to them by a telephone interviewer. Further, data from the two sources will need to be integrated into a single data set, so much care must be taken to ensure the data are compatible.

Mixed-mode data collection is quite common in global marketing research surveys, especially if the countries or regions involved differ in terms of infrastructure. Some countries, such as the United States or Australia, have excellent transportation systems as well as well-developed telephone and Internet systems; other countries, such as India or China, do not. When marketing research companies must survey consumers in multiple countries, often the data-collection methods must differ as a function of differences in infrastructure.

Comparisons of the Four Data-Collection Modes

No doubt you are now suffering information overload about data-collection modes, and this is understandable given that the modes and issues we have discussed are mostly new topics for you. As a convenient way to compare the pros and cons of the four data-collection modes, we have created Table 9.2, which simplifies the many points in this section. Use Table 9.2 to review the various data-collection types and their advantages and disadvantages, as well as to compare them to one another.

TABLE 9.2   Pros and Cons of Basic Data-Collection Modes

Factor	In-Person	Via Computer	Self-Administered	Mixed-Mode
Feedback	☺	☹	☹	☺
Rapport	☺	☹	☹	☺
Quality control	☺	😐	☹	☺
Adaptability	☺	☹	☹	☺
Interviewer mistakes	☹	☺	☺	☺
Speed	☹	☺	☹	☺
Cost	☹	😐	☺	☺
Respondent apprehension	☹	☺	☺	☺
Complexity	😐	☺	☺	☹

Note 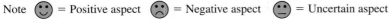 ☺ = Positive aspect   ☹ = Negative aspect   😐 = Uncertain aspect

DESCRIPTIONS OF DATA-COLLECTION METHODS

Now that you have an understanding of the pros and cons of personal, computer, self-administered, and mixed-mode survey methods, we can describe the various interviewing techniques used in each mode. Excluding mixed-mode surveys, marketing researchers can use several different data-collection methods (Table 9.3):

Person-administered surveys:

1. In-home survey
2. Mall-intercept survey
3. In-office survey
4. Telephone survey (central location or Computer-assisted telephone survey (CATI))

Computer-administered surveys:

5. Fully automated survey
6. Online and other Internet-based survey

TABLE 9.3   Various Ways to Gather Data

Data-Collection Method	Description
In-home interview	The interviewer conducts the interview in the respondent's home. Appointments may be made ahead by telephone.
Mall-intercept interview	Shoppers in a mall are approached and asked to take part in the survey. Questions may be asked in the mall or in the mall-intercept company's facilities located at the mall.
In-office interview	The interviewer makes an appointment with business executives or managers to conduct the interview at the respondent's place of work.
Central location telephone interview	Interviewers work in a data-collection company's office using cubicles or work areas for each interviewer. Often the supervisor has the ability to "listen in" to interviews to check that they are being conducted correctly.
Computer-assisted telephone interview	With a central location telephone interview, the questions are programmed for a computer screen and the interviewer then reads them off. Responses are entered directly into the computer program by the interviewer.
Fully automated interview	A computer is programmed to administer the questions. Respondents interact with the computer and enter their own answers by using a keyboard, by touching the screen, or by using some other means.
Online or other Internet-based survey	Respondents fill out a questionnaire that resides on the Internet or otherwise accesses it via the Internet, such as through an e-mail attachment or downloading the online file.
Group self-administered survey	Respondents take the survey in a group context. Respondents work individually, but they meet as a group, which allows the researcher to economize.
Drop-off survey	Questionnaires are left with the respondent to fill out. The administrator may return at a later time to pick up the completed questionnaire, or the respondent may mail it in.
Mail survey	Questionnaires are mailed to prospective respondents who are asked to fill them out and return them by mail.

Self-administered surveys:

7. Group self-administered survey
8. Drop-off survey
9. Mail survey

Person-Administered Interviews

At least four variations of person-administered interviews are commonly used; their differences are based largely on the location of the interview. These methods include the in-home interview, the mall-intercept interview, the in-office interview, and the central location telephone interview.

IN-HOME SURVEYS. Just as the name implies, an **in-home survey** is conducted by an interviewer who enters the home of the respondent. It takes longer to recruit participants for in-home interviews and researchers must travel to and from respondents' homes. Therefore, the cost per interview is relatively high. Two important factors must be satisfied to justify the high cost of in-home interviews. First, the marketing researcher must believe that personal contact is essential to the success of the interview. Second, the researcher must be convinced that the in-home environment is conducive to the questioning process. In-home interviews are useful when the research objective requires respondents' physical presence to see, read, touch, use, or interact with the research object, such as a product prototype, *and* the researcher believes that the security and comfort of respondents' homes is an important element affecting the quality of the data collected. For example, the Yankelovich Youth MONITOR conducts in-home interviews of children 6 years old and older so that both parents and children are comfortable with the interviewing process.[25]

> In-home interviews are used when the survey requires respondents to see, read, touch, use, or interact with a product prototype *and* the researcher believes that the security and comfort of respondents' homes is important to the quality of the data collected.

For instance, a company develops a new type of countertop toaster oven that is designed to remain perfectly clean. However, in order to get the benefit of clean cooking, the oven must be set up according to different cooking applications (pizza versus bacon, for example) and the throw-away "grease-catch foil" must be placed correctly at the bottom of the unit to work properly. Will consumers be able to follow the setup instructions? This is a study that would require researchers to conduct surveys in the home kitchens of respondents. Researchers would observe respondents open the box, unwrap and assemble the device, read the directions, and cook a meal. All of this may take an hour or more. Respondents may not be willing to travel somewhere and spend an hour on this research project, but they would be more likely to do it in their own home.

MALL-INTERCEPT SURVEYS. Although the in-home interview has important advantages, it has the significant disadvantage of cost. The expense of in-home interviewer travel is high, even for local surveys. Patterned after "man-on-the-street" interviews pioneered by opinion-polling companies and other "high-traffic" surveys conducted in settings where crowds of pedestrians pass by, the **mall-intercept survey** is one in which respondents are encountered and questioned while they are visiting a shopping mall. A mall-intercept company generally is located within a large shopping mall, usually one that draws from a regional rather than a local market area. Typically, the interview company negotiates exclusive rights to do interviews in the mall and, thus, forces all marketing research companies that wish to do mall intercepts in that area to use that interview company's services. In any case, the travel costs are eliminated because the respondents incur the costs themselves by traveling to the mall.

> Mall-intercept interviews are conducted in large shopping malls; they cost less per interview than in-home interviews.

Mall-intercept interviewing has become a major survey method due to its ease of implementation,[26] and it is available in many countries.[27] Shoppers are intercepted in the pedestrian traffic areas of shopping malls and either interviewed on the spot or asked to move to a permanent interviewing facility located in the mall office. Although some

The representativeness of mall interview samples is always an issue.

The representativeness of mall interview samples is always an issue.

Mall interview companies use rooms in their small headquarters areas to conduct private interviews in a relaxed setting.

In-office interviews are conducted at executives' or managers' places of work because they are the most suitable locations.

malls do not allow interviewing because they view it as a nuisance to shoppers, many do permit mall-intercept interviews and may rely on the data themselves to fine-tune their own marketing programs. Mall-intercept companies are adopting high-tech techniques, such as electronic pads, and are experimenting with kiosks to attract respondents.[28]

In addition to costing less, mall interviews also have many of the benefits associated with in-home interviewing, among them the important advantage of the presence of an interviewer who can interact with the respondent.[29] However, it is necessary to point out a few drawbacks specifically associated with mall interviewing. First, sample representativeness is an issue, for most malls draw from a relatively small area in close proximity to their location. If researchers are looking for a representative sample of some larger area, such as the county or Metropolitan Statistical Area (MSA), they should be wary of using the mall-intercept technique. Some people shop at malls more frequently than others and, therefore, have a greater chance of being interviewed.[30] The recent growth in non-mall retailing—catalogs and stand-alone discounters such as Wal-Mart, for example—means that more mall visitors are recreational shoppers rather than convenience-oriented shoppers. Thus, mall-intercept samples need to be scrutinized to determine what consumer groups they actually represent.[31] Also, many shoppers refuse to take part in mall interviews for various reasons. Nevertheless, special selection procedures called *quotas*, which are described in Chapter 12, may be used to counter the problem of nonrepresentativeness.

A second shortcoming of mall-intercept interviewing is that a shopping mall is not a comfortable home environment that is conducive to rapport and close attention to detail. The respondents may feel uncomfortable because passersby stare at them; they may be pressed for time or otherwise preoccupied by various distractions outside the researcher's control. These factors may adversely affect the quality of the interview. Some interview companies attempt to counter this problem by taking respondents to special interview rooms located in the company's mall offices. This minimizes distractions and encourages respondents to be more relaxed. Some mall interviewing facilities have kitchens and rooms with one-way mirrors.

Recently, a panel of mall-intercept company owners and managers was convened by the Marketing Research Association to discuss trends in mall data collection. Marketing Research Insight 9.2 summarizes the essence of the panel's findings.

IN-OFFICE SURVEYS. Although the in-home and mall-intercept interview methods are appropriate for a wide variety of consumer goods, marketing research conducted in the business-to-business or organizational market typically requires interviews with business executives, purchasing agents, engineers, or other managers. Normally, **in-office surveys** take place in person in the respondent's office or perhaps in a company lounge area. Interviewing businesspersons face-to-face has essentially the same advantages and drawbacks as in-home consumer interviewing. For example, if Knoll, Inc. wanted information regarding user preferences for different adjustment features that might be offered in an ergonomic office chair, it would make sense to interview prospective users or purchasers of these chairs. It would also be logical to interview these people at their places of business.

MARKETING RESEARCH INSIGHT | Practical Application

9.2 Has the Mall Intercept Become a Dinosaur?

The status and utilization of mall data-collection companies are declining. This is the conclusion of a recent panel[32] comprised of a number of data-collection professionals. Historically, the popularity of mall-intercept data collection, whereby face-to-face interviewers had permission to roam the mall and ask shoppers to take part in surveys, crested in the 1990s. Thus, the heyday of mall intercept data collection in the United States occurred in the 1980s, a time when large numbers of consumers flocked to huge regional shopping malls. During this decade, prospective mall-intercept survey respondents were plentiful and mall-intercept companies proliferated.

The 1990s, however, saw a turnaround in the mall-intercept business. Three trends converged to greatly diminish the importance of mall intercepts. First, malls themselves became less desirable shopping venues because of travel costs, the advent of online shopping, and the desire of shoppers to have a "shopping experience." Second, the marketing research industry came to realize that online surveys had significant cost and other advantages, and third, the technique became more complex and difficult as marketing researchers increasingly used them for surveys that were longer, had more stringent participant qualifications, and faster turnaround requirements. As a consequence, the number of mall-intercept interviews fell dramatically.

So, are mall intercepts now dinosaurs? The panel members did not believe this to be the case. They did agree that mall intercepts have an "image" problem now precisely for the reasons just listed. However, mall-intercept companies can adopt some strategies to make this data-collection method more attractive to the marketing research industry. These strategies include:

1. Adopt and keep pace with mobile data-collection technology, such as laptops, tablets, electronic pads, and handheld devices.
2. Establish kiosk locations in malls where they are more visible and more in tune with the "shopping experience" atmosphere desired by mall shoppers.
3. Work with marketing research buyers to make incentives more substantial and attractive to mall shoppers, thus recruiting higher-quality respondents.
4. Work with marketing research buyers to reduce interview length and/or create an understanding of the amount of time necessary to obtain high-quality mall intercept interviews.
5. Partner with full-service marketing research companies and thus become the preferred provider of mall-intercept interviews.
6. Tighten quality assurance systems for interviewers, interview quality, time management, and close communications with marketing research buyers.
7. Publicize the fact that respondents typically experience more enjoyment and involvement with face-to-face interviews compared to self-administered ones.

As you might imagine, in-office personal interviews incur relatively high costs. The researcher must first locate those executives qualified to give opinions on a specific topic or individuals who would be involved in product purchase decisions. Sometimes names can be obtained from industry directories or trade association membership lists. More often, the researcher must conduct screening over the telephone by calling a particular company believed to have executives of the type needed. However, locating those people within a large organization may be time-consuming. Once a qualified person is located, the next step is to persuade that person to agree to an interview and then set up a time, which may require a sizeable incentive. Finally, an interviewer must go to the particular place at the appointed time. Even with appointments, long waits are sometimes encountered and cancellations are not uncommon because businesspeople's schedules sometimes shift unexpectedly. Added to these cost factors is the fact that interviewers who specialize in business interviews are generally paid more due to their specialized knowledge and abilities. They have to navigate around gatekeepers such as administrative assistants, learn technical jargon, and be cognizant of product features

In-office personal interviews incur costs due to the difficulty of gaining access to qualified respondents.

when respondents ask detailed questions or even criticize the questions being posed in the interview.

TELEPHONE SURVEYS. As we have mentioned, the need for a face-to-face interview is often predicated on the necessity of the respondent's actually seeing a product, advertisement, or packaging sample. Or it may be vital for the interviewer to watch the respondent to ensure that correct procedures are followed or otherwise to verify something about the respondent or the respondent's reactions. However, if physical contact is not necessary, telephone interviewing is an attractive option; it has a number of advantages, as well as disadvantages.[33]

Advantages of telephone interviews are cost, quality, and speed.

The advantages of telephone interviewing are many, and they explain why phone surveys are commonly used for marketing surveys. First, the telephone is a relatively inexpensive way to collect survey data. Long-distance telephone charges are much lower than the cost of a face-to-face interview. A second advantage of the telephone interview is that it has the potential to yield a very high quality sample. If the researcher employs random dialing procedures and proper callback measures, the telephone approach may produce a better sample than any other survey procedure. A third and very important advantage is that telephone surveys have very quick turnaround times. Most telephone interviews are of short duration anyway, but a good interviewer may complete several interviews per hour. Conceivably, the data-collection phase of a study could be completed in a few days with telephone interviews. In fact, in political polling, in which real-time information on voter opinions is essential, it is not unusual to have national telephone polls completed in a single night.

Unfortunately, the telephone survey has several inherent shortcomings. First, the respondent cannot see anything or physically interact with the research object, which ordinarily eliminates the telephone survey as an alternative in situations requiring that the respondent view product prototypes, advertisements, packages, or anything else. A second disadvantage is that the telephone interview does not permit the interviewer to make the various judgments and evaluations that the in-person interviewer can, for example, judgments regarding respondents' income based on the home they live in and other outward signs of economic status. Similarly, the telephone does not allow for the observation of body language and facial expressions, nor does it permit eye contact.

On the other hand, some may argue that the lack of face-to-face contact is an advantage. Self-disclosure studies have indicated that respondents do provide more information in personal interviews, except when the topics are threatening or potentially embarrassing. The relative anonymity of the telephone will probably generate more valid responses to questions about alcohol consumption, contraceptive methods, racial issues, or income tax reporting than face-to-face interviews.[34] A recent review article concluded that telephone interviews elicit more suspicion and less cooperation, generate more "no" opinions and socially desirable answers, and foster more dissatisfaction with long interviews than do face-to-face interviews with the same questions.[35]

A third disadvantage of the telephone interview is that the quantity and types of information that can be obtained are more limited. Very long interviews are inappropriate for the telephone, as are questions with lengthy lists of response options that respondents will have difficulty remembering. Respondents short on patience may hang up during interviews, or they may utter short and convenient responses just to speed up the interview. Obviously, the telephone is a poor choice for conducting an interview with many open-ended questions where respondents make comments or give statements, because these will be difficult for the interviewer to record.

The telephone is a poor choice for conducting a survey with many open-ended questions.

A last, and most significant, problem with the telephone survey is increasing noncooperation from the public, a situation compounded by consumer adoption of answering machines, caller i.d., and call-blocking devices.[36] Concerned about these gatekeeping methods, the research industry is, just beginning to study ways around them.[37] Another difficulty is that legitimate telephone interviewers must contend with the negative impression people have of telemarketers.[38] However, in spite of their shortcomings and the declining response rates, telephone surveys remain popular in the industry. In fact, according to one study that was conducted in New Zealand, when monetary incentives, assurance that it is not a sales call, and a short survey are involved, response rates are quite good.[39]

> Telephone interviewers must contend with the negative impression people have of telemarketers.

Central location telephone surveying involves the installation of several telephone lines at one location so that interviewers make calls from a central location; it is the research industry's current standard practice. Usually, interviewers have separate, enclosed work spaces and wear lightweight headsets to free both hands so that they can record responses. Everything is done from the central location, and the advantages of operating from a central location account for the popularity of this type of organization. For example, resources and expenses are pooled and interviewers can handle multiple surveys, such as calling plant managers in the afternoon and households during the evening hours, thus achieving both efficiency and control.

> Central location interviewing is the current telephone survey standard because it affords efficient control of interviewers.

Apart from cost savings, perhaps the most important reason for using a central location is quality control. Recruitment and training are uniform. Interviewers can be oriented to the equipment, they can study the questionnaire and its instructions, and they can practice the interview among themselves over their phone lines. And the actual interviewing process can be monitored. Most telephone interviewing facilities have monitoring equipment that permits a supervisor to listen in on interviews. They can easily spot interviewers who are not doing the interview properly and can take the necessary corrective action. Ordinarily, each interviewer will be monitored at least once per shift,[40] but the supervisor may focus attention on newly hired interviewers to make sure they are doing their work correctly. The fact that interviewers never know when the supervisor will listen in guarantees more overall diligence. Completed questionnaires are checked on the spot as a further quality-control measure, and interviewers can be immediately informed of any deficiencies. Finally, the company has control over interviewers' schedules. Interviewers report in and out, work regular hours. and make calls during the time periods stipulated by the researcher as appropriate interviewing times.

 ## Setting Up Controls for a Telephone Interview

For this active learning exercise, assume your marketing research course requires team projects and your team decides to research why students at your university chose to attend it. Your five-member team will conduct telephone interviews of 200 students selected at random from the university's student directory, with each team member responsible for completing 40 interviews by calling from his or her apartment or dorm room. You have volunteered to supervise the telephone interviewing. You have read about the tight controls in effect at central telephone interview companies, and you realize that quality assurance procedures should be in place for your student telephone interviewers. In order to satisfy each of the following telephone quality issues, what procedure would you use and how do you propose to use it?

You may want to review the descriptions of how central location telephone surveys are conducted to see if your answers to these questions about your team research project are consistent with standard practices in marketing research. After you complete this exercise, explain how your control of your fellow team members would be easier if done in a central location telephone facility.

Quality Assurance Procedure
The student team member interviewers should call the right students at the proper times of the day.
Ensure that they conduct the interviews correctly, meaning read the instructions and "skip" questions as required by the respondent's answers.
The 40 interviews should be conducted on schedule.
How to handle "no" answers and answering machines.
Make sure that their completed interviews are not bogus, that is, that they do not cheat.

Computer-Administered Interviews

Computer technology has significantly impacted the telephone data-collection industry. Two variations of computer-administered telephone interview systems are (1) using a human interviewer and (2) using a computer, sometimes with a synthesized or recorded voice. The Internet-based interview has become one of the most popular survey techniques, and we describe online surveys in this section as well.

COMPUTER-ASSISTED TELEPHONE INTERVIEW (CATI). The most advanced telephone interview companies have computerized the central location telephone interviewing process; such systems are called **computer-assisted telephone interviews (CATI)**. Each of these systems is unique, and new variations appear almost daily, but we can describe a typical system.

With CATI, the interviewer reads the questions from a computer screen and enters respondents' answers directly into the computer program.

Each interviewer is equipped with a hands-free headset and is seated in front of a computer screen connected to the company's computer system. Often, the computer dials the prospective respondent's telephone automatically, and the computer screen provides the interviewer with the introductory comments. As the interview progresses, the interviewer moves through the questions by pressing a key or a series of keys on the keyboard. Some systems use light pens or pressure-sensitive screens.

The questions and possible responses appear on the screen one at a time. The interviewer reads the question to the respondent, enters the response code, and the computer moves on to the next appropriate question. For example, an interviewer might ask if the respondent owns a dog. If the answer is "yes," a series of questions regarding what type of dog food the dog owner buys might appear. If the answer is "no," these questions would be inappropriate, so the computer program skips to the next appropriate question, which might be "Do you own a cat?" In other words, the computer eliminates the potential for human error that would exist if the survey were done via non-CATI interviewing. The human interviewer is just the "voice" of the computer; because telephone communication is used, the respondent usually has no clue that a computer is involved.

With CATI, the interviewer is the "voice" of the computer.

With CATI, the computer can be used to customize questions. For example, in the early part of a long interview the interviewer might ask a respondent about the year, make, and model of each car he or she owns. Later in the interview, the interviewer might ask questions about each specific car. The question might come up on the interviewer's screen as follows: "You said you own a Lexus. Who in your family drives this car most often?" Other questions about the other cars would appear in similar fashion. These types of questions can, of course, be asked in a manual interview, but they can be handled much more efficiently in a computerized interview because the interviewer does not have to physically flip questionnaire pages back and forth or remember previous responses.

The CATI approach also eliminates the need for editing completed questionnaires and creating computer data files by later manually entering every response from a keyboard.

There is no need to check for errors in completed questionnaires because there is no physical questionnaire. And most computerized interview systems do not permit entering an "impossible" answer. For example, if a question has three possible answers with codes A, B, and C, and the interviewer enters a D by mistake, the computer will ask for the answer to be reentered until an acceptable code is used. If a combination or pattern of answers is impossible, the computer will not accept an answer or it may alert the interviewer to the inconsistency and move to a series of questions that will resolve the discrepancy. The CATI system also eliminates data entry for completed questionnaires because data are entered directly into a computer file as the interview is conducted.

Most CATI systems are programmed to make wrong answers impossible.

This second operation brings to light another advantage of computer-administered interviewing. Tabulations may be run at any point in the study. Such real-time reporting is impossible with pencil-and-paper questionnaires in which there can be a wait of several days following interview completion before detailed tabulations of the results are available. Instantaneous results available with computerized telephone interviewing provide some real advantages. Based on preliminary tabulations, certain questions may be dropped, saving time and money in subsequent interviewing. If, for example, over 90% of those interviewed answered a particular question in the same manner, there may be no need to continue asking the question.

CATI systems permit tabulation in midsurvey.

Tabulations may also suggest the addition of questions to the survey. If an unexpected pattern of product use is uncovered in the early interviewing stages, questions can be added to further delve into this behavior. So the computer-administered telephone survey affords an element of flexibility unavailable in the traditional paper-and-pencil survey methods. Finally, managers may find the early reporting of survey results useful in preliminary planning and strategy development. Sometimes survey project deadlines run very close to managers' presentation deadlines, and advance indications of the survey's findings permit them to organize their presentations in advance rather than all in a rush the night before. The many advantages and quick turnaround of CATI and CAPI (computer-assisted personal interviewing) make them mainstay data-collection methods for many syndicated omnibus survey services.[41,42]

In sum, computer-assisted telephone interviewing options are very attractive to marketing researchers because of the advantages of cost savings, quality control, and time savings over the paper-and-pencil method.[43] But you are no doubt wondering why we have not mentioned wireless telephones. After all, everyone you know has one. If fact, many people no longer own land-line telephones. Yes, the wireless, mobile, or cell phone is on the minds of marketing researchers. There are some fantastic opportunities here, but there are some significant obstacles as well.

FULLY AUTOMATED SURVEY. Some companies have developed **fully automated surveys**, in which the survey is administered completely by a computer, but not online. With one such system, a computer dials a phone number and a recording is used to introduce the survey. The respondent then uses the push buttons on the telephone to make responses, thereby interacting directly with the computer. In the research industry, this approach is known as **completely automated telephone survey (CATS)**. CATS has been successfully employed for customer-satisfaction studies, service-quality monitoring, election day polls, product/warranty registration, and even in-home product tests with consumers who have been given a prototype of a new product.[44]

In another system, the respondent sits or stands in front of the computer unit and reads the instructions off the screen. Each question and its various response options appear on the screen, and the respondent answers by pressing a key or touching the screen. For example, the question may ask the respondents to rate how satisfied, on a scale of 1 to 10 (where 1 is very unsatisfied and 10 is very satisfied), they were the last time they used a travel agency to plan a family vacation. The instructions would tell the respondent to press the key with the number appropriate to the degree of satisfaction. So, respondents might press a "2" or a "7," depending on their experience and expectations. If, however, a "0" or some other ineligible key were pressed, the computer could be programmed to beep, indicating that the response was inappropriate, and instruct the respondent to make another entry.

This approach has all of the advantages of computer-driven interviewing, plus it eliminates the interviewer expense or extra cost of human voice communication. Because respondents' answers are saved in a file during the interview itself, tabulation can take place on a daily basis, and it is a simple matter for the researcher to access the survey's data at practically any time. Some researchers believe that the research industry should move to replace pencil-and-paper questionnaires with computer-based ones.[45]

ONLINE INTERVIEWS. The **Internet-based questionnaire**, in which the respondent answers questions online, has become the industry standard for surveys in virtually all countries with high Internet penetration. Internet-based online surveys are fast, easy, and inexpensive.[46] These questionnaires accommodate all of the standard question formats and are very flexible, including the ability to present pictures, diagrams, or displays to respondents. As an example, take a look at the products offered by Greenfield Online-Ciao! (www.greenfield-ciaosurveys.com), some of which place respondents in a virtual shopping trip situation and let them select and inspect various products on the shelf. In fact, the graphics capability is a major reason why researchers tracking advertising effects prefer online surveys to telephone surveys, which for a great many years have been the standard data-collection method for tracking advertising.[47] The researcher can check the website for current tabulations whenever desired, and respondents can access the online survey at any time of the day or night.

Fully computerized interviews allow respondents to work at their own pace in a comfortable setting.

Online data collection has profoundly changed the marketing research landscape,[48] particularly in the case of online panels.[49] For instance, instead of "episodic" research on customer satisfaction in which a company does a large study once a year, online data collection allows the gathering of "continuous market intelligence." The survey is posted permanently on the Web and modified as the company's strategies are implemented. Company managers can download tabulated customer reactions on a daily basis.[50] Some researchers refer to this advantage of online surveys as "real-time research."[51] The speed, convenience, and flexibility of online surveys make them very attractive.[52] Online surveys are also generally believed to achieve response quality equal to that of telephone or mail surveys, although, research to this effect is only now becoming evident.[53] One serendipitous effect of online surveys is that, because the researcher can monitor the progress of the online survey on a continual basis, they make it possible to spot problems with the survey quickly and make adjustments.

We would be remiss if we did not point out that in each country the technology infrastructure as well as cultural aspects completely dictate the data-collection method of choice. For example, Intercampo, a data-collection company located in Madrid, Spain conducts 10,000 personal interviews each year with Spanish consumers. It has no plans to shift away from this data-collection method because Spaniards are highly conversational and, while the Internet is well accepted in Spain, still greatly prefer personal conversations. Another country where culture and infrastructure dictate the data-collection method is China. Read our Marketing Research Insight 9.3 about the "flip-flop" in data-collection methods in China.

MARKETING RESEARCH INSIGHT   **Global Application**

9.3 The Flip-Flop Data-Collection Landscape in China

Marketing research is a very new phenomenon in China. Formal marketing research companies have been operating in the People's Republic of China for only about 20 years. In fact, the first Chinese marketing research company was established in 1988.[54] In the past two decades, the marketing research industry in China has skyrocketed. Current estimates are in excess of $600 million in revenue with a 20% annual growth rate. The industries for which marketing research is commonly undertaken in China are automobiles, petroleum, information technology, telecommunications, pharmaceuticals and medical, and financial. With respect to size, marketing research providers in China form a pyramid. There are only a very few huge national marketing research companies and a great many regional marketing research organizations. The latter group is very tiny and largely comprised of "one-man" operations. One tier above these entities is a large number of regional companies and many of these are field service companies, meaning that they specialize in data collection.

Unlike the case in Western and European countries, the bulk of data collection in China is conducted in the form of face-to-face interviews. The tide is changing, however. As little as ten years ago, nine-tenths of all data collection in China was achieved through face-to-face interviews, but today, that figure is more like a slight majority. On the surface, it appears that Chinese respondents are acting like Western and European respondents; that is, they decline to take part in surveys. But this is not the case. Instead, Chinese

respondents are becoming more comfortable with marketing research, and they are becoming increasingly willing to answer surveys on the telephone. In other words, from a cultural standpoint, Chinese respondents were originally willing to provide sensitive information only in a face-to-face context, but they have learned that the telephone is an efficient communication medium and now they are willing to provide the same information over the telephone. It is also important to note that Chinese markets did not "open up" to private business practices until the 1980s, and Chinese consumers have not had to endure the telemarketing campaigns that have spoiled the response rates in Western and European counties.

But what about Internet surveys? The rush to online research in the West is not being paralleled in the East because the penetration of the Internet in China is low, with the exception of the largest cities such as Beijing, Shanghai, or Guangzhou.

Thus, the data-collection landscape of China is a flip-flop to that in Western and European countries. Face-to-face, personal interviews are still highly acceptable in China, whereas they are far less popular in the West. Telephone interviewing is on the rise and predicted to continue to be a significant data-collection method in China, whereas it is on a sharp decline in the West and Europe. Finally, in contrast to pronounced shifts to Internet and online surveys in the West, online surveys in China are not now prevalent outside major Chinese cities, although online surveys are forecast to be significant data-collection methods in the near future when Internet penetration begins to match the penetration levels in the West and Europe.

Returning to the topic at hand, the online survey is no cure-all for a marketing researcher's data-collection woes, for the marketing research industry quickly learned that the honeymoon of Internet surveys was, indeed, very short. Their novelty soon wore off, and Internet surveys quickly began exhibiting the same symptoms of low cooperation rates that diminish the quality of telephone and mail surveys. Marketing researchers were quick to realize that online surveys presented design challenges and opportunities related to fostering cooperation in potential respondents.

> Online surveys have the important advantages of speed and low cost, plus real-time access to data; however, drawbacks include difficulty achieving sample representativeness, respondent validation, and asking probing questions.

Self-Administered Surveys

Recall that a self-administered survey is one in which the respondent is in control, often deciding when to take the survey, where to take it, and how much time and attention to devote to it. Plus with a self-administered survey, respondents can always decide what questions they will or will not answer; that is, respondents fill in answers to a static copy of the questionnaire (what we have referred to as a "paper-and-pencil" questionnaire).

Probably the most popular type of self-administered survey is the mail survey, but there are other variations that researchers consider from time to time: the group self-administered survey and the drop-off survey.

Before continuing, we need to address a question that may have occurred to you, namely, Why aren't Internet-based interviews categorized as "self-administered"? This is an excellent question, and our answer is that the sophistication of Internet-based questionnaire design software does not allow respondents to avoid answering key questions. For example, the program may be set up to remind a respondent that a certain question was not answered. This prompt continues until the question is answered. Because we consider the ability of Internet surveys to stop respondents from "opting out" of questions to be a significant quality-control feature, we have not included Internet-based interviews in the self-administered group.

GROUP SELF-ADMINISTERED SURVEYS. Basically, a **group self-administered survey** entails administering a questionnaire to respondents in groups, rather than individually, for convenience and to gain economies of scale. For example, 20 or 30 people might he recruited to view a TV program sprinkled with test commercials. All respondents would be seated in a viewing facility with a large television projection screen. Then they would be given a questionnaire to fill out regarding their recall of test ads, their reactions to the ads, and so on. As you would suspect, the survey is handled in a group context primarily to reduce costs and to provide the opportunity to interview a large number of people in a short time.

The variety of groups with which self-administered surveys can be used is limitless. Students can be given surveys in their classes; church groups can be given surveys during meetings; social clubs and organizations, company employees, movie theater patrons, and any other group can be surveyed during meetings, work, or leisure time. Often, the researcher will pay the group to secure the support of the group's leaders. In all of these cases, respondents work through the questionnaire at their own pace. A survey administrator may be present, so there is some opportunity for interaction concerning instructions or how to respond, but the group context often discourages respondents from asking all but the most pressing questions.

DROP-OFF SURVEYS. Another variation of the self-administered survey is the **drop-off survey**, sometimes called "drop and collect," in which the survey representative approaches a prospective respondent, introduces the general purpose of the survey, and leaves it with the respondent to fill out. Essentially, the objective is to gain the prospective respondent's cooperation. Respondents are told the questionnaire is self-explanatory and it will be left with them to fill out at leisure. Perhaps the representative will return to pick up the questionnaire at a certain time on the same day or the next day, or the respondent may be instructed to complete and return it by prepaid mail. In this way, a representative can cover a number of residential areas or business locations in a single day with an initial drop-off pass and a later pick-up pass.

Drop-off surveys are especially appropriate for local market research in which travel is necessary but limited. Reports are that they have quick turnaround, high response rates, minimal interviewer influence on answers, and good control over how respondents are selected—plus, they are inexpensive.[55] Studies also have shown that the drop-off survey improves response rates from business or organizational respondents.[56]

Variations of the drop-off method include handing out the surveys to people at their places of work and asking them to fill them out at home and return them the next day. Some hotel chains leave questionnaires in their rooms with an invitation to fill them out and turn them in at the desk on checkout. Stores sometimes hand out short surveys on customer demographics, media habits, purchase intentions, or other information that customers are asked to fill out at home and return on their next shopping trip and may use a

---

Group self-administered surveys economize in time and money because all respondents participate at the same time.

Drop-off surveys must be self-explanatory because they are left with the respondents who fill them out without assistance.

gift certificate drawing as an incentive to participate. As you can see, the term *drop-off* can be stretched to cover any situation in which the prospective respondent encounters the survey as though it were "dropped off" by a research representative.

MAIL SURVEYS.   A **mail survey** is one in which the questions are mailed to prospective respondents, who are asked to fill them out and return them to the researcher by mail.[57] Part of the attractiveness of this type of survey stems from its self-administered aspect: There are no interviewers to recruit, train, monitor, and compensate. Also, mailing lists are readily available from companies that specialize in this business, which makes it possible to access very specific groups of target respondents. For example, it is possible to obtain a list of physicians specializing in family practice who operate clinics in cities larger than 500,000 people. One may also opt to purchase computer files, printed labels, or even labeled envelopes from these companies. In fact, some mailing list companies will even provide insertion and mailing services. A number of companies sell mailing lists and most, if not all, can provide these online. On a per-item basis, mail surveys are very inexpensive, but they do have all of the problems associated with not having an interviewer present, which we discussed earlier in this chapter.

> Mail surveys suffer from nonresponse and self-selection bias.

Despite the American Statistical Association's description of the mail survey as "powerful, effective, and efficient,"[58] it has two major problems. The first is **nonresponse**, that is, questionnaires that are not returned.[59] The second is **self-selection bias**, which means that those who do respond are probably different from those who do not fill out and return the questionnaire. Therefore, the sample collected through this method may be nonrepresentative of the general population. Research has shown that self-selected respondents can be more interested and involved in the study topic.[60] To be sure, the mail survey is not the only method that suffers from nonresponse and self-selection bias.[61] Response failures occur in all types of surveys, and marketing researchers must be constantly alert to the possibility that final samples are somehow different from the original set of potential respondents due to some systematic tendency or latent pattern of response, such as being more involved with the product, having more education, being more or less dissatisfied, or even being more opinionated in general than the target population.[62]

> Self-selection bias means respondents who return surveys by mail may differ from the original sample.

But nonresponse and the subsequent danger of self-selection bias are greatest with mail surveys, for they typically achieve response rates of less than 20%. Researchers have tried various tactics to increase response rates, such as using registered mail, color, money, personalization, reminder postcards, and so on.[63,64] However, even when researchers experiment with prenotifications, incentives, or other stimuli, response rates remain low.[65] Special types of mail surveys *are* viable in countries with high literacy rates and dependable postal systems, however,[66] and there is some evidence that mail surveys of business respondents using prenotifications, incentives, and various other strategies lessen the nonresponse problem to some extent.[67] Marketing Research Insight 9.4 offers recommendations for mail surveys based on the experience of a company that has achieved a good deal of success with this data-collection method.

When informing clients about data-collection alternatives, market researchers should discuss the nonresponse problems and biases inherent in each method being considered. For example, as we have mentioned, mail surveys are notorious for low response, and those respondents who do fill out and return a mail questionnaire are likely to be different from those who do not. There are people who refuse to answer questions over the telephone, and consumers who like to shop are more likely to he encountered in mall-intercept interviews than are those who do not like to shop. For each data-collection method, a conscientious researcher will help the client understand its particular nonresponse and bias problems.

> When informing clients of data collection alternatives, market researchers should inform them of the nonresponse problems and biases inherent in each one being considered.

MARKETING RESEARCH INSIGHT

Practical Application

9.4 Mail Surveys Can Work!

You may have the impression that mail surveys do not work well because of their large nonresponse factor, but there are some success stories. The following set of recommendations is provided by Jack Semler,[68] President and CEO, Readex Research, located in Stillwater, Minnesota.

Generally speaking, the mail survey method works best in situations where highly representative results are required, complex or lengthy questionnaires are to be deployed, or sensitive issues need to be explored. When an appropriate mailing series is used, supported by response-enhancing tactics, response rates of 30%–50% and better are not unusual. This can be true even when very long questionnaires are sent as part of the survey process. It's also easier to gather information on such things as salary, personal data, and opinions on charged social issues using the mail survey.

Mail can prove advantageous when used in circumstances where potential respondents are hard to reach. For example, since a mail survey can be answered at the respondent's convenience, a busy retail store manager can participate after hours or a doctor when doing paperwork. As well, there is no worry of interviewer bias or interviewer quality.

Most mail surveys are optimized by using three elements to the mailing series. The first is an alert letter, followed very shortly by the survey kit, which includes the actual questionnaire, introduction letter, reply envelope, and incentive. After some period of time (usually two to three weeks) a follow-up survey is sent to nonresponders. However, the actual mailing series can be varied depending on the nature of the target audience, i.e., how responsive they may be or based on the length and complexity of the questionnaire.

One way research companies have sought to cope with the low response to mail surveys is to create a mail panel in which respondents agree to respond to several questionnaires mailed to them over time. Some see this approach as a preferred option.[69] Others are shifting to Internet communication systems that are faster and cheaper; that is, they are using electronic mail systems of various types to reach their panels. Of course, the panel members are carefully prescreened to ensure that it represents the company's target market or consumers of interest.

CHOICE OF SURVEY METHOD

In selecting a data-collection method, the researcher balances quality against cost, time, and other special considerations.

How does a marketing researcher decide what survey method to use? Since you have read this far in the chapter, you now know that each data-collection method has unique advantages, disadvantages, and special features. As a quick reference tool, we have summarized these for you in Table 9.4. The table reveals that there is no "perfect" data-collection method. The marketing researcher is faced with the problem of selecting the one survey mode that is most suitable in a given situation.

But how does a researcher decide which is the best survey mode for a particular research project? When answering this question, the researcher should always have foremost concern for the overall quality of the data collected. Even the most sophisticated techniques of analysis cannot make up for poor data. So, the researcher must strive to choose a survey method that achieves the highest quality of data allowed by time, cost, and other special considerations[70] of the research project at hand.

We wish we could provide you with a set of questions the answers to which would reveal the most appropriate data-collection method. However, this is not possible, because situations are unique and researchers have to apply good judgment to select the method that best fits the circumstances. In some cases, the decision is obvious, but others require some careful thinking. Also, as we have indicated in our descriptions, new data-collection methods are emerging[71] as are improvements to old ones, so the researcher must constantly keep up-to-date. Nevertheless, there are some general, recurring considerations; we have summarized in the following descriptions.

TABLE 9.4 Major Advantages and Disadvantages of Alternative Data-Collection Methods

Method	Major Advantages	Major Disadvantages	Comment
In-home interview	Conducted in privacy of the home, which facilitates interviewer–respondent rapport	Cost per interview can be high; interviewers must travel to respondent's home	Often much information per interview is gathered
Mall-intercept interview	Fast and convenient data-collection method	Only mall patrons are interviewed; respondents may feel uncomfortable answering questions at the mall	Mall-intercept company often has exclusive interview rights for that mall
In-office interview	Useful for interviewing busy executives or managers	Relatively high cost per interview; gaining access is sometimes difficult	Useful when respondents must examine prototypes or samples of products
Central location telephone interview	Fast turnaround; good quality control; reasonable cost	Restricted to telephone communication	Long-distance calling is not a problem
CATI	Computer eliminates human interviewer error; simultaneous data input to computer file; good quality control	Setup costs can be high	Losing ground to online surveys and panels
Fully automated interview	Respondent responds at his or her own pace; computer data file results	Respondent must have access to a computer and be computer literate	Many variations; an emerging data-collection method with exciting prospects
Online survey	Ease of creating and posting; fast turnaround; computer data file results	Respondent must have access to the Internet	Fastest-growing data-collection method; very flexible; online analysis available
Mail survey	Low cost	Slow response and self-selection bias	Once popular but now rarely used
Group self-administered survey	Cost of interviewer eliminated; economical for assembled groups of respondents	Must find groups and secure permission to conduct the survey	Prone to errors of self-administered surveys; good for pretests or pilot tests
Drop-off survey	Cost of interviewer eliminated; appropriate for local market surveys	Generally not appropriate for large-scale national surveys	Many variations exist with respect to logistics and applications

How Much Time Is There for Data Collection?

Sometimes data must be collected within some very close time frames. There are many reasons for tight deadlines: A national campaign is set to kick off in four weeks and one component of it needs to be tested; a trademark infringement trial is coming up in four weeks and requires a survey of the awareness of the company's trademark; an application for a radio license with

A short deadline may dictate which data-collection method to use.

the FCC deadline is six weeks away and a listenership study of other stations in the area must be conducted; and so on. In the past, telephone surveys, due to their speed, were often selected if there was a very short time horizon. Today, the online survey is an exceptionally fast data-collection alternative. Magazine ads, logos, and other marketing stimuli may be evaluated in online surveys. Poor choices under the condition of a short time horizon would be in-home interviews or mail surveys, because their logistics require long time periods.

How Much Money Is There for Data Collection?

With a generous budget, any appropriate data-collection method may be considered, but with a tight budget, the more costly data-collection methods must be eliminated. With technology costs dropping and Internet access becoming more and more common, online survey research options have become attractive when the data-collection budget is limited. For example, some online survey companies allow the client to design the questionnaire and select the target sample type and number from their panels. In this way, surveys can be completed for a few hundred or a few thousand dollars, which, most researchers would agree, is a small cost for data collection. Of course, the researcher must be convinced that the panel members are those desired for the survey. Other considerations, such as respondent interaction, incidence rate, or any other "cultural" factors, may have a bearing on the selection of the data-collection method.

What Type of Respondent Interaction Is Required?

Most certainly, the selection of method may be influenced by any special requirements that are vital to the survey. One requirement might be that the respondent inspect an advertisement, package design, or logo. Or, the researcher may want respondents to handle a prototype product, taste formulas, or watch a video. When there are requirements such as these built into the survey, the researcher typically has discussed data-collection issues early on with the client and has reached an agreement that time and money will not be paramount and that the data-collection method selected will accommodate the requirements.

If respondents need to see, handle, or experience something, the data-collection mode must accommodate these requirements.

For example, if the respondent needs to view photos of a logo or magazine ad, mail surveys or online surveys may be considered. If the respondent needs to observe a short video or moving graphic, online surveys may be considered. If the respondent needs to watch a 20-minute infomercial, mailed videos (with a considerable incentive!), mall intercepts, or special online techniques can be considered. If the respondent is required to handle, touch, feel, or taste a product, mall-intercept company services are reasonable. If a respondent is required to actually use a product in a realistic setting, in-home interviews may be the only data-collection method that will work.

What Is the Incidence Rate?

The incidence rate, the percentage of the population that possesses some characteristic necessary to be included in the survey, affects the data-collection mode decision.

By **incidence rate** we are referring to the percentage of the population that possesses some characteristic necessary to be included in the survey. Rarely are research projects targeted to "everyone." In most cases, there are qualifiers for being included in a study. Examples are registered voters, persons owning and driving their own automobile, persons 18 years of age and older, and so on. Sometimes the incidence rate is very low. A drug company may want to interview only men above 50 with medicated cholesterol above the 250 level. A cosmetics firm may only want to interview women who are planning facial cosmetic surgery within the next six months. In low-incidence situations such as these, certain precautions must be taken in selecting the data-collection method. For example, in either of these examples, it would be foolishly time-consuming and expensive to send out interviewers door-to-door looking for members who have the qualifications to participate in the study. A data-collection method that can easily and inexpensively screen respondents is desirable for a low-incidence-rate situation because a great many potential respondents must be contacted and a large percentage of these would not qualify to take the survey. Of course, the marketing research industry has worked with low-incidence populations for a long time, and online panels that are maintained by research providers are often touted as affordable ways for researchers to access the low-incidence panel members who are pre-identified.[72]

Are There Cultural and/or Infrastructure Considerations?

Finally, on occasion, the choice of the data-collection method is shaped by cultural norms and/or the communication or other systems that are in place. These considerations have become more of an issue as increasing numbers of marketing research companies operate around the globe. For example, in Scandinavia, residents are uncomfortable allowing strangers into their homes. Therefore, telephone and online surveying is more popular than door-to-door interviewing. On the other hand, in India fewer than 10% of the residents have a telephone and online access is very low. Door-to-door interviewing is used often there.[73] Telephone surveys are used heavily in Canada, where incentives are typically not offered to prospective respondents; online research there is growing slowly.[74] A global marketing research study might be conducted across 100 countries via both online and mail surveys to compensate for differences in Internet access and to obtain a representative sample.[75] It would be very important for a firm conducting a study in a culture with which it is unfamiliar to consult local research firms before deciding on a data-collection method.

It is interesting to note that even the marketing researcher's perceptions of infrastructure or cultural considerations will affect the choice of the data-collection method. Marketing researchers in Spain, for example, have traditionally refrained from using mail surveys in favor of face-to-face interviews. However, a recent study has revealed that the quality of mail surveys of Spanish respondents is equal to that of face-to-face interviews.[76]

Cultural norms and/or limitations of communications systems may limit the choice of data-collection method.

SPSS Student Assistant: Milk Bone Biscuits: Modifying Variables and Values

---

Summary

In this chapter, you learned about the data-collection step in the marketing research process. The four basic survey methods are (1) person-administered surveys, (2) computer-assisted surveys, (3) self-administered surveys and (4) mixed-mode, sometimes called "hybrid," surveys.

Person-administered survey methods have the advantages of allowing feedback, permitting rapport building, facilitating certain quality controls, and capitalizing on the adaptability of a human interviewer. However, they are prone to human error and are slow and costly and sometimes produce the respondent reaction known as "interview evaluation."

Computer-administered interviews are faster, error-free, can show pictures or graphics, allow for real-time capture of data, and may make respondents feel more at ease because another person is not listening to their answers. The disadvantages are that they require technical skills and possibly incur high setup costs.

Self-administered surveys have the advantages of reduced cost, respondent control, and no interview-evaluation apprehension. Their disadvantages include respondent control, in that respondents may not complete the task or make errors, lack of a monitor to help guide respondents, and requirements for a perfect questionnaire.

Finally, mixed-mode surveys, sometimes referred to as "hybrid" surveys, use multiple data-collection methods. In mixed-mode surveys, researchers can take advantage of aspects of each of the various methods to achieve their data-collection goals. However, the different modes employed may produce different responses to the same research question. Because of this, multimode methods are more complex, requiring researchers to design different questionnaires for each mode and make certain that data from the different sources can all be compiled in a common database for analysis.

We described ten different survey data-collection methods: (1) in-home interviews, which are conducted in respondents' homes; (2) mall-intercept interviews, conducted by approaching shoppers in a mall; (3) in-office interviews, conducted with executives or managers in their places of work; (4) telephone interviews, normally conducted from a central location by workers in a telephone interview company's facilities; (5) computer-assisted telephone interviews, in which the interviewer reads questions from a computer screen and enters responses directly into the program; (6) fully automated interviews, in which the respondent interacts directly with a computer; (7) online surveys; (8) group self-administered surveys, in which the questionnaire is handed out to a group for individual response; (9) drop-off surveys, in which the questionnaire is left with the respondent to be completed and picked up or returned at a later time; and (10) mail surveys, in which questionnaires are mailed to prospective respondents who are requested to fill them out and mail them back. Each data-collection method has specific advantages and disadvantages.

The chapter noted that researchers must take into account several considerations when deciding on what survey data-collection method to use. The major concerns are (1) the survey time horizon, (2) the survey budget, (3) the type of respondent interaction required, (4) incidence rate, and (5) cultural and infrastructure considerations. All should be considered, but one or more factors may be paramount because each data-collection situation is unique. Ultimately, the researcher will select a method with which he or she feels comfortable and one that will result in the desired quality and quantity of information without exceeding time or budget constraints.

Key Terms

Survey 240
Person-administered survey 245
Interview evaluation 247
Computer-administered survey 247
Self-administered survey 248
Mixed-mode survey 249
In-home survey 253
Mall-intercept survey 253

In-office survey 254
Central location telephone survey 257
Computer-assisted telephone
   interviews (CATI) 258
Fully automated survey 259
Completely automated survey
   (CATS) 259

Internet-based questionnaire 260
Group self-administered survey 262
Drop-off survey 262
Mail survey 263
Nonresponse 263
Self-selection bias 263
Incidence rate 266

Review Questions/Applications

1. List the major advantages of survey research methods over qualitative methods. Can you think of any drawbacks, and if so, what are they?
2. What aspects of computer-administered surveys make them attractive to marketing researchers?
3. What are the advantages of person-administered surveys over computer-administered ones?
4. What would be the reasons for a researcher to consider a mixed-mode survey?
5. Indicate the differences among (a) in-home surveys, (b) mall-intercept surveys, and (c) in-office surveys. What do they share in common?
6. Why are telephone surveys popular?
7. Name the pros and cons of self-administered surveys.
8. What advantages do online surveys have over other types of self-administered surveys?
9. What are the major disadvantages of a mail survey?
10. How does a drop-off survey differ from a regular mail survey?
11. How does the incidence rate affect the choice of a data-collection method?
12. Is a telephone interview inappropriate for a survey that has as one of its objectives a complete listing of all possible advertising media a person was exposed to in the last week? Why or why not?
13. NAPA Car Parts is a retail chain specializing in stocking and selling both domestic and foreign automobile parts. It is interested in learning about its customers, so the marketing director instructs all 2,000 store managers that whenever a customer makes a purchase of $150 or more, they are to write down a description of the customer who made that purchase. They are to do this just for the second week in October, writing each description on a separate sheet of paper. At the end of the week, they are to send all sheets to the marketing director. Comment on this data-collection method.
14. For each of the following cases, discuss the feasibility of each of the types of survey modes:
   a. Fabergé, Inc. wants to test a new fragrance called "Lime Brut."
   b. Kelly Services needs to determine how many businesses expect to hire temporary secretaries to fill in for those who go on vacation during the summer months.
   c. The Encyclopaedia Britannica requires information on the degree to which mothers of elementary school-aged children see encyclopedias as worthwhile purchases for their children.
   d. AT&T is considering a television screen phone system and wants to know people's reaction to it.
15. With a telephone survey, when a potential respondent refuses to take part, has changed his or

her telephone number, or has moved away, it is customary to simply try another prospect until a respondent is secured. It is not standard practice to report the number of refusals or noncontacts. What are the implications of this policy for the reporting of nonresponse?

16. Compu-Ask Corporation has developed a stand-alone computerized interview system that can be adapted to almost any type of survey. It can fit on a handheld computer, and the respondent answers questions directly using a stylus once the interviewer has turned on the computer and started up the program. Indicate the appropriateness of this interviewing system in each of the following cases:

    a. A survey of plant managers concerning a new type of hazardous waste disposal system.

    b. A survey of high school teachers to see if they are interested in a company's videotapes of educational public broadcast television programs.

    c. A survey of consumers to determine their reactions to a nonrefrigerated variety of yogurt.

17. A researcher is pondering what survey method to use for a client who markets a home security system for apartment dwellers. The system is comprised of sensors that are pressed onto all of the windows and magnetic strips that are glued to each door. Once plugged into an electric socket and activated with a switch box, the system emits a loud alarm and simulates a barking guard dog when an intruder trips one of the sensors. The client wants to know how many apartment dwellers in the United States are aware of the system, what they think of it, and how likely they are to buy it in the coming year. Which factors are positive and which ones are negative for each of the following survey methods: (a) in-home interviews, (b) mall intercepts, (c) online survey, (d) drop-off survey, and (e) CATI survey?

CASE 9.1

STEWARD RESEARCH, INC.

Joe Steward is president of Steward Research, Inc. The firm specializes in customized research for clients in a variety of industries. The firm has a centralized location telephone facility and a division, "Steward Online," that specializes in online surveys. However, Joe often calls on the services of other research firms in order to provide his client with the most appropriate data-collection method. In a meeting with four project directors, Joe discusses each client's special situation.

Client 1: A small tools manufacturer has created a new device for sharpening high-precision drill bits. High-precision drill bits are used to drill near perfect holes in devices such as engine blocks. Such applications have demanding specifications, and drill bits may be used only a few times before being discarded. However, the new sharpening device returns the bits to original specifications and they can then be resharpened and used as many as a dozen times. After testing the device and conducting several focus groups in order to get suggestions for modifications, the client now wants more information on presentation methods. The project director and the client have developed several different presentation formats. The client wishes to have some market evaluation of these presentations before launching a nationwide training program of the company's 125-person salesforce.

Client 2: A regional bakery markets several brands of cookies and crackers to supermarkets throughout California, Nevada, Arizona, and New Mexico. The product category is very competitive and competitors use a great deal of newspaper and TV advertising. The bakery's V.P. of marketing desires more analytics to make the promotional decisions for the firm. She has lamented that though she spends several million dollars a year on promotions in the four states, she has no analytic upon which to evaluate the effectiveness of the expenditures. Steward's project director has recommended a study that will establish some baseline measures of attitudes, preferences, top-of-mind brand awareness (called TOMA, this is a measure of brand awareness achieved by asking respondents to name the first three brands that come to mind when thinking of a product or a service category such as "cookies").

Client 3: An inventor has developed a new device that sanitizes a toothbrush each time the brush is used and replaced in the device. The device uses steam to sanitize the brush, and lab tests have shown the mechanism to be very effective at killing virtually all germs and viruses. The inventor has approached a large manufacturer who is interested in buying the rights to the device but would like some information first. The manufacturer wants to know if people have any concerns about toothbrush sanitization and whether or not they would be willing to purchase a countertop, plug-in device to keep their toothbrush sterile. The project director states that the manufacturer is not interested in a representative sample, just what a few hundred people think about these issues. The inventor is anxious to supply this information very quickly before the manufacturer loses interest in the idea.

1. For each of the three clients, suggest one or more data-collection methods that would be appropriate.
2. For each data-collection method you select in Question 1, discuss the rationale for your choice.
3. What disadvantages are inherent in the data-collection methods you have recommended?

CASE 9.2

MACHU PICCHU NATIONAL PARK SURVEY

There are many ruins of the temples and palaces in Peru built by the Incas, who attained what some historians consider to be the highest accomplishments in the Americas in agriculture, engineering, monument building, and craftsmanship. Unfortunately, the Incas were no match for the Spanish, who, with firearms and horses, defeated the entire Inca empire in a matter of a few years in the 1560s.

In 1913, Hirram Bingham discovered the Inca complex called Machu Picchu. Having avoided plunder by the Spanish Conquistadors, it is the best preserved Inca ruin of its type. Located at 8,000 feet above sea level on a moutain at the border of the Andes mountains and the Peruvian jungle, Machu Picchu is still very difficult to access; to reach it requires a three-hour mountain train ride from Cusco, Peru, the closest city. Normally, tourists board the train very early in the morning in Cusco and arrive at the Machu Picchu village train station around 10 am. They then board buses that take 30 minutes to climb up the 6-mile switchback dirt road to the entrance of Machu Picchu. With guides or on their own, tourists wander the expansive Machu Picchu ruins, have lunch at the Machu Picchu lodge located at the top of the mountain, and hurry to catch the bus down the mountain so they will not miss the one train that leaves around 3 pm to return to Cusco. Some tourists stay overnight at the Machu Picchu Lodge or in one of the six hotels located at the base in Machu Picchu village. At peak season, approximately 1,000 tourists visit Machu Picchu daily.

Machu Picchu is a Peruvian national park, and since it is one of the top tourist attractions in the world, the national park department wishes to conduct a survey to research tourists' satisfaction with the park's many features as well as their total experience on their visit to Peru. With the help of a marketing researcher who specializes in tourism research, the park department officials have created a self-administered questionnaire for its survey. Now, there is the question of how to gather the data, and some alternatives have been suggested. Using concepts in this chapter and your knowledge of data-collection methods and issues, answer each of the following questions.

1. If the questionnaire is an online survey, would it be successful? Why or why not?
2. If the park department uses a mail survey, what issues must be resolved? Would it be successful? Why or why not?
3. If the six hotels in the Machu Picchu area each desired to know how its customers felt about the hotel's services, prices, and accomodations, how might both the park department and the hotels work together on data collection to effect a mutually beneficial survey?
4. Using the knowledge that the Peru national park department has very meager resources for marketing research, suggest a different method (not online, not mail, and not partnering with the local hotels) with the potential for achieving a high response rate and high-quality responses.

Your Integrated Case

ADVANCED AUTOMOBILE CONCEPTS

Cory Rogers presented his interpretations of the focus groups he had subcontracted for Nick Thomas of Advanced Automobile Concepts to get a feel for how American consumers felt about global warming initiatives, gasoline prices, alternative fuels, hybrid automobiles, and other aspects of the AAC division's mission. Nick was impressed with the amount of information that had been collected from just a few focus groups. "Of course," noted Cory, "we have to take all of this information as tentative because we talked with so few folks, and there is a good chance that they are just a part of your target market. But we do have some good exploratory research that will guide us in the survey." Nick agreed with Cory's assessment and asked, "What's next?" Cory said, "I need to think about how we will gather the survey data. That is, in order to make an informed decision as to the type(s) of new automobiles to manufacture and market, it is important to understanding the worries, beliefs, preconceptions, and preferences of potential automobile buyers. In other words, there must be a survey of prospective automobile purchasers, and it is time to start thinking about the method of data collection."

Although specifics were still to be hammered out, everyone involved agreed that a survey should be conducted that would reach a large number of American households, perhaps one to two thousand. Again, with the details to come, the survey would include anywhere from 40 to 75 questions on a variety of topics, including demographics of the household, inventory of currently owned automobiles, beliefs about global warming, gasoline usage, reactions to various "new technology" automobiles, and all of the other constructs and questions identified in the research project objectives. The survey would be directed to either the male or female head of household using a 50–50 split so both genders are equally represented. Other than this factor, the overriding objective is to choose a method that will ultimately yield a respondent profile that reflects the demographic and automobile ownership profile of the American public. It is possible to purchase lists of American households in just about any quantity desired—hundreds, thousands, or even tens of thousands. These lists can be in the form of mailing addresses, e-mail addresses, telephone numbers, or any combination. Here are some of the questions that Cory Rogers must answer.

1. If a mail survey were used, what would be the pros, cons, and special considerations associated with achieving the overriding objective of the survey?
2. Many telephone data-collection companies offer national coverage. Some have centralized telephone interview facilities and some offer CATI services. If a telephone survey were used employing one of these companies, what would be the pros, cons, and special considerations associated with achieving the overriding objective of the survey?
3. The following data collection methods are not likely to achieve the overriding objective. For each one, indicate why not.
   a. Drop-off survey
   b. Group-administered survey
   c. Mall-intercept survey
4. Compare the use of an in-home method to the use of an online method for the Advanced Automobile Concepts survey. What are the relevant pros and cons for each? Indicate which one you would recommend and why.

Learning Objectives

- To learn about basic question–response formats
- To appreciate the considerations used by the researcher to determine which question format will be used for a particular question
- To understand the basics of measurement regarding people, places, and things
- To recognize the four types of scales used by marketing researchers
- To examine question formats commonly used in marketing research
- To comprehend why reliability and validity are concerns when designing and administering questions intended to measure concepts

Where We Are

1 Establish the need for marketing research
2 Define the problem
3 Establish research objectives
4 Determine research design
5 Identify information types and sources
6 Determine methods of accessing data
▶ 7 Design data-collection forms
8 Determine the sample plan and size
9 Collect data
10 Analyze data, and
11 Prepare and present the final research report.

Why is Measurement Important?

William D. Neal, Senior Partner SDR Consulting, by permission, SDR Consulting

In most cases, we must actually measure higher-order constructs that we are studying as we conduct marketing research. How we measure "loyalty," "satisfaction," "sales potential," "demand," "brand value," and "brand equity," for example, is very important and seldom involves just a single question, but multiple measures. The way the researcher decides how to measure these constructs impacts what he or she can or cannot say about them and their impact on the development of successful marketing strategy and

Visit SDR Consulting at www.sdr-consulting.com

tactics. For instance, brand loyalty can be defined as the brand purchased most often, or it can be defined as the person's most preferred brand. The measure of "brand purchased most often" is behavioral and may be highly influenced by costs, convenience, and availability. The "brand most preferred" is attitudinal and may be highly influenced by perceptions of brand quality and esteem. "Most preferred" may not reflect what is actually bought.

A second consideration in determining how to measure constructs is the "level of measurement." The "level of measurement" is determined by the researcher and it is extremely important because it determines what statistical analyses may be performed. If the research objective, for example, calls for determining the "mean number of units forecast," a level of measurement necessary for calculating a mean must be selected by the researcher. You will learn about "levels of measurement," how they are determined, and what statistical analyses are appropriate for each level in this chapter.

William D. Neal

This chapter is the first of two devoted to the questionnaire design phase of the marketing research process. Its primary goal is to develop the foundation for understanding measurement in marketing research. As can be seen in William Neal's comments you have just read, measurement includes a definition of the concept you are studying and application of certain principles that you will learn in this chapter. Our chapter first describes six question–response formats, defining basic concepts in measurement, and then explains the various scale formats commonly used in marketing research. Next, we describe some "workhorse" scale formats that are often used by marketing researchers. Finally, we offer some recommendations as to what scale format to use when you are measuring various constructs typically included in marketing research projects.

BASIC QUESTION–RESPONSE FORMATS

Question–response formats can be open-ended, categorical, or scaled.

Designing a questionnaire from the ground up is akin to a composer creating a song, an author writing a novel, or an artist painting a landscape. That is, it requires creativity. Still, there are some basic aspects of questionnaire design that can be described. This chapter is concerned with the response side of questions on a questionnaire, and it will introduce you to measurement issues. To begin, you should be aware of the three basic question–response formats from which a researcher has to choose: open-ended, categorical, and scaled-response questions. Figure 10.1 illustrates the three types and indicates two variations for each one. Pros and cons of each format are provided in Table 10.1 on page 275. A description of each format follows.

Open-Ended Response Format Questions

With an **open-ended question**, the respondents are instructed to respond in their own words. The response depends, of course, on the topic. An **unprobed format** seeks no additional information from the respondent. With an unprobed response format, the researcher wants a simple comment or statement from the respondent, or perhaps the researcher simply wants the respondent to indicate the name of a brand or a store.[1] On the other hand, the researcher may use a **probed format**, which includes follow-up question(s) instructing the interviewer to ask for additional information, saying, for instance, "Can you think of anything more?" The intent here is to encourage the respondent to provide information beyond the initial and possibly superficial first comments.

Six basic response format options are available to the researcher.

FIGURE 10.1

Diagram of Six Alternative Question-Response Formats

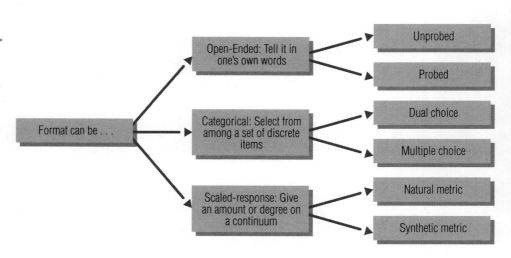

Format can be . . .

- Open-Ended: Tell it in one's own words
  - Unprobed
  - Probed
- Categorical: Select from among a set of discrete items
  - Dual choice
  - Multiple choice
- Scaled-response: Give an amount or degree on a continuum
  - Natural metric
  - Synthetic metric

TABLE 10.1 **Pros and Cons of Alternative Response Formats**

Response Format	Example Question	Pros	Cons
Unprobed open-ended	*"What was your reaction to the Sony Blu-Ray disc player advertisement you saw on television last?"*	+ Allows respondent to use his or her own words.	− Difficult to code and interpret. − Respondents may not give complete answers.
Probed open-ended	*"Did you have any other thoughts or reactions to the advertisement?"*	+ Elicits complete answers.	− Difficult to code and interpret.
Categorical dual-choice	*"Do you think that Sony Blu-Ray players are better than Panasonic Blu-ray disc players?" (Answer yes or no.)*	+ Simple to administer and code.	− May oversimplify response options.
Categorical multiple-choice	*"If you were to buy a Blu-Ray disc player tomorrow, which brand would you be most likely to purchase? Would it be:* *a. Panasonic* *b. General Electric* *c. Sony* *d. JVC, or* *e. Some other brand?"*	+ Allows for broad range of possible responses. Simple to administer and code.	− May alert respondents to response options of which they were unaware. − Must distinguish "pick one" from "pick all that apply."
Metric natural scale	*"About how many times per week do you use your Blu-Ray disc player?"*	+ Respondents can relate to the scale. + Simple to administer and code.	− Respondents may not be able to give exact answers using the scale.
Metric synthetic scale	*"Do you disagree strongly, disagree, agree, or agree strongly with the statement 'Sony Blu-Ray disc players are a better value than General Electric Blu-Ray disc players'?"*	+ Allows for degree of intensity/feelings to be expressed. + Simple to administer and code	− Scale may be "forced" or overly detailed

Categorical Response Format Questions

The **categorical question** lists response options on the questionnaire that can be answered quickly and easily.[2] A **dual-choice categorical question** has only two response options, such as "yes" or "no." If there are more than two options for the response, then the researcher is using a **multiple-choice categorical question**. Both the dual-choice and multiple-choice categorical question formats are very common on questionnaires because they facilitate the answering process as well as data entry. They also standardize response options to these questions on the questionnaire.

Scaled-Response Questions

The **scaled-response question** utilizes a continuum chosen by the researcher to measure the attributes of some construct under study. The response options are identified on the questionnaire. With a **natural scaled-response format**, the researcher asks the respondent to use an appropriate and readily understood measure, such as years, times, dollars, or the like. With a **synthetic scaled-response format**, the respondent must use a made-up continuum, such as a 7-point scale, an amount of agreement or disagreement, an intention to purchase expressed as a percentage, or some other similar response to indicate opinons or feelings. We describe both of these formats in detail later in this chapter.

CONSIDERATIONS IN CHOOSING A QUESTION–RESPONSE FORMAT

All of the six different question formats we have just described are possible response formats for questions on a questionnaire. So how does the researcher decide on which option to use? At least four considerations serve to narrow down the choice: (1) the nature of the property being measured, (2) previous research studies, (3) the ability of the respondent, and (4) the scale level desired.

Nature of the Property Being Measured

As will become clear later in the chapter when we describe basic concepts in measurement, the inherent nature of the property of a construct often determines the question–response format. For example, if Alka Seltzer wants to know if respondents have bought its brand of flu relief medicine in the last month, the only answers are "yes," "no," or, perhaps, "do not recall." If we ask marital status, a woman is married, separated, divorced, widowed, or single or she may be cohabitating. But when we ask how much a person likes Hershey's chocolate, we can use a scaled-response approach, because "liking" is a subjective property with varying degrees. So, some properties are preset as to appropriate responses, whereas others are amenable to scales that indicate gradations or levels.

The properties of the construct being measured often determine the appropriate response format.

Previous Research Studies

On some occasions, a survey follows an earlier one, and there may be a desire to explicitly compare the new findings with the previous survey. In this case, it is customary to simply adopt the question format used in the initial study. On the other hand, a particular scale or question–response format may have been developed by others who have measured the construct. Some scales are published or available for use by marketing researchers at no cost, whereas others may reside within the researcher's own company as a result of its work with several clients over time. For instance, some research companies specialize in customer satisfaction studies, and they have refined their own scales tapping this construct.[3] In any case, if a researcher believes a question format to be suitable for the purpose of the study at hand, it is good practice to adopt or adapt it rather than inventing a new one.

Researchers strive to use question formats that are tried and true.

Ability of the Respondent

It is advantageous to match the question format with the abilities of the respondents. For instance, if a researcher feels that the respondents in a particular study are not articulate or that they will be reluctant to verbalize their opinions, the open-ended option is not a good choice. Similarly, if the respondent, such as a child, is unable to rate objects on natural scales, it is appropriate to perhaps move back to a dual-choice categorical question format in which the respondent simply indicates "agree" or "disagree."[4]

Some respondents may relate better to one type of response format than another.

Scale Level Desired

You will learn in subsequent chapters that certain statistical analyses incorporate assumptions about the nature of the measures being analyzed, so the researcher must bear these requirements in mind when selecting a question format. For example, if the response options are simply "yes" or "no," the researcher can report the percentage of respondents who answered in each way, but if the question asks how many times respondents used an ATM machine in the past month, the researcher could calculate an average number of times. An average is different from a percent, one reason being that a dual-choice yes–no response option is less informative than a scaled-response option such as "0," "1," "2," and so on. If a researcher desires to use higher-level statistical analyses, the question must have a scaled-response format. This point brings us to the concepts involved with measurement.

BASIC CONCEPTS IN MEASUREMENT

Questionnaires are designed to collect information gathered via **measurement**, which is defined as determining the nature of some characteristic of interest to the researcher. For instance, a marketing manager may wish to know how a person feels about a certain product, or how much of the product he or she uses in a certain time period. This information, once compiled, can help answer specific research objectives such as determining product opinions and usage.

> Measurement is determining if and how much of a property is possessed by an object.

But what are we really measuring? We are measuring properties—sometimes called *attributes* or *qualities*—of objects. Objects include consumers, brands, stores, advertisements, or whatever construct is of interest to the researcher working with a particular manager. **Properties** are the specific features or characteristics of an object that can be used to distinguish it from another object. For example, assume the object we want to research is a consumer. As depicted in Figure 10.2, the properties of interest to a manager who is trying to define who buys a specific product are a combination of demographics, such as age and gender, as well as buyer behavior, which includes such things as the buyer's preferred brand and perceptions of various brands. In the figure, note that the measurement process is embodied in the response format presented in the question dealing with each property. Once the object's designation on a property has been determined, we say that the object has been measured on that property. Measurement underlies marketing research to a very great extent because researchers are keenly interested in describing marketing phenomena. Furthermore, researchers are often given the task of finding relevant differences in the profiles of various customer types, and measurement is a necessary first step in this task.

Measurement is a very simple process as long as we are measuring **objective properties**, which are physically verifiable characteristics such as age, income, number of bottles purchased, store last visited, and so on. They are observable and tangible. Typically, objective

FIGURE 10.2

How Measurement Works in Marketing Research

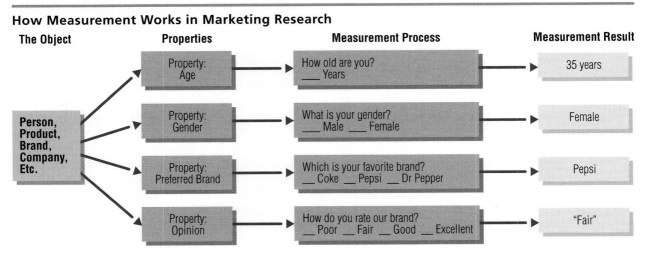

Automobiles have several properties that can be measured.

Objective properties are observable and tangible. Subjective properties are unobservable and intangible, and they must be translated onto a rating scale through the process of scale development.

properties, such as gender, are the ones that are preset as to appropriate response options, such as "male" or "female." However, marketing researchers often desire to measure **subjective properties**, which cannot be directly observed because they are mental constructs, such as a person's attitude or intentions. Subjective properties are unobservable and intangible. In this case, the marketing researcher must ask respondent to translate their mental constructs onto a continuum of intensity, which is not an easy task. To do this, the marketing researcher must adapt or develop rating-scale formats—referred to as "synthetic metric" scales in Table 10.1—that are very clear and that are used identically by the respondents. This process is known as "scale development."

SCALE CHARACTERISTICS

Scale characteristics are description, order, distance, and origin.

Scale development is designing questions and response formats to measure the subjective properties of an object. There are various types of scales, each of which possesses different characteristics. The characteristics of a scale determine the scale's level of measurement. The level of measurement, as you shall see, is very important. First, however, you must learn about the four characteristics of scales: description, order, distance, and origin.

Description

Description refers to the use of a unique descriptor, or label, to stand for each designation in the scale. For instance, "yes" and "no," "agree" and "disagree," and the number of years of a respondent's age are descriptors of three different scales. All scales include description in the form of unique labels that are used to define the response options in the scale.

Order

An ordered scale has descriptors that are "greater than," "less than," and "equal to" one another.

Order refers to the relative sizes of the descriptors. Here, the key word is *relative,* which includes such distinctions as "greater than," "less than," and "equal to." Respondents' least-preferred brand is "less than" their most-preferred brand, and respondents who check the same income category are the same ("equal to"). Not all scales possess order characteristics. For instance, is a "buyer" greater than or less than a "nonbuyer"? We have no way of making a relative size distinction.

Distance

A scale has the characteristic of **distance** when differences between the descriptors are known and may be expressed in units. The respondent who purchases three bottles of diet cola buys two more than the one who purchases only one bottle; a three-car family owns one more automobile than a two-car family. Note that when the characteristic of distance exists, we are also given order. We know not only that the three-car family has "more than" the number of cars of the two-car family but we also know the distance between the two (1 car).

Origin

A scale is said to have the characteristic of **origin** if there is a true zero point for the scale. Thus, 0 is the origin for an age scale just as it is for the number of miles traveled to the store or for the number of bottles of soda consumed. Not all scales have a true zero point for the property they are measuring. In fact, many scales used by marketing researchers have arbitrary neutral points, but they do not possess origins. For instance, when a respondent says, "No opinion," to the question "Do you agree or disagree with the statement, the Lexus is the best car on the road today?" we cannot say that the person has a true zero level of agreement.

A neutral category is not a true zero value for a scale.

Perhaps you noticed that each scale characteristic builds on the previous one. That is, description is the most basic and is present in every scale. If a scale has order, it also possesses description. If a scale has distance, it also possesses order and description, and if a scale has origin, it also has distance, order, and description. In other words, if a scale has a higher-level property, it also has all lower-level properties. But the opposite is not true, as is explained in the next section.

LEVELS OF MEASUREMENT SCALES

You may ask, "Why is it important to know the characteristics of scales?" The answer is that the characteristics possessed by a scale determine that scale's level of measurement. Throughout this chapter, we try to convince you that it is very important for a marketing researcher to understand the level of measurement of the scale selected. Let us now examine the four levels of measurement. They are nominal, ordinal, interval, and ratio. Table 10.2 shows how each scale type differs with respect to the scaling characteristics we have just discussed.

Table 10.2 uses two concepts introduced to you in Figure 10.1: categorical versus metric scales. A **categorical scale** is one that is typically composed of a small number of distinct values or categories, such as "male" versus "female" or "married," versus "single," versus "widowed." As you can see in the figure, there are two categorical scale types: nominal and ordinal. These will be described in detail in this section. The other concept is a **metric scale**, which is composed of numbers or labels that have an underlying measurement continuum. We also describe two metric scales in this section: interval and ratio scales.

There is a hierarchy of scales; ratio scales are the "highest" and nominal scales are the "lowest."

Nominal Scales

Nominal scales are defined as those that use only labels; that is, they possess only the characteristic of description. Examples include designations of race, religion, type of dwelling, gender, brand last purchased, buyer/nonbuyer; answers that involve yes–no, agree–disagree; or any other instance in which the descriptors cannot be differentiated except qualitatively. If you describe respondents in a survey according to their occupation—banker, doctor, computer programmer—you have used a nominal scale. Note that these examples of a nominal scale only label the consumers. They do not provide other information such as "greater than," "twice as large," and so forth. Examples of nominal-scaled questions are found in Table 10.3A on page 281.

Nominal scales simply label objects.

TABLE 10.2   Measurement Scales Differ by What Scale Characteristics They Possess

Level of Measurement		Scale Characteristic				Example
		Description	Order	Distance	Origin	
Categorical scale	Nominal	✔	⊘	⊘	⊘	**Which brand or brands do you use?**
	Ordinal	✔	✔	⊘	⊘	**Rank the brands as to 1st, 2nd, etc. choice.**
Metric scale	Interval	✔	✔	✔	⊘	**Rate each brand on a scale of 1–7.**
	Ratio	✔	✔	✔	✔	**How many times do you use each brand?**

✔ = does possess this characteristic   ⊘ = does *not* possess this characteristic

Ordinal Scales

Ordinal scales permit the researcher to rank-order the respondents or their responses. For instance, if respondents are asked to indicate their first, second, third, and fourth choices of brands, the results would be ordinally scaled. Similarly, if one respondent checked the category "Buy every week or more often" on a purchase-frequency scale and another checked the category "Buy once per month or less," the result would be an ordinal measurement. Ordinal scales indicate only relative size differences among objects. They possess description and order, but we do not know how far apart the descriptors are on the scale because ordinal scales do not possess distance or origin. Examples of ordinal-scaled questions are found in Table 10.3B.

Interval Scales

Interval scales use descriptors that are equal distances apart.

Interval scales are those in which the distance between each descriptor is known. For adjacent descriptors, the distance is normally defined as one scale unit. For example, a coffee brand rated "3" in taste is one unit away from one rated "4." Sometimes the researcher must impose a belief that equal intervals exist between the descriptors. That is, if you were asked to evaluate a store's salespeople by selecting a single designation from a list of "extremely friendly," "very friendly," "somewhat friendly," "somewhat unfriendly," "very unfriendly," or "extremely unfriendly," the researcher would probably assume that each designation was one unit away from the preceding one. In these cases, we say that the scale is "assumed interval." As shown in Table 10.3C, these descriptors are evenly spaced on a questionnaire; as such, the labels connote a continuum and the check lines are equal distances apart. By wording or spacing the response options on a scale so they appear to have equal intervals between them, the researcher achieves a higher level of measurement than ordinal or nominal, and a higher-level measure allows the researcher to see finer distinctions among respondents' properties.

TABLE 10.3   Examples of the Use of Different Scaling Assumptions in Questions

A. Nominal-Scaled Questions (descriptors with no order, distance, or origin)

1. Please indicate your gender: ___Male ___Female
2. Check all the brands you would consider purchasing. (Check all that apply.)

    ____ Sony

    ____ LG

    ____ RCA

    ____ Samsung

3. Do you recall seeing a Delta Airlines advertisement for "carefree vacations" in the past week?

    ____ Yes ____No

B. Ordinal-Scaled Questions (descriptors with order, but no distance or origin)

1. Please rank each brand in terms of your preference. Place a "1" by your first choice, a "2" by your second choice, and so on.

    ____ Arrid

    ____ Right Guard

    ____ Mennen

2. For each pair of grocery stores, circle the one you would be more likely to patronize.

    Kroger versus First National

    First National versus A&P

    A&P versus Kroger

3. In your opinion, would you say the prices at Wal-Mart are

    _____ Higher than Sears,

    _____ About the same as Sears, or

    _____ Lower than Sears?

C. Interval-Scaled Questions (descriptors with order and distance but no origin)

1. Please rate each brand in terms of its overall performance.

Brand	Rating (Circle One) Very Poor									Very Good
Mont Blanc	1	2	3	4	5	6	7	8	9	10
Parker	1	2	3	4	5	6	7	8	9	10
Cross	1	2	3	4	5	6	7	8	9	10

2. Indicate your degree of agreement with the following statements by circling the appropriate number.

Statement	Strongly Agree				Strongly Disagree
a. I always look for bargains.	1	2	3	4	5
b. I enjoy being outdoors.	1	2	3	4	5
c. I love to cook.	1	2	3	4	5

TABLE 10.3 (*Continued*)

3. Please rate **Pontiac Vibe** by checking the line that best corresponds to your evaluation of each item listed.

Slow pickup _____ _____ _____ _____ _____ _____ _____ Fast pickup

Good design _____ _____ _____ _____ _____ _____ _____ Bad design

Low price _____ _____ _____ _____ _____ _____ _____ High price

D. Ratio-Scaled Questions (descriptors with order, distance, and origin)

1. Please indicate your age.
   ____Years

2. Approximately how many times in the last month have you purchased something over $10 in price at a 7–11 store?
   0 1 2 3 4 5 More (specify:____)

3. How much do you think a typical purchaser of a $250,000 term life insurance policy pays per year for that policy?
   $_____

4. What is the probability that you will use a lawyer's services when you are ready to make a will?
   _____ percent

Ratio Scales

Ratio scales have a true zero point.

Ratio scales are ones in which a true zero origin exists—such as an actual number of purchases in a certain time period, dollars spent, miles traveled, number of children in the household, or years of college education. This characteristic allows us to construct ratios when comparing results of the measurement. One person may spend twice as much as another or travel one-third as far. Such ratios are inappropriate for interval scales, so we are not allowed to say that one store was one-half as friendly as another. Examples of ratio-scaled questions are presented in Table 10.3D.

 Active Learning Element

See if you can use the following template to figure out the scaling characteristics and scale type of a question. For each question in the first column, circle your answer to each of the questions along its row. Use these answers and the information in Figure 10.2 to identify and write in the scale type.

| Question | Answer each question by circling "Yes" or 'No" | | | | |
	Is there an origin?	Is there equal distance between adjacent labels?	Is each label greater than or less than its adjacent label(s)?	There are labels. (Note: all scales have labels.)	Write in the name of the type of scale in the question.
Do you own an Nintendo Wii home video game console? ___ Yes ___ No	Yes? No?	Yes? No?	Yes? No?	Yes? No?	_____

Question	Answer each question by circling "Yes" or 'No'				Write in the name of the type of scale in the question.
	Is there an origin?	Is there equal distance between adjacent labels?	Is each label greater than or less than its adjacent label(s)?	There are labels. (Note: all scales have labels.)	
About how many times per week do you use your Wii? ____ Times	Yes? No?	Yes? No?	Yes? No?	Yes? No?	_____
"I enjoy playing the sports games on my Wii." ___ Strongly Agree ___ Agree ___ No Opinion ___ Disagree ___ Strongly Disagree	Yes? No?	Yes? No?	Yes? No?	Yes? No?	_____
For a new Wii game, would you prefer to buy one that is primarily: ___ Educational ___ Amusement ___ Sports skill	Yes? No?	Yes? No?	Yes? No?	Yes? No?	_____

WHY THE MEASUREMENT LEVEL OF A SCALE IS IMPORTANT

Why all the fuss over scale characteristics and the level of measurement? There are two important reasons. First, the level of measurement determines what information you will have about the object of study; it determines what you can say and what you cannot say about the object. For example, nominal scales measure the lowest information level, and therefore they are sometimes considered the crudest scales. Nominal scales allow us to do nothing more than identify our object of study on some property. Ratio scales, however, contain the greatest amount of information; they allow us to say many things about our object, such as how different it is from another object quantitatively. A second important reason for understanding the level of measurement the scale possesses is that the level of measurement dictates what type of statistical analyses you may or may not perform. Low-level scales necessitate low-level analyses, such as simple percentages, whereas high-level scales permit much more sophisticated analyses, such as correlations. In other words, the amount of information contained in the scale dictates the limits of statistical analysis. You will read more about this topic in Chapters 15 through 18.

As a general recommendation, it is desirable to use a scale at the highest appropriate level of measurement possible. Of course, appropriateness is determined by the properties of the object being measured and to some extent by the mental abilities of your respondents. As we have pointed out, some characteristics are inherently qualitative and can be measured only with a nominal scale, while other characteristics can be quantified and measured with a metric scale. We have prepared Marketing Insight 10.1 to help you understand the use of interval scales in marketing research.

Measurement level is important because it determines (1) what you can or cannot say about your object and (2) which statistical analysis you may use.

MARKETING RESEARCH INSIGHT   Practical Application

10.1 Measuring Brand Attitudes and Emotions with a Marketing Event

A rapidly growing phenomenon is special-event marketing where a company, brand, or group of companies sponsors some sort of short-term happening that attracts a significant number of potential customers. This event can take on any of a variety of forms; it can be as large as a festival or a fair; it can be as exciting as a concert with famous music stars; it can be as small as a reception before a sports event; or it can be as local as a company picnic. Regardless of the event, it will have the potential to stir some emotions and to change attitudes in consumers. That is, it will impact subjective properties of the attendees, and there is good reason to believe that these unobservable changes will translate into opinions about the brand and/or intentions to purchase the sponsoring brand.

Here is a diagram of the possible factors associated with and impacted by a marketing event that were investigated in a recent study on event marketing.[5]

On the top half of the diagram, is the "brand-attitude route"; in the bottom half is the "event-related route." Both routes are comprised of unobservable constructs that are suspected to have some role in the consumer's intention to buy the sponsoring brand ("Buying intentions"). The brand-attitude route is the typical way that traditional marketing efforts work. Specifically, through advertising, free samples, coupons, and the like, consumers become interested in the brand (Brand involvement) and this leads to brand-related emotions and attitudes. These, in turn, affect intentions to buy the brand. In the study, all of the constructs were measured with 5- or 7-point synthetic metric intervals scales. Brand involvement was measured by interest such as degree of importance of the brand to the person;

brand emotion was feelings such as degree of joy or worry about the brand; and brand attitude was the degree of "goodness" of the brand. As can be seen by looking at the arrows in the figure, traditional marketing efforts heighten brand involvement, which stimulates brand emotion and increases brand attitude. Brand emotion, in turn, affects brand attitude, which increases intentions to buy the brand.

The marketing event path takes place when the brand or company sponsors some special event. Here, a critical consideration is the fit of the event with the brand's identity. For example, if there is a natural and logical connection—such as the John Deere company, which markets mainly argicultural equipment, sponsoring a tractor pull—the perceived fit is high; whereas if John Deere sponsored a golf tournament, the fit would surely be low. Fit and event involvement (importance of the event to the person) impact event emotions (how much happiness or excitement was experienced), and these affect the person's attitudes and opinions about how good the event was. Note that the event-related route directly impacts the brand attitude in its route. In other words, if the event successfully fits the image of the sponsoring brand, and it is imporant, exciting, and valuable to the consumer, experiencing the event will increase the consumer's opinions of the goodness of the sponsoring brand, and we already know that increased brand attitude will generate more intentions to buy the brand.

So, by mapping and measuring unobservable, subjective properties of fit, involvement, emotions, attitudes, and intentions with interval scales, the researchers were able to investigate the relationships indicated by the arrows in the diagram. Using interval scales allowed the reseachers to apply sophisticated statistical techniques to confirm these relationships and to expand our understanding of how event marketing affects consumers' ultimate brand choices.

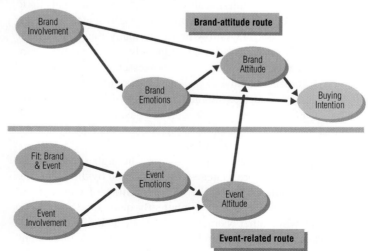

WORKHORSE SCALES USED IN MARKETING RESEARCH

We noted in our opening comments that marketing researchers often measure the subjective properties of consumers. There are many variations of these properties, but usually they are concerned with the psychological aspects. Various terms and labels are given to these constructs: attitudes, opinions, evaluations, beliefs, impressions, perceptions, feelings, and intentions. Because these constructs are unobservable, the marketing researcher must develop some means of allowing respondents to express the direction and the intensity of their impressions in a convenient and understandable manner. To do this, the marketing researcher uses scaled-response questions, which are designed to measure unobservable constructs. In Figure 10.1, we identifed these as "synthetic scale-response" format questions because the researcher uses a tailor-made scale. In this section, we will describe the basic scale formats that are most common in marketing research practice. That is, you will find these scale formats time and again on questionnaires; hence, we refer to them as **"workhorse scales"** because they do the bulk of the measurement work in marketing research.

Workhorse scales are standard ones that marketing researchers rely on time and again.

Synthetic scaled-response questions are used to measure unobservable constructs.

The Intensity Continuum Underlying Workhorse Scales

Because most psychological properties exist on a continuum ranging from one extreme to another in the mind of the respondent, it is common practice to use scaled-response questions with an interval scale format. In other words, they are metric. Sometimes numbers are used to indicate a single unit of distance between each position on the scale. Usually, but not always, the scale ranges from an extreme negative, through a neutral, and to an extreme positive designation. The neutral point is not considered zero, or an origin; instead, it is considered a point along a continuum. Take a look at the examples in Table 10.4, and you will see that all of them span a continuum ranging

TABLE 10.4   The Intensity Continuum Underlying Scaled-Response Question Forms

Extremely Negative			Neutral		Extremely Positive	
	Strongly Disagree	Somewhat Disagree	Neither Agree nor Disagree	Somewhat Agree	Strongly Agree	
	1	2	3	4	5	
Extremely Dissatisfied	Very Dissatisfied	Somewhat Dissatisfied	No Opinion	Somewhat Satisfied	Very Satisfied	Extremely Satisfied
1	2	3	4	5	6	7
Extremely Unfavorable	Very Unfavorable	Somewhat Unfavorable	No Opinion	Somewhat Favorable	Very Favorable	Extremely Favorable
1	2	3	4	5	6	7

from extremely negative to extremely positive with a "no opinion" position in the middle of the scale.

As we noted earlier, it is not good practice to invent a novel scale format with every questionnaire. Instead, marketing researchers often fall back on standard types used by the industry. These workhorse scales include the Likert scale, the lifestyle inventory, and the semantic differential, all three of which we describe next. Of course, sometimes no previous applicable scale exists; or if one exists, it may have been developed in a context different from the one the researcher has in mind.

Marketing researchers use standard scales rather than inventing new ones for each research project.

The Likert Scale

The Likert scale format measures intensity of agreement or disagreement.

A synthetic scaled-response form commonly used by marketing researchers[6] is the **Likert scale,** in which respondents are asked to indicate their degree of agreement or disagreement on a symmetric agree–disagree scale for each of a series of statements. That is, the scale captures the intensity of their feelings toward the statement's claim or assertion because respondents are asked how much they agree or disagree with the statement. With this scale, it is best to use "flat" or plain statements and let respondents indicate the intensity of their feelings by using the agree–disagree response continuum position. Table 10.5 presents an example of this use of this scale in a telephone interview. You should notice the directions given by the interviewer to ensure proper administration of this scale.

The Likert-type of response format, borrowed from Rensis Likert's formal scale development approach, has been extensively modified and adapted by marketing researchers, so much, in fact, that its definition varies from researcher to researcher. Some assume that any intensity scale using descriptors such as "strongly," "somewhat," "slightly," or the like is a Likert variation. Others use the term only for questions with agree–disagree response options. We tend to agree with the second opinion and prefer to refer to any scaled measurement other than an agree–disagree dimension as a "sensitivity"

TABLE 10.5   **The Likert Question Format Can Be Used in Telephone Surveys, but Respondents Must Be Briefed on Its Format or Otherwise Prompted**

(INTERVIEWER: READ) I have a list of statements that I will read to you. As I read each one, please indicate whether you agree or disagree with it.
Are the instructions clear? (IF NOT, REPEAT)
(INTERVIEWER: READ EACH STATEMENT. WITH EACH RESPONSE, ASK) Would you say that you (dis)agree STRONGLY or (dis)agree SOMEWHAT?

Statement	Strongly Agree	Agree	Neutral	Disagree	Strongly Disagree
Levi's Engineered jeans are good-looking.	1	2	3	4	5
Levi's Engineered jeans are reasonably priced.	1	2	3	4	5
Your next pair of jeans will be Levi's Engineered jeans.	1	2	3	4	5
Levi's Engineered jeans are easy to identify on someone.	1	2	3	4	5
Levi's Engineered jeans make you feel good.	1	2	3	4	5

or "intensity" scale. But this convention is only our preference, and you should be aware that different researchers embrace other designations.

The Lifestyle Inventory

There is a special application of the Likert question form called the **lifestyle inventory**, which takes into account the values and personality traits of people as reflected in their unique activities, interests, and opinions (AIOs) toward their work, leisure time, and purchases. The technique was originated by advertising strategists who wanted to obtain descriptions of groups of consumers as a means of developing more effective advertising. The underlying belief is that knowledge of consumers' lifestyles, as opposed to just demographics, offers direction for marketing decisions. Many companies use psychographics as a market targeting tool.[7]

Lifestyle questions measure consumers' unique ways of living. These questions can be used to distinguish among types of purchasers, such as heavy versus light users of a product, store patrons versus nonpatrons, or other customer types. They can assess the degree to which a person is, for example, price-conscious, fashion-conscious, an opinion giver, a sports enthusiast, child-oriented, home-centered, or financially optimistic. These attributes are measured by a series of AIO statements, usually in the form presented in Table 10.6.[8] Each respondent indicates degree of agreement or disagreement by responding to the agree–disagree scale positions. In some applications, the questionnaire may contain a large number of different lifestyle statements, ranging from very general descriptions of the

Lifestyle inventories measure a person's activities, interests, and opinions with a Likert scale.

A consumer's lifestyle may be measured in terms of activities, interests, and opinions using a Likert scale.

TABLE 10.6   Examples of Lifestyle Statements on a Questionnaire

Please respond by circling the number that best corresponds to how much you agree or disagree with each statement.

Statement	Strongly Disagree	Disagree	Neither Agree Nor Disagree	Agree	Strongly Agree
I shop a lot for "specials."	1	2	3	4	5
I usually have one or more outfits that are of the very latest style.	1	2	3	4	5
My children are the most important thing in my life.	1	2	3	4	5
I usually keep my house very neat and clean.	1	2	3	4	5
I would rather spend a quiet evening at home than go out to a party.	1	2	3	4	5
It is good to have a charge account.	1	2	3	4	5
I like to watch or listen to baseball or football games.	1	2	3	4	5
I think I have more self-confidence than most people.	1	2	3	4	5
I sometimes influence what my friends buy.	1	2	3	4	5
I will probably have more money to spend next year than I have now.	1	2	3	4	5

person's AIOs to very specific statements concerning particular products, brands, services, or other items of interest to the marketing researcher.

 Construct a College Student Lifestyle Inventory

Since you are a college student, you can easily relate to the dimensions of college student lifestyle. In this active learning exercise, for each of the following college student activities write the Likert scale statement that could appear on a college student lifestyle inventory questionnaire. Be sure to model your statements on our descriptions recommended in the Likert scale workhorse scale format.

College Lifestyle Dimension	Write Your Statement Below
Studying	
Going out	
Working	
Exercising	
Shopping	
Dating	
Spending money	

The Semantic Differential Scale

The semantic differential scale is a good way to measure a brand, company, or store image.

A specialized scaled-response question format that has sprung directly from the problem of translating a person's qualitative judgments into metric estimates is the **semantic differential scale**. Like the Likert scale, this one has been borrowed from another area of research, namely, semantics. The semantic differential scale contains a series of bipolar adjectives for the various properties of the object under study, and respondents indicate their impressions of each property by indicating locations along its continuum. The focus of the semantic differential is on the measurement of the meaning of an object, concept, or person. Because many marketing stimuli have meaning, mental associations, or connotations, this type of synthetic scale works very well when the marketing researcher is attempting to determine brand, store, or other images.[9]

The construction of a semantic differential scale begins with the determination of a concept or object to be rated. The researcher then selects bipolar pairs of words or phrases that could be used to describe the object's salient properties. Depending on the object, some examples might be "friendly–unfriendly," "hot–cold," "convenient–inconvenient," "high quality–low quality," or "dependable–undependable." The opposites are positioned at the endpoints of a continuum of intensity, and it is customary to use five or seven separators between each point. Respondents then check their evaluation of the performance of the object, say a brand, by checking the appropriate line. The closer respondents checks to an endpoint on a line, the more intense is their evaluation of the object being measured.

Table 10.7 shows how this was done in a survey for Red Lobster. The respondents also rated Jake's Seafood Restaurant on the same survey. You can see that each respondent has been instructed to indicate his or her impression of various restaurants, such as Red Lobster, by checking the appropriate line between the several bipolar adjective phrases. As

TABLE 10.7   The Semantic Differential Scale Is Useful when Measuring Store, Company, or Brand Images

Indicate your impression of *Red Lobster* restaurant by checking the line corresponding to your opinion for each pair of descriptors.

High prices	— — — — — — —	Low prices
Inconvenient location	— — — — — — —	Convenient location
For me	— — — — — — —	Not for me
Warm atmosphere	— — — — — — —	Cold atmosphere
Limited menu	— — — — — — —	Wide menu
Fast service	— — — — — — —	Slow service
Low-quality food	— — — — — — —	High-quality food
A special place	— — — — — — —	An everyday place

Presentation of the Results

High prices		Low prices
Inconvenient location		Convenient location
For me		Not for me
Warm atmosphere		Cold atmosphere
Limited menu		Wide menu
Fast service		Slow service
Low-quality food		High-quality food
A special place		An everyday place

●———● *Red Lobster*

●┄┄┄┄● *Jake's Seafood Restaurant*

you look at the phrases, you should note that they have been randomly flipped to avoid having all of the "good" ones on one side. This flipping procedure is used to avoid the **halo effect**,[10] which is a general feeling about a store or brand that can bias a respondent's impressions of its specific properties.[11] For instance, if you had a very positive image of Red Lobster and all of the positive items were on the right-hand side and all the negative ones were on the left-hand side, you might be tempted to just check all of the answers on the right-hand side without reading each characteristic carefully. But it is entirely possible that some specific aspect of the Red Lobster might not be as good as the others. Perhaps the restaurant is not located in a very convenient place, or the menu is not as broad as you would like. Randomly flipping favorable and negative ends of the descriptors in a semantic differential scale minimizes the halo effect.[12] Also, there is some evidence that when respondents are ambivalent about the survey topic, it is best to use a balanced set of negatively and positively worded questions.[13]

When using the semantic differential scale, you should control for the "halo effect."

One of the most appealing aspects of the semantic differential scale is that from it the researcher can compute averages and then plot a "profile" of the brand or company image. Each check line is assigned a number for coding. Usually, the numbers are 1, 2, 3, and so on, beginning from the left side. Then, because a metric scale is used, an average may be computed for each bipolar pair. The averages are plotted as you see them in Table 10.7, and the marketing researcher has a very nice graphic with which to report the findings to the client.

With a semantic differential scale, a researcher can plot the average evaluation on each set of bipolar descriptors.

TABLE 10.8 **Scaled-Response Question Formats Can Have Various Forms**

Scale Name	Description and Examples
Graphic rating scale	Use of a line or pictorial representation to indicate intensity of response:

unimportant ◄- - - - - - - - - - - - - - - - - ► **extremely important**

☺ ☺ ☺ ☺ ☺

Scale Name	Description and Examples
Itemized rating scale	Use of a numbered or labeled continuous scale to indicate intensity of response:

___ 1	___ 2	___ 3	___ 4	___ 5
			Very	
Poor	Fair	Good	Good	Excellent
_____	_____	_____	_____	_____

Stapel scale	Use of numbers, usually −5 to +5 to indicate the intensity of response:
	Fast checkout service −5 −4 −3 −2 −1 +1 +2 +3 +4 +5
Percentage scale	Use of percentages to indicate the intensity of response:

Unlikely to purchase   Likely to purchase

| 0% | 10% | 20% | 30% | 40% | 50% | 60% | 70% | 80% | 90% | 100% |

Very dissatisfied   Very satisfied

| 0% | | 25% | | 50% | | 75% | | 100% |

Other Synthetic Scaled-Response Question Formats

A great many variations of synthetic scaled-response question formats are used in marketing research. If you choose a career in this field, you will realize that each marketing research company or marketing research department tends to rely on "tried-and-true" formats that they apply in study after study. Several examples are provided in Table 10.8.

Researchers tend to rely on "tried-and-true" scale formats.

There are very good reasons for this practice of adopting a preferred question format. First, it expedites the questionnaire design process. That is, by selecting a standardized scaled-response form that has been used in several studies, there is no need to be creative and to invent a new form. This saves both time and money.[14] Second, by testing a synthetic scaled-response format across several studies, there is opportunity to assess its reliability as well as its validity. Both of these topics are discussed in detail in the next sections of this chapter, which introduce the basic concepts involved with reliability and validity of measurements and illustrate the methods used to assess reliability and validity.

Issues in the Use of Synthetic Scaled-Response Formats

Use a neutral response option when you think respondents have a valid "no opinion" response.

Using synthetic scaled-response formats requires the researcher to answer two questions. First is whether or not to include the middle, neutral response option. Our Likert scale, lifestyle, and semantic differential examples all have a neutral point, but some researchers prefer to leave out the neutral option on their scales. There are valid arguments for both options.[15] Those arguing for the inclusion of a neutral option believe that some respondents have not formed opinions on that item, and they must be given the opportunity to indicate their ambivalence. Proponents of not including a neutral position, however, believe that respondents may use the neutral option as a dodge or a way to hide their opinions.[16] Eliminating the neutral position forces these respondents to indicate their opinions or feelings.

The second question concerns whether or not to use a completely symmetric scale. Sometimes, common sense causes the researcher to conclude that only the positive side is appropriate. For example, when you think of how important something is to you, you do not usually think in terms of degrees of "unimportance." In fact, for many constructs symmetric scales are awkward or nonintuitive and should not be used.[17] Consequently, some scales contain only the positive side, because very few respondents would make use of the negative side.

When in doubt, a researcher can pretest both the complete and the one-sided versions to see whether the negative side will be used by respondents. As a general rule, it is best to pretest a sensitivity scale to make sure it is being used in its entirety. Some groups, such as Hispanics, have a tendency to use only one end of a scale,[18] and pretests should be used to find a scale that will be used appropriately.

A sometimes troublesome issue that global marketing reseachers encounter is cultural differences among respondents. In some cultures extremism is valued, and in some others moderation or "going along with the crowd" is expected. That is, just because a scale represents a complete range of intensities along a continuum does not guarantee that the complete range will be used. Read Marketing Reseach Insight 10.2, which describes what researchers found when they examined how respondents in 26 different countries compared with respect to their use of the full range of a scale.[19]

> Use common sense in deciding whether to have a completely symmetric scale.

MARKETING RESEARCH INSIGHT   Global Application

10.2 How Cultural Differences Affect Respondents' Use of the Extreme Ends of Scales

Whenever a marketing researcher undertakes global studies, a host of considerations must be considered. Typically, language differences alone are a great concern, for often a literal translation of questions fails to include nuances, idioms, and subtleties that are built into the initial question's wording. Often two or three iterations of translations, interpretations, and pretests are necessary for the researcher to feel confident that the various language versions are equivalent.

However, even when the questions are equivalent, there is the possibility that cultural response styles will come into play. A cultural response style is a tendency among members of a cultural group to use the scale in a particular way. For instance, cultures where indivdualism and dogmatism are valued are perhaps more likely to use the extreme ends of scales than are cultures where collectivism and cooperation are valued. In the collective cultures, extremism is avoided, and one would expect that respondents in these cultures would tend to respond with more "middle-of-the-road" responses to the scales posed on a questionnaire.

This line of thinking was validated to some extent by a study. As can be seen in the following figure, respondents from Thailand and Taiwan, which are collective, communal cultures, exhibited a relatively strong middle-of-the-road response tendency. That is, they tended not to use the extreme end response options such as "very strongly agree" or "very strongly disagree" in the test surveys. Chinese respondents, also representing a communal society, were found to have middle-of-the-road response propensities as well. In contrast, Russian respondents displayed very pronounced extreme response tendencies, meaning that they used the "very strongly agree" and "very strongly disagree" endpoints of the scales in the study a great deal, and much more so than respondents in any other countries. Romanian and Argentinian respondents also displayed extreme response tendencies, although these were somewhat less pronounced.

The majority of countries in the study fell into a range of response moderation rather than response extremism, as can be seen by the clustering of many countries close to the "0" response-style demarcation in the figure, which indicates neither high numbers of extreme responses nor unusually large numbers of middle-of-the-road responses were found.

This figure and findings from other studies that have corroborated these differences in cultural response tendencies are a cautionary warning to any researcher undertaking global marketing research, and the warning is especially relevant to marketing researchers who are investigating countries whose cultures are strongly individualistic or largely collective in nature.

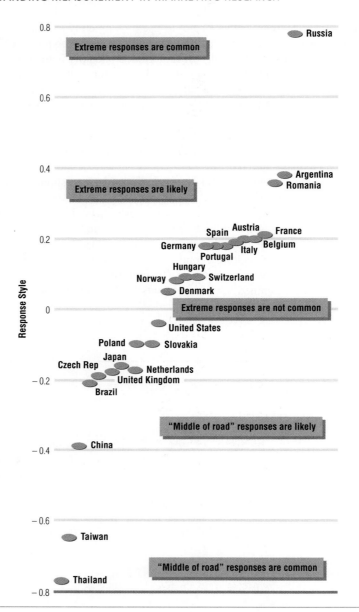

WHAT SCALE TO USE WHEN

It has been our experience that when you study each workhorse scale and the other scaled-response question formats described in this chapter, each one makes sense. However, when faced with the actual decision as to what scale to recommend in a given situation, neophyte marketing researchers find it difficult to sort these scales out.

As we indicated in Chapter 4, market researchers' mindset is geared toward the actual survey steps, and questionnaire design is a vital step that they must think about when formulating the marketing research proposal. We indicated in Chapter 4 that market researchers use "constructs," or standard marketing concepts, and, more important, we indicated that researchers typically have a mental vision of how each construct will be measured. This mental vision, we indicated, is called an *operational definition*.

Since you now understand the basic concepts of measurement and have become acquainted with the workhorse scales and other scales used by market researchers, we have provided Table 10.9 as a quick reference to appropriate scales pertaining to the constructs most often measured by market researchers. You will notice that most of the scales in Table 10.9 are interval scaled because most of the constructs are attitudinal or intensity scales, and the general recommendation is to use the highest-level scale possible.[20] Of course, the table is not a complete listing of marketing constructs, but those included are the ones that are often involved in marketing research undertakings.

We have included some nominally scaled constructs in Table 10.9; that is, the awareness, possession, recall, and recognition constructs are measured with yes/no scales. If there is a list, and the respondent checks all that apply, the researcher can use a **summated scale**, meaning that the number of checks will be counted for each respondent and that number will stand as the metric measure of the construct. For example, in a list of 10 appliances that a person could have in a kitchen, those respondents with many appliances will have high summated scale numbers; those with few will have low summated scale numbers.

If you are still confused about what scale to use when, do not feel badly, as scales are not an easy concept to understand at first reading. We did not include as one of our "workhorse" scales the simple, commonly used 5-point anchored scale.[21] An **anchored scale** is one where the endpoints are identified by the opposite ends of the measurement continuum and are associated with the beginning and ending numbers of the scale. For example, a telephone interviewer might say, "Please tell me how satisfied you were with your cable televison service where a 1 means 'unsatisfied' and a 5 means 'very satisfied.' Another example is "Please rate the music quality of your HDTV's audio system where 1 means 'poor' and 5 means 'excellent.'" An **unanchored scale** is one where the endpoints are not identified, as in "Please indicate on a scale of 1–5 how satisfied you were with your automobile's gas mileage." It is implicit in an unanchored scale that as the scale numbers rise, the evaluation is more postive. So a 1 would be the least postive response, and a 5 would be the most postive response. Nevertheless, it is important to indicate how the numbers relate to the respondent's evaluation in the instructions for that rating scale.

Figuring out what scale to use and when is challenging for a neophyte marketing researcher.

RELIABILITY AND VALIDITY OF MEASUREMENTS

Ideally, a measurement used by a market researcher should be reliable and valid. A **reliable measure** is one in which a respondent answers in the same or in a very similar manner to an identical or near-identical question. Obviously, if a question elicits wildly different answers from the same person, and you know that circumstances have not changed between administrations of the question, there is something very wrong with the question. It is unreliable.[22]

Validity, on the other hand, operates on a completely different plane than reliability; it is possible to have perfectly reliable measurements that are invalid. Validity is defined as the accuracy of the measurement: It is an assessment of the exactness of the measurement relative to what actually exists. So a **valid measure** is one that is truthful. To illustrate this concept and its difference from reliability, think of a respondent who is embarrassed by a

Reliable measures obtain identical or very similar responses from the same respondent.

Validity is the truthfulness of responses to a measure.

TABLE 10.9 Commonly Used Scales for Selected Constructs

Construct	Response Scale
Awareness (or Possession)	Yes–No OR check one from a list of items Example: *Which of the following kitchen appliances do you own ? (check all that apply.)*
Brand/Store image	Semantic differential (with 4 or 7 scale points) using a set of bipolar adjectives Example: *Refer to example on page 279.*
Demographics	Standard demographic questions (gender, age range, income range, etc.) Examples: *Indicate your gender ___ Male ___ Female* *What is your age range?* *___ 20 or younger* *___ 21–30* *___ 31–40* *___ 41–50* *___ 51 or older*
Frequency of use	Labeled (Never, Rarely, Occasionally, Often, Quite Often, Very Often) OR # times per relevant time period (e.g., month) Example: *How often do you buy takeout Chinese dinners?*
Importance	Labeled (Unimportant, Slightly Important, Important, Quite Important, Very Important) OR numbered rating using 5 scale points Example: *How important is it to you that your dry cleaning service has same-day service?*
Intention to purchase	Labeled (Unlikely, Somewhat Likely, Likely, Quite Likely, Very likely) OR 100% probability Example: *The next time you buy cookies, how likely are you to buy a fat-free brand?*
Lifestyle/Opinion	Likert (Strongly Disagree–Strongly Agree with 5 scale points) using a series of lifestyle statements Example: *Indicate how much you agree or disagree with each of the following statements.* *1. I have a busy schedule.* *2. I work a great deal.*
Performance or Attitude	Labeled (Poor, Fair, Good, Very Good, Excellent) OR numbered rating scale using 5 scale points OR Stapel scale using −3 to +3 Example: *Indicate how well you think Arby's performs on each of the following features.* *1. Variety of items on the menu* *2. Reasonable price* *3. Location convenient to your home*
Recall or recognition	Yes–No OR check one from a list of items Example: *Where have you seen or heard an ad for Pets-R-Us in the past month? (check all that apply).*
Satisfaction	Labeled (Not at all Satisfied, Slightly Satisfied, Somewhat Satisfied, Very Satisfied, Completely Satisfied) OR 10-point satisfaction scale where 1 = "not at all satisfied" and 10 = "completely satisfied" *Note*: if there is reason to believe that an appreciable number of respondents are not satisfied, the recommendation is for a symmetric balanced scale to measure the degree of dissatisfaction (Completely Dissatisfied; Slightly Dissatisfied; Neither Dissatisfied nor Satisfied; Slightly Satisfied; Completely Satisfied) Example: *Based on your experience with Federal Express, how satisfied have you been with its overnight delivery service?*

Not at all Satisfied	Slightly Satisfied	Somewhat Satisfied	Somewhat Satisfied	Completely Satisfied
☐	☐	☐	☐	☐

question about his income. This person makes under $40,000 per year, but he does not want to tell that to the interviewer. Consequently, he responds with the highest category, "Over $100,000." In a retest of the questions, the respondent persists in his lie by stipulating the highest income level again. Here, the respondent has been perfectly consistent (that is, reliable), but he has also been completely untruthful (that is, invalid). Of course, lying is not the only reason for invalidity. The respondent may have a faulty memory, may have a misconception, or may even be a bad guesser, which causes his responses to depart from reality.[23]

When developing questions for a questionnaire, a researcher uses an intuitive form of judgment called *face validity* to evaluate the validity of each question. Face validity is concerned with the degree to which a measurement "looks like" it measures that which it is designed to measure.[24] Thus, as each question is developed, there is an implicit assessment of its face validity. Often, a researcher will ask colleagues to look at the questions to see if they agree with the researcher's face validity judgments. Revisions strengthen the face validity of the question until it passes the researcher's subjective evaluation. Unfortunately, face validity is considered by academic marketing researchers to be a very weak test, so marketing research practitioners are faced with an ethical dilemma when they work with scales. We describe this ethical dilemma in our Marketing Research Insight 10.3.

Face validity: Does the question "look like" it measures what it is supposed to measure?

MARKETING RESEARCH INSIGHT — Ethical Application

10.3 Why Marketing Researchers Face Ethical Issues in Scale Development

Scale development poses an ethical dilemma for researchers. The proper development of a scale is a very lengthy and expensive process because several different criteria must be satisfied in assessing the quality of a scale. To meet these criteria, a scale should be developed over a series of administrations. After each one, statistical tests are used to refine the scale, and each subsequent administration tests the new version, which leads to further refinement. It is not unusual for scales that are published in academic journals to go through three or four administrations involving hundreds of respondents. To say this more pointedly, when a marketing researcher must develop a scale to measure a marketing construct, doing it properly may take several months or even years of work.

The few marketing research firms who have pursued scale development have developed proprietary instruments that are protected by copyright. That is, they have invested time and money in scale development so that scale will be part of the marketing research services they offer, and they will enjoy a competitive advantage over other marketing research firms because of the legal protection afforded their work by a copyright.

As you would expect, the vast majority of marketing research practitioners do not have the time, and their clients are unwilling to supply the monetary resources necessary, to thoroughly develop scales. So there is an ethical dilemma when a marketing researcher must measure some marketing phenomenon but does not have the luxury of time nor the resources necessary to do so properly. Proper scale development simply cannot take place due to the fact that clients do not appreciate the time and cost factors. In fact, they may not even believe these procedures are warranted and will refuse to pay for them, meaning that if such tests are performed, the marketing researcher's profits will be reduced. Consequently, the vast majority of marketing researchers are forced to design their measures by relying on face validity alone, meaning that the researcher, and perhaps the client if inclined to take part, simply judges that the question developed to measure the marketing construct at hand "looks like" an adequate measure.

The unfortunate truth is that most marketing research practitioners cannot concern themselves at all with rigorous scale development that relies on time-consuming reliability or validity measurements. The standard procedure is to use measures that are well known through the company's experience, through the researcher's own experience, or available in the marketing research literature. On the other hand, it is unethical for a researcher to discover reliability and/or validity problems and not strive to resolve them. A conscientious market researcher will devote as much time and energy as possible to ensure the reliability and validity of the research throughout the entire process.

The formal development of reliable and valid measures is a long and complicated process that is largely entrusted to academic marketing researchers.[25] In other words, marketing professors who work on the cutting edge of research often labor for months and sometimes years to develop reliable and valid measures of the marketing constructs with which they are working. Fortunately, these labors are ultimately published in academic journals, which puts these measures in the public domain, meaning that marketing research practitioners can use them freely. The *Marketing Scales Handbooks* edited by Gordon C. Bruner II, Karen E. James, and Paul J. Hensel contain hundreds of scales (available at their Office of Scales Research, www.siu.edu/departments/coba/osr/index.html). These handbooks save time and effort in searching for scales in journal articles or other similar academic sources.

SPSS Student Assistant:
Coca-Cola: Sorting,
Searching, and Inserting
Variables and Cases

Summary

This chapter discussed the concepts involved in the measurement of the subjective properties of marketing phenomena. We began by reviewing the three basic question–response option formats—open-ended, categorical, and scaled-response—and then we introduced you to the four types of scales used in marketing research: (1) nominal or simple classification; (2) ordinal or rank order; (3) interval scales, which include number scales and other scales that appear to be equally spaced; and (4) ratio scales, which have a true zero point. As you move from the lowest (nominal) to the highest (ratio) type of scale, you gain more information from the measurement.

Marketing researchers use common set of scale types, and the chapter included descriptions of three of these. First is the Likert scale, which appears as an agree–disagree continuum with five to seven positions.

Next, are lifestyle questions, which use a Likert approach to measure people's attitudes, interests, and opinions. Third, the semantic differential scale uses bipolar adjectives to measure the image of a brand or a store. We also listed a number of other scaled-response question formats that are popular with marketing reseachers and recommended ways a neophyte marketing researcher should measure each of 10 commonly researched marketing constructs, such as awareness or satisfaction.

Finally, we discussed measurement reliability and validity. Reliability is the degree to which a respondent's answers are consistent. Validity, on the other hand, applies to the accuracy of responses. It is possible to have reliable measures that are inaccurate. Researchers use face validity, or intuitive judgment, when developing questions that "look like" they elicit valid answers.

Key Terms

Review Questions/Applications

1. List each of the three basic question–response formats. Indicate the two variations for each one and provide an example for each.

2. Identify at least three considerations that determine the format of a question and indicate how each one would affect the format.

3. What is measurement? In your answer, differentiate an object from both its objective and subjective properties.

4. Name the four characteristics that determine the level of measurement of a scale.

5. Define the four types of scales and indicate the types of information contained in each.

6. Explain what is meant by a continuum along which a subjective property of an object can be measured.

7. What are the arguments for and against the inclusion of a neutral response position in a symmetric scale?

8. Distinguish among a Likert scale, a lifestyle scale, and a semantic differential scale.

9. What is the halo effect, and how does a researcher control for it?

10. What is an operational definition? Provide operational definitions for the following constructs:
    a. Brand loyalty
    b. Intention to purchase
    c. Importance of "value for the price"
    d. Attitude toward a brand
    e. Recall of an advertisement
    f. Past purchases

11. How does reliability differ from validity? In your answer, define each term.

12. Mike, the owner of Mike's Market, a convenience store, is concerned about low sales. He reads in a marketing textbook that the image of a store often has an impact on its ability to attract its target market. He contacts the All-Right Research Company and commissions it to conduct a study that will shape his store's image. You are charged with the responsibility of developing the store image part of the questionnaire.

    Design a semantic differential scale that will measure the relevant aspects of Mike's Market's image. In your work on this scale, you must do the following: (a) brainstorm the properties to be measured, (b) determine the appropriate bipolar adjectives, (c) decide on the number of scale points, and (d) indicate how the scale controls for the halo effect.

13. Each of the examples listed next involves a marketing researcher's need to measure some construct. Devise an appropriate scale for each one. Defend the scale in terms of its scaling assumptions, number of response categories, use or nonuse of a "no opinion" or neutral response category, and face validity.
    a. Mattel wants to know how preschool children react to a sing-along video game in which the child must sing along with an animated character and guess the next word in the song at various points in the video.
    b. TCBY is testing five new flavors of yogurt and wants to know how its customers rate each one on sweetness, flavor strength, and richness of taste.
    c. A pharmaceutical company wants to find out how much a new federal law eliminating doctors' dispensing of free sample prescription drugs will affect their intentions to prescribe generic versus brand-name drugs for their patients.

14. Harley-Davidson is the largest American motorcycle manufacturer and has been in business for several decades. Several years ago, Harley-Davidson expanded into "signature" products, such as shirts that prominently display the Harley-Davidson logo. Some people have a negative image of Harley-Davidson because it was the motorcycle favored by the Hell's Angels and other motorcycle gangs. There are two research questions here. First, do consumers have a negative feeling toward Harley-Davidson, and, second, are they disinclined to purchase Harley-Davidson signature products such as shirts, belts, boots, jackets, sweatshirts, lighters, and key chains? Design a Likert measurement scale that can be used in a nationwide telephone study to address these two issues.

15. In conducting a survey for the Equitable Insurance Company, Burke Marketing Research assesses reliability by calling back a small group of respondents to readminister five questions. One question asks, "If you were going to buy life insurance sometime this year, how likely would you be to consider the Equitable Company?" Respondents indicate the likelihood on a probability scale (0% to 100% likely). Typically, this test–retest approach finds that respondents are within 10% of their initial response. That is, if respondents indicated that they were 50% likely in the initial survey, they responded in the 45% to 55% range on the retest.

The survey has been going on for four weeks, and it will be two more weeks before the data collection is completed. Respondents who are retested are called back exactly one week after the initial survey. In the last week, reliability results have been very different. Now Burke is finding that the retest averages are 20% higher than the initial test. Has the scale become unreliable? If so, why has its previous good reliability changed? If not, what has happened, and how can Burke still claim that it has a reliable measure?

16. General Foods Corporation includes Post, which is the maker of Fruit and Fibre Cereal. The brand manager is interested in determining how much Fruit and Fibre consumers think is helping them toward a healthier diet. But the manager is very concerned that respondents in a survey may not be entirely truthful about health matters. They may exaggerate what they really believe so they "sound" more health conscious than they really are, and they may say they have healthy diets when they really do not.

The General Foods Corporation marketing research director has come up with a unique way to overcome the problem. He suggests that they conduct a survey of Fruit and Fibre customers in Pittsburgh, Atlanta, Dallas, and Denver. Fifty respondents who say that Fruit and Fibre is helping them toward a healthier diet and who also say they are more health conscious than the average American will be selected, and General Foods will offer to "buy" their groceries for the next month. To participate, the chosen respondents must submit their itemized weekly grocery trip receipts. By reviewing the items bought each week, General Foods can determine what they are eating and make judgments on how healthy their diets really are. What is your reaction to this approach? Will General Foods be able to assess the validity of its survey this way? Why or why not?

CASE 10.1

METRO TOYOTA

The Metro Toyota dealership, located on the south side of a major metropolitan area, wanted to know how people who intended to buy a new automobile in the next 12 months view their purchase. The general sales manager called the marketing department at the local university and arranged for a class project to be undertaken by undergraduate marketing research students. The professor had a large class that semester, so she decided to divide the project into two groups and to have each group compete against the other to see which one designed and executed the better survey.

Both groups worked diligently on the survey over the semester. They met with the Metro Toyota general sales manager, discussed the dealership with his managers, conducted focus groups, and consulted the research literature on brand, store, and company image. Both teams conducted telephone surveys, whose findings are presented in their final reports.

The marketing research professor offered to grant extra credit to each team if it gave a formal presentation of its research design, findings, and recommendations.

Findings of Marketing Research Teams
Team One's Findings for Metro Toyota Importance
of Features of Dealership in Deciding to Buy There

Feature	Percent Indicating "Yes"[a]
Competitive prices	86%
No high pressure	75%
Good service facilities	73%
Low-cost financing	68%
Many models in stock	43%
Convenient location	35%
Friendly salespersons	32%

[a] Based on responses to the question "Is _(insert feature)___ important to you when you decide on a dealership from which to purchase your new automobile?"

Perception of Metro Toyota Dealership Percent Responding "Yes"

Feature	Percent Indicating "Yes"[b]
Competitive prices	45%
No high pressure	32%
Good service facilities	80%
Low-cost financing	78%
Many models in stock	50%
Convenient location	81%
Friendly salespersons	20%

[b] Based on responses to the question "Were you satisfied with Metro Toyota's _(insert feature)___ when you purchased your new automobile there?"

Team Two's Findings for Metro Toyota Importance and Image of Metro Toyota Dealership

Feature	Importance[c]	Satisfaction[d]
Competitive prices	6.5	1.3
No high pressure	6.2	3.6
Good service facilities	5.0	4.3
Low-cost financing	4.7	3.9
Many models in stock	3.1	3.0
Convenient location	2.2	4.1
Friendly salespersons	2.0	1.2

[c] Based on a 7-point scale where 1 = "unimportant" and 7 = "extremely important."
[d] Based on a 5-point scale where 1 = "completely unsatisfied" and 5 = "completely satisfied."

1. Describe the different ways these findings can be presented in graphical form to the Metro Toyota management group. Which student team has the ability to present its findings more effectively? How and why?

2. What are the managerial implications apparent in each team's findings? Identify the implications and recommendations for Metro Toyota that are evident in each team's findings.

CASE 10.2

EXTREME EXPOSURE ROCK CLIMBING CENTER FACES THE KRAG

For the past five years, Extreme Exposure Rock Climbing Center has enjoyed a monopoly. Located in Sacaramento, California, Extreme Exposure was the dream of Kyle Anderson, an avid participant in freesyle extreme sports of various types, including outdoor rock climbing, hang gliding, skydiving, mountan biking, snowboarding, and a number of other adrenalin-pumping sports. Now in his mid-30s, Kyle came to realize at the age of 30 that after three leg fractures, two broken arms, and numerous dislocations, he could not participate on the extreme edge as he used to. So, he found an abandoned warehouse, recruited two investors and a friendly banker, and opened up Extreme Exposure.

Kyle's rock climbing center has over 6,500 square feet of simulated rock walls to climb, with about 100 different routes up to a maximum of 50 vertical feet. Extreme Exposure's design permits the four major climbing types: top-roping, where the climber climbs up with a rope anchored at the top; lead-climbing, where the climber clips a rope to the wall while ascending; bouldering, where the climber has no rope but stays near the ground; and rapelling, where the person descends quickly by sliding down a rope. Climbers can buy day passes or month-long or annual memberships. Shoes and harnesses can be rented cheaply, and helmets are available free of charge as all climbers must wear protective helmets. In addition to individual and group climbing classes, Extreme Exposure has several group programs, including birthday parties, a kids' summer camp, and corporate team-building classes.

A newspaper article has reported that another rock climbing center, to be called "The Krag," will be built in Sacramento in the next six months. Kyle notes the following items about The Krag that are different from Extreme Exposure: (1) The Krag will have climbs up to a maximum of 60 vertical feet, (2) it will have a climber certification program, (3) there will be day trips to outdoor rock-climbing areas, (4) there will be group overnight and extended-stay rock-climbing trips to the Canadian Rockies, and (5) The Krag's annual membership fee will be about 20% lower than Extreme Exposure's.

Kyle chats with Dianne, one of his Extreme Exposure members who is in marketing, during a break in one of her climbing visits, Dianne summarizes what she believes Kyle needs to find out about his current members. Dianne's list follows.

1. What is the demographic and rock-climbing profile of Extreme Exposure's members?
2. How satisfied are the members with Extreme Exposure's climbing facilities?
3. How interested are its members in (a) day trips to outdoor rock-climbing areas, (b) group overnight and/or extended-stay rock-climbing trips to the Canadian Rockies, and (c) a rock-climber certification program?
4. What are members' opinions of the annual membership fee charged by Extreme Exposure?
5. Will members consider leaving Extreme Exposure to join a new rock-climbing center with climbs that are 10 feet higher than the maximum climb at Extreme Exposure?
6. Will members consider leaving Extreme Exposure to join a new rock-climbing center with climbs that are 10 feet higher than the maximum climb at Extreme Exposure and whose annual membership fee is 20% lower than Extreme Exposure's?

For each of Dianne's questions, identify the relevant construct and indicate how is should be measured.

CASE 10.3 Your Integrated Case

ADVANCED AUTOMOBILE CONCEPTS

Cory Rogers of CMG Research has talked on the phone with Nick Thomas, CEO of Advanced Automobile Concepts at Zen Motors, and, although they have not completely decided on the survey data-collection method to be used in the AAC survey, they both agree that an online survey seems most attractive. There are a few issues, such as the specific online questionnaire system and the sample, to be decided, but Nick gives Cory the go-ahead to begin the questionnaire design process. Being a good marketing researcher, Cory knows that the first step in the process is to come up with operational definitions, meaning the appropriate measurement scale, for the constructs in the survey.

There are several constructs involved with the research desired by Advanced Automobile Concepts. Each one is briefly described here. In each case, provide the operational definition, that is, identify what you think is the most appropriate scale format for Cory to use. You are not being asked to develop the precise questions, but you are being asked to recommend a response scale. In thinking about your recommendations, you should keep the following facts in mind: (1) A very wide variety of individuals will be responding; (2) the questionnaire will undoubtedly be quite long, meaning that the best types of response scale will be those that are intuitive and easy for respondents to relate to; and (3) insofar as possible, it is desirable to use metric scales.

1. Current vehicle ownership (size and type of vehicle)
2. Beliefs about global warming and the effects of the use of gasoline on global warming
3. Beliefs about gasoline price levels and trends
4. Opinions as to the impact of alternative-fuel automobiles (such as hybrids, synthetic fuels, electric, etc.) on global warming
5. Intentions to buy an alternative-fuel automobile
6. Preferences for various sizes of alternative-fuel automobiles (such as mini, economy 2-door, economy 4-door, standard)
7. Preferred television show type (e.g., drama, mini-series, sports), magazine type (e.g., business and finance, family living, travel), radio music genre (e.g., rock, jazz, easy listening), and newspaper section (e.g., local news, sports, editorial).

11 Developing Questions and Designing the Questionnaire

Learning Objectives

- To appreciate the basic functions of a questionnaire
- To learn the "Do's" and "Do Not's" of wording questions
- To learn the basics of questionnaire organization
- To comprehend coding of questionnaires
- To understand the advantages of computer-assisted questionnaire design software
- To learn how to use Qualtrics

Where We Are

1. Establish the need for marketing research
2. Define the problem
3. Establish research objectives
4. Determine research design
5. Identify information types and sources
6. Determine methods of accessing data
7. Design data-collection forms
8. Determine the sample plan and size
9. Collect data
10. Analyze data, and
11. Prepare and present the final research report.

Since Most Consumers Want a Car with Excellent Fuel Economy, Wouldn't You Agree Your Next Car Will Be a Hybrid?

Clifford D. Scott, Associate Professor of Marketing, University of Arkansas, Fort Smith, has many years of research experience in high-tech, biotech, and consulting.

Lawyers and market researchers both ask leading questions, and both do it for the same two reasons. First, leading questions are easier. A single leading question can cut right to the point. ("Did you see Carrie Bradshaw steal a pair of Fendi pumps from Bergdorf's on Tuesday?") Getting the same information without putting words in the respondent's mouth requires a series of organized, interlocking, nonleading questions: "Did you leave home on Tuesday?" "Can you tell us where you went?" "Did you see anyone you knew there?" "What, if anything, did she do that you found to be unusual?"

Second, leading questions bolster your case. A skilled questioner, whether in court or in a market study, can usually get the answers she wants. For a lawyer, that approach is fine: a lawyer is supposed to be an advocate. But a researcher is supposed to be a scientist. People risk their careers and their fortunes on the outcome of a study. If they take those risks and lose, they will look for someone to blame. The researcher makes an excellent target IF the study shows evidence of bias, such as leading questions. The faulty study can, and often will, come back to haunt the researcher.

This chapter will teach you how to identify and eliminate leading questions, one of the most common, and most damning, sources of bias. Looking at the question at the top of this page, clearly you would want to be "like all those other smart consumers" and buy a hybrid! Wording a question in this way would guarantee that you will get a larger percentage of respondents indicating they will buy a hybrid than if you had just asked: "If you had to select your next car today, what brand of car would you buy?" In this chapter you will learn more about the "dos and don'ts" of designing a questionnaire to avoid biased questions.

Clifford D. Scott, Ph.D., J.D.

*Y*ou are now ready to learn about questionnaire design. In this chapter you will learn the functions of a questionnaire and the process of designing questionnaires. We give you guidelines on how to word questions so they are focused and clear, and we show you how to avoid biased questions. You will also learn how to organize a questionnaire and how to apply codes, plus you will hear about the importance of pretesting your questionnaire. We introduce you to computer-assisted questionnaire design programs, and we will show you how to use Qualtrics, a popular computer program that is used to develop a questionnaire that can be published online for use by respondents and that generates a downloadable computer file of all respondents' answers.

THE FUNCTIONS OF A QUESTIONNAIRE

A questionnaire presents the survey questions to respondents.

A **questionnaire** is the vehicle used to present the questions that the researcher desires respondents to answer. Surely, you realize that questionnaires are important elements in surveys, but it might surprise you to learn that a questionnaire serves six key functions. (1) It translates the research objectives into specific questions that are asked of the respondents. (2) It standardizes those questions and the response categories so every participant responds to identical stimuli. (3) By its wording, question flow, and appearance, it fosters cooperation and keeps respondents motivated throughout the interview. (4) Questionnaires serve as enduring records of the research. (5) Depending on the type of questionnaire used, a questionnaire can speed up the process of data analysis. Online questionnaires, for example, can be transmitted to thousands of potential respondents in seconds, and their submitted responses are available for analysis almost instantaneously. (6) Finally, questionnaires contain the information on which reliability assessments may be made, and they are used in follow-up validation of respondents' participation in the survey. In other words, questionnaires are used by researchers for quality control.

Given that it serves all of these functions, the questionnaire is indeed a very important ingredient in the research process. In fact, studies have shown that a questionnaire's design directly affects the quality of the data collected. Even experienced interviewers cannot compensate for questionnaire defects.[1] The time and effort invested in developing a good questionnaire are well spent.[2]

THE QUESTIONNAIRE DESIGN PROCESS

Questionnaire design is a systematic process that requires the researcher to go through a series of decisions.

As you will soon learn, **questionnaire design** is a systematic process in which the researcher contemplates various question formats, considers a number of factors characterizing the survey at hand, ultimately words the various questions very carefully, and organizes the questionnaire's layout. It is a process that requires the researcher to go through a series of interrelated steps.

Figure 11.1 is a flowchart of the various phases in a typical questionnaire design process. As you can see, a significant part of questionnaire design involves the development of individual questions in the survey—identified as "Question Development" in the figure. We have expanded and highlighted the question development steps so you can see that there are some specific activities the researcher must execute before any question is acceptable.

As you can see in Figure 11.1, a question will ordinarily go through a series of drafts before it is in acceptable final form. In fact, even before the question is constructed, the researcher mentally reviews alternative question response-scale formats to decide which ones are best suited to the survey's respondents and circumstances. As the question begins to take shape, the researcher continually evaluates the question and its response options.

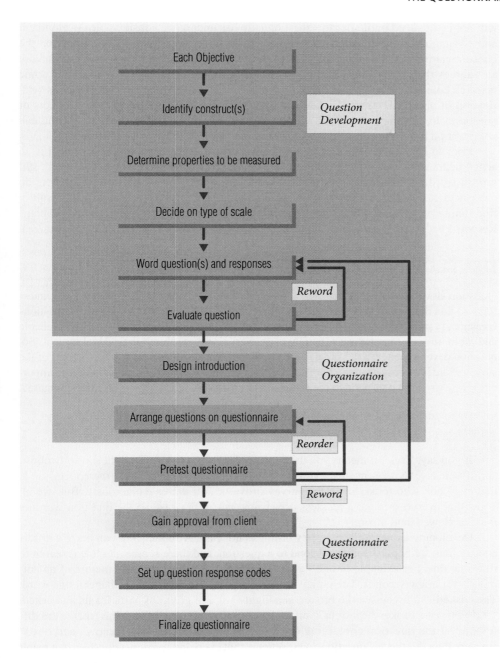

FIGURE 11.1
Question Development and Questionnaire Design Process

Changes are made, and the question's wording is reevaluated to make sure that it is asking what the researcher intends. Also, the researcher strives to minimize **question bias**, defined as the ability of a question's wording or format to influence respondents' answers.[3] It is important to point out that question development takes place for every question pertaining to each research objective. We elaborate on question development and the minimization of question bias very soon.

With regard to questionnaires for a custom-designed research study, it is important only that you realize the questions on the questionnaire, along with its instructions, introduction, and general layout, are all systematically evaluated for potential error and revised accordingly. Generally, this evaluation takes place at the researcher's end, and the client

Question bias occurs when the question's wording or format influences the respondent's answer.

will not be involved until after the questionnaire has undergone considerable development and evaluation by the researcher. The client is given the opportunity to comment on the questionnaire during the client approval step, in which the client reviews the questionnaire and agrees that it covers all of the appropriate issues. This step is essential, and some research companies require the client to sign or initial a copy of the questionnaire as verification of approval. Granted, clients may not appreciate all of the technical aspects of questionnaire design, but they are vitally concerned with the survey's objectives and can comment on the degree to which the questions appear to address these objectives.

Prior to client approval, the questionnaire normally undergoes a pretest, which is an actual field test using a very limited sample in order to reveal any difficulties that might still lurk in wording, instructions, administration, and so on. However, some researchers do pretests after client approval or in concert with client approval. Pretests normally result in fine-tuning of the questionnaire. We describe pretesting more fully later in this chapter.[4] Response codes, to be described later as well, are decided, and the questionnaire is finalized.

DEVELOPING QUESTIONS

Question development is the practice of selecting appropriate response formats and wording questions that are understandable, unambigous, and unbiased.

Question development involves selecting appropriate response formats and wording questions so that they are understandable, unambiguous, and unbiased. Because research questions measure (1) attitudes, (2) beliefs, (3) behaviors, and (4) demographics[5] and must elicit reliable and valid answers, marketing researchers are very concerned with their development. So, question development is a tall order, so to speak, but it is absolutely vital to the success of the survey. Here is a corny example to make our point that the wording of questions is very important. How would you respond to the following question that might appear on a questonnaire?

Have you stopped trying to beat red traffic lights when you think you have the chance?   _____ Yes   _____ No

If you say, "Yes," it means you used to speed up when the traffic light showed yellow, and if you say, "No," it means you are still taking chances. Either way, the conclusion is that everyone who took part in the survey drove or still drives dangerously. But, we all know that everyone is not a reckless driver now nor in the past, so the question wording must be flawed, and it surely is.[6]

Developing a question's precise wording is not easy. A single word can make a difference in how study participants respond to a question, and there is considerable research to illustrate this. For example in one study, researchers let subjects view a picture of an automobile for a few seconds. Then, they asked a single question, but they changed one word. They asked, "Did you see <u>the</u> broken headlight?" of one group of participants and asked, "Did you see <u>a</u> broken headlight?" of another group. Only the "a" and the "the" were different, yet the question containing the "the" produced more "don't know" and "Yes" answers than did the "a" question.[7] Our point is that even one word in a question can result in bias that will distort the findings of the survey.

Unfortunately, words that we use commonly in speaking to one another sometimes encourage biased answers when they appear on a questionnaire. We have created Table 11.1 listing "Ten Words to Avoid in Question Development."[8] Again, the point to remember is that although we use these words every day, they can introduce an element of bias when they are used in a questionnaire because respondents may interpret them literally when answering the questions.

Some words, when taken literally, introduce question bias.

As you can see by reading Table 11.1, it is important that questions do not contain subtle cues, signals, or interpretations that lead respondents to give answers that are innacurate. Granted, not all respondents will be influenced by the wording, but if a significant minority is affected, this bias can cause the findings to be distorted or mixed, as you saw in

TABLE 11.1   Ten Words to Avoid in Question Development: Example in a Survey Performed with Home Theater System Purchasers

Word*	Poor Wording	Why the Wording Is Poor	Better Wording
All	Did you consider **all** the options before you decided to purchase your home theater system?	There may be a huge number of options or too many for a consumer to even know about, let alone consider one by one.	What options did you consider when you decided to purchase your home theater system?
Always	Do you **always** buy audio products from Bose?	"Always" means every purchase every time with no exceptions.	How often do you buy audio products from Bose?
Any	Did you have **any** concerns about the price?	Even the smallest concern qualifies as "any;" and small concerns are usually insignificant.	To what extent was the price a concern for you?
Anybody	Did you talk to **anybody** about home theater systems before you made your decision?	This includes family, friends, coworkers, sales personnel, neighbors, parents, teachers, and anybody else on the planet.	Which of the following people did you talk with about home theater systems before you made your decision? (Likely parties such as spouse, coworkers, etc. are listed.)
Best	What is the **best** feature on your new home theater system?	"Best" infers that there is a single feature that stands out, but it is possible that features were of equal importance or combinations of features are important.	Please rate the following features of our new home theater system on their performance for you using "poor," "fair," "good," or "excellent."
Ever	Have you **ever** seen a home theater system?	"Ever" means on any occasion in one's past lifetime.	Have you seen a home theater system in the past 30 days?
Every	Do you consult *Consumer Reports* **every** time you purchase a major item?	"Every" means without fail, or otherwise no way without doing this.	How often do you consult *Consumer Reports* when you purchase a major item?
Most	What was the **most** important factor that convinced you it was time to make this purchase?	There may not be a single most important factor; there may be factors of equal importance or there may be combinations of factors that are relevant.	Please rate the following factors on their importance in convincing you it was time to purchase a home theater system using "unimportant," "slightly important," or "very important."
Never	Would you say that you **never** think about an extended warranty when making a major electronics purchase?	"Never" means not ever, without fail.	How often do you consider an extended warranty when making a major electronics purchase?
Worst	Is the high price the **worst** aspect of purchasing a home theater system?	There may not be a single bad or worst factor; there may be ties for last place or combinations of factors that make for "worst" aspects.	To what extent did the high price concern you when you were considering the purchase of your home theater system?

*Why avoid these words?** The words are ***extreme absolutes***, meaning that they place respondents in a situation where they must either agree fully or completely disagree with the extreme position in the question.

our broken headlight example. You should notice from the "Better Wording" column in Table 11.1 that these questions do not place respondents in the awkward position of responding to extreme absolutes. The better wording questions give respondents latitude to respond in degrees (such as how often, how important, etc.) that are more consistent with their actual deliberations or actions than are the extreme absolute versions.

Asking, "Did you consider **all** the options before you decided ..." is not advisable.

Four "Do's" of Question Wording

The researcher uses question evaluation to scrutinize a possible question for its question bias.

Question evaluation amounts to scrutinizing the wording of a question to ensure that question bias is minimized and that the question is worded such that respondents understand it and can respond to it with relative ease. As we noted earlier, question bias occurs when the phrasing of a question influences a respondent to answer wrongly or with other than perfect accuracy. Ideally, every question should be examined and tested according to a number of crucial factors known to be related to question bias. To be sure, question evaluation is a judgment process, but we can offer four simple guidelines or "Do's" for question wording. We strongly advise that you do ensure that the question is (1) focused, (2) simple, (3) brief, and (4) crystal clear. A discussion of these four guidelines follows.

A question should be focused.

THE QUESTION SHOULD BE FOCUSED ON A SINGLE ISSUE OR TOPIC. To the greatest extent possible, the researcher must stay focused on the specific issue or topic.[9] For example, the focus of the question "What type of hotel do you usually stay in when on a trip?" is hazy because it does not narrow down the type of trip or when the hotel is being used. For example, is it a business or a pleasure trip? Is the hotel at a place en route or at the final destination? A more focused version is "When you are on a family vacation and stay in a hotel at your destination, what type of hotel do you typically use?" As a second example, consider how "unfocused" the following question is: "When do you typically go to work?" Does this mean when do you leave home for work or when do you actually begin work once at your workplace? A better question would be "At what time do you ordinarily leave home for work?"

A question should be brief.

THE QUESTION SHOULD BE BRIEF. Unnecessary and redundant words should always be eliminated. This requirement is especially important when designing questions that will be administered verbally, such as over the telephone. Brevity will help the respondent to comprehend the central question and reduce the distraction of wordiness. Here is a question that suffers from a lack of brevity: "What are the considerations that would come to your mind while you are confronted with the decision to have some type of repair done on the automatic icemaker in your refrigerator assuming that you noticed it was not making ice cubes as well as it did when you first bought it?" A better, brief form would be

"If your icemaker was not working right, how would you correct the problem?" One source recommends that a brief question is no more than 20 words in length.[10]

THE QUESTION SHOULD BE A GRAMMATICALLY SIMPLE SENTENCE IF POSSIBLE. A simple sentence is preferred because it has only a single subject and predicate, whereas compound and complex sentences are busy with multiple subjects, predicates, objects, and complements. The more complex the sentence, the greater the potential for respondent error. With more conditions to remember, there is more information to consider simultaneously, so respondents' attention may wane or they may concentrate on only one part of the question.

> A question should be grammatically simple.

To avoid these problems, the researcher should strive to use only simple sentence structure[11]—even if two separate sentences are necessary to communicate the essence of the question. A simple approach to the question "If you were looking for an automobile that would be used by the head of your household who is primarily responsible for driving your children to and from school, music lessons, and friends' houses, how much would you and your spouse discuss the safety features of one of the cars you took for a test drive?" is "Would you and your spouse discuss the safety features of a new family car?" followed by (if yes), "Would you discuss safety 'very little,' 'some,' 'a good deal,' or 'to a great extent'?"

THE QUESTION SHOULD BE CRYSTAL CLEAR.[12,13] Forgive us for stealing one of Tom Cruise's movie lines, but it is essential that all respondents "see" the question identically. For example, the question "How many children do you have?" is unclear because it can be interpreted in various ways. One respondent might think of only those children living at home, whereas another might include children from a previous marriage. A better question is "How many children under the age of 18 live with you in your home?"

> A question should be crystal clear.

One tactic for achieving clarity is to use words that are in respondents' core vocabularies. It is best to avoid words that are vague or open to misinterpretations. To develop a crystal clear question, the reseacher may be forced to slightly abuse the previous guideline of simplicity, but with a bit of effort, question clarity can be obtained with an economical number of words.[14] One author has nicely summarized this guideline: "The question should be simple, intelligible, and clear."[15]

Question wording is difficult when survey reseach is conducted in a foreign country. Many countries have unique cultures—some with several different languages—and so creating a questionnaire is an exceptionally challenging undertaking.[16] There are, however, ways to address the wording and translation issues confronting researchers who find themselves engaged in global research projects. You will find these guidelines in Marketing Research Insight 11.1.

Four "Do Not's" of Question Wording

There are four situations in which question bias is practically assured, and it is important that you learn about these so you can avoid them or spot them when you are reviewing a questionnaire draft. Specifically, the question should not be (1) leading, (2) loaded, (3) double-barreled, or (4) overstated.

DO NOT "LEAD" THE RESPONDENT TO A PARTICULAR ANSWER. A **leading question** gives the respondent a strong cue or expectation as to how to answer.[17] Therefore, it biases responses. Consider this question "Don't you see problems with using your credit card for an online purchase?" The respondent is being led here because the question wording stresses one side (in this case, the negative side) of the issue. Therefore, the question "leads" respondents to the conclusion that there must be some problems, and, therefore, they will likely agree with the question, particularly respondents who have no opinion.

> Do not use leading questions that have strong cues for how to answer.

MARKETING RESEARCH INSIGHT   **Global Application**

11.1 New Guidelines for Developing a Questionnaire in a Foreign Language

What about question wording in global marketing research situations where the researcher must create questionnaires in diverse languages? How can question bias be avoided when the researcher does not speak the language of the respondents? For example, a researcher working with Burger King might need to design a survey for respondents who speak only one of the following languages: English, Chinese, Spanish, Italian, Tamil, German, or Russian. One possible solution is to design the questionnaire in some "common" language and then survey only bilingual respondents.[18] However, this approach is generally unsatisfactory because of the many opportunities for miscomprehension. Instead, global marketing researchers use the following "back translation approach"[19] when attempting to do across-the-globe research:

Create the questionnaire in the researcher's native language (e.g., English).[20]

- Translate the questionnaire into the other language (e.g., German).
- Have independent translators translate it back into the native language (e.g., from German to English) to check that the first translation was accurate.

- Revise the questionnaire based on the "back translation" (into a better German version).
- If an online survey is involved, make sure that the letters and characters (such as Chinese, Japanese, or Arabic) are accurate to the language being used.
- Carefully pretest the revised questionnaire using individuals whose native tongue is the other language (e.g., natives of Germany).

Even with these precautions, translation errors may occur when idioms or concepts do not cross over well from one culture into the other.

The back translation approach is not completely successful, however, in making the wording in one language equivalent to that in another. For instance, "doing laundry" means something very different to respondents who must use the local river (Thailand) than to those with washer and dryer units in their basements (United States), and "having wine for dinner" is not an equivalent expression in a country where wine is consumed with every dinner (France) compared to one where wine is consumed only on special occasions (China).

One suggestion for addressing this problem is to use a systematic process and a committee to collaborate in the questionnaire translation effort. The following diagram shows how this process should work.

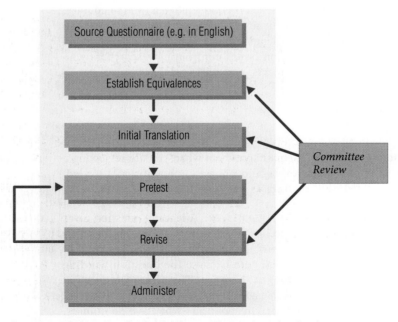

Recommended process for foreign language questionnaire development.

Ideally, the committee would be comprised of multilingual individuals with expertise in translations and questionnaire design. The first task is to address the equivalences of words, behaviors, idioms, and other nuances between the languages. The committee translates the questionnaire in various ways and decides on the best version. Then it is pretested with a small sample of native-speaking respondents who are debriefed as to difficulties, and, if possible, statistical comparisons are made as to equivalence. The pretest results are reviewed by the committee, which makes subsequent revisions and may require additional pretesting of the revisions until the questionnaire is ready for administration.

Rephrasing the question as "Do you see any problems with using your credit card for an online purchase?" is a much more objective request of the respondent. Here the respondent is free—that is, not led—to respond "yes" or "no." The following are other forms of leading questions:

As a Cadillac owner, you are satisfied with your car, aren't you?	This is a leading question because the wording presupposes that all Cadillac owners are satisfied. It places the respondent in a situation where disagreement is uncomfortable and singles him or her out as an outlier.
Have you heard about the satellite radio system that everyone is talking about?	This is a leading question due to its possessing the ability to condition the respondent in terms of answering in a socially desirable manner. In other words, few people would want to admit they are clueless about something "everybody is talking about."[21]

While you may think that leading questions are very easy to identify, and that they do not trick any intelligent person into a biased answer, we have just scratched the surface of this form of bias. Read Marketing Research Insight 11.2 to gain an understanding the various forms of leading questions.

DO NOT USE "LOADED" WORDING OR PHRASING. Whereas leading questions are typically obvious, loaded questions are stealthy. That is, a **loaded question** has buried in its wording elements that make reference to universal beliefs or rules of behavior. It may even elicit emotions or touch on a person's inner fears. Some researchers refer to a loaded question simply as a "biased question."[22] Identifying this type of bias in a question requires more judgment, For example, a company marketing Mace for personal use may use the question "Should people be allowed to protect themselves from harm by using a taser for self-defense?" Obviously, most respondents will agree with the need to protect oneself from harm and self-defense is acceptable, but these are loaded concepts because no one wants to be harmed and self-defense is only legal if one is attacked. Eliminating the loaded aspect of this question would result in "Do you think carrying a taser is acceptable for someone who believes it is needed?" As you can see, the phrasing of each question should be examined thoroughly to guard against the various sources of bias error, for with the new wording we do not load the question with mention of harm or self-defense.

Do not use loaded questions that have emotional overtones.

DO NOT USE A "DOUBLE-BARRELED" QUESTION. A **double-barreled question** is really two different questions posed in one question.[23] When two questions are asked together, it is difficult for a respondent to answer either one directly.[24] Consider a question asked of patrons at a restaurant, "Were you satisfied with the restaurant's food and service?" How do repondents answer? If they say "yes," does it mean they were satisfied with the food? The service? A combination? The question would be much improved by asking about a

Do not use double-barreled questions that ask two questions at the same time.

MARKETING RESEARCH INSIGHT

Ethical Application

11.2 The Many Ways That a Question Can Be Leading

Marketing and public opinion research associations hold deceptive practices such as leading questions to be unethical. Actually, our definition of a leading question is rather simple, and some authors have recently come up with a more complete definition.

A leading question is an interrogatory making use of a biasing mechanism. This mechanism may come in any one of, or any combination of, three forms: question structure; question content; question delivery.

This more formal definition of a leading question reveals that there are three different ways that a question can lead or strongly influence the respondent to give a particular answer. It can lead with form, facts, or phonics. Each is described in the following table. For each type, we have provided an example using the subject of fast-food and overweight consumers.

As can be seen from the expanded definition of a "leading question" and these examples, there are many obvious as well as many subtle ways a question may lead a respondent to answer in a particular way. From an ethical point of view, it is vital that marketing researchers examine their questions carefully and remove any elements of bias such as these.

Leading by *Form* (Question Structure)

Common ways to make the form of the question leading include crafting a question that:

1. *Includes the answer in the question*

2. *Uses logic or apparent logic to steer the respondent to an answer (parallel examples)*

3. *Presumes the truth of an answer, or the truth of something logically leading to an answer*

Examples

1. *Don't you think that fast foods have too many calories?*

2. *Since most fast foods are fried, shouldn't these companies put warnings on their labels?*

3. *Since McDonald's is the largest fast-food company, shouldn't it set the example for more nutritious meals?*

Leading with *Facts* (Question Content)

Common ways to use facts to make a question leading would be to include:

1. *Unsupported assertions presented as facts*

2. *Supported facts (or points presented as supported) presented in an unbalanced fashion*

3. *Loaded words/broadly held beliefs that generate an emotional/cognitive impetus toward an answer*

Examples

1. *Since everyone buys fast foods, shouldn't everyone be concerned about nutrition?*

2. *Since studies have shown that overweight children buy fast foods, shouldn't "kids meals" be healthier?*

3. *Do you think that Kentucky Fried Chicken should have warnings for obese people suffering from deadly diseases such as diabetes?*

Leading with *Phonics* (Question Delivery)

Common ways to use phonics (or context) to make a question leading include:

1. *Make respondents aware of the desired outcome of, or "purpose" for, the survey*

2. *Make respondents aware of the sponsor*

3. *Use preceding questions to set up assumptions in the mind of the respondent*

Examples

1. *Will you take part in our survey that will alert consumers to the dangers of fast food?*

2. *Our survey is sponsored by the Vegetarian Council.*

3. *Since you have agreed that fast-food consumption contributes to eating disorders, shouldn't fast-food companies take responsibility for correcting them?*

"Don't you think that fast foods have too many calories?" is a leading question.

single item: one question for food and another question for service. Sometimes double-barreled questions are not as obvious. Look at the following question designed to ask about occupational status:

_____ Full-time employment

_____ Full-time student

_____ Part-time student

_____ Unemployed

_____ Retired

How does one who is retired and a full-time student answer the question? An improvement would be to ask one question about occupational status and another about student status.[25]

DO NOT USE WORDS THAT OVERSTATE THE CONDITION. An **overstated question** is one that places undue emphasis on some aspect of the topic. It uses what might be considered "dramatics" to describe the topic. Avoid words that overstate conditions. It is better to present the question in a neutral tone rather than in a strong positive or negative tone. Here is an example that might be found in a survey conducted for Ray-Ban sunglasses. An overstated question might ask, "How much do you think you would pay for a pair of sunglasses that will protect your eyes from the sun's harmful ultraviolet rays, which are known to cause blindness?" As you can see, the overstatement concerns the effects of ultraviolet rays, and because of this overstatement, respondents will be compelled to think about how much they would pay for something that can prevent blindness and not about how much they would really pay for the sunglasses. A more toned-down and acceptable wording would be "How much would you pay for sunglasses that will protect your eyes from the sun's glare?"

Do not use overstated questions with words that overemphasize the case.

To be sure, there are other question wording pitfalls.[26] For example, it is nonsensical to ask respondents about details they don't recall (How many and what brands of aspirin did you see last time you bought some?); for guesses (What is the price per gallon of premium gasoline at the Exxon station on the corner?); or for predictions about their actions in circumstances they cannot fathom (How often would you go out to eat at this new, upscale restaurant that will be built 10 miles from your home?). Our advice to you is if you use common sense in developing questions for your questionnaire, you will probably avoid most other sources of question wording bias.

Can You Identify What Is "Bad" about a Question and Correct It?

Here are some questions that might appear on a questionnaire. Each one has violated one of the "do's" or "do not's" of question wording that you just read about. For each "Bad" question, write in what is bad about it—that is, decide on which "do" or "do not" is violated—and write a bettter version of the question, eliminating the error.

Bad Version of the Question	What's the Error?	Good Version of the Question
How do you feel about car seats for infants?		
When your toddler wants to ride in the car with you as you run errands or pick up your older children at school, practice, or some friend's home, do you use an infant car seat?		
If using an infant car seat is not convenient for you to use, or when you are in a hurry and your toddler is crying, do you still go ahead and use the infant car seat?		
How much do you think you should have to pay for an infant seat that restrains and protects your toddler in case someone runs into your car or you lose control of your car and run into a light post or some other object?		
Shouldn't concerned parents of toddlers use infant car seats?		
Since infant car seats are proven to be exceptionally valuable, do you agree that infant car seats should be used for your loved ones?		
Do you think that parents who are responsible citizens and who are aware of driving dangers use infant car seats?		
If you had an accident with your toddler on board, do you believe an infant car seat could protect your child from being maimed?		

We have prepared Table 11.2 as a convenient summary of the "Do's" and "Do Not's" of question wording containing some questions that might be developed for a survey on automobile global positioning systems (GPS). In the table, we have created examples of bad questions that violate the recommended question wording, and we have provided a "good" example that abides by the recommendation. Use Table 11.2 as a handy study guide or to otherwise keep our wording recommendations foremost in your mind when you are involved in question development.

Seasoned researchers develop a sixth sense about the "Do's" and "Do not's" we have just described; however, because the researcher can become caught up in the research process, slips do occur. This possibility explains why many researchers use "experts" to review drafts of their questionnaires. For example, it is common for the questionnaire to be designed by one employee of the research company and then be given to another employee

TABLE 11.2   Examples of Do's and Do Not's for Question Wording

Do or Do Not Guideline	Bad Question	Good Question
Do: Be Focused	How do you feel about your automobile's GPS system?	Please rate your automobile's GPS system on each of the following features. (Features are listed.)
Do: Be Brief	When traffic conditions are bad, do you or do you not rely on your automobile's GPS system to find the fastest way to work?	Does your autmobile GPS system help you arrive at work on time?
Do: Use Simple Structure	If you needed to find your child's best friend's house that was over 10 miles from your house for your child to attend a birthday party, would you rely on your autmobile GPS system to get you there?	To what extent would you rely on your automobile GPS system to find a friend's house?
Do: Be Crystal Clear	Is your automobile GPS system useful?	How useful is your automobile GPS system for each of the following occasions? (Occasions are listed.)
Do Not: Lead	Shouldn't everyone have a GPS system in their automobile?	In your opinion, how helpful is an automobile GPS system?
Do Not: Load	If GPS systems were shown to help us decrease our depletion of world oil reserves, would you purchase one?	How much do you think an automobile GPS system might save you on gasoline?
Do Not: Double-Barrel	Would you consider purchasing an automobile GPS system if it saved you time, money, and worry?	Would you consider buying an automobile GPS system if you believed it would reduce your commuting time by 10%? (Separate questions about money and worry savings.)
Do Not: Overstate	Do you think that an autobile GPS system can help you avoid traffic jams that may last for hours?	To what extent do you believe an automobile GPS system will help you avoid traffic congestion?

who understands questionnaire design for a thorough inspection for question bias as well as **face validity**, that is, whether the questions "look right."

QUESTIONNAIRE ORGANIZATION

Now that you have learned about question development, and the guidelines and specific things to avoid when wording questions, we can turn to the organization of the questionnaire. Normally, the researcher creates questions by taking the research objectives in turn and developing the questions that relate to each objective. In other words, the questions are developed but not as yet arranged on the questionnaire.

Questionnaire organization refers to the sequence of statements and questions that make up a questionnaire. Organization is an important concern because the questionnaire's arrangement and the ease with which respondents can complete the questions have potential to affect the quality of the information gathered. Well-organized questionnaires motivate respondents to be conscientious and complete, whereas poorly organized ones discourage and frustrate respondents and may even cause them to stop answering questions in the middle of the survey. We will describe two critical aspects of questionnaire organization: the introduction and the actual flow of questions in the questionnaire body.

Questionnaire organization pertains to the introduction and the actual flow of questions on the questionnaire.

The Introduction

The introduction is very important in questionnaire design.[27] An introduction written to accompany a mail survey or online survey is normally referred to as a **cover letter**. If the introduction is to be verbally presented to a potential respondent, as in the case of a personal interview, it may be referred to as the "opening comments." Of course, each survey and its target respondent group are unique, so a researcher cannot use a standardized introduction. In this section, we discuss the five functions of the introduction, which are listed in Table 11.3. The table provides examples of the sentences you might find in a survey on personal money management software. As you read our descriptions of each function, refer to the example in Table 11.3 and the brief explanation.

First, it is common courtesy for interviewers to introduce themselves at the beginning of a survey. Note in Table 11.3 that the interviewer has done so and the prospective respondent has been made aware that this is a bona fide survey, not a sales pitch. Additionally, the sponsor of the survey should be identified. There are two options with respect to sponsor identity. In an **undisguised survey**, the sponsoring company is identified, but in a **disguised survey**, the sponsor's name is not divulged to respondents. The choice of approach rests with the survey's objectives or with the researcher and client, who agree whether disclosure of the sponsor's name or true intent can in some way influence respondents' answers. Another reason for disguise is to prevent alerting competitors to the survey.

Whether or not to use a disguised survey depends on the survey's objectives, possible undue influence from knowledge of the client, or desire to not alert competitors to the survey.

Second, the general purpose of the survey should be described clearly and simply. In a cover letter, the purpose may be expressed in one or two sentences. Typically, respondents are not informed of the several specific purposes of the survey, as listing all the research objectives might bore them and perhaps be intimidating. Consider a survey being conducted for a bank by a marketing research firm. The actual purpose of the survey is to determine the bank's image relative to that of its competitors. However, the research firm need only say, "We are conducting a survey on customers' perceptions of financial institutions in this area." This satisfies the respondent's curiosity and does not divulge the name of the bank.

The introduction should indicate to respondents how they were selected.

TABLE 11.3   The Functions of the Questionnaire Introduction

Function	Example	Explanation
Identifies the surveyor/ sponsor	"Hello, my name is _____, and I am a telephone interviewer working with Nationwide Opinion Research Company here in Milwaukee. I am not selling anything."	The sponsor of the survey is identified, plus the prospective respondent is made aware that this is a bona fide survey and not a sales pitch.
Indicates the purpose of the survey	"We are conducting a survey on Internet browsers, sometimes called 'Web browsers.'"	Informs prospective respondent of the topic and the reason for the call.
Explains how the respondent was selected	"Your telephone number was generated randomly by a computer."	Notifies prospective respondents how they were chosen to be in the survey.
Requests for/provides incentive for participation	"This is an anonymous survey, and I would now like to ask you a few questions about your experiences with your Web browser program. Is now a good time?"	Asks for prospective respondent's agreement to take part in the survey at this time. (Also notes here anonymity to gain cooperation.)
Qualifies (or disqualifies) individual to be a respondent in the survey	"Do you use Internet Explorer, Firefox, or Opera?"	Determines if prospective respondent is qualified to take part in the survey; those who do not use one of these programs will be screened out.

Third, prospective respondents must be made aware of how and why they were selected. Just a short sentence to answer the respondent's mental question of "Why me?" will suffice. Telling respondents that they were "selected at random" usually is sufficient. Of course, you should be ethical and tell them the actual method used. If their selection wasn't random, you should inform them as to which method was used, but in a nontechnical manner.

Fourth, you must ask prospective respondents for their participation in the survey. With a mail survey, the cover letter might end with "Will you please take ten minutes to complete the attached questionnaire and mail it back to us in the postage-paid, preaddressed envelope provided?" If you are conducting a personal interview or a telephone interview, you might say something like "I would now like to ask you a few questions about your experiences with automotive repair shops. OK?" You should be as brief as possible, yet let respondents know that you are getting ready for them to participate by answering questions.

This is also the appropriate time to offer an incentive to participate. **Incentives** are offers to do something for the respondent in order to increase the probability that the respondent will participate in the survey. Researchers may use various incentives to encourage participation. As consumers have become more resistant to telemarketers and marketing researchers' pleas for information, researchers are reporting they must offer increased incentives. Offering a monetary incentive, a sample of a product, or a copy of study results are examples. Other incentives encourage respondent participation by letting them know the importance of their participation: "You are one of a select few, randomly chosen, to express your views on a new type of automobile tire." Or the topic itself can be highlighted for importance: "It is important that consumers let companies know whether or not they are satisfied."

Other forms of incentives address respondent anxieties concerning privacy. Here again, there are methods that tend to reduce these anxieties and, therefore, increase participation. As you can see in Table 11.3, one is **anonymity**, in which the respondent is assured that neither the respondent's name nor any identifying details will be associated with the responses. The second method is **confidentiality**,[28] which means that the respondent's name is known by the researcher but is not divulged to a third party, namely, the client. Anonymous surveys are most appropriate in data-collection modes where the respondent responds directly on the questionnaire. Any self-administered survey qualifies for anonymity as long as respondents do not reveal their identity and provided the questionnaire does not have any covert identification tracing mechanism. However, in cases when an interviewer is used, appointments and/or callbacks are usually necessary, so there typically is an explicit designation of

Anonymity means the respondent is never identified by the data collected; confidentiality means that the respondent is not to be identified to a client or any other third party.

Incentives entice respondents to take part in a survey when they otherwise would have declined.

the respondent's name, address, telephone number, and so forth on the questionnaire. In this case, confidentiality may be required. Often questionnaires have a callback notation area for interviewer notes indicating, for instance, whether the phone is busy, whether the respondent is not at home, or when the respondent will be available for a callback. For this information, the respondent will ordinarily receive an assurance of confidentiality, and it is vital that the researcher guard against the violation of that confidentiality.

A fifth function of the introduction is to qualify prospective respondents. Respondents are screened for their appropriateness to take part in the survey. **Screening questions** are used to ferret out respondents who do not meet the necessary qualifications.[29] Whether you screen respondents depends on the research objectives. If the survey's objective is to determine the factors used by consumers to select an automobile dealer for the purpose of purchasing a new car, you may want to screen out those who have never purchased a new car or those who have not purchased a new car within, say, the last two years. "Have you purchased a new car within the last two years?" For all those who answer "no," the survey is terminated with a polite "Thank you for your time." Some would argue that you should ask the screening question early on so as not to waste the time of the researcher or the respondent, something that should be considered with each survey. We place screening questions last in the introduction because we have found it awkward to begin a conversation with a prospective respondent without first taking care of the first four items just discussed.

Creating the introduction should entail just as much care and effort as the development of the questionnaire questions. The first words heard or read by prospective respondents will largely determine whether they will take part in the survey. It makes sense, therefore, for the researcher to labor over a cover letter or opening until it has a maximum chance of eliciting respondents cooperation.[30] If the researcher is unsuccessful in persuading prospective respondents to take part in the survey, all of the work on the questionnaire itself will have been in vain.[31]

Question Flow

Question flow pertains to the sequencing of questions or blocks of questions, including any instructions, on the questionnaire. Each research objective gives rise to a question or a set of questions. As a result, as indicated in Figure 11.1, questions are usually developed on an objective-by-objective basis. However, to facilitate respondents' ease in answering questions, the organization of these sets of questions should follow some understandable logic insofar as possible. A sequence of questions commonly found in questionnaires is presented in Table 11.4, and, as the table title notes, there should be a logical or commonsense order to the questions.[32]

Of course, it should be obvious that one objective is to keep the questionnaire as short as possible, as long questionnaires have a negative effect on the response rate.[33] The table points out that the first few questions are normally screening questions, which will determine whether the potential respondent qualifies to participate in the survey based on certain selection criteria that the researcher has deemed essential. Not all surveys, of course, have screening questions. A survey of charge account customers for a department store, for example, may not require screening questions. This is true because, in a sense, all potential respondents have already been qualified by virtue of having a charge account with the store.

Once the individual is qualified by the screening questions, the next questions may serve a "warm-up" function. **Warm-up questions** are simple and easy-to-answer questions that are used to get the respondents' interest[34] and to demonstrate the ease of responding to the research request. Ideally, warm-up questions pertain to the research objectives, but the researcher may opt for a few quick and easy superfluous questions to heighten respondents' interest so that they will be more inclined to deal with the harder questions that follow.

Transitions are statements or questions used to let the respondent know that changes in question topic or format are about to happen. A statement such as "Now, I would like to

TABLE 11.4   The Location of Questions on a Questionnaire Is Logical

Question Type	Location	Examples	Rationale
Screens	First questions asked	"Have you shopped at Old Navy in the past month?" "Is this your first visit to this store?"	Used to select the respondent types desired by the researcher to be in the survey.
Warm-ups	Immediately after any screens	"How often do you go shopping for casual clothes?" "On what days of the week do you usually shop for casual clothes?"	Easy to answer; shows respondent that survey is easy to complete; generates interest.
Transitions (statements and questions)	Prior to major sections of questions or changes in question format	"Now, for the next few questions, I want to ask about your family's TV viewing habits." "Next, I am going to read several statements and, after each, I want you to tell me if you agree or disagree with this statement."	Notifies respondent that the subject or format of the following questions will change.
Complicated and difficult-to-answer questions	Middle of the questionnaire; close to the end	"Rate each of the following 10 stores on the friendliness of their salespeople on a scale of 1 to 7." "How likely are you to purchase each of the following items in the next three months?"	Respondent has committed to completing the questionnaire; can see (or is told) that there are not many questions left.
Classification and demographic questions	Last section	"What is the highest level of education you have attained?"	Questions that are "personal" and possibly offensive are placed at the end of the questionnaire.

ask you a few questions about your family's TV viewing habits" is an example of a transition statement. Such statements aid in making certain that the respondent understands the line of questioning. Transitions include "skip" questions. A **skip question** is one to which the answer affects what will be asked next. For example, a skip question may be "When you buy groceries, do you usually use coupons?" If the response is that the respondent does not use coupons, questions asking for the details of coupon usage are not appropriate, and the questionnaire will instruct the respondent (or the interviewer, if one is involved) to skip over or to bypass those questions. If there are a great number of transition and skip questions, the researcher can consider making a flowchart of the questions to ensure that there are no errors in the instructions.[35] Online questionnaires typically have a skip logic function that handles these transitions.

As Table 11.4 reveals, it is good practice to "bury" complicated and difficult-to-answer questions deep in the questionnaire. Scaled-response questions such as semantic differential scales, Likert-type response scales, or other questions that require some degree of mental activity such as evaluation, voicing opinions, recalling past experiences, indicating intentions, or responding to "what-if" questions are found there—for at least two good reasons. First, by the time respondents have arrived at these questions, they have answered several relatively easy questions and are now caught up in a responding mode in which they feel some sort of commitment. Thus, even though the questions in this section require more mental effort, respondents will feel more compelled to complete the questionnaire than to break it off. Second, if the questionnaire is self-administered or online, respondents will see that only a few sections of questions remain to be answered—the end is in sight, so to speak. If the survey is being administered by an interviewer, the questionnaire will typically include prompts for the interviewer to notify respondents that the interview is in its last stages. Also, experienced interviewers can sense when respondents' interest levels sag, and they may voice their own prompts, if permitted, to keep respondents on task.

The more complicated and difficult-to-answer questions are placed deep in the questionnaire.

Demographics questions, sometimes called classification questions, are used to classify respondents into various groups for purposes of analysis.

For some people, age is a personal question, so it is best to ask it at the end of the interview.

The last section of a questionnaire is traditionally reserved for classification questions. **Classification questions**, which almost always include demographic questions, are used to classify respondents into various groups for purposes of analysis. For instance, the researcher may want to classify respondents into categories based on age, gender, income level, and so on. The placement of classification questions such as these at the end of the questionnaire is useful because some respondents will consider certain demographic questions "personal," and they may refuse to give answers to questions about the highest level of education they attained, their age, their income level, or marital status.[36] In these cases, if the respondent refuses to answer, the refusal comes at the very end of the questioning process. If it occurred at the very beginning, the interview would begin with a negative tone, perhaps causing the person to think that the survey will be asking any number of personal questions, and the respondent may very well object to taking part in the survey at that point.[37]

Most researchers agree in principle to these question flow recommendations, but some prefer to think about questionnaire organization a bit differently. That is, they tend to envision the questionnaire as comprised of areas or blocks or elements that can be arranged efficiently and logically while still following the basic question flow suggestions you have just read. Read Marketing Research Insight 11.3 to learn about the three different alternatives for questionnaire organization.

 ## Work with Questionnaire Flow

The following table identifies each of the research objectives for a survey to determine the attractiveness of a possible new restaurant, as well as a possible measurement scale to be used with each research objective. Using your newly acquired knowledge of question flow and questionnaire organization, indicate for each objective in the following table where on the questionnaire you recommend placing the question(s) pertaining to that objective. Jot down your reasons for your recommendation as well.

Research Objective and Description	How to Measure?	Location on the Questionnaire and Reason(s) for This Location
Will the restaurant be successful? Will a sufficient number of people patronize the restaurant?	Describe the restaurant concept and ask about intentions to purchase there on a scale.	
How should the restaurant be designed? What about décor, atmosphere, specialty entrées and desserts, waitstaff uniforms, reservations, special seating, and so on?	Determine respondents' preferences for each of the several possible design features on a preference scale.	
What should be the average price of entrées? How much are potential patrons willing to pay for the entrées as well as for the house specials?	Describe standard entrees and sample house specials and find out how much respondents are willing to pay using price ranges.	
What is the optimum location? How far from their homes are patrons willing to drive, and are there any special location features (such as waterfront deck seating, free valet parking, no reservations, etc.) to take into consideration?	Determine furthest driving distance respondents are willing to drive to the new restaurant for each location feature.	
What is the profile of the target market?	Ask for demographics of the respondents.	

Research Objective and Description	How to Measure?	Location on the Questionnaire and Reason(s) for This Location
What are the best promotional media? What advertising media should be used to reach the target market most effectively?	Determine normal use of such various local media as newspaper, radio, television, and obtain specifics, such as what newspaper sections are read, what radio programming, and what local television news times watched.	

MARKETING RESEARCH INSIGHT   Practical Application

11.3 Approaches to Question Block Organization on a Questionnaire

The flow of questions we have described in this chapter is generally used by questionnaire designers. Given a great many questions, it is often possible to think of the questionnaire in terms of "blocks" of similar questions, such as demographic questions, usage questions, opinion questions, and so forth. We will describe three of the approaches to block organization: the funnel approach, the work approach, and the sections approach.

The **funnel approach** is the simplest and uses a wide-to-narrow or general-to-specific flow of questions that places general inquiries at the beginning of a topic on the questionnaire and those requiring more specific and detailed responses later on.[38] That is, the questionnaire begins (after the screens) with a block of general and easy-to-answer questions and proceeds to a block of more detailed questions.[39] The most specific questions are personal demographic questions located at the end of the questionnaire.

The **work approach** is employed when the researcher realizes that respondents will need to apply a different amount of mental effort to various blocks of questions. When questions tap responses that are deeper than simple recall, respondents must apply a higher degree of concentration in answering them. As we have specified in our recommendations on question flow, difficult questions are placed deep in the questionnaire. As a rule, nominal-scale questions are easier to answer than either scaled-response or open-ended questions. Open-ended questions are thought to be the most taxing questions for respondents. In fact, some researchers recommend rarely using open-ended questions or using a minimum of open-ended questions.[40] As just noted, when respondents encounters the work question block(s), they should be caught up in the responding mode or otherwise committed to completing the questionnaire. If this is the case, respondents will be more inclined to expend the extra effort necessary to answer them.

Another organization scheme is to arrange the questions in logical sets on the questionnaire, which is referred to as the sections approach. A **sections approach** organizes questions into sets based on the common objective of the questions in the set. This approach is particularly useful when the researcher is investigating several topics with a block of questions for each topic. By using sections, the researcher has a structure to cover all the topics, and the respondent's focus is concentrated on that topic in the section question block. For example, several questions may measure media habits, others may measure frequency of purchasing different products, and other sets of questions may measure preferences for restaurant services and features. Sometimes the research objectives define the sections. Sections could also be based on question format, for example, placing all Likert questions in one section.

Which approach is best? There is no single format that fits all cases. In fact, the three approaches we have just described are not mutually exclusive, and a researcher may use a combination of approaches in a single questionnaire. A researcher may find that the survey topics influence the placement or approach used in question flow.[41] However, although any one or a combination of these approaches may be used, the guiding principle should be which approach best facilitates respondents in answering the questions. Researchers can analyze questions in any sequence they wish; it's the respondents who are important here.

As we indicated earlier, designing a questionnaire is a blend of creativity and adherence to simple, commonsense guidelines. The most important idea to keep in mind, though, is to design the questionnaire's flow of questions so as to make it respondent-friendly[42] by minimizing the amount of effort necessary to respond while maximizing the probability that each respondent will fill it out reliably, accurately, and completely.[43] To achieve these results, the researcher selects logical response formats, provides clear directions, makes the questionnaire visually appealing, and numbers all sections plus all items in each section.[44]

COMPUTER-ASSISTED QUESTIONNAIRE DESIGN

Computer-assisted questionnaire design is easy, fast, friendy, and flexible.

Computer-assisted questionnaire design refers to software programs that allow users to develop and disseminate questionnaires and, in most cases, to retrieve and analyze data gathered by the questionnaire. Several companies have developed computer software that bridges the gap between composing questions on a word processor and generating the final, polished version complete with checkboxes, radio circles, coded questions, graphics of various types, and a variety of specialized features. These software programs allow researchers to publish questionnaires on the Internet and enable respondents to enter data on the Internet. The data are then downloaded and made available for analysis. Practically all of these special-purpose personal computer programs generate data files that can be exported in a format that SPSS can import.

The following paragraphs illustrate how these computer-assisted questionnaire design programs work. First, however, we should point out at least four distinct advantages of these software packages: They are easier, faster, and friendlier and provide significant functionality beyond what is available with a traditional word processor.[45] With this in mind, here are descriptions of the basic functions of a computer-assisted questionnaire design program.

Questionnaire Creation

The typical questionnaire design program will query the user on, for example, type of question, number of response categories, whether multiple responses are permitted, if skips are to be used, and how response options will appear on the questionnaire. Usually, the program offers a list of question types for selection, such as closed-ended, open-ended, numeric, or scaled-response questions. The program may even have a question library[46] feature that provides "standard" questions on constructs that researchers often measure, such as demographics, importance, satisfaction, performance, or usage. Plus, the researcher can upload graphic files of various types if these are part of the research objectives. Most computer-assisted questionnaire design programs are quite flexible and allow the user to modify question formats, build blocks or matrices of questions with the identical response format, include an introduction and instructions for specific questions, and to move the location of questions with great ease. Often, the appearance can be modified to the designer's preferences for font, background, color, and more.

Data Collection and Creation of Data Files

Computer-assisted questionnaire design programs have question types, question libraries, real-time data capture, and downloadable data sets.

Computer-assisted questionnaire design programs create online survey questionnaires. Once online, the survey is ready for respondents, who are alerted to the online survey by whatever communication methods the researcher wishes to use. Normally, a data file is built as respondents take part, that is, in real time.

To elaborate, each respondent accesses the online questionnaire, registers responses to the questions, and, typically, clicks on a "Submit" button at the end of the questionnaire. The submit signal prompts the program to write the respondent's answers into a data file, so the data file grows in direct proportion to and at the same rate as respondents submit their surveys. Features, such as requesting an e-mail address, are often available to block multiple submissions by the same respondent. The data file can be downloaded in several formats at the researchers discretion, including Excel-readable ones.

Data Analysis and Graphs

Many of the questionnaire design software programs have provisions for data analysis, graphics presentation, and report formats. Some packages offer only simplified graphing capabilities; others offer different statistical analysis options. In fact, it is very useful to researchers to monitor the survey's progress with these features. Some of the programs enable users to create professional-quality graphs that can be saved and/or embedded in word processor report files.

How to Use Qualtrics

Students whose instructors have adopted this textbook can use Qualtrics to perform online surveys. To register, access www.qualtrics.com and enter the coupon code provided by your instructor under the "Free Account." Once registered, simply use the "Create Survey" option to design your questionnaire with the "Quick Survey Builder" feature, which is exceptionally easy to use.

We have provided screen captures from Qualtrics with some annotations so you can see how this software works. You will find these along with explanations in Marketing Research Insight 11.4.

MARKETING RESEARCH INSIGHT   Practical Application

11.4 How to Use Qualtrics to Design an Online Questionnaire

After you have completed the simple registration process to access Qualtrics, click "Create Survey" and then use the Quick Survey Builder. Give your survey a name, such as "My First Questionnaire," and begin the process of building your questionnaire.

Question development in Qualtrics is a simple process. As we indicated in Figure 11.1, for each research objective the researcher will have a question or set of questions, along with the response format(s), in mind. To develop a question, use the "Create a New Question" function, which will create a default question you can modify into the type desired (the response format). The annotated screen capture of Qualtrics shows a first question. Notice the 12 basic question type options (the green pop-up panel in the figure). However, by clicking on the "Show All Question Types" link, you will see over 80 different types, some of which are highly specialized.

In the figure, we have selected the "Multiple Choice" question type. To begin question development, simply type or paste in the question in the text editor area that opens when you click on it. Next, type in the various responses in the response categories area. If there are not enough categories, use the "Choices" feature to add to the number of choices.

Notice that you can also make the question a "check all that apply" with the "Multiple Answer" feature.

The second figure shows how Qualtrics enables the development of a "matrix table" question. In this example, there are five different possible specials being considered by the pizza delivery company, and respondents will be asked to indicate how likely they are to purchase each one. Notice that 5 scale points or gradations are specified. With the "Automatic Scale Points" feature, Qualtrics will generate an appropriate label for each level depending on the scale selected. In the figure, the "Likely-Unlikely" scale has been selected.

Questionnaire design with Qualtrics is also made very simple because questions or question blocks can be easily moved around on the questionnaire. The second figure, which shows several developed questions, illustrates questionnaire design and flow. There is a single-answer (yes/no) question about using Papa John's Pizza in the past month, a synthetic metric scale question about evaluations of various aspects of Papa John's Pizza, and an overall satisfaction question that uses a graphic rating scale. Notice that in Qualtrics the evaluations (Q7) are in a "matrix table" question format. The number of features or statements can be expanded, as can the number of scale points.

This figure also shows "skip logic" or internal instructions for Qualtrics to skip over certain question(s) based on the answer to a particular question. If the respondent

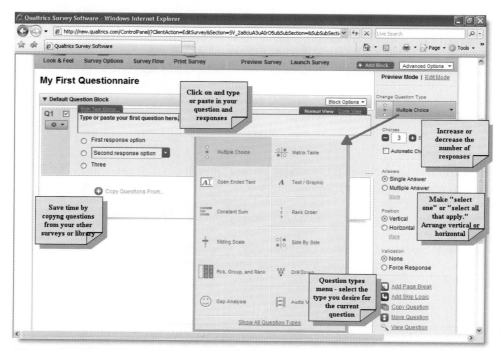

Creating a question in Qualtrics.

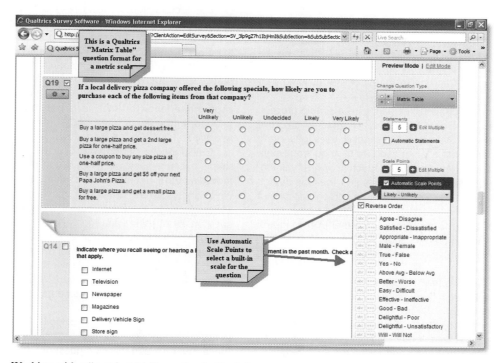

Working with a "matrix table" question in Qualtrics.

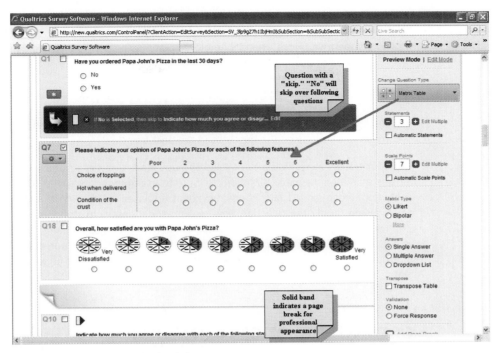

Skip logic and page breaks in Qualtrics.

indicates "No" to the question "Have you ordered Papa John's Pizza in the last 30 days," the questionnaire will skip over the evaluations and satisfaction question because the researcher only wants recent customers to answer these questions.

A simple page break is used after the overall satisfaction question to enhance the appearance of the questionnaire. Qualtrics also has a "Look and Feel" feature that offers selections of colors, fonts, and background for the questionnaire. When the questionnaire is ready, Qualtrics lets the user preview what the online survey will look like.

Question development and questionnaire design is exceptionally easy with Qualtrics because its interface is largely a "point-and-click" platform. There are tutorials and examples available for users, and after a quick orientation, most users are able to negotiate the basic features of Qualtrics to develop questions and design and launch an online questionnaire with a highly professional appearance. To be sure, there are many advanced features, such as downloading responses, which are not covered here. However, with this introduction, you are ready to begin experimenting with Qualtrics question development and questionnaire design.

Use Qualtrics to Design an Online Questionnaire

This active learning exercise will allow you to experiment with and learn how to use Qualtrics. Select any business (for example: restaurant, store, service provider) and investigate the consumer behavior of your fellow university students with respect to this business.

1. How much do they use it?
   a. How often do they use it per month?
   b. How much do they typically spend (individually) when they use it?
   c. Which of its aspects do they typically use (e.g., if the topic is a restaurant, do they typically purchase appetizer, main course, alcoholic beverage, dessert, take-out, and so on)?
   d. Did they use it in the past month?

2. For those who have used it in the past month …
   a. How do they rate its performance according to various aspects, such as location, competitive prices, friendly employees, and so on. (You must decide these based on the type of business and your knowledge of its operations.)
   b. Overall, how satisfied are they with it?
3. What advertising do they recall, and/or where do they recall seeing or hearing it? (You must identify the relevant advertising media used by the business.)
4. Provide a demographic profile of the sample, that is, both those who have not used and those who have used the business in the past month.

Use your access to Qualtrics to develop the questions and design the online questionnaire for this marketing research situation. Be sure to use appropriate scales (Chapter 10) and to apply knowledge gained in this chapter about unbiased wording. With respect to questionnaire design, apply the question flow recommendations in this chapter. Use Qualtrics for skip logic and to create a professional appearance for the questionnaire. As an extra benefit, your access to Qualtrics includes the ability to publish or post your questionnaire on the Internet, and you can pretest your questionnaire by asking some of your friends or classmates to respond to it online.

CODING THE QUESTIONNAIRE

Codes are numbers associated with question responses to facilitate data entry and analysis.

A final task in questionnaire design is **coding** questions, which is the use of numbers associated with question response options to facilitate data analysis after the survey has been conducted. The logic of coding is simple once you know the ground rules, and we have incorporated the basic rules in Table 11.5. The primary objective of coding is to represent each possible response with a unique number because numbers are easier and faster to use in computer tabulation programs.

Here are the basic rules for questionnaire coding:

■ Every closed-ended question should have a code number associated with every possible response.
■ Use single-digit code numbers, beginning with "1," incrementing them by 1 and using the logical direction of the response scale.
■ Use the same coding system for questions with identical response options regardless of where these questions are positioned in the questionnaire.
■ Remember that a "check all that apply" question is just a special case of a "yes" or "no" question, so use a "1" (= "yes") and "0" (= "no") coding system.
■ Whenever possible, set up the coding system before the questionnaire is finalized.

Table 11.5 illustrates code designations for selected questions to exemplify our code system guidelines. For a "hard-copy" questionnaire, codes are normally placed in parentheses, as you see in Table 11.5 (except for the "all that apply" question). In an online questionnaire, the codes are set up internally and not displayed. As you can see, when words such as "yes" and "no" are used as literal response categories, codes are normally placed alongside each response and in parentheses. For labeled scales, we recommend that the numbers match the direction of the scale. For example, notice in Question 3 in Table 11.5, that the codes are 1–5 and match the Poor–Excellent direction of the scale. If we happened to have a 5-point Likert scale with a Strongly Disagree to Strongly Agree response option in our questoinnaire, the codes would be 1–5. For scaled-response questions in which

TABLE 11.5 Examples of Codes on the Final Questionnaire

1. Have you purchased a Papa John's pizza in the last month?

   _____ Yes (1)   _____ No (2)   _____ Unsure (3)

2. The last time you bought a Papa John's pizza, did you (check only one):

   _____ Have it delivered to your house?   (1)

   _____ Have it delivered to your place of work?   (2)

   _____ Pick it up yourself?   (3)

   _____ Eat it at the pizza parlor?   (4)

   _____ Purchase it some other way?   (5)

3. In your opinion, the taste of a Papa John's pizza is (check only one):

   _____ Poor   (1)

   _____ Fair   (2)

   _____ Good   (3)

   _____ Very Good   (4)

   _____ Excellent   (5)

4. Which of the following toppings do you typically have on your pizza? (Check all that apply.)

   _____ Green pepper (0;1)   (Note: The 0;1 indicates the coding system that will be
                                     used. Typically, no precode such as this is placed on the
   _____ Onion (0;1)   questionnaire. Each response category must be defined as
                                     a separate question.)
   _____ Mushroom (0;1)

   _____ Sausage (0;1)

   _____ Pepperoni (0;1)

   _____ Hot peppers (0;1)

   _____ Black olives (0;1)

   _____ Anchovies (0;1)

5. How do you rate the speediness of Papa John's delivery service once you have ordered? (Circle the appropriate number.)

Very Slow	1	2	3	4	5	6	7	Very Fast

6. Please indicate your age: _____ Years (*Note:* No precode is used as the respondent will write in a number.)

7. Please indicate your gender.

   _____ Male (1)   _____ Female (2)

numbers are used as the response categories, the numbers are already on the questionnaire, so there is no need to use codes for these questions.

As you examine Table 11.5, please notice the one instance (Question 4, the "Check all that apply" question) in which coding becomes slightly complicated; but, again, once you learn the basic rules, the coding is fairly easy to understand. Occasionally, a researcher uses an **"all that apply" question** that asks the respondent to select more than one item from a list of possible responses.[47] This is the case in Question 4 in Table 11.5. With "all that apply" questions, the standard approach is to have each response category option coded with a 0 or a 1. The designation "0" will be used if the category is not checked, whereas a "1" is used if it is checked by a respondent. It is as though the researcher asked for a yes/no response for each item in the list (e.g, Do you usually order green peppers as topping? ____ No(0) ____ Yes(1)), but by listing them and asking "all that apply," the questionnaire is less cluttered and more efficient.

> The codes for an "all that apply" question are set up as though each possible response was answered with "yes" or "no."

PERFORMING THE PRETEST OF THE QUESTIONNAIRE

In referring back to Figure 11.1, you will find that as part of the questionnaire design process the entire questionnaire should be pretested.[48] A **pretest** involves conducting a dry run of the survey on a small, representative set of respondents in order to discover errors before the survey is launched.[49] It is very important that pretest participants be in fact representative, that is, selected from the target population under study. Before the questions are administered, participants are informed that it is a pretest and their cooperation is requested in spotting words, phrases, instructions, question flow, or other aspects of the questionnaire that appear confusing, difficult to understand, or otherwise a problem.

> A pretest is a dry run of a questionnaire to find and repair difficulties that respondents encounter while taking the survey.

Normally, from 5 to 10 respondents are involved in a pretest, and the researcher looks for common problems across this group.[50] For example, if only one pretest respondent indicates some concern about a question, the researcher probably would not modify its wording, but if three mention the same concern, the researcher would be alerted to the need for revision. Ideally, when making revisions, researchers should place themselves in the respondent's shoes and ask the following questions: "Is the meaning of the question clear?" "Are the instructions understandable?" "Are the terms precise?" and "Are there any loaded or charged words?"[51] However, because researchers can never completely replicate the respondent's perspective, pretesting is extremely valuable.[52]

SPSS Student Assistant: Coca-Cola: Sorting, Searching, and Inserting Variables and Cases

 Synthesize Your Learning

This exercise will require you to consider concepts and material taken from these three chapters:

Chapter 9	Evaluating Survey Data-Collection Methods
Chapter 10	Understanding Measurement in Marketing Research
Chapter 11	Developing Questions and Designing the Questionnaire

Moe's Tortilla Wraps

Moe's is a sandwich shop that sells wraps, which are sandwiches made with tortilla bread rather than regular sandwich bread. There are seven Moe's units located in the greater San Diego, California area, and Moe is thinking about setting up a franchise system to go "big time" with statewide coverage. Moe hires a marketing strategy consultant who recommends that he conduct a baseline survey of his seven San Diego units to better understand his customers and to spot strengths and weaknesses that he might not be aware of. The consultant recommends that Moe also do a survey of consumers in the San Diego, California area who are not Moe's Tortilla Wraps customers or who are infrequent customers to see if there are weaknesses or factors that are preventing them from being loyal customers. Finally, the consultant recommends that surveys be done in three of the possible expansion metropolitan areas of San Francisco, Sacramento, and Los Angeles to ascertain the attractiveness of and market potential for Moe's Tortilla Warps to sandwich shop users in these cities. The consultant mentions that, ideally, the three surveys would have some equivalent or highly similar questions that would facilitate comparisons of the findings among the surveys.

Together Moe and the consultant agree on the following research objectives.

Research Objectives for Users of Moe's Tortilla Wraps Survey in San Diego, California

1. How often do users purchase a sandwich at Moe's?
2. Overall, how satisfied are users with Moe's Tortilla Wraps?
3. How do they rate Moe's Tortilla Wraps performance on the following various aspects?
   a. Competitive price
   b. Convenience of locations
   c. Variety of sandwiches
   d. Freshness of sandwich fillings
   e. Speed of service
   f. Taste of wraps
   g. Uniqueness of sandwiches
4. Obtain a demographic profile of the sample.

Research Objectives for Nonusers of Moe's Tortilla Wraps Survey in San Diego, California

1. How often do people purchase sandwiches from sandwich shops?
2. Overall, how satisfied are they with the sandwich shop they use most often?
3. Have they heard of Moe's Tortilla Wraps?
4. If so, have they used Moe's in the past 6 months?
5. If so, how do they rate Moe's Tortilla Wraps performance on the following various aspects?
   a. Competitive price
   b. Convenience of locations
   c. Variety of sandwiches
   d. Freshness of sandwich fillings
   e. Speed of service
   f. Taste of wraps
   g. Uniqueness of sandwiches
6. Obtain a demographic profile of the sample.

Research Objectives for Potential Users of Moe's Tortilla Wraps Survey in San Francisco, Sacramento, and Los Angeles, California

1. How often do people purchase sandwiches from sandwich shops?
2. How do they rate the sandwich shop they use most often on the following various aspects?
   a. Competitive price
   b. Convenience of locations
   c. Variety of sandwiches
   d. Freshness of sandwich fillings
   e. Speed of service
   f. Taste of wraps
   g. Uniqueness of sandwiches

3. Given the following description...

   A sandwich shop that uses tortillas rather than bread for its sandwiches. It specializes in Southwest-flavored beef, chicken, ham, or processed meat sandwiches dressed with cheese, chopped lettuce, tomato, onions, and/or peppers and topped with salsa or a spicy chipotle dressing, and all priced at about the same you would pay for a sandwich at Jack in the Box.

4. What is their reaction to the use of a tortilla in place of bread in a sandwich?

5. How likely are they to use this sandwich shop if it was at a convenient location in their city?

6. Obtain a demographic profile of the sample.

   For each set of objectives associated with each target group of consumers, decide and justify a data-collection method. Given your chosen data-collection method, design the full questionnaire, that is, select measurement scales, develop questions, and finalize the appearance of the questionnaire for each of the three Moe's Tortilla Wraps surveys. In your deliberations, keep in mind that cost is a concern, as Moe does not have deep pockets to finance this research. However, his expansion plans are not on a fast timetable, so the completion time of the surveys is not especially critical. Of course, it is important to have survey findings that are representative of the respective target consumers for each survey.

Summary

This chapter described questionnaire design and some of the activities that are involved in the design process. We noted that questionnaires serve several functions. We also advocated that the designer follow a step-by-step development process that begins with question development, includes question evaluation, client approval, and a pretest to ensure that the questions and instructions are understandable to respondents. Certain words should be avoided in wording questions, and we provided a list of "top ten" words you should definitely avoid because they are absolute extremes that force respondents to totally agree or totally disagree with the question. The objective of question development is to create questions that minimize question bias, and the four "do's" in question development stress that the ideal question is focused, simple, brief, and crystal clear. Question bias is most likely to occur when question wording is leading, loaded, double-barreled, or overstated.

The organization of questions on the questionnaire is critical, including the first statements, or introduction to the survey. The introduction should identify the sponsor of the survey, relate its purpose, explain how respondents were selected, solicit their cooperation, and, if appropriate, qualify them for taking part in the survey. We next provided general guidelines for the flow of questions in the questionnaire and pointed out the location and role of screens, warm-ups, transitions, "difficult" questions, and classification questions. The chapter also introduced you to the notion of coding and placing the codes to be used in the computer data file on the questionnaire itself. In addition, we described Qualtrics, a software system that aids in questionnaire design, and briefly described the features of this and similar programs. Finally, you learned the function of and details about pretesting a questionnaire.

Key Terms

Questionnaire   304
Questionnaire design   304
Question bias   305
Question development   306
Question evaluation   308
Leading question   309

Loaded question   311
Double-barreled question   311
Overstated question   313
Face validity   315
Questionnaire organization   315
Cover letter   316

Undisguised survey   316
Disguised survey   316
Incentives   317
Anonymity   317
Confidentiality   317
Screening questions   318

Review Questions/Applications

1. What is a questionnaire and what are its functions?
2. What is meant by the statement that questionnaire design is a systematic process?
3. What is meant by question bias? Write two biased questions using some of the words to avoid described in Table 11.1. Rewrite each question without using the problem word.
4. What are the four guidelines, or "Do's," for question wording?
5. What are the four "Do Not's" for question wording. Describe each Do Not.
6. What is the purpose of a questionnaire introduction, and what things should it accomplish?
7. Distinguish anonymity from confidentiality.
8. Indicate the functions of (a) screening questions, (b) warm-ups, (c) transitions, (d) "skip" questions, and (e) classification questions.
9. List at least three features of computer-assisted questionnaire design programs that are more advantageous to a questionnaire designer than a word processor program.
10. What is coding and why is it used? Relate the special coding need with "all that apply" questions.
11. What is the purpose of a pretest of the questionnaire, and how does a reseacher go about conducting a pretest?
12. Listed here are five different aspects of a questionnaire to be designed for the crafts guild of Maui, Hawaii. It is to be administered by personal interviewers who will intercept tourists as they are waiting at their departing flight gates at the Maui Airport. Indicate a logical question flow for the questionnaire using the guidelines in Table 11.3.
    a. Determine how they selected Maui as a destination.
    b. Discover what places they visited in Maui and how much they liked each one.
    c. Describe what crafts they purchased, where they purchased them, when they bought them, how much they paid, who made the selection, and why they bought those particular items.
    d. Specify how long they stayed and where they stayed while on Maui.
    e. Provide a demographic profile of each tourist interviewed.
13. The Marketing Club at your university is thinking about undertaking a money-making project. Coeds will be invited to compete and 12 will be selected to be in the "Girls of (insert your school) University" calendar. All photographs will be taken by a professional photographer and tastefully done. Some club members are concerned about the reactions of other students who might think that the calendar will degrade women. Taking each of the "Do Not's" of question wording into consideration, write a question that would tend to bias answers such that the responses would tend to support the view that the calendar would be degrading. Indicate how the question is in error, and provide a version that is in better form.
14. Using the Internet, find a downloadable trial version of a computer-assisted questionnaire design program other than Qualtrics and become familiar with it. For each of the following possible features of computer-assisted questionnaire design programs, briefly relate the specifics on how the program you have chosen provides the feature:
    a. Question type options
    b. Question library
    c. Font and appearance
    d. Web uploading (sometimes called "publishing")
    e. Analysis, including graphics
    f. Download file format options
15. Panther Martin invents and markets various types of fishing lures. In an effort to survey the reactions of potential buyers, it hires a research company to intercept fishermen at boat launches, secure their cooperation to use a Panther Martin lure under development sometime during their fishing trip that day, meet them when they return, and verbally administer questions to them. As an

incentive, each respondent will receive three lures to try that day, and five more will be given to each fisherman who answers the questions at the end of the fishing trip.

What opening comments should be verbalized when approaching fishermen who are launching their boats? Draft a script to be used when asking these fishermen to take part in the survey.

CASE 11.1

PARK PLACE PSYCHIATRIC HOSPITAL

Park Place Psychiatric Hospital opened a few years ago in Tucson, Arizona. It specializes in psychiatric care and mental health services for both inpatients and outpatients, although the hospital is quite small and can only accommodate up to 40 inpatients at any one time. The hospital is located in the desert, approximately 40 miles from downtown Tucson and 20 to 50 miles away from upscale subdivisions, which are its target market. It has invested in an extensive advertising campaign using billboards, newspaper, Yellow Pages, radio spots, and a website. By the end of last year, Park Place had experienced only 45% occupancy, but it is optimistic about the future.

The management of Park Place has decided that in order to grow, it must reach out to its patient population in Tucson through more aggressive program offerings. Among the services being considered is a series of seminars on selected mental health care problems and a set of companion programs that will cover the various topics more extensively. The marketing manager contacts a local research company and works with some of its personnel to formulate a list of research objectives. These objectives address his concerns about the effectiveness of the marketing program, the hospital's location, the decision-making process of a family member who detects another family member having a problem, and an interest in various programs and seminars. The hospital management also desires to know where Tucson residents will turn for help when a family member exhibits symptoms of minor or major mental health problems.

These research objectives are specified as follows:

- To determine the level of interest in participating in each of the following one-time, two-hour evening group seminars costing $100 each to take place at the Park Place Psychiatric Hospital weight control, stress management, substance abuse, Alzheimers disease, understanding anxiety, living with an autistic child, and coping with teenagers.
- To assess the degree of interest in enrolling in any two-month-long group programs costing $1500 each previously listed (weight control, stress management, etc.). The programs involve two 2-hour sessions per week for 8 weeks that take place at the Park Place Hospital location.
- To evaluate where a person or family would likely seek help if a minor mental health problem possibly requiring professional counseling were evident with some family member (a minor mental health problem would be depression, stress, lethargy, sleeping problems, anger, or some other problem such that the person is undependable, erratic, or disoriented). The possible places to seek assistance include religious counselor such as minister or pastor, knowledgeable friends and acquaintances, family lawyer, family doctor, psychiatric care facility, psychologist, social worker, local police, or some other form of assistance.
- To evaluate where a person or family would likely seek help if a major mental health problem possibly requiring professional counseling were evident with some family member (a major mental health problem would be severe depression, violence, bizarre behavior, self-abuse, or some other problem such that the person's well-being is in danger and/or that he or she may harm others). The possible places to seek assistance include religious counselor such as minister or pastor, knowledgeable friends and acquaintances, family lawyer, family doctor, psychiatric care facility, psychologist, social worker, local police, or some other form of assistance.
- To determine if prospective clients recall Park Place Psychiatric Hospital recent advertising and, if so, in which advertising medium.

- To evaluate the importance of location in the selection of a mental health care facility for a family member, either as an inpatient or an outpatient.
- To determine how Park Place Psychiatric Hospital's location is perceived.
- To obtain target market information.

Random telephone calls will be used to select prospective respondent households from the upscale neighborhoods that Park Place Psychiatric Hospital has identified as its target market.

1. Design a questionnaire suited for a telephone survey of 500 Tucson households to be conducted with the "adult head of the household who is responsible for the family's health care."
2. Justify your choice of the type of question response format for each question. If you have used the same format for a group of related questions, you should indicate your rationale for the group rather than for each question in the group.
3. Identify the organization aspects of your questionnaire. Identify the question flow approach you have used and indicate why. That is, identify all screening questions, warm-ups, transition questions, and skip questions that you have used.

CASE 11.2

THE STEAKSTOP RESTAURANT: WHAT IS WRONG WITH THESE QUESTIONS?

Note: this case was contributed by Tulay Girard, Ph.D., Assistant Professor of Marketing, Pennsylvania State University–Altoona

The SteakStop is a (fictitious) chain restaurant located in the southeastern United States. Working for its headquarters, the marketing manager, Brenda Bauer, hired you as a marketing intern to work on a customer satisfaction survey. On average, the 20 chain restaurants will receive about 150 phone surveys per store per month. Brenda would like to receive weekly, monthly, and quarterly reports generated from the customer feedback received. She drafted an automated telephone survey to collect information on customer satisfaction with the menu items and service in the restaurant. Below are the script and the questions that Brenda wants you to improve.

While looking at the survey questions, you noticed violations of the basic questionnaire design rules based on what you learned from your marketing research course. Among such violations are double-barreled, loaded, leading, overstated or vague questions, and questions with bad scales.

Professor Tulay Girard

The SteakStop Restaurant Phone Survey Script

"Welcome to our customer feedback system. Please enter your access code followed by the pound sign. It is located on your purchase receipt next to the toll-free phone number you've just dialed."

Introduction Script

"Thank you for participating in SteakStop's customer satisfaction survey. By participating in this survey you will have a chance to win a $50 gift certificate. Winners will be notified by telephone. You must complete the entire survey to have a chance to win the gift certificate."

"If at any time during this survey you wish to repeat a question, just press the star key. Your feedback is important to us. Now, we will ask you questions regarding your latest dining experience at SteakStop."

Main Survey

1. "**What meal did you choose?** If steak, press 1. If seafood, press 2. If chicken, press 3. If sandwich, press 4."
2. "**Did you order one of our fantastic appetizers that everyone is raving about?** If yes, press 1. If no, press 2."
   (If the answer is yes, continue with 2a; if no, skip to 3)
   2a. "**How would you rate the quality of our appetizers?** If good press 1, if very good press 2, if excellent press 3, if exceptional press 4."

3. **"Were you pleased with the exceptional taste of your meal?** If yes press 1. If no, press 2."
4. **"Please rate your hot and tasty meal based on your satisfaction?** If good press 1, if very good press 2, if excellent press 3, if exceptional press 4."
5. **"All of our health-conscious customers consider the portion size of our meals to be ideal, do you?** If yes press 1. If no, press 2."
6. **"Was your server attentive and responsive to your needs?** If yes, press 1. If no, press, 2."
7. **"What does our competitor, Beef-O-Rama, charge for a complete meal?** If under $15, press 1. If between $15 and $20, press 2. If over $20, press 3."
8. "Now that you've completed the survey, please enter your 10-digit phone number followed by the pound key so we can notify you if you are a winner of the $50 gift certificate. If you prefer not to enter the drawing, press the pound key to skip this step."

Closing Statement

"Thank you for participating in our survey! We look forward to hearing from you each time you eat at SteakStop."

"Remember, "When it's time to stop for a steak, stop at SteakStop!""

Case Question

1. Carefully go over each question and identify what type of error was made. Then, correct the errors using "Do's" and "Do Not's" for wording questions.

CASE 11.3 Your Integrated Case

ADVANCED AUTOMOBILE CONCEPTS

(*Note:* This case requires that you have read and answered Case 10.3, Advanced Automotive Concepts.)

Cory Rogers now felt he had a good grasp of the research objectives needed in order to conduct the research study for Nick Thomas of Advanced Automobile Concepts. Furthermore, he had taken some time to write operational definitions of the constructs, so he had done most of the preliminary work on the questionnaire. He sat down and started working on the questionnaire that he would need. Cory and Nick have decided that the most reasonable approach to the survey is to use an online panel. This alternative, while somewhat expensive, will guarantee that the final sample is representative of the market. That is, companies that operate such panels assure buyers of their services that the sample will represent any general target market that a buyer may desire to have represented. In the case of Advanced Automotive Concepts, the market of interest is "all automobile owners," meaning that practically all adults qualify.

Consequently, it is time to design a questionnaire suitable for administration to an online panel of adult consumers. The survey objectives have been agreed to, and the ones relevant to questionnaire design for this phase of the research project are listed here.

1. What are (prospective) automobile buyers' attitudes toward . . .
   a. Global warming (do consumers believe it is real and will affect their choice of car power source),
   b. Fuel prices (do they believe they will remain high for several years),
   c. Very small autos (1 seat) with very high mpg ratings,
   d. Small autos (2 seat) with high mpg ratings, and
   e. Hybrid compact-size autos with moderately high mpg ratings?
2. Do attitudes (in Question 1) vary by market segment? Market segments are defined by . . .
   a. Demographics,
      i. Age
      ii. Income
      iii. Education
      iv. Gender
   b. Life style

3. What are consumer preferences and intentions for various types and combinations of fuel-efficient automobiles?
   a. Very small (1 seat), no trunk space, and very high mpg
   b. Small (2 seat), very limited trunk space, and high mpg
   c. Hybrid models (compact and moderately high mpg)
      i. Synthetic fuel hybrids
      ii. Electric hybrids
   d. Alternative-fuel models
4. What are media habits of those who prefer the new automobile types?
   a. Reading newspaper (local, state, national)
   b. Watching local news on TV (6 am, 8 am, 6 pm, 10 pm)
   c. Listening to FM radio (talk, easy listening, country, top 40, oldies)
   d. Reading magazine types (general interest, business, science, sports)

Go over the needed integrated case facts and information imparted to you in previous chapters and design an online survey questionnaire for Advanced Automotive Concepts. Naturally, you are responsible for proper construct measurement, clear question wording, appropriate question flow, and all other principles of good questionnaire design. (Your instructor may or may not want you to use Qualtrics for this assignment, so be sure to check on the desired format.)

Learning Objectives

- To become familiar with sample design terminology
- To understand the differences between "probability" and "nonprobability" sampling methods
- To learn how to take four types of probability samples: simple random samples, systematic samples, cluster samples, and stratified samples
- To learn how to take four types of nonprobability samples: convenience samples, purposive samples, referral samples, and quota samples
- To acquire the skills to administer different types of samples, including online samples
- To be able to develop a sample plan

Where We Are

1 Establish the need for marketing research
2 Define the problem
3 Establish research objectives
4 Determine research design
5 Identify information types and sources
6 Determine methods of accessing data
7 Design data-collection forms
▶ 8 Determine the sample plan and size
9 Collect data
10 Analyze data, and
11 Prepare and present the final research report.

A Survey That Changed Survey Sampling Practice

The *Literary Digest*, an influential general-interest magazine started in 1890, correctly predicted several presidential campaigns using surveys. The world was becoming accustomed to viewing surveys as accurate predictors of future events. But the prediction the magazine made in the 1936 election was so bad that it is given credit for not only causing the collapse of the magazine (it was purchased by Time, Inc. in 1938) but for stirring interest in refining survey sampling techniques.

Alf Landon, the Republican candidate and governor of Kansas, was running against Democratic President Franklin D. Roosevelt. The *Literary Digest* used three lists as its sample frame for polling American voters. First, it sent a postcard to all of its 2 million subscribers. Second, it added to this sample with sample frames composed of lists of telephone owners and automobile owners. The *Digest*'s survey predicted Landon would win overwhelmingly. Roosevelt won in a landslide, taking 46 of 48 states. Only Maine and New Hampshire voted for Landon. What could have gone wrong? The *Literary Digest* had used an unusually large sample yet the results were terribly wrong. The answer: The sampling method was wrong.

Literary Digest's famous blunder was due to using a poor sampling method.

Remember, 1936 was the depth of the Great Depression. Those who could afford a magazine subscription, telephone, or automobile were much better off than the general public, and these "better-off" citizens were much more likely to be Republicans. So the *Digest* was surveying, in very large numbers, voters who were mostly Republican. The magazine didn't use a sampling method that would guarantee that Democrats would be just as likely to be surveyed.

What this story illustrates is that you must have a good sampling method. With a poor sampling method, even very large sample sizes will not produce good survey results. In contrast, other surveys using much smaller sample sizes predicted Roosevelt would win. These were ridiculed for using small samples, but their predictions were correct because they used sound sampling methods. Among those producing accurate predictions was a young man named George Gallup. The Gallup Company exists today and is still conducting accurate surveys.

In this chapter, you will learn how the sampling method is important in producing representative results and how the sample size is important in producing accurate survey results.[1]

International markets are measured in hundreds of millions of people, national markets comprise millions of individuals, and even local markets may constitute hundreds of thousands of households. To obtain information from every single person in a market is usually impossible and obviously impractical. For these reasons, marketing researchers make use of a sample. This chapter describes how researchers go about taking samples. As can be seen in our account of the Literary Digest survey, the consequences of making an error when taking a sample can be quite severe. Despite the fact that the Literary Digest error was made several years ago, the dangers lurking in the sample selection step of the marketing research process have not diminished.

We begin with definitions of such basic concepts as population, sample, and census. Then we discuss the reasons for taking samples. From there, we distinguish the four types of probability sampling methods from the four types of nonprobability sampling methods. Because online surveys are popular, we discuss sampling aspects of these surveys. Last, we present a step-by-step procedure for taking a sample, regardless of the sampling method used.

BASIC CONCEPTS IN SAMPLES AND SAMPLING

To begin, we acquaint you with some basic terminology used in sampling. The terms we discuss here are *population, census, sample, sample unit, sample frame, sample frame error,* and *sample error.* As we describe these concepts, it will be useful to refer to Figure 12.1, which depicts them in a way that might help you to learn how they relate to one another.

Population

The population is the entire group under study as defined by research objectives.

A **population** is defined as the entire group under study as specified by the objectives of the research project. As can be seen in Figure 12.1, the shape labeled population is the largest and most encompassing. Managers tend to have a less specific definition of the population than do researchers because the researcher must define the population very precisely, whereas the manager defines it in a more general way.

For instance, let us examine a research project performed for Terminix Pest Control. If Terminix were interested in determining how prospective customers were combating roaches, ants, spiders, and other insects in their homes, the Terminix manager would probably define the population as "everybody who might use our services." However, the researcher in charge of sample design would use a definition such as

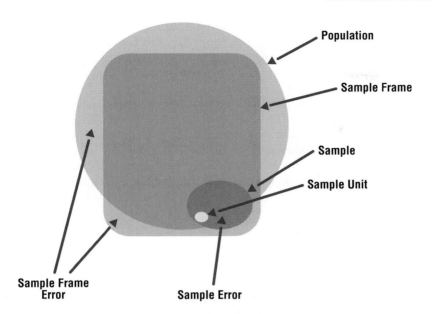

FIGURE 12.1

Basic Sampling Concepts

"heads of households in those metropolitan areas served by Terminix who are responsible for insect pest control." Notice that the researcher has converted "everybody" to "households" and has indicated more precisely who the respondents will be in the form of "heads of households." The definition is also made more specific by the requirement that the household be in a metropolitan Terminix service area. Just as problem definition error can be devastating to a survey, so can population definition error because a survey's findings are applicable only to the population from which the survey sample is drawn. For example, if the Terminix population is "everybody who might use our services," it would include industrial, institutional, and business users as well as households. If a large national chain such as Hilton Hotels or Olive Garden Restaurants were included in the survey, then the findings could not be representative of households alone.

Census

A **census** is defined as an accounting of the complete population. In other words, if you wanted to know the average age of members of a population, you would have to ask each and every population unit his or her age and compute the average. You can therefore see the impracticalities associated with a census, particularly when you think about target markets that have millions of consumers in them.

Perhaps the best example of a census is the U.S. census taken every 10 years by the U.S. Census Bureau (www.census.gov). The target population in the case of the U.S. census is all households in the United States. In truth, this definition of the population constitutes an "ideal" census, for it is virtually impossible to obtain information from every single household in the United States. At best, the Census Bureau can reach only

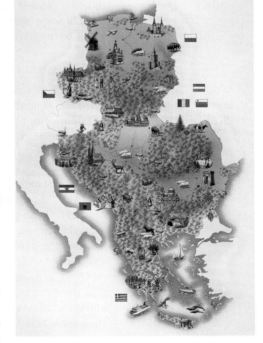

The population is the entire group under study.

A census requires information from everyone in the population.

a certain percentage of households, obtaining a census that provides information within the time period of the census-taking activity. Even with a public-awareness promotional campaign budget of several hundred thousand dollars that covers all of the major advertising media—television, newspaper, and radio—and an elaborate follow-up procedure, the Census Bureau admits that its numbers are inaccurate.[2]

The difficulties encountered by U.S. census takers are identical to those encountered in marketing research. For example, individuals may be in transition between residences, without places of residence, illiterate, incapacitated, illegally residing in the United States, or unwilling to participate. Marketing researchers undertaking survey research face all of these problems and a host of others. In fact, researchers long ago realized the impracticality and outright impossibility of taking a census of a population. Consequently, they turned to the use of subsets, or samples chosen to represent the target population.

Sample and Sample Unit

The sample is a subset of the population, and the sample unit pertains to the basic level of investigation.

Both a sample and a sample unit are depicted in Figure 12.1. A **sample** is a subset of the population that suitably represents that entire group.[3] Once again, there is a difference between how a manager uses this term and how it is used by the researcher. The manager will often overlook the "suitability" aspect of this definition and assume that any sample is a representative sample. However, the researcher is trained to detect sample errors and is very careful to assess the degree of representativeness of the subgroup selected to be the sample.

As you would expect, a **sample unit** is the basic level of investigation. In the Terminix example, the unit is a household. For a Weight Watchers survey, the unit would be one person, but for a survey of hospital purchases of laser surgery equipment, the sample unit would be hospital purchasing agents.

Sample Frame and Sample Frame Error

A sample frame is a master list of the entire population.

You should notice in Figure 12.1 that the sample and sample unit exist within the area called the "sample frame." A **sample frame** is some master list of all the sample units in the population. You will see in Figure 12.1 that the sample frame shape does not take in all of the population shape and, further, that it takes in some area that is outside the population's boundary. In other words, the sample frame does not always correspond perfectly to the population.

For instance, if a population is defined to be all automobile dealers in the state of Wyoming, the researcher would need a master list as a frame from which to sample. Similarly, if the population being researched is certified public accountants (CPAs), the researcher would need a sample frame for this group. In the case of automobile dealers, a list might be purchased from a service such as American Business Lists of Turnersville, New Jersey, which has compiled a list of automobile dealers from Yellow Pages listings. For CPAs, the researcher could purchase a list of members who have passed the CPA exam from the American Institute of Certified Public Accountants, located in New York City. Sometimes the researcher cannot find a list, and the sample frame becomes a matter of whatever access to the population the researcher can think up, such as "all shoppers who purchase at least $50 worth of merchandise at a Radio Shack store during the second week of March." Here, because some shoppers pay by credit card, some by check, and some with cash, there is no physical master list of qualified shoppers, but there is a stream of shoppers that can be sampled.

A listing of the population may be inaccurate and thus contain sample frame error.

We have made you aware that a sample frame invariably contains **sample frame error**, which is the degree to which the sample frame fails to account for all of the population. A way to envision sample frame error is by matching the list with the population and seeing to what degree the list adequately matches the targeted population. What do you think is the sample frame in our Wyoming automobile dealers sample? The primary error involves using only Yellow Pages listings. Not all dealers are listed in the Yellow Pages, as some have gone out of business, some have come into being since the publication of the Yellow Pages, and some decline to be listed. The same type of error exists for CPAs, and the researcher would have to determine how current the list is.[4]

Whenever a sample is drawn, the researcher should judge the amount of potential sample frame error.[5] One should not become enamoured by sheer numbers alone. Marketing Research Insight 12.1 demonstrates how sampling Internet users in a particular country may incur considerable sample frame error even though it gives access to millions of potential respondents. Sometimes the only available sample frame contains much potential sample frame error, but it is used due to the lack of any other. It is a researcher's responsibility to seek out a sample frame that provides the least amount of error at a reasonable cost.

Sampling Error

Sampling error is any error in a survey due to the fact that a sample is used[6] and is caused by two factors. First is the sample selection method, including sample frame error, as you will learn later in this chapter. In Figure 12.1, the sample shape is contained within the sample frame shape but includes some area outside the population shape. This is a type of sample error caused by the sample frame, which is not completely faithful to the population definition. You will learn in this chapter that some sampling methods minimize this

Whenever a sample is taken, the survey will reflect sampling error.

MARKETING RESEARCH INSIGHT

Global Application

12.1 Use Caution and Judgment When Using Internet Users as a Sample Frame

There is, perhaps, a tendency to think that the entire planet is on the Internet and that samples of Internet users adequately represent the populations of countries. This line of thinking is entirely fallacious, for the level of penetration of the Internet varies dramatically from country to country. That is, there is considerable sample frame error, even though the sheer numbers of Internet users may be quite high, if the general population of the country is to be sampled. A recent article by Kira Singer[7] described the penetration rates and special types of Internet users in many different countries. The following table, summarizing only Asia-Pacific countries, is taken from this article.

The table demonstrates that it is easy to be misled by the number of Internet users in any single country. For example, there are an estimated 55 million Internet users in India. However, the percentage figures communicate something about the sample frame error. An estimated 95% of India's citizens do not have Internet access, so choosing Internet users as a sample frame for this country incurs a huge amount of

Country	Estimated Internet Users (millions)	Internet Penetration	Special Aspects of Internet Users
Australia	*13.9*	*68%*	*Broadly representative*
China	*117.0*	*9%*	*Small percentage that is educated and urban*
India	*54.8*	*5%*	*Tiny percentage that is educated and urban*
Japan	*85.8*	*67%*	*Younger and urban*
Singapore	*2.3*	*67%*	*Home users, under government scrutiny*
South Korea	*33.4*	*67%*	*Low representation of older citizens*
Taiwan	*13.7*	*60%*	*Broadly representative*
Thailand	*8.5*	*13%*	*Wealthier citizens*

sample frame error. The table also notes that in low-Internet-penetration countries, certain types of citizens are more likely to be encountered when choosing Internet users as a sample frame. If a marketing researcher intended to specifically target these consumers—for instance, wealthier citizens of Thailand—then there would be less sample frame error.

error factor, whereas others do not control it well at all. The second factor is the the size of the sample. In Chapter 13, we show you the relationship between sample size and sampling error.

REASONS FOR TAKING A SAMPLE

Taking a sample is less expensive than taking a census.

By now you may have surmised at least two general reasons why a sample is almost always more desirable than a census. First, there are practical considerations, such as cost and population size, that make a sample more desirable than a census. Taking a census is expensive—consumer populations may number in the millions. Even if the population is restricted to a medium-sized metropolitan area, hundreds of thousands of individuals can be involved. Even when using a mail survey, accessing the members of a large population is cost-prohibitive.

Second, the typical research firm and the typical researcher cannot analyze the huge amounts of data generated by a census. Although computer statistical programs can handle thousands of observations with ease, they slow down appreciably with hundreds of thousands, and most are unable to accommodate millions of observations. In fact, even before considering the size of the computer or tabulation equipment to be used, a researcher must consider the various data preparation procedures involved in just handling the questionnaires or responses and transferring these responses into computer files. If "hard-copy" questionnaires are to be used, the sheer physical volume can easily overwhelm the researcher's capabilities.

Defending the use of samples from a different tack, we can turn to an informal cost–benefit analysis to defend the use of samples. If the project director of our Terminix household survey had chosen a sample of 500 households at a cost of $10,000 and had determined that 20% of those surveyed "would consider" switching from their current pest control provider to Terminix, what would be the result if a completely different sample of the same size were selected in identical fashion to determine the same characteristic? For example, suppose the second sample resulted in an estimate of 22%. The project would cost $10,000 more, but what has been gained with the second sample?

Common sense suggests that very little additional information has been gained, for if the project director combined the two samples he or she would come up with an estimate of 21%. In effect, $10,000 more has been spent to gain 1% more information. It is extremely doubtful that this additional precision offsets the additional cost. We will develop this notion in more detail in Chapter 13 on sample size determination.

PROBABILITY VERSUS NONPROBABILITY SAMPLING METHODS

With probability sampling, the chances of selection are "known," but with nonprobability sampling, they are "unknown."

All sample designs fall into one of two general categories: probability or nonprobability. **Probability samples** are those in which members of the population have a known chance (probability) of being selected into the sample. **Nonprobability samples**, on the other hand, are those where the chances (probability) of selecting members from the population into the sample are unknown. Unfortunately, the terms *known* and *unknown* are misleading, for in order to calculate a precise probability, one would need to know the exact size of the population, and it is impossible to know the exact size of the population in most marketing research studies. If we were targeting readers of the magazine *People*, for example, the exact size of the population changes from week to week as a result of new subscriptions, old ones running out, and fluctuations in counter sales as a function of whose picture is on the cover. You would be hard-pressed, in fact, to think of cases in which the population size is known and stable enough to be associated with an exact number.

The essence of a "known" probability rests in the sampling method rather than in knowing the exact size of the population. Probability sampling methods are those that ensure that the probability of any member of the population being selected into the sample could be calculated if the exact size of the population were known for the moment in time that sampling took place. In other words, the probability value is really never calculated in actuality, but we are assured by the sample method that the chances of any one population member being selected into the sample could be computed. This is an important theoretical notion underlying probability sampling.

With nonprobability methods there is no way to determine the probability even if the population size is known, because the selection technique is subjective. As one author has described the difference, nonprobability sampling uses human intervention, whereas probability sampling does not.[8] Nonprobability sampling is sometimes called "haphazard sampling" because it is prone to human error and even subconscious biases.[9] The following descriptions will illustrate that it is the sampling method that determines whether the sample is a probability or nonprobability sample.

> With probability sampling, the method determines the chances of a sample unit being selected into the sample.

Probability Sampling Methods

There are four probability sampling methods: simple random sampling, systematic sampling, cluster sampling, and stratified sampling (Table 12.1). A discussion of each method follows.

TABLE 12.1   Four Different Probability Sampling Methods

Simple Random Sampling

The researcher uses random numbers from a computer, random digit dialing, or some other random selection procedure that guarantees each member of the population in the sample frame has an identical chance of being selected into the sample.

Systematic Sampling

Using a sample frame that lists members of the population, the researcher selects a random starting point for the first sample member. A constant "skip interval," calculated by dividing the number of population members in the sample frame by the sample size, is then used to select all other sample members from the sample frame. A skip interval must be used such that the entire list is covered, regardless of the starting point. This procedure accomplishes the same end as simple random sampling, and it is more efficient.

Cluster Sampling

The sample frame is divided into groups called *clusters*, each of which must be considered very similar to the others. The researcher can then randomly select a few clusters and perform a census of each one (one stage). Alternatively, the researcher can randomly select more clusters and take samples from each one (two stage). This method is desirable when highly similar clusters can be easily identified, such as subdivisions spread across a wide geographic area.

Stratified Sampling

If the population is believed to have a skewed distribution for one or more of its distinguishing factors (e.g., income or product usage), the researcher identifies subpopulations in the sample frame called *strata*. A simple random sample is then taken of each stratum. Weighting procedures may be applied to estimate population values such as the mean. This approach is better suited than other probability sampling methods to populations that are not distributed in a bell-shaped pattern (i.e., that are skewed).

SIMPLE RANDOM SAMPLING. With **simple random sampling**, the probability of being selected into the sample is equal for all members of the population. This probability is expressed by the following formula:

Formula for simple random sample selection probability   Probability of selection $=$ sample size/population size

With simple random sampling, the probability of selection into the sample is "known" for all members of the population.

So, with simple random sampling, if the researcher is surveying a population of 100,000 recent purchasers Blu-Ray DVD players with a sample size of 1,000 respondents, the probability of selection of any single population member into this sample would be 1,000 divided by 100,000, or 1 out of 100, calculated to be 1%.

There are a number of approaches to simple random sampling, including the random device method and the random numbers method.

The "random device" is a form of simple random sampling.

The Random Device Method.   The **random device method** involves using an apparatus of some sort that guarantees that every member of the population has the same chance of being selected into the sample. Examples of the random device method with which you are familiar are flipping a coin to decide heads or tails, lottery numbers selected by numbered ping-pong balls, a roulette wheel in a casino, and being dealt a hand in a poker game. In every case, every member of the population has the same probability of being selected as every other member of that population: 1/2; for the coin toss, 1/59 for any Powerball number, 1/37 for the roulette numbers, or 5/52 for the cards.

For sampling purposes, you can create a device for randomly choosing participants by using their names or some other unique designation. For example, suppose you wanted to determine the attitudes of students in your marketing research class toward a career in marketing research. Assume that the particular class you have chosen as your population has 30 students enrolled. To do a "**blind draw**," you first write the name of every student on a 3-by-5 index card, then take all of these cards and put them inside a container of some sort. Next, you place a top on the container and shake it very vigorously. This procedure ensures that the names are thoroughly mixed. You then ask some person to draw the sample. This individual is blindfolded so that he or she cannot see inside the container. You would instruct the person to take out 10 cards as the sample. (For now, let us just concentrate on sample selection methods. We cover sample size determination in the next chapter.) In this sample, every student in the class has an equal chance of being selected with a probability of 10/30, or 33%, or 1 out of 3.

A random number embodies simple random sampling assumptions.

The Random Numbers Method.   All of our random device examples involve small populations that are easily accommodated by the physical aspects of the device. With large populations, random devices become cumbersome (just try shuffling a deck of 1,000 playing cards). A tractable and more sophisticated application of simple random sampling is to use computer-generated numbers based on the concept of **random numbers**, which are numbers whose random nature is assured. Computer programs have the ability to generate numbers without any systematic sequence to them whatsoever—that is, they are random. A computer easily handles data sets of hundreds of thousands of individuals; it can quickly label each one with a unique number or designation; it can generate a set of random numbers; and it can match the random numbers with the unique designations of the individuals in the data set to select or "pull" the sample. Using random numbers, a computer system can draw a huge random sample from a gigantic population in a matter of minutes and guarantee that every population member in the computer's files has the same chance of being selected.

Marketing Research Insight 12.2 shows the steps involved in using random numbers generated by a spreadsheet program to select students from a 30-member population.

MARKETING RESEARCH INSIGHT

Practical Application

12.2 How to Use Random Numbers to Select a Simple Random Sample

Step 1: Assign all members of the population a unique number.

Name	Number
Adams, Bob	1
Baker, Carol	2
Brown, Fred	3
Chester, Harold	4
Downs, Jane	5
. . .	↓
Zimwitz, Roland	30

Step 2: Generate random numbers in the range of 1 to *N* (30 in this case) by using the random number function in a spreadsheet program such as Microsoft Excel.[10] Excel generates random numbers from 0.0 to 1.0, so if you multiply the random number by *N* and format the result as an integer, you will have random numbers in the range of 1 to *N*. The following set of 10 random numbers was generated this way.

23	12	8	4	22	17	6	23	14	2	13

Select the first random number and find the corresponding population member. In the following example, number 23 is the first random number.

Step 3: Select the person corresponding to that number into the sample.

#23—Stepford, Ann

Step 4: Continue to the next random number and select that person into the sample.

#12—Fitzwilliam, Roland

Step 5: Continue on in the same manner until the full sample is selected. If you encounter a number selected earlier, such as the 23 that occurs at the eighth random number, simply skip over it because you have already selected that population member into the sample. (This explains why 11 numbers were drawn.)

Beginning with the first generated random number, you would progress through the set of random numbers to select members of the population into the sample. If you encounter the same number twice within the same sample draw, the number is skipped over, because it is improper to collect information twice from the same person.

 ### Are Random Numbers Really Random?

Some people do not believe that random numbers are actually random. These individuals sometimes point out that certain numbers seem to repeat more frequently than other numbers in lotteries, or they claim that they have a "favorite" or "lucky" number that wins for them when gambling or taking a chance of some sort. You can test the randomness of random numbers by creating an Excel spreadsheet and using its random number function. Use the following steps to perform this test.

Games of chance such as roulette are based on random numbers, which underlie random sampling.

1. First, open Excel and place numbers 1 to 100 in column cells A2–A101, with 1 in A2, 3 in A2, etc.

2. Place numbers 1 to 100 in roll cells C1–CX1, respectively.

3. Next, in cells C3–CX101, enter the Excel function =INT(RAND()*100)+1. (Note: you can enter this formula into cell C3, then copy it and paste the copy into block cells C3–CX101. You should see numbers that are whole intergers ranging from 1 to 100 in cells C3–CX101.)

4. Next in cell B1, enter =COUNTIF(C2:CX2,A2). Copy this formula and paste it into cells B2–B101. You will now see integers such as 0, 1, 2, 3, etc. in column B2–B101.

5. Finally, in cell B102, enter in the formula =AVERAGE(B2:B101). Format cell B102 to be a number with 1 decimal place.

6. Cell B102 is the average number of times that the number in column A2–A101 appears in the corresponding row, meaning row C2–CX2 for A2 or 1, C3–CX3 for A3 or 2, and so on.

What is in cell B102? It is the average number of times out of 100 times that each number from 1 to 100 appeared in its respective row. In other words, if the average in cell B102 is 1, then every number from 1 to 100 had an equal chance of being in its respective row. Stated differently, B102 is the number of chances out of 100 for any number from 1 to 100 to be selected by Excel's random number function.

You can "redraw" all 1,000 random numbers in Excel by simply entering a blank-Return anywhere in the spreadsheet. Try this with cell 103 several times; you will see that the average changes slightly, but it will tend to "hover" around 1.0.

You can test the "lucky number" theory by copying row 101 into rows 105–114, and placing the lucky number into cells A105–A114. Create an average of cells B105:B114 in cell B115. Then do several repetitions by entering a "space-enter" in any cell outside of your working cell and keep track of the numbers that appear in cell B115. You will find that it is typically 1, meaning that the lucky number has no more chance of being drawn than any of the 99 other random numbers.

Advantages and Disadvantages of Simple Random Sampling.   Simple random sampling is an appealing sampling method simply because it embodies the requirements necessary to obtain a probability sample and, therefore, to derive unbiased estimates of the population's characteristics. This sampling method guarantees that every member of the population has an equal chance of being selected into the sample; therefore, the resulting sample, no matter what the size, will be a valid representation of the population.

> Using random numbers to draw a simple random sample requires a complete accounting of the population.

However, there are some slight disadvantages associated with simple random sampling. To use either the random device or the random numbers approach, it is necessary to predesignate each population member. In the blind draw example, each student's name was written on an index card, whereas in the random numbers example, every population member was assigned a unique label or number. In essence, simple random sampling necessarily begins with a complete listing of the population, and current and complete listings are sometimes difficult to obtain. Incomplete or inaccurate listings of populations, of course, contain sample frame error. If the population does not exist as an electronic list, it can be cumbersome as we indicated to manually provide unique designations for each population member.

Simple Random Sampling Used in Practice.   There are two practical applications in which simple random sample designs are employed quite successfully: random digit dialing and computer-based random samples. In fact, these two general cases constitute the bulk of the use of simple random sampling in marketing research.

> Random digit dialing overcomes problems of unlisted and new telephone numbers.

One application in which simple random sampling is commonly employed is random digit dialing. **Random digit dialing (RDD)** is used in telephone surveys to overcome the problems of unlisted and new telephone numbers. Unlisted numbers are a growing concern not only for researchers in the United States but in all industrialized countries.[11,12] A current challenge to RDD is cell phone ownership.[13]

> Plus-one dialing is a convenient variation of random digit dialing.

In random digit dialing, telephone numbers are generated randomly with the aid of a computer. Telephone interviewers call these numbers and administer the survey to the respondent once the person has been qualified.[14] However, random digit dialing may result in a large number of calls to nonexistent telephone numbers. A popular variation of random digit dialing that reduces this problem is the **plus-one dialing procedure**, in which numbers are selected from a telephone directory and a digit, such as a "1," is added to each number to determine which telephone number is then dialed. Alternatively, a random number can be substituted for the last digit.[15]

Random digit dialing was the marketing research industry's first widespread use of random sampling. With current computer technology, it is feasible to use random sampling in a great variety of situations. For example, often companies possess computer lists, company files, or commercial listings that have been converted into databases. Practically every database software program has a random number selection feature, so simple random sampling is very easy to achieve if the researcher has a computerized database of the population. The database programs can work with random numbers of as many digits as are necessary, so even Social Security numbers with nine digits are no problem. Companies with credit files, subscription lists, or marketing information systems present the greatest opportunity for using this approach, or a research company may turn to a specialized sampling company, such as Survey Sampling, and have it draw a random sample of households or businesses in a certain geographic area using its extensive databases.

In our chapter on the marketing research industry, we made note of the many companies that maintain consumer and business panels of various types, and practically every one of these companies sells access to random samples of their panels. That is, these panels, which sometimes number in the tens of thousands of individuals, are really megasamples of various types of populations. The panels operate as sample frames from which the panel company draws smaller random samples according to the specifications of their clients.

SYSTEMATIC SAMPLING. In the special situation of a large population list that is not in the form of a computer database, such as a telephone book or a directory, the time and expense required to use simple random sampling are daunting. Fortunately, there is an economical alternative that can be used. At one time, **systematic sampling**, which is a way to select a random sample from a directory or a list that is much more efficient (uses less effort) than simple random sampling, was the most prevalent type of sampling technique. However, its popularity has declined as computerized databases and generated random number features have become widely available. But in the special case of a physical listing of the population, such as a membership directory or a telephone book, systematic sampling is often chosen over simple random sampling primarily because of its economic efficiency. Systematic sampling can be applied to physical listings with less difficulty and be accomplished in a shorter time than can simple random sampling, and it has the potential in these cases to create a sample that is almost identical in quality to samples created from simple random sampling.

Systematic sampling is more efficient than simple random sampling.

To use systematic sampling, it is necessary to obtain a hard-copy listing of the population. As noted earlier, the most common listing is a directory of some sort. The researcher decides on a **skip interval**, which is calculated by dividing the number of names on the list by the sample size, as can be seen in the following formula:

One must calculate a "skip interval" to use systematic sampling.

Formula for skip interval   Skip interval = population list size/sample size

Names are selected based on this skip interval. For example, if the skip interval is 250, every 250th name would be selected into the sample. The use of the skip interval formula ensures that the entire list will be covered. Marketing Research Insight 12.3 shows how to take a systematic sample.

Why Systematic Sampling Is Efficient.   Systematic sampling is probability sampling because it employs a random starting point, which ensures there is sufficient randomness in the systematic sample to approximate an equal probability of any member of the population being selected into the sample. In essence, systematic sampling envisions the list as made up of the skip interval number of mutually exclusive samples, each one of which is representative of the listed population. The random starting point guarantees that the selected sample is selected randomly.

MARKETING RESEARCH INSIGHT

Practical Application

12.3 How to Take a Systematic Sample

Step 1: Identify a listing of the population that contains an acceptable level of sample frame error. **Example:** The telephone book for your city.

Step 2: Compute the skip interval by dividing the number of names on the list by the sample size. **Example:** 25,000 names in the phone book, sample size of 500, so skip interval = every 50th name.

Step 3: Using random number(s), determine a starting position for sampling the list. **Example:** *Select:* random number for page number. *Select:* random

number for the column on that page. *Select:* random number for name position in that column (say, Jones, William P.).

Step 4: Apply the skip interval to determine which names on the list will be in the sample. **Example:** Jones, William P. (skip 50 names) Lathum, Ferdinand B.

Step 5: Treat the list as "circular." That is, the first name on the list is now the initial name you selected, and the last name is now the name just prior to the initially selected one. **Example:** When you come to the end of the phone book names (Zs), just continue on through to the beginning.

How is the random starting point chosen? With a directory or physical list as the sample frame, the efficient approach is to first generate a random number between 1 and the number of pages to determine the page on which you will start. Suppose page 53 is drawn. Another random number would be drawn between 1 and the number of columns on a page to decide the column on that page. Assume the third column is drawn. A final random number between 1 and the number of names in a column would be used to determine the actual starting position in that column. Let us say the 17th name is selected. From that beginning point, the skip interval would be employed. The skip interval would ensure that the entire list is covered, and the final name selected would be approximately one skip interval before the starting point. It is convenient to think of the listing as circular, such that A actually follows Z if the list is alphabetized, and the random starting point determines where the list "begins."

The essential difference between systematic sampling and simple random sampling is apparent in the use of the words *systematic* and *random*. The system used in systematic sampling is the skip interval, whereas the randomness in simple random sampling is determined through the use of successive random draws. Systematic sampling skips its way through the entire population list from random beginning point to the end, whereas random sampling guarantees that the complete population will be covered by successive random draws. The efficiency in systematic sampling is gained from two features: (1) the skip interval and (2) the need to draw a random number(s) only at the beginning.

> Systematic sampling is more efficient than simple random sampling because only one or a very few random numbers need to be drawn at the beginning.

 Take a Systematic Sample Using Your Telephone Book

This Active Learning Exercise will give you experience in taking a systematic sample from a "hard-copy" list such as a telephone book. For this exercise, you will use the telephone book for your localilty, and you will apply systematic sampling steps as though you were selecting a sample of 1,000 households. Use the following steps:

1. Estimate the total number of households listed in the telephone book. You can do this estimate by:
   a. Determine the total number of pages of household listings:
      _____ pages
   b. Determine the number of columns of numbers per page:
      _____ columns

c. Determine the average number of household listings per column (if there are business telephone numbers mixed with the household ones, you will need to make an adjustment for this factor):

_____ household listings

d. Determine the estimated total number of households in your sample frame (the telephone book) by mutiplying the number of pages times the number of columns times the number of household listings per column.

_____ household numbers

2. Determine the skip interval by dividing the number of household numbers by the sample size, 1,000.

_____ skip interval

3. Now, using some sort of random number generator such as an Excel function or a table of random numbers (typically found in a statitics textbook) select a random starting point in either of two ways:

(1) Select a random number between 1 and the total number of households in your sample frame, or

(2) Select a random page from 1 to the number of pages in the telephone book and turn to that page. Then, select a random column from 1 to the number of columns per page, and go to that column. Finally, select a random household in that column with a random number from 1 to the number of households per column.

4. Using your skip interval, you can now select the 1,000 household telephone listings.

The procedure you have used here assumes that every one of your 1,000 randomly selected households will particpate in the survey (100% response rate); however, this assumption is unrealistic. Assume that you expect a 50% response rate. What adjustment in the skip interval calculation can you make to accommodate the fact every other prospective respondent will refuse to take part in the survey when asked?

Disadvantage of Systematic Sampling. The greatest danger in the use of systematic sampling lies in the listing of the population (sample frame). Sample frame error is a major concern with telephone directories because of unlisted numbers. It is also a concern for lists that are not current. In both instances, the sample frame will not include certain population members, and these members have no chance of being selected into the sample because of this fact.

CLUSTER SAMPLING Another form of probability sampling is known as **cluster sampling**, in which the population is divided into subgroups, called *clusters*, each of which could represent the entire population. Note that the basic concept behind cluster sampling is very similar to the one behind systematic sampling, but the implementation differs. The procedure uses some convenient means that identifies clusters that are theoretically identical, such as the pages of listings in a hard-copy directory. Any one cluster, or page, therefore, could be a representation of the population. Cluster sampling can even be applied to an electonic database (the clusters can be everyone whose name begins with a "A," "B," "C," etc.). It is easy to administer, and cluster sampling goes a step further in striving to gain economic efficiency over systematic sampling by simplifying the sampling procedure used.[16] We illustrate by describing a type of cluster sampling known as area sampling.

A cluster sampling method divides the population into groups, any one of which can be considered a representative sample.

Area Sampling as a Form of Cluster Sampling. In **area sampling**, the researcher subdivides the population to be surveyed into geographic areas, such as census tracts, cities, neighborhoods, or any other convenient and identifiable geographic designation. The researcher has two options at this point: a one-step approach or a two-step approach.

Area sampling employs either a one-step or a two-step approach.

In the **one-step area sample** approach, the researcher may believe the various geographic areas (clusters) to be sufficiently identical to permit concentrating attention on just one area and then generalizing the results to the full population. But the researcher would need to select that one area randomly and perform a census of its members. Alternatively, the researcher may employ a **two-step area sample** approach to the sampling process. That is, for the first step, the researcher could select a random sample of areas and then, for the second step, the researcher could decide on a probability method to sample individuals within the chosen areas. The two-step area sample approach is preferable to the one-step approach because there is always the possibility that a single cluster may be less representative than the researcher believes. But the two-step method is more costly because more areas and time are involved. Marketing Research Insight 12.4 illustrates how to take an area sample using subdivisions as the clusters.[17]

A two-step area sample involves a sample of areas and then a sample of individual within the selected areas.

Area grid sampling is a variation of the area sampling method. To use it, the researcher imposes a grid over a map of the area to be surveyed. Each cell within the grid then becomes a cluster. The difference between area grid sampling and area sampling lies primarily in the use of a grid framework, which cuts across natural or artificial boundaries such as streets, rivers, city limits, or other separations normally used in area sampling. Geodemography has been used to describe the demographic profiles of the various clusters.[18] Regardless of how the population is sliced up, the researcher has the option of a one-step or a two-step approach.[19]

Disadvantage of Cluster (Area) Sampling.   The greatest danger in cluster sampling is cluster specification error, which occurs when the clusters are not homogeneous. For example, if a subdivision association used area sampling to survey its members using its streets as cluster identifiers, and one street circumnavigated a small lake in the back of the subdivision, the "Lake Street" homes might be more expensive and luxurious than most of the other homes in the subdivision. If by chance Lake Street was selected as a cluster in the survey, it would most likely bias the results toward the opinions of the relatively few wealthy subdivision residents. In the case of one-step area sampling, this bias could be severe.

STRATIFIED SAMPLING.   All of the sampling methods we have described thus far implicitly assume that the population has a normal, or bell-shaped, distribution for its key properties. That is, there is the assumption that every potential sample unit is a fairly good representation of the population and any who are extreme in one way are perfectly counterbalanced by potential sample units at the opposite extreme. Unfortunately, it is

---

MARKETING RESEARCH INSIGHT   Practical Application

12.4 How to Take a Two-Step Area Sampling Using Subdivisions

Step 1: Determine the geographic area to be surveyed and identify its subdivisions. Each subdivision cluster should be highly similar to all others. **Example:** 20 subdivisions within 5 miles of the proposed site for our new restaurant; assign each a number.

Step 2: Decide on the use of one-step or two-step cluster sampling. **Example:** Use two-step cluster sampling.

Step 3: (Assuming two-step): Using random numbers, select the subdivisions to be sampled. **Example:** Select four subdivisions randomly, say numbers 3, 15, 2, and 19.

Step 4: Using some probability method of sample selection, select the members of each chosen subdivision to be included in the sample. **Example:** Identify a random starting point; instruct field-workers to drop off the survey at every fifth house (systematic sampling).

common to work with populations in marketing research that contain unique
subgroupings; you might encounter a population that is not distributed symmetrically
across a normal curve. In this situation, unless you make adjustments in your sample
design, you will end up with a sample described as "statistically inefficient" or, in other
words, inaccurate. One solution is **stratified sampling**, which separates the population
into different subgroups and then samples all of these subgroups.

With stratified sampling,
the population is
separated into different
strata and a sample is
taken from each stratum.

Working with Skewed Populations.   A **skewed population** has a long tail on one side and
a short tail on the opposite end. As such, it deviates greatly from the bell-shaped
distribution that is assumed to be the case in the use of simple random, systematic, or
cluster sampling. So, if any of these methods is used to draw the sample from a skewed
distribution, it most certainly would be inaccurate.

For example, let's take the case of a college that is attempting to assess how its students perceive the quality of its educational programs. A researcher has formulated the
question "To what extent do you value your college degree?" The response options are
along a 5-point scale, where 1 equals "not valued at all" and 5 equals "very highly valued."
The population of students is stratified or divided by year: freshman, sophomore, junior,
and senior. That is, the researcher identifies four strata that comprise the complete population of the college's students. We would expect the response to differ by stratum (the
respondent's year status) because seniors probably value a degree more than do juniors
who value a degree more than do sophomores, and so on. At the same time, you would
expect that seniors would be more in agreement (have less variability) than would the
underclass students. This belief comes from the fact that freshmen are students who are
trying out college, some of whom are not serious about completing it and do not value it
highly but some of whom are intending to become doctors, lawyers, or professionals
whose training will include graduate work as well as their present college work. The serious freshmen students would value a college degree highly, whereas the less serious ones
would not. So, we would expect much variability in the freshmen students, less in sophomores, still less in juniors, and the least with college seniors. The situation might be something similar to the distributions illustrated in Figure 12.2. Notice in Figure 12.2, we have
portrayed each of the four class strata distributions as a normal curve, and the entire college
population of all four classes as a skewed curve.

Stratified sampling
is appropriate when we
expect that responses will
vary across strata, or
groups, in the population.

FIGURE 12.2

Stratified Simple Random Sampling

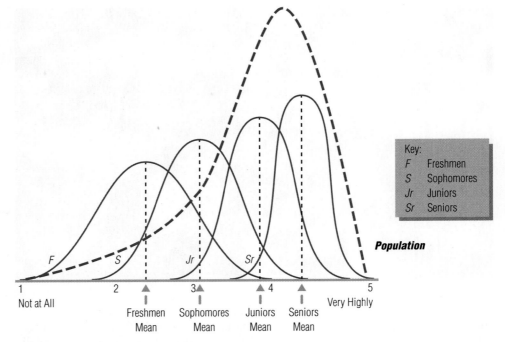

"To what extent do you value a college degree?"

Stratified sampling is used when the researcher is working with a "skewed" population divided into strata and wishes to achieve high statistical efficiency.

    With stratified random sampling, one takes a skewed population and identifies the subgroups or **strata** contained within it. Simple random sampling, systematic sampling, or some other type of probability sampling procedure is then applied to draw a sample from each stratum because we typically believe that the individual strata have bell-shaped distributions. So, it is a "divide and conquer" approach to sampling.

Accuracy of Stratified Sampling. How does stratified sampling result in a more accurate overall sample? Actually, there are two ways this accuracy is achieved. First, stratified sampling allows for explicit analysis of each stratum. Our college degree example (Figure 12.2) illustrates why a researcher would want to know about the distinguishing differences among the strata in order to assess the true picture. Each stratum represents a different response profile, and by recognizing this, stratified sampling is a more accurate sample design.

A stratified sample may require the calculation of a weighted mean to achieve accuracy.

    Second, there is a procedure that allows the estimation of the overall sample mean by use of a **weighted mean**, whose formula takes into consideration the sizes of the strata relative to the total population size and applies those proportions to the strata's means. The population mean is calculated by multiplying each stratum by its proportion and summing the weighted stratum means. This formula results in an estimate that is consistent with the true distribution of the population. Here is the formula that is used for two strata:

Formula for weighted mean

$$\text{Mean}_{\text{population}} = (\text{mean}_A)(\text{proportion}_A) + (\text{mean}_B)(\text{proportion}_B)$$

where A signifies stratum A, and B signifies stratum B.

    Here is an example of the use of weighted mean. A researcher separated a population of households that rent DVDs on a regular basis into two strata. Stratum A was families without young children, and stratum B was families with young children. When asked to use a scale of 1 = "poor," 2 "fair," 3 = "good," 4 = "very good, and 5 = "excellent" to rate their video/DVD rental store on its DVD selection, the means were computed to be 2.0 ("fair") for the "with young children" stratum B sample and 4.0 ("very good") for the "without young children" stratum A sample. The researcher knew from census information that families without young children accounted for 70% of the population, whereas families with young children accounted for the remaining 30%. The weighted mean rating for video selection was then computed as $(0.7)(4.0) + (0.3)(2.0) = 3.4$ (between "fair" and "good").

How to Apply Stratified Sampling. Stratified sampling is used in a number of instances in marketing research because skewed populations are often encountered. Prior knowledge of populations under study, augmented by research objectives sensitive to subgroupings, sometimes reveals that the population is not normally distributed. Under these circumstances, it is advantageous to apply stratified sampling to preserve the diversity of the various subgroups. Usually, a **surrogate measure**, which is some observable or easily determined characteristic of each population member, is used to help partition or separate the population members into their various subgroupings. For example, in the instance of the college, the year classification of each student is a handy surrogate. Of course, the researcher has the opportunity to divide the population into as many relevant strata as necessary to capture different subpopulations. For instance, the college might want to further stratify on college of study or on ranges in grade point average (GPA). Perhaps professional school students value their degrees more than do liberal arts students or high GPA students more than average GPA or failing students. The key issue is that the researcher should use some basis for dividing the population into strata that results in different responses across strata. Also, there should be some logic or usefullness to the stratification system.

> Researchers should select a basis for stratification that reveals different responses across the strata.

If the strata sample sizes are faithful to their relative sizes in the population, you have what is called a **proportionate stratified sample** design. Here you do not need to use the weighted formula because each stratum's weight is automatically accounted for by its sample size. But think for a moment about proportionate sampling: It erroneously assumes that the variability of each stratum is related to its size, that is, larger strata have more variability than small ones. But a large stratum could be composed of very homogeneous individuals, which translates to a relatively small stratum sample size, and a small stratum could be composed of very different individuals, which translates to a relative large stratum sample size. So some researchers opt to use the stratum relative variability, rather than the relative size, as a factor in deciding stratum sample size. This approach is called *disproportionate stratified sampling,* and a weighted formula needs to be used because the strata sizes do not reflect their relative proportions in the population. We have provided a step-by-step description of stratified sampling in Marketing Research Insight 12.5.

> An advantage of the disproportionate method is that smaller samples may be assigned to strata with lower variance. These "extra" sample elements may be assigned to strata with higher variance. Thus accurate estimates of each strata may be achieved without increasing the total sample size.

PICTORIAL REPRESENTATIONS OF PROBABILITY SAMPLING METHODS. The claim is that a picture is worth 1,000 words, so we have created some "pictures" or graphical representations of the various probability sampling methods in Figure 12.3, which contains representations of each of the four types of probability sample methods used in a fictitious satisfaction survey. The population in every instance is comprised of 25 consumers. One-fifth (20%) of the consumers are unsatisfied, two-fifths (40%) are satisfied, and two-fifths (40%) are indifferent or neutral about our brand. With each probability sample method (simple random sample, systematic sample, cluster sample, and stratified random sample), the resulting sample's satisfaction profile is consistent

MARKETING RESEARCH INSIGHT   Practical Application

12.5 How to Take a Stratified Sample

Step 1: Be certain that the population's distribution for some key factor is *not* bell-shaped and that separate subpopulations exist. **Example:** Condominium owners differ from apartment dwellers in their homeowner's insurance needs, so stratify by condo ownership and apartment dwelling.

Step 2: Use this factor or some surrogate variable to divide the population into strata consistent with the separate subpopulations identified. **Example:** Use a screening question on condo ownership/apartment dwelling. This may require a screening survey using random digit dialing to identify respondent pools for each stratum.

Step 3: Select a probability sample from each stratum. **Example:** Use a computer to select simple random samples for each stratum.

Step 4: Examine each stratum for managerially relevant differences. **Example:** Do condo owners differ from apartment dwellers in the value of the furniture they own (and need covered by insurance)? Answer: Condo owners have an average of $15,000 in owned furniture value; apartment dewellers have an average of $5,000 in owned furniture value.

Step 5: If stratum sample sizes are not proportionate to the stratum sizes in the population, use the weighted mean formula to estimate the population value(s). **Example:** If condo owners are 30% and apartment dwellers are 70% of the population, the estimate of the average is ($15,000)(0.30) + ($5,000)(0.70) = $8,000 owned furniture value.

with the population. That is, each probability sample has five consumers, with one unsatisfied (20%), two satisfied (40%), and two indifferent (40%). Again, the reason the samples are faithful to the population is that in all cases, every member of the population has an equal chance of being selected into the sample, assuming that there is no sample frame error.

Nonprobability Sampling Methods

All of the sampling methods we have described thus far embody probability sampling assumptions. In each case, the probability of any unit being selected from the population into the sample is known, even though it cannot be calculated precisely. The critical difference between probability and nonprobability sampling methods is the mechanics used in the sample design. With a nonprobability sampling method, selection is not based on chance or randomness. Instead, a nonprobability sample is based on an inherently biased selection process, typically in order to reduce the cost of sampling.[20] So, with a nonprobability sample, the reseacher achieves some savings, but at the expense of using a sample that is not truly representative of the population.[21] There are four nonprobability sampling methods: convenience samples, purposive samples, referral samples, and quota samples (Table 12.2). A discussion of each method follows.

CONVENIENCE SAMPLES. **Convenience samples** are samples drawn at the convenience of the interviewer. Accordingly, the most convenient areas to a researcher in terms of reduced time and effort turn out to be high-traffic areas such as shopping malls or busy pedestrian intersections. The selection of the place and, consequently, prospective respondents is subjective rather than objective. Certain members of the population are automatically eliminated from the sampling process.[22] For instance, there are those people who may be infrequent visitors or even nonvisitors to the particular high-traffic

With nonprobability sampling methods, some members of the population do not have any chance of being included in the sample.

Convenience samples may misrepresent the population.

area used. On the other hand, in the absence of strict selection procedures, there are members of the population who may be omitted because of their physical appearance, general demeanor, or the fact that they are in a group rather than alone. One author states, "Convenience samples . . . can be seriously misleading."[23] You can appreciate how these samples can be misleading if you complete the Active Learning Exercise about convenience sampling.

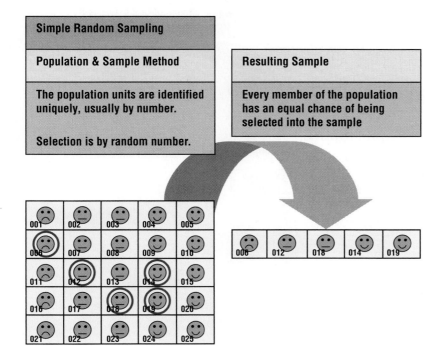

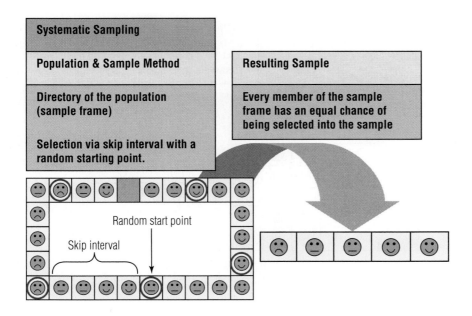

FIGURE 12.3

Pictorial Representations of Probability Sampling Methods

FIGURE 12.3

(Continued)

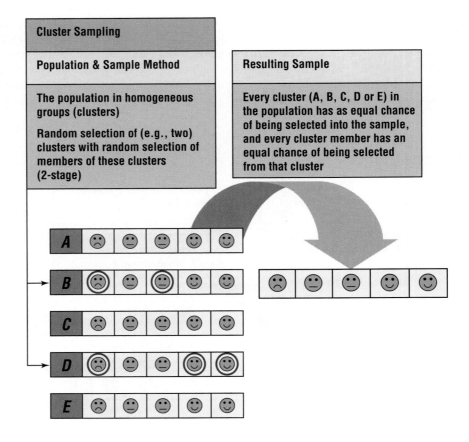

Cluster Sampling

Population & Sample Method

The population in homogeneous groups (clusters)

Random selection of (e.g., two) clusters with random selection of members of these clusters (2-stage)

Resulting Sample

Every cluster (A, B, C, D or E) in the population has as equal chance of being selected into the sample, and every cluster member has an equal chance of being selected from that cluster

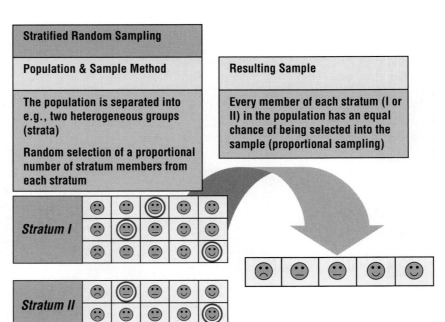

Stratified Random Sampling

Population & Sample Method

The population is separated into e.g., two heterogeneous groups (strata)

Random selection of a proportional number of stratum members from each stratum

Resulting Sample

Every member of each stratum (I or II) in the population has an equal chance of being selected into the sample (proportional sampling)

**TABLE 12.2   Four Different Types of Nonprobability Sampling
Methods**

Convenience Sampling

The researcher or interviewer uses a high-traffic location such as a busy pedestrian area or a shopping mall as the sample frame from which to intercept potential respondents. Sample frame error occurs in the form of members of the population who are infrequent or nonusers of that location. Other errors may result from any arbitrary way that the interviewer selects respondents from the sample frame.

Purposive Sampling

The researcher uses personal judgment or that of some other knowledgeable person to identify who will be in the sample. Subjectivity and convenience enter in here; consequently, certain members of the population will have a smaller chance of selection than will others.

Referral Sampling

Respondents are asked for the names or identities of others like themselves who might qualify to take part in the survey. Members of the population who are less well known, disliked, or whose opinions conflict with the selected respondents' have a low probability of being selected.

Quota Sampling

The researcher identifies quota characteristics such as demographic or product use factors and uses these to set up quotas for each class of respondent. The sizes of the quotas are determined by the researcher's belief about the relative size of each class of respondent in the population. Often, quota sampling is used as a means of ensuring that convenience samples will have the desired proportion of different respondent classes.

 Assess the Representativeness of Various Convenience Samples

Suppose the athletic department at your university is disappointed at student attendance of its "minor" collegiate sports events, such as wrestling, cross country, and softball. It wants to learn why students do not attend them. Listed here are possible locations for a convenience sample. For each one, indicate what types of students would be overrepresented in the sample and what types would be underrepresented in the sample versus the population of students at your university.

Convenience Sample Location	What Students Would Be Overrepresented?	What Students Would Be Underrepresented?
The university recreation center		
The university commons		
The library		
Physics 401 (advanced class for physics majors)		

Mall intercepts are convenience samples.

It should be obvious that mall-intercept companies use convenience sampling to recruit respondents. For example, shoppers are encountered at large shopping malls and are quickly qualified with screening questions. For those satisfying the desired population characteristics, a questionnaire or a taste test may be administered. Alternatively, the respondents may be given a test product and asked if they would use it at home. A follow-up telephone call some days later solicits the reaction to product performance. In this case, the convenience extends beyond easy access of respondents into considerations of setup for taste tests, storage of products to be distributed, and control of the interviewer workforce. Additionally, large numbers of respondents can be recruited in a matter of days. The screening questions and geographic dispersion of malls may appear to reduce the subjectivity inherent in the sample design, but in fact the vast majority of the population was not there and could not be approached to take part. There are ways of reducing convenience sample selection error using a quota system, which we discuss shortly.

With a purposive sample, one "judges" the sample to be representative.

PURPOSIVE SAMPLES. **Purposive samples** are quite different from convenience samples in concept because they require a judgment or an "educated guess" as to who should represent the population. Often, the researcher or some individual helping the researcher who has considerable knowledge about the population will choose those types of individuals that he or she feels constitute the sample. This practice is sometimes called a "judgment sample" or an "exemplar sample." It should be apparent that purposive samples are highly subjective and, therefore, prone to much error.

A referral sample asks respondents to provide the names of additional respondents.

Focus group studies use purposive sampling rather than probability sampling. In a recent focus group concerning the need for a low-fat yet nutritious snacks, 12 mothers of preschool children were selected as representative of the present and prospective market. Six of the women also had school-age children, while the other six had only preschoolers. That is, the researcher purposively included the two types of focus group participants because in his judgment, these 12 women represented the population adequately for the purposes of the research. We must quickly point out, however, that the intent of this focus group was far different from that of a survey. Consequently, the use of a purposive sample was considered satisfactory for this particular phase in the research process for the snacks. The focus group findings served as the foundation for a large-scale regional survey conducted 2 months later that relied on a probability sampling method.

It might be surprising to learn that there are marketing research circumstances where nonprobability sampling is more appropriate than probability sampling. Marketing Research Insight 12.6 describes why purposive sampling is preferred and how it is applied in B2B marketing research situations.

REFERRAL SAMPLES. **Referral samples**, sometimes called "snowball samples," require respondents to provide the names of prospective respondents. Such samples begin when the researcher compiles a short list of possible respondents that is smaller than the total sample desired for the study. After respondents are interviewed, each is queried about the names of other possible respondents.[24] In this manner, additional respondents are referred by previous respondents. Or, as the other name implies, the sample grows just as a snowball grows when it is rolled downhill.

Referral samples are most appropriate when there is a limited and disappointingly short sample frame and when respondents can provide the names of others who would qualify for the survey. The nonprobability aspects of referral sampling come from the selectivity used throughout.

In a referral sample, respondents provide the names of their acquaintances.

The initial list may also be special in some way, and the primary means of adding people to the sample is by tapping the memories of those on the original list. Even though they rely heavily on social networks,[25] referral samples are often useful in industrial marketing research situations.[26]

MARKETING RESEARCH INSIGHT   Practical Application

12.6 Why Purposive Samples Are Appropriate for B2B Marketing Research

Most marketing research is consumer research where the focus is on individuals or households and their purchases of goods and services. In marketing jargon, this is "B2C" marketing, or business-to-consumers marketing. B2B marketing, or business-to-business marketing is a separate world. Because of the special characteristics and circumstances of B2B marketing research, nonprobability sampling is often the norm.[27] First, consider the special nature of B2B markets:

1. B2B markets exist on derived demand, meaning that it is important to comprehend the dynamics of end-user consumer markets for goods and services that underlie the ebb and flow of demand in the B2B market.
2. B2B markets are highly concentrated, meaning that the populations of buyers is small; a few firms account for a large majority of the sales, and information about the market is closely guarded by a few firms.
3. B2B markets have complex buying processes, meaning that it is absolutely critical to gather information from the "right" and most informative respondents.

These three characteristics argue loudly for the use of purposive sampling rather than random sampling. With purposive sampling, the B2B marketing researcher seeks to identify the most knowledgeable managers, executives, buyers, or persons in order to learn about the B2B market under study. Using the following approach of purposive sampling and feedback, the B2B market researcher can obtain information that converges on his or her critical questions:

1. Purposive sampling is done with the use of experts, meaning that the B2B marketing researcher seeks out those individuals who are judged knowledgeable about the B2B market in question. Because of the small industry size and its concentration, experts or otherwise highly informed individuals are often relatively easy to identify and approach.
2. Feedback is used to obtain a consensus. That is, the marketing research can identify a pool or small group of knowledgeable individuals with purposive sampling and through the following iterative process, fathom the general pattern or set of opinions that are agreed to by the experts. The process involves first gathering information from the experts and then creating a brief summary, including notations of differences of opinion. This summary is then communicated to the experts in the sample who modify, revise, or reaffirm their views. When the marketing researcher judges that sufficient consensus is reached, the information is generally believed to be reliable and valid even though only very small samples are used in this B2B research.

QUOTA SAMPLES. The **quota sample** establishes a specific quota—or percentage of the total sample—for various types of individuals to be interviewed. For example, a researcher may desire the sample to be 50% male and 50% female. As we indicated earlier, quota samples are commonly used by marketing researchers who rely on mall intercepts, a convenience sample method. The quotas are determined by the research objectives and are defined by the key characteristics used to identify the population. In quota sampling, a fieldworker is provided with screening criteria that will classify the potential respondent into a particular quota group. For example, if the interviewer is assigned to obtain a sample quota of 50 each for black females, black males, white females, and white males, the qualifying characteristics would be race and gender. If the fieldworkers are working mall intercepts, each would determine through visual inspection into which quota the prospective respondent falls and work toward filling the quota in each of the four groups. So a quota system reduces some of the nonrepresentativeness inherent in convenience samples.

Quota samples rely on key characteristics to define the composition of the sample.

Quota samples are best used by companies that have a firm grasp of the features characterizing the individuals they wish to study in a particular marketing research project. A large bank, for instance, might stipulate that the final sample be one-half adult males and one-half adult females because in the bank's understanding of its market, the customer base is equally divided between males and females. When done conscientiously and with a firm understanding of the population's quota characteristics, some researchers feel quota sampling can rival probability sampling. One researcher has commented, "Probability sampling is the recommended

Quota samples are appropriate when you have a detailed demographic profile of the population on which to base the sample.

method, but in the 'real world,' statistical inferences are often based on quota samples and other nonrandom sampling methods. Strangely, these heretical uses of statistical theory, in my experience, seem to work just as well as they do for 'purist' random samples."[28]

PICTORIAL REPRESENTATIONS OF NONPROBABILITY SAMPING METHODS. Figure 12.4 contains representations of each of the four types of nonprobability sample methods used in our fictitious satisfaction survey. Recall that the population in every instance is comprised of 25 consumers. One-fifth (20%) of the consumers are unsatisfied, two-fifths (40%) are satisfied,

FIGURE 12.4

Pictorial Representations of Nonprobability Sampling Methods

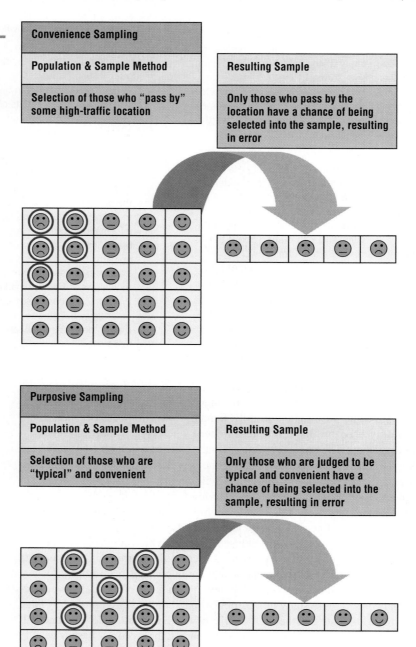

Convenience Sampling

Population & Sample Method

Selection of those who "pass by" some high-traffic location

Resulting Sample

Only those who pass by the location have a chance of being selected into the sample, resulting in error

Purposive Sampling

Population & Sample Method

Selection of those who are "typical" and convenient

Resulting Sample

Only those who are judged to be typical and convenient have a chance of being selected into the sample, resulting in error

FIGURE 12.4

(Continued)

Referral Sampling

Population & Sample Method

Selection based on the refererals of respondents who are selected arbitrarily

Resulting Sample

Only those who are in the social network have a chance of being selected into the sample, resulting in error

Quota Sampling

Population & Sample Method

Population distribution is classified by demographics and/or some consumer behavior variable(s).

Selection based on a quota system that ensures the population distribution, but from a convenient location like a shopping mall

Resulting Sample

Only those who pass by the convenient location have a chance of being selected into the sample, resulting in error

Men

Women

and two-fifths (40%) are indifferent or neutral about our brand. However, for each of the nonprobability sample methods (convenience sample, purposive sample, referral sample, and quota sample), the resulting satisfaction profile is a poor representation of the population. If you look at the selection specifics of any nonprobability sample method, the selections concentrate in specific areas of the population, which means that some members of the population have a disproportionate chance of being selected into the sample, resulting in sample selection error.

ONLINE SAMPLING TECHNIQUES

Because there has been so much emphasis on online surveys, some claim that they are unique. To be sure, the sampling done for Internet surveys poses special opportunities and challenges, but most of the issues can be addressed in the context of our probability and nonprobability sampling concepts.[29] The trick is to understand how the online sampling method works and to interpret the sampling procedure correctly with respect to basic sampling concepts.[30] Unfortunately, online sampling procedures are often not apparent or obvious until one delves into the mechanics of the sample selection process. To illustrate, we describe four types of online sampling: (1) random online intercept sampling, (2) invitation online sampling, (3) online panel sampling, and (4) other online sampling types.

Random Online Intercept Sampling

Random online intercept sampling relies on a random selection of website visitors. There are a number of Java-based or other html-embedded routines that will select website visitors on a random basis, such as time of day or random selection from the stream of site visitors. If the population is defined as website visitors, then this is a simple random sample of these visitors within the time frame of the survey. If the sample selection program starts randomly and incorporates a skip interval system, it is a systematic sample,[31] and if the sample program treats the population of website visitors like strata, it uses stratified simple random sampling as long as random selection procedures are faithfully followed. However, if the population is other than website visitors, and the site is used because there are many visitors, the sample is akin to a mall-intercept sample (convenience sample).

Invitation Online Sampling

Invitation online sampling alerts potential respondents that they may fill out a questionnaire hosted at a specific website.

Invitation online sampling alerts potential respondents that they may fill out a questionnaire hosted at a specific website.[32] For example, a retail store chain may hand out a notice to customers with their receipts notifying them that they may go online to fill out the questionnaire. However, to avoid spam, online researchers must have an established relationship with potential respondents who expect to receive an e-mail survey. If the retail store uses a random sampling approach such as systematic sampling, a probability sample will result. Similarly, if the e-mail list is a truly representative group of the population, and the procedures embody random selection, it will constitute a probability sample. However, if in either case there is some aspect of the selection procedure that eliminates population members or otherwise overrepresents elements of the population, the sample will be a nonprobability sample.[33]

A good example of a sampling system that overcomes this problem is Opinion Place[sm]. It uses a proprietary sampling method by which visitors learn about Opinion Place[sm] through promotions placed throughout America Online (AOL) properties, the Internet, and various rewards programs. Additionally, AOL members can access the area quickly through a permanent placement in AOL Member Perks or through AOL Keyword: Opinion Place. Visitors to Opinion Place[sm] proceed through a complex, sophisticated screening process to ensure random representation across all surveys.[34]

Online Panel Sampling

Online panel sampling involves representative samples of consumers organized by marketing research companies for the purpose of conducting online surveys.

Online panel sampling refers to consumer or other respondent panels that are set up by marketing research companies for the explicit purpose of conducting online surveys with representative samples.[35] Several companies conduct this type of survey using these preselected panels, which afford fast, convenient, and flexible access to the sample.[36] Typically, the panel company enlists several thousand individuals who are representative of a large geographic area; the market researcher can specify sample parameters, such as specific geographic representation, income, education, family characteristics, and so forth. The panel company then uses its database on its panel members to broadcast an e-mail notification to those panelists who qualify according to the sample parameters specified by the market researcher. Although online panel samples are not probability samples, they are used extensively by the marketing research industry.[37] One of the greatest pluses of online panels is the high response rate, which ensures that the final sample closely represents the population targeted by the researcher.

Other Online Sampling Approaches
Other online sampling approaches are feasible and limited only by the creativity of the sample designers. To identify the underlying sample method, you simply need to analyze the specifics of how potential respondents are selected. For instance, a respondent may be asked to forward the survey site to friends (referral sampling), or a survey page may pop up after every customer makes an online purchase (census). Regardless of the approach, if analyzed carefully in the context of the basic sampling techniques described in this chapter, you should be able to determine if the sample is a probability or a nonprobability sample.

DEVELOPING A SAMPLE PLAN

Up to this point, we have discussed various aspects of sampling as though they were discrete and seemingly unrelated decisions. However, they are logically joined together and there is a definite sequence of steps, called the **sample plan**, that the researcher goes through in order to draw and ultimately arrive at the final sample.[38] These steps are illustrated in Figure 12.5. Now that you are acquainted with the basic terms, definitions, and concepts involved with sampling, we can describe these steps in detail.

Step 1: Define the Population
As you know, the very first step to be considered in the sampling process requires a definition of the target population under study. We indicated earlier in the chapter that the target population is identified by the marketing research study objectives; however, typically at the beginning of the sampling phase of a research project, the focus on the relevant population

A sample plan begins with the population definition.

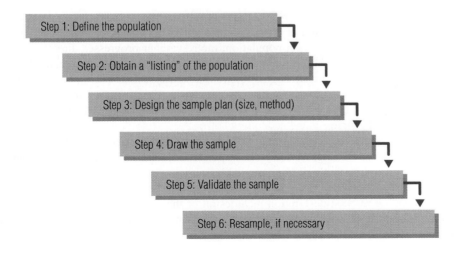

FIGURE 12.5

Steps in the Sampling Process

is necessarily sharpened. This sharpening involves the translation of vague descriptions of the target population into fairly specific demographic or other characteristics that separate the target population from other populations. The task here is for the researcher to specify the sample unit in the form of a precise description of the type of person to be surveyed.

For example, in an awareness survey of in-home Nordic Track treadmill models, the assumption might be that important descriptors helping to define the relevant population are that its members (1) own their own homes and (2) do not belong to fitness centers. A population description can result from previous studies, or it may be the result of the collective wisdom of marketing decision makers who have catered to a particular population for a number of years and have had the opportunity to observe members' behaviors and listen to their comments.

Step 2: Obtain a Listing of the Population (Sample Frame)

Once the population has been defined, the researcher begins searching for a suitable list to serve as the sample frame. In some studies, candidate lists are readily available in the form of databases of various sorts—company files or records, either public or private, that are made available to the researcher. In other instances, the listing is available at a price from a third party. Unfortunately, it is rare that a listing is perfectly faithful to the target population. Most lists suffer from sample frame error; or, as we noted earlier, the database does not contain a complete enumeration of members of the population. Alternatively, the listing may be a distorted accounting of the population in that some of those listed may not belong to it.

As a example, consider the use of a voter registration list as a sample frame for a survey about automobile driving. Refer back to Figure 12.1 and you will realize that the key to assessing sample frame error lies in two factors: (1) judging how different the people listed in the sample frame are from the population and (2) estimating what kinds of people in the population are not listed in the sample frame. With the first factor, screening questions at the beginning of an interview will usually suffice as a means of disqualifying those contacted who are not consistent with the population definition. As we noted in an earlier chapter, the percentage of people on a list who qualify as members of the population is referred to as the **incidence rate**. In our voter registration list example, it is a simple matter to use a qualifier question about whether or not the individual has a driver's license. Since most people in the United States drive, there should be a high incidence rate. However, not every driver is registered to vote, so some drivers would not be in the sample frame, but the sample frame error would be small. So voter registration records would serve as an acceptable sample frame for this survey. If the population is global and has a low incidence rate, researchers typically turn to compiled lists. Sampling companies such as Survey Sampling, Inc. have developed services to accommodate this especially problematic aspect of global marketing research.

Step 3: Design the Sample Plan (Size and Method)

Armed with a precise definition of the population and an understanding of the availability and condition of lists of the target population, the researcher progresses directly into the design of the sample itself. At this point, the costs of various data-collection methods come into play. That is, the researcher begins to simultaneously balance sample design, data-collection costs, and sample size. We discuss sample size determination in the next chapter, and you will learn that it is a trade-off between the desire for statistical precision and the requirements of efficiency and economy.

Regardless of the size of the sample, the specific sampling method or combination of sampling methods to be employed must be stipulated in detail by the researcher. There is no one "best" sampling method. The sample plan varies according to the objectives of the survey and its constraints.[39]

The sampling method description includes all of the steps necessary for drawing the sample. For instance, if we decided to use systematic sampling, the sampling method would detail the sample frame, the sample size, the skip interval, how the random starting point is

Lists to be considered as sample frames should be assessed in terms of sample frame error.

The percentage of people on a list who qualify as members of the population is referred to as the incident rate.

Sample size and sample method are separate steps in the sample plan.

to be determined, qualifying questions, recontacts, and replacement procedures. That is, all eventualities and contingencies should be foreseen and provisions should be made for each of them. These contingency plans are most apparent in the directions given to interviewers or provided to the data-collection company. Obviously, it is vital to the success of the survey that the sampling method be adhered to throughout the entire sampling process.

Step 4: Draw the Sample

Drawing the sample is a two-phase process. First, the sample unit must be selected. Second, information must be gained from that unit. Simply put, you need to choose a person and ask some questions. However, the question of substitutions arises.[40] Substitutions occur whenever an individual who was qualified to be in the sample proves to be unavailable, unwilling to respond, or unsuitable. The question here is "How is the substitution respondent determined?" If the marketing research project director wishes to ensure that a particular sampling method is used faithfully, the question of substitutions must be addressed. In practice, there are three substitution methods: drop-downs, oversampling, and resampling.

The **drop-down substitution** is used when the researcher has a convenient listing of the entire population. Let us say that we are using a telephone directory as our sample frame, and you are the interviewer who is instructed to call every 100th name. On your first call, the person qualifies but refuses to take part in the survey. If the drop-down method of substitution is in effect, you are trained to call the name immediately following the one you just called. You will not skip 100 names but just drop down to the next one below the refusal. If that person refuses to take part, you will drop down another name and so on until you find a cooperative respondent. Then you will resume the 100 skip interval, using the original name as your beginning point. Obviously, interviewers must be provided with the complete sample frame to use drop-down substitution.

Oversampling is an alternative substitution method, and it is used based on the researcher's knowledge of incidence rates, nonresponse rates, and unusable responses. For example, if the typical response rate for a mail survey questionnaire hovers around 20%, 1,000 potential respondents must be drawn into the mail-out sample in order to obtain a final sample of 200 respondents. Each data-collection method has its own separate oversampling implications, and it is up to the marketing research project director to apply wisdom and experience to determine the appropriate degree of oversampling. Otherwise, resampling will be necessary at a later point in the marketing research study in order to obtain the desired sample size.

Resampling constitutes a third means of respondent substitution. It is a procedure in which the sample frame is tapped for additional names after the initial sample is drawn. Here the response rate may turn out to be much lower than anticipated, and more prospective respondents must be drawn. Of course, ways must be found to avoid including in the resample prospective respondents who appeared in the original sample.

Substitutions in the sample may be effected with "drop-downs," oversampling, or resampling.

Incidence rates and response rates determine the need for sample substitutions.

Step 5: Validate the Sample

Typically, the final activity in the sampling process is the validation stage. **Sample validation** is a process whereby the researcher inspects some characteristic(s) of the sample to judge how well it represents the population. Sample validation can take a number of forms, one of which is to compare the sample's demographic profile with a known profile, such as the census. With quota sample validation, of course, the researcher must use a demographic characteristic other than those used to set up the quota system. The essence of sample validation is to assure the client that the sample is, in fact, a representative sample of the population about which the decision maker wishes to make decisions. Although not all researchers perform sample validation, it is recommended when prior knowledge exists about the population's demographic profile. When no such prior information exists, validation is not possible, and the sample selection method bears the full burden of convincing clients that the sample is representative of the population.

Sample validation assures the client that the sample is representative, but sample validation is not always possible.

SPSS Student Assistant:
Red Lobster: Recoding
and Computing Variables

Step 6: Resample If Necessary

When a sample fails the validation assessment, it means that it does not adequately represent the population. This problem may arise even when sample substitutions are incorporated.[41] Sometimes when this condition occurs, the researcher can use a weighting scheme in the tabulations and analyses to compensate for the misrepresentation. On the other hand, it is sometimes possible to perform resampling by selecting more respondents and adding them to the sample until a satisfactory level of validation is reached.

Summary

This chapter described various sampling methods. It began by acquainting you with various terms, such as *population, census,* and *sample frame.* A sample is taken because it is too costly to perform a census, and there is sufficient information in a sample to allow it to represent the population. We described four probability sampling methods in which there is a known chance of a member of the population being selected into the sample: (1) simple random sampling, (2) systematic sampling, (3) cluster sampling (using area sampling as an example), and (4) stratified sampling. We also described four nonprobability sampling methods: (1) convenience sampling, (2) purposive sampling, (3) referral sampling, and (4) quota sampling. Finally, we described six steps needed to develop a sample plan: (1) define the relevant population; (2) obtain a listing of the population; (3) design the sample plan (size and methods); (4) access the population; (5) draw the sample; (6) validate the sample; and (7) resample if necessary.

Key Terms

Population 338
Census 339
Sample 340
Sample unit 340
Sample frame 340
Sample frame error 340
Sampling error 341
Probability samples 342
Nonprobability samples 342
Simple random sampling 344
Random device method 344
Blind draw method 344
Random numbers 344
Random digit dialing (RDD) 346
Plus-one dialing procedure 346

Systematic sampling 347
Skip interval 347
Cluster sampling 349
Area sampling 349
One-step area sample 350
Two-step area sample 350
Stratified sampling 351
Skewed population 351
Strata 352
Weighted mean 352
Surrogate measure 353
Proportionate stratified sample 353
Disproportionate stratified sampling 353
Convenience samples 354

Purposive samples 358
Referral samples 358
Quota sample 359
Random online intercept sampling 362
Invitation online sampling 362
Online panel sampling 362
Sample plan 363
Incidence rate 364
Drop-down substitution 365
Oversampling 365
Resampling 365
Sample validation 365

Review Questions/Applications

1. Distinguish between a nonprobability and a probability sampling method. Which one is the preferable method and why? Indicate the pros and cons associated with probability and nonprobability sampling methods.

2. List and describe briefly each of the probability sampling methods described in the chapter.

3. What is meant by the term *random*? Explain how each of the following embodies randomness: (a) a blind draw, (b) random digit dialing, and (c) use of a computer to generate random numbers.

4. In what ways is a systematic sample more efficient than a simple random sample? In what way is systematic sampling less representative of the population than simple random sampling?

5. Distinguish cluster sampling from simple random sampling. How are systematic sampling and cluster sampling related?

6. Differentiate one-step from two-step area sampling and indicate when each one is preferred.

7. What is meant by a "skewed" population? Illustrate what you think is a skewed population distribution variable and what it looks like.

8. What are some alternative online sampling methods? Describe each one.

9. Briefly describe each of the four nonprobability sampling methods.

10. Why is quota sampling often used with a convenience sampling method such as mall intercepts?

11. Describe each of the three methods of substitution for individuals who are selected into the sample but refuse to participate in the survey or who did not qualify.

12. Provide the marketing researcher's definitions for each of the following populations:

 a. Columbia House, a mail-order house specializing in movies and television DVDs and music CDs, wants to determine interest in a 12-for-1 offer on its CDs to new members.

 b. The manager of your student union is interested in determining if students desire a "universal" debit ID card that will be accepted anywhere on campus and in many stores off campus.

 c. Joy Manufacturing Company decides to conduct a survey to determine the sales potential of a new type of air compressor used by construction companies.

13. Here are four populations and a potential sample frame for each one. For each pair, identify (1) members of the population who are not in the sample frame and (2) sample frame items that are not part of the population. Also, for each one, would you judge the amount of sample frame error to be acceptable or unacceptable?

Population	Sample Frame
a. Buyers of Scope mouthwash	Mailing list of *Consumer Reports* subscribers
b. Listeners to a particular FM radio classical music station	Telephone directory in your city
c. Prospective buyers of a new day planner and prospective clients tracking kit	Members of Sales and Marketing Executives International (a national organization of sales managers)
d. Users of weatherproof decking materials (to build outdoor decks)	Individuals' names registered at a recent home and garden show

14. A market researcher is proposing a survey for the Big Tree Country Club, a private country club that is contemplating several changes in its layout to make the golf course of championship caliber. The researcher is considering three different sample designs as a way to draw a representative sample of the club's golfers. The three alternative designs are:

 a. Station an interviewer at the tee on the first hole on one day chosen at random, with instructions to ask every 10th golfer to fill out a self-administered questionnaire.

 b. Put a stack of questionnaires on the counter where golfers check in and pay for their golf carts. There would be a sign above the questionnaires, and there would be an incentive of a "free dinner in the clubhouse" for three players who fill out the questionnaires and whose names are selected by a lottery.

 c. Using the city telephone directory and a plus-one dialing procedure, a random page in the directory and a name on that page would be selected, both by means of a table of random numbers. The plus-one system would be applied to that name and every name listed after it until 1,000 golfers are identified and interviewed by telephone.

 Assess representativeness and other issues associated with this sample problem. Be sure to identify the sample method being contemplated in each case. Which sample method do you recommend using and why?

15. A researcher has the task of estimating how many units of a new, revolutionary photocopy machine (it does not require ink cartridges and is guaranteed not to jam) will be purchased by business firms in Cleveland, Ohio for the upcoming annual sales forecast. She is going to ask about their likelihood of purchasing the new device, and for those "very likely" to purchase, she wants respondents to estimate how many machines their company will buy. She has data that will allow her to divide the companies into small, medium, and large firms based on number of employees at the Cleveland office.

 a. What sampling plan should be used?

 b. Why?

16. Honda USA is interested in learning what its 550 U.S. dealers think about a new service program Honda provided to the dealers at the beginning of last year. Honda USA wants to know if the dealers

are using the program and, if so, what they like and dislike about the program. Honda USA does not want to survey all 550 dealers but wants to ensure that the results are representative of all the dealers.

a. What sampling plan should be used?

b. Why?

17. Applebee's Restaurants has spent several thousand dollars advertising the restaurant during the last 2 years. The company wishes to get some information about what effect the advertising has had and decides to measure TOMA (Top of Mind Awareness). A TOMA "score" for such a restaurant is the ranking a firm has as a result of asking a representative sample of consumers in the service area to "name a non–fast-food restaurant." The restaurant named by the most persons has the #1 TOMA score and so on. It is important that Applebee's management conduct the TOMA survey with a representative sample in the metropolitan area.

a. What sampling plan should be used?

b. Why?

18. Belk has a chain of department stores in the United States. Top management requires that each store manager collect, maintain, and respond to customer complaint letters and calls. Each store keeps a file of these complaint letters. Top management is *considering* establishing a more formalized method of monitoring and evaluating the responses managers make to the complaint letters. Management wants some information that will indicate whether or not it needs to develop a formalized program or if it can leave well enough alone and allow store managers to use their discretion in handling the complaints. So top management wants to review a sample of these complaint letters and the responses to them.

a. What sampling plan should be used?

b. Why?

19. Jetadiah Brown wants to establish a pet store, to be called "Jet's Pets." Jet thinks there is an opportunity in the south side of the city because he knows that many new subdivisions have been built and many families have bought homes there. Plus, he knows that there are no pet stores located on the south side. The growth in the number of families and the fact that there are no competitors strongly suggest a marketing opportunity for Jet's Pets.

Jet wants to survey the families in two ZIP code areas. Of course, he cannot survey all of them, so he must use a sample. Below are possible ways of selecting a sample of the families living in several subdivisions in the two ZIP code areas. For each one: (1) identify the type of sample method, (2) identify the sample frame, (3) indicate the sample frame error, if any, and (4) indicate the degree to which the resulting sample will be representative of all families living in the two ZIP code areas.

a. Place questionnaires in veterinarian clinics located in the two ZIP code areas for patient owners to fill out while they are waiting for the doctor to examine their pet.

b. Select every 100th name in the city telephone book; call and interview only those who live in the two ZIP code areas.

c. Use a random number system to select a single subdivision located somewhere in the two ZIP code areas, and then place questionnaires in the mailboxes of every home in the selected subdivision.

d. Announce in the local newspaper a "Cutest Dog Contest" and have contestants send in a photo and address information. Use the contestants who live in the two ZIP code areas as the sample.

e. Get the addresses of past pet adopters who live in the two ZIP code areas from the local animal shelter. Send a mail survey to the nearest neighbor's address for each of the addresses obtained from the animal shelter. For example, if the adopter lives at 1 Green Street, send the mail questionnaire to the occupants at 2 Green Street.

CASE 12.1

PEACEFUL VALLEY SUBDIVISION: TROUBLE IN SUBURBIA

Located on the outskirts of a large city, the suburb of Peaceful Valley contains approximately 6,000 upscale homes. The subdivision came about 10 years ago when a developer built an earthen dam on Peaceful River and created Peaceful Lake, a meandering 20-acre body of water. The lake became the centerpiece of the development, and the first 1,000 one-half acre lots were sold as lakefront property.

Now Peaceful Valley is fully developed with 50 streets, all approximately the same length, with approximately 120 houses on each street. Peaceful Valley's residents are primarily young, professional, dual-income families with one or two school-age children.

But controversy has come to Peaceful Valley. The Suburb Steering Committee has recommended that the community build a swimming pool, tennis court, and a meeting room facility constructed on four adjoining vacant lots in the back of the subdivision. Construction cost estimates range from $1.5 million to $2 million, depending on how large the facility will be. Currently, every Peaceful Valley homeowner is billed $100 annually for maintenance, security, and upkeep of Peaceful Valley. About 75% of the residents pay this fee. To construct the proposed recreational facility, every Peaceful Valley household would be expected to pay a one-time fee of $500, and annual fees would increase to $250 based on facility maintenance cost estimates.

Objections to the recreational facility come from various quarters. For some, the one-time fee is unacceptable; for others, the notion of a recreational facility is not appealing. Some residents have their own swimming pools, belong to local tennis clubs, or otherwise have little use for a meeting room facility. Other Peaceful Valley homeowners see the recreational facility as a wonderful addition where their children could learn to swim, play tennis, or just hang out under supervision.

The president of the Peaceful Valley Suburb Association has decided to conduct a survey to poll the opinions and preferences of Peaceful Valley homeowners regarding the swimming pool, tennis court, and meeting room facility concept. Below are some possible sample methods. Indicate your reactions and answers to the questions associated with each one.

1. There is only one street into/out of the subdivision. The president is thinking that he can pay his teenage daughter to stand at the stoplight at the entrance to Peaceful Valley next week between the hours of 7 am and 8:30 am and hand out questionnaires to exiting drivers while they wait for the red light to change. The handouts would include addressed, postage-paid envelopes for returns. Identify what sample method the president would be using, list the pros and cons, and indicate how representative the resulting sample would be.

2. The chairperson of the Suburb Steering Committee thinks the 1,000 homeowners whose houses are on the waterfront properties of Peaceful Lake are the best ones to survey because they paid more for their lots; their houses are bigger, and they tend to have lived in Peaceful Valley longer than other residents. If these 1,000 homeowners are used for the sample, what would be the sample method involved, what are its pros and cons, and how representative would the resulting sample be?

3. Assume that the Steering Committee chairperson's point that the 1,000 waterfront owners are not the same as the 5,000 other Peaceful Valley Subdivision homeowners is true. How should this fact be used to draw a representative sample of the entire subdivision? Identify the probability sampling method that is most appropriate, and indicate, step-by-step, how it should be applied here.

4. How would you select a simple random sample of those Peaceful Valley homeowners who paid their subdivision association dues last year? What, if any, sample bias might result from this approach?

5. How could a two-step cluster sample be used here? Describe this sample method and how it could be used to select a representative sample of Peaceful Valley households.

HOW TO BECOME INVOLVED IN POLITICS USING A SAMPLING DESIGN

Note: this case is provided by Dr. Robert W. Armstrong, Professor of Marketing, University of North Alabama.

After graduating from North Alabama University, Jeff Jackson decided that he should use some of his marketing education and become involved in political polling research. Jeff had found to his surprise that his favorite course was marketing research. He had always viewed research as a painful experience where you would do some worthless literature review on some topic that held little interest. However, at UNA, Jeff found that if he did research in areas in which he was interested in the topic, he quite enjoyed

Dr. Robert W. Armstrong

the study. Jeff also had an interest in politics. He ran for student senate and was elected in his senior year. He also held office in his fraternity, Sigma Chi.

Since graduation, Jeff had not found a job in marketing research. His professor, Dr. Armstrong, recommended going to larger cities where demand would be greater. But Jeff had a local girlfriend and most of his family lived in the Florence area. So he really wanted to stay. One afternoon, Jeff received a call from a friend who worked for a law firm in Florence who wanted to talk to him about a short-run job. Jeff was intrigued. He knew nothing about law but a job is a job. He met with Jodie Powell, a local lawyer, who was fresh out of the University of Alabama.

At the meeting, Jodie told Jeff that his senior partner, Bob Steel, was thinking about running for mayor in the next election but was not sure how he would poll in the region. Jodie knew that Jeff was interested in politics and that he was good at marketing research, so he asked Jeff if he wanted to help with the election polling research. Jeff stated that he did not know very much about polling but was willing to learn and get some experience that may help his chances at a future job. Jodie asked Jeff to come in on Friday to meet with Bob Steel to discuss the necessary research.

After leaving Jodie's office, Jeff realized that he knew nothing about polling. He decided to call up his marketing research professor, Dr. Armstrong, to ask what he needed to learn to become a political researcher. Dr. Armstrong told him that he knew a great deal about political research in that it was a direct application of the marketing research method. He told Jeff that the key to good political research was a good sampling method. Also, Jeff needed to learn more about validity, both external and internal. Jeff studied these topics before his meeting with Bob Steel.

Bob Steel was a very nice man, who, like most politicians, had a way of making you like him right away. Bob talked to Jeff a few minutes about job hunting and the frustration and then got down to business. Bob asked Jeff what research he would conduct to determine his electability. This puzzled Jeff—he had expected Bob to give him explicit instructions on what he wanted researched. Jeff asked Bob who he wanted polled. Bob responded that he wanted to know if he would get elected if he ran against the current incumbent mayor. Bob told Jeff that he was happy to have him on the team and that they could meet next week to have further discussion on what needed to be done.

After Bob left the room, Jodie asked Jeff what ideas he had for the polling research. Jeff was somewhat confused; in class, Dr. Armstrong had told them what he wanted researched and gave out somewhat detailed research problems. Now it seems that Jeff would have to drive this project much more than he expected.

Jeff called another meeting with Dr. Armstrong, who was not at all surprised by the lack of direction and ambiguity of the politician. Dr. Armstrong told Jeff that he would have to diplomatically give guidance to Jodie and Bob regarding the polling research but to get much more specific regarding what they actually wanted researched.

In the week that followed, Jeff prepared for the meeting by researching the incumbent mayor's relative strengths and weaknesses based on in-depth interviews with some city officials and reviewing the last election's results. Jeff found the following:

1. The incumbent mayor was strong with higher socioeconomic status voters.
2. The incumbent mayor was strong with Baptist voters but did not fare as well with other religious groups.
3. The incumbent mayor was relatively weak in the county or in neighborhoods further from the city center.

The meeting day arrived and Jeff felt ready to do a better job. Bob asked Jeff to go over his findings and to recommend a polling research plan. Jeff said that given his preliminary results, they should use the voter registration lists to do a random sample of voters, asking whether voters would vote for Bob Steel and about their incomes, their religion, and address as given in the voter registration lists. Bob said that sounded great and asked Jeff to begin the research as soon as possible.

Jeff was pleased and developed a short, one-page questionnaire that asked the following questions:

1. Would you vote for Bob Steel for mayor in the next election?
2. What is your current family income?
3. What religious group do you belong to?

Jeff decided to do the survey over the phone since Bob wanted the results in 3 weeks so that he could decide whether to draw up a candidacy petition for the next election or not. Jeff went back to his frat to get a few volunteers to help him call. Jodie gave him a computer printout of the registered voters.

Jeff then was left with the problem of how to select a random sample. The printout had 20,000 names. Jeff had used a random number generator for a marketing research project at UNA and could not really enter all the names into the computer in 3 weeks and still do the survey. So, Jeff had a brilliant epiphany—he decided to throw a dart without looking at the computer readout and then drill a hole with an electric drill where the dart landed. He would survey every name above the hole; the total came to 133 names. He and his friends spent the next three nights surveying these names.

Jeff and friends found that many people would not answer the income question but would answer the other two questions. Jeff found that Bob Steel had a good chance, with 61% saying they would vote for him, and that religion did not matter much regarding voting preference. He reported this information to Bob Steel, who was excited and used this information to start his candidacy petition.

Questions

1. Critique Jeff's qualitative research on the incumbent's weaknesses.
2. What could Jeff have done to improve the quality of the questions in the questionnaire? What questions needed to be asked?
3. Was telephone data gathering the best way to conduct this research?
4. What sampling method was used? What sampling method should have been used? How could Jeff improve his technique?
5. Critique the findings.

CASE 12.3 Your Integrated Case

ADVANCED AUTOMOBILE CONCEPTS

After some deliberation, Cory Rogers of CMG Research and Nick Thomas of AAC have narrowed the data-collection method for Advanced Automobile Concepts survey down to the use of an online panel. With the data-collection method and questionnaire design settled, Advance Automobile Concepts is now confronted with the sample selection step in the marketing research process. Although the size of the sample is not precisely known, it is understood that it will be "quite large." However, the principals involved realize that a large sample size will be useless if the sample selection process fails to garner a representative sample.

With some thought and a bit of discussion, the principals have come to agreement that the population is all households in the United States. The major issue to be resolved in these population definition debates was whether or not to include individuals who do not own vehicles. Eventually, it was decided to include the nonowners, as the development and ultimate manufacture of the alternative-fuel models has a 5-year horizon, and it is possible that in that time period, the nonowners could move into the vehicle owner category. At the same time, the attractiveness of alternative-fuel vehicles may be great for vehicle nonowners, and it did not seem prudent to leave out this possibly significant segment of the potential vehicle-buying public. Recent census estimates are that the number of U.S. households is approximately 111 million units.

1. Specify the population definition.
2. If a probability sampling method is to be used, what would be a reasonable sample frame for:
   a. A telephone survey
   b. A mail survey
   c. An online survey
3. What are the practical problems involved with drawing a simple random sample of American households (regardless of the survey method)?
4. If random digit dialing was used for the sample plan, what are the advantages and disadvantages of this sample method?
5. Should Advanced Automobile Concept use a probability online panel such as the one maintained by Knowledge Networks, Inc? With respect to sample design, what are the advantages and disadvantages involved with using this approach? (You may want to review Knowledge Networks, Inc. services by visiting its website at www.knowledgenetworks.com.)

Learning Objectives

- To understand the eight axioms underlying sample size determination with a probability sample

- To know how to compute sample size using the confidence interval approach

- To become aware of practical considerations in sample size determination

- To be able to describe different methods used to decide sample size, including knowing whether or not a particular method is flawed

Doing a Telephone Survey? How Many Phone Numbers Will You Need?

Jim Follet, Survey Sampling International SSI by permission.

I n this chapter, you are going to learn how to determine an appropriate sample size, *n*. If you are doing a telephone survey, how many numbers will you need in order to obtain your desired *n*? To answer this question, we asked an expert, Jim Follet, at Survey Sampling International to tell you how it's done at the leading sample provider in the world.

You are going to learn how to calculate the size of a sample in this chapter. But, for a given sample size *n*, how many telephone numbers are you going to need? This may seem like a difficult task, but by following a few basic rules, it can become quite simple. To start, two pieces of information are required. The first is an estimate of the incidence of qualified individuals in the particular geographic frame you've selected. The second is an idea of how many qualified individuals contacted will actually complete the interview. We call these two pieces of information the "incidence rate" and the "completion rate." It's useful to be somewhat conservative in projecting these rates, since these figures are rarely known as facts until the survey has been completed.

Next, you must know the number of completed interviews required, or the *n*. Then, it's necessary to have information on what we call the "working phones rate." The working phones rate varies with the type of sample being used.

The equation we use to calculate the number of phone numbers needed for a project starts with the number of completed interviews required, *n*, divided by the working phones rate. That result is then divided by the incidence rate. Then, that quotient is divided by the contact and cooperation rates to determine the total number of numbers you will need for your project.

Survey Sampling International
Visit SSI at www.ssi.com.

SSI's Formula for Determining the Number of Telephone Numbers Needed

$$\text{Number of telephone numbers needed} = \frac{\text{completed interviews}}{\text{working phone rate} \times \text{incidence} \times \text{completion rate}}$$

where:

completed interviews = number of interviews required for a survey (*n*).

completion rate = percent of qualified respondents who complete the interview (taking into account circumstances such as refusals, answering machines, no answers, and busy signals).

working phone rate = percent of working residential telephone numbers for the entire sample. Rate varies by country and also depends on the selection methodology. Typically, in the United States, working phone rate ranges from 40% to 75%.

incidence = the percent of a group which qualifies to be selected into a sample (to participate in a survey). Qualification may be based on one or many criteria, such as age, income, product use, or where the respondent lives. The incidence varies depending on three factors specified by the client:

$$\text{Incidence} = \text{product incidence} \times \text{geographic incidence} \times \text{demographic incidence}$$

product incidence = percentage of respondents that qualify for a survey based on screening for things like product use, ailments, or a particular behavior.

geographic = likelihood of a respondent actually living in the targeted geographic area, incidence expressed as a percentage.

demographic incidence = percentage of respondents that qualify for a survey based on demographic criteria. The most common targets include age, income, and race.

For example, if 800 completed interviews are needed, the working phone rate is 60%, the incidence is 70%, and the completion rate is estimated to be 40%, 4,762 numbers should be ordered (800 / 0.60 / 0.70 / 0.40).

Marketing managers typically confuse sample size with sample representativeness.

In the previous chapter, you learned that the method of sample selection determines its representativeness. Unfortunately, many managers falsely believe that sample size and sample representativeness are related, but they are not. By studying this chapter, you will learn that the size of a sample directly affects its accuracy or error, which is completely different from representativeness.

Here is a way to convince yourself that there is no relationship between the size of a sample and its representativeness of the population from which it is drawn. Suppose we want to find out what percentage of the U.S. workforce dresses "business casual" most of the workweek. So we take a convenience sample by standing on a corner of Wall Street in New York City, and we ask everyone who will talk to us about whether or not they come to work in business casual dress. At the end of 1 week, we have questioned over 5,000 respondents in our survey. Are these people representative of the U.S. workforce population? No, of course they are not. In fact, they are not even representative of New York City workers because a nonprobability sampling method was used. What if we surveyed 10,000 New Yorkers with the same sample method? No matter what its size, the sample would still be unrepresentative for the same reason.

The selection method determines a sample's representativeness, not the size of the sample.

There are two important points. First, only a probability sample, typically referred to as a "random sample," is truly representative of the population, and second, the size of that random sample determines the sample's accuracy of findings.[1] **Sample accuracy** refers to how close a random sample's statistic (for example, percentage of "yes" answers to a particular question) is to the population's value (that is, the true percentage of agreement in the population) it represents. Sample size has a direct bearing on how accurate the sample's findings are relative to the true values in the population. If a random sample has

The accuracy of a sample is a measure of how closely it reports the true values of the population it represents.

5 respondents, it is more accurate than if it had only 1 respondent; 10 respondents are more accurate than 5 respondents; and so forth. Common sense tells us that larger random samples are more accurate than smaller random samples. But, as you will learn in this chapter, 5 is not 5 times more accurate than 1, and 10 is not twice as accurate as 5. The important points to remember at this time are that (1) sample method determines a sample's representativeness, while (2) sample size determines a random sample's accuracy. Precisely how accuracy is affected constitutes a major section of this chapter.

This chapter is concerned with methods of determining random sample size. To be sure, sample size determination can be a complicated process,[2,3,4] but we have tried to make it uncomplicated and intuitive. To begin, we share with you some axioms about sample size. These statements serve as the basis for the confidence interval approach, which is the best sample size determination method, so we describe its underlying notions of variability, allowable sample error, and level of confidence. These are combined into a simple formula to calculate sample size, and we give some examples of how the formula works. Next, we describe four other popular, but mostly incorrect, methods used to decide on a sample's size. Last, there are practical considerations and special situations that affect the final sample size, and we briefly mention some of these.

SAMPLE SIZE AXIOMS

How to determine the number of respondents in a particular sample is actually one of the simplest decisions within the marketing research process;[5] however, because formulas are used, it often appears bewildering. In reality, a sample size decision is usually a compromise between what is theoretically perfect and what is practically feasible. Although it is not the intent of this chapter to make you a sampling expert, it is important that you understand the fundamental concepts that underlie sample size decisions.[6]

There are two good reasons a marketing researcher should have a basic understanding of sample size determination. First, many practitioners have a **large sample size bias**, which is a false belief that sample size determines a sample's representativeness. Such practitioners ask questions such as "How large a sample should we have to be representative?" However, as you just learned, there is no relationship between sample size and representativeness. So, you already know one of the basics of sample size determination. Second, a marketing manager should have a basic understanding of sample size determination because the size of the sample is often a major cost factor, particularly for personal interviews but even with telephone surveys. Consequently, understanding how sample size is determined will help the manager better manage available resources.

The size of a sample has nothing to do with its representativeness. Sample size affects the sample accuracy.

TABLE 13.1   The Axioms of Random Sample Size and Sample Accuracy

1. The only perfectly accurate sample is a census.
2. A random sample will always have some inaccuracy, which is referred to as "sample error."
3. The larger a random sample is, the more accurate it is, meaning the less sample error it has.
4. Random sample accuracy (sample error) can be calculated with a simple formula and expressed as a ± % number.
5. You can take any finding in the survey, replicate the survey with the same random sample size, and "very likely" find the same results within the ± % range of the original sample's finding.
6. In almost all cases, the accuracy (sample error) of a random sample is independent of the size of the population.
7. A random sample size can be a very tiny percentage of the population size and still be very accurate (have little sample error).
8. The size of a random sample depends on the client's desired accuracy (acceptable sample error) balanced against the cost of data collection for that sample size.

We wish to contradict the large sample size bias of many marketing research clients with Table 13.1, which lists eight axioms about sample size and how this size relates to the accuracy of that sample. An axiom is a universal truth, meaning that the statement will always be correct. However, we must point out that these axioms pertain only to probability samples, so they are true only as long as the sample in question is a random one. Remember, no matter how any one of our statements astonishes you, it will always be true when dealing with a random sample. As we describe the confidence interval method of sample size determination, we will refer to each axiom in turn and help you understand it.

THE CONFIDENCE INTERVAL METHOD OF DETERMINING SAMPLE SIZE

The confidence interval approach is the most correct method by which to determine sample size.

The most correct method of determining sample size is the **confidence interval approach**, which applies the concepts of accuracy (sample error), variability, and confidence interval to create a "correct" sample size. It is the one used by national opinion polling companies and most marketing researchers. To describe the confidence interval approach to sample size determination, we first must describe the four underlying concepts.

Sample Size and Accuracy

The only perfectly accurate sample is a census.

The first axiom, "***The only perfectly accurate sample is a census***," is easy to understand. Accuracy is the complement of "sample error," meaning that with more accuracy, you have less error. So with perfect accuracy, you have zero sample error. You should be aware that a survey has two types of error: nonsampling error and sampling error. **Nonsampling error** pertains to all sources of error other than the sample selection method and sample size, so nonsampling error includes things such as problem specification mistakes, question bias, or incorrect analysis. In Chapter 12, you learned that **sampling error** involves sample selection method and sample size.[7] With a census, every member of the population is selected, so there is no error in selection. Because a census accounts for every single individual, it is perfectly accurate, meaning that it has no sample error whatsoever.

However, a census is almost always infeasible due to cost and for practical reasons. This fact brings us to the second axiom, "*A random sample will always have some inaccuracy which is referred to as 'sample error.'*" This axiom notifies you that no random sample is a perfect representation of the population. However, it is important to remember that a random sample is nonetheless a *very good* representation of the population, even if it is not perfectly accurate.

The third axiom, "*The larger a random sample is, the more accurate it is, meaning the less sample error it has*," serves notice that there is a relationship between sample size and the accuracy of that sample. This relationship is presented graphically in Figure 13.1.

FIGURE 13.1

Relationship between Sample Size and Sample Error

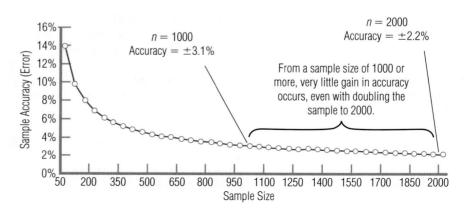

In the figure, sample accuracy (error) is listed on the vertical axis and sample size is noted on the horizontal one. The graph shows the accuracy levels of samples ranging in size from 50 to 2,000. The shape of the graph is consistent with the third axiom, as the sample error decreases the sample size increases. However, you should immediately notice that the graph is not a straight line. In other words, doubling sample size does not result in halving the sample error. The relationship is a curved one. It looks a bit like a ski jump lying on its back.

The larger the size of the (probability) sample, the less its sample error.

There is another important property of the sample error graph. As you look at the graph, note that at a sample size of around 1,000, the accuracy level is about ±3% (actually ±3.1%), and it decreases at a very slow rate with larger sample sizes. In other words, once a sample is greater than, say, 1,000, large gains in accuracy are not realized with large increases in the size of the sample. In fact, if it is already ±3.1% in accuracy, not much more accuracy is possible.

At the lower end of the sample size axis, however, large gains in accuracy can be made with a relatively small sample size increase. You can see this clearly by looking at the sample errors associated with smaller sample sizes in Table 13.2. For example, with a sample size of 50, the accuracy level is ±13.9%, whereas with a sample size of 200 it is ±6.9%, meaning the accuracy of the 200 sample is roughly double that of the 50 sample. But as was just described, such huge gains in accuracy are not the case at the other end of the sample size scale because of the nature of the curved relationship. You will see this fact if you compare the sample error of a sample size of 2,000 (±2.2%) to that of a sample size of 10,000 (±1.0%): With 8,000 more in the sample, we have improved the accuracy by only 1.2%. So, while the accuracy surely does increase with larger and larger sample sizes, there is only a minute gain in accuracy when these sizes are more than 1,000 respondents.

With a sample size of 1,000 or more, very little gain in accuracy occurs even with doubling or tripling the sample to 2,000 or 3,000.

The sample error values and the sample error graph were produced via the fourth axiom[8]: *"Probability sample accuracy (error) can be calculated with a simple formula, and expressed as a ± % number."* The formula follows:

Sample error formula $\pm \text{ Sample error } \% = 1.96 \times \sqrt{\dfrac{p*q}{n}}$

Yes, this formula is simple; "*n*" is the sample size, and there is a constant, 1.96. But what are *p* and *q*?

TABLE 13.2   Sample Sizes and Sample Error

Sample Size (n)	Sample Error (accuracy level)
10	±31.0%
50	±13.9%
100	±9.8%
200	±6.9%
400	±4.9%
500	±4.4%
750	±3.6%
1,000	±3.1%
1,500	±2.5%
2,000	±2.2%
5,000	±1.4%
10,000	±1.0%

p and *q*: The Concept of Variability

Let's set the scene. We have a population and we want to know what percentage of the population responds with a "yes" to a particular question. We will use a random sample to estimate the population percentage of "yes" answers. What are the possibilities? We might find 100% "yes's" in the sample; we might find 0% "yes's"; or we might find something in between, say, 50% "yes's" in the sample.

When we find a wide dispersion of responses—that is, when we do not find one response option accounting for a large number of respondents relative to the other items— we say that the results have much variability. **Variability** is defined as the amount of dissimilarity (or similarity) in respondents' answers to a particular question. If most respondents indicate the same answer on the response scale, the distribution has little variability because respondents are highly similar. On the other hand, if respondents are evenly spread across the question's response options, there is much variability because respondents are quite dissimilar. So, the cases of 100% and the 0% agreement have little variability because everyone answers the same, while the 50% in-between case has a great deal of variability because with any two respondents, one answers "yes" and the other answers "no."

You should realize that our sample error formula pertains only to nominal data, or data in which the response items are categorical. We recommend that you always think of a yes/no question such as we have described here. The greater the similarity, meaning the more that you find people saying "yes" in the population, the less the variability in the responses. For example, we may find that the question "The next time you order a pizza, will you use Domino's?" yields a 90% to 10% distribution split between "yes" versus "no." In other words, most of the respondents give the same answer, meaning that there is much similarity in the responses, and the variability is low. In contrast, if the question results in a 50–50 split, the overall response pattern is (maximally) dissimilar, and there is much variability. You can see the variability of responses in Figure 13.2. With the 90% to 10% split, the graph has one high side (90%) and one low side (10%), meaning almost everyone agrees on Domino's; with disagreement or much variability in people's answers, both sides are at even levels (50%–50%).

The Domino's Pizza example relates to *p* and *q* in the following way:

$$p = \text{percent saying "yes"}$$

$$q = 100\% - p, \text{ or percent saying "no"}$$

Variability refers to how similar or dissimilar responses are to a given question.

A 50–50 split in response signifies maximum variability (dissimilarity) in the population, whereas a 90–10 split signifies little variability.

The more variability in the population, the larger will be the required sample size.

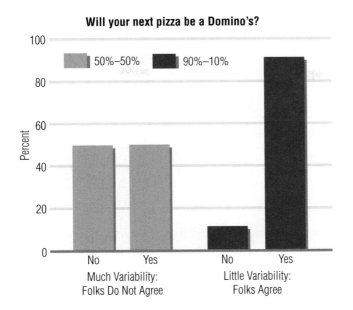

FIGURE 13.2

Amount of Variability is Reflected in the Spread of the Distribution

In other words, p and q will always sum to 100%, as in the cases of 90% + 10% and 50% + 50%.

In our sample error fomula, p and q are multiplied together. The largest possible product of p times q is 2,500, or 50% times 50%. You can verify this fact by multiplying other combinations of p and q, such as 90×10 (900), 80×20 (1,600), or 60×40 (2,400). Every one will have a result smaller than 2,500, and, in fact, the most lopsided combination of 99×1 (99) yields the smallest product. So, if we assume the worst possible case of maximum variability or 50–50 disagreement, the sample error formula becomes even simpler and can be given with two constants, 1.96 and 2,500, as follows:

Sample error fomula with $p = 50\%$ and $q = 50\%$ $\pm$ Sample error % = $1.96 \times \sqrt{\dfrac{2,500}{n}}$

This is the formula we used to create the sample error graph in Figure 13.1 and the sample error percentages in Table 13.2. To determine how much sample error is associated with a random sample of a given size, all you need to do is to "plug in" the sample size in this fomula.

The Concept of a Confidence Interval

The fifth sample size axiom states, *"You can take any finding in the survey, replicate the survey with the same random sample size, and "very likely" find the same results within the $\pm \%$ range of the original finding."* This axiom is based on the concept of a "confidence interval."

A **confidence interval** is a range whose endpoints define a certain percentage of the responses to a question. A confidence interval is based on the normal, or bell-shaped, curve commonly found in statistics. Figure 13.3 reveals that the properties of the normal curve are such that 1.96 times the standard deviation theoretically defines the endpoints for 95% of the distribution.

The theory called the **central limit theorem** underlies many statistical concepts, and it is the basis of the fifth axiom. A replication is a repeat of the original, so if we repeated our Domino's survey a great many times—perhaps 1,000—with a fresh random sample of the same size, and we made a bar chart of all 1,000 "yes" results, the central limit theorem

A confidence interval defines endpoints based on knowledge of the area under a bell-shaped curve.

FIGURE 13.3

Normal Curves with its 95% Properties

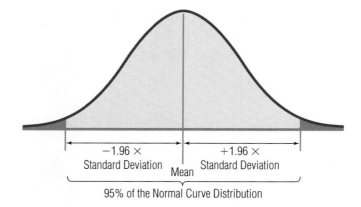

holds that our bar chart would look like a normal curve. Figure 13.4 illustrates how the bar chart would look if 50% of our population members intended to use Domino's the next time they ordered a pizza.

Figure 13.4 reveals that 95% of the replications fall within ±1.96 times the sample error. In our example, 1,000 random samples, each with sample size (n) equal to 100, were taken, the percentage of "yes" answers was calculated for each sample, and all of these were plotted in a line chart. The sample error for a sample size of 100 is calculated as follows:

Sample error formula with $p = 50\%$, $q = 50\%$, and $n = 100$

$$\pm \text{Sample error } \% = 1.96 \times \sqrt{\frac{2{,}500}{n}}$$
$$= 1.96 \times \sqrt{\frac{2500}{100}}$$
$$= 1.96 \times \sqrt{25}$$
$$= 1.96 \times 5$$
$$= \pm 9.8\%$$

which means that the limits of the 95% confidence interval in our example are 50% ± 9.8%, or 40.2% to 59.8%.

The confidence interval is calculated as follows:

Confidence interval formula   Confidence interval $= p \pm$ sample error

How can a researcher use the confidence interval? This is a good time to leave the theoretical and move to the practical aspects of sample size. The confidence interval

FIGURE 13.4

Plotting the Findings of 1,000 Replications of the Domino's Pizza Survey

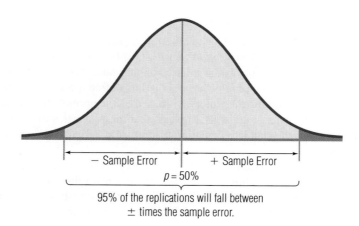

Sample Size   Sampling Distribution (Reflective of Sample Error)

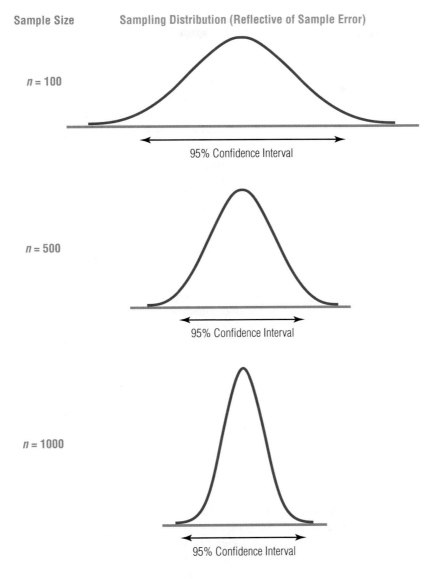

approach allows the researcher to predict what would be found if a survey were replicated many, many times. Of course, no client would agree to the cost of 1,000 replications, but the researcher can say, "I found that 50% of the sample intends to order Domino's the next time. I am very confident that the true population percentage is between 40.2% and 59.8%; in fact, I am confident that if I did this survey over 1,000 times, 95% of the findings will fall in this range." Notice that the 1,000 replications are never done; the researcher just uses one random sample, uses this sample's accuracy information from p and q, and applies the central limit theorem assumptions to calculate the confidence intervals.

What if the confidence interval was too wide? That is, what if the client felt that a range from about 40% to 60% was not precise enough? Figure 13.5 shows how the sample size affects the shape of the theoretical sampling distribution, and, more important, the confidence interval range. Notice in Figure 13.5 that the larger the sample, the smaller the range of the confidence interval. Why? Because larger sample sizes have less sample error, meaning that they are more accurate, and the range or width of the confidence interval is the smaller than with more accurate samples.

The confidence interval gives the range of findings if the survey were replicated many, many times with the identical sample size.

**How Does the Level of Confidence
Affect the Sample Accuracy Curve?**

Thus far, the sample error formula has used a constant of 1.96 which corresponds to the statistician's "z" value for a 95% level of confidence. However, there is another level of confidence sometimes used by marketing researchers, and this is the 99% level of confidence with the corresponding z value of 2.58. For this active learning exercise, use the sample error formula with $p = 50\%$ and $q = 50\%$, but use a z value of 2.58, and calculate the sample error associated with sample sizes of:

Sample size (n)	Sample error (e)
100	±_____%
500	±_____%
1,000	±_____%
2,000	±_____%

Plot your computed sample error ± numbers that correspond to 99% confidence level sample sizes of 100, 500, 1,000, and 2,000 in Figure 13.1. Connect your four plotted points with a curved line similar to the one already in the graph. Use the percentages in Table 13.2 to draw a similar line for the 95% confidence level sample error values. Using your computations and the drawing you have just made, write down two things you can conclude about the effect of a level of confidence different from 95% on the amount of sample error with samples in the range of the horizontal axis in Figure 13.3.

1. _____

2. _____

How Population Size (*N*) Affects Sample Size

Perhaps you noticed something that is absent in all of these discussions and calculations, and that element is mentioned in the sixth sample size axiom, *"In almost all cases, the accuracy (sample error) of a random sample is independent of the size of the population."* Our formulas do not include *N*, the size of the population! We have been calculating sample error and confidence intervals without taking the size of the population into account. Does this mean that a sample of 100 will have the same sample error and confidence interval of ±9.8% for a population of 20 million people who watched the last SuperBowl, 2 million Kleenex tissue buyers, and 200,000 Scottish Terrier owners? Yes, it does. The only time that the population size is a consideration in sample size determination[9] is in the case of a "small population," and this possibility is discussed in the last section in this chapter.

With few exceptions, sample size and the size of the population are not related to each other.

Because the size of the sample is independent of the population size, the seventh sample size axiom, *"A random sample size can be a very tiny percentage of the population size and still be very accurate (have little sample error),"* can now be understood. National opinion polls tend to use sample sizes ranging from 1,000 to 1,200 people, meaning that the sample error is around ±3%, or highly accurate. In Table 13.2, you saw that a sample size of 5,000 yields an error of ±1.4%, which is a very small error level, yet 5,000 is less than 1% of 1 million, and a great many consumer markets—cola drinkers, condominium owners, debit card users, allergy sufferers, home gardners, Internet surfers, and so on—are each comprised of many millions of customers. Here is one more example to drive our point home: A sample of 500 is just as accurate for the entire population of China (1.3 billion people) as it is for Montgomery, Alabama (225,000 people) as long as a random sample is taken in both cases. In both cases, the sample error is $\pm 4.4\%$.

THE SAMPLE SIZE FORMULA

You are now acquainted with the basic concepts essential for understanding sample size determination using the confidence interval approach. To calculate the proper sample size for a survey, only three items are required: (1) the variability believed to be in the population, (2) the acceptable sample error, and (3) the level of confidence required in your estimates of the population values. This section will describe the formula used to compute sample size via the **Confidence Interval Method**. As we describe the formula, we will present some of the concepts you learned earlier a bit more formally.

To compute sample size, only three items are required: variability, acceptable sample error, and confidence level.

Determining Sample Size via the Confidence Interval Formula

As you would expect, there is a formula that includes our three required items.[10] When considering a percentage, the formula is as follows[11]:

Standard sample size formula $\quad n = \dfrac{z^2(pq)}{e^2}$

where
- $n =$ the sample size
- $z =$ standard error associated with the chosen level of confidence (typically, 1.96)
- $p =$ estimated percent in the population
- $q = 100 - p$
- $e =$ acceptable sample error expressed as a percent

VARIABILITY: $p \times q$. This sample size formula is used if we are focusing on some nominally scaled question in the survey. For instance, when conducting our Domino's Pizza survey, our major concern might be the percentage of pizza buyers who intend to buy Domino's. If no one is uncertain, there are two possible answers: those who do and those who do not. Earlier, we illustrated that if our pizza buyers population has very little variability, that is, if almost everyone, say 90%, is a Domino's Pizza-holic, this belief will be reflected in the sample size formula calculation. With little variation in the population, we know that we can take smaller samples because this is accommodated in the formula by $p \times q$. The estimated percent in the population, p, is the mechanism that performs this translation along with q, which is always determined by p, as $q = 100\% - p$.

The standard sample size formula is applicable if you are concerned with the nominally scaled questions in the survey such as "yes or no" questions.

ACCEPTABLE SAMPLE ERROR: e. The formula includes another factor—acceptable sample error. **Acceptable sample error** is the term e, which is the amount of sample error that the researcher will permit to be associated with the survey. Notice that since we are calulating the sample size n, the sample error is treated as a variable, meaning that the researcher (and client) will decide on some desirable or allowable level of sample error and then calculate the sample size that will guarantee that the acceptable sample error will be delivered. Recall that sample error is used to indicate how closely to the population percentage you want the many, many replications, if you were to take them.

That is, if we performed any survey with a p value that was to be estimated—who intends to buy from Wal-Mart, IBM, Shell, Allstate, or any other vendor versus any other vendor—the acceptable sample error notion would hold. Small acceptable sample error translates into a low percentage, such as $\pm 3\%$ or less, whereas high acceptable sample error translates into a large percentage, such as $\pm 10\%$ or higher.

Managers sometimes find it unbelievable that a sample can be small yet highly accurate.

In marketing research, a 95% or 99% level of confidence is standard practice.

LEVEL OF CONFIDENCE: *z*. Last, we need to decide on a level of confidence, or, to relate to our previous section, the percentage of area under the normal curve described by our calculated confidence intervals. Thus far, we have used the constant 1.96, because 1.96 is the z value that pertains to 95% confidence intervals. Researchers typically only worry about the 95% or 99% level of confidence. The 95% level of confidence is by far the most common, so we used 1.96 in the examples earlier and referred to it as a constant because it is the chosen z in most cases. Also, 1.96 rounds up to 2, which is convenient in case you do not have a calculator handy and you want to do a quick approximation of the sample size.

Actually, any level of confidence ranging from 1% to 100% is possible, but you would need to consult a z table in order to find the corresponding value. Marketing researchers almost never deviate from 95%, but if they do, 99% is the level likely to be used. We have listed the z values for the 99% and 95% levels of confidence in Table 13.3 so you can turn to it quickly if you need to.

We are now finally ready to calculate sample size. Let us assume there is great expected variability ($p = 50\%$, $q = 50\%$) and we want $\pm 10\%$ acceptable sample error at the 95% level of confidence ($z = 1.96$). To determine the sample size needed, we calculate as follows:

Sample size computed with $p = 50\%$, $q = 50\%$, and $e = \pm 10\%$

$$n = \frac{1.96^2(50 \times 50)}{10^2}$$

$$= \frac{3.84(2,500)}{100}$$

$$= \frac{9,600}{100}$$

$$= 96$$

Just to convince you of the usefulness of the confidence interval approach, recall our previous comment that most national opinion polls use sample sizes of about 1,100 and they claim about $\pm 3\%$ accuracy (allowable sample error). Using the 95% level of confidence, the computations would be:

Sample size computed with $p = 50\%$, $q = 50\%$, and $e = 3\%$

$$n = \frac{1.96^2(50 \times 50)}{3^2}$$

$$= \frac{3.84(2,500)}{9}$$

$$= \frac{9,600}{9}$$

$$= 1067$$

TABLE 13.3   Values of z for 95% and 99% Levels of Confidence

Level of Confidence	z
95%	1.96
99%	2.58

In other words, if these national polls were to be ±3% percent accurate at the 95% confidence level, they would need to have sample sizes of 1,067 (or about 1,100 respondents). The next time you read in the newspaper or see on television something about a national opinion poll, check the sample size and look to see if there is a footnote or reference on the "margin of error." It is a good bet that you will find the error to be somewhere close to ±3% and the sample size to be in the 1,100 range.

What if the researcher wanted a 99% level of confidence in the estimates? The computations would be as follows:

99% confidence interval sample size computed with $p = 50\%$, $q = 50\%$, and $e = 3\%$

$$
\begin{aligned}
n &= \frac{2.58^2(50 \times 50)}{3^2} \\
&= \frac{6.66(2,500)}{9} \\
&= \frac{16,650}{9} \\
&= 1,850
\end{aligned}
$$

Thus, if a survey were to have ±3% allowable sample error at the 99% level of confidence, it would need to have a sample size of 1,850, assuming the maximum variability (50%).

 ## Sample Size Calculations Practice

While you surely can mentally follow the step-by-step sample size calculations examples we have just described, it is always more insightful for someone just learning about sample size to perform the calculations themselves. In this Active Learning exercise, refer back to the standard sample size formula and use it to calculate the appropriate sample size for each of the following five cases.

Case	Confidence Level	Value of p	Allowable Error	Sample Size (write your answer below)
A	95%	65%	±3.5%	_____
B	99%	75%	±3.5%	_____
C	95%	60%	±5%	_____
D	99%	70%	±5%	_____
E	95%	50%	±2%	_____
F	99%	55%	±2%	_____

A researcher can calculate sample size using either a percentage or a mean. We have just described and you have just used in the Active Learning exercises, the percentage approach to computing sample size. To learn how to determine sample size using a mean, study Marketing Research Insight 13.1. Although the formulas are different, the basic concepts involved are identical.

MARKETING RESEARCH INSIGHT   Practical Application

13.1 Determining Sample Size Using the Mean: An Example of Variability of a Scale

We have presented the standard sample size formula in this chapter, and it assumes that the researcher is working with a case of percentages (*p* and *q*). However, there are instances when the reseacher is more concerned with the mean of a variable, in which case the percentage sample size formula does not fit. Instead, the researcher must use a different formula for sample size that includes the variability expressed as a standard deviation. That is, this situation calls for the use of the standard deviation to indicate the amount of variation. In this case, the sample size formula changes slightly to the following:

Sample size formula for a mean

$$n = \frac{s^2 z^2}{e^2}$$

where:

    n = the sample size
    z = standard error associated with the chosen level of
        confidence (typically, 1.96)
    s = variability indicated by an estimated standard
        deviation
    e = the amount of precision or allowable error in the
        sample estimate of the population

    Although this formula looks different from the one for a percentage, it applies the same logic and key concepts in an identical manner.[12] As you can see, the formula determines sample size by multiplying the squares of the variability(*s*) and

level of confidence values (*z*) and dividing that product by the square of the desired precision value (*e*). First, let us look at how variability of the population is a part of the formula. It appears in the form of *s*, or the estimated standard deviation of the population. This means that, because we are going to estimate the population mean, we need to have some knowledge of, or at least a good guess at, how much variability there is in the population. We must use the standard deviation because it expresses this variation. Unfortunately, unlike our percentage sample size case, there is no "50% equals the most variation" counterpart, so we have to rely on some prior knowledge about the population for our estimate of the standard deviation.

    Next, we must express *e*, which is the acceptable error around the sample mean when we ultimately estimate the population mean from our survey. If information on the population variability is truly unknown and a pilot study is out of the question, a researcher can use a range estimate and knowledge that the range is approximated by the mean ±3 standard deviations. On occasion, marketing researchers find themselves working with metric scale data, not nominal data. For instance, the researcher might have a 10-point importance scale or a 7-point satisfaction scale that is the critical variable with respect to determining sample size.

    Suppose, for example, that a critical question on the survey involved a scale in which respondents rated their satisfaction with the client company's products on a scale of 1 to 10. If respondents use this scale, the theoretical range would be 10, and 10 divided by 6 (+ or −3 standard deviations approximates the range) equals a standard deviation of 1.7, which would be the variability estimate. Note that this would be a conservative estimate, as respondents might not use the entire 1–10 scale or the mean might not equal 5, the midpoint, meaning that 1.7 is the largest variability estimate possible in this case.[13]

PRACTICAL CONSIDERATIONS IN SAMPLE SIZE DETERMINATION

Although we have discussed how variability, acceptable sample error, and confidence level are used to calculate sample size, we have not discussed the criteria used by the marketing manager and researcher to determine these factors. General guidelines follow.

How to Estimate Variability in the Population

When using the standard sample size formula using percentages, there are two alternatives here: (1) expect the worst case or (2) guesstimate what the actual variability is. We have shown you that with percentages, the **worst case**, or most, **variability** is 50%/50%. This assumption is the most conservative one, and it will result in the calculation of the largest possible sample size.

The worst case, or most, variability is 50% for *p* and 50% for *q*.

On the other hand, a researcher may want to use an educated guess about p, or the percentage, in order to lower the sample size. Remember that any p/q combination other than 50%/50% will result in a lower calculated sample size because p times q is in the numerator of the formula. A lower sample size means less effort, time, and cost, so there are good reasons for a researcher to try to estimate p rather than to take the worst case.

Surprisingly, information about the target population often exists in many forms. There are census descriptions available in the form of secondary data, and there are compilations and bits of information that may be gained from groups such as chambers of commerce, local newspapers, state agencies, groups promoting commercial development, and a host of other similar organizations. Moreover, many populations under study by firms are known to them either formally through prior research studies or informally through prior business experiences. All of this information combines to help the research project director to grasp the variability in the population. If the project director has conflicting information, or is worried about the timeliness or some other aspect of the information about the population's variability, the director may conduct a pilot study in order to estimate p more confidently.[14,15]

By estimating p to be other than 50%, the researcher can reduce the sample size and save money.

To estimate variability, you can use prior research, experience, and/or intuition.

How to Determine the Amount of Acceptable Sample Error

The marketing manager intuitively knows that small samples are less accurate, on the average, than are large samples. But it is rare for a marketing manager to think in terms of sample error. So, it is almost always up to the researcher to educate the manager on what might be acceptable or "standard" sample error.

Translated in terms of accuracy, the more accurate the marketing decision maker desires the estimate to be, the larger must be the sample size. So, it is the task of the marketing research director to extract from the marketing decision maker the acceptable range of allowable error sufficient to make a decision. As you have learned, the acceptable sample error is specified as a plus or minus percent. That is, the researcher might say to the marketing decision maker, "I can deliver an estimate that is within ±10% of the actual figure." If the marketing manager is confused by this, the researcher can next say, "This means that if I find that 45% of the sample is thinking seriously about leaving your competitors and buying your brand, I will be telling you that I estimate that between 35% and 55% of your competitors' buyers are thinking about jumping over to be your customers." The conversation would continue until the marketing manager feels comfortable with the confidence interval range.

Marketing researchers often must help decision makers understand the implications of sample size in their requests for high precision, expressed as acceptable sample error.

How to Decide on the Level of Confidence

All marketing decisions are made under a certain amount of risk, and it is mandatory to incorporate the estimate of risk, or at least some sort of a notion of uncertainty, into sample size determination. Because sample statistics are estimates of population values, the proper approach is to use the sample information to generate a range in which the population value is anticipated to fall. Because the sampling process is imperfect, it is appropriate to use an estimate of sampling error in the calculation of this range. Using proper statistical terminology, the range is what we have called the confidence interval. The researcher reports the range and the confidence he or she has that the range includes the population figure.

As we have indicated, the typical approach in marketing research is to use the standard confidence interval of 95%. As we have also indicated, this level translates into a z of 1.96. As you may recall from your statistics course, any level of confidence between 1% and 99.9% is possible, but the only level of confidence that marketing researchers may consider is the 99% level. With the 99% level of confidence, the corresponding z value is 2.58. The 99% level of confidence means that if the survey were replicated many, many times with the sample size determined by using 2.58 in the sample size formula, 99% of the sample p's would fall in the sample error range.

Use of a 95% or 99% level of confidence is standard in sample size determination.

However since, the z value is in the numerator of the sample size formula, an increase from 1.96 to 2.58 will increase the sample size. In fact, for any given sample error, the use of a 99% level of confidence will increase the sample size by about 74%. So, using the 99% confidence level has profound effects on the calculated sample size. Are you surprised that most marketing researchers opt for a z of 1.96?

How to Balance Sample Size with the Cost of Data Collection

Perhaps you thought we had forgotten to comment on the last sample size axiom: *"The size of a random sample depends on the client's desired accuracy (acceptable sample error) balanced against the cost of data collection for that sample size."* This is a very important axiom because it describes the reality of almost all sample size determination decisions. We hope you will remember that in one of the very early chapters of this textbook, we commented on the cost of the research versus the value of the research, and that there was always a need to make sure that the cost of the research did not exceed the value of the information expected from that research.

In situations where data collection costs are significant, such as with personal interviews or in the case of buying access to online panel respondents, cost and value issues come into play vividly with sample size determination.[16] You just learned that using the 99% level confidence impacts the sample size considerably, and you also learned that for this reason marketing researchers almost always use the 95% level of confidence.

In order to help you understand how to balance sample size and cost, let's consider the typical sample size determination case. First, a 95% level of confidence is used, so z = 1.96. Next, the $p = q = 50\%$ situation is customarily assumed, as it is the worst possible case of variabilty. Then, the researcher and marketing manager decide on a *preliminary* acceptable sample error level. As an example, let's take the case of a researcher and a client initially agreeing to a $\pm 3.5\%$ sample error.

Using the sample size formula, the sample size, n, is calculated as follows:

Sample size computed with $p = 50\%$, $q = 50\%$, and $e = 3.5\%$

$$n = \frac{1.96^2(50 \times 50)}{3.5^2}$$
$$= \frac{3.84(2{,}500)}{12.25}$$
$$= \frac{9{,}600}{12.25}$$
$$= 784 \text{ (rounded up)}$$

If the cost per completed interview averages around $20, then the cost of data collection for a sample size is 784 times $20, which equals $15,680. The client now knows the sample size necessary for a $\pm 3.5\%$ sample error and that it will cost $15,680 for these interviews. If the client has issues with this cost, the researcher may create a table with alternative accuracy levels and their associated sample sizes based on knowledge of the standard sample size formula. The table could also include the data-collection cost estimates so that the client can make an informed decision on the acceptable sample size. Although not every researcher creates a table such as this, the acceptable sample errors and the costs of various sample sizes are most certainly discussed in order to come to an agreement on the survey's sample size. In most cases, the final agreed-to sample size is a trade-off between the acceptable error and the cost of the research. We have prepared Marketing Research Insight 13.2 as a lifelike depiction of how this trade-off occurs.

The researcher must take cost into consideration when determining sample size.

A table that relates data-collection cost and sample error is a useful tool when deciding the survey sample size.

MARKETING RESEARCH INSIGHT   Practical Insight

13.2 How the Clients and Marketing Researchers Agree on Sample Size

In this fictitious example, we describe how a sample size was determined for a survey for a water park that is thinking about adding an exciting new ride to be called "The Frantic Flume."

Larry, our marketing researcher, has worked with Dana, the water park owner, to develop the research objectives and basic research design for a survey to see if there is sufficient interest in the Frantic Flume ride. Yesterday, Dana indicated that she wanted to have an accuracy level of ±3.5% because this was "just a little less accurate than your typical national opinion poll."

Larry has done some calculations and created a table that he faxed to Dana. The table looks like this:

"The Frantic Flume" Survey: Sample Size, Sample Error and Sample Data Collection Cost

Sample Size	Sample Error	Sample Cost*
784	±3.5%	$15,680
600	±4.0%	$12,000
474	±4.5%	$9,480
384	±5.0%	$7,680
317	±5.5%	$6,340
267	±6.0%	$5,340

*Estimated at $20 per completed inverview.

The following telephone conversation now takes place:

LARRY: "Did the fax come through okay?"

DANA: "Yes, but maybe I wish it didn't."

LARRY: "What do you mean?"

DANA: "There is no way I am going to pay over $15,000 just for the data collection."

LARRY: "Yes, I figured this when we talked yesterday, but we were thinking about the accuracy of a national opinion poll then, but we are talking about your water park survey now. So, I prepared a schedule with some alternative sample sizes, their accuracy levels, and their costs."

DANA: "Gee, can you really get an accuracy level of ±6% with just 267 respondents? That seems like a very small sample."

LARRY: "Small in numbers, but it is still somewhat hefty in price, as the data-collection company will charge $20 per completed telephone interview. You can see that it will still amount to over $5,000."

DANA: "Well, that's nowhere near $15,000! What about the 384 size? It will come to $7,680 according to your table, and the accuracy is ±5%. How does the accuracy thing work again?"

LARRY: "If I find that, say 70% of the respondents in the random sample of your customers want The Frantic Flume at your water park, then you can be assured that between 65% to 75% of all of your customers want it."

DANA: "And with $7,680 for data collection, the whole survey comes in under $15,000?"

LARRY: "I am sure it will. If you want me to, I can calculate a firm total cost using the 384 sample size."

DANA: "Sounds like a winner to me. When can you get it to me?

LARRY: "I'll have the proposal completed by Friday. You can study it over the weekend."

DANA: "Great. I'll set up a tentative meeting with the investors for the middle of next week."

OTHER METHODS OF SAMPLE SIZE DETERMINATION

In practice, a number of different methods are used to determine sample size, including some that are beyond the scope of this textbook.[17] The more common methods are described briefly in this section. As you will soon learn, most have critical flaws that make them undesirable, even though you may find instances in which they are used and proponents who argue for their use. Since you are acquainted with the eight sample size axioms, and you know how to calculate sample size using the Confidence Interval Method formula, you should comprehend the flaws as we point each one out.

Arbitrary "Percent Rule of Thumb" Sample Size

Arbitrary sample size approaches rely on erroneous rules of thumb.

The **arbitrary approach** may take on the guise of a "percent rule of thumb" statement regarding sample size: "A sample should be at least 5% of the population in order to be accurate." In fact, it is not unusual for a marketing manager to respond to a marketing researcher's sample size recommendation by saying, "But that is less than 1% of the entire population!"

You must agree that the arbitrary percent rule-of-thumb approach certainly has some intuitive appeal in that it is very easy to remember and it is simple to apply. Surely, you will not fall into the seductive trap of the percent rule of thumb, for you understand that sample size is not related to population size at all. Just to convince youself, consider these sample sizes. If you take 5% samples of populations with sizes 10,000, 1,000,000, and 10,000,000, the *n*'s will be 500, 50,000, and 500,000, respectively. Now, think back to the sample accuracy graph (Figure 13.1). The highest sample size on that graph was 2,000, so obviously the percent rule-of-thumb method can yield sample sizes that are absurd with respect to accuracy. Further, you have also learned from the sample size axioms that a sample can be a very, very small percentage of the total population and have very great accuracy.

Arbitrary sample sizes are simple and easy to apply, but they are neither efficient nor economical.

In sum, arbitrary sample sizes are simple and easy to apply, but they are neither efficient nor economical. With sampling, we wish to draw a subset of the population in an thrifty manner and to estimate the population values with some predetermined degree of accuracy. Percent rule-of-thumb methods lose sight of the accuracy aspect of sampling; they certainly violate some of the axioms about sample size, and, as you just saw, they certainly are not cost-effective when the population under study is large.

Conventional Sample Size Specification

Using conventional sample size can result in a sample that may be too small or too large.

The **conventional approach** follows some "convention," or number believed somehow to be the right sample size. A manager may be knowledgeable about national opinion polls and notice that they often involve sample sizes of between 1,000 and 1,200 respondents. This may appear to be the "conventional" number, and the manager may question a marketing researcher whose sample size recommendation varies from this convention. On the other hand, the survey may be one in a series of studies a company has undertaken on a particular market, and the same sample size may be applied each succeeding year simply because it was used last year. The convention might be an average of the sample sizes of similar studies, it might be the largest sample size of previous surveys, or it might be equal to the sample size of a competitor's survey that the company somehow discovered.

Conventional sample sizes ignore the special circumstances of the survey at hand.

The basic difference between an "percent rule of thumb" and a "conventional" sample size determination is that the first approach has no defensible logic, whereas the conventional approach appears logical. However, the logic is faulty. We just illustrated how a percent rule-of-thumb approach, such as a 5% rule of thumb, explodes into huge sample sizes very quickly; however, the national opinion poll convention of 1,200 respondents would be constant regardless of the population size. Still, this characteristic is one of this method's weaknesses, for it assumes that the manager wants an accuracy of around ±3% and it assumes that there is maximum variability in the population.

Adopting past sample sizes or taking those used by other companies can be criticized as well, for both approaches assume that whoever determined sample size in the previous studies did so correctly (that is, not with a flawed method). If a flawed method was used, you simply perpetuate the error by copying it, and if the sample size method used was not flawed, the circumstances and assumptions surrounding the predecessor's survey may be very different from those encompassing the present one. So, the conventional sample size approach ignores the circumstances surrounding the study at hand and may well prove to be much more costly than would be the case if the sample size were determined correctly.

Statistical Analysis Requirements for Sample Size Specification

Sometimes the researcher's desire to use particular statistical techniques influences sample size.

On occasion, a sample's size will be determined using a **statistical analysis approach**, meaning that the researcher wishes to perform a particular type of data analysis that has

The conventional approach wrongly uses a "cookie cutter," resulting in the same sample size for every survey.

sample size requirements.[18] In truth, the sample size formulas in this chapter are appropriate for the simplest data analyses.[19] We have not discussed statistical procedures as yet in this text, but we can assure you that some advanced techniques require certain minimum sample sizes in order to be reliable or to safeguard the validity of their statistical results.[20] Sample sizes based on statistical analysis criteria can be quite large.[21]

Sometimes a research objective is to perform "subgroup analysis,"[22] which is an investigation of subsegments within the population. As you would expect, the desire to gain knowledge about subgroups has direct implications for sample size.[23] It should be possible to look at each subgroup as a separate population and to determine sample size for each subgroup, along with the appropriate methodology and other specifics to gain knowledge about that subgroup. That is, if you were to use the standard sample size formula described in this chapter to determine the sample size and more than one subgroup was to be analyzed fully, this objective would require a total sample size equal to the number of subgroups times the standard sample size formula's computed sample size.[24] Once this is accomplished, all of the subgroups can be combined into a large group in order to obtain a complete population picture.

Cost Basis of Sample Size Specification

Sometimes termed the **"all you can afford" approach**, cost can be the overriding basis for sample size. As you learned with our presentation of the eighth sample-size axiom, managers and marketing research professionals are vitally concerned with the costs of data collection, because they can mount quickly, particularly for personal interviews, telephone surveys, and even for mail surveys in which incentives are included in the envelopes mailed out. So it is not surprising that cost sometimes becomes the only basis for sample size.

Exactly how the "all you can afford" approach is applied varies a great deal. In some instances, the marketing research project budget is determined in advance, and set amounts are specified for each phase. The budget may provide, for instance, $10,000 for "interviewing," or it might specify $5,000 for "data collection." A variation is for the amount of the entire year's marketing research budget to be set, with each project receiving a slice of that total. With this approach, the marketing research project director is forced to stay within the total project budget but can allocate the money across the various cost elements. The sample size ends up being whatever is affordable within the budget.

But using the "all you can afford" sample size specification is a case of the tail wagging the dog. That is, instead of the value of the information to be gained from the survey being a

Using cost as the sole determinant of sample size may seem wise, but it is not.

MARKETING RESEARCH INSIGHT   Ethical Application

13.3 The Ethics of Sample Size

Marketing managers and other clients of marketing researchers do not have a thorough understanding of sample size. In fact, they tend to have a belief in a false "law of large sample size." That is, they often confuse the size of the sample with the representativeness of the sample. As you know from learning about sample selection procedures, the way the sample is selected determines its representativeness, not its size. Also, as you have just learned, the benefits of excessively large samples are typically not justified by their increased costs.

It is an ethical marketing researcher's responsibility to try to educate a client on the wastefulness of excessively large samples. Occasionally, there are good reasons for having a very large sample, but whenever the sample size exceeds that of a typical national opinion poll (1,200 respondents), justification is required. Otherwise, the manager's cost will be unnecessarily inflated. Unethical researchers may recommend very large samples as a way to increase their profits, which may be set at a percentage of the total cost of the survey. They may even have ownership in the data-collection company slated to gather the data at a set cost per respondent. It is important, therefore, that marketing managers know the motivations underlying the sample size recommendations of the researchers they hire.

The appropriateness of using cost as a basis for sample size depends on when cost factors are considered.

primary consideration in the sample size, the sample size is determined by budget factors that usually ignore the value of the survey's results to management, and this approach certainly does not consider sample accuracy at all. In fact, because many managers harbor a large sample size bias, it is possible that their marketing research project costs are overstated for data collection when smaller sample sizes could have sufficed quite well. As can be see in our Marketing Research Insight 13.3, unconscionable marketing researchers can use this bias selfishly.

Still, you know from the last sample size axiom, that you cannot decide on sample size without taking cost into consideration. The key is to remember *when* to consider cost. In the "all you can afford" examples just described, cost drives the sample size completely. When the researcher has $5,000 for interviewing and a data-collection company charges $25 per completed interview, the sample is set at 200 respondents. However, the correct approach is to consider cost relative to the value of the research to the manager. If the manager requires extremely precise information, the researcher will surely suggest a large sample and then estimate the cost of obtaining the sample. The manager, in turn, should then consider this cost in relation to how much the information is actually worth. Using the cost schedule concept, the researcher and manager can then discuss alternative sample sizes, different data-collection modes, costs, and other considerations. This is a healthier situation, for now the manager is assuming some ownership of the survey and a partnership arrangement is being forged between the manager and the researcher. The net result will be a better understanding on the part of the manager as to how and why the final sample size was determined. This way, cost will not be the only means of determining sample size, but it will be given the consideration it deserves.

TWO SPECIAL SAMPLE SIZE DETERMINATION SITUATIONS

The final section of this chapter takes up two special cases: sample size when sampling from small populations and sample size when using a nonprobability sampling method.

Sampling from Small Populations

Implicit to all sample size discussions thus far in this chapter is the assumption that the population is very large. This assumption is reasonable because there are multitudes of households in the United States, millions of registered drivers, hundreds of thousands of persons over the age of 65, and so forth. So it is common, especially with consumer goods and services marketers, to draw samples from very large populations. Occasionally, however, the population is much smaller, which is not unusual in the case of B2B marketers. This case is addressed by the condition stipulated in our sixth sample size axiom, "*In almost all cases, the accuracy (sample error) of a random sample is independent of the size of the population.*"

As a general rule, a **small population** situation is one in which the sample exceeds 5% of the total population size. Notice that a small population is defined by the size of the sample under consideration. If the sample is less than 5% of the total population, you can consider the population to be of large size, and you can use the procedures described earlier in this chapter. On the other hand, if it is a small population, the sample size formula needs some adjustment with what is called a "**finite multiplier**," which is an adjustment factor that is approximately equal to the square root of that proportion of the population not included in the sample. For instance, suppose our population size was considered to be 1,000 companies and we decided to take a sample of 500. That would result in a finite multiplier of about 0.71, or the square root of 0.5, which is calculated as (1,000 − 500)/1,000. We could use a sample of only 355 (or 0.71 times 500) companies, and it would be just as accurate as one of size 500 if we had a large population.

The formula for computation of a sample size using the finite multiplier is as follows:

Even with Survey Sampling's B2B service, the population may be small.

Small population sample size formula   Small population sample size = sample size formula $n \times \sqrt{\dfrac{N - n}{N - 1}}$

Here is an example using the 1,000-company population. Let us suppose we want to know the percentage of companies that are interested in a substance abuse counseling program for their employees offered by a local hospital. We are uncertain about the variability, so we use our 50–50 "worst case" approach. We decide to use a 95% level of confidence, and the director of counseling services at Claremont Hospital would like the results to be accurate to ±5%. The computations are as follows:

With small populations, you should use the finite multiplier to determine sample size.

Sample size computed with $p = 50\%$, $q = 50\%$, and $e = 5\%$

$$n = \frac{1.96^2(pq)}{e^2}$$
$$= \frac{1.96^2(50 \times 50)}{5^2}$$
$$= \frac{3.84(2{,}500)}{25}$$
$$= \frac{9{,}600}{25}$$
$$= 384$$

Now, applying the finite multiplier to adjust the sample size for a small population:

**Example:
Sample size formula to adjust for a small population size**

$$\text{Small size population sample} = n\sqrt{\frac{N - n}{N - 1}}$$
$$= 384\sqrt{\frac{1{,}000 - 384}{1{,}000 - 1}}$$
$$= 384\sqrt{\frac{616}{999}}$$
$$= 384\sqrt{0.62}$$
$$= 384 \times 0.79$$
$$= 303$$

In other words, we need a sample size of 303, not 384, because we are working with a small population. By applying the finite multiplier, we can reduce the sample size by 81 respondents and achieve the same accuracy level. If this survey required personal interviews, we would gain a considerable cost savings.

Appropriate use of the finite multiplier formula will reduce a calculated sample size and save money when performing research on small populations.

Sample Size Using Nonprobability Sampling

All sample size formulas and other statistical considerations treated in this chapter assume that some form of probability sampling method has been used. In other words, the sample must be random with regard to selection, and the only sampling error present is due to sample size. Remember, sample size determines the accuracy, not the representativeness, of the sample. The sampling method determines the representativeness. All sample size formulas assume that representativeness is guaranteed with use of a random sampling procedure.

The only reasonable way of determining sample size with nonprobability sampling is to weigh the benefit or value of the information obtained with that sample against the cost of gathering that information. Ultimately, this is a very subjective exercise, as the manager may place significant value on the information for a number or reasons. For instance, the information may crystallize the problem, it may open the manager's eyes to vital additional considerations, or it might even make him or her aware of previously unknown market segments. But because of the unknown bias introduced by a haphazard sample selection[25] process, it is inappropriate to apply sample size formulas. For nonprobability sampling, sample size is a judgment based almost exclusively on the value of the biased information to the manager, rather than desired precision, relative to cost.

> When using nonprobability sampling, sample size is unrelated to accuracy, so cost–benefit considerations must be used.

SPSS Student Assistant:
Noxzema Skin Cream:
Selecting Cases

 Synthesize Your Learning

This exercise will require you to take into consideration concepts and material from these two chapters:

Chapter 12	Determining How to Select a Sample
Chapter 13	Determining the Size of a Sample

Niagara Falls Tourism Association

One of the most popular tourist destinations in the United States is Niagara Falls, located on the U.S.–Canada border in northern New York. An estimated 10 to 12 million visitors see Niagara Falls per year. However, although its attractiveness has not changed, environmental factors have recently threatened to significantly decrease these numbers. There are at least three factors at work: (1) the sharp increase in gasoline prices, (2) the substantial weakening of the U.S. economy, and (3) increased competition from beefed-up marketing efforts of other tourist attractions in the United States who are experiencing declines due to factors (1) and (2).

A large majority of Niagara Falls visitors are Americans who drive to the location, so gasoline costs and family financial worries have the Niagara Falls Tourism Association especially concerned. The association represents all types of businesses in the greater Niagara area that rely on tourism to survive. Among their members are 80 hotels that account for approximately 16,000 rooms. The hotels have anywhere from 20 to 600 rooms, with a large majority (about 80%, accounting for 30% of the rooms) being local and smaller, and the larger ones (the remaining 20%, accounting for 70% of the rooms) being national chains and larger. For all hotels in the area, occupancy at peak season (June 15–September 15) averages around 90%. The association wants to conduct a survey of present visitors to find out their overall satisfaction with the visit to the Niagara area and their intentions to tell their friends, relatives, and coworkers to visit Niagara Falls. The association has designed a face-to-face interview questionnaire, and it has issued a Request for Proposals for sample design. It has received three bids, and each one is described below.

Bid #1. The Maid of the Mist union—employees of the company that operates the boats the take tourists on the Niagara River to view and experience the falls—proposes to do the interviews with tourists who are waiting for the Maid boats to return and load up. Union employees will conduct interviews with 1,000 adult American tourists (1 per family group) during a 1-week period in July at $3 per completed interview.

Bid #2. The Simpson Research Company—a local marketing research company—proposes to take a sample of the five of the largest association member hotels and conduct 200 interviews in the lobbies of these hotels with American tourists (1 per family) during the months of July and August at a cost of $5 per completed interview.

Bid #3. The SUNY–Niagara Marketing Department—an academic unit in the local university—proposes to randomly select 20 hotels from *all* the hotels in the area (not just those belonging to the Tourism Association) and to then select a proportional random sample of rooms, using room numbers, from each selected hotel based on hotel room capacities. It will interview 750 American tourists (1 per family) in their rooms during the time period of June 15–September 15 at a cost of $10 per completed interview.

Questions

1. What is the sample frame in each bid?
2. Identify the type of sample method and assess the representativeness of the sample with respect to American tourists visiting the Niagara Falls area.
3. Evaluate the accuracy (sample error) with each bid.
4. The Niagara Falls Tourism Association has budgeted $5,000 for data collection in this survey. Using information from your answers to Questions 1–3, and further considering the total cost of data collection, which one of the proposals do you recommend that the Niagara Falls Tourist Association accept? Justify your recommendation

Summary

We began this chapter by notifying you of the "large sample size" bias that many managers hold. To counter this myth, we listed eight sample size axioms that relate the size of a random sample to its accuracy, or closeness of its findings to the true population value. These axioms were used to describe the method of confidence interval sample size determination, which is the most correct method because it relies on statistical concepts of variability, confidence intervals, and sample error. From the descriptions of these concepts, we moved to the standard sample size formula used by market researchers. This formula uses variability ($p \times q$), level of confidence (z), and acceptable sample error (e) to compute the sample size, n. We indicated that for the confidence level, typically 95% or 99% levels are applied. These equate to z values of 1.96 and 2.58, respectively. For variability with percentage estimates, the researcher can fall back on a 50–50 split, which is

the greatest variability case possible. The standard sample size formula is best considered a starting point for deciding the final sample size, for data collection costs must be taken into consideration. Normally, the researcher and manager will discuss the alternative sample error levels and their associated data-collection costs to come to agreement on a final acceptable sample size.

Although most are flawed, there are other methods of determining sample size: (1) designating size arbitrarily, (2) using a "conventional" size, (3) basing size on the requirements of statistical procedures to be used, and (4) letting cost determine the size. Finally, the chapter discussed two special sampling situations. With a small population, the finite multiplier should be used to adjust the sample size determination formula. Last, with nonprobability sampling, a cost–benefits analysis should take place.

Key Terms

Sample accuracy 374
Large sample size bias 375
Confidence interval approach 376
Nonsampling error 376
Sampling error 376
Variability 378

Confidence interval 379
Central limit theorem 379
Confidence Interval Method 383
Acceptable sample error 383
Worst case variability 386
Arbitrary approach 390

Conventional approach 390
Statistical analysis approach 390
"All you can afford" approach 391
Small population 393
Finite multiplier 393

Review Questions/Applications

1. Describe each of the following methods of sample size determination and indicate a critical flaw in the use of each one.
   a. Using a "rule of thumb" percentage of the population size.
   b. Using a "conventional" sample size such as the typical size pollsters use.
   c. Using the amount in the budget allocated for data collection to determine sample size.

2. Describe and provide illustrations of each of the following notions: (a) variability, (b) confidence interval, and (c) acceptable sample error.

3. What are the three fundamental considerations involved with the confidence interval approach to sample size determination?

4. When calculating sample size, how can a researcher decide on the level of accuracy to use? What about level of confidence? What about variability with a percentage?

5. Using the formula provided in your text, determine the approximate sample sizes for each of the following cases, all with precision (allowable error) of ±5%:

   a. Variability of 30%, confidence level of 95%.

   b. Variability of 60%, confidence level of 99%.

   c. Unknown variability, confidence level of 95%.

6. Indicate how a pilot study can help a researcher understand variability in the population.

7. Why is it important for the researcher and the marketing manager to discuss the accuracy level associated with the research project at hand?

8. What are the benefits to be gained by knowing that a proposed sample is more than 5% of the total population's size? In what marketing situation might this be a common occurrence?

9. A researcher knows from experience the average costs of various data collection alternatives:

Data Collection Method	Cost/Respondent
Personal interview	$50
Telephone interview	$25
Mail survey	$0.50 (per mailout)

   If $2,500 is allocated in the research budget for data collection, what are the levels of accuracy for the sample sizes allowable for each data-collection method? Based on your findings, comment on the inappropriateness of using cost as the only means of determining sample size.

10. Last year, Lipton Tea Company conducted a mall-intercept study at six regional malls around the country and found that 20% of the public preferred tea over coffee as a midafternoon hot drink. This year, Lipton wants to have a nationwide telephone survey performed with random digit dialing. What sample size should be used in this year's study in order to achieve an accuracy level of ±2.5% at the 99% level

of confidence? What about at the 95% level of confidence?

11. Allbookstores.com has a used-textbook division. It buys its books in bulk from used-book buyers who set up kiosks on college campuses during final exams, and it sells the used textbooks to students who log on to the allbookstores.com website via a secured credit card transaction. The used texts are then sent by United Parcel Service to the student.

    The company has conducted a survey of used-book buying by college students each year for the past 4 years. In each survey, 1,000 randomly selected college students have been asked to indicate whether or not they bought a used textbook in the previous year. The results are as follows:

	Years Ago			
	1	2	3	4
Percent buying used text(s)	45%	50%	60%	70%

    What are the sample size implications of these data?

12. American Ceramics, Inc. (ACI) has been developing a new form of ceramic that can stand high temperatures and sustained use. Because of its improved properties, the project development engineer in charge of this project thinks that the new ceramic will compete as a substitute for the ceramics currently used in spark plugs. She talks to ACI's market research director about conducting a survey of prospective buyers of the new ceramic material. During their phone conversation, the research director suggests a study using about 100 companies as a means of determining market demand. Later that day, the research director does some background using the Thomas Register as a source of names of companies manufacturing spark plugs. A total of 312 companies located in the continental United States are found in the register. How should this finding impact the final sample size of the survey?

13. Here are some numbers that you can use to sharpen your computational skills for sample size determination. Crest toothpaste is reviewing plans for its annual survey of toothpaste purchasers. With each case below, calculate the sample size pertaining to the key variable under consideration. Where information is missing, provide reasonable assumptions.

Case	Key Variable	Variability	Acceptable Error	Confidence Level
a.	Market share of Crest toothpaste last year	23% share	4%	95%
b.	Percent of people who brush their teeth per week	Unknown	5%	99%
c.	How likely Crest buyers are to switch brands	30% switched last year	5%	95%
d.	Percent of people who want tartar-control features in their toothpaste	20% two years ago; 40% one year ago	3.5%	95%
e.	Willingness of people to adopt the toothpaste brand recommended by their family dentist	Unknown	6%	99%

14. Do managers really have a "large sample size bias"? Because you cannot survey managers easily, this exercise will use surrogates. Ask any five seniors majoring in business administration who have not taken a marketing research class the following questions. Indicate whether each of the following statements is true or false.

   a. A random sample of 500 is large enough to represent all of the full-time college students in the United States.

   b. A random sample of 1,000 is large enough to represent all of the full-time college students in the United States.

   c. A random sample of 2,000 is large enough to represent all of the full-time college students in the United States.

   d. A random sample of 5,000 is large enough to represent all of the full-time college students in the United States.

   What have you found out about sample size bias?

15. The following items pertain to determining sample size when a mean is involved. Calculate the sample size for each case.

Case	Key Variable	Standard Deviation	Acceptable Error	Confidence Level
A	Number of car rentals per year for business trip usage	10	2	95%
B	Number of songs downloaded with iTunes per month	20	2	95%
C	Number of miles driven per year to commute to work	500	50	99%
D	Use of a 9-point scale measuring satisfaction with the brand	2	0.3	95%

16. The Andrew Jergens Company markets a "spa tablet" called ActiBath, which is a carbonated moisturizing treatment for use in a bath. From previous research, Jergens management knows that 60% of all women use some form of skin moisturizer and 30% believe their skin is their most beautiful asset. There is some concern among management that women will associate the drying aspects of taking a bath with ActiBath and not believe that it can provide a skin moisturizing benefit. Can these facts about use of moisturizers and concern for skin beauty be used in determining the size of the sample in the ActiBath survey? If so, indicate how. If not, indicate why and how sample size can be determined.

17. Donald Heel is the Microwave Oven Division Manager of Sharp Products. Don proposes a $40 cash rebate program as a means of promoting Sharp's new crisp-broil-and-grill microwave oven. However, the Sharp president wants evidence that the program would increase sales by at least 25%, so Don applies some of his research budget to a survey. He uses the National Phone Systems Company to conduct a nationwide survey using random digit dialing. National Phone Systems is a fully integrated telephone polling company, and it has the capability of providing daily tabulations. Don decides to use this option, and instead of specifying a final sample size, he chooses to have National Phone Systems perform 50 completions each day. At the end of 5 days of fieldwork, the daily results are as follows:

Day	1	2	3	4	5
Total sample size	50	100	150	200	250
Percentage of respondents who would consider buying a Sharp microwave with a $40 rebate	50%	40%	35%	30%	33%

For how much longer should Don continue the survey? Indicate your rationale.

CASE 13.1

PEACEFUL LAKE SUBDIVISION REVISITED: SAMPLE SIZE

The details about the Peaceful Lake Subdivision survey are found in Case 12.1 on pages 368–369.

Recall that the president of this subdivision has decided to conduct a survey to determine how Peaceful Lake's 6,000 homeowners feel about the recreation complex that some of the residents want built. The complex will require up to $2 million in construction costs. To construct the proposed recreational facility, every Peaceful Valley household would be expected to pay a one-time fee of $500, and annual fees would increase to $200 based on facility maintenance cost estimates. The president has decided on a probability sampling method, but he is reconsidering the sample size based on his recent Internet search of sample sizes.

1. What is the expected level of sample error (accuracy level) for a sample size of 3,000? Is this a large or a small error level, and why do you judge it to be small or large?
2. If the president desires the survey to be accurate to ±5% and at a 95% level of confidence, what sample size should be used? How would you adjust this sample size if the president believes that there will be a 75% response rate to the survey?
3. Should the survey be a sample or a census of Peaceful Lake Subdivision homeowners? Defend your choice. Be certain to discuss any practical considerations that enter into your choice.

CASE 13.2

TARGET: DECIDING ON THE NUMBER OF TELEPHONE NUMBERS

Target is a major retail store chain specializing in good-quality merchandise and good values for its customers. Currently, Target operates about 1,700 stores, including over 200 "Super Targets," in major metropolitan areas in 48 of the 50 states in America. One of the core marketing strategies employed by Target is to ensure that shoppers have a special experience every time they shop at Target. This special shopping experience is enhanced by Target's department arrangements that are intuitive. For example, toys are next to sporting goods. Another shopping experience feature is the "racetrack," or extra-wide center aisle that helps shoppers navigate the store easily and quickly. A third feature is the aesthetic appearance of its shelves, product displays, and seasonal specials. Naturally, Target continuously monitors the opinions and satisfaction levels of its customers because competitors are constantly trying to outperform Target and/or customers preferences change.

Target management has committed to an annual survey of 1,000 of its customers to determine these very issues and to provide for a constant tracking and forecasting system of its cusomers' opinions. The survey will include customers of Target's competitors, such as Wal-Mart, Kmart, and Sears. In other words, the population under study is all consumers who shop in mass-merchandise stores throughout Target's geographic markets. The marketing research project director has decided on the use of a telephone survey to be conducted by a national telephone survey data-collection company, and he is currently working with Survey Sampling, Inc. to purchase the telephone numbers of consumers residing in Target's metropolitan target markets. The SSI personnel have informed him of the basic formula they use to determine the number of telephone numbers needed. (You learned about this formula in the opening vignette in this chapter provided by Jim Follet, Survey Sampling International.)

The formula is as follows:

Telephone numbers needed = completed interviews/(working phone rate × incidence × completion rate)

where

working phone rate = percentage of telephone numbers that are "live."
incidence = percentage of those reached that will take part in the survey.
completion rate = percentage of those willing to take part in the survey that actually complete the survey.

As a matter of convenience, Target identifies four different regions that are roughly equal in sales volume: North, South, East, and West.

Region	North		South		East		West	
	Low	High	Low	High	Low	High	Low	High
Working Rate	70%	75%	60%	65%	65%	75%	50%	60%
Incidence	65%	70%	70%	80%	65%	75%	40%	50%
Completion Rate	50%	70%	50%	60%	80%	90%	60%	70%

1. With a desired final sample size of 250 for each region, what is the lowest total number of telephone numbers that should be purchased for each region?
2. With a desired final sample size of 250 for each region, what is the highest total number of telephone numbers that should be purchased for each region?
3. What is the lowest and highest total number of telephone numbers to be purchased for the entire survey?

CASE 13.3 Your Integrated Case

ADVANCED AUTOMOBILE CONCEPTS

As you know, Nick Thomas, CEO, Advanced Automobile Concepts, has agreed with Cory Rogers of CMG Research to use an online survey for the research. In particular, the decision has been made to purchase panel access, meaning that the online survey, developed with the use of *Qualtrics*, will be completed by individuals who have joined the ranks of the panel data company and agreed to periodically answer surveys online. These individuals are compensated by their panel companies, but the companies claim that their panel members are highly representative of the general population. Also, because the panel members have provided extensive information about themselves, such as demographics, lifestyles, product ownership, and so on, that is stored in the panel company databanks, a client can purchase the data without having to ask these questions on its survey.

Cory's CMG Research team has done some investigation and have concluded that there are several panel companies that can provide a representative sample of American households. Among these are Knowledge Networks, e-Rewards, and Survey Sampling International, and their costs and services seem comparable: For a "blended" online survey of 50 questions, the cost is roughly $10 per complete response. "Blended" means a combination of stored database information and answers to online survey questions. Thus, the costs of these panel company services are based on the number of respondents, and each company will bid on the work based on the nature and size of the sample.

Cory knows that his Advanced Automobile Concepts client is operating under two constraints. First, Zen Motors top management has agreed to a total cost for all of the research, and it is up to Nick Thomas to spend this budget prudently. If a large portion of the budget is expended on a single activity—such as paying for an online panel sample—then there is less available for other research activities. Second, Cory Rogers knows from his extensive experience with clients that both Nick Thomas and Zen Motors top management will expect this project to have a large sample size. Of course, as a marketing researcher, Cory realizes that large sample sizes are generally not required from a sample error standpoint, but he must be prepared to respond to any of Nick Thomas's or Zen Motors' top management questions, reservations, or objections when the sample size is proposed. As preparation for the possible need to convince top management that his recommendation is the right decision for the sample size for the Advanced Automobile Concepts survey, Cory decides to make a table that specifies sample error and cost of the sample.

For each of the following possible sample sizes listed, calculate the associated expected cost of the panel sample and the sample error:

1. 20,000
2. 10,000
3. 5,000
4. 2,500
5. 1,000
6. 500

Learning Objectives

- To learn about total error and how nonsampling error is related to it
- To understand the sources of data-collection errors and how to minimize them
- To learn about the various types of nonresponse error and how to calculate response rate in order to measure nonresponse error
- To read about questionnaire inspection procedures used during and after data collection

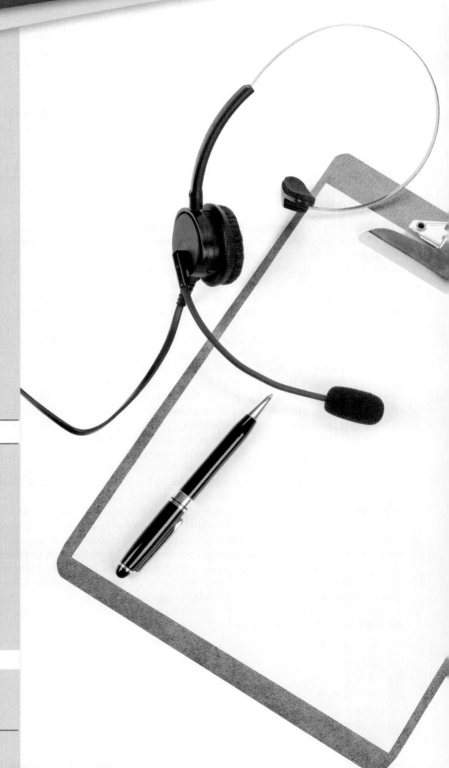

Dealing with Falling Response Rates

Mr. Patrick Glaser,
Director of Respondent
Cooperation, CMOR

Respondent cooperation refers to the general willingness of people to participate in research. Participation is a crucial concern of marketing researchers because a majority of popular marketing research techniques involve collecting information from people, be it ordinary consumers, specialized professionals, business leaders, or some other group of interest. Unfortunately, researchers have found it increasingly difficult to convince people to participate in research.

CMOR

Shielding the Profession

Response rates have been falling in all of marketing research. We asked Mr. Patrick Glaser, Director of Respondent Cooperation at CMOR, to open this chapter with a few remarks about this important issue.

Many theories have been put forth as to why people have become less willing to participate in research. One widely held notion links the cooperation problem with the growing popularity of marketing research. The public may be weary of participating in research projects simply because the number of surveys, focus groups and other studies has increased. Another popular theory posits that the public feels intruded upon due to an increasing expectation of personal privacy. Privacy concerns are paramount in modern times due to the incidence of fraud and identity theft through credit cards, the Internet, and in other areas of people's everyday lives. These and other situations may all be contributing to problems of low respondent cooperation.

Two principal concerns to research are fostered by low cooperation. First, the cost of conducting research has risen as people have become resistant to participating in studies. As respondent cooperation decreases, greater levels of resources must be committed to recruit comparable numbers of respondents for surveys, focus groups, and other types of research projects. In practice, this may mean offering monetary incentives or placing additional telephone calls, mailings or letters, or other techniques in order to bolster participation. Second, low respondent cooperation can threaten data quality in research. Marketing research surveys, for example, may be subject to a phenomenon known as nonresponse bias, or error. This problem occurs when research findings become inaccurate due to the researcher's inability to interview every person that was selected to participate in their project. This may occur both because of a lack of cooperation or because the respondent was not able to be reached, or contacted by the researcher.

Sometimes, respondents who *do* participate in a research project may exhibit significantly different patterns of behavior, opinions, or other characteristics from those that *do not* participate. This can skew some or all of the research project results, and it is generally difficult to predict when this problem will occur. Because of this, researchers may commit substantial resources to convincing those people who have been selected to participate in their study to cooperate.

CMOR, the Council for Marketing & Opinion Research, was found in 1992 to implement government affairs activities as well as to improve respondent cooperation. CMOR's Respondent Cooperation activities include:

A multifaceted research program designed to study the scope of the respondent cooperation problem, understand the public's perceptions of research, and develop solutions to improve cooperation;

- Public relations efforts to communicate the value of research to the public;
- Efforts to assist the research profession in maintaining the highest ethical standards when interacting with the public; and
- Developing and promoting best practices in respondent cooperation.

CMOR also works to disseminate information regarding respondent cooperation throughout the survey research profession as well as encourage industry dialogue on cooperation issues. For example, the annual CMOR Respondent Cooperation Workshop brings together researchers from marketing research, academia, polling, and government policy backgrounds to present ideas, debate techniques, and share information. It is greatly important that best practices are adopted by researchers throughout the survey research profession. Since a single bad research experience can taint a respondent's opinion about future participation, it falls to the entire research profession to maintain the highest professional and ethical standards when communicating and interacting with the public.

T*his chapter deals with data-collection issues, including, as you have just read, factors that stimulate individuals to participate in sureys. You learned about sample error in the previous chapter, and you will learn about another source of research error in this chapter. Early on we remind you that there are two kinds of error in survey research. The first is sampling error, which arises from the fact that we have taken a sample. But what about the error that arises from a respondent who does not listen carefully to the question or an interviewer who is almost burned out from listening to answering machines or having prospective respondents hang up? This is the second type of error, called* nonsampling error.

This chapter teaches you the sources of nonsampling errors, and along with a discussion of each source of error, we make suggestions on how you can minimize the negative effect of each error type. We also teach you how to calculate the response rate in order to measure the amount of nonresponse error. We relate what a researcher looks for in preliminary questionnaire screening after the survey has been completed in order to spot respondents whose answers may exhibit bias, such as always responding positively or negatively to questions.

DATA COLLECTION AND NONSAMPLING ERROR

In the two previous chapters, you learned that the sample plan and sample size are important in predetermining the amount of sampling error that you will experience. The significance of understanding sampling is that we can control sampling error.[1] However, as we indicated to you, sampling error is only one of the two components of total error in a survey. The counterpart to sampling error is **nonsampling error**, which is defined as all errors in a survey *except* those attributable to the sample plan and the sample size. Nonsampling error includes the following: (1) all types of nonresponse error, (2) data-gathering errors, (3) data-handling errors, (4) data analysis errors, and (5) interpretation errors. It also includes errors in problem definition, question wording, and, in fact, anything other than sampling error.

Generally, the greatest potential for large nonsampling error occurs during the data-collection stage, so we discuss errors that can occur during this stage at some length. **Data collection** is the phase of the marketing research process during which respondents provide their answers or information to inquiries posed to them by the researcher. These inquiries may be direct questions asked by a live, face-to-face interviewer; they may be posed over the telephone; they may be self-administered by the respondent such as with an online survey; or they may take some other form of solicitation that the researcher has decided to use. Because nonsampling error cannot be measured by a formula as sampling error can, we describe the various controls that can be imposed on the data-collection process to minimize the effects of nonsampling error.[2]

> Nonsampling error is defined as all errors in a survey except those due to the sample plan and the sample size.

> Data collection has the potential to greatly increase the amount of nonsampling error in a survey.

POSSIBLE ERRORS IN FIELD DATA COLLECTION

A wide variety of nonsampling errors can occur during data collection. To help you learn about them, we divide these errors into two general types and further specify errors within each general type. The first general type is **fieldworker error**, defined as errors committed by the individuals who administer questionnaires, typically interviewers.[3] The quality of fieldworkers can vary dramatically depending on the researcher's resources and the circumstances of the survey, but it is important to keep in mind that fieldworker error can occur with professional data-collection workers as well as with do-it-yourselfers. Of course, the potential for fieldworker error is less with professionals than with first-timers or part-timers. The other general type is **respondent error**, which refers to errors on the part of the respondent. These, of course, can occur regardless of the method of data collection, but some data-collection methods have greater potential for respondent error than others. Within each general type, we identify two classes of error: intentional errors, or errors that are committed deliberately, and unintentional errors, or errors that occur without willful intent.[4]

> Nonsampling errors are committed by fieldworkers and respondents.

Figure 14.1 lists the various errors described in this section under each of the four headings. In the early sections of this chapter, we will describe these data-collection errors, and later, we will discuss the standard controls that marketing researchers employ in order to minimize these errors.

Intentional Fieldworker Errors

Intentional fieldworker errors occur whenever a data collector willfully violates the data-collection requirements set forth by the researcher. We describe two variations of intentional fieldworker error: interviewer cheating and leading the respondent. Both are constant concerns of all researchers.

Interviewer cheating occurs when the interviewer intentionally misrepresents respondents. You might think to yourself, "What would induce an interviewer to intentionally falsify responses?" The cause is often found in the compensation system.[5] Interviewers may work by the hour, but a common compensation system is to reward them by completed

> Interviewer cheating is a concern, especially when compensation is based on a per-completion basis.

FIGURE 14.1

**Data-Collection
Errors Can Occur
with Fieldworkers
or Responders**

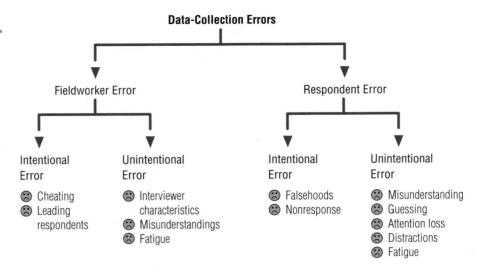

interviews. That is, a telephone interviewer or a mall-intercept interviewer may be paid at a rate of $7.50 per completed interview, so at the end of an interview day, the interviewer simply turns in the completed questionnaires (or data files, if the interviewer uses a laptop, tablet, or PDA system), and the number is credited to the interviewer. Or interviewers may cheat by interviewing someone who is convenient instead of a person designated by the sampling plan. Again, the by-completed-interview compensation may provide the incentive for this type of cheating.[6] At the same time, most interviewers are not full-time employees,[7] and their conscientiousness may be diminished as a result.

You might ask, "Why not just change the compensation system for interviewers and 'fix' this problem?" There is some defensible logic for a paid-by-completion compensation system. Interviewers do not always work like production-line workers. With mall intercepts, for instance, there are periods of inactivity, depending on mall shopper flow and respondent qualification requirements. Telephone interviewers are often instructed to call only during a small number of "prime-time" hours in the evening, or they may be waiting for periods of time in order to satisfy a particular survey's policy for the number of call-backs. Also, as you may already know, the compensation levels for fieldworkers are low, the hours are long, and the work is frustrating at times.[8] So the temptation to turn in bogus completed questionnaires is certainly present, and some interviewers give in to this temptation.

 ## What Type of Cheater are You?

Students who read about the fieldworker cheating error we have just described are sometimes skeptical that such cheating goes on. However, if you are a "typical" college student, you probably have cheated to some degree in your academic experience. Surprised? Take the following test and for each statement, circle "Yes" or "No" under the "I have done this" heading.

Statement	I have done this.	
Copied another student's homework or assignments.	Yes	No
Allowed someone else to copy my homework/assignments.	Yes	No
Collaborated on take-home exams I was supposed to do alone.	Yes	No
Used an unauthorized cheat sheet on an exam.	Yes	No
Looked at or copied from someone else's exam during a test.	Yes	No

Statement	I have done this.	
Allowed someone else to copy from my exam during a test.	Yes	No
Found out what is on an exam before taking it.	Yes	No
Told another student what was on an exam before s/he took it.	Yes	No
Programmed extra help or information into a calculator that I then used on an exam.	Yes	No
Copied information from a source for a paper without properly citing the source.	Yes	No
Copied information from the Web for a paper without properly citing the source.	Yes	No
Obtained research paper(s) from the Web and handed in as my own.	Yes	No

If you circled "Yes" at least one time, you are like most business students who have answered a variation of this test.[9] If you indicated "Yes" from 2 to 5 times, you are still consistent with about 50% of college students. Now, if you and the majority of univeristy students in general believe that fellow students are cheating on examinations and assignments, don't you think that interviewers who may be in financially tight situations are tempted to cheat on their interviews?

The second error that we are categorizing as intentional on the part of the interviewer is **leading the respondent**, which is defined as occurring when the interviewer influences the respondent's answers through wording, voice inflection, or body language. In the worst case, the interviewer may actually reword a question so it is leading. For instance, consider the question "Is conserving electricity a concern for you?" An interviewer can influence the respondent by changing the question to "Isn't conserving electricity a concern for you?"

There are other, less obvious ways of leading the respondent. One way is to subtly signal the type of response that is expected. If, for example, a respondent says "yes" in response to our question, the interviewer might say, "I thought you would say 'yes' as over 90% of my respondents have agreed on this issue." A comment such as this plants a seed in the respondent's head that he or she should continue to agree with the majority. Another method of subtle leading is through interviewer cues. In a personal interview, for instance, the interviewer might ever so slightly shake his or her head "no" to questions the interviewer disagrees with and "yes" to those the interviewer agrees with while posing the question. The respondent may perceive these cues and begin responding in the expected manner signaled by head movements while the interviewer reads the questions. Over the telephone, an interviewer might give verbal cues such as "uh-huh" to responses the interviewer disagrees with or "okay" to responses the interviewer agrees with, and this continued reaction pattern may subtly influence the respondent's answers. Again, we have categorized this example as an intentional error because professional interviewers are trained to avoid them, and if they commit them, they should be aware of their violations.

Interviewers should not influence respondents' answers.

Unintentional Fieldworker Errors

An **unintentional interviewer error** occurs whenever an interviewer commits an error while believing that he or she is performing correctly.[10] There are three general sources of unintentional interviewer error: personal characteristics, misunderstandings, and fatigue. Unintentional interviewer error can arise from the interviewer's **personal characteristics**, such as accent, sex, and demeanor. Under some circumstances, the interviewer's voice,[11] gender,[12] or lack of experience[13] can be a source of bias. In fact, just the presence of an interviewer, regardless of personal characteristics, may be a source of bias. Marketing

Interviewer errors can occur without the interviewer's being aware of them.

MARKETING RESEARCH INSIGHT   Global Application

14.1 Which Causes More Response Bias with Dutch Respondents: CAPI, CASI, or CATI?[14]

As in many other countries, marketing researchers in the Netherlands have noticed dramatic declines in cooperation rates and sharp increases in interviewing costs. Advances in computer technology have enticed some marketing researchers to gravitate to "interviewer-less" surveys. In other words, there has been a movement toward self-administered online surveys and away from personal or telephone interviews that require the use of a trained interviewer. In a nutshell, there are three popular alternatives, and each one is briefly described here.

- **CATI**—computer-assisted telephone interviews where the survey is programmed into a computer and the interviewer reads the questions to the respondent over the telephone.
- **CASI**—computer-assisted self-interviews where the respondent takes part in an online survey without any interviewer present.
- **CAPI**—computer-assisted personal interview where the interviewer conducts a face-to-face interview while using a laptop, handheld, or other computerized device to administer the survey.

Among other questions, the Dutch researchers wondered whether and to what extent the presence (either face-to-face or over the telephone) of an interviewer caused response biases such as underreporting socially undesirable or overreporting socially desirable behaviors. An example of a socially undesirable behavior underreporting bias is not admitting to or not truthfully divulging how many traffic violations you comitted in the past year. A socially acceptable behavior overreporting bias example is overstating one's income. As you would expect, the Dutch researchers hypothesized that face-to-face interviews would be associated with more bias whereas self-administered surveys would be associated with less bias of both types.

The Dutch researchers used these three variations of the same survey with equivalent Dutch respondent samples. They found that CASI provided respondents with more privacy and anonymity, which translated into more "honest" or accurate reports of socially undesirable behaviors. Similarly, the CASI respondents gave more truthful responses when answering questions about socially desirable topics. Surprisingly, there were minimal differences between CAPI and CATI. This finding strongly suggests that even a "remote" interviewer engenders some sort of "evaluation apprehension" in respondents, meaning that they may be worrying about how the interviewer regards their answers. So, the use of an interviewer, regardless whether a face-to-face or a telephone interview is used, will most certainly sway some respondents to be untruthful in that they may understate their socially undesirable behaviors and overstate their socially desirable behaviors. Researchers working with such sensitive topics should take the interviewer out of the equation to the extent possible.

Research Insight 14.1 describes how, in certain situations, self-administered surveys are an improvement in this regard over telephone surveys or personal interviews.

Unintentional interviewer errors include misunderstandings and fatigue.

Interviewer misunderstanding occurs when interviewers believe they know how to administer a survey but, instead, do it incorrectly. As we have described, a questionnaire may include various types of instructions for the interviewer, a variety of response-scale types, directions on how to record responses, and other complicated guidelines that must be adhered to by the interviewer. As you can guess, there is a considerable education gap between marketing researchers who design questionnaires and interviewers who administer them. This gap can easily become a communication problem in which the instructions on the questionnaire are confusing to the interviewer. Studies have shown that interviewer experience cannot overcome poor questionnaire instructions.[15] Under this circumstance, the interviewer will usually struggle to comply with the researcher's wishes but may fail to do so to some degree or another.[16]

The third type of unintentional interviewer error pertains to **fatigue-related mistakes**, which can occur when an interviewer becomes tired. You may be surprised that fatigue can enter into something as simple as asking questions and recording answers, but interviewing is labor-intensive,[17] and it can become tedious and monotonous. It is repetitive at best, and it is especially demanding when respondents are uncooperative. Toward the end of a long interviewing day, the interviewer may be less mentally alert than earlier in the day, and this condition can cause slipups and mistakes to occur. The interviewer may fail to obey a skip pattern, might forget to check the respondent's reply to a question, might hurry through a section of the questionnaire, or might appear or sound weary to a potential respondent, who refuses to take part in the survey as a result.

Intentional Respondent Errors

Intentional respondent errors occur when respondents willfully misrepresent themselves in surveys. There are at least two major intentional respondent errors that require discussion: falsehoods and refusals. **Falsehoods** occur when respondents fail to tell the truth in surveys. They may feel embarrassed, they might want to protect their privacy, or they may even suspect that the interviewer has a hidden agenda, such as suddenly turning the interview into a sales pitch.[18] Certain topics have greater potential for misrepresentation. For instance, the income level of the respondent is a sensitive topic for many people, disclosure of marital status is a concern for women living alone, age is a delicate topic for some, and personal hygiene questions may offend some respondents. For more information on the tendencies of respondents to not tell the truth when asked sensitive questions, we have prepared Marketing Research Insight 14.2. Alternatively, respondents may become bored; the interview process may become burdensome; respondents may find the interviewer irritating; or for some reason, respondents may want to end the interview in a hurry. So falsehoods may be motivated by a desire on the part of the respondent to deceive, or they may be mindless responses uttered just to complete the interview as quickly as possible.

Personal characteristics such as appearance, dress, or accent, although unintentional, may cause fieldworker errors.

Sometimes respondents do not tell the truth.

 MARKETING RESEARCH INSIGHT   Practical Application

14.2 Under What Circumstances Are Respondents Least Likely to Tell Lies?

Falsehoods are a type of respondent error that appears to be influenced by type of survey administration. This is the conclusion of researchers[19] who recently investigated how respondents answered various sensitive questions in surveys. A "sensitive" question may be one of three types. First, it may be a topic that is intrusive or embarrassing for the respondent to comment on. Second, the respondent may be concerned about the disclosure or loss of privacy of this information to third parties. Third, it might be a topic that relates to socially desirable (or undesirable) behavior.

The researchers claim that falsehoods—that is, lies—are known to exist on surveys, but the questions they sought to answer were why and under what circumstances. The "why" is simple: Respondents lie to avoid embarrassment and/or to

steer clear of consequences from the disclosures. Thus, respondents lie on surveys for the same reasons they lie in real life. However, lying on surveys seems to be more deliberate in that respondents who lie actively edit or script their responses according to survey circumstances. Survey conditions under which respondents lie less are with self-administered surveys, in cases where the respondent believes that the truth will be learned, and when privacy is assured.

Thus, to minimize respondent falsehoods on surveys, marketing researchers should, to the extent possible, use the following tactics:

1. Whenever possible and reasonable, use self-administered surveys.
2. Strongly suggest or imply that respondents' answers will be verified or validated.
3. Assure confidentiality. (Recall that with confidentiality, the respondent's identity may be known to the researcher, but it is not divulged to any third parties.)

Nonresponse is defined as failure on the part of a prospective respondent to take part in a survey or to answer a question.

The second type of intentional respondent error is nonresponse, which we have referred to at various times in this book. Recall that **nonresponse** is either a failure on the part of a prospective respondent to take part in the survey, premature termination of the interview, or refusal to answer specific questions on the questionnaire. In fact, nonresponse of various types is probably the most common intentional respondent error that researchers encounter. Some observers believe that survey research is facing tough times ahead because of a growing distaste for survey participation, increasingly busy schedules, and a desire for privacy.[20] By one estimate, the refusal rate of U.S. consumers is almost 50%.[21] Telephone surveyors are most concerned.[22]

While most agree that declining cooperation rates present a major threat to the industry,[23] some believe the problem is not as severe as many think.[24] Nonresponse in general, and refusals in particular, are encountered in virtually every survey conducted. While you may think that this is a difficult state of affairs, there is an even more challenging situation with business-to-business (B2B) marketing research, where there are different "hurdles" that have to be cleared just to find the right person to take part in the survey. Read Marketing Research Insight 14.3 to learn about the hurdles in B2B marketing research. We devote an entire section to nonresponse error in a following section of this chapter.

 MARKETING RESEARCH INSIGHT   Practical Application

14.3 B2B Respondent Recruiting Hurdles: Gatekeepers, Voice Mail, and Timing

Business-to-business (B2B) marketing research always represents special challenges because the respondents are business executives, managers, or other professionals whose availability is very limited. Unlike consumers, who are easily contacted with random digit dialing, mall intercepts, or broadcast e-mail solicitations, B2B respondents typically must be searched for and found deep in the bowels of multilayered corporations or complex organizations, and there may be precious few prospective B2B sample frames because B2B populations are often quite small. Recently, the vice president of a successful research call center commented on her company's tactics for jumping over the three B2B marketing research hurdles of gatekeepers, voice mail, and timing.[25]

Hurdling Gatekeepers
A gatekeeper is an administrative assistant or secretary who will be the first relevant contact in attempting to reach a prospective B2B respondent. Gatekeepers are responsible for screening contacts so their bosses will not be bothered with trivial and time-consuming meetings or calls, and surveys are usually at the top of the "do not bother the boss" list. Successful tactics are to be honest and recruit gatekeepers as allies. Explain quickly and convincingly that this is bona fide marketing research that may eventually help the boss on the job. Alternatively, quickly tell the gatekeeper about the type of

individual being sought and solicit cooperation in finding that person in the company.

Hurdling Voice Mail
Often, when the right B2B respondents are reached, they do not answer the telephone and the message rolls over to voice mail. To leave or not to leave a message is currently in debate. Those marketing researchers who opt to leave a message advocate a quick, no-nonsense, strictly business message to convince listeners of the importance of the research and the critical role they will play by taking part. If the message must be long and complicated, it is best to not leave it.

Hurdling Timing
B2B research interviews are rarely short by corporate standards. Instead, they often take 10 or 20 minutes, which is close to an eternity on the corporate clock. The way to clear this hurdle is to convince the B2B prospect of the importance of participation and to "book" a time on the prospect's calendar for the necessary time block. Sometimes, these time slots are very early in the morning or quite late in the afternoon or into the evening, so the research data-collection company must be prepared to do the interview when the respondent is available and not just on the standard 8-to-5 workday.

After Clearing the Hurdles . . .
Even after clearing these hurdles, successful B2B surveys always require special interviewer qualities because B2B respondents are generally highly educated, quick-thinking multitaskers. So the interviewer characteristics that work best with B2B respondents are patience, professionalism, and adaptability.

Unintentional Respondent Errors

An **unintentional respondent error** occurs whenever a respondent gives a response that is not valid but believes it is the truth. There are five types of unintentional respondent errors: respondent misunderstanding, guessing, attention loss, distractions, and respondent fatigue.

First, **respondent misunderstanding** is defined as situations in which a respondent gives an answer without comprehending the question and/or the accompanying instructions. Potential respondent misunderstandings exist in all surveys. Such misunderstandings range from simple errors, such as checking two responses to a question when only one is called for, to complex errors, such as misunderstanding terminology.[26] For example, a respondent may think in terms of net income for the past year rather than income before taxes as desired by the researcher. Any number of misunderstandings such as these can plague a survey.

A second form of unintentional respondent error is **guessing**, in which a respondent gives an answer when uncertain of its accuracy. Occasionally, respondents are asked about topics they have little knowledge of or low recall about, but they feel compelled to provide an answer to the questions being posed. Here, the respondent might guess the answer. All guesses are likely to contain errors. Here is an example of guessing. If you were a respondent and were asked to estimate the amount of electricity in kilowatt hours you used last month, how many would you say you used?

A third unintentional respondent error occurs when a respondent's interest in the survey wanes, which is known as **attention loss**. The typical respondent is not as excited about the survey as is the researcher, and some respondents will find themselves less and less motivated to take part in the survey as they work their way through the questionnaire. With attention loss, respondents do not attend carefully to questions, they issue superficial and perhaps mindless answers, and they may refuse to continue taking part in the survey.

Fourth, **distractions**, such as interruptions, may occur while the questionnaire administration takes place. For example, during a mall-intercept interview, a respondent may be distracted when an acquaintance walks by and says hello. A parent answering questions on the telephone might have to attend to a fussy toddler, or an online survey respondent might be prompted that an e-mail message has just arrived. A distraction may cause the respondent to get "offtrack" or otherwise not take the survey as seriously as is desired by the researcher.

Fifth, unintentional respondent error can take the form of **respondent fatigue**, in which the respondent becomes tired of participating in the survey. Whenever a respondent tires of a

Unintentional respondent errors include misunderstanding, guessing, attention loss, distractions, and fatigue.

Sometimes a respondent will answer without understanding the question.

Whenever a respondent guesses, error is likely.

Guesses are a form of unintentional respondent error.

survey, deliberation and reflection will diminish. Exasperation will mount and cooperation will diminish. Respondents might even opt for the "no opinion" response category just as a means of quickly finishing the survey because they have grown tired of answering questions.

 What Type of Error Is It?

It is sometimes confusing to students when they first read about intentional and unintentional errors and that errors may be attributed to interviewers or interviewees (respondents). To help you learn and remember these various types of data-collection errors, see if you can correctly identify the type for each of the following data-collection situations. Place an "X" in the cell that corresponds to the type of error that pertains to the situation.

Situation	Interviewer Error		Interviewee Error	
	Intentional	Unintentional	Intentional	Unintentional
A respondent says "no opinion" to every question asked.				
When a mall-intercept interviewer is suffering from a bad cold, few people want to take the survey.				
Because a telephone respondent has an incoming call, he asks his wife to take the phone and answer the rest of the interviewer's questions.				
A respondent grumbles about doing the survey, so an interviewer decides to skip asking the demographic questions.				
A respondent who lost her job last year gives her last year's income level rather than the much lower one she will earn for this year.				

FIELD DATA-COLLECTION QUALITY CONTROLS

There are precautions and procedures that can be implemented to minimize the effects of the various types of errors just described. Please note that we said "minimize" and not "eliminate," as the potential for error always exists. However, by instituting the following controls a researcher can be assured that the nonsampling error factor involved with data collection will be diminished. The field data-collection quality controls we describe are listed in Table 14.1.

Control of Intentional Fieldworker Error

There are two general strategies to guard against cases in which the interviewer might intentionally commit an error. These strategies are supervision and validation.[27]

Supervision uses administrators to oversee the work of field data-collection workers.[28] Most centralized telephone interviewing companies have a "listening-in" capability

Intentional fieldworker error can be controlled with supervision and validation procedures.

TABLE 14.1 How to Control Data-Collection Errors

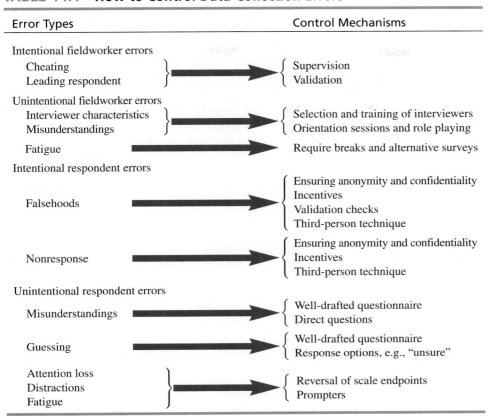

Error Types	Control Mechanisms
Intentional fieldworker errors	
Cheating	Supervision
Leading respondent	Validation
Unintentional fieldworker errors	
Interviewer characteristics	Selection and training of interviewers
Misunderstandings	Orientation sessions and role playing
Fatigue	Require breaks and alternative surveys
Intentional respondent errors	
Falsehoods	Ensuring anonymity and confidentiality
	Incentives
	Validation checks
	Third-person technique
Nonresponse	Ensuring anonymity and confidentiality
	Incentives
	Third-person technique
Unintentional respondent errors	
Misunderstandings	Well-drafted questionnaire
	Direct questions
Guessing	Well-drafted questionnaire
	Response options, e.g., "unsure"
Attention loss	Reversal of scale endpoints
Distractions	Prompters
Fatigue	

that the supervisor can use to tap into and monitor any interviewer's line during an interview. The respondent and the interviewer may be unaware of the monitoring, so the "listening in" samples a representative interview performed by that interviewer. If the interviewer is leading or unduly influencing respondents, this procedure will spot the violation, and the supervisor can take corrective action such as reprimanding that interviewer. With personal interviews, the supervisor might accompany an interviewer to observe while that interviewer administers a questionnaire in the field. Because "listening in" without the consent of the respondent could be considered a breach of privacy, many companies now inform respondents that all or part of the call may be monitored and/or recorded.

Validation verifies that the interviewer did the work. This strategy is aimed at the falsification/cheating problem. There are various ways to validate the work. One is for the supervisor to recontact respondents to find out whether they took part in the survey. An industry standard is to randomly select 10% of the completed surveys for purposes of making a call-back to validate that the interview was actually conducted. A few sample questions might even be readministered for comparison purposes. In the absence of call-back validation, some supervisors will inspect completed questionnaires; with a trained eye, they may spot patterns in an interviewer's completions that raise suspicions of falsification. Interviewers who turn in bogus completed questionnaires are not always careful about simulating actual respondents. The supervisor might find inconsistencies, such as very young respondents with large numbers of children, that raise doubts as to a questionnaire's authenticity.

An industry standard is verification of 10% of the completed surveys.

Control of Unintentional Fieldworker Error

The supervisor is instrumental in minimizing unintentional interviewer error. We describe three mechanisms commonly used by professional field data-collection companies in this regard: selection and training, orientation sessions, and role playing.[29]

Interviewer personal characteristics that can cause unintentional errors are best taken care of by careful selection of interviewers. Following selection, it is important to train them well so as to avoid any biases resulting from manner, appearance, and so forth. **Orientation sessions** are meetings in which the supervisor introduces the survey and questionnaire administration requirements to the fieldworkers.[30] The supervisor might highlight qualification or quota requirements, note skip patterns, or go over instructions to the interviewer that are embedded throughout the questionnaire in order to standardize the interview across interviewers.[31] Finally, often as a means of becoming familiar with a questionnaire's administration requirements, interviewers will conduct **role-playing sessions**, which are dry runs or dress rehearsals of the questionnaire with the supervisor or some other interviewer playing the respondent's role. Successive role-playing sessions serve to familiarize interviewers with the questionnaire's special administration aspects. To control for interviewer fatigue, some researchers require interviewers to take frequent breaks and/or alternate surveys, if possible. In short, the more competent the field interverview is through training, supervision, and personal skills, the lower the potential for interviewer error.[32]

Unintentional fieldworker errors can be reduced with supervised orientation sessions and role playing.

Control of Intentional Respondent Error

To control intentional respondent error, it is important to minimize respondent falsehoods and nonresponse tendencies. Tactics useful in minimizing intentional respondent error include anonymity, confidentiality, incentives, validation checks, and third-person technique.[33]

Anonymity is assuring the respondent that his or her name will not be associated with the answers. **Confidentiality** is assuring the respondent that his or her answers will remain private. Both assurances are believed to be helpful in forestalling falsehoods. The belief here is that when respondents are guaranteed they will remain nameless, they will be more comfortable in self-disclosure and will refrain from lying or misrepresenting themselves.[34]

Tactics useful in minimizing intentional respondent error include anonymity, confidentiality, validation checks, and third-person technique.

Confidentiality and/or anonymity may reduce refusals to take part in a survey.

Another tactic for reducing falsehoods and nonresponse error is the use of **incentives**, which are cash payments, gifts, or something of value promised to respondents in return for their participation.[35] For participating in a survey, the respondent may be paid in cash or provided with a redemption coupon or might be given a gift such as a ballpoint pen or a T-shirt. Here, in a sense, the respondent is being induced to tell the truth by direct payment. Respondents may now feel morally obligated to tell the truth because they will receive compensation. Or, they may feel guilty about receiving an incentive and then not answering truthfully. Unfortunately, practitioners and academic researchers are only beginning to understand how to entice prospective respondents to take part in a survey.[36] For instance, only recently has relevance been documented to increase response rates.[37]

A different approach for reducing falsehoods is the use of **validation checks**, in which information provided by a respondent is confirmed during the interview. For instance, in an in-home survey on Leap Frog educational products for preschool children, the interviewer might ask to see the respondent's Leap Frog unit and modules as a verification or validation check. A more unobtrusive validation is to have the interviewer, who is trained to be alert to untrue answers, check for old-appearing respondents who say they are young, shabbily dressed respondents who say they are wealthy, and so on. A well-trained interviewer will make a note of suspicious answers in the margin of the questionnaire.[38]

Finally, a researcher can use a questionnaire design feature to reduce intentional respondent errors. Sometimes the opportunity arises where a **third-person technique** can be used in a question; that is, instead of directly quizzing the respondent, the question can be couched in terms of a third person who is similar to the respondent. For instance, a question posed to a middle-aged man might be "Do you think a person such as yourself uses Viagra?" Here, the respondent will most probably think in terms of his own circumstances, but because the subject of the question is some unnamed third party, the question is not seen as personal. In other words, he will not be divulging some personal and private information by talking about this fictitious other person. The third-person technique may be used to reduce both falsehoods and nonresponse.

Incentives sometimes compel respondents to be more truthful, and they also discourage nonresponse.

With an embarrassing question, the third-person technique may make the situation less personal.

Control of Unintentional Respondent Error

The control of unintentional respondent error takes various forms as well, including well-drafted questionnaire instructions and examples, reversals of scale endpoints, and use of prompters. With regard to misunderstanding, well-drafted **questionnaire instructions and examples** are commonly used as a way of avoiding respondent confusion. We described these in Chapter 11 on questionnaire design. Also, researchers sometimes resort to direct questions to assess respondent understanding. For example, after describing a 5-point agree–disagree response scale in which 1 = strongly agree, 2 = agree, 3 = neither agree nor disagree, 4 = disagree, and 5 = strongly disagree, the interviewer might be instructed to ask, "Are these instructions clear?" If the respondent answers in the negative, the instructions are repeated until the respondent understands them. Guessing may be reduced by alerting respondents to response options such as "no opinion," "do not recall," or "unsure."

A tactic we described when we discussed the semantic differential is **reversals of scale endpoints,** in which instead of putting all of the negative adjectives on one side and all the positive ones on the other side, a researcher will switch the positions of a few items. Such reversals are intended to warn respondents that they must respond to each bipolar pair individually. With agree–disagree statements, this tactic is accomplished by negatively wording a statement every now and then to induce respondents to attend to each statement individually. Both of these tactics are intended to heighten the respondent's attention.

Finally, long questionnaires often use "**prompters**," such as "We are almost finished," or "That was the most difficult section of questions to answer," or other statements strategically

Ways to combat unintentional respondent error include well-drafted questionnaire instructions and examples, reversals of scale endpoints, and use of "prompters."

"Prompters" are used to keep respondents on task and alert.

located to encourage the respondent to remain on track. Sometimes interviewers will sense an attention lag or fatigue on the part of the respondent and provide their own prompters or comments intended to maintain the respondent's full participation in the survey.

Final Comment on the Control of Data-Collection Errors with Traditional Surveys

As you can see, a wide variety of nonsampling errors can occur on the part of both interviewers and respondents during the data-collection stage of the marketing research process. Similarly, a variety of precautions and controls are used to minimize nonsampling error. Each survey is unique, of course, so we cannot provide universally applicable guidelines. We will, however, stress the importance of good questionnaire design in reducing these errors. Also, researchers, who understand the true value of their services, commonly rely on professional field data-collection companies whose existence depends on how well they can control interviewer and respondent error. Finally, technology is dramatically changing data collection and helping in the control of its errors.[39] For example, in certain research situations, there is good opportunity to use multiple data-collection methods that, in combination, derive an accurate picture of the topic being researched.

NONRESPONSE ERROR

Although nonresponse was briefly described earlier in our discussion of mail surveys, we will now describe the nonresponse issue more fully, including various types of nonresponse, how to assess the degree of this error, and some ways of adjusting or compensating for nonresponse in surveys. Nonresponse was defined earlier as a failure on the part of a prospective respondent to take part in the survey or to answer specific questions on the questionnaire. Nonresponse has been labeled the marketing research industry's biggest problem,[40,41] and it is multinational in scope.[42] Compounding the problem has been the increase in the numbers of surveys, which means the likelihood of being asked to participate in a survey has increased. With several researchers chasing the same population, there is always a constant battle to keep response rates from dropping. Some industry observers believe that the major problems leading to nonresponse are caused by fears of invasion of privacy, consumer skepticism regarding the benefits of participating in research, and the use of research as a guise for telemarketing.

A reliable measure of the declining response rate is that experienced by the University of Michigan's Survey of Consumer Attitudes telephone surveys over the past two decades.[43] The decrease prior to 1996 was about 1% per year, but since 1996, the decline has been 1.5% per year and the decline rate is accelerating. This pattern has prompted the authors of this study to state, ". . . the long-term future of telephone interviewing does not appear promising." As one would expect, nonresponse rates differ by demographic characteristics. Figure 14.2 is based on findings from the American Time Use Survey conducted annually by the U.S. Bureau of the Census with over 25,000 American households.[44] This survey is currently experiencing a response rate of about 55%, or a 45% nonresponse rate. In Figure 14.2 you can see how various demographic characteristics are associated with greater- or less-than-average nonresponse rates. The figure identifies types of potential respondents who are less (postive percents) or more likely (negative percents) to cooperate in a survey.

The identification, control, and adjustments necessary for nonresponse are critical to the success of a survey. There are at least three different types of potential nonresponse error lurking in any survey: refusals to participate in the survey, break-offs during the interview, and refusals to answer specific questions, or item omission. Table 14.2 briefly describes each type of nonresponse.

There are three types of nonresponse error: refusals to participate in the survey, break-offs during the interview, and refusals to answer specific questions (item omissions).

FIGURE 14.2

Nonresponse to Telephone Surveys Varies by Demographic Characteristics

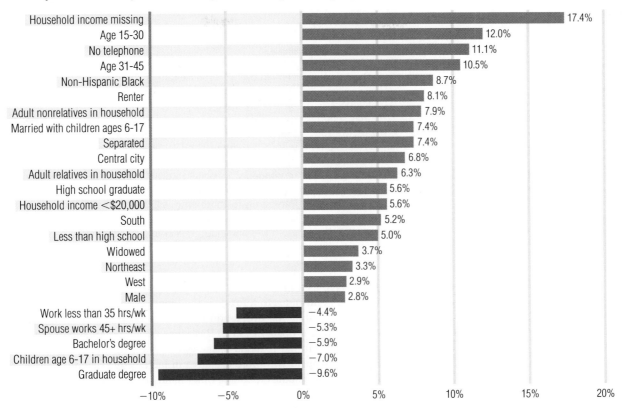

Refusals to Participate in the Survey

A **refusal** occurs when a potential respondent declines to take part in the survey. Refusal rates differ by area of the country as well as by demographic differences. The reasons for refusals are many and varied.[45] The person may be busy, he or she may have no interest in the survey, something about the interviewer's voice or approach may have turned the person off, the survey topic may be overly sensitive,[46] or the refusal may simply reflect how that person always responds to surveys. We have prepared Marketing Research Insight 14.4 so that you can learn about the effect of topic interest in gaining a potential respondent's cooperation. Part of the problem for a refusal to participate is because the respondents do not want to take the time or because they regard it as an intrusion of their privacy. Refusals are a concern even with panels.[47]

As we previously mentioned, one way to overcome refusals is to use incentives as a token of appreciation. In a review of 15 different mail surveys, researchers found that

Refusals to participate in surveys are increasing worldwide.

TABLE 14.2   The Three Types of Nonresponses with Surveys

Name	Description
Refusal	The prospective respondent declines to participate in the survey.
Break-off	The respondent stops answering in the middle of the survey.
Item Omission	The respondent does not answer a particular question but does answer questions after that question.

MARKETING RESEARCH INSIGHT   Practical Application

14.4 Do Respondents Participate in Surveys Due to Topic Interest?

There is a commonly held belief that survey respondents are more inclined to take part in a survey if the topic has some high level of interest to them. Three researchers[48] set out to test this belief. They employed four different surveys, each on a different topic and each with a different household population. The populations were teachers, new parents, senior citizens, and political contributors. The topics were education and schools, child care and parenting, Medicare and health issues, voting and elections, and issues facing the nation. Respondents were selected with random sampling methods,

and all those selected were approached with a telephone survey. A total of 2,330 respondents participated in the surveys, with an overall response rate of 63%.

The results: People do cooperate more with surveys that have high topic interest to them. In fact, the researchers found that with a survey topic of high interest to the person, the chances of that person taking part are 40% higher than with a low-interest topic. Clearly, if a marketing researcher believes the survey topic will be interesting to potential respondents, it is vital to divulge the topic very early in the introduction. Alternatively, if the survey topic is not highly interesting to those who will be asked to participate in the survey, the researcher should give strong consideration to incentives and inducements for individuals who participate.

inclusion of a small gift, such as a $1.50 rollerball pen, increased response rates by nearly 14%. A second feature that contributes to refusals is the length of the questionnaire.[49] The study previously cited found that for every additional minute it takes to fill out the questionnaire, the response rate drops by 0.85%. Response rates to mail surveys are also influenced by the type of appeal that is made in the cover letter. Results from one study indicated that a social utility appeal was more effective in increasing response rates when an educational institution was the sponsor. On the other hand, an egoistic appeal was more effective when the sponsor was a commercial organization. An egoistic appeal is a suggestion that the respondent's individual responses are highly important in completing the research task.[50]

Break-Offs During the Interview

If tired, confused, or uninterested, respondents may "break off" in the middle of an interview.

A **break-off** occurs when a respondent reaches a certain point and then decides not to answer any more questions for the survey. As you would expect, there are many reasons for break-offs. For instance, the interview may take longer than the respondent initially believed; the topic and specific questions may prove to be distasteful, too personal, or boring; the instructions may be confusing; or a sudden interruption may occur. Sometimes with self-administered surveys, a researcher will receive a partially completed questionnaire that the respondent simply stopped filling out.

It is critical that well-trained interviewers be employed to carry out the surveys. In a discussion on how to improve respondent cooperation, Howard Gershowitz, senior vice president of MKTG, said, "I think the interviewers have to be taken out of the vacuum and be included in the process. Companies that are succeeding right now realize that the interviewers are the key to their success."[51] Increasingly, research providers are focusing on improved training techniques and field audits.

Refusals to Answer Specific Questions (Item Omission)

Occasionally, a respondent will refuse to answer a particular question that he or she considers too personal or a private matter.

Even if a refusal or break-off situation does not occur, a researcher will sometimes find that specific questions have lower response rates than others. In fact, if a marketing researcher suspects ahead of time that a particular question, such as the respondent's annual income for last year, will have some degree of refusal, it is appropriate to include the designation

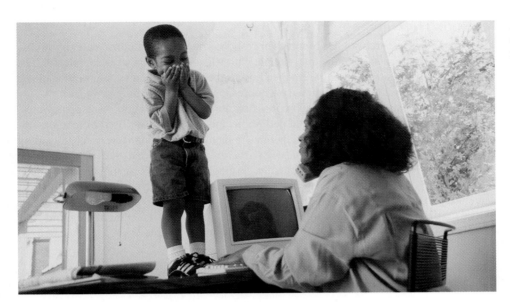

A break-off may occur at any time during an interview.

"refusal" on the questionnaire. Of course, it is not wise to put these designations on self-administered questionnaires because respondents may use this option simply as a cop-out, when they might have provided accurate answers if the designation were not there. "**Item omission**" is the phrase sometimes used to identify the percentage of the sample that did not answer a particular question.[52] Research has shown that sensitive questions elicit more item omissions and questions that require more mental effort garner more "don't know's."[53] So it is useful for a researcher to offer the "don't know" option with the latter type of questions to reduce item omissions.

What is a Completed Interview?

As we learned earlier, you will experience both break-offs and item omissions. At which point does a break-off still constitute a completed interview? At which level of item omission do we deem a survey to be incomplete? In other words, a researcher must have a definition or otherwise specify the criteria for a "completed interview."

Almost all surveys will have some item omissions and break-offs. However, simply because a few questions remain unanswered does not mean you do not have a completed interview. But, how many questions must be answered before you have a completed interview? The answer to this question is a judgment call, and it will vary with each marketing research project. Only in rare cases will it be necessary that all respondents answer all of the questions. In most others, the researcher will adopt some decision rule that defines completed versus not completed interviews. For example, in most research studies there are questions directed at the primary purpose of the study. Also, there are usually questions asked for purposes of adding additional insights into how respondents answered the primary questions. Such secondary questions often include a list of demographic questions. Demographics, because they are more personal in nature, are typically placed at the end of the questionnaire. Because they are not the primary focus of the study, a **completed interview** may be defined as one in which all the primary questions have been answered. In this way, you will have data for your primary questions and most of the data for your secondary questions. Interviewers can then be given a specific statement as to what constitutes a completed survey, such as "If the respondent answers through Question 18, you may count it as a completion." (The demographics begin with Question 19.) Likewise, the researcher must adopt a decision rule for determining the extent of item omissions necessary to invalidate a survey or a particular question.

You must define a "completed" interview.

Measuring Nonresponse Error in Surveys

Most marketing research studies report their response rates. The **response rate** essentially enumerates the percentage of the total sample with which interviews were completed. It is, therefore, the opposite of the nonresponse rate (a measure of nonresponse error). If you have a 75% response rate, then you have a nonresponse error of 25%.

The research industry has an accepted way to calculate a survey's response rate.

For many years, there was much confusion about the calculation of response rates. There was no one universally accepted definition, and different firms used different methods to calculate response rates. In fact, there were many terms in common usage, including *completion rate*, *cooperation rate*, *interview rate*, *at-home rate*, and *refusal rate*, among others. In 1982, however, CASRO (Council of American Survey Research Organizations) published a special report in an attempt to provide a uniform definition and method for calculating the response rate.[54]

According to the CASRO report, response rate is defined as the ratio of the number of completed interviews to the number of eligible units in the sample.[55] Or,

CASRO Response Rate Formula (simple form)

$$\text{Response rate} = \frac{\text{number of completed interviews}}{\text{number of eligible units in sample}}$$

In many studies, eligible respondents are determined by screening or qualifying questions. For example, if we were working with a department store that was specifically concerned with its kitchenwares department, we would determine respondents' eligibility for the survey by asking them the screening question, "Do you shop at Acme Department Store regularly?" If the person answers "yes," then we would ask, "Have you shopped in the kitchenwares department at any time during the last 3 months?" If the person answers "yes" to this question, then he or she is eligible to take part in the survey.

Ineligible people, those who refuse the survey, and those who cannot be reached are included in the formula for response rate.

Let's assume that we have a sample of 1,000 shoppers and the results of the survey are:

Completions = 400

Ineligible = 300

Refusals = 100

This information allows you to calculate the number of sample units that are (a) eligible, (b) noneligible, and (c) not ascertained.

When calculating the response rate, we have the number of completions in the numerator (as usual). However, in the denominator we have the number of completions plus the percentage of those who refused, who were busy, and eligible not-at-homes. Because we do not talk to those who refuse (before the screening question), don't answer, have busy signals, or who are not at home, how do we determine the percentage of these people that would have been eligible? We multiply their number by the percentage of those that we did talk with that are eligible. By doing this, we are assuming that the same percentage of eligibles exist in the population of those that we did talk with (of the 700 we talked with, 0.57 were eligible) as exist in the population of those that we did not get to talk with (due to refusals, no answers, busy, or not-at-homes).

The formula for calculating the response rate for this situation is:

CASRO Response Rate Fomula (Expanded Form)

$$\text{Response rate} = \frac{\text{completions}}{\text{completions} + \left(\dfrac{\text{completions}}{\text{completions} + \text{ineligible}}\right) \times (\text{refusals} + \text{not reached})}$$

Here are the calculations:

Calculation of CASRO Response Rate (Expanded Form)

$$\text{Response rate} = \frac{400}{400 + \left(\dfrac{400}{400 + 300}\right)(100 + 200)}$$

$$= \frac{400}{400 + (0.57)(300)}$$

$$= 70.0\%$$

How to Calculate a Response Rate Using the CASRO Formula

Although the CASRO formulas seem simple and straightforward, questions arise as to exactly how to interpret them when dealing with individual research projects. We have created this Active Learning exercise so you can appreciate what goes into the proper calculation of a response rate.

We are providing you with this example of a generic telephone survey because it seems that all research projects are unique when trying to calculate a response rate. For example, although the situation we present here is fairly common, we use two of the response rate formulas discussed in this chapter in an attempt to provide you with as much detail as possible so that you will understand how to calculate a response rate.

> **Population:** Survey of car-buying attitudes and behavior in households with telephones in Anytown, USA.
>
> **Sampling Frame:** Telephone directory.
>
> **Eligibility of Respondents:** The survey seeks information about car dealers and recent car-purchasing behavior. Your client wants information collected *only from individuals who have purchased an automobile within the last yea*r. Consequently, a screening question was asked at the beginning of the survey to determine if the respondent, or anyone in the household, had purchased a car within the last year.

Assume you are doing this survey as a class project and you have been assigned the task of conducting telephone interviews. You are given a list of randomly selected telephone numbers and told to fill a quota of five completions. You are instructed to make at least three contact attempts before giving up on a telephone number. Also, you are given a call record sheet where you are to write in the result of each and every call attempt that you make. So, as you call each number, you record one of the following outcomes by the telephone number and in the column corresponding to which contact attempt pertained to that particular call. The results that you can record are as follows:

> **Disconnected (D):** Message from phone company stating number no longer in service.
>
> **Wrong Target (WT):** (Ineligible) number is a business phone and you are interested only in residences.
>
> **Ineligible Respondent (IR):** No one in household has purchased an automobile within last year.
>
> **Refusal (R):** Subject refuses to participate.
>
> **Terminate (T):** Subject begins survey but stops before completing all questions.
>
> **Completed (C):** Questionnaire is completed.
>
> **Busy (BSY):** Phone line is busy; attempt call-back at later time unless this is your third attempt.
>
> **No Answer (NA):** No one anwers or you encounter a telephone answering device. You may leave a message and state that you will call back later unless this is your third attempt.

Call Back (CB):   Subject has instructed you to call back at a more convenient time; record call-back time and date and return call unless this is your third attempt.

Let us assume that your list of numbers and codes looks like the following:

Telephone Number	1st Attempt	2nd Attempt	3rd Attempt
474-2892	No Answer	No Answer	Completed
474-2668	Busy	Ineligible Respondent	
488-3211	Disconnected		
488-2289	Completed		
672-8912	Wrong Target		
263-6855	Busy	Busy	Busy
265-9799	Terminate		
234-7160	Refusal		
619-6019	Call Back	Busy	Busy
619-8200	Ineligible Respondent		
474-2716	Ineligible Respondent		
774-7764	No Answer	No Answer	
474-2654	Disconnected		
488-4799	Wrong Target		
619-0015	Busy	Completed	
265-4356	No Answer	No Answer	Completed
265-4480	Wrong Target		
263-8898	No Answer	No Answer	No Answer
774-2213	Completed		

You should note that you completed your quota of five completed interviews with 19 telephone numbers. So, the response rate computation should not include anything about any telephone numbers that you did not have to call in your part of the survey even if these numbers were provided to you.

Look at the last code you recorded for each number and count the number of each code. Insert these numbers into the following response-rate formula to determine your correctly computed response rate:

$$\text{Response rate} = \frac{C}{C + \left(\dfrac{C}{C + IR + WT}\right)(BSY + D + T + R + NA)}$$

$$= \underline{\hspace{2cm}} \%$$

Note how ineligibles were handled in the formula. Both IR and WT were counted as ineligibles. The logic is that the percentage of eligibles among those who were talked with is the same as among those not talked with (BSY, D, T, R, and NA).

Reducing Nonresponse Error

We have now learned the three types of nonresponse error as well as the various factors that are included in the calculation of the response rate. Obviously, marketing researchers cannot eliminate nonresponse, but they do endeavor to minimize nonresponse. One set of tactics is aimed at reducing the number of refusals. Each survey data-collection mode represents a unique potential for nonresponse. Mail surveys historically represent the worst case, but even with these, there are many strategies employed by marketing researchers to increase response rates.[56] Such strategies include **advance notification**[57] via postcard or telephone, **monetary incentives**,[58] and **follow-up contacts**. Identification of respondents prior to mailing the survey can increase response rates for a 10-minute survey from 27.5% to 33.7%. In addition to respondent identification, if respondent cooperation can be secured in advance, the response rate can be improved to 40%. Researchers are now experimenting with other data-collection methods such as faxes, e-mail, and so on as means of increasing response rates. However, one has to contend with other problems, such as a restricted population, loss of anonymity, and shorter questionnaires.[59]

Tactics such as advance notification, monetary incentives, and follow-up mailings are used to increase response rates.

Other tactics are aimed at reducing the not-at-homes, busy signals, and no answers. For instance, several **call-back attempts** should be made. Interviewers should be trained to write the time and date when the respondent is not at home, the phone is busy, or there is no answer. Call-back attempts, usually three or four, should be made at a later time and/or date. Marketing research firms have designed special forms that can keep track of the several call-back attempts that may be made to obtain a completed survey from a particular respondent. Usually, this sheet allows for a total of four call-back attempts. There are provisions to mark the time and date of the call as well as the result. The results are coded so that the data analyst can find out whether the nonresponse was due to a disconnected number, language problems, refusal to answer, and so on.

Call-back forms are essential tools for tracking attempts to reduce nonresponses.

The CASRO response-rate formula was developed for "landline" telephone surveys. As you know, many people have shifted a large portion of all of their telephone communications to cellular or wireless telephones. Marketing researchers are wrestling with ways to access potential respondents who are totally wireless or otherwise more accessible on their wireless telephones. However, there are at least four thorny ethical issues that accompany this strategy. Read Marketing Research Insight 14.5 to learn about these ethical considerations.

We discussed using replacement samples in Chapter 12. There are many methods for replacing samples. Essentially, they all strive to replace a nonrespondent (noncontact or refusal) with an equivalent respondent during the survey. For instance, a telephone interviewer using a telephone book to interview every twenty-fifth name may find that one of these people refuses to participate in the survey. To replace the nonrespondent, the interviewer can be directed to use a "drop-down" replacement procedure. That is, the interviewer will call the next name below that one rather than skipping to the next twenty-fifth name. The interviewer can continue calling names in this manner until a replacement is secured for the refusal. On finding a replacement, the original 25-name skip interval would be resumed. The basic strategy for treating nonresponse error during the conduct of the survey involves a combination of judicious use of incentives and persuasion to cooperate and repeated attempts to reach the original prospective respondent. Systematic replacement of those respondents who, for whatever reason, do not take part in the survey, helps achieve desired levels of allowable error.

Adjusting Results to Reduce the Effects of Nonresponse Error

Nonresponse error should always be measured, and if we assess the degree of nonresponse to be a problem, we are obliged to make adjustments. Of course, if we do not find significant nonresponse error, there is no reason to make adjustments. But, if some exists, there are at least two methods of compensating for its presence[60]: weighted averages and oversampling.[61]

MARKETING RESEARCH INSIGHT   Ethical Application

14.5 Ethical Considerations in Surveys Using Cell Phones

Worldwide, the "cell phone" generation continues to grow, and, in some cases, it is larger than the "landline" population of potential survey respondents. On the surface, it might seem that accessing cell phone users would be just the same as accessing landline users for surveys; however, there are at least four thorny ethical aspects[62] accompanying cell phone surveys that marketing researchers should consider as they increasingly rely on cell phone populations.

1. **Cell phone surveys are inherently unsafe.**   While the typical landline telephone survey respondent is comfortably situated at home, the typical cell phone survey respondent is more likely to be engaged in some multitasking activity: driving a car, negotiating a busy sidewalk or stairway, operating machinery, exercising on a treadmill, or even catching a train. So, it is up to the ethical marketing reseacher to include simple questions about the reasonableness of the respondent taking part in a survey that may distract from the primary task. If sufficient danger exists, the survey should be postponed.
2. **Cell phone surveys are unevenly expensive for respondents.**   Depending on calling plans and other factors, there may be a cost applied to the cell phone

respondent for the time used on the cell phone for the survey. This cost varies by respondent, and the ethical marketing researcher will build into the survey an offer for remuneration of the expense incurred by taking part in the survey. Of course, some respondents will decline this offer because it would require disclosure of personal information such as name and mailing address.

3. **Most cell phone surveys are not brief.**   The general use and expectation of cell phone users is that calls will be short and to the point. Granted, some cell phone users do not have this expectation, but the general belief is that most are not expecting a long phone call. The ethical marketing researcher will therefore strive to make the cell phone survey as brief as possible.
4. **Cell phone users are disproportionately nonadults.**   While practically no underaged individuals own landline telephones, the number of underaged/nonadult cell phone owners is immense. This situation means that random cell phone calls are guaranteed to access teenagers and even preteens. Nonadults are more susceptible to question bias and far less sophisticated than adults in their approach to surveys. The ethical marketing researcher will take precautions that ensure that interviewers can detect when a nonadult has been contacted and not include such underage individuals if they are not consistent with the objectives of the survey.

Weighting responses by subgroup sizes is a way to compensate for nonresponse error.

WEIGHTED AVERAGES. Weighted averages involve applying weights that are believed to accurately reflect the proportions that subgroups represent in the population to the subgroup means to compute an overall score that adjusts for the nonresponse differences in the subgroups. This way, a weighted average is applied to adjust a sample's results to be consistent with the believed true demographic profile.

Caution should be used in weighting responses, and it should be done only in unusual situations.

For example, if we believed the target market for a sunblock spray was really 50% married and 50% single, but an online survey sample contained 25% married and 75% single, we could adjust the results using a 50:50 weighted average. One question on the survey may have asked, "On the average, how much would you expect to pay for a 4-oz bottle of NoSun Sunblock Spray?" We find that the married respondents' average answer is $2.00, whereas the singles' average is $3.00. If we were to take the overall average of the online survey (25:75) sample, it would be computed as $2.75 ($0.25 \times \$2.00 + 0.75 \times \$3.00$), but if we applied the 50:50 true ratio, the average price would turn out to be $2.50 ($0.5 \times \$2.00 + 0.5 \times \$3.00$). Nonresponse error distorted the average price, but we have adjusted using the believed true demographic profile to eliminate that source of error.

If a researcher believes that nonresponse will be a problem, oversampling can be used in order to compensate.

OVERSAMPLING. The second general strategy for dealing with nonresponse error in a survey is typically more expensive, but it is applied under certain circumstances. With the second strategy, the marketing researcher uses **oversampling**, which involves drawing a sample that is larger than the group to be analyzed. Please note that we are referring to an instance in which the final sample will be a good deal larger than the target sample size, and not a case of drawing a large number of potential respondents in order to achieve the target sample size. The researcher then draws a subsample of respondents to match the believed profile of the target group. Alternatively, with high refusal rates for specific questions, oversampling may generate sufficient numbers of respondents who do answer these questions.

For example, using the sunblock spray example, we might post the survey online for a longer time and receive 2,000 responses, but still with the incorrect 75% singles and 25% married distribution. Now, we would use our computer capabilities to randomly select a 50:50 sample of marrieds to singles (that is, 500 of each type) out of our respondent group data set. We would not need to perform the weighted averaging because the sample being analyzed is in the proper proportions. In essence, however, we would be throwing away 1,000 responses returned by marrieds to bring our sample into conformity with the married:single population ratio. In fact, if we greatly oversampled, we would have the opportunity to draw a subsample from the respondents that matched our believed population along several demographic factors, such as gender, age, education, income, and so forth.

But with more factors, the final sample size could decrease, and more returned questionnaires would be left out of our analyses. Obviously, it is the best policy to strive to reduce nonresponse errors of all types to as low a level as possible by appropriate survey method choice, use of incentives, and whatever other inducements are available to the researcher so that adjustments are not necessary. As a rule of thumb, such adjustments, though sometimes appropriate, should be avoided.

PRELIMINARY QUESTIONNAIRE SCREENING

As we have indicated, nonresponses appear in practically every survey. At the same time, there are respondents whose answers have a suspicious pattern to them. Both of these occurences necessitate a separate phase of the data-collection stage in the marketing research process that involves the inspection of questionnaires as they are being prepared for entry into a computer file for tabulation and analysis. Alternatively, the responses may automatically be placed in a file, such as with an online survey. Some data-collection companies allow direct entry of responses into a computer file, and this option is becoming commonplace. It is in these cases that the researcher should screen the responses for problems prior to analysis.

Completed questionnaires should be screened for errors.

Researchers develop a sixth sense about the quality of responses, and they can often spot errors just by inspecting raw questionnaires or questionnaire files. So, it may be that a stack of completed questionnaires is sent to the researcher whose office might be in Omaha, Little Rock, or Boston. Regardless of the format, it is good practice to perform a screening step to catch respondent errors before tabulation of the data takes place. So when inspecting individual respondents' answers, the reseacher may be looking at a hard-copy questionnaire or may be scrutinizing the code numbers in a row of a computer file.

What to Look for in Questionnaire Inspection

What is the purpose of questionnaire checks? Despite all of the precautions described thus far, the danger still exists that problem questionnaires are included in the completions. The purpose of inspecting completed questionnaires is to determine the degree of "bad" questionnaires and, if deemed advisable, to pull the ones with severe problems.

Problem questionnaires are ones that fall into the following categories: They have questionable validity; they have unacceptable patterns of incompleteness; they have unacceptable amounts of apparent respondent misunderstanding; or they have other complications

TABLE 14.3   Types of Response Problems Found During Questionnaire Inspection

Problem Type	Description
Incomplete questionnaire	Questionnaire is incompletely filled out. The respondent stopped answering questions at some point (break-off).
Nonresponse to specific question	The respondent refused to answer particular question(s), but answered others before and after it (item omission).
Yea- or nay-saying pattern	Respondent exhibits a persistent tendency to respond favorably or unfavorably, respectively, regardless of the questions.
Middle-of-the-road pattern	Respondent indicates "no opinion" to most questions.
Unreliable responses	Respondent is not consistent on a reliability check.

such as illegible writing, damage in transit, or some other obvious problem. Five different problems that can be identified by screening completed questionnaires are incomplete questionnaires, nonresponses to specific questions, yea- or nay-saying patterns, middle-of-the-road patterns, and unreliable responses. We describe each problem and summarize each one in Table 14.3. In industry jargon, these are "exceptions," and they signal possible field data-collection errors to a researcher.

INCOMPLETE QUESTIONNAIRES. Incomplete questionnaires are those in which the later questions or pages of a questionnaire are left blank. We just described this type of nonresponse error as a "break-off," which is its common label with personal or telephone interviews. That is, the researcher might find that a respondent answered the first three pages of questions, and then, for some reason, the respondent stopped. As we noted earlier, perhaps the respondent became bored, or the questions might have been too complicated, or perhaps the respondent thought the topic was too personal. The reason that the questionnaire was not completed may never be known.

Some questionnaires may be only partially completed.

NONRESPONSES TO SPECIFIC QUESTIONS—(ITEM OMISSIONS). Also, as we noted in our descriptions of the various types of nonresponse, for whatever reasons, respondents will sometimes leave a question blank. In a telephone interview, they may decline answering a question, and the interviewer might note this occurrence with the designation "ref" (refused) or some other code to indicate that the respondent failed to answer the question.

When a respondent does not answer a particular question, it is referred to as an "item omission."

YEA- OR NAY-SAYING PATTERNS. Even when questions are answered, there can be signs of problems. A **yea-saying** pattern may be evident on one questionnaire in the form of all "yes" or "strongly agree" answers.[63] The yea-sayer has a persistent tendency to respond in the affirmative regardless of the question, and yea-saying implies that the responses are not valid. The negative counterpart to the yea-saying is **nay-saying**, identifiable as persistent responses in the negative.

Yea-saying and nay-saying are seen as persistent tendencies on the parts of some respondents to agree or disagree, respectively, with most of the questions asked.

MIDDLE-OF-THE-ROAD PATTERNS. The **middle-of-the-road pattern** is seen as a preponderance of "no opinion" responses. No opinion is in essence no response, and the prevalence of no opinion on a questionnaire may signal low interest, lack of attention, or even objections to being involved in the survey. True, a respondent may not have an opinion on a topic, but if one gives a great many no-opinion answers, questions arise as to how useful that respondent is to the survey.

Some respondents will hide their opinions by indicating "no opinion" throughout the survey.

UNRELIABLE RESPONSES. We defined reliability in a previous chapter as the consistency in a respondent's answers. Sometimes a researcher will deliberately include a consistency check. For instance, if a respondent encountered the question "Is the amount of electricity used by your electric appliances a concern to you?" the person might respond with a "yes." Later in the survey, this question appears: "When you use your electric coffee maker, toaster, or electric can opener, do you think about how much electricity is being used?" Now suppose that the respondent answers with a "no" to this question. This signals an inconsistent or **unreliable respondent** who should be eliminated from the sample.

There are other bothersome problems that can pop up during questionnaire screening. For example, you might find that a respondent has checked more than one response option when only one was supposed to be checked. Another respondent may have failed to look at the back of a questionnaire page and thus missed all of the questions there. A third respondent may have ignored the agree–disagree scale and written in comments about energy conservation. Usually, detecting these errors requires physically examining the questionnaires. With surveys that are done online, however, these problems can usually be blocked by selecting options or requirements in the online questionnaire program that will prevent such errors from occuring.

> Problems found when screening completed questionnaires include incomplete questionnaires, nonresponses to specific questions, yea- or nay-saying patterns, middle-of-the-road patterns, and unreliable responses.

SPSS Student Assistant: Getting SPSS Help

Summary

Total error in survey research is a combination of sampling error and nonsampling error. Sampling error may be controlled by the sample plan and the sample size. Researchers must know both the sources of nonsampling error and how to minimize the effect on total errors. The data-collection phase of marketing research holds great potential for nonsampling errors. There are intentional as well as unintentional errors on the part of both interviewers and respondents that must be regulated. Dishonesty, misunderstanding, and fatigue affect fieldworkers; whereas falsehoods, refusals, misunderstanding, and fatigue affect respondents. We described the several controls and procedures used to overcome these sources of error.

At the same time, nonresponse errors of various types are encountered in the data-collection phase. Nonresponse error is measured by the calculation of the response rate. There are several methods for improving the response rate and thereby lowering nonresponse error. A weighted average method or oversampling may be applied to bring the sample back into alignment with the population. Once the interviews are completed, the researcher must screen them for errors. Invariably, incomplete questionnaires and refusals are present, and tendencies such as yea-saying may be seen as well.

Key Terms

Nonsampling error 403
Data collection 403
Fieldworker error 403
Respondent error 403
Intentional fieldworker errors 403
Interviewer cheating 403
Leading the respondent 405
Unintentional interviewer
   errors 405
Personal characteristics 405
Interviewer misunderstanding 406
Fatigue-related mistakes 406
Intentional respondent errors 407

Falsehoods 407
Nonresponse 408
Unintentional respondent error 409
Respondent misunderstanding 409
Guessing 409
Attention loss 409
Distractions 409
Respondent fatigue 409
Supervision 410
Validation 411
Orientation sessions 412
Role-playing sessions 412
Anonymity 412

Confidentiality 412
Incentives 413
Validation checks 413
Third-person technique 413
Questionnaire instructions and
   examples 413
Reversals of scale endpoints 413
Prompters 413
Refusals 415
Break-offs 416
Item omission 417
Completed interview 417
Response rate 418

Review Questions/Applications

1. Distinguish sampling error from nonsampling error.

2. Because we cannot easily calculate nonsampling errors, how must the prudent researcher handle nonsampling error?

3. Identify different types of intentional fieldworker error and the controls used to minimize them. Identify different types of unintentional fieldworker error and the controls used to minimize them.

4. Identify different types of intentional respondent error and the controls used to minimize them. Identify different types of unintentional respondent error and the controls used to minimize them.

5. Define "nonresponse." List three types of nonresponse found in surveys.

6. If a survey is found to have resulted in significant nonresponse error, what should the researcher do?

7. Why is it necessary to perform preliminary screening of completed questionnaires?

8. Identify five different problems that a researcher might find while screening completed questionnaires.

9. What is an "item omission," and how do marketing researchers handle the case?

10. Your church is experiencing low attendance with its Wednesday-evening Bible classes. You volunteer to design a telephone questionnaire aimed at finding out why church members are not attending these classes. Because the church has limited funds, members will be used as telephone interviewers. List the steps necessary to ensure good data quality in using this "do-it-yourself" option for field data collection.

11. A new mall-intercept company opens its offices in a nearby discount mall, and its president calls on the insurance company where you work to solicit business. It happens that your company is about to do a study on the market reaction to a new whole-life insurance policy it is considering adding to its line. Make an outline of the information you would want from the mall-intercept company president in order to assess the quality of its services.

12. Acme Refrigerant Reclamation Company performs large-scale reclamation of contaminated refrigerants as mandated by the U.S. Environmental Protection Agency. It wishes to determine what types of companies will use this service, so the marketing director designs a questionnaire intended for telephone administration. Respondents will be plant engineers, safety engineers, or directors of major companies throughout the United States. Should Acme use a professional field data-collection company to gather the data? Why or why not?

13. You work part-time in a telemarketing company. Your compensation is based on the number of credit card applicants you sign up with the telemarketing approach. The company owner has noticed that the credit card solicitation business is slowing down, and so she decides to take on some marketing research telephone interview business. When you start work on Monday, she says that you are to do telephone interviews and gives you a large stack of questionnaires to have completed. What intentional fieldworker errors are possible under the circumstances described here?

14. Indicate what specific intentional and unintentional respondent errors are likely with each of the following surveys:

    a. The Centers for Disease Control sends out a mail questionnaire on attitudes and practices concerning prevention of AIDS.

    b. Eyemasters has a mall-intercept survey performed to determine opinions and users of contact lenses.

    c. Boy Scouts of America sponsors a telephone survey on American's views on humanitarian service agencies.

15. How do you define a "completion," and how does this definition help a researcher deal with "incomplete questionnaires"?

16. What is nay-saying and how does it differ from yea-saying? What should a researcher do if a respondent is suspected of being a nay-sayer?

17. On your first day as a student marketing intern at the O-Tay Research Company, the supervisor hands you a list of yesterday's telephone interviewer records. She tells you to analyze them and to give her a report by 5 pm. Well, get to it!

	Ronnie	Mary	Pam	Isabelle
Completed	20	30	15	19
Refused	10	2	8	9
Ineligible	15	4	14	15
Busy	20	10	21	23
Disconnected	0	1	3	2
Break-off	5	2	7	9
No answer	3	2	4	3

CASE 14.1

CASS CORRIDOR FOOD CO-OP

Founded in the 1960s, Cass Corridor Food Co-Op is a small, mostly organic or naturally grown fruits and vegetables retailer, located in Detroit, Michican on Cass Avenue. At one time, Cass Avenue and the "corridor" of streets parallel to it was a prestigious location for the wealthiest citizens of Detroit to live, but Cass Corridor fell on very hard times in the 1960s, when it earned a reputation as being one of the most dangerous neighborhoods in the United States. Drug sellers and users, criminals and homeless people, and gangs roamed the area until the late 1980s, when demolition and rebuilding dramatically changed the enviroment for the better. Now called "Midtown" by the new residents who are trying to revitalize it as a thriving community, it is still referred to as "Cass Corridor" by some Detroit residents who remember its ugly past.

Cass Corridor Co-Op was founded to help the poor and unfortunate residents of this area during its worst times, so it is essentially a "bare-bones" operation. Most of the new "Midtown" residents do not use the co-op, so the organizers and operators of Cass Corridor Co-Op have talked to a professor of marketing from Wayne State University, which is located directly north of the Cass Corridor area, who recommended that the co-op conduct a survey of the Midtown residents to see if the co-op's mission and approach fit the new consumers who are living there. Because he realized that Cass Corridor Co-Op operates on a meager budget, he recommends as a means of holding costs down that it use the American Marketing Association (AMA) student chapter for data collection via a telephone survey.

While the Cass Corridor Co-Op folks were excited, they were skeptical of the ability of students to execute this survey, so the professor proposed a meeting with Cass Corridor Co-Op officials, the marketing research projects director of the student AMA chapter, and himself to discuss the matter. When he returned to campus, he informed the AMA student chapter president of the opportunity and told her to have the marketing research projects director draft a list of the quality-control safeguards that would be used in a Cass Corridor Co-Op community telephone survey in which 20 AMA student chapter member interviewers would be calling from their apartments or dorm rooms.

1. Take the role of the marketing research projects director and draft all of the interviewer controls you believe are necessary to effect data collection comparable in quality to that gathered by a professional telephone interviewing company.

2. The American Marketing Association student chapter president calls the marketing research projects director and says, "I'm concerned about the questionnaire's length. It will take over 20 minutes for the typical respondent to complete over the phone. Isn't the length going to cause problems?" Again, take the role of the marketing research projects director. Indicate what non-response problems might result from the questionnaire's length, and recommend ways to counter each of these problems.

CASE 14.2

BIG WEST RESEARCH: CATI OR ONLINE PANEL?

Big West Research, Inc. is a full-service interview company located in 10 regional malls throughout the West, extending as far south as San Diego. Each location is equipped with a complete focus group facility that accounts for approximately 25% of Big West's revenues. Another 25% is derived from Big West's mall-intercept interviewing, and the remaining 50% of the business is obtained from centralized telephone interview services. Work has been reasonably steady in all three areas over the past 5 years; although, the mall-intercept interviewing seems to be on a decline. Big West Research has continually wrestled with quality problems in its telephone interview business. The major difficulty is retention of interviewers. An internal study has revealed that the average location needs six telephone interviewers to work full-time and another three part-timers who are hired as the volume of work requires. When work is slack, the part-time interviewers are laid off, and when the workload increases beyond the ability of the full-time interviewers, the part-timers are used for the time they are needed. The average length of time full-time telephone interviewers work for Big West is just under 6 months.

Quality-control problems have affected business. It is increasingly more difficult to hire good telephone interviewers. One major account recently informed Big West that it would no longer use its services when a major error was found in how Big West's interviewers administered a critical question on its survey. Other accounts have complained that Big West is slow in turning telephone interview work around, and they have also noted errors in the work that has been done. At the same time, marketing research trade publications are reporting a general decline in telephone research due to nonresponse problems, issues of privacy, and various "call-blocking" systems that consumers can use to screen their incoming calls.

Ned Allen, the manager responsible for telephone interviewing, has met with various computer services companies about the problem. Ned is thinking of recommending that Big West move away from centralized telephone interviewing and to computer-assisted telephone interviewing (CATI). Ned has done some preliminary analysis, and he figures that CATI would greatly eliminate interviewer errors while speeding up interviews. He thinks that the ease of a CATI system will probably entice interviewers to stay with Big West longer. Also, because CATI can be integrated across all 10 locations, it would serve to spread the work evenly across the full-time interviewers. Right now, each location operates like a stand-alone data-collection company, but work is allocated to each through Big West's main office located in San Francisco.

Ned finds that a fully integrated CATI system would require somewhere around $250,000 in installation costs, and annual maintenance/upgrading is going to be about $150,000. Also Big West would need to levy a setup charge of $250 per page on clients to convert questionnaires to a CATI format.

Ned is also comtemplating dropping the telephone interview business completely and establishing an online panel that would be representative of the "Upscale West USA." It would consist of 20,000 online panelists with 1,000 in each of the 20 largest cities in the "Upscale West" (California, Oregon, Washington, Arizona, and Nevada). The panel respondents would be upscale consumers who would be compensated with catalog buying points for responding to at least three online surveys per month. Ned estimates the annual panelist compensation cost alone would be $2 million. The progamming of the online service will cost about $250,000, and the Internet fees to maintain the online panel is estimated to be about the same amount.

1. Using your knowledge of the data-collection concepts and issues described in this chapter, make a pro and con list for Ned concerning the CATI system.
2. What is your advice concerning the online panel system that is a great deal more expensive than the CATI system? Should Ned just focus his attention on the CATI system, or should he pursue the online panel idea? Why?

CASE 14.3 Your Integrated Case

ADVANCED AUTOMOBILE CONCEPTS

It has been decided to use an online panel company as the specific data-collection method for the Advanced Automobile Concepts survey. Among the reasons for this decision are (1) use of an online questionnaire; (2) assurance of a random sample that represents U.S. households; (3) high response rate; (4) quick survey data collection; (5) low refusals to particular questions; (6) demographic, automobile ownership, and media preference responses in the online panel company's database so no need to ask these questions; and (7) reasonable total cost. Nick Adams of AAConcepts has agreed that the selection of the online panel company is entirely up to CMG Research.

Cory Rogers's team at CMG Research has narrowed the choice down to two different online panel companies that have made the "final cut," meaning that inspections of their website descriptions, e-mail and telephone communications, and other factors have narrowed the set of possible providers down. The costs of using either of these companies are highly comparable, so no single provider is favored at this time.

Cory's team is aware of a set of questions published by ESOMAR (European Society for Opinion and Marketing Research) entitled "26 Questions to Help Research Buyers of Online Samples,"[64] and they decide to select five questions that are geared toward data quality. Each competing online panel company had prepared a short response to each of the five questions, which are listed here.

Question 1. What experience does your company have with providing online samples for market research?

Company A: We have conducted market research since 1999. We are the only panel company to take advantage of computer technology and provide a truly nationally representative U.S. sample online.

Company B: We have supplied online U.S. samples since 1990, European samples since 2000, and our Asian Panel went "live" in 2005. We have supplied approximately 5,000 online samples to our clients in the past 10 years.

Question 2. What are the people told when they are recruited?

Company A: Individuals volunteer for our online panel via our website, where they are informed that they will be compensated with redemption points based on the number of surveys in which they take part.

Company B: We recruit household members by asking them to join our panel, telling them they can have a say in the development of new products and services. They are rewarded with "credits" that they can use to claim products.

Question 3. If the sample comes from a panel, what is your annual panel turnover/attrition/retention rate?

Company A: Our voluntary drop-out rate is approximately 5% per month. If a panelist misses 10 consecutive surveys, he/she loses panel membership.

Company B: We do a 1-for-1 replacement for each panel member who drops out voluntarily (about 3% per year) or is removed due to nonparticipation (about 2% per year).

Question 4. What profile data is kept on panel members? For how many members is this data collected and how often is this data updated?

Company A: We maintain extensive individual-level data, in the form of about 1,000 variables, including demographics, household characteristics, financials, shopping and ownership, lifestyles, and more. All are updated every other year.

Company B: For each panelist, we have about 2,500 data points on demographics, assortment of goods and services owned, segmentation/lifestyle factors, health-related matters, political opinions, travel, financials, Internet usage, leisure activities, memberships, etc. Our updating is done annually.

Question 5. Explain how people are invited to take part in a survey.

Company A: Typically a survey invitation is sent via e-mail and posted on every selected panel member's personal member page. In either case, we have a link to the online survey location: "Click here to start your survey." The e-mail invitation is sent daily to selected panelists until the survey quota is filled.

Company B: Based on the client's sample requirements, we e-mail selected panelists with a link to the online survey. After 48 hours, if the panelist has not participated, we send a reminder, and again 48 hours after the reminder.

Keeping the quality of the data as a foremost concern, compare the practices of these two competing panel companies and recommend one that you think CMG research should use for the Advanced Automobile Concepts survey. Why have you selected your choice over the competitor?

Chapter
15 Using Basic Descriptive Analysis

Learning Objectives

- To understand data coding and the data code book
- To learn about the concept of data summarization and the functions it provides
- To appreciate the five basic types of statistical analysis used in marketing research
- To use measures of central tendency and dispersion customarily used in describing data
- To learn how to obtain descriptive statistics with SPSS

Where We Are

Would You Say You Already Know What Basic Descriptive Statistics Are?

When asked what is meant by basic descriptive statistics most students start trying to recall some of those concepts they learned back in the elementary statistics course. "Er, uhhh, are they *t* tests? Or, uhh, are they standard deviations?" A few of you already know what is meant by basic descriptive statistics, are but we will surprise you by telling you *all* of you know what they are! That's correct. You already know. "How can that be possible?"

Think about it this way. What is the first or second question students ask their professors when they return to class after a test and the professor is preparing to hand the graded tests out? Let's see what you think the questions may be? Go ahead, tell us.

"What was the average score on the test?"

You are right! That is the first question asked. Let's suppose that your professor answers "75." Now, some of you were hoping to make much higher than a C and others of you may wonder "Wow! I hope I made a 75 but I wonder how many scored below the average." This is why the second question is . . . go ahead, give it a shot.

"What was the grade distribution? How many A's, B's, C's and so on?"

Correct again! There, we told you that you already knew what basic descriptive statistics are. Basic descriptive statistics answer two fundamental questions: (1) How did the average person respond? and (2) How different are the others from this average? So, when your professor says the average grade was a 75, she is answering the first question. When she gives you the number, or percentage, of letter grades (A through F), she is answering the second question.

Note that it was important to you to know answers to *both* questions. Knowing only the first does tell you the average performance of the class. You do know that a 75 is better than a 55 and it is less than a 90 average. It certainly

What is the first question you ask your professor just before she hands back your graded tests?

tells you something of value, doesn't it? But by only knowing the average, you still don't know how different the other scores are. It is possible that everyone scored a 75! It is also possible that no one scored a 75; some scored very high and some scored very low! Note how different this makes the interpretation of the 75 for the professor. In the first case, everyone is doing "average." In the second case, she has some outstanding students and some who need immediate resuscitation! Again, we see why it is important to look at both these questions.

Let's think of a marketing research application of basic descriptive statistics. In our Applied Automotive Concepts case, we have asked a sample of consumers many questions about their lifestyles, demographics, magazine readership, automobile ownership, and type of new, high-mpg automobile most preferred. After making certain that all the data have been correctly entered into a computer program such as SPSS, the marketing researcher will run basic descriptive statistics. You will have the opportunity to work with this SPSS data set as you read and do the Active Learning and Integrated Case exercises in this chapter. For now, simply read our example.

We will look at the question: "What is your preference for a standard-size, 4-seat hybrid automobile that gets 60 mpg in the city and 50 mpg on the highway?" The answers are measured on a 1–7 scale ranging from "Very undesirable" (1) to "Very desirable" (7). Now we are ready to answer our two questions: What was the average response to the question? Since we have an interval scale, "average" may be an arithmetic mean. As you will learn in this chapter, when you want to calculate an arithmetic mean, you run the SPSS command "Descriptives," which gives you the following output:

SPSS

Descriptive Statistics					
	N	Minimum	Maximum	Mean	Std. Deviation
Preference for 4 seat standard-size hybrid fuel automobile	1000	1	7	4.96	1.626
Valid N (listwise)	1000				

We see our average as 4.96 on a 7-point scale. This is akin to knowing our average test score was 75, and it alone gives us some information. We know there is some preference for this auto; we don't have a real low score nor do we have an extremely high score. Now, what about our second question? How different are those who didn't have this "average" score? Statisticians use the term *variance* to describe the degree to which data vary. One measure of variance is the "standard deviation," which is reported to us in the table as 1.626. The higher this number, the more people differ from the average; the lower the number, the less they differ. Another measure of variance is the "range." We see in the table that some scored the minimum (1) and some scored the maximum (7). If we want to know how many scored in each of the seven different scale categories, we would run another SPSS command, "Frequencies." The output is shown next.

| | | | | Cumulative |
Valid	Frequency	Percent	Valid Percent	Percent
1	31	3.1	3.1	3.1
2	48	4.8	4.8	7.9
3	117	11.7	11.7	19.6
4	175	17.5	17.5	37.1
5	209	20.9	20.9	58.0
6	203	20.3	20.3	78.3
7	217	21.7	21.7	100.0
Total	1000	100.0	100.0	

Table title: **Preference for 4 seat standard-size hybrid fuel automobile**

With these two tables alone, the marketing researcher has provided the client with all the basic descriptive statistics the client needs to understand the responses to this question. In this chapter, you will learn when and how to run "Descriptives" and "Frequencies" in SPSS. When you finish the chapter, you will be able to do more than just articulate what is meant by basic descriptive statistics. You will know how to use the powerful SPSS tool to generate them for you. You will also learn that basic descriptive statistics are the "bread and butter" of most marketing research projects.

T his chapter begins our discussion of the various statistical techniques available to the marketing researcher. As you will soon learn, these really are devices to convert formless data into valuable information just as was done in the "Would you Say You Already Know What Basic Descriptive Statistics Are?" example that you just read. These techniques summarize and communicate patterns found in the data sets marketing researchers analyze. We begin the chapter by describing data coding and the code book. Then we introduce data summarization and the four functions it accomplishes. Here we preview five different types of statistical analyses commonly used by marketing researchers. Next, we define descriptive analysis and discuss descriptive measures, such as the mode, median, and mean. We also discuss measures of variability, including the frequency distribution, range, and standard deviation. It is important to understand when each measure is appropriate, so this topic is addressed. Last, we show you how to obtain the various descriptive statistics available in SPSS.

CODING DATA AND THE DATA CODE BOOK

After questionnaires are screened and exceptions are dealt with, the researcher moves to the data entry stage of the data analysis process. **Data entry** refers to the creation of a computer file that holds the raw data taken from all of the questionnaires deemed suitable for analysis.

Data entry refers to the creation of a computer file that holds the raw data taken from all of the questionnaires deemed suitable for analysis.

A number of data entry options exist, ranging from manual keyboard entry of each and every piece of data to online questionnaire programs and services whereby respondents' responses are stored into a data file immediately after they complete the online survey. Most online systems like Qualtrics have simple data analysis and basic graphical presentation capabilities that can be used while the survey is in progress. Here, the data entry is handled "behind the scenes" and often without the need for a marketing researcher's conscious involvement.

Researchers utilize data coding when preparing and working with a computer data file.

However, data entry requires an operation called **data coding**, defined as the identification of codes that pertain to the possible responses for each question on the questionnaire. Marketing researchers must be aware of data coding and often take an active part in establishing the coding system because data coding has direct consequences for data analysis. Typically, these codes are numeric because numbers are quick and easy to input and computers work with numbers more efficiently than they do with alphanumeric codes. Recall that we discussed precoding the questionnaire in Chapter 11. In large-scale projects, and especially in cases in which the data entry is performed by a subcontractor, researchers utilize a **data code book**, which identifies all of the variable names and code numbers associated with each possible response to each question that makes up the data set. With a code book that describes the data file, any researcher can work on the data set, regardless of whether or not that researcher was involved in the research project during its earlier stages.

With online surveys, such as with Qualtrics, the data file "builds" or "grows" as respondents submit their completed online questionnaires. That is, the codes are programmed into the questionnaire file, but they do not appear as code numbers like those customarily placed on a paper-and-pencil questionnaire. So, in the case of Web-based surveys, the code book is vital, as it is the researcher's only map to decipher the numbers found in the data file and to correlate them to the answers to the questions on the questionnaire.

With SPSS, it is easy to obtain the coding after the SPSS data set has been set up. With the data file opened, and all of the variables and their variable labels defined, use the "Utilities-Variables" command, which brings up a window that isolates each variable's information, such as labels and codes, one-by-one (see Figure 15.1).

FIGURE 15.1

SPSS Variable View and Variables Window Reveal the Underlying Code Book

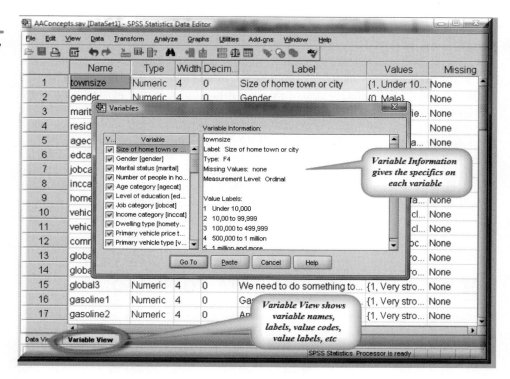

TYPES OF STATISTICAL ANALYSES USED IN MARKETING RESEARCH

As you have learned by using SPSS, experimenting with the data sets we have provided, and becoming familiar with how SPSS works, marketing researchers work with data matrices. A **data matrix** is the coded raw data from a survey. You also know that these data are arranged in columns, which represent answers to the various questions on the survey questionnaire, and rows, which represent each respondent or case. The problem confronting the marketing researcher when faced with a data matrix is **data summarization**, which is defined as the process of describing a data matrix by computing a small number of measures that characterize the data set. Data summarization condenses the data matrix while retaining enough information so the client can mentally envision its salient characteristics.[1] Data summarization is actually any statistical analysis that accomplishes one or more of the following functions: (1) It condenses the data; (2) it applies understandable conceptualizations; (3) it communicates underlying patterns; and (4) it generalizes sample findings to the population.[2] Refer to Table 15.1.

Marketing researchers can use five basic types of statistical analyses to reduce a data matrix: descriptive analysis, inferential analysis, differences analysis, associative analysis, and predictive analysis (Table 15.2). Each one has a unique role in the data analysis process; moreover, they are usually combined into a complete analysis of the information in order to satisfy the research objectives. As you can see in Figure 15.2, these techniques are progressively more complex, but at the same time, they convert raw data into increasingly more useful information as they increase in complexity.

These introductory comments will provide a preview of the subject matter that will be covered in this and other chapters. Because this is an introduction, we use the names of statistical procedures, but we do not define or describe them here. The specific techniques are all developed later. It is important, however, that you understand each of the various categories of analysis available to the marketing researcher and comprehend generally what each is about.

Descriptive Analysis

Certain measures such as the mean, mode, standard deviation, and range are forms of **descriptive analysis** that is used by marketing researchers to describe the sample data matrix in such a way as to portray the "typical" respondent and to reveal the general pattern

Descriptive analysis is used to describe the variables (question responses) in a data matrix (all respondents' answers).

TABLE 15.1 The Four Functions of Data Analysis

Function	Description	Example
Summarization	Use of measures and statistical values to describe the data matrix	The *average* respondent's age is 44.
Conceptualization	Use of words or graphics that managers can relate to	*The pie graph shows that few respondents are younger than 30 years of age.*
Communication	Describes underlying patterns or relationships	Most *satisfied customers recommend our brand* to their friends.
Generalization	Indicates how sample findings relate to the population	This means that *from 32% to 40% of the target market* purchases our brand on a regular basis.

TABLE 15.2   Five Types of Statistical Analyses Used by Marketing Researchers

Type	Description	Example	Statistical Concepts
Descriptive analysis (Chapter 15)	Summarize basic findings for the sample	Describe the typical respondent, describe how similar respondents are to the typical respondent	Mean, median, mode, frequency distribution, range, standard deviation
Inferential analysis (Chapter 16)	Determine population parameters, test hypotheses	Estimate population values	Confidence interval, hypothesis test
Differences analysis (Chapter 17)	Determine if differences exist; evaluate statistical significance of difference in the means of two or more groups in a sample	Evaluate the statistical significance of difference in the means of two or more groups in a sample	t test of differences, analysis of variance
Associative analysis (Chapter 18)	Determine associations	Determine if two variables are related in a systematic way	Correlation, cross-tabulation
Predictive analysis (Chapter 19)	Find complex relationships within the variables in the data set	Determine the dispositions of several variables' influences on a key variable	Multiple regression

FIGURE 15.2

Levels of Analysis Used in Marketing Research

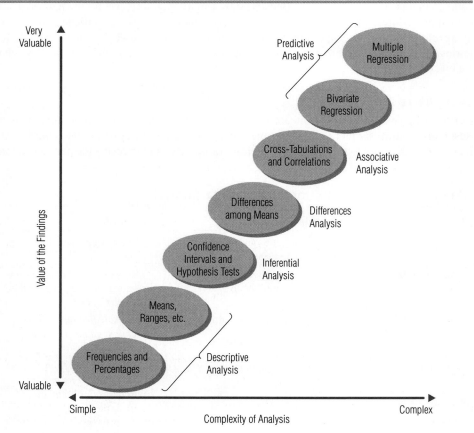

of responses. Descriptive measures are typically used early in the analysis process and become foundations for subsequent analysis.[3]

Inferential Analysis

When statistical procedures are used by marketing researchers to generalize the results of the sample to the target population that it represents, the process is referred to as **inferential analysis**. In other words, such statistical procedures allow a researcher to draw conclusions about the population based on information contained in the data matrix provided by the sample. Inferential statistics include hypothesis testing and estimating true population values based on sample information. We describe basic statistical inference in Chapter 16.

Inferential analysis is used to generate conclusions about the population's characteristics based on the sample data.

Differences Analysis

Occasionally, a marketing researcher needs to determine whether two groups are different. For example, the researcher may be investigating credit card usage and may want to see if high-income earners differ from low-income earners in how often they use an American Express card. The researcher may statistically compare the average annual dollar expenditures charged on an American Express card by high- versus low-income buyers. Important market segmentation information may come from this analysis. Or the researcher may run an experiment to see which of several alternative advertising themes garners the most favorable impression from a sample of target audience members. The researcher uses **differences analysis** to determine the degree to which real and generalizable differences exist in the population in order to help the manager make an enlightened decision on which advertising theme to use. Statistical differences analyses include the *t* test for significant differences between groups and analysis of variance. We define and describe them in Chapter 17.

Difference analysis is used to compare the mean of the responses of one group to that of another group, such as satisfaction ratings for "heavy" users versus "light" users.

Associative Analysis

Other statistical techniques are used by researchers to determine systematic relationships among variables. **Associative analysis** investigates if and how two variables are related. For instance, are advertising recall scores positively associated with intentions to buy the advertised brand? Are expenditures on salesforce training positively associated with salesforce performance? Depending on the statistic used, the analysis may indicate the strength of the association and/or the direction of the association between two questions on a questionnaire in a given study. We devote Chapter 18 to descriptions of cross-tabulations and correlations, which are basic associative analysis methods used in marketing research.

Differences analysis may reveal important distinctions among various types of credit card users.

Associative analysis determines the strength and direction of relationships between two or more variables (questions in the survey).

Predictive Analysis

Techniques are also available that will help the researcher in determining more complex patterns of associations, but most of these procedures are beyond the scope of this textbook, with one exception. Statistical procedures and models are available to help make forecasts about future events, and these fall under the category of **predictive analysis**. Regression analysis is commonly used by the marketing researcher to enhance prediction capabilities. Because marketing managers are typically worried about what will happen in the future given certain conditions, such as a price increase, prediction is very desirable. Predictive analysis can provide valuable insight into the nature of multiple relationships among the variables in a data matrix. Regression analysis is described in depth in Chapter 19.

Predictive analysis allows insights into multiple relationships among variables.

It is not our intention to make you an expert in statistical analysis. Rather, the primary objective of our chapters on statistical analysis is to acquaint you with the basic concepts involved in each of the selected measures. You will certainly do basic statistical analysis throughout your marketing career, and it is very likely that you will encounter information summarized in statistical terms. So it is important for you to have a conceptual understanding of the commonly used statistical procedures. Our descriptions are intended to show you when and where each measure is appropriately used and to help you interpret the meaning of the statistical result once it is reported. We also rely heavily on computer statistical program output because you will surely encounter statistical program output in your company's marketing information system and/or summarized in a marketing research study report.

UNDERSTANDING DATA VIA DESCRIPTIVE ANALYSIS

The Advanced Automobile Concepts SPSS Data Set

We now turn to the several tools in descriptive analysis available to the researcher to summarize the data obtained from a sample of respondents. In this chapter and in all other data analysis chapters, we are going to use The Advanced Automobile Concepts survey data set. That way, you can reconstruct the data analysis on your own with your Student Version of SPSS using the data set. To download this data set, go to the website (www.pearsonhighered.com/Burns) and find the data set download area.

For your information and as a quick review, the questionnaire was posted online and with the aid of a panel company, and qualified respondents answered the questions and submitted their questionnaires in the time period allotted for the survey. Certain data, such as demographics and automobile ownership, were purchased from the panel company's database. The survey and database data were combined and set up in SPSS, with variable names and value labels, and cleaned. The final data set has a total of 1,000 respondents and 50 variables, and it exists as an SPSS data file called "AAConcepts.sav." At your earliest convenience, you should download the "AAConcepts.sav" file and use SPSS to examine the questions and response formats that were used in The Advanced Automobile Concepts survey. We will refer to some of these as we instruct you on the use of SPSS for various types of analyses described in this chapter and other chapters that follow.

From now on, you are going to "watch over the shoulder" of the marketing researcher confronted with analyzing this data set. As you know, an SPSS data set is made up of rows and columns (in the data view window). The columns are the variables that correspond to the questions and parts of questions on the questionnaire, and the individual rows represent each respondent. Refer to Figure 15.3 to see The Advanced Automobile Concepts survey data in their row and column arrangement in SPSS. Of course, it is not possible to show all of the variables (columns) and respondents (rows), and Figure 15.3 shows only the first several respondents in the data set with the questions (variables) visible.

Commonly used descriptive analysis measures reveal central tendency (typical response) and variability (similarity of responses).	Two sets of measures are used extensively to describe the information obtained in a sample. The first set involves measures of central tendency, or measures that describe the "typical" respondent or response. The second set involves measures of variability, or measures that describe how similar (dissimilar) respondents or responses are to (from) "typical" respondents or responses. Other types of descriptive measures are available, but they are not as popular as central tendency and variability. In fact, they are rarely reported to clients.

Measures of Central Tendency: Summarizing the "Typical" Respondent

Three measures of central tendency are the mode, the median, and the mean.	The basic data summarization goal involved in all **measures of central tendency** is to report a single piece of information that describes the most typical response to a question. The term *central tendency* applies to any statistical measure used that somehow reflects a typical or frequent response.[4] Three such measures of central tendency are commonly used as data summarization devices[5]: the mode, the median, and the mean. We describe each one in turn.

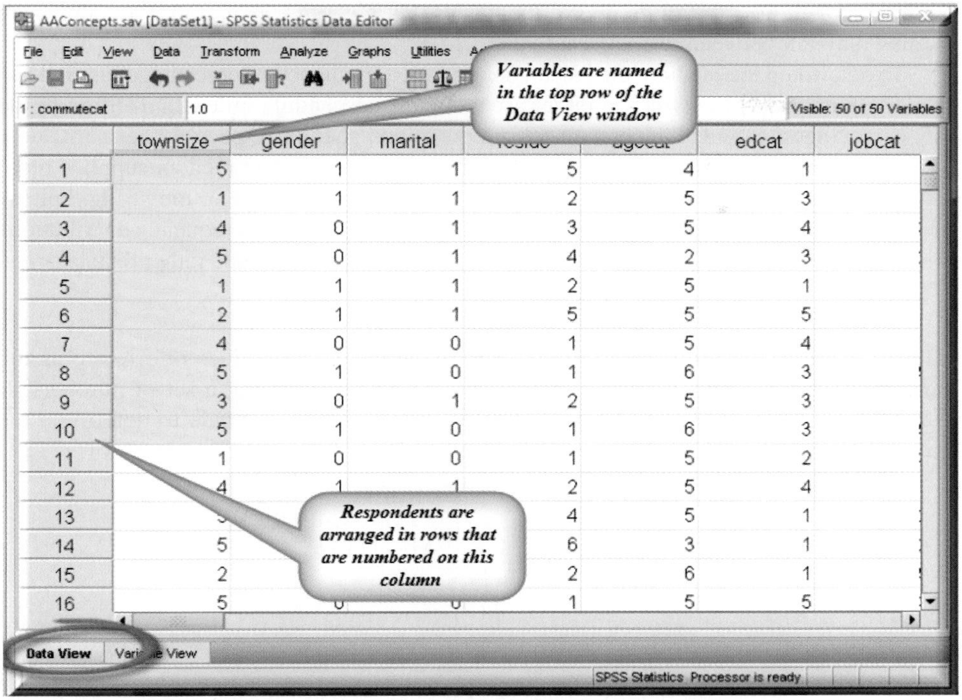

FIGURE 15.3

**SPSS Data View
Window Shows
the Advanced
Automobile
Concepts Survey
Data Matrix**

MODE. The **mode** is a descriptive analysis measure defined as that value in a string of numbers that occurs most often. In other words, if you scanned a list of numbers constituting a field in a data matrix, the mode would be the number that appeared more than any other. For example, in Figure 15.3, the first variable, "townsize," pertains to the size category for the respondent's town or city of residence. The response options and their codes are (1) Under 10,000, (2) 10,000 to 99,999, (3) 100,000 to 499,999, (4) 500,000 to 1 million, and (5) over 1 million. A simple method of finding the mode is, first, tabulating the frequency or percentage distribution for each number in the string, and then scanning for the largest incidence or using a bar chart or histogram as a visual aid. If you do a quick count using just the codes for the first ten respondents that are highlighted in yellow in Figure 15.3, you will find that there are two, one 2, one 3, and two 4s, and four 5s. Since 5 is the most prevalent, then "Over 1 million" is the mode. Naturally, we do not know if this is the mode for the entire data set, for there are 984 respondent townsizes that we cannot see in this figure.

You should note that the mode is a relative measure of central tendency, for it does not require that a majority of responses had this value. Instead, it simply specifies the value that occurs most frequently, and there is *no* requirement that this happened in 50% or more cases. The mode can take on any value as long as it is the most frequently occurring number. If a tie for the mode occurs, the distribution is considered to be "bimodal." Or it might even be "trimodal" if there is a three-way tie.

MEDIAN. An alternative measure of central tendency is the **median**, which expresses that value whose occurrence lies in the middle of an ordered set of values. That is, it is the value such that one-half of all of the other values are greater than the median and one-half of the remaining values are less than the median. Thus, the median tells us the approximate halfway point in a set or string of numbers that are arranged in ascending or descending order by taking into account the frequencies of all value. With an odd number of values,

With a string of numbers, the mode is that number appearing most often.

The median expresses the value whose occurrence lies in the middle of a set of ordered values.

the median will always fall on one of the values, but with an even number of values, the median may fall between two adjacent values.

To determine the median, the researcher creates a frequency or percentage distribution with the numbers in the string in either ascending or descending order. In addition to the raw percentages, cumulative percentages are computed and, by inspecting these, the location of the 50–50 break is determined. You should notice that the median supplies more information than does the mode, for a mode may occur anywhere in the string, but the median must be at the halfway point. We should point out that most frequency distributions are not symmetric, and the 50–50 point often falls on a particular value rather than between two adjacent ones.

MEAN. A third measure of central tendency is the mean, sometimes referred to as the "arithmetic mean." The **mean** is the average value characterizing a set of numbers. It differs from the mode and the median in that a computation is made to determine the average through the use of the following formula:

The mean is the arithmetic average of a set of numbers.

Formula for a Mean

$$\text{Mean } (\bar{x}) = \frac{\sum_{i=1}^{n} x_i}{n}$$

where

$n =$ the number of cases
$x_i =$ each individual value
$\sum$ signifies that all the x_i values are summed.

As you can see, all of the members in the set of n numbers, each designated by x_i, are summed and that total is divided by the number of members in that set. The resulting number is the mean, a measure that indicates the central tendency of those values. It approximates the typical value in that set of values. Because the mean is determined by taking every member of the set of numbers into account through this formula, it is more informative than the median. Means communicate a great deal of information, and they can be plotted for quick interpretations as illustrated in Marketing Research Insight 15.1.

Measures of Variability: Visualizing the Diversity of Respondents

Although they are extremely useful, measures of central tendency are incomplete descriptors of the variety of values in a particular set of numbers. That is, they do not indicate the variability of responses to a particular question or, alternatively, the diversity of respondents on some characteristic measured in a survey. To gain a sense of the diversity or variability of values, the marketing researcher must turn to measures of variability. All **measures of variability** are concerned with depicting the "typical" difference between the values in a set of values.

Measures of variability reveal the typical difference between the values in a set of values.

It is one matter to know the mode or some other measure of central tendency, but it is quite another matter to be aware of how close to the mean or measure of central tendency the rest of the values fall. For example, earlier, using only the first ten respondents in our Advanced Automobile Concepts SPSS data set shown in Figure 15.3, we discovered that the mode for the size of the hometown was "Over 1 million." However, there were 2 respondents in the "Under 10,000" size category, 1 in the "10,000 to 99,999" category, 1 in the "100,000 to 499,999" category, and two in the "500,000 to 1 million" category. So, we have a good sense of the variability of the hometown sizes as they range from very small towns to medium- and large-sized cities. In other words, we do not just have mega-city dwellers as the mode suggests. Instead, we have a good cross section of different-sized American cities and towns in our sample.

MARKETING RESEARCH INSIGHT

Global Application

15.1 Marketing Research Reveals Unique Australian Wine Lifestyle Segments

Marketing researchers investigating wine drinkers in Australia have created a scale that can be used to identify different wine consumer segments.[6] Lifestyle can be measured a number of ways, and these researchers have developed a wine-drinking-specific lifestyle measure that captures how wine drinkers behave and think in situations such as (1) wine-drinking occasions, (2) wine shopping, (3) wine qualities, (4) wine-drinking rituals, and (5) consequences of wine drinking.

The most recent in a series of surveys has revealed five segments. For illustration purposes, the following figure uses the averages for three very different wine lifesyle segments, and it illustrates the communication power of averages.

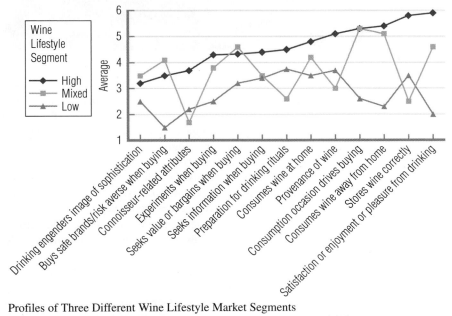

Profiles of Three Different Wine Lifestyle Market Segments

The graph immediately and vividly depicts high, low, and "mixed" segments. Segment #1, the "high" segment, is consistently higher in wine-related lifestyle than is segment #2, the "low" segment. To say this differently, the averages for the "high" segment reveal that it has integrated wine consumption into its lifestyle quite deeply, whereas the "low" segment drinks wine but has not embraced the various nuances of wine consumption to the great extent evident with the high segment. The "mixed" wine-related lifesyle segment is clearly not like either the high or the low segments. Sometimes the mixed segment's average is above the high segment average; sometimes it is below the low segment's average, and on some of the wine-related lifestyle aspects, the mixed segment's average is between the low and high segments' averages. Thus, the average, when presented visually such as has been done here, is a very valuable data summarization concept.

Thus, knowing the variability of the data could greatly impact a marketing decision based on the data because it expresses how similar the respondents are to one another on the topic under examination. There are three measures of variability: frequency distribution, range, and standard deviation. Each measure provides its own unique information that helps to describe the diversity of responses.

Measures of variability include frequency distribution, range, and standard deviation.

FREQUENCY DISTRIBUTION. A **frequency distribution** is a tabulation of the number of times that each different value appears in a particular set of values. Frequencies themselves

Variability indicates how different (or similar, in this case) respondents are on a topic, such as what model of automobile is preferred.

are raw counts, and normally these frequencies are converted into percentages for ease of comparison. The conversion is arrived at very simply through a quick division of the frequency for each value by the total number of observations for all of the values, resulting in a percent, called a **percentage distribution**. For instance, if you count the ten respondents in our SPSS data set in Figure 15.3, in the "gender" column, you will find six 1s and four 0s. The value codes are 0 = male and 1 = female, so the frequency distribution is 6 female and 4 male respondents. For the marital status ("marital" column), there are seven 1s (married) and three 0s (unmarried), so the marital status distribution is 7 married and 3 unmarried respondents. These are frequency distributions, and to determine the percentage distribution, each frequency must be divided by the number of respondents, or 10 in this case. So the percentage distributions are 60% females and 40% males with 70% married and 30% unmarried.

A frequency (percentage) distribution reveals the number (percent) of occurrences of each number in a set of numbers.

To review, a frequency distribution affords an accounting of the responses to values in a set. It quickly communicates all of the different values in the set, and it expresses how similar the values are. The percentage distribution is often used here because most people can easily relate to percentages. Plus, percentage distributions are easily presented as pie or bar charts,[7] which are convenient graphical representations of these distributions that researchers find very helpful when communicating findings to clients or others.

The range identifies the maximum and minimum values in a set of numbers.

RANGE. The **range** identifies the distance between the lowest value (minimum) and the highest value (maximum) in an ordered set of values. Stated somewhat differently, the range specifies the difference between the endpoints in a set of values arranged in order. The range does not provide the same amount of information supplied by a frequency distribution; however, it identifies the interval in which the set of values occurs. The range also does not tell you how often the maximum and minimum occurred, but it does provide some information on the dispersion by indicating how far apart the extremes are.

A standard deviation indicates the degree of variation in a way that can be translated into a bell-shaped curve distribution.

STANDARD DEVIATION. The **standard deviation** indicates the degree of variation or diversity in the values in such a way as to be translatable into a normal, or bell-shaped curve, distribution. Although marketing researchers do not always rely on the normal curve interpretation of the standard deviation, they often encounter the standard deviation

TABLE 15.3 Normal Curve Interpretation of Standard Deviation

Number of Standard Deviations from the Mean	Percent of Area under Curve*	Percent of Area to Right (or Left)†
±1.00	68%	16.0%
±1.64	90%	5.0%
±1.96	95%	2.5%
±2.58	99%	0.5%
±3.00	99.7%	0.1%

*This is the area under the curve with the number of standard deviations as the lower (left-hand) and upper (right-hand) limits and the mean equidistant from the limits.

†This is the area left outside of the limits described by plus or minus the number of standard deviations. Because of the normal curve's symmetric properties, the area remaining below the lower limit (left-hand tail) is exactly equal to the area remaining above the upper limit (right-hand tail).

when performing basic analyses, and they usually report it in their tables. So it is worthwhile to digress for a moment to describe this statistical concept.

Table 15.3 shows the properties of a bell-shaped, or normal, distribution of values. As we have indicated in our chapter on sample size determination, the usefulness of this model is apparent when you realize that it is a symmetric distribution: Exactly 50% of the distribution lies on either side of the midpoint (the apex of the curve). With a normal curve, the midpoint is also the mean. Standard deviations are standardized units of measurement that are located on the horizontal axis. They relate directly to assumptions about the normal curve. For example, the range of 1 standard deviation above and 1 standard deviation below the midpoint includes 68% of the total area underneath that curve. Because the bell-shaped distribution is a theoretical or ideal concept, this property never changes. Moreover, the proportion of area under the curve and within plus or minus any number of standard deviations from the mean is perfectly known. For the purposes of this presentation, normally only two or three of these values are of interest to marketing researchers. Specifically, ±2.58 standard deviations describes the range in which 99% of the area underneath the curve is found, ±1.96 standard deviations is associated with 95% of the area underneath the curve, and ±1.64 standard deviations corresponds to 90% of the bell-shaped curve's area. Remember, we must assume that the shape of the frequency distribution of the numbers approximates a normal curve, so keep this in mind during our following examples.

It is now time to review the calculation of the standard deviation. The equation typically used for the standard deviation is as follows:

The standard deviation embodies the properties of a bell-shaped distribution of values.

Formula for a Standard Deviation

$$\text{Standard deviation } (s) = \sqrt{\frac{\sum_{i=1}^{n}(x_i - \bar{x})^2}{n - 1}}$$

In this equation, x_i stands for each individual observation and $\bar{x}$ stands for the mean, as indicated earlier. The standard deviation is a measure of the differences of all observations from the mean, expressed as a single number. To compute the standard deviation, you must begin with the mean and then compare each observation to the mean by subtracting and squaring the difference. It may seem strange to square differences, add them up, divide them by $(n - 1)$, and then take the square root. If we did not square the differences, we

The squaring operation in the standard deviation formula is used to avoid the cancellation effect.

would have positive and negative values; and if we summed them, there would be a cancellation effect. That is, large negative differences would cancel out large positive differences, and the numerator would end up being close to zero. But this result is contrary to what we know is the case with large differences: There is variation, which should be expressed by the standard deviation.

The formula remedies this problem by squaring the subtracted differences before they are summed. Squaring converts all negative numbers to positives and, of course, leaves the positives positive. Next, all of the squared differences are summed and divided by 1 less than the number of total observations in the string of values; 1 is subtracted from the number of observations to achieve what is typically called an "unbiased" estimate of the standard deviation. But we now have an inflation factor to worry about because every comparison has been squared. To adjust for this, the equation specifies that the square root be taken after all other operations are performed. This final step adjusts the value back down to the original measure (that is, units rather than squared units). By the way, if you did not take the square root at the end, the value would be referred to as the **variance.** In other words, the variance is the standard deviation squared.

Now, whenever a standard deviation is reported along with a mean, a specific picture should appear in your mind. Assuming that the distribution is bell-shaped, the size of the standard deviation number helps you envision how similar or dissimilar the typical responses are to the mean. If the standard deviation is small, the distribution is greatly compressed. On the other hand, with a large standard deviation value, the distribution is consequently stretched out at both ends.

We have prepared Marketing Research Insight 15.2 as a means of helping you remember the various descriptive statistics concepts that are commonly used by marketing researchers.

> With a bell-shaped distribution, 95% of the values lie within ±1.96 times the standard deviation away from the mean.

WHEN TO USE A PARTICULAR DESCRIPTIVE MEASURE

> The scaling assumptions underlying a question determine which statistic is appropriate.

In Chapter 10, you learned that the level of measurement for a scale affects how it may be statistically analyzed. Remember, for instance, that nominal question forms contain much less information than do those questions with interval scaling assumptions. Similarly, the amount of information provided by each of the various measures of central tendency and dispersion differs. As a general rule, statistical measures that communicate the most amount of information should be used with scales that contain the most amount of information, and measures that communicate the least amount of information should be used with scales that contain the least amount of information. The level of measurement determines the appropriate measure; otherwise, the measure will be uninterpretable.

At first reading, this rule may seem confusing, but on reflection it should become clear that the level of measurement of each question dictates the measure that should be used. It is precisely at this point that you must remember the arbitrary nature of coding schemes. For instance, if on a demographic question concerning religious preference, "Catholic" is assigned a "1," "Protestant" is assigned a "2," "Jewish" is assigned a "3," and so forth, a mean could be computed. But what would be the interpretation of an average religion of 2.36? It would have no practical interpretation because the mean assumes interval or ratio scaling, whereas the religion categories are nominal. The mode would be the appropriate central tendency measure for these responses.

Table 15.4 indicates how the level of measurement relates to each of the three measures of central tendency and measures of variation. The table should remind you that a clear understanding of the level of measurement for each question on the questionnaire is essential because the researcher must select the statistical procedure and direct the computer to

MARKETING RESEARCH INSIGHT

Practical Insights

15.2 Descriptive Statistics: What They Mean and How to Compute Them

Invariably, a researcher has to make "sense" out of a set of numbers that represents the ways respondents answered the questions in the survey by using the process we have termed, "data summarization." The answers to survey questions are normally coded; that is, they are converted to numbers such as 1 for "yes," 2 for "no," and 3 for "maybe." Sometimes the numbers pertain to responses on a scale such as when a respondent indicates that a wireless phone company rates a "4" on a 5-point scale where 1 means "poor," 2 means "fair," 3 means "good," 4 means "very good," and a 5 means "excellent" service. We are using the responses to this scale in our example here.

Descriptive statistics are basic to marketing research and essential to the researcher's understanding of how the respondents answered each question. Here is a data set comprising the answers ten different respondents gave when asked to rate the quality of their wireless phone company's service.

Respondent	Rating	Respondent	Rating
1	4	6	4
2	5	7	3
3	4	8	4
4	2	9	5
5	3	10	4

To illustrate the nine descriptive statistics concepts, the ratings of our ten respondents are analyzed in the following table. For each finding, the poor–excellent scale is used to aid in the interpretation.

STATISTICAL CONCEPT	WHAT IS IT?	HOW DO YOU COMPUTE IT?	USING THE RATINGS EXAMPLE AND INTERPRETATION		
Frequency	The number of times a number appears in the data set	Count the number of times the number appears in the set of numbers.	As an example, the number 4's frequency is 5, so 5 respondents gave a "very good" rating.		
Frequency distribution	The number of times each different number in the set appears	Count the number of times each different number appears in the set and make a table that shows each number, its count, and the total count (all counts totaled).	Rating 2/fair 3/good 4/very good 5/excellent Total	Count 1 2 5 2 10	
Percentage distribution	The presence of each different number expressed as a percent	Divide each frequency count for each rating number by the total count, and report the result as a percent.	Rating 2/fair 3/good 4/very good 5/excellent Total	Percent 10% 20% 50% 20% 100%	
Cumulative distribution (frequency or percentage)	A running total of the counts or percentages	Arrange all the different numbers in order and indicate the sum of the counts (percentages) of all preceding numbers plus the present one.	Rating 2/fair 3/good 4/very good 5/excellent Total	Percent 10% 20% 50% 20% 100%	Cum. Percent 10% 30% 80% 100%
Median	The number in the set of numbers such that 50% of the other numbers are larger, and 50% of the other numbers are smaller	Use the cumulative percentage distribution to locate where the cumulative percent equals 50% or where it includes 50%.	Rating 2/fair 3/good 4/very good 5/excellent	Cum. Percent 10% 30% 80% ⟵ Median 100%	

(continued)

STATISTICAL CONCEPT	WHAT IS IT?	HOW DO YOU COMPUTE IT?	USING THE RATINGS EXAMPLE AND INTERPRETATION
Mode	*In a frequency or a percentage distribution, the number that has the largest count or percentage (ties are acceptable)*	*By inspection, determine which number has the largest frequency or percentage in the distribution.*	*The number 4 (very good) accounts for 50%, the largest of any other rating.*
Mean	*The arithmetic average of the set of numbers*	*Add up all the numbers and divide this sum by the total number of numbers in the set.*	*$(4 + 5 + 4 + 2 + 3 + 4 + 3 + 4 + 5 + 4)/10 = 3.8$ so the mean is just a bit below "very good."*
Range	*An indication of the "spread" or span covered by the numbers*	*Find the lowest and highest numbers in the set and identify them as the minimum and maximum, respectively.*	*The minimum is 2 and the maximum is 5, so the range is $5 - 2$, or 3. Respondents rate it from "fair" to "excellent."*
Standard deviation	*An indication of how similar or dissimilar the numbers are in the set, interpretable under the assumptions of a normal curve of that result*	*Sum the square of each number subtracted from the mean, divide that sum by the total number of numbers less 1, and then take the square root.*	*$\{((4 - 3.8)^2 + (5 - 3.8)^2 + \cdots + (4 - 3.8)^2)/10 - 1)\}^{1/2} = 0.92$ 95% of the respondents are within ± 1.6 (1.96 times 0.84) ratings away from average of 3.8, or between "fair" and "excellent."*

perform the procedure. The computer cannot distinguish the level of measurement because we typically store and handle our data as numbers as a matter of convention and convenience.

As you might suspect, there is much potential for misunderstanding when a researcher communicates the results of descriptive analyses to the marketing manager. We have noted some of the common misconceptions held by managers in Marketing Research Insight 15.3. A researcher who knowingly allows these misunderstandings to exist is acting unethically.

TABLE 15.4   What Descriptive Statistic to Use When

Example Question	Measurement Level	Central Tendency (the most typical response)	Variability (how similar the responses are)
What is your gender?	Nominal scale	Mode	Frequency and/or percentage distribution
Rank these 5 brands from your 1st choice to your 5th choice	Ordinal scale	Median	Cumulative percentage distribution
On a scale of 1 to 5, how does Starbucks rate on variety of its coffee drinks?	Interval scale	Mean	Standard deviation and/or range
About how many times did you buy fast food for lunch last week?	Ratio scale	Mean	Standard deviation and/or range

MARKETING RESEARCH INSIGHT   Ethical Application

15.3 Ethical Issues in Descriptive Data Analysis

The adage that "perception is reality" raises some ethical issues when marketing researchers use the terminology of descriptive statistics to communicate their findings to marketing managers. Actually, in this case we should change the adage to "misperception is reality," for the typical marketing manager, who is broadly familiar with the precise meanings of statistical concepts, may well have misperceptions about them that can greatly distort how the manager understands what the marketing researcher is reporting. Here are some statements that might be made by a researcher, what each statement means in terms of descriptive analysis, and possible misperceptions that a manager might have who is not accustomed to working with statistical terminology.

WHAT THE MARKETING RESEARCHER SAYS	WHAT THE MARKETING RESEARCHER MEANS	LIKELY MISPERCEPTION BY THE MARKETING MANAGER
"The modal answer was. . . ."	*The answer given by more respondents than any other answer.*	*Most or all of the respondents gave this answer.*
"A majority responded. . . ."	*Over 50% of the respondents answered this way.*	*Most or all of the respondents gave the answer.*
"A plurality responded. . . ."	*The answer was given by more respondents than any other answer, but less than 50% gave that answer.*	*A majority of respondents gave the answer.*
"The median response was. . . ."	*The answer such that 50% answered above it and 50% answered below it*	*Most respondents gave this answer.*
"The mean response was. . . ."	*The arithmetic average of all respondents' answers or responded very close to this answer*	*Most respondents gave this answer.*
"There was some variability in the responses. . . ."	*Respondents gave a variety of responses with some agreement*	*There was no agreement among the respondents.*
"The standard deviation was. . . ."	*The value was computed by applying the standard deviation formula*	*No comprehension.*

Remember, these are basic statistical concepts. There are a great many more sophisticated statistics that a researcher may use to completely analyze a data set, so there is ample opportunity for a marketing manager to miscomprehend what a marketing researcher is communicating about the statistical findings. Here are some approaches that can be used to make certain that the audience will not misunderstand the researcher's words.

1. Some companies have prepared handbooks or glossaries that define marketing research terms, including statistical concepts. They are given to clients at the onset of work. Alternatively, they may be on the marketing research company's website for easy reference.

2. Some researchers include an appendix in the final report that defines and illustrates the statistical concepts mentioned in the report.
3. Definitions of statistical concepts are included in the text of the final report where the concept is first mentioned.
4. Footnotes and annotations are included in the tables and figures that explain the statistical concepts used.

No ethical researcher would intentionally mislead a client in reporting findings, and because statistical concepts have high potential for misperceptions like those illustrated here, ethical researchers go to considerable lengths to prevent such misunderstandings.

Compute Measures of Central Tendency and Variability

The chapter has described measures of central tendency—mean, median, mode—as well as measures of variability—precentage distribution, range, and standard deviation. At the same time, you should realize that certain measures are appropriate for some scales, but inappropriate for other scales. Following is a data set of respondents who answered questions on a survey about the propane gas grills they own:

Respondent	For How Many Years Have You Owned Your Gas Grill?	Where Did You Purchase Your Gas Grill?	About How Much Did Your Pay for Your Gas Grill?
1	2	Department store	$200
2	7	Hardware store	$500
3	8	Department store	$300
4	4	Specialty store	$400
5	2	Specialty store	$600
6	1	Department store	$300
7	3	Department store	$400
8	4	Department store	$300
9	6	Specialty store	$500
10	8	Department store	$400
11	5	Department store	$600
12	6	Department store	$400
13	4	Hardware store	$800
14	4	Specialty store	$1000
15	3	Department store	$200
16	8	Hardware store	$600
17	5	Specialty store	$800
18	10	Specialty store	$1200
19	2	Hardware store	$400
20	6	Specialty store	$900
Mean	—	—	—
Standard Deviation	—	—	—
Range: Maximum & Minimum	—	—	—
Frequency Distribution			
Median	—	—	—
Mode	—	—	—

For your Active Learning exercise here, you must determine what measure(s) of central tendency and what measures of variability are appropriate and compute them. We have identified the relevant measures under the "Respondent" column of the data set, and your task is to write in the proper answer under each of the three questions in the survey.

Your Integrated Case

THE ADVANCED AUTOMOBILE CONCEPTS SURVEY: OBTAINING DESCRIPTIVE STATISTICS WITH SPSS

Beginning with this chapter and all subsequent chapters dealing with statistical analyses, we provide illustrations for the use of SPSS, in two ways. First, in the textbook descriptions, we indicate step-by-step the procedures used with SPSS to obtain the statistical analyses being described. Plus, we have included examples of SPSS output in these sections. The second way we illustrate SPSS is with your SPSS Student Assistant. By now, you are well acquainted with the Student Assistant. We urge you to look at these statistical analysis sections that illustrate how to operate SPSS as well as how to find specific statistical results in SPSS output.

Descriptive statistics are needed to see The Advanced Automobile Concepts survey's basic findings.

Obtaining a Frequency Distribution and the Mode with SPSS

There were many questions on The Advanced Automobile Concepts survey that had categorical response options and, thus, embodied nominal scaling assumptions. With a nominal scale, the mode is the appropriate measure of central tendency, and variation must be assessed by looking at the distribution of responses across the various response categories.

A frequency distribution and mode are appropriate for nominal scales.

Earlier, to illustrate how to determine the mode of our 10-respondent Advanced Automobile Concepts data set, we used the size of hometown variable, as it is a nominal scale. We will now use this variable with the entire 1,000-completions data set to illustrate how to instruct SPSS to create a frequency distribution and find the mode.

Figure 15.4 shows the clickstream sequence to find a mode for the size of hometown using the entire Advanced Automobile Concepts survey data set. As you can see, the

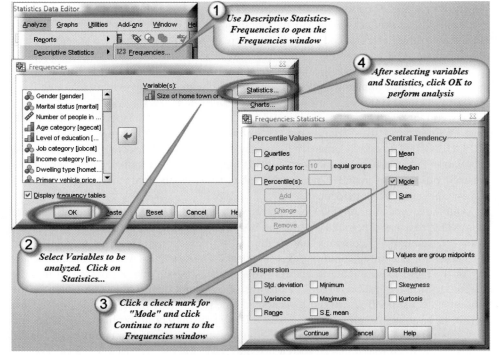

FIGURE 15.4

SPSS Clickstream to Obtain a Frequency Distribution and the Mode

FIGURE 15.5

**SPSS Output
for a Frequency
Distribution
and the Mode**

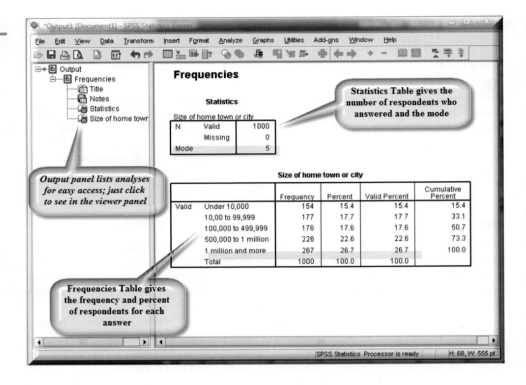

Use the ANALYZE–
DESCRIPTIVE
STATISTICS–
FREQUENCIES
procedure to produce
descriptive statistics for
variables with nominal
or ordinal scaling.

primary menu sequence is ANALYZE–DESCRIPTIVE STATISTICS–FREQUENCIES. This sequence opens up the variable selection window, where you specify the variable(s) to be analyzed, and the Statistics . . . button opens up the Statistics window that has several statistical concepts as options. Since we are working only with the mode, you would click in the checkmark box beside the Mode. "Continue" will close this window and "OK" will close the variable selection and cause SPSS to create a frequency distribution and to identify the mode. You can see this output in Figure 15.5, where the code number of "5" is specified as the mode response and the frequency distribution shows that "1 million and more" is the largest hometown/city size represented, with 267 respondents selecting it, or 26.7% of the total 100%.

As you look at the output, you should notice that the variable labels and value labels were defined, and they appear on the output. The DESCRIPTIVE STATISTICS–FREQUENCIES procedure creates a frequency distribution and associated percentage distribution of the responses for each question. Its output includes a statistics table and a table for each variable that includes the variable label, value labels, frequencies, percent, valid percent, and cumulative percent.

Our Advanced Automobile Concepts survey data set is *not* typical, because there are no missing answers. There are no missing responses because the data set was purchased from a consumer panel company that guaranteed 100% response. However, as you learned in Chapter 14, it is not uncommon for respondents to refuse to answer a question in a survey or for them to be unable to answer a question. Alternatively, a respondent may be directed to skip a question if the previous answer does not qualify the respondent for the subsequent question. If any of these occurs, and the respondent is still included in the data set, we have an instance of "missing data." This is absolutely no problem for SPSS and most other data analysis programs, but the output will be adjusted to compensate for the missing data. Read Marketing Research Insight 15.4 to learn about what SPSS specifies as "valid percent."

MARKETING RESEARCH INSIGHT

Practical Application

15.4 How SPSS Handles Missing Data

When a researcher conducts a survey, and the data set is inspected, it is not uncommon to discover some questions where respondents have failed to answer. The reasons for these omissions are varied. The respondent may have refused to answer the question, perhaps the respondent was interrupted and did not return to the last question answered, or there might even have been a data entry error of some sort. Regardless of the reason, the researcher is now confronted with the problem of "missing data," or cases where fewer respondents than the entire sample answered a question.

SPSS has a built-in procedure for missing data. First, by its convention, SPSS will denote any missing data cell in its data matrix with a "." In other words, a researcher can locate any missing data in the Data Editor by looking for a period or dots in the place of numbers. Second, SPSS is programmed to omit any missing data from its analysis. That is, the SPSS output first reports in its Statistics table the "N" which is comprised of "Valid" responses and "Missing" responses, if any missing data is found. In a frequencies table, SPSS reports the Frequency counts and "Percent" values, and in both columns, the Missing System or Missing values are counted. Then SPSS reports a "Valid Percent" column that does not include the missing values.

Should you use the "Percent" or the "Valid Percent?" It is up to the researcher; however, the vast majority of researchers chose to report the "Valid Percent" numbers in their reports. When they choose this option, they are explicitly assuming that if the missing data respondents had responded to the question, their answers would be distributed exactly as they are distributed among those respondents who did answer the question.

Active Learning

Use your SPSS Advanced Automobile Concepts data set to compute the frequency distribution and percentage distribution and to identify the mode as we have just described. Use Figure 15.4 to direct your mouse clicks and selections using the hometown size variable in the data set. Compare the SPSS output that you obtain with Figure 15.5 and make sure that you can identify the mode of 5 (1 million and more). Also, if you want to understand the "Valid Percent" output provided by SPSS for its Frequencies analysis, use your cursor and block the first ten respondents on the Data View of the SPSS Data Editor. With a right-click of your mouse, use the "clear" function to set these ten town-size numbers to blanks. Then rerun the frequencies for the hometown size variable.

You will now see that the SPSS frequencies table reports the ten "Missing System" respondents. (Missing System means that it found blanks, which are the SPSS system default for missing data.) If your understanding of missing data and SPSS valid percents is still a bit muddled, reread Marketing Research Insight 15.4 to gain the proper understanding of valid percents. Although missing data is not a concern in the Advanced Automobile Concepts survey data set, you most certainly will encounter it if your marketing research course includes an actual survey that you perform as part of the course requirements.

Wait! Don't save your AAConcepts data set with the missing data unless you give it a new SPSS data set name such as "AAConceptswithMissingData.sav."

SPSS Student Assistant:
Descriptive Statistics
for Nominal Data:
Frequencies, Percents,
Mode

Finding the Median with SPSS

It is also a simple matter to determine the median using the ANALYZE–DESCRIPTIVE STATISTICS–FREQUENCIES menu sequence. As we indicated, in order for the median to be a sensible measure of central tendency, the values must, at minimum, have ordinal scale properties. The size of town variable uses the following codes: (1) "Under 10,000," (2) "10,000 to 99,999," (3) "100,000 to 499,999," (4) "500,000 to 1 million," and (5) "over 1 million." The codes have ordinal properties as a "1" size is smaller than a "2"

size and so on through a "5" size city. It is a simple matter to use the Advanced Automobile Concepts to obtain the size of hometown median from the full data set. The procedure is very similar to the mode procedure, as first, the "size of hometown or city" variable is selected in the variable selection window, but, second, the median, rather than the mode, is checked in the statistics window. Refer to Figure 15.4 and just imagine that the size of hometown or city is the chosen variable and that the median is checked instead of the mode.

The resulting SPSS output will have the frequency distribution of our likelihood variable, and it will show that code number 3, pertaining to "100,000 to 499,999" is the 50–50 location in the scale, or the median.

When using SPSS DESCRIPTIVES, always bear in mind the variables being analyzed should be interval or ratio scaled.

SPSS Student Assistant: Descriptive Statistics for Scaled Data: Mean, Standard Deviation, Median, Range.

 Find a Median with SPSS

Use your SPSS Advanced Automobile Concepts data set to find the median size on the hometown variable in the Advanced Automobile Concepts survey. Again, use Figure 15.4 as your clickstream guide but select the income variable for the analysis and place a checkmark in the median checkbox. If you do not find that the code number 2, pertaining to "between $25,000 and $49,000" is the 50–50 location in the scale, or the median, redo your work carefully to correct any errors you may have made.

Finding the Mean, Range, and Standard Deviation with SPSS

As we have mentioned, computer statistical programs cannot distinguish the level of measurement of various questions. Consequently, it is necessary for the analyst to discern the level of measurement and to select the correct procedure(s). There are several questions in the Advanced Automobile Concepts survey that asked respondents to use a 7-point Likert (very strongly disagree–to–very strongly agree) response scale, so we have an interval scale.

For quick data summarization of these variables, we do not want frequency tables, for two reasons. First, the Likert scale variables are interval scaled and, second, the frequency tables would be full of percents of all sizes, and their modes and medians would be very confusing, to say the least. But, we can turn to the mean and other summarization statistics for interval or ratio data for help here. Specifically, we will use the ANALYZE–DESCRIPTIVE STATISTICS–DESCRIPTIVES commands, and click on the Options button after we have selected "Gasoline emissions contribute to global warming" as the variable for analysis. In the Options panel, you can select the mean, standard deviation, range, and so forth. Refer to Figure 15.6 for the SPSS clickstream sequence.

Figure 15.7 presents the output generated from this option. In our Advanced Automobile Concepts survey, the output reveals that the average reaction to the statement "Gasoline emissions contribute to global warming" is 4.82. Recalling the interval scale used (1 = Very strongly disagree, 2 = Strongly disagree, 3 = Disagree, 4 = Neither disagree nor agree, 5 = Agree, 6 = Strongly agree, and 7 = Very strongly agree), a 4.8 is very close to 5, meaning that, on average, our survey respondents "agree" with this statement. The standard deviation is 2.3 (rounded), meaning there was much variability, and you can also see that the lowest response (minimum) was 1 and the highest (maximum) was 6, meaning that the entire range of the scale was used by the sample of respondents.

While consumers agree that fuel emissions contribute to global warming, will they be receptive to a radically new way to conserve fuel?

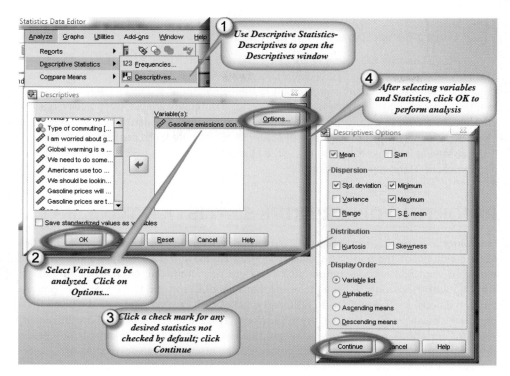

FIGURE 15.6

SPSS Clickstream to Obtain a Mean, Standard Deviation, and the Range

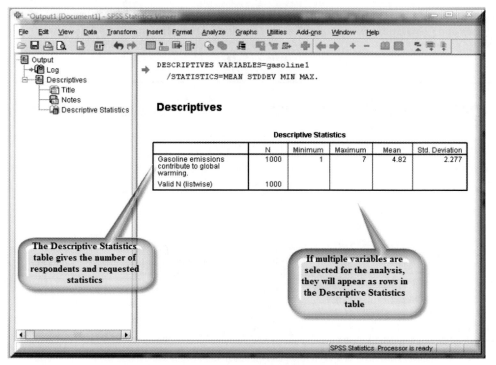

FIGURE 15.7

SPSS Output for a Mean, Standard Deviations, and the Range

Using SPSS for a Mean and Related Descriptive Statistics

In this Active Learning exercise, you are being asked to stretch your learning a bit, for instead of simply repeating what has just been described for how to obtain the mean, range, and standard deviation with SPSS and comparing it to the SPSS output in this chapter, we want you to find the mean, range, and standard deviation for a different variable. Specifically, use the clickstream shown in Figure 15.6, on page 453, but select the question that pertains to "Number of people in household" and direct SPSS to compute these descriptive statistics.

You should find that the mean is 2.21, a standard deviation is 1.381, and the range has a minimum of 1 and a maximum of 9.

REPORTING DESCRIPTIVE STATISTICS TO CLIENTS

How does a marketing researcher report the findings of the various descriptive statistics used to summarize the findings of a survey? After all, the various descriptive measures are buried in statistical analysis output tables that are very confusing to anyone untrained in working with these tools. It is on the researcher's shoulders to build tables or other presentation methods, such as graphs, to efficiently and effectively communicate the basic findings to the manager. For instance, the researcher may use a table format to show the means, standard deviations, and perhaps the ranges that have been found for a variable or a group of related variables. If percentages are computed, the researcher can develop or "lift" a percentages table from the statistical output.

SPSS Student Assistant:
Working with SPSS
Output.

Guidelines for the preparation of presentation graphs are contained in our chapter on report writing, Chapter 20. However, while you have a clear understanding of the several descriptive measures as well as how to obtain them with SPSS, we believe that now is a good time to instruct you on how to prepare their associated presentation tables. Consequently, we have prepared Marketing Research Insight 15.5, which describes guidelines and gives examples of tables for data summarizations findings.

 MARKETING RESEARCH INSIGHT   **Practical Application**

15.5 Guidelines for the Presentation of Data Summarizations

A table is the most common vehicle for presenting summarizations of data. That is, the researcher has used knowledge of data reduction concepts and identified the measures of central tendency and variability that best communicate the essence of the findings. The most useful tables are those where quick inspection will reveal the basic pattern(s) or the essence of the findings. Readers of these tables will greatly appreciate any and all efforts that the researcher can put into their construction that facilitates their quick detection of the researcher's findings. This means that the researcher must worry about the communication aspects of the tables. Here are some table organization guidelines.[8]

Keep tables as simple as possible.

- Use rows for the variables (metric data) or the categories (categorical data) being presented in the table.
- Use columns for measures of central tendency and variability.
- Use highly descriptive and self-explanatory labels.
- Use only variables with identical response scales in a single table.
- If appropriate, arrange the variables (rows) in logical order, usually ascending or descending, based on the descriptive measure being used.
- Highlight key measures.

Beyond organization, there are cosmetic or appearance guidelines that will ensure that the table strongly implies that it is credible and should be taken very seriously.

Use one decimal place unless convention (for example, currency requires two decimal places for cents) or the nature of the data (for example, numbers "tied" with one decimal place may require two decimal places to show that they are different) demands otherwise.

- With scales, include a table footnote that describes the scale.
- Do not report measures that are largely redundant.
- Only report findings that are meaningful or useful.
- Use a conservative, professional format.

Reporting Metric Data (Ratio and Interval Scales)
Metric data is summarized with the following descriptive measures: average, median, mode, standard deviation, minimum, and maximum. Typically, the researcher works with several variables or questions in the survey that are related either by the research objectives or logically. Often these questions have the same underlying response scales. For example, there may be a dozen attitude-related questions or several frequencies of product usage questions. It is often natural and efficient to combine the findings of related questions into a single table. Recommendations for what to include in standard metric variable tables are as follows:

Descriptive Measure	For a Standard Metric Variables Table . . .	Comment
Average (mean)	Absolutely included as averages are the most commonly used central tendency measure for metric data.	Place averages in a column very close to the variable descriptions and arrange variables in ascending or descending order of the averages.
Median	Do not include.	Managers do not relate to medians of metric data.
Mode	Do not include.	Managers do not relate to modes of metric data.
Standard deviation	Typically include in the table.	If most standard deviations are approximately equal, do not include as redundancy would result.
Minimum	Include if the data have several different minimums.	Reporting the same minimum several times is redundant.
Maximum	Include if the data have several different maximums.	Reporting the same maximum several times is redundant.

Here is a "model" metric variables table. Notice that the labels are self-explanatory and the averages are highlighted to

indicate their importance. The features are arranged in descending order of the averages so it is easy to identify the highest-performing feature (assortment of breads) and the lowest performer (distinctive taste). The standard deviations are reported as they vary, but the minimum and maximum values are not reported, as they are 1 or 5 in almost all cases. You should also note that an informative table footnote describes the scale used in these ratings.

Performance of the Subshop

Feature of the Subshop	Average*	Standard Deviation
Assortment of breads	4.5	0.5
Variety of subs	4.3	0.7
Variety of toppings	4.0	0.8
Freshness of bread	3.9	0.8
Freshness of toppings	3.8	0.7
Promptness of service	3.7	1.0
Cleanliness of facility	3.7	0.9
Value for the price	3.6	1.1
Generosity of toppings	3.5	1.0
Distinctive taste	3.2	1.3

*Based on a scale where 1 = "poor" and 5 = "excellent."

Reporting Nominal or Categorical Data
Nominal data is summarized with the following descriptive measures: frequencies, frequency distribution, percents, percent distribution, and mode. It is important to note that usually only one categorical variable is summarized in each table because the categories are unique to the variable (such as male and female for gender or buyer and nonbuyer for type of customer). Recommendations for what to put in standard categorical data tables are as follows:

Descriptive Measure	For a Standard Categorical Variable Table . . .	Comment
Frequencies, frequency distribution	Include if the researcher wants the reader to note something about the sample, such as a very small sample where percents are greatly affected by a few respondents.	Place frequencies in a column very close to the variable group labels (such as male, female). If appropriate, arrange the categories in ascending or descending order of the percents. Include a total of the frequencies at the bottom.
Percents, percent distribution	Absolutely include, as percents are the most commonly used descriptive measure for nominal data.	Place percents in a column close to the variable group labels (such as male, female) and beside the frequencies, if used. If appropriate, arrange the

(continued)

Descriptive Measure	For a Standard Categorical Variable Table . . .	Comment
		categories in ascending or descending order of the percents. Include a 100% total at the bottom.
Mode	*Highlight, but if obvious, do not report in the table.*	*The largest percentage group is usually readily apparent in a percent distribution and especially if ascending or descending order can be used.*

Here is a "model" nominal (or categorical) variable table. The frequencies are not included, as a large number of respondents answered this question. Each time period is listed chronologically and the mode is identified with the percentage in bold. The 100% total is included to indicate that all time periods are included in this table.

What time in the day do you typically visit the Subshop?

Time Period	Percent
Before 12 pm	*5.3%*
Between 12 pm to 3 pm	**56.8%**
Between 3pm to 6 pm	*24.2%*
After 6 pm	*13.7%*
Total	*100.0%*

Special Case: Reporting Short Metric Scales

On occasion, a marketing researcher may notice something about a short metric variable (that is, an interval or a ratio scale) that seems important to communicate to the client but that will not be communicated effectively with average, median, mode, standard deviation, minimum, and maximum. In the Subshop example that we are using here, the marketing researcher notices something unusual about the overall satisfaction variable—a 7-point interval scale. Specifically, as can be seen in the following percentage table, there is bimodal distribution, meaning that there is a large group at the "very satisfied" rating and another large group at the "neutral" rating. The percentage distribution table expresses this finding quickly and effectively to the client.

Overall, how satisfied are you with the Subshop?

Satisfaction Level	Percent
Delighted	*10.1%*
Very satisfied	*40.8%*
Satisfied	*10.6%*
Neutral	*30.7%*
Unsatisfied	*5.2%*
Very unsatisfied	*2.6%*
Total	*100.0%*

Summary

This chapter introduced you to the descriptive statistics researchers use to inspect basic patterns in data sets. These measures help researchers summarize, conceptualize, and generalize their findings. We also previewed the five types of statistical analysis: descriptive, inferential, differences, associative, and predictive. Descriptive analysis is performed with measures of central tendency such as the mean, mode, or median, each of which portrays the typical respondent or the typical answer to the question being analyzed. The chapter contained formulas and examples of how to determine these central tendency measures. Measures of variability, including the frequency distribution, range, and standard deviation, provide bases for envisioning the degree of similarity of all respondents to the typical respondent. The chapter also contained instructions and formulas for key variability measures. Basically, descriptive analysis yields a profile of how respondents in the sample answered the various questions in the survey. The chapter also provides information on how to instruct SPSS to compute descriptive analyses with SPSS using The Advanced Automobile Concepts survey data set. Clickstream sequences for setting up the analyses and the resulting output are both shown.

Key Terms

Data entry 433
Data coding 434
Data code book 434
Data matrix 435

Data summarization 435
Descriptive analysis 435
Inferential analysis 437
Differences analysis 437

Associative analysis 437
Predictive analysis 437
Measures of central tendency 438
Mode 439

Median 439
Mean 440
Measures of variability 440

Frequency distribution 441
Percentage distribution 442
Range 442

Standard deviation 442
Variance 444

Review Questions/Applications

1. Indicate what data summarization is and why it is useful.
2. Define and differentiate each of the following: (a) descriptive analysis, (b) inferential analysis, (c) associative analysis, (d) predictive analysis, and (e) differences analysis.
3. Indicate why a researcher might refrain from reporting the use of highly sophisticated statistical analyses and opt for simpler forms of analysis.
4. What is a data matrix and how does it appear?
5. What is a measure of central tendency and what does it describe?
6. Indicate the concept of variability and relate how it helps in the description of responses to a particular question on a questionnaire.
7. Using examples, illustrate how a frequency distribution (or a percentage distribution) reveals the variability in responses to a Likert-type question in a lifestyle study. Use two extreme examples of much variability and little variability.
8. Indicate what a range is and where it should be used as an indicator of the amount of dispersion in a sample.
9. With explicit reference to the formula for a standard deviation, show how it measures how different respondents are from one another.
10. Why is the mean an inappropriate measure of central tendency in each of the following cases: (a) gender of respondent (male or female); (b) marital status (single, married, divorced, separated,

widowed, other); (c) a taste test in which subjects indicate their first, second, and third choices of Miller Lite, Bud Light, and Coors Light.
11. For each of the cases in Question 10, what is the appropriate central tendency measure?
12. In a survey on magazine subscriptions, respondents write in the number of magazines they subscribe to regularly. What measures of central tendency can be used? Which is the most appropriate and why?
13. If you use the standard deviation as a measure of the variability in a sample, what statistical assumptions have you implicitly adopted?
14. A manager has commissioned research on a special marketing problem. He is scheduled to brief the board of directors on the problem's resolution in a meeting in New York tomorrow morning. Unfortunately, the research has fallen behind schedule, but the research director works late that night in the downtown San Francisco headquarters and completes the basic data analysis, which will be sufficient for the presentation. However, he now has stacks of computer output and less than an hour before the manager calls him for an early-morning briefing on the survey's basic findings. The researcher looks around at the equipment in his office and an idea flashes into his head. He immediately grabs a blank questionnaire. What is he about to do to facilitate the quick communication of the study's basic findings to the manager?

CASE 15.1

SAFESCOPE CASE STUDY: MARKET RESEARCH TO VALIDATE A NEW BUSINESS

Note: This case is contributed by U.N. Umesh, Professor of Marketing and Entrepreneurship, Washington State University, Vancouver, and Ash Gupte, Partner, Key West Technologies, LLC. It is much more comprehensive than most end-of-chapter cases in this textbook. There are two sets of questions at the end of the case: (1) questions pertaining to central tendency and variability—topics in Chapter 15—and (2) comprehensive case questions. Your instructor will tell you which set of questions to answer.

SafeScope, Inc. is a start-up company. Its founders are executives with successful track records in industry, representing business, technology, and marketing experience in their careers, primarily with large companies. Now as entrepreneurs, they realize the different way in which they have to operate—with significantly fewer people and financial resources as well as under great pressure of

Professor U.N. Umesh

Mr. Ash Gupte

time to strike within a market window for the opportunity they have identified. However, their career training and methodical approach continue to motivate them to use some of the critical tools, such as market research, that they depended on in their prior business lives.

SafeScope has identified an opportunity to create and offer a service by utilizing existing and new technology to present its users with a continuous view and monitoring of their family assets—both property and people. These assets might include, for example, a family's home, a couple of school-age children, a distant vacation home, aged parents in a different city, and a boat moored at a nearby marina. The service would provide users on-demand visibility into the status of any asset as well as alert them in the event of certain critical situations arising relevant to those assets, such as an impending hurricane, a sick child, an aged parent who has "fallen and cannot get up," etc., which would require some action on their part. The service would primarily be targeted at economically well-off, urban, typically two-income families with children.

Ash Gupte, the president of SafeScope, felt that relationships in society and families had changed over the years. Family members had become more independent and mobile. Although cell phones and e-mail have made it easier to stay in touch, there was a greater need to do so because everyone seemed to have their own plans and independent activities. Older grandparents lived far away and had increasing life expectancies—and there was a need to make sure they were all right every day. Parents could feel comfortable if they knew where their child was at any time, particularly if they were unavailable for many hours. Communicating by cell phone and e-mail still left out the monitoring of pets, vacation homes, boats, etc. Further, it would be time-consuming to check daily on every person and asset that mattered, as it would require disparate and numerous communications. An easy-to-read dashboard that displayed all persons, activities, and assets at one glance would be a boon to the time-strapped and anxious potential customer. The following table gives a comprehensive view of the service capabilities.

Service Delivery	Assets			
Interface/Access	*Home*	*People*	*Vacation Home*	*Other Assets*
Phone/PDA: ***Text/e-mail*** ***messages*** • Voice calls • Pictures • Streaming video	***Status of security*** ***system*** • Video feeds • On-demand contact • Exception/ emergency/ alarm reporting	• Where they are • On demand contact • Exception/ emergency/ alarm reporting	• Status of security system • Video feeds • Exception/ emergency/ alarm reporting	• Monitoring as appropriate • Video feeds • Exception/ emergency/ alarm reporting
Web Interface: • Complete dashboard view (SafeScope) • Pop-up notification • Drill down • Related resources • Hot Links	• Pet monitoring • Remote appointments • Neighbor link	• Emergency response • Appointment reminders • Health monitoring • Neighbor, school, doctor Hot Links	• Neighbor link • Weather alerts	• Any of the other tools applicable from the service

In a general sense, SafeScope desired to aggregate and enhance the monitoring and information tools that were already in use by customers. Hence, some parts of the service solution would integrate existing capabilities—for example, GPS—while others would be new tools and services that would enhance the scope, depth, and timeliness of asset monitoring. All of these service components would be brought under a single, intelligent dashboard via the Web interface and coordinated with the user's phone/PDA for mobile communication and visibility.

As the company founders developed their ideas for the SafeScope service, they drew on their own views of what was not yet available and what would be valuable. They also consulted several friends and business acquaintances and online and other information sources and progressively refined their thoughts as they went along. All of this amounted to smart, experienced, but anecdotal, market research further qualified by some practical considerations relative to the technologies available, scale of opportunity the founders wanted to pursue, and so on.

As a next step, each founder conducted in-depth interviews of five two-income professionals apiece—although these were friends and associates—to get some preliminary views on the feasibility of this project. They recognized the shortcomings of not surveying the general population, but they wanted to know if the idea was appealing to at least some people. About half of those interviewed were quite positive about the idea and felt that they might subscribe to such a service when offered; the rest were supportive of the idea in terms of appealing to one segment of the population but did not plan to personally pay for such a service when offered.

The founders recognized that such a limited survey was probably a great way to build a straw man for addressing a business opportunity, but what they needed was objective and statistically relevant validation from a cross section of their prospective customers. So they decided to acquire that market research before dedicating the next few years of their lives to this entrepreneurial opportunity. They hired a well-established local marketing research firm that one of them had worked with before to conduct a survey.

The other founders agreed with Ash on the importance of the service to the busy professional but also noted that there were some real unknowns about their proposition. For example, was the service most critical while customers were out of town on extended vacation or business trips? Was it valuable on a day-to-day basis? Would customers pay differently for each scenario? And how much would they be willing to pay? What would customers compare the SafeScope service to in determining their willingness to pay? Although confident that its basic offering was compelling, marketing research would drive many decisions for the young company. For example, the variety of mobile PDA/phone operating systems to be supported would imply greater software development cost, whereas supporting PC platforms would be much less expensive.

SafeScope hired the marketing research firm to determine the potential demand for these services and their perceived value. Respondents were asked to rate the likelihood of purchasing these services when presented with their monthly cost using a 7-point scale: "would definitely purchase" = 7 to "would definitely not purchase" = 1. The top box rating of 7, "definitely purchase," was viewed as an important measure of the likelihood that someone would purchase the service and is reported separately in the following table The prices per month of the services proposed by SafeScope during the survey were:

Monitoring a home (5 cameras and sensors): $40
Monitoring a single moveable asset e.g., a boat: $20
Tracking per child: $40
Monitoring aged or infirm parent: $25
Monitoring vacation home: $25

SafeScope received detailed feedback from respondents about the pricing of each service but felt it was very important to know what would be the maximum amount customers were likely to spend on the bundle of SafeScope services that they subscribed to, since bringing multiple services under one dashboard was the company's primary goal.

Selected Survey Results from 200 Individuals and Families (Respondents)

	Average Likelihood of Purchase	Proportion of Respondents Rating a 7	Maximum Purchase If Suitable (Bundled)	Average Likelihood to Purchase Multiple Services	Proportion of Respondents Rating a 7
Use during absence from hometown	2.5	15%	$35	2.0	8%
Use anytime	5.5	45%	$88	5.0	31%
Use on PDA/ phone only	5.0	45%	$62	3.5	28%
Use on PC only	5.8	55%	$51	5.1	45%
Use on PC and PDA/phone	6.1	75%	$85	5.8	60%

At the end of the survey, respondents were asked to provide open-ended comments. The most significant comment was that the prices of individual services were high.

Questions Specifically Related to Material in Chapter 15

1. Interpret the averages found in the survey.
2. Indicate how "top-box" scores can be used as a measure of variability, and interpret the "Proportion of Respondents Rating 7" value findings.

Comprehensive Case Questions

1. What decision(s) are the founders seeking to make with the market research they are about to have done?
2. If the founders had to use a step-by-step approach to commercializing this service, starting with the idea, what would they be?
3. If the survey is focused on a "cross section of their prospective customers," identify some of the important groups or segments that they should include in their research and identify some good sources for gaining access to some of these segments.
4. Is the emphasis of their survey likely to be precision in the results or directionality of the results?
5. Since there are several service components being considered and some already exist, how important is it for SafeScope to validate the value of the new services?
6. Assess the value of the in-depth interview conducted by the team in deciding on the next steps.
7. Assuming that the core effort of the market research is to establish the relative value of the various services, what questions would be included in a typical survey to yield a clear idea?
8. In your opinion which type of service offer has greater value—high visibility while customers travel or routine visibility anytime? Why?
9. Why is the top rating of 7 an important statistic in determining a launch decision for a service?
10. Is there a real demand for this service?
11. Should the management team of the start-up reconsider any of their assumptions about the business?
12. Based on the market research report, which service would be the most desirable to introduce?
13. Is it wise to introduce the product/service that is most demanded by the market? What impact would serving this market have on SafeScope's development burden?
14. Would it make sense to provide bundled pricing for these services, for example, a discount when respondents purchase a set of services?

CASE 15.2

THE HOBBIT'S CHOICE RESTAURANT SURVEY DESCRIPTIVE ANALYSIS

In addition to the Advanced Automobile Concepts survey, Cory Rogers of CMG Research was working with Jeff Dean, who believed that there was an opportunity to build an upscale restaurant, possibly to be called "The Hobbit's Choice," somewhere in the metropolitan area. Cory's team had designed an online questionnaire and gathered a representative sample. The questionnaire with its associated value codes follows.

The Hobbit's Choice Restaurant Survey Questionnaire

1. Do you eat at an upscale restaurant at least once every 2 weeks?

   1. Yes (Continue)   2. No (Terminate)

2. How many total dollars do you spend per month in restaurants (for your meals only)?

   $_____

3. Now please read the description of <u>another type</u> of restaurant below and answer the following questions.

A restaurant with a very elegant decor, offering very personal service in a spacious, semiprivate atmosphere, featuring menu items, traditional and unusual, prepared by chefs with international reputations. The atmosphere, food, and service at this restaurant meet a standard equal to that of the finest restaurants in the world. Menu items are priced separately, known as "a la carte," and the prices are what one would expect for a restaurant meeting or surpassing the highest restaurant standards in the world.

How likely would it be for you to patronize this restaurant?

   1. Very Likely

   2. Somewhat Likely

   3. Neither Likely Nor Unlikely

   4. Somewhat Unlikely

   5. Very Unlikely

4. Thinking again of the restaurant just described and remembering that drinks, appetizers, entrées, and desserts are priced separately (a la carte), what would you expect an average evening meal entrée item alone to be priced?

   $ _____

5. Would you describe yourself as one who listens to the radio?

   1. Yes

   2. No (Go to Question 7)

6. To which type of radio programming do you most often listen?

   1. Country & Western

   2. Easy Listening

   3. Rock

   4. Talk/News

   5. No Preference

7. Would you describe yourself as a viewer of TV local news?

   1. Yes

   2. No (Go to Question 9)

8. Which newscast do you watch most frequently?

   1. 7:00 am News

   2. Noon News

   3. 6:00 pm News

   4. 10:00 pm News

9. Do you read the newspaper?

   1. Yes

   2. No (Go to Question 11)

10. Which section of the local newspaper would you say you read most frequently?

    1. Editorial

    2. Business

    3. Local

    4. Classifieds

5. Life, Health & Entertainment

6. No Preference

11. Do you subscribe to *City Magazine*?

   1. Yes

   2. No

We are going to describe some characteristics of restaurants and we want you to tell us how strongly you would prefer each characteristic in a restaurant of your choice.

12. Waterfront view

13. Located less than a 30-minute drive from your home

14. A formal waitstaff wearing tuxedos

15. Unusual desserts such as "Baked Alaska" and "Flaming Bananas Foster"

16. A large variety of entrées

17. Unusual entrées such as moose, bison, venison, and pheasant

18. Simple decor: tables, chairs, and a few wall decorations

19. Elegant decor: curtains, original paintings, fine furniture

20. A string quartet for background music

21. A jazz combo for background music

Response scale for
Questions 12 through 21

1. Very Strongly Not Prefer

2. Somewhat Not Prefer

3. Neither Prefer Nor Not Prefer

4. Somewhat Prefer

5. Very Strongly Prefer

   The following questions are asked for classification purposes only.

22. In which year were you born?

   _____

23. What is your highest level of education?

   1. Less Than High School

   2. Some High School

   3. High School Graduate

   4. Some College (No Degree)

   5. Associate Degree

   6. Bachelor's Degree

   7. Master's Degree

   8. Doctorate Degree

24. What is your marital status?

   1. Single

   2. Married

   3. Other

25. Including children under 18 years of age living with you, what is your family size?

   _____

26. Please check the letter that includes the zip code in which you live.

   A. (1 & 2)

   B. (3, 4, & 5)

   C. (6, 7, 8, & 9)

   D. (10, 11, & 12)

27. Which of the following categories best describes your before-tax household income?

   1. Household Earning < $15,000

   2. Household Earning $15,000–$24,999

   3. Household Earning $25,000–$49,999

   4. Household Earning $50,000–$74,999

   5. Household Earning $75,000–$99,999

    6. Household Earning $100,000–$149,999

    7. Household Earning $150,000+

28. What is your gender?

    1. Male

    2. Female

Cory had other marketing research projects and meetings scheduled with present and prospective clients, so he called in his marketing intern, Christine Yu. Christine was a senior marketing major at Able State University, and she had studied marketing research in the previous semester. Cory called Christine into his office, and said, "Christine, it is time to do some analysis on the survey we did for Jeff Dean. For now, let's just get a feel for what the data look like. I'll leave it up to your judgment as to what basic analysis to run. Let's meet tomorrow at 2:30 pm to see what you have found."

Your task in Case 15.2 is to take the role of Christine Yu, marketing intern. The file name is Hobbit.sav, and it is in SPSS data file format. Your instructor will provide this SPSS data file to you or tell you how you can obtain it.

1. Determine what variables are categorical (either nominal or ordinal scales), perform the appropriate descriptive analysis, and interpret it.
2. Determine what variables are metric scales (either interval or ratio scales), perform the appropriate descriptive analysis, and interpret it.

CASE 15.3 Your Integrated Case

ADVANCED AUTOMOBILE CONCEPTS DESCRIPTIVE ANALYSIS

SPSS

Cory Rogers was happy to call Nick Thomas to inform him that Advanced Automobile Concepts survey data were collected and ready for analysis. Of course, Cory had other marketing research projects and meetings scheduled with present and prospective clients, so he called in his data analyst, Celeste Brown. Celeste was a recently graduated marketing major who had worked as a marketing intern at CMG Research last year. Celeste had worked on a few small CMG survey data sets, but she had not yet tackled any large projects. Cory called Celeste into his office and said, "Celeste, it is time to do some analysis on the survey we did for Nick Thomas of Advanced Automobile Concepts. I am going to assign you primary responsibility for all data analysis on this important project. For now, let's just get a feel for what the data look like. I'll leave it up to your judgment as to what analyses to run, but for now, do some summarizations in order to reveal the basic patterns and to gain an understanding of the nature of the variability in the data. Let's meet on Thursday at 2:30 pm to see what you have found."

Your task in Case 15.3 is to take the role of Celeste Brown, marketing analyst. The data set for the Advanced Automobile Concepts survey is now ready for descriptive analysis. The file name is AAConcepts.sav, and it is in SPSS data file format. The instructor of your marketing research course will tell you how to access this SPSS data set. The data set sample represents American households, and it includes owners as well as nonowners of vehicles because the market for the hybrid vehicles to be developed and marketed by the Advanced Automobile Concepts division of ZEN Motors will not "hit" the market for 3 to 5 years from now.

The AAConcepts SPSS data set defines the variables, but for easy reference, here is a list of the major variables in the survey.

For the demographic and automobile ownership variables coding, see the SPSS code sheet (the Variable View function of SPSS). All of the attitude variables are measured with a 7-point Likert scale, where 1 = "very strongly disagree" and 7 = "very strongly agree." The likelihoods of buying new automobile types are measured on a 100-point probability scale. The lifestyle types are measured on a 1–10 scale, where 1 = "does not describe me at all," and 10 = "describes me almost perfectly." The preferences scale is 1–7 with 1 = "very undesirable" and 7 = "very desirable."

Demographics

- Hometown size
- Gender
- Marital status
- Number of people in family
- Age category
- Education category
- Job type category
- Income category
- Dwelling type

Attitudes: Global Warming (Measure: 1–7)

- I am worried about global warming.
- Global warming is a real threat.
- We need to do something to slow global warming.

Attitudes: Gasoline Prices (Measure: 1–7)

- Gasoline prices will remain high in the future.
- Gasoline prices are too high now.
- High gasoline prices will impact what type of autos are purchased.

Probabilities of Buying Hybrid Automobile Types (Measure: 0–100%)

- Probability of buying a very small (1-seat) hybrid auto within 3 years?
- Probability of buying a small (2-seat) hybrid auto within 3 years?
- Probability of buying an economy-size hybrid auto within 3 years?
- Probability of buying a standard-size hybrid auto within 3 years?
- Probability of buying a large-size hybrid auto within 3 years?

Automobile Ownership

- Primary vehicle price category
- Primary vehicle type
- Type of commuting

Attitudes: Gasoline Usage (Measure: 1–7)

- Gasoline emissions contribute to global warming.
- Americans use too much gasoline.
- We should be looking for gasoline substitutes.

Attitudes: Effects of New Automobile Types (Measure: 1–7)

- Very small autos with very high mpg will reduce fuel emissions.
- Very small autos with very high mpg will keep gas prices stable.
- Very small autos with very high mpg will slow down global warming.
- Small autos with high mpg will reduce fuel emissions.
- Small autos with high mpg will keep gas prices stable.
- Small autos with high mpg will slow down global warming.
- Hybrid autos that use alternative fuels will reduce fuel emissions.
- Hybrid autos that use alternative fuels will keep gas prices down.
- Hybrid autos that use alternative fuels will slow down global warming.

Preferences for Various Types of Hybrid Automobile Models (Measure: 1–7)

- Super cycle 1-seat; 120+ mpg city
- Runabout Sport 2-seat; 90 mpg city, 80 mpg highway
- Runabout with Luggage 2-seat; 80 mpg city, 70 mpg highway
- Economy 4-seat; 70 mpg city; 60 mpg highway
- Standard 4-seat; 60 mpg city, 50 mpg highway

Lifestyle Type (Measure: 1–10)

- **Novelist**—very early adopter, risk taker, "way out," "show off," want to be unique and special
- **Innovator**—Early adopter, less a risk taker than novelist, but into new technology; likes new products, but not a "show off"
- **Trendsetter**—Opinion leaders, well off financially and educationally, often the first adopters of new trends that are adopted by most of society
- **Forerunner**—Early majority of population, respected and fairly well off; not opinion leaders, but adopt new products before the "average" person
- **Mainstreamer**—Late majority of population, "average people," who are reserved and deliberate
- **Classic**—Laggards who cling to "old" ways

Favorite TV Show Type

- Comedy
- Drama
- Movies/Mini-series
- News/Documentary
- Reality, Science Fiction
- Sports

Favorite Magazine Type

- Business & Money
- Music & Entertainment
- Family & Parenting
- Sports & Outdoors
- Home & Garden
- Cooking–Food & Wine
- Trucks–Cars & Motorcycles
- News–Politics & Current Events

Favorite Radio Genre

- Classic Pop & Rock
- Country
- Easy listening
- Jazz & Blues
- Pop & Chart
- Talk

Favorite Local Newspaper Section

- Editorial
- Business
- Local news
- National news
- Sports
- Entertainment

For each of the following questions, it is your task to determine the type of scale for each variable, so that you can conduct the proper descriptive analysis with SPSS, and to interpret it.

1. What is the demographic composition of the sample?
2. What is the automobile ownership profile of respondents in the survey?
3. How do respondents feel about (1) global warming and (2) the use of gasoline?
4. What are the respondents' opinions about the effects of the use of various kinds of hybrid vehicles?
5. What size of "new" automobile (very small with very high mpg, small with high mpg, and hybrid using alternative fuels) do people in the sample believe are likely to have the most positive effects?
6. What type of hybrid automobile is the most attractive to people in the sample in terms of likelihood of purchase in the next 3 years? What type is the least attractive?

Learning Objectives

- To distinguish statistics from parameters
- To understand the concept of statistical inference
- To learn how to estimate a population mean or percentage
- To test a hypothesis about a population mean or percentage
- To learn how to perform and interpret statistical inference with SPSS

Where We Are

1 Establish the need for marketing research
2 Define the problem
3 Establish research objectives
4 Determine research design
5 Identify information types and sources
6 Determine methods of accessing data
7 Design data-collection forms
8 Determine the sample plan and size
9 Collect data
10 Analyze data, and
11 Prepare and present the final research report.

Answering Clients' Questions About the Applicability of Research Findings

Richard Homans, Senior Vice President and Managing Director, Ipsos Forward Research

www.ipsos.com

Ipsos Forward Research

Clients can benefit by understanding the basics of some of the tools of statistical inference you will learn about in this chapter. For example, let's suppose you've conducted some research and measured likelihood to purchase your proposed new product. You've set an action standard that if the mean on the 7-point scale is above 5.5, you will take the product to the next stage of product development. The results come in and the mean is 6.0. That's great news! This means you can start planning for that next stage in the development of this product.

But, a wise client would ask: "What would that number be if we did the research over again tomorrow?" This is indeed a wise question to ask because every measure we take in research is subject to sampling error. We will always have sampling error; it is inherent in the sampling process. This means the answer to the client's question is "Yes, that number will likely vary if we conducted the research study over again tomorrow." In fact, because sampling error exists in every sample, that number is going to vary virtually every time we conduct a study. This is where confidence intervals can be very important to the client. A confidence interval will give the client a range within which we can expect the sample statistic, in this case, a mean, to vary if we conducted the study over many, many times. A confidence interval would allow us to make a statement such as: "If we conducted this study over 100 times, 95 times out of the 100 studies, the mean to this question will fall between 5.7 and 6.3." Now, our client has some measure of the reliability of our first estimate. Even if we did many, many studies, it is not likely that the mean will fall below 5.7. Since this is above our action standard of 5.5, the client can feel more assured in the decision to move forward in developing the new product.

While the tools of statistical inference can be helpful, we must remember that other errors, nonsampling errors, must be controlled in order for us to have valid and reliable results. A good marketing research professional will know what the sources of those errors are and will have taken the steps necessary to control them. Also, clients should understand the impact of sample size on confidence intervals. The smaller the sample size, given the same variance in the data, the wider the confidence interval, and the larger the sample size, the more narrow the confidence interval. You will learn about confidence intervals and other tools of statistical inference in this chapter.

A s you learned in Chapter 15, descriptive measures of central tendency and measures of variability adequately summarize the findings of a survey. However, whenever a probability sample is drawn from a population, it is not enough to simply report the sample's descriptive statistics, for these measures contain a certain degree of error due to the sampling process. Every sample provides some information about its population, but there is always some sample error that must be taken into account. That is what Richard Homans is talking about in our opening case. By reading the material in this chapter, you should be able to understand the nuances of Mr. Homans's comments.

We begin the chapter by noting that the term statistic applies to a sample, whereas the term parameter pertains to the related population value. Next, we describe the concept of logical inference and show how it relates to statistical inference. There are two basic types of statistical inference, and we discuss both cases. First, there is parameter estimation in which a value, such as the population mean, is estimated based on a sample's mean and its size. Second, there is hypothesis testing where an assessment is made as to how much of a sample's findings support a manager's or researcher's a priori belief regarding the size of a population value. We provide formulas and numerical examples and also show you examples of SPSS procedures and output using the Advanced Automobile Concepts survey data.

SAMPLE STATISTICS AND POPULATION PARAMETERS

Statistics are sample values, whereas parameters are corresponding population values.

We begin this chapter by defining the concepts of statistics and parameters. There is a fundamental distinction you should keep in mind. Values that are computed from information provided by a sample are referred to as the sample's **statistics**, whereas values that are computed from a complete census, which are considered to be precise and valid measures of the population, are referred to as **parameters**. Statisticians use Greek letters—α (alpha), β (beta), etc.—when referring to population parameters and Roman letters—a, b, etc.—when referring to statistics. Every sample statistic has a corresponding population parameter. As you can see in Table 16.1, the notation used for a percentage is p for the statistic and π for the parameter, the notations for standard deviation are s (statistic) and σ (parameter), and the notations for the mean are $\bar{x}$ (statistic) and μ (parameter). Because a census is impractical, the sample statistic is used to estimate the population parameter. This chapter describes the procedures used when estimating various population parameters.

THE CONCEPTS OF INFERENCE AND STATISTICAL INFERENCE

Inference is drawing a conclusion based on some evidence.

We will start by defining "inference" because an understanding of this concept will help you understand what statistical inference is all about. **Inference** is a form of logic in which you make a general statement (a generalization) about an entire class based on what you

TABLE 16.1 **Population Parameters and Their Corresponding Sample Statistics**

Statistical Concept	Population Parameter (Greek Letters)	Sample Statistic (Roman Letters)
Average	μ (mu)	$\bar{x}$
Standard deviation	σ (sigma)	s
Percentage	π (pi)	p
Slope	β (beta)	b

How many of your friends having car problems with the same manufacturer would it take for you to generalize that the company makes defective cars?

have observed about a small set of members of that class. When you infer, you draw a conclusion from a small amount of evidence. For example, if two of your friends each bought a new Dodge sedan and they both complained about their cars' performances, you might infer that *all* new Dodges perform poorly. On the other hand, if one of your friends complained about his Dodge, whereas the other friend did not, you might infer that *some* new Dodge cars have performance problems.

Inferences are greatly influenced by the amount of evidence in support of the generalization. So, if 20 of your friends bought new Dodge cars, and they all complained about poor performance, your inference would naturally be stronger or more certain than it would be in the case of only two friends' complaining.

Statistical inference is a set of procedures in which the sample size and sample statistic are used to make an estimate of the corresponding population parameter. That is, statistical inference has formal steps for estimating the population parameter (the generalization) based on the evidence of the sample statistic and taking into account the sample error based on sample size. For now, let us concentrate on the percentage, p, as the sample statistic we are using to estimate the population percentage, π, and see how sample size enters into statistical inference. Suppose that Dodge suspected that there were some dissatisfied customers and it commissioned two independent marketing research surveys to determine the amount of dissatisfaction that existed in its customer group. (Of course, our Dodge example is entirely fictitious. We don't mean to imply that Dodge cars perform in an unsatisfactory way.)

In the first survey, 100 customers who had purchased a Dodge in the last 6 months were called on the telephone and asked, "In general, would you say that you are 'satisfied' or 'dissatisfied' with the performance of your Dodge since you bought it?" The survey found that 30 respondents (30%) are dissatisfied. This finding could be inferred to be total population of Dodge owners who had bought a car in the last 6 months, and we would say that there is 30% dissatisfaction. However, we know that our sample, which, by the way, was a probability sample, must contain some sample error, and in order to reflect this you would have to say that there was *about* 30% dissatisfaction in the population. In other words, the total might actually be more or less than 30% if we did a census because the sample provided us with only an estimate.

In the second survey, 1,000 respondents—that's 10 times more than in the first survey—were called on the telephone and asked the same question. This survey found that 35% of the respondents are "dissatisfied." Again, we know that the 35% is an estimate containing

Statistical inference takes into account that large random samples are more accurate than are small ones.

Statistical inference is based on sample size and variability, which then determine the amount of sampling error.

TABLE 16.2   **Two Types of Statistical Inference: Results of Online Music Listeners Survey Conducted for iTunes™**

Type	Description	Example*
Parameter estimation	Estimate the population value (parameter) through the use of confidence intervals	The percentage of PC users who listen to music online is 30% ± 10%, or from 20% to 40%.
Hypothesis test	Compare the sample statistic with what is believed (hypothesized) to be the population value prior to undertaking the study	Online music listeners listen an average of 45 ± 15 minutes per day, not 90 as believed by iTunes managers.

*Note: The examples are fictitious.

sampling error, so now we would also say that the population dissatisfaction percentage was *about* 35%. This means that we have two estimates of the degree of dissatisfaction with Dodges. One is about 30%, whereas the other is about 35%.

How do we translate our answers (remember they include the word *about*) into more accurate numerical representations? Let us say you could translate them into ballpark ranges. That is, you could translate them so we could say "30% plus or minus x%" for the sample of 100 and "35% plus or minus y%" for the sample of 1,000. How would x and y compare? To answer this question, think back on how your logical inference was stronger with 20 friends than it was with 2 friends with Dodges. To state this in a different way, with a larger sample (or more evidence), we have agreed that you would be more certain that the sample statistic was accurate with respect to estimating the true population value. In other words, with a larger sample size you should expect the range used to estimate the true population value to be smaller. Intuitively, you should expect the range for y to be smaller than the range for x because you have a large sample and less sampling error.

As these examples reveal, with statistical inference for estimates of population parameters such as the percentage or mean, the sample statistic is used as the beginning point, and then a range is computed in which the population parameter is estimated to fall. The size of the sample, or n, plays a crucial role in this computation, as you will see in all of the statistical inference formulas we present in this chapter.

The two types of statistical inference are parameter estimation and hypothesis testing.

Two types of statistical inferences often used by marketing researchers will be described: parameter estimates and hypothesis tests. **Parameter estimation** is used to estimate the population value (parameter) through the use of confidence intervals. **Hypothesis testing** is used to compare the sample statistic with what is believed (hypothesized) to be the population value prior to undertaking the study. For quick reference, we have listed and described these two types of statistical inference in Table 16.2 with examples of findings from an online survey conducted for iTunes™.

PARAMETER ESTIMATION

To estimate a population parameter you need a sample statistic (mean or percentage), the standard error of the statistic, and the desired level of confidence (95% or 99%).

Estimation of population parameters is a common type of statistical inference used in marketing research survey analysis. As was indicated earlier, inference is largely a reflection of the amount of sampling error believed to exist in the sample statistic. When the *New York Times* conducts a survey and finds that readers spend an average of 45 minutes daily reading the *Times*, or when McDonald's determines through a nationwide sample that 78% of all Egg McMuffin Breakfast buyers buy a cup of coffee, both companies may want to determine more accurately how close these estimates are to what the actual population parameter is.

Parameter estimation is the process of using sample information to compute an interval that describes the range of a parameter such as the population mean (μ) or the population percentage (π). It involves the use of three values: the sample statistic (such as the mean or the percentage), the standard error of the statistic, and the desired level of confidence (usually 95% or 99%). A discussion of how each value is determined follows.

Sample Statistic

The mean, you should recall from the formula provided in Chapter 15, is the average of a set of interval- or ratio-scaled numbers. For example, you might be working with a sample of golfers and researching the average number of golf balls they buy per month. Or you might be investigating how much high school students spend, on average, on fast foods between meals. For a percentage, you could be examining what percentage of golfers buy only Maxfli Gold balls, or you might be looking at what percentage of high school students buy from Taco Bell between meals. In either case, the mean or percentage is derived from a sample, so it is the sample statistic.

In parameter estimation, the sample statistic is usually a mean or a percentage.

Standard Error

There usually is some degree of variability in the sample. That is, our golfers do not all buy the same number of golf balls per month and they do not all buy Maxfli. Not all of our high school students eat fast food between meals and not all of the ones who do go to Taco Bell. In Chapter 15, we introduced you to variability with a mean by describing the standard deviation, and we used the percentage distribution as a way of describing variability when percentages are being used. Also, in Chapter 13, we described how, if you theoretically took many, many samples and plotted the mean or percentage as a frequency distribution, it would approximate a bell-shaped curve called the sampling distribution.

The **standard error** is a measure of the variability in the sampling distribution based on what is theoretically believed to occur were we to take a multitude of independent samples from the same population. We described the standard error formulas in Chapter 13, but we repeat them here because they are vital to statistical inference as they tie together the sample size and its variability.

The standard error is a measure of the variability in a sampling distribution.

The formula for the standard error of the mean is as follows:

Formula for Standard Error of the Mean
$$s_{\bar{x}} = \frac{s}{\sqrt{n}}$$

where

$s_{\bar{x}}$ = standard error of the mean
s = standard deviation
n = sample size.

The formula for the standard error of the percentage is as follows:

The formula for mean standard error differs from a percentage standard error.

Formula for Standard Error of the Percentage
$$s_p = \sqrt{\frac{p \times q}{n}}$$

where

s_p = standard error of the percentage
p = the sample percentage
$q = (100 - p)$
n = sample size

In both equations, the sample size n is found in the denominator. This means that the standard error will be smaller with larger sample sizes and larger with smaller sample sizes. At the same time, both of these formulas for the standard error reveal the impact of the variation found in the sample. Variation is represented by the standard deviation s for a mean and by ($p \times q$) for a percentage. In either equation, the variation is in the numerator, so the

The standard error takes into account sample size and the variability in the sample.

greater the variability, the greater the standard error. Thus, the standard error simultaneously takes into account both the sample size and the amount of variation found in the sample. The following examples illustrate this fact.

Suppose that the *New York Times* survey on the amount of daily time spent reading the *Times* had determined a standard deviation of 20 minutes and used a sample size of 100. The resulting standard error of the mean would be as follows:

Notice how sample variability affects the standard error in these two examples.

Calculation of Standard Error of the Mean with Standard Deviation = 20 and Sample Size = 100

$$s_{\bar{x}} = \frac{s}{\sqrt{n}}$$

$$s_{\bar{x}} = \frac{20}{\sqrt{100}}$$

$$= \frac{20}{10}$$

$$= 2 \text{ minutes}$$

Notes: Std. dev. = 20
n = 100

On the other hand, if the survey had determined a standard deviation of 40 minutes, the standard error would be as follows:

Calculation of Standard Error of the Mean with Standard Deviation = 40 and Sample Size = 100

$$s_{\bar{x}} = \frac{s}{\sqrt{n}}$$

$$s_{\bar{x}} = \frac{40}{\sqrt{100}}$$

$$= \frac{40}{10}$$

$$= 4 \text{ minutes}$$

Notes: Std. dev. = 40
n = 100

As you can see, the standard error of the mean from a sample with little variability (20 minutes) is smaller than the standard error of the mean from a sample with much variability (40 minutes), as long as both samples have the same size. In fact, you should have noticed that when the variability was doubled from 20 to 40 minutes, the standard error also doubled, given identical sample sizes. (Refer to Figure 16.1.)

The standard error of a percentage mirrors this logic, although the formula looks a bit different. In this case, as we indicated earlier, the degree of variability is inherent in the $(p \times q)$ aspect of the equation. Very little variability is indicated if p and q are very different

Statistical inference can be used to estimate how many minutes people read their daily newspaper.

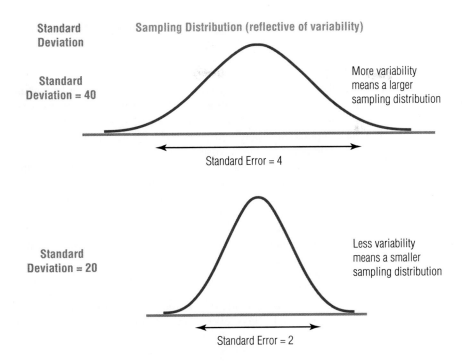

in size. For example, if a survey of 100 McDonald's breakfast buyers determined that 90% of the respondents ordered coffee with their Egg McMuffin and 10% of the respondents did not, there would be very little variability because almost everybody orders coffee with breakfast. On the other hand, if the sample determined that there was a 50–50 split between those who had and those who had not ordered coffee, there would be a great deal more variability because any two customers would probably differ in their drink orders.

With a 50–50 percent split there is great variability.

We can apply these two results to the standard error of percentage for a comparison. Using a 90–10 percent split, the standard error of percentage is as follows:

**Calculation of Standard
Error of the Percent with
$p = 90$ and $q = 10$ and
Sample Size $= 100$**

$$s_p = \sqrt{\frac{p \times q}{n}}$$

$$= \sqrt{\frac{(90)(10)}{100}}$$

$$= \sqrt{\frac{900}{100}}$$

$$= \sqrt{9}$$

$$= 3\%$$

*Notes: $p = 90$
        $q = 10$
        $n = 100$*

Using the 50–50 percent split, the standard error of the percentage is as follows:

**Calculation of Standard
Error of the Percentage with
$p = 50$ and $q = 50$ and
Sample Size $= 100$**

$$s_p = \sqrt{\frac{p \times q}{n}}$$

$$= \sqrt{\frac{(50)(50)}{100}}$$

$$= \sqrt{\frac{2500}{100}}$$

$$= \sqrt{25}$$

$$= 5\%$$

*Notes: $p = 50$
        $q = 50$
        $n = 100$*

A 50–50 percent split has a larger standard error than a 90–10 one when sample size is the same.

Again, these examples show that greater variability in responses results in a larger standard error of the percentage at a given sample size.

Confidence Intervals

Population parameters are estimated with the use of confidence intervals.

Confidence intervals are the degree of accuracy desired by the researcher and stipulated as a level of confidence in the form of a range with a lower boundary and an upper boundary. You may recall that we described sample accuracy in Chapter 13 as a ±% value, and we are using this concept in the computation of confidence intervals. Because there is always some sampling error when a sample is taken, it is necessary to estimate the population parameter with a range. We did this in the Dodge owners' example earlier. One factor affecting the size of the range is how confident the researcher wants to be that the range includes the true population percentage (parameter). Normally, the researcher first decides on how confident he or she wants to be; that is, the researcher formally selects a level of confidence. The sample statistic is the beginning of the estimate, but because there is sample error present, a "plus" amount and an identical "minus" amount is added and subtracted from the sample statistic to determine the maximum and minimum, respectively, of the range.

The range of your estimate of the population mean or percentage depends largely on the sample size and the variability found in the sample.

Typically, marketing researchers rely only on the 99%, 95%, or 90% levels of confidence, which correspond to ±2.58, ±1.96, and ±1.64 standard errors, respectively. They are designated z_α, so $z_{0.99}$ is ±2.58 standard errors. By far, the **most commonly used level of confidence** in marketing research is the 95% level,[1] corresponding to 1.96 standard errors. In fact, the 95% level of confidence is usually the default level found in statistical analysis programs such as SPSS. Now that the relationship between the standard error and the measure of sample variability—be it the standard deviation or the percentage—is apparent, it is a simple matter to determine the range in which the population parameter will be estimated. We use the sample statistics $\overline{x}$ or p to compute the standard error and then apply our desired level of confidence. In notation form these are as follows:

$$\overline{x} \pm z_\alpha s_{\overline{x}}$$

Formula for Confidence Interval for a Mean

where

$\overline{x}$ = sample mean
z_α = z value for 95% or 99% level of confidence
$s_{\overline{x}}$ = standard error of the mean.

Confidence intervals are estimated using these formulas.

$$p \pm z_\alpha s_p$$

Formula for Confidence Interval for a Percentage

where

p = sample percentage
z_α = z value for 95% or 99% level of confidence
s_p = standard error of the percentage.

If you wanted to be 99% confident that your range included the true population percentage, for instance, you would multiply the standard error of the percentage s_p by 2.58 and add that value to the sample finding percentage p to obtain the upper limit, and you would subtract it from that percentage to find the lower limit. Notice that you have now taken into consideration the sample statistic p, the variability that is in the formula for s_p; the sample size n, which is also in the formula for s_p; and the degree of confidence in your estimate.

Marketing researchers typically use only 95 or 99% confidence intervals.

How do these formulas relate to inference? Recall that we are estimating a population parameter. That is, we are indicating a range into which it is believed that the true population parameter falls. The size of the range is determined by those pieces of information we have about the population on hand as a result of our sample. The final ingredient is our level of confidence or the degree to which we want to be correct in our estimate of the population parameter. If we are conservative and wish to assume the 99% level of confidence, then the range would be more encompassing than if we are less conservative and assume only the 95% level of confidence because 99% is associated with ± 2.58 standard errors and 95% is associated with ± 1.96 standard errors.

Using these formulas for the sample of 100 *New York Times* readers with a mean reading time of 45 minutes and a standard deviation of 20 minutes, the 95% and the 99% confidence interval estimates would be calculated as follows.

Calculation of a 95% Confidence Interval for a Mean

$$\overline{x} \pm 1.96 \times s_{\overline{x}}$$

$$45 \pm 1.96 \times \frac{20}{\sqrt{100}}$$

$$45 \pm 1.96 \times 2$$

$$45 \pm 3.9$$

$$41.1 - 48.9 \text{ minutes}$$

Notes: Mean $= 45$
Std. dev. $= 20$
$z = 1.96$

Here are two examples of confidence interval computations with a mean.

Calculation of a 99% Confidence Interval for a Mean

$$\overline{x} \pm 2.58 \times s_{\overline{x}}$$

$$45 \pm 2.58 \times \frac{20}{\sqrt{100}}$$

$$45 \pm 2.58 \times 2$$

$$45 \pm 5.2$$

$$39.8 - 50.2 \text{ minutes}$$

Notes: Mean $= 45$
Std. dev. $= 20$
$z = 2.58$

If 50% of the 100 Egg McMuffin eaters orders coffee, the 95% and 99% confidence intervals would be computed using the percentage formula.

Calculation of a 95% Confidence Interval for a Percentage

$$p \pm 1.96 \times s_p$$

$$p \pm 1.96 \times \sqrt{\frac{p \times q}{n}}$$

$$50 \pm 1.96 \times \sqrt{\frac{50 \times 50}{100}}$$

$$50 \pm 1.96 \times 5$$

$$50 \pm 9.8$$

$$40.2\% - 59.8\%$$

Notes: $p = 50$
$q = 50$
$n = 100$
$z = 1.96$

Here are two examples of confidence interval computations with a percentage.

Calculation of a 99% Confidence Interval for a Percentage

$$p \pm 2.58 \times s_p$$

$$p \pm 2.58 \times \sqrt{\frac{p \times q}{n}}$$

$$50 \pm 2.58 \times \sqrt{\frac{50 \times 50}{100}}$$

$$50 \pm 2.58 \times 5$$

$$50 \pm 12.9$$

$$37.1\% - 62.9\%$$

Notes: $p = 50$
$q = 50$
$n = 100$
$z = 2.58$

Notice that the only thing that differs when you compare the 95% confidence interval computations to the 99% confidence interval computations in each case is z_{α}. It is 1.96 for 95% and 2.58 for 99% of confidence. The confidence interval is always wider for 99% than it is for 95% when the sample size is the same and variability is equal.

A 99% confidence interval is always wider than a 95% confidence interval if all other factors are equal.

Calculate Some Confidence Intervals

This Active Learning section will give you some practice in calculating confidence intervals. For this set of exercises, you are working with a survey of 1,000 people who responded to questions about satellite radio. The questions, sample statistics, and other pertinent information are listed below. Compute the 95% confidence interval for the population parameter in each case. Be certain to follow the logic of the questions, as it has implications for the sample size pertaining to each question.

Question	Sample Statistic(s)	95% Confidence Interval	
		Lower Boundary	Upper Boundary
Have you heard of satellite radio?	500/1,000 = 50% responded "yes."		
If yes, do you own a satellite radio?	150/500 = 30% responded "yes."		
If you own satellite radio, about how many minutes of satellite radio did you listen to last week?	Average of 100.7 minutes; standard deviation of 25.0 minutes for the 150 satellite radio owners.		

How to Interpret an Estimated Population Mean or Percentage Range

How are these ranges interpreted? The interpretation is quite simple when you remember that the sampling distribution notion is the underlying theoretical concept. If we were using a 99% level of confidence, and if we repeated the sampling process and computed the sample statistic many times, their frequency distribution (the sampling distribution) would comprise a bell-shaped curve. A total of 99% of these repeated samples results would produce a range that includes the population parameter.

Obviously, a marketing researcher would take only one sample for a particular marketing research project, and this restriction explains why estimates must be used. Furthermore, it is the conscientious application of probability sampling techniques that allows us to make use of the sampling distribution concept. So, statistical inference procedures are the direct linkages between probability sample design and data analysis. Do you remember that you had to grapple with confidence levels when we determined sample size? Now we are on the other side of the table, so to speak, and we must use the sample size for our inference procedures. Confidence intervals must be used when estimating population parameters, and the size of the random sample used is always reflected in these confidence intervals.

There are five steps to computing a confidence interval.

There are five steps involved in computing confidence intervals for a mean or a percentage (Table 16.3): (1) Determine the sample statistic; (2) identify the sample size; (3) determine the variability in the sample for the statistic; (4) decide on the level of confidence; (5) perform the computations to determine the upper and lower boundaries of the confidence interval range.

As a final note, we want to remind you that the logic of statistical inference is identical to the reasoning process you go through when you weigh evidence to make a generalization or conclusion of some sort. The more evidence you have, the more precise you will be in your generalization. The only difference is that with statistical inference we must follow certain rules that require the application of formulas so our inferences will be consistent

TABLE 16.3 **How to Compute Confidence Intervals for a Mean or a Percentage**

Step 1 Find the sample statistic, either the mean, $\bar{x}$, or the percentage, p.

Step 2 Identify the sample size, n.

Step 3 Determine the amount of variability found in the sample in the form of standard error of the mean, $s_{\bar{x}}$:

$$s_{\bar{x}} = \frac{s}{\sqrt{n}}$$

or standard error of the percentage, s_p:

$$s_p = \sqrt{\frac{p \times q}{n}}$$

Step 4 Decide on the desired level of confidence to determine the value for z:

$$z_{.95}(1.96) \text{ or } z_{.99}(2.58)$$

Step 5 Compute your (95%) confidence interval as $\bar{x} \pm 1.96 s_{\bar{x}}$ or $p \pm 1.96 s_p$.

with the assumptions of statistical theory. When you make a nonstatistical inference, your judgment can be swayed by subjective factors, so you may not be consistent with others who are making an inference with the same evidence. But in statistical inference, the formulas are completely objective and perfectly consistent. Plus, they are based on accepted statistical concepts.

Your Integrated Case

THE ADVANCED AUTOMOBILE CONCEPTS SURVEY

SPSS

How to Obtain a Confidence Interval for a Percentage with SPSS

Your SPSS program will not calculate the confidence intervals for a percentage. This is because with a categorical variable such as the programming format of the Advanced Automobile Concepts survey, there may be many different categories. But you know now that the computation is fairly easy, and all you need to know is the value of p and the sample size, both of which you can obtain using the "Frequencies" procedure in SPSS.

Here is an example using the Advanced Automobile Concepts data set. We found in our descriptive analysis that "1 million and more" was the largest hometown size category and 26.7% of the respondents live in cities of this size. We can calculate the confidence intervals at a 95% level of confidence easily because we know that the sample size was 1,000. Here are the calculations.

Calculation of a 95% Confidence Interval for the "1 million and more" Hometown Size Percentage in the Advanced Automobile Concepts Population

$$p \pm 1.96 \times s_p$$

$$p \pm 1.96 \times \sqrt{\frac{p \times q}{n}}$$

$$26.7 \pm 1.96 \times \sqrt{\frac{26.7 \times 73.3}{1000}}$$

$$26.7 \pm 1.96 \times 1.4$$

$$26.7 \pm 2.7$$

$$24.0\% - 29.4\%$$

Notes: $p = 26.7\%$
$q = 73.3\%$
$n = 1,000$
$z = 1.96$

Luckily, confidence intervals are easy to calculate for percentages. So all you need to do is a FREQUENCIES analysis to obtain the target percentage and a sample size value to go into the formula to calculate these confidence intervals.

How to Obtain and Use a Confidence Interval for a Mean with SPSS

Obtaining and Interpreting a Confidence Interval for a Mean

Fortunately, because the calculations are a bit more complicated and tedious, your SPSS program will calculate the confidence interval for a mean. To illustrate this feature, we will revisit a critical comment that Nick Thomas, CEO of Advanced Automobile Concepts, made to Cory Rogers of CMG Research early in their association. Nick indicated that Zen Motors would need some compelling evidence that the general public was of the opinion that gasoline usage was detrimental. You should recall that in our descriptive analysis example of a mean, we found that the average disagree–agree response to the statement "Gasoline emissions contribute to global warming" was 4.8, or "agree."

To determine the 95% confidence interval for this average, examine Figure 16.2 which shows the clickstream sequence to accomplish a 95% confidence interval estimate using SPSS. As you can see, the correct SPSS procedure is a "One Sample *t*-test," and you use the ANALYZE–COMPARE MEANS–ONE SAMPLE T TEST menu clickstream sequence to open up the proper window. Refer to Figure 16.2 to see that all you need to do is to select the "Gasoline emissions contribute to global warming" variable into the Test Variables area, and then click "OK."

Figure 16.3 shows the results of ANALYZE–COMPARE MEANS–ONE SAMPLE T TEST for our "Gasoline emissions contribute to global warming" variable. As you can see, the average is 4.8, and the 95% confidence interval is 4.68 – 4.96. Although a "5" is the code for "Agree," this confidence interval is sufficiently close so we can claim that it amounts to "Agree." Our interpretation

SPSS Student Assistant:
Establishing Confidence
Intervals for Means

FIGURE 16.2

**SPSS Clickstream
to Obtain a 95%
Confidence
Interval
for a Mean**

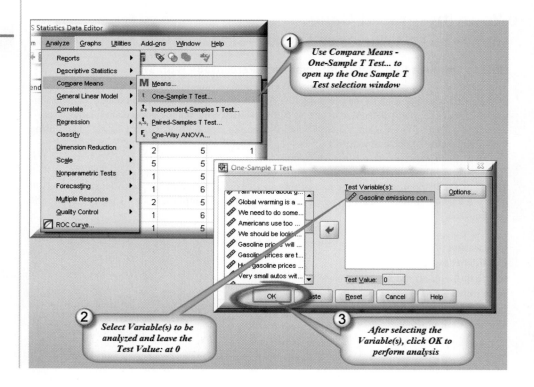

FIGURE 16.3

SPSS Output for a 95% Confidence Interval for Mean

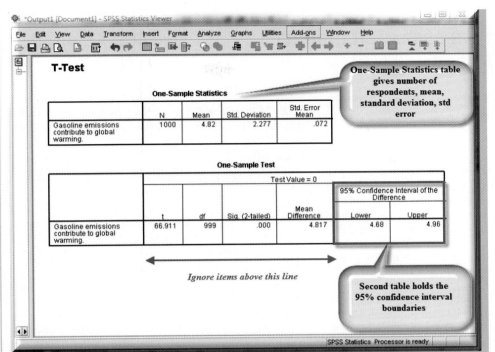

of this finding: If we conducted a great many replications of this survey using the same sample size, we would find that 95% of the sample averages for the statement "Gasoline emissions contribute to global warming" to be in the range of 4.68 and 4.96.

 ## Establishing Confidence Interval for Means

You have just learned that the 95% confidence interval for the "Gasoline emissions contribute to global warming" variable would include an average of 4.8, with a lower boundary of 4.68 and an upper boundary of 4.96. What about the statement. "We should be looking for gasoline substitutes"?

To answer this question, you must use SPSS to compute the 95% confidence interval for the mean of this variable. Use the clickstream identified in Figure 16.2 and use the annotations in Figure 16.3 to find and interpret your 95% confidence interval for the public's opinion on this topic. How do you interpret this finding, and how does this confidence interval compare to the one we found for "Global warming is a real threat"?

Using a Confidence Interval to Estimate Market Potential

A confidence interval for the public's opinion of the statement "Gasoline emissions contribute to global warming" is certainly useful; however, it is not especially persuasive from a business standpoint. Business decisions are based on estimates of financial barometers such as sales or profit. A confidence interval for a value on a disagree–agree measurement scale cannot be translated into a financial measure. When you read Marketing Research Insight 16.1, you will learn how we can take one of the survey questions and make some market potential estimates.

MARKETING RESEARCH INSIGHT   Practical Application

16.1 How to Estimate Market Potential Using a Survey's Findings

A common way to estimate total market potential is to use buying intentions, which are personal assessments of buyers about how likely they are to purchase some item in the future. Naturally, some consumers who say they will buy do not, but then some who say they will not buy do actually buy, so there is some degree of compensation in the data. Regardless, a marketing researcher knows from experience and common sense that an exact estimate of market potential is not possible, so he or she will use a range. The confidence interval range is highly acceptable and often used.

A question format used in the Advanced Automobile Concepts survey that can be related to sales potential is the probability measure. The survey asked respondents to indicate the probability (on a 0% to 100% scale) of buying certain types of hybrid automobiles in the next 3 years. For our illustration, here, we will take the very small, 3-wheel, 1-seat commuter "cycle" hybrid model. Although the question was asked about each respondent's probability, we can combine them and apply the findings to the population. There are an estimated 111,617,402 American households (U.S. Census, 2006 estimate), and the survey is a probability sample of this population, so confidence intervals can be applied as follows:

Pessimistic Estimate	Best Estimate	Optimistic Estimate
	111,617,402 households	
12.35% = *1,378,475*	*13.78% =* *1,538,088*	*15.21% =* *1,697,701*
	÷ 3 years	
= 459,492	*= 512,696*	*= 565,900*

We use the lower confidence interval figure for the "pessimistic" estimate, the upper confidence interval value for the "optimistic" estimate, and the average probability value for the "best" estimate. Notice that the question was for a 3-year time period, and since most business decisions are based on annual estimates, the estimated market potential per year is indicated in this table. The 95% confidence interval estimates are possible, but if many, many replications of the survey were to take place, most of the average probabilities of purchasing this hybrid model would fall between about 12% and about 15%.

REPORTING CONFIDENCE INTERVALS TO CLIENTS

You are now well versed on the computation and interpretation of the generalization known as confidence intervals. So, how do marketing researchers report confidence intervals to their clients? It may surprise you to learn that detailed confidence intervals are typically not reported. Just think about all of the numbers that would have to be computed and reported to clients if confidence intervals were reported for every finding—it would require two more numbers per finding: the lower boundary and the upper boundary. So there is a dilemma: Clients do not want to wade through so much detail, yet researchers must somehow inform clients that there is sample error in the findings. The solution to this dilemma is really quite simple, and you will learn about it by reading Marketing Research Insight 16.2.

HYPOTHESIS TESTS

A hypothesis is what the manager or researcher expects the population mean (or percentage) to be.

Sometimes, someone, such as the marketing researcher or marketing manager, offers an expectation about the population parameter (either the mean or the percentage) based on prior knowledge, assumptions, or intuition. This expectation, called a **hypothesis**, most commonly takes the form of an exact specification as to what the population parameter value is.

A **hypothesis test** is a statistical procedure used to "accept" or "reject" the hypothesis based on sample information.[2] With all hypothesis tests, you should keep in mind that the sample is the only source of current information about the population. Because our sample is random and representative of the population, the sample results are used to determine if the hypothesis about the population parameter is accepted or rejected.[3]

MARKETING RESEARCH INSIGHT | Practical Application

16.2 Guidelines for the Presentation of Confidence Intervals

Whereas generalization of findings requires the use of confidence intervals, researchers have two options when it comes to reporting confidence intervals to clients or readers of their marketing research reports. These options are (1) the general case and (2) findings-specific confidence intervals.

The General Case

This is the industry standard; it is used almost unanimously with opinion polling, and it is by far the most popular approach used by marketing researchers. The General Case is merely to state the sampling error associated with the survey sample size. For example, the report may say "findings are accurate to ±4%," or "the survey has an error of ±3.5%." This sample error, of course, is calculated using the sample error formula (refer to Chapter 13), typically at the 95% level of confidence with $p = q = 50\%$ and $z = 1.96$.

Sample Error Formula $\pm$ Sample error % = $1.96 \times \sqrt{\dfrac{p * q}{n}}$

The Findings-Specific Case

Since you have studied the sample error formula in Chapter 13, you realize that $p = q = 50\%$ is the most conservative sample error estimate, for any combination of p and q other than $p = q = 50\%$ will result in a smaller numerator in the sample size formula, and, thus, a smaller sample size. Also, this formula only pertains to percentage findings, as the confidence intervals for findings about averages require the use of a different formula.

To decide whether or not to use the findings-specific approach, the researcher must answer the following question:

"Are there findings that require more than the general case of reporting sample error?" For instance, there may be findings that the client will use to answer critical questions or on which to base important decisions. If the answer is no, the researcher will just report the general case. If yes, the next step is to identify all of the findings that the researcher believes absolutely require the reporting of findings-specific confidence intervals. To present the confidence intervals for each relevant finding, the researcher can provide a table that lists the 95% confidence interval lower and upper boundaries, which must be computed either by the researcher's statistical analysis program or by the use of some other computational aid in the researcher's tool kit. The following table illustrates how a researcher can efficiently accommodate the confidence intervals for diverse variables in a single table. Most likely, these findings will have been reported elsewhere in the report with other informative summary statistics, such as standard deviations and sample sizes for respondents answering various questions.

95% Confidence Intervals for Key Findings

	Sample Finding	Lower Boundary	Upper Boundary
Used the Subshop in the past 60 days.	*30%*	*26.0%*	*34.0%*
Used a Subshop coupon in the past 30 days.	*12%*	*9.2%*	*14.8%*
Number of Subshop visits in the past 60 days.	*1.5*	*1.4*	*1.6*
Overall satisfaction with the Subshop*	*5.6*	*5.4*	*5.8*

*Based on a scale where 1 = very dissatisfied and 5 = very satisfied

---

All of this might sound frightfully technical, but it is a form of inference that you do every day. You just do not use the words *hypothesis* or *parameter* when you do it. Here is an example to show how hypothesis testing occurs naturally. Your friend, Bill, does not use an automobile seat belt because he thinks only a few drivers actually wear them. But Bill's car breaks down, and he has to ride with his coworkers to and from work while it is being repaired. Over the course of a week, Bill rides with five different coworkers, and he notices that four out of the five buckle up. When Bill begins driving his own car the next week, he begins fastening his seat belt.

This is intuitive hypothesis testing in action; Bill's initial belief that few people wear seat belts was his hypothesis. **Intuitive hypothesis testing** (as opposed to statistical hypothesis testing) occurs when someone uses something he or she has observed to see if it agrees with or refutes a belief about that topic. Everyone uses intuitive hypothesis testing; in fact, we rely on it constantly. We just do not call it hypothesis testing, but we are

People test and revise intuitive hypotheses often without thinking about it.

People engage in intuitive hypothesis testing constantly.

constantly gathering evidence that supports or refutes our beliefs, and we reaffirm or change our beliefs based on our findings. Read Marketing Research Insight 16.3 to see that you perform intuitive hypothesis testing a great deal.

Obviously, if you had asked Bill before his car went into the repair shop, he might have said that only a small percentage, perhaps as low as 10%, of drivers wear seat belts. His week of car rides is analogous to a sample of 5 observations, and he observes that 4 out of 5 (80%) of his coworkers buckle up. Now his initial hypothesis is not supported by the evidence. So Bill realizes that his hypothesis is in error, and it must be revised. If you asked Bill what percentage of drivers wears seat belts after his week of observations, he undoubtedly would have a much higher percentage in mind than his original estimate. The fact that Bill began to fasten his seat belt suggests he perceives his behavior to be out of the norm, so he has adjusted his belief and his behavior as well. In other words, his hypothesis was not supported, so Bill revised it to be consistent with what is actually the case. The logic of statistical hypothesis testing is very similar to this process Bill has just exhibited.

Here are five steps in hypothesis testing.

There are five basic steps involved in hypothesis testing, and we have listed them in Table 16.4. We have also described with each step how Bill's hypothesis that only 10% of drivers buckle their seat belts is tested via intuition.

MARKETING RESEARCH INSIGHT   Practical Application

16.3 Intuitive Hypothesis Testing: We Do It All the Time!

People do intuitive hypothesis testing all the time to reaffirm their beliefs or to re-form them to be consistent with reality. The following diagram illustrates how you perform intuitive hypothesis testing.

Here is an everyday example. As a student studying marketing research, you believe that you will "ace" the first exam if you study hard the night before the exam. You take the exam, and you score a 70%. Ouch! You now realize that your belief was wrong, and you need to study more for the next exam. So your hypothesis was not supported, and you now have to come up with a new one.

You ask the student beside you who did ace the exam, how much study time he put in. He says he studied for the three nights before the exam. Notice that he has found evidence (his A grade) that supports his hypothesis, so he will not change his study habits belief. You, on the other hand, must change your hypothesis or suffer the consequences.

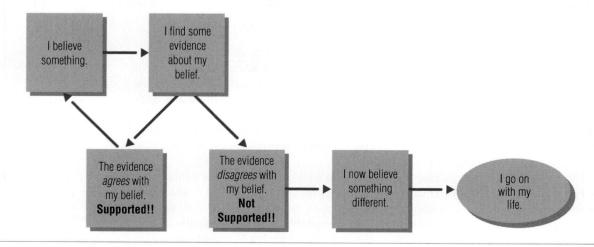

TABLE 16.4   The Five Basic Steps Involved in Hypothesis Testing (Using Bill's Seat Belt Hypothesis)

The Steps	Bill's Intuitive Hypothesis Test
Step 1 Begin with a statement about what you believe exists in the population, that is, the population mean or percentage.	Bill believes only 10% of drivers buckle their seat belts.
Step 2 Draw a random sample and determine the sample statistic.	In a sample of 5 rides with coworkers, Bill finds that 80% of them buckled up.
Step 3 Compare the statistic to the hypothesized parameter.	Bill notices that 80% is different from 10%.
Step 4 Decide whether or not the sample supports the hypothesis.	The observed 80% of drivers does not support Bill's hypothesis that 10% buckle up.
Step 5 If the sample does not support the hypothesis, revise the hypothesis to be consistent with the sample's statistic.	The actual incidence of drivers who buckle their seat belts is about 80%. (*Bill, your hypothesis of 10% is not supported; you need to buckle up like just about everyone else.*)

However, due to the variation that we know will be caused by sampling, it is impossible to be absolutely certain that our assessment of the acceptance or rejection of the hypothesis will be correct if we simply compare our hypothesis arithmetically to the sample finding, as was done in Bill's seatbelt example. Therefore, you must fall back on the sample size concepts discussed in Chapter 13 and rely on the use of probabilities. The statistical concept underlying hypothesis testing permits us to say that if many, many samples were drawn, and a comparison made for each one, a true hypothesis would be accepted, for example, 99% of these times.

Statistical hypothesis testing involves the use of four ingredients: the sample statistic, the standard error of the statistic, the desired level of confidence, and the hypothesized population parameter value.[4] The first three values were discussed in the section on parameter estimation. The final value is simply what the client or researcher believes the population parameter (π or μ) to be before the research is undertaken.

Statisticians often refer to the **alternative hypothesis** when performing statistical tests. This concept is important for you to know about. We have included Marketing Research Insight 16.4 as a way of introducing you to the idea of an alternative hypothesis and to understand how it is used in statistical hypothesis tests.

Bill found that his hypothesis about seat belts was not supported, so he started buckling up.

A hypothesis test gives you the probability of support for your hypothesis based on your sample evidence and sample size.

There is always an alternative hypothesis.

Test of the Hypothesized Population Parameter Value

The **hypothesized population parameter** value can be determined using either a percentage or a mean. The equation used to test the hypothesis of a population percentage is as follows:

Formula for Test of a Hypothesis About a Percentage

$$z = \frac{p - \pi_H}{s_p}$$

where

p = the sample percentage
π_H = the hypothesized percentage
s_p = the standard error of the percentage.

MARKETING RESEARCH INSIGHT · Practical Application

16.4 What Is an Alternative Hypothesis?

Whenever you test a stated hypothesis, you always automatically test its alternative. The alternative hypothesis takes in all possible cases that are not treated by the stated hypothesis. For example, if you hypothesize that 50% of all drivers fasten their seat belts, you are saying that the population percentage is equal to 50% (stated hypothesis), and the alternative hypothesis is that the population percent is not equal to 50%. To say this differently, the alternative hypothesis is that the population percentage can be any percentage other than 50%, the stated hypothesis. The alternative hypothesis is always implicit, but sometimes statisticians will state it along with the stated hypothesis.

To avoid confusion, we do not formally present alternative hypotheses in this textbook. But here are some stated hypotheses and their alternatives. You may want to refer back to this exhibit if the alternative hypothesis is important to your understanding of the concepts being described.

The importance of knowing what the alternative hypothesis is stems from the fact that it is a certainty that the sample

The Stated Hypothesis	The Alternative Hypothesis
Population Parameter Hypothesis	
The population mean is equal to $50.	*The population mean is not equal to $50.*
The population percentage is equal to 60%.	*The population percentage is not equal to 60%.*
Directional Hypothesis	
The population mean is greater than 100.	*The population mean is less than or equal to 100.*
The population percentage is less than 70%.	*The population percentage is greater than or equal to 70%.*

results must support either the stated hypothesis or the alternative hypothesis. There is no other outcome possible. If the findings do not support the stated hypothesis, then they must support the alternative hypothesis because it covers all possible cases not specified in the stated hypothesis. Of course, if the stated hypothesis is supported by the findings, the alternative hypothesis is not supported.

The equation used to test the hypothesis of a mean is identical in logic, except it uses the mean and standard error of the mean.

Here are formulas used to test a hypothesized population parameter.

Formula for Test of a Hypothesis About a Mean

$$z = \frac{\bar{x} - \mu_H}{s_{\bar{x}}}$$

where

$\bar{x}$ = the sample mean
μ_H = the hypothesized mean
$s_{\bar{x}}$ = standard error of the mean.

To a statistician, "compare means" amounts to "take the difference."

Tracking the logic of these equations, one can see that the sample mean ($\bar{x}$), is compared to the hypothesized population mean (μ_H). Similarly, the sample percentage (p) is compared to the hypothesized percentage (π_H). In this case, "compared" means "take the difference." This difference is divided by the standard error to determine how many standard errors away from the hypothesized parameter the sample statistic falls. The standard error, you should remember, takes into account the variability found in the sample as well as the sample size. A small sample with much variability yields a large standard error, so our sample statistic could be quite far away from the mean arithmetically but still less than 1 standard error away in certain circumstances. All the relevant information about the population as found by our sample is included in these computations. Knowledge of areas under the normal curve then come into play to translate this distance into a probability of support for the hypothesis.

An example of no support for Bill's seat belt hypothesis.

Here is a simple illustration using Bill's seat belt hypothesis. Let us assume that instead of observing his friends buckling up, Bill reads that a Harris Poll finds that 80% of respondents in a national sample of 1,000 wear their seat belts. The hypothesis test would be computed as follows (notice we substituted the formula for s_p in the second step):

Calculation of a Test of Bill's Hypothesis That Only 10% of Drivers "Buckle Up." Sorry, Bill. No support for you.

$$z = \frac{p - \pi_H}{s_p}$$

$$= \frac{p - \pi_H}{\sqrt{\dfrac{p \times q}{n}}}$$

$$= \frac{80 - 10}{\sqrt{\dfrac{80 \times 20}{1,000}}}$$

$$= \frac{70}{\sqrt{\dfrac{1,600}{1,000}}}$$

$$= \frac{70}{\sqrt{1.6}}$$

$$= 55.3$$

Notes:
Hypothesized percent $= 10$
Sample percent $(p) = 80$
Sample $q = 20$
$n = 1,000$

The crux of statistical hypothesis testing is the **sampling distribution concept**. Our actual sample is one of the many, many theoretical samples comprising the assumed bell-shaped curve of possible sample results using the hypothesized value as the center of the bell-shaped distribution. There is a greater probability of finding a sample result close to the hypothesized mean, for example, than of finding one that is far away. But, there is a critical assumption working here. We have conditionally accepted from the outset that the person who stated the hypothesis is correct. So, if our sample mean turns out to be within ± 2.58 standard errors of the hypothesized mean, it supports the hypothesis maker at the 99% level of confidence because it falls within 99% of the area under the curve.

The sampling distribution concept says that our sample is one of many, many theoretical samples that comprise a bell-shaped curve with the hypothesized value as the mean.

But what if the sample result is found to be outside this range? Which is correct—the hypothesis or the researcher's sample results? The answer to this question is always the same: Sample information is invariably more accurate than a hypothesis. Of course, the sampling procedure must adhere strictly to probability sampling requirements and assure representativeness. As you can see, Bill was greatly mistaken because his hypothesis of 10% of drivers wearing seat belts was 55.3 standard errors away from the 80% finding of the national poll.

You always assume the sample information to be more accurate than any hypothesis.

The following example serves to describe the hypothesis testing process with a mean. Northwestern Mutual Life Insurance Company has a college student internship program. The program allows college students to participate in an intensive training program and to become field agents in one academic term. Arrangements are made with various universities in the United States whereby students will receive college credit if they qualify for and successfully complete this program. Rex Reigen, district agent for Idaho, believed, based on his knowledge of other programs in the country, that the typical college agent will be able to earn about $2,750 in the first semester of participation in the program. He hypothesizes that the population parameter, that is, the mean, will be $2,750. To check Rex's hypothesis, a survey was taken of current college agents, and 100 of these individuals were contacted through telephone calls. Among the questions posed was an estimate of the amount of money made in their first semester of work in the program. The sample mean is determined to be $2,800 and the standard deviation is $350.

Does the sample support Rex's hypothesis that student interns make $2,750 in the first semester?

In essence, the amount of $2,750 is the hypothesized mean of the sampling distribution of all possible samples of the same size that can be taken of the college agents in the country. The unknown factor, of course, is the size of the standard error in dollars. Consequently, although it is assumed that the sampling distribution will be a normal curve with the mean

How many standard errors is $2,800 away from $2,750?

of the entire distribution at $2,750, we need a way to determine how many dollars are within ±1 standard error of the mean, or any other number of standard errors of the mean for that matter. The only information available that would help to determine the size of the standard error is the standard deviation obtained from the sample. This standard deviation can be used to determine a standard error with the application of the standard error formula.

The amount of $2,800 found by the sample differs from the hypothesized amount of $2,750 by $50. Is this amount a sufficient enough difference to cast doubt on Rex's estimate? Or, in other words, is it far enough from the hypothesized mean to reject the hypothesis? To answer these questions, we compute as follows (note that we have substituted the formula for the standard error of the mean in the second step):

Calculation of a Test of Rex's Hypothesis That Northwestern Mutual Interns Make an Average of $2,750 in Their First Semester of Work. Rex is right!

$$z = \frac{\bar{x} - \mu_H}{s_{\bar{x}}}$$

$$= \frac{\bar{x} - \mu_H}{\dfrac{s}{\sqrt{n}}}$$

$$= \frac{2,800 - 2,750}{\dfrac{350}{\sqrt{100}}}$$

$$= \frac{50}{35}$$

$$= 1.43$$

Notes:
Hypothesized mean = 2,750
Sample mean = 2,800
Std. dev. = 350
$n = 100$

The *z* is calculated to be 1.43 standard errors. What does this mean?

The sample variability and the sample size have been used to determine the size of the standard error of the assumed sampling distribution. In this case, 1 standard error of the mean is equal to $35 (standard error of the mean formula: $350/\sqrt{100}$). When the difference of $50 is divided by $35 to determine the number of standard errors away from which the hypothesized mean the sample statistic lies, the result is 1.43 standard errors. As is illustrated in Figure 16.4, 1.43 standard errors is within ±1.96 standard errors of Rex's hypothesized mean. It also reveals that the hypothesis is supported because it falls in the acceptance region.

A computed of 1.43 is less than 1.96, so the hypothesis is supported.

Although the exact probability of support for the hypothesized parameter can be determined from the use of a table, it is often handy just to recall the two numbers 1.96 and 2.58; as we have said, these two are directly associated with the intervals of 95% and 99%, respectively, which are the "standards" of the marketing research industry. Any time that the computed *z* value falls outside 2.58, the resulting probability of support for the hypothesis is 0.01 or less. Of course, computer statistical programs such as SPSS will provide the exact probability because they are programmed to look up the probability in the *z* table just as you would have to do if you did the test by hand calculations and you wanted the exact probability.

FIGURE 16.4

Sample Findings Support the Hypothesis in This Example

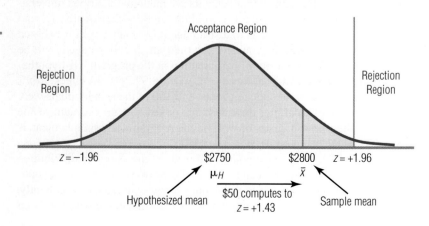

Directional Hypotheses

It is sometimes appropriate to indicate a directional hypothesis. A **directional hypothesis** is one that indicates the direction in which you believe the population parameter falls relative to some target mean or percentage. That is, the owner of a toy store might not be able to state the exact number of dollars parents spend each time they buy a toy in that store, but the owner might say, "They spend under $100." A directional hypothesis is usually made with a "more than" or "less than" statement. For example, Rex Reigen might have hypothesized that the average college agent working for Northwestern Mutual Life earns *more than* $2,750. In both the "more than" case and the "less than" case, identical concepts are brought into play, but one must take into account that only one side (one tail) of the sampling distribution is being used.

There are only two differences to keep in mind for directional hypothesis tests. First, you must be concerned with the sign determined for the *z* value as well as its size. When you subtract the hypothesized mean from the sample mean, the sign will be positive with "greater than" hypotheses, whereas the sign will be negative for "less than" hypotheses if the hypothesis is true. To use Rex's example again, the hypothesized target of $2,750 would be subtracted from the sample mean of $2,800 yielding a +$50, so the positive sign does support the "greater than" hypothesis. But is the difference statistically significant?

To answer this question requires our second step: to divide the difference by the standard error of the mean to compute the *z* value. We did this earlier and determined the *z* value to be 1.43. Because we are working with only one side of the bell-shaped distribution, you need to adjust the critical *z* value to reflect this fact. As Table 16.5 shows, a *z* value of ±1.64 standard errors defines the endpoints for 95% of the normal curve, and a *z* value of ±2.33 standard errors defines the endpoints for 99% confidence levels. Now the directional hypothesis is supported at that level of confidence if the computed *z* value is larger than the critical cut point, *and*, of course, its sign is consistent with the direction of the hypothesis. Otherwise, the directional hypothesis is not supported at your chosen level of confidence. Although the computed *z* value is close (1.43), it is not equal to or greater than 1.64, so Rex's directional hypothesis is not supported.

How to Interpret Hypothesis Testing

How do you interpret hypothesis tests? The interpretation of a hypothesis test is again directly linked to the sampling distribution concept. If the hypothesis about the population parameter is correct or true, then a high percentage of sample means must fall close to this value. In fact, if the hypothesis is true, then 99% of the sample results will fall between ±2.58 standard errors of the hypothesized mean. On the other hand, if the hypothesis is incorrect, there is a strong likelihood that the computed *z* value will fall outside ±2.58 standard errors. In other words, must adjust the "standard" number of standard errors (1.96 or 2.58) for directional hypothesis tests. We have done this for you in Table 16.5.

With the directional hypothesis test *z* values, the interpretation remains the same. The further away the hypothesized value is from the actual case, the more likely the computed

> A directional hypothesis is one in which you specify the hypothesized mean (or percentage) to be less than or greater than some amount.

> When testing a directional hypothesis, you must look at the sign as well as the size of the computed *z* value.

> If a hypothesis is not supported by a random sample finding, use the sample statistic and estimate the population parameter with a confidence interval.

TABLE 16.5 With a Directional Hypothesis Test, the Critical Points for *z* Must Be Adjusted, and the Sign (+ or −) Is Important

Level of Confidence	Direction of Hypothesis*	z Value
95%	Greater than	+1.64
	Less than	−1.64
99%	Greater than	+2.33
	Less than	−2.33

*Subtract the sample statistic (mean or percentage) from the hypothesized parameter (μ or π).

z value will not fall in the critical range. Failure to support the hypothesis essentially tells the hypothesizer that the assumptions about the population are in error and that they must be revised in light of the evidence from the sample. This revision is achieved through estimates of the population parameter just discussed in the previous section. These estimates can be used to provide the manager or researcher with a new mental picture of the population through confidence interval estimates of the true population value.

Your Integrated Case

ADVANCED AUTOMOBILE CONCEPTS

How to Use SPSS to Test a Hypothesis for a Percentage

SPSS does not perform percentages hypothesis tests, but you can use it to obtain the necessary information to do one by hand calculation.

As you found out earlier, SPSS does not perform statistical tests on percentages, so if you have a hypothesis about a percentage, you are required to do the calculations with your handy calculator. You should use the SPSS "Frequencies" procedure to have it calculate the sample p value and to determine the sample size if you do not know it precisely. Then apply the percentage hypothesis test formula to calculate the z value. If the value is inside the range of ± 1.96, the hypothesized percent is supported at the 95% level of confidence, and if it is inside ± 2.58, it is supported at the 99% level. You will have an opportunity to use SPSS and do these calculations in exercises at the end of this chapter.

How to Use SPSS to Test a Hypothesis for a Mean

We can test the hypothesized mean of any metric variable (interval or ratio scale) in our Advanced Automobile Concepts survey. As an illustration, we will hypothesize that the general public "agrees" to the statement "Hybrid autos that use alternative fuels will slow down global warming." You should recall that on our scale, the "agree" position corresponds to the value code of 5. Your SPSS software can be easily directed to make a mean estimation or to test a hypothesis for a mean.

To test a hypothesis about a mean with SPSS, use the ANALYZE–COMPARE MEANS–ONE SAMPLE T TEST command sequence.

To perform a mean hypothesis test, SPSS provides a Test Value box in which the hypothesized mean can be entered. As you can see in Figure 16.5, you get to this box by using the ANALYZE–COMPARE MEANS–ONE SAMPLE T TEST command sequence. You then select the variable "Hybrid autos that use alternative fuels will slow down global warming." Next, enter a "5" as the Test Value and click on the OK button.

The resulting output is contained in Figure 16.6. When you look at it, you will notice that the information layout for the output is identical to the previous output table. The output indicates our

Do people think that hybrid cars using synthetic fuels will slow down global warming?

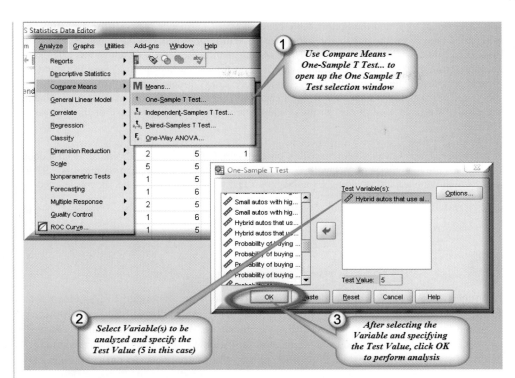

FIGURE 16.5

SPSS Clickstream to Test a Hyposthesis about a Mean

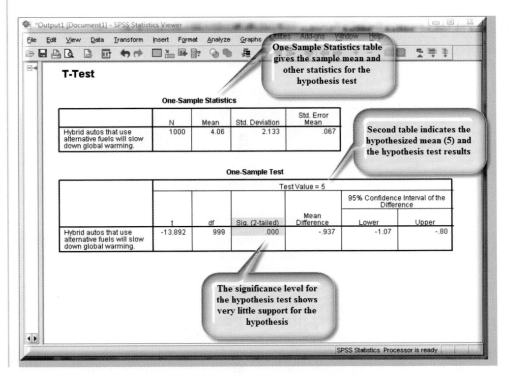

FIGURE 16.6

SPSS Output for the Test of a Hyphothesis about a Mean

test value equal to 5, and the bottom table contains 95% confidence intervals for the estimated population parameter (the population parameter is the difference between the hypothesized mean and the sample mean, expected to be 0). There is a mean difference of −.937, which was calculated by subtracting the hypothesized mean value (5) from the sample mean (4.06), and the standard error is provided in the upper half (.067). A t value of −13.892 is determined by dividing −.937 by .067. It is associated with a two-tailed significance level of 0.000. (For now, assume the t value is the z value we have used in our formulas and explanations. We describe use of the t value in Chapter 17.)

In other words, our Advanced Automobile Concepts sample finding of an average of about 4 does not support the hypothesis of 5. The 95% confidence interval for the population mean is 3.93 to 4.20, which we obtained by doing a one-sample t test to estimate this range, as you learned to do earlier.

SPSS Student Assistant:
Testing a Hypothesis
for a mean.

 Use SPSS for a Hypothesis Test for a Mean

Although it is easy to follow our descriptions and look at the annotated SPSS screen captures, it is something altogether different to actually work with SPSS. For this Active Learning Exercise, replicate the test of the hypothesis test that the general public "agrees" with the statement "Hybrid autos that use alternative fuels will slow down global warming." To do this, you will need to start SPSS and open up the AAConcepts.sav data set. Then perform the hypothesis test for a mean exactly as we have just described. Compare your SPSS output with that provided in Figure 16.6.

Now that you are more experienced in the test of a hypothesis about a mean, experiment with different hypotheses about the population mean for the statement "Hybrid autos that use alternative fuels will slow down global warming" by trying a "6" and then a "7." Compare the following aspects of the SPSS output for the three hypothesis tests—5, 6, and 7.

Computed Values (below)	Hypothesis: Mean = 5	Hypothesis: Mean = 6	Hypothesis: Mean = 7
Mean difference	_____	_____	_____
Std. error mean	_____	_____	_____
t	_____	_____	_____
Sig. (2-tailed)	_____	_____	_____

Two of the computed values change with the means, whereas two do not. Use a graph such as the one in Figure 16.4 to show how these three hypothesis tests would appear relative to one another.

REPORTING HYPOTHESIS TESTS TO CLIENTS

Explicit hypotheses are sometimes encountered by marketing researchers. When this happens, the marketing researcher is well equipped to perform the appropriate hypothesis test. The steps involved are straightforward and are listed in Marketing Research Insight 16.5.

MARKETING RESEARCH INSIGHT

Practical Application

16.5 Guidelines for the Presentation of Hypothesis Tests

The step-by-step approach to the presentation of hypothesis tests is as follows:

Step 1 State the hypothesis.

Step 2 Perform appropriate hypothesis test computations. That is, if the hypothesis test is stated as a percent, the percent formula should be used; if it is stated as an average, the average formula should be used.

Step 3 Determine if the hypothesis is supported or not supported. That is, compare the computed z value to the critical z value (normally 1.96 for a 95% level of confidence nondirectional hypothesis)

Step 4 If the hypothesis is not supported, compute confidence intervals to provide the client with the appropriate confidence intervals.

These steps are followed for each explicitly stated hypothesis. An example of how to present hypothesis tests in a research report follows:

Results of Hypothesis Tests

Hypothesis	Result of Test
Hypothesis 1: 60% of consumers buy from a fast-food location at least 1 time per month	*This hypothesis was supported at the 95% level of confidence by the findings of the survey.*
Hypothesis 2: In a typical month, those consumers who purchase from a fast-food outlet, spend about $45 on themselves for food, drinks, snacks, etc.	*The average was found to be $31.87, and the hypothesis of $45 was not supported. The 95% confidence interval computations determined the range to be between $28.50 and $35.24.*

 Synthesize Your Learning

This exercise will require you to take into consideration concepts and material from these three chapters.

Chapter 14	Dealing with Fieldwork and Data Quality Issues
Chapter 15	Using Basic Descriptive Analysis
Chapter 16	Performing Population Estimates and Hypothesis Tests

Blood Bank of Delmarva and Optimal Strategix, LLC

This case is provided by

Anu Sivaraman, Assistant Professor of Marketing, Alfred Lerner College of Business & Economics, University of Delaware

R. Sukumar, President and CEO, Optimal Strategix Group, Inc., Newtown, PA

The Blood Bank of Delmarva (BBD) (www.bbd.org) is a nonprofit community service program that provides blood and blood products to the 17 hospitals in the Delaware, Maryland, and Virginia (Delmarva) Peninsula. About 76,000 blood donations are needed in this area each year for more than 20,000 patients across the Delmarva Peninsula. BBD understands the importance of identifying drivers of donor behavior and studying donor motivations. In particular, BBD wanted to design and execute a survey that would capture the attributes that donors value most. To conduct this study, BBD employed the Optimal Strategix Group (www.optimalstrategix.com), a market research firm located in Newtown, Pennsylvania. The firm's specialty is its customized and advanced analytics capabilities that include a proprietary technology that can identify an optimal combination of donor values.

Dave Bonk, director of public relations for BBD and Bob Travis, the CEO of BBD, met and discussed the following objectives:

Determine blood donation frequency and amount

- Identify BBD usage and membership aspects
- Assess opinions about blood donation
- Evaluate overall satisfaction with BBD
- Identify salient characteristics and evaluate BBD's performance on them
- Gather demographic information about BBD blood donors

Optimal Strategix designed a survey and posted it online for donors of BBD. An abbreviated version of the questionnaire is detailed here. A portion of the SPSS data set (200 respondents) is included with the case.

Blood Bank of Delmarva Online Questionnaire

Please answer the following questions to the best of your ability. When you have answered all questions, click on the "submit" button at the end.

1. How often do you donate blood?

_____More often than every 6 months (1)   _____Once every 6 months (2)
_____Once every 12 months   (3)   _____Once every 18 months (4)
_____Once every 24 months   (5)   _____Once every 48 months (6)
_____Not Sure/Don't Know, but I have donated previously (97)
_____I have never donated blood (99)

2. How many times have you donated blood in the last 2 years (to any blood bank)? _____

3. Have you donated blood at the Blood Bank of Delmarva?
_____Yes (1) _____No (2)

4. (Select only one) When you donate blood, **typically** do you:
_____Walk in (without appointment) (1)
_____Wait until the blood bank contacts me to schedule an appointment (2)
_____Schedule an appointment ahead of time (without a request from the blood bank) (3)

5. Are you a member of the Blood Bank of Delmarva?
_____Yes (1) _____No (2) _____Not sure/Don't know (99)

6. (If yes) What motivated you to become a member of the Blood Bank of Delmarva? (Check all that apply.)
_____Assurance that blood will be there for me when I need/when my family needs it
_____BBD makes me feel appreciated for donating blood
_____Coverage for blood costs
_____Community support/Someone else needs it

7. On a scale of 1 to 7, where 1 = "Completely disagree" and 7 = "Completely agree," please indicate the degree to which you agree or disagree with each of the following statements about blood donation at BBD:

Statement	Completely Disagree (1)	Disagree (2)	Somewhat Disagree (3)	Neither Disagree nor Agree (4)	Somewhat Agree (5)	Agree (6)	Completely Agree (7)	Not Sure/ Don't Know (99)
When I call to make an appointment at the Blood Bank, they get me an appointment as fast as I want.	1	2	3	4	5	6	7	99

Statement	Completely Disagree (1)	Disagree (2)	Somewhat Disagree (3)	Neither Disagree nor Agree (4)	Somewhat Agree (5)	Agree (6)	Completely Agree (7)	Not Sure/ Don't Know (99)
When I go to the Blood Bank to donate blood, I don't have to wait too long for the receptionist to sign me in.	1	2	3	4	5	6	7	99
After the receptionist has signed me in, I don't have to wait too long for my screening interview.	1	2	3	4	5	6	7	99
The staff makes me feel at ease when I give blood.	1	2	3	4	5	6	7	99
The needle used during my blood donation does not concern me too much.	1	2	3	4	5	6	7	99
The Blood Bank of Delmarva (BBD) has been very informative about the membership program.	1	2	3	4	5	6	7	99
I am confident that the blood I donate is going to good use.	1	2	3	4	5	6	7	99
I am not discouraged from donating blood even if I don't always qualify.	1	2	3	4	5	6	7	99
I do not have trouble finding time during the day to donate blood.	1	2	3	4	5	6	7	99
I feel like I belong to a special group when I donate blood.	1	2	3	4	5	6	7	99
When I donate blood, I feel that the staff is focused on me.	1	2	3	4	5	6	7	99
Being a member of the BBD makes me feel like I am appreciated.	1	2	3	4	5	6	7	99
I feel like I am part of a special community as a member of the BBD	1	2	3	4	5	6	7	99

(continued)

Statement	Completely Disagree (1)	Disagree (2)	Somewhat Disagree (3)	Neither Disagree nor Agree (4)	Somewhat Agree (5)	Agree (6)	Completely Agree (7)	Not Sure/ Don't Know (99)
Even if the $5 ($2 for 65 or older) yearly fee to belong to the BBD was higher, I would not cancel my membership.	1	2	3	4	5	6	7	99
My membership with the BBD would become more important if the cost of blood at the hospital goes up.	1	2	3	4	5	6	7	99

8. Overall, how satisfied are you with **the Blood Bank of Delmarva?**

_____ Very Satisfied (1)
_____ Somewhat Dissatisfied (2)
_____ Neutral (3)
_____ Somewhat Satisfied (4)
_____ Very Satisfied (5)
_____ Not sure/Don't know (99)

9. Below is a list of over 20 different attributes pertaining to donating blood. Thinking about the last time you donated blood, select up to 8 attributes. With each one indicate how would you rate the experience based on a scale of 1–5, where 1 = Extremely Poor Performance and 5 = Extremely Good Performance.

The Top 8 Attributes are Listed Below.*	Extremely Poor Performance	Somewhat Poor Performance	Neither Poor nor Good Performance	Somewhat Good Performance	Extremely Good Performance
Feeling that many people are helped with one donation	1	2	3	4	5
Supporting a good cause by donating blood	1	2	3	4	5
Giving back to community by donating blood	1	2	3	4	5
Feeling that my donation is making a difference	1	2	3	4	5
Blood donation is used for a good cause	1	2	3	4	5
Ensuring blood availability for my community	1	2	3	4	5
Ensuring blood availability for my family/friends	1	2	3	4	5
The staff at the donation site is experienced	1	2	3	4	5

* Note: only the top 8 based on number of respondents who answered these questions are listed in the table above and in the SPSS data set.

10. Are you male or female?

_____Male (1)   _____Female (2)

11. How old are you? _____

12. What is your race/ethnicity? (Please select one)

_____Asian/Pacific Islander (1)   _____African American (2)
_____Hispanic (3)   _____Native American/Alaskan Native (4)
_____Caucasian (5   _____Other (98)
_____I prefer not to answer (99)

13. What is the highest level of education you have completed?

_____Some High School (1)   _____High School (2)
_____Some College (3)   _____Associates Degree (4)
_____Bachelors Degree (5)   _____Masters/MBA (6)
_____MD/PhD (7)   _____I prefer not to answer (99)

14. What is your household income before taxes?

_____Less than $20,000 (1)   _____$20,000 to $39,999 (2)
_____$40,000 to $59,999 (3)   _____$60,000 to $79,999 (4)
_____$80,000 to $99,000 (5)   _____$100,000 or more (6)
_____I prefer not to answer (99)

15. Are you currently: (Select one)

_____Single (1)   _____Never Married (2)
_____Married (3)   _____Currently Separated (4)
_____Divorced (5)   _____Widowed (6)
_____I prefer not to answer (99)

16. Please specify your household family size (including yourself)?

_____1 (1)   _____2–3 (2)   _____4–6 (3)
_____7–9 (4)   _____10 or more (5)   _____I prefer not to answer (99)

17. Please indicate the length of time you have lived in the community?

_____< 1 year (1)   _____1–2 yrs (2)   _____3–5 yrs (3)
_____6–10 years (4)   _____> 10 yrs (5)   _____I prefer not to answer (99)

18. Are you currently employed?

_____Yes   _____No (2)   _____I prefer not to answer (99)

19. Are you currently: (Select one)

_____Single (1)   _____Never Married (2)
_____Married (3)   _____Currently Separated (4)
_____Divorced (5)   _____Widowed (6)
_____I prefer not to answer (99)

Use the BBDDonor.sav SPSS dataset to answer the following questions. In this SPSS data set there are various instances of "missing data," meaning cases where respondents possibly did not provide an answer, did not wish to provide that answer, or were directed not to answer. In the data set, these cases appear as a "99," and most variables are coded with the 99 = "I prefer not to answer," or "Not sure/don't know." All such cases appear as "Missing System" in SPSS tables.

1. What is the profile of this sample? That is, summarize the findings for
   a. Demographics
   b. Blood donation
   c. Blood Bank of Delmarva membership and usage
   d. Attitudes toward blood donation
   e. Satisfaction with Blood Bank of Delmarva
   f. Performance of Blood Bank of Delmarva

2. For each of the following questions on the survey, indicate (1) the nature of the missing data (refusal, item omission, or other), (2) what the survey authors did to make respondents who feel uncomfortable about that question and might refuse to

answer, and (3) the impact of the missing data on the findings of those questions where missing data occurs to a high degree.

   a. Questions 5 and 6
   b. Question 7 (all parts)
   c. Question 8
   d. Question 9 (all parts)
   e. Question 14

3. Assume that the 200 respondents are a random sample of BBD users.

   a. What percentage of BBD users donates blood more often than every 6 months?
   b. On average, how many times have BBD users donated blood in the past 2 years?
   c. Test the hypothesis that BBD users "agree" with each of the statements in Question 7.
   d. Test the hypothesis that BBD users are "very satisfied" overall with BBD.
   e. Test the hypothesis that the average BBD user is 50 years old.

Summary

This chapter began by distinguishing a sample statistic from its associated population parameter. We then introduced you to the concept of statistical inference, which is a set of procedures for generalizing the findings from a sample to the population. A key factor in inference is the sample size, n. It appears in statistical inference formulas because it expresses the amount of sampling error: Large samples have less sampling error than do small samples given the same variability. We illustrated the three inference types commonly used by marketing researchers. First, we described how a population parameter, such as a mean, can be estimated by using confidence intervals computed by application of the standard error formula. Second, we related how a researcher can use the sample findings to test a hypothesis about a mean or a percentage.

We used SPSS and the Advanced Automobile Concepts data to illustrate how you can direct SPSS to calculate 95% confidence intervals for the estimation of a mean as well as how to test a hypothesis about a mean. Both are accomplished with the SPSS menu item—One-Sample T Test procedure. For parameter estimation or for the test of a hypothesis with a percentage, you can use SPSS to determine the percent, but you must use the formulas in this chapter to calculate the confidence interval or perform the significance test.

Key Terms

Statistics 468
Parameters 468
Inference 468
Statistical inference 469
Parameter estimation 470
Hypothesis test 470
Standard error 471
Standard error of a mean 471

Standard error of a percentage 471
Confidence intervals 474
Most commonly used level of confidence 474
Hypothesis 480
Hypothesis testing 480
Intuitive hypothesis testing 481
Alternative hypothesis 483

Hypothesized population parameter 483
Sampling distribution concept 485
Directional hypothesis 487

Review Questions/Applications

1. What essential factors are considered when statistical inference takes place?
2. What is meant by "parameter estimation," and what function does it perform for a researcher?
3. How does parameter estimation for a mean differ from that for a percentage?
4. List the steps in statistical hypothesis testing. List the steps in intuitive hypothesis testing. How are they similar? How are they different?
5. When a researcher's sample evidence disagrees with a manager's hypothesis, which is right?

6. What does it mean when a researcher says that a hypothesis has been supported at the 95% confidence level?
7. Distinguish a directional from a nondirectional hypothesis and provide an example of each one.
8. Here are several computation practice exercises to help you identify which formulas pertain and to learn how to perform the necessary calculations. In each case, perform the necessary calculations and write your answers in the column identified by a question mark.
   a. Determine confidence intervals for each of the following:

Sample Statistic	Sample Size	Confidence Level	Your Confidence Intervals?
Mean: 150 Std. Dev: 30	200	95%	_____
Percent: 67%	300	99%	_____
Mean: 5.4 Std. Dev: 0.5	250	99%	_____
Percent: 25.8%	500	99%	_____

   b. Test the following hypothesis and interpret your findings:

Hypothesis	Sample Findings	Confidence Level	Your Test Results?
Mean = 7.5	Mean: 8.5 Std. Dev: 1.2 $n = 670$	95%	_____
Percent = 86%	$p = 95$ $n = 1000$	99%	_____
Mean >125	Mean: 135 Std. Dev: 15 $n = 500$	95%	_____
Percent <33%	$p = 31$ $n = 120$	99%	_____

9. The manager of the aluminum recycling division of Environmental Services wants a survey that will tell him how many households in the city of Seattle, Washington, (approximately 500,000 households) will voluntarily wash out, store, and then transport all of their aluminum cans to a recycling center located in the downtown area and open only on Sundays. A random survey of 500 households determines that 20% of households would do so and that each participating household expects to recycle about 100 cans monthly with a standard deviation of 30 cans. What is the value of parameter estimation in this instance?
10. It is reported in the newspaper that a survey sponsored by *Forbes* magazine with *Fortune* 500 company executives has found that 75% believe that the United States trails Japan and Germany in automobile engineering. The article notes that executives were interviewed at a recent "Bring the U.S. Back to Competitiveness" symposium held on the campus of the University of Southern California. Why would it be incorrect for the article to report confidence intervals?
11. Alamo Rent-A-Car executives believe that Alamo accounts for about 50% of all Cadillacs that are rented. To test this belief, a researcher randomly identifies 20 major airports with on-site rental car lots. Observers are sent to each location and instructed to record the number of rental company Cadillacs observed in a 4-hour period. About 500 are observed, and 30% are observed being returned to Alamo Rent-A-Car. What are the implications of this finding for the Alamo executives' belief?

CASE 16.1

THE PETS, PETS, AND PETS TEAM PROJECT (PART 1)

Marsha and Josh are members of a marketing research class team that is doing its semester project for Pets, Pets, and Pets, a local pet shop. While Marsha and Josh are not dating, there is definitely some chemistry going on with them. Josh is a student-athlete, and he devotes much more time to his baseball training and practice than he does to his classes. Marsha is a straight "A" student, valedictorian of her high school graduating class, who studies 10 hours a day, just about every day.

Marsha and Josh are in Dr. Z's marketing research class (they call him Dr. Z, because no one can figure out how to pronounce his name correctly). Dr. Z requires that each team select some local company and perform a survey for it. Pets, Pets, and Pets is a local pet shop that sells pets and pet supplies. Marsha and Josh have struggled with the project, but they have succeeded in collecting a sample of about 160 Pets, Pets, and Pets customers, and it is now in the form of an SPSS data set. Dr. Z requires that each team give a "briefing" of its findings for the various types of required statistical analyses. The statistical inference analyses briefings are due today.

After pulling an all-nighter for her managerial economics paper, Marsha opens up an e-mail that Josh sent her with the analyses he has performed for the presentation. The arrangement was that Josh would do the analyses, and Marsha would prepare the PowerPoint slides and make the presentation. The e-mail reads:

> Marsh:
>
> *All I could do is the "frequencies" on SPSS, and I clicked on the output items that seemed right. Then I saved it and I am e-mailing it to you from the computer lab since I do not own a computer. Breakfast training table is at 7:30, and Coach Laval wants me in the batting cage at 9. I need to get my ankle taped up by the trainers at 8:30. So I am busy until Dr. Z's class at 10:30. So, I will see you in class.*
>
> Josh

Marsh sighs and opens up this SPSS output file.

Statistics

		Times Visited PPP in Past Year	Amount Spent on Last Visit to PPP	How Likely to Buy at PPP Next Time (1–7 scale)	Number of Pets Owned
N	Valid	162	162	162	162
	Missing	0	0	0	0
Mean		4.4	$18.2	5.3	1.64
Mode		4	15	4	1
Std. Deviation		4.98	.85	1.50	.770
Std. Error of Mean		.39	.30	.118	.061

Use Pets, Pets, & Pets how often?

		Frequency	Percent	Valid Percent	Cumulative Percent
Valid	Do Not Use Regularly	90	55.6	55.6	55.6
	Use Regularly	72	44.4	44.4	100.0
	Total	162	100.0	100.0	

Recommended PPP to a friend?

		Frequency	Percent	Valid Percent	Cumulative Percent
Valid	No	29	17.9	17.9	17.9
	Yes	133	82.1	82.1	100.0
	Total	162	100.0	100.0	

Recall seeing a PPP newspaper ad in the past month?

		Frequency	Percent	Valid Percent	Cumulative Percent
Valid	Yes	76	46.9	46.9	46.9
	No	86	53.1	53.1	100.0
	Total	162	100.0	100.0	

1. Dr. Z's requirement is for each team to present its "statistical inference" findings in class today. What analysis or analyses should Josh have done?
2. It is possible to make the presentation on the variables in the output file. Do what Marsha needs to do, now.

CASE 16.2

THE HOBBIT'S CHOICE RESTAURANT SURVEY INFERENTIAL ANALYSIS

(For necessary background on this case, read Case 15.2, The Hobbit's Choice Restaruant Survey Descriptive Analysis, on pages 460–463.)

Cory Rogers was pleased with the descriptive analysis performed by his marketing intern, Christine Yu. Christine had done all of the proper descriptive analyses, and she had copied the relevant tables and findings into a Word document with notations that Cory could refer to quickly.

Cory says, "Christine, this is great work. Our client's name is Jeff Dean, and I am going to meet with him in an hour to show him what we have found. In the meantime, I want you to look a bit deeper into the data. I have jotted down some items that I want you to analyze. This is the next step in understanding how the sample findings generalize to the population of the greater metropolitan area."

Your task here is to again take the role of Christine Yu, marketing intern. Using The Hobbit's Choice Restaurant survey SPSS data set, perform the proper analysis and interpret the findings for each of the following questions specified by Cory Rogers.

1. What are the population estimates for each of the following?
   a. Preference for "easy-listening" radio programming
   b. Viewing of 10 p.m. local news on TV
   c. Subscribe to City Magazine
   d. Average age of heads of households
   e. Average price paid for an evening meal entrée
2. Because Jeff Dean's restaurant will be upscale, it will appeal to high-income consumers. Jeff hopes that at least 25% of the households have an income level of $100,000 or higher. Test this hypothesis.
3. With respect to those who are "very likely" to patronize The Hobbit's Choice Restaurant, Jeff believes that they will either "very strongly" or "somewhat" prefer each of the following: (a) waitstaff with tuxedos, (b) unusual desserts, (c) large variety of entrées, (d) unusual entrées, (e) elegant décor, and (f) jazz combo music. Does the survey support or refute Jeff's hypotheses? Interpret your findings.

CASE 16.3 Your Integrated Case

THE ADVANCED AUTOMOBILE CONCEPTS SURVEY GENERALIZATION ANALYSIS

Cory Rogers was pleased with Celeste Brown's descriptive analysis. Celeste had done all of the proper descriptive analyses, and she had copied the relevant tables and findings into a Word document with notations that Cory could refer to quickly. Cory says, "Celeste, this is great work. I am going to meet Nick Thomas tomorrow to show him what we have found. In the meantime, here are some things to analyze. We need to generalize the findings to the U.S. population. I also have some hypotheses that I want to you test."

In the way of background, the data set for the Advanced Automobile Concepts survey was described in Case 15.3, beginning on page 463. There are 50 variables that pertain to the following topics:

Demographics

Vehicle ownership

Probabilities of buying various types of hybrid vehicles in the next 3 years

Preferences for specific types of hybrid vehicles

Lifestyle

Favorite television show type

Favorite radio genre

Favorite magazine type

Favorite local newspaper section

Refer to Case 15.3 for specific items used to measure each of these topics and the scales used for the items. This SPSS data set, called AAConcepts.sav, is comprised of 1,000 respondents who are a representative sample of American households. There are an estimated 111,617,402 American households (U.S. Census, 2006 estimate).

Your task here is to again take the role of Celeste Brown, marketing analyst. Using The Advanced Automobile Concepts SPSS data set, perform the proper analysis and interpret the findings for each of the following questions specified by Cory Rogers.

1. What percentage of the American public owns
   a. Standard vehicle
   b. Luxury vehicle
   c. SUV or van

2. How does the American public feel about the following statements:
   a. Hybrid autos that use alternative fuels will reduce fuel emissions.
   b. Hybrid autos that use alternative fuels will keep gas prices down.
   c. Hybrid autos that use alternative fuels will slow down global warming.

3. The Advanced Automobile Concepts principals fully understand that there is resistance to change at Zen. Some senior executives grew up during America's "romance with the automobile" era of the 1950s and 1960s and believe that most Americans want a large and powerful automobile. These executives point out that SUVs are extremely popular despite global warming warnings that have been issued for the past decade and numerous gasoline price surges during which filling up the gas tank of an SUV or a luxury automobile approached the $100 mark. These executives further believe that hybrid and alternative-fuel automobiles are generally regarded by the American public as undesirable because they are perceived to be unattractive, boxy in appearance, and sluggish in acceleration. In fact, some of these senior executives believe that the probability of the American public buying the various hybrid vehicles in the next 3 years is something like the following:

Hybrid Vehicle Type	**Probability**
• Probability of buying a very small (1-seat) hybrid auto within 3 years?	• 5%
• Probability of buying a small (2-seat) hybrid auto within 3 years?	• 5%
• Probability of buying an standard-size hybrid auto within 3 years?	• 15%
• Probability of buying a standard-size synthetic fuel auto within 3 years?	• 15%
• Probability of buying a standard-size electric auto within 3 years?	• 20%

Test these hypotheses with the findings from the survey.

4. Using the findings from the survey, estimate the number of vehicles of each of the following hybrid types that are expected to be purchased over the next 3 years:

   a. Very small (1-seat) hybrid auto
   b. Small (2-seat) hybrid auto
   c. Standard-size hybrid auto
   d. Standard-size electric auto
   e. Standard-size synthetic fuel auto

Learning Objectives

- To learn how differences are used for market segmentation decisions

- To understand when *t* tests or *z* tests are appropriate and why you do not need to worry about this issue

- To be able to test the differences between two percentages or means for two independent groups

- To know what is a paired samples difference test and when to use it

- To comprehend ANOVA and how to interpret ANOVA output

- To learn how to perform differences tests for means using SPSS

Where We Are

1 Establish the need for marketing research

2 Define the problem

3 Establish research objectives

4 Determine research design

5 Identify information types and sources

6 Determine methods of accessing data

7 Design data-collection forms

8 Determine the sample plan and size

9 Collect data

▶ 10 Analyze data, and

11 Prepare and present the final research report.

A Marketing Research Professional Comments on the Importance of Differences Analysis

William H. MacElroy,
President, Socratic
Technologies

The following quote about differences analysis is provided by William H. MacElroy, President, Socratic Technologies.

Over the years, I've seen many instances where true insights can be concealed by looking at just the simple average (mean). Consider the example where one group of people really likes a new product concept and another group of equal size dislikes it as passionately. If you just look at the mean purchase interest of both groups, you will be "averaging out" all the interesting findings and—even more importantly—will be looking at a level of interest that doesn't really represent anyone at all. Obviously, understanding the differences between groups and the "lay of the data" will highly influence who we recommend for the targeting of the new product.

To increase the usefulness of our analysis, we can examine differences between two proportions, differences between two means, or differences between more than two means. In order to find valuable insights for our clients, it is important for marketing researchers to know the appropriate statistical tests to run and how the structure of the data distribution influences the correct choice of method. In this chapter you will learn all the tests that are appropriate for the three situations described above. You will also learn how to run these tests using SPSS and you will learn how to interpret the results.

Visit Socratic Technologies
at www.sotech.com/

A s you learned in Chapter 16, it is possible to make inferences about measures of cen-tral tendency such as means and percentages found in a random sample survey. These inferences take the form of confidence intervals or tests of hypotheses. A different type of inference concerns differences. That is, as William MacElroy described in his opening comments, the researcher can ask, "Are there statistically significant differences between two or more groups, and, if so, what are they?" In this chapter, we describe the logic of differ-ences tests, and we show you how to use SPSS to conduct various types of differences tests.[1]

We begin this chapter discussing why differences are important to marketing man-agers, and we give some guidelines to researchers and managers for interpreting differ-ences tests. Next, we introduce you to differences (percentages or means) between two independent groups, such as a comparison of high-speed cable versus DSL telephone Internet users on how satisfied they are with their Internet connection service. Next, we introduce you to ANOVA, a scary name, but a simple way to compare the means of several groups simultaneously and to quickly spot patterns of significant differences. We provide numerical examples and also show you examples of SPSS procedures and output using the Advanced Automobile Concepts survey data. Finally, we show you that it is possible to test differences between the averages of two similarly scaled questions. For instance, do buyers rate a store higher in "merchandise selection" than they rate its "good values?"

WHY DIFFERENCES ARE IMPORTANT

Market segmentation is based on differences between groups of consumers.

Perhaps one of the most useful marketing management concepts is market segmentation. Basically, market segmentation holds that different types of consumers have different requirements, and these differences can form the bases of marketing strategies. For exam-ple, the Iams Company, which markets pet foods, sells over 20 different varieties of dry dog food geared to a dog's age (puppy, adult, senior), weight situation (small, medium, large), and activity (reduced, normal, moderate, high). Toyota Motors markets 20 models, including 8 car models, 2 truck models, 7 SUV/Van models, and 3 hybrid models. Even Boeing Airlines has five different types of commercial jets and a separate business jets division for corporate travel.

Let's look at differences from the consumer's side. Everyone washes their hands, but the kind of soap required differs for weekend gardeners with potting soil under their fin-gernails, factory workers whose hands are dirty with solvents, preschoolers who have sticky drink residue on their hands and faces, or aspiring beauty princesses who wish their hands to look absolutely flawless. The needs and requirements of each of these market seg-ments differ greatly from the others, and an astute marketer will customize the marketing mix to each target market's unique situation.[2]

These differences, of course, are quite obvious, but as competition becomes more intense with prolific market segmentation and target marketing being the watchword of most companies in an industry, there is a need to investigate differences among consumer groups (for consumer marketers) and business establishments (for B2B marketers). One common basis for market segmentation is the discovery of (1) statistically significant, (2) meaningful, (3) stable, and (4) actionable differences. Unique market segments exist even for the common cold; we have illustrated the four segmentation requirements for cold sufferers with a brief explanation of each one in Table 17.1.

We will discuss each requirement briefly. In our comments, we will assume that we are working with a pharmaceuticals company that markets cold remedies.

To be potentially useful to the marketing researcher or manager, differences must, at minimum, be statistically significant.

THE DIFFERENCES MUST BE SIGNIFICANT. As you know, the notion of statistical signifi-cance underpins marketing research.[3] **Statistical significance of differences** means that the differences found in the sample(s) truly exist in the population(s) from which the

TABLE 17.1 The Four Contingent Requirements of Differences Between Groups to Be Useful for Market Segmentation

Requirement	Explanation	Cold Remedy Example
First, the differences must be statistically significant.	Statistically significant differences should be demonstrated between the groups.	On a scale of 1 to 10, how important is it to you that your cold medicine relieves your . . .

Group	Congestion?*	Muscle Aches?*
1	8.2	5.3
2	5.4	9.1

*Average rating

Requirement	Explanation	Cold Remedy Example
Second, the differences must be meaningful.	The differences between the market segments should be of such a magnitude that the marketer can target them individually.	Group 1 suffers greatly from *congestion problems* when they have colds; Group 2 suffers from *muscle aches and pains* to a great extent. A congestion relief additive will not reduce aches, nor will a pain relief additive reduce congestion with cold sufferers.
Third, the differences must be stable.	The differences should not be short-term or transitory.	Group 1, *congestion sufferers,* have respiratory weaknesses or situations that are aggravated when they suffer from colds, whereas Group 2, *muscle aches and pains*, does not have these preconditions but are physically more active, so muscle aches and pains are more of a concern to them.
Fourth, the differences must be actionable.	The market segment groups should be identified and suitable for target marketing.	The history of Group 1's, *congestion sufferers*, respiratory problems makes it identifiable: This group will be vigilant for congestion relief. The physical activity profile of Group 2, *muscle aches and pains,* is identifiable, and since they value physical activity, they will be looking for cold remedies that allow them to remain as active as their cold infections permit.

random samples are drawn. So, the apparent differences between and among market segments must be subjected to tests that assess the statistical significance of these differences. This is the topic of this chapter, and we will endeavor to teach you here how to perform and interpret tests of the statistical significance of differences. With our cold remedy marketer, we could ask cold sufferers, "How important is it that your cold remedy relieves your. . . ." The respondents would respond using a scale of 1 = "not important" to 10 = "very important" for each cold symptom (fever, sore throat, congestion, aching muscles, and so on) and statistical tests such as those described in this chapter would determine if the responses were significantly different. In Table 17.1, we noted two groups (1 and 2) that have statistically significant differences. Group 1, *congestion sufferers*, greatly desires breathing congestion relief; Group 2, *muscle aches and pains*, desires relief from musculoskeletal aches and pains associated with their colds.

THE DIFFERENCES MUST BE MEANINGFUL. A finding of statistical significance in no way guarantees "meaningful" difference. In fact, owing to the proliferation of analysis based on the data mining of tens of thousands of records, online surveys that garner thousands of respondents, and other ways to capture very large samples, there is a very real danger of finding a great deal of statistical significance that is not meaningful. The reason for this is that statistical significance is determined to a very great extent by the sample size.[4] By examining the formulas we provide in this chapter, you will see that the sample size, n, is instrumental in the calculation of z, the determinant of the significance level. Large samples, those in excess of 1,000 per sample group, often yield statistically significant results when the absolute differences between the groups are quite small. A **meaningful difference** is one that the marketing manager can potentially use as a basis for marketing decisions.

In our common cold example, there are some meaningful implications to be drawn from the fact that one group cannot breathe easily and the other group has aches and pains because there are some cold remedy ingredients that reduce congestion and others that diminish pain. Granted, the pharmaceuticals company could include both ingredients, but the congestion sufferers do not want an ingredient that might make them drowsy from the strong pain relief ingredient, and the aches and pains sufferers do not want their throats and nasal passages to feel dry and uncomfortable from the decongestant ingredient. These differences are meaningful both to the customer groups as well as to the pharmaceuticals manufacturer. We will offer some guidelines on what might be statistically significant and what are "meaningful" differences later in the chapter.

> To be useful to the marketing researcher or manager, differences must, if statistically significant, be meaningful.

THE DIFFERENCES SHOULD BE STABLE. Stability refers to the requirement that we are not working with a short-term or transitory set of differences. Thus, a **stable difference** is one that will be in place for the foreseeable future. The persistent problem experienced by Group 1, *congestion sufferers*, is most probably due to some respiratory weakness or condition. They may have preconditions such as allergies or breathing problems, or they may be exposed to heavy pollution or some other factor that affects their respiration in general. Group 2, *aches and pains sufferers*, may be very active people who do not have respiration weaknesses, but who value active lifestyle activities such as regular exercise, or may have occupations that require a good deal of physical activity. In either case, there is a very good possibility that when a cold strikes, the sufferer will experience the same discomfort, either congestion or muscle aches, time and time again. That is, the differences between the two groups are stable. The pharmaceuticals company can develop custom-designed versions of its cold relief product because it knows from experience and research that certain consumers will be consistent (stable) in seeking certain types of relief or specific product benefits when they suffer from colds.

> To be useful to the marketing researcher or manager, differences must, if statistically significant and meaningful, be stable.

THE DIFFERENCES MUST ACTIONABLE. Market segmentation requires that standard or innovative market segmentation bases be used, and that these uniquely identify the various groups so they can be analyzed and incorporated into the marketer's targeting mechanisms. An **actionable difference** means that the marketer can focus various marketing strategies and tactics, such as product design or advertising, on the market segments to accentuate the differences between the segments. There are a great many segmentation bases that are actionable, such as demographics, lifestyles, and product benefits. In our example, among the many symptoms manifest by colds sufferers, we have identified two meaningful and stable groups, so a cold remedy product line that concentrates on each one of these separately is possible. A quick glance at the cold remedies section of your local drug store will verify the actionability of these cold symptoms market segments.

> To be useful to the marketing researcher or manager, differences must, if statistically significant, meaningful, and stable, be actionable.

You may be confused about meaningful and actionable differences. Recall that "potentially use" was part of our definition of a meaningful difference. With our cold remedies example, a pharmaceuticals company could potentially develop and market a cold remedy that was specific to every type of cold symptom as experienced by every demographic group and further identified by lifestyle differences. For example, there could be a cold medicine to alleviate the runny noses of teenage girls who participate in high school athletics and a different one for the sniffles of teenage boys who play high school sports. But it would be economically unjustifiable to offer so many different cold medicines, so all marketers must assess actionability based on market segment size and profitability considerations. Nevertheless, the fundamental differences are based on statistical significance, meaningfulness, and stability assessments.

To be sure, the bulk of this chapter deals strictly with statistically significant differences, because it is the beginning point for market segmentation and savvy target marketing. Meaningfulness, stability, and actionability are not statistical issues; rather, they are marketing manager judgment calls.

Because cold sufferers consistently have different symptoms such as runny noses, congestion, and achy muscles, pharmaceutical companies have identified different market segments.

SMALL SAMPLE SIZES: THE USE OF A *t* TEST OR A *z* TEST AND HOW SPSS ELIMINATES THE WORRY

Most of the equations described in this chapter will lead to the computation of a *z* value; as we pointed out in the previous chapter, computation of the *z* value makes the assumption that the raw data for most statistics under scrutiny have normal, or bell-shaped, distributions. However, statisticians have shown that this normal curve property does not hold when the sample size is 30 observations or less.[5] In this instance, a *t* value is computed instead of a *z* value.

The ***t* test** is the statistical inference test to be used with small samples sizes ($n \leq 30$). Instead of relying on a constant normal distribution, the *t* test relies on Student's *t* distribution. The *t* distribution's shape is determined by the number of degrees of freedom, defined as the sample size minus the number of population parameters estimated, which is $(n - 1)$ here because the population parameter is the difference between the two population means. The smaller the number of degrees of freedom, the more spread out the curve becomes. It still retains a bell shape, but it flattens out a little bit with each successive loss of a sample unit below 30. Any instance when the sample size is 30 or greater requires the use of a *z* **test**.

All of this is surely very confusing to you, but the great advantage to using computerized statistical analysis routines is that they are programmed to compute the correct statistic. In other words, you do not need to decide whether you want the program to compute a *t* value, a *z* value, or some other value. With SPSS, the analyses of differences are referred to as "*t* tests," but since SPSS will always determine the correct significance level, whether it is a *t* or a *z*, you do not need to worry about which statistic to use. The talent you need to acquire is how to interpret the significance level that is reported by SPSS. We have provided Marketing Research Insight 17.1 to introduce you to a "flag-waving" analogy that students have told us is helpful in this regard.

The *t* test should be used when the sample size is 30 or less.

Most computer statistical programs report only the *t* value because it is identical to the *z* value with large samples.

MARKETING RESEARCH INSIGHT   Practical Application

17.1 Signal Flag Waving and Significance in Statistical Analysis

The output from statistical procedures in all software programs can be envisioned as "signal-flag-waving" devices. When the signal flag is waving briskly, statistical significance is present. Then, and only then, is it warranted to look at the findings more closely to determine the pattern of the findings; but if the flag is not waving, you will waste your time by looking any further. To read statistical flags, you need to know two things. First, where is the flag located? Second, how vigorously does it need to wave for you to pay attention to it and to delve further into the analysis in order to interpret it?

Where Is the Flag?

Virtually every statistical test or procedure involves the computation of some critical statistic, and that statistic is used to determine the statistical significance of the findings. The critical statistic's name changes depending on the procedure and its underlying assumptions, but usually the statistic is identified as a letter: z, t, F, or something similar. Statistical analysis computer programs will automatically identify and compute the correct statistic, so although it is helpful to know ahead of time what statistic will be computed, it is not essential to know it. Moreover, the statistic is not the flag; rather, it is just a computation necessary to raise the flag. You might think of the computed statistic as the flagpole.

The computer program will also raise the flag on the flagpole, but its name changes a bit depending on the procedure.

The flags, called "p values" by statisticians, are identified on computer output by the terms "significance" or "probability." Sometimes abbreviations such as "Sig" or "Prob" are used to economize on the output. To find the flag, locate the "Sig" or "Prob" designation in the analysis, and look at the number that is associated with it. The number will be a decimal, perhaps as low as 0.000 but ranging to as high as 1.000. When you locate it, you have found the statistical significance flag.

How Much Is the Flag Waving?

If the National Hurricane Center announced that there is a 95% chance that a hurricane will make landfall in the location where you are staying, you would definitely know that hurricane-force winds are imminent. That is, gentle winds blow all the time, and we are not concerned about them; but when hurricane-force winds build, we become concerned, and we pay a great deal of attention to the weather. For the purposes of this textbook, we have adopted the 95% level of confidence. That is, if you were 95% confident that a hurricane was imminent, you would take significant steps to avoid being in harm's way. In other words, it would definitely get your attention.

As we noted above, the significance or probability values reported in statistical analysis output range from 0.000 to 1.000, and they indicate the degree of support for the null hypothesis (no differences). If you just compute 1 minus the reported significance level—for example, if the sig level is 0.03, you would use 1 minus 0.03 to come up with 0.97, or 97%—that is the level of confidence for the finding. Any time this value is 95% or greater, you should know that the flag is waving frantically to catch your attention.

TESTING FOR SIGNIFICANT DIFFERENCES BETWEEN TWO GROUPS

There are statistical tests for comparing the means or percentages of two different groups or samples.

Often, as we have done in our cold remedy example, a researcher will want to compare two groups of interest. That is, the researcher may want to compare the answers of two independent groups, such as walk-ins versus loyal customers, to the same question. The question may be either on a categorical scale or a metric scale. A categorical scale requires that the researcher compare percentages; when a metric scale is involved the researcher will compare means. As you know by now, the formulas differ depending on whether percentages or means are being tested.

Differences Between Percentages with Two Groups (Independent Samples)

Independent samples are treated as representing two potentially different populations.

When a marketing researcher is interested in making comparisons between two groups of respondents to determine whether or not there are statistically significant differences between them, the researcher is considering them, in concept, as two potentially different populations. The question to be answered then becomes whether or not their respective population parameters are different. But, as always, a researcher can only work with the sample results. Therefore, the researcher must fall back on statistical significance to determine whether the difference that is found between the two sample statistics is a true population difference. You will shortly discover that the logic of differences test is very similar to the logic of hypothesis testing that you learned about in the previous chapter.

Again, we refer to the intuitive approach you use every day when comparing two things to make an inference. Let us assume you have read a *BusinessWeek* article about college recruiters that quotes a Lou Harris poll of 100 randomly selected companies, indicating that 65% of them will be visiting college campuses to interview business majors. The article goes on to say that a similar poll taken last year with 300 companies found only 40% for the sample percentage. This is great news: More companies will be coming to your campus this year for job interviews. However, you cannot be completely confident of your joyous conclusion because of sampling error. If the difference between the percentages was very large, say 80% for this year and 20% for last year, you would be more inclined to believe that a true change had occurred. But if you found out the difference was based on small sample sizes, you would be less confident of your inference that last year's and this year's college recruiting are different. Intuitively, you have taken into account two critical factors in determining whether statistically significant differences exist between a percentage or a mean compared between two samples: the magnitude of the difference between the compared statistic (65% versus 40%) and sample sizes (100 versus 300).

To test whether a true difference exists between two group percentages, we test the **null hypothesis**, or the hypothesis that the difference in their population parameters is equal to zero. The alternative hypothesis is that there is a true difference between them. To perform the test of **significance of differences between two percentages**, each representing a separate group (sample), the first step requires a "comparison" of the two percentages, that is, finding the arithmetic difference between them. The second step requires that this difference be translated into a number of standard errors away from the hypothesized value of zero. Once the number of standard errors is known, knowledge of the area under the normal curve will yield an assessment of the probability of support for the null hypothesis.

We realize that it is confusing to keep in mind the null hypothesis, the alternative hypothesis, and all these equations as well. Just as in Chapter 16, where we provided a Marketing Research Insight on what an alternative hypothesis is for a hypothesis test, we have provided one in this chapter that describes what the alternative hypothesis is in the differences tests that are described here.

For a difference between two percentages test, the equation is as follows:

Formula for Significance of the Difference Between Two Percentages
$$z = \frac{p_1 - p_2}{s_{p_1 - p_2}}$$

where

p_1 = percentage found in sample 1

p_2 = percentage found in sample 2

$s_{p_1 - p_2}$ = standard error of the difference between two percentages.

The standard error of the difference between two percentages combines the standard error of the percentage for both samples, and it is calculated with the following formula:

Formula for the Standard Error of the Difference Between Two Percentages
$$s_{p_1 - p_2} = \sqrt{\frac{p_1 \times q_1}{n_1} + \frac{p_2 \times q_2}{n_2}}$$

Again, if you compare these formulas to the ones we used in hypothesis testing in Chapter 16, you will see that the logic is identical. First, in the numerator, we subtract one sample's statistic (p_2) from the other sample's statistic (p_1) just as we subtracted the hypothesized percentage from the sample percentage in hypothesis testing. You should have

With a differences test, the null hypothesis states there is no difference between the percentages (or means) being compared.

With a differences test, you test the null hypothesis that no differences exist between the two group means (or percentages).

MARKETING RESEARCH INSIGHT   Practical Application

17.2 What Is the Alternative Hypothesis for a Differences Test?

In Chapter 16, we introduced you to the concept of an alternative hypothesis. To refresh your memory, the alternative hypothesis takes in all possible cases that are not treated by the stated hypothesis.

With differences tests, the stated hypothesis, called the "null hypothesis," is that the arithmetic difference between one parameter (for example, percentage or mean for Group 1) and another one (for example, percentage or mean for Group 2) is zero. That is, the statistical test begins with the assumption that the two percentages (means) are exactly the same value. So the alternative hypothesis of a differences test is that they are not the same value. In other words, the difference is not equal to zero.

Here are the stated and alternative hypotheses for the two types of differences tests described in this chapter.

Stated Hypothesis	Alternative Hypothesis
Differences Between Two Groups	
No difference exists between the percents (means) of two groups (populations).	*A difference does exist between the percents (means) of two groups (populations).*
The percentage (mean) of one group (population) is greater than the mean of another group (population).	*The percentage (mean) of one group (population) is less than or equal to the percentage (mean) of another group (population).*
Differences in Means Among More Than Two Groups (Note: Only differences in means can be tested here)	
No difference exists between the means of all paired groups (populations).	*A difference exists between the means of at least one pair of groups (populations).*

noticed that we use the subscripts 1 and 2 to refer to the two different sample statistics. Second, the sampling distribution is expressed in the denominator. However, the sampling distribution under consideration now is the assumed sampling distribution of the differences between the percentages rather than the simple standard error of a percentage used in hypothesis testing. That is, the assumption has been made that the differences have been computed for comparisons of the two sample statistics for many repeated samplings.

If the null hypothesis is true, this distribution of differences follows the normal curve with a mean equal to 0 and a standard error equal to 1. Stated somewhat differently, the procedure requires us, as before, to accept the (null) hypothesis as true unless it lacks support from the statistical test. Consequently, the differences of a multitude of comparisons of the two sample percentages generated from many, many samplings would average 0. In other words, our sampling distribution is now the distribution of the difference between one sample and the other, taken over many, many times.[6] The following example will walk you through the point we just made.

Here is how you would perform the calculations for the Harris poll on companies coming to campus to hire college seniors. Recall that last year's poll with 300 companies reported 40% were coming to campus and this year's poll with 100 companies reported that 65% were visiting campuses.

Computation of the Significance of the Difference Between Two Percentages

$$z = \frac{p_1 - p_2}{s_{p_1-p_2}}$$

$$= \frac{65 - 40}{\sqrt{\dfrac{65 \times 35}{100} + \dfrac{40 \times 60}{300}}}$$

$$= \frac{25}{\sqrt{22.75 + 8.0}}$$

$$= \frac{25}{5.55}$$

$$= 4.5$$

Notes:
$p_1 = 65$
$p_2 = 40$
$n_1 = 100$
$n_2 = 300$

We compare the computed z value with our standard z of 1.96 for the 95% level of confidence; the computed z of 4.5 is larger than 1.96. A computed z value that is larger than the standard z value of 1.96 amounts to *no support* for the null hypothesis at the 95% level of confidence. So there is a statistically significant difference between the two percentages, and we are confident that if we repeated this comparison many, many times with a multitude of independent samples, we would conclude that there is a significant difference in at least 95% of these replications. Of course, we would never do many, many replications, but this is the statistician's basis for the level of significance.

It is a simple matter to apply the formulas to percentages to determine the significance of their differences, for all that is needed is the sample size of each group. We have provided Marketing Research Insight 17.3, which relies on the significance of the difference between percentages tests. The Insight highlights the significantly different distinctions between two very different, and stable, consumer groups.

Our percentages differences test begins with the assumption that there will be no change in the job market for college graduates over last year's level.

Calculations to Determine Significant Differences Between Percentages

You can now perform your own tests of the differences between two percentages using the formulas we have provided and described. A local health club has just finished a media blitz for new memberships. Over the past month, the health club has run advertisements in the newspaper, on the local television news channels, on its website, on two different FM radio stations, and in the Yellow Pages. Whenever a prospective new member visited one of the health club's facilities, the person was asked to fill out a short questionnaire in which one question asked what ads the person saw in the past month. Some of these prospects joined the health club and some did not, meaning that we have two populations: those who joined the health club and those who did not. At the end of the 30 days, a staff member performed the following tabulations:

	Joined the Health Club	Did Not Join the Health Club
Total visitors	100	30
Recalled newspaper ads	45	15
Recalled FM radio station ads	89	20
Recalled Yellow Pages ads	16	5
Recalled local TV news ads	21	6

Use your knowledge of the formula and the test of the significance of the differences between two percentages to ascertain if there are any significant differences in this data. What are the implications of your findings with respect to the effectiveness of the various advertising media used during the membership recruitment ad blitz?

MARKETING RESEARCH INSIGHT

Practical Application

17.3 Do Spendthrifts Spend, and Are Tightwads Tight?

Since the beginning of commerce, it has been observed that some consumers spend extravagantly while some are quite miserly. However, are these spur-of-the-moment phenomena, or are they patterns that persist over time?

Researchers sought to identify and classify consumers on a scale that identifies spendthrifts versus tightwads.[7] In an attempt to study the spendthrift/tightwad trait, they compared credit card usage and debt and the amount of savings of spendthrifts and tightwads. Performing percentage differences tests using the published data produced the following two graphs, which show where the significant differences were found.

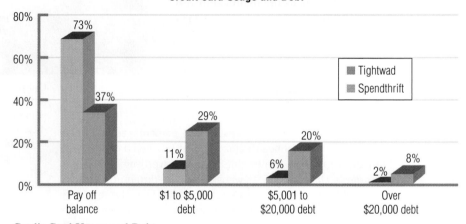

Credit Card Usage and Debt

Amount of savings

The graphs illustrate that spendthrifts have greater credit card debt and less life savings, whereas tightwads have less credit card debt and greater life savings accounts. One striking difference is that almost three-quarters of the tightwads pay off their credit card balances every month, but only about one-third of the spendthrifts are able to keep a zero credit card debt. The findings confirm that "tight" consumers actively manage their credit card debt and garner savings accounts benefits, and "spend" consumers experience credit management issues and endure the worries of meager savings to fall back on in the case of financial emergencies.

Using SPSS for Differences Between Percentages of Two Groups

As is the case with most statistical analysis programs, SPSS does not perform tests of the significance of the differences between the percentages of two groups. You can, however, use SPSS to determine the sample percentage on your variable of interest along with its sample size. Repeat this descriptive analysis for the other sample, and you will have all the values required (p_1, p_2, n_1, and n_2) to perform the calculations by hand or in a spreadsheet program. (Recall that you can compute q_1 and q_2, based on the "$p + q = 100$" relationship.)

SPSS

SPSS does not perform tests of the significance of the differences between the percentages of two groups, but you can use SPSS to generate the relevant information and perform a hand calculation.

Differences Between Means with Two Groups (Independent Samples)

The procedure for testing the **significance of differences between two means** from two different groups (either two different samples or two different groups in the same sample) is identical to the procedure used in testing two percentages. As you can easily guess, however, the equations differ because a metric scale is involved.

Here is the equation for the test of difference between two sample means:

Formula for Significance of the Differences Between Two Means

$$z = \frac{\bar{x}_1 - \bar{x}_2}{s_{\bar{x}_1 - \bar{x}_2}}$$

If the null hypothesis is true, when you subtract one group mean from the other, the result should be about zero.

where

$\bar{x}_1 =$ mean found in sample 1
$\bar{x}_2 =$ mean found in sample 2
$s_{\bar{x}_1 - \bar{x}_2} =$ standard error of the difference between two means.

The standard error of the difference is easy to calculate and again relies on the variability that has been found in the samples and their sizes. Because we are working with means, we use the standard deviations in the formula for the standard error of a difference between two means:

Formula for the Standard Error of the Differences Between Two Means

$$s_{\bar{x}_1 - \bar{x}_2} = \sqrt{\frac{s_1^2}{n_1} + \frac{s_2^2}{n_2}}$$

Here is the formula for the standard error of the difference between two means.

where

$s_1 =$ standard deviation in sample 1
$s_2 =$ standard deviation in sample 2
$n_1 =$ size of sample 1
$n_2 =$ size of sample 2.

To illustrate how significance of differences computations are made, we use the following example that answers the question "Do male teens and female teens drink different amounts of sports drinks?" In a recent survey, teenagers were asked to indicate how many 20-ounce bottles of sports drinks they consume in a typical week. The descriptive statistics revealed that males consume 9 bottles on average and females consume 7.5 bottles of sports drinks on average. The respective standard deviations were found to be 2 and 1.2.

Is there a difference in the average number of soft drinks consumed by males versus the average number of soft drinks consumed by females?

Both samples were of size 100. Applying this information to the formula for the test of statistically significant differences, we get the following:

Here are the calculations for a test of the differences between the means of two groups.

Computation of the Significance of the Differences Between Two Means

$$z = \frac{\overline{x}_1 - \overline{x}_2}{\sqrt{\dfrac{s_1^2}{n_1} + \dfrac{s_2^2}{n_2}}}$$

$$= \frac{9.0 - 7.5}{\sqrt{\dfrac{2^2 100}{} + \dfrac{1.2^2}{100}}}$$

Notes:

$$= \frac{1.5}{\sqrt{0.04 + 0.144}}$$

$\overline{x}_1 = 9.0$
$\overline{x}_2 = 7.5$
$s_1 = 2.0$

$$= \frac{1.5}{0.233}$$

$s_2 = 1.2$
$n_1 = 100$

$$= 6.43$$

$n_2 = 100$

Figure 17.1 indicates how these two samples compare on the sampling distribution assumed to underlie this particular example. At the bottom of the figure, we have provided the bell-shaped curve of the standard error of the differences with 0 as its mean (the null hypothesis). By looking at the computed z value, labeled on the graph, you know the probability of support for the null hypothesis of no difference between the two means is less than 0.001 because the large number of standard errors (6.43) calculated to exist for this example is much greater than 2.58.

How do you interpret this test for significance of differences? As always, the sampling distribution concept underlies our interpretation. If the null hypothesis was true, and we drew many, many samples and did this explicit comparison each time, then 95% of the differences would fall within ±1.96 standard errors of zero. Of course, only one comparison can be made, and you have to rely on the sampling distribution concept and its attendant assumptions to determine whether this one particular instance of information supports or refutes the hypothesis of no significant differences found between the means of your two groups. To learn about how a bank in Finland used differences of means to discover the reasons for its "older" customers resisting the adoption of mobile banking, read Marketing Research Insight 17.4.

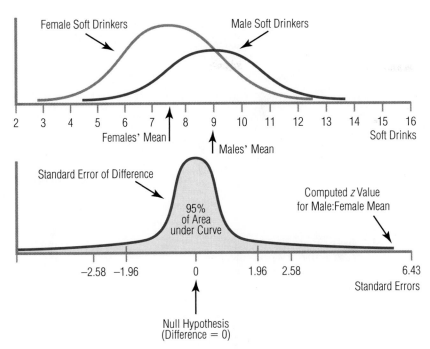

FIGURE 17.1

A Significant Difference Exists between the Two Means Because *z* Is Calculated to Be Greater Than 1.96

Directional hypotheses are also feasible in the case of tests of statistically significant differences. The procedure is identical to directional hypotheses that are stipulated in hypothesis tests. That is, you must first look at the sign of the computed z value to check that it is consistent with your hypothesized direction. Then, you would use a cutoff z value, such as 2.33 standard errors for 99% level of confidence, because only one tail of the sampling distribution is being used.

Your Integrated Case

ADVANCED AUTOMOBILE CONCEPTS: HOW TO PERFORM AN INDEPENDENT SAMPLES SIGNIFICANCE OF DIFFERENCES BETWEEN MEANS TEST WITH SPSS

To demonstrate an independent samples significance test, we will take up the question of whether or not market segmentation is relevant to Advanced Automobile Concepts. We will take it up very slowly looking at just gender as a possible segmentation variable and only one of the possible hybrid models: the one-seat, three-wheel model. So we have two groups: males and females. We can test the mean of the preference for the one-seat, three-wheel hybrid vehicle, which was measured on a 1-point scale where 1 = "very undesirable" and 7 = "very desirable."

The clickstream that directs SPSS to perform an independent samples t test of the significance of the differences between means is displayed in Figure 17.2. As you can see, you begin with the ANALYZE–COMPARE MEANS–INDEPENDENT SAMPLES T-TEST . . . menu sequence. This sequence opens up the selection menu, and the "Preference: Super Cycle 1 seat hybrid" preference is clicked into the "Test variable" area, and the "Gender" variable is clicked into the "Grouping Variable" box. Using the "Define Groups" button, a window opens to let us identify the codes of the two groups (0 = male and 1 = female). This sets up the t test, and a click on OK executes it.

The annotated output is found in Figure 17.3. The first table reveals that the mean of the 505 males is 3.50, and the mean for the 495 females is 3.09.

The statistical test for the differences between the two means is given next. However, SPSS computes the results two different ways. One is identified as the "equal variances assumed," and the other

SPSS Student Assistant: Assessing Differences Between Means for Two Groups (Independent)

To determine the significance of the difference in the means of two groups with SPSS, use the ANALYZE– COMPARE MEANS– INDEPENDENT SAMPLES T-TEST . . . menu sequence.

FIGURE 17.2

SPSS Clickstream to Obtain an Independent Samples t-Test

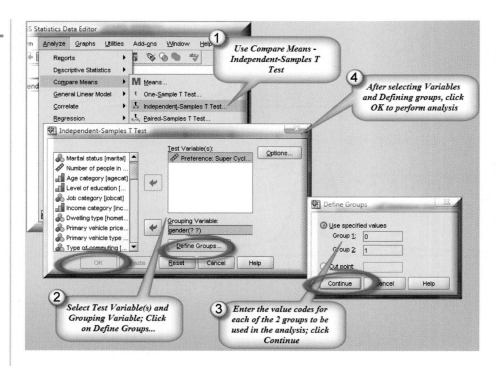

is called the "equal variances not assumed." In our previous descriptions, we omitted a detail involved in tests for the significance of differences between two means. In some cases, the variances (standard deviations) of the two samples are about the same; that is, they are not significantly different. If so, you can use the formula pertaining to the equal variances (same variance for both samples), but if the standard deviations are statistically significant in their differences, you should use the unequal variances line on the output.

FIGURE 17.3

SPSS Output for an Independent Sample t-Test

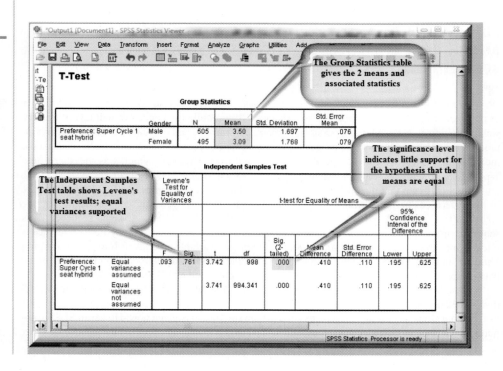

How do you know which one to use? The null hypothesis here is that there is no difference between the variances (standard deviations), and it is tested with an F value printed in the top row of the independent samples test table. The F test is just another statistical test, and it is the proper one here. (Recall that we stated earlier that SPSS will always select and compute the correct statistical test.) The F value is based on a procedure called "Levene's Test for Equality of Variances." In our output, the F value is identified as .093 with a Sig (probability) of .761. The probability reported here is the probability that the variances are equal, so any time the probability is *greater than*, say 0.05, then you would use the equal variance line on the output. If the probability associated with the F value is *small,* say 0.05 or less, then the variances null hypothesis is not supported, and you should use the unequal variance line. If you forget this rule, then just look at the standard deviations and try to remember that if they are about the same size, you would use the equal variances t value.

Using the equal variance estimate information, you will find that the computed t value is 3.742, and the associated probability of support for the null hypothesis of no difference between the males' preference mean and the females' preference mean is 0.000. In other words, they differ significantly. Males prefer the one-seat, three-wheel hybrid model more than do females, and Nick could use this finding as a basis for segmenting this model's market using gender. However, Nick should bear in mind that either gender's mean is somewhat negative and not past the neutral rating, so perhaps other segmentation bases will derive more useful findings.

Perform Means Differences Analysis with SPSS

You have just observed how to perform an Independent Samples T-Test with SPSS using your Advanced Automobile Concepts survey data. For this Active Learning exercise, determine if there is a difference in the preferences for the various possible hybrid models based on gender. That is, redo the one-seat, three-wheel hybrid model just to make sure that you can find and execute the analysis. Then use the clickstream instructions in Figure 17.2 to direct SPSS to perform this analysis for each of the other possible hybrid models, and use the annotations on the Independent Samples T-Test output provided in Figure 17.3 to interpret your findings.

TESTING FOR SIGNIFICANT DIFFERENCES IN MEANS AMONG MORE THAN TWO GROUPS: ANALYSIS OF VARIANCE

As you have learned, it is fairly easy to test for the significance of the differences between means for two groups. But, sometimes a researcher will want to compare the means of three, four, five, or more different groups. Analysis of variance, sometimes called ANOVA, should be used to accomplish such multiple comparisons.[8] The use of the word *variance* is misleading, for it is not an analysis of the standard deviations of the groups. To be sure, the standard deviations are taken into consideration, and so are the sample sizes, as you just saw in all of our differences between means formulas. Fundamentally, **ANOVA (analysis of variance)** is an investigation of the differences between the group means to ascertain whether sampling errors or true population differences explain their failure to be equal.[9] That is, "variance" signifies for our purposes differences between two or more groups' means—do they vary from one another significantly? Although a term such as "Analysis of Variance" or "ANOVA" sounds frightfully technical, it is nothing more than a statistical procedure that allows you to compare the means of several groups. As we noted in our discussion on market segmentations, markets are often comprised of a number of market segments, not just two, so ANOVA is a valuable tool for discovering differences between and among multiple market segments. The following sections explain to you the basic concepts involved with analysis of variance and also how it can be applied to marketing research situations.

ANOVA is used when comparing the means of three or more groups.

MARKETING RESEARCH INSIGHT   Global Application

17.4 How Differences of Means Analysis Helped a Scandinavian Bank with its "Mature" Customers

Computer technology has significantly impacted some sectors of the economy, and one area that is changing dramatically is personal banking. Not only can customers bank online, they can also perform many banking services on their wireless phones. In Europe, where wireless telephones are very prevalent, a bank in Finland worried about how its "elderly" customers would relate to mobile banking using one's wireless phone. Older consumers are slow to adopt new technology for a number of reasons, including (1) usage barriers: not being able to operate the technology; (2) value barriers: not seeing the added value; (3) risk barriers: worries about personal or financial risks; (4) tradition barriers: wanting to retain old, face-to-face, banking practices; or (5) image barriers: the perception that the technology is too complicated to use. Researchers sought to compare younger bank customers who were using the mobile banking services to older customers who were less inclined to use it.[10] They administered several Likert statements to both groups of the bank's customers and compared the group averages. The findings are listed in the following table:

Opinion of Mobile Banking	Young Customers	Old Customers
Usage Barriers		
In my opinion, mobile banking services are easy to use.		n.s.
In my opinion, the use of mobile banking services is convenient.		n.s.
In my opinion, mobile banking services are fast to use.		n.s.
In my opinion, progress in mobile banking services is clear.		n.s.
The use of changing PIN codes in mobile banking services is convenient. (reverse scored)	4.65	4.88
Value Barriers		
The use of mobile banking services is economical.		n.s.
In my opinion, mobile banking does not offer any advantage compared to handling my financial matters in other ways.		n.s.
In my opinion, the use of mobile banking services increases my ability to control my financial matters by myself.		n.s.
Risk Barriers		
I fear that while I am paying a bill by mobile phone, I might make mistakes since the correctness of the inputted information is difficult to check from the screen.	4.64	5.04
I fear that while I am using mobile banking services, the battery of the mobile phone will run out or the connection will otherwise be lost.	4.22	4.67
I fear that while I am using a mobile banking service, I might tap out the information on the bill wrongly.	4.26	4.72
I fear that the list of PIN codes will be lost and end up in the wrong hands.	3.56	4.24
I trust that while I am using mobile banking services, third parties are not able to use my account or see my account information.		n.s.
Tradition Barriers		
Patronizing the banking office and chatting with the teller is a nice occasion on a weekday.		n.s.
I find self-service alternatives more pleasant than personal customer service.		n.s.
Image Barriers		
I have a very positive image of mobile banking services.		n.s.
In my opinion, new technology is often too complicated to be useful.	3.47	3.91
I have such an image that mobile banking services are difficult to use.		n.s.

*Based on a scale where 1 = totally disagree and 7 = totally agree; n.s.= not significant at the 95% level of confidence.

The differences tests reveal that usage, value, tradition, and image barriers are not appreciably different (the "n.s." designations mean "not significant") in comparing the opinions of older and younger bank customers. However, the older customers do have substantial worries about the security of their transactions, and specifically concerns about inputting incorrect information, connection breakdowns, wireless phone power loss, and security of their PINs. Accordingly, the Scandinavian bank was advised to launch a promotional campaign aimed at its "55+" customers to convince them of the security of mobile banking and safeguards against customer input errors and connection losses in midtransaction.

Basic Logic in Analysis of Variance

In using analysis of variance there is a desire on the part of a researcher to determine whether a statistically significant difference exists between the means for *any two groups* in the sample for a given variable regardless of the number of groups. The end result of analysis of variance is an indication to the marketing researcher of whether a significant difference at some chosen level of statistical significance exists between *at least* two group means. Significant differences may exist between all of the group means, but analysis of variance results alone will not communicate how many pairs of means are statistically significant in their differences.

To elaborate, ANOVA is a **"signal-flag" procedure**, meaning that if at least one pair of means has a statistically significant difference, ANOVA will signal this by indicating significance. (We introduced you to the flag-waving notion in Marketing Research Insight 17.1 on page 508.) Then, it is up to the researcher to conduct further tests (called "post hoc" tests) to determine precisely how many statistically significant differences actually exist and which ones they are. Of course, if the signal flag does not pop up, the researcher knows that no significant differences exist.

ANOVA will "flag" when at least one pair of means has a statistically significant difference, but it does not tell which pair.

Let us elaborate just a bit on how ANOVA works. ANOVA uses some complicated formulas, and we have found from experience that market researchers do not memorize them. Instead, a researcher understands the basic purpose of ANOVA and is adept at interpreting ANOVA output. Let's assume that we have three groups, A, B, and C. In concept, ANOVA performs all possible independent samples *t* tests for significant differences between the means, comparing, in our A, B, C example, A:B, A:C, and B:C. ANOVA is very efficient because it makes these comparisons simultaneously, not individually as you would need to do if you were running independent samples *t* tests. ANOVA's null hypothesis is that no single pair of means is significantly different. Because multiple pairs of group means are being tested, ANOVA uses the *F* test statistic, and the significance level (sometimes referred to as the *p value*) that appears on the output in this *F* test, is the probability of support for the null hypothesis.

Here is an example that will help you to understand how ANOVA works and when to use it. A major department store conducts a survey, and one of the questions on the survey is "In what department did you last make a purchase for over $250?" There are four departments where significant numbers of respondents made these purchases: (1) electronics, (2) home & garden, (3) sporting goods, and (4) automotive. Another question on the survey is "How likely are you to purchase another item for over $250 from that department the next time?" The respondents indicate how likely they are to do this on a 7-point scale where 1 = "very unlikely" and 7 = "very likely." It is easy to calculate the mean of how likely each group is to return to the department store and purchase another major item from that same department.

ANOVA is a "flag-waving" procedure that signals when at least one pair of means is significantly different.

The researcher who is doing the analysis decides to compare these means statistically, so five different independent samples *t* tests of the significance of the differences are

TABLE 17.2 Results of Five Independent Samples *t* tests of How Likely Customers Are to Return to the Same Department to Make Their Next Major Purchase

Groups Compared	Group Means*	Significance	
Electronics:Home & Garden	5.1:5.3	.873	
Electronics:Sporting Goods	5.1:5.6	.469	
Electronics:Automotive	5.1:2.2	(.000)	Significant difference between the two departments
Home & Garden:Sporting Goods	5.3:5.6	.656	
Home & Garden:Automotive	5.3:2.2	(.000)	
Sporting Goods:Automotive	5.6:2.2	(.000)	

*Based on a scale where 1= "very unlikely" and 7= "very likely."

performed. Table 17.2 summarizes the findings. It may take a few minutes, but if you examine Table 17.2, you will see that the automotive department's mean is significantly different and lower than the repurchase likelihood means of the other three departments. Also, there is no significant difference in the other three department patrons' means. In other words, there is a good indication that the patrons who bought an item for more than $250 from the department store's automotive department are not as satisfied with the product as are customers who bought large-ticket items from any other department.

> The Sig. value in the ANOVA table indicates the level of significance.

Now, look at Table 17.3. It is an abbreviated ANOVA output. Instead of looking at several *p* values as in Table 17.2, all the researcher needs to do is to look at the significance level (Sig.) for the *F* test, our signal flag. It is .000, which is less than .05, meaning that there is at least one significant difference. So now it is worth the researcher's time and effort to look at the next table to find the significant difference(s). This table is arranged so that the means that are not significantly different fall in the same column, while those that are significantly different fall in separate columns, and each column is identified as a unique subset. The means are arranged in the second table from the lowest mean to the highest mean, and it is immediately apparent that the automotive department has a problem.

> ANOVA is much more advantageous than running multiple *t* tests of the significance of the differences between means.

ANOVA has two distinct advantages over performing multiple *t* tests of the significance of the differences between means. First, it immediately notifies the researcher if there is any significant difference because all the researcher needs to do is to look at the "Sig."

TABLE 17.3 Results of ANOVA of How Likely Customers Are to Return to the Same Department to Make Their Next Major Purchase

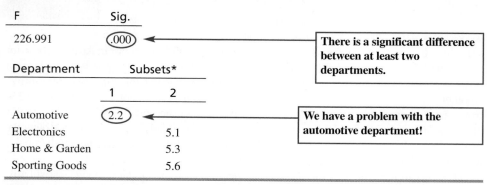

F	Sig.		
226.991	(.000)		There is a significant difference between at least two departments.

Department	Subsets*		
	1	2	
Automotive	(2.2)		We have a problem with the automotive department!
Electronics		5.1	
Home & Garden		5.3	
Sporting Goods		5.6	

*Means in the same column are not significantly different; means in different columns are significantly different.

value, our signal flag. Second, in our example, it arranges the means so the significant differences can be located and interpreted easily.

To elaborate, this Sig(nificance) value is the flag that we referred to earlier and in Marketing Research Insight 17.1. When the flag is waving, the researcher is then justified at looking at each pair of means to find which one(s) are significantly different. Once you learn how to read SPSS ANOVA output, it is quite easy to identify these cases. Of course, if the *F* statistic *p* value flag is not waving, meaning that the *p* value is *greater than .05*, it is a waste of time to look at the differences between the pairs of means, as no difference will be statistically significant at the 95% level of confidence.

How to Determine Statistically Significant Differences Among Group Means

As we mentioned in passing earlier, there are **"post hoc" tests**, which are options that are available to determine where the pair(s) of statistically significant differences between the means exist(s). As you will soon see in our SPSS example, there are over a dozen of these to choose from, including Scheffe's and Tukey's that you may recognize from a statistics course. It is beyond the scope of this book to provide a complete delineation of the various types of tests. Consequently, only one test, Duncan's multiple range test, will be used as an illustration of how the differences may be determined. **Duncan's multiple range test** provides output that is mostly a "picture" of what pair(s) of means are significantly different, and it is much less statistical than most of the other post hoc tests, so we have chosen to use it here for this reason. The picture provided by the Duncan's post hoc test is the arrangement of the means as you saw them in Table 17.3.

The Duncan multiple range test is our preferred post hoc test because its output is easy to interpret.

Your Integrated Case

ADVANCED AUTOMOBILE CONCEPTS: HOW TO RUN ANALYSIS OF VARIANCE WITH SPSS

In The Advanced Automobile Concepts survey, there are several categorical variables that have more than two groups. For example, there are five age categories: between 18 and 24, between 25 and 34, between 35 and 49, between 50 and 64, and 65 and over.

One-way ANOVA in this case is done under the ANALYZE–COMPARE MEANS–ONE-WAY ANOVA menu command sequence illustrated in Figure 17.4. A window opens to set up the ANOVA analysis. The "Dependent list' is where you click in the variable(s) pertaining to the means, and the "Factor" variable is the grouping variable. In our example, the preference for the one-seat, three-wheel hybrid model is our dependent variable, and the "Age Category" is the grouping variable. Figure 17.4 also shows how to select the Duncan's Multiple Range option under the Post Hoc . . . Tests menu. Returning to the selection window and clicking on OK commences the ANOVA procedure.

To run analysis of variance with SPSS, use the ANALYZE–COMPARE MEANS–ONE-WAY ANOVA menu command sequence.

Figure 17.5 is an annotated ANOVA output. The first table contains a number of intermediate and additional computational results, but our attention should be focused on the "Sig." column. Here is the support for the null hypothesis that not one pair of means is significantly different. Since, the Sig. value is .000, we are assured that there is at least one significantly different pair. The next table is the Duncan's test output. Specifically, the table is arranged so the means ascend in size from top left to right bottom, and the columns represent subsets of groups that are significantly different from groups in the other columns. You can immediately see that "between 50 and 64" (2.55), is the lowest group average, and it is significantly different from all other age groups. At the same time, it can be seen that "between 35 and 49," "65 and older," and "between 25 and 34" are all in the same column, signifying that their means are not significantly different from one another. Finally, the "between 18 and 24" age group (4.94) occupies a column by itself, indicating that it is significantly different from all other group means. Plus, since this column is the one on the far right, it is the one with the highest average. We have found that the "late-teens and early twenties" is the age market segment that most prefers the one-seat, three-wheel hybrid model.

FIGURE 17.4

SPSS Clickstream to Perform Analysis of Variance

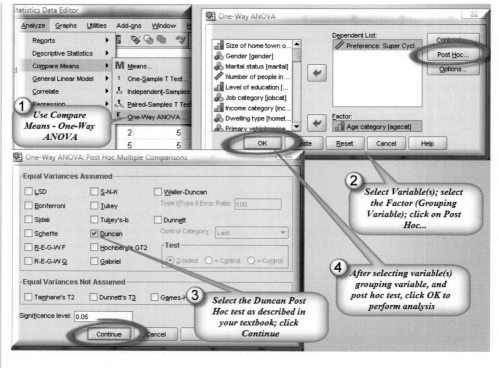

SPSS

SPSS Student Assistant:
Applying ANOVA
(Analysis of Variance)

Interpreting ANOVA (Analysis of Variance)

How do we interpret this finding? The answer lies in our knowledge that if we replicated this survey hundreds of times, we would find these age-group differences exactly as we have found them with this one survey. Granted, the averages' numbers might shift slightly up or down, but the pattern portrayed in the Duncan's multiple range test table in Figure 17.5 would appear in at least 95% of these

FIGURE 17.5

SPSS Output for ANOVA

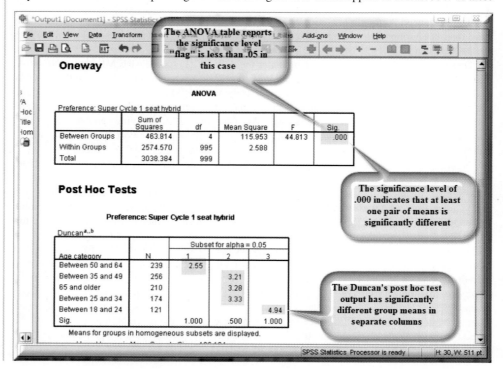

replications. Further, we can say that we have discovered a meaningful differences finding with the "between 18 and 24" age group's mean of 4.94, which is on the positive side of the preference scale and quite a bit higher than the 3.33 range of the next highest group.

There are several "post hoc" tests with ANOVA, and we have used Duncan's multiple range test as an illustration with the Advanced Automobile Concepts survey data.

 ### Perform Analysis of Variance with SPSS

Let's investigate for age-group means differences across all of the hybrid models under consideration at this time by Advanced Automobile Concepts. We recommend that you use the AAConcepts.sav data set and run the ANOVA just described. Make sure that your SPSS output looks like that in Figure 17.5. Then investigate the preference mean differences for the other hybrid models by age group.

n-Way ANOVA

The Advanced Automobile Concepts survey example illustrates what is normally termed **one-way ANOVA** because only one independent factor is used to set up the groups. However, it is not unusual to look at two or more grouping factors simultaneously, in which case one would use **_n_-way ANOVA**. For example, a manager might decide to use age groups and occupation classifications at the same time to test for differences. Or, with a test market experiment, the researcher might want to see the effect of a high versus a low price in newspaper versus billboard advertising. The overlaying of various independent factors permits the marketing researcher to investigate "interaction effects." **Interaction effects** are cases in which the independent factors are operating in concert and are simultaneously affecting the means of the groups. Conceptually, *n*-way ANOVA operates identically to the one-way ANOVA regardless of the number of treatment classification schemes being used. Of course, the formulas and computations are more complicated. We suggest that you refer to more advanced sources if you are interested in using *n*-way ANOVA.

n-way ANOVA allows you to test multiple grouping variables at the same time.

REPORTING GROUP DIFFERENCES TESTS TO CLIENTS

Finding significant differences is exciting to marketing researchers because it means that the researcher will have something that is potentially very useful to report to the client. Remember, market segmentation is very prevalent, and whenever significant differences are found, they may represent important market segmentation implications. However, in the bowels of a long marketing research report, differences may not be obvious to the client, especially if the researcher does not take care to highlight them. Marketing Research Insight 17.5 describes how researchers can use table organization and arrangement to present differences findings in a succinct and useful manner.

DIFFERENCES BETWEEN TWO MEANS WITHIN THE SAME SAMPLE (PAIRED SAMPLE)

Statisticians developed differences tests long before marketers adopted market segmentation, and there is a final difference test to describe in this chapter that is not used for market segmentation purposes. Occasionally, a researcher will want to test for differences between the *means for two variables* within the same sample. For example in our pharmaceuticals company cold remedy situation described earlier in this chapter, a survey can be

MARKETING RESEARCH INSIGHT   Practical Application

17.5 Guidelines for the Reporting of Differences Tests

In reporting group differences to clients, marketing researchers usually construct a **group comparison table** that summarizes the significant differences in an efficient manner. In the case of two-group comparison tables, the presentation is made side-by-side where the groups are columns and the rows are the variables where significant differences are found. Depending on the objectives of the research, it is perfectly acceptable to combine percentage differences and mean differences in the same table. Of course, it is incumbent on the marketing researcher to design a table that communicates the differences with a minimum of confusion. Study the following example of two-group differences found in a survey for the Subshop.

Differences Between Female and Male Customers of the Subshop

Item	Females	Males
Menu Items Typically Purchased		
Alcoholic beverage	*14%*	*37%*
Large-size sandwich	*24%*	*59%*
Salad	*53%*	*13%*
Rating of the Subshop*		
Value for the price	*5.2*	*6.1*
Fast service	*4.5*	*5.2*
Overall satisfaction with the Subshop**	*4.9*	*5.5*
Use Subshop Promotions		
Use Subshop coupons	*23%*	*5%*
Belong to Subshop frequent-buyer club	*33%*	*12%*

*Based on a rating scale where 1 = "poor" and 7 = "excellent."
**Based on rating scale where1 = "very unsatisfied" and 7 = "very satisfied."

In this group comparison table, it can be immediately seen that male and female customers of the Subshop are being compared and that there are four areas of comparison: menu items purchased, ratings of the Subshop's features, overall satisfaction, and use of promotions. There would be an indication in the text of the report or perhaps a footnote to the table relating that only differences at the (for example) 95% level of significance are reported in the table.

When the researcher is reporting differences found from ANOVA, the table presentation becomes more challenging as there can be overlaps between nonsignificant differences and significant differences. For the purposes of this textbook, we recommend that the researcher use a modification of the Duncan's multiple range post hoc table.

Subshop Performance Differences Between Customer Types

Subshop Feature*	Sit-down Customers	Take-out Customers	Drive-through Customers
Fast service	*5.4*	*6.2*	
Value for the price	*6.2*	*5.5*	*5.0*
Friendly waitstaff	*5.1*	*4.0*	

*Based on a rating scale where 1 = "poor" and 7 = "excellent."

In this group comparison table, three types of customers are being compared, and the researcher has found significant differences for three different Subshop features. In the fast-service rating, the Take-out and Drive-through customer groups are not different, but the Sit-down customers rate the service slower than either of the other groups. In the value-for-the-price rating, all three group means are significantly different. The Sit-down customers' average rating for friendly waitstaff is higher than the average for the Take-out and Drive-through customers, which are not significantly different. Notice that where nonsignificant differences are reported, the group cells are merged and the average of the two groups combined is indicated so that the client will not focus on nonsignificant arithmetic differences.

You can test the significance of the difference between two means for two different questions answered by the same respondents using the same scale.

used to determine "How important is it that your cold remedy relieves your . . ." using an scale of 1 = "not important" and 10 = "very important" for each cold symptom. The question then becomes are any two average importance levels significantly different? To determine the answer to this question, we must perform a **paired samples test for the differences between two means**, which is a test to determine if two means of two different questions using the same scale format, and answered by the same respondents in the sample, are significantly different. Of course, the *variables must be measured on the same metric scale*; otherwise, the test would be analyzing differences between variables that are logically incomparable such as the number of dollars spent versus the number of miles driven.

But the same respondents answered both questions, so you do not have two independent groups. Instead, you have two independent questions with one group. The logic and equations we have described still apply, but there must be an adjustment factor because only one sample is involved. We do not provide the equations, but in the following SPSS section we describe how to perform and to interpret a paired samples *t* test.[11]

Your Integrated Case

THE ADVANCED AUTOMOBILE CONCEPTS SURVEY: HOW TO PERFORM A PAIRED SAMPLES SIGNIFICANCE OF DIFFERENCES BETWEEN MEANS TEST WITH SPSS

With the paired samples test, we can test the significance of the difference between the mean of any two questions by the same respondents in our sample. Let's take a critical decision that Nick Thomas may have to address, namely, if Zen Motors agrees to fund the development of only one of the four-door Advanced Automobile Concepts hybrids, which one is more popular? On the surface, it looks like the standard-size four-door model is the winner, with an average preference of 4.96, whereas the economy-size four-door model hybrid's preference average is 3.50. However, if this difference is not statistically significant, the apparent difference will evaporate in the face of a single replication of the survey. Using a paired samples differences test, one can determine the statistical significance.

The SPSS clickstream sequence to perform a paired samples *t* test of the significance of the differences between means is displayed in Figure 17.6. As you can see, you begin with the ANALYZE–COMPARE MEANS–PAIRED SAMPLES T-TEST . . . menu sequence. This sequence opens up the selection menu, and via cursor clicks, you can select "Preference: Standard 4 seat hybrid" and "Preference: Economy 4 seat hybrid" as the variable pair to be tested. This sets up the *t* test, and a click on OK executes it.

To test the significance of difference between two means for questions answered by the same respondents, use the SPSS ANALYZE–COMPARE MEANS– PAIRED SAMPLES T-TEST . . . menu sequence.

FIGURE 17.6

Clickstream to Obtain a Paired Samples *t*-Test

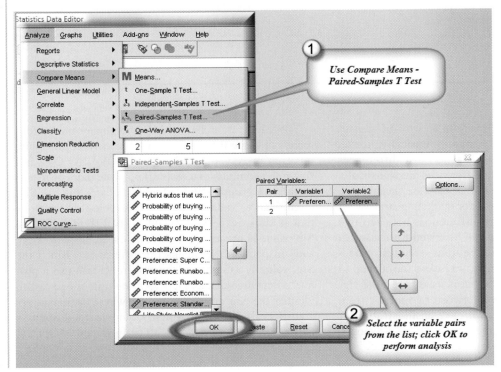

FIGURE 17.7

SPSS Output for a Paired Samples *t*-Test

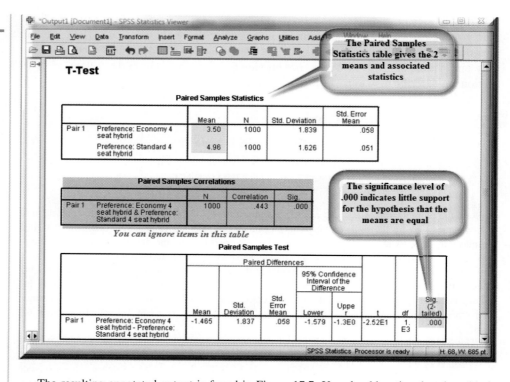

The resulting annotated output is found in Figure 17.7. You should notice that the table is similar, but not identical, to the independent samples output. The relevant information includes (1) 1,000 respondents gave answers to each statement and were analyzed; (2) the means for standard size and economy size are 4.96 and 3.50, respectively; (3) the computed *t* value is -25.221; and (4) the two-tailed significance level is 0.000. In other words, the test gives almost no support for the null hypothesis that the means are equal. The standard size is definitely preferred over the economy size.

SPSS Student Assistant: Assessing Differences Between Means for 2 Questions (Paired)

Summary

The chapter began with a discussion on why differences are important to marketing managers. Basically, market segmentation implications underlie most differences analyses. It is important that differences are statistically significant, but it is also vital that they are meaningful, stable, and an actionable basis for marketing strategy.

We then described how differences between two percentages in two samples can be tested for statistical significance. Then we described the same test procedure using means. In addition, you were introduced to the *t* test procedure in SPSS that is used to test the significance of the differences between two means from two independent samples. We gave an illustration of how to use SPSS for this analysis using the Advanced Automobile Concepts data set.

When a researcher wishes to compare the various means of more than two groups, the correct procedure involves analysis of variance, or ANOVA. ANOVA is a flagging technique that tests all possible pairs of means for all the groups involved and indicates via the Sig. (significance) value in the ANOVA table if at least one pair is statistically significant in its difference. If the Sig. value is greater than .05, the researcher will waste time inspecting the means for differences. But if the Sig. value is .05 or less, the researcher can use a post hoc procedure such as Duncan's multiple range test to identify the pair or pairs of groups where the means are significantly different. Finally, you learned about a paired samples test and how to perform and interpret it using SPSS.

Key Terms

Statistical significance of
   differences 504
Meaningful difference 506
Stable difference 506
Actionable difference 506
t test 507
z test 507
Null hypothesis 509

Significance of differences between
   two percentages 509
Significance of differences between
   two means 513
ANOVA (analysis of variance) 517
Signal-flag procedure 519
Post hoc tests 521
Duncan's multiple range test 521

One-way ANOVA 523
n-way ANOVA 523
Interaction effects 523
Group comparison table 524
Paired samples test for the
   differences between two
   means 524

Review Questions/Applications

1. What are differences and why should market researchers be concerned with them? Why are marketing managers concerned with them?

2. What is considered to be a "small sample," and why is this concept of concern to statisticians? To what extent do market researchers concern themselves with small samples? Why?

3. When a market researcher compares the responses of two identifiable groups with respect to their answers to the same question, what is this called?

4. With regard to differences tests, briefly define and describe each of the following:
   a. Null hypothesis
   b. Sampling distribution
   c. Significant difference

5. Relate the formula and identify each formula's components in the test of significant differences between two groups when the question involved is
   a. A "yes/no" type
   b. A metric scale-type question

6. Are the following two sample results significantly different?

Sample One	Sample Two	Confidence Level	Your Finding?
Mean: 10.6	Mean: 11.7	95%	
Std. dev.: 1.5	Std. dev.: 2.5		
$n = 150$	$n = 300$		
Percent: 45%	Percent: 54%	99%	
$n = 350$	$n = 250$		
Mean: 1,500	Mean: 1,250	95%	
Std. dev.: 550	Std. dev.: 500		
$n = 1,200$	$n = 500$		

7. When should one-way ANOVA be used and why?

8. When a researcher finds a significant F value in analysis of variance, why can it be considered a "signal-flag" device?

9. What is a paired samples test? Specifically how are the samples "paired"?

10. The circulation manager of the *Daily Advocate* commissions a market research study to determine what factors underlie the attrition in circulation. Specifically, the survey is designed to compare current *Daily Advocate* subscribers with those who have dropped their subscriptions in the past year. A telephone survey is conducted with both sets of individuals. Following is a summary of the key findings from the study.

Item	Current Subscribers	Lost Subscribers	Significance
Length of residency in the city	20.1 yrs	5.4 yrs	.000
Length of time as a subscriber	27.2 yrs	1.3 yrs	.000
Watch local TV news program(s)	87%	85%	.372
Watch national news program(s)	72%	79%	.540
Obtain news from the Internet	13%	23%	.025

(*continued*)

Item	Current Subscribers	Lost Subscribers	Significance
Satisfaction* with . . .			
Delivery of newspaper	5.5	4.9	.459
Coverage of local news	6.1	5.8	.248
Coverage of national news	5.5	2.3	.031
Coverage of local sports	6.3	5.9	.462
Coverage of national sports	5.7	3.2	.001
Coverage of local social news	5.8	5.2	.659
Editorial stance of the newspaper	6.1	4.0	.001
Value for subscription price	5.2	4.8	.468

*Based on a 7-point scale where 1 = "very dissatisfied" and 7 = "very satisfied."

Interpret these findings for the circulation manager.

11. A researcher is investigating different types of customers for a sporting goods store. In a survey, respondents have indicated how much they exercise in approximate minutes per week. These respondents have also rated the performance of the sporting goods store across 12 difference characteristics, such as good value for the price, convenience of location, helpfulness of the sales clerks, and so on. The researcher used a 1–7 rating scale for these 12 characteristics where 1 = "poor performance" and 7 = "excellent performance." How can the researcher investigate differences in the ratings based on the amount of exercise reported by the respondents?

12. A marketing manager of *Collections, Etc.,* a Web-based catalog sales company, uses a segmentation scheme based on the incomes of target customers. The segmentation system has four segments: (1) low income, (2) moderate income, (3) high income, and (4) wealthy. The company database holds information on every customer's purchases over the past several years, and the total dollars spent at *Collections, Etc.* is one of the prominent variables. Using Microsoft Excel on this database, the marketing manager finds that the average total dollar purchases for the four groups are as follows:

Market Segment	Average Total Dollar Purchases
Low Income	$101
Moderate Income	$120
High Income	$231
Wealthy	$595

Construct a table based on the Duncan's multiple range test table concept discussed in the chapter illustrating that the Low and Moderate Income groups are not different from each other, but the other groups are significantly different from one another.

13. How would a grocery store chain company go about constructing and validating a market segmentation system? Take the possible segmentation variables of family type (single, couple, or with children) and occupation (skilled labor, professional, or retired). Indicate the steps you would follow and any considerations you would take into account as a researcher investigating whether using these two demographic variables as the basis is a useful segmentation system for the grocery store chain company.

CASE 17.1

THE PETS, PETS, AND PETS TEAM PROJECT (PART II)

(Part I (Case 16.1) of this case is on pages 497. You do not need to read Part I to answer Part II.)

Marsha and Josh are working on the differences analysis of the marketing research team project survey they did for Pets, Pets, and Pets. However, Josh, the student-athlete, blew out his knee running bases, and he is scheduled for reconstructive surgery. Because Josh is on crutches, he and Marsha are communicating by cell phone. Josh says, "I have been missing Dr. Z's marketing research class because of doctor appointments. But I bought a laptop and installed SPSS, so I am good to go on our analysis."

Marsha responds, "Great, I'll e-mail over the SPSS file and a document indicating what we have decided to do for analysis. It is due tomorrow morning with another presentation. You do the analysis, interpret it, and send it back to me to put into the PowerPoint file."

Josh says, "Okay, send it on over."

Thirty minutes later, Marsha's cell phone chirps with Josh calling. Josh says, "Uh, Marsh, I guess I don't understand the differences stuff in our marketing research textbook. Can you give me some help?"

Marsha's File Sent to Josh

Variable Code Book for Pets, Pets, & Pets SPSS File

Variable	Response Scale
Times visited PPP in past year	Actual number of times
Amount spent on last visit to PPP	Actual dollar amount rounded to dollars
How likely to buy at PPP next time (1–7 scale)	1–7 scale where:1 = unlikely, 7 = very likely
Number of pets owned	Actual number of pets
Use Pets, Pets, & Pets how often?	1 = do not use regularly; 2 = use regularly
Recall seeing a PPP newspaper ad in the past month?	1 = yes; 2 = no
Income level	1 = below $20,000
	2 = between $20,000 and $40,000
	3 = between $40,000 and $60,000
	4 = between $60,000 and $80,000
	5 = between $80,000 and $100,000
	6 = greater than $100,000

Research Questions

1. Do regular PPP patrons differ from those who are not regular patrons, and if so, how?
2. Do regular PPP patrons recall seeing PPP newspaper advertising more or less than those who do not use PPP regularly?
3. Do PPP customers differ by household income level, and if so how?

Indicate the specific differences statistical tests that should be conducted to answer each of research questions 1, 2, and 3 in the e-mail attachment Marsha sent to Josh. In each of your answers, tell precisely what the grouping variable is, what the variable being used to compare the groups to each other is, and if percentages or means are to be compared.

CASE 17.2

THE HOBBIT'S CHOICE RESTAURANT SURVEY DIFFERENCES ANALYSIS

SPSS

(For necessary background on this case, read Case 15.2 on pages 460 and Case 16.2, The Hobbit's Choice Restaurant Survey Inferential Analysis, on pages 499)

Cory Rogers called a meeting with Jeff Dean, which marketing intern Christine Yu attended. At the beginning of the meeting, Cory's wife called with news that their 5-year-old son was having a stomach ache at school, and Cory had to pick him up and take him to the doctor. Cory excused himself, saying, "I am sorry about this, but these things happen when you are a dual-career household.

Christine, sit with Jeff for a bit and find out what questions he has about the survey findings. Then take a shot at the analysis, and we'll meet about it tomorrow afternoon. I am sure that Cory Junior will be over his stomach ailment by then."

After meeting for about 20 minutes, Christine had a list of six questions that Jeff Dean was especially interested in. Christine's notes are below.

Your task in Case 17.2 is to take Christine's role, using The Hobbit's Choice Restaurant survey SPSS data set, perform the proper analysis, and interpret the findings for each of the following questions.

1. Jeff wonders if The Hobbit's Choice Restaurant is more appealing to women than it is to men, or vice versa. Perform the proper analysis, interpret it, and answer Jeff's question.
2. With respect to the location of The Hobbit's Choice Restaurant, is a waterfront view preferred more than a drive of less than 30 minutes?
3. With respect to the restaurant's atmosphere, is a string quartet preferred over a jazz combo?
4. What about unusual entrées versus unusual desserts?
5. In general, elegant restaurants are appealing to higher-income households and are less appealing to lower-income households. Is this pattern the case for The Hobbit's Choice Restaurant?
6. Jeff and Cory speculated that the different geographic areas that they identified by ZIP codes would have different reactions to the prospect of patronizing a new upscale restaurant. Are these anticipated differences substantiated by the survey? Perform the proper analysis and interpret your findings.

CASE 17.3 **Your Integrated Case**

THE ADVANCED AUTOMOBILE CONCEPTS SURVEY
DIFFERENCES ANALYSIS

Cory Rogers called a meeting with Nick Thomas and Celeste Brown attended it. After meeting for about 20 minutes, Celeste understood that the Advanced Automobile Concepts division principals were encouraged by the findings of the survey, which indicated that there is substantial demand for the various types of high-mileage hybrid automobiles under consideration. Depending on development costs, prices, and other financial considerations, it seems that any one or any combination of the hybrid automobiles could be a viable product. The next step in their planning is to identify the target market for each hybrid automobile type under consideration. This step is crucial to market strategy, as it is known that the more precise the target market definition, the more specific and pinpointed can be the marketing strategy. For a first cut at the market segment descriptions, the survey included a number of commonly used demographic factors, which are

*   Gender
*   Marital status
*   Age category
*   Education category
*   Income category
*   Hometown size category

The survey measured the likelihood of buying each hybrid type, but Celeste learned that Nick Thomas of Advanced Automobile Concepts considers preferences to be a better measure because the hybrid model descriptions included seat size, miles per gallon estimates, and some notions about the styling.

Your task is to apply appropriate differences analysis to your AAConcepts.sav SPSS data set to determine the target market descriptions for each of the five possible hybrid models:

1. Super cycle one-seat; 120+ mpg city
2. Runabout Sport two-seat; 90 mpg city, 80 mpg highway
3. Runabout with Luggage two-seat; 80 mpg city, 70 mpg highway
4. Economy four-seat; 70 mpg city, 60 mpg highway
5. Standard four-seat; 60 mpg city, 50 mpg highway

Learning Objectives

- To learn what is meant by an "association" between two variables

- To examine various relationships that may be construed as associations

- To understand where and how cross-tabulations with chi-square analysis are applied

- To become familiar with the use and interpretation of correlations

- To learn how to obtain and interpret cross-tabulations, chi-square findings, and correlations with SPSS

Where We Are

1 Establish the need for marketing research
2 Define the problem
3 Establish research objectives
4 Determine research design
5 Identify information types and sources
6 Determine methods of accessing data
7 Design data-collection forms
8 Determine the sample plan and size
9 Collect data
▶ 10 Analyze data, and
11 Prepare and present the final research report.

How Qualtrics Provides the "Total" Package

Scott Smith, Ph.D., the founder of Qualtrics.

We help many of our clients at Qualtrics with their marketing research projects. We do much more than help with the design of their questionnaires. In working closely with our clients, we often see that they are interested in knowing answers to such questions as "Which package design is most effective in increasing awareness of our product on supermarket shelves?" "What type of pre-store opening promotion is most effective in producing sales during Grand Openings?" "Which customer demographic is most strongly related to product purchase/nonpurchase?" "Which type of sales training method results in the least salesforce turnover?" These are just a few of the questions our clients have in which they are really asking to understand the association between two variables. Which

Visit Qualtrics at www.qualtrics.com.

"type of pre-store promotion" is associated with "sales"? "Which package design is associated with the level of awareness?" In these examples, we have two variables and we wish to know if they are associated.

Marketing research projects can be conducted that will answer these questions. When marketing researchers collect the data needed to answer the questions, they want to know if the pattern of association revealed in the data, if any, is statistically significant. That is, does the pattern revealed in the sample data, exist in the population? Fortunately, statisticians have given us some tools to answer this question. You will learn about these tools in this chapter.

—Scott Smith, Ph.D.
Founder, Qualtrics, Inc.

This chapter illustrates the usefulness of statistical analyses beyond simple descriptive measures, statistical inference, and differences tests. Often, as described in the opening comments by Qualtrics founder Scott Smith, marketers are often interested in relationships among variables. For example, Frito-Lay wants to know what kinds of people, and under what circumstances, choose to buy Cheetos, Fritos, Lay's potato chips, and any of the other items in the Frito-Lay line. The Pontiac Division of General Motors wants to know what types of individuals would respond favorably to the various style changes proposed for the Solstice. A newspaper wants to understand the lifestyle characteristics of its subscribers so that it can modify or change sections in the newspaper to better suit its audience. Furthermore, the newspaper desires information about various types of subscribers in order to communicate to its advertisers and help them in designing copy and placing advertisements within the various newspaper sections. For all of these cases, statistical procedures, termed associative analyses, are available to determine the answers to these questions. **Associative analyses** determine whether stable relationships exist between two variables; they are the central topic of this chapter.

We begin the chapter by describing the four different types of relationships possible between two variables. Then we describe cross-tabulations and indicate how a cross-tabulation can be used to determine whether or not a statistically significant association exists between the variables. From cross-tabulations, we move to a general discussion of correlation coefficients, and we illustrate the use of Pearson product moment correlations. As in our previous analysis chapters, we show you SPSS steps to perform these analyses and the resulting output.

Associative analyses determine whether stable relationships exist between two variables.

TYPES OF RELATIONSHIPS BETWEEN TWO VARIABLES

In order to describe a relationship between two variables, we must first remind you of the scale characteristic called *description* that we introduced to you in Chapter 10. Every scale has unique descriptors, sometimes called *levels*, that identify the different locations on that scale. The term *levels* implies that the scale is metric—namely, interval or ratio—whereas the term *labels* implies that the scale is not metric—typically, nominal. A simple label is a "yes" or a "no"; for instance, a respondent is labeled as a buyer (yes) or a nonbuyer (no) of a particular product or service. Of course, if the researcher measured how many times a respondent bought a product, the level would be the number of times and the scale would be metric, because this scale would satisfy the assumptions of a ratio scale.

A **relationship** is a consistent and systematic linkage between the levels or labels for two variables. This linkage is statistical, not necessarily causal. A causal linkage is one in which one variable has certainly affected the other one, but with a statistical linkage the relationship is not certain, because some other variable might have had some influence. Nonetheless, statistical linkages or relationships often provide us with insights that lead to understanding even though they are not cause-and-effect relationships. For example, if we found a relationship that 9 out of 10 bottled water buyers purchased "Vitaminwater," we understand that the ingredients are important to these buyers.

Associative analysis procedures are useful because they determine if there is a consistent and systematic relationship between the presence (label) or amount (level) of one variable and the presence (label) or amount (level) of another variable. There are four basic types of relationships between two variables: nonmonotonic, monotonic, linear, and curvilinear. A discussion of each follows.

A relationship is a consistent and systematic linkage between the levels or labels for two variables.

The fact that most tourists at sunny beach resorts use sun block is a nonmonotonic relationship.

Nonmonotonic Relationships

A **nonmonotonic relationship** is one in which the presence (or absence) of one variable is systematically associated with the presence (or absence) of another variable. The term *nonmonotonic* means essentially that although there is no discernible direction to the relationship, a relationship does exist. For example, McDonald's, Burger King, and Wendy's all know from experience that morning customers typically purchase coffee, whereas noon customers typically purchase soft drinks. The relationship is in no way exclusive—there is no guarantee that a morning customer will always order a coffee or that an afternoon customer will always order a soft drink. In general, though, this relationship exists, as can be seen in Figure 18.1. The nonmonotonic relationship is simply that the morning customer tends to purchase breakfast foods such as eggs, biscuits, and coffee, and the afternoon customers tends to purchase lunch items such as burgers, fries, and soft drinks.

In other words, with a nonmonotonic relationship, the presence of one label for a variable tends to indicate the presence of another specific label of another variable: Breakfast diners typically order coffee. Here are some other examples of nonmonotonic relationships: (1) People who live in the suburbs tend to buy lawn mowers but inner-city dwellers do not; (2) tourists in the Florida Keys tend to use sun block, whereas tourists in Anchorage, Alaska typically do not; and (3) Disney movie audience members are typically families, not college students. Again, each example indicates that the presence (absence) of one aspect of some object tends to be joined to the presence (absence) of an aspect of some other object. But the association is very general, and we must state each one by spelling it out verbally. In other words, we know only the general pattern of presence or nonpresence with a nonmonotonic relationship.

A nonmonotonic relationship means two variables are associated, but only in a very general sense.

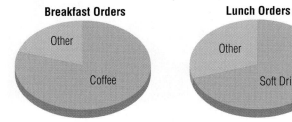

FIGURE 18.1

McDonald's Example of Nonmonotonic Relationship for the Type of Drink Ordered at Breakfast and for Lunch

Monotonic Relationships

A monotonic relationship is one in which the general direction of the relationship between two variables is known.

Monotonic relationships are ones in which the researcher can assign a general direction to the association between the two variables. There are two types of monotonic relationships: increasing and decreasing. Monotonic increasing relationships are those in which one variable increases as the other variable increases. As you would guess, monotonic decreasing relationships are those in which one variable increases as the other variable decreases. You should note that in neither case is there any indication of the exact amount of change in one variable as the other changes. "Monotonic" means that the relationship can be described only in a general directional sense. Beyond this, precision in the description is lacking. The following example should help to explain this concept.

Monotonic relationships can be increasing or decreasing.

It is common knowledge that there is a a monotonic increasing relationship between a child's age and the amount of involvement the child has in the purchase of shoes. As Figure 18.2 illustrates, very young children often have virtually no input into the purchase decision, whereas older children tend to gain more and more control over the purchase decision process until they ultimately become adults and have complete control over the decision. However, no universal rule operates as to the amount of parental influence or the point in time at which the child becomes independent and gains complete control over the decision-making process. It is simply known that younger children have less influence in the decision-making process, and older children have more influence in the shoe purchase decision.

Linear Relationships

A linear relationship means the two variables have a "straight-line" relationship.

Next, we turn to a more precise relationship, and one that is very easy to envision. A **linear relationship** is a "straight-line association" between two variables. Here, knowledge of the amount of one variable will automatically yield knowledge of the amount of the other variable as a consequence of applying the linear or straight-line formula that is known to exist between them. In its general form, a **straight-line formula** is as follows:

Formula for a Straight Line $y = a + bx$

where

y = the dependent variable being estimated or predicted
a = the intercept
b = the slope
x = the independent variable used to predict the dependent variable.

FIGURE 18.2

A Child's Control of His or Her Shoe Purchases

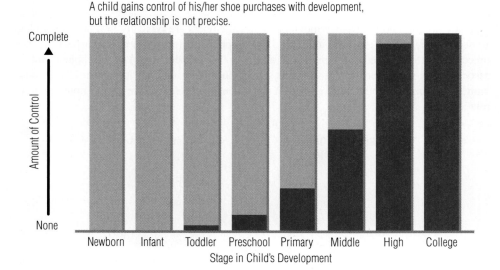

A child gains control of his/her shoe purchases with development, but the relationship is not precise.

Amount of Control — Complete ... None

Stage in Child's Development: Newborn Infant Toddler Preschool Primary Middle High College

The terms *intercept* and *slope* should be familiar to you, but if you are a bit hazy, we describe the straight-line formula in detail in the next chapter. We also clarify the terms *independent* and *dependent* in Chapter 19.

It should be apparent to you that a linear relationship is much more precise and contains a great deal more information than does a monotonic relationship. By simply substituting the values of *a* and *b*, an exact amount can be determined for *y* given any value of *x*. For example, if Jack-in-the-Box estimates that every customer will spend about $5 per lunch visit, it is easy to use a linear relationship to estimate how many dollars of revenue will be associated with the number of customers for any given location. The following equation would be used:

> Linear relationships are quite precise.

Straight-Line Formula Example $y = \$0 + \$5$ times number of customers

So if 100 customers come to a Jack-in-the-Box location, the associated expected total revenues would be $0 plus $5 times 100, or $500 dollars. If 200 customers were expected to visit the location, the expected total revenue would be $0 plus $5 times 200, or $1,000. To be sure, the Jack-in-the-Box location would not derive exactly $1,000 for 200 customers, but the linear relationship shows what is expected to happen, on average.

Curvilinear Relationships

Finally, we turn to **curvilinear relationships**, or those in which one variable is associated with another variable, but the relationship is described by a curve rather than a straight line. In other words, the formula for a curved relationship is used rather than the formula for a straight line. Many curvilinear patterns are possible. For example, the relationship may be an S-shape, a J-shape, or some other curved-shape pattern. An example of a curvilinear relationship with which you should be familiar is the product life-cycle curve that describes the sales pattern of a new product over time, growing slowly during its introduction and then spurting upward rapidly during its growth stage and finally plateauing or slowing down considerably as the market becomes saturated. Curvilinear relationships are beyond the scope of this text; nonetheless, it is important to know they are a type of relationship that can be investigated through the use of special-purpose statistical procedures.

> A curvilinear relationship is some smooth curve pattern that describes an association.

CHARACTERIZING RELATIONSHIPS BETWEEN VARIABLES

Depending on its type, a relationship can usually be characterized in three ways: by its presence, direction, and strength of association. We need to describe these before taking up specific statistical analyses of associations between two variables.

Presence

Presence refers to the finding that a systematic relationship exists between the two variables of interest in the population. Presence is a statistical issue. By this statement, we mean that the marketing researcher relies on statistical significance tests to determine if there is sufficient evidence in the sample to support that a particular association is present in the population. The previous chapter on statistical inference introduced the concept of a null hypothesis. With associative analysis, the null hypothesis states there is no association present in the population and the appropriate statistical test is applied to test this hypothesis. If the test results reject the null hypothesis, then we can state that an association is present in the population (at a certain level of confidence). We describe the statistical tests used in associative analysis later in this chapter.

> The presence of a relationship between two variables is determined by a statistical test.

Direction (or Pattern)

You have seen that in the cases of monotonic and linear relationships, associations may be described with regard to direction. As we indicated earlier, a monotonic relationship may

> Direction is an aspect of a relationship that is positive or negative; pattern refers to the general nature of the relationship.

be increasing or decreasing. For a linear relationship, if *b* (the slope) is positive, then the linear relationship is increasing; and if *b* is negative, then the linear relationship is decreasing. So the direction of the relationship is straightforward with linear and monotonic relationships.

For nonmonotonic relationships, speaking of a positive or a negative direction is inappropriate because we can only describe the general pattern of the relationship in words.[1] It will soon become clear to you that the scaling assumptions of variables having a nonmonotonic association take the place of directional aspects of the relationship. Nevertheless, we can verbally describe the pattern of the association, as we have in our examples, and this takes the place of the concept of direction. Finally, with curvilinear relationships, we can use a formula; however, the formula will define a pattern, such as an S-shape, to characterize the nature of the relationship.

Strength of Association

Strength indicates how consistent the relationship is.

Finally, when present—that is, statistically significant—the association between two variables can be described in terms of its strength, commonly using words such as *strong*, *moderate*, *weak*, or some similar characterization. That is, when a consistent and systematic association is found to be present between two variables, it is then up to the marketing researcher to ascertain the strength of the association. Strong associations are those in which there is a high probability of the two variables' exhibiting a dependable relationship, regardless of the type of relationship being analyzed. A low degree of association, on the other hand, is one in which there is a low probability of the two variables' exhibiting a dependable relationship. The relationship exists between the variables, but it is less evident.

There is an orderly procedure for determining the presence, direction, and strength of a relationship, which is outlined in Table 18.1. As you can see in the table, you must first decide what type of relationship can exist between the two variables of interest. The answer to this question depends on the scaling assumptions of the variables: Low-level (nominal) scales can embody only imprecise, patternlike, relationships, but high-level (interval or ratio) scales can incorporate very precise linear relationships.

Based on scaling assumptions, first determine the type of relationship and then perform the appropriate statistical test.

Once you identify the appropriate relationship type as either monotonic, nonmonotonic, or linear, the next step is to determine whether that relationship actually exists in the population you are analyzing. This step requires a statistical test; we describe the proper test for each of these three relationship types beginning with the next section of this chapter.

TABLE 18.1   Step-by-Step Procedure for Analyzing Relationships

Step	Description
1. **Choose variables to analyze.**	Identify which variables you think might be related.
2. **Determine the scaling assumptions of the chosen variables.**	For purposes of this chapter, both must be either metric (interval or ratio) or categorical (nominal).
3. **Use the correct relationship analysis.**	For two nominal variables, use cross-tabulation; for two metric variables, use correlation.
4. **Determine if the relationship is present.**	If the analysis shows that the relationship is statistically significant, it is present.
5. **If present, determine the direction of the relationship.**	A monotonic (metric scales) relationship will be either increasing or decreasing; a nonmonotonic relationship (nominal scales) will require looking for a pattern.
6. **If present, assess the strength of the relationship.**	With correlation, the size of the coefficient denotes strength; with cross-tabulation, the pattern is subjectively assessed.

After determining that a true relationship does exist in the population by means of the correct statistical test, you then establish its direction or pattern. Again, the type of relationship dictates how you describe its direction. You might have to inspect the relationship in a table or graph, or you might only need to look for a positive or negative sign before the computed statistic.

Finally, the strength of the relationship remains to be judged. Some associative analysis statistics, such as correlations, indicate the strength in a very straightforward manner—that is, just by absolute size. With nominal-scaled variables, however, you must inspect the pattern to judge the strength. We describe this procedure—the use of cross-tabulations—next, and we describe correlation analysis later in this chapter.

CROSS-TABULATIONS

Cross-tabulation and the associated chi-square value that we are about to explain are used to assess if a nonmonotonic relationship exists between two nominal-scaled variables. Remember that nonmonotonic relationships are those in which the presence of one nominal-scaled variable coincides with the presence of another nominal-scaled variable, such as lunch buyers ordering soft drinks with their meals.

Cross-Tabulation Analysis

A researcher investigating the relationship between two nominal-scaled variables typically uses "cross-tabs," or **cross-tabulation table**, defined as a table in which data are compared using a row and column format. A cross-tabulation table is sometimes referred to as an "r × c" (r-by-c) table because it is comprised of rows by columns. The intersection of a row and a column is called a **cross-tabulation cell**.

A cross-tabulation consists of rows and columns defined by the categories classifying each variable.

As an example, let's take a survey where there are two types of individuals: buyers of Michelob Light Beer and nonbuyers of Michelob Light Beer. There are also two types of occupations: professional workers, who might be called "white-collar" employees, and manual workers, who are sometimes referred to as "blue-collar" workers. There is no requirement that the number of rows and columns be equal; we are just using a 2 × 2 cross-tabulation to keep the example as simple as possible. A cross-tabulation table for our Michelob Light beer survey is presented in Table 18.2. Notice that we have identified the four cells by lines for the rows and columns. The columns are in vertical alignment and are indicated in this table as either "Buyer" or "Nonbuyer" of Michelob Light, whereas the rows are indicated as "White Collar" or "Blue Collar" for occupation.

Types of Frequencies and Percentages in a Cross-Tabulation Table

Look at the frequencies table, Table 18.2A. We have annotated the table to help you learn the terminology and to understand how the numbers are computed. The **frequencies table** contains the raw numbers determined from the preliminary tabulation.[2] The upper-left-hand cell is a frequency cell that counts people in the sample who are both white-collar workers and buyers of Michelob Light (152), and the frequency cell to its right identifies the number of individuals who are white-collar workers who do not buy Michelob Light (8). These cell numbers represent raw counts, or frequencies, that is, the number of respondents who possess the quality indicated by the row label as well as the quality indicated by the column label. The cell frequencies can be summed to determine the row totals and the column totals. For example, Buyer/White Collar (152) and Nonbuyer/White Collar (8) sum to 160, and Buyer/White Collar (152) and Buyer/Blue Collar (14) sum to 166. Similarly, the row and column totals sum to equal the grand total of 200. Take a few minutes to become familiar with the terms and computations in the frequencies table, as they will be referred to in the following discussion.

A cross-classification table can have four types of numbers in each cell: frequency, raw percentage, column percentage, and row percentage.

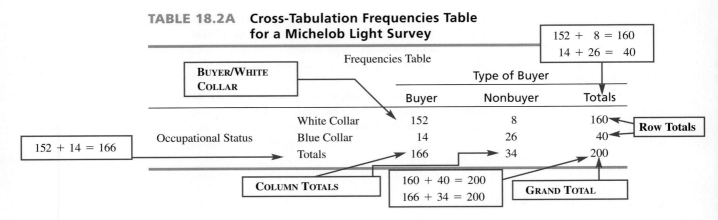

TABLE 18.2A Cross-Tabulation Frequencies Table for a Michelob Light Survey

Table 18.2B illustrates how at least three different sets of percentages can be computed for the cells in the table: raw percentages, column percentages, and row percentages.

The first table in Table 18.2B shows that the raw frequencies can be converted to raw percentages by dividing each by the grand total. The **raw percentages table** contains the percentages of the raw frequency numbers just discussed. The grand total location now has 100% (or 200/200) of the grand total. Above it are 80% and 20% for the raw percentages

Raw percentages are cell frequencies divided by the grand total.

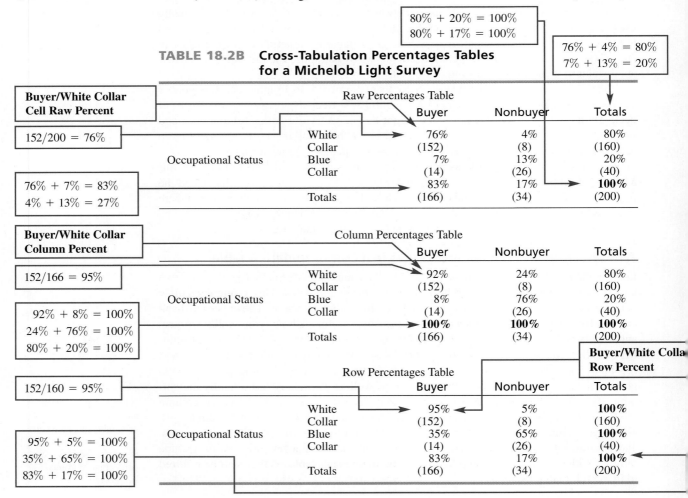

TABLE 18.2B Cross-Tabulation Percentages Tables for a Michelob Light Survey

of white-collar occupation respondents and blue-collar occupation respondents, respectively, in the sample. Divide a couple of the cells by 2000 just to verify that you understand how they are derived. For instance, 152 ÷ 200 = 76%.

Two additional cross-tabulation tables that are more valuable in revealing underlying relationships can be derived. The **column percentages table** divides the raw frequency by its column total raw frequency, as follows:

Formula for a Column Cell Percentage

$$\text{Column cell percentage} = \frac{\text{cell frequency}}{\text{total of cell frequencies in that column}}$$

For instance, it is apparent that of the nonbuyers, 24% were white-collar but 76% were blue-collar respondents. Note the reverse pattern for the buyers group: 92% of white-collar respondents were Michelob Light buyers and 8% were blue-collar buyers. You are beginning to see the nonmonotonic relationship.

The **row percentages table** presents the data with the row totals as the 100% base for each. A row cell percentage is computed as follows:

Formula for a Row Cell Percentage

$$\text{Row cell percentage} = \frac{\text{cell frequency}}{\text{total of cell frequencies in that row}}$$

Now it is possible to see that of the white-collar respondents, 95% were buyers and 5% were nonbuyers. As you compare the row percentages table to the column percentages table, you should detect the relationship between occupational status and Michelob Light beer preference. Can you state it at this time?

Unequal percentage concentrations of individuals in a few cells, as we have in this example, illustrates the possible presence of a nonmonotonic association. If approximately 25% of the sample had fallen in each of the four cells, no relationship would be found to exist—it would be equally probable for any person to be a Michelob Light buyer or nonbuyer and a white- or a blue-collar worker. However, the large concentrations of individuals in two particular cells here suggests that there is a high probability that a buyer of Michelob Light beer is also a white-collar worker, and there is also a tendency for nonbuyers to work in blue-collar occupations. In other words, there is probably an association between occupational status and the beer-buying behavior of individuals in the population represented by this sample. However, as noted in Step 4 of our procedure for analyzing relationships (Table 18.1), we must test the statistical significance of the apparent relationship before we can say anything more about it.

Row (column) percentages are row (column) cell frequencies divided by the row (column) total.

CHI-SQUARE ANALYSIS

Chi-square (χ^2) analysis is the examination of the frequencies of two nominal-scaled variables in a cross-tabulation table to determine whether the variables have a nonmonotonic relationship.[3] The formal procedure for chi-square analysis begins when the researcher formulates a statistical null hypothesis that the two variables under investigation are *not* associated in the population. Actually, it is not necessary for the researcher to state this hypothesis in a formal sense, for chi-square analysis always implicitly takes this hypothesis into account. In other words, whenever we use chi-square analysis with a cross-tabualtion, we always begin with the assumption that no association exists between the two nominal-scaled variables under analysis.[4]

Chi-square analysis assesses nonmonotonic associations in cross-tabulation tables.

Observed and Expected Frequencies

The statistical procedure is as follows. The cross-tabulation table in Table 18.2A contains **observed frequencies**, which are the actual cell counts in the cross-tabulation table. These observed frequencies are compared to **expected frequencies**, which are defined as the

Observed frequencies are the counts for each cell found in the sample.

theoretical frequencies that are derived from this hypothesis of no association between the two variables. The degree to which the observed frequencies depart from the expected frequencies is expressed in a single number called the *chi-square statistic*. The computed chi-square statistic is then compared to a table chi-square value (at a chosen level of significance) to determine whether the computed value is significantly different from zero.

Here's a simple example to help you understand what we just stated. Suppose you perform a blind taste test with 10 of your friends. First, you pour Diet Pepsi in 10 paper cups with no identification on the cup. Next, you assemble your ten friends, and you let each one try a taste from his or her paper cup. Then, you ask each friend to guess whether it is Diet Pepsi or Diet Coke. If your friends guessed randomly, you would expect 5 to guess Diet Pepsi and 5 to guess Diet Coke. This is your null hypothesis: There is no relationship between the diet brand being tested and the guess. But you find that 9 of your friends correctly guess Diet Pepsi, and 1 incorrectly guesses Diet Coke. In other words, you have found a departure from the expected frequencies in your observed frequencies. It looks like your friends can correctly identify Diet Pepsi about 90% of the time. There *seems* to be a relationship, but we are not certain of its statistical significance because we have not done any significance tests. The chi-square statistic is used to perform such a test. We will describe the chi-square test and then apply it to your blind taste test using Diet Pepsi.

> Expected frequencies are calculated based on the null hypothesis of no association between the two variables under investigation.

The expected frequencies are those that would be found if there were no association between the two variables. Remember, this is the null hypothesis. About the only "difficult" part of chi-square analysis is in the computation of the expected frequencies. The computation is accomplished using the following equation:

Formula for an Expected Cross-Tabulation Cell Frequency

$$\text{Expected cell frequency} = \frac{\text{cell row total} \times \text{cell column total}}{\text{grand total}}$$

The application of this equation generates a number for each cell that would have occurred if the study had taken place and no associations existed. Returning to our Michelob Light beer example, you were told that 160 white-collar and 40 blue-collar consumers had been sampled, and it was found that there were 166 buyers and 34 nonbuyers of Michelob Light. The expected frequency for each cell, assuming no association, calculated with the expected cell frequency, is as follows:

Calculations of Expected Cell Frequencies Using the Michelob Beer Example

$$\text{White-collar buyer} = \frac{160 \times 166}{200} = 132.8$$

$$\text{White-collar nonbuyer} = \frac{160 \times 34}{200} = 27.2$$

$$\text{Blue-collar buyer} = \frac{40 \times 166}{200} = 33.2$$

$$\text{Blue-collar nonbuyer} = \frac{40 \times 34}{200} = 6.8$$

Notes:
Buyers total = 166
Nonbuyers total = 34
White-collar total = 160
Blue-collar total = 40
Grand total = 200

The Computed χ^2 Value

> The computed chi-square value compares observed to expected frequencies.

Next, compare the observed frequencies to these expected frequencies. The formula for this computation is as follows:

Chi-square Formula

$$\chi^2 = \sum_{i=1}^{n} \frac{(\text{Observed}_i - \text{Expected}_i)^2}{\text{Expected}_i}$$

where

Observed_i = observed frequency in cell i
Expected_i = expected frequency in cell i
n = number of cells.

Applied to our Michelob beer example,

Calculation of Chi-Square Value (Michelob Example)

$$\chi^2 = \frac{(152 - 132.8)^2}{132.8} + \frac{(8 - 27.2)^2}{27.2}$$
$$+ \frac{(14 - 33.2)^2}{33.2} + \frac{(26 - 6.8)^2}{6.8} = 81.64$$

Notes:
Observed frequencies are in Table 18.2A. Expected frequencies are computed above.

You can see from the equation that each expected frequency is compared to the observed frequency and squared to adjust for any negative values and to avoid the cancellation effect. This value is divided by the expected frequency to adjust for cell size differences, and these amounts are summed across all of the cells. If there are many large deviations of observed frequencies from the expected frequencies, the computed chi-square value will increase; but if there are only a few slight deviations from the expected frequencies, the computed chi-square number will be small. In other words, the computed chi-square value is really a summary indication of how far away from the expected frequencies the observed frequencies are found to be. As such, it expresses the departure of the sample findings from the null hypothesis of no association.

> The chi-square statistic summarizes how far away from the expected frequencies the observed cell frequencies are found to be.

Some researchers think of an expected-to-observed comparison analysis as a "goodness-of-fit" test. It assesses how closely the actual frequencies fit the pattern of expected frequencies. We have provided Marketing Research Insight 18.1 as an illustration of the goodness-of-fit notion.[5]

> Chi-square analysis is sometimes referred to as a "goodness-of-fit" test.

Let us apply this equation to the example of your ten friends guessing about Diet Pepsi or Diet Coke. We already agreed that if they guessed randomly, you would find 5 guessing for each brand, on a 50–50 split. But if we found an 19–10 vote for Diet Pepsi, you would be inclined to conclude that they could recognize Diet Pepsi. That is, most recognized the cola taste, so they gave the name, Diet Pepsi, that is related to it. Let's use the chi-square formula with observed and expected frequencies to see if the relationship is statistically significant.

To determine the chi-square value, we calculate as follows:

Calculation of Chi-Square Value Using Diet Pespi Taste Test

$$\chi^2 = \sum_{i-1}^{n} \frac{(\text{Observed}_i - \text{Expected}_i)^2}{\text{Expected}_i}$$
$$= \frac{(9 - 5)^2}{5} + \frac{(1 - 5)^2}{5}$$
$$= 6.4$$

Notes:
Observed 9 Correct and 1 Incorrect guess
Expected 5 Correct and 5 Incorrect guesses
(random chance)

Remember, you need to use the frequencies, not the percentages.

Should this boss reward his blue-collar workers with Michelob Light? Cross-tabulation can answer this question.

MARKETING RESEARCH INSIGHT

Practical Application

18.1 "Zeroing in" on Goodness-of-Fit

Can you guess the next number based on the apparent pattern of 1, 3, 5? Okay, what about this series: 1, 6, 11, 16?

In the first series, you realize that 2 was added to determine the next number (1, 3, 5, 7, 9, and so on). You looked at the series and noticed the equal intervals of 2. You then created a mental expectation of the series based on your suspected pattern.

Let us study the second series, which is a bit more difficult. Suppose your first intuition was to add a 3 to the previous number. Here is your expected series and the actual one compared:

Expected	1	4	7	10
Actual	1	6	11	16
Difference	**0**	**2**	**4**	**6**

Oops, not much of a match here. So let's try a 4:

Expected	1	5	9	13
Actual	1	6	11	16
Difference	**0**	**1**	**2**	**3**

Getting closer, but still not there. Now try a 5:

Expected	1	6	11	16
Actual	1	6	11	16
Difference	**0**	**0**	**0**	**0**

You have been performing "goodness-of-fit" tests. Notice that the differences became smaller as you zeroed in on the true pattern. (Catch the pun?) In other words, when the actual numbers are equal to the expected numbers, there is no difference, and the fit is perfect. This is the concept used in chi-square analysis. When the differences are small, you have a good fit to the expected values. When the differences are larger, you have a poor fit, and your hypothesis (the expected number sequence) is incorrect.

The Chi-Square Distribution

Now that you've learned how to calculate a chi-square value, you need to know if it is statistically significant. In previous chapters, we described how the normal curve or z distribution, the F distribution, and Student's t distribution, all of which exist in tables, are used by a computer statistical program to determine level of significance. Chi-square analysis requires the use of a different distribution. The **chi-square distribution** is skewed to the right and the rejection region is always at the right-hand tail of the distribution. It differs from the normal and t distributions in that it changes its shape depending on the situation at hand, but it does not have negative values. Figure 18.3 shows examples of two chi-square distributions.

The chi-square distribution's shape changes depending on the number of degrees of freedom.

FIGURE 18.3

Chi-Square Curve's Shape Depends on its Degrees of Freedom

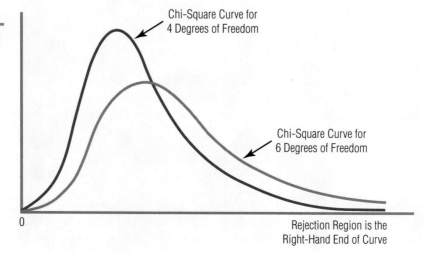

Chi-Square Curve for 4 Degrees of Freedom

Chi-Square Curve for 6 Degrees of Freedom

0

Rejection Region is the Right-Hand End of Curve

The chi-square distribution's shape is determined by the number of degrees of freedom. The figure shows that the more the degrees of freedom, the more the curve's tail is pulled to the right. Or, in other words, the more the degrees of freedom, the larger the calculated chi-square value must be to fall in the rejection region for the null hypothesis.

It is a simple matter to determine the number of degrees of freedom. In a cross-tabulation table, the degrees of freedom are found through the following formula:

Formula for Chi-Square Degrees of Freedom

$$\text{Degrees of freedom} = (r - 1)(c - 1)$$

where

r = the number of rows, and
c = the number of columns.

A table of chi-square values contains critical points that determine the break between acceptance and rejection regions at various levels of significance. It also takes into account the numbers of degrees of freedom associated with each curve. That is, a computed chi-square value says nothing by itself—you must consider the number of degrees of freedom in the cross-tabulation table, because more degrees of freedom are indicative of higher critical chi-square table values for the same level of significance. The logic of this situation stems from the number of cells. With more cells, there is more opportunity for departure from the expected values. The higher table values adjust for potential inflation due to chance alone. After all, we want to detect real nonmonotonic relationships, not phantom ones.

SPSS and virtually all computer statistical analysis programs have chi-square tables in memory and print out the probability of the null hypothesis. Let us repeat this point: The program itself will take into account the number of degrees of freedom and determine the probability of support for the null hypothesis. This probability is the percentage of the area under the chi-square curve that lies to the right of the computed chi-square value. When rejection of the null hypothesis occurs, we have found a statistically significant nonmonotonic association existing between the two variables.

For managers, cross-tabulations are extremely valuable analyses because they very quickly and often clearly communicate the patterns of relationships in the data. When you read Marketing Research Insight 18.2 notice how the patterns are easy to see even in the case of a survey performed in a country whose culture and circumstances are largely unknown to you.

How to Interpret a Chi-Square Result

How does one interpret a chi-square result? Chi-square analysis yields the amount of support for the null hypothesis as if the researcher repeated the study many, many times with independent samples. By now, you should be well acquainted with the concept of many, many independent samples. For example, if the chi-square analysis yielded a 0.02 signficiance level for the null hypothesis, the researcher would conclude that evidence to support the null hypothesis would be found in only 2% of the many, many samples. Since the null hypothesis is not supported, this means there is a significant association.

It must be pointed out that chi-square analysis is simply a method to determine whether a nonmonotonic association exists between two variables. Chi-square does not indicate the nature of the association, and it indicates only roughly the strength of the

The computed chi-square value is compared to a table value to determine statistical significance.

Computer statistical programs look up table chi-square values and print out the probability of support for the null hypothesis.

A significant chi-square means the researcher should look at the cross-tabulation row and column percentages to "see" the association pattern.

In a "blind" taste test, can your friends identify the cola brand, or is it a matter of guessing? Chi-square analysis will answer this question.

MARKETING RESEARCH INSIGHT   **Global Application**

18.2 Use of Exercise Equipment by Women in the United Arab Emirates

Most Westerners have a vague understanding of Arab countries, and it probably surprises you to learn that home exercise equipment is experiencing a mini-boom in at least one Arab country, the UAE. In what might be the first survey on this topic, marketing researchers administered a questionnaire to 400 women living in Dubai, UAE.[6] They used cross-tabulations and chi-square analysis to identify the following significant relationships. Their data have been reworked to create these three cross-tabulation findings.

The cross-tabulations show the relationships between the primary reason for purchasing home exercise equipment (lose weight, look good, or get fit) with three demographic factors.

Cross-Tabulations of Reasons Why Women in the United Arab Emirates Purchase Exercise Equipment

	Primary Reason			
	Lose Weight	Look Good	Get Fit	Total
Occupation				
Students	*73%*	*23%*	*4%*	*100%*
Employees	*11%*	*66%*	*23%*	*100%*
Housewives/other	*63%*	*6%*	*31%*	*100%*
Businesswomen	*8%*	*38%*	*54%*	*100%*

	Primary Reason			
	Lose Weight	Look Good	Get Fit	Total
Religion				
Muslim	*47%*	*31%*	*22%*	*100%*
Christian	*22%*	*55%*	*23%*	*100%*
Hindu	*100%*	*0%*	*0%*	*100%*
Nationality				
Middle East	*57%*	*26%*	*17%*	*100%*
European	*22%*	*61%*	*17%*	*100%*
North American	*7%*	*79%*	*14%*	*100%*
Subcontinent	*41%*	*34%*	*25%*	*100%*

Occupation is commonly used in Western research, and the finding is that UAE female students and housewives buy exercise equipment to lose weight, whereas employees do so to look good, and businesswomen buy the equipment to get fit. The religion and nationality cross-tabulations demographics are unique to many Arab countries that are a mixture of relations and nationalities. The patterns for religion are that Hindu and Muslim women purchase exercise equipment to lose weight, and Christian women in the UAE are purchasing this equipment to look good. Finally, the "to look good" buyers tend to be Europeans or North Americans, while the "to lose weight" buyers tend to be Middle Eastern or Subcontinent citizens.

association by its size. It is best interpreted as a prerequisite to looking more closely at the two variables to discern the nature of the association that exists between them. That is, the chi-square test is another one of our "flags" that tell us whether or not it is worthwhile to inspect all those row and column percentages.

When the computed chi-square value is small, then the null hypothesis, or the hypothesis of independence between the two variables, is generally assumed to be true. It is not worth the marketing researcher's time to focus on such associations because they are more a function of sampling error than they are of meaningful relationships between the two variables. However, when chi-square analysis identifies a relationship with a significance level of .05 or less (the flag is waving), the researcher can be assured that he or she is not wasting time and is actually pursuing a real association, a relationship that truly exists between the two variables in the population. In our Diet Pepsi blind taste test, the chi-square table value for the 95% level of significance is 3.841, and the computed value is 6.4, so the computed value is larger than the critical value. If we used SPSS, the significance level would be reported as .0001, indicating that the relationship is statistically significant.

MARKETING RESEARCH INSIGHT

Practical Application

18.3 Cross-Tabulations Reveal Differences Between Gen X and Gen Y Sports Spectating

Researchers were interested in comparing the way Generation X (people born in the time period of 1965 to 1980) differed from Gen Y (people born in the 1980s and 1990s) with respect to watching professional sports on television.[7] They asked a large sample comprised of both types of individuals if they watched Gravity Games, X Games, Major League Baseball, Gorge Games, the Olympics, boxing, National Football League (NFL) games, golf, NBA games, and so on.

The cross-tabulation tables that resulted for two of these sports follow:

	NFL Games	
	Generation X	Generation Y
Watch	406	713
Do Not Watch	255	779

	NBA Games	
	Generation X	Generation Y
Watch	219	524
Do Not Watch	443	969

For NFL games, the computed chi-square value was large and statistically signficant, meaning that there is a relationship between watching this professional sport on television and the generation: Proportionately, Gen Xer's watch it more (by about 61% to about 48%). But with NBA games, the computed chi-square value was small and not statistically significant, meaning there is no relationship between watching this professional sport on television and the generation: About 33–35% of either generation watch NBA games on television.

 Compute Chi-Square Values

We have described the concepts of observed frequencies, expected frequencies, and computed chi-square value. Plus, we have provided formulas for the latter two concepts. Your task in this Active Learning exercise will be to compute the expected frequencies and chi-square values for two different cross-tabulation tables. Marketing Research Insight 18.3 has a cross-tabulation for a sports marketing survey that compared Generation X with Generation Y television viewers of professional sports. Compute the expected frequencies and chi-square values for each one.

Your Integrated Case

ADVANCED AUTOMOBILE CONCEPTS: ANALYZING CROSS-TABULATIONS FOR SIGNIFICANT ASSOCIATIONS BY PERFORMING CHI-SQUARE ANALYSIS WITH SPSS

We are going to use our Advanced Automobile Concepts survey data to demonstrate how to perform and interpret cross-tabulation analysis with SPSS. You should recall that we have several demographic variables, including gender and marital status. We will take gender as one of the nominal variables. For the second nominal variable, we will take the preferred magazine type. Thus,

FIGURE 18.4

SPSS Clickstream to Create Cross Stabulation Tabulations with Chi-Square Analysis

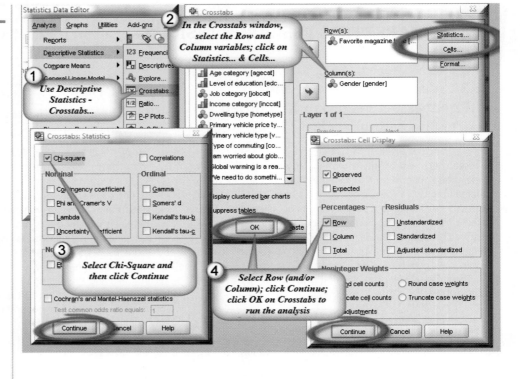

With SPSS, chi-square is an option under the "Crosstabs" analysis routine.

we are investigating the possible association of gender (male versus female) and favorite magazine type (Business & Money, Music & Entertainment, Family & Parenting, Sports & Outdoors, Home & Garden, Cooking, Food, & Wine, Trucks, Cars, & Motorcycles, or News, Politics, & Current Events).

The clickstream command sequence to perform a chi-square test with SPSS is ANALYZE–DESCRIPTIVE STATISTICS–CROSSTABS, which leads to a dialog box in which you can select the variables for chi-square analysis. In our example in Figure 18.4, we have selected Gender as the column variable, and Favorite Magazine type as the row variable. There are three options buttons at the bottom of the box. The Cells . . . option leads to the specification of observed frequencies, expected frequencies, row percentages, column percentages, and so forth. We have opted for just the observed frequencies (raw counts) and the row percentages. The Statistics . . . button opens up a menu of statistics that can be computed from cross-tabulation tables. Of course, the only one we want is the chi-square option.

The resulting output is found in Figure 18.5. In the top table, you can see that we have variable and value labels, and the table contains the raw frequency as the first entry in each cell. Also, the row percentages are reported along with each row and column total. In the second table, there is information on the chi-square analysis result. For our purposes, the only relevant statistic is the "Pearson chi-square," which you can see has been computed to be 23.272. The df column pertains to the number of degrees of freedom, which is 7, and the Asymp. Sig. corresponds to the probability of support for the null hypothesis. Significance in this example is 0.002, which means that there is practically no support for the null hypothesis that Gender and Favorite Magazine type are not associated. In other words, they are related.

With chi-square analysis, interpret the SPSS significance level as the amount of support for *no* association between the two variables being analyzed.

So, SPSS has effected the first step in determining a nonmonotonic association. Through chi-square analysis, it has signaled that a statistically significant association actually exists. The next step is to fathom the nature of the association. Remember that with a nonmonotonic relationship, you must inspect the pattern and describe it verbally. We can ask the question "Which gender is reading what magazine type?" Remember that the pattern is a matter of degree, not "on versus off." If you look at the column percentages in Figure 18.5, you will see some magazine types that garner proportionally more male readers: Business & Money, Home & Garden, and Trucks, Cars, & Motorcycles. Similarly, the magazine type that has proportionately more female readers is Music & Entertainment.

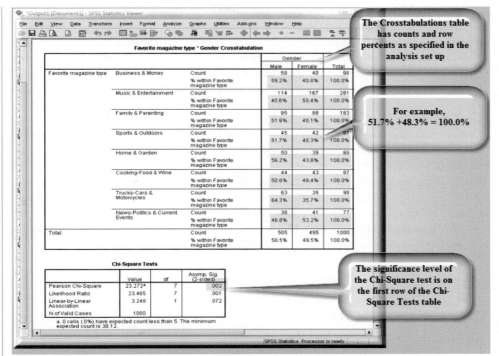

FIGURE 18.5

SPSS Output for Cross Stabulations Tabulations with Chi-Square Analysis

You can interpret this finding in the following way. If Advanced Automobile Concepts wants to communicate to prospective male hybrid automobile buyers, it should use the magazine types they prefer, and if it desires to communicate to prospective female hybrid automobile buyers, it should use the type that they prefer.

In other words, because the significance was less than 0.05, it was worthwhile to inspect and interpret the percentages in the cross-tabulation table. By doing this, we can discern the pattern or nature of the association, and the percentages indicate its relative strength. More importantly, because the relationship was determined to be statistically significant, you can be assured that this association and the relationship you have observed will hold for the population that this sample represents.

SPSS Student Assistant:
Setting Up and Analyzing
Cross tabulations

 Setting up and Analyzing Cross-Tabulations

To make certain that you can perform SPSS cross-tabulation with chi-square analysis, use the Advanced Automobile Concepts SPSS data set and replicate the Gender–Favorite magazine type analysis just described. When you are convinced that you can do this analysis correctly, and interpret the output, use it to see if there is an association between marital status and favorite magazine type. What about marital status and favorite television show type?

REPORTING CROSS-TABULATION FINDINGS TO CLIENTS

It is important to remind you that in Step 4 of the procedure for analyzing relationships outlined in Table 18.1, the researcher must test to determine whether or not a relationship exists. In the present case, this test requires the application of cross-tabulation and chi-square analysis. Practically all statistical analysis programs will perform this test, but with the many cross-tabulations that can be computed quickly by such programs, the neophyte marketing researcher sometimes loses sight of this critical step. So, we will underscore the requirement that the researcher find a statistically significant cross-tabulation relationship before moving on to the presentation phase.

Bar charts can be used to "see" a nonmonotonic relationship.

When we introduced the notion of relationship or association analysis, we noted that characterizing the direction and strength of nonmonotonic relationships that are detected in cross-tabulations with chi-square analysis are not possible because nominal scales are involved. Nominal scales do not have order or magnitude: They are simply categories or labels that uniquely identify the data. As you have learned in our descriptions of the various tables possible with cross-tabulations, percentages are easily prepared and they can usually depict nonmonotonic relationships quite well. In addition, to reveal the nonmonotonic relationships found significant in cross-tabulation tables, researchers often turn to graphical presentations, as pictures will show the relationships very adequately. We have created Marketing Research Insight 18.4 to describe alternative ways to present the findings of cross-tabulation relationships analyses to clients.

MARKETING RESEARCH INSIGHT   Practical Application

18.4 Guidelines for the Reporting of Cross-Tabulation Findings

Using Column and Row Percentages

A question that quickly arises whenever a researcher finds a statistically significant relationship in a cross-tabulation analysis is "Should I report the row percentages, or should I report the column percentages?" The answer to this question depends on the research objective that fostered the nominal questions on the survey. Take, for instance, the following significant cross-tabulation finding for the Subshop:

Column Percentages Table

Size of Sandwich Ordered	Males	Females
Xtr-Large size	*50%*	*5%*
Large size	*40%*	*20%*
Regular size	*10%*	**75%**
Total	*100%*	*100%*

Rows Percentages Table

Size of Sandwich Ordered	Males	Females	Total
Xtr-Large size	**90%**	*10%*	*100%*
Large size	**67%**	*33%*	*100%*
Regular size	*13%*	**87%**	*100%*

If the research question is "Who orders what size of sandwich," the rows percentages table is appropriate, as it indicates that males tend to order the Xtr-Large size and the

Large size (90% and 67%, respectively), whereas females tend to be the ones who order the Regular size (87%). On the other hand, if the research question is "What do males versus females order," then the column percentages table is appropriate, as it indicates that males order Xtr-Large and Large sizes (50% and 40%), whereas females order the Regular size (70%). You should remember that we described a nonmonotonic relationship as an identifiable association where the presence of one variable is paired with the presence (or absence) of another, so the relationships are not 100% versus 0%; rather, it is a degree or relative presence that exists in the population. Study our two presentation tables, and you will notice that we have used shading to help the reader understand how the percentages are computed. That is, the male and female columns are different shades as they express percents within each gender. Similarly, the sandwich size rows are different shades, representing percentages within each sandwich size. We have also used a bold font to emphasize where the percentages reveal especially strong relationships.

Using Stacked Bar Charts

A handy graphical tool that illustrates a nonmonotonic relationship is a stacked bar chart. With a stacked bar chart, two variables are accommodated simultaneously in the same bar graph. Each bar in the stacked bar chart stands for 100%, and it is divided proportionately by the amount of relationship that one variable shares with the other variables. Thus, a stacked bar chart is an excellent visual display of row or column percentages in a cross-tabulation table. For instance, you can see in the following figures that the two Subshop cross-tabulation tables have been used to create the visual displays.

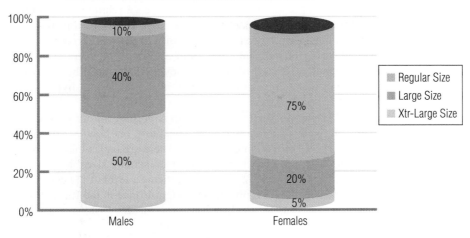

What Sandwich Size do Males and Females Order?

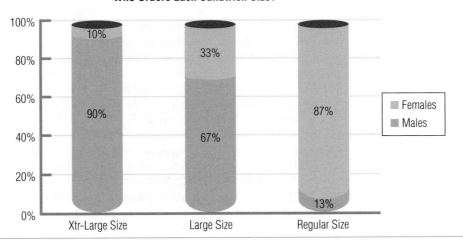

Who Orders Each Sandwich Size?

CORRELATION COEFFICIENTS AND COVARIATION

We now move to the relationship between two metric variables. The **correlation coefficient** is an index number, constrained to fall between the range of −1.0 and +1.0, that communicates both the strength and the direction of a linear relationship between two metric variables. The strength of association between two variables is communicated by the absolute size of the correlation coefficient, and its sign communicates the direction of the association. Stated in a slightly different manner, a correlation coefficient indicates the degree of "covariation" between two variables. **Covariation** is defined as the amount of change in one variable systematically associated with a change in another variable. The greater the absolute size of the correlation coefficient, the greater is the covariation between the two variables, or the stronger their relationship.[8]

Let us take up the statistical significance of a correlation coefficient first. Regardless of its absolute value, a correlation that is not statistically significant has no meaning at all. This is because of the null hypothesis, which states that the population correlation coefficient is equal to zero. If this null hypothesis is rejected (statistically

A correlation coefficient standardizes the covariation between two variables into a number ranging from −1.0 to +1.0.

To use a correlation, you must first establish that it is statistically significant from zero.

significant correlation), then you can be assured that a correlation other than zero will be found in the population. But if the sample correlation is found to be not significant, the population correlation will be zero. Here is a question; if you can answer it correctly, you understand the statistical significance of a correlation: If you repeated a correlational survey many, many times and computed the average for a correlation that was not significant across all of these surveys, what would be the result? (The answer is zero because if the correlation is not significant, the null hypothesis is presumed to be true, and the population correlation is zero.)

Step 4 (Determine if the relationship is present) in our procedure for analyzing relationships in Table 18.1 requires a statistical test, but how do you determine the statistical significance of a correlation coefficient? There are tables that give the lowest value of the significant correlation coefficients for given sample sizes, but most computer statistical programs will indicate the statistical significance level of the computed correlation coefficient. Your SPSS program provides the significance in the form of the probability that the null hypothesis is supported. In SPSS, this is a "Sig." value that we will identify for you when we show you SPSS correlation output. In addition, it will also allow you to indicate a directional hypothesis about the size of the expected correlation just as with a directional means hypothesis test.

Rules of Thumb for Correlation Strength

Rules of thumb exist concerning the strength of a correlation based on its absolute size.

After we have established that a correlation coefficient is statistically significant, we can talk about some general rules of thumb concerning the strength of association. Correlation coefficients that fall between +1.00 and +.81 or between −1.00 and −.81 are generally considered to be "strong." Those correlations that fall between +.80 and +.61 or −.80 and −.61 generally indicate a "moderate" association. Those that fall between +.60 and +.41 or −.60 and −.41 are typically considered to be "low," and they denote a weak association. Finally, any correlation that falls between the range of ±.21 and ±.40 is usually considered indicative of a very weak association between the variables. Next, any correlation that is equal to or less than ±.20 is typically uninteresting to marketing researchers because it rarely identifies a meaningful association between two variables. We have provided Table 18.3 as a reference on these rules of thumb. As you use these guidelines, remember two things. First, we are assuming that the statistical significance of the correlation has been established. Second, researchers make up their own rules of thumb, so you may encounter someone whose guidelines differ slightly from those in the table.[9]

In any case, it is helpful to think in terms of the closeness of the correlation coefficient to 0 or to ±1.00. Statistically significant correlation coefficients that are close to 0 show that there is no systematic association between the two variables, whereas those that are closer to +1.00 or −1.00 express that there is some systematic association between the variables.

TABLE 18.3   **Rules of Thumb about Correlation Coefficient Size***

Coefficient Range	Strength of Association*
±.81 to ±1.00	Strong
±.61 to ±.80	Moderate
±.41 to ±.60	Weak
±.21 to ±.40	Very weak
±.00 to ±.20	None

*Assuming the correlation coefficient is statistically significant.

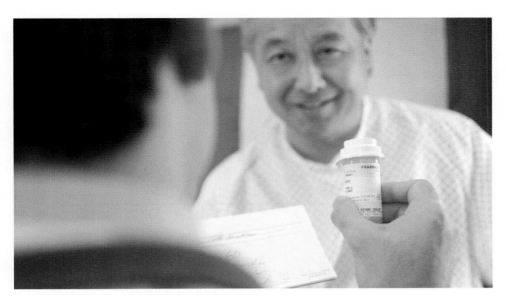

The success of a prescription drug pharmaceutical company may be correlated with how many salespersons it has in the field to talk with doctors.

The Correlation Sign: The Direction of the Relationship

But what about the sign of the correlation coefficient? The sign indicates the direction of the relationship. A positive sign indicates a positive direction; a negative sign indicates a negative direction. For instance, if you found a significant correlation of 0.83 between years of education and hours spent reading *National Geographic* magazine, it would mean that people with more education spend more hours reading this magazine. But if you found a significant negative correlation between years of education and frequency of cigarette smoking, it would mean that more educated people smoke less.

A correlation indicates the strength of association between two variables by its size. The sign indicates the direction of the association.

Graphing Covariation Using Scatter Diagrams

We addressed the concept of covariation between two variables in our introductory comments on correlations. It is now time to present covariation in a slightly different manner. Here is an example: A marketing researcher is investigating the possible relationship between total company sales for Novartis, a leading pharmaceuticals sales company, in a particular territory and the number of salespeople assigned to that territory. At the researcher's fingertips are the sales figures and number of salespeople assigned for each of 20 different Novartis territories in the United States.

It is possible to depict the raw data for these two variables on a scatter diagram such as the one in Figure 18.6. A **scatter diagram** plots the points corresponding to each matched pair of *x* and *y* variables. In this figure, the vertical axis is Novartis sales for the territory, and the horizontal axis contains the number of salespeople in that territory. The arrangement or scatter of points appears to fall in a long ellipse. Any two variables that exhibit systematic covariation will form an ellipse-like pattern on a scatter diagram. Of course, this particular scatter diagram portrays the information gathered by the marketing researcher on sales and the number of salespeople in each territory, and only that information. In actuality, the scatter diagram could have taken any shape, depending on the relationship between the points plotted for the two variables concerned.[10]

A number of different types of scatter diagram results are portrayed in Figure 18.7. Each of these scatter diagram results is indicative of a different degree of covariation. For instance, you can see that the scatter diagram depicted in Figure 18.7(a) is one in which there is no apparent association or relationship between the two variables. The points fail to create any identifiable pattern; instead, they are clumped into a large, formless shape.

Covariation can be examined with use of a scatter diagram.

FIGURE 18.6

**A Scatter
Diagram Showing
Covariation**

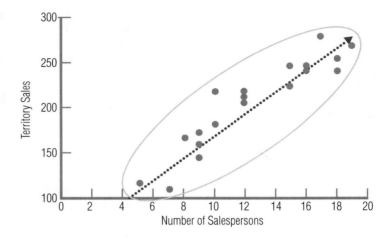

The points in Figure 18.7(b) indicate a negative relationship between variable x and variable y; higher values of x tend to be associated with lower values of y. The points in Figure 18.7(c) are fairly similar to those in Figure 18.7(b), but the angle or the slope of the ellipse is different. This slope indicates a positive relationship between x and y because larger values of x tend to be associated with larger values of y.

Two highly correlated variables will appear on a scatter diagram as a tight ellipse pattern.

What is the connection between scatter diagrams and correlation coefficients? The answer to this question lies in the linear relationship described earlier in this chapter. Look at Figures 18.6 and 18.7(b) and 18.7(c). All form ellipses. Imagine taking an ellipse and pulling on both ends. It would stretch out and become thinner until all of its points fall on a straight line. If you happened to find some data that formed an ellipse with all of its points falling on the axis line and you computed a correlation, you would find it to be exactly 1.0 (+1.0 if the ellipse went up to the right and −1.0 if it went down to the right). Now imagine pushing the ends of the ellipse until it became the pattern in Figure 18.7(a). There would be no identifiable straight line. Similarly, there would be no systematic covariation. The correlation for a ball-shaped scatter diagram is zero because there is no discernable linear relationship. In other words, a correlation coefficient indicates the degree of covariation between two variables, and you can envision this relationship as a scatter diagram. The form and angle of the scatter pattern is revealed by the size and sign, respectively, of the correlation coefficient.

THE PEARSON PRODUCT MOMENT CORRELATION COEFFICIENT

The Pearson product moment correlation coefficient measures the degree of linear association between two variables.

The **Pearson product moment correlation** measures the linear relationship between two interval- and/or ratio-scaled variables such as those depicted conceptually by scatter diagrams. The correlation coefficient that can be computed between the two

FIGURE 18.7

**Scatter Diagrams
Illustrating Various
Relationships**

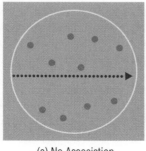
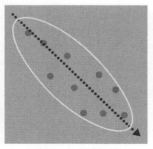
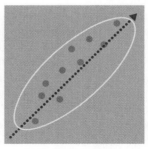

(a) No Association   (b) Negative Association   (c) Positive Association

variables is a measure of the "tightness" of the scatter points to the straight line. You already know that in a case in which all of the points fall exactly on the straight line, the correlation coefficient indicates this as a plus or minus 1. In the case in which it was impossible to discern an ellipse, such as in scatter diagram Figure 18.7(a), the correlation coefficient approximates zero. Of course, it is extremely unlikely that you will find perfect 1.0 or 0.0 correlations. Usually, you will find some value in between that could be interpreted as "strong," "moderate," or "weak" correlation using the rules of thumb given earlier.

The formula for calculating a Pearson product moment correlation is complicated, and researchers never compute it by hand, for they invariably find these on computer output. However, some instructors believe that students should understand the workings of the correlation coefficient formula. We have described this formula and provided an example in Marketing Research Insight 18.5.

MARKETING RESEARCH INSIGHT   *Practical Application*

18.5 How to Compute a Pearson Product Moment Correlation Coefficient

Marketing researchers almost never compute statistics such as chi-square or correlation, but it is insightful to learn about this computation.

The computational formula for Pearson product moment correlations is as follows:

Formula for Pearson Product Moment Correlation

$$r_{xy} = \frac{\sum\limits_{n}^{i=1}(x_i - \bar{x})(y_i - \bar{y})}{n s_x s_y}$$

where

x_i = each x value
$\bar{x}$ = mean of the x values
y_i = each y value
$\bar{y}$ = mean of the y values
n = number of paired cases
s_x, s_y = standard deviations of x and y, respectively.

We briefly describe the components of this formula to help you see how the concepts we just discussed fit in. In the statistician's terminology, the numerator represents the cross-products sum and indicates the covariation or "covariance" between x and y. The cross-products sum is divided by n to scale it down to an average per pair of x and y values. This average covariation is then divided by both standard

deviations to adjust for differences in units. The result constrains r_{xy} to fall between −1.0 and +1.0.

Here is a simple computational example. You have some data on population and retail sales by county for ten counties in your state. Is there a relationship between population and retail sales? You do a quick calculation and find the average number of people per county is 690,000 and the average retail sales are $9.54 million. The standard deviations are 384.3 and 7.8, respectively, and the cross-products sum is 25,154. The computations to find the correlation are:

Calculation of a Correlation Coefficient

$$r_{xy} = \frac{\sum\limits_{i-1}^{n}(x_i - \bar{x})(y_i - \bar{y})}{n s_x s_y}$$

$$= \frac{25{,}154}{10 \times 7.8 \times 384.3}$$

$$= \frac{25{,}154}{29{,}975.4}$$

$$= 0.84$$

Notes:
Cross-products sum = 25,154
$n = 10$
Std. dev. of $x = 7.8$
Std. dev. of $y = 384.3$

A correlation of 0.84 is a high positive correlation coefficient for the relationship. This value reveals that the greater the number of citizens living in a county, the greater the county's retail sales.

A positive correlation signals an increasing linear relationship, whereas a negative correlation signals a decreasing one.

Pearson product moment correlation and other linear association correlation coefficients indicate not only the degree of association but the direction as well, because as we described in our introductory comments on correlations, the sign of the correlation coefficient indicates the direction of the relationship. Negative correlation coefficients reveal that the relationship is opposite: As one variable increases, the other variable decreases. Positive correlation coefficients reveal that the relationship is increasing: Larger quantities of one variable are associated with larger quantities of another variable. It is important to note that the angle or the slope of the ellipse has nothing to do with the size of the correlation coefficient. Everything hinges on the width of the ellipse. (The slope will be considered in Chapter 19 under regression analysis.)

 Date.net: Male Users Chat Room Phobia

Date.net is an online meeting service. It operates a virtural meeting place for men seeking women and women seeking men. Date.net's public chat room is where its members first become aquainted, and if a couple wishes to move into its own private chat room, Date.net creates one and assesses a fee for each minute that the couple is chatting in this private chat room. Recent internal analysis has revealed that women chat room users are considerably less satisfied with Date.net's public chat room than are its male chat room users. This is frustrating to Date.net principals because they know that disappointing public chats will not lead to private chats.

The company commissions an online marketing research company to design a questionnaire that was posted on the Date.net website for 15 days. The marketing research company asked a number of demographic, online chatting, Date.net services usage, and personal satisfaction questions. The survey was a success, as over 5,000 Date.net users filled it out in the time period. Date.net executives requested a separate analysis of male members who use the public chatroom. The research company reported all correlations that are significant at the 0.01 level. Here is a summary of the correlation analysis findings.

Factor		Correlation with Amount of Date.net Chat Room Use
Demographics:	Age	−.68
	Income	−.76
	Education	−.78
	Number of years divorced	+.57
	Number of children	+.68
	Years at present address	−.90
	Years at present job	−.85
Satisfaction with:	Relationships	−.76
	Job/career	−.86
	Personal appearance	−.72
	Life in general	−.50

Factor		Correlation with Amount of Date.net Chat Room Use
Online behavior:	Minutes online daily	+.90
	Online purchases	−.65
	Other chatting time/month	+.86
	Number of e-mail accounts	+.77
Use of Date.net (where 1 = not important and 5 = very important)	Meet new people	+.38
	Only way to talk to women	+.68
	Looking for a life partner	−.72
	Not much else to do	+.59

For each factor, use your knowledge of correlations and provide a statement of how it characterizes the typical Date.net male chat room user. Given your findings, what tactics do you recommend to Date.net to address the low satisfaction with Date.net's public chat room that has been expressed by its female members?

Your Integrated Case

ADVANCED AUTOMOBILE CONCEPTS: HOW TO OBTAIN PEARSON PRODUCT MOMENT CORRELATION(S) WITH SPSS

With SPSS, correlations are computed with the CORRELATE–BIVARIATE feature.

With SPSS, it takes only a few clicks to compute correlation coefficients. Once again, we will use the Advanced Automobile Concepts survey case study. In the survey, we measured preferences for each of the five possible hybrid automobile models on a 7-point interval scale. CMG Research also purchased the lifestyle measures of the respondents. There are six different lifestyles: Novelist, Innovator, Trendsetter, Forerunner, Mainstreamer, and Classic. Each lifestyle type is measured with a 10-point interval scale, where 1 = "does not describe me at all," and 10 = "describes me perfectly." Correlation analysis can be used to find out which lifestyle profile is associated with which hybrid automobile model preference. That is, high positive correlations would indicate that people wanted that hybrid model and that they scored high on the lifestyle type. Conversely, low or negative correlations would signal that people did not match up well at all. We'll only do one of the hybrid model preferences here; you can do the rest in your SPSS integrated case analysis work at the end of the chapter.

So, we need to perform correlation analysis with the preference for the one-seat, three-wheel hybrid model and the six lifestyle types to determine which, if any, lifestyle type is associated with preference for this hybrid model. The clickstream sequence is ANALYZE–CORRELATE–BIVARIATE that leads, as can be seen in Figure 18.8, to a selection box to specify which variables are to be correlated. Note that we have selected the one-seat, three-wheel hybrid model preference and all six lifestyle types. Different types of correlations are optional, so we have selected Pearson's, and the two-tailed test of significance is the default.

The output generated by this command is provided in Figure 18.9. Whenever you instruct SPSS to compute correlations, its output is a symmetric correlation matrix composed of rows and columns that pertain to each of the variables. Each cell in the matrix contains three items (1) the correlation coefficient, (2) the significance level, and (3) the sample size. You can see in Figure 18.9 the computed correlations between "Preference: Super Cycle 1-seat hybrid" and the six lifestyles of Novelist, Innovator, Trendsetter, Forerunner, Mainstreamer, and Classic.

A correlation matrix is symmetric with 1s on the diagonal.

FIGURE 18.8

SPSS Clickstream to Obtain Correlations

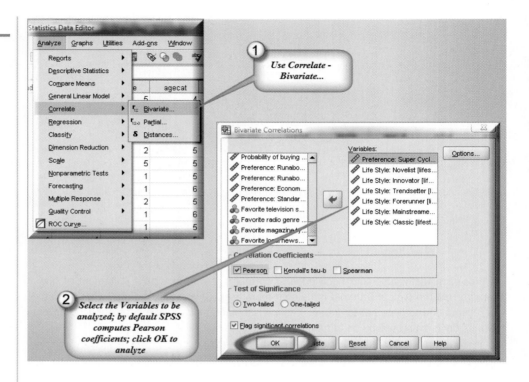

FIGURE 18.9

SPSS Output for Correlations

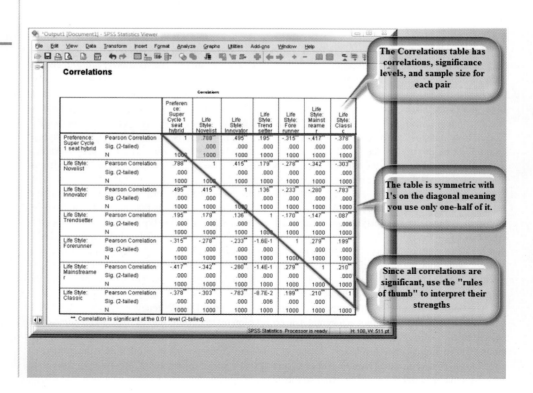

If you look at our correlation printout, you will notice that a correlation of 1.000 is reported where a variable is correlated with itself. This reporting may seem strange, but it serves the purpose of reminding you that the correlation matrix generated with this procedure is symmetric. In other words, the correlations in the matrix above the diagonal 1s are identical to those correlations below the diagonal. With only a few variables, this fact is obvious; however, sometimes several variables are compared in a single run, and the 1s on the diagonal are handy reference points. They all have a "Sig." value of .000 that translates into a .001 or less probability that the null hypothesis of zero correlation is supported.

Since we now know that the correlations are statistically significant, or significantly different from zero, we can assess their strengths. Only one—the .788 for Novelist—approaches .80, which, according to our rules of thumb on correlation size, indicates a moderately strong association. In other words, we only have one lifestyle-type relationship that is stable and fairly strong. The interpretation of this finding is that those who prefer the one-seat, three-wheel, "super cycle" hybrid model are people who tend to buy new products for their novelty and to make themselves seem unique—to "show off" a bit. And, yes, a vehicle like the "super cycle" would certainly be a novelty, turning heads and gaining attention for the owner.

> With correlation analysis, each correlation will have a unique significance level.

Special Considerations in Linear Correlation Procedures

Perhaps because the word *correlation* is used in everyday language, statistical correlations are sometimes misunderstood by clients.[11] Consequently, we have prepared Table 18.4 to summarize and remind you of four cautions to keep in mind when working with correlations. We will discuss each of these cautions in turn.

> **SPSS Student Assistant:** Working with Correlations

To begin, the scaling assumptions underlying linear correlation should be apparent to you, but it does not hurt to reiterate that the correlation coefficient discussed in this section assumes that both variables share interval-scaling assumptions at minimum. If the two variables have nominal-scaling assumptions, the researcher would use cross-tabulation analysis; and if the two variables have ordinal-scaling assumptions, the researcher would opt to use a rank order correlation procedure. (We do not discuss rank order correlation in this chapter, as its use is relatively rare.)

Next, the correlation coefficient takes into consideration only the relationship between two variables. It does not take into consideration interactions with any other variables. In fact, it explicitly assumes that they do not have any bearing on the relationship between the two variables of interest. All other factors are considered to be constant or "frozen" in their bearing on the two variables under analysis.

Third, the correlation coefficient explicity does not assume a **cause-and-effect relationship**, which is a condition of one variable bringing about the other variable. Although you might be tempted to believe that more company salespeople cause more company sales or that an increase in the competitor's salesforce in a territory takes away sales, correlation should not be interpreted to demonstrate such cause-and-effect relationships. Just think of all of the other factors that affect sales: price, product quality, service policies, population, advertising, and more. It would be a mistake to assume that just one factor causes sales. Instead, a correlation coefficient merely investigates the presence, strength, and direction of a linear relationship between two variables.

> Correlation does not demonstrate cause and effect.

TABLE 18.4　Four Cautions When Using Correlation

1. Use correlations only for metric variables (interval or ratio scaling).
2. Correlation assumes that only the two variables involved are relevant: All other variables and factors are considered to be constant.
3. Correlation does not indicate cause and effect, only covariance between the two variables being analyzed.
4. Correlation expresses only the linear relationship between two variables.

Correlation will not detect nonlinear relationships between variables.

Last, the Pearson product moment correlation expresses only linear relationships. Consequently, a correlation coefficient result of approximately zero does not necessarily mean that the scatter diagram that could be drawn from the two variables defines a formless ball of points. Instead, it means that the points do not fall in a well-defined elliptical pattern. Any number of alternative, curvilinear patterns, such as an S-shape or a J-shape pattern, are possible, and the linear correlation coefficient would not be able to communicate the existence of these patterns to the marketing researcher. Any one of several other systematic but nonlinear patterns is entirely possible and would not be indicated by a linear correlation statistic. Only those cases of linear or straight-line relationships between two variables are identified by the Pearson product moment correlation. In fact, when a researcher does not find a significant or strong correlation, but still believes some relationship exists between two variables, he or she may resort to running a scatter plot. This procedure allows the researcher to visually inspect the plotted points and possibly to spot a systematic nonlinear relationship. You already know that your SPSS program has a scatter plot option that will provide a scatter diagram that you can use to obtain a sense of the relationship, if any, between two variables.

REPORTING CORRELATION FINDINGS TO CLIENTS

We again remind you that in Step 4 of the procedure for analyzing relationships outlined in Table 18.1, the researcher must test to determine that a significant correlation has been found before reporting it. Losing sight of this step is entirely possible when a statistical

---

MARKETING RESEARCH INSIGHT   Practical Application

18.6 Guidelines for the Reporting of Correlation Findings

To begin, marketing researchers usually have a "target" or a "focal" variable in mind, and they look at correlations of other variables of interest with this target variable. As an illustration, we will say that in our fictitious Subshop survey, the researcher decides that the target variable is the number of times Subshop customers used the Subshop in the past 2 months. This is a metric variable where respondents have given a number such as 0, 3, 10, and so on. The researcher has found six other variables with statistically significant correlations with the target in the analysis of the Subshop survey data. Naturally, some of these have negative correlations, and the correlations range in size or strength. Study how these findings are arranged in the following table.

Variables Correlated with Subshop Patronage

Variable	Correlation
*Variables positively correlated with patronage:**	
I tend to use the same sandwich shop.	*.76*
I worry about calories.	*.65*
Age	*.55*
Number of years with present company	*.40*

Variable	Correlation
*Variables negatively correlated with patronage:**	
I "do" lunch at the place closest to my work.	*−.71*
Years of education	*−.51*

*Subshop patronage (number of times used in past 2 months).

Notice in the table (our recommendations), the target variable is clearly indicated and the positive and negative correlations are identified and separated. Also, in each case, the correlations are reported in descending order based on the absolute size. In this way, the client's attention is drawn first to the positively related variables and can see the pattern from strong to weak positive correlations. Next, the client's attention is drawn to the negatively associated variables and, again, can see the pattern from strong to weak negative correlations. If the researcher thinks it appropriate, a third column can be added to the table, and the designations of "Strong," "Moderate," "Weak," and so on can be placed beside each correlation according to the rules of thumb listed in Table 18.3. Alternatively, these designations can be specified as in a table footnote or otherwise noted in the text that describes the findings verbally.

analysis program issues a great many correlations, often in a layout that is confusing to first-time data analysts. To our knowledge, there is no marketing research industry standard on how to report statistically significant correlations to clients. But we do have a recommended approach that takes into account correlation signs and sizes. Our recommendation is in Marketing Research Insight 18.6.

Summary

This chapter dealt with instances in which a marketing researcher wants to see if there is a relationship between the responses to one question and the responses to another question in the same survey. Four different types of relationship are possible. First, there is a nonmonotonic relationships where the presence (or absence) of one variable is systematically associated with the presence (or absence) of another. Second, a monotonic relationship indicates the direction of one variable relative to the direction of the other variable. Third, a linear relationship is characterized by a straight-line appearance if the variables are plotted against one other on a graph. Fourth, a curvilinear relationship means the pattern has a definite curved shape. Associative analyses are used to assess these relationships statistically.

Associations can be characterized by presence, direction, and strength, depending on the scaling assumptions of the questions being compared. With chi-square analysis, a cross-tabulation table is prepared for two nominal-scaled questions, and the chi-square statistic is computed to determine whether the observed frequencies (those found in the survey) differ significantly from what would be expected if there were no nonmonotonic relationship between the two. If the null hypothesis of no relationship is rejected, the researcher then looks at the cell percentages to identify the underlying pattern of association.

A correlation coefficient is an index number, constrained to fall between the range of +1.0 to −1.0, that communicates both the strength and the direction of association between two variables. The sign indicates the direction of the relationship and the absolute size indicates the strength of the association. Normally, correlations in excess of ±0.8 are considered high. With two questions that are interval and/or ratio in their scaling assumptions, the Pearson product moment correlation coefficient is appropriate as the means of determining the underlying linear relationship. A scatter diagram can be used to inspect the pattern.

Key Terms

Associative analyses 534
Relationship 534
Nonmonotonic relationship 535
Monotonic relationships 536
Linear relationship 536
Straight-line formula 536
Curvilinear relationship 537
Cross-tabulation table 539

Cross-tabulation cell 539
Frequencies table 539
Raw percentages table 540
Column percentages table 541
Row percentages table 541
Chi-square (χ^2) analysis 541
Observed frequencies 541
Expected frequencies 541

Chi-square formula 542
Chi-square distribution 544
Correlation coefficient 551
Covariation 551
Scatter diagram 553
Pearson product moment
    correlation 554
Cause-and-effect relationship 559

Review Questions/Applications

1. Explain the distinction between a statistical relationship and a causal relationship.
2. Define and provide an example for each of the following types of relationship: (a) nonmonotonic, (b) monotonic, (c) linear, and (d) curvilinear.
3. Relate the three different aspects of a relationship between two variables.
4. What is a cross-tabulation? Give an example.
5. With respect to chi-square analysis, describe or identify each of the following: (a) r-by-c table,

(b) frequencies table, (c) observed frequencies, (d) expected frequencies, (e) chi-square distribution, (f) significant association, (g) scaling assumptions, (h) row percentages versus column percentages, and (i) degrees of freedom.

6. What is meant by the term *significant correlation*?

7. Briefly describe the connections among the following: covariation, scatter diagram, correlation, and linear relationship.

8. Indicate, with the use of a scatter diagram, the general shape of the scatter of data points in each of the following cases: (a) a strong positive correlation, (b) a weak negative correlation, (c) no correlation, (d) a correlation of $-.98$.

9. What are the scaling assumptions involved in the Pearson product moment correlation?

10. Listed below are various factors that may have relationships that are interesting to marketing managers. For each one, (1) identify the type of relationship, (2) indicate its nature or direction, and (3) specify how knowledge of the relationship could help a marketing manager in designing marketing strategy.

    a. Readership of certain sections of the Sunday newspaper and age of the reader for a sporting goods retail store.

    b. Ownership of a telephone answering machine and household income for a telemarketing service being used by a public television broadcasting station soliciting funds.

    c. Number of miles driven in company cars and need for service such as oil changes, tune-ups, or filter changes for a quick auto service chain attempting to market fleet discounts to companies.

    d. Plans to take a 5-day vacation to Jamaica and the exchange rate of the Jamaican dollar to that of other countries for Sandals, an all-inclusive resort located in Montego Bay.

    e. Amount of do-it-yourself home repairs and the declining state of the economy (for example, a recession) for Ace Hardware stores.

11. Indicate the presence, nature, and strength of the relationship involving purchases of intermediate-size automobiles and each of the following factors: (a) price, (b) fabric versus leather interior, (c) exterior color, and (d) size of rebate.

12. For each of the following examples, compose a reasonable statement of an association you would expect to find existing between the factors involved, and construct a stacked bar chart expressing that association.

    a. Wearing of braces to straighten teeth by children attending expensive private schools versus those attending public schools.

    b. Having a Doberman pinscher as a guard dog, use of a home security alarm system, and ownership of rare pieces of art.

    c. Adherence to the "diet pyramid" recommended by the Surgeon General of the United States for healthful living and family history of heart disease.

    d. Purchases of toys as gifts during the Christmas buying season versus other seasons of the year by parents of preschool-aged children.

13. Below is some information about ten respondents to a mail survey concerning candy purchasing. Use SPSS to construct the four different types of cross-tabulation tables that are possible. Label each table, and indicate what you perceive to be the general relationship apparent in the data.

Respondent	Buy Plain M&Ms	Buy Peanut M&Ms
1	Yes	No
2	Yes	No
3	No	Yes
4	Yes	No
5	No	No
6	No	Yes
7	No	No
8	Yes	No
9	Yes	No
10	No	Yes

14. Morton O'Dell is the owner of Mort's Diner, which is located in downtown Atlanta, Georgia. Mort's opened up about 12 months ago, and it has experienced success, but Mort is always worried about what food items to order as inventory on a weekly basis. Mort's daughter, Mary, is an engineering student at Georgia Tech, and she offers to help her father. She asks him to provide sales data for the past 10 weeks in terms of pounds of food bought by customers. With some difficulty, Mort comes up with the following list:

Week	Meat	Fish	Fowl	Vegetables	Desserts
1	100	50	150	195	50
2	91	55	182	200	64
3	82	60	194	209	70
4	75	68	211	215	82
5	66	53	235	225	73
6	53	61	253	234	53
7	64	57	237	230	68
8	76	64	208	221	58
9	94	68	193	229	62
10	105	58	181	214	62

Mary uses these sales figures to construct scatter diagrams that illustrate the basic relationships among the various types of food items purchased at Mort's Diner over the past 10 weeks. She tells her father that the diagrams provide some help in his weekly inventory ordering problem. Construct Mary's scatter diagrams with your SPSS to indicate what assistance they are to Mort. Perform the appropriate associate analysis with SPSS and interpret your findings.

CASE 18.1

THE PETS, PETS, AND PETS TEAM PROJECT (PART III)

(Part I (Case 16.1) of this case is on pages 497–499, and Part II (Case 17.1) of this case is on pages 528–529.)

This is the ongoing saga of the Pets, Pets, and Pets team marketing research project undertaken by Josh and Marsha this semester. Marsha has been carrying most of the load while Josh recuperates from surgery on his knee that he blew out while practicing on the baseball team. At least, this is Josh's story and he is sticking to it.

At 10:01 pm, in an apartment north of campus, a cell phone suddenly blasts out the school's fight song. After checking the incoming number, Josh answers: "Hey, Marsh. What's up?"

MARSHA: It is after 10 p.m. and I am looking for our Pets, Pets & Pets marketing research data analysis that you said you would e-mail to me by 10 tonight.

JOSH: Jeeze, Marsh, I am studying for that big finance test that we both have tomorrow. Finance has, like, numbers and equations, and I am really spooked about it.

MARSHA: I am done studying finance, and I need to prepare the relationships analysis presentation that we—or should I say "I"—have to give in Dr. Z's marketing research tomorrow morning. I need that analysis now!

JOSH: Okay, okay, I will do it right away and e-mail you the file. Just keep checking for it. Bye.

At 12:13 a.m. an e-mail from Josh arrives at Marsha's computer. She opens up the file and finds . . .

Correlations

		Times used PPP in the past year	Dollar amount spent at PPP on last visit	How likely to revisit PPP	Number of pets	Use PPP regularly or not?	Recall seeing PPP newspaper in the past month	Income level
Times used PPP in the past year	Pearson Correlation	1	.403**	.382**	.778**	.702**	.310**	−.067
	Sig. (2-tailed)		.000	.000	.000	.000	.000	.412
	N	152	99	150	152	152	152	152
Dollar amount spent PPP on last visit	Pearson Correlation	.403**	1	.604**	−.226*	.398**	.165	.228*
	Sig. (2-tailed)	.000		.000	.024	.000	.102	.023
	N	99	99	99	99	99	99	99
How likely to revisit PPP	Pearson Correlation	.382**	.604**	1	.009	.490**	.011	.115
	Sig. (2-tailed)	.000	.000		.910	.000	.890	.163
	N	150	99	150	150	150	150	150

(continued)

		Times used PPP in the past year	Dollar amount spent at PPP on last visit	How likely to revisit PPP	Number of pets	Use PPP regularly or not?	Recall seeing PPP newspaper in the past month	Income level
Number of pets	Pearson Correlation	.778**	−.226*	.009	1	.490**	.271**	.331**
	Sig. (2-tailed)	.000	.024	.910		.000	.001	.000
	N	152	99	150	152	152	152	152
Use PPP regularly or not	Pearson Correlation	.702**	.398**	.490**	.490**	1	.241**	−.126
	Sig. (2-tailed)	.000	.000	000	000		.003	.123
	N	152	99	150	152	152	152	152
Recall seeing PPP newspaper in the past month	Pearson Correlation	.310**	.165	.011	.271**	.241**	1	.173*
	Sig. (2-tailed)	.000	.102	.890	.001	.003		.033
	N	152	99	150	152	152	152	152
Income level	Pearson Correlation	−.067	.228*	.115	−.331**	−.126	.173**	1
	Sig. (2-tailed)	.412	.023	.163	.000	.123	.033	
	N	152	99	150	152	152	152	152

**Correlation is significant at the 0.01 level (2-tailed).
*Correlation is significant at the 0.05 level (2-tailed).

Marsha immediately calls Josh. "Were you like completely unconscious when Dr. Z went over cross-tabulations and the data scaling assumptions for cross-tabs versus correlations?"

JOSH: Oh, you mean the matrix stuff with the formulas for types of frequencies and the chi-square value? Hey, I told you that I don't do numbers and formulas well. But the correlations with the cool rules of thumb made a lot sense to me, so I did them.

Marsha is silent for several seconds, so Josh says: "Um, so maybe I did some of it not quite right? Look, I am coming right over to your apartment and will do it right if you tell me what to do. Besides, I need some help with studying for our finance test. I will pick up a pizza and be there in 30 minutes. What type of cold drink do you want me to pick up for you?"

Marsha sighs loudly and says: "Never mind the cold drink, I will be drinking a lot of coffee for sure."

Here is the code book and variable definitions for the Pets, Pets, and Pets marketing research study that Josh and Marsha are working on.

Variable Code Book for Pets, Pets, and Pets SPSS File

Variable	Response Scale
Times visited PPP in past year	Actual number of times
Amount spent on last visit to PPP	Actual dollar amount rounded to dollars
How likely to buy at PPP next time (1–7 scale)	1–7 scale where
	1 = unlikely, 7 = very likely
Number of pets owned	Actual number of pets
Use Pets, Pets, & Pets how often?	1 = do not use regularly
	2 = use regularly
Recall seeing a PPP newspaper ad in the past month?	1 = yes
	2 = no
Income level	1 = below $20,000
	2 = between $20,000 and $40,000
	3 = between $40,000 and $60,000
	4 = between $60,000 and $80,000
	5 = between $80,000 and $100,000
	6 = greater than $100,000

What associative analysis is appropriate and why is it appropriate to answer each of the following questions?

1. Is the number of visits to Pets, Pets, and Pets in the past year related to the dollar amount that buyers spent there in the last purchase?
2. Is the number of visits related to being likely to buy at Pets, Pets, and Pets next time?
3. Is recall of Pets, Pets, and Pets newspaper advertisements related to shoppers being regular users of Pets, Pets, and Pets?
4. Do higher-income buyers spend more at Pet, Pets, and Pets?
5. Are specific income groups more or less likely to be regular users of Pets, Pets, and Pets, and if so, which one(s)?

CASE 18.2

THE HOBBIT'S CHOICE RESTAURANT SURVEY ASSOCIATIVE ANALYSIS

(For necessary background, read Case 15.2 on pages 460–463, Case 16.2 on pages 499, and Case 17.2, The Hobbit's Choice Restaurant Survey Differences Analysis, on pages 529–530).

Cory Junior's stomach ailment turned out to be much worse than Cory Rogers expected, and Cory Senior, called in to inform his marketing intern, Christine Yu, that it would probably be several days before he would be able to get back to the office. Cory says to Christine, "I know you are a bit lost with The Hobbit's Choice Restaurant project, but why don't you take a look at the proposal and see if there is any further analysis that you can do while I am out. Have Tonya pull the proposal from the file."

Christine looks at the research proposal, and she jots down some notes with respect to research questions that need to be addressed. Her notes are below.

Your task in Case 18.2 is to use The Hobbit's Choice Restaurant SPSS data set and perform the proper analysis. You will also need to interpret the findings.

1. Perform the correct analysis and interpret your findings with regard to The Hobbit's Choice Restaurant menu, décor, and atmosphere for those people who prefer to drive less than 30 minutes to get to the restaurant.
2. Do older or younger people want unusual desserts and/or unusual entrées?
3. Use the variable that distinguishes the "Probable patrons" (likely to patronize Hobbit's Choice = 1 or = 2) for the "Not probable patrons" (likely to patronize Hobbit's Choice = 3, = 4, or = 5). If the probable patrons constitute The Hobbit's Choice Restaurant target market, what is the demographic makeup of this target market? Use the demographics of household income, education level, gender, and zip code.
4. Is the *City Magazine* a viable advertising medium for Jeff Dean to use? Apart from this question, are there other viable promotion vehicles that Jeff should know about?

CASE 18.3

FRIENDLY MARKET VERSUS CIRCLE K

Friendly Market is a convenience store located directly across the street from a Circle K convenience store. Circle K is a national chain, and its stores enjoy the benefits of national advertising campaigns, particularly the high visibility these campaigns bring. All Circle K stores have large red-and-white store signs, identical merchandise assortments, and standardized floor plans, and they are open around the clock. Friendly Market, in contrast, is a one-of-a-kind "mom-and-pop" variety convenience store owned and managed by Bobby Jones. Bobby's parents came to the United States from Palestine when Bobby was 15 years old. The family members became American citizens and adopted the last name of Jones. Bobby had difficulty making the transition to U.S. schools, and he dropped out without finishing high school. For the next 10 years of his life, Bobby worked in a variety of jobs, both full- and part-time, and for most of the past 10 years, Bobby has been a Circle K store employee.

Three years ago, Bobby made a bold move to open his own convenience store. Don's Market, a mom-and-pop convenience store across the street from the Circle K where Bobby was working at the time, had closed 6 months before, and Bobby watched it month after month as it remained boarded up with a for-sale sign on the front door and no apparent interested parties. Bobby gathered up his life savings and borrowed as much money as he could from friends, relatives, and banks. He bought the old Don's Market building and equipment, renamed it Friendly Market, and opened its doors for business. Bobby's core business philosophy was to greet everyone who came in and to get to know all his customers on a first-name basis. He also watched Circle K's prices closely and sought to have lower prices on at least 50% of merchandise sold by both stores.

To the surprise of the manager of the Circle K across the street, Friendly Market prospered. Recently, Bobby's younger sister, who had gone on to college and earned an MBA degree at Indiana University, conducted a survey of Bobby's target market to gain a better understanding of why Friendly Market was successful. She drafted a simple questionnaire and did the telephone interviewing herself. She used the local telephone book and called a random sample of over 150 respondents whose residences were listed within 3 miles of Friendly Market. She then created an SPSS data set with the following variables name and values:

Variable Name	Value Labels
FRIENDLY	0 = Do not use Friendly Market regularly; 1 = Use Friendly Market regularly
CIRCLE K	0 = Do not use Circle K regularly; 1 = Use Circle K regularly
DWELL	1 = Own home; 2 = Rent
SEX	1 = Male; 2 = Female
WORK	1 = Work full-time; 2 = Work part-time; 3 = Retired or Do not work
COMMUTE	0 = Do not pass by Friendly Market/Circle K corner on way to work; 1 = Do pass by Friendly Market/Circle K corner on way to work

In addition to these demographic questions, respondents were asked if they agreed (= 3), disagreed (= 1), or neither agreed nor disagreed (= 2) with each of five different lifestyle statements. The variable names and questions follow:

Variable Name	Lifestyle Statement
BARGAIN	I often shop for bargains.
CASH	I always pay cash.
QUICK	I like quick, easy shopping.
KNOW ME	I shop where they know my name.
HURRY	I am always in a hurry.

The data set, named "Friendly.sav," is available, and your instructor will direct you on how to obaitn it. Use SPSS to perform the relationship analyses necessary to answer the following questions.

1. Do Friendly Market and Circle K have the same customers?
2. What is the demographic profile associated with Friendly Market's customers?
3. What is the demographic profile associated with Circle K's customers?
4. What is the lifestyle profile associated with Friendly Market's customers?

THE ADVANCED AUTOMOBILE CONCEPTS SURVEY
ASSOCIATIVE ANALYSIS

Cory Rogers was very pleased with the way the Advanced Automobile Concepts project was shaping up. Celeste Brown, the CMG data analyst, had applied differences analysis using the preferences for the various hybrid models that might be developed, and she had found a unique demographic target market profile for each model. Celeste had summarized her findings in a professional PowerPoint presentation that Cory and Celeste presented to Nick Thomas and his assembled managers just yesterday. The presentation was one of the smoothest possible, and Nick's development team members became very excited and animated when they realized that Advanced Automobile Concepts had a possibility of five "winner" hybrid model vehicles to work with. In fact, at the end of the meeting, Nick had decided to go ahead with a preliminary marketing plan for each model.

Nick informed Cory and Celeste that Zen Motors places a huge amount of emphasis on its communications, investing millions of dollars every year in many different types of advertising to convince prospective customers that Zen Motors models are the best possible choices. Nick explained, "Zen does not shotgun its advertising. Everything is based on solid marketing research that reveals the media usage characteristics of each target market. That is why I insisted on including the media usage information in our AAC survey. Zen corporate will most certainly shoot us down if we come to it with any preliminary marketing plan for any hybrid model that does not have advertising recommendations based on media usage research. I did not realize at the time that we would be working on all five hybrid models, but each of my development teams will need whatever media usage findings you can come up with for its particular model."

Cory and Celeste are in a meeting the following day to discuss further analysis for the Advanced Automobile Concepts project. Cory says, "I recall that we have a lot of detail on the media habits of the AAC survey respondents. Let's see—it includes favorite television show type, radio genre, magazine type, and local newspaper section. Nick Thomas called this morning and asked if we could have our findings to him inside of a week, so I guess he and his team are moving very fast. Nick also told me that he spoke to the Zen Motors advertising group, and they have strong preferences for what demographic factors should be used for each type of media. Nick says that for television, they prefer to use age; for newspaper and television, they prefer to use education; and for magazines, they prefer to use income."

Celeste says, "Needs it yesterday, so what is new? Seriously, I can get to it by the end of this week and have it ready to present early next week, assuming no glitches." Cory concludes the meeting with "Great, just let me know on Friday morning how it is coming, as I told Nick I will call him on that day to set up the presentation."

Your task in Case 18.4 is to revisit Case 17.3 where Celeste (you) used differences analyses to find the unique demographic profiles for each of the five possible new hybrid models.

- Super Cycle one-seater; 120+ mpg city
- Runabout Sport two-seater; 90 mpg city, 80 mpg highway
- Runabout with Luggage two-seater; 80 mpg city, 70 mpg highway
- Economy four-seater; 70 mpg city, 60 mpg highway
- Standard four-seater; 60 mpg city, 50 mpg highway

1. Use each unique hybrid model demographic profile to determine whether or not statistically significant associations exist, and if they do, recommend the specific media vehicles for radio, newspaper, television, and magazines.
2. What is the lifestyle of each of the possible target markets, and what are the implications of this finding for the advertising message that would "speak" to this market segment when the hybrid model is introduced?

Learning Objectives

- To understand the basic concept of prediction

- To learn how marketing researchers use regression analysis

- To learn how marketing researchers use bivariate regression analysis

- To see how multiple regression differs from bivariate regression

- To appreciate various types of stepwise regression, how they are applied, and the interpretation of their findings

- To learn how to obtain and interpret regression analyses with SPSS

Where We Are

1 Establish the need for marketing research

2 Define the problem

3 Establish research objectives

4 Determine research design

5 Identify information types and sources

6 Determine methods of accessing data

7 Design data-collection forms

8 Determine the sample plan and size

9 Collect data

▶ 10 Analyze data, and

11 Prepare and present the final research report.

Predicting Height and Beyond . . .

Sir Francis Galton
(1822–1911)

In 1885, Sir Francis Galton wrote a paper entitled "Regression toward mediocrity in hereditary stature."[1] The theory presented in the paper was that the physical characteristics of offspring, while related to their parents, are less extreme. Tall parents tend to produce children less tall than themselves. Short parents tend to produce children taller than themselves. The physical characteristics of the children tend to "regress" toward the average of the population. Galton plotted the median heights of many pairs of parents and their offspring. By drawing a line through his data, Galton was able to use the line to predict the height of offspring given the height of the parents. Galton's line became known by statisticians as the "regression line." Galton's early work has been improved upon greatly over the years, and the result has given us the tool of linear regression. With knowledge of one variable, bivariate linear regression allows us to predict another variable. With knowledge of multiple variables, multiple linear regression allows us to predict another variable. Regression can not only teach us what variables are important in prediction but also their relative importance.

Imagine almost any variable of importance in business, and someone has most likely used regression to try to predict it. Examples would include advertising readership, brand name awareness, brand loyalty, attitudes, word-of-mouth communications, intention to purchase a new product, market share, and sales. Regression is an important tool in marketing research. You will learn the basics of understanding both bivariate and multiple linear regression in this chapter, and you will also learn how to run both of these techniques using SPSS.

T*his chapter is the last one in which we discuss statistical procedures frequently used by marketing researchers. A researcher sometimes wishes to predict what might result if the manager were to implement a certain alternative. Alternatively, the researcher may be seeking a parsimonious way to describe market segments or the differences between various types of consumers. In this chapter, we will describe regression analysis. Although it may seem like an intimidating procedure, we will show you how regression relates directly to the scatter diagrams and linear relationships you learned about in the previous chapter.*

We describe three types of regression analysis. The first, bivariate regression, simply takes correlation analysis between two variables into the realm of prediction. Next, multiple regression analysis introduces the concept of simultaneously using two or more variables to make a prediction about a target variable such as sales. Finally, we will briefly introduce you to stepwise regression. This is a technique used by a researcher when faced with a large number of candidate predictors and when seeking the subset of these that best predicts or describes the phenomenon under study, just as was the situation in our introductory case.

UNDERSTANDING PREDICTION

> Prediction is a statement of what is believed will happen in the future based on past experience or prior observation.

A **prediction** is a statement of what is believed will happen in the future based on past experience or prior observation. We are confronted with the need to make predictions on a daily basis. For example, you must predict whether it will rain to decide whether to carry an umbrella. You must predict how difficult an examination will be in order to properly study. You must predict how heavy the traffic will be in order to decide what time to start driving to be on time for your dentist appointment.

Marketing managers are also constantly faced with the need to make predictions, and the stakes are much higher than in the three examples just cited. That is, instead of getting caught in a downpour, receiving a disappointingly low grade, or missing a dentist appointment, the marketing manager has to worry about competitors' reactions, changes in sales, wasted resources, and whether profitability objectives will be achieved. Making accurate predictions is a vital part of the marketing manager's workaday world.

Two Approaches to Prediction

> The two approaches to prediction are extrapolation and predictive modeling.

There are two ways of making a prediction: extrapolation and predictive modeling. In **extrapolation**, you can use past experience as a means of predicting the future. This process identifies a trend or a regular pattern over time and forecasts that pattern into the future. For example, if the weather forecaster has predicted an 80% chance of rain every day for the past week and it had rained every day, you would expect it to rain if the forecaster predicted an 80% chance of rain today. Similarly, if the last two exams you took under a certain professor were quite easy, you would predict the next one would be easy as well. Of course, it might not rain or the professor might administer a hard exam, but the observed patterns argue for rain today and an easy next exam. In both cases, you have detected a consistent pattern over time and based your predictions on this pattern. Forecasts based on extrapolation are beyond the scope of this textbook, so we will simply mention them and then move on to the central topics of this chapter.

In the other case, prediction relies on an observed relationship believed to exist between the factor you are predicting and some condition you judge to influence the factor. For example, how do weather forecasters make predictions? They inspect several pieces of evidence, such as wind direction and velocity, barometric pressure changes, humidity, jet stream configuration, and temperature. That is, they go far beyond taking what happened yesterday and forecasting that it will happen today. They build a predictive model, using the relationships believed to exist among variables to make a prediction. A **predictive model** relates the condition or conditions that are expected to be in place and that will influence the factor you are predicting. It is not an extrapolation of a consistent pattern over time; rather, it is an observed relationship that exists across time.

Extrapolation detects a pattern in the past and projects it into the future. Predictive modeling uses relationships found among variables to make a prediction.

How to Determine the "Goodness" of Your Predictions

Regardless of the method of prediction, you will always want to judge the "goodness" of your predictions, which is how good your method is at making those predictions. The acid test for a predictive model is to compare its predictions to what actually happened and to decide on the accuracy or "goodness" of its predictions.

All predictions should be judged as to their "goodness" (accuracy).

Here is a simple example that will explain the basic approach. Imagine that while you are away at college, your little brother, who is a high school sophomore, works part-time at the movie theater in your hometown. He is rather conceited, and this irks you a bit. When you come home for a school vacation, he claims that he can predict the theater's popcorn sales for each day in the week. It turns out that you also worked at the theater while in high school, and you know the theater manager very well. She agrees to keep a record of popcorn sales and to provide the daily amount to you for the next week. So you challenge your little brother to write down the sales for the next 7 days. After the week passes, how would you determine the accuracy of your brother's prediction?

The easiest way would be to compare the predictions for each day's popcorn sales to the actual amount sold. We have done this in Table 19.1. When you look at the table, you will see that we have calculated the difference between your brother's prediction and the actual sales for each evening. Notice that for some days, the predictions were high, whereas for others, the predictions were low. When you compare how far the predicted values are from the actual or observed values, you are performing **analysis of residuals**. Stated differently, assessment of the goodness of a prediction requires you to compare the pattern of errors in the predictions to the actual data. Analysis of residuals underlies all assessments of the accuracy of a forecasting method, and because researchers cannot wait a month, a quarter, or a year to compare a prediction with what actually happens, they fall back on past data. In other words, they select a predictive model and apply it to the past data. Then, they examine the residuals to assess the model's predictive accuracy.

The goodness of a prediction is based on examination of the residuals.

Residuals are the errors: comparisons of predictions to actual values.

There are many ways to examine residuals. For example, in the case of your little brother's forecast, you could judge it either on a total basis or an individual basis. On a

TABLE 19.1   Weekly Popcorn Sales: Using Residual Errors to Assess the Goodness of a Forecast

Day of Week	Your Brother's Prediction	Actual Sales	Residual (Difference)	Type of Error: Prediction was . . .
Monday	$100	$125	−25	Very low
Tuesday	$115	$130	−15	Low
Wednesday	$120	$135	−15	Low
Thursday	$125	$125	0	Exact
Friday	$260	$225	+35	Very high
Saturday	$300	$250	+50	Very high
Sunday	$275	$235	+40	Very high
Averages	**$185**	**$175**	**+10**	**High**

Analysis of residuals reveals how well your little brother can forecast a movie theater's popcorn sales.

total basis, you might compute the average as we have done in the table, or you could sum all of the daily residuals. Of course, you would need to square the daily residuals or use the absolute values to avoid cancellation of the positive differences by the negative differences. (You have seen the necessary squaring operation before, for instance, in the formula for a standard deviation we described in Chapter 15.) For the individual error, you might look for some pattern.[2] On an individual basis, you might notice a pattern: Your little brother tends to underestimate how much popcorn will be bought on weekdays, which are low-sales days; whereas he overestimates it for Friday through Sunday, which are high-sales days. As you can see, the goodness of a prediction approach depends on how closely it predicts a set of representative values judged by examining the residuals (or errors).

Now that you have a basic understanding of prediction and how you determine the goodness of your predictions, we turn our attention to regression analysis.

BIVARIATE LINEAR REGRESSION ANALYSIS

In this chapter on predictive analysis, we will deal exclusively with linear regression analysis, a predictive model technique often used by marketing researchers. However, regression analysis, particularly "multiple" regression, which is described later, is a complex statistical technique with a large number of requirements and nuances.[3] Consequently, we will begin with a very simple form of regression to introduce you to basic concepts, and after you have completed this introduction, we will move to complicated notions. Still, our chapter is basically an introduction to this area, and as we will warn you toward the end of the chapter, there are a great many aspects of regression analysis that are beyond the scope of this book.

With bivariate regression, one variable is used to predict another variable using the formula for a straight line.

We first define **bivariate regression analysis** as a predictive analysis technique in which one variable is used to predict the level of another by use of the straight-line formula. "Bivariate" means "two variables," and researchers sometimes refer to this case as "simple regression." We review the equation for a straight line and introduce basic terms used in regression. We also describe basic computations and significance with bivariate regression. We show how a regression prediction is made, and we illustrate how to perform this analysis with SPSS.

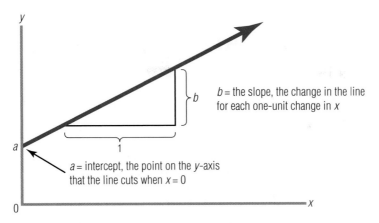

FIGURE 19.1

General Equation for a Straight Line in Graph Form

A straight-line relationship underlies regression, and it is a powerful predictive model. Figure 19.1 illustrates a straight-line relationship; you should refer to it as we describe the elements in a general straight-line formula. The formula for a straight line is:

Formula for a Straight-Line Relationship $y = a + bx$

The straight-line equation is the basis of regression analysis.

where

y = the predicted variable
x = the variable used to predict y
a = the **intercept**, or point where the line cuts the y axis when $x = 0$
b = the **slope** or the change in y for any 1-unit change in x.

You should recall the straight-line relationship we described underlying the correlation coefficient: When the scatter diagram for two variables appears as a thin ellipse, there is a high correlation between them. Regression is directly related to correlation. In fact, we will shortly use one of our correlation examples to illustrate the application of bivariate regression.

Regression is directly related to correlation by the underlying straight-line relationship.

Basic Concepts in Bivariate Regression Analysis

We now define the independent and dependent variables and show how the intercept and slope are computed. Then we use SPSS output to show how tests of significance are interpreted.

INDEPENDENT AND DEPENDENT VARIABLES. As we indicated, bivariate regression analysis is a case in which only two variables are involved in the predictive model. When we use only two variables, one is termed dependent and the other is termed independent. The **dependent variable** is that which is predicted, and it is customarily termed y in the regression straight-line equation. The **independent variable** is that which is used to predict the dependent variable, and it is the x in the regression formula. We must quickly point out that the terms "dependent" and "independent" are arbitrary designations and are customary to regression analysis. There is no cause-and-effect relationship or true dependence between the dependent and the independent variable. It is strictly a statistical relationship, not causal, that may be found between these two variables.

In regression, the independent variable is used to predict the dependent variable.

COMPUTING THE SLOPE AND THE INTERCEPT. To compute a (intercept) and b (slope), you must work with a number of observations of the various levels of the dependent variable paired with different levels of the independent variable, identical to the scatter diagrams we illustrated previously when we were demonstrating how to perform correlation analysis.

The formulas for calculating the slope (b) and the intercept (a) are rather complicated, but some instructors are in favor of their students learning these formulas, so we have included them in Marketing Research Insight 19.1.

MARKETING RESEARCH INSIGHT   Practical Application

19.1 How to Calculate the Intercept and Slope of a Bivariate Regression

In the example below, we are using the Novartis pharmaceuticals company sales territory and number of salespersons data found in Table 19.2, which includes intermediate regression calculations.

TABLE 19.2   Bivariate Regression Analysis Data and Intermediate Calculations

Territory (I)	Sales ($ millions) (y)	Number of Salespersons (x)	xy	x^2
1	102	7	714	49
2	125	5	625	25
3	150	9	1350	81
4	155	9	1395	81
5	160	9	1440	81
6	168	8	1344	64
7	180	10	1800	100
8	220	10	2200	100
9	210	12	2520	144
10	205	12	2460	144
11	230	12	2760	144
12	255	15	3825	225
13	250	14	3500	196
14	260	15	3900	225
15	250	16	4000	256
16	275	16	4400	256
17	280	17	4760	289
18	240	18	4320	324
19	300	18	5400	324
20	310	19	5890	361
Sums	**4,325**	**251**	**58,603**	**3,469**
	(Average = 216.25)	(Average = 12.55)		

The formula for computing the regression parameter *b* is:

Formula for *b*, the slope, in Bivariate Regression

$$b = \frac{n\sum_{i=1}^{n}x_i y_i - \left(\sum_{i=1}^{n}x_i\right)\left(\sum_{i=1}^{n}y_i\right)}{n\sum_{i=1}^{n}x_i^2 - \left(\sum_{i=1}^{n}x_i\right)^2}$$

where

x_i = an x variable value
y_i = a y value paired with each x_i value
n = the number of pairs.

The calculations for b, the slope, are as follows:

Calculation of b, the Slope, in Bivariate Regression Using Novartis Sales Territory Data

$$b = \frac{n \sum_{i=1}^{n} x_i y_i - \left(\sum_{i=1}^{n} x_i\right)\left(\sum_{i=1}^{n} y_i\right)}{n \sum_{i=1}^{n} x_i^2 - \left(\sum_{i=1}^{n} x_i\right)^2}$$

$$= \frac{20 \times 58{,}603 - 251 \times 4{,}325}{20 \times 3{,}469 - 251^2}$$

$$= \frac{1{,}172{,}060 - 1{,}085{,}575}{69{,}380 - 63{,}001}$$

$$= \frac{86{,}485}{6{,}379}$$

$$= 13.56$$

Notes:
$n = 20$
Sum $xy = 58{,}603$
Sum $x = 251$
Sum $y = 4{,}325$
Sum $x^2 = 3{,}469$

The formula for computing the intercept is:

Formula for a, the Intercept, in Bivariate Regression

$$a = \bar{y} - b\bar{x}$$

The computations for a, the intercept, are as follows:

Calculation of a, the Intercept, in Bivariate Regression Using Novartis Sales Territory Data

$a = \bar{y} - b\bar{x}$
$= 216.25 - 13.56 \times 12.55$
$= 216.25 - 170.15$
$= 46.10$

Notes:
$\bar{y} = 216.25$
$\bar{x} = 12.55$

In other words, the bivariate regression equation has been found to be:

Novartis Sales Regression Equation $y = 46.10 + 13.56x$

The interpretation of this equation is as follows. Annual sales in the average Novartis sales territory are $46.10 million, and they increase $13.56 million annually with each additional salesperson.

When SPSS or any other statistical analysis program computes the intercept and the slope in a regression analysis, it does so on the basis of the "least-squares criterion." The **least-squares criterion** is a way of guaranteeing that the straight line that runs through the points on the scatter diagram is positioned so as to minimize the vertical distances away from the line of the various points. In other words, if you draw a line where the regression line is calculated and measure the vertical distances of all the points away from that line, it would be impossible to draw any other line that would result in a lower total of all of those vertical distances. Or, to state the least-squares criterion using residuals analysis, the line is the one with the lowest total squared residuals.

The least-squares criterion used in regression analysis guarantees that the "best" straight-line slope and intercept will be calculated.

A Step-by-Step Method to Evaluating Regression Findings

By now, you realize that every statistical analysis beyond simple descriptive ones involves some sort of statistical test, and the complexity of regression analysis requires multiple tests. These tests are considered in a step-by-step manner by the marketing researcher, and we have listed and described these steps in Table 19.3. The formulas for these tests are quite complicated, so rather than detailing the formulas, we will describe the tests and then use SPSS Advanced Automobile Concepts survey data output to identify where to look and how to interpret them.

TABLE 19.3   Step-by-Step Procedure for Regression Analysis Using SPSS

Step	Description
1. **Choose the dependent variable and independent variable(s) to analyze. Run SPSS basic regression "Enter" method on SPSS.**	The dependent variable (y) is the predicted variable, and the independent variable (x) is the variable used to predict y. Typically, both y and x variables are metric (interval or ratio scales).
2. **Determine whether or not a linear relationship exists in the population (using a 95% level of confidence).**	From the initial SPSS output, the ANOVA table reports a computed F value and associated Sig. level. a. If the Sig. value is .05 or less, there is a linear relationship among the chosen variables in the propulation. Go to Step 3. b. If the Sig. value is more than 0.05, there is no linear relationship among the chosen variables in the population. Return to Step 1 with a new set of variables, or stop.
3. **Determine whether or not the chosen independent variable(s) are statistically significant (using a 95% level of confidence).**	In the SPSS coefficients table, look at the Sig. level for the t value for the constant. If Sig. is 0.05 or less, use the constant with the $y = a + bx$ linear equation. If not, $a = 0$ in the equation. Also look at the Sig. level for each computed b coefficient for the associated independent variable. a. If the Sig. level is 0.05 or less, it is permissible to use the associated independent variable to predict the dependent variable with the $y = a + bx$ linear equation. b. If the Sig. level is more than 0.05, it is not permisssible to use the associated independent variable to predict the dependent variable. c. If you find a mixture of (a) and (b), you may want to do "trimmed" or stepwise multiple regression analysis (see the text for these techniques).
4. **Determine the strength of the relationship(s) in the linear model.**	In the SPSS output, R Square is the square of the correlation coefficient, the Adjusted R Square reduces the R^2 by taking into account the sample size and number of parameters estimated. Use Adjusted R Square as a measure of the "percent variance explained" in the y variable using the linear equation to predict y.
5. **If desired, make a prediction of y, using the significant linear relationship that has been determined.**	Select a value for x, and use the equation Predicted $y = (a + bx)^* \pm z_\alpha \times$ standard error of the estimate, to determine the predicted y and the upper and lower boundaries for a 95% confidence interval.

*For multiple regression, $y = a + b_1x_1 + b_2x_2 + b_3x_3 + \cdots + b_mx_m$

Following are descriptions of each of the steps in Table 19.3. We will provide an actual example from the Advanced Automobile Concepts survey SPSS data set after the descriptions.

Step 1 In bivariate regression, the researcher identifies the dependent and independent variable pair and instructs SPSS or some other statistical analysis program to perform a regression analysis.

Step 2 Immediately, the researcher must find out whether or not a linear relationship exists in the population. This step is analogous to determining the statistical significance of the correlation between the two variables. You should recall that if a correlation coefficient is not statistically significant, then the population correlation is zero. In other words, there is no intercept and no slope for the population correlation scatter diagram. This first step is one of our "flag" notions, for if there is no significant correlation, then there is no reason to continue and examine the intercept or slope on the computer output.

However, when the overall relationship is statistically significant, the researcher can move to the third step.

Step 3   The next step involves determining the statistical significance of the intercept (a) and the slope (b). Here, as will be described using the Advanced Automobile Concepts survey data, the researcher must assess individually whether or not the intercept and the slope are statistically significant from zero.

Step 4   As you learned with correlations, there is a strength of relationship measure associated with linear models. The correlation coefficient is modified with regression analysis. First, it can be squared, called R^2, to express the strength, and it can be adjusted, Adjusted R^2, for the multiple regression case, to yield a value that can be related to "percent of variance explained."

Step 5   Finally, the researcher can use the regression analysis finding to predict a level of y, given levels of the independent variable(s). Because the regression prediction applies to what would be found in the population, the researcher computes a chosen level of confidence's confidence interval limits in making this prediction.

To avoid getting lost in the regression output maze, we recommend our step-by-step procedure to negotiate it.

Your Integrated Case

ADVANCED AUTOMOBILE CONCEPTS: HOW TO RUN AND INTERPRET BIVARIATE REGRESSION ANALYSIS WITH SPSS

Now let us illustrate bivariate regression with SPSS using The Advanced Automobile Concepts survey data with which you are well acquainted. Our purpose here is to help you learn the basic SPSS commands for bivariate regression and to familiarize you with the SPSS output and various regression statistics found on it.

Choosing the Variables to Be Analyzed

The first step in bivariate regression analysis is to identify the dependent and independent variables. For our example, we will use the "probability of buying a standard-size hybrid auto within 3 years" as our dependent variable. Logically, we would expect this probability to be related to demographics, beliefs, and attitudes. For illustration, we will select income level as the independent variable.

Checking That Variables Are Metric and Recoding When Necessary

A requirement of regression is that the dependent variable be metric, meaning interval or ratio scaled. Our "probability of buying . . ." satisfies this requirement for the dependent variable. However, if you review the questionnaire and coding system used for the income as well as for hometown size, age, and education, you will come to realize that the codes define ordinal scales. For instance, a "5" pertains to hometowns of 1 million and more, a "4" corresponds to 500,000 to 1 million, and a "3" designates a hometown of between 100,000 and 499,999 people. Because the size ranges are not equal, the code numbers are not metric; rather, they are ordinal. In any regression, it is best to use realistic values because realistic values are easiest to interpret. Consequently, we will recode the hometown size, age, education, and income values to represent the midpoints of the various ranges designated on the questionnaire. Naturally, not every respondent's value falls on the midpoint, but we can make the assumption that while some have actual values above the midpoint and some have actual values below the midpoint, these will average to be the midpoint or very close to it for all respondents who fall into that particular range. SPSS has a very handy function for recoding under the TRANSFORM–RECODE command, with which you can recode the numbers into new values. The operation of this feature is shown in Figure 19.2.

In any regression, it is best to use realistic values because realistic values are easiest to interpret.

FIGURE 19.2

How to Recode Variables in SPSS

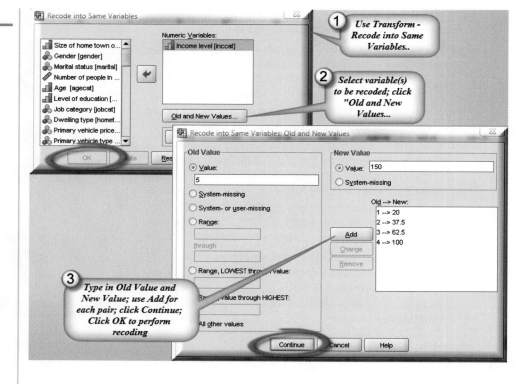

When working with ranges of a metric variable (such as income) in regression analysis, we recommend using the midpoints.

Here are the recode values that we will use to convert our four demographic variables into values that are metric. For hometown size, we will use thousands: $1 = 5, 2 = 55, 3 = 300, 4 = 750$, and $5 = 1500$. For years of age, $1 = 17, 2 = 21, 3 = 30, 4 = 42, 5 = 57$, and $6 = 70$. For years of education, $1 = 9, 2 = 12, 3 = 14, 4 = 16$, and $5 = 18$, and for \$10,000 of income, $1 = 20$, $2 = 37.5, 3 = 62.5, 4 = 100$, and $5 = 150$ (shown in Figure 19.2). If you are tracking this recoding carefully, you no doubt have noted that we have cases where the lower or upper limit of the range is not specified, such as "\$125,000 and higher" for income. In these cases, we choose a value that is reasonable. If you wish to work with our recoded variables, you may recode your AAConcepts.sav data set, or you can choose to use the SPSS data set named, AAConcepts.Recoded.sav.

Running the Regression

Because we are using bivariate regression as an introduction to regression, we will illustrate how to use the Advanced Automobile Concepts survey data set for this analysis. As you can see in Figure 19.3, the SPSS menu clickstream command to run bivariate regression is ANALYZE–REGRESSION–LINEAR. This opens up the linear regression selection window, where you would indicate which variable is the dependent variable and which the independent variable. In our example, we are investigating what you would expect to be a linear relationship between the probability of buying a standard-size electric auto within three years (dependent variable) and income level. When these variables are clicked into their respective locations on the SPSS linear regression setup window, clicking on OK will generate the SPSS output we are about to describe.

The annotated SPSS linear regression output is shown in Figure 19.4. There are several pieces of information provided with a regression analysis such as this. In the Model Summary table, three types of "Rs" are indicated. For bivariate regression, R Square (.021 on the output) is the square of the correlation coefficient 0.146. The Adjusted R Square (.020) reduces the R^2 by taking into account the sample size and number of parameters estimated. This R Square value is very important because it reveals how well the straight-line model fits the scatter of points. Because a correlation coefficient ranges from -1.0 to $+1.0$, its square will range from 0 to $+1.0$. The higher the R Square value, the better is the straight line's fit to the elliptical scatter of points. A standard error value is reported, and we explain its use later.

SPSS Student Assistant: Running and Interpreting Bivariate Regression.

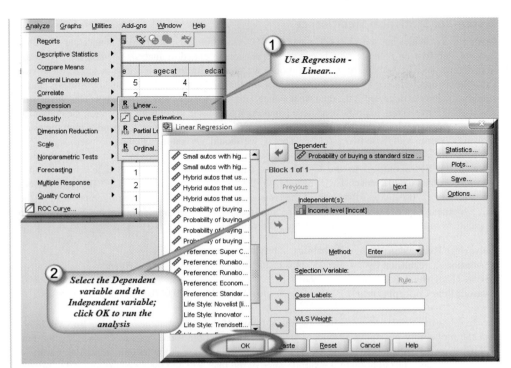

FIGURE 19.3

SPSS Clickstream for Bivariate Regression Analysis

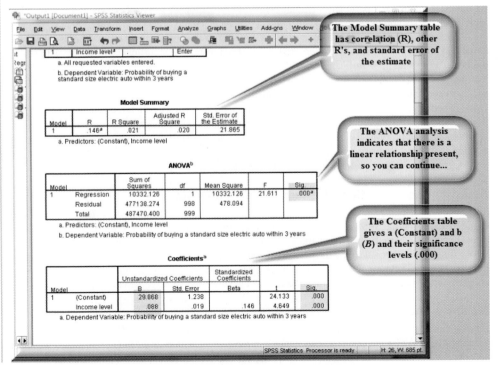

FIGURE 19.4

SPSS Output for Bivariate Regression Analysis

Testing for Statistical Significance

Next, SPSS provides an Analysis of Variance (ANOVA) section; this information is necessary for Step 2 in our step-by-step process. As you can see, regression is related to analysis of variance.[4] We must first determine whether the straight-line model we are attempting to apply to describe these two variables is appropriate. The F value is significant (.000), so we reject the null hypothesis that a straight-line model does *not* fit the data we are analyzing. Just as in ANOVA, as we have described, this test is a flag, and the flag has now been raised, making it justifiable to continue inspecting the output for more significant results. If the ANOVA F test is not significant, we would have to abandon our regression analysis attempts with these two variables. That is, we should not continue to the third step.

Since the ANOVA significance is .05 or less, we can move to Step 3. This step involves the next table in the SPSS output. In the Coefficients Table, the values of b and a are listed under "Unstandardized Coefficients." The constant (a) is 29.868, whereas b, identified as "B," is .088. Both Sig. values are .000 and less than .05, so the constant and the b coefficient are not equal to zero (the null hypothesis). In other words, rounding to hundredths, the regression equation has been found to be identical in form to the one we calculated before:

Bivariate Regression Equation Determined by SPSS Using the Advanced Automobile Concepts Data

Probability of buying a standard size electric auto within three years
$$= 29.868$$
$$+ .088 \times \text{income level (in \$10,000s)}$$

Notes:
Intercept (a) = 29.868
b = .088

To relate this finding to our regression line in Figure 19.1, it says that the regression line will intercept the probability of buying a standard-size hybrid auto within three years at 29.868, and the line will increase .088 percentage points for each $10,000 unit increase in the income scale (the x axis).

You must always test the regression model, intercept, and slope for statistical significance.

Because the determination of the significance of the intercept and the slope are so vital to bivariate regression analysis, we will elaborate on this aspect. Simply computing the values for a and b is not sufficient for regression analysis because the two values must be tested for statistical significance. The intercept and slope that are computed are sample estimates of population parameters of the true intercept, α (alpha), and the true slope, β (beta). The tests for statistical significance are tests as to whether the computed intercept and computed slope are significantly different from zero (the null hypothesis). To determine statistical significance, regression analysis requires that a t test be undertaken for each parameter estimate. The interpretation of these t tests is identical to other significance tests you have seen.

In our example, you would look at the Sig. column in the Coefficients table. This is where the slope and intercept t test results are reported. Both of our tests have significance levels of .000, which are below our standard significance level cutoff of .05, so our computed intercept and slope are valid estimates of the population intercept and slope. If x and y do not share a linear relationship, the population regression slope will equal zero and the t test result will support the null hypothesis. However, if a systematic linear relationship exists, the t test result will force rejection of the null hypothesis, and the researcher can be confident that the calculated slope estimates the true one that exists in the population. Remember, we are dealing with a statistical concept, and you must be assured that the straight-line parameters α and β really exist in the population before you can use your regression analysis findings as a prediction device.

Assessing the Strength of the Regression Relationship

Regression analysis predictions are estimates that have some amount of error in them.

To assess the strength of the regression relationship (Step 4), examine the R Square value of .021 found in the first table on the SPSS regression output. This is the appropriate measure for bivariate regression as is our situation here. It means that about 2% of the probability of buying a standard-size electric auto within three years is explained by the person's income level. Gadzooks! This finding means that income predicts very little future automobile purchasing, but purchasing a new-technology vehicle is a very complicated process, and it is unrealistic to expect any single independent variable to explain it.

Making a Prediction and Accounting for Error

Finally, there is Step 5, the last step, to relate, and it is the most important one. How do you make a prediction? The fact that the line is a best-approximation representation of all the points means we must account for a certain amount of error when we use the line for our predictions. The true advantage of a significant bivariate regression analysis result lies in the ability of the marketing researcher to use the information gained about the regression line through the points on the scatter diagram and to estimate the value or amount of the dependent variable based on some level of the independent variable. For example, with our regression result calculated for the relationship between probability of buying a standard-size electric auto within three years and average income level of some possible target of consumers, it is now possible to estimate the probability predicted to be associated with specific attitude levels. However, we know that the scatter of points does not describe a perfectly straight line because the correlation is .146 and nowhere near 1.0. So our regression prediction can only be a very crude estimate.

Generating a regression prediction is conceptually identical to estimating a population mean. That is, it is necessary to express the amount of error by estimating a range rather than stipulating an exact estimate for your prediction. Regression analysis provides for a **standard error of the estimate**, which is a measure of the accuracy of the predictions of the regression equation. This standard error value is listed in the top half of the SPSS output and just beside the Adjusted R Square in Figure 19.4. It is analogous to the standard error of the mean you used in estimating a population mean from a sample, but it is based on the residuals, or how far away each predicted value is from the actual value. Do you recall the popcorn sales example of residuals we described earlier in this chapter? SPSS does the same comparison by using the regression equation it computed to predict the probability value for each respondent, and this predicted value is compared to the actual amount given by the respondent. The differences, or residuals, are translated into a standard error of estimate value. In our Advanced Automobile Concepts survey example, the standard error of the estimate was found to be 18.278.

Regression analysis can be used to predict the expected sales of new automobile models such as the Tata Nano.

The standard error of the estimate is used to calculate a range of the prediction made with a regression equation.

The use of a 95% or 99% confidence interval is standard.

One of the assumptions of regression analysis is that the plots on the scatter diagram will be spread uniformly and in accord with the normal curve assumptions over the regression line. Figure 19.5 illustrates how this assumption might be depicted graphically. The points are congregated close to the line and then become more diffuse as they move away from the line. In other words, a greater percentage of the points is found on or close to the line than is found further away. The great advantage of this assumption is that it allows the marketing researcher to use knowledge of the normal curve to specify the range in which the dependent variable is predicted to fall. For example, if the researcher used the predicted dependent value result ±1.96 times the standard error of the estimate, that would be stipulating a range with a 95% level of confidence; whereas if the researcher uses ±2.58 times the standard error of the estimate, that would be stipulating a range with a 99% level of confidence. The interpretation of these confidence intervals is identical to interpretations for previous confidence intervals: Were the prediction made many times and an actual result determined each time, the actual results would fall within the range of the predicted value 95% or 99% of these times.

Figure 19.6 illustrates how you can envision a regression prediction. Let us use the regression equation to make a prediction about the probability of buying a standard-size electric auto within

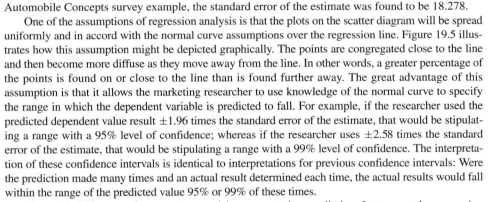

FIGURE 19.5

Regression Assumes That Data Points Form a Bell-Shaped Curve Around the Regression Line

FIGURE 19.6

To Predict with Regression, Apply Levels of Confidence Around the Regression Line

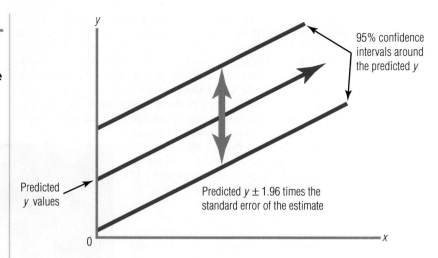

three years that would be associated with consumers whose income is approximately $75,000. Applying the regression formula, we have the following:

Calculation of Purchase Probability Predicted with an Income Level of $75,000

$y = a + bx$

Probability of buying a standard-size
electric auto within 3 years

$= 29.868 + .088 \times$ income level (in $10,000s)

$= 29.868 + .088 \times 75$

$= 29.868 + 6.6$

$= 36.468\%$

$= 36.5\%$ (rounded)

Notes:
Intercept $(a) = 29.868$
$b = .088$
$x = \$75,000$

Regression predictions are made with confidence intervals.

Next, to reflect the imperfect aspects of the predictive tool being used, we must apply confidence intervals. If the 95% level of confidence were applied, the computations would be:

Calculation of 95% Confidence Intervals for the Predicted Purchase Probability

Predicted $y \pm z_\alpha$ Standard error of the estimate
$36.5\% \pm 1.96 \times 21.865$
$36.5\% \pm 42.8554$
0.0% to 79.4% (rounded)
(A negative probability is not possible, so the lower
limit is set at 0.0%.)

The precision of a prediction based on a regression analysis finding depends on the size of the standard error of the estimate.

You may be troubled at the large range of our confidence intervals—and well you should be. If you recall our popcorn sales estimation example at the beginning of the chapter, you should remember that it is important to assess the precision of the predictions generated by a predictive model. How precisely a regression analysis finding predicts is determined by the size of the standard error of the estimate, a measure of the variability of the predicted dependent variable. In our Advanced Automobile Concepts survey case, the probability of purchasing a standard-size electric automobile in the next three years may be predicted by income level with our bivariate regression findings; however, if we repeated the survey many, many times, and made our $75,000 income prediction of the average dollars spent every time, 95% of these predictions would fall between 0% and 79%. There is no way to make this prediction more exact because its precision is dictated by the variability in the data.

But there is a lesson here, as our bivariate regression analysis is actually quite typical for survey data. With surveys, variables are usually measured on limited and arbitrary scales. For instance, in the Advanced Automobile Concepts survey, there are only five levels of income! So, the variability of the independent variable in our example is very restricted. This situation translates into low correlations, which, as you know, indicate that the linear relationship assumed in regression analysis is weak. It is statistically significant due to sample size, but it is quite weak. ∎

Perform a Bivariate Regression with SPSS

You have just observed how to perform a bivariate regression using the probability of buying a standard-size electric automobile in the next three years as the dependent variable, and income, recoded using midpoints of the ranges, as the independent variable. Now you have an opportunity to apply your knowledge. Using the clickstream and annotated SPSS output in Figures 19.3 and 19.4, respectively, and the Advanced Automobile Concepts survey data set provided to you, perform three bivariate regression analyses, each using the probability of purchasing a synthetic-fuel vehicle in the next three years with these independent variables: (1) income level, (2) age, and (3) education level. When you have determined statistically significant results, make a prediction and apply 95% confidence intervals.

How to Improve a Regression Analysis Finding

There are two situations when a researcher would desire to improve a regression analysis. In the second step of our step-by-step method, the researcher may find that the overall test (the flag) is not significant, while in the fourth step, the researcher may find that the correlation (R^2) between the independent and dependent variables is lower than desired. In either case, the researcher can use a scatter diagram to identify outlier pairs of points.

An **outlier**[5] is a data point that is substantially outside the normal range of the data points being analyzed. As one author has noted, outliers "stick out like sore thumbs."[6] When using a scatter diagram to identify outliers,[7] draw an ellipse that encompasses most of the points that appear to be in an elliptical pattern.[8] As noted in Figure 19.7, there are two outlier points, so the researcher would eliminate them from the regression analysis and rerun it. Generally, this approach will improve the regression analysis results, meaning that the R^2 value will increase and the standard error of the estimate will decrease, so the predictions will have narrower confidence intervals.

MULTIPLE REGRESSION ANALYSIS

Now that you are familiar with bivariate regression analysis, you are ready to step up to a higher level: multiple regression analysis. You will find that all of the concepts in bivariate regression apply to multiple regression, except you will be working with more than one independent variable.

An Underlying Conceptual Model

In Chapter 4 where you learned about marketing research problem definition, we referred to a model as a structure that ties together various constructs and their relationships. In that

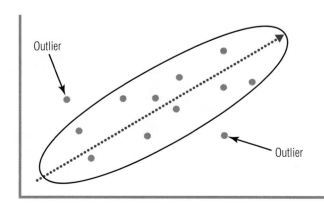

FIGURE 19.7

How to Identify Outliers in Regression Analysis

chapter, we indicated that it is beneficial for the marketing manager and the market researcher to have some sort of model in mind when designing the research plan. The bivariate regression equation that you just learned about is a model that ties together an independent variable and its dependent variable. The dependent variables that market researchers are interested in are typically sales, potential sales, or some attitude held by those who make up the market. For example, in the Novartis example, the dependent variable was territory sales. If Dell computers commissioned a survey, it might want information on those who intend to purchase a Dell computer, or it might want information on those who intend to buy a competing brand as a means of understanding these consumers and perhaps dissuading them. The dependent variable would be purchase intentions for Dell computers. If Maxwell House Coffee was considering a line of gourmet iced coffee, it would want to know how coffee drinkers feel about gourmet iced coffee; that is, their attitudes toward buying, preparing, and drinking it would be the dependent variable.

Figure 19.8 provides a general conceptual model that fits many marketing research situations, particularly those that are investigating consumer behavior. A **general conceptual model** identifies independent and dependent variables and shows their expected basic relationships to one another. In Figure 19.8, you can see that purchases, intentions to purchase, and preferences are in the center, meaning they are dependent. The surrounding concepts are possible independent variables. That is, any one could be used to predict any dependent variable. For example, one's intentions to purchase an expensive automobile like a Lexus could depend on one's income. It could also depend on friends' recommendations (word of mouth), one's opinions about how a Lexus would enhance one's self-image or experiences riding in or driving a Lexus.

In truth, consumers' preferences, intentions, and actions are potentially influenced by a great number of factors, as would be very evident if you listed all of the subconcepts that make up each concept in Figure 19.8. For example, there are probably a dozen different demographic variables, there could be dozens of lifestyle dimensions, and a person is exposed to a great many types of advertising media every day. Of course, in the problem definition stage, the researcher and manager slice the myriad of independent variables down to a manageable number to be included on the questionnaire. That is, they have the general model structure in Figure 19.8 in mind, but they identify and measure specific variables that pertain to the problem at hand. Because bivariate regression analysis treats only dependent-independent pairs, it would take a great many bivariate regression analyses to account for possible relevant dependent-independent pairs of variables in a general model such as Figure 19.8. Fortunately, there is no need to perform a great many bivariate regressions, as there is a much better tool called multiple regression analysis, a technique we are about to describe in some detail.

Our underlying conceptual model example is one of many different conceptual models that researchers have available to them. In truth, every research project has a unique

---

There is an underlying general conceptual model in multiple regression analysis.

The researcher and the manager identify, measure, and analyze specific variables that pertain to the general conceptual model they have in mind.

FIGURE 19.8

A Conceptual Model for Multiple Regression Analysis

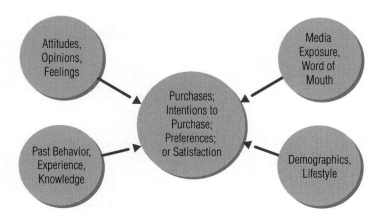

MARKETING RESEARCH INSIGHT   **Global Application**

19.2 Regression Analysis Tests a Model of the Predictors of Bank Switching in New Zealand

Compared to many other countries, there are few banks in New Zealand. This situation places keen interest on customers who switch banks. Researchers working on this problem conceived of a model with several reasons that could possibly predict bank switching.[9] The model listed the following possible reasons as independent variables:

- High prices
- Poor reputation
- Inconvenience
- Products not matching customers' needs
- Low reliability
- Low-performing employees
- Poor responses to redressing poor service quality
- Overall customer dissatisfaction

They also suspected that personal characteristics of New Zealand bank customers would tend to predict bank switching. These demographic factors were:

- Age
- Gender
- Education
- Income

They conducted a mail survey of a probability sample of households in Christchurch, New Zealand. After performing a special application of multiple regression analysis, the researchers concluded that the reasons underlying New Zealand bank switching were the following:

- Poor bank reputation
- Poor bank service quality
- Low customer satisfaction
- Low commitment to the bank on the part of the customer
- Younger-aged bank customers
- Lower-educated bank customers

New Zealand banks now know that the bank customers who switch are younger and less educated and do not have much commitment to the bank from which they switch. Additionally, they are leaving the bank due to its poor reputation, poor bank service, and low overall satisfaction with the bank.

Multiple regression analysis found out why customers switch banks in New Zealand.

conceptual model that depends entirely on the research objectives. Regression analysis can be used to test a model of possible explanations, that is, a conceptual model. Marketing Research Insight 19.2 shows how researchers discovered the key factors that explained why New Zealand bank customers switch banks.

The General Conceptual Model for Advanced Automobile Concepts

Understandably, Nick Thomas, CEO of Advanced Automobile Concepts (AAC), a new division of a large automobile manufacturer, ZEN Motors, wants everyone to intend to purchase a new gasoline alternative-technology automobile; however, this will not be the case due to different beliefs and predispositions in the driving public. Regression analysis will assist Nick by revealing what variables are good predictors of intentions to buy the various new-technology automobile models under consideration at Advanced Automobile Concepts. What is the general conceptual model apparent in the Advanced Automobile Concepts survey data set?

In order to answer this question and to portray the general conceptual model in the format of Figure 19.8, you must inspect the several variables in this SPSS data set or otherwise come up with a list of the variables in the survey. A handy list of all these variables is Case 15.3 on page 463. Using the variable labeled "Probability of buying a standard-size hybrid auto within three years" as the dependent variable, diagram the general types of independent or predictor variables that are apparent in this study. Comment on the usefulness of this general conceptual model to Nick Thomas; that is, assuming that the regression results are significant, what marketing strategy implications will become apparent?

Multiple Regression Analysis Described

> Multiple regression means that you have more than one independent variable to predict a single dependent variable.

Multiple regression analysis is an expansion of bivariate regression analysis in that more than one independent variable is used in the regression equation. The addition of independent variables complicates the conceptualization by adding more dimensions, or axes, to the regression situation. But it makes the regression model more realistic because, as we have just explained in our general model discussion, predictions normally depend on multiple factors, not just one.

BASIC ASSUMPTIONS IN MULTIPLE REGRESSION. Consider our example with the number of salespeople as the independent variable and territory sales as the dependent variable. A second independent variable, such as advertising levels, can be added to the equation. The addition of a second variable turns the regression line into a regression plane because there are three dimensions if we were to try to graph it: territory sales (y), number of salespeople (x_1), and advertising level (x_2). A **regression plane** is the shape of the dependent variable in multiple regression analysis. If other independent variables are added to the regression analysis, it would be necessary to envision each one as a new and separate axis existing at right angles to all other axes. Obviously, it is impossible to draw more than three dimensions at right angles. In fact, it is difficult to even conceive of a multiple dimension diagram, but the assumptions of multiple regression analysis require this conceptualization.

> With multiple regression, you work with a regression plane rather than a line.

Everything about multiple regression is essentially equivalent to bivariate regression except you are working with more than one independent variable. The terminology is slightly different in places, and some statistics are modified to take into account the multiple aspect, but for the most part, concepts in multiple regression are analogous to those in the simple bivariate case. We note these similarities in our description of multiple regression. The equation in multiple regression has the following form:

> A multiple regression equation has two or more independent variables (x's).

$$\text{Multiple Regression Equation} \qquad y = a + b_1x_1 + b_2x_2 + b_3x_3 + \cdots + b_mx_m$$

where

$y =$ the dependent, or predicted, variable
$x_i =$ independent variable i
$a =$ the intercept
$b_i =$ the slope for independent variable i
$m =$ the number of independent variables in the equation.

As you can see, the addition of other independent variables has done nothing more than to add b_ix_i's to the equation. We still have retained the basic $y = a + bx$ straight-line formula, except now we have multiple x variables, and each one is added to the equation, changing y by its individual slope. The inclusion of each independent variable in this manner preserves the straight-line assumptions of multiple regression analysis. This is sometimes known as **additivity** because each new independent variable is added on to the regression equation.

Let's look at a multiple regression analysis result so you can better understand the multiple regression equation. Here is a possible result using our Lexus example:

Notes:

Lexus Purchase Intention Multiple Regression Equation Example

Intention to purchase a Lexus = 2
+ 1.0 × attitude toward Lexus (1–5 scale)
− .5 × attitude toward current auto (1–5 scale)
+ 1.0 × income level (1–10 scale)

$a = 2$
$b_1 = 1.0$
$b_2 = -.5$
$b_3 = 1.0$

This multiple regression equation says that you can predict the level of a consumer's intention to buy a Lexus if you know three variables: (1) attitude toward Lexus, (2) attitude toward the automobile owned now, and (3) income level using a scale with 10 income grades. Further, we can see the impact of each of these variables on Lexus purchase intentions.

Here is how to interpret the equation. First, the average person has a "2" intention level, or some small propensity to want to buy a Lexus. Attitude toward Lexus is measured on a 1–5 scale, and with each attitude scale point, intention goes up 1 point. That is, an individual with a strong positive attitude of "5" will have a greater intention than one with a strong negative attitude of "1." With attitude toward the current automobile owned (for example, a potential Lexus buyer may currently own a Cadillac or a BMW), the intention *decreases* by .5 for each level on the 5-point scale. Of course, we are assuming that these potential buyers own automobile makes other than a Lexus. Finally, the intention increases by 1 with each increasing income grade. Here is a numerical example for a potential Lexus buyer whose Lexus attitude is 4, current automobile make attitude is 3, and income is 5:

Notes:

Calculation of Lexus Purchase Intention Using the Multiple Regression Equation

Intention to purchase a Lexus = 2
+ 1.0 × 4
− .5 × 3
+ 1.0 × 5
= 9.5

Intercept = 2
Attitude toward Lexus $(x_1) = 4$
Attitude toward current auto $(x_2) = 3$
Income level $(x_3) = 5$

Multiple regression is a very powerful tool because it tells us what factors are related to the dependent variable, which way (the sign) each factor influences the dependent variable, and how much (the size of b_i) each factor influences it.

Just as was the case in bivariate regression analysis in which we used the correlation between y and x, it is possible to inspect the strength of the linear relationship between the independent variables and the dependent variable with multiple regression. Multiple R, also called the **coefficient of determination**, is a handy measure of the strength of the overall linear relationship. Just as was the case in bivariate regression analysis, the multiple regression analysis model assumes that a straight-line (plane) relationship exists among the variables. Multiple R ranges from 0 to +1.0 and represents the amount of the dependent variable "explained," or accounted for, by the combined independent variables. High multiple R values indicate that the regression plane applies well to the scatter of points, whereas low values signal that the straight-line model does not apply well. At the same time, a multiple regression result is an estimate of the population multiple regression equation, and, just as was the case with other estimated population parameters, it is necessary to test for statistical significance.

Multiple R indicates how well the independent variables can predict the dependent variable in multiple regression.

Although determining the strength of the relationship is the Step 4 in our step-by-step procedure for using regression analysis, multiple R is like a lead indicator of the multiple regression analysis findings. As you will see soon, it is one of the first pieces of information provided in a multiple regression output. Many researchers mentally convert the multiple R into a percentage. For example a multiple R of .75 means that the regression findings will explain 75% of the dependent variable. The greater the explanatory power of the multiple regression finding, the better and more useful it is for the researcher.

Let us issue a caution before we show you how to run a multiple regression analysis using SPSS. The **independence assumption** stipulates that the independent variables must be statistically independent and uncorrelated with one another. The independence assumption is very important because if it is violated, the multiple regression findings are untrue. The presence of moderate or stronger correlations among the independent variables is termed **multicollinearity** and will violate the independence assumption of multiple regression analysis results when it occurs.[10] It is up to the researcher to test for and remove multicollinearity if it is present.

The way to avoid the multicollinearity problem is to use warnings statistics issued by most statistical analysis programs to identify this problem. One commonly used method is the **variance inflation factor**, sometimes referred to as **VIF**. The VIF is a single number, and a rule of thumb is that as long as the VIF is less than 10, multicollinearity is not a concern. With a VIF of greater than 10 associated with any independent variable in the multiple regression equation, it is prudent to remove that variable from consideration or to otherwise reconstitute the set of independent variables.[11] In other words, when examining the output of any multiple regression, the researcher should inspect the VIF number associated with each independent variable that is retained in the final multiple regression equation by the procedure. If the VIF is greater than 10, the researcher should remove that variable from the independent variable set and rerun the multiple regression.[12] This iterative process is used until only independent variables that are statistically significant and that have acceptable VIFs are in the final multiple regression equation.

> With multiple regression, the independent variables should have low correlations with one another.
>
> Multicollinearity can be assessed and eliminated in multiple regression with the VIF statistic.

Your Integrated Case

ADVANCED AUTOMOBILE CONCEPTS: HOW TO RUN AND INTERPRET MULTIPLE REGRESSION ANALYSIS WITH SPSS

Running multiple regression is almost identical to performing simple bivariate regression with SPSS. The only difference is that you will select more than one independent variable for the analysis. Let's think about a general conceptual model that might predict how likely people are to be buying a hybrid automobile in the future. We already know from basic marketing strategy that demographics are often used for target marketing, and we have age, income, education, and household size. Also, beliefs are often useful for predicting market segments, and we have some variables that pertain to beliefs about the future and effects of gasoline prices. To summarize, we have determined our conceptual model: the probability of buying a standard-size hybrid automobile in the next three years may be predicted by (1) household demographics and (2) beliefs about gasoline prices.

Just as with bivariate regression, the ANALYZE–REGRESSION–LINEAR command sequence is used to run a multiple regression analysis, and the variable, probability of buying a standard-size hybrid automobile in the next three years, is selected as the dependent variable, while the other seven are specified as the independent variables. You will find this annotated SPSS clickstream in Figure 19.9.

As the computer output in Figure 19.10 shows, the Multiple R value (Adjusted R Square in the Model Summary table) indicating the strength of the relationship between the independent variables and the dependent variable is .282, signifying that there is some linear relationship present. Next, the printout reveals that the ANOVA *F* is significant, signaling that the null hypothesis of no linear relationship is rejected and it is justifiable to use a straight-line relationship to model the variables in this case.

Just as we did with bivariate regression, it is necessary in multiple regression analysis to test for statistical significance of the b_i's (betas) determined for the independent variables. Once again, you must determine whether sampling error is influencing the results and giving a false reading. You should recall that this test is a test for significance from zero (the null hypothesis) and is achieved through the use of separate *t* tests for each b_i. The SPSS output in Figure 19.10 indicates the levels of statistical significance. In this particular example, it is apparent that education, age, and income and the belief that "high gasoline prices will impact what type of autos are purchased" are significant, as all have significance levels of less than .05. However, the number of people in the household independent variable is not significant, as its significance level is .274 and above our standard cutoff value of .05. Similarly, the beliefs regarding

> The SPSS ANALYZE– REGRESSION–LINEAR command is used to run multiple regression.

> **SPSS Student Assistant:** Running and Interpreting Multiple Regression.

> With multiple regression, look at the significance level of each calculated beta.

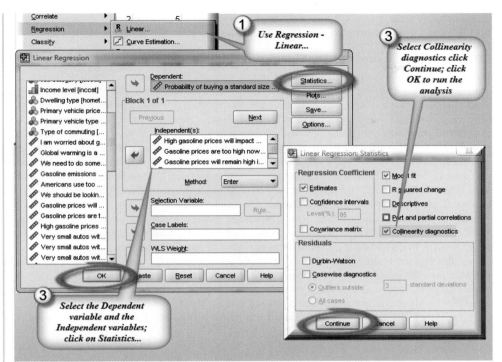

FIGURE 19.9

SPSS Clickstream for Multiple Regression Analysis

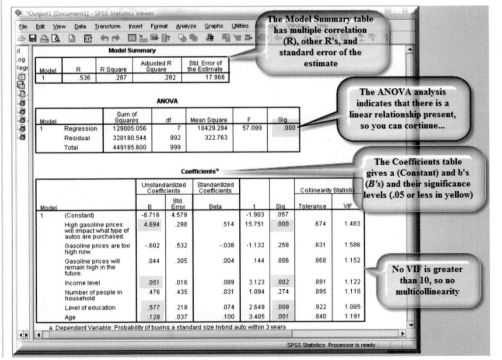

FIGURE 19.10

SPSS Output for Multiple Regression Analysis

"gasoline prices are too high now," and "gasoline prices will remain high in the future" are not significant. No VIF value is greater than the problem level of 10, so multicollinearity is not a concern here.

"Trimming" the Regression for Significant Findings

A trimmed regression means that you eliminate the nonsignificant independent variables and rerun the regression.

What do you do with the mixed significance results we have just found in our multiple regression analysis? Before we answer this question, you should be aware that this mixed result is very likely, so handling it is vital to your understanding of how to perform multiple regression analysis successfully. Here is the answer: It is standard practice in multiple regression analysis to systematically eliminate those independent variables that are shown to be insignificant through a process called "trimming." You then rerun the trimmed model and inspect the significance levels again. This series of eliminations or iterations helps to achieve the simplest model by eliminating the nonsignificant independent variables. The trimmed multiple regression model with all significant independent variables is found in Figure 19.11. Notice that the VIF diagnostics were not selected, as they were examined on the untrimmed SPSS output and found to be acceptable.

Run trimmed regressions iteratively until all betas are significant.

This additional run enables the marketing researcher to think in terms of fewer dimensions within which the dependent variable relationship operates. Generally, successive iterations sometimes cause the Multiple R to decrease somewhat, and it is advisable to scrutinize this value after each run. You can see that the new Multiple R is still .282, so in our example, there has been no decrease. Iterations will also cause the beta values and the intercept value to shift slightly; consequently, it is necessary to inspect all significance levels of the betas once again. Through a series of iterations, the marketing researcher finally arrives at the final regression equation expressing the salient independent variables and their linear relationships with the dependent variable. A concise predictive model has been found.

Using Results to Make a Prediction

We are now ready to illustrate the last step in our step-by-step process for regression analysis—making a prediction. The use of a multiple regression result is identical in concept to the application of a bivariate regression result—that is, it relies on an analysis of residuals that reflect the amount of error in its predictions. Remember, we began this chapter with a description of residuals and indicated that residuals analysis is a way to determine the goodness of a prediction. Ultimately, the marketing researcher wishes to predict the dependent variable based on assumed or known values of the independent variables that are

FIGURE 19.11

SPSS Output for Trimmed Multiple Regression Analysis

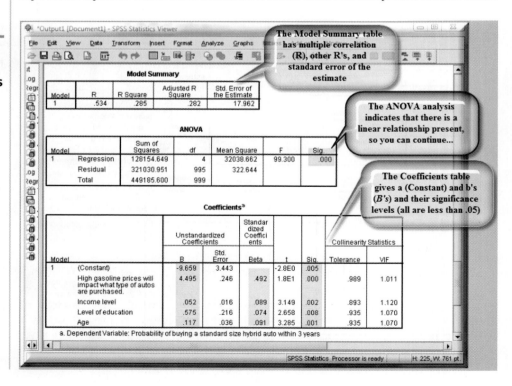

found to have significant relationships within the multiple regression equation. The standard error of the estimate is provided on all regression analysis programs, and it is possible to apply this value to forecast the ranges in which the dependent variable will fall, given levels of the independent variables.

Making a prediction with multiple regression is simple: All you need to do is to apply the final (significant) multiple regression intercept and various coefficients. For a numerical example, let us assume that we are interested in predicting the probability of purchasing a standard-size hybrid vehicle in the next three years for this type of consumer: college graduate (16 years of education), 50 years old, making $100,000 in income, and agreeing that "high gasoline prices will impact what type of autos are purchased" with a "6." The calculations follow. Remember the constant and betas are from the trimmed multiple regression output in Figure 19.11.

Once the multiple regression equation coefficients are determined, one can make a prediction of the dependent variable using independent variable values.

Calculation of probability of Purchasing a Standard-Size Hybrid Vehicle in the Next 3 Years for a Specific Attitude, Income, Education, and Age	$y = a + b_1x_1 + b_2x_2 + b_3x_3$ $= -9.659$ $+4.495 \times 6$ $+.052 \times 100$ $+.575 \times 16$ $+.117 \times 50$ $= -9.659 + 26.97 + 5.2$ $+ 9.2 + 5.85$ $= 37.56\%$ (rounded)

Notes:

Intercept $= -9.659$
$b_1 = 4.495 \times$ attitude $(x_1) = 6$
$b_2 = .052 \times$ income $(x_2) = \$100,000$
$b_3 = .575 \times$ education $(x_3) = 16$
$b_4 = .117 \times$ age $(x_4) = 50$

The calculated prediction is about 37.56%; however, we must take into consideration the sample error and variability of the data with a confidence interval, that is, the predicted probability of purchasing a standard size hybrid vehicle in the next three years ±1.96 times the standard error of the estimate.

Here is an example of a prediction using multiple regression.

Calculation of 95% Confidence Interval for a Prediction Based on Multiple Regression Findings with The Advanced Automobile Concepts Survey	Predicted $y \pm 1.96 \times$ standard error of the estimate $37.56 \pm 1.96 \times 17.966$ 37.56 ± 35.2 2.36% to 72.76%

Again we have found that survey data does not yield precise predictions because of the restrictions on the variability of the data. The confidence interval range is quite large, but it is perfectly reflective of the variability in the data and in no way a flaw in the multiple regression analysis. Soon we will describe how it is best to use multiple regression as a "screening" device with survey data. ∎

Special Uses of Multiple Regression Analysis

There are a number of special uses and considerations to keep in mind when running, multiple regression analysis. These include using a "dummy" independent variable, using standardized betas to compare the importance of independent variables, and using multiple regression as a screening device.

USING A "DUMMY" INDEPENDENT VARIABLE. A **dummy independent variable** is defined as one that is scaled with a nominal 0-versus-1 coding scheme. The 0-versus-1 code is traditional, but any two adjacent numbers could be used, such as 1 versus 2. The scaling assumptions that underlie multiple regression analysis require that the independent and dependent variables both be at least interval scaled. However, there are instances in which a marketing researcher may want to use an independent variable that does not embody interval-scaling assumptions. It is not unusual, for instance, for the marketing researcher to wish to use a dichotomous, or two-level, variable as an independent variable in a multiple regression analysis. Some commonly used dummy variables are gender (male versus female), purchasing (buyer versus nonbuyer), advertising exposure (recalled versus not recalled), or purchase history (first-time

The interval-at-minimum scaling assumption requirement of multiple regression may be relaxed by use of a dummy variable.

MARKETING RESEARCH INSIGHT   Ethical Application

19.3 What Factors Predict the Success of Business Ethics Taught in MBA Programs?

Researchers sampled students from 75 different MBA programs across the United States. They wished to identify aspects of these programs that were related to the perceived effectiveness of the incorporation of ethics into these MBA programs.[13] Using the effectiveness of ethics incorporation as the dependent variable, they found eight independent variable factors that were related at the .01 level of significance or lower. The factors and their standardized beta coefficients are listed next.

Factor	Standardized Beta
Number of incorporation methods used	.260
Required core course(s)	.152
Quality of program management	.149

Factor	Standardized Beta
Integrated case studies within most courses	.145
Referred to in most courses	.120
Willingness to recommend school	.081
Quality of curriculum	.075
Quality of faculty	.062

The table reveals that the most important factor was the teaching of business ethics using a variety of methods, including speakers, required core course(s), integrated case studies within some courses, referred to in most courses, elective course(s), and workshops. The next three factors, in terms of importance were: teaching business ethics as a required core course, overall quality of the MBA program's management, and integration of business ethics case studies with most of the courses in the MBA program. Of the eight statistically significant factors, the quality of the MBA faculty was the least important aspect.

buyer versus repeat buyer). For instance, with gender, a researcher may want to use a "0" for male and "1" for female as an independent variable. In these instances, it is usually permissible to go ahead and slightly violate the assumption of metric scaling for the independent variable to come up with a result that is in some degree interpretable.

USING STANDARDIZED BETAS TO COMPARE THE IMPORTANCE OF INDEPENDENT VARIABLES. Regardless of the application intentions, it is usually of interest to the marketing researcher to determine the relative importance of the independent variables in the multiple regression result. Because independent variables are often measured with different units, it is erroneous to make direct comparisons between the calculated betas. For example, it is improper to directly compare the *b* coefficient for family size to another for money spent per month on personal grooming because the units of measurement are so different (people versus dollars). The most common approach is to standardize the independent variables through a quick operation that involves dividing the difference between each independent variable value and its mean by the standard deviation of that independent variable. This results in what is called the **standardized beta coefficient**. In other words, standardization translates each independent value into the number of standard deviations away from its own mean. Essentially, this procedure transforms these variables into a set of values with a mean of zero and a standard deviation equal to 1.0.

> The researcher can compare standardized beta coefficients' sizes directly, but comparing unstandardized betas is like comparing apples and oranges.
>
> Standardized betas indicate the relative importance of alternative predictor variables.

When they are standardized, direct comparisons may be made between the resulting betas. The larger the absolute value of a standardized beta coefficient, the more relative importance it assumes in predicting the dependent variable. SPSS and most other statistical programs provide the standardized betas automatically. An example of the use of standardized beta coefficients is a recent study, described in Marketing Research Insight 19.3, that looked at the effectiveness of ethics coverage in MBA programs.

If you review the SPSS output in Figure 19.11, you will find the standardized values under the column designated "Standardized Coefficients." It is important to note that this operation has no effect on the final multiple regression result. Its only function is to allow direct comparisons of the relative impact of the significant independent variables on the dependent variable. As an example, if you look at the "Standardized Coefficients" reported in our Advanced Automobile Concepts regression printout (Figure 19.11), you will see that the attitude "high gasoline prices will impact what type of autos are purchased" is the most important variable (.492), whereas level of education, age, and income level (.074, .091, and .088, respectively) are much less important. We have highlighted these numbers with a light blue color so you can identify them easily.

 Segmentation Associates, Inc.

Segmentation Associates, Inc. is a marketing research company that specializes in market segmentation studies. It has access to large and detailed databases on demographics, lifestyles, asset ownership, consumer values, and a number of other consumer descriptors. It has developed a reputation for reducing these large databases into findings that are managerially relevant to its clients. That is, Segmentation Associates is known for its ability to translate its findings into market segmentation variables for its clients to use in their marketing strategies.

In the past year, Segmentation Associates has conducted a great many market segmentation studies for a number of automobile manufacturers. The company has agreed to provide disguised findings of some of its work. In the following table, segmentation variables are identified, and each of three different types of automobile buyer is identified. For each segmentation variable, Segmentation Associates has provided the results of its multiple regression findings. The values are the standardized beta coefficients of those segmentation variables found to be statistically significant. Where a dash ("—") appears, that regression coefficient was not statically significant.

Segmentation Variable	Economy Automobile Buyer	Sports Car Buyer	Luxury Automobile Buyer
Demographics			
Age	−.28	−.15	+.59
Education	−.12	+.38	—
Family size	+.39	−.35	—
Income	−.15	+.25	+.68
Lifestyle/Values			
Active	—	+.59	−.39
American Pride	+.30	—	+.24
Bargain Hunter	+.45	−.33	—
Conservative	—	−.38	+.54
Cosmopolitan	−.40	+.68	—
Embraces Change	−.30	+.65	—
Family Values	+.69	—	+.21
Financially Secure	−.28	+.21	+.52
Optimistic	—	+.71	+.37

Here are some questions to answer.

1. What is the underlying conceptual model used by Segmentation Associates that is apparent in these three sets of findings?
2. What are the segmentation variables that distinguish economy automobile buyers, and in what ways?
3. What are the segmentation variables that distinguish sports car buyers, and in what ways?
4. What are the segmentation variables that distinguish luxury automobile buyers, and in what ways?

USING MULTIPLE REGRESSION AS A SCREENING DEVICE. Another important application of multiple regression analysis is as a screening or identifying device. That is, the marketing researcher faced with a large number and variety of prospective independent variables may use multiple regression as a **screening device** or a way of spotting the salient (statistically significant) independent variables for the dependent variable at hand. In this instance, the intent is *not* to determine some sort of a prediction of the dependent variable; rather, it may be to search for clues as to what factors help the researcher understand the behavior of this particular dependent variable. For instance, the researcher might be seeking market segmentation bases and could use regression to spot which demographic variables are related to the consumer behavior variable under study. Recall that our examples of the use of bivariate and multiple regression with our Advanced Automobile Concepts survey data set have yielded very large confidence intervals when we applied the findings to make predictions. Although we illustrated how to make predictions from our regression analysis results, predictions are not the goal of our survey. Rather, the true purpose is to identify segments of the car-buying public that are more likely to purchase hybrid vehicles in the future, and this goal is usually well served when multiple regression is used as a screening device to identify the salient segmentation factors.

STEPWISE MULTIPLE REGRESSION

When the researcher is using multiple regression as a screening tool or is otherwise faced with a large number of independent variables in the conceptual model that are to be tested by multiple regression, it can become tedious to narrow down the independent variables by manual trimming. Fortunately, there is a type of multiple regression, called stepwise multiple regression, that does the trimming operation automatically.

Here is a simple explanation. With **stepwise multiple regression**, the one independent variable that is statistically significant and explains the most variance in the dependent variable is determined, and it is entered into the multiple regression equation. Then the statistically significant independent variable that contributes most to explaining the remaining unexplained variance in the dependent variable is determined and entered. This process is continued until all statistically significant independent variables have been entered into the multiple regression equation.[14] In other words, all of the insignificant independent variables are eliminated from the final multiple regression equation based on the level of significance stipulated by the researcher in the multiple regression options. The final output contains only statistically significant independent variables. Stepwise regression is used by researchers when they are confronted with a large number of competing independent variables and they do want to narrow down the analysis to a set of statistically significant independent variables in a single regression analysis. With stepwise multiple regression, there is no need to trim and rerun the regression analysis because SPSS does the trimming automatically based on the stepwise method selected by the researcher.

Researchers recently used stepwise multiple regression in an attempt to understand the factors that predict satisfaction of season ticket holders for selected Australian professional sports teams. As illustrated in Marketing Research Insight 19.4, this technique effectively reduced a large number of possible explanatory (independent) variables down to a very small set.

Stepwise regression is useful if a researcher has many independent variables and wants to narrow the set down to a smaller number of statistically significant variables.

How to Do Stepwise Multiple Regression with SPSS

A researcher executes stepwise multiple regression by using the ANALYZE–REGRESSION–LINEAR command sequence precisely as was described for multiple regression. The dependent variable and many independent variables are selected into their respective windows as before. To direct SPSS to perform stepwise multiple regression, one uses the

MARKETING RESEARCH INSIGHT   Practical Application

19.4 Stepwise Regression Finds Key Drivers of Australian Sports League Team Satisfaction

In Australia, two leagues dominate the professional sports landscape—the Australian Football League (AFL) Clubs and the National Rugby League (NRL). It is estimated that between 20,000 and 50,000 Australian sports fans are season ticket holders, or "members" of a team's fan support group. There are many benefits to season ticket membership, including discounts, memorabilia and souvenirs, special seating, privileged information about the team and its players, and more. In fact, researchers came up with at least 18 different reasons why Australian professional sports team season ticket holders might be satisfied with their chosen team.[15]

Overall satisfaction with the team was measured on an 11-point scale, and each of the 18 reasons or characteristics of the team's season ticket holder membership was measured on a 7-point Likert scale ranging from "poor" to "excellent." That is, there were 18 possible independent variables competing to predict overall satisfaction with the club's membership system. The researchers performed key driver analysis,[16] which is the application of multiple regression to narrow down a large number of possible determinants of overall satisfaction with a brand, company, or store into a small and tractable set of statistically significant ones. In particular, the researchers applied stepwise regression analysis.

They found the following five key drivers to overall satisfaction with the Australian team season ticket membership:

- The way contributions members are recognized by the club
- The service provided to members by the staff of the club
- The savings on game entry fees from being a member
- The way members are valued by the club
- The number of games won during year of membership

The adjusted R^2 was .541, meaning that these five aspects of the professional sports clubs accounted for 54% of the variance. So, slightly more than one-half of the overall satisfaction was explained or accounted for by only five factors. Notice that only one factor pertains to the team's win-loss record! Even a losing team in the Australian Football League (AFL) Clubs and the National Rugby League (NRL) can retain its season ticket holders if it pays attention to and delivers the desired service quality levels desired by them in the areas of: recognition of their loyalty, providing excellent customer service, providing discounts for season ticket holders, and expressing how much they value their season ticket holders.

Stepwise multiple regression analysis discovers why fans of Australian Football teams such as the Sydney Swans, who play at Moore Park, "stick with" their teams.

"Method" selection menu to select "Stepwise." The findings will be the same as those arrived at by a researcher who uses iterative trimmed multiple regressions. Of course, with stepwise multiple regression output, there will be information on those independent variables that are taken out of the multiple regression equation based on nonsignificance, and, if the researcher wishes, SPSS stepwise multiple regression will also take into account the VIF statistic to assure that multicollinearity is not an issue.

We do not have screenshots of stepwise multiple regression, as this technique is quite advanced. In fact, we do not recommend that you use stepwise multiple regression unless you gain a good deal more background on multiple regression because you may encounter findings that are difficult to understand or are even counterintuitive.[17]

THREE WARNINGS REGARDING MULTIPLE REGRESSION ANALYSIS

Regression is a statistical tool, not a cause-and-effect statement.

Before leaving our description of multiple regression analysis, we must issue a warning about your interpretation of regression. We all have a natural tendency to think in terms of causes and effects, and regression analysis invites us to think in terms of a dependent variable's resulting or being caused by an independent variable's actions. This line of thinking is absolutely incorrect: Regression analysis is nothing more than a statistical tool that assumes a linear relationship between two variables. It springs from correlation analysis, which is, as you will recall, a measure of the linear association and not the causal relationship between two variables. Consequently, even though two variables, such as sales and advertising, are logically connected, a regression analysis does not permit the marketing researcher to make cause-and-effect statements because other independent variables are not controlled.

The second warning we have is that you should not apply regression analysis to predict outside of the boundaries of the data used to develop your regression model. That is, you may use the regression model to interpolate within the boundaries set by the range (lowest value to highest value) of your independent variable(s), but if you use it to predict for independent values outside those limits, you have moved into an area that is not accounted for by the raw data used to compute your regression line. For this reason, you are not assured that the regression equation findings are valid. For example, it would not be correct to use our probability of buying a standard-size hybrid auto in the next three years–income regression equation findings on individuals who are wealthy and have annual incomes in the millions of dollars because these individuals were not represented in The Advanced Automobile Concepts survey.

Our last warning concerns the small amount of knowledge you have gained about multiple regression analysis in this chapter. You may be surprised that we say you have learned little about regression, but there is a great deal more to multiple regression analysis that is beyond the scope of this book. Our coverage in this chapter introduces you to regression analysis, and it provides you with enough information about it to run uncomplicated regression analyses with SPSS, identify the relevant aspects of the SPSS output, and to interpret the findings. As you will see when you work with the SPSS regression analysis procedures, we have only scratched the surface of this topic.[18] There are many more options, statistics, and considerations involved.[19] In fact, there is so much material that whole textbooks on regression exist. Our purpose has been to teach you the basic concepts and to help you to interpret the statistics associated with these concepts as you encounter them in statistical analysis program output. Our descriptions are merely an introduction to multiple regression analysis to help you comprehend the basic notions, common uses, and interpretations involved with this predictive technique.[20]

Despite our simple treatment of it, we fully realize that even simplified regression analysis is very complicated and difficult to learn and that we have showered you with a great many statistical regression terms and concepts in this chapter. Seasoned researchers are intimately acquainted with them and very comfortable in using them. However, as a student encountering them for the first time, you undoubtedly feel very intimidated. Although we may not be able to reduce your anxiety, we have created Table 19.4, which lists all of the regression analysis concepts we have described in this chapter and provides an explanation of each one. At least you will not need to search through the chapter to find these concepts when you are trying to learn or use them.

TABLE 19.4   Regression Analysis Concepts

Concept	Explanation
Regression analysis	A predictive model using the straight-line relationship of $y = a + bx$
Intercept	The constant, or "a," in the straight-line relationship that is the value of y when $x = 0$.
Slope	The "b," or the amount of change in y for a 1-unit change in x
Dependent variable	y, the variable that is being predicted by the x(s) or independent variable(s)
Independent variable(s)	The x variable or variables that are used in the straight-line equation to predict y
Least-squares criterion	A statistical procedure that assures the computed regression equation is the best one possible
R Square	A number ranging from 0 to 1.0 that reveals how well the straight-line model fits the scatter of points—the higher, the better
Standard error of the estimate	A value that is used to make a prediction at the (for example) 95% level of confidence with the formula $y \pm z \times s_e$
Multiple regression analysis	A powerful form of regression where more than one x variable is in the regression equation
Additivity	A statistical assumption that allows the use of more than one x variable in a multiple regression equation: $y = a + b_1x_1 + b_2x_2 + \cdots + b_mx_m$
Independence assumption	A statistical requirement that when more than one x variable is used, no pair of x variables has a high correlation
Multiple R	Also called the coefficient of determination, a number that ranges from 0 to 1.0 that indicates the strength of the overall linear relationship in a multiple regression, the higher the better
Multicollinearity	The term used to denote a violation of the independence assumption that causes regression results to be in error
Variance inflation factor (VIF)	A statistical value that identifies what x variable(s) contributes to multicollinearity and should be removed from the analysis to eliminate multicollinearity. Any variable with a VIF of 10 or greater should be removed.
Trimming	Removing an x variable in multiple regression because it is not statistically significant, rerunning the regression, and repeating until all remaining x variables are significant
Beta coefficients and standardized beta coefficients	Beta coefficients are the slopes (b values) determined by multiple regression for each independent variable, x. These are standardized to be in the range of .00 to .99 so they can be compared directly to determine their relative importance in y's prediction
Dummy independent variable	Use of an x variable that has a 0, 1 or similar coding, used sparingly when nominal variables must be in the independent variables set
Stepwise multiple regression	A specialized multiple regression that is appropriate when there is a large number of independent variables that need to be trimmed down to a small, significant set and the researcher wishes the statistical program to do this automatically

REPORTING REGRESSION FINDINGS TO CLIENTS

As we indicated in this chapter, there are two basic uses of regression analysis: as a screening device and as a prediction generator. We show the recommended presentation formats for each case.

Reporting Regression Used as a Screening Device

The objective of a screening mechanism is to identify the relevant or meaningful variables as they relate to some dependent variable of interest. For most clients, the dependent variable of interest is sales, purchases, intentions to purchase, satisfaction, or some other variable that translates in some way how customers regard or behave toward the company or brand. Normally, the researcher is faced with a large number of possible factors, any combination of which might relate to the dependent variable. The situation is identical to that described in our presentation on a general conceptual model and embodied in our Marketing Research Insight 19.2, "Regression Analysis Tests a Model of the Predictors of Bank Switching in New Zealand," as well as Marketing Research Insight 19.4, "Stepwise Regression Finds Key Drivers of Australian Sports League Team Satisfaction."

When regression is used as a screening device, the items to report are (1) dependent variable, (2) statistically significant independent variables, (3) signs of beta coefficients, and (4) standardized beta coefficients for the significant variables. Here is a table that reports the use of regression analysis to determine the target market profile of the Subshop.

Factors Related to Number of Visits to the Subshop (Stepwise Regression Analysis Results)

Dependent Variable		
How many times have you eaten at the Subshop in the past 30 days?	288 Total Cases	
Independent Variable(s)	**Coefficient***	**Standardized**
Demographic Factors		
Gender**	−3.02	−.43
Age	4.71	.35
Education	−7.28	−.12
*Lifestyle Factors***		
I typically go to restaurants that have good prices.	.32	.35
Eating at restaurants is a large part of my diet.	−.21	−.27
I usually buy the "special of the day" at lunch.	−.17	−.20
Intercept	2.10	

*95% level of confidence
**Dummy variable coded 0 = female and 1 = male
***Based on a scale where 1 = strongly disagree and 7 = strongly agree

We will point out a number of nuances in the presentation table. First, the method of multiple regression (stepwise) is reported. Second, only the statistically significant (95% level of confidence) independent variables are reported. Third, the types of independent variables (here, demographics and lifestyle) are separated. Fourth, within each type, the independent variables are arranged in descending order according to the absolute values of their standardized beta coefficients. Fifth, where the coding of the independent variable is pertinent to proper interpretation, the measurement scale is reported as a footnote to the table. Note, in particular, that gender was used as a dummy variable, so it is important that the reader know the code in order to realize that the finding denotes that the Subshop's target market is skewed toward women.

Reporting Regression Used as a Predictive Tool

Using regression as a predictive tool is very different from its use as a screening device. To properly apply the regression result as a predictive equation, the following aspects are necessary: (1) dependent variable; (2) statistically significant independent variables; (3) intercept; (4) beta coefficients, including signs; (5) adjusted R^2; and (6) standard error of the estimate. A preferred format for reporting the statistically significant findings of the use of multiple regression as a predictive tool is a multiple regression equation such as the following:

$$\text{Predicted sales} = \textbf{305.3} \times \textbf{population} + \textbf{76.3} \times \textbf{income} - \textbf{200.3} \\ \times \textbf{\# competitors} \pm \textbf{6,359.6}$$

This equation could be used to estimate the sales of a new Subshop located in a particular geographic area. The equation says that the expected average sales would be equal to 305.3 times the population (in 10,000s) plus 76.3 times income (in $10,000s) minus 200.3 times the number of relevant competitors (other sandwich shops and fast-food restaurants located in the target area). The 95% confident interval would be computed by using this equation and then subtracting 6,359.6 to obtain the lower limit and adding 6,359.6 to calculate the upper limit.

If the Subshop had three new locations under consideration, the researcher could apply this regression equation to the known or estimated independent variable levels and make predictions of the expected sales levels for each. This presentation would provide the client with sufficient information for its new location decision.

Predicted Sales for Each of Three Possible New Locations for the Subshop

	Location 1 **Main &** **Fourth** **Streets**	**Location 2** **Commerce &** **Congress** **Streets**	**Location 3** **Red Brook** **Shopping** **Center**
Population in 10,000s	100	120	85
Average income in $10,000s	100	75	50
Number of competitors	12	15	8
Expected sales	**$35,756**	**$39,354**	**$28,163**
Lower C.I.	$29,397	$32,994	$21,804
Upper C.I.	$42,116	$45,714	$34,523

Synthesize Your Learning

This exercise will require you to take into consideration concepts and material from these three chapters:

Chapter 17	Implementing Basic Differences Tests
Chapter 18	Making Use of Associations Tests
Chapter 19	Understanding Regression Analysis Basics

Alpha Airlines

In the middle of the first decade of the 21st century, many airlines found themselves in a very unfortunate situation. On the supply side, prices rose at an unusually high rate. Aviation fuel, in particular, rose at an alarming rate, and other costs—employee wages and salaries, supplies, services, rent, and repairs—rose faster than ever before. Unable to counter these price increases, most airlines slowly instituted price increases and unbundled some of their services, such as charging $15 per checked-in bag. On the demand side, in the face of a recession and rising costs of many goods and services, business flyers reduced their flying and consumers cut back on their travel plans or turned to less expensive travel methods such as trains or personal automobiles. Reports by ticket sales agencies confirmed that many international vacationers and tourists had cancelled or indefinitely postponed their plans.

Alpha Airlines, a major international airline, felt the squeeze of both sides of the equation during this time as passenger miles and revenues began to fall in what some airline industry analysts characterized as a "death spiral." However, marketing executives at Alpha Airlines vowed not to give up without putting up a very good fight, and they designed a questionnaire to obtain some baseline data as well as to assess the reactions of Alpha Airlines customers to possible changes in Alpha Airline's services and prices. An abbreviated version of the questionnaire follows.

1. Approximately how many of the following trips have you taken on Alpha Airlines this year?

    a. Domestic business _____
    b. Domestic tourist _____
    c. International business _____
    d. International tourist _____

2. Do you . . . (check all that apply)

    _____ Belong to Alpha Airlines frequent-flyer program?

    _____ Belong to Alpha Airlines Prestige Club (private lounge areas in some airports)?

    _____ Use Alpha Airlines website to book most of your flights?

    _____ Usually travel business class (including first class) on Alpha Airlines?

3. Indicate from 1 to 7, where 1 = do not want at all and 7 = desire very much, how desirable is each of the following potential new Alpha Airline services is to you.

    _____ Double Alpha Airlines frequent-flyer miles for any trips after you have earned 25,000 miles in that year

    _____ From 33% to 50% savings air fare for a second family member on any international flight with you

    _____ No $15 checked-in bag charge if you belong to the Alpha Airlines Prestige Club

    _____ Priority boarding on international Alpha Airlines flights if you belong to the Alpha Airlines Frequent-Flyer program

    _____ Free wireless Internet service while in flight

In addition to the answers to these questions, the questionnaire also gathered information on the following: gender, education level (highest level in years), income level (in $10,000 increments), age (actual years), marital status, approximate number of air flight (any airline) trips taken for each of the past three years, some lifestyle dimensions.[21] [For example: From my experience, I have found that the larger the airline company the lower the actual cost of travel has been; I generally call several airlines or travel agents to get price quotes and routing before I decide on a paricular airline; The price I pay for my ticket is more important to me than the service I receive prior to and during the flight; I choose to travel by airline because my time is very valuable to me; I feel that the services I receive during the flight are good; I feel that the preflight services (i.e., baggage handling, ticket processing, etc.) are good; and Normally, I fly with one particular airline company.]

The self-administered questionnaire is handed out by flight attendants to all Alpha Airlines passengers traveling on domestic or international flights during the first week of the month, resulting in over 20,000 completed and useable questionnaires. The Alpha Airlines marketing executives have a number of questions that they hope will be answered by this survey.

For each of the following questions, indicate the specific questions or variables in the survey that should be analyzed, paying close attention to the scale properties of each variable. Specify the type of statistical analysis that is appropriate and how SPSS output would indicate whether or not statistically significant findings are present.

1. What is the target market profile of each of the following types of Alpha Airlines traveler? That is, what demographic and lifestyle factors are related to the number of miles traveled on Alpha Airlines for each of the following types?

   a. Domestic business traveler
   b. Domestic tourist traveler
   c. International business traveler
   d. International tourist traveler

2. Are there differences in the desirabilities of each of the five potential new Alpha Airlines services with respect to:

   a. Gender?
   b. Belonging (or not) to Alpha Airlines frequent-flyer program?
   c. Belonging (or not) to Alpha Airlines Prestige Club (private lounge areas in some airports)?
   d. Use or nonuse of Alpha Airlines' website to book most of your flights?
   e. Usual class of seating (business versus economy class) on Alpha Airlines?

3. Do relationships exist for estimated number of air flight trips in each of the past three years on any airline with . . .

   a. Age?
   b. Income?
   c. Education?
   d. Any of the lifestyle dimenstions?

4. Do associations exist for (1) participating or not in Alpha Airlines frequent-flyer program, (2) membership or not to Alpha Airlines Prestige Club (private lounge areas in some airports), and/or (3) use or not of Alpha Airlines website to book most flights with

   a. Gender,
   b. Marital status, or
   c. Usual class of seating (business versus economy class) on Alpha Airlines?

5. Based on total Alpha Airlines miles traveled this year, what is the prediction for total Alpha Airlines miles expected to travel next year using all of the information gathered in the survey? What is the most critical assumption underlying this prediction?

Summary

Predictive analyses are methods used to forecast the levels of a variable, such as sales. Model building and extrapolation are two general options available to market researchers. In either case, it is important to assess the goodness of the prediction. This assessment is typically performed by comparing the predictions against the actual data with procedures called residuals analyses.

Market researchers use regression analysis to make predictions. The basis of this technique is an assumed straight-line relationship existing between the variables. With bivariate regression, one independent variable, x, is used to predict the dependent variable, y, using the straight-line formula of $y = a + bx$. A high R^2 and a statistically significant slope indicate that the linear model is a good fit. With multiple regression, the underlying conceptual model specifies that several independent variables are to be used, and it is necessary to determine which ones are significant. By systematically eliminating the non-significant independent variables in an iterative manner, a process called "trimming," a researcher will ultimately derive a set of significant independent variables that yield a significant predictive model. The standard error of the estimate is used to compute a confidence interval range for a regression prediction.

Seasoned researchers may opt to use stepwise multiple regression if faced with a large number of candidate independent variables, such as several demographic, lifestyle, and buyer-behavior characteristics. With stepwise multiple regression, only statistically significant independent variables are entered into the multiple regression equation.

Key Terms

Prediction 570	Independent variable 573	Coefficient of determination 587
Extrapolation 570	Least-squares criterion 575	Independence assumption 588
Predictive model 571	Standard error of the estimate 581	Multicollinearity 588
Analysis of residuals 571	Outlier 583	Variance inflation factor (VIF) 588
Bivariate regression analysis 572	General conceptual model 584	Dummy independent variable 591
Intercept 573	Multiple regression analysis 586	Standardized beta coefficient 592
Slope 573	Regression plane 586	Screening device 594
Dependent variable 573	Additivity 586	Stepwise multiple regression 594

Review Questions/Applications

1. Construct and explain a reasonably simple predictive model for each of the following cases:
   a. What is the relationship between gasoline prices and distance traveled for family automobile touring vacations?
   b. How do hurricane-force warnings relate to purchases of flashlight batteries in the expected landfall area?
   c. What do florists do with regard to inventory of flowers for the week prior to and the week following Mother's Day?

2. Indicate what the scatter diagram and probable regression line would look like for two variables that are correlated in each of the following ways (in each instance, assume a negative intercept): (a) −.89 (b) +.48, and (c) − .10

3. Circle K runs a contest inviting customers to fill out a registration card. In exchange, they are eligible for a grand prize drawing of a trip to Alaska. The card asks for the customer's age, education, gender, estimated weekly purchases (in dollars) at that Circle K, and approximate distance of the Circle K is from home. Identify each of the following if a multiple regression analysis were to be performed: (a) independent variable, (b) dependent variable, (c) dummy variable.

4. Explain what is meant by the independence assumption in multiple regression. How can you examine your data for independence, and what statistic is issued by most statistical analysis programs? How is this statistic interpreted? That is, what would indicate the presence of multicollinearity, and what would you do to eliminate it?

5. What is multiple regression? Specifically, what is "multiple" about it, and how does the formula for multiple regression appear? In your formula, identify the various terms and also indicate the signs (positive or negative) that they may take on.

6. If one uses the "enter" method for multiple regression analysis, what statistics on an SPSS output should be examined to assess the result? Indicate how you would determine each of the following:
   a. Variance explained in the dependent variable by the independent variables
   b. Statistical significance of each of the independent variables.
   c. Relative importance of the independent variables in predicting the dependent variable

7. Explain what is meant by the notion of "trimming" a multiple regression result. Use the following example to illustrate your understanding of this concept.

   A bicycle manufacturer maintains records over 20 years of the following: retail price in dollars, cooperative advertising amount in dollars, competitors' average retail price in dollars, number of retail locations selling the bicycle manufacturer's brand, and whether or not the winner of the Tour de France was riding the manufacturer's brand (coded as a dummy variable where $0 =$ no and $1 =$ yes).

The initial multiple regression result determines the following:

Variable	Significance Level
Average retail price in dollars	.001
Cooperative advertising amount in dollars	.202
Competitors' average retail price in dollars	.028
Number of retail locations	.591
Tour de France	.032

Using the "enter" method, what would be the trimming steps you would expect to undertake to identify the significant multiple regression result? Explain your reasoning.

8. Using the bicycle example in Question 7, what do you expect would be the sequence in the elimination of variables using stepwise multiple regression? Explain your reasoning with respect to the operation of each step of this technique.

9. Using SPSS graphical capabilities, diagram the regression plane for the following variables:

Number of Gallons of Gasoline Used per Week	Miles Computed for Work per Week	Number of Riders in Carpool
5	50	4
10	125	3
15	175	2
20	250	0
25	300	0

10. The Maximum Amount is a company that specializes in making fashionable clothes in large sizes for large people. Among its customers are Queen Latifah and Shaquille O'Neal. A survey was performed for the Maximum Amount, and a regression analysis was run on some of the data. Of interest in this analysis was the possible relationship between self-esteem (dependent variable) and number of Maximum Amount articles purchased last year (independent variable). Self-esteem was measured on a 7-point scale in which 1 signifies very low and 7 indicates very high self-esteem. Following are some items that have been taken from the output.

Pearson product moment correlation $= +0.63$
Intercept $= 3.5$
Slope $= +0.2$
Standard error $= 1.5$

All statistical tests are significant at the 0.01 level or less. What is the correct interpretation of these findings?

11. Wayne LaTorte is a safety engineer who works for the U.S. Postal Service. For most of his life, Wayne has been fascinated by UFOs. He has kept records of UFO sightings in the desert areas of Arizona, California, and New Mexico over the past 15 years and he has correlated them with earthquake tremors. A fellow engineer suggests that Wayne use regression analysis as a means of determining the relationship. Wayne does this and finds a "constant" of 30 separate earth tremor events and a slope of 5 events per UFO sighting. Wayne then writes an article for the *UFO Observer*, claiming that earthquakes are largely caused by the subsonic vibrations emitted by UFOs as they enter Earth's atmosphere. What is your reaction to Wayne's article?

CASE 19.1

THE PETS, PETS, AND PETS TEAM PROJECT (PART IV)

A cell phone chirps at 9:13 p.m. in an apartment just off campus. Marsha checks the caller identification, presses the On button, and says, "Josh! What a surprise. Are you calling to say that you did that regression analysis for our Pets, Pets, and Pets marketing research project that you promised to send me by 7 p.m. tonight?"

JOSH: Boy, are you heartless, and after I brought pizza to your place last week.
MARSHA: Yeah, right, and you kept me up all night going over that present value finance stuff that was on our finance class test the next day. Then, you said you couldn't stay awake and crashed on my couch at 3 am. I could hardly finish our marketing research presentation on cross-tabs and correlations for Dr. Z's class because of your loud snoring.

JOSH: Well, anyway, I did pass that test, and I did the regression analysis just like we agreed. I used the evaluations of Pets, Pets, and Pets that we added plus some of the lifestyle statements that we added in the regressions. Plus, I even summarized them into tables. I just e-mailed them to you. So, the ball is in your court.

MARSHA: Hey, wait! Hang on while I look at them in case I have any questions.

Marsha checks her e-mail and opens up Josh's document. The document follows.

TABLE 1

Number of Times Visited PPP in Past Year	
Independent Variable(s)	Standardized
I usually purchase pet supplies from the same company.*	.31
Pets, Pets, and Pets helps me stretch my wallet.*	−.25
Buying pet supplies at Pets, Pets, and Pets gives me time to do more important things.*	.25
My pet is a large part of my life.*	.30
I am pleased with my pet right now.*	.13
I enjoy taking care of my pet.*	.15
How many miles do you live from Pets, Pets, and Pets?	−.19
Indicate your gender (1 = male, 2 = female).	−.18

TABLE 2

How Likely to Buy at PPP Next Time (1–7 scale)	
Independent Variable(s)	Standardized
There is a wide variety of pet supplies at Pets, Pets, and Pets.*	−.25
There are good values at Pets, Pets, and Pets.*	.49
There are helpful employees at Pets, Pets, and Pets.*	.33

TABLE 3

Amount Spent at PPP Last Time	
Independent Variable(s)	Standardized
Number of pets owned	−.17
Recall seeing a PPP newspaper ad in the past month? (1 = yes, 2 = no)	−.21
Family income level	.38

*Based on a scale where 1 = strongly disagree and 5 = strongly agree

MARSHA: All right, I see three tables with the multiple regression findings. You did separate ones for how many times they visited PPP in the past year, how likely they are to use PPP the next time, and the amount they spent the last time they visited PPP. Your tables have the standardized beta coefficients for the statistically significant independent variables, right?

JOSH: Um, yeah, right.

MARSHA: What I mean is that you used trimming or stepwise multiple regression. Right?

JOSH: Yep, I did the stepwise regression just like Dr. Z showed us in class.

MARSHA: Okay. I should have the presentation done in plenty of time for our marketing research class tomorrow. Bye!

1. Describe how the stepwise multiple regression approach that Josh used resulted in the significant independent variables reported in each of his three tables.
2. Describe the relationships revealed in each table, and indicate the implications of these relationships that Marsha can work with in making recommendations for Pets, Pets, and Pets marketing strategy.

CASE 19.2

THE HOBBIT'S CHOICE RESTAURANT SURVEY PREDICTIVE ANALYSIS

SPSS

Jeff Dean, the aspiring restaurant owner, was a very happy camper. He had learned that his dream of The Hobbit's Choice Restaurant could be a reality. Through the research conducted under Cory Rogers's expert supervision and Celeste Brown's SPSS analysis, Jeff had a good idea of what features were desired, where it should be located, and even what advertising media to use to promote it. He believed he had all the information he needed to obtain the financing necessary to design and build The Hobbit's Choice Restaurant.

Jeff called Cory on Friday morning and said, "Cory, I am very excited about everything that your work has found about the good prospects of The Hobbit's Choice Restaurant. I want to set up a meeting with my banker next week to pitch it to him for the funding. Can you get me the final report by then?"

Cory was silent for a moment and then he said, "Celeste is doing the final figures and dressing up the tables so we can paste them into the report document. But I think you have forgotten about the last research objective. We still need to address the target market definition with a final set of analyses. I know that Celeste just finished another important project, and she has been asking if there is any work she can do this week. I'll give her this task. Why don't you plan on coming over at 11:00 a.m. on Monday. Celeste and I will show you what we have found."

Your task in Case 19.3 is to take Celeste's role, use The Hobbit's Choice Restaurant SPSS data set, and perform the proper analysis. You will also need to interpret the findings.

1. What is the demographic target market definition for The Hobbit's Choice Restaurant?
2. What is the target market definition of restaurant spending behavior for The Hobbit's Choice Restaurant?
3. Develop a general conceptual model of market segmentation for The Hobbit's Choice Restaurant. Test it using multiple regression analysis and interpret your findings for Jeff Dean.

CASE 19.3 Your Integrated Case

ADVANCED AUTOMOBILE CONCEPTS SEGMENTATION ANALYSIS

SPSS

It is Monday, and today is your first day in your new marketing internship. After a rigorous application and review process, including two grueling interviews with Cory Rogers and Celeste Brown, you have been hired by CMG Research.

It is 9:00 am, and you are in Cory Rogers's office along with Celeste Brown. Cory says, "We know that it is just your first day as the CMG Research marketing intern, but we are getting bogged down with a lot of work that must be completed very quickly or our clients will be unhappy. As I indicated to you a few days ago when I let you know that we chose you to be this year's marketing intern, Celeste and I were very impressed with your command of SPSS and your understanding of more advanced statistical analyses such as regression and analysis of variance. So, we are going to let you show us your stuff right away."

Cory continues, "We are in the final stages of a major survey that we conducted for Advanced Automobile Concepts. They have five hybid-model automobiles under consideration for multimillion-dollar development. We have provided them with a great deal of analysis, and they are in the process of narrowing down the development list. I would like to give them one more set of findings. Specifically, I would like to give them target market definitions for each of the possible models. That is, using multiple regression analysis as a screening device, we need to identify the significant demographics, beliefs about global warming and gasoline prices, and attitudes toward hybrid-vehicle factors that uniquely define these preference segments."

Celeste then says, "I have prepared a list of the five types as well as all of the demographic, belief, and attitude variables that we want analyzed. After our meeting, I will take you to my office and orient you on the survey, sample, prior findings, the SPSS data set, and anything else that you have questions about."

Cory ends the meeting with, "Great. I am sure that you will do a fantastic job with this assignment. Celeste and I have to catch a flight in a couple of hours, and we will be out of town for the next 3 days. But, you can call, text, or e-mail. Let's set a meeting for 9:00 am on Thursday so you can show us what you have found."

Preferences for Each of Five Possible Hybrid Automobiles (1–7 scale)

- Super Cycle one-seat hybrid
- Runabout Sport two-seat hybrid
- Runabout with Luggage two-seat hybrid
- Economy four-seat hybrid
- Standard four-seat hybrid

Demographics (See SPSS data file for levels and coding)	Beliefs about Global Warming and Gasoline Prices (1–7 agreement scale)	Attitudes toward Hybrid Automobiles (1–7 agreement scale)
• Size of hometown or city • Gender • Marital status • Number of people in household • Age • Level of education • Income level	• I am worried about global warming. • Global warming is a real threat. • We need to do something to slow global warming. • Gasoline emissions contribute to global warming. • Americans use too much gasoline. • We should be looking for gasoline substitutes. • Gasoline prices will remain high in the future. • Gasoline prices are too high now. • High gasoline prices will impact what type of autos are purchased.	• Hybrid autos that use alternative fuels will reduce fuel emissions. • Hybrid autos that use alternative fuels will keep gas prices down. • Hybrid autos that use alternative fuels will slow down global warming.

On the way to her office for your orientation to the Advanced Automobile Concepts project and its SPSS data set, Celeste, says, "For sure this is pretty confusing, but when we quizzed you during your interview, we asked specific questions about multiple regression and how it can be used for market segmentation analyses. Your answers were right on. Just remember that we are using the preferences data for the segments and not the probabilities of purchasing these types of vehicles. The preferences questions used descriptions of the vehicle features and characteristics that the Advanced Automobile Concepts folks are considering, while the probabilities questions were just to get rough indications of how the respondents felt about the various technologies."

Your task as the new CMG marketing intern: Use the AAConcepts.sav data file, or your AAConcepts.Recoded.sav data file if you do not want to do the recoding operations. Perform the proper analyses to identify the salient demographic, belief, and/or attitude factors that are related to preferences for each of the five different hybrid models under consideration. With each hybrid automobile model, prepare a summary that does the following:

1. Lists the statistically significant independent variables (use 95% level of confidence),
2. Interprets the directional of the relationship of each statistically significant independent variable with respect to the preference for the hybrid model concerned,
3. Identifies or distinguishes the relative importance of each of the statistically significant independent variables, and
4. Assesses the strength of the statistically significant independent variables as they join to predict the preferences for the hybrid model concerned.

Learning Objectives

- To appreciate the importance of the marketing research report

- To learn a new online report-writing tool, the *iReportWriter Assistant*, that will help you write better reports

- To know what material should be included in each part of the marketing research report

- To learn the basic guidelines for writing effective marketing research reports

- To know how to use visuals such as figures, tables, charts, and graphs

- To learn how to make visuals such as tables and figures such as pie charts and bar charts using SPSS

- To learn the basic principles for presenting your report orally

Communication Works for Those Who Work at It

Heather Howard
Donofrio, Ph.D.,
Business Communications

Interpersonal communication? Why should I study that? I talk to people all the time; I've done it all my life. I communicate with people all day. I write papers and e-mails all the time. I don't need to be taught something that just comes naturally. Do you feel that way about communication? If so, let's explore a couple of other questions.

Have you ever listened to an entire presentation only to wonder what the point of the speech was? Do you find yourself carrying on a conversation with someone only to realize you don't know what the person has been talking about for the last five minutes? Have you ever read a report to find you have learned nothing from it? If you answered yes to any of these questions, you see the importance of learning effective interpersonal communication.

Communication is an essential tool for your success in business. But don't be fooled into thinking it will be any easier to attain than any other business fundamental. As John Powell said, Communication works for those who work at it.[1]

And William B. Chiasson, CFO of Leapfrog Enterprises and former Senior Vice President and CFO of Levi Strauss and Company, gave the following statement as advice for MBA graduates: "Anyone pursuing an MBA should emphasize communication and interpersonal skills, the ability to work in small and large teams, and the ability to work with people in a multidisciplinary capacity."[2] The business world is without a doubt calling out for good communicators. If you want to be prepared for your career, you must ensure that you have the needed communication skills.

A career in marketing requires a variety of communication skills, including the ability to present research results in a spoken and written manner. But writing a marketing research report for the first time can be a bit daunting and confusing. The authors of your textbook recognize the sometimes overwhelming job of the research report and have provided an online tool to help you understand this job.

In this chapter, you will be introduced

609

to a new online report writing tool. We will refer to this tool as the iReporting Assistant, which will be explained in detail for you in the chapter. The iReporting Assistant takes you through the whole process of writing the report. You begin with the prewriting steps of analyzing your purpose, anticipating your audience, and adapting the message to the audience. Then, you research your topic—a process discussed in great detail in this text—organize your information into a workable outline, and compose your first draft. Much of the work is done after these six steps, after which you revise, proofread, and evaluate whether your report will accomplish your purpose.[3]

Other aspects of the report to consider are the citations (the style to be used), grammar, and professional graphics. All parts of the report should be as flawless as possible for the report to be effective. (Your product is a reflection of you and your company.) The online writing tool will ensure that you have the information needed to create a masterful marketing research report that can contribute to a successful business career.

—Heather Howard Donofrio

*W*e asked Dr. Heather Donofrio to introduce you to this chapter in our opening vignette. One of the points she makes clearly is how important it is for you to be an effective communicator, both written and oral. If you have been following our integrated case, *Advanced Automotive Concepts,* you know that the data analysis for Nick Thomas's project is finished. Cory Rogers and his CMG Research team have worked diligently to investigate the market potential of hybrid cars for Advanced Automotive Concepts, and they are ready to prepare their findings and recommendations for presentation. You might think the bulk of their work is finished, but that is not the case. Now begins the task of sifting through the hundreds of pages of printouts and other information to determine what to present and then how to present it clearly and effectively. When the members of the team have prepared the written report, they will also need to decide which elements are critical to include in the oral presentation to the client.

Compiling a market research report is a challenging (and sometimes daunting) task. Cory and his team meet to discuss what parts need to be in the report, what content needs to be in each part, what kinds of visuals to include, and what format to follow for headings and subheadings. Then they assign responsibilities to the members of the team and agree on a timetable. When they have a common understanding of what their objectives are and what each team member will do, they are ready to strike out on their individual tasks, meeting frequently to ensure that all tasks will be completed on time and to maintain consistency in their ideas and understandings.

It is very likely that you have worked on a team project and have been required to assemble a report representing your team's work. Determining objectives and organizing the team members to carry out specific responsibilities are key to successful team management, and marketing researchers use these same techniques to assemble final reports for their clients. Although report writing is our final chapter, this does not indicate that it is less important than our other topics have been.[4] On the contrary, it means that communicating the results of your research is the culmination of the entire process. Being able to do so effectively and efficiently is critical to your success. In fact, all of your outstanding data and significant findings and recommendations are meaningless if you cannot communicate them in such a way that the client knows what you have said, understands your meaning, and responds appropriately. Michael A. Lotti, marketing researcher at Eastman

Writing a research report is like any other endeavor; teams should be well organized with clear responsibilities.

Kodak Company, has stated that even the best research will not drive the appropriate action unless the audience understands the outcomes and implications.[5] It is important that you be able to transfer exactly what is in your mind to the mind of the receiver of your message. The ultimate result of your hard labor is communication with your client.

*The **marketing research report** is a factual message that transmits research results, vital recommendations, conclusions, and other important information to the client, who in turn bases decisions on the contents of the report. This chapter deals with the essentials of writing and presenting the marketing research report.*

THE IMPORTANCE OF THE MARKETING RESEARCH REPORT

Researchers must provide value to clients in the research report. The marketing research report is the product that represents the efforts of the marketing research team, and it may be the only part of the project that the client will see. If the report is poorly written, riddled with grammatical errors, sloppy, or inferior in any way, the quality of the research (including its analysis and information) becomes suspect and its credibility is reduced. If organization and presentation are faulty, the reader may never reach the intended conclusions. The time and effort expended in the research process are wasted if the report does not communicate effectively.

If, on the other hand, all aspects of the report are done well, the report will not only communicate properly but will also serve to build credibility. Marketing research users,[6] as well as marketing research suppliers,[7] agree that reporting the research results is one of the most important aspects of the marketing research process. Many managers will not be involved in any aspect of the research process but will use the report to make business decisions. Effective reporting is essential, and all of the principles of organization, formatting, good writing, and good grammar must be used.

IMPROVING THE EFFICIENCY OF REPORT WRITING

So far, we have tried to explain to you just how important the report is to the success of the research project. You are probably thinking, based on the report writing (term papers!) you have done thus far in your college career, that writing a marketing research report is a

The marketing research report is a factual message that transmits research results, vital recommendations, conclusions, and other important information to the client, who in turn bases decisions on the contents of the report.

The time and effort expended in the research process are wasted if the report does not communicate effectively.

Report writing can be complex, involved, and time-consuming. However, if you read this chapter closely, you will take a big step toward being a more effective and efficient report writer!

formidable task. You are right. It is complex and involved and very time-consuming. However, in recent years several technological advances have greatly improved report writing. There are several software tools now available to help researchers gain efficiency in report writing. Burke, Inc. provides its clients access to its online reporting tool, *DigitalDashboard*. This service allows clients to watch data come in as they are being collected and organizes data into presentation-quality tables. Readers can examine total results or conduct their own subgroup analysis, even down to examining the results from individual respondents. Because the reports are available online, different client users can access them and conduct analyses that are important to their unit or division of the company. **Online reporting software** electronically distributes marketing research reports to selected managers in an interactive format that allows each user to conduct individual analyses.

E-Tabs has an award-winning software product that allows users to create standard tables and headings for repetitive reports, as is the case with tracking studies. Once banners, titles, and table formats are created, the report-writing task becomes more efficient by eliminating these steps for future reports. Of course, online reporting not only aids in the dissemination and use of reports but also avoids the expensive process of producing and storing paper reports. We've tried to make your report writing more efficient as well by preparing the *iReportWriter Assistant*, which you can access on the website for this textbook. The *iReportWriter Assistant* is explained in more detail in Marketing Research Insight 20.1.

There are several software tools now available to help researchers gain efficiency in report writing.

Online reporting software electronically distributes marketing research reports to selected managers in an interactive format that allows each user to conduct individual analyses.

We have prepared the iReportWriter Assistant, which you can access on the website for this textbook. The iReportWriter Assistant is explained in more detail in Marketing Research Insight 20.1.

Take a Tour of an Online Marketing Research Report Service

Burke's Digital Dashboard helps clients analyze and interpret research reports more efficiently.

For our active learning exercise we will take a closer look at Burke, Inc.'s online reporting writing software, Digital Dashboard. Go to www.digitaldashboard.com and click on "About Digital Dashboard." Read about the features and take a look at the example output pages. (Don't run the demonstration yet!) Note the features "In the Customer's Words," "Individual Reports," and "Data Collection Status Report." When you have read all the features, it is time to take the tour, noted at the bottom of the screen. (The program will run automatically—just give it a few seconds.) Watch for features such as the data filter, executive summary, trends over time, comparisons of the results of significant subgroups, the ability to filter to examine any subgroup results desired, the ability to search for verbatim comments, the ability to conduct statistical testing using the report software, and the ability to create your own charts and titles and transfer data to spreadsheets. Do you see how such tools can make the reporting process more efficient and the report more usable for clients?

ORGANIZING THE WRITTEN REPORT

Marketing research reports are tailored to specific audiences and purposes, and you must consider both in all phases of the research process, including planning the report. Before you begin writing, then, you must answer some questions:

- What message do you want to communicate?
- What is your purpose?

MARKETING RESEARCH INSIGHT

Practical Application

20.1 Your *iReportWriter Assistant*

It's easy to think that you are done with your marketing research when you complete data collection, but your work has just begun. Preparing reports is an in-depth process that requires time and effort, but it is well worth doing properly. The skill with which you complete reports will represent your own abilities as a researcher.

What to Do Prior to Writing?

Because report preparation is so critical to the marketing researcher, we have provided a tool to guide you through the marketing research report-writing process. This tool, the **iReporting Assistant**, is an overall discussion of the research report from the prewriting step (analyzing your purpose, anticipating your audience, and adapting the message to the audience) through research (including the research steps you have learned about in this text, the organization of your information into a workable outline, and the composition of your first draft), and finally to the revision step (revision, proofreading, and evaluation of whether or not your report will accomplish your purpose).

Templates to Help You Get Started

Knowledge of the writing process will prepare you to publish reports, but the actual course of action can be a bit more daunting. For example, what should the title page look like? How do you construct a list of illustrations? This text's *iReporting Assistant* helps solve these concerns by providing templates for the title page and list of illustrations along with letters of authorization and transmittal, the table of contents, the research objectives, and the method. Headings and subheadings are also explained so that the information you provide in a report is clear and flows well.

Help with Grammar

Well, so far, the writing process is taken care of, but two more areas are of great concern—grammar and citations. Despite the statistical accuracy and thorough coverage you may provide in your report, if your grammar is lacking, readers may question your ability, dedication, and effectiveness. An online grammar help is also provided by the *iReporting Assistant.*

Proper Citations

Finally, though you have done much research for your report, chances are that you have used information from other sources. Proper citation is not only polite, it is a requirement in order to avoid plagiarism (also discussed in the *iReportWriter Assistant*). You will probably be using one of two citation styles: APA (from the American Psychological Association) or MLA (from the Modern Language Association). Either is an acceptable citation form, but they differ in rules of formatting. After determining which style you should use for your report (whether required by a professor, organization, client, etc.), you must follow the rules of the chosen style. Some report writers find this part of the report a bit confusing, but never fear—the *iReportWriter Assistant* will assist you in securing the information needed for citing sources, including online sources.

An Example Report

As a final help to budding research report writers, an example of a proper marketing research report is provided. Check it out before writing or compare your own report to it during the revision step. In either case, good luck and happy report writing!

To access the *iReporting Assistant*, go to www.pearsonhighered.com/burns and click on the Companion Website link for this text.

- Who is the audience?
- If there are multiple audiences, who is your primary audience? Your secondary audience?
- What does your audience know?
- What does your audience need to know?
- Are there cultural differences you need to consider?
- What biases or preconceived notions of the audience might serve as barriers to your message?
- What strategies can you use to overcome these negative attitudes?
- Do your audience's demographic and lifestyle variables affect attitudes toward your research?
- What are your audience's interests, values, and concerns?

These and other questions must be addressed before you know how to structure your report.

When you are preparing the final report, it is often helpful "to get on the other side of the desk." Assume you are the reader instead of the sender.

When you are preparing the final report, it is often helpful "to get on the other side of the desk." Assume you are the reader instead of the sender. Doing so will help you see things through the eyes of your audience and increase the success of your communication. This is your opportunity to ask that basic (and very critical) question from the reader's point of view: "What's in it for me?"

Once you have answered these questions, you need to determine the format of your document. If the organization for which you are conducting the research has specific guidelines for preparing the document, you should follow them. However, even if no specific guidelines are provided, there are certain elements that must be considered when you are preparing the report. These elements can be grouped in three sections: front matter, body, and end matter. Table 20.1 lists these three sections and the elements they include.

iReportWriter Assistant: Visit the online report-writing guide for a discussion of the parts of the marketing research report. Templates for many of the report parts are provided.

Front matter consists of all pages that precede the first page of the report.

Front Matter

The **front matter** consists of all pages that precede the first page of the report—the title page, letter of authorization (optional), letter/memo of transmittal, table of contents, list of illustrations, and abstract/executive summary.

Title Page

The **title page** (Figure 20.1) contains four major items of information: (1) the title of the document, (2) the organization/person(s) for whom the report was prepared, (3) the organization/person(s) who prepared the report, and (4) the date of submission. If names of individuals appear on the title page, they may be in either alphabetical order or some other agreed-upon order; each individual should also be given a designation or descriptive title.

The document title should be as informative as possible. It should include the purpose and content of the report, such as "An Analysis of the Demand for a Branch Office of the CPA Firm of Saltmarsh, Cleaveland & Gund" or "Alternative Advertising Copy to

---

TABLE 20.1   The Elements of a Marketing Research Report

A. Front Matter
    1. Title Page
    2. Letter of Authorization
    3. Letter/Memo of Transmittal
    4. Table of Contents
    5. List of Illustrations
    6. Abstract/Executive Summary

B. Body
    1. Introduction
    2. Research Objectives
    3. Method
    4. Results
    5. Limitations
    6. Conclusions or Conclusions and Recommendations

C. End Matter
    1. Appendices
    2. Endnotes

FIGURE 20.1

Title Page

ADVANCED AUTOMOTIVE CONCEPTS:

A MARKETING RESEARCH STUDY

TO DETERMINE CAR MODEL PREFERENCES

AND PROFILE MARKET SEGMENTS

Prepared for
Mr. Nick Thomas

Prepared by
Cory Rogers
CMG Research, Inc.

July, 2010

Introduce the New M&M/Mars Low-Fat Candy Bar." The title should be centered and printed in all uppercase (capital) letters. Other items of information on the title page should be centered and printed in uppercase and lowercase letters. The title page is counted as page i of the front matter; however, no page number is printed on it. (See Figure 20.1.) On the next page, a printed page number, ii, will appear.

Some experts recommend that if you are making a presentation on the survey results, you change the title to a brief and understandable one.[8] For example, "An Analysis of the Demand for a Branch Office of the CPA Firm of Saltmarsh, Cleaveland & Gund" would be changed to simply "Demand for a Branch Office of Saltmarsh, Cleaveland & Gund." We provide you with some additional insights on preparing for an oral presentation later in the chapter.

Letter of Authorization

The **letter of authorization** is the marketing research firm's certification to do the project, and it is optional. It includes the name and title of the persons authorizing the research to be performed, and it may also include a general description of the nature of the research project, completion date, terms of payment, and any special conditions of the research project requested by the client or research user. If you allude to the conditions of your authorization in the letter/memo of transmittal, it is not necessary to include the letter of authorization in the report. However, if your reader may not know the conditions of authorization, inclusion of this document is helpful.

Letter/Memo of Transmittal

Use a letter for transmittal outside your organization and a memo within your own organization.

Use a **letter of transmittal** to release or deliver the document to an organization of which you are not a regular employee. Use a **memo of transmittal** to deliver the document within your own organization. The letter/memo of transmittal describes the general nature of the research in a sentence or two and identifies the individual who is releasing the report. The primary purpose of the letter/memo of transmittal is to orient the reader to the report and to build a positive image of the report. It should establish rapport between the writer and receiver. It gives the receiver a person to contact if questions arise.

Writing style in the letter/memo of transmittal should be personal and slightly informal. Some general elements that may appear in the letter/memo of transmittal are a brief identification of the nature of the research, a review of the conditions of the authorization to do the research (if no letter or authorization is included), comments on findings, suggestions for further research, and an expression of interest in the project and further research. It should end with an expression of appreciation for the assignment, acknowledgment of assistance from others, and suggestions for following up. Personal observations, unsupported by the data, are appropriate. Figure 20.2 presents an example of a letter of transmittal.

Table of Contents

The **table of contents** (Figure 20.3) helps the reader locate information in the research report. It should list all sections of the report that follow; each heading should read exactly as it appears in the text and should include the page number on which it appears. If a section is longer than one page, list the page on which it begins. Indent subheadings under headings. All items except the title page and the table of contents are listed with page numbers in the table of contents. Front-matter pages are numbered with lowercase Roman numerals: i, ii, iii, iv, and so on. Arabic numerals (1, 2, 3) begin with the introduction section of the body of the report.

List of Illustrations

If the report contains tables and/or figures, include in the table of contents a **list of illustrations** with page numbers on which they appear. All tables and figures should be included in this list, which helps the reader find specific illustrations that graphically portray the information. **Tables** are words or numbers that are arranged in rows and columns; **figures** are graphs, charts, maps, pictures, and so on. Because tables and figures are numbered independently, you may have both a Figure 1 and a Table 1 in your list of illustrations. Give each a name, and list each in the order in which it appears in the report.

Abstract/Executive Summary

Abstracts are "skeletons" of reports.

Your report may have many readers. Some of them will need to know the details of your report, such as the supporting data on which you base your conclusions and recommendations. Others will not need as many details, but will want to read the conclusions and recommendations. Still others with a general need to know may read only the executive summary. Therefore, the **abstract** or **executive summary** is a "skeleton" of your report. It serves as a summary for the

FIGURE 20.2

Letter of Transmittal

CMG Research, Inc.
1100 St. Louis Place
St. Louis, MO

July 21, 2010

Nick Thomas
Advanced Automotive Concepts
Anytown, USA 00000

Dear Mr. Thomas:

As you requested in your letter of authorization dated February 25, 2010, I have completed the marketing research analysis for Advanced Automotive Concepts. The results are contained in the report entitled "Advanced Automotive Concepts: A Marketing Research Study to Determine Car Model Preferences and Profile Market Segments."

The complete methodology is described in the report. Standard marketing research practices were used throughout the research project. You will find that the results of the report provide the information necessary to achieve the research objectives we set out for this project. These results represent "the voice of your future consumers," and we trust you will be able to use these results to make the best decisions for Advanced Automotive Concepts.

Should you need further assistance, please do not hesitate to call me at (877) 492-2891. I enjoyed working with you on this project, and I look forward to working with you again in the future.

Sincerely,

Cory Rogers

Cory Rogers

busy executive or a preview for the in-depth reader. It provides an overview of the most useful information, including the conclusions and recommendations. The abstract or executive summary should be very carefully written and convey the information as concisely as possible. It should be single-spaced and should briefly cover the general subject of the research, the scope of the research (what the research covers/does not cover), identification of the methods used (for example, a mail survey of 1,000 homeowners), conclusions, and recommendations.

Body

The **body** is the bulk of the report. It contains an introduction to the report, an explanation of your methods, a discussion of your results, a statement of limitations, and a list of conclusions and recommendations. Do not be alarmed by the repetition that may

FIGURE 20.3

Table of Contents

Table of Contents

ii

appear in your report. Only a few people will read it in its entirety. Most will read the executive summary, conclusions, and recommendations. Therefore, formal reports are repetitious. For example, you may specify the research objectives in the executive summary and refer to them again in the findings section as well as in the conclusions section. Also, do not be concerned that you use the same terminology to introduce the tables and/or figures. In many lengthy reports, repetition actually enhances reader comprehension.

The first page of the body contains the title, centered at the top of the page; this page is counted as page 1, but no page number is printed on it. All other pages throughout the document are numbered consecutively.

Introduction

The **introduction** to the marketing research report orients the reader to the contents of the report. It may contain a statement of the background situation leading to the problem, a statement of the problem, and a summary description of how the research process was initiated. It should contain a statement of the general purpose of the report and also the specific objectives for the research.

Research objectives may be listed either in a separate section (See Table 20.1) or within the introduction section. The listing of research objectives should follow the statement of the problem, since the two concepts are closely related. The list of specific research objectives often serves as a good framework for organizing the results section of the report.

Listing of research objectives should follow the statement of the problem.

Method

The **method** section describes, in as much detail as necessary, how you conducted the research, who (or what) your subjects were, and what tools or methods were used to achieve your objectives. Supplementary information should be placed in an appendix. If you used secondary information, you will need to document your sources (provide enough information so that your sources can be located).[9] You do not need to document facts that are common knowledge or can be easily verified. But if you are in doubt, document! **Plagiarism** refers to representing the work of others as your own. Plagiarism is a serious offense; it can cost you your job. Make certain you read Marketing Research Insight 20.2 carefully.

In most cases, the method section does not need to be long. It should, however, provide the essential information your reader needs to understand how the data were collected and how the results were achieved. It should be detailed enough that the data collection could be replicated by others for purposes of reliability. In other words, the method section should be clear enough that other researchers could conduct a similar study.

In some cases, the needs of the research user may dictate a very extensive method section. A client may, for example, want the researcher to not only thoroughly describe the method that was used but also discuss why other methods were not selected. For example, in situations in which research information will be provided in litigation, where there is certain to be an adversary, a researcher may be asked to provide an exhaustive description of the methods used in conducting the study and the methods that were not chosen.

The method section describes in detail how the research was conducted, who (or what) the subjects were, and what tools or methods were used to achieve the objectives.

Make sure you understand what plagiarism means. If in doubt, provide a reference to the source and put the citation in the proper format.

iReportWriter Assistant: See the online report writing guide for more information on plagiarism.

Method or Methodology?

You will note that we have named the section of the research report that describes the details of the procedures and tools used as the "method" section. However, in many cases, you will see the word *methodology* used as the title for this section of the report. You should use the word *method*. Why? The two terms have different meanings. Even though so many people use them interchangeably, that does not mean such usage is correct. **Methodology** refers to the science of determining appropriate methods to conduct research. The *American Heritage Dictionary* defines it as "the theoretical analysis of the methods appropriate to a field of study or to the body of methods and principles particular to a branch of knowledge."[10] Therefore, it would be appropriate to say that there are "objections to the methodology of a consumer survey" (that is, objections dealing with the appropriateness of the methods used in the survey) or to say "the methodology of modern marketing research" (that is, the principles and practices that underlie research in the field of marketing research).[11] Consequently, there is an important conceptual distinction between methodology and method. "Method" refers to the tools of scientific investigation (and the tools used in a marketing research project are described in detail in the method section of the report). "Methodology" refers to the principles that *determine how* such tools are deployed and interpreted. Marketing research *methodology* prescribes, for example, that we must use

The section of the report in which you describe the details of the procedures and tools used in the research project should be called the "method" section. Do not use the term *methodology*.

MARKETING RESEARCH INSIGHT

Ethical Issue

20.2 Do You Feel Like This About Documentation?

"It's just a few words."
"It's just a document for my office."
"I'm not making money off it."
"The information is from the Web; everyone can find it and use it."
"I could never say it better."
"The words are perfect; who cares who wrote it?"
"A bunch of citations just makes the report more difficult to read."
"Nobody expects me to reinvent the wheel."

Plagiarism is derived from a Latin word for kidnapping a Roman citizen's slave.[12] Words can be thought of as property. Avoiding plagiarism involves respect for the original author's work and respect for your audience's needs or desire to trace data and learn more from the source.

Just as all printed sources must be documented, so must information found online. In a letter to the *New York Times*, Marilyn Bergman, the president of the American Society of Composers, Authors, and Publishers, expressed a disturbing trend of online theft of words when she said that Americans are prompted by a "free for the taking" feeling about information on the Web.[13] The Internet is not in the public domain. Proper documentation of all sources helps a writer avoid public humiliation and maintain professional integrity.

Documentation of Online Sources: Why and How?

Copyright laws provide four general types of rights for an author:

1. The right to produce copies of the document
2. The right to sell or distribute document
3. The right to create new works based on the copyrighted work
4. The right to perform a work in public

The APA (American Psychological Association) and the MLA (Modern Language Association) offer two different formats for citation. Generally, the APA style is used in business fields, and the MLA style is used in the humanities. Style books and university websites offer examples of documentation for a range of sources, including electronic formats. For example, the preceding information was found on the library services website of the University of Maryland University College (UMUC). The source citation and format follow:

University of Maryland University College (1998). "Citing Internet Resources: APA Style," [On-line]. Available: http://www.umuc.edu/library/apa.html [2/4/99].

Format:

Author, I., Author, I., & Author, I. (Year, month date). Title, [Type of medium]. Available: Site/Path/File [Access date].

UMUC library services explains each field as follows:

Author—The creator or compiler of the information on the Web page. This can be the Web master or the name of the organization that is responsible for the page.
Year, month date—The date that the Web page was put online; it should be the same as the "last updated" date if available.
Title—The title of the document. Often, this can be found at the top of the Web page.
Type of medium—The way the document was accessed. If the document was found on the Web or through another Internet service, this field should read "Online."
Site/Path/File—The address or URL of the website.
Access date—The date that you viewed the Web page or accessed the information.

---

probability samples if we desire to have a sample that is representative of some population. Researchers would describe their use of their probability sample for a particular study in the *method* section of their paper. Use "method" not "methodology."

Results

The results section is the most important portion of your report and should present the findings of the research in a logical manner.

The **results** section is the most important portion of your report. Some researchers prefer the use of the term *findings*. This section should present the findings of your research in a logical manner and be organized around your objectives for the study. The results should be presented in narrative form and accompanied by tables, charts, figures, and other appropriate visuals that support and enhance the explanation of results. Tables and figures are supportive material; they should not be overused or used as filler. Each should contain a number and title and should be referred to in the narrative.

Outline your results section before you write the report. The survey questionnaire itself can serve as a useful aid in organizing your results because the questions are often grouped in a logical order or in purposeful sections. Another useful method for organizing your results is to individually print all tables and figures and arrange them in a logical sequence. Once you have the results outlined properly, you are ready to write the introductory sentences, definitions (if necessary), review of the findings (often referring to tables and figures), and transition sentences to lead into the next topic.

Limitations

Do not attempt to hide or disguise problems in your research; no research is faultless. Always be above board, and open regarding all aspects of the research. To avoid discussion of limitations often renders suspect your integrity and your research. Suggest what the limitations are or may be and what impact they have on the results. You might also suggest opportunities for further study based on the limitations. Typical **limitations** in research reports often focus on but are not limited to factors such as time, money, size of sample, and personnel. Consider the following example: "The reader should note that this study was based on a survey of graduating students at a mid-sized public university in the Southeast United States. Budget constraints limited the sample to this university and this region of the country. Care should be exercised in generalizing these findings to other populations."

> Do not attempt to hide or disguise problems in your research. Suggest what the limitations are or may be and what impact they have on the results.

Conclusions and Recommendations

Conclusions and recommendations may be listed together or in separate sections, depending on the amount of material you have to report. In any case, you should note that conclusions are not the same as recommendations. **Conclusions** are the outcomes and decisions you have reached based on your research results. **Recommendations** are suggestions for how to proceed based on the conclusions. Unlike conclusions, recommendations may require knowledge beyond the scope of the research findings themselves, for example, information on conditions within the company, the industry, and so on. Therefore, researchers should exercise caution in making recommendations. The researcher and the client should determine prior to the study whether the report is to contain recommendations. A clear understanding of the researcher's role will result in a smoother process and will help avoid conflict. Although a research user may desire the researcher to provide specific recommendations, both parties must realize that the researcher's recommendations are based solely on the knowledge gained from the research report, not familiarity with the client. Other information, if made known to the researcher, could totally change the researcher's recommendations.

> Conclusions are the outcomes and decisions you have reached based on your research results. Recommendations are suggestions for how to proceed based on the conclusions.

If recommendations are required and if a report is intended to initiate further action, however, recommendations are the important map to the next step. Writing recommendations in a bulleted list and beginning each with an action verb helps to direct the reader to the logical next step.

End Matter

The **end matter** comprises the **appendices**, which contain additional information to which the reader may refer for further reading but that is not essential to reporting the data, and the end notes. Appendices contain the "nice-to-know" information, not the "need-to-know." Therefore, the body of the report should not be cluttered with this information; it should instead be inserted at the end for the reader who desires or requires additional information. Tables, figures, additional reading, technical descriptions, data-collection forms, and appropriate computer printouts are some elements that may appear in an appendix. (If they are critical to the reader, however, they may be included in the report itself.) Each appendix should be labeled with both a letter and a title, and each should appear in the table of contents.

> End matter contains additional information to which the reader may refer for further reading, but that is not essential to reporting the data.

A reference page or endnotes (if appropriate) should precede the appendix. A reference page contains all of the sources from which information was collected for the report.

The references should be complete, so a reader could retrieve the source if needed. End notes are notes at the end of a document that provide supplementary information or comments for ideas provided in the body of the report.

GUIDELINES AND PRINCIPLES FOR THE WRITTEN REPORT

We have described the parts of the research report. However, you should also consider their form and format and their style.

Form and Format

Form and format concerns include headings and subheadings and visuals.

HEADINGS AND SUBHEADINGS. In a long report, your reader needs signals and signposts to serve as a road map. Headings and subheadings perform this function. **Headings** indicate the topic of each section. All information under a specific heading should relate to that heading, and **subheadings** should divide that information into segments. A new heading should introduce a change of topic. Choose the kind of heading that fits your purpose—single word, phrase, sentence, question—and consistently use that form through-out the report. If you use subheadings within the divisions, the subheadings must be parallel in form to one another but not to the main headings. Learn how to use headings and subheadings and you will improve your writing skills. Marketing Research Insight 20.3 will give you the information you need to create headings and subheadings.

Visuals

Visuals are tables, figures, charts, diagrams, graphs, and other graphic aids. Used properly, they can dramatically and concisely present information that might otherwise be difficult to comprehend. Tables systematically present numerical data or words in columns and rows. Figures translate numbers into visual displays so that relationships and trends become comprehensible. Examples of figures are graphs, pie charts, and bar charts.

Visuals should tell a story; they should be uncluttered and self-explanatory, but even though they are self-explanatory, the key points of all visuals should be explained in the text. Refer to visuals by number: ". . . as shown in Figure 1." Each visual should be titled and numbered. If possible, place the visual immediately below the paragraph in which its first reference appears. Or, if sufficient space is not available, continue the text and place the visual on the next page. Visuals can also be placed in an appendix. Additional informa-tion on preparing visuals is presented later in this chapter.

Style

Consider stylistic devices when you are actually writing the sentences and paragraphs in your report. These can make the difference in whether or not your reader receives the mes-sage as you intended. Therefore, consider the following "tips" for the writer:

1. A good paragraph has one main idea, and a topic sentence should state that main idea. As a general rule, begin paragraphs with topic sentences; however, topic sentences can appear in the middle or at the end of a paragraph. See Marketing Research Insight 20.4 to help you become a better paragraph writer.
2. Avoid long paragraphs (usually those with more than nine printed lines). Long paragraphs are a strategy for burying a message—most readers do not read the middle contents of long paragraphs.
3. Capitalize on white space. Immediately before and immediately after white space (the beginning and the end of a paragraph) are points of emphasis. So are the beginning and the end of a page. Therefore, place more important information at these strategic points.

Headings and subheadings act as signals and signposts to serve as a road map in a long report.

iReportWriter Assistant: The online report writer provides examples of proper heading and subheading formats.

Visuals can dramatically and concisely present information that might otherwise be difficult to comprehend.

iReportWriter Assistant: For an in-depth discussion of the construction of visuals, see the online report-writing guide.

Stylistic devices can make the difference in whether or not your reader receives the message as you intended.

MARKETING RESEARCH INSIGHT   Practical Insights

20.3 How Headings Can Help You Write a Professional Report

Most students have difficulty organizing their reports. Yet rarely will they take the time to outline the report as they were taught to do in grade school. There are few more effective methods to improving your writing skills than properly outlining before you begin writing. Here we provide you with a few key thoughts that will help you improve your writing skills through the proper use of headings.

First, before you can outline, you must do some basic planning. Go back to your research objectives. Make certain that your report addresses the research objectives that were identified at the beginning of the research project.

Second, read the information you have! Many students just start writing without reading over the information they have generated either from secondary data or even from an analysis of the results of their primary data collection.

Third, what information has been gathered for each of the research objectives? Organize your information into separate areas based on how it addresses a particular research objective. For example, if one objective is to gather information on the likelihood to subscribe to a new service, find that information and file it under the research objective. Was any other information gathered that addresses this objective?

Fourth, now that you are familiar with your research objectives and the information gathered for each, start outlining the information gathered by using headings. Headings are the *most useful* way a writer can organize a paper, and they are very useful to readers because they serve as guideposts telling readers where they are, where they've been, and where they are headed.

Fifth, understand your format for headings before you begin to write. We provide the following to help you with your headings. Read this and use it!

TITLE

Titles are centered at the top of the page and are either bold-faced or underlined. Titles are normally in a larger font than the rest of the paper.

FIRST-LEVEL HEADING

First-level headings indicate what the following section, usually consisting of several subdivisions, is about. First-level headings are centered, bold, and all caps and are usually in larger font sizes than the other material but smaller than the title.

Second-Level Heading

Second-level headings are centered and bold, with capitals used only for the first letter of each word. Font size may be the same as that of the rest of the report. Try to always use more than one second-level heading if you are going to use them following a first-level heading.

Third-Level Heading

Left-justified, third-level headings should be bold and in the same font size as the rest of the report.

Fourth-Level Heading. These are left-justified and on the same line as the first sentence in the paragraph. Use bold and the same-sized font as the remainder of the report.

Fifth-level headings are in bold and are part of a sentence. These are generally the lowest level of outline you will use, but you can go further by using indention and numbering of ideas or italicizing the first word in each item of a list.

Source: Portions of the above adapted from Bovée, C. and Thill, J. (2000). *Business Communication Today*, 6th ed. Upper Saddle River, NJ: Prentice Hall, 499.

4. Use jargon sparingly. Some of your audience may understand technical terms; others may not. When in doubt, properly define the terms for your readers. If many technical terms are required in the report, consider including a glossary of terms in an appendix to assist the less-informed members of your audience.

5. Use strong verbs to carry the meaning of your sentences. Instead of "making a recommendation," "recommend." Instead of "performing an investigation," "investigate."

6. As a general rule, use the active voice. Voice indicates whether the subject of the verb is doing the action (active voice) or receiving the action (passive voice). For example, "The marketing research was conducted by Judith" uses the passive voice. "Judith conducted the marketing research" uses the active voice. Active voice is direct and forceful, and the active voice uses fewer words.

7. Eliminate extra words. Write your message clearly and concisely. Combine and reword sentences to eliminate unnecessary words. Remove opening fillers and eliminate unnecessary redundancies. For example, instead of writing, "There are 22 marketing research firms in Newark," remove the opening filler by writing, "Twenty-two

MARKET RESEARCH INSIGHT

Practical Application

20.4 Developing Logical Paragraphs

"**A** paragraph** is a group of related sentences that focus on one main idea."[a] The first sentence should be a **topic sentence**, which identifies the main idea of the paragraph. For example: "To assess whether residents would patronize an upscale restaurant, respondents were asked their likelihood of patronizing an upscale restaurant." Next, the **body of the paragraph** supports the main idea of the topic sentence by giving more information, analysis, or examples. For example, continuing from the topic sentence example just given: "A description of an upscale restaurant was read to all respondents. The description was as follows:. . . . The respondents were then asked to indicate their likelihood of patronizing an upscale restaurant by selecting a choice on a 5-point response rating scale ranging from 'Very likely to patronize' to 'Very unlikely to patronize.' The actual scale was as follows:. . . ."

Paragraphs should close with a sentence that signals the end of the topic and indicates where the reader is headed. For example: "How respondents answered the likelihood-to-patronize scale is discussed in the following two paragraphs." Note this last sentence contains a **transitional expression**. A transitional expression is a word, or group of words, that tells readers where they are heading. Some examples include *following, next, second, third, at last, finally, in conclusion, to summarize, for example, to illustrate, in addition, so, therefore*, and so on.[b]

Controlling the **length of paragraphs** should encourage good communication. As a rule, paragraphs should be short. Business communication experts believe most paragraphs should be under or around the 100-word range.[c] This is long enough to express the topic sentence and include three or four sentences in the body of the paragraph. The paragraph should never cover more than one main topic. Complex topics should be broken into several paragraphs.

[a]Ober, S. (1998). *Contemporary Business Communication*, 3rd ed. Boston: Houghton Mifflin, 121.
[b]Ober, S. (1998). *Contemporary Business Communication*, 3rd ed. Boston: Houghton Mifflin, 123.
[c]Bovee, C. and Thill, J. (2000) *Business Communication Today*, 6th ed. Upper Saddle River, NJ: Prentice Hall, 153.

marketing research firms are located in Newark." Instead of saying, "the end results," say, "the results."

8. Avoid unnecessary changes in tense. Tense tells if the action of the verb occurred in the past (past tense—*were*), is happening right now (present tense—*are*), or will happen in the future (future tense—*will be*). Changing tenses within a document is an error writers frequently make.

9. In sentences, keep the subject and verb close together. The farther apart they become, the more difficulty the reader has understanding the message and the greater the chance for errors in subject/verb agreement.

10. Vary the length and structure of sentences and paragraphs.

11. Use faultless grammar. If your grammar is in any way below par, you need to take responsibility for finding ways to improve. Poor grammar can result in costly errors and the loss of your job. It can jeopardize your credibility and the credibility of your research. There is no acceptable excuse for poor grammar.

12. Maintain 1-inch side margins. If your report will be bound, use a 1½-inch left margin.

13. Follow the organization's preference for double- or single-spacing.

14. Edit carefully. Your first draft is not a finished product; neither is your second. Edit your work carefully, rearranging and rewriting until you communicate the intent of your research as efficiently and effectively as possible. Some authors suggest that as much as 50% of your production time should be devoted to improving, editing, correcting, and evaluating an already written document.[14]

15. Proofread! Proofread! Proofread! After you have finished a product, check it carefully to make sure everything is correct. Double-check names and numbers, grammar, spelling, and punctuation. Although spell-checkers and grammar-checkers are useful, you cannot rely on them to catch all errors. One of the best ways to proofread is to read a document aloud, preferably with a reader following along on the original.

An alternative is to read the document twice—once for content and meaning and once for mechanical errors. The more important the document is, the more time and readers you need to use for proofreading.

USING VISUALS: TABLES AND FIGURES

Visuals assist in the effective presentation of numerical data. The key to a successful visual is a clear and concise presentation that conveys the message of the report. The selection of the visual should match the presentation purpose for the data. Common visuals include the following[15]:

- *Tables*, which identify exact values (see Marketing Research Insight 20.5)
- *Graphs* and *charts*, which illustrate relationships among items
- *Pie charts*, which compare a specific part of the whole to the whole (see Marketing Research Insight 20.6)
- *Bar charts* (see Marketing Research Insight 20.7) and *line graphs*, which compare items over time or show correlations among items
- *Flow diagrams*, which introduce a set of topics and illustrate their relationships (see Figure 20.7)
- *Maps*, which define locations
- *Photographs*, which have an aura of legitimacy because they are not "created" in the sense that other visuals are created; photos depict factual content
- *Drawings*, which focus on visual details

A discussion of some of these visuals follows.

Tables

Tables allow the reader to compare numerical data. Effective table guidelines are as follows:

1. Do not allow computer analysis to imply a level of accuracy that is not achieved. Limit your use of decimal places (12% or 12.2% instead of 12.223%).
2. Place items you want the reader to compare in the same column, not the same row.
3. If you have many rows, shade alternating entries or double-space after every five entries to assist the reader in accurately lining up items.
4. Total columns and rows when relevant.

Marketing Research Insight 20.5 gives you the necessary keystroke instructions to create tables using SPSS.

Tables allow the reader to compare numerical data.

Pie Charts

When you want to illustrate the *relative* sizes or *proportions* of one component versus others, pie charts are useful. For example, if you wanted to illustrate to your reader the proportions of consumers that preferred different types of radio programming, a pie chart would be an excellent tool for showing the relative sizes of each type of programming preference. The **pie chart** is a circle divided into sections. Each section represents a percentage of the total area of the circle associated with one component. Today's data analysis programs easily and quickly make pie charts. Your SPSS 17.0 program, for example, allows you to build customized pie charts.

Most experts agree that the pie chart should have a limited number of segments (four to eight, at most). If your data have many small segments, consider combining the smallest or the least important into an "other" or "miscellaneous" category. Because internal labels are difficult to read for small sections, labels for the sections should be placed outside the circle.

Marketing Research Insight 20.6 gives you the keystroke instructions for creating pie charts using SPSS 17.0.

When you want to illustrate the relative sizes or proportions of one component versus others, pie charts are useful.

The pie chart is a circle divided into sections. Each section represents a percentage of the total area of the circle associated with one component.

MARKETING RESEARCH INSIGHT

Practical Application

20.5 How to Create a Table Using SPSS

We will use the Integrated Case Advanced Automotive Concepts data set (AAConcepts.sav) that you are familiar with, as we have been using it for all of the statistical analysis examples in previous chapters. Let's say we wish to find out the type of car preferred by respondents. To do this, we create a simple frequency table for responses to the question "What is your primary vehicle type?"

1. The first step is to create a frequency table for responses to the question using ANALYZE–DESCRIPTIVE STATISTICS–FREQUENCIES and selecting the variable corresponding to the preference for primary vehicle type. The resulting frequency table is displayed in the SPSS output Viewer.
2. To edit the table, put the cursor anywhere on the table and double-click. This activates the table editor, which is indicated by a shaded highlight box appearing around the table, and a red arrow pointing to the selected table. A toolbar will also appear on your screen.
3. Figure 20.4 illustrates how to change the format of the table (after you have double-clicked on it). Select FORMAT–TABLELOOKS.
4. To select a particular table format, browse through the directory and select one that suits your needs. In this case, we used Boxed (VGA) format. However, because

we want to change the fonts, we have to edit the format we selected.

5. To edit an already available format, click EDIT LOOK while in TABLELOOKS. To change the fonts, alignment, margins, and so on, click on CELL FORMATS. Change the fonts, size, style, and so on to suit your needs. To change borders, click on BORDERS and select appropriate borders. An example of a finished table is within Figure 20.4. You can hide categories by shading all the data in a column, right-clicking, and selecting CLEAR. You can also do this by moving your cursor to the right side of the border of a column and dragging the border to close the column.
6. After adjusting the table properties for the attributes you want, save your customized table format by clicking on SAVE AS within the TABLELOOKS dialog box and saving the table under a new file name. Keep reading. We show you how to recall this new table format for all the tables you make without having to reedit each new table. You can use this customized table look for any future tables you create. After you click SAVE AS and name the table format to be saved, click SAVE–OK.
7. You are now back in the table edit mode. The next step is to change the text in specific cells. To do this, double-click on the cell in which you want to change the text. The selected text will be highlighted. Simply type over and press Enter when you are done.

FIGURE 20.4

With an Output Table/Table Builder

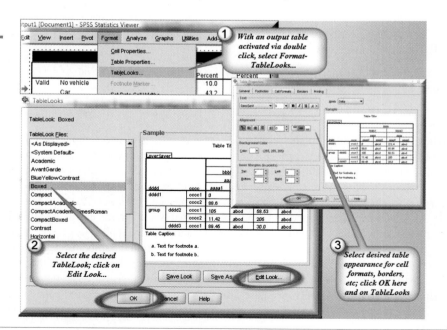

MARKETING RESEARCH INSIGHT

Practical Application

20.6 How to Create a Pie Chart Using SPSS

We again use data from the Advanced Automotive Concepts survey (AAConcepts.sav) to demonstrate the creation of a simple pie graph using SPSS. Let's say we want to show responses to the question "Primary vehicle price type?" in the form of a pie chart.

1. Create a pie chart for responses to the question "Primary vehicle price type?"

   Figure 20.5 shows that you use the Command sequence of GRAPHS–LEGACY DIALOGS–PIE. Click Summaries for Groups of Cases and then Define.

   The next screen allows you to choose the variable that you want to graph. Select the variable corresponding to the question on the questionnaire, click the button for Define Slices By, and the variable will be entered.

   You can choose what you want your slices to represent. In this case, we selected the slices to represent % of cases.

2. At this stage, you can also enter the titles and footnotes for the chart by clicking on TITLES and entering the appropriate labels.

   Using the command OPTIONS, you can decide how you want missing values to be treated. Here we have not included missing values in the chart by clicking *off* the checkmark (3) on the Display Groups Defined by Missing Values.

   Click OK and the resulting pie chart will appear in the SPSS Viewer. SPSS 17.0 displays a legend with the pie chart. You are now ready to edit the chart.

   (If you have an existing template of a pie graph, you can request the output to be formatted according to template specifications by double-clicking anywhere on the chart; go to FILE–APPLY CHART TEMPLATE and select the saved file name.)

3. Scroll down to the pie chart. To edit the chart, double-click anywhere on the chart. This takes you to the SPSS Chart Editor screen. You will do all your editing in this screen.

4. In the Chart Editor screen, click on the area you wish to edit. This puts a border around the area to be edited; it also changes the editing tools available to you in Chart Editor. Click once on the title. You can now edit the font. Right-click once on the pie. Go to SHOW DATA LABELS. A Properties prompt screen will appear.

FIGURE 20.5

Use Graphs-Legacy Dialogs-Pie/Pie Chart Builder

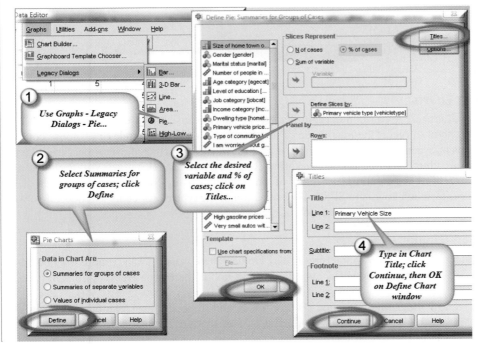

To place a descriptive label on each slice as well as the value, click on the description under Not Displayed and click the green upward arrow. Click Apply and Close. This places values and corresponding descriptive labels within each slice. Click once on the Standard slice such that *only* the Standard slice is highlighted with a border. Right-click and go to EXPLODE SLICE.

5. Still in Chart Editor, right-click on the pie chart, as shown in Figure 20.6. Choose PROPERTIES WINDOW. Select DEPTH & ANGLE-3-D for EFFECT, move the slide bar down to −60 for ANGLE, 3 for DISTANCE. APPLY & CLOSE.

6. You can add text *anywhere* on the chart in SPSS 17.0. Click the TEXT icon in Chart Editor (or go to the OPTIONS–TEXT BOX).

7. After making all the changes, you can save your customized chart by using command options FILE–SAVE CHART TEMPLATE. For future charts, you can call up the customized template, avoiding the need for you to edit every pie chart you create.

8. The chart is now ready to be transferred to a word processing document.

FIGURE 20.6

In the Chart Editor/ Pie Chart Editor

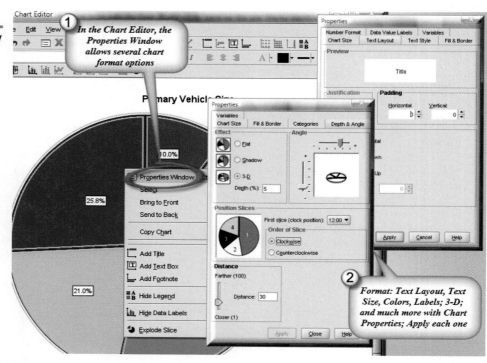

Bar Charts

Bar charts are used often in reporting survey data because they are easy to interpret. They are useful to report the magnitude of response or to show magnitude or response comparisons between groups. They are also useful for illustrating change over time.

Bar charts are used often in reporting survey data because they are easy to interpret. They are useful to report the magnitude of response or to show magnitude or response comparisons between groups. They are also useful for illustrating change over time. Several types of **bar charts** can be used. Marketing Research Insight 20.7 gives you the keystroke instructions for creating bar charts of various types using SPSS. Study the types of bar charts available to you in SPSS. Your selection of the type of bar chart will depend on what you are trying to communicate to your reader.

Line Graphs

Flow diagrams introduce a set of topics and illustrate their relationships.

Line graphs are easy to interpret if they are designed properly. Line graphs may be drawn in SPSS using the GRAPHS option. You will notice there are several options in types of line graphs.

Flow diagrams introduce a set of topics and illustrate their relationships. Flow diagrams are particularly useful to illustrate topics that are sequential, for example, step 1, step 2, and so on. (See Figure 20.7.)

FIGURE 20.7

A Flow Diagram Introduces Topics

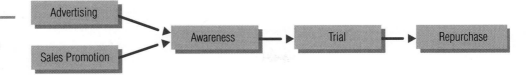

MARKETING RESEARCH INSIGHT Online Application

20.7 How to Create a Bar Chart Using SPSS

We use data from the Advanced Automotive Concepts data (AAConcepts.sav) to demonstrate the creation of a simple bar graph using SPSS. Let's say we want to show graphically the frequency distribution of the level of education.

1. Create a bar chart for responses to question 6 on the questionnaire: "Level of Education?"

   As you can see in Figure 20.8, after opening the data file, use the Command GRAPHS–LEGACY DIALOGS–BAR. You have the option of choosing from three different styles of bar charts. In this case, we used the Simple chart. Click Summaries for Groups of Cases and then Define.

   The next screen allows you to choose the variable that you want to graph. Select the variable "Level of Education," highlight the variable, and click on the Category Axis button.

   You can choose what you want your bars to represent. In this case, we selected the bars to represent % of cases because we want to know the percentages of respondents' level of education.

2. At this stage, you can also enter the titles and footnotes for the chart by clicking on TITLES. Also, by selecting OPTIONS, you can decide how you want missing values to be treated. Here, we have not included missing

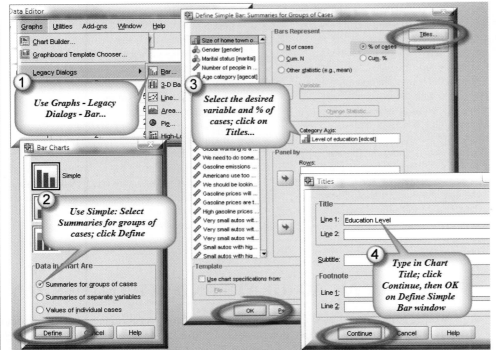

FIGURE 20.8

Use Graphs-Legacy Dialogs/Bar Chart Builder

FIGURE 20.9

In the Chart Editor, the Properties Window/Bar Chart Editor

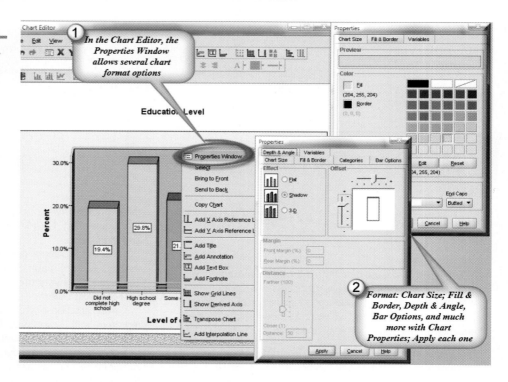

values in the chart by clicking *off* the checkmark (3) on the Display Groups Defined by Missing Values.

Click OK and the bar chart will appear in the SPSS Viewer. You are now ready to edit the chart.

(If you have an existing template of a bar graph, while in the Define Simple Bar Summaries for Groups of Cases box, you can request the output to be formatted according to template specifications by clicking on Use Chart Specifications From, and selecting the saved file name.)

3. To edit the chart, double-click anywhere on the chart. This opens the SPSS Chart Editor screen. You will do all your editing in this screen. Figure 20.9 shows the operation of the SPSS Chart Editor screen with our bar chart.

4. In the Chart Editor screen, click on the area you wish to edit. This puts a border around the area to be edited. It also changes the editing tools available to you in Chart Editor. Click once on the title. You can now edit the title in several ways by using the tools in the menu bar. You can change fonts, font size, color, fill, alignment, and so on.

5. Click once on one of the bars. All the bars should now be highlighted with a border around them. Notice the tools available to you on the menu bar. Go to the PROPERTIES icon (or go to EDIT–PROPERTIES). Select

DEPTH & ANGLE, choose SHADOW for EFFECT, and set OFFSET to +15 by moving the slide bar. APPLY–CLOSE. Again, click on a bar and then the PROPERTIES icon. Select FILL & BORDER and select a pattern and fill color for your bars. *(Note:* Click the fill button to change the color of the bars. The border button allows you to change the color of the border line of the bars.)

6. Still in Chart Editor, click anywhere other than a bar. Select PROPERTIES WINDOW–FILL & BORDER. Change the color of the background.

7. To edit the textual content of the chart, select the TEXT icon in Chart Editor (or go to OPTIONS–TEXT BOX). A box and a set of markers will appear. Insert your text and then drag the box where you want the text to appear.

8. After making all the changes, you can save your customized chart by using the command FILE–SAVE CHART TEMPLATE. For future charts, you can call up the customized template, avoiding the need for you to edit every bar chart you create.

9. The chart is now ready to be transferred to a word processing document.

PRODUCING AN ACCURATE AND ETHICAL VISUAL

An ethical visual is one that is totally objective in terms of how information is presented in the research report.

A marketing researcher should always follow the doctrine of full disclosure. An **ethical visual** is one that is totally objective in terms of how information is presented in the research report. Sometimes misrepresenting information is intentional (as when a client asks a researcher to misrepresent the data in order to promote a "pet project") or it may be unintentional. In the latter case, those preparing a visual are sometimes so familiar with the material being presented that they falsely assume the graphic message is apparent to all who view it.

Now look at Figure 20.10(a) and Figure 20.10(b). We see in both line graphs that sales are plotted over time. Wouldn't you really prefer to be the CEO of the company represented in (b) rather than (a)? Look again. The data are exactly the same! However, by changing the scale we are easily able to alter the appearance of the line graphs such that one looks much more desirable than the other. We prepared both these graphs by first making a single graph

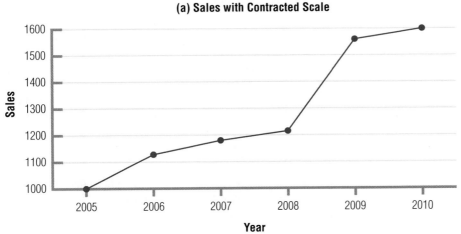

FIGURE 20.10

Ethical Graphs

using SPSS 17.0. Then we copied the graph twice in a Word® document. Compressing the graph shown in (a) vertically resulted in contracting the scale such that the change in sales is much less pronounced than it is in (b). In (b) we did the opposite; we enlarged the same graph vertically resulting in an expansion of the scale. The point is to make certain that your scale is set to display the results in as fair and objective a manner as possible. You don't want to understate negatives or overstate positives in your report. It is unethical to change the scale within the body of the report without informing the reader and making sure the reader understands the reason for and the effect of the change. SPSS will automatically assign a range for your scale. Unless there is some justifiable reason for doing so, it's best to not change the scales at all!

To ensure that you have objectively and ethically prepared your visuals you should do the following:

1. Double- and triple-check all labels, numbers, and visual shapes. A faulty or misleading visual discredits your report and work.
2. Exercise caution if you use three-dimensional figures. They may distort the data by multiplying the value by the width and the height.
3. Make sure all parts of the scales are presented. Truncated graphs (having breaks in the scaled values on either axis) are acceptable only if the audience is familiar with the data.

PRESENTING YOUR RESEARCH ORALLY

The purpose of the oral presentation is to succinctly present the information and to provide an opportunity for questions and discussion.

You may be asked to present an oral summary of the recommendations and conclusions of your research. The purpose of the **oral presentation** is to succinctly present the information and to provide an opportunity for questions and discussion. The presentation may be accomplished through a simple conference with the client, or it may be a formal presentation to a roomful of people. In any case, says Jerry W. Thomas, CEO of Decision Analyst, research reports should "be presented orally to all key people in the same room at the same time." He believes this is important because many people do not read the research report, and others may not understand all the details of the report. "An oral presentation ensures that everyone can ask questions to allow the researchers to clear up any confusion."[16] It also ensures that everyone hears the same thing.

To be adequately prepared when you present your research orally, follow these steps:

A good oral presentation is the result of good organization and practice.

1. Identify and analyze your audience. Consider the same questions you addressed at the beginning of the research process and at the beginning of this chapter.
2. Find out the expectations your audience has for your presentation. Is the presentation formal or informal? Does your audience expect a graphical presentation?
3. Determine the key points your audience needs to hear.
4. Outline the key points, preferably on 3-by-5 cards to which you can easily refer.
5. Present your points succinctly and clearly. The written report will serve as a reference for further reading.
6. Make sure your visuals graphically and ethically portray your key points.
7. Practice your presentation. Be comfortable with what you are going to say and how you look. The more prepared you are and the better you feel about yourself, the less you will need to worry about jitters.
8. Check out the room and media equipment prior to the presentation.
9. Arrive early.

10. Be positive and confident. You are the authority; you know more about your subject than anyone else.
11. Speak loudly enough for all in the room to hear. Enunciate clearly. Maintain eye contact and good posture. Dress professionally.

Summary

The preparation and presentation of the marketing research report is the final stage of the marketing research process. This stage is as important as, if not more important than, any other stage in the research process. This importance is attributed to the fact that, regardless of the care in the design and execution of the research project itself, if the report does not adequately communicate the project to the client, all is lost.

We have prepared on online report writing tool for you in this course. We call it the *iReportWriter Assistant* and you can access it by going to www.pearsonhighered.com/burnsbush and clicking on the Companion Website link for this text. The *iReportWriter Assistant* will teach you what to consider before you write, provide you with some templates to show you how to start writing sections of the report, give you links to help you with grammar, show you how to properly cite your reference sources, and show you an actual finished marketing research report.

While preparing and writing the report may be time-consuming, advances are being made to make report writing more efficient. Online reporting software is an efficient tool that assists marketing researchers in monitoring data collection and disseminating research results. It also allows data users to interact with the reports and to massage data. Burke, Inc.'s DigitalDashboard is a good example of an online reporting system that allows clients to interact with the report.

Marketing research reports should be tailored to their audiences. They are typically organized into the categories of front matter, body, and end matter. Each of these categories has subparts, with each subpart having a different purpose. Conclusions are based on the results of the research, and recommendations are suggestions based on conclusions. Guidelines for writing the marketing research report include proper use of headings and subheadings, which serve as signposts and signals to the reader, and proper use of visuals such as tables and figures. Style considerations include paragraphs beginning with topic sentences, spare use of jargon, strong verbs, active voice, consistent tense, conciseness, and varied sentence structure and length. Editing and proofreading, preferably by reading the report aloud, are important steps in writing the research report.

Care should be taken to ensure that all presentations to the reader are clear and objective. Many visual aids may be distorted so that they have a different meaning to the reader. This means that ethical considerations must be taken into account in the preparation of the research report. Reports rely on tables, figures, and graphical displays of various types. SPSS includes routines for creating report tables and graphs. We describe step-by-step commands on how to use SPSS to make professional-appearing tables and graphs.

In some cases, marketing researchers are required to present the findings of their research project to the client orally. Guidelines for making an oral presentation include knowing the audience and its expectations and the key points you wish to make; correctly preparing visuals; practicing; checking out presentation facilities and equipment prior to the presentation; and being positive.

Key Terms

Review Questions/Applications

1. Discuss the relative importance of the marketing research report to the other stages in the marketing research process.
2. What is the *iReportWriter Assistant*?
3. What are the main functions provided by the *iReportWriter Assistant*?
4. How can you access the *iReportWriter Assistant*?
5. What are the components of the marketing research report?
6. When should you include or omit a letter of authorization?
7. When should you write a memo? When should you write a letter?
8. Where is the derivation of the word *plagiarism*?
9. Should you use "Method" or "Methodology" to describe how the research was conducted? Why?
10. Distinguish among results, conclusions, and recommendations.
11. When should you acknowledge you have a limitation(s) in your report?
12. When should you use a subheading?
13. What are the components of a good, logical paragraph?
14. What are some elements of good style in report writing?
15. What makes a table a table?
16. What are the first few keystrokes in making a table using SPSS?
17. What are the first few keystrokes in making a pie chart using SPSS?
18. What visual would be the best at displaying the relative changes in spending between four promotion mix variables over time?
19. What kind of visual would you create if you wanted to use images of people to illustrate the differences in employment levels among three industries?
20. Why do you think we included a discussion of ethics in preparing visuals? Can you illustrate how a visual could present data in an unethical fashion?
21. Go online and search for examples of marketing research reports. Or, visit your library and ask the reference librarian if any marketing research reports that have been placed in the library. Chances are good that you will be able to find several reports of various kinds. Examine the reports. What commonalities do they have in terms of the sections that the authors have created? Look at the sections carefully. What types of issues were addressed in the introduction section? The method section? How did the authors organize all of the information reported in the results section? Are recommendations different from conclusions?

CASE 20.1 ## Your Integrated Case

ADVANCED AUTOMOTIVE CONCEPTS: USING *iREPORTWRITER ASSISTANT*

Cory Rogers was about to write up the first draft of the final report for Advanced Automotive Concepts (AAC). He decided to go to the online report-writing module he learned when he took his first marketing research course in college. Since the *iReportWriter Assistant* is constantly updated, Cory knew he would have access to the latest links and information that would assist him in writing his report. Nick Thomas of AAC had told Cory that ZEN Motors had their own marketing research department and that they were eager to read his report. Cory knew that they would be particularly interested in technical issues, such as how the sample size was determined and the margin of error. Cory had also had a frank discussion with Nick Thomas about conclusions and recommendations. Nick had told him: "Cory I want to know what the numbers say. What are the conclusions based on those numbers? In terms of how to proceed, I will meet with my top staff members and we will make those decisions. We have to factor in many constraints that, frankly, I am not even aware of at this point."

As a trained marketing researcher, Cory was very familiar with the steps in the marketing research process. Knowledge of these steps was useful in writing the "method" section of his marketing research reports. For example, Cory knew that he should address the types and sources of information used in the report; he should also address the research design and why it was chosen over other designs; and he knew the sampling plan and sample size should also be included in the "method" section. Cory made a list of topics he should cover and he started organizing these topics in terms of headings and subheadings that would eventually be used in the final report.

Cory thought, "Ah, yes! I have to properly cite every source I have used in this report." He dreaded this part. As many times as he had written a report, remembering every detail that goes into a reference was just something that would not stay in Cory's memory bank. Yet he knew it was important to use the proper form for his reference list.

Before you start on the questions that follow, access the *iReportWriter Assistant* by going to www.pearsonhighered.com/burnsbush and click on the Companion Website link for this text. Now read over the major topics covered in the *iReportWriter Assistant* before you read the following questions. Once you are finished reviewing the contents of the *iReportWriter Assistant*, you should be ready to answer the following questions.

1. What is it about the information in this case that Cory should consider doing before he actually begins to write the report? Name some specific issues Cory should address.
2. Should Cory include the standard "Conclusions and Recommendations" section of the report? Why or why not?
3. We are told that Cory has made a list of issues to include in the "Method" section of the report. What, if anything, is included in the *iReportWriter Assistant* that could help Cory ensure that he has included everything he needs to include?
4. What section of the *iReportWriter Assistant* should Cory seek out to help him with properly citing the secondary sources used in the marketing research report?

CASE 20.2 Your Integrated Case

ADVANCED AUTOMOBILE CONCEPTS: MAKING A POWERPOINT® PRESENTATION

Cory Rogers completed the report for Advanced Automotive Concepts. He decided he wanted to make some PowerPoint slides to use in his presentation of the findings. Working in Word, he wrote a title for his presentation: "Advanced Automotive Concepts: A Marketing Research Study To Determine Car Model Preferences and Profile Market Segments." Then he wrote out several other comments that he wanted to include in the beginning of his presentation, such as the research objectives and several issues dealing with the method used including the sample plan and the sample size. When Cory wrote out a number of the statements that he thought would help him communicate the purpose and method of the study, he turned his attention to presenting the findings.

Cory thought he would begin his presentation of the study with a description of the sample, often referred to as a "profile of the sample." He noticed that for Gender and Marital Status there were only two categories (male, female; and married, unmarried) for each question. He decided to just orally report the percentages of the categories. However, for some of the other variables, there were several categories of response and he felt he would communicate the results better by showing the frequency distribution table. He prepared a frequency distribution of the responses to these questions using SPSS. He continued by making several key analyses of the data using SPSS.

1. Using a word processing program, write out several of the statements that you think would be appropriate to present to the client, Nick Thomas, for an oral presentation.
2. Import the statements you prepared in Question 1 into PowerPoint using Copy and Paste. Experiment with different text colors and font sizes and styles.
3. Using SPSS, run several frequency distributions. Using TABLELOOKS, select an output format you like and import that output into PowerPoint.
4. Using SPSS, make a bar chart of the answers to the question regarding the variable "Americans use too much gasoline." Experiment with the different options of bar charts available to you in SPSS. Select a bar chart and import that chart into PowerPoint using Copy and Paste. Experiment with making edits on your slide.

Endnotes

Chapter 1

1. Kotler, P. and Keller, K. L. (2006). *Marketing Management*, 12th ed. Upper Saddle River, NJ: Prentice Hall, 5.
2. Keefe, L. M. (2004, September 15). What is the meaning of 'marketing'? *Marketing News*. Chicago: American Marketing Association, 17–18.
3. Vargo, S. L. and Lusch, R. F. (2004). Evolving to a new dominant logic for marketing. *Journal of Marketing*, 68, 1, 1–17.
4. Shostack, G. L. (1977). Breaking free from product marketing. *Journal of Marketing*, 41, 2, 74. Shostack's original example used General Motors.
5. Drucker, Peter (1973). *Management: Tasks, Responsibilities, Practices*. New York: Harper & Row, 64–65.
6. Students will recognize these philosophies as the product concept and the selling concept. See Kotler, Philip and Armstrong, Gary (2001). *Principles of Marketing*, 9th ed. Upper Saddle River, NJ: Prentice Hall, 18.
7. Kotler, P. (2003). *Marketing Management*, 11th ed. Upper Saddle River, NJ: Prentice Hall, 19.
8. For additional reading on this topic, see: Kotler, P. and Keller, K. L. (2006). *Marketing Management*, 12th ed. Upper Saddle River, NJ: Prentice Hall, 15–23.
9. Bennett, P. D. (Ed.) (1995). *Dictionary of Marketing Terms*, 2nd ed. Chicago: American Marketing Association, 169.
10. Bennett, P. D. (Ed.) (1995). *Dictionary of Marketing Terms*, 2nd ed. Chicago: American Marketing Association, 165.
11. Without insights we cannot keep customers loyal. (2004, February 26). *Marketing*, 20.
12. Clancy, K. and Krieg, P. C. (2000). *Counterintuitive Marketing: Achieve Great Results Using Uncommon Sense*. New York: The Free Press.
13. Merritt, N. J. and Redmond, W. H. (1990). Defining marketing research: perceptions vs. practice. *Proceedings: American Marketing Association*, 146–150.
14. Market research: pre-testing helps ad effectiveness. (2003, May 8). *Marketing*, 27.
15. Tracy, K. (1998). *Jerry Seinfeld: The Entire Domain*. Secaucus, NJ: Carol Publishing, 64–65.
16. Marconi, J. (1998, June 8). What marketing aces do when marketing research tells them, "don't do it!" *Marketing News*; and Zangwill, W. (1993, March 8). When customer research is a lousy idea. *The Wall Street Journal*, A12.
17. Hodock, C. L. (2007). *Why Smart Companies Do Dumb Things*. Amherst, N.Y.: Prometheus Books, p. 157.
18. Market research: pre-testing helps ad effectiveness. (2003, May 8). *Marketing*, 27.
19. Hise, P. (1998). Grandma got run over by bad research. *Inc.*, 20, 1, 27.
20. Heilbrunn, J. (1989, August). Legal lessons from the Delicare affair—1. United States. *Marketing and Research Today*, 17(3),156–160. Also see Frederickson, P. and Totten, J. W. (1990). "Marketing Research Projects in the Academic Setting: Legal Liability after Beecham vs. Yankelovich." In: Capella, L. M., et al., eds., Progress in Marketing Thought, *Proceedings of the Southern Marketing Association*, 250–253.
21. Communication to the authors from Kimberly-Clark Worldwide on March 15, 2005. Visit the Kotex website at www.kotex.com.
22. Business ignorance (2004, August). *Industrial Engineer*, 36(8),12.

23. The description of the MIS is adapted from Kotler, P. and Keller, K. L. (2006). *Marketing Management*, 12th ed. Upper Saddle River, NJ: Prentice Hall.
24. Bakker, Gerben. (2003, January). Building knowledge about the consumer: the emergence of market research in the motion picture industry. Industry Overview. *Business History*, 45, 1, 101 (29).

Chapter 2

1. Others have broken the marketing research process down into different numbers of steps. Regardless, there is widespread agreement that using a step-process approach is a useful tool for learning marketing research.
2. Neal, William D. (2002). "Linking Marketing Strategy and Marketing Research." In: *Decisions that Click*. Chuck Chakrapani, ed. Toronto: Professional Marketing Research Society.
3. Goodman, J. and Beinhacker, D. (October, 2003). By the numbers: Stop wasting money! *Quirk's Marketing Research Review*. Retrieved from Quirks.com on December 12, 2008.
4. Adapted from Adler, L. (1979, September 17). Secrets of when, and when not to embark on a marketing research project. *Sales & Marketing Management Magazine*, 123, 108.
5. Adapted from Adler, L. (1979, September 17). Secrets of when, and when not to embark on a marketing research project, *Sales & Marketing Management Magazine*, 123, 108.
6. Wellner, A. S. (2001, April). Research on a shoestring. *American Demographics*, 38–39.
7. Lohse, G. L. and Rosen, D. L. (2001, Summer). Signaling quality and credibility in Yellow Pages advertising: the influence of color and graphics on choice. *Journal of Advertising*, 73–85.
8. Wilson, S. and Macer, T. *The 2007 Confirmit Annual Market Research Software Survey*. London: Meaning Limited, 6.
9. Clancy, K. J. and Shulman, R. S. (1994). *Marketing Myths That Are Killing Business*. New York: McGraw Hill, 63.
10. Information for this case was excerpted from "Profile of Hybrid drivers." Retrieved from www.hybridcars.com on December 16, 2008.

Chapter 3

1. Bartels, R. (1976). *The History of Marketing Thought*, 2nd ed. Columbus, OH: Grid, 124–125.
2. Hardy, H. (1990). *The Politz Papers: Science and Truth in Marketing Research*. Chicago: American Marketing Association.
3. Bartels, *The history of Marketing Thought*, 125.
4. Jack J. Honomichl received a B.S. degree from Northwestern University and a Master's degree from the University of Chicago; Mr. Honomichl has spent a good part of his life in the research industry. He has held executive positions with the Marketing Information Center, a subsidiary of Dun & Bradstreet; Audits & Surveys, Inc.; the MRCA; and the *Chicago Tribune*. He frequently contributes to *Advertising Age* and the American Marketing Association's *Marketing News*. His book on the industry, entitled *Honomichl on Marketing Research*, is published by National Textbook Company, Lincolnwood, IL. He has published nearly 400 articles in the trade and the academic press. He was inducted into the Market Research Council's Hall of Fame at the Yale Club in New York in 2002. Other members of the Hall of Fame include such notables as Arthur C. Nielsen, Sr., George Gallup, Sr., David Ogilvy, Marion Harper, Daniel Yankelovich, Daniel Starch, Ernest Dicter, Alfred Politz, and Elmo Roper.

5. Much of the following was excerpted from Honomichl, J. "Jack J. Honomichl on the Marketing Research Industry," in Burns, A. C. and R. F. Bush (2006). *Marketing Research*, 5th ed. Upper Saddle River, NJ: Pearson/Prentice Hall, 40–41.

6. Honomichl, J. (2008, August 15). Top firms consolidated grip on industry. *Marketing News*, H2–H3 and ff.

7. Honomichl, J. (2008, June 15). Economy stunts industry growth. *Marketing News*, H2–H3 and ff.

8. Honomichl, J. (2008, June 15). Economy stunts industry growth. *Marketing News*, H4.

9. Honomichl, J. (2008, June 15). Economy stunts industry growth. *Marketing News*, H7.

10. Honomichl, J. (2008, June 15). Economy stunts industry growth. *Marketing News*, H22.

11. Malhotra, N. K. (2007). *Marketing Research*, 5th ed. Upper Saddle River, NJ: Prentice Hall, 17.

12. Kinnear, T. C. and Root, A. R. (1994). *Survey of Marketing Research: Organization Function, Budget, and Compensation.* Chicago: American Marketing Association, 38.

13. Kinnear and Root, *Survey of Marketing Research*, 12.

14. ORC International. Retrieved from ORC.co.UK on December 19, 2008.

15. Honomichl, J. (2007, June 15). Economy stunts industry growth. *Marketing News*, H6.

16. Honomichl, J. (2007, June 15). Economy stunts industry growth. *Marketing News*, H11.

17. Honomichl, J. (2007, June 15). Economy stunts industry growth. *Marketing News*, H12.

18. Honomichl, J. (2004, August 15). Despite acquisitions, firms' revenue dips. *Marketing News*, H28.

19. Honomichl, J. (2004, August 15). Despite acquisitions, firms' revenue dips. *Marketing News*, H19.

20. Personal communication with Creative & Response Research Service, Inc., August 12, 2003.

21. Krum, J. R. (1978, October). B for marketing research departments. *Journal of Marketing*, 42:8–12; Krum, J. R., Rau, P. A., and Keiser, S. K. (1987–1988, December–January). The marketing research process: role perceptions of researchers and users. *Journal of Advertising Research*, 27, 9–21; Dawson, S., Bush, R. F. and Stern, B. (1994, October). An evaluation of services provided by the marketing research industry. *Service Industries Journal*, 14, 4, 515–526; Austin, J. R. (1991). An exploratory examination of the development of marketing research service relationships: an assessment of exchange evaluation dimensions. In M. C. Gilly, et al. (Eds.), *Enhancing Knowledge Development in Marketing*, 1991 AMA Educators' Conference *Proceedings* Chicago, IL: American Marketing Associations, 133–141; Swan, J. E., Trawick, I. F. and Carroll, M. G. (1981, August). Effect of participation in marketing research on consumer attitudes toward research and satisfaction with a service. *Journal of Marketing Research*, 356–363; also see Malholtra, N. K., Peterson, M. and Kleiser, S. B. (1999, Spring). Marketing research: a state-of-the-art review and directions for the 21st century. *Journal of the Academy of Marketing Science*, 27, 2, 160–183.

22. See Neal, W. D. (2002, September 16). Shortcomings plague the industry. *Marketing Research*, 36, 19, 37ff.

23. See, for example: McManus, J. (2004, April 1). Stumbling into intelligence: market research organizations are trying to grab a bigger piece of the pie. *American Demographics*, 26, 3.

24. Bush, Ronald F. (2008, December). Quote provided for *Insight Express*, marketing research firm.

25. Wilson, Sheila and Macer, Tim (2007). *The 2007 Confirmit Annual Market Research Software Survey.* London, UK: Meaning Limited, 19.

26. How can we increase our email marketing response rates? (2002). *CRM Magazine*. Retrieved from DestinationCRM.com.

27. See a review of this in Braunsberger, K., Wybenga, H. and Gates, R. (2007). A comparison of reliability between telephone and web-based surveys. *Journal of Business Research,* 60, 758–764.

28. Fienberg, H. (2008, January). Do not call registry update. *Alert!* 46, 1, 14–15.

29. Berkowitz, D. (2003, October 24). Harsh realities for marketing research. Retrieved from eMarketer.com on October 27, 2003.

30. Fienberg, H. (2008, May). "New FCC ruling on autodialer calls to cell phones: are you in compliance? *Alert!* 46, 5, 38–39.

31. Schultz, D. E. (2005, February 15). MR deserves blame for marketing's decline. *Marketing News*, 7; and Schultz, D. E., Schultz, H. F. and Haigh, D. (2004, September). A roadmap for developing an integrated, audience-focused, market research-driven organization. *ESOMAR World Congress.* Readers seeking more information on Schultz's suggested remedy are encouraged to read the ESOMAR paper.

32. The following paragraphs are based on: Mahajan, V. and Wind, J. (1999, Fall). Rx for marketing research: a diagnosis of and prescriptions for recovery of an ailing discipline in the business world. *Marketing Research*, 7–13.

33. Baker, S. and Mouncey, P. (2003). The market researcher's manifesto. *International Journal of Market Research*, 45, 4, 415ff.

34. Honomichl, J. (2003). *The Marketing Research Industry: As Old Order Crumbles a New Vision Takes Shape.* Barrington, IL: Marketing Aid Center,

35. Mahajan, V. and Wind, J. (1999, Fall). Rx for marketing research: a diagnosis of and prescriptions for recovery of an ailing discipline in the business world. *Marketing Research*, 7–13.

36. Schultz, D. E. (2005, February 15). MR deserves blame for marketing's decline. *Marketing News*, 7; and Schultz, D. E., Schultz, H. F. and Haigh, D. (2004, September). A roadmap for developing an integrated, audience-focused, market research-driven organization. *ESOMAR World Congress.* Readers seeking more information on Schultz's suggested remedy are encouraged to read the ESOMAR paper.

37. Schultz, D. E. (2005, February 15). MR deserves blame for marketing's decline. *Marketing News* , 7; and Schultz, D. E., Schultz, H. F. and Haigh, D. (2004, September). A roadmap for developing an integrated, audience-focused, market research-driven organization. *ESOMAR World Congress.* Readers seeking more information on Schultz's suggested remedy are encouraged to read the ESOMAR paper.

38. Blackwell, R. D. (1998). Why the new market research? An interview appearing in *Inc.*, 20, 10, 86.

39. Clancy, K. and Krieg, P. C. (2000). *Counterintuitive Marketing: Achieve Great Results Using Uncommon Sense.* New York: The Free Press.

40. Witt, L. (2004, March). Inside intent. *American Demographics*, 26, 2.

41. Honomichl, J. (2003). *The Marketing Research Industry: As Old Order Crumbles a New Vision Takes Shape.* Barrington, IL: Marketing Aid Center; Krum, J. R. (1978, October). B for marketing research departments. *Journal of Marketing*, 42, 8–12; Krum, J. R., Rau, P. A. and Keiser, S. K. (1987–1988, December–January). The marketing research process: role perceptions of researchers and users. *Journal of Advertising Research*, 27, 9–21; Dawson, S., Bush, R. F. and Stern, B. (1994, October). An evaluation of services provided by the marketing research

industry. *Service Industries Journal*, 14, 4, 515–526; also see Austin, J. R. (1991). "An Exploratory Examination of the Development of Marketing Research Service Relationships: An Assessment of Exchange Evaluation Dimensions." In M. C. Gilly, et al. (eds.), *Enhancing Knowledge Development in Marketing*. 1991 AMA Educators' Conference Proceedings, 133–141; also see Swan, J. E., Trawick, I. F. and Carroll, M. G. (1981, August). Effect of participation in marketing research on consumer attitudes toward research and satisfaction with a service. *Journal of Marketing Research*, 356–363; also see Malholtra, N. K., Peterson, M. and Kleiser, S. B. (1999, Spring). Marketing research: a state-of-the-art review and directions for the 21st century. *Journal of the Academy of Marketing Science*, 27, 2, 160–183.

42. Quoted in Chakrapani, C. (2001, Winter). From the editor. *Marketing Research*, 13, 4, 2.

43. What's wrong with marketing research? (2001, Winter). *Marketing Research*, 13, 4.

44. Dawson, S., Bush, R. F. and Stern, B. (1994, October). An evaluation of services provided by the market research industry. *Service Industries Journal*, 144, 515–526.

45. Consensus eludes certification issue (1989, September 11). *Marketing News*, 125, 127; Stern, B. and Crawford, T. (1986, September 12). It's time to consider certification of researchers. *Marketing News*, 20–21; Stern, B. L. and Grubb, E. L. (1991). Alternative solutions to the marketing research industry's "quality control" problem. In: R. L. King (ed.). *Marketing: Toward the Twenty-First Century*. Proceedings of the Southern Marketing Association, 225–229; Jones, M. A. and McKinney, R. (1993). The need for certification in marketing research. In: D. Thompson (Ed.), *Marketing and Education: Partners in Progress* Proceedings of the Atlantis Marketing Association, 224–229. Also, for an excellent review of the pros and cons of certification, see Rittenburg, T. L. and Murdock, G. W. (1994, Spring). Highly sensitive issue still sparks controversy within the industry. *Marketing Research*, 6, 2, 5–10. Also see Giacobbe, R. W. and Segel, M. N. (1994). Credentialing of marketing research professionals: an industry perspective. In R. Archoll and A. Mitchell (eds.), *Enhancing Knowledge Development in Marketing*. A.M.A Educators' Conference Proceedings, 229–301.

46. Achenbaum, A. A. (1985, June–July). Can we tolerate a double standard in marketing research? *Journal of Advertising Research*, 25, RC3–RC7.

47. Murphy, P. E. and Laczniack, G. R. (1992, June). Emerging ethical issues facing marketing researchers. *Marketing Research*, 4, 2, 6–11.

48. This paper is updated from an original version written by Jessica Wilson and was adapted from information provided by the MRA, particularly from materials posted on its website at www.mra-net.org Retrieved on December 19, 2008. Also, much of the material was adapted from the writings of Joan Burns of Teradyne, Inc., who was the chair of the Certification Workgroup. See, for example: Burns, J. (2005). Certification: the five key questions. Retrieved April 19, 2005, from the Marketing Research Association website at www.mra-net.org.

49. See Steinberg, M. S. (1992, June). The "profesionalization" of marketing. *Marketing Research*, 4, 2, 56. Also see McDaniel, S. W. and Solano-Mendez, R. (1993). Should marketing researchers be certified? *Journal of Advertising Research*, 33, 4, 20–31.

50. McDaniel, S. W. (2006). "Should Marketing Researchers Be Certified?" in Burns, A. C. and Bush, R. F. *Marketing Research*, 5th ed. Upper Saddle River, NJ: Pearson/Prentice Hall, 58–59.

51. McDaniel, S., Verille, P. and Madden, C. S. (1985, February). The threats to marketing research: an empirical reappraisal. *Journal of Marketing Research*, 74–80; Akaah, I. P. and Riordan, E. A.

(1989, February). Judgements of marketing professionals about ethical issues in marketing research. *Journal of Marketing Research*, 112–120; Laczniak, G. R. and Murphy, P. E. *Marketing Ethics*. Lexington, MA: Lexington Books; Ferrell, O. C. and Gresham, L. G. (1985, Summer). A contingency framework for understanding ethical decision making in marketing. *Journal of Marketing Research*, 87–96; Reidenbach, R. E. and Robin, D. P. (1990). A partial testing of the contingency framework for ethical decision making: a path analytical approach. In L. M. Capella, H. W. Nash, J. M. Starling, and R. D. Taylor (eds.), *Progress in Marketing Thought*. Proceedings of the Southern Marketing Association, 121–128; LaFleur, E. K. and Reidenbach, R. E. (1993). A taxonomic construction of ethics decision rules: an agenda for research. In T. K. Massey, Jr. (ed.), *Marketing: Satisfying a Diverse Customerplace*. Proceedings of the Southern Marketing Association, 158–161; Reidenbach, R. E., LaFleur, E. K., Robin, D. P. and Forest, P. J. (1993). Exploring the dimensionality of ethical judgements made by advertising professionals concerning selected child-oriented television advertising practices. In T. K. Massey, Jr. (ed.), *Marketing: Satisfying a Diverse Customerplace*. Proceedings of the Southern Marketing Association, 166–170; Klein, J. G. and Smith, N. C. (1994). Teaching marketing research ethics in business school classroom. In R. Achrol and A. Mitchell (eds.), *Enhancing Knowledge Development in Marketing*. A.M.A Educators' Conference Proceedings, 92–99.

52. Dolliver, M. (2000, July 10). Keeping honest company. *Adweek*, 41, 28, 29.

53. Hodcock, C. L. (2007). *Why Smart Companies Do Dumb Things*. Amherst, NY: Prometheus Books. 319.

54. See Kelley, S., Ferrell, O. C. and Skinner, S. J. (1990). Ethical behavior among marketing researchers: an assessment. *Journal of Business Ethics*, 9, 8, 681ff.

55. See Whetstone, J. T. (2001, September). How virtue fits within business ethics. *Journal of Business Ethics*, 33, 2, 101–114; and Pallister, J., Nancarrow, C. and Brace, I. (1999, July). Navigating the righteous course: a quality issue. *Journal of the Market Research Society*, 41, 3, 327–342.

56. Hunt, S. D., Chonko, L. B. and Wilcox, J. B. (1984, August). Ethical problems of marketing researcher. *Journal of Marketing Research*, 21, 309–324.

57. For an excellent article on ethics, see Hunt, S. D. and Vitell, S. (1986). A general theory of marketing ethics. *Journal of Macromarketing*, 6, 1, 5–16.

58. Hunt, S. D., Chonko, L. B. and Wilcox, J. B. (1984). Ethical problems of marketing researcher. *Journal of Marketing Research*, 21, 309–324.

59. For an excellent discussion of these two philosophies relative to marketing research, see Kimmel, A. J. and Smith, N. C. (2001, July). Deception in marketing research: ethical, methodological, and disciplinary implications. *Psychology & Marketing*, 18, 7, 672–680.

60. Bowers, D. K. (1995, Summer). Confidentiality challenges. *Marketing Research*, 7, 3, 34–35.

61. Hunt, S. D., Chonko, L. B. and Wilcox, J. B. Ethical problems of marketing researcher. *Journal of Marketing Research*, 21, 309–324.

62. Hoffman, T. (2003). Market research providers confront credibility concerns; IT chiefs say they want ethics policies and disclosures stated more clearly. *Computerworld*, 37, 41, 4ff.

63. Hodock, C. L. (2007). *Why Smart Companies Do Dumb Things*. Amherst, NY: Prometheus Books. 318–19.

64. Ensing, D. (2008, October). Let me help you with that. *Quirk's Marketing Research Review*, 30–36.

65. Kiecker, P. L. and Nelson, J. E. (1989). Cheating behavior by telephone interviewers: a view from the trenches. In P. Bloom, et al.

(eds.), *Enhancing Knowledge Development in Marketing*. A.M.A. Educators' Conference Proceedings, Chicago, IL 182–188.

66. Hunt, S. D., Chonko, L. B. and Wilcox, J. B., Ethical problems of marketing researcher. *Journal of Marketing Research*, 21, 309–324.

67. Ibid.

68. Jarvis, S. (2002, February 4). CMOR finds survey refusal rate still rising. *Marketing News*, 36, 3, 4. Also see Bowers, D. K. (1997). CMOR's first four years. *Marketing Research*, 9, 44–45; Shea, C. Z. and LeBourveau C. (2000, Fall). Jumping the "hurdles" of marketing research. *Marketing Research*, 12, 3, 22–30.

69. Oliver, J. and Eales K. (2008). Re-evaluating the consequentialist perspective of using covertparticipant observation in management research. *Qualitative Market Research: An International Journal*, 11, 3, 344–357.

70. Kimmel, A. J. and Smith, N. C. (2001, July). Deception in marketing research: ethical, methodological, and disciplinary implications. *Psychology & Marketing*, 18, 7, 663–689.

71. Shing, M. and Spence, L. (2002). Investigating the limits of competitive intelligence gathering: is mystery shopping ethical? *Business Ethics: A European Review*, 11, 4, 343ff.

72. Chavez, J. (2003, October 19). Do-not-call registry contains loopholes for some businesses. Knight Ridder/Tribune Business News. Retrieved on December 7, 2003, from BusinessFile ASAP.

73. Mail abuse prevention system definition of spam. Retrieved March 1, 2002, from www.mailabuse.org/standard.html.

74. New law: Is Spam on the lam? *Managing Technology*. Retrieved on December 6, 2003, from knowledge.wharton.upenn.edu; Galgano, M. (2004, August 16). Spam wars. *The Edge: IMRO's Quarterly Newsletter for the Online Research Industry*.

75. Galgano, M. (2004, August 16). Spam wars. *The Edge: IMRO's Quarterly Newsletter for the Online Research Industry*.

76. *National Do Not Email Registry: A Report to Congress* (2004, June). Washington, DC: Federal Trade Commission; and FTC declines to create do not spam registry. Retrieved from www.cmor.org on April 10, 2005.

77. Baldinger, A. and Perterson, B. (1993, August 16). CMOR concentrates on six key areas to improve cooperation. *Marketing News*, 27, 17, A15.

78. The author makes no pretense that this is an original case. Rather, this case has been adapted from Sparks, J. R. and Hunt, S. D. (1998). Marketing researcher ethical sensitivity; conceptualization, measurement, and exploratory investigation. *Journal of Marketing*, 62, 2, 92–109.

79. See www.bls.gov/oco/home.htm. Retrieved on September 25, 2008.

80. See www.bls.gov/oco/home.htm. Retrieved on September 25, 2008.

81. Jarvis, S. (2001, August 14). Compensation prize. *Marketing News*. Retrieved from www.marketingpower.com on December 19, 2001.

Chapter 4

1. Personal communication with Lawrence D. Gibson. Also see: Gibson, L.D. (1998, Spring). Defining marketing problems: don't spin your wheels solving the wrong puzzle. *Marketing Research*, 10, 3, 5–12.

2. Getzels, J. W. and Csikszentmihalyi, M. (1975). *Perspectives in creativity*. Chicago: Aldine Publishing Co.

3. Raiffa, H. (1968). *Decision Analysis*. Reading, MA: Addison-Wesley Publishing Co.

4. The Operative Product Word: Ambitiousness. *Advertising Age*, December 21, 1996, 14; Murtaugh, P. (1998, May). Consumer research: the big lie. *Food & Beverage Marketing*, 16; and Parasuraman, A., Grewal, D. and Krishnan, R. (2004). *Marketing Research*. Boston: Houghton Mifflin, 41–42.

5. See Allen, F. (1994). *Secret Formula*. New York: HarperCollins, Inc.

6. Koten, J. and Kilman, S. (1985, July 15). Marketing classic; how Coke's decision to offer 2 colas undid 4½ years of planning—after successful introduction of New Coke, firm began to see market slip away—which one will be flagship? *The Wall Street Journal*, 1.

7. Gibson, Defining marketing problems: don't spin your wheels solving the wrong puzzle.

8. Gibson, L. D. (1998, Spring). Defining marketing problems: don't spin your wheels solving the wrong puzzle. *Marketing Research*, 10, 4, 7.

9. Retrieved from www.dictionary.com on November 13, 2003.

10. Kotler, P. (2003). *Marketing Management: Analysis, Planning, Implementing, and Control*, 11th ed. Upper Saddle River, NJ: Prentice Hall, 102.

11. For example, see: Gordon, G. L., Schoenbachler, D. D., Kaminski, P. F. and Brouchous, K. A. (1997). New product development: using the salesforce to identify opportunities. *Business and Industrial Marketing*, 12, 1, 33; and Ardjchvilj, A., Cardozo, R. and Ray, S. (2003, January). A theory of entrepreneurial opportunity identification and development. *Journal of Business Venturing*, 18, 1, 105.

12. Kotler, *Marketing Management*, 103.

13. Personal communication with Lawrence D. Gibson. Also see Gibson, Defining marketing problems.

14. Semon, T. (1999, June 7). Make sure the research will answer the right question. *Marketing News*, 33, 12, H30.

15. Hodock, C. L. (2007). *Why Smart Companies Do Dumb Things*. Amherst, N.Y.: Prometheus Books, 227–232.

16. "Students may be surprised to learn that there is little agreement in the advertising industry as to what constitutes a "better" advertising claim at the testing stage. The researcher is often saddled with the task of measuring the quality of the claims and with defining what a better claim should be. It would be helpful if the firm has a history of testing claims and has reached agreement on what constitutes a "better" claim. In the end, the definition of "better" must be based on consensus or the decision cannot be made." Quote provided to the authors by Ron Tatham, Ph.D.

17. Adapted from Dictionary.com. Retrieved on November 15, 2003. Also see Bagozzi, R. P. and Phillips, L. W. (1982, September). Representing and testing organizational theories: a holistic construal. *Administrative Science Quarterly*, 27, 3, 459.

18. Adapted from Dictionary.com. Retrieved on November 15, 2003. Also see Bagozzi, R. P. and Phillips, L. W. (1982, September). Representing and testing organizational theories: a holistic construal. *Administrative Science Quarterly*, 27, 3, 459.

19. Smith, S. M. and Albaum, G. S. (2005). *Fundamentals of Marketing Research*. Thousand Oaks, CA: Sage Publications, Inc., 349.

20. Dictionary. American Marketing Association. Retrieved on December 10, 2003 from www.marketingpower.com.

21. Bearden, W. O., Netemeyer, R. G.and Mobley, M. F. (1993). *Handbook of Marketing Scales*. Newberry Park, CA: Sage Publications, Inc.; Bearden, W. O. and Netemeyer, R. G. (1999). *Handbook of Marketing Scales: Multi-item measures for Marketing and Consumer Behavior Research*. Thousand Oaks, CA: Sage Publications, Inc.; and Bruner, G. C., Hensel, P.J. and James, K. E. (2005). *Marketing Scales Handbook: A Compilation of Multi-Item Measures for Consumer Behavior and Advertising*. Chicago, IL: American Marketing Association.

22. Moser, A. (2005). Take steps to avoid misused research pitfall. *Marketing News*, 39, 15, 27.

23. See Insights based on 30 years of defining the problem and research objectives. In Burns, A. C and Bush, R. F. *Marketing Research*, 5th ed. Upper Saddle River, NJ: Pearson Prentice Hall, 92–93.

24. See: Evgeniou, T. and Cartwright, P. (2005). Barriers to information management. *European Management Journal*, 23, 3, 293–299.

25. See Jones, S. (2006). Problem-definition in marketing research: facilitating dialog between clients and researcher. *Psychology and Marketing*, 2, 2, 83–92.

26. Jones, S. (1985). Problem-definition in marketing research: facilitating dialog between clients and researchers. *Psychology and Marketing, 2*, 2, 83.

27. Kane, C. (1994, November 28). New product killer: the research gap. *Brandweek*, 35, 46, 12.

28. Rogers, K. (1970). The identity crisis of the marketing researcher. In J. Siebert and G. Wills, (eds.), *Marketing Research*. Middlesex: Penguin; Small, R. J. and Rosenberg, L. J. (1975). The marketing researcher as a decision-maker: Myth or reality? *Journal of Marketing*, 39, 1, 2–7; Crawford, C. M. (1977). Marketing research and the new product failure rate. *Journal of Marketing*, 41, 2, 51–61; and Channon, C. (1982). What do we know about how research works. *Journal of the Market Research Society*, 24, 4, 241–315.

29. For more information on proposals and reports, see Carroll, N., Mohn, M., and Land, T. H. (1989, January/February/March). A guide to quality marketing research proposals and reports. *Business*, 39, 38–40.

Chapter 5

1. Momentum Market Intelligence performs both quantitative and qualitative research. It also offer a complete marketing intelligence system to clients. On their web page, at www.mointel.com, go to "Capabilities" to read more about the services the company offers.

2. Singleton, D. (2003, November 24). Basics of good research involve understanding six simple rules. *Marketing News*, 22–23.

3. For an excellent in-depth treatment of research design issues, see Creswell, J. (2003). *Research Design; Qualitative, Quantitative, and Mixed Methods Approaches*. Thousand Oaks, CA: Sage.

4. Burns, A. C. and Bush, R. F. (2005). *Basic Marketing Research Using Microsoft Excel Data Analysis*. Upper Saddle River, NJ: Prentice Hall, 100–102.

5. Personal communication with Holly McLennan, Marketing Director, 1-800-GOT-JUNK? on April 27, 2005; and Martin, J. (2003, October 27). Cash from trash: 1-800-Got Junk? *Fortune*, 148, , , 196.

6. For one example, see Parasuraman, A., Berry, L. L. and Zeithaml, V. A. (1991, Winter). Refinement and reassessment of the SERVQUAL scale. *Journal of Retailing*, 67, 4, 420ff. A small effort in exploratory research on this topic will uncover many references on measuring service quality.

7. Stewart, D. W. (1984). *Secondary Research: Information Sources and Methods*. Newbury Park, CA: Sage; Davidson, J. P. (1985, April). Low cost research sources. *Journal of Small Business Management*, 23, , , , 73–77.

8. Knox, N. (2003, December 16). Volvo teams up to build what women want. *USA Today*, 1B.

9. Bonoma, T. V. (1984). Case research in marketing: Opportunities, problems, and a process. *Journal of Marketing Research*, 21, 199–208.

10. Myers, J. Wireless for the 21st century. *Telephony*, 231, 6, 24–26.

11. Greenbaum, T. I. (1988). *The Practical Handbook and Guide in Focus Group Research*. Lexington, MA: D.C. Heath.

12. Stoltman, J. J. and Gentry, J. W. (1992). Using focus groups to study household decision processes and choices. In R. P. Leone and V. Kumar (eds.). AMA *Educator's Conference Proceedings:*

Vol. 3: *Enhancing knowledge development in marketing*. Chicago: American Marketing Association, 257–263.

13. Miller, C. (1991, May 27). Respondents project let psyches go crazy. *Marketing News*, 25, 11, 1, 3.

14. See Churchill, G. A., Jr., and Iacobucci, D. (2005). *Marketing Research: Methodological Foundations*. Mason, OH: Thomson/South-Western, 679.

15. Kinnear, T. C. and Taylor, J. R. (1991). *Marketing Research: An Applied Approach*. New York: McGraw-Hill, 142.

16. Sudman, S. and Wansink, B. (2002). *Consumer Panels*, 2nd ed. Chicago: American Marketing Association. This book is recognized as an authoritative source on panels.

17. Personal communication with Allison Groom, American Heart Association, March 12, 2002.

18. Lohse, G. L. and Rosen, D. L. (2002, Summer). Signaling quality and credibility in Yellow Pages advertising: the influence of color and graphics on choice. *Journal of Advertising*, 30, 2, 73–85.

19. Wyner, G. (2000, Fall). Learn and earn through testing on the Internet: the Web provides new opportunities for experimentation. *Marketing* Research, 12, 3, 37–38.

20. For example, see Montgomery, D. (2001). *Design and Analysis of Experiments*. New York: Wiley; and Kerlinger, F. N. (1986). *Foundation of Behavioral Research*, 3rd ed. New York: Holt, Rinehart, and Winston.

21. Campbell, D. T. and Stanley, J. C. (1963). *Experimental and Quasi-experimental Designs for Research*. Chicago: Rand McNally.

22. Calder, B. J., Phillips, L. W. and Tybout, A. M. (1992, December). The concept of external validity. *Journal of Consumer Research*, 9, 240–244.

23. Gray, L. R. and Diehl, P. L. (1992). *Research Methods for Business and Management*. New York: Macmillan, 387–390.

24. Doyle, J. (1994, October). In with the new, out with the old. *Beverage World*, 113 , 1576, 204–205.

25. Brennan, L. (1988, March). Test marketing. *Sales & Marketing Management Magazine*, 140, , 50–62.

26. Miles, S. (2001). MyTurn is cutting back in unusual way. *The Wall Street Journal*, Eastern Edition.

27. A root beer float in a bottle? (2003, June 19). *The Columbus Dispatch*. Retrieved on December 19, 2003, from Lexis-Nexis.

28. Kaushik, N. (2003, July 23). Thai co introduces children's furniture. *Businessline*, 1.

29. Liddle, A. (2002, May 20). DQ field tests irradiated burgers as farm bill relaxes labeling law. *Nation's Restaurant News*, 36, 20, 3ff.

30. Keep jellyfish at bay. (2003, April 1). *Community Pharmacy,* 26.

31. Thompson, S. (2003, November 11). Snacks take flight. *Advertising Age*, 73, 45, 6.

32. Churchill, G. A., Jr. (2001). *Basic Marketing Research*, 4th ed. Fort Worth, TX: The Dryden Press, 144–145.

33. Saab plots device that detects early stages of tiredness. (2007, November 8) *Marketing Week, London*. Retrieved August 6, 2008 from ProQuest.

34. Ebenkamp, B. (2008, June 2). What can you do with a dollar? Go e.l.f. yourself. *Brandweek*, 49, 22. Retrieved August 6, 2008 from ProQuest.

35. Wapshott, Nicholas (2008, April 14). My baby maybe. *New Statesman*, 137, 4892, 20. Retrieved August 27, 2008 from ProQuest.

36. Walkup, C. and Martin, R. (2007, October 15). McD thirsts for $1B in new beverage sales. *Nation's Restaurant News*, 41. Retrieved August 6, 2008 from ProQuest; Weird Facts. (2008, August 5). McDonald's tests changes. Retrieved

August 6, 2008 from weirdfactshere.blogspot.com/2008/08/mcdonalds-tests-changes-weird-facts.html.

37. Spethmann, B. (1985, May 8). Test market USA. *Brandweek*, 36, 40–43.

38. Clancy, K. J. and Shulman, R. S. (1995, October). Test for success. *Sales & Marketing Management Magazine*, 147, 10, 111–115.

39. Melvin, P. (1992, September). Choosing simulated test marketing systems. *Marketing Research*, 4, 3, 14–16.

40. Ibid. Also see Turner, J. and Brandt, J. (1978, Winter). Development and validation of a simulated market to test children for selected consumer skills. *Journal of Consumer Affairs*, 266–276.

41. Blount, S. (1992, March). It's just a matter of time. *Sales & Marketing Management*, 144, 3, 32–43.

42. Power, C. (1992, August 10). Will it sell in Podunk? Hard to say. *BusinessWeek*, 46–47.

43. Nelson, E. (2001, February 2). Colgate's net rose 10 percent in period, new products helped boost sales. *The Wall Street Journal*, Eastern edition, B6.

44. Ihlwan, M. (2002, February 4). A nation of digital guinea pigs: Korea is a hotbed of such experiments as a cash-free city. *BusinessWeek*, 50.

45. Greene, S. (1996, May 4). Chattanooga chosen as test market for smokeless cigarette. *Knight-Ridder/Tribune Business News*, 5040084.

46. Hayes, J. (1995, January 3). McD extends breakfast buffet test in south-east markets. *National Restaurant News*, 29, 4, 3.

47. Kotler, P. (1991). *Marketing Management: Analysis, Planning, Implementation, and Control.* Upper Saddle River, NJ: Prentice Hall, 335.

48. Syms, P. (2007, December–January). Testing time for brands. *Brand Strategy*, 36–37.

49. Power, C. (1992, August 10). Will it sell in Podunk? Hard to say. *BusinessWeek*, 46–47.

50. Murphy, P. and Laczniak, G. (1992, June). Emerging ethical issues facing marketing researchers. *Marketing Research*, 6.

Chapter 6

1. For an example of using secondary data for a marketing research project, see Castleberry, S. B. (2001, December). Using secondary data in marketing research: a project that melds Web and off-Web sources. *Journal of Marketing Education*, 23, 3, 195–203.

2. For a comparison of three search engines see: www.lib.berkeley.edu/TeachingLib/Guides/Internet/SearchEngines.html.

3. Ritchie, K. (2002). *Marketing to Generation X.* New York: Simon and Schuster.

4. Portions adapted from Social and Demographic Trends, Pew Research Center. Retrieved on January 2, 2009 from www.pewsocialtrends.org; Weiss, M. J. (2003, September 1). To be or not to be. *American Demographics.* Retrieved from LexisNexis on October 30, 2003.

5. Kotler, P. (2003). *Marketing Management*, 11th ed. Upper Saddle River, NJ: Prentice Hall, 53.

6. Senn, J. A. (1988). *Information Technology in Business: Principles, Practice, and Opportunities.* Upper Saddle River, NJ: Prentice Hall, 66.

7. Grisaffe, D. (2002, January 21). See about linking CRM and MR systems. *Marketing News*, 36, 2, 13.

8. Drozdenko, R. G. and Drake, P. D. (2002). *Optimal Database Marketing.* Thousand Oaks, CA: Sage.

9. Lewis, L. (1996, November). Retailers begin tracking consumer purchases and recording consumer preferences and demographic data. *Progressive Grocer*, 75, 11, 18.

10. McKim, R. (2001, September). Privacy notices: what they mean and how marketers can prepare for them. *Journal of Database Marketing*, 9, 1, 79–84.

11. See, for example, U.S. *Industrial Outlook 1999.* (1999). Washington, DC: International Trade Administration, U.S. Department of Commerce.

12. The evolution of the standards for defining MAs was discussed in detail in OMB's *Federal Register* Notice of December 21, 1998, "Alternative Approaches to Defining Metropolitan and Nonmetropolitan Areas" (63 FR 70526–70561). Table 1 of the December Notice summarized the evolution of MA standards since 1950. (The December Notice is available on the OMB website.)

13. Gordon, L. P. (1995). *Using Secondary Data in Marketing Research: United States and Worldwide.* Westport, CT: Quorum Books, 24.

14. These questions and much of the following discussion is taken from Stewart, D. W. (1984). *Secondary Research: Information Sources and Methods.* Newbury Park, CA: Sage.

15. Murray, D., Schwartz, J. and Lichter, S. R. (2001). *It Ain't Necessarily So: How Media Make and Unmake the Scientific Picture of Reality.* Lanham, MD: Rowman & Littlefield.

16. Ibid., 71–76.

17. Ibid., vii–ix.

18. Crossen, C. (1994). *Tainted Truth: The Manipulation of Fact in America.* New York: Simon & Schuster, 140.

19. See: Goldberg, B. (2002). *Bias.* Washington, DC: Regnery Publishing; and Best, J. (2001). *Damned Lies and Statistics.* Berkeley, CA: University of California Press.

20. Chapman, J. (1987, February). Cast a critical eye: small area estimates and projections sometimes can be dramatically different. *American Demographics*, 9, 30.

21. These steps are updated and adapted from Stewart, D. W. *Secondary Research*, 20–22, by Ms. Peggy Toifel, MSLS, MBA, University Librarian, University of West Florida, 2004.

22. America's experience with Census 2000. (2000, August). *Direct Marketing*, 63, 4, 46–51.

23. Researchers wishing to use SIC codes should refer to the *Standard Industrial Classification Manual 1987*, rev. ed. (1987). Executive office of the President, Office of Management and Budget, Washington, DC: Government Printing Office.

24. Winchester, J. (1998, February). Marketers prepare for switch from SIC codes. *Business Marketing*, 1, 34.

25. Boettcher, J. (1996, April–May). NAFTA prompts a new code system for industry—the death of SIC and birth of NAICS. *Database*, 42–45.

Chapter 7

1. Actually, virtually all these firms offer some customization of data analysis, and many offer varying methods of collecting data. Still, although customization is possible, these same companies provide standardized processes and data.

2. See: *Rocking the ages: the Yankelovich perspective on generational marketing.* (1997). New York: Harper Business.

3. Solutions & Services/consumer trends research/monitor annually. Retrieved from www.yankelovich.com on September 6, 2002.

4. Retrieved from www.yankelovich.com/monitor on May 10, 2005.

5. Retrieved from www.yankelovich.com on May 10, 2005.

6. Abate, P. Senior Vice President, Ipsos Public Relations. Personal communication with the authors, September 12, 2008.

7. Harris poll. Retrieved from www.HarrisInteractive.com on May 10, 2005.

8. What does America think about? (undated publication). Wilmington, DE: Scholarly Resources.

9. Welcome to VALS™. Retrieved from www.sric-bi.com/VALS/ on January 12, 2009. Also see: Fish, D. (2000, November). Untangling psychographics and lifestyle. *Quirk's Marketing Research Review*, 138ff.

10. *Tapestry Segmentation, Segment Summaries (2009)*. Redlands, CA: ESRI. Also taken from *Tapestry Segmentation Handbook*. Undated. Redlands, CA: ESRI.

11. See: Seal, J. and Moody, M. (2008, Spring). The hidden limitations of tracking research. *Marketing Research*, 20, 1, 17–21.

12. Stolzenberg, M. (2000, February). 10 tips on tracking research. *Quirk's Marketing Research Review*, 20–24.

13. The information in this section was edited by J. Frighetto, The Nielsen Company, and communicated to the authors on January 13, 2009.

14. The information in this section was edited by Ms. Shelley L. Hughes, IRI, and communicated to the authors on January 15, 2009. Also see: Custom store tracking (2004). Retrieved on January 10, 2004 from www.infores.com.

15. The information in this section was edited by Ms. Shelley L. Hughes, IRI, and communicated to the authors on January 15, 2009. See also: Retrieved from www.infores.com/ on May 10, 2005.

16. NPD group, food and beverages worldwide. (2002). Retrieved from www.npd.com on May 16, 2002.

17. Retrieved from: usa.infores.com/productssolutions/allproducts/tabid/156/default.aspx/ on January 12, 2009.

18. CBP, Category Business Planner (2009). Retrieved from us.nielsen.com/products/rs_cbp.shtml on January 12, 2009. The information in this section was edited by J. Frighetto, The Nielsen Company, and communicated to the authors on January 13, 2009.

19. Nielsen SoundScan. Retrieved online from www.soundscan.com on January 12, 2009.

20. Nielsen VideoScan. Retrieved from www.nielsen.com/solutions/videoscan.html on January 12, 2009.

21. BookScan—the world's first and largest continuous sales monitoring service. Retrieved from www.bookscan.com on January 12, 2009.

22. Retrieved on May 13, 2005 from Nielsen Media Research website at www.nielsenmedia.com.

23. Repeat-viewing with people meters. *Journal of Advertising Research*, 9–13; Stoddard, L. R., Jr. (1987, October). The history of people meters. *Journal of Advertising Research*, 10–12.

24. Material for this section on the NTI was edited by Ms. Sandra Parrelli of The Nielsen Company and communicated to the authors on January 13, 2009.

25. You can see the schedule at www.arbitron.com. Go to Portable People Meter and then "PPM Markets." Retrieved on January 14, 2009.

26. See Arbitron.com.

27. See mediamark.com.

28. The most comprehensive overview of print advertising in one book. (2009). Retrieved from mediamark.com/starch/MRI Starch Adnorms on January 14, 2009.

29. About Consumer Generated Media (CGM). (2009).Retrieved from www.nielsen-online.com. Go to "Resources" and then "About Consumer Generated Media."

30. Simmons National Consumer Study. (2009). Retrieved from www.smrb.com on January 13, 2009. Go to "Core Solutions" and go to "National Consumer Study".

31. Patchen, R. H. and Kolessar, R. S. (1999, August). Out of the lab and into the field: a pilot test of the Personal Portable Meter. *Journal of Advertising Research*, 39, 4, 55–68. Also see: Moss, L. (2002, February 11). A constant companion. *Broadcasting & Cable*, 132, 6, 17.

32. Hughes, L. Q. (2001, June 18). Buyers demand more data. *Advertising Age*, 72, 25, T2.

33. Retrieved from usa.infores.com on January 14, 2009. Go to "Products Solutions," "All Products," "All products Detail."

34. Reid, A. (2000, January 28). Is ITV's tvSPAN the holy grail adland has been waiting for? *Campaign*, 20.

35. For a review of these discussions, see Peters, B. (1990, December). The brave new world of single-source information. *Marketing Research*, 2, 4, 16; Churchill, V. B. (1990, December). The role of ad hoc survey research in a single source world. *Marketing Research*, 2, 4, 22–26; and Metzger, G. D. (1990, December). Single source: yes and no (the backward view). *Marketing Research*, 2, 4, 29.

Chapter 8

1. Ezzy, D. (2001, August). Are qualitative methods misunderstood? *Australian and New Zealand Journal of Public Health*, 25, 4, 294–297.

2. Clark, A. (2001, September 13). Research takes an inventive approach, *Marketing*, 25–26.

3. DeNicola, N. (2002, March 4). Casting finer net not necessary. *Marketing News, 36*, 5, 46.

4. Griffen, D. S. and Duley, R. (2000, July/August). Read all about it. *Quirks Marketing Research Review, 14*, 7, 20–21, 104-106.

5. Smith, S. M., and Whitlark, D. B. (2001, Summer). Men and women online: what makes them tick? *Marketing Research, 13*(2):20–25.

6. Piirto, R. (1991, September). Socks, ties and videotape. *American Demographics*, 6.

7. Fellman, M. W. (1999, Fall). Breaking tradition. *Marketing Research, 11*, 3, 20–34.

8. For some guidelines to direct observation, see Becker, B. (1999, September 27). Take direct route when data-gathering. *Marketing News, 33*(20):29, 31.

9. Modified from Tull, D. S. and Hawkins, D. I. (1987). *Marketing Research*, 4th ed. New York: Macmillan, 331.

10. Rust, L. (1993, November/December). How to reach children in stores: marketing tactics grounded in observational research. *Journal of Advertising Research, 33*, 6, 67-72; and Rust, L. (1993, July/August). Parents and children shopping together: a new approach to the qualitative analysis of observational data. *Journal of Advertising Research, 33*, 4, 65–70.

11. Thomas, J. (1999, February). Motivational research. *Quirks Marketing Research Review, 12*, 2, 40–43.

12. Viles, P. (1992, August 24). Company measures listenership in cars. *Broadcasting, 122*, 35, 28.

13. Kephart, P. (1996, May). The spy in aisle 3. *American Demographics Marketing Tools*, www.marketingtools.com/Publications/MT/96_mt/9605MD04.htm.

14. Del Vecchio, E. (1988, Spring). Generating marketing ideas when formal research is not available. *Journal of Services Marketing, 2*, 2, 71–74.

15. Mariampolski, H. (1988, January 4). Ethnography makes comeback as research tool. *Marketing News, 22*, 1, 32, 44; Peñaloza, L. (1994, June). Atravesando Fronteras/Border Crossings: a critical ethnographic study of the consumer acculturation of Mexican immigrants. *Journal of Consumer Research*, 21, 32–53; Peñaloza, L. (2006). Researching ethnicity and consumption. In: Russell W. Belk, ed., *Handbook of Qualitative Research*

Techniques in Marketing. Cheltenham: Edward Elgar, 547–549; Carlon, M. (2008, April). Evolving ethnography. *Quirk's Marketing Research Review*, 22, 4, 18, 20.

16. Hellebusch, S. J. (2000, September 11). Don't read research by the numbers. *Marketing News, 34*, 19, 25.

17. Greenbaum, T. I. (1988). *The Practical Handbook and Guide in Focus Group Research*. Lexington, MA: D. C. Heath.

18. Stoltman, J. J. and Gentry, J. W. (1992). Using focus groups to study household decision processes and choices. In R. P. Leone and V. Kumar, eds., *AMA Educator's Conference Proceedings*, Vol. 3. Enhancing knowledge development in marketing. Chicago: American Marketing Association, 257–263.

19. Last, J. and Langer, J. (2003, December). Still a valuable tool. *Quirk's Marketing Research Review, 17*, 11, 30.

20. Kahn, A. (1996, September 6). Focus groups alter decisions made in business, politics. *Knight-Ridder/Tribune Business News*, 916.

21. Wellner, A. (2003, March). The new science of focus groups. *American Demographics, 25*, 2, 29ff.

22. Langer, J. (2001). *The Mirrored Window: Focus Groups from a Moderator's Viewpoint*. New York: Paramount Market Publishing, 4.

23. Greenbaum, T. L. (1993, March 1). Focus group research is not a commodity business. *Marketing News, 27*, 5, 4.

24. Greenbaum, T. L. (1991, May 27). Answer to moderator problems starts with asking right questions. *Marketing News, 25*, 11, 8–9; and Fern, E. F. (1982, February). The use of focus groups for idea generation: the effects of group size, acquaintanceship, and moderator on response quantity and quality. *Journal of Marketing Research*, 1–13.

25. Greenbaum, T. L. (1991). Do you have the right moderator for your focus groups? Here are 10 questions to ask yourself. *Bank Marketing, 23*, 1, 43.

26. Based on Henderson, N. R. (2000, December). Secrets of our success: insights from a panel of moderators. *Quirk's Marketing Research Review, 14*, 11, 62–65.

27. For guidelines for "backroom observers," see Langer, J. (2001, September 24). Get more out of focus group research. *Marketing News, 35*, 20, 19–20.

28. Grinchunas, R. and Siciliano, T. (1993, January 4). Focus groups produce verbatims, not facts. *Marketing News, 27*, 1, FG-19.

29. Zinchiak, M. (2001, July/August). Online focus groups FAQs. *Quirk's Marketing Research Review, 15*, 7, 38–46.

30. Lonnie, K. (2001, November 19). Combine phone, Web for focus groups. *Marketing News, 35*, 24, 15–16.

31. For interesting comments, see DeNicola, N. and Kennedy, S. (2001, November 19). Quality inter(net)action. *Marketing News, 35*, 24, 14.

32. Jarvis, S. and Szynal, D. (2001, November 19). Show and tell. *Marketing News, 35*, 24, 1, 13.

33. Adapted from Zinchiak, Online focus group FAQs.

34. Langer, J. (2001). *The Mirrored Window: Focus Groups from a Moderator's Viewpoint*. New York: Paramount Market Publishing, 11.

35. Quinlan, P. (2000, December). Insights on a new site. *Quirk's Marketing Research Review, 15*, 11, 36–39.

36. Hines, T. (2000). An evaluation of two qualitative methods (focus group interviews and cognitive maps) for conducting research into entrepreneurial decision making. *Qualitative Market Research, 3*, 1, 7–16; Quinlan, P. (2008, June). Let the maps be your guide. *Quirk's Marketing Research Review*, 22, 6, 74, 76, 78.

37. Berlamino, C. (1989, December/January). Designing the qualitative research project: addressing the process issues. *Journal of Advertising Research, 29*, 6, S7-S9; Johnston, G. (2008, June).

Qualtitatively speaking. *Quirk's Marketing Research Review*, 22, 6, 18, 20; *Alert! Magazine*. (2007, September). Special Expanded Qualitative Research Issue, 45, 9; Brownell, L. (2008, April). Chief executive column. *Alert! Magazine*, 46, 4,11, 23.

38. Flores Letelier, M., Spinosa, C. and Calder, B. (2000, Winter). Taking an expanded view of customers' needs: qualitative research for aiding innovation. *Marketing Research, 12*, 4, 4–11.

39. Kahan, H. (1990, September 3). One-on-ones should sparkle like the gems they are. *Marketing News, 24*, 18, 8–9.

40. Roller, M. R. (1987, August 28). A real in-depth interview wades into the stream of consciousness. *Marketing News, 21*, 18, 14.

41. Kahan, One-on-ones should sparkle like the gems they are.

42. An interesting article on recent developments in depth interviewing is Wansink, B. (2000, Summer). New techniques to generate key marketing insights. *Marketing Research, 12*, 2, 28–36.

43. Kates, B. (2000, April). Go in-depth with depth interviews. *Quirk's Marketing Research Review, 14*, 4, 36–40.

44. Mitchell, V. (1993, First Quarter). Getting the most from in-depth interviews. *Business Marketing Digest, 18*, 1, 63–70.

45. Reynolds, T. J. and Gutman, J. (1988). Laddering, method, analysis, and interpretation. *Journal of Advertising Research, 28*, 1, 11–21.

46. Qualitative Research Services, Word Association Tests. Retrieved from www.decisionanalyst.com on May 20, 2005.

47. Qualitative Research Services, Sentence Completion Tests. Retrieved from www.decisionanalyst.com on May 20, 2005.

48. An example is Piirto, R. (1990, December). Measuring minds in the 1990s. *American Demographics, 12*, 12, 30–35.

49. Dictionary. American Marketing Association. Retrieved on December 16, 2003 from www.marketingpower.com.

50. Dictionary. American Marketing Association. Retrieved on December 16, 2003 from www.marketingpower.com.

51. Taylor, C. (2003, December). What's all the fuss about? *Quirk's Marketing Research Review, 17*, 11, 40–45.

52. Miles, L. (2003, December 11). Market research: living their lives. *Marketing. Market Research Bulletin*. Retrieved online from www.brandrepublic.com on May 20, 2005.

53. Marshall, S., Drapeau, T. and DiSciullo, M. (2001, July/August). An eye on usability. *Quirk's Marketing Research Review, 15*, 7, 20-21, 90–92.

54. Allmon, D. E. (1988). Voice stress and Likert scales: a paired comparison. In: David L. Moore, ed., Marketing: Forward Motion. *Proceedings of the Atlantic Marketing Association* (1988), 710–714.

55. Green, P., Wind, Y., Krieger, A. and Saatsoglou, P. (2000, Spring). Applying qualitative data. *Marketing Research, 12*, 1, 17–25.

56. Clarke, A. (2001, September 13). Research takes an inventive approach. *Marketing*, 2–26.

57. Wellner, A. S. (2001, April). Research on a shoestring. *American Demographics, 23*, 4, 38–39.

Chapter 9

1. Malhotra, N. (1999). *Marketing Research: An Applied Orientation*, 3rd ed. Upper Saddle River, NJ: Prentice Hall, 125.

2. Tourangeau, R. (2004). Survey research and societal change. *Annual Review of Psychology*, 55, 1, 775–802.

3. Cuneo, A. Z. and Bulik, B. S. (2003, February). Unified voice at risk as HP CEO departs. *Advertising Age*, 76, 7, 3–5.

4. Blyth, B. (2008). Mixed mode: the only "fitness" regime. *International Journal of Market Research*, 50, 2, 241–266.

5. Curtin, R., Presser, S. and Singer, E. (2005, Spring). Changes in telephone survey nonresponse over the past quarter century. *Public Opinion Quarterly*, 69, 1, 87–98.

6. See: Oishi, S. M. (2003). *How to Conduct In-Person Interviews for Surveys*. Thousand Oaks, CA: Sage Publications, 6.

7. Tourangeau, R. (2004). Survey research and societal change. *Annual Review of Psychology*, 55, 1, 775–802.

8. Fielding, M. (2004, November). Recent converts. *Marketing News*, 38, 19, 21–22.

9. Tourangeau, R. (2004). Survey research and societal change. *Annual Review of Psychology*, 55, 1, 775–802.

10. Cleland, K. (1996, May). Online research costs about one-half that of traditional methods. *Business Marketing,* 81, 4, B8–B9.

11. See, for example, Dudley, D. (2001, January). The name collector. *New Media Age*, 18–20; Kent, R. and Brandal, H. (2003, Quarter 4). Improving email response in a permission marketing context. *International Journal of Market Research*, 45, 4, 489–540; or Agrawal, A., Basak, J., Jain, V., Kothari, R., Kumar, M., Mittal, P. A., Modani, N., Ravikumar, K., Sabharwal, Y. and Sureka, R. (2004, September/October). Online marketing research. *IBM Journal of Research & Development*, 48, 5/6, 671–677.

12. See: Macer, T. (2002, December). CAVI from OpinionOne. *Quirk's Marketing Research Review*.

13. Bourque, L. and Fielder, E. (2003*). How to Conduct Self-administered and Mail Surveys*, 2nd ed. Thousand Oaks, CA: Sage Publications.

14. Jang, H., Lee, B., Park, M. and Stokowski, P. A. (2000, February). Measuring underlying meanings of gambling from the perspective of enduring involvement. *Journal of Travel Research*, 38, 3, 230–238.

15. Ericson, P. I. and Kaplan, C. P. (2000, November). Maximizing qualitative responses about smoking in structured interviews. *Qualitative Health Research*, 10, 6, 829–840.

16. Bronner, F. and Kuijlen, T. (2007). The live or digital interviewer. *International Journal of Market Research*, 49, 2, 167–190.

17. Haynes, D. (2005, February). Respondent goodwill is a cooperative activity. *Quirk's Marketing Research Review*, 19, 2, 30–32.

18. Macer, T. and Wilson, S. (2007, February). Online makes more inroads. *Quirk's Marketing Research Review*, 23, 2, 50–55; and Westergaard, J. (2005, November). Your survey, our needs. *Quirk's Marketing Research Review*, 19, 10, 64–66.

19. Some authors restrict the definition only to cases where two or more data-collection methods are used in the same phase of the study. See: Hogg, A. (2002, July), Multi-mode research dos and don'ts. *Quirk's Marketing Research Review*, electronic archive.

20. Cuneo, A. Z. (2004, November). Researchers flail as public cuts the cord. *Advertising Age*, 75, 46–48.

21. See, for example, www.uwf.edu/panel.

22. Fricker, S., Galesic, M., Tourangeau, R. and Ting Yan. (2005, Fall). An experimental comparison of web and telephone surveys. *Public Opinion Quarterly*, 69, 3, 370–392.

23. See Roy, A. (2003). Further issues and factors affecting the response rates of e-mail and mixed-mode studies. In M. Barone, et. al. (eds.), *Enhancing Knowledge Development in Marketing*. Proceedings: AMA Educator's Conference. Chicago, IL: American Marketing Association, 338–339; and Bachmann, D., Elfrink, J. and Vazzana, G. (1999). E-mail and snail mail face off in rematch. *Marketing Research*, 11, 4, 11–15.

24. Hogg, A. (2002, July). Multi-mode research dos and don'ts. *Quirk's Marketing Research Review*, electronic archive.

25. Roy, S. (2004, July). The littlest consumers. *Display & Design Ideas*, 16, 7, 18–21.

26. See Jacobs, H. (1989, Second Quarter). Entering the 1990s—the state of data collection from a mall perspective. *Applied Marketing Research,* 30, 2, 24–26; Lysaker, R. L. (1989, October). Data collection methods in the U.S. *Journal of the Market Research Society*, 31, 4, 477–488; Gates, R. and Solomon, P. J. (1982, August/September). Research using the mall intercept: state of the art. *Journal of Advertising Research,* 43–50; Bush, A. J., Bush, R. F. and Chen, H. C. (1991). Method of administration effects in mall intercept interviews. *Journal of the Market Research Society*, 33, 4, 309–319.

27. See, for example, Ghazali, E., Mutum, A. D. and Mahbob, N. A. (2006). Attitude towards online purchase of fish in urban Malaysia: an ethnic comparison. *Journal of Food Products Marketing*, 12, 4, 109–128; or Yun Wang and Heitmeyer, J. (2006, January). Consumer attitude toward US versus domestic apparel in Taiwan. *International Journal of Consumer Studies*, 30, 1, 64–74.

28. Frost-Norton, T. (2005, June). The future of mall research: current trends affecting the future of marketing research in malls. *Journal of Consumer Behaviour*, 4, 4, 293–301.

29. Hornik, J. and Eilis, S. (1989, Winter). Strategies to secure compliance for a mall intercept interview. *Public Opinion Quarterly,* 52, 4*,* 539–551.

30. At least one study refutes the concern about shopping frequency. See DuPont, T. D. (1987, August/September). Do frequent mall shoppers distort mall-intercept results? *Journal of Advertising Research*, 27, 4, 45–51.

31. Bush, A. J. and Grant, E. S. (1995, Fall). The potential impact of recreational shoppers on mall intercept interviewing: an exploratory study. *The Journal o f Marketing Theory and Practice,* 3, 4, 73–83.

32. Frost-Norton, T. (2005). The future of mall research: current trends affecting the future of marketing research firms in malls. *Journal of Consumer Behavior*, 4, 4, 293–302.

33. Bourque, L. and Fielder, E. (2003). *How to Conduct Telephone Interviews*, 2nd ed. Thousand Oaks, CA: Sage Publications.

34. Bush, A. J. and Hair, J. F. (1983, May). An assessment of the mall intercept as a data collection method. *Journal of Marketing Research*, 22, 158–167.

35. Holbrook, A. L., Green, M. C. and Krosnick, J. A. (2003, Spring). Telephone versus face-to-face interviewing of national probability samples with long questionnaires. *Public Opinion Quarterly*, 67, 1, 79–126.

36. Sheppard. J. (2000, April). Half-empty or half-full? *Quirk's Marketing Research Review*, 14, 4, 42–45.

37. See, for example, Xu, M., Bates, B. J. and Schweitzer, J. C. (1993). The impact of messages on survey participation in answering machine households. *Public Opinion Quarterly*, 57, 232–237; Meinert, D. B., Festervand, T. A. and Lumpkin, J. R. (1992). Computerized questionnaires: pros and cons, in Robert L. King, ed., "Marketing: Perspectives for the 1990s." *Proceedings of the Southern Marketing Association*, 201–206.

38. Remington, T. D. (1993). Telemarketing and declining survey response rates. *Journal of Advertising Research*, 32, 3, RC-6, RC-7.

39. Brennan, M., Benson, S. and Kearns, Z. (2005 Quarter 1). The effect of introductions on telephone survey participation rates. *International Journal of Market Research*, 47 1, 65 (10 pp.).

40. At the extreme, it is reported that Chinese research companies monitor at least 50% of all telephone interviews. See: Harrison, M. (2006,Winter). Learning the language. *Marketing Research*, 18, 4, 10–16.

41. Bos, R. (1999, November). A new era in data collection. *Quirk's Marketing Research Review*, 12, 10, 32–40.

42. Fletcher, K. (1995, June 15). Jump on the omnibus. *Marketing*, 25–28.

43. Gates, R. H. and Jarboe, G. R. (Spring). Changing trends in data acquisition for marketing research. *Journal of Data Collection*, 27, 1, 25–29; also see Synodinos, N. E. and Brennan, J. M. (1998, Summer). Computer interactive interviewing in survey research. *Psychology and Marketing*, 117–138.

44. DePaulo, P. J. and Weitzer, R. (1994, January 3). Interactive phone technology delivers survey data quickly. *Marketing News*, 28, 1, 15.

45. Jones, P. and Palk, J. (1993). Computer-based personal interviewing: State-of-the-art and future prospects. *Journal of the Market Research Society*, 35, 3, 221–233.

46. For a "speed" comparison, see Cobanouglu, C., Warde, B. and Moeo, P. J. (2001, Fourth Quarter). A comparison of mail, fax and Web-based survey methods. *International Journal of Market Research*, 43, 3, 441–452.

47. Bruzzone, D. and Shellenberg, P. (2000, July/August). Track the effect of advertising better, faster, and cheaper online. *Quirk's Marketing Research Review*, 14, 7, 22–35.

48. Not all observers agree that this trend is positive. See: Lauer, H. (2005, July/August). You say evolution, I say devolution. *Quirk's Marketing Research Review*, 19, 7, 82–88.

49. Miles, L. (2004, June 16). Online market research panels offer clients high response rates at low prices. *Marketing*, 39.

50. Grecco, C. (2000, July/August). Research non-stop. *Quirk's Marketing Research Review*, 14, 7, 70–73.

51. Greenberg, D. (2000, July/August). Internet economy gives rise to real-time research. *Quirk's Marketing Research Review*, 14, 7, 88–90.

52. Frazier, D. and Rohmund, I. (2007, July/August). The real-time benefits of online surveys. *Electric Perspectives*, 32, 4, 88–91.

53. See, for example, Deutskens, E., Jong, A,, Ruyter, K. and Wetzels, M. (2006, April). Comparing the generalizability of online and mail surveys in cross-national service quality research. *Marketing Letters*, 17, 2, 119–136; Coderre, F., St-Laurent, N. and Mathieu, A. (2004, Quarter 3). Comparison of the quality of qualitative data obtained through telephone, postal and email surveys. *International Journal of Market Research*, 46, 3, 347–357; or Kaplowitz, M. D., Hadlock, T. D. and Levine, R. (2004, Spring). A comparison of web and mail survey response rates. *Public Opinion Quarterly*, 68, 1, 94-1-1; Sparrow, N. and Curtice, J. (2004), Measuring the attitudes of the general public versus Internet polls: an evaluation. *International Journal of Market Research*, 46, 1, 23–44.

54. Information in this Marketing Research Insight is based on: Harrison, Matthew (2006, Winter). Learning the language. *Marketing Research*, 18, 4, 10–16.

55. Brown, S. (1987). Drop and collect surveys: a neglected research technique? *Journal of the Market Research Society*, 5, 1, 19–23.

56. See: Ibeh, K. I. N., Brock, J. K.-U. (2004, Quarter 3). Conducting survey research among organisational populations in developing countries. *International Journal of Market Research*, 46, 3, 375–383; Ibeh, K., Brock, J. K.-U. and Zhou, Y. J. (2004, February). The drop and collect survey among industrial populations: theory and empirical evidence. *Industrial Marketing Management*, 33, 2, 155–165.

57. See: Bourque, L. and Fielder, E. (2003). *How to Conduct Self-Administered and Mail Surveys*, 2nd ed. Thousand Oaks, CA: Sage Publications.

58. American Statistical Association (1997). More about mail surveys. ASA Series: What is a survey?

59. Nonresponse is a concern with any survey, and our understanding of refusals is minimal. See, for example, Groves, R. M.,

Cialdini, R. B. and Couper, M. P. (1992). Understanding the decision to participate in a survey. *Public Opinion Quarterly*, 56, 475–495.

60. Anderson, R. C., Fell, D., Smith, R. L.; Hansen, E. N. and Gomon, S. (2005, January). Current consumer behavior research in forest products. *Forest Products Journal*, 55, 1, 21–27.

61. Grandcolas, U., Rettie, R. and Marusenko, K. (2003). Web survey bias: sample or mode effect? *Journal of Marketing Management*, 19, 541–561.

62. See, for example, McDaniel, S. W. and Verille, P. (1987, January). Do topic differences affect survey nonresponse? *Journal of the Market Research Society*, 29, 1, 55–66; or Whitehead, J. C. (1991, Winter), Environmental interest group behavior and self-selection bias in contingent valuation mail surveys. *Growth & Change*, 22, 1, 10–21.

63. A large number of studies have sought to determine response rates for a wide variety of inducement strategies. See, for example, Fox, R. J., Crask, M. and Kim, J. (Winter). Mail questionnaires in survey research: a review of response inducement techniques. *Public Opinion Quarterly*, 52, 4, 467–491.

64. Yammarino, F., Skinner, S. and Childers, T. (1991). Understanding mail survey response behavior. *Public Opinion Quarterly*, 55, 613–639.

65. See: Conant, J., Smart, D. and Walker, B. (1990). Mail survey facilitation techniques: an assessment and proposal regarding reporting practices. *Journal of the Market Research Society*, 32, 4, 369–380; Kaplowitz, M. D. and Lupi, F. (2004, Summer), Color photographs and mail survey response rates. *Journal of Public Opinion Research*, 16, 2, 199–206; or Trussell, N. and Lavrakas, P. I. (2004, Fall). The influence of incremental increases in token cash incentives on mail survey response. *Public Opinion Quarterly*, 68, 3, 349–367.

66. Jassaume R. A., Jr. and Yamada, Y. (1990, Summer). A comparison of the viability of mail surveys in Japan and the United States. *Public Opinion Quarterly*, 54, 2, 219–228.

67. Newby, R., Watson, J. and Woodliff, D. (2003, Winter). SME survey methodology: response rates, data quality, and cost effectiveness. *Entrepreneurship: Theory & Practice*, 28, 2, 163–172.

68. Provided by permission of Jack Semler, President and CEO, Readex Research.

69. Arnett, R. (1990, Second Quarter). Mail panel research in the 1990s. *Applied Marketing Research*, 30, 2, 8–10.

70. A recent industry study identified effectiveness, demand for a specific modality, cost, speed of data collection, and available resources as the top five selection criteria when selecting a data collection modality. *Source*: Research industry trends: 2004 report (2004, April). Prepared by Pioneer Marketing Research for Dialtek L.P. (available at www.dialtek.com).

71. For an example of a new data-collection method, see: Wentz, L. (2004, April 12). Mindshare to read 20,000 media minds. *Advertising Age*, 75, 15, 1.

72. Philpott, G. (2005, February). Get the most from net-based panel research. *Marketing News*, 39, 2, 58.

73. Gerlotto, C. (2003, November). Learning on the go: tips on getting international research right. *Quirk's Marketing Research Review*, 44.

74. Weiss, L. (2002, November). Research in Canada. *Quirk's Marketing Research Review*, 40.

75. Ilieva, J., Baron, S. and Healey, N. M. (2002, Quarter 3). Online surveys in marketing research: pros and cons. *International Journal of Market Research*, 44, 3, 361–376.

76. De Rada, V. D. (2005, Quarter 1). Response effects in a survey about consumer behaviour. *International Journal of Market Research*, 47, 1, 45–64.

Chapter 10

1. Sometimes open-ended questions are used to develop categorical questions that are used later. See, for example, Erffmeyer, R. C. and Johnson, D. A. (2001, Spring). An exploratory study of sales force automation practices: expectations and realities. *The Journal of Personal Selling & Sales Management*, 21, 2, 167–175.

2. Fox, S. (2001, May). Market research 101. *Pharmaceutical Executive*, Supplement: Successful product management: a primer, 34.

3. Honomichl, J. (1994). Satisfaction measurement jump-starts survey research. *Marketing News*, 25, 14, 15.

4. See, for example, Leigh, J. H. and Martin C. R., Jr. (1987). "Don't know" item nonresponse in a telephone survey: effects of question form and respondent characteristics. *Journal of Marketing Research*, 29, 3, 317–339.

5. Martensen, A., Grønholdt, L., Bendtsen, L., and Jensen, M. J. (September, 2007). Application of a model for the effectiveness of event marketing. *Journal of Advertising Research*, 47, 3, 283–301. Readers should note that the textbook authors have simplified the original model for pedagogical purposes.

6. See for example, Yoon, S. and Kim, J. (2001, Nov./Dec.). Is the internet more effective than traditional media? Factors affecting the choice of media. *Journal of Advertising Research*, 41, 6, 53–60; Donthu, N. (2001, Nov./Dec.). Does your web site measure up? *Marketing Management*, 10, 4, 29–32; or Finn, A., McFadyen, S., Hoskins, C. and Hupfer, M. (2001, Fall). Quantifying the sources of value of a public service. *Journal of Public Policy & Marketing*, 20, 2, 225–239.

7. See, for example, Wellner, A. S. (2002, February). The female persuasion. *American Demographics*, 24, 2, 24–29; Wasserman, T. (2002, January 7). Color me bad. *Brandweek*, 43, 1, 2; or Wilke, M. and Applebaum, M. (2001, November 5). Peering out of the closet. *Brandweek*, 42, 41, 26–32.

8. Statements are taken from Wells, W. D. and Tigert, D. J. (1971). Activities, interests, and opinions. *Journal of the Advertising Research*, reported in Kassarjian, H. H. and Robertson, T. S. *Perspectives in Consumer Behavior*. Glenview, IL: Scott Foresman, 1973, 175–176.

9. Other methods of brand image measurement have been been found to be comparable. See: Driesener, C. and Romaniuk, J. (2006). Comparing methods of brand image measurement. *International Journal of Market Research*, 48, 6, 681–698.

10. Another way to avoid the halo effect is to have subjects rate each stimulus on the same attribute and then move to the next attribute. See Wu, B. T. W. and Petroshius, S. (1987). The halo effect in store image management. *Journal of the Academy of Marketing Science*, 15, 1, 44–51.

11. The halo effect is real and used by companies to good advantage. See, for example, Moukheiber, Z. and Langreth, R. (2001, December 10). The halo effect. *Forbes*, 168, 15, 66; or Anonymous. (2002, March 11). Sites seeking advertising (the paid kind). *Advertising Age*, 73, 10, 38.

12. Some authors recommend using negatively worded statements with Likert scales to avoid the halo effect; however, recent evidence (Swain, S. D., Weathers, D. and Niedrich, R. W. (February, 2007). Assessing three sources of misresponse to reversed Likert items. *Journal of Marketing Research*, 45, 1, 116–131) argues convincingly against this recommendation.

13. Garg, R. K. (1996, July). The influence of positive and negative wording and issue involvement on responses to Likert scales in marketing research. *Journal of the Marketing Research Society*, 38, 3, 235–246.

14. Scale development requires rigorous research. See, for example, Churchill, G. A. (1979, February). A paradigm for developing better measures of marketing constructs. *Journal of Marketing Research*, 16, 64–73, for method; or Ram, S. and Jung, H. S. (1990). The conceptualization and measurement of product usage. *Journal of the Academy of Marketing Science*, 18, 1, 67–76, for an example;

15. See, for example, Bishop, G. F. (1985, Summer). Experiments with the middle response alternative in survey questions. *Public Opinion Quarterly*, 51, 220–232; or Schertizer, C. B. and Kernan, J. B. (1985, October). More on the robustness of response scales. *Journal of the Marketing Research Society*, 27, 262–282.

16. See also: Duncan, O. D. and Stenbeck, M. (1988, Winter). No opinion or not sure? *Public Opinion Quarterly*, 52, 513–525; and Durand, R. M. and Lambert, Z. V. (1988, March). Don't know responses in survey: analyses and interpretational consequences. *Journal of Business Research*, 16, 533–543.

17. Semon, T. T. (2001, October 8). Symmetry shouldn't be goal for scales. *Marketing News*, 35, 21, 9.

18. Elms. P. (2000, April). Using decision criteria anchors to measure importance among Hispanics. *Quirk's Marketing Research Review*, XV, 4, 44–51.

19. de Jong, M. G., Steenkamp, J.-B. E. M., Fox, J.-P. and Baumgartner, H. (2008, February). Using item response theory to measure extreme response style in marketing research: a global investigation. *Journal of Marketing Research*, 45, 1, 104–115. The figure in the Marketing Research Insight is an adaptation of Figure 3 in this article.

20. Ashley, D. (2003, February). The questionnaire that launched a thousand responses. *Quirk's Marketing Research Review*, electronic archive.

21. At least one recent study has found favor for a 10-point scale. See: Coelho, P. S. and Esteves, S. P. (2007). The choice between a five-point and a ten-point scale in the framework of customer satisfaction measurement. *International Journal of Market Research*, 49, 3, 313–339.

22. The topic of internal consistency of multiple-item measures is too advanced for this basic textbook. Also, recent research touts single-item measures in certain instances. See: Bergkvist, L. and Rossiter, J. (2007, May). The predictive validity of multiple-item versus single-item measures of the same constructs. *Journal of Marketing Research*, 44, 2, 175–184.

23. For example, bogus recall was found negatively related to education, income, and age, but positively related to "yea-saying" and attitude toward the slogan. See: Glassman, M. and Ford, J. B. (1988, Fall). An empirical investigation of bogus recall. *Journal of the Academy of Marketing Science*, 16, 3–4, 38–41; Raghav, S. Reliability and validity of survey research in marketing: the state of the art. In R. L. King, ed., *Marketing: Toward the Twenty-First Century*. Proceedings of the Southern Marketing Association (1991), 210–213; Milton, M. P., Strutton, H. D. and Dunn, M. G. Demographic sample reliability among selected telephone sampling replacement techniques. In R. L. King, ed., *Marketing: Toward the Twenty-First Century*. Proceedings of the Southern Marketing Association (1991), 214–219; Babin, B. J., Darden, W. R. and Griffin, M. A note on demand artifacts in marketing research. In R. L. King, ed., *Marketing: Perspectives for the 1990s*. Proceedings of the Southern Marketing Association (1992), 227–230; Dunipace, R. A., Mix, R. A. and Poole, R. R. Overcoming the failure to replicate research in marketing: a chaotic explanation. In T. K. Massey, Jr., ed.,

Marketing: Satisfying a Diverse Customerplace. Proceedings of the Southern Marketing Association (1993), 194–197; Malawian, K. P. and Butler, D. D. The semantic differential: is it being misused in marketing research? In R. Achrol and A. Mitchell, eds., *Enhancing Knowledge Development in Marketing.* A.M.A. Educators' Conference Proceedings (1994), 19.

24. Statistical analysis can sometimes be used to assist in estabishing face validity. See, for example, Wolburg, J. M. and Pokrywczynski, J. (2002, Sept./Oct.). A psychographic analysis of Generation Y college students. *Journal of Advertising Research*, 41, 5, 33–52.

25. For an example, see: Russell, C., Norman, A. and Heckler, S. (2004, June). The consumption of television programming: development and validation of the connectedness scale. *Journal of Consumer Research*, 31, 1, 150–161, or Terblanceh, N. S. and Boshoff, C.(2008). Improved scale development in marketing. *International Journal of Market Research*, 50, 1, 105–119.

Chapter 11

1. Susan, C. (1994). Questionnaire design affects response rate. *Marketing News,* 28, H25, and Sancher, M. E. (1992). Effects of questionnaire design on the quality of survey data. *Public Opinion Quarterly*, 56, 206–217.

2. For a more comprehensive coverage of this topic, see Baker, M. J. (2003, Summer). Data collection—questionnaire design. *Marketing Review*, 3, 3, 343–370.

3. Babble, E. (1990). *Survey Research Methods,* 2nd ed. Belmont, CA: Wadsworth Publishing Co., 131–132.

4. Hunt, S. D., Sparkman, R. D. and Wilcox, J. (1982, May). The pretest in survey research: issues and preliminary findings. *Journal of Marketing Research*, 26, 4, 269–273.

5. Dillman, D. A. (1978). *Mail Telephone Surveys: The Total Design Method.* New York: John Wiley & Sons, Inc.

6. Interested readers may wish to read: Wood, Robert T. and Williams, Robert J. (February, 2007). "How much money do you spend on gambling?" The comparative validity of question wordings used to assess gambling expenditure. *International Journal of Social Research Methodology*, 10, 1, 63–77.

7. Loftus, E. and Zanni, G. (1975). Eyewitness testimony: the influence of the wording of a question. *Bulletin of the Psychonomic Society*, 5, 86–88.

8. Adapted and modified from Payne, S. L. (1951). *The Art of Asking Questions.* First printing, 1951, Princeton University Press. Current source is the 1980 edition, Chapter 10.

9. Several other marketing research textbooks advocate question focus. See Baker, Michael J. (2003, Summer). Data collection—questionnaire design. *Marketing Review*, 3, 3, 343–370. Practioners also recommend sharp focus. See Anonymous (February, 2008). Do's and Don'ts. *CRM Magazine*, 12, 2, Special section, 13-13.

10. Webb, John (2000, Winter). Questionnaires and their design. *Marketing Review*,. 1 2, 197–218.

11. Ibid.

12. Question clarity must be achieved for respondents of different education levels, ages, socioeconomic strata, and even intelligence: Noelle-Neumann, Elisabeth (1970, Summer). Wanted: rules for wording structured questionnaires. *Public Opinion Quarterly*, 34, 2, 191–201.

13. Webb, John (2000, Winter). Questionnaires and their design. *Marketing Review*, 1, 2, 197–218.

14. For memory questions, it is advisable to have respondents recontruct specific events. See, for example, Cook, W A. (1987,

February–March). Telescoping and memory's other tricks. *Journal of Advertising Research*, 27, 1.

15. Baker, M. J. (2003, Summer). Data collection—questionnaire design. *Marketing Review*, 3 3, 343–370.

16. Connell, S. (2002, Winter), Travel broadens the mind: the case for international research. *International Journal of Marketing Research*, 44, 1, 97–108.

17. Baker, M. J. (2003, Summer). Data collection—questionnaire design. *Marketing Review*, 33, 343–370.

18. Lerman, D., Maxwell, S., Jallat, F. and Reed, G. (2006). Single language surveys: an efficient method for researching cross-cultural differences. *Advances in Consumer Research—Latin American Conference Proceedings*, Vol. 1, 63–64.

19. Sinickas, A. (2005, December/January). Cultural differences and research. *Strategic Communication Management*, 9, 1, 12.

20. For tips on using a translation service, see: Podrovitz, B. and Stejskal, J. (November 2005). Success in any language. *Quirk's Marketing Research Review*, 19, 10, 38–42.

21. Peterson, R. A. (2000). Constructing effective questionnaires, Thousand Oaks, CA: Sage Publications, Inc., 58.

22. Webb, J. (2000, Winter). Questionnaires and their design. *Marketing Review*, 1, 2, 197–218.

23. Baker, M. J. (2003, Summer). Data collection—questionnaire design. *Marketing Review*, 3, 3, 343–370.

24. Webb, J. (2000, Winter). Questionnaires and their design. *Marketing Review*, 1, 2, 197–218.

25. Patten, M. (2001). *Questionnaire Research*. Los Angeles, CA: Pyrczak Publishing, 9.

26. See, for example, Anonymous (May, 2008). More ways to build a better survey. *HR Focus*, 85, 5, 13–14.

27. Brennan, M., Benson, S. and Kearns, Z. (2005, Quarter 1). The effect of introductions on telephone survey participation rates. *International Journal of Market Research*, 47,1, 65–74.

28. There is some evidence that mention of confidentiality has a negative effect on response rates, so the researcher should consider not mentioning it in the introduction even if confidentiality is in place. See: Brennan, M., Benson, S. and Kearns, Z. (2005, Quarter 1). The effect of introductions on telephone survey participation rates. *International Journal of Market Research*, 2005, 47, 1, 65–74.

29. Screens can be used to quickly identify respondents who will not answer honestly. See: Waters, K. M. (1991, Spring–Summer). Designing screening questionnaires to minimize dishonest answers. *Applied Marketing Research*, 31, 1, 51–53.

30. The Marketing Research Association offers recommendations and model introduction, closing, and validation scripts on its website (http://cmor.org/resp_coop_tools.htm).

31. For recommended guidelines for introductions in "b-to-b" surveys, see Durkee, A. (2005, March). First impressions are everything in b-to-b telephone surveys. *Quirk's Marketing Research Review*, XIX, 3, 30–32.

32. While we advocate common sense, reseachers are mindful of question order effects. See for instance, Latflin, L. and Hansen, M. (October 2006). *Quirk's Marketing Research Review*, 20, 9, 40–44.

33. Smith, R., Olah, D., Hansen, B. and Cumbo, D. (2003, November/December). The effect of questionnaire length on participant response rate: a case study in the U.S. cabinet industry. *Forest Products Journal*, 53, 11/12, 33–36.

34. Webb, J. (2000, Winter). Questionnaires and their design. *Marketing Review*, 1, 2, 197–218.

35. Bethlehem, J. (1999/2000, Winter). The routing structure of questionnaires. *International Journal of Market Research*, 42, 1, 95–110.

36. Baker, M. J. (2003, Summer). Data collection—questionnaire design. *Marketing Review*, 3, 3, 343–370.

37. At least one group-administered survey found that question sequence had no effect on cooperation rate. See: Roose, H., De Lange, D., Agneessens, F. and Waege, H. (2002, May). Theatre audience on stage: three experiments analysing the effects of survey design features on survey response in audience research. *Marketing Bulletin*, 13, 1–10.

38. Based on Sudman, S. and Bradhurn, N. (1982). *Asking Questions*. San Francisco: Jossey-Bass, 219–221.

39. Webb, J. (2000, Winter). Questionnaires and their design. *Marketing Review*, 1, 2, 197–218.

40. Patten, M. (2001). Questionnaire research: A practical guide, 2nd edition. Los Angeles, CA: Pyrczak Publishing, 19.

41. Blunch, N. J. (1984, November). Position bias in multiple choice questions. *Journal of Marketing Research*, 21, 216–220; Welch, J. L. and Swift, C. O. (1992, Summer). Question order effects in taste testing of beverages. *Journal of Academy of Marketing Science*, 265–268; Bickatt, B. A. (1993, February). Carryover and backfire effects in marketing research. *Journal of Marketing Research*, 52–62.

42. Dillman, D. A., Sinclair, M. D. and Clark, J. R. (1993). Effects of questionnaire length, respondent-friendly design, and a difficult question on response rates for occupant-addressed census mail surveys. *Public Opinion Quarterly*, 57, 289–304.

43. Question order may also affect responses. See, for example, Ayidiya, S. A. and McClendon, M. J. (1990, Summer). Response effects in mail surveys. *Public Opinion Quarterly*, 54, 2, 229–247.

44. Carroll, S. (1994). Questionnaire design affects response rate. *Marketing News*, 25, 14, 23.

45. They also represent new presentation and format considerations that need to be researched. See, for example, Healey, B., Macpherson, T. and Kuijten, B. (2005, May). An empirical evaluation of three web survey design principles. *Marketing Bulletin*, 16, 1–9; or Christian, L. M., Dillman, D. A. and Smyth, J.D. (2007, Spring). Helping respondents get it right the first time: the influence of words, symbols, and graphics in web surveys. *Public Opinion Quarterly*, 71, 1, 113–125.

46. Highly sophisticated questionnaire design systems have a great many question formats and types in their libraries, and they sometimes have algorithms built into them to arrange the questions into a logical format. See Jenkins, S. and Solomonides, T. (1999/2000, Winter). Automating questionnaire design and construction. *International Journal of Market Research*, 42, 1, 79–95.

47. Although very efficient, "check all that apply" questions have recently been found to be slighly less effective than "forced choice" or "yes/no" question formats. See: Smyth, J. D., Christian, L. M. and Dillman, D. A. (Spring, 200*). Does "Yes or No" on the telephone mean the same as "check-all-that-apply" on the web? *Public Opinion Quarterly*, 72, 1, 103–113.

48. At least one author says to not pretest is foolhardy: Webb, J. (2000, Winter). Questionnaires and their design. *Marketing Review*, 1, 2, 197–218.

49. Some authors refer to "pretesting" as "piloting" the questionnaire, meaning "pilot testing" the questionniare. See: Baker, M. J. (2003, Summer). Data collection—questionnaire design. *Marketing Review*, 3, 3, 343–370.

50. Normally, pretests are done individually, but a focus group could be used. See Long, S. A. (1991, May 27). Pretesting questionnaires minimizes measurement error. *Marketing News*, 25, 11, 12.

51. For a detailed description of the goals and procedures used in pretesting, see Czaja, R. (1998, May). Questionnaire pretesting comes of age. *Marketing Bulletin*, 9, 52–64.

52. For a comprehensive article on pretesting, see Presser, S., Couper, M. P., Lessler, J. T., Martin, E., Martin, J., Rothgeb, J. M. and Singer, E. (2004, Spring). Methods for testing and evaluating survey questions. *Public Opinion Quarterly*, 68, 1, 109–130.

Chapter 12

1. See Bradburn, N. M. and Sudman, S. (1988). Polls and surveys: understanding what they tell us; Cantril, A. H. (1991). The opinion connection: polling, politics, and the press; Cantril, A. H. Public opinion polling. Retrieved from Answers.com on April 29, 2007; Landon in a landslide: the poll that changed polling. Retrieved from www.historymatter.gmu.edu on April 29, 2007.

2. Garland, S. (1990, September 19). Money, power and numbers: a firestorm over the census. *BusinessWeek*, 45.

3. Wyner, G. A. (2001, Fall). Representation, randomization, and realism. *Marketing Research*, 13, 3, 4–5.

4. Sample frame error is especially a concern in business samples. See, for example, Macfarlene, P. (2002, First Quarter). Structuring and measuring the size of business markets. *International Journal of Market Research*, 44, 1, 7–30.

5. See, for example, Stephen, E. H. and Soldo, B. J. (1990, April). How to judge the quality of a survey. *American Demographics*, 12, 4, 42–43.

6. Wyner, G. A. (Spring 2007). Survey errors. *Marketing Research*, 19, 1, 6–8.

7. Singer, K. (July/August 2006). One billion and growing, *Quirk's Marketing Research Review*, 20, 7, 62–67.

8. Bradley, N. (1999, October). Sampling for Internet surveys: an examination of respondent selection for internet research. *Journal of the Market Research Society*, 41, 4, 387.

9. Hall, T. W., Herron, T. L. and Pierce, B. J. (January 2006). How reliable is haphazard sampling? *CPA Journal*, 76, 1, 26–27.

10. The Excel cell entry is ROUND(RAND()*30,1), meaning a random number from 0 to .9999 times 30, rounded to no decimal, generating random numbers from 0 to 30.

11. Foreman, J. and Collins, M. (1991, July). The viability of random digit dialing in the UK. *Journal of the Market Research Society*, 33, 3, 219–227; Hekmat, F. and Segal, M. (1984). Random digit dialing: some additional empirical observations. In David M. Klein and Allen E. Smith, eds., "Marketing Comes of Age," *Proceedings of the Southern Marketing Association*, 176–180.

12. A recent change in the British telephone system has greatly increased the ability of RDD to access a representative sample. See: Nicolaas, G. and Lynn, P. (2002, August). Random-digit dialing in the UK: viability revisited. *Journal of the Royal Statistical Society*: Series A (Statistics in Society), 165, 2, 297–316.

13. See: Tucker, C., Brick, J. M. and Meekins, B. (Spring 2007). Household telephone service and usage patterns in the United Stated in 2004: implications for telephone samples. *Public Opinion Quarterly*, 71, 1, 3–22; Link, M. W., Battaglia, M. P., Frankel, M. R., Osborn, L., and Mokdad, A. H. (Spring 2008). A comparison of address-based sampling (ABS) versus random-digit dialing (RDD) for general population surveys. *Public Opinion Quarterly*, 72, 1, 6–27.

14. Random digit dialing is used by the major Web traffic monitoring companies. See: Fatth, H. (2000, November 13). The metrics system. *Adweek*, 41, 46, 98–102.

15. Tucker, C., Lepkowski, J. M. and Piekarski, L. (2002), The current efficiency of list-assisted telephone sampling designs, *Public Opinion Quarterly*, 66, 3, 321–338.

16. Economy is dependent on the number of clusters. See: Zelin, A., and Stubbs, R. (2005), Cluster sampling: a false economy? *International Journal of Market Research*, 47, 5, 503–524.

17. See also Sudman, S. (1985, February). Efficient screening methods for the sampling of geographically clustered special populations. *Journal of Marketing Research*, 22, 20–29.

18. Cronish, P. (1989, January). Geodemographic sampling in readership surveys. *Journal of the Market Research Society*, 31, 1, 45–51.

19. For a somewhat more technical description of cluster sampling, see Carlin, J. B. and Hocking, J. (1999, October). Design of cross-sectional surveys using cluster sampling: an overview with Australian case studies. *Australian and New Zealand Journal of Public Health*, 23, 5, 546–551.

20. Academic global business researchers often use nonprobability samples for cost savings. See: Yang, Z., Wang, X. and Su, C. (December 2006). A review of research methodologies in international business. *International Business Review*, 15, 6, 601–617.

21. Thomas, J. S., Reinartz, W. and Kumar, V. (2004, July/August). Getting the most out of all your customers. *Harvard Business Review*, 82, 7/8, 116–124.

22. Academic marketing researchers often use convenience samples of college students. See Peterson, R. A. (2001, December). On the use of college students in social science research: insights from a second-order meta-analysis. *Journal of Consumer Research*, 28, 3, 450–461.

23. Wyner, G. A. (2001, Fall). Representation, randomization, and realism. *Marketing Research*, 13, 3, 4–5.

24. A variation of the snowball sample is found in Eaton, J. and Struthers, C. W. (2002, August). Using the Internet for organizational research: a study of cynicism in the workplace. *CyberPsychology & Behavior*, 5, 4, 305–313, where university students were required to return surveys completed by family, friends, and coworkers.

25. Browne, K. (February 2005). Snowball sampling: using social networks to research non-heterosexual women. *Journal of Social Research Methodology*, 8, 1, 47–60.

26. For an application of referral sampling, see: Moriarity, R. T., Jr., and Spekman, R. E. (1984, May). An empirical investigation of the information sources used during the industrial buying process. *Journal of Marketing Research*, 21, 137–147.

27. This MRI is based on the article by Ptacek, C. H. (March 2008). Nonprobability sampling assures representation and validity with B2B universes. *Quirk's Marketing Research Review*, 22, 3, 16–18.

28. Thomas, Jerry W., President/CEO, Decision Analyst, Inc., personal communication.

29. For an historical perspective and prediction about online sampling, see Sudman, S. and Blair, E. (1999, Spring). Sampling in the twenty-first century. *Academy of Marketing Science*, 27, 2, 269–277.

30. Internet surveys can access hard-to-reach groups. See Anonymous (1999, Summer). Pro and con: Internet interviewing. *Marketing Research*, 11, 2, 33–36.

31. See as an example: Dahlen, M. (2001, July/August). Banner advertisements through a new lens. *Journal of Advertising Research*, 41, 4, 23–30.

32. For a comparison of online sampling to telephone sampling, see: Couper, M. P. (2000, Winter). Web surveys: a review of issues and approaches. *Public Opinion Quarterly*, 64, 4, 464–494.

33. For a comparison of an invitation online sample to a RDD sample for a low incidence population, see: Mathy, R. M., Schillace, M., Coleman, S. M. and Berquist, B. E. (2002, June). Methodological rigor with Internet samples: new ways to reach underrepresented populations. *CyberPsychology & Behavior*, 5, 3, 253–266.

34. Provided by DMS, by permission.

35. For recommendations about online panel management, see: Miles, L. (2004, June 16). Online on tap. *Marketing* , 39–40.

36. Grossnickle, J. and Raskin, O. (2001, Summer). What's ahead on the Internet. *Marketing Research*, 13, 2, 8–13.

37. Miller, T. W. (2001, Summer). Can we trust the data of online research? *Marketing Research,* 13, 2, 26–32.

38. Sample plans are useful wherever someone desires to draw a representative group from a population. For an auditing example, see: Martin, J. (2004, August). *The Internal Auditor*, 61, 4, 21–23.

39. Rothman, J. and Mitchell, D. (1989, October). Statisticians can be creative too. *Journal of the Market Research Society*, 31, 4, 456–466.

40. The need for substitutions can be affected by the respondent selection procedure. See, for example: Hagen, D. E. and Collier, C. M. (1982, Winter). Must respondent selection procedures for telephone surveys be so invasive? *Public Opinion Quarterly*, 47, 547–556.

41. Cooperation is known to vary across demographic groups. See: Guggenheim, B. (1989, February/March). All research is not created equal! *Journal of Advertising Research*, 29, 1, RC7–RC11.

Chapter 13

1. One author refers to these as "quality" and "quantity." See Hellebusch, Stephen J, (September 2006), Know sample quantity for clearer results, *Marketing News*, Vol. 40, No. 15, 23–26.

2. Lenth, R. (2001, August), Some Practical Guidelines For Effective Sample Size Determination, *The American Statistician*; Vol. 55, No. 3, 187–193.

3. Williams, G. (1999, April) What Size Sample Do I Need? *Australian and New Zealand Journal of Public Health*; Vol. 23, No. 2, 215-217.

4. Cesana, B. M, Reina, G. and Marubini, E. (2001, November) Sample Size For Testing A Proportion In Clinical Trials: A "Two-Step" Procedure Combining Power And Confidence Interval Expected Width, *The American Statistician*, Vol. 55, No. 4, 288–292.

5. Our chapter simplifies a complex area. See for example, Williams, G. (1999, April), What size sample do I need? *Australian and New Zealand Journal of Public Health*, Vol. 21, No. 2, 215-217.

6. This chapter pertains to quantiative marketing reseach samples. For qualitative research situations, see for example, Christy, R. and Wood, M. (1999,) Researching possibilities in marketing, *Qualitative Market Research*; Vol. 2, No. 3, 189-196.

7. Frendberg, Norman (1992, June), Increasing Survey Accuracy, *Quirk's Marketing Research Review*, electronic archive.

8. One author has simply said, ". . . sampling error has the unique distinction of being a measurable source of error in survey research . . .", Frendberg, Norman (1992, June), Increasing Survey Accuracy, *Quirk's Marketing Research Review*, electronic archive.

9. We realize that some researchers prefer to always use the sample size formula that includes N; however, since N does not affect sample size unless N is small (or n is large relative to N), we have opted for simplicity and to use the sample size formula without N.

10. Xu, Gang (1999, June), Estimating Sample Size for a Descriptive Study in Quantitative Research, *Quirk's Marketing Research Review*, electonic archive.

11. For a similar, but slightly different treatment, see Sangren, Susie (1999, January), A Simple Solution to Nagging Questions About Survey, Sample Size and Validity, *Quirk's Marketing Research Review*, electonic archive.

12. For a different formula that uses the difference between two means, see Minchow, Don (2000, June), How large did You say

the Sample has to be?, *Quirk's Marketing Research Review*, electronic archive.

13. For a caution on this approach, see Browne, R. H. (2001, November), Using the sample range as a basis for calculating sample size in power calculations, *The American Statistician,* Vol. 55, No. 4, 293–298.

14. See Shiffler, R. E., & Adams, A. J. (1987, August). A Correction for Biasing Effects of Pilot Sample Size on Sample Size Determination. *Journal of Marketing Research*, 24, 3, 319–321.

15. For more information see, Lenth. R. V (2001, August), Some practical guidelines for effective sample size determination, *The American Statistician*, Vol. 55, No. 3, 187–193.

16. There are, of course, other factors that affect the final sample size, see for example, Sangren, Susie (2000, April), Survey and Sampling in an Imperfect World, *Quirk's Marketing Research Review*, electronic archive.

17. See, for example, Cesana, B. M, Reina, G. and Marubini, E. (2001, November) Sample size for testing a proportion in clinical trials: A "two-step" procedure combining power and confidence interval expected width, *The American Statistician,* Vol 55, No. 4, 288–192.

18. To see how simple crosstabulations can increase the required sample size, see Sangren, Susie (2000, April), Survey and Sampling in an Imperfect World, *Quirk's Marketing Research Review*, electronic archive.

19. Kupper, Lawrence L., Hafner, Kerby B. (1989, May), How Appropriate Are Popular Sample Size Formulas? *American Statistician*, Vol. 43, Issue 2, p. 101–195.

20. Barlet, J, Kotrlik, J. and Higgins, C. (2001, Spring), Organizational Research: Determining Appropriate Sample Size In Survey Research, *Information Technology, Learning, and Performance Journal*, Vol. 19, No.1, 43–50.

21. Hunter, J. E. (2001, June), The desperate need for replications, *Journal of Consumer Research*; Vol. 28, No. 1, 149–158.

22. A different statistical analysis determination of sample size is through use of estimated effect sizes. See, for example, Semon, T. T. (1994). Save a Few Bucks on Sample Size, Risk Millions in Opportunity Cost. *Marketing News*, 28, 1, 19.

23. Ball, Jason (February 2004), Simple rules shape proper sample size, *Marketing News*, 2/1/2004, Vol. 38, No. 2, 38–38.

24. Ball, Jason, (2004, February 1), A Numbers Game: Simple Rules Shape Proper Sample Size, *Marketing News* (Special Report), pg 38.

25. See, for example, Hall, T. W, Herron, T. L. Pierce, B. J, and Witt, T. J. (2001, March) The effectiveness of increasing sample size to mitigate the influence of population characteristics in haphazard sampling, *Auditing*; Vol. 20, No. 1, 169–185.

Chapter 14

1. In Chapter 13 you learned to control sampling error by using a sample size formula that allowed you to determine the sample size required in order to control for the amount of sample error (*e*) you are willing to accept.

2. For a breakdown of the types of nonsampling errors encountered in business-to-business marketing research studies, see: Lilien, G., Brown, R. and Searls, K. (1991, January 7). Cut errors, improve estimates to bridge biz-to-biz info gap. *Marketing News*, 25, 1, 20–22.

3. Interviewer errors have been around for a very long time. See: Snead, Roswell, (1942). Problems of field interviewers. *Journal of Marketing*, 7, 2, 139–145.

4. Intentional errors are especially likely when data is supplied by competitors. See: Croft, R. (1992, Third Quarter). How to minimize the problem of untruthful response. *Business Marketing Digest*, 17, 3, 17–23.

5. To better understand this area, see: Barker, R. A. (1987, July). A demographic profile of marketing research interviewers. *Journal of the Market Research Society*, 29, 279–292.

6. For some interesting theories on interviewer cheating, see: Harrison, D. E. and Krauss, S. I. (2002, October). Interviewer cheating: implications for research on entrepreneurship in Africa. *Journal of Developmental Entrepreneurship*, 7, 3, 319–330.

7. Peterson, B. (1994, Fall). Insight into consumer cooperation. *Marketing Research*, 6, 4, 52–53.

8. These problems are international in scope. For the United Kingdom, see: Kreitzman, L. (1990, February 22). Market research: virgins and groupies. *Marketing*, 35–38.

9. The items are based on items developed and the research reported by: Klein, H., Levenburg, N., McKendall, M. and Mothersell, W. (May 2007). Cheating during the college years: how do business school students compare? *Journal of Business Ethics*, 72, 2, 197–206.

10. Collins, M. (1997, January). Interviewer variability: a review of the problem. *Journal of the Market Research Society*, 39, 1, 67–84.

11. See: Flores-Macias, F. and Lawson, C. (Spring 2008). Effects of interviewer gender on survey responses: findings from a household survey in Mexico. *International Journal of Public Opinion Research*, 20, 1, 100–110; or Oksenberg, L., Coleman, L. and Cannell, C. F. (1986, Spring). Interviewers' voices and refusal rates in telephone surveys. *Public Opinion Quarterly*, 50, 1, 97–111.

12. Pol, L. G. and Ponzurick, T. G. (1989, Spring). Gender of interviewer/gender of respondent bias in telephone surveys. *Applied Marketing Research*, 29, 2, 9–13.

13. See: Hansen, K. M. (Spring 2007). The effects of incentive, interview length, and interviewer characteristics on response rates in a CATI study. *International Journal of Public Opinion Research*, 19, 1, 112–121; or Olson, K. and Peytchev, A. (2007, Summer). Effect of interviewer experience on interview pace and interviewer attitudes. *Public Opinion Quarterly*, 71, 2, 273–286.

14. Based on: Bronner, F. and Kuijlen, T. (2007). The live or digital interviewer. *International Journal of Market Research*, 49, 2, 167–190.

15. Sanchez, M. E. (1992, Summer). Effects of questionnaire design on the quality of survey data. *Public Opinion Quarterly*, 56, 2, 206–217.

16. Kiecker, P. and Nelson, J. E. (1996, April). Do interviewers follow telephone survey instructions? *Journal of the Market Research Society*, 38, 2, p161–173.

17. Loosveldt, G., Carton, A. and Billiet, J. (2004, Quarter 1). Assessment of survey data quality: a pragmatic approach focused on interviewer tasks. *International Journal of Market Research*, 46, 1, 65–82.

18. Epstein, W. M. (January 2006). Response bias in opinion polls and American social welfare. *Social Science Journal*, 43, 1, 99–110.

19. Tourangeau, R. and Yan, T. (September 2007). Sensitive questions in surveys. *Psychological Bulletin*, 133, 5, 859–883.

20. Honomichl, J. (1991, June 24). Legislation threatens research by phone. *Marketing News*, 25, 13, 4; Webster, C. (1991). Consumers' attitudes toward data collection methods. In Robert L. King, ed., "Marketing: Toward the Twenty-First Century," *Proceedings of the Southern Marketing Association* (1991), 220–224.

21. Jarvis, S. (2002, February 4). CMOR finds survey refusal rate still rising. *Marketing News*, 36, 3, 4.

22. See, for example: Honomichl, J. (1991, May 27). Making a point—again—for an "industry identifier." *Marketing News*, 25, 11, H35; or Spethmann, B. (1991, June 10). Cautious consumers have surveyors wary. *Advertising Age*, 62, 24, 34.

23. Arnett, R. (1990, Second Quarter). Mail panel research in the 1990s. *Applied Marketing Research*, 30, 2, 8–10.

24. Not all observers share this view. See: Schlossberg, H. (1991, January 7). Research's image better than many think. *Marketing News*, 25, 1, 24–25.

25. Vanthuyne, J. (March 2006). Overcoming the hurdles. *Quirk's Marketing Research Review*, 20, 3, 46–49.

26. One author refers to responses to questions on a survey as "hearsay," which includes potential for misunderstanding: Semon, T. (2003). Settle for personal truth vs. facts in surveys. *Marketing News*, 37, 2, 17.

27. Of course, eliminating the interviewer entirely may be an option. See: Horton, K. (1990, February). Disk-based surveys: new way to pick your brain. *Software Magazine*, 10, 2, 76–77.

28. For early articles on interviewers and supervision, see: Clarkson, E. P. (1949, January). Some suggestions for field research supervisors. *Journal of Marketing*, 13, 3, 321–329; and Reed, V. D., Parker, K. G. and Vitriol, H. A. (1948, January). Selection, training, and supervision of field interviewers in marketing research. *Journal of Marketing*, 12, 3, 365–378.

29. For a book on interviewer error reduction, see: Fowler, F. and Mangione, T. (1990). *Standardized Survey Interviewing: Minimizing Interviewer-Related Error*. Newbury Park: Sage Publications.

30. There is a move in the UK for interviewer certification. See: Hemsley, S. (2000, August 17). Acting the part. *Marketing Week*, 23, 28, 37–40.

31. For an argument against interviewer standardization, see: Gobo, G. (October 2006). Set them free: improving data quality by broadening the interviewer's tasks. *International Journal of Social Research Methodology*, 9, 4, 279–301.

32. Tucker, C. (1983, Spring). Interviewer effects in telephone surveys. *Public Opinion Quarterly*, 47. 1, 84–95.

33. See: Childers, T. and Skinner, S. (1985, January). Theoretical and empirical issues in the identification survey respondents. *Journal of the Market Research Society*, 27, 39–53; Jim L., Finlay, J. L. and Seyyet, F. J. (1988). The impact of sponsorship and respondent attitudes on response rate to telephone surveys: an exploratory investigation. In David L. Moore, ed., Marketing: Forward Motion, *Proceedings of the Atlantic Marketing Association* (1988), 715–721; Goldsmith, R. E. Spurious response error in a new product survey. In J. Joseph Cronin, Jr. and Melvin T. Stith, eds., "Marketing: Meeting the Challenges of the 1990s," *Proceedings of the Southern Marketing Association* (1987), 172–175; Downs P. E. and Kerr, J. R. Recent evidence on the relationship between anonymity and response variables. In John H. Summey, Blaise J. Bergiel, and Carol H. Anderson, eds., A Spectrum of Contemporary Marketing Ideas, *Proceedings of the Southern Marketing Association* (1982), 258–264; Glisan, G. and Grimm, J. L., Improving response rates in an industrial setting: will traditional variables work? In John H. Summey, Blaise J. Bergiel, and Carol H. Anderson, eds., A Spectrum of Contemporary Marketing Ideas, *Proceedings of the Southern Marketing Association* (1982), 265–268; Taylor, R. D., Beisel, J. and Blakney, V. The effect of advanced notification by mail of a forthcoming mail survey on the response rates, item omission rates, and response speed. In David M. Klein and Allen E. Smith, eds., Marketing Comes of Age, *Proceedings of the Southern Marketing Association* (1984), 184–187; Friedman, H. H. (1979, Spring). The effects of a monetary incentive and the ethnicity of

the sponsor's signature on the rate and quality of response to a mall survey. *Journal of the Academy of Marketing Science*, 95–100; Goldstein, L. and Friedman, H. H. (1975, April). A case for double postcards in surveys. *Journal of Advertising Research*, 43–49; Hubbard, R. and Little, E. L. (1988, Fall). Cash prizes and mail response rates: a threshold analysis. *Journal of the Academy of Marketing Science*, 42–44; Childers, T. L. and Ferrell, O. C. (1979, August). Response rates and perceived questionnaire length in mail surveys. *Journal of Marketing Research*, 429–431; Childers, T. L., Pride, W. M. and Ferrell, O. C. (1980, August). A reassessment of the effects of appeals on response to mail surveys. *Journal of Marketing Research*, 365–370; Steele, T., Schwendig, W. and Kilpatrick, J. (1992, March/April). Duplicate responses to multiple survey mailings: a problem? *Journal of Advertising Research*, 26–33; Wilcox, J. B. (1977, November). The interaction of refusal and not-at-home sources of nonresponse bias. *Journal of Marketing Research*, 592–597.

34. An opposite view is expressed by Pruden and Vavra who believe it is important to identify participants and provide some sort of follow-up acknowledgement of their participation in the survey: Pruden, D. R. and Vavra, T. G. (2000, Summer). Customer research, not marketing research. *Marketing Research*, 12, 2, 14–19.

35. See, for example: Lynn, P. (2002, Autumn). The impact of incentives on response rates to personal interview surveys: role and perceptions of interviewers. *International Journal of Public Opinion Research*, 13, 3, 326–336.

36. A comparison on nonresponse errors under different incentives is Barsky, J. K. and Huxley, S. J. (1992, December). A customer-survey tool: using the "quality sample." *The Cornell Hotel and Restaurant Administration Quarterly*, 33, 6, 18–25.

37. Derham, P. (October 2006). Increase response rates by increasing relevance. *Quirk's Marketing Research Review*, 20, 9, 26–30.

38. Screening questionnaires can also be used. See: Waters, K. M. (1991, Spring/Summer). Designing screening questionnaires to minimize dishonest answers. *Applied Marketing Research*, 31, 1, 51–53.

39. For examples, see: Prete, D. D. (1991, September 2). Clients want more specific research—and faster. *Marketing News*, 25, 18, 18; Hawk, K. (1992, November 12). More marketers going online for decision support. *Marketing News*, 24, 23, 14; Riche, M. F. (1990). Look before leaping. *American Demographics*, 12, 2, 18–20; or Wolfe, M. J. (1989, September 11). New way to use scanner data and demographics aids local marketers. *Marketing News*, 23, 19, 8–9.

40. Coleman, L. G. (1991, January 7). Researchers say nonresponse is single biggest problem. *Marketing News*, 25, 1, 32–33.

41. Landler, M. (1991, February 11). The "bloodbath" in market research. *Business Week*, 72, 74.

42. Baim, J. (1991, June). Response rates: a multinational perspective. *Marketing & Research Today*, 19, 2, 114–119.

43. Source: Curtin, R., Presser, S. and Singer, E. (2005, Spring). Changes in telephone survey nonresponse over the past quarter century. *Public Opinion Quarterly*, 69, 1, 87–108.

44. Abraham, K. G., Maitland, A. and Bianchi, S. M. (2006 Special Issue). Nonresponse in the American time use survey. *Public Opinion Quarterly*, 70, 5, 676–703.

45. Groves, R. M., Couper, M. P., Presser, S., Singer, E., Tourangeau, R., Acosta, G. P. and Nelson, L. (2006, First Quarter). Experiments in producing nonresponse bias. *Public Opinion Quarterly*, 2006 Special Issue, 70, 5, 720–736.

46. Tourangeau, R. and Yan, T. (September 2007). Sensitive questions in surveys. *Psychological Bulletin*, 133, 5, 859–883.

47. Vogt, C. A. and Stewart, S. I. (2001). Response problems in a vacation panel study. *Journal of Leisure Research*, 33, 1, 91–105.

48. Groves, R. M., Presser, S. and Dipko, S. (2004, Spring). The role of topic interest in survey participation decisions. *Public Opinion Quarterly*, 68, 1, 2–31.

49. Farrell, B. and Elken, T. (1994, August 29). Adjust five variables for better mail surveys. *Marketing News*, 20.

50. Tyagi, P. K. (1989, Summer). The effects of appeals, anonymity, and feedback on mail survey response patterns from salespeople. *Journal of the Academy of Marketing Science*, 17, 3, 235–241.

51. Anonymous. (1993, August 16). The researchers' response: four industry leaders tell how to improve cooperation. *Marketing News*, A12.

52. Some authors use the term *unit nonresonse* to refer to item omissions. See, for example: Hudson, D., Seah, L.-H., Hite, D. and Haab, T. (2004). Telephone presurveys, self-selection, and non-response bias to mail and Internet surveys in economic research. *Applied Economics Letters*, 11, 4, 237–240.

53. Shoemaker, P. J., Eichholz, M. and Skewes, E. A. (2002, Summer). Item nonresponse: distinguishing between don't know and refuse. *International Journal of Public Opinion Research*, 14, 2, 193–201.

54. Frankel, L. R. On the definition of response rates. A Special Task Force Report Published by the Council of American Survey Research Organizations, 3 Upper Devon, Belle Terre, Port Jefferson, NY 11777.

55. The CASRO formula pertains to telephone surveys. For Web-based surveys, see: preview by Michael Bowling, J., Rimer, B. K., Lyons, E. J., Golin, C. E., Frydman, G. and Ribisl, K. M. (November 2006). Methodologic challenges of e-health research. *Evaluation and Program Planning*, 29, 4, 390–396.

56. A different approach is to measure nonresponse and make adjustments with weights. See: Colombo, R. (2000, January/April). A model for diagnosing and reducing nonresponse bias, *Journal of Advertising Research*, 40, 1/2, 85–93.

57. De Leeuw, E., Callegaro, M., Hox, J., Korendijk, E. and Lensvelt-Mulders, G. (Fall 2007). The influence of advance letters on response in telephone surveys. *Public Opinion Quarterly*, 71, 3, 413–443.

58. See for example: Brazil, J., Jue, A., Mulins, C. and Plunkett, J. (2006, July/August). Capture their interest. *Quirk's Marketing Research Review*, 20, 7, 46–54; or Jobber, D., Saunders, J. and Mitchell, V.-W. (2004, April). Prepaid monetary incentive effects on mail survey response. *Journal of Business Research*, 57, 4, 347–350.

59. For a comparison of response rates by mail versus fax, see: Dickson, J. P. and MacLachlan, D. L. (1996, February). Fax surveys: Return Patterns and Comparison with Mail Surveys. *Journal of Marketing Research*, 33, 1, 108–113.

60. There are more complex methods. See, for example: Bollinger, C. R. and Martin, H. D. (2001, April). Estimation with response error and nonresponse: food-stamp participation in the SIPP. *Journal of Business & Economic Statistics*, 19, 2, 129–141.

61. For more complex procedures, see: Armstrong, J. S. and Overton, T. S. (1977, August). Estimating nonresponse bias in mail surveys. *Journal of Marketing Research*, 14, 396–402; Pearl, D. K. and Fairley, D. (1985, Winter). Testing for the potential of nonresponse bias in sample surveys. *Public Opinion Quarterly*, 49, 553–560; or Sharlot, T. (1986, July). Weighting the survey results. *Journal of the Market Research Society*, 28, 363–366.

62. Based on: Lavrakas, P. J., Shuttles, C. D., Steeh, C. and Fienberg, H. (2007, Special Issue). The state of surveying cell phone numbers in the United States. *Public Opinion Quarterly*, 71, 5, 840–854.

63. For yea-saying and nay-saying, see: Bachman, J. G. and O'Malley, P. M. (1985, Summer). Yea-saying, nay-saying, and going to extremes: black–white differences in response styles. *Public Opinion Quarterly*, 48, 491–509; and Greenleaf, E. A. (1992, May). Improving rating scale measures by detecting and correcting bias components in some response styles. *Journal of Marketing Research*, 29, 2, 176–188.

64. www.esomar.org/index.php/26-questions.html

Chapter 15

1. It is important for the researcher and client to have a partnership during data analysis. See, for example: Fitzpatrick, M. (2001, August). Statistical analysis for direct marketers—in plain English. *Direct Marketing*, 64, 4, 54–56.

2. For an alternative presentation, see: Ehrenberg, A. (2001, Winter). Data, but no information. *Marketing Research*, 13, 4, 36–39.

3. The use of descriptive statistics is sometimes called "data reduction," although some authors term any appropriate analysis that makes sense as data "data reduction." See: Vondruska, R. (1995, April). The fine art of data reduction. *Quirk's Marketing Research Review*, online archive.

4. Some authors argue that central tendency measures are too sterile. See, for example: Pruden, D. R. and Vavra, T. G. (2000, Summer). Customer research, not marketing research. *Marketing Research*, 12, 2, 14–19.

5. For an illustrative article on central tendency measures used in business valuation, see: Sellers, K., Yingping, H. and Campbell, S. (2008, Jan./Feb.). Measures of central tendency in business valuation. *Value Examiner*, 7–18.

6. Based on Bruwer, J. and Li, E. (200&). Wine-related lifestyle (WRL) market segmentation: demographic and behavioural factors. *Journal of Wine Research*, 18, 1, 19–34.

7. Gutsche, A. (2001, September 24). Visuals make the case. *Marketing News*, 35, 20, 21–23.

8. Some guidelines are drawn from: Ehrenberg, A. (2001, Winter). Data, but no information. *Marketing Research*, 13, 2, 36–39.

Chapter 16

1. The 95% level is standard in academic research and commonly adopted by practitioners; however, some authors prefer to use the "probability" or 1 minus the discovered significance level of a finding being true. See: Zucker, Hank (1994). What is Significance? *Quirk's Marketing Research Review*, electronic archive.

2. It has been well documented that tests of statistical significance are often misused in the social sciences, including the field of marketing research. Critics note that researchers endow the tests with more capabilities than they actually have and rely on them as the sole approach for analyzing data (Sawyer and Peter, 1983). Other critics note that combining p values with alpha levels in the often-used model $p \geq \alpha$ = significance is inappropriate since the two concepts arise from incompatible philosophies (Hubbard and Bayarri, 2003). Users of statistical tests should be familiar with these arguments and other writings noting misinterpretations of statistical significance testing (Carver, 1978). See: Sawyer, Alan G. and Peter, J. P. (1983, May). The significance of statistical significance tests in marketing research. *Journal of Marketing Research*, 20, 122–133; Hubbard, R. and Bayarri, M. J. (2003, August). Confusion over measures of evidence (p's) versus errors (α's) in classical statistical testing (with comments). *The American Statistician*, 57, 171–82; and Carver, R. P. (1978, August). The case against statistical significance testing. *Harvard Educational Review*, 48, 278–399.

3. Some disciplines, such as psychology and medicine, encourage their researchers to refrain from performing hypothesis tests and to report confidence intervals instead. See: Fidler, F., Cumming, G., Burgman, M. and Thomason, N. (2004, November). Statistical reform in medicine, psychology and ecology. *Journal of Socio-Economics*, 33, 5, 615–630; or Fidler, F., Thomason, N., Cumming, G., Finch, S. and Leeman, J. (2004, February). Research article editors can lead researchers to confidence intervals, but can't make them think: statistical reform lessons from medicine. *Psychological Science*, 15, 2, 119–126.

4. Some researchers believe that strict use of statistical tests obviates "important" or "meaningful" findings. See, for example: Kirk, J. M. (2006). Thoughts on our overreliance on statistical testing in deriving consumer insights. *Quirk's Marketing Research Review*, 20, 3, 22–25.

Chapter 17

1. One author considers *t* tests (differences tests) to be one of the most important statistical procedures used by marketing researchers. See: Migliore, V. T. (1996). If you hate statistics. . . . *Quirk's Marketing Research Review*, electronic archive.

2. For a contrary view, see Mazur, L. (2000, June 8), The only truism in marketing is they don't exist. *Marketing*, 20.

3. Unfortunately, the nature of statistical significance is not a matter of universal agreement. See: Hubbard, R. and Armstrong, J. S. (2006). Why we don't really know what statistical significance means: implications for educators. *Journal of Marketing Education*, 28, 2, 114–120.

4. Meaningful difference is sometimes called "practical significance." See: Thompson, B. (2002, Winter). "Statistical," "practical," and "clinical": how many kinds of significance do counselors need to consider? *Journal of Counseling and Development*, 30, 1, 64–71.

5. This is common, but controversial. See: Ozgur, C. and Strasser, S. (2004). A study of the statistical inference criteria: can we agree on when to use *z* versus *t*? *Decision Sciences Journal of Innovative Education*, 2, 2, 177–192.

6. For some cautions about differences tests, see: Helgeson, N. (1999). The insignificance of significance testing. *Quirk's Marketing Research Review*, electronic archive.

7. Rick, S., Cryder, C. and Loewenstein, G. (2008). Tightwads and spendthrifts. *Journal of Consumer Research*, 34, 6, 767–782.

8. Hellebusch, S. J. (2001, June 4). One chi square beats two *z* tests. *Marketing News*, 35, 12, 11, 13.

9. For illumination, see: Burdick, R. K. (1983, August). Statement of hypotheses in the analysis of variance. *Journal of Marketing Research*, 20, 320–324.

10. Laukkanen,T., Sinkkonen, S., Kivijarvi,M. and Laukkanen, P. (2007). Innovation resistance among mature consumers. *Journal of Consumer Marketing*, 24, 7, 419–427.

11. For an example of the use of paired samples *t* tests, see: Ryan, C. and Mo, X. (2001, December). Chinese visitors to New Zealand: demographics and perceptions. *Journal of Vacation Marketing*, 8, 1, 13–27.

Chapter 18

1. For elaboration and an example, see: Semon, T. (1999, August). Use your brain when using a chi-square. *Marketing News*, 33, 16, 6.

2. It is not advisable to use cross-tabulations analysis with chi-square when there are cases of cell frequencies of less than 5 cases. See: Migliore, V. (1998). *Quirk's Marketing Research Review*, electronic archive.

3. For advice on when to use chi-square analysis, see: Hellebusch, S. J. (2001, June 4). One chi square beats two *z* tests. *Marketing News*, 35, 12, 11, 13.

4. An alternative view is that the researcher is testing multiple cases of percentage differences (analogous to multiple independent group means tests) in a cross-tabulation table, and use of the chi-square test compensates for Type I error that reduces the confidence level. See: Neal, W. (1989, March). The problem with multiple paired comparisons in crosstabs. *Marketing Research*, 1, 1, 52–54.

5. Here are some articles that use cross-tabulation analysis: Burton, S. and Zinkhan, G. M. (1987, Fall). Changes in consumer choice: further investigation of similarity and attraction effects. *Psychology in Marketing*, 4, 255–266; Bush, A. J. and Leigh, J. H. (1984, April/May). Advertising on cable versus traditional television networks. *Journal of Advertising Research*, 24, 33–38; and Langrehr, F. W. (1985, Summer). Consumer images of two types of competing financial institutions. *Journal of the Academy of Marketing Science*, 13, 248–264.

6. McKechnie, D., Grant, J., Korepina, V. and Sadykova, N. (2007). Women: segmenting the home fitness equipment market. *Journal of Consumer Marketing*, 24, 1, 18–26.

7. Bennett, G., Sagas, M. and Dees, W. (2006). Media preferences of action sports consumers: differences between generation X and Y. *Sports Marketing Quarterly*, 15, 1, 40–49.

8. Garee, M. (1997, September). Statistics don't lie if you know what they're really saying. *Marketing News*, 31, 9, 11.

9. Correlation is sensitive to the number of scale points, especially in instances when variables have fewer than 10 scale points. See: Martin, W. (1978, May). Effects of scaling on the correlation coefficient: additional considerations. *Journal of Marketing Research*, 15, 2, 304–308.

10. For a more advanced treatment of scatter diagrams, see: Goddard, B. L. (2000, April). The power of computer graphics for comparative analysis. *The Appraisal Journal*, 68, 2, 134–141.

11. See also: Gibson, L. (2007). Irreverent thoughts: just what are correlation and regression? *Marketing Research*, 19, 2, 30–33.

Chapter 19

1. Galton, F. (1886). Regression toward mediocrity in hereditary stature. *Journal of the Anthropological Institute,* 15, 246–253.

2. Residual analysis can take many forms. See, for example: Dempster, A. P. and Gasko-Green, M. (1981). New tools for residual analysis. *Annals of Statistics*, 9, 945–959.

3. At least one marketing researcher thinks that regression analysis is so complex that it actually clouds reality. See: Semon, Thomas T (2006). Complex analysis masks real meaning. *Marketing News*, 40, 12, 7.

4. See: Melnick, E. L. and Shoaf, F. R. (1977, June). Regression equals analysis of variance. *Journal of Advertising Research*, 17, 27–31.

5. There are, of course, other and more acceptable ways of identifying outliers. However, our approach relates to the graphical presentation we have used for visualizing linear relationships existing in correlations and regression. At best, our approach simply introduces students to outlier analysis and helps them identify the most obvious cases.

6. Semon, T. (1999, June 23). Outlier problem has no practical solution. *Marketing News*, 31, 16, 2.

7. A well-known marketing academic has recommended graphing to researchers: Zinkhan, G. (1993). Statistical inference in advertising research. *Journal of Advertising*, 22, 3, 1.

8. For more sophisticated handling of outliers, see: Clark, T. (1989, June). Managing outliers: qualitative issues in the han-

dling of extreme observations in marketing research, *Marketing Research*, 2, 2, 31–48.

9. Clemes, M., Gan, C, and Zheng, L. Y. (2007). Customer switching behavior in the New Zealand banking industry. *Banks and Bank Systems*, 2, 4, 50–65.

10. For more information, see, for example: Grapentine, T. (1997, Fall). Managing multicollinearity. *Marketing Research*, 9, 3, 11–21; and Mason, R. L., Gunst, R. F. and Webster, J. T. (1986). Regression analysis and problems of multicollinearity in marketing models: diagnostics and remedial measures. *International Journal of Research in Marketing*, 3, 3, 181–205.

11. For a graphical presentation, see Stine, R. (1995, February). Graphical interpretation of variance inflation factors. *The American Statistician*, 49, 1, 53–56.

12. For alternatives see: Wang, G. (1996, Spring). How to handle multicollinearity in regression modeling. *The Journal of Business Forecasting*, 14, 4, 23–27.

13. Grady B. and Edgington, R. (2008). Ethics education in MBA programs: effectiveness and effects. *International Journal of Management and Marketing Research*, 1, 1, 49–69.

14. Our description pertains to "forward" stepwise regression. We admit that this is a simplification of stepwise multiple regression.

15. McDonald, H. and Stavros, C. (2007). A defection analysis of lapsed season ticket holders: a consumer and organizational study. *Sport Marketing Quarterly*, 16, 4, 218–229.

16. Willson, E. and Wragg, T. (2001). We cannot diagnose the patient's illness . . . but experience tells us what treatment works. *International Journal of Market Research*, 43, 2, 189–215.

17. See for example: Kennedy, P. (2005, Winter). Oh No! I got the wrong sign! What should I do? *Journal of Economic Education*, 36, 1, 77–92.

18. We admit that our description of regression is introductory. Two books that expand our description are: Lewis-Beck, M. S. *Applied Regression: An Introduction* (1980); and Schroeder, L. D., Sjoffquist, D. L. and Stephan, P. E. *Understanding Regression Analysis: An Introductory Guide* (1986), both published by Sage Publications, Inc., Newbury Park, California.

19. For readable treatments of problems encountered in multiple regression applied to marketing research, see: Mullet, G. (1994, October). Regression, regression. *Quirk's Marketing Research Review*, electronic archive; Mullet, G. (1998, June). Have you ever wondered. . . . *Quirk's Marketing Research Review*, electronic archive; Mullet, G. (2003, February). Data abuse. *Quirk's Marketing Research Review*, electronic archive.

20. Regression analysis is commonly used in academic marketing research. Here are some examples: Callahan, F. X. (1982, April/May). Advertising and profits 1969–1978. *Journal of Advertising Research*, 22, 17–22; Dubinsky, A. J. and Levy, M. (1989, Summer). Influence of organizational fairness on work outcomes of retail salespeople. *Journal of Retailing*, 65, 221–252; Frieden, J. B. and Downs, P. E. (1986, Fall). Testing the social involvement model in an energy conservation context. *Journal of the Academy of Marketing Science*, 14, 13–20; and Tellis, G. J. and Fornell, C. (1988, February). The relationship between advertising and product quality over the product life cycle: a contingency theory. *Journal of Marketing Research*, 25, 64–71. For an alternative to regression analysis, see:

Quaintance, B. S. and Franke, G. R. (1991). Neural networks for marketing research. In Robert L. King, ed., "Marketing: Toward the Twenty-First Century," *Proceedings of the Southern Marketing Association* (1991), 230–235.

21. Taken from: Bruning, E. R., Kovacic, M.L. and Oberdick, L. E. (1985). Segmentation analysis of domestic airline passenger markets. *Journal of the Academy of Marketing Science*, 13, 1, 17–31.

Chapter 20

1. Powell, J. (1995). *Will the Real Me Please Stand Up?: 25 Guidelines for Good Communication.* Notre Dame, IN: Ave Maria Press, 6.

2. Owens, J. (2003). The moral high ground. *Marshall News,* 50–51.

3. The source for this description of the writing process is Mary Ellen Guffey's (2006) *Essentials of Business Communication,* 7th ed. Florence, KY: South-Western College Publishing.

4. We wish to acknowledge that this chapter was originally written by M. Howard, Ph.D., and H. Donofrio, Ph.D., assisted us in updating the chapter. Both Dr. Howard and Dr. Donofrio are experts in business communications.

5. Burns, A. and Bush, R. (2005). *Marketing Research: Online Research Applications,* 4th ed. Upper Saddle River, NJ: Prentice Hall, 580.

6. Deshpande, R. and Zaltman, G. (February 1982). Factors affecting the use of market research information: a path analysis. *Journal of Marketing Research, 19.* 14–31.

7. Deshpande, R. and Zaltman, G. (February 1984). A comparison of factors affecting researcher and manager perceptions of market research use. *Journal of Marketing Research, 21,* 32–38.

8. Fink, A. (2003). *How to Report on Surveys,* 2nd ed. Thousand Oaks, CA: Sage, 35.

9. To properly cite your sources, see: *MLA Handbook for Writers of Research Papers,* 5th ed. (2001). New York: The Modern Language Association of America; or *Publication Manual of the American Psychological Association,* 5th ed. Washington, DC: The American Psychological Association.

10. *The American Heritage Dictionary of the English Language,* 4th ed. (2000). Boston: Houghton Mifflin. Retrieved from www.dictionary.com on May 24, 2005.

11. *The American Heritage Dictionary of the English Language,* 4th ed. (2000). Boston: Houghton Mifflin. Retrieved from www.dictionary.com on May 24, 2005. See "methodology."

12. Jameson, D. A. (1993, June). The ethics of plagiarism: how genre affects writers' use of source materials. *The Bulletin,* 2, 18–27.

13. Imperiled copyrights, *New York Times* (1998, April 15), A24.

14. Guffey, M. E. (2000). *Business Communication: Process and Product,* 3rd ed. Cincinnati: South-Western College Publishing, 103.

15. Tufte, E. R. (1983). *The Visual Display of Quantitative Information.* Cheshire, CT: Graphics Press.

16. Thomas, J. (2001, November). Executive excellence. *Marketing research,* 13, 11–12.

Credits

Chapter 1
Page 3 (photo and logo): Golf Digest. Page 3 (logo): Marketing Research Association. Page 7 (Marketing Research Insight 1.1 and photos): Penny Wamback, NewProductWorks®, the innovation resource center of GFK Strategic Innovation (formerly Arbor Strategy Group). Page 8 (photo): Penny Wamback, NewProductWorks®, the innovation resource center of GFK Strategic Innovation (formerly Arbor Strategy Group). Page 10 (ad): By permission of Golf Digest Publications, Jon Last.

Chapter 2
Page 23 (opening vignette, logo and photo): Colleen Moore. Page 32 (ad): www.census.gov. Page 34 (logo): www.qualtrics.com, Ryan Smith. Page 35 (logo) Diane Urso, SSI.

Chapter 3
Page 41 (opening vignette, logo and photo): Larry Brownell, Marketing Research Association. Page 43 (photo): Jack Honomichl, Laurence Gold. Page 44 (Table 3.1): Jack Honomichl, Laurence Gold. Page 45 (Table 3.2): Jack Honomichl, Laurence Gold. Page 49 (Market Research Insight 3.1 and photo): Jeff Minier. Page 51 (ad): By permission of Ted Donnelly. Page 52 (logo): Bill Neal. Page 52 (ad): Kathryn Blackburn. Page 53 (Marketing Research Insight 3.2, logo and photo): Janice Caston. Page 54 (ad): Diane Urso. Page 60 (Marketing Research Insight 3.3 and logo): Jennifer Cattel, Marketing Research Association. Page 62 (photo): Madhav Segal. Page 63 (Marketing Research Insight 3.4 and photos): Michael Brereton. Page 65 (ad and photo): Ted Donnelly. Page 74 (Case 3.1): Harriette Bettis-Outland. Page 77 (logo): Nick Thomas. Page 79 (photo and logo): Matthew Senger. Page 81 (photo and Director's Welcome): Madhav Segal.

Chapter 4
Page 83 (photo and logo): Ron Tatham. Page 106 (ad): Cristi Allen. Page 110 (Case 4.1 and photo): Pushkala Ramen.

Chapter 5
Page 115 (opening vignette and photos): Doss Struse. Page 122 (Marketing Research Insight 5.1 and ad): Molly Lammers. Page 125 (Marketing Research Insight 5.2 and logo): Erica Demme. Page 126 (ad): Alison Babcock. Page 127 (logo): Alison Babcock. Page 134 (Marketing Research Insight 5.4): Herb Sorenson. Page 135 (photo): Herb Sorenson.

Chapter 6
Page 147 (photo and logo): Cristi Allen. Page 148 (logo): Cristi Allen. Page 152 (ad): James Quirk. Pages 162–163 (screen): www.proquest.com, Tina Taylor. Page 168 (ad): www.census.gov, U.S. Census Bureau.

Chapter 7
Page 177 (photo and logo): Tom Evans. Pages 182–183 (ad): Paul Abbate, Ipsos. Page 186 (Marketing Research Insight 7.2 and photo): Fred Miller. Page 187 (art): Fred Miller. Page 188 (Table 7.3): Fred Miller. Page 190 (Market Research Insight 7.3 and photo): Steve Moore. Page 190 (logo and art): Brent Roderick. Page 191 (art): Brent Roderick. Page 191 (Nielsen info): Jennifer Frighetto. Page 192 (Infoscan info): Shelley Hughes. Page 194 (logo): Alana Johnson. Page 195 (photo): Anne Donohoe. Page 197 (Marketing Research

Insight 7.4 and logo): Sandra Parrelli. Page 201 (Case 7.1): Sandra Parrelli. Page 201 (photo): Anthony Pantino. Page 202 (photos): Anthony Patino.

Chapter 8
Page 207 (photo): Marketing Research Association. Page 210 (Marketing Research Insight 8.1): Marketing Research Association. Page 216 (photo): Holly Ford. Page 225 (Marketing Research Insight 8.3 and photo): Philip Trocchia. Page 226 (photo and logo): Holly O'Neill. Page 230 (Marketing Research Insight 8.5, photo and logo): Farnaz Badie. Page 235 (photos): Wendy Wilhelm. Page 237 (Case 8.2): Philip Trocchia.

Chapter 9
Page 239 (opening vignette): By permission of TaiCompanies, Hal Meier. Page 240 (ad): TaiCompanies, Hal Meier. Page 264 (Marketing Research Insight 9.4): Carl Brennan.

Chapter 10
Page 273 (photo and logo): Bill Neal.

Chapter 11
Page 303 (opening vignette and photo): Clifford D. Scott. Page 323 (Marketing Research Insight 11.1): Clifford D. Scott. Page 324 (screens): Ryan Smith, Qualtrics. Page 325 (screen): Ryan Smith, Qualtrics. Page 333 (Case 11.2 and photo): Dr. Tulay Girard, PhD, Assistant Professor of Marketing, Pennsylvania State University—Altoona.

Chapter 12
Page 369 (photo): Dr. Robert W. Armstrong. Pages 369–371 (Case 12.2): Dr. Robert W. Armstrong, Professor of Marketing, University of North Alabama.

Chapter 13
Page 373 (photo and logo): Diane Urso, SSI. Page 393 (ad): Diane Urso, SSI.

Chapter 14
Page 401 (opening vignette, photo and logo): Patrick Glaser.

Chapter 15
Page 457 (Case 15.1): U.N. Umesh. Page 458 (photos): U.N. Umesh.

Chapter 16
Page 467 (photo and logo): Richard Homans. Page 488 (case): Anu Sivaraman.

Chapter 17
Page 503 (photo and logo): William MacElroy.

Chapter 18
Page 533 (photo and logo): Ryan Smith, Qualtrics.

Chapter 20
Page 609 (opening vignette and photo): Heather Donofrio. Page 612 (ad): Andrea Fisher.

Name Index

Miles, S., 137*n*26
Mill, John Stuart, 59
Miller, C., 123*n*13
Miller, Fred L., 185–89
Miller, T. W., 363*n*37
Minchow, D., 386*n*12
Minier, Jeff, 49
Mitchell, A., 63*n*51, 295*n*23
Mitchell, D., 364*n*39
Mitchell, V., 224*n*44
Mitchell, V., W., 421*n*58
Mittal, P. A., 248*n*11
Mix, R., 295*n*23
Mo, X., 525*n*11
Mobley, M. F., 103*n*19
Modani, N., 248*n*11
Moeo, P. J., 260*n*46
Mokdad, A. H., 346*n*13
Montgomery, D., 133*n*20
Moody, M., 191*n*11
Moore, David L., 232*n*54, 412*n*33
Moore-Mezler, Colleen, 23–24
Moriarity, R. T., Jr., 358*n*27
Moser, A., 104*n*20
Mothersell, W., 405*n*9
Moukheiber, Z., 289*n*11
Mulins, C., 421*n*58
Mullet, G., 596*n*19
Murphy, Patrick E., 59*n*47, 63*n*51, 141*n*50
Murray, D., 159*n*15
Murtaugh, P., 87*n*2
Mutum, A. D., 253*n*27
Myers, J., 121*n*10

Nancarrow, C., 64*n*55
Nash, H. W., 63*n*51
Neal, W., 541*n*4
Neal, William D., 26–27, 27*n*2, 55*n*22, 273
Nelson, E., 140*n*43
Nelson, J. E., 68*n*65, 406*n*16
Nelson, L., 415*n*45
Netemeyer, R., 103*n*19
Newby, R., 263*n*67
Nicolaas, G., 346*n*12
Niedrich, R.W., 289*n*12
Nielsen, A. C., 42
Noelle-Neumann, E., 309*n*12
Norman, A., 296*n*25

O'Malley, P. M., 421*n*63
O'Neill, Holly M., 226–29
Ober, S., 624*n*
Oberdick, L. E., 600*n*21
Oishi, S. M., 245*n*6
Oksenberg, L., 405*n*11
Olah, D., 318*n*33
Oliver, J., 69*n*69
Olson, K., 405*n*13
Osborn, L., 346*n*13
Osbourne, Ozzie, 150
Overton, T. S., 421*n*62
Owens, J., 609*n*2
Ozgur, C., 507*n*5

Palk, J., 260*n*45
Pallister, J., 64*n*55
Parasuraman, A., 87*n*2, 119*n*6
Park, M., 249*n*14
Parker, K. G., 410*n*28

Parlin, Charles Coolidge, 42
Parrelli, Sandra, 194*n*24
Patchen, R. H., 196*n*31
Patten, M., 313*n*25, 321*n*40
Payne, S. L., 306*n*8
Pearl, D. K., 421*n*62
Peñaloza, L., 215*n*15
Peter, J. P., 480*n*2
Peters, B., 199*n*35
Peterson, B., 404*n*7
Peterson, M., 55*n*21, 59*n*41
Peterson, R. A., 310*n*21, 354*n*22
Petroshius, S., 289*n*10
Peytchev, A., 405*n*13
Phillips, L. W., 102*n*15, 102*n*16, 135*n*22
Philpott, G., 267*n*72
Piekarski, L., 347*n*15
Pierce, B. J., 343*n*9, 394*n*25
Piirto, R., 211*n*7, 229*n*48
Plunkett, J., 421*n*58
Podrovitz, B., 310*n*19
Pol, L. G., 405*n*12
Politz, Alfred, 42
Ponzurick, T. G., 405*n*12
Poole, R. R., 295*n*23
Powell, John, 609
Power, C., 140*n*42, 141*n*49
Presley, Elvis, 149
Presser, S., 244*n*5, 328*n*52, 414*n*43, 415*n*45, 416*n*48
Prete, D. D., 414*n*39
Price, Keith, 53
Pruden, D. R., 412*n*34, 438*n*4
Ptacek, C. H., 359*n*24

Quaintance, B. S., 596*n*20
Quinlan, P., 220*n*35, 220*n*36
Quirk, Tom, 152

Raghav, S., 295*n*23
Raiffa, H., 87*n*1
Ram, S., 290*n*14
Raskin, O., 363*n*36
Rau, P. A., 55*n*21, 59*n*41
Ravikumar, N., 248*n*11
Ray, S., 90*n*9
Redmond, W. H., 11*n*13
Reed, G., 310*n*17
Reed, V. D., 410*n*28
Reid, A., 199*n*34
Reidenbach, R. E., 63*n*51
Reigen, Rex, 485
Reina, G., 375*n*4, 389*n*17
Reinartz, W., 354*n*21
Remington, T. D., 257*n*38
Rettie, R., 263*n*61
Ribisl, K. M., 418*n*55
Richardson, Steve, 207–210
Riche, M. F., 414*n*39
Rick, S., 512*n*7
Rimer, B. K., 418*n*55
Riordan, E. A., 63*n*51
Ritchie, K., 149*n*3
Robertson, T. S., 287*n*8
Robin, D. P., 63*n*51
Rogers, K., 107*n*26
Rohmund, I., 260*n*52
Roller, M. R., 223*n*40
Romaniuk, J., 288*n*9

Roose, H., 319*n*37
Roosevelt, Franklin D., 337–40
Root, A. R., 47*n*12, 48*n*13
Rosen, D. L., 31*n*7, 129*n*18
Rosenberg, L. J., 107*n*26
Rossiter, J., 295*n*22
Rothgeb, J. M., 328*n*52
Rothman, J., 364*n*39
Roy, A., 250*n*23
Roy, S., 253*n*25
Russell, C., 296*n*25
Rust, L., 213*n*10
Ruyter, K., 260*n*53
Ryan, C., 525*n*11

Saatsoglou, P., 232*n*55
Sabharwal, Y., 248*n*11
Sadykova, N., 546*n*6
Sagas, M., 547*n*7
Sanchez, M. E., 406*n*15
Sangren, S., 383*n*11, 388*n*16, 391*n*18
Saunders, J., 421*n*58
Sawyer, A. G., 480*n*2
Schertizer, C. B., 290*n*15
Schillace, M., 362*n*33
Schlossberg, H., 408*n*24
Schoenbachler, D. D., 90*n*9
Schroeder, L. D., 596*n*18
Schultz, Don E., 56, 58*n*37
Schwartz, J., 159*n*15
Schweitzer, J. C., 257*n*37
Schwendig, W., 412*n*33
Scott, Clifford D., 303
Scudamore, Brian, 119
Seah, L.-H., 417*n*52
Seal, J., 191*n*11
Searles, K., 403*n*2
Segal, Madhav N., 81, 346*n*11
Seinfeld, Jerry, 11
Sellers, K., 438*n*5
Semler, Jack, 264
Semon, Thomas T., 97*n*12, 291*n*17, 391*n*22, 409*n*26, 538*n*1, 572*n*3, 583*n*6
Senger, Matt, 79–81
Senn, J. A., 150*n*6
Seyyet, F. J., 412*n*33
Shellenberg, P., 260*n*47
Sheppard, J., 257*n*36
Shiffler, R. E., 387*n*14
Shing, M., 69*n*71
Shoaf, F. R., 580*n*4
Shoemaker, P. J., 417*n*53
Shostack, G. L., 5*n*4
Shulman, R. S., 34*n*9, 139*n*38
Shuttles, C. D., 422*n*60
Siciliano, T., 217*n*27
Sinatra, Frank, 149
Sinclair, M. D., 321*n*42
Singer, E., 244*n*5, 328*n*52, 414*n*43, 415*n*45
Singer, K., 341*n*6
Singleton, David, 117
Sinickas, A., 310*n*18
Sinkkonen, S., 518*n*8
Sjoffquist, D. L., 596*n*18
Skewes, E. A., 417*n*53
Skinner, S., 64*n*54, 263*n*64, 412*n*33
Small, R. J., 107*n*26

Subject Index

Selected Formulas

Chapter 13 Determining the Size of a Sample

p. 373: Survey Sampling, International Formula for Determining the Number of Telephone Numbers Needed

$$\text{Number of Telephone Numbers Needed} = \frac{\text{Completed Interviews}}{\text{Working Phone Rate} \times \text{Incidence} \times \text{Completion Rate}}$$

$$\pm \text{ Sample Error Percent} = 1.96\sqrt{\frac{pq}{n}}$$

p. 383: Standard sample size formula for a proportion

$$n = \frac{z^2(pq)}{e^2}$$

Where

- n = the sample size
- z = standard error associated with the chosen level of confidence (typically, 1.96)
- p = estimated percent in the population
- q = $100 - p$
- e = acceptable sample error

p. 386: Sample size formula for a mean

$$n = \frac{z^2 s^2}{e^2}$$

Where

- n = the sample size
- z = standard error associated with the chosen level of confidence (typically, 1.96)
- s = variability indicated by an estimated standard deviation
- e = the amount of precision or allowable error in the sample estimate of the population

Chapter 15 Using Basic Descriptive Analysis

p. 440: Formula for a sample mean

$$\text{Mean } (\bar{x}) = \frac{\sum_{i=1}^{n} x_i}{n}$$

Where

- n = the number of cases
- x_i = each individual value
- $\sum$ signifies that all the x_i values are summed

p. 443: Formula for a sample standard deviation

$$\text{Standard deviation } (s) = \sqrt{\frac{\sum_{i-1}^{n}(x_i - \bar{x})^2}{n-1}}$$

Where

- x_i = each individual observation
- $\bar{x}$ = the sample mean

Chapter 16 Performing Population Estimates and Hypothesis Tests

p. 471: Formula for standard error of the mean

$$s_{\bar{x}} = \frac{s}{\sqrt{n}}$$

where

- $s_{\bar{x}}$ = standard error of the mean
- s = sample standard deviation
- n = sample size

p. 471: Formula for standard error of the percentage

$$s_p = \sqrt{\frac{pq}{n}}$$

where

- s_p = standard error of the percentage
- p = the sample percentage
- q = $(100 - p)$
- n = sample size

p. 474: Formula for confidence interval for a Mean

$$\bar{x} \pm z_\alpha s_{\bar{x}}$$

Where

- $\bar{x}$ = sample mean
- z_α = z value for 95% or 99% level of confidence
- $s_{\bar{x}}$ = standard error of the mean

p. 474: Formula for confidence interval for a Percentage

$$p \pm z_\alpha s_p$$

Where

- p = sample percentage
- z_α = z value for 95% or 99% level of confidence
- s_p = standard error of the percentage

p. 483: Formula for test of a hypothesis about a percent

$$z = \frac{p - \pi_H}{s_{\bar{x}}}$$

Where

- p = the sample percentage
- π_H = the hypothesized population percentage
- s_p = the standard error of the percentage

p. 484: Formula for test of a hypothesis about a mean

$$z = \frac{\bar{x} - \mu_H}{s_{\bar{x}}}$$

where

- $\bar{x}$ = the sample mean
- μ_H = the hypothesized population mean
- $s_{\bar{x}}$ = standard error of the mean

Chapter 17 Implementing Basic Differences Tests

p. 509: Formula for significance of the difference between two percentages

$$z = \frac{p_1 - p_2}{s_{p_1 - p_2}}$$

Where

- p_1 = percentage found in sample 1
- p_2 = percentage found in sample 2